Unit Conversions (Equivalents)

Length

1 in. = 2.54 cm (defined)
1 cm = 0.3937 in.
1 ft = 30.48 cm
1 m = 39.37 in. = 3.281 ft
1 mi = 5280 ft = 1.609 km
1 km = 0.6214 mi
1 nautical mile (U.S.) = 1.151 mi = 6076 ft = 1.852 km
1 fermi = 1 femtometer (fm) = 10^{-15} m
1 angstrom (Å) = 10^{-10} m = 0.1 nm
1 light-year (ly) = 9.461×10^{15} m
1 parsec = 3.26 ly = 3.09×10^{16} m

Volume

1 liter (L) = 1000 mL = 1000 cm^3 = 1.0×10^{-3} m^3 =
   1.057 qt (U.S.) = 61.02 $in.^3$
1 gal (U.S.) = 4 qt (U.S.) = 231 $in.^3$ = 3.785 L =
   0.8327 gal (British)
1 quart (U.S.) = 2 pints (U.S.) = 946 mL
1 pint (British) = 1.20 pints (U.S.) = 568 mL
1 m^3 = 35.31 ft^3

Speed

1 mi/h = 1.4667 ft/s = 1.6093 km/h = 0.4470 m/s
1 km/h = 0.2778 m/s = 0.6214 mi/h
1 ft/s = 0.3048 m/s (exact) = 0.6818 mi/h = 1.0973 km/h
1 m/s = 3.281 ft/s = 3.600 km/h = 2.237 mi/h
1 knot = 1.151 mi/h = 0.5144 m/s

Angle

1 radian (rad) = 57.30° = 57°18′
1° = 0.01745 rad
1 rev/min (rpm) = 0.1047 rad/s

Time

1 day = 8.640×10^4 s
1 year = 3.156×10^7 s

Mass

1 atomic mass unit (u) = 1.6605×10^{-27} kg
1 kg = 0.06852 slug
[1 kg has a weight of 2.20 lb where $g = 9.80$ m/s^2.]

Force

1 lb = 4.44822 N
1 N = 10^5 dyne = 0.2248 lb

Energy and Work

1 J = 10^7 ergs = 0.7376 ft·lb
1 ft·lb = 1.356 J = 1.29×10^{-3} Btu = 3.24×10^{-4} kcal
1 kcal = 4.19×10^3 J = 3.97 Btu
1 eV = 1.6022×10^{-19} J
1 kWh = 3.600×10^6 J = 860 kcal
1 Btu = 1.055×10^3 J

Power

1 W = 1 J/s = 0.7376 ft·lb/s = 3.41 Btu/h
1 hp = 550 ft·lb/s = 746 W

Pressure

1 atm = 1.01325 bar = 1.01325×10^5 N/m^2
   = 14.7 $lb/in.^2$ = 760 torr
1 $lb/in.^2$ = 6.895×10^3 N/m^2
1 Pa = 1 N/m^2 = 1.450×10^{-4} $lb/in.^2$

SI Derived Units and Their Abbreviations

Quantity	Unit	Abbreviation	In Terms of Base Units[†]
Force	newton	N	$kg·m/s^2$
Energy and work	joule	J	$kg·m^2/s^2$
Power	watt	W	$kg·m^2/s^3$
Pressure	pascal	Pa	$kg/(m·s^2)$
Frequency	hertz	Hz	s^{-1}
Electric charge	coulomb	C	$A·s$
Electric potential	volt	V	$kg·m^2/(A·s^3)$
Electric resistance	ohm	Ω	$kg·m^2/(A^2·s^3)$
Capacitance	farad	F	$A^2·s^4/(kg·m^2)$
Magnetic field	tesla	T	$kg/(A·s^2)$
Magnetic flux	weber	Wb	$kg·m^2/(A·s^2)$
Inductance	henry	H	$kg·m^2/(s^2·A^2)$

[†] kg = kilogram (mass), m = meter (length), s = second (time), A = ampere (electric current).

Metric (SI) Multipliers

Prefix	Abbreviation	Value
yotta	Y	10^{24}
zeta	Z	10^{21}
exa	E	10^{18}
peta	P	10^{15}
tera	T	10^{12}
giga	G	10^9
mega	M	10^6
kilo	k	10^3
hecto	h	10^2
deka	da	10^1
deci	d	10^{-1}
centi	c	10^{-2}
milli	m	10^{-3}
micro	μ	10^{-6}
nano	n	10^{-9}
pico	p	10^{-12}
femto	f	10^{-15}
atto	a	10^{-18}
zepto	z	10^{-21}
yocto	y	10^{-24}

Douglas C. Giancoli

Physics
Physics 3 B

Custom Edition for University of California, Irvine

Taken from:
Physics for Scientists and Engineers with Modern Physics, Fourth Edition
by Douglas C. Giancoli

Cover Art: Courtesy of Photodisc/Getty Images and Corbis.

Taken from:

Physics for Scientists and Engineers with Modern Physics, Fourth Edition
by Douglas C. Giancoli
Copyright © 2009, 2000, 1989, 1984 by Douglas C. Giancoli, Inc.
Published by Prentice Hall
Upper Saddle River, New Jersey 07458

Pearson Learning Solutions, 501 Boylston Street, Suite 900, Boston, MA 02116
A Pearson Education Company
www.pearsoned.com

Printed in the United States of America

7 8 9 10 11 V0UD 19 18 17 16 15

000200010270758332

SS

ISBN 10: 1-256-36374-X
ISBN 13: 978-1-256-36374-3

MasteringPhysics® Instructions for Physics 2, Physics 3 and Physics 7 students.

MasteringPhysics® will be used for online homework and tutorial for Physics 2, Physics 3 and Physics 7.
- All Physics 2, Physics 3 and Physics 7 students are **required to have a student access code** for MasteringPhysics®.
- Once you **purchase** a MasteringPhysics® student access code, it is **valid for 2 years** and may be used every quarter (including summer) during that time.
- Each student access code may only be used **for one course per quarter**.

What You Need:
- ♦ **A valid email address:** <u>it is recommended that you use your uci.edu email address</u>. Your MasteringPhysics® access code is linked to the email address you enter.
- ♦ **Student access code**: included in the Student Access Kit that is packaged with your new textbook.
- ♦ **The ZIP code for UCI: 92697**
- ♦ **Your 8-digit UCI student ID number**
- ♦ **A Course ID:** _____ (Instructor provides this)

Register
- Go to http://www.masteringphysics.com
- Under "Students" Click **Register.**
- To register using the Student Access Code inside the MasteringPhysics® Student Access Kit, select **Yes, I have an access code**. Click **Continue.**
- **License Agreement and Privacy Policy:** Click **I Accept** to indicate that you have read and agree to the license agreement and privacy policy.
- Select the appropriate option under "Do you have a Pearson Education account?" and supply the requested information. Upon completion, the **Confirmation & Summary** page confirms your registration. This information will also be emailed to you for your records. You can either click **Log In Now** or return to www.masteringphysics.com later.

Log In
- Go to http://www.masteringphysics.com
- Click **Login to MasteringPhysics.**
- Enter your Login Name and Password and click **Log In**.

Enroll in Your Instructor's Course and/or Access the Self-Study Area
Upon first login, you'll be prompted to do one or more of the following:
- **Join your MasteringPhysics course** by entering the **MasteringPhysics Course ID** provided by your instructor.
- **Enter your 8-digit UCI student ID number when prompted**. If you don't use your correct student ID to enroll, you won't get credit for the homework you do. So check this carefully.

Click **Save** and **OK.**

Note: When assignments are created, you may access them in the Assignments Due Soon area, or by clicking the "Assignments" tab. Otherwise, click on Study Area to access self-study material.

Keyboard shortcuts for entering mathematical expressions

When you finish adding values in any of the math templates:
Press the right or left arrow keys to move outside of the specially formatted area and to exit template insertion mode.

To move between the top and bottom parts of a fraction: Use the up and down arrow keys.

For this Math Format Template	Type this...	For this Greek Letter/ Symbol	Type this...	For this Greek Letter/ Symbol	Type this...	For Special Functions, type...
2.56	. (Period)	α	\alpha	τ	\tau	acos
y_1	_ (Underscore)	β	\beta	ϕ	\phi	acot
x^2	^	γ	\gamma	χ	\chi	acsc
$\sin(\theta)$	(and)	δ	\delta	ψ	\psi	asec
$[2\pi r]$	[and]	ϵ	\epsilon	ω	\omega	asin
$K+U$	+	η	\eta	$\hbar$	\hbar	atan
$x_f - x_i$	— (Hyphen)	θ	\theta	Δ	\Delta	cos
$7 \cdot 10^{-8}$	*	κ	\kappa	Σ	\Sigma	cot
$\frac{1}{2}mv^2$	/	λ	\lambda	Φ	\Phi	csc
		μ	\mu	Ψ	\Psi	e
$\sqrt{2gh}$	\sqrt	ν	\nu	Ω	\Omega	ln
$\sqrt[n]{x}$	\nrt	π	\pi	$\mathcal{E}$	\EMF	log
$|\vec{a}|$	|	ρ	\rho			sec
$\vec{V}$	\vec	σ	\sigma			sin
$\hat{j}$	\hat					tan

Contents

13 FLUIDS   339

17 TEMPERATURE, THERMAL EXPANSION, AND THE IDEAL GAS LAW   454

18 KINETIC THEORY OF GASES   476

Volume 2

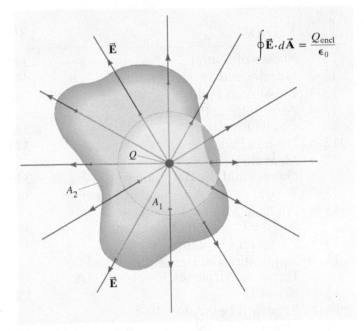

$$\oint \vec{E} \cdot d\vec{A} = \frac{Q_{encl}}{\epsilon_0}$$

APPLICATIONS (SELECTED)

Preface

I was motivated from the beginning to write a textbook different from others that present physics as a sequence of facts, like a Sears catalog: "here are the facts and you better learn them." Instead of that approach in which topics are begun formally and dogmatically, I have sought to begin each topic with concrete observations and experiences students can relate to: start with specifics and only then go to the great generalizations and the more formal aspects of a topic, showing *why* we believe what we believe. This approach reflects how science is actually practiced.

Why a Fourth Edition?

Two recent trends in physics texbooks are disturbing: (1) their revision cycles have become short—they are being revised every 3 or 4 years; (2) the books are getting larger, some over 1500 pages. I don't see how either trend can be of benefit to students. My response: (1) It has been 8 years since the previous edition of this book. (2) This book makes use of physics education research, although it avoids the detail a Professor may need to say in class but in a book shuts down the reader. And this book still remains among the shortest.

This new edition introduces some important new pedagogic tools. It contains new physics (such as in cosmology) and many new appealing applications (list on previous page). Pages and page breaks have been carefully formatted to make the physics easier to follow: no turning a page in the middle of a derivation or Example. Great efforts were made to make the book attractive so students will want to *read* it.

Some of the new features are listed below.

What's New

Chapter-Opening Questions: Each Chapter begins with a multiple-choice question, whose responses include common misconceptions. Students are asked to answer before starting the Chapter, to get them involved in the material and to get any preconceived notions out on the table. The issues reappear later in the Chapter, usually as Exercises, after the material has been covered. The Chapter-Opening Questions also show students the power and usefulness of Physics.

APPROACH paragraph in worked-out numerical Examples: A short introductory paragraph before the Solution, outlining an approach and the steps we can take to get started. Brief NOTES after the Solution may remark on the Solution, may give an alternate approach, or mention an application.

Step-by-Step Examples: After many Problem Solving Strategies (more than 20 in the book), the next Example is done step-by-step following precisely the steps just seen.

Exercises within the text, after an Example or derivation, give students a chance to see if they have understood enough to answer a simple question or do a simple calculation. Many are multiple choice.

Greater clarity: No topic, no paragraph in this book was overlooked in the search to improve the clarity and conciseness of the presentation. Phrases and sentences that may slow down the principal argument have been eliminated: keep to the essentials at first, give the elaborations later.

$\vec{F}, \vec{v}, \vec{B}$ ***Vector notation, arrows***: The symbols for vector quantities in the text and Figures now have a tiny arrow over them, so they are similar to what we write by hand.

Cosmological Revolution: With generous help from top experts in the field, readers have the latest results.

Page layout: more than in the previous edition, serious attention has been paid to how each page is formatted. Examples and all important derivations and arguments are on facing pages. Students then don't have to turn back and forth. Throughout, readers see, on two facing pages, an important slice of physics.

New Applications: LCDs, digital cameras and electronic sensors (CCD, CMOS), electric hazards, GFCIs, photocopiers, inkjet and laser printers, metal detectors, underwater vision, curve balls, airplane wings, DNA, how we actually *see* images. (Turn back a page to see a longer list.)

Examples modified: more math steps are spelled out, and many new Examples added. About 10% of all Examples are Estimation Examples.

This Book is Shorter than other complete full-service books at this level. Shorter explanations are easier to understand and more likely to be read.

Content and Organizational Changes

- **Rotational Motion**: Chapters 10 and 11 have been reorganized. All of angular momentum is now in Chapter 11.

- **First law of thermodynamics**, in Chapter 19, has been rewritten and extended. The full form is given: $\Delta K + \Delta U + \Delta E_{int} = Q - W$, where internal energy is E_{int}, and U is potential energy; the form $Q - W$ is kept so that $dW = P\,dV$.

- Kinematics and Dynamics of Circular Motion are now treated together in Chapter 5.

- Work and Energy, Chapters 7 and 8, have been carefully revised.

- Work done by friction is discussed now with energy conservation (energy terms due to friction).

- Chapters on Inductance and AC Circuits have been combined into one: Chapter 30.

- Graphical Analysis and Numerical Integration is a new optional Section 2–9. Problems requiring a computer or graphing calculator are found at the end of most Chapters.

- Length of an object is a script ℓ rather than normal l, which looks like 1 or I (moment of inertia, current), as in $F = I\ell B$. Capital L is for angular momentum, latent heat, inductance, dimensions of length $[L]$.

- Newton's law of gravitation remains in Chapter 6. Why? Because the $1/r^2$ law is too important to relegate to a late chapter that might not be covered at all late in the semester; furthermore, it is one of the basic forces in nature. In Chapter 8 we can treat real gravitational potential energy and have a fine instance of using $U = -\int \vec{\mathbf{F}} \cdot d\vec{\boldsymbol{\ell}}$.

- New Appendices include the differential form of Maxwell's equations and more on dimensional analysis.

- Problem Solving Strategies are found on pages 30, 58, 64, 96, 102, 125, 166, 198, 229, 261, 314, 504, 551, 571, 600, 685, 716, 740, 763, 849, 871, and 913.

Organization

Some instructors may find that this book contains more material than can be covered in their courses. The text offers great flexibility. Sections marked with a star * are considered optional. These contain slightly more advanced physics material, or material not usually covered in typical courses and/or interesting applications; they contain no material needed in later Chapters (except perhaps in later optional Sections). For a brief course, all optional material could be dropped as well as major parts of Chapters 1, 13, 16, 26, 30, and 35, and selected parts of Chapters 9, 12, 19, 20, 33, and the modern physics Chapters. Topics not covered in class can be a valuable resource for later study by students. Indeed, this text can serve as a useful reference for years because of its wide range of coverage.

Versions of this Book

Complete version: 44 Chapters including 9 Chapters of modern physics.

Classic version: 37 Chapters including one each on relativity and quantum theory.

3 Volume version: Available separately or packaged together (Vols. 1 & 2 or all 3 Volumes):

Volume 1: Chapters 1–20 on mechanics, including fluids, oscillations, waves, plus heat and thermodynamics.

Volume 2: Chapters 21–35 on electricity and magnetism, plus light and optics.

Volume 3: Chapters 36–44 on modern physics: relativity, quantum theory, atomic physics, condensed matter, nuclear physics, elementary particles, cosmology and astrophysics.

Thanks

Many physics professors provided input or direct feedback on every aspect of this textbook. They are listed below, and I owe each a debt of gratitude.

Mario Affatigato, Coe College
Lorraine Allen, United States Coast Guard Academy
Zaven Altounian, McGill University
Bruce Barnett, Johns Hopkins University
Michael Barnett, Lawrence Berkeley Lab
Anand Batra, Howard University
Cornelius Bennhold, George Washington University
Bruce Birkett, University of California Berkeley
Dr. Robert Boivin, Auburn University
Subir Bose, University of Central Florida
David Branning, Trinity College
Meade Brooks, Collin County Community College
Bruce Bunker, University of Notre Dame
Grant Bunker, Illinois Institute of Technology
Wayne Carr, Stevens Institute of Technology
Charles Chiu, University of Texas Austin
Robert Coakley, University of Southern Maine
David Curott, University of North Alabama
Biman Das, SUNY Potsdam
Bob Davis, Taylor University
Kaushik De, University of Texas Arlington
Michael Dennin, University of California Irvine
Kathy Dimiduk, University of New Mexico
John DiNardo, Drexel University
Scott Dudley, United States Air Force Academy
John Essick, Reed College
Cassandra Fesen, Dartmouth College
Alex Filippenko, University of California Berkeley
Richard Firestone, Lawrence Berkeley Lab
Mike Fortner, Northern Illinois University
Tom Furtak, Colorado School of Mines
Edward Gibson, California State University Sacramento
John Hardy, Texas A&M
J. Erik Hendrickson, University of Wisconsin Eau Claire
Laurent Hodges, Iowa State University
David Hogg, New York University
Mark Hollabaugh, Normandale Community College
Andy Hollerman, University of Louisiana at Lafayette
William Holzapfel, University of California Berkeley
Bob Jacobsen, University of California Berkeley
Teruki Kamon, Texas A&M
Daryao Khatri, University of the District of Columbia
Jay Kunze, Idaho State University

Jim LaBelle, Dartmouth College
M.A.K. Lodhi, Texas Tech
Bruce Mason, University of Oklahoma
Dan Mazilu, Virginia Tech
Linda McDonald, North Park College
Bill McNairy, Duke University
Raj Mohanty, Boston University
Giuseppe Molesini, Istituto Nazionale di Ottica Florence
Lisa K. Morris, Washington State University
Blaine Norum, University of Virginia
Alexandria Oakes, Eastern Michigan University
Michael Ottinger, Missouri Western State University
Lyman Page, Princeton and WMAP
Bruce Partridge, Haverford College
R. Daryl Pedigo, University of Washington
Robert Pelcovitz, Brown University
Vahe Peroomian, UCLA
James Rabchuk, Western Illinois University
Michele Rallis, Ohio State University
Paul Richards, University of California Berkeley
Peter Riley, University of Texas Austin
Larry Rowan, University of North Carolina Chapel Hill
Cindy Schwarz, Vassar College
Peter Sheldon, Randolph-Macon Woman's College
Natalia A. Sidorovskaia, University of Louisiana at Lafayette
James Siegrist, UC Berkeley, Director Physics Division LBNL
George Smoot, University of California Berkeley
Mark Sprague, East Carolina University
Michael Strauss, University of Oklahoma
Laszlo Takac, University of Maryland Baltimore Co.
Franklin D. Trumpy, Des Moines Area Community College
Ray Turner, Clemson University
Som Tyagi, Drexel University
John Vasut, Baylor University
Robert Webb, Texas A&M
Robert Weidman, Michigan Technological University
Edward A. Whittaker, Stevens Institute of Technology
John Wolbeck, Orange County Community College
Stanley George Wojcicki, Stanford University
Edward Wright, UCLA
Todd Young, Wayne State College
William Younger, College of the Albemarle
Hsiao-Ling Zhou, Georgia State University

I owe special thanks to Prof. Bob Davis for much valuable input, and especially for working out all the Problems and producing the Solutions Manual for all Problems, as well as for providing the answers to odd-numbered Problems at the end of this book. Many thanks also to J. Erik Hendrickson who collaborated with Bob Davis on the solutions, and to the team they managed (Profs. Anand Batra, Meade Brooks, David Currott, Blaine Norum, Michael Ottinger, Larry Rowan, Ray Turner, John Vasut, William Younger). I am grateful to Profs. John Essick, Bruce Barnett, Robert Coakley, Biman Das, Michael Dennin, Kathy Dimiduk, John DiNardo, Scott Dudley, David Hogg, Cindy Schwarz, Ray Turner, and Som Tyagi, who inspired many of the Examples, Questions, Problems, and significant clarifications.

Crucial for rooting out errors, as well as providing excellent suggestions, were Profs. Kathy Dimiduk, Ray Turner, and Lorraine Allen. A huge thank you to them and to Prof. Giuseppe Molesini for his suggestions and his exceptional photographs for optics.

For Chapters 43 and 44 on Particle Physics and Cosmology and Astrophysics, I was fortunate to receive generous input from some of the top experts in the field, to whom I owe a debt of gratitude: George Smoot, Paul Richards, Alex Filippenko, James Siegrist, and William Holzapfel (UC Berkeley), Lyman Page (Princeton and WMAP), Edward Wright (UCLA and WMAP), and Michael Strauss (University of Oklahoma).

I especially wish to thank Profs. Howard Shugart, Chair Frances Hellman, and many others at the University of California, Berkeley, Physics Department for helpful discussions, and for hospitality. Thanks also to Prof. Tito Arecchi and others at the Istituto Nazionale di Ottica, Florence, Italy.

Finally, I am grateful to the many people at Prentice Hall with whom I worked on this project, especially Paul Corey, Karen Karlin, Christian Botting, John Christiana, and Sean Hogan.

The final responsibility for all errors lies with me. I welcome comments, corrections, and suggestions as soon as possible to benefit students for the next reprint.

D.C.G.

email: Paul.Corey@Pearson.com

Post: Paul Corey
One Lake Street
Upper Saddle River, NJ 07458

About the Author

Douglas C. Giancoli obtained his BA in physics (summa cum laude) from the University of California, Berkeley, his MS in physics at the Massachusetts Institute of Technology, and his PhD in elementary particle physics at the University of California, Berkeley. He spent 2 years as a post-doctoral fellow at UC Berkeley's Virus lab developing skills in molecular biology and biophysics. His mentors include Nobel winners Emilio Segrè and Donald Glaser.

He has taught a wide range of undergraduate courses, traditional as well as innovative ones, and continues to update his textbooks meticulously, seeking ways to better provide an understanding of physics for students.

Doug's favorite spare-time activity is the outdoors, especially climbing peaks (here on a dolomite summit, Italy). He says climbing peaks is like learning physics: it takes effort and the rewards are great.

Online Supplements (partial list)

MasteringPhysics™ (www.masteringphysics.com)
is a sophisticated online tutoring and homework system developed specially for courses using calculus-based physics. Originally developed by David Pritchard and collaborators at MIT, MasteringPhysics provides **students** with individualized online tutoring by responding to their wrong answers and providing hints for solving multi-step problems when they get stuck. It gives them immediate and up-to-date assessment of their progress, and shows where they need to practice more. MasteringPhysics provides **instructors** with a fast and effective way to assign tried-and-tested online homework assignments that comprise a range of problem types. The powerful post-assignment diagnostics allow instructors to assess the progress of their class as a whole as well as individual students, and quickly identify areas of difficulty.

WebAssign (www.webassign.com)

CAPA and LON-CAPA (www.lon-capa.org)

Student Supplements (partial list)

Student Study Guide & Selected Solutions Manual (Volume I: 0-13-227324-1, Volumes II & III: 0-13-227325-X) by Frank Wolfs

Student Pocket Companion (0-13-227326-8) by Biman Das

Tutorials in Introductory Physics (0-13-097069-7)
by Lillian C. McDermott, Peter S. Schaffer, and the Physics Education Group at the University of Washington

Physlet® Physics (0-13-101969-4)
by Wolfgang Christian and Mario Belloni

Ranking Task Exercises in Physics, Student Edition (0-13-144851-X)
by Thomas L. O'Kuma, David P. Maloney, and Curtis J. Hieggelke

E&M TIPERs: Electricity & Magnetism Tasks Inspired by Physics Education Research (0-13-185499-2) by Curtis J. Hieggelke, David P. Maloney, Stephen E. Kanim, and Thomas L. O'Kuma

Mathematics for Physics with Calculus (0-13-191336-0)
by Biman Das

To Students

HOW TO STUDY

1. Read the Chapter. Learn new vocabulary and notation. Try to respond to questions and exercises as they occur.
2. Attend all class meetings. Listen. Take notes, especially about aspects you do not remember seeing in the book. Ask questions (everyone else wants to, but maybe you will have the courage). You will get more out of class if you read the Chapter first.
3. Read the Chapter again, paying attention to details. Follow derivations and worked-out Examples. Absorb their logic. Answer Exercises and as many of the end of Chapter Questions as you can.
4. Solve 10 to 20 end of Chapter Problems (or more), especially those assigned. In doing Problems you find out what you learned and what you didn't. Discuss them with other students. Problem solving is one of the great learning tools. Don't just look for a formula—it won't cut it.

NOTES ON THE FORMAT AND PROBLEM SOLVING

1. Sections marked with a star (*) are considered **optional**. They can be omitted without interrupting the main flow of topics. No later material depends on them except possibly later starred Sections. They may be fun to read, though.
2. The customary **conventions** are used: symbols for quantities (such as m for mass) are italicized, whereas units (such as m for meter) are not italicized. Symbols for vectors are shown in boldface with a small arrow above: $\vec{F}$.
3. Few equations are valid in all situations. Where practical, the **limitations** of important equations are stated in square brackets next to the equation. The equations that represent the great laws of physics are displayed with a tan background, as are a few other indispensable equations.
4. At the end of each Chapter is a set of **Problems** which are ranked as Level I, II, or III, according to estimated difficulty. Level I Problems are easiest, Level II are standard Problems, and Level III are "challenge problems." These ranked Problems are arranged by Section, but Problems for a given Section may depend on earlier material too. There follows a group of General Problems, which are not arranged by Section nor ranked as to difficulty. Problems that relate to optional Sections are starred (*). Most Chapters have 1 or 2 Computer/Numerical Problems at the end, requiring a computer or graphing calculator. Answers to odd-numbered Problems are given at the end of the book.
5. Being able to solve **Problems** is a crucial part of learning physics, and provides a powerful means for understanding the concepts and principles. This book contains many aids to problem solving: (a) worked-out **Examples** and their solutions in the text, which should be studied as an integral part of the text; (b) some of the worked-out Examples are **Estimation Examples**, which show how rough or approximate results can be obtained even if the given data are sparse (see Section 1–6); (c) special **Problem Solving Strategies** placed throughout the text to suggest a step-by-step approach to problem solving for a particular topic—but remember that the basics remain the same; most of these "Strategies" are followed by an Example that is solved by explicitly following the suggested steps; (d) special problem-solving Sections; (e) "Problem Solving" marginal notes which refer to hints within the text for solving Problems; (f) **Exercises** within the text that you should work out immediately, and then check your response against the answer given at the bottom of the last page of that Chapter; (g) the Problems themselves at the end of each Chapter (point 4 above).
6. **Conceptual Examples** pose a question which hopefully starts you to think and come up with a response. Give yourself a little time to come up with your own response before reading the Response given.
7. **Math** review, plus some additional topics, are found in Appendices. Useful data, conversion factors, and math formulas are found inside the front and back covers.

USE OF COLOR

Vectors

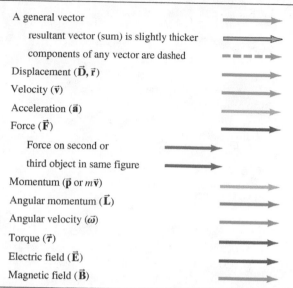

A general vector

    resultant vector (sum) is slightly thicker

    components of any vector are dashed

Displacement ($\vec{\mathbf{D}}, \vec{\mathbf{r}}$)

Velocity ($\vec{\mathbf{v}}$)

Acceleration ($\vec{\mathbf{a}}$)

Force ($\vec{\mathbf{F}}$)

    Force on second or

    third object in same figure

Momentum ($\vec{\mathbf{p}}$ or $m\vec{\mathbf{v}}$)

Angular momentum ($\vec{\mathbf{L}}$)

Angular velocity ($\vec{\omega}$)

Torque ($\vec{\tau}$)

Electric field ($\vec{\mathbf{E}}$)

Magnetic field ($\vec{\mathbf{B}}$)

Electricity and magnetism

Electric field lines

Equipotential lines

Magnetic field lines

Electric charge (+)   +   or   ● +

Electric charge (–)   –   or   ● –

Electric circuit symbols

Wire, with switch S

Resistor

Capacitor

Inductor

Battery

Ground

Optics

Light rays

Object

Real image (dashed)

Virtual image (dashed and paler)

Other

Energy level (atom, etc.)

Measurement lines |←1.0 m→|

Path of a moving object

Direction of motion or current

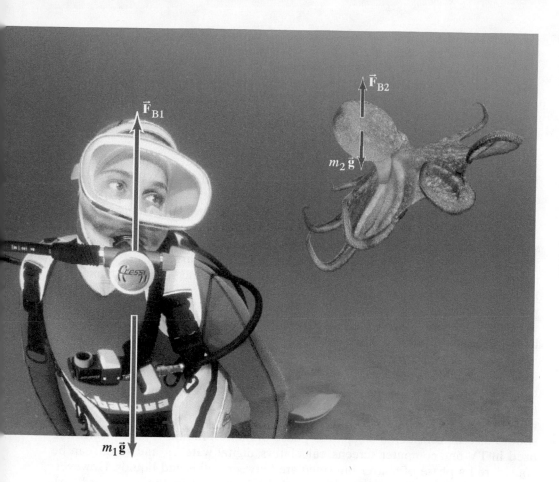

Underwater divers and sea creatures experience a buoyant force $(\vec{F}_B)$ that closely balances their weight $m\vec{g}$. The buoyant force is equal to the weight of the volume of fluid displaced (Archimedes' principle) and arises because the pressure increases with depth in the fluid. Sea creatures have a density very close to that of water, so their weight very nearly equals the buoyant force. Humans have a density slightly less than water, so they can float.

When fluids flow, interesting effects occur because the pressure in the fluid is lower where the fluid velocity is higher (Bernoulli's principle).

C H A P T E R

13

Fluids

CHAPTER-OPENING QUESTIONS—Guess now!

1. Which container has the largest pressure at the bottom? Assume each container holds the same volume of water.

(a)   (b)   (c)   (d)   (e)

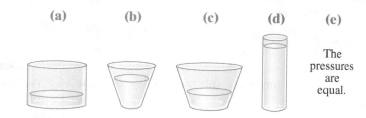

The pressures are equal.

2. Two balloons are tied and hang with their nearest edges about 3 cm apart. If you blow between the balloons (not *at* the balloons, but at the opening between them), what will happen?
(a) Nothing.
(b) The balloons will move closer together.
(c) The balloons will move farther apart.

CONTENTS

I n previous Chapters we considered objects that were solid and assumed to maintain their shape except for a small amount of elastic deformation. We sometimes treated objects as point particles. Now we are going to shift our attention to materials that are very deformable and can flow. Such "fluids" include liquids and gases. We will examine fluids both at rest (fluid statics) and in motion (fluid dynamics).

13–1 Phases of Matter

The three common **phases**, or **states**, of matter are solid, liquid, and gas. We can distinguish these three phases as follows. A **solid** maintains a fixed shape and a fixed size; even if a large force is applied to a solid, it does not readily change in shape or volume. A **liquid** does not maintain a fixed shape—it takes on the shape of its container—but like a solid it is not readily compressible, and its volume can be changed significantly only by a very large force. A **gas** has neither a fixed shape nor a fixed volume—it will expand to fill its container. For example, when air is pumped into an automobile tire, the air does not all run to the bottom of the tire as a liquid would; it spreads out to fill the whole volume of the tire. Since liquids and gases do not maintain a fixed shape, they both have ability to flow; they are thus often referred to collectively as **fluids**.

The division of matter into three phases is not always simple. How, for example, should butter be classified? Furthermore, a fourth phase of matter can be distinguished, the **plasma** phase, which occurs only at very high temperatures and consists of ionized atoms (electrons separated from the nuclei). Some scientists believe that so-called colloids (suspensions of tiny particles in a liquid) should also be considered a separate phase of matter. **Liquid crystals**, which are used in TV and computer screens, calculators, digital watches, and so on, can be considered a phase of matter intermediate between solids and liquids. However, for our present purposes we will mainly be interested in the three ordinary phases of matter.

13–2 Density and Specific Gravity

It is sometimes said that iron is "heavier" than wood. This cannot really be true since a large log clearly weighs more than an iron nail. What we should say is that iron is more *dense* than wood.

The **density**, ρ, of a substance (ρ is the lowercase Greek letter rho) is defined as its mass per unit volume:

$$\rho = \frac{m}{V}, \tag{13–1}$$

where m is the mass of a sample of the substance and V is its volume. Density is a characteristic property of any pure substance. Objects made of a particular pure substance, such as pure gold, can have any size or mass, but the density will be the same for each.

We will sometimes use the concept of density, Eq. 13–1, to write the mass of an object as

$$m = \rho V,$$

and the weight of an object as

$$mg = \rho V g.$$

The SI unit for density is kg/m^3. Sometimes densities are given in g/cm^3. Note that since $1\,kg/m^3 = 1000\,g/(100\,cm)^3 = 10^3\,g/10^6\,cm^3 = 10^{-3}\,g/cm^3$, then a density given in g/cm^3 must be multiplied by 1000 to give the result in kg/m^3. Thus the density of aluminum is $\rho = 2.70\,g/cm^3$, which is equal to $2700\,kg/m^3$. The densities of a variety of substances are given in Table 13–1. The Table specifies temperature and atmospheric pressure because they affect the density of substances (although the effect is slight for liquids and solids). Note that air is roughly 1000 times less dense than water.

TABLE 13–1
Densities of Substances†

Substance	Density, $\rho\ (kg/m^3)$
Solids	
Aluminum	2.70×10^3
Iron and steel	$7.8\ \times 10^3$
Copper	$8.9\ \times 10^3$
Lead	$11.3\ \times 10^3$
Gold	$19.3\ \times 10^3$
Concrete	$2.3\ \times 10^3$
Granite	$2.7\ \times 10^3$
Wood (typical)	$0.3-0.9 \times 10^3$
Glass, common	$2.4-2.8 \times 10^3$
Ice (H_2O)	0.917×10^3
Bone	$1.7-2.0 \times 10^3$
Liquids	
Water (4°C)	$1.00\ \times 10^3$
Blood, plasma	$1.03\ \times 10^3$
Blood, whole	$1.05\ \times 10^3$
Sea water	1.025×10^3
Mercury	$13.6\ \times 10^3$
Alcohol, ethyl	$0.79\ \times 10^3$
Gasoline	$0.68\ \times 10^3$
Gases	
Air	1.29
Helium	0.179
Carbon dioxide	1.98
Steam (water, 100°C)	0.598

†Densities are given at 0°C and 1 atm pressure unless otherwise specified.

EXAMPLE 13–1 Mass, given volume and density. What is the mass of a solid iron wrecking ball of radius 18 cm?

APPROACH First we use the standard formula $V = \frac{4}{3}\pi r^3$ (see inside rear cover) to obtain the volume of the sphere. Then Eq. 13–1 and Table 13–1 give us the mass m.

SOLUTION The volume of the sphere is

$$V = \frac{4}{3}\pi r^3 = \frac{4}{3}(3.14)(0.18\,\text{m})^3 = 0.024\,\text{m}^3.$$

From Table 13–1, the density of iron is $\rho = 7800\,\text{kg/m}^3$, so Eq. 13–1 gives

$$m = \rho V = (7800\,\text{kg/m}^3)(0.024\,\text{m}^3) = 190\,\text{kg}.$$

The **specific gravity** of a substance is defined as the ratio of the density of that substance to the density of water at 4.0°C. Because specific gravity (abbreviated SG) is a ratio, it is a simple number without dimensions or units. The density of water is $1.00\,\text{g/cm}^3 = 1.00 \times 10^3\,\text{kg/m}^3$, so the specific gravity of any substance will be equal numerically to its density specified in g/cm^3, or 10^{-3} times its density specified in kg/m^3. For example (see Table 13–1), the specific gravity of lead is 11.3, and that of alcohol is 0.79.

The concepts of density and specific gravity are especially helpful in the study of fluids because we are not always dealing with a fixed volume or mass.

13–3 Pressure in Fluids

Pressure and force are related, but they are not the same thing. **Pressure** is defined as force per unit area, where the force F is understood to be the magnitude of the force acting perpendicular to the surface area A:

$$\text{pressure} = P = \frac{F}{A}. \tag{13–2}$$

Although force is a vector, pressure is a scalar. Pressure has magnitude only. The SI unit of pressure is N/m^2. This unit has the official name **pascal** (Pa), in honor of Blaise Pascal (see Section 13–5); that is, $1\,\text{Pa} = 1\,\text{N/m}^2$. However, for simplicity, we will often use N/m^2. Other units sometimes used are dynes/cm^2, and lb/in.^2 (abbreviated "psi"). Several other units for pressure are discussed, along with conversions between them, in Section 13–6 (see also the Table inside the front cover).

⚠ CAUTION

Pressure is a scalar, not a vector

EXAMPLE 13–2 Calculating pressure. The two feet of a 60-kg person cover an area of 500 cm². (*a*) Determine the pressure exerted by the two feet on the ground. (*b*) If the person stands on one foot, what will the pressure be under that foot?

APPROACH Assume the person is at rest. Then the ground pushes up on her with a force equal to her weight mg, and she exerts a force mg on the ground where her feet (or foot) contact it. Because $1\,\text{cm}^2 = (10^{-2}\,\text{m})^2 = 10^{-4}\,\text{m}^2$, then $500\,\text{cm}^2 = 0.050\,\text{m}^2$.

SOLUTION (*a*) The pressure on the ground exerted by the two feet is

$$P = \frac{F}{A} = \frac{mg}{A} = \frac{(60\,\text{kg})(9.8\,\text{m/s}^2)}{(0.050\,\text{m}^2)} = 12 \times 10^3\,\text{N/m}^2.$$

(*b*) If the person stands on one foot, the force is still equal to the person's weight, but the area will be half as much, so the pressure will be twice as much: $24 \times 10^3\,\text{N/m}^2$.

FIGURE 13–1 Pressure is the same in every direction in a nonmoving fluid at a given depth. If this weren't true, the fluid would be in motion.

Pressure is particularly useful for dealing with fluids. It is an experimental observation that *a fluid exerts pressure in any direction*. This is well known to swimmers and divers who feel the water pressure on all parts of their bodies. At any depth in a fluid at rest, the pressure is the same in all directions at a given depth. To see why, consider a tiny cube of the fluid (Fig. 13–1) which is so small that we can consider it a point and can ignore the force of gravity on it. The pressure on one side of it must equal the pressure on the opposite side. If this weren't true, there would be a net force on the cube and it would start moving. If the fluid is not flowing, then the pressures must be equal.

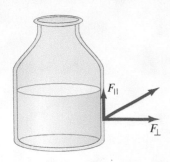

FIGURE 13-2 If there were a component of force parallel to the solid surface of the container, the liquid would move in response to it. For a liquid at rest, $F_\parallel = 0$.

FIGURE 13-3 Calculating the pressure at a depth h in a liquid.

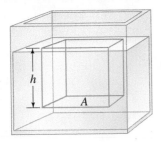

FIGURE 13-4 Forces on a flat, slablike volume of fluid for determining the pressure P at a height y in the fluid.

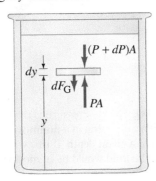

For a fluid at rest, the force due to fluid pressure always acts *perpendicular* to any solid surface it touches. If there were a component of the force parallel to the surface, as shown in Fig. 13-2, then according to Newton's third law the solid surface would exert a force back on the fluid that also would have a component parallel to the surface. Such a component would cause the fluid to flow, in contradiction to our assumption that the fluid is at rest. Thus the force due to the pressure in a fluid at rest is always perpendicular to the surface.

Let us now calculate quantitatively how the pressure in a liquid of uniform density varies with depth. Consider a point at a depth h below the surface of the liquid, as shown in Fig. 13-3 (that is, the surface is a height h above this point). The pressure due to the liquid at this depth h is due to the weight of the column of liquid above it. Thus the force due to the weight of liquid acting on the area A is $F = mg = (\rho V)g = \rho A h g$, where Ah is the volume of the column of liquid, ρ is the density of the liquid (assumed to be constant), and g is the acceleration of gravity. The pressure P due to the weight of liquid is then

$$P = \frac{F}{A} = \frac{\rho A h g}{A}$$

$$P = \rho g h. \qquad \text{[liquid]} \quad \textbf{(13-3)}$$

Note that the area A doesn't affect the pressure at a given depth. The fluid pressure is directly proportional to the density of the liquid and to the depth within the liquid. In general, the pressure at equal depths within a uniform liquid is the same.

EXERCISE A Return to Chapter-Opening Question 1, page 339, and answer it again now. Try to explain why you may have answered differently the first time.

Equation 13-3 tells us what the pressure is at a depth h in the liquid, due to the liquid itself. But what if there is additional pressure exerted at the surface of the liquid, such as the pressure of the atmosphere or a piston pushing down? And what if the density of the fluid is not constant? Gases are quite compressible and hence their density can vary significantly with depth. Liquids, too, can be compressed, although we can often ignore the variation in density. (One exception is in the depths of the ocean where the great weight of water above significantly compresses the water and increases its density.) To cover these, and other cases, we now treat the general case of determining how the pressure in a fluid varies with depth.

As shown in Fig. 13-4, let us determine the pressure at any height y above some reference point[†] (such as the ocean floor or the bottom of a tank or swimming pool). Within this fluid, at the height y, we consider a tiny, flat, slablike volume of the fluid whose area is A and whose (infinitesimal) thickness is dy, as shown. Let the pressure acting upward on its lower surface (at height y) be P. The pressure acting downward on the top surface of our tiny slab (at height $y + dy$) is designated $P + dP$. The fluid pressure acting on our slab thus exerts a force equal to PA upward on our slab and a force equal to $(P + dP)A$ downward on it. The only other force acting vertically on the slab is the (infinitesimal) force of gravity dF_G, which on our slab of mass dm is

$$dF_G = (dm)g = \rho g\, dV = \rho g A\, dy,$$

where ρ is the density of the fluid at the height y. Since the fluid is assumed to be at rest, our slab is in equilibrium so the net force on it must be zero. Therefore we have

$$PA - (P + dP)A - \rho g A\, dy = 0,$$

which when simplified becomes

$$\frac{dP}{dy} = -\rho g. \qquad \textbf{(13-4)}$$

This relation tells us how the pressure within the fluid varies with height above any reference point. The minus sign indicates that the pressure decreases with an increase in height; or that the pressure increases with depth (reduced height).

[†]Now we are measuring y positive upwards, the reverse of what we did to get Eq. 13-3 where we measured the depth (i.e. downward as positive).

If the pressure at a height y_1 in the fluid is P_1, and at height y_2 it is P_2, then we can integrate Eq. 13–4 to obtain

$$\int_{P_1}^{P_2} dP = -\int_{y_1}^{y_2} \rho g \, dy$$

$$P_2 - P_1 = -\int_{y_1}^{y_2} \rho g \, dy, \qquad \text{(13–5)}$$

where we assume ρ is a function of height y: $\rho = \rho(y)$. This is a general relation, and we apply it now to two special cases: (1) pressure in liquids of uniform density and (2) pressure variations in the Earth's atmosphere.

For liquids in which any variation in density can be ignored, $\rho = $ constant and Eq. 13–5 is readily integrated:

$$P_2 - P_1 = -\rho g (y_2 - y_1). \qquad \text{(13–6a)}$$

For the everyday situation of a liquid in an open container—such as water in a glass, a swimming pool, a lake, or the ocean—there is a free surface at the top exposed to the atmosphere. It is convenient to measure distances from this top surface. That is, we let h be the *depth* in the liquid where $h = y_2 - y_1$ as shown in Fig. 13–5. If we let y_2 be the position of the top surface, then P_2 represents the atmospheric pressure, P_0, at the top surface. Then, from Eq. 13–6a, the pressure $P (= P_1)$ at a depth h in the fluid is

$$P = P_0 + \rho g h. \qquad \text{[}h \text{ is depth in liquid]} \quad \text{(13–6b)}$$

Note that Eq. 13–6b is simply the liquid pressure (Eq. 13–3) plus the pressure P_0 due to the atmosphere above.

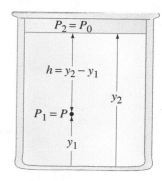

FIGURE 13–5 Pressure at a depth $h = (y_2 - y_1)$ in a liquid of density ρ is $P = P_0 + \rho g h$, where P_0 is the external pressure at the liquid's top surface.

EXAMPLE 13–3 **Pressure at a faucet.** The surface of the water in a storage tank is 30 m above a water faucet in the kitchen of a house, Fig. 13–6. Calculate the difference in water pressure between the faucet and the surface of the water in the tank.

APPROACH Water is practically incompressible, so ρ is constant even for $h = 30$ m when used in Eq. 13–6b. Only h matters; we can ignore the "route" of the pipe and its bends.

SOLUTION We assume the atmospheric pressure at the surface of the water in the storage tank is the same as at the faucet. So, the water pressure difference between the faucet and the surface of the water in the tank is

$$\Delta P = \rho g h = (1.0 \times 10^3 \, \text{kg/m}^3)(9.8 \, \text{m/s}^2)(30 \, \text{m}) = 2.9 \times 10^5 \, \text{N/m}^2.$$

NOTE The height h is sometimes called the **pressure head**. In this Example, the head of water is 30 m at the faucet. The very different diameters of the tank and faucet don't affect the result—only pressure does.

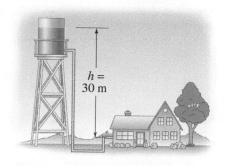

FIGURE 13–6 Example 13–3.

EXAMPLE 13–4 **Force on aquarium window.** Calculate the force due to water pressure exerted on a 1.0 m $\times$ 3.0 m aquarium viewing window whose top edge is 1.0 m below the water surface, Fig. 13–7.

APPROACH At a depth h, the pressure due to the water is given by Eq. 13–6b. Divide the window up into thin horizontal strips of length $\ell = 3.0$ m and thickness dy, as shown in Fig. 13–7. We choose a coordinate system with $y = 0$ at the surface of the water and y is positive downward. (With this choice, the minus sign in Eq. 13–6a becomes plus, or we use Eq. 13–6b with $y = h$.) The force due to water pressure on each strip is $dF = P \, dA = \rho g y \ell \, dy$.

SOLUTION The total force on the window is given by the integral:

$$\int_{y_1 = 1.0\,\text{m}}^{y_2 = 2.0\,\text{m}} \rho g y \ell \, dy = \tfrac{1}{2} \rho g \ell (y_2^2 - y_1^2)$$

$$= \tfrac{1}{2}(1000 \, \text{kg/m}^3)(9.8 \, \text{m/s}^2)(3.0 \, \text{m})[(2.0 \, \text{m})^2 - (1.0 \, \text{m})^2] = 44{,}000 \, \text{N}.$$

NOTE To check our answer, we can do an estimate: multiply the area of the window $(3.0 \, \text{m}^2)$ times the pressure at the middle of the window ($h = 1.5$ m) using Eq. 13–3, $P = \rho g h = (1000 \, \text{kg/m}^3)(9.8 \, \text{m/s}^2)(1.5 \, \text{m}) \approx 1.5 \times 10^4 \, \text{N/m}^2$. So $F = PA \approx (1.5 \times 10^4 \, \text{N/m}^2)(3.0 \, \text{m})(1.0 \, \text{m}) \approx 4.5 \times 10^4 \, \text{N}$. Good!

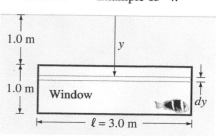

FIGURE 13–7 Example 13–4.

EXERCISE B A dam holds back a lake that is 85 m deep at the dam. If the lake is 20 km long, how much thicker should the dam be than if the lake were smaller, only 1.0 km long?

Now let us apply Eq. 13–4 or 13–5 to gases. The density of gases is normally quite small, so the difference in pressure at different heights can usually be ignored if $y_2 - y_1$ is not large (which is why, in Example 13–3, we could ignore the difference in air pressure between the faucet and the top of the storage tank). Indeed, for most ordinary containers of gas, we can assume that the pressure is the same throughout. However, if $y_2 - y_1$ is very large, we cannot make this assumption. An interesting example is the air of Earth's atmosphere, whose pressure at sea level is about $1.013 \times 10^5 \, \text{N/m}^2$ and decreases slowly with altitude.

EXAMPLE 13–5 **Elevation effect on atmospheric pressure.** (a) Determine the variation in pressure in the Earth's atmosphere as a function of height y above sea level, assuming g is constant and that the density of the air is proportional to the pressure. (This last assumption is not terribly accurate, in part because temperature and other weather effects are important.) (b) At what elevation is the air pressure equal to half the pressure at sea level?

APPROACH We start with Eq. 13–4 and integrate it from the surface of the Earth where $y = 0$ and $P = P_0$, up to height y at pressure P. In (b) we choose $P = \frac{1}{2} P_0$.

SOLUTION (a) We are assuming that ρ is proportional to P, so we can write

$$\frac{\rho}{\rho_0} = \frac{P}{P_0},$$

where $P_0 = 1.013 \times 10^5 \, \text{N/m}^2$ is atmospheric pressure at sea level and $\rho_0 = 1.29 \, \text{kg/m}^3$ is the density of air at sea level at 0°C (Table 13–1). From the differential change in pressure with height, Eq. 13–4, we have

$$\frac{dP}{dy} = -\rho g = -P\left(\frac{\rho_0}{P_0}\right) g,$$

so

$$\frac{dP}{P} = -\frac{\rho_0}{P_0} g \, dy.$$

We integrate this from $y = 0$ (Earth's surface) and $P = P_0$, to the height y where the pressure is P:

$$\int_{P_0}^{P} \frac{dP}{P} = -\frac{\rho_0}{P_0} g \int_{0}^{y} dy$$

$$\ln \frac{P}{P_0} = -\frac{\rho_0}{P_0} gy,$$

since $\ln P - \ln P_0 = \ln(P/P_0)$. Then

$$P = P_0 e^{-(\rho_0 g/P_0)y}.$$

So, based on our assumptions, we find that the air pressure in our atmosphere decreases approximately exponentially with height.

NOTE The atmosphere does not have a distinct top surface, so there is no natural point from which to measure depth in the atmosphere, as we can do for a liquid.

(b) The constant $(\rho_0 g/P_0)$ has the value

$$\frac{\rho_0 g}{P_0} = \frac{(1.29 \, \text{kg/m}^3)(9.80 \, \text{m/s}^2)}{(1.013 \times 10^5 \, \text{N/m}^2)} = 1.25 \times 10^{-4} \, \text{m}^{-1}.$$

Then, when we set $P = \frac{1}{2} P_0$ in our expression derived in (a), we obtain

$$\frac{1}{2} = e^{-(1.25 \times 10^{-4} \, \text{m}^{-1})y}$$

or, taking natural logarithms of both sides,

$$\ln \frac{1}{2} = (-1.25 \times 10^{-4} \, \text{m}^{-1})y$$

so (recall $\ln \frac{1}{2} = -\ln 2$, Appendix A–7, Eq. ii)

$$y = (\ln 2.00)/(1.25 \times 10^{-4} \, \text{m}^{-1}) = 5550 \, \text{m}.$$

Thus, at an elevation of about 5500 m (about 18,000 ft), atmospheric pressure drops to half what it is at sea level. It is not surprising that mountain climbers often use oxygen tanks at very high altitudes.

13–4 Atmospheric Pressure and Gauge Pressure

Atmospheric Pressure

The pressure of the air at a given place on Earth varies slightly according to the weather. At sea level, the pressure of the atmosphere on average is $1.013 \times 10^5 \, N/m^2$ (or 14.7 lb/in.²). This value lets us define a commonly used unit of pressure, the **atmosphere** (abbreviated atm):

$$1 \, atm = 1.013 \times 10^5 \, N/m^2 = 101.3 \, kPa.$$

Another unit of pressure sometimes used (in meteorology and on weather maps) is the **bar**, which is defined as

$$1 \, bar = 1.000 \times 10^5 \, N/m^2.$$

Thus standard atmospheric pressure is slightly more than 1 bar.

The pressure due to the weight of the atmosphere is exerted on all objects immersed in this great sea of air, including our bodies. How does a human body withstand the enormous pressure on its surface? The answer is that living cells maintain an internal pressure that closely equals the external pressure, just as the pressure inside a balloon closely matches the outside pressure of the atmosphere. An automobile tire, because of its rigidity, can maintain internal pressures much greater than the external pressure.

✖ PHYSICS APPLIED
Pressure on living cells

CONCEPTUAL EXAMPLE 13–6 | **Finger holds water in a straw.** You insert a straw of length ℓ into a tall glass of water. You place your finger over the top of the straw, capturing some air above the water but preventing any additional air from getting in or out, and then you lift the straw from the water. You find that the straw retains most of the water (see Fig. 13–8a). Does the air in the space between your finger and the top of the water have a pressure P that is greater than, equal to, or less than the atmospheric pressure P_0 outside the straw?

RESPONSE Consider the forces on the column of water (Fig. 13–8b). Atmospheric pressure outside the straw pushes upward on the water at the bottom of the straw, gravity pulls the water downward, and the air pressure inside the top of the straw pushes downward on the water. Since the water is in equilibrium, the upward force due to atmospheric pressure P_0 must balance the two downward forces. The only way this is possible is for the air pressure inside the straw to be *less than* the atmosphere pressure outside the straw. (When you initially remove the straw from the glass of water, a little water may leave the bottom of the straw, thus increasing the volume of trapped air and reducing its density and pressure.)

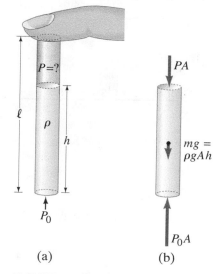

FIGURE 13–8 Example 13–6.

Gauge Pressure

It is important to note that tire gauges, and most other pressure gauges, register the pressure above and beyond atmospheric pressure. This is called **gauge pressure**. Thus, to get the **absolute pressure**, P, we must add the atmospheric pressure, P_0, to the gauge pressure, P_G:

$$P = P_0 + P_G.$$

If a tire gauge registers 220 kPa, the absolute pressure within the tire is 220 kPa + 101 kPa = 321 kPa, equivalent to about 3.2 atm (2.2 atm gauge pressure).

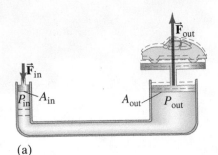

(a)

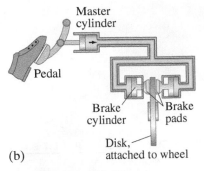

Master cylinder

Pedal

Brake cylinder

Brake pads

Disk, attached to wheel

(b)

FIGURE 13–9 Applications of Pascal's principle: (a) hydraulic lift; (b) hydraulic brakes in a car.

PHYSICS APPLIED

Hydraulic lift

PHYSICS APPLIED

Hydraulic brakes

13–5 Pascal's Principle

The Earth's atmosphere exerts a pressure on all objects with which it is in contact, including other fluids. External pressure acting on a fluid is transmitted throughout that fluid. For instance, according to Eq. 13–3, the pressure due to the water at a depth of 100 m below the surface of a lake is $P = \rho g h = (1000 \, \text{kg/m}^3)(9.8 \, \text{m/s}^2)(100 \, \text{m}) = 9.8 \times 10^5 \, \text{N/m}^2$, or 9.7 atm. However, the total pressure at this point is due to the pressure of water plus the pressure of the air above it. Hence the total pressure (if the lake is near sea level) is 9.7 atm + 1.0 atm = 10.7 atm. This is just one example of a general principle attributed to the French philosopher and scientist Blaise Pascal (1623–1662). **Pascal's principle** states that *if an external pressure is applied to a confined fluid, the pressure at every point within the fluid increases by that amount.*

A number of practical devices make use of Pascal's principle. One example is the hydraulic lift, illustrated in Fig. 13–9a, in which a small input force is used to exert a large output force by making the area of the output piston larger than the area of the input piston. To see how this works, we assume the input and output pistons are at the same height (at least approximately). Then the external input force F_{in}, by Pascal's principle, increases the pressure equally throughout. Therefore, at the same level (see Fig. 13–9a),

$$P_{\text{out}} = P_{\text{in}}$$

where the input quantities are represented by the subscript "in" and the output by "out." Since $P = F/A$, we write the above equality as

$$\frac{F_{\text{out}}}{A_{\text{out}}} = \frac{F_{\text{in}}}{A_{\text{in}}},$$

or

$$\frac{F_{\text{out}}}{F_{\text{in}}} = \frac{A_{\text{out}}}{A_{\text{in}}}.$$

The quantity $F_{\text{out}}/F_{\text{in}}$ is called the **mechanical advantage** of the hydraulic lift, and it is equal to the ratio of the areas. For example, if the area of the output piston is 20 times that of the input cylinder, the force is multiplied by a factor of 20. Thus a force of 200 lb could lift a 4000-lb car.

Figure 13–9b illustrates the brake system of a car. When the driver presses the brake pedal, the pressure in the master cylinder increases. This pressure increase occurs throughout the brake fluid, thus pushing the brake pads against the disk attached to the car's wheel.

13–6 Measurement of Pressure; Gauges and the Barometer

Many devices have been invented to measure pressure, some of which are shown in Fig. 13–10. The simplest is the open-tube *manometer* (Fig 13–10a) which is a U-shaped tube partially filled with a liquid, usually mercury or water. The pressure P being measured is related to the difference in height Δh of the two levels of the liquid by the relation

$$P = P_0 + \rho g \, \Delta h,$$

where P_0 is atmospheric pressure (acting on the top of the liquid in the left-hand tube), and ρ is the density of the liquid. Note that the quantity $\rho g \, \Delta h$ is the gauge pressure—the amount by which P exceeds atmospheric pressure P_0. If the liquid in the left-hand column were lower than that in the right-hand column, P would have to be less than atmospheric pressure (and Δh would be negative).

Instead of calculating the product $\rho g \, \Delta h$, sometimes only the change in height Δh is specified. In fact, pressures are sometimes specified as so many "millimeters of mercury" (mm-Hg) or "mm of water" (mm-H_2O). The unit mm-Hg is equivalent to a pressure of 133 N/m², since $\rho g \, \Delta h$ for 1 mm = 1.0×10^{-3} m of mercury gives

$$\rho g \, \Delta h = (13.6 \times 10^3 \, \text{kg/m}^3)(9.80 \, \text{m/s}^2)(1.00 \times 10^{-3} \, \text{m}) = 1.33 \times 10^2 \, \text{N/m}^2.$$

The unit mm-Hg is also called the **torr** in honor of Evangelista Torricelli (1608–1647), a student of Galileo's who invented the barometer (see next page).

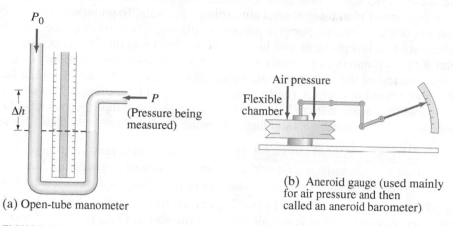

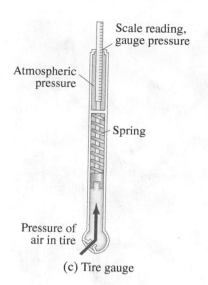

FIGURE 13–10 Pressure gauges: (a) open-tube manometer, (b) aneroid gauge, and (c) common tire-pressure gauge.

In the figure:
- P_0
- Δh
- P (Pressure being measured)
- (a) Open-tube manometer
- Air pressure
- Flexible chamber
- (b) Aneroid gauge (used mainly for air pressure and then called an aneroid barometer)
- Scale reading, gauge pressure
- Atmospheric pressure
- Spring
- Pressure of air in tire
- (c) Tire gauge

Conversion factors among the various units of pressure (an incredible nuisance!) are given in Table 13–2. It is important that only $N/m^2 = Pa$, the proper SI unit, be used in calculations involving other quantities specified in SI units.

TABLE 13–2 Conversion Factors Between Different Units of Pressure

In Terms of $1\ Pa = 1\ N/m^2$	$1\ atm$ in Different Units
$1\ atm = 1.013 \times 10^5\ N/m^2$	$1\ atm = 1.013 \times 10^5\ N/m^2$
$= 1.013 \times 10^5\ Pa = 101.3\ kPa$	
$1\ bar = 1.000 \times 10^5\ N/m^2$	$1\ atm = 1.013\ bar$
$1\ dyne/cm^2 = 0.1\ N/m^2$	$1\ atm = 1.013 \times 10^6\ dyne/cm^2$
$1\ lb/in.^2 = 6.90 \times 10^3\ N/m^2$	$1\ atm = 14.7\ lb/in.^2$
$1\ lb/ft^2 = 47.9\ N/m^2$	$1\ atm = 2.12 \times 10^3\ lb/ft^2$
$1\ cm\text{-}Hg = 1.33 \times 10^3\ N/m^2$	$1\ atm = 76.0\ cm\text{-}Hg$
$1\ mm\text{-}Hg = 133\ N/m^2$	$1\ atm = 760\ mm\text{-}Hg$
$1\ torr = 133\ N/m^2$	$1\ atm = 760\ torr$
$1\ mm\text{-}H_2O\ (4°C) = 9.80\ N/m^2$	$1\ atm = 1.03 \times 10^4\ mm\text{-}H_2O\ (4°C)$

Another type of pressure gauge is the aneroid gauge (Fig. 13–10b) in which the pointer is linked to the flexible ends of an evacuated thin metal chamber. In an electronic gauge, the pressure may be applied to a thin metal diaphragm whose resulting distortion is translated into an electrical signal by a transducer. A common tire gauge is shown in Fig. 13–10c.

Atmospheric pressure can be measured by a modified kind of mercury manometer with one end closed, called a mercury **barometer** (Fig. 13–11). The glass tube is completely filled with mercury and then inverted into the bowl of mercury. If the tube is long enough, the level of the mercury will drop, leaving a vacuum at the top of the tube, since atmospheric pressure can support a column of mercury only about 76 cm high (exactly 76.0 cm at standard atmospheric pressure). That is, a column of mercury 76 cm high exerts the same pressure as the atmosphere[†]:

$$P = \rho g\, \Delta h$$
$$= (13.6 \times 10^3\ kg/m^3)(9.80\ m/s^2)(0.760\ m) = 1.013 \times 10^5\ N/m^2 = 1.00\ atm.$$

FIGURE 13–11 A mercury barometer, invented by Torricelli, is shown here when the air pressure is standard atmospheric, 76.0 cm-Hg.

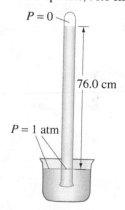

In figure: $P = 0$; $76.0\ cm$; $P = 1\ atm$

[†]This calculation confirms the entry in Table 13–2, $1\ atm = 76.0\ cm\text{-}Hg$.

A calculation similar to what we just did will show that atmospheric pressure can maintain a column of water 10.3 m high in a tube whose top is under vacuum (Fig. 13–12). No matter how good a vacuum pump is, water cannot be made to rise more than about 10 m using normal atmospheric pressure. To pump water out of deep mine shafts with a vacuum pump requires multiple stages for depths greater than 10 m. Galileo studied this problem, and his student Torricelli was the first to explain it. The point is that a pump does not really suck water up a tube—it merely reduces the pressure at the top of the tube. Atmospheric air pressure *pushes* the water up the tube if the top end is at low pressure (under a vacuum), just as it is air pressure that pushes (or maintains) the mercury 76 cm high in a barometer. [Force pumps (Section 13–14) that push up from the bottom can exert higher pressure to push water more than 10 m high.]

CONCEPTUAL EXAMPLE 13–7 | Suction. A student suggests suction-cup shoes for Space Shuttle astronauts working on the exterior of a spacecraft. Having just studied this Chapter, you gently remind him of the fallacy of this plan. What is it?

RESPONSE Suction cups work by pushing out the air underneath the cup. What holds the suction cup in place is the air pressure outside it. (This can be a substantial force when on Earth. For example, a 10-cm-diameter suction cup has an area of $7.9 \times 10^{-3} \, \text{m}^2$. The force of the atmosphere on it is $(7.9 \times 10^{-3} \, \text{m}^2)(1.0 \times 10^5 \, \text{N/m}^2) \approx$ 800 N, about 180 lbs!) But in outer space, there is no air pressure to push the suction cup onto the spacecraft.

We sometimes mistakenly think of suction as something we actively do. For example, we intuitively think that we pull the soda up through a straw. Instead, what we do is lower the pressure at the top of the straw, and the atmosphere *pushes* the soda up the straw.

13–7 Buoyancy and Archimedes' Principle

Objects submerged in a fluid appear to weigh less than they do when outside the fluid. For example, a large rock that you would have difficulty lifting off the ground can often be easily lifted from the bottom of a stream. When the rock breaks through the surface of the water, it suddenly seems to be much heavier. Many objects, such as wood, float on the surface of water. These are two examples of *buoyancy*. In each example, the force of gravity is acting downward. But in addition, an upward *buoyant force* is exerted by the liquid. The buoyant force on fish and underwater divers (as in the Chapter-Opening photo) almost exactly balances the force of gravity downward, and allows them to "hover" in equilibrium.

The buoyant force occurs because the pressure in a fluid increases with depth. Thus the upward pressure on the bottom surface of a submerged object is greater than the downward pressure on its top surface. To see this effect, consider a cylinder of height Δh whose top and bottom ends have an area A and which is completely submerged in a fluid of density ρ_F, as shown in Fig. 13–13. The fluid exerts a pressure $P_1 = \rho_F g h_1$ at the top surface of the cylinder (Eq. 13–3). The force due to this pressure on top of the cylinder is $F_1 = P_1 A = \rho_F g h_1 A$, and it is directed downward. Similarly, the fluid exerts an upward force on the bottom of the cylinder equal to $F_2 = P_2 A = \rho_F g h_2 A$. The net force on the cylinder exerted by the fluid pressure, which is the **buoyant force**, $\vec{F}_B$, acts upward and has the magnitude

$$\begin{aligned} F_B &= F_2 - F_1 = \rho_F g A (h_2 - h_1) \\ &= \rho_F g A \, \Delta h \\ &= \rho_F V g \\ &= m_F g, \end{aligned}$$

where $V = A \, \Delta h$ is the volume of the cylinder, the product $\rho_F V$ is the mass of the fluid displaced, and $\rho_F V g = m_F g$ is the weight of fluid which takes up a volume equal to the volume of the cylinder. Thus the buoyant force on the cylinder is equal to the weight of fluid displaced by the cylinder.

FIGURE 13–12 A water barometer: a full tube of water is inserted into a tub of water, keeping the tube's spigot at the top closed. When the bottom end of the tube is unplugged, some water flows out of the tube into the tub, leaving a vacuum between the water's upper surface and the spigot. Why? Because air pressure can not support a column of water more than 10 m high.

FIGURE 13–13 Determination of the buoyant force.

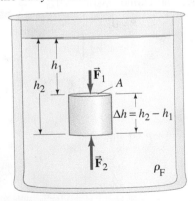

This result is valid no matter what the shape of the object. Its discovery is credited to Archimedes (287?–212 B.C.), and it is called **Archimedes' principle**: *the buoyant force on an object immersed in a fluid is equal to the weight of the fluid displaced by that object.*

By "fluid displaced," we mean a volume of fluid equal to the submerged volume of the object (or that part of the object that is submerged). If the object is placed in a glass or tub initially filled to the brim with water, the water that flows over the top represents the water displaced by the object.

We can derive Archimedes' principle in general by the following simple but elegant argument. The irregularly shaped object D shown in Fig. 13–14a is acted on by the force of gravity (its weight, $m\vec{g}$, downward) and the buoyant force, $\vec{F}_B$, upward. We wish to determine F_B. To do so, we next consider a body (D′ in Fig. 13–14b), this time made of the fluid itself, with the same shape and size as the original object, and located at the same depth. You might think of this body of fluid as being separated from the rest of the fluid by an imaginary membrane. The buoyant force F_B on this body of fluid will be exactly the same as that on the original object since the surrounding fluid, which exerts F_B, is in exactly the same configuration. This body of fluid D′ is in equilibrium (the fluid as a whole is at rest). Therefore, $F_B = m'g$, where $m'g$ is the weight of the body of fluid. Hence the buoyant force F_B is equal to the weight of the body of fluid whose volume equals the volume of the original submerged object, which is Archimedes' principle.

Archimedes' discovery was made by experiment. What we have done in the last two paragraphs is to show that Archimedes' principle can be derived from Newton's laws.

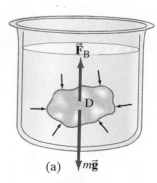
(a)

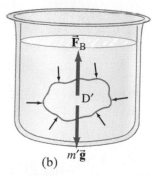
(b)

FIGURE 13–14
Archimedes' principle.

CONCEPTUAL EXAMPLE 13–8 **Two pails of water.** Consider two identical pails of water filled to the brim. One pail contains only water, the other has a piece of wood floating in it. Which pail has the greater weight?

RESPONSE Both pails weigh the same. Recall Archimedes' principle: the wood displaces a volume of water with weight equal to the weight of the wood. Some water will overflow the pail, but Archimedes' principle tells us the spilled water has weight equal to the weight of the wood object; so the pails have the same weight.

EXAMPLE 13–9 **Recovering a submerged statue.** A 70-kg ancient statue lies at the bottom of the sea. Its volume is $3.0 \times 10^4 \, \text{cm}^3$. How much force is needed to lift it?

APPROACH The force F needed to lift the statue is equal to the statue's weight mg minus the buoyant force F_B. Figure 13–15 is the free-body diagram.

SOLUTION The buoyant force on the statue due to the water is equal to the weight of $3.0 \times 10^4 \, \text{cm}^3 = 3.0 \times 10^{-2} \, \text{m}^3$ of water (for seawater, $\rho = 1.025 \times 10^3 \, \text{kg/m}^3$):

$$F_B = m_{H_2O}g = \rho_{H_2O}Vg$$

$$= (1.025 \times 10^3 \, \text{kg/m}^3)(3.0 \times 10^{-2} \, \text{m}^3)(9.8 \, \text{m/s}^2)$$

$$= 3.0 \times 10^2 \, \text{N}.$$

The weight of the statue is $mg = (70 \, \text{kg})(9.8 \, \text{m/s}^2) = 6.9 \times 10^2 \, \text{N}$. Hence the force F needed to lift it is $690 \, \text{N} - 300 \, \text{N} = 390 \, \text{N}$. It is as if the statue had a mass of only $(390 \, \text{N})/(9.8 \, \text{m/s}^2) = 40 \, \text{kg}$.

NOTE Here $F = 390 \, \text{N}$ is the force needed to lift the statue without acceleration when it is under water. As the statue comes *out* of the water, the force F increases, reaching $690 \, \text{N}$ when the statue is fully out of the water.

FIGURE 13–15 Example 13–9. The force needed to lift the statue is $\vec{F}$.

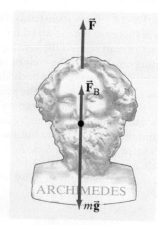

Archimedes is said to have discovered his principle in his bath while thinking how he might determine whether the king's new crown was pure gold or a fake. Gold has a specific gravity of 19.3, somewhat higher than that of most metals, but a determination of specific gravity or density is not readily done directly because, even if the mass is known, the volume of an irregularly shaped object is not easily calculated. However, if the object is weighed in air ($= w$) and also "weighed" while it is under water ($= w'$), the density can be determined using Archimedes' principle, as the following Example shows. The quantity w' is called the *apparent weight* in water, and is what a scale reads when the object is submerged in water (see Fig. 13–16); w' equals the true weight ($w = mg$) minus the buoyant force.

EXAMPLE 13–10 Archimedes: Is the crown gold? When a crown of mass 14.7 kg is submerged in water, an accurate scale reads only 13.4 kg. Is the crown made of gold?

APPROACH If the crown is gold, its density and specific gravity must be very high, SG = 19.3 (see Section 13–2 and Table 13–1). We determine the specific gravity using Archimedes' principle and the two free-body diagrams shown in Fig. 13–16.

SOLUTION The apparent weight of the submerged object (the crown) is w' (what the scale reads), and is the force pulling down on the scale hook. By Newton's third law, w' equals the force F'_T that the scale exerts on the crown in Fig. 13–16b. The sum of the forces on the crown is zero, so w' equals the actual weight w ($= mg$) minus the buoyant force F_B:

$$w' = F'_T = w - F_B$$

so

$$w - w' = F_B.$$

Let V be the volume of the completely submerged object and ρ_O its density (so $\rho_O V$ is its mass), and let ρ_F be the density of the fluid (water). Then $(\rho_F V)g$ is the weight of fluid displaced ($= F_B$). Now we can write

$$w = mg = \rho_O V g$$
$$w - w' = F_B = \rho_F V g.$$

We divide these two equations and obtain

$$\frac{w}{w - w'} = \frac{\rho_O V g}{\rho_F V g} = \frac{\rho_O}{\rho_F}.$$

We see that $w/(w - w')$ is equal to the specific gravity of the object if the fluid in which it is submerged is water ($\rho_F = 1.00 \times 10^3 \text{ kg/m}^3$). Thus

$$\frac{\rho_O}{\rho_{H_2O}} = \frac{w}{w - w'} = \frac{(14.7 \text{ kg})g}{(14.7 \text{ kg} - 13.4 \text{ kg})g} = \frac{14.7 \text{ kg}}{1.3 \text{ kg}} = 11.3.$$

This corresponds to a density of 11,300 kg/m³. The crown is not gold, but seems to be made of lead (see Table 13–1).

FIGURE 13–16 (a) A scale reads the mass of an object in air—in this case the crown of Example 13–10. All objects are at rest, so the tension F_T in the connecting cord equals the weight w of the object: $F_T = mg$. We show the free-body diagram of the crown, and F_T is what causes the scale reading (it is equal to the net downward force on the scale, by Newton's third law). (b) Submerged, the crown has an additional force on it, the buoyant force F_B. The net force is zero, so $F'_T + F_B = mg$ ($= w$). The scale now reads $m' = 13.4$ kg, where m' is related to the effective weight by $w' = m'g$. Thus $F'_T = w' = w - F_B$.

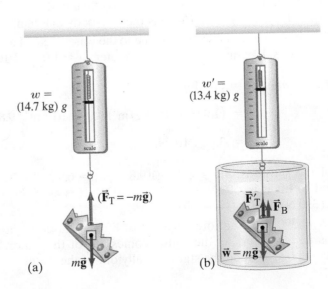

Archimedes' principle applies equally well to objects that float, such as wood. In general, *an object floats on a fluid if its density* (ρ_O) *is less than that of the fluid* (ρ_F). This is readily seen from Fig. 13–17a, where a submerged log will experience a net upward force and float to the surface if $F_B > mg$; that is, if $\rho_F V g > \rho_O V g$ or $\rho_F > \rho_O$. At equilibrium—that is, when floating—the buoyant force on an object has magnitude equal to the weight of the object. For example, a log whose specific gravity is 0.60 and whose volume is 2.0 m³ has a mass $m = \rho_O V = (0.60 \times 10^3 \text{ kg/m}^3)(2.0 \text{ m}^3) = 1200 \text{ kg}$. If the log is fully submerged, it will displace a mass of water $m_F = \rho_F V = (1000 \text{ kg/m}^3)(2.0 \text{ m}^3) = 2000 \text{ kg}$. Hence the buoyant force on the log will be greater than its weight, and it will float upward to the surface (Fig. 13–17). The log will come to equilibrium when it displaces 1200 kg of water, which means that 1.2 m³ of its volume will be submerged. This 1.2 m³ corresponds to 60% of the volume of the log $(1.2/2.0 = 0.60)$, so 60% of the log is submerged.

In general when an object floats, we have $F_B = mg$, which we can write as (see Fig. 13–18)

$$F_B = mg$$
$$\rho_F V_{\text{displ}} g = \rho_O V_O g,$$

where V_O is the full volume of the object and V_{displ} is the volume of fluid it displaces (= volume submerged). Thus

$$\frac{V_{\text{displ}}}{V_O} = \frac{\rho_O}{\rho_F}.$$

That is, the fraction of the object submerged is given by the ratio of the object's density to that of the fluid. If the fluid is water, this fraction equals the specific gravity of the object.

EXAMPLE 13–11 Hydrometer calibration.

A **hydrometer** is a simple instrument used to measure the specific gravity of a liquid by indicating how deeply the instrument sinks in the liquid. A particular hydrometer (Fig. 13–19) consists of a glass tube, weighted at the bottom, which is 25.0 cm long and 2.00 cm² in cross-sectional area, and has a mass of 45.0 g. How far from the end should the 1.000 mark be placed?

APPROACH The hydrometer will float in water if its density ρ is less than $\rho_w = 1.000 \text{ g/cm}^3$, the density of water. The fraction of the hydrometer submerged $(V_{\text{displaced}}/V_{\text{total}})$ is equal to the density ratio ρ/ρ_w.

SOLUTION The hydrometer has an overall density

$$\rho = \frac{m}{V} = \frac{45.0 \text{ g}}{(2.00 \text{ cm}^2)(25.0 \text{ cm})} = 0.900 \text{ g/cm}^3.$$

Thus, when placed in water, it will come to equilibrium when 0.900 of its volume is submerged. Since it is of uniform cross section, $(0.900)(25.0 \text{ cm}) = 22.5 \text{ cm}$ of its length will be submerged. The specific gravity of water is defined to be 1.000, so the mark should be placed 22.5 cm from the weighted end.

EXERCISE C On the hydrometer of Example 13–11, will the marks above the 1.000 mark represent higher or lower values of density of the liquid in which it is submerged?

Archimedes' principle is also useful in geology. According to the theories of plate tectonics and continental drift, the continents float on a fluid "sea" of slightly deformable rock (mantle rock). Some interesting calculations can be done using very simple models, which we consider in the Problems at the end of the Chapter.

Air is a fluid, and it too exerts a buoyant force. Ordinary objects weigh less in air than they do if weighed in a vacuum. Because the density of air is so small, the effect for ordinary solids is slight. There are objects, however, that *float* in air—helium-filled balloons, for example, because the density of helium is less than the density of air.

EXERCISE D Which of the following objects, submerged in water, experiences the largest magnitude of the buoyant force? (*a*) A 1-kg helium balloon; (*b*) 1 kg of wood; (*c*) 1 kg of ice; (*d*) 1 kg of iron; (*e*) all the same.

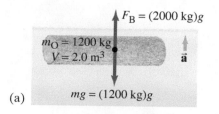

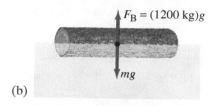

(a) $F_B = (2000 \text{ kg})g$ $m_O = 1200 \text{ kg}$ $V = 2.0 \text{ m}^3$ $\vec{a}$ $mg = (1200 \text{ kg})g$

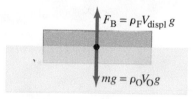

(b) $F_B = (1200 \text{ kg})g$ mg

FIGURE 13–17 (a) The fully submerged log accelerates upward because $F_B > mg$. It comes to equilibrium (b) when $\Sigma F = 0$, so $F_B = mg = (1200 \text{ kg})g$. Thus 1200 kg, or 1.2 m³, of water is displaced.

FIGURE 13–18 An object floating in equilibrium: $F_B = mg$.

$F_B = \rho_F V_{\text{displ}} g$

$mg = \rho_O V_O g$

FIGURE 13–19 A hydrometer. Example 13–11.

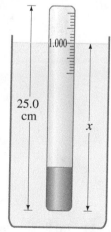

1.000

25.0 cm

x

EXAMPLE 13–12 **Helium balloon.** What volume V of helium is needed if a balloon is to lift a load of 180 kg (including the weight of the empty balloon)?

APPROACH The buoyant force on the helium balloon, F_B, which is equal to the weight of displaced air, must be at least equal to the weight of the helium plus the weight of the balloon and load (Fig. 13–20). Table 13–1 gives the density of helium as 0.179 kg/m³.

SOLUTION The buoyant force must have a minimum value of

$$F_B = (m_{He} + 180 \text{ kg})g.$$

This equation can be written in terms of density using Archimedes' principle:

$$\rho_{air} V g = (\rho_{He} V + 180 \text{ kg})g.$$

Solving now for V, we find

$$V = \frac{180 \text{ kg}}{\rho_{air} - \rho_{He}} = \frac{180 \text{ kg}}{(1.29 \text{ kg/m}^3 - 0.179 \text{ kg/m}^3)} = 160 \text{ m}^3.$$

NOTE This is the minimum volume needed near the Earth's surface, where $\rho_{air} = 1.29 \text{ kg/m}^3$. To reach a high altitude, a greater volume would be needed since the density of air decreases with altitude.

FIGURE 13–20 Example 13–12.

13–8 Fluids in Motion; Flow Rate and the Equation of Continuity

We now turn to the subject of fluids in motion, which is called **fluid dynamics**, or (especially if the fluid is water) **hydrodynamics**.

We can distinguish two main types of fluid flow. If the flow is smooth, such that neighboring layers of the fluid slide by each other smoothly, the flow is said to be **streamline** or **laminar flow**.† In streamline flow, each particle of the fluid follows a smooth path, called a **streamline**, and these paths do not cross one another (Fig. 13–21a). Above a certain speed, the flow becomes turbulent. **Turbulent flow** is characterized by erratic, small, whirlpool-like circles called *eddy currents* or *eddies* (Fig. 13-21b). Eddies absorb a great deal of energy, and although a certain amount of internal friction called **viscosity** is present even during streamline flow, it is much greater when the flow is turbulent. A few tiny drops of ink or food coloring dropped into a moving liquid can quickly reveal whether the flow is streamline or turbulent.

†The word *laminar* means "in layers."

FIGURE 13–21 (a) Streamline, or laminar, flow; (b) turbulent flow. The photos show airflow around an airfoil or airplane wing (more in Section 13–10).

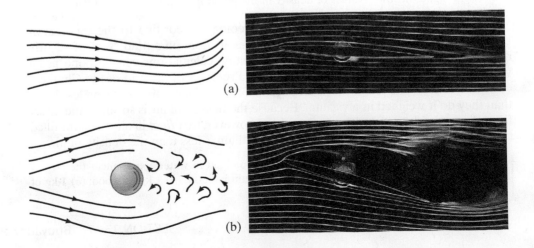

(a)

(b)

Let us consider the steady laminar flow of a fluid through an enclosed tube or pipe as shown in Fig. 13–22. First we determine how the speed of the fluid changes when the size of the tube changes. The mass **flow rate** is defined as the mass Δm of fluid that passes a given point per unit time Δt:

$$\text{mass flow rate} = \frac{\Delta m}{\Delta t}.$$

In Fig. 13–22, the volume of fluid passing point 1 (that is, through area A_1) in a time Δt is $A_1 \Delta \ell_1$, where $\Delta \ell_1$ is the distance the fluid moves in time Δt. Since the velocity† of fluid passing point 1 is $v_1 = \Delta \ell_1 / \Delta t$, the mass flow rate through area A_1 is

$$\frac{\Delta m_1}{\Delta t} = \frac{\rho_1 \Delta V_1}{\Delta t} = \frac{\rho_1 A_1 \Delta \ell_1}{\Delta t} = \rho_1 A_1 v_1,$$

where $\Delta V_1 = A_1 \Delta \ell_1$ is the volume of mass Δm_1, and ρ_1 is the fluid density. Similarly, at point 2 (through area A_2), the flow rate is $\rho_2 A_2 v_2$. Since no fluid flows in or out the sides, the flow rates through A_1 and A_2 must be equal. Thus, since

$$\frac{\Delta m_1}{\Delta t} = \frac{\Delta m_2}{\Delta t},$$

then

$$\rho_1 A_1 v_1 = \rho_2 A_2 v_2. \tag{13–7a}$$

This is called the **equation of continuity**.

If the fluid is incompressible (ρ doesn't change with pressure), which is an excellent approximation for liquids under most circumstances (and sometimes for gases as well), then $\rho_1 = \rho_2$, and the equation of continuity becomes

$$A_1 v_1 = A_2 v_2. \qquad [\rho = \text{constant}] \tag{13–7b}$$

The product Av represents the *volume rate of flow* (volume of fluid passing a given point per second), since $\Delta V / \Delta t = A \Delta \ell / \Delta t = Av$, which in SI units is m^3/s. Equation 13–7b tells us that where the cross-sectional area is large, the velocity is small, and where the area is small, the velocity is large. That this is reasonable can be seen by looking at a river. A river flows slowly through a meadow where it is broad, but speeds up to torrential speed when passing through a narrow gorge.

EXAMPLE 13–13 **ESTIMATE** **Blood flow.** In humans, blood flows from the heart into the aorta, from which it passes into the major arteries. These branch into the small arteries (arterioles), which in turn branch into myriads of tiny capillaries, Fig. 13–23. The blood returns to the heart via the veins. The radius of the aorta is about 1.2 cm, and the blood passing through it has a speed of about 40 cm/s. A typical capillary has a radius of about 4×10^{-4} cm, and blood flows through it at a speed of about 5×10^{-4} m/s. Estimate the number of capillaries that are in the body.

APPROACH We assume the density of blood doesn't vary significantly from the aorta to the capillaries. By the equation of continuity, the volume flow rate in the aorta must equal the volume flow rate through *all* the capillaries. The total area of all the capillaries is given by the area of one capillary multiplied by the total number N of capillaries.

SOLUTION Let A_1 be the area of the aorta and A_2 be the area of *all* the capillaries through which blood flows. Then $A_2 = N \pi r_{\text{cap}}^2$, where $r_{\text{cap}} \approx 4 \times 10^{-4}$ cm is the estimated average radius of one capillary. From the equation of continuity (Eq. 13–7b), we have

$$v_2 A_2 = v_1 A_1$$
$$v_2 N \pi r_{\text{cap}}^2 = v_1 \pi r_{\text{aorta}}^2$$

so

$$N = \frac{v_1}{v_2} \frac{r_{\text{aorta}}^2}{r_{\text{cap}}^2} = \left(\frac{0.40 \text{ m/s}}{5 \times 10^{-4} \text{ m/s}} \right) \left(\frac{1.2 \times 10^{-2} \text{ m}}{4 \times 10^{-6} \text{ m}} \right)^2 \approx 7 \times 10^9,$$

or on the order of 10 billion capillaries.

---

†If there were no viscosity, the velocity would be the same across a cross section of the tube. Real fluids have viscosity, and this internal friction causes different layers of the fluid to flow at different speeds. In this case v_1 and v_2 represent the average speeds at each cross section.

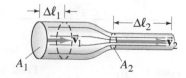

FIGURE 13–22 Fluid flow through a pipe of varying diameter.

PHYSICS APPLIED
Blood flow

FIGURE 13–23
Human circulatory system.

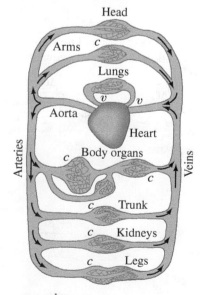

v = valves
c = capillaries

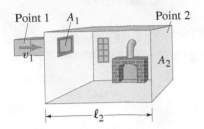

FIGURE 13–24 Example 13–14.

EXAMPLE 13–14 Heating duct to a room. What area must a heating duct have if air moving 3.0 m/s along it can replenish the air every 15 minutes in a room of volume 300 m³? Assume the air's density remains constant.

APPROACH We apply the equation of continuity at constant density, Eq. 13–7b, to the air that flows through the duct (point 1 in Fig. 13–24) and then into the room (point 2). The volume flow rate in the room equals the volume of the room divided by the 15-min replenishing time.

SOLUTION Consider the room as a large section of the duct, Fig. 13–24, and think of air equal to the volume of the room as passing by point 2 in $t = 15\,\text{min} = 900\,\text{s}$. Reasoning in the same way we did to obtain Eq. 13–7a (changing Δt to t), we write $v_2 = \ell_2/t$ so $A_2 v_2 = A_2 \ell_2/t = V_2/t$, where V_2 is the volume of the room. Then the equation of continuity becomes $A_1 v_1 = A_2 v_2 = V_2/t$ and

$$A_1 = \frac{V_2}{v_1 t} = \frac{300\,\text{m}^3}{(3.0\,\text{m/s})(900\,\text{s})} = 0.11\,\text{m}^2.$$

If the duct is square, then each side has length $\ell = \sqrt{A} = 0.33\,\text{m}$, or 33 cm. A rectangular duct 20 cm × 55 cm will also do.

13–9 Bernoulli's Equation

Have you ever wondered why an airplane can fly, or how a sailboat can move against the wind? These are examples of a principle worked out by Daniel Bernoulli (1700–1782) concerning fluids in motion. In essence, **Bernoulli's principle** states that *where the velocity of a fluid is high, the pressure is low, and where the velocity is low, the pressure is high.* For example, if the pressures in the fluid at points 1 and 2 of Fig. 13–22 are measured, it will be found that the pressure is lower at point 2, where the velocity is greater, than it is at point 1, where the velocity is smaller. At first glance, this might seem strange; you might expect that the greater speed at point 2 would imply a higher pressure. But this cannot be the case. For if the pressure in the fluid at point 2 were higher than at point 1, this higher pressure would slow the fluid down, whereas in fact it has sped up in going from point 1 to point 2. Thus the pressure at point 2 must be less than at point 1, to be consistent with the fact that the fluid accelerates.

To help clarify any misconceptions, a faster fluid *would* exert a greater force on an obstacle placed in its path. But that is not what we mean by the pressure in a fluid, and besides we are not considering obstacles that interrupt the flow. We are examining smooth streamline flow. The fluid pressure is exerted on the walls of a tube or pipe, or on the surface of any material the fluid passes over.

Bernoulli developed an equation that expresses this principle quantitatively. To derive Bernoulli's equation, we assume the flow is steady and laminar, the fluid is incompressible, and the viscosity is small enough to be ignored. To be general, we assume the fluid is flowing in a tube of nonuniform cross section that varies in height above some reference level, Fig. 13–25. We will consider the volume of fluid shown in color and calculate the work done to move it from the position shown in Fig. 13–25a to that shown in Fig. 13–25b. In this process, fluid entering area A_1 flows a distance $\Delta\ell_1$ and forces the fluid at area A_2 to move a distance $\Delta\ell_2$. The fluid to the left of area A_1 exerts a pressure P_1 on our section of fluid and does an amount of work

$$W_1 = F_1 \Delta\ell_1 = P_1 A_1 \Delta\ell_1.$$

At area A_2, the work done on our cross section of fluid is

$$W_2 = -P_2 A_2 \Delta\ell_2.$$

The negative sign is present because the force exerted on the fluid is opposite to the motion (thus the fluid shown in color does work on the fluid to the right of point 2). Work is also done on the fluid by the force of gravity. The net effect of the process shown in Fig. 13–25 is to move a mass m of volume $A_1 \Delta\ell_1$ ($= A_2 \Delta\ell_2$, since the

FIGURE 13–25 Fluid flow: for derivation of Bernoulli's equation.

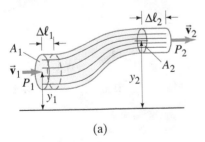

(a)

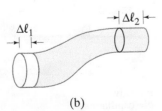

(b)

fluid is incompressible) from point 1 to point 2, so the work done by gravity is

$$W_3 = -mg(y_2 - y_1),$$

where y_1 and y_2 are heights of the center of the tube above some (arbitrary) reference level. In the case shown in Fig. 13–25, this term is negative since the motion is uphill against the force of gravity. The net work W done on the fluid is thus

$$W = W_1 + W_2 + W_3$$

$$W = P_1 A_1 \Delta\ell_1 - P_2 A_2 \Delta\ell_2 - mgy_2 + mgy_1.$$

According to the work-energy principle (Section 7–4), the net work done on a system is equal to its change in kinetic energy. Hence

$$\tfrac{1}{2}mv_2^2 - \tfrac{1}{2}mv_1^2 = P_1 A_1 \Delta\ell_1 - P_2 A_2 \Delta\ell_2 - mgy_2 + mgy_1.$$

The mass m has volume $A_1 \Delta\ell_1 = A_2 \Delta\ell_2$ for an incompressible fluid. Thus we can substitute $m = \rho A_1 \Delta\ell_1 = \rho A_2 \Delta\ell_2$, and then divide through by $A_1 \Delta\ell_1 = A_2 \Delta\ell_2$, to obtain

$$\tfrac{1}{2}\rho v_2^2 - \tfrac{1}{2}\rho v_1^2 = P_1 - P_2 - \rho gy_2 + \rho gy_1,$$

which we rearrange to get

$$P_1 + \tfrac{1}{2}\rho v_1^2 + \rho gy_1 = P_2 + \tfrac{1}{2}\rho v_2^2 + \rho gy_2. \qquad \textbf{(13–8)} \qquad \textit{Bernoulli's equation}$$

This is **Bernoulli's equation**. Since points 1 and 2 can be any two points along a tube of flow, Bernoulli's equation can be written as

$$P + \tfrac{1}{2}\rho v^2 + \rho gy = \text{constant}$$

at every point in the fluid, where y is the height of the center of the tube above a fixed reference level. [Note that if there is no flow $(v_1 = v_2 = 0)$, then Eq. 13–8 reduces to the hydrostatic equation, Eq. 13–6a: $P_2 - P_1 = -\rho g(y_2 - y_1)$.]

Bernoulli's equation is an expression of the law of energy conservation, since we derived it from the work-energy principle.

EXERCISE F As water in a level pipe passes from a narrow cross section of pipe to a wider cross section, how does the pressure against the walls change?

EXAMPLE 13–15 **Flow and pressure in a hot-water heating system.** Water circulates throughout a house in a hot-water heating system. If the water is pumped at a speed of 0.50 m/s through a 4.0-cm-diameter pipe in the basement under a pressure of 3.0 atm, what will be the flow speed and pressure in a 2.6-cm-diameter pipe on the second floor 5.0 m above? Assume the pipes do not divide into branches.

APPROACH We use the equation of continuity at constant density to determine the flow speed on the second floor, and then Bernoulli's equation to find the pressure.

SOLUTION We take v_2 in the equation of continuity, Eq. 13–7, as the flow speed on the second floor, and v_1 as the flow speed in the basement. Noting that the areas are proportional to the radii squared $(A = \pi r^2)$, we obtain

$$v_2 = \frac{v_1 A_1}{A_2} = \frac{v_1 \pi r_1^2}{\pi r_2^2} = (0.50\,\text{m/s})\frac{(0.020\,\text{m})^2}{(0.013\,\text{m})^2} = 1.2\,\text{m/s}.$$

To find the pressure on the second floor, we use Bernoulli's equation (Eq. 13–8):

$$\begin{aligned}
P_2 &= P_1 + \rho g(y_1 - y_2) + \tfrac{1}{2}\rho(v_1^2 - v_2^2) \\
&= (3.0 \times 10^5\,\text{N/m}^2) + (1.0 \times 10^3\,\text{kg/m}^3)(9.8\,\text{m/s}^2)(-5.0\,\text{m}) \\
&\quad + \tfrac{1}{2}(1.0 \times 10^3\,\text{kg/m}^3)\big[(0.50\,\text{m/s})^2 - (1.2\,\text{m/s})^2\big] \\
&= (3.0 \times 10^5\,\text{N/m}^2) - (4.9 \times 10^4\,\text{N/m}^2) - (6.0 \times 10^2\,\text{N/m}^2) \\
&= 2.5 \times 10^5\,\text{N/m}^2 = 2.5\,\text{atm}.
\end{aligned}$$

NOTE The velocity term contributes very little in this case.

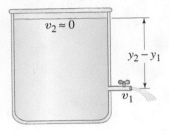

FIGURE 13-26 Torricelli's theorem: $v_1 = \sqrt{2g(y_2 - y_1)}$.

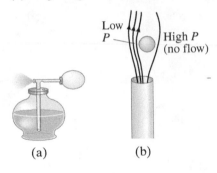

FIGURE 13-27 Examples of Bernoulli's principle: (a) atomizer, (b) Ping-Pong ball in jet of air.

(a)   (b)

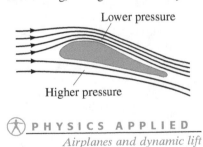

FIGURE 13-28 Lift on an airplane wing. We are in the reference frame of the wing, seeing the air flow by.

Lower pressure

Higher pressure

⊕ P H Y S I C S   A P P L I E D
Airplanes and dynamic lift

13–10 Applications of Bernoulli's Principle: Torricelli, Airplanes, Baseballs, TIA

Bernoulli's equation can be applied to many situations. One example is to calculate the velocity, v_1, of a liquid flowing out of a spigot at the bottom of a reservoir, Fig. 13–26. We choose point 2 in Eq. 13–8 to be the top surface of the liquid. Assuming the diameter of the reservoir is large compared to that of the spigot, v_2 will be almost zero. Points 1 (the spigot) and 2 (top surface) are open to the atmosphere, so the pressure at both points is equal to atmospheric pressure: $P_1 = P_2$. Then Bernoulli's equation becomes

$$\tfrac{1}{2}\rho v_1^2 + \rho g y_1 = \rho g y_2$$

or

$$v_1 = \sqrt{2g(y_2 - y_1)}. \tag{13–9}$$

This result is called **Torricelli's theorem**. Although it is seen to be a special case of Bernoulli's equation, it was discovered a century earlier by Evangelista Torricelli. Equation 13–9 tells us that the liquid leaves the spigot with the same speed that a freely falling object would attain if falling from the same height. This should not be too surprising since Bernoulli's equation relies on the conservation of energy.

Another special case of Bernoulli's equation arises when a fluid is flowing horizontally with no significant change in height; that is, $y_1 = y_2$. Then Eq. 13–8 becomes

$$P_1 + \tfrac{1}{2}\rho v_1^2 = P_2 + \tfrac{1}{2}\rho v_2^2, \tag{13–10}$$

which tells us quantitatively that the speed is high where the pressure is low, and vice versa. It explains many common phenomena, some of which are illustrated in Figs. 13–27 to 13–32. The pressure in the air blown at high speed across the top of the vertical tube of a perfume atomizer (Fig. 13–27a) is less than the normal air pressure acting on the surface of the liquid in the bowl. Thus atmospheric pressure in the bowl pushes the perfume up the tube because of the lower pressure at the top. A Ping-Pong ball can be made to float above a blowing jet of air (some vacuum cleaners can blow air), Fig. 13–27b; if the ball begins to leave the jet of air, the higher pressure in the still air outside the jet pushes the ball back in.

EXERCISE G Return to Chapter-Opening Question 2, page 339, and answer it again now. Try to explain why you may have answered differently the first time. Try it and see.

Airplane Wings and Dynamic Lift

Airplanes experience a "lift" force on their wings, keeping them up in the air, if they are moving at a sufficiently high speed relative to the air and the wing is tilted upward at a small angle (the "attack angle"), as in Fig. 13–28, where streamlines of air are shown rushing by the wing. (We are in the reference frame of the wing, as if sitting on the wing.) The upward tilt, as well as the rounded upper surface of the wing, causes the streamlines to be forced upward and to be crowded together above the wing. The area for air flow between any two streamlines is reduced as the streamlines get closer together, so from the equation of continuity $(A_1 v_1 = A_2 v_2)$, the air speed increases above the wing where the streamlines are squished together. (Recall also how the crowded streamlines in a pipe constriction, Fig. 13–22, indicate the velocity is higher in the constriction.) Because the air speed is greater above the wing than below it, the pressure above the wing is less than the pressure below the wing (Bernoulli's principle). Hence there is a net upward force on the wing called **dynamic lift**. Experiments show that the speed of air above the wing can even be double the speed of the air below it. (Friction between the air and wing exerts a *drag force*, toward the rear, which must be overcome by the plane's engines.)

A flat wing, or one with symmetric cross section, will experience lift as long as the front of the wing is tilted upward (attack angle). The wing shown in Fig. 13–28 can experience lift even if the attack angle is zero, because the rounded upper surface deflects air up, squeezing the streamlines together. Airplanes can fly upside down, experiencing lift, if the attack angle is sufficient to deflect streamlines up and closer together.

Our picture considers streamlines; but if the attack angle is larger than about 15°, turbulence sets in (Fig. 13–21b) leading to greater drag and less lift, causing the wing to "stall" and the plane to drop.

From another point of view, the upward tilt of a wing means the air moving horizontally in front of the wing is deflected downward; the change in momentum of the rebounding air molecules results in an upward force on the wing (Newton's third law).

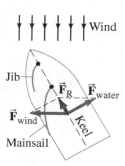

Sailboats

A sailboat can move *against* the wind, with the aid of the Bernoulli effect, by setting the sails at an angle, as shown in Fig. 13–29. The air travels rapidly over the bulging front surface of the sail, and the relatively still air filling the sail exerts a greater pressure behind the sail, resulting in a net force on the sail, $\vec{F}_{wind}$. This force would tend to make the boat move sideways if it weren't for the keel that extends vertically downward beneath the water: the water exerts a force ($\vec{F}_{water}$) on the keel nearly perpendicular to the keel. The resultant of these two forces ($\vec{F}_R$) is almost directly forward as shown.

FIGURE 13–29 Sailboat sailing against the wind.

Baseball Curve

Why a spinning pitched baseball (or tennis ball) curves can also be explained using Bernoulli's principle. It is simplest if we put ourselves in the reference frame of the ball, with the air rushing by, just as we did for the airplane wing. Suppose the ball is rotating counterclockwise as seen from above, Fig. 13–30. A thin layer of air ("boundary layer") is being dragged around by the ball. We are looking down on the ball, and at point A in Fig. 13–30, this boundary layer tends to slow down the oncoming air. At point B, the air rotating with the ball adds its speed to that of the oncoming air, so the air speed is higher at B than at A. The higher speed at B means the pressure is lower at B than at A, resulting in a net force toward B. The ball's path curves toward the left (as seen by the pitcher).

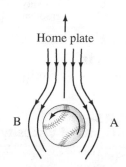

FIGURE 13–30 Looking down on a pitched baseball heading toward home plate. We are in the reference frame of the baseball, with the air flowing by.

Lack of Blood to the Brain—TIA

In medicine, one of many applications of Bernoulli's principle is to explain a TIA, a transient ischemic attack (meaning a temporary lack of blood supply to the brain). A person suffering a TIA may experience symptoms such as dizziness, double vision, headache, and weakness of the limbs. A TIA can occur as follows. Blood normally flows up to the brain at the back of the head via the two vertebral arteries—one going up each side of the neck—which meet to form the basilar artery just below the brain, as shown in Fig. 13–31. The vertebral arteries issue from the subclavian arteries, as shown, before the latter pass to the arms. When an arm is exercised vigorously, blood flow increases to meet the needs of the arm's muscles. If the subclavian artery on one side of the body is partially blocked, however, as in arteriosclerosis (hardening of the arteries), the blood velocity will have to be higher on that side to supply the needed blood. (Recall the equation of continuity: smaller area means larger velocity for the same flow rate, Eqs. 13–7.) The increased blood velocity past the opening to the vertebral artery results in lower pressure (Bernoulli's principle). Thus blood rising in the vertebral artery on the "good" side at normal pressure can be *diverted down* into the other vertebral artery because of the low pressure on that side, instead of passing upward to the brain. Hence the blood supply to the brain is reduced.

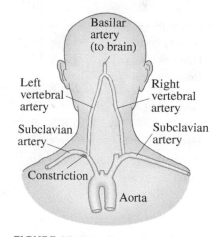

FIGURE 13–31 Rear of the head and shoulders showing arteries leading to the brain and to the arms. High blood velocity past the constriction in the left subclavian artery causes low pressure in the left vertebral artery, in which a reverse (downward) blood flow can then occur, resulting in a TIA, a loss of blood to the brain.

Other Applications

A **venturi tube** is essentially a pipe with a narrow constriction (the throat). The flowing fluid speeds up as it passes through this constriction, so the pressure is lower in the throat. A *venturi meter*, Fig. 13–32, is used to measure the flow speed of gases and liquids, including blood velocity in arteries.

Why does smoke go up a chimney? It's partly because hot air rises (it's less dense and therefore buoyant). But Bernoulli's principle also plays a role. When wind blows across the top of a chimney, the pressure is less there than inside the house. Hence, air and smoke are pushed up the chimney by the higher indoor pressure. Even on an apparently still night there is usually enough ambient air flow at the top of a chimney to assist upward flow of smoke.

FIGURE 13–32 Venturi meter.

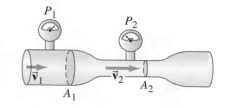

Bernoulli's equation ignores the effects of friction (viscosity) and the compressibility of the fluid. The energy that is transformed to internal (or potential) energy due to compression and to thermal energy by friction can be taken into account by adding terms to Eq. 13–8. These terms are difficult to calculate theoretically and are normally determined empirically. They do not significantly alter the explanations for the phenomena described above.

*13–11 Viscosity

Real fluids have a certain amount of internal friction called **viscosity**, as mentioned in Section 13–8. Viscosity exists in both liquids and gases, and is essentially a frictional force between adjacent layers of fluid as the layers move past one another. In liquids, viscosity is due to the electrical cohesive forces between the molecules. In gases, it arises from collisions between the molecules.

The viscosity of different fluids can be expressed quantitatively by a *coefficient of viscosity*, η (the Greek lowercase letter eta), which is defined in the following way. A thin layer of fluid is placed between two flat plates. One plate is stationary and the other is made to move, Fig. 13–33. The fluid directly in contact with each plate is held to the surface by the adhesive force between the molecules of the liquid and those of the plate. Thus the upper surface of the fluid moves with the same speed v as the upper plate, whereas the fluid in contact with the stationary plate remains stationary. The stationary layer of fluid retards the flow of the layer just above it, which in turn retards the flow of the next layer, and so on. Thus the velocity varies continuously from 0 to v, as shown. The increase in velocity divided by the distance over which this change is made—equal to v/ℓ—is called the *velocity gradient*. To move the upper plate requires a force, which you can verify by moving a flat plate across a puddle of syrup on a table. For a given fluid, it is found that the force required, F, is proportional to the area of fluid in contact with each plate, A, and to the speed, v, and is inversely proportional to the separation, ℓ, of the plates: $F \propto vA/\ell$. For different fluids, the more viscous the fluid, the greater is the required force. Hence the proportionality constant for this equation is defined as the coefficient of viscosity, η:

$$F = \eta A \frac{v}{\ell}. \tag{13–11}$$

Solving for η, we find $\eta = F\ell/vA$. The SI unit for η is $\mathrm{N \cdot s/m^2} = \mathrm{Pa \cdot s}$ (pascal·second). In the cgs system, the unit is $\mathrm{dyne \cdot s/cm^2}$, which is called a *poise* (P). Viscosities are often given in centipoise $(1\ \mathrm{cP} = 10^{-2}\ \mathrm{P})$. Table 13–3 lists the coefficient of viscosity for various fluids. The temperature is also specified, since it has a strong effect; the viscosity of liquids such as motor oil, for example, decreases rapidly as temperature increases.[†]

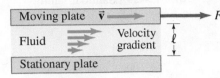

FIGURE 13–33
Determination of viscosity.

TABLE 13–3
Coefficients of Viscosity

Fluid (temperature in °C)	Coefficient of Viscosity, η (Pa·s)[†]
Water (0°)	1.8×10^{-3}
(20°)	1.0×10^{-3}
(100°)	0.3×10^{-3}
Whole blood (37°)	$\approx 4 \times 10^{-3}$
Blood plasma (37°)	$\approx 1.5 \times 10^{-3}$
Ethyl alcohol (20°)	1.2×10^{-3}
Engine oil (30°) (SAE 10)	200×10^{-3}
Glycerine (20°)	1500×10^{-3}
Air (20°)	0.018×10^{-3}
Hydrogen (0°)	0.009×10^{-3}
Water vapor (100°)	0.013×10^{-3}

[†] 1 Pa·s = 10 P = 1000 cP.

*13–12 Flow in Tubes: Poiseuille's Equation, Blood Flow

If a fluid had no viscosity, it could flow through a level tube or pipe without a force being applied. Viscosity acts like a sort of friction (between fluid layers moving at slightly different speeds), so a pressure difference between the ends of a level tube is necessary for the steady flow of any real fluid, be it water or oil in a pipe, or blood in the circulatory system of a human.

The French scientist J. L. Poiseuille (1799–1869), who was interested in the physics of blood circulation (and after whom the poise is named), determined how the variables affect the flow rate of an incompressible fluid undergoing laminar flow in a cylindrical tube. His result, known as *Poiseuille's equation*, is:

$$Q = \frac{\pi R^4 (P_1 - P_2)}{8\eta\ell}, \tag{13–12}$$

where R is the inside radius of the tube, ℓ is the tube length, $P_1 - P_2$ is the pressure

[†]The Society of Automotive Engineers assigns numbers to represent the viscosity of oils: 30 weight (SAE 30) is more viscous than 10 weight. Multigrade oils, such as 20–50, are designed to maintain viscosity as temperature increases; 20–50 means the oil is 20 wt when cool but is like a 50-wt pure oil when it is hot (engine running temperature).

difference between the ends, η is the coefficient of viscosity, and Q is the volume rate of flow (volume of fluid flowing past a given point per unit time which in SI has units of m^3/s). Equation 13–12 applies only to laminar flow.

Poiseuille's equation tells us that the flow rate Q is directly proportional to the "pressure gradient," $(P_1 - P_2)/\ell$, and it is inversely proportional to the viscosity of the fluid. This is just what we might expect. It may be surprising, however, that Q also depends on the *fourth* power of the tube's radius. This means that for the same pressure gradient, if the tube radius is halved, the flow rate is decreased by a factor of 16! Thus the rate of flow, or alternately the pressure required to maintain a given flow rate, is greatly affected by only a small change in tube radius.

An interesting example of this R^4 dependence is *blood flow* in the human body. Poiseuille's equation is valid only for the streamline flow of an incompressible fluid. So it cannot be precisely accurate for blood whose flow is not without turbulence and that contains blood cells (whose diameter is almost equal to that of a capillary). Nonetheless, Poiseuille's equation does give a reasonable first approximation. Because the radius of arteries is reduced as a result of arteriosclerosis (thickening and hardening of artery walls) and by cholesterol buildup, the pressure gradient must be increased to maintain the same flow rate. If the radius is reduced by half, the heart would have to increase the pressure by a factor of about $2^4 = 16$ in order to maintain the same blood-flow rate. The heart must work much harder under these conditions, but usually cannot maintain the original flow rate. Thus, high blood pressure is an indication both that the heart is working harder and that the blood-flow rate is reduced.

⊛ PHYSICS APPLIED
Blood flow

*13–13 Surface Tension and Capillarity

The *surface* of a liquid at rest behaves in an interesting way, almost as if it were a stretched membrane under tension. For example, a drop of water on the end of a dripping faucet, or hanging from a thin branch in the early morning dew (Fig. 13–34), forms into a nearly spherical shape as if it were a tiny balloon filled with water. A steel needle can be made to float on the surface of water even though it is denser than the water. The surface of a liquid acts like it is under tension, and this tension, acting along the surface, arises from the attractive forces between the molecules. This effect is called **surface tension**. More specifically, a quantity called the *surface tension*, γ (the Greek letter gamma), is defined as the force F per unit length ℓ that acts perpendicular to any line or cut in a liquid surface, tending to pull the surface closed:

$$\gamma = \frac{F}{\ell}. \tag{13–13}$$

To understand this, consider the U-shaped apparatus shown in Fig. 13–35 which encloses a thin film of liquid. Because of surface tension, a force F is required to pull the movable wire and thus increase the surface area of the liquid. The liquid contained by the wire apparatus is a thin film having both a top and a bottom surface. Hence the total length of the surface being increased is 2ℓ, and the surface tension is $\gamma = F/2\ell$. A delicate apparatus of this type can be used to measure the surface tension of various liquids. The surface tension of water is $0.072\ \text{N/m}$ at 20°C. Table 13–4 gives the values for several substances. Note that temperature has a considerable effect on the surface tension.

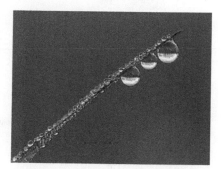

FIGURE 13–34 Spherical water droplets, dew on a blade of grass.

**TABLE 13–4
Surface Tension of Some Substances**

Substance (temperature in °C)	Surface Tension (N/m)
Mercury (20°)	0.44
Blood, whole (37°)	0.058
Blood, plasma (37°)	0.073
Alcohol, ethyl (20°)	0.023
Water (0°)	0.076
(20°)	0.072
(100°)	0.059
Benzene (20°)	0.029
Soap solution (20°)	≈ 0.025
Oxygen (−193°)	0.016

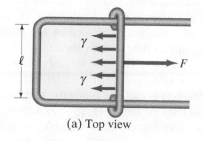

(a) Top view

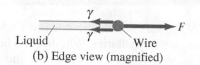

Liquid   Wire
(b) Edge view (magnified)

FIGURE 13–35 U-shaped wire apparatus holding a film of liquid to measure surface tension ($\gamma = F/2\ell$).

FIGURE 13–36 A water strider.

Because of surface tension, some insects (Fig. 13–36) can walk on water, and objects more dense than water, such as a steel needle, can float on the surface. Figure 13–37a shows how the surface tension can support the weight w of an object. Actually, the object sinks slightly into the fluid, so w is the "effective weight" of that object—its true weight less the buoyant force.

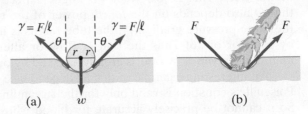

FIGURE 13–37 Surface tension acting on (a) a sphere, and (b) an insect leg. Example 13–16.

EXAMPLE 13–16 ESTIMATE Insect walks on water.

The base of an insect's leg is approximately spherical in shape, with a radius of about 2.0×10^{-5} m. The 0.0030-g mass of the insect is supported equally by its six legs. Estimate the angle θ (see Fig. 13–37) for an insect on the surface of water. Assume the water temperature is 20°C.

APPROACH Since the insect is in equilibrium, the upward surface tension force is equal to the pull of gravity downward on each leg. We ignore the buoyant force for this estimate.

SOLUTION For each leg, we assume the surface tension force acts all around a circle of radius r, at an angle θ, as shown in Fig. 13–37a. Only the vertical component, $\gamma \cos \theta$, acts to balance the weight mg. So we set the length ℓ in Eq. 13–13 equal to the circumference of the circle, $\ell \approx 2\pi r$. Then the net upward force due to surface tension is $F_y \approx (\gamma \cos \theta)\ell \approx 2\pi r \gamma \cos \theta$. We set this surface tension force equal to one-sixth the weight of the insect since it has six legs:

$$2\pi r \gamma \cos \theta \approx \tfrac{1}{6}mg$$
$$(6.28)(2.0 \times 10^{-5}\,\text{m})(0.072\,\text{N/m})\cos\theta \approx \tfrac{1}{6}(3.0 \times 10^{-6}\,\text{kg})(9.8\,\text{m/s}^2)$$
$$\cos\theta \approx \frac{0.49}{0.90} = 0.54.$$

So $\theta \approx 57°$. If $\cos \theta$ had come out greater than 1, the surface tension would not be great enough to support the insect's weight.

NOTE Our estimate ignored the buoyant force and ignored any difference between the radius of the insect's "foot" and the radius of the surface depression.

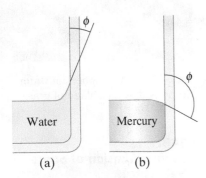

FIGURE 13–38 (a) Water "wets" the surface of glass, whereas (b) mercury does not "wet" the glass.

FIGURE 13–39 Capillarity.

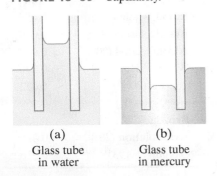

(a) Glass tube in water   (b) Glass tube in mercury

Soaps and detergents lower the surface tension of water. This is desirable for washing and cleaning since the high surface tension of pure water prevents it from penetrating easily between the fibers of material and into tiny crevices. Substances that reduce the surface tension of a liquid are called *surfactants*.

Surface tension plays a role in another interesting phenomenon, capillarity. It is a common observation that water in a glass container rises up slightly where it touches the glass, Fig. 13–38a. The water is said to "wet" the glass. Mercury, on the other hand, is depressed when it touches the glass, Fig. 13–38b; the mercury does not wet the glass. Whether a liquid wets a solid surface is determined by the relative strength of the cohesive forces between the molecules of the liquid compared to the adhesive forces between the molecules of the liquid and those of the container. *Cohesion* refers to the force between molecules of the same type, whereas *adhesion* refers to the force between molecules of different types. Water wets glass because the water molecules are more strongly attracted to the glass molecules than they are to other water molecules. The opposite is true for mercury: the cohesive forces are stronger than the adhesive forces.

In tubes having very small diameters, liquids are observed to rise or fall relative to the level of the surrounding liquid. This phenomenon is called **capillarity**, and such thin tubes are called **capillaries**. Whether the liquid rises or falls (Fig. 13–39) depends on the relative strengths of the adhesive and cohesive forces. Thus water rises in a glass tube, whereas mercury falls. The actual amount of rise (or fall) depends on the surface tension—which is what keeps the liquid surface from breaking apart.

*13–14 Pumps, and the Heart

We conclude this Chapter with a brief discussion of pumps, including the heart. Pumps can be classified into categories according to their function. A *vacuum pump* is designed to reduce the pressure (usually of air) in a given vessel. A *force pump*, on the other hand, is a pump that is intended to increase the pressure—for example, to lift a liquid (such as water from a well) or to push a fluid through a pipe. Figure 13–40 illustrates the principle behind a simple reciprocating pump. It could be a vacuum pump, in which case the intake is connected to the vessel to be evacuated. A similar mechanism is used in some force pumps, and in this case the fluid is forced under increased pressure through the outlet.

A centrifugal pump (Fig. 13–41), or any force pump, can be used as a *circulating pump*—that is, to circulate a fluid around a closed path, such as the cooling water or lubricating oil in an automobile.

The heart of a human (and of other animals as well) is essentially a circulating pump. The action of a human heart is shown in Fig. 13–42. There are actually two separate paths for blood flow. The longer path takes blood to the parts of the body, via the arteries, bringing oxygen to body tissues and picking up carbon dioxide, which it carries back to the heart via veins. This blood is then pumped to the lungs (the second path), where the carbon dioxide is released and oxygen is taken up. The oxygen-laden blood is returned to the heart, where it is again pumped to the tissues of the body.

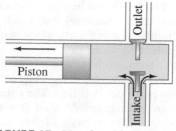

FIGURE 13–40 One kind of pump: the intake valve opens and air (or fluid that is being pumped) fills the empty space when the piston moves to the left. When the piston moves to the right (not shown), the outlet valve opens and fluid is forced out.

FIGURE 13–41 Centrifugal pump: the rotating blades force fluid through the outlet pipe; this kind of pump is used in vacuum cleaners and as a water pump in automobiles.

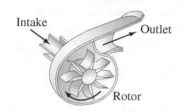

FIGURE 13–42 (a) In the diastole phase, the heart relaxes between beats. Blood moves into the heart; both atria fill rapidly. (b) When the atria contract, the systole or pumping phase begins. The contraction pushes the blood through the mitral and tricuspid valves into the ventricles. (c) The contraction of the ventricles forces the blood through the semilunar valves into the pulmonary artery, which leads to the lungs, and to the aorta (the body's largest artery), which leads to the arteries serving all the body. (d) When the heart relaxes, the semilunar valves close; blood fills the atria, beginning the cycle again.

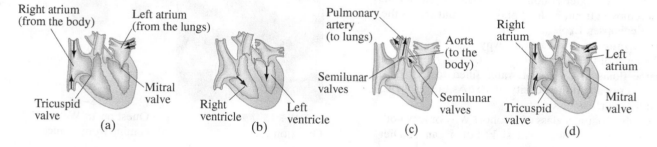

Summary

The three common phases of matter are **solid**, **liquid**, and **gas**. Liquids and gases are collectively called **fluids**, meaning they have the ability to flow. The **density** of a material is defined as its mass per unit volume:

$$\rho = \frac{m}{V}. \tag{13–1}$$

Specific gravity is the ratio of the density of the material to the density of water (at 4°C).

Pressure is defined as force per unit area:

$$P = \frac{F}{A}. \tag{13–2}$$

The pressure P at a depth h in a liquid is given by

$$P = \rho g h, \tag{13–3}$$

where ρ is the density of the liquid and g is the acceleration due to gravity. If the density of a fluid is not uniform, the pressure P varies with height y as

$$\frac{dP}{dy} = -\rho g. \tag{13–4}$$

Pascal's principle says that an external pressure applied to a confined fluid is transmitted throughout the fluid.

Pressure is measured using a manometer or other type of gauge. A **barometer** is used to measure atmospheric pressure. Standard **atmospheric pressure** (average at sea level) is $1.013 \times 10^5 \, \text{N/m}^2$. **Gauge pressure** is the total (absolute) pressure less atmospheric pressure.

Archimedes' principle states that an object submerged wholly or partially in a fluid is buoyed up by a force equal to the weight of fluid it displaces $\left(F_B = m_F g = \rho_F V_{\text{displ}} g \right)$.

Fluid flow can be characterized either as **streamline** (sometimes called **laminar**), in which the layers of fluid move smoothly and regularly along paths called **streamlines**, or as **turbulent**, in which case the flow is not smooth and regular but is characterized by irregularly shaped whirlpools.

Fluid flow rate is the mass or volume of fluid that passes a given point per unit time. The **equation of continuity** states that for an incompressible fluid flowing in an enclosed tube, the product of the velocity of flow and the cross-sectional area of the tube remains constant:

$$Av = \text{constant}. \qquad (13\text{--}7b)$$

Bernoulli's principle tells us that where the velocity of a fluid is high, the pressure in it is low, and where the velocity is low, the pressure is high. For steady laminar flow of an incompressible and nonviscous fluid, **Bernoulli's equation**, which is based on the law of conservation of energy, is

$$P_1 + \tfrac{1}{2}\rho v_1^2 + \rho g y_1 = P_2 + \tfrac{1}{2}\rho v_2^2 + \rho g y_2, \qquad (13\text{--}8)$$

for two points along the flow.

[***Viscosity** refers to friction within a fluid and is essentially a frictional force between adjacent layers of fluid as they move past one another.]

[***Liquid surfaces hold together as if under tension (**surface tension**), allowing drops to form and objects like needles and insects to stay on the surface.]

Questions

1. If one material has a higher density than another, must the molecules of the first be heavier than those of the second? Explain.

2. Airplane travelers sometimes note that their cosmetics bottles and other containers have leaked during a flight. What might cause this?

3. The three containers in Fig. 13–43 are filled with water to the same height and have the same surface area at the base; hence the water pressure, and the total force on the base of each, is the same. Yet the total weight of water is different for each. Explain this "hydrostatic paradox."

FIGURE 13–43
Question 3.

4. Consider what happens when you push both a pin and the blunt end of a pen against your skin with the same force. Decide what determines whether your skin is cut—the net force applied to it or the pressure.

5. A small amount of water is boiled in a 1-gallon metal can. The can is removed from the heat and the lid put on. As the can cools, it collapses. Explain.

6. When blood pressure is measured, why must the cuff be held at the level of the heart?

7. An ice cube floats in a glass of water filled to the brim. What can you say about the density of ice? As the ice melts, will the water overflow? Explain.

8. Will an ice cube float in a glass of alcohol? Why or why not?

9. A submerged can of Coke® will sink, but a can of Diet Coke® will float. (Try it!) Explain.

10. Why don't ships made of iron sink?

11. Explain how the tube in Fig. 13–44, known as a **siphon**, can transfer liquid from one container to a lower one even though the liquid must flow uphill for part of its journey. (Note that the tube must be filled with liquid to start with.)

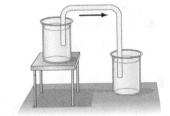

FIGURE 13–44
Question 11. A siphon.

12. A barge filled high with sand approaches a low bridge over the river and cannot quite pass under it. Should sand be added to, or removed from, the barge? [*Hint*: Consider Archimedes' principle.]

13. Explain why helium weather balloons, which are used to measure atmospheric conditions at high altitudes, are normally released while filled to only 10–20% of their maximum volume.

14. A row boat floats in a swimming pool, and the level of the water at the edge of the pool is marked. Consider the following situations and explain whether the level of the water will rise, fall, or stay the same. (*a*) The boat is removed from the water. (*b*) The boat in the water holds an iron anchor which is removed from the boat and placed on the shore. (*c*) The iron anchor is removed from the boat and dropped in the pool.

15. Will an empty balloon have precisely the same apparent weight on a scale as a balloon filled with air? Explain.

16. Why do you float higher in salt water than in fresh water?

17. If you dangle two pieces of paper vertically, a few inches apart (Fig. 13–45), and blow between them, how do you think the papers will move? Try it and see. Explain.

FIGURE 13–45
Question 17.

FIGURE 13–46
Question 18. Water coming from a faucet.

18. Why does the stream of water from a faucet become narrower as it falls (Fig. 13–46)?

19. Children are told to avoid standing too close to a rapidly moving train because they might get sucked under it. Is this possible? Explain.

20. A tall Styrofoam cup is filled with water. Two holes are punched in the cup near the bottom, and water begins rushing out. If the cup is dropped so it falls freely, will the water continue to flow from the holes? Explain.

21. Why do airplanes normally take off into the wind?

22. Two ships moving in parallel paths close to one another risk colliding. Why?

23. Why does the canvas top of a convertible bulge out when the car is traveling at high speed? [*Hint*: The windshield deflects air upward, pushing streamlines closer together.]

24. Roofs of houses are sometimes "blown" off (or are they pushed off?) during a tornado or hurricane. Explain using Bernoulli's principle.

Problems

13-2 Density and Specific Gravity

1. (I) The approximate volume of the granite monolith known as El Capitan in Yosemite National Park (Fig. 13–47) is about $10^8\,\text{m}^3$. What is its approximate mass?

FIGURE 13–47 Problem 1.

2. (I) What is the approximate mass of air in a living room $5.6\,\text{m} \times 3.8\,\text{m} \times 2.8\,\text{m}$?

3. (I) If you tried to smuggle gold bricks by filling your backpack, whose dimensions are $56\,\text{cm} \times 28\,\text{cm} \times 22\,\text{cm}$, what would its mass be?

4. (I) State your mass and then estimate your volume. [*Hint:* Because you can swim on or just under the surface of the water in a swimming pool, you have a pretty good idea of your density.]

5. (II) A bottle has a mass of 35.00 g when empty and 98.44 g when filled with water. When filled with another fluid, the mass is 89.22 g. What is the specific gravity of this other fluid?

6. (II) If 5.0 L of antifreeze solution (specific gravity = 0.80) is added to 4.0 L of water to make a 9.0-L mixture, what is the specific gravity of the mixture?

7. (III) The Earth is not a uniform sphere, but has regions of varying density. Consider a simple model of the Earth divided into three regions—inner core, outer core, and mantle. Each region is taken to have a unique constant density (the average density of that region in the real Earth):

Region	Radius (km)	Density (kg/m³)
Inner Core	0–1220	13,000
Outer Core	1220–3480	11,100
Mantle	3480–6371	4,400

(a) Use this model to predict the average density of the entire Earth. (b) The measured radius of the Earth is 6371 km and its mass is $5.98 \times 10^{24}\,\text{kg}$. Use these data to determine the actual average density of the Earth and compare it (as a percent difference) with the one you determined in (a).

13-3 to 13-6 Pressure; Pascal's Principle

8. (I) Estimate the pressure needed to raise a column of water to the same height as a 35-m-tall oak tree.

9. (I) Estimate the pressure exerted on a floor by (a) one pointed chair leg (66 kg on all four legs) of area = $0.020\,\text{cm}^2$, and (b) a 1300-kg elephant standing on one foot (area = $800\,\text{cm}^2$).

10. (I) What is the difference in blood pressure (mm-Hg) between the top of the head and bottom of the feet of a 1.70-m-tall person standing vertically?

11. (II) How high would the level be in an alcohol barometer at normal atmospheric pressure?

12. (II) In a movie, Tarzan evades his captors by hiding underwater for many minutes while breathing through a long, thin reed. Assuming the maximum pressure difference his lungs can manage and still breathe is −85 mm-Hg, calculate the deepest he could have been.

13. (II) The maximum gauge pressure in a hydraulic lift is 17.0 atm. What is the largest-size vehicle (kg) it can lift if the diameter of the output line is 22.5 cm?

14. (II) The gauge pressure in each of the four tires of an automobile is 240 kPa. If each tire has a "footprint" of $220\,\text{cm}^2$, estimate the mass of the car.

15. (II) (a) Determine the total force and the absolute pressure on the bottom of a swimming pool 28.0 m by 8.5 m whose uniform depth is 1.8 m. (b) What will be the pressure against the *side* of the pool near the bottom?

16. (II) A house at the bottom of a hill is fed by a full tank of water 5.0 m deep and connected to the house by a pipe that is 110 m long at an angle of 58° from the horizontal (Fig. 13–48). (a) Determine the water gauge pressure at the house. (b) How high could the water shoot if it came vertically out of a broken pipe in front of the house?

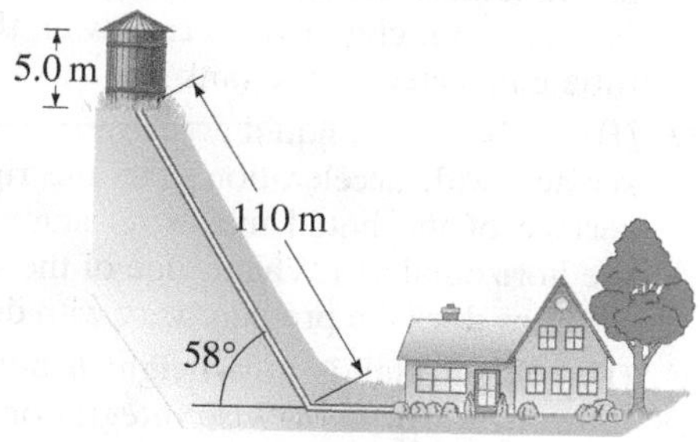

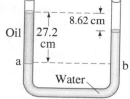

FIGURE 13–48 Problem 16.

17. (II) Water and then oil (which don't mix) are poured into a U-shaped tube, open at both ends. They come to equilibrium as shown in Fig. 13–49. What is the density of the oil? [*Hint:* Pressures at points a and b are equal. Why?]

FIGURE 13–49 Problem 17.

18. (II) In working out his principle, Pascal showed dramatically how force can be multiplied with fluid pressure. He placed a long, thin tube of radius $r = 0.30\,\text{cm}$ vertically into a wine barrel of radius $R = 21\,\text{cm}$, Fig. 13–50. He found that when the barrel was filled with water and the tube filled to a height of 12 m, the barrel burst. Calculate (a) the mass of water in the tube, and (b) the net force exerted by the water in the barrel on the lid just before rupture.

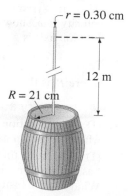

FIGURE 13–50 Problem 18 (not to scale).

19. (II) What is the normal pressure of the atmosphere at the summit of Mt. Everest, 8850 m above sea level?

20. (II) A hydraulic press for compacting powdered samples has a large cylinder which is 10.0 cm in diameter, and a small cylinder with a diameter of 2.0 cm (Fig. 13–51). A lever is attached to the small cylinder as shown. The sample, which is placed on the large cylinder, has an area of 4.0 cm². What is the pressure on the sample if 350 N is applied to the lever?

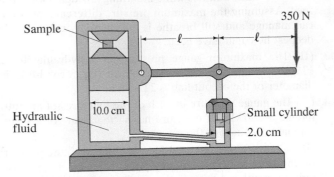

FIGURE 13–51 Problem 20.

21. (II) An open-tube mercury manometer is used to measure the pressure in an oxygen tank. When the atmospheric pressure is 1040 mbar, what is the absolute pressure (in Pa) in the tank if the height of the mercury in the open tube is (a) 21.0 cm higher, (b) 5.2 cm lower, than the mercury in the tube connected to the tank?

22. (III) A beaker of liquid accelerates from rest, on a horizontal surface, with acceleration a to the right. (a) Show that the surface of the liquid makes an angle $\theta = \tan^{-1}(a/g)$ with the horizontal. (b) Which edge of the water surface is higher? (c) How does the pressure vary with depth below the surface?

23. (III) Water stands at a height h behind a vertical dam of uniform width b. (a) Use integration to show that the total force of the water on the dam is $F = \frac{1}{2}\rho g h^2 b$. (b) Show that the torque about the base of the dam due to this force can be considered to act with a lever arm equal to $h/3$. (c) For a freestanding concrete dam of uniform thickness t and height h, what minimum thickness is needed to prevent overturning? Do you need to add in atmospheric pressure for this last part? Explain.

24. (III) Estimate the density of the water 5.4 km deep in the sea. (See Table 12–1 and Section 12–4 regarding bulk modulus.) By what fraction does it differ from the density at the surface?

25. (III) A cylindrical bucket of liquid (density ρ) is rotated about its symmetry axis, which is vertical. If the angular velocity is ω, show that the pressure at a distance r from the rotation axis is

$$P = P_0 + \frac{1}{2}\rho\omega^2 r^2,$$

where P_0 is the pressure at $r = 0$.

13–7 Buoyancy and Archimedes' Principle

26. (I) What fraction of a piece of iron will be submerged when it floats in mercury?

27. (I) A geologist finds that a Moon rock whose mass is 9.28 kg has an apparent mass of 6.18 kg when submerged in water. What is the density of the rock?

28. (II) A crane lifts the 16,000-kg steel hull of a sunken ship out of the water. Determine (a) the tension in the crane's cable when the hull is fully submerged in the water, and (b) the tension when the hull is completely out of the water.

29. (II) A spherical balloon has a radius of 7.35 m and is filled with helium. How large a cargo can it lift, assuming that the skin and structure of the balloon have a mass of 930 kg? Neglect the buoyant force on the cargo volume itself.

30. (II) A 74-kg person has an apparent mass of 54 kg (because of buoyancy) when standing in water that comes up to the hips. Estimate the mass of each leg. Assume the body has SG = 1.00.

31. (II) What is the likely identity of a metal (see Table 13–1) if a sample has a mass of 63.5 g when measured in air and an apparent mass of 55.4 g when submerged in water?

32. (II) Calculate the true mass (in vacuum) of a piece of aluminum whose apparent mass is 3.0000 kg when weighed in air.

33. (II) Because gasoline is less dense than water, drums containing gasoline will float in water. Suppose a 230-L steel drum is completely full of gasoline. What total volume of steel can be used in making the drum if the gasoline-filled drum is to float in fresh water?

34. (II) A scuba diver and her gear displace a volume of 65.0 L and have a total mass of 68.0 kg. (a) What is the buoyant force on the diver in seawater? (b) Will the diver sink or float?

35. (II) The specific gravity of ice is 0.917, whereas that of seawater is 1.025. What percent of an iceberg is above the surface of the water?

36. (II) Archimedes' principle can be used not only to determine the specific gravity of a solid using a known liquid (Example 13–10); the reverse can be done as well. (a) As an example, a 3.80-kg aluminum ball has an apparent mass of 2.10 kg when submerged in a particular liquid: calculate the density of the liquid. (b) Derive a formula for determining the density of a liquid using this procedure.

37. (II) (a) Show that the buoyant force F_B on a partially submerged object such as a ship acts at the center of gravity of the fluid before it is displaced. This point is called the **center of buoyancy**. (b) To ensure that a ship is in stable equilibrium, would it be better if its center of buoyancy was above, below, or at the same point as, its center of gravity? Explain. (See Fig. 13–52.)

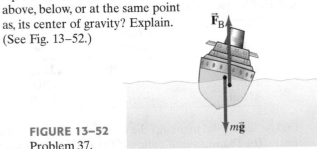

FIGURE 13–52
Problem 37.

38. (II) A cube of side length 10.0 cm and made of unknown material floats at the surface between water and oil. The oil has a density of 810 kg/m³. If the cube floats so that it is 72% in the water and 28% in the oil, what is the mass of the cube and what is the buoyant force on the cube?

39. (II) How many helium-filled balloons would it take to lift a person? Assume the person has a mass of 75 kg and that each helium-filled balloon is spherical with a diameter of 33 cm.

40. (II) A scuba tank, when fully submerged, displaces 15.7 L of seawater. The tank itself has a mass of 14.0 kg and, when "full," contains 3.00 kg of air. Assuming only a weight and buoyant force act, determine the net force (magnitude and direction) on the fully submerged tank at the beginning of a dive (when it is full of air) and at the end of a dive (when it no longer contains any air).

41. (III) If an object floats in water, its density can be determined by tying a sinker to it so that both the object and the sinker are submerged. Show that the specific gravity is given by $w/(w_1 - w_2)$, where w is the weight of the object alone in air, w_1 is the apparent weight when a sinker is tied to it and the sinker only is submerged, and w_2 is the apparent weight when both the object and the sinker are submerged.

42. (III) A 3.25-kg piece of wood (SG = 0.50) floats on water. What minimum mass of lead, hung from the wood by a string, will cause it to sink?

13–8 to 13–10 Fluid Flow, Bernoulli's Equation

43. (I) A 15-cm-radius air duct is used to replenish the air of a room 8.2 m × 5.0 m × 3.5 m every 12 min. How fast does the air flow in the duct?

44. (I) Using the data of Example 13–13, calculate the average speed of blood flow in the major arteries of the body which have a total cross-sectional area of about 2.0 cm².

45. (I) How fast does water flow from a hole at the bottom of a very wide, 5.3-m-deep storage tank filled with water? Ignore viscosity.

46. (II) A fish tank has dimensions 36 cm wide by 1.0 m long by 0.60 m high. If the filter should process all the water in the tank once every 4.0 h, what should the flow speed be in the 3.0-cm-diameter input tube for the filter?

47. (II) What gauge pressure in the water mains is necessary if a firehose is to spray water to a height of 18 m?

48. (II) A $\frac{5}{8}$-in. (inside) diameter garden hose is used to fill a round swimming pool 6.1 m in diameter. How long will it take to fill the pool to a depth of 1.2 m if water flows from the hose at a speed of 0.40 m/s?

49. (II) A 180-km/h wind blowing over the flat roof of a house causes the roof to lift off the house. If the house is 6.2 m × 12.4 m in size, estimate the weight of the roof. Assume the roof is not nailed down.

50. (II) A 6.0-cm-diameter horizontal pipe gradually narrows to 4.5 cm. When water flows through this pipe at a certain rate, the gauge pressure in these two sections is 32.0 kPa and 24.0 kPa, respectively. What is the volume rate of flow?

51. (II) Estimate the air pressure inside a category 5 hurricane, where the wind speed is 300 km/h (Fig. 13–53).

FIGURE 13–53 Problem 51.

52. (II) What is the lift (in newtons) due to Bernoulli's principle on a wing of area 88 m² if the air passes over the top and bottom surfaces at speeds of 280 m/s and 150 m/s, respectively?

53. (II) Show that the power needed to drive a fluid through a pipe with uniform cross-section is equal to the volume rate of flow, Q, times the pressure difference, $P_1 - P_2$.

54. (II) Water at a gauge pressure of 3.8 atm at street level flows into an office building at a speed of 0.68 m/s through a pipe 5.0 cm in diameter. The pipe tapers down to 2.8 cm in diameter by the top floor, 18 m above (Fig. 13–54), where the faucet has been left open. Calculate the flow velocity and the gauge pressure in the pipe on the top floor. Assume no branch pipes and ignore viscosity.

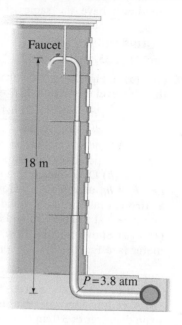

FIGURE 13–54
Problem 54.

55. (II) In Fig. 13–55, take into account the speed of the top surface of the tank and show that the speed of fluid leaving the opening at the bottom is

$$v_1 = \sqrt{\frac{2gh}{(1 - A_1^2/A_2^2)}},$$

where $h = y_2 - y_1$, and A_1 and A_2 are the areas of the opening and of the top surface, respectively. Assume $A_1 \ll A_2$ so that the flow remains nearly steady and laminar.

FIGURE 13–55
Problems 55, 56, 58, and 59.

56. (II) Suppose the top surface of the vessel in Fig. 13–55 is subjected to an external gauge pressure P_2. (a) Derive a formula for the speed, v_1, at which the liquid flows from the opening at the bottom into atmospheric pressure, P_0. Assume the velocity of the liquid surface, v_2, is approximately zero. (b) If $P_2 = 0.85$ atm and $y_2 - y_1 = 2.4$ m, determine v_1 for water.

57. (II) You are watering your lawn with a hose when you put your finger over the hose opening to increase the distance the water reaches. If you are pointing the hose at the same angle, and the distance the water reaches increases by a factor of 4, what fraction of the hose opening did you block?

58. (III) Suppose the opening in the tank of Fig. 13–55 is a height h_1 above the base and the liquid surface is a height h_2 above the base. The tank rests on level ground. (a) At what horizontal distance from the base of the tank will the fluid strike the ground? (b) At what other height, h_1', can a hole be placed so that the emerging liquid will have the same "range"? Assume $v_2 \approx 0$.

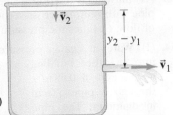

FIGURE 13–55 (repeated)
Problems 55, 56, 58, and 59.

59. (III) (a) In Fig. 13–55, show that Bernoulli's principle predicts that the level of the liquid, $h = y_2 - y_1$, drops at a rate

$$\frac{dh}{dt} = -\sqrt{\frac{2gh A_1^2}{A_2^2 - A_1^2}},$$

where A_1 and A_2 are the areas of the opening and the top surface, respectively, assuming $A_1 \ll A_2$, and viscosity is ignored. (b) Determine h as a function of time by integrating. Let $h = h_0$ at $t = 0$. (c) How long would it take to empty a 10.6-cm-tall cylinder filled with 1.3 L of water if the opening is at the bottom and has a 0.50-cm diameter?

60. (III) (a) Show that the flow speed measured by a venturi meter (see Fig. 13–32) is given by the relation

$$v_1 = A_2\sqrt{\frac{2(P_1 - P_2)}{\rho(A_1^2 - A_2^2)}}.$$

(b) A venturi meter is measuring the flow of water; it has a main diameter of 3.0 cm tapering down to a throat diameter of 1.0 cm. If the pressure difference is measured to be 18 mm-Hg, what is the speed of the water entering the venturi throat?

61. (III) *Thrust of a rocket.* (a) Use Bernoulli's equation and the equation of continuity to show that the emission speed of the propelling gases of a rocket is

$$v = \sqrt{2(P - P_0)/\rho},$$

where ρ is the density of the gas, P is the pressure of the gas inside the rocket, and P_0 is atmospheric pressure just outside the exit orifice. Assume that the gas density stays approximately constant, and that the area of the exit orifice, A_0, is much smaller than the cross-sectional area, A, of the inside of the rocket (take it to be a large cylinder). Assume also that the gas speed is not so high that significant turbulence or nonsteady flow sets in. (b) Show that the thrust force on the rocket due to the emitted gases is

$$F = 2A_0(P - P_0).$$

62. (III) A fire hose exerts a force on the person holding it. This is because the water accelerates as it goes from the hose through the nozzle. How much force is required to hold a 7.0-cm-diameter hose delivering 450 L/min through a 0.75-cm-diameter nozzle?

*13–11 Viscosity

*63. (II) A viscometer consists of two concentric cylinders, 10.20 cm and 10.60 cm in diameter. A liquid fills the space between them to a depth of 12.0 cm. The outer cylinder is fixed, and a torque of 0.024 m·N keeps the inner cylinder turning at a steady rotational speed of 57 rev/min. What is the viscosity of the liquid?

*64. (III) A long vertical hollow tube with an inner diameter of 1.00 cm is filled with SAE 10 motor oil. A 0.900-cm-diameter, 30.0-cm-long 150-g rod is dropped vertically through the oil in the tube. What is the maximum speed attained by the rod as it falls?

*13–12 Flow in Tubes; Poiseuille's Equation

*65. (I) Engine oil (assume SAE 10, Table 13–3) passes through a fine 1.80-mm-diameter tube that is 8.6 cm long. What pressure difference is needed to maintain a flow rate of 6.2 mL/min?

*66. (I) A gardener feels it is taking too long to water a garden with a $\frac{3}{8}$-in.-diameter hose. By what factor will the time be cut using a $\frac{5}{8}$-in.-diameter hose instead? Assume nothing else is changed.

*67. (II) What diameter must a 15.5-m-long air duct have if the ventilation and heating system is to replenish the air in a room 8.0 m × 14.0 m × 4.0 m every 12.0 min? Assume the pump can exert a gauge pressure of 0.710×10^{-3} atm.

*68. (II) What must be the pressure difference between the two ends of a 1.9-km section of pipe, 29 cm in diameter, if it is to transport oil $(\rho = 950\,\text{kg/m}^3, \eta = 0.20\,\text{Pa·s})$ at a rate of 650 cm³/s?

*69. (II) Poiseuille's equation does not hold if the flow velocity is high enough that turbulence sets in. The onset of turbulence occurs when the **Reynolds number**, Re, exceeds approximately 2000. Re is defined as

$$Re = \frac{2\bar{v}r\rho}{\eta},$$

where $\bar{v}$ is the average speed of the fluid, ρ is its density, η is its viscosity, and r is the radius of the tube in which the fluid is flowing. (a) Determine if blood flow through the aorta is laminar or turbulent when the average speed of blood in the aorta $(r = 0.80\,\text{cm})$ during the resting part of the heart's cycle is about 35 cm/s. (b) During exercise, the blood-flow speed approximately doubles. Calculate the Reynolds number in this case, and determine if the flow is laminar or turbulent.

*70. (II) Assuming a constant pressure gradient, if blood flow is reduced by 85%, by what factor is the radius of a blood vessel decreased?

*71. (III) A patient is to be given a blood transfusion. The blood is to flow through a tube from a raised bottle to a needle inserted in the vein (Fig. 13–56). The inside diameter of the 25-mm-long needle is 0.80 mm, and the required flow rate is 2.0 cm³ of blood per minute. How high h should the bottle be placed above the needle? Obtain ρ and η from the Tables. Assume the blood pressure is 78 torr above atmospheric pressure.

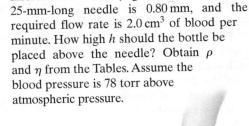

FIGURE 13–56
Problems 71 and 79.

*13–13 Surface Tension and Capillarity

*72. (I) If the force F needed to move the wire in Fig. 13–35 is $3.4 \times 10^{-3}\,\text{N}$, calculate the surface tension γ of the enclosed fluid. Assume $\ell = 0.070$ m.

*73. (I) Calculate the force needed to move the wire in Fig. 13–35 if it is immersed in a soapy solution and the wire is 24.5 cm long.

*74. (II) The surface tension of a liquid can be determined by measuring the force F needed to just lift a circular platinum ring of radius r from the surface of the liquid. (a) Find a formula for γ in terms of F and r. (b) At 30°C, if $F = 5.80 \times 10^{-3}\,\text{N}$ and $r = 2.8$ cm, calculate γ for the tested liquid.

*75. (III) Estimate the diameter of a steel needle that can just "float" on water due to surface tension.

*76. (III) Show that inside a soap bubble, there must be a pressure ΔP in excess of that outside equal to $\Delta P = 4\gamma/r$, where r is the radius of the bubble and γ is the surface tension. [*Hint*: Think of the bubble as two hemispheres in contact with each other; and remember that there are two surfaces to the bubble. Note that this result applies to any kind of membrane, where 2γ is the tension per unit length in that membrane.]

*77. (III) A common effect of surface tension is the ability of a liquid to rise up a narrow tube due to what is called capillary action. Show that for a narrow tube of radius r placed in a liquid of density ρ and surface tension γ, the liquid in the tube will reach a height $h = 2\gamma/\rho gr$ above the level of the liquid outside the tube, where g is the gravitational acceleration. Assume that the liquid "wets" the capillary (the liquid surface is vertical at the contact with the inside of the tube).

General Problems

78. A 2.8-N force is applied to the plunger of a hypodermic needle. If the diameter of the plunger is 1.3 cm and that of the needle 0.20 mm, (*a*) with what force does the fluid leave the needle? (*b*) What force on the plunger would be needed to push fluid into a vein where the gauge pressure is 75 mm-Hg? Answer for the instant just before the fluid starts to move.

79. Intravenous infusions are often made under gravity, as shown in Fig. 13–56. Assuming the fluid has a density of 1.00 g/cm^3, at what height h should the bottle be placed so the liquid pressure is (*a*) 55 mm-Hg, and (*b*) 650 mm-H_2O? (*c*) If the blood pressure is 78 mm-Hg above atmospheric pressure, how high should the bottle be placed so that the fluid just barely enters the vein?

80. A beaker of water rests on an electronic balance that reads 998.0 g. A 2.6-cm-diameter solid copper ball attached to a string is submerged in the water, but does not touch the bottom. What are the tension in the string and the new balance reading?

81. Estimate the difference in air pressure between the top and the bottom of the Empire State building in New York City. It is 380 m tall and is located at sea level. Express as a fraction of atmospheric pressure at sea level.

82. A hydraulic lift is used to jack a 920-kg car 42 cm off the floor. The diameter of the output piston is 18 cm, and the input force is 350 N. (*a*) What is the area of the input piston? (*b*) What is the work done in lifting the car 42 cm? (*c*) If the input piston moves 13 cm in each stroke, how high does the car move up for each stroke? (*d*) How many strokes are required to jack the car up 42 cm? (*e*) Show that energy is conserved.

83. When you ascend or descend a great deal when driving in a car, your ears "pop," which means that the pressure behind the eardrum is being equalized to that outside. If this did not happen, what would be the approximate force on an eardrum of area 0.20 cm^2 if a change in altitude of 950 m takes place?

84. Giraffes are a wonder of cardiovascular engineering. Calculate the difference in pressure (in atmospheres) that the blood vessels in a giraffe's head must accommodate as the head is lowered from a full upright position to ground level for a drink. The height of an average giraffe is about 6 m.

85. Suppose a person can reduce the pressure in his lungs to -75 mm-Hg gauge pressure. How high can water then be "sucked" up a straw?

86. Airlines are allowed to maintain a minimum air pressure within the passenger cabin equivalent to that at an altitude of 8000 ft (2400 m) to avoid adverse health effects among passengers due to oxygen deprivation. Estimate this minimum pressure (in atm).

87. A simple model (Fig. 13–57) considers a continent as a block (density $\approx 2800 \text{ kg/m}^3$) floating in the mantle rock around it (density $\approx 3300 \text{ kg/m}^3$). Assuming the continent is 35 km thick (the average thickness of the Earth's continental crust), estimate the height of the continent above the surrounding rock.

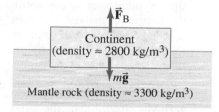

FIGURE 13–57
Problem 87.

88. A ship, carrying fresh water to a desert island in the Caribbean, has a horizontal cross-sectional area of 2240 m^2 at the waterline. When unloaded, the ship rises 8.50 m higher in the sea. How many cubic meters of water was delivered?

89. During ascent, and especially during descent, volume changes of trapped air in the middle ear can cause ear discomfort until the middle-ear pressure and exterior pressure are equalized. (*a*) If a rapid descent at a rate of 7.0 m/s or faster commonly causes ear discomfort, what is the maximum rate of increase in atmospheric pressure (that is, dP/dt) tolerable to most people? (*b*) In a 350-m-tall building, what will be the fastest possible descent time for an elevator traveling from the top to ground floor, assuming the elevator is properly designed to account for human physiology?

90. A raft is made of 12 logs lashed together. Each is 45 cm in diameter and has a length of 6.1 m. How many people can the raft hold before they start getting their feet wet, assuming the average person has a mass of 68 kg? Do *not* neglect the weight of the logs. Assume the specific gravity of wood is 0.60.

91. Estimate the total mass of the Earth's atmosphere, using the known value of atmospheric pressure at sea level.

92. During each heartbeat, approximately 70 cm^3 of blood is pushed from the heart at an average pressure of 105 mm-Hg. Calculate the power output of the heart, in watts, assuming 70 beats per minute.

93. Four lawn sprinkler heads are fed by a 1.9-cm-diameter pipe. The water comes out of the heads at an angle of 35° to the horizontal and covers a radius of 7.0 m. (*a*) What is the velocity of the water coming out of each sprinkler head? (Assume zero air resistance.) (*b*) If the output diameter of each head is 3.0 mm, how many liters of water do the four heads deliver per second? (*c*) How fast is the water flowing inside the 1.9-cm-diameter pipe?

94. A bucket of water is accelerated upward at $1.8\,g$. What is the buoyant force on a 3.0-kg granite rock (SG = 2.7) submerged in the water? Will the rock float? Why or why not?

95. The stream of water from a faucet decreases in diameter as it falls (Fig. 13–58). Derive an equation for the diameter of the stream as a function of the distance y below the faucet, given that the water has speed v_0 when it leaves the faucet, whose diameter is d.

FIGURE 13–58   Problem 95.
Water coming from a faucet.

96. You need to siphon water from a clogged sink. The sink has an area of $0.38\,\text{m}^2$ and is filled to a height of 4.0 cm. Your siphon tube rises 45 cm above the bottom of the sink and then descends 85 cm to a pail as shown in Fig. 13–59. The siphon tube has a diameter of 2.0 cm. (a) Assuming that the water level in the sink has almost zero velocity, estimate the water velocity when it enters the pail. (b) Estimate how long it will take to empty the sink.

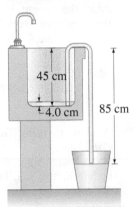

FIGURE 13–59
Problem 96.

97. An airplane has a mass of 1.7×10^6 kg, and the air flows past the lower surface of the wings at 95 m/s. If the wings have a surface area of $1200\,\text{m}^2$, how fast must the air flow over the upper surface of the wing if the plane is to stay in the air?

98. A drinking fountain shoots water about 14 cm up in the air from a nozzle of diameter 0.60 cm. The pump at the base of the unit (1.1 m below the nozzle) pushes water into a 1.2-cm-diameter supply pipe that goes up to the nozzle. What gauge pressure does the pump have to provide? Ignore the viscosity; your answer will therefore be an underestimate.

99. A hurricane-force wind of 200 km/h blows across the face of a storefront window. Estimate the force on the $2.0\,\text{m} \times 3.0\,\text{m}$ window due to the difference in air pressure inside and outside the window. Assume the store is airtight so the inside pressure remains at 1.0 atm. (This is why you should not tightly seal a building in preparation for a hurricane).

100. Blood from an animal is placed in a bottle 1.30 m above a 3.8-cm-long needle, of inside diameter 0.40 mm, from which it flows at a rate of $4.1\,\text{cm}^3/\text{min}$. What is the viscosity of this blood?

101. Three forces act significantly on a freely floating helium-filled balloon: gravity, air resistance (or drag force), and a buoyant force. Consider a spherical helium-filled balloon of radius $r = 15$ cm rising upward through 0°C air, and $m = 2.8$ g is the mass of the (deflated) balloon itself. For all speeds v, except the very slowest ones, the flow of air past a rising balloon is turbulent, and the drag force F_D is given by the relation

$$F_D = \tfrac{1}{2} C_D \rho_{air} \pi r^2 v^2$$

where the constant $C_D = 0.47$ is the "drag coefficient" for a smooth sphere of radius r. If this balloon is released from rest, it will accelerate very quickly (in a few tenths of a second) to its terminal velocity v_T, where the buoyant force is cancelled by the drag force and the balloon's total weight. Assuming the balloon's acceleration takes place over a negligible time and distance, how long does it take the released balloon to rise a distance $h = 12$ m?

*102. If cholesterol buildup reduces the diameter of an artery by 15%, by what % will the blood flow rate be reduced, assuming the same pressure difference?

103. A two-component model used to determine percent body fat in a human body assumes that a fraction $f\,(< 1)$ of the body's total mass m is composed of fat with a density of $0.90\,\text{g/cm}^3$, and that the remaining mass of the body is composed of fat-free tissue with a density of $1.10\,\text{g/cm}^3$. If the specific gravity of the entire body's density is X, show that the percent body fat $(= f \times 100)$ is given by

$$\% \text{ Body fat} = \frac{495}{X} - 450.$$

*## Numerical/Computer

*104. (III) Air pressure decreases with altitude. The following data show the air pressure at different altitudes.

Altitude (m)	Pressure (kPa)
0	101.3
1000	89.88
2000	79.50
3000	70.12
4000	61.66
5000	54.05
6000	47.22
7000	41.11
8000	35.65
9000	30.80
10,000	26.50

(a) Determine the best-fit quadratic equation that shows how the air pressure changes with altitude. (b) Determine the best-fit exponential equation that describes the change of air pressure with altitude. (c) Use each fit to find the air pressure at the summit of the mountain K2 at 8611 m, and give the % difference.

Answers to Exercises

A: (d).

B: The same. Pressure depends on depth, not on length.

C: Lower.

D: (a).

E: (e).

F: Increases.

G: (b).

Heating the air inside a "hot-air" balloon raises the air's temperature, causing it to expand, and forces air out the opening at the bottom. The reduced amount of air inside means its density is lower than the outside air, so there is a net buoyant force upward on the balloon. In this Chapter we study temperature and its effects on matter: thermal expansion and the gas laws.

17

Temperature, Thermal Expansion, and the Ideal Gas Law

CONTENTS

CHAPTER-OPENING QUESTION—Guess now!

A hot-air balloon, open at one end (see photos above), rises when the air inside is heated by a flame. For the following properties, is the air inside the balloon higher, lower, or the same as for the air outside the balloon?

(i) Temperature,
(ii) Pressure,
(iii) Density.

I n the next four Chapters, Chapters 17 through 20, we study temperature, heat and thermodynamics, and the kinetic theory of gases.

We will often consider a particular **system**, by which we mean a particular object or set of objects; everything else in the universe is called the "environment." We can describe the **state** (or condition) of a particular system—such as a gas in a container—from either a microscopic or macroscopic point of view. A **microscopic** description would involve details of the motion of all the atoms or molecules making up the system, which could be very complicated. A **macroscopic** description is given in terms of quantities that are detectable directly by our senses and instruments, such as volume, mass, pressure, and temperature.

The description of processes in terms of macroscopic quantities is the field of **thermodynamics**. Quantities that can be used to describe the state of a system are called **state variables**. To describe the state of a pure gas in a container, for example, requires only three state variables, which are typically the volume, the pressure, and the temperature. More complex systems require more than three state variables to describe them.

The emphasis in this Chapter is on the concept of temperature. We begin, however, with a brief discussion of the theory that matter is made up of atoms and that these atoms are in continual random motion. This theory is called *kinetic theory* ("kinetic," you may recall, is Greek for "moving"), and we discuss it in more detail in Chapter 18.

17–1 Atomic Theory of Matter

The idea that matter is made up of atoms dates back to the ancient Greeks. According to the Greek philosopher Democritus, if a pure substance—say, a piece of iron—were cut into smaller and smaller bits, eventually a smallest piece of that substance would be obtained which could not be divided further. This smallest piece was called an **atom**, which in Greek means "indivisible."[†]

Today the atomic theory is universally accepted. The experimental evidence in its favor, however, came mainly in the eighteenth, nineteenth, and twentieth centuries, and much of it was obtained from the analysis of chemical reactions.

We will often speak of the relative masses of individual atoms and molecules—what we call the **atomic mass** or **molecular mass**, respectively.[‡] These are based on arbitrarily assigning the abundant carbon atom, ^{12}C, the atomic mass of exactly 12.0000 **unified atomic mass units** (u). In terms of kilograms,

$$1\,u = 1.6605 \times 10^{-27}\,kg.$$

The atomic mass of hydrogen is then 1.0078 u, and the values for other atoms are as listed in the Periodic Table inside the back cover of this book, and also in Appendix F. The molecular mass of a compound is the sum of atomic masses of the atoms making up the molecules of that compound.[§]

An important piece of evidence for the atomic theory is called **Brownian motion**, named after the biologist Robert Brown, who is credited with its discovery in 1827. While he was observing tiny pollen grains suspended in water under his microscope, Brown noticed that the tiny grains moved about in tortuous paths (Fig. 17–1), even though the water appeared to be perfectly still. The atomic theory easily explains Brownian motion if the further reasonable assumption is made that the atoms of any substance are continually in motion. Then Brown's tiny pollen grains are jostled about by the vigorous barrage of rapidly moving molecules of water.

In 1905, Albert Einstein examined Brownian motion from a theoretical point of view and was able to calculate from the experimental data the approximate size and mass of atoms and molecules. His calculations showed that the diameter of a typical atom is about 10^{-10} m.

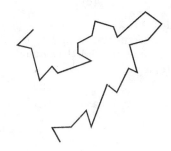

FIGURE 17–1 Path of a tiny particle (pollen grain, for example) suspended in water. The straight lines connect observed positions of the particle at equal time intervals.

[†]Today we do not consider the atom as indivisible, but rather as consisting of a nucleus (containing protons and neutrons) and electrons.

[‡]The terms *atomic weight* and *molecular weight* are sometimes used for these quantities, but properly speaking we are comparing masses.

[§]An *element* is a substance, such as gold, iron, or copper, that cannot be broken down into simpler substances by chemical means. *Compounds* are substances made up of elements, and can be broken down into them; examples are carbon dioxide and water. The smallest piece of an element is an atom; the smallest piece of a compound is a molecule. Molecules are made up of atoms; a molecule of water, for example, is made up of two atoms of hydrogen and one of oxygen; its chemical formula is H_2O.

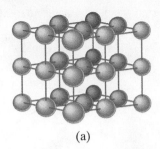

(a)

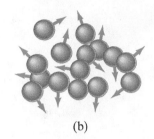

(b)

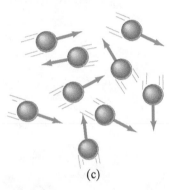

(c)

FIGURE 17–2
Atomic arrangements in
(a) a crystalline solid, (b) a liquid,
and (c) a gas.

At the start of Chapter 13, we distinguished the three common phases (or states) of matter—solid, liquid, gas—based on **macroscopic**, or "large-scale," properties. Now let us see how these three phases of matter differ, from the atomic or **microscopic** point of view. Clearly, atoms and molecules must exert attractive forces on each other. For how else could a brick or a block of aluminum hold together in one piece? The attractive forces between molecules are of an electrical nature (more on this in later Chapters). When molecules come too close together, the force between them must become repulsive (electric repulsion between their outer electrons), for how else could matter take up space? Thus molecules maintain a minimum distance from each other. In a solid material, the attractive forces are strong enough that the atoms or molecules move only slightly (oscillate) about relatively fixed positions, often in an array known as a crystal lattice, as shown in Fig. 17–2a. In a liquid, the atoms or molecules are moving more rapidly, or the forces between them are weaker, so that they are sufficiently free to pass around one another, as in Fig. 17–2b. In a gas, the forces are so weak, or the speeds so high, that the molecules do not even stay close together. They move rapidly every which way, Fig. 17–2c, filling any container and occasionally colliding with one another. On average, the speeds are sufficiently high in a gas that when two molecules collide, the force of attraction is not strong enough to keep them close together and they fly off in new directions.

EXAMPLE 17–1 **ESTIMATE** **Distance between atoms.** The density of copper is $8.9 \times 10^3 \, \text{kg/m}^3$, and each copper atom has a mass of 63 u. Estimate the average distance between the centers of neighboring copper atoms.

APPROACH We consider a cube of copper 1 m on a side. From the given density ρ we can calculate the mass m of a cube of volume $V = 1 \, \text{m}^3$ ($m = \rho V$). We divide this by the mass of one atom (63 u) to obtain the number of atoms in $1 \, \text{m}^3$. We assume the atoms are in a uniform array, and we let N be the number of atoms in a 1-m length; then $(N)(N)(N) = N^3$ equals the total number of atoms in $1 \, \text{m}^3$.

SOLUTION The mass of 1 copper atom is $63 \, \text{u} = 63 \times 1.66 \times 10^{-27} \, \text{kg} = 1.05 \times 10^{-25} \, \text{kg}$. This means that in a cube of copper 1 m on a side (volume = $1 \, \text{m}^3$), there are

$$\frac{8.9 \times 10^3 \, \text{kg/m}^3}{1.05 \times 10^{-25} \, \text{kg/atom}} = 8.5 \times 10^{28} \, \text{atoms/m}^3.$$

The volume of a cube of side ℓ is $V = \ell^3$, so on one edge of the 1-m-long cube there are $(8.5 \times 10^{28})^{\frac{1}{3}}$ atoms = 4.4×10^9 atoms. Hence the distance between neighboring atoms is

$$\frac{1 \, \text{m}}{4.4 \times 10^9 \, \text{atoms}} = 2.3 \times 10^{-10} \, \text{m}.$$

NOTE Watch out for units. Even though "atoms" is not a unit, it is helpful to include it to make sure you calculate correctly.

FIGURE 17–3 Expansion joint on a bridge.

17–2 Temperature and Thermometers

In everyday life, **temperature** is a measure of how hot or cold something is. A hot oven is said to have a high temperature, whereas the ice of a frozen lake is said to have a low temperature.

Many properties of matter change with temperature. For example, most materials expand when their temperature is increased.[†] An iron beam is longer when hot than when cold. Concrete roads and sidewalks expand and contract slightly according to temperature, which is why compressible spacers or expansion joints (Fig. 17–3) are placed at regular intervals. The electrical resistance of matter changes with temperature (Chapter 25). So too does the color radiated by objects, at least at high temperatures: you may have noticed that the heating element of an electric stove glows with a red color when hot.

[†]Most materials expand when their temperature is raised, but not all. Water, for example, in the range 0°C to 4°C contracts with an increase in temperature (see Section 17–4).

At higher temperatures, solids such as iron glow orange or even white. The white light from an ordinary incandescent lightbulb comes from an extremely hot tungsten wire. The surface temperatures of the Sun and other stars can be measured by the predominant color (more precisely, wavelengths) of light they emit.

Instruments designed to measure temperature are called **thermometers**. There are many kinds of thermometers, but their operation always depends on some property of matter that changes with temperature. Many common thermometers rely on the expansion of a material with an increase in temperature. The first idea for a thermometer, by Galileo, made use of the expansion of a gas. Common thermometers today consist of a hollow glass tube filled with mercury or with alcohol colored with a red dye, as were the earliest usable thermometers (Fig. 17–4).

Inside a common liquid-in-glass thermometer, the liquid expands more than the glass when the temperature is increased, so the liquid level rises in the tube (Fig. 17–5a). Although metals also expand with temperature, the change in length of a metal rod, say, is generally too small to measure accurately for ordinary changes in temperature. However, a useful thermometer can be made by bonding together two dissimilar metals whose rates of expansion are different (Fig. 17–5b). When the temperature is increased, the different amounts of expansion cause the bimetallic strip to bend. Often the bimetallic strip is in the form of a coil, one end of which is fixed while the other is attached to a pointer, Fig. 17–6. This kind of thermometer is used as ordinary air thermometers, oven thermometers, automatic off switches in electric coffeepots, and in room thermostats for determining when the heater or air conditioner should go on or off. Very precise thermometers make use of electrical properties (Chapter 25), such as resistance thermometers, thermocouples, and thermistors, often with a digital readout.

Temperature Scales

In order to measure temperature quantitatively, some sort of numerical scale must be defined. The most common scale today is the **Celsius** scale, sometimes called the **centigrade** scale. In the United States, the **Fahrenheit** scale is also common. The most important scale in scientific work is the absolute, or Kelvin, scale, and it will be discussed later in this Chapter.

One way to define a temperature scale is to assign arbitrary values to two readily reproducible temperatures. For both the Celsius and Fahrenheit scales these two fixed points are chosen to be the freezing point and the boiling point[†] of water, both taken at standard atmospheric pressure. On the Celsius scale, the freezing point of water is chosen to be 0°C ("zero degrees Celsius") and the boiling point 100°C. On the Fahrenheit scale, the freezing point is defined as 32°F and the boiling point 212°F. A practical thermometer is calibrated by placing it in carefully prepared environments at each of the two temperatures and marking the position of the liquid or pointer. For a Celsius scale, the distance between the two marks is divided into one hundred equal intervals representing each degree between 0°C and 100°C (hence the name "centigrade scale" meaning "hundred steps"). For a Fahrenheit scale, the two points are labeled 32°F and 212°F and the distance between them is divided into 180 equal intervals. For temperatures below the freezing point of water and above the boiling point of water, the scales may be extended using the same equally spaced intervals. However, thermometers can be used only over a limited temperature range because of their own limitations—for example, the liquid mercury in a mercury-in-glass thermometer solidifies at some point, below which the thermometer will be useless. It is also rendered useless above temperatures where the fluid, such as alcohol, vaporizes. For very low or very high temperatures, specialized thermometers are required, some of which we will mention later.

[†]The freezing point of a substance is defined as that temperature at which the solid and liquid phases coexist in equilibrium—that is, without any net liquid changing into the solid or vice versa. Experimentally, this is found to occur at only one definite temperature, for a given pressure. Similarly, the boiling point is defined as that temperature at which the liquid and gas coexist in equilibrium. Since these points vary with pressure, the pressure must be specified (usually it is 1 atm).

FIGURE 17–4 Thermometers built by the Accademia del Cimento (1657–1667) in Florence, Italy, are among the earliest known. These sensitive and exquisite instruments contained alcohol, sometimes colored, like many thermometers today.

FIGURE 17–5 (a) Mercury- or alcohol-in-glass thermometer; (b) bimetallic strip.

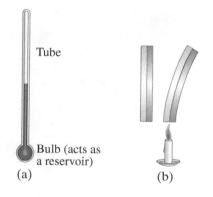

Tube

Bulb (acts as a reservoir)

(a)   (b)

FIGURE 17–6 Photograph of a thermometer using a coiled bimetallic strip.

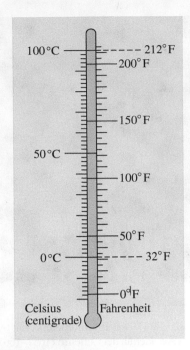

FIGURE 17–7 Celsius and Fahrenheit scales compared.

⚠ **C A U T I O N**

Convert temperature by remembering 0°C = 32°F *and a change of* 5 C° = 9 F°

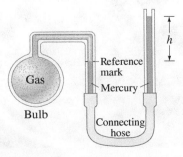

FIGURE 17–8 Constant-volume gas thermometer.

Every temperature on the Celsius scale corresponds to a particular temperature on the Fahrenheit scale, Fig. 17–7. It is easy to convert from one to the other if you remember that 0°C corresponds to 32°F and that a range of 100° on the Celsius scale corresponds to a range of 180° on the Fahrenheit scale. Thus, one Fahrenheit degree (1 F°) corresponds to $100/180 = \frac{5}{9}$ of a Celsius degree (1 C°). That is, $1\,F° = \frac{5}{9}\,C°$. (Notice that when we refer to a specific temperature, we say "degrees Celsius," as in 20°C; but when we refer to a *change* in temperature or a temperature interval, we say "Celsius degrees," as in "2 C°.") The conversion between the two temperature scales can be written

$$T(°C) = \tfrac{5}{9}[T(°F) - 32]$$

or

$$T(°F) = \tfrac{9}{5}T(°C) + 32.$$

Rather than memorizing these relations (it would be easy to confuse them), it is usually easier simply to remember that 0°C = 32°F and that a change of 5 C° = a change of 9 F°.

EXAMPLE 17–2 **Taking your temperature.** Normal body temperature is 98.6°F. What is this on the Celsius scale?

APPROACH We recall that 0°C = 32°F and 5 C° = 9 F°.

SOLUTION First we relate the given temperature to the freezing point of water (0°C). That is, 98.6°F is 98.6 − 32.0 = 66.6 F° above the freezing point of water. Since each F° is equal to $\frac{5}{9}$ C°, this corresponds to $66.6 \times \frac{5}{9} = 37.0$ Celsius degrees above the freezing point. The freezing point is 0°C, so the temperature is 37.0°C.

EXERCISE A Determine the temperature at which both scales give the same numerical reading $(T_C = T_F)$.

Different materials do not expand in quite the same way over a wide temperature range. Consequently, if we calibrate different kinds of thermometers exactly as described above, they will not usually agree precisely. Because of how we calibrate them, they will agree at 0°C and at 100°C. But because of different expansion properties, they may not agree precisely at intermediate temperatures (remember we arbitrarily divided the thermometer scale into 100 equal divisions between 0°C and 100°C). Thus a carefully calibrated mercury-in-glass thermometer might register 52.0°C, whereas a carefully calibrated thermometer of another type might read 52.6°C. Discrepancies below 0°C and above 100°C can also be significant.

Because of such discrepancies, some standard kind of thermometer must be chosen so that all temperatures can be precisely defined. The chosen standard for this purpose is the **constant-volume gas thermometer**. As shown in the simplified diagram of Fig. 17–8, this thermometer consists of a bulb filled with a dilute gas connected by a thin tube to a mercury manometer (Section 13–6). The volume of the gas is kept constant by raising or lowering the right-hand tube of the manometer so that the mercury in the left-hand tube coincides with the reference mark. An increase in temperature causes a proportional increase in pressure in the bulb. Thus the tube must be lifted higher to keep the gas volume constant. The height of the mercury in the right-hand column is then a measure of the temperature. This thermometer gives the same results for all gases in the limit of reducing the gas pressure in the bulb toward zero. The resulting scale serves as a basis for the standard temperature scale (Section 17–10).

17–3 Thermal Equilibrium and the Zeroth Law of Thermodynamics

We are all familiar with the fact that if two objects at different temperatures are placed in thermal contact (meaning thermal energy can transfer from one to the other), the two objects will eventually reach the same temperature. They are then said to be in **thermal equilibrium**. For example, you leave a fever thermometer in your mouth until it comes into thermal equilibrium with that environment, and then you read it. Two objects are defined to be in thermal equilibrium if, when placed in thermal contact, no net energy flows from one to the other, and their temperatures don't change. Experiments indicate that

> **if two systems are in thermal equilibrium with a third system, then they are in thermal equilibrium with each other.**

This postulate is called the **zeroth law of thermodynamics**. It has this unusual name because it was not until after the great first and second laws of thermodynamics (Chapters 19 and 20) were worked out that scientists realized that this apparently obvious postulate needed to be stated first.

Temperature is a property of a system that determines whether the system will be in thermal equilibrium with other systems. When two systems are in thermal equilibrium, their temperatures are, by definition, equal, and no net thermal energy will be exchanged between them. This is consistent with our everyday notion of temperature, since when a hot object and a cold one are put into contact, they eventually come to the same temperature. Thus the importance of the zeroth law is that it allows a useful definition of temperature.

17–4 Thermal Expansion

Most substances expand when heated and contract when cooled. However, the amount of expansion or contraction varies, depending on the material.

Linear Expansion

Experiments indicate that the change in length $\Delta\ell$ of almost all solids is, to a good approximation, directly proportional to the change in temperature ΔT, as long as ΔT is not too large. The change in length is also proportional to the original length of the object, ℓ_0. That is, for the same temperature increase, a 4-m-long iron rod will increase in length twice as much as a 2-m-long iron rod. We can write this proportionality as an equation:

$$\Delta\ell = \alpha\ell_0\Delta T, \tag{17–1a}$$

where α, the proportionality constant, is called the *coefficient of linear expansion* for the particular material and has units of $(C°)^{-1}$. We write $\ell = \ell_0 + \Delta\ell$, Fig. 17–9, and rewrite this equation as $\ell = \ell_0 + \Delta\ell = \ell_0 + \alpha\ell_0\Delta T$, or

$$\ell = \ell_0(1 + \alpha\,\Delta T), \tag{17–1b}$$

where ℓ_0 is the length initially, at temperature T_0, and ℓ is the length after heating or cooling to a temperature T. If the temperature change $\Delta T = T - T_0$ is negative, then $\Delta\ell = \ell - \ell_0$ is also negative; the length shortens as the temperature decreases.

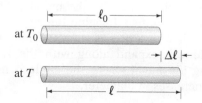

FIGURE 17–9 A thin rod of length ℓ_0 at temperature T_0 is heated to a new uniform temperature T and acquires length ℓ, where $\ell = \ell_0 + \Delta\ell$.

TABLE 17–1 Coefficients of Expansion, near 20°C

Material	Coefficient of Linear Expansion, α $(C°)^{-1}$	Coefficient of Volume Expansion, β $(C°)^{-1}$
Solids		
Aluminum	25×10^{-6}	75×10^{-6}
Brass	19×10^{-6}	56×10^{-6}
Copper	17×10^{-6}	50×10^{-6}
Gold	14×10^{-6}	42×10^{-6}
Iron or steel	12×10^{-6}	35×10^{-6}
Lead	29×10^{-6}	87×10^{-6}
Glass (Pyrex®)	3×10^{-6}	9×10^{-6}
Glass (ordinary)	9×10^{-6}	27×10^{-6}
Quartz	0.4×10^{-6}	1×10^{-6}
Concrete and brick	$\approx 12 \times 10^{-6}$	$\approx 36 \times 10^{-6}$
Marble	$1.4\text{–}3.5 \times 10^{-6}$	$4\text{–}10 \times 10^{-6}$
Liquids		
Gasoline		950×10^{-6}
Mercury		180×10^{-6}
Ethyl alcohol		1100×10^{-6}
Glycerin		500×10^{-6}
Water		210×10^{-6}
Gases		
Air (and most other gases at atmospheric pressure)		3400×10^{-6}

The values of α for various materials at 20°C are listed in Table 17–1. Actually, α does vary slightly with temperature (which is why thermometers made of different materials do not agree precisely). However, if the temperature range is not too great, the variation can usually be ignored.

PHYSICS APPLIED

Expansion in structures

EXAMPLE 17–3 **Bridge expansion.** The steel bed of a suspension bridge is 200 m long at 20°C. If the extremes of temperature to which it might be exposed are −30°C to +40°C, how much will it contract and expand?

APPROACH We assume the bridge bed will expand and contract linearly with temperature, as given by Eq. 17–1a.

SOLUTION From Table 17–1, we find that $\alpha = 12 \times 10^{-6}(C°)^{-1}$ for steel. The increase in length when it is at 40°C will be

$$\Delta\ell = \alpha\ell_0\Delta T = (12 \times 10^{-6}/C°)(200\,\text{m})(40°C - 20°C) = 4.8 \times 10^{-2}\,\text{m},$$

or 4.8 cm. When the temperature decreases to −30°C, $\Delta T = -50\,C°$. Then

$$\Delta\ell = (12 \times 10^{-6}/C°)(200\,\text{m})(-50\,C°) = -12.0 \times 10^{-2}\,\text{m},$$

or a decrease in length of 12 cm. The total range the expansion joints must accommodate is 12 cm + 4.8 cm ≈ 17 cm (Fig. 17–3).

CONCEPTUAL EXAMPLE 17–4 **Do holes expand or contract?** If you heat a thin, circular ring (Fig. 17–10a) in the oven, does the ring's hole get larger or smaller?

RESPONSE You might guess that the metal expands into the hole, making the hole smaller. But it is not so. Imagine the ring is solid, like a coin (Fig. 17–10b). Draw a circle on it with a pen as shown. When the metal expands, the material inside the circle will expand along with the rest of the metal; so the circle expands. Cutting the metal where the circle is makes clear to us that the hole in Fig. 17–10a increases in diameter.

FIGURE 17–10 Example 17–4.

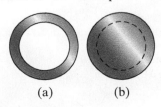

(a)   (b)

EXAMPLE 17–5 **Ring on a rod.** An iron ring is to fit snugly on a cylindrical iron rod. At 20°C, the diameter of the rod is 6.445 cm and the inside diameter of the ring is 6.420 cm. To slip over the rod, the ring must be slightly larger than the rod diameter by about 0.008 cm. To what temperature must the ring be brought if its hole is to be large enough so it will slip over the rod?

APPROACH The hole in the ring must be increased from a diameter of 6.420 cm to 6.445 cm + 0.008 cm = 6.453 cm. The ring must be heated since the hole diameter will increase linearly with temperature (Example 17–4).

SOLUTION We solve for ΔT in Eq. 17–1a and find

$$\Delta T = \frac{\Delta \ell}{\alpha \ell_0} = \frac{6.453 \text{ cm} - 6.420 \text{ cm}}{(12 \times 10^{-6}/\text{C}°)(6.420 \text{ cm})} = 430 \text{ C}°.$$

So it must be raised at least to $T = (20°C + 430 \text{ C}°) = 450°C$.

NOTE In doing Problems, do not forget the last step, adding in the initial temperature (20°C here).

CONCEPTUAL EXAMPLE 17–6 **Opening a tight jar lid.** When the lid of a glass jar is tight, holding the lid under hot water for a short time will often make it easier to open (Fig. 17–11). Why?

RESPONSE The lid may be struck by the hot water more directly than the glass and so expand sooner. But even if not, metals generally expand more than glass for the same temperature change (α is greater—see Table 17–1).

NOTE If you put a hard-boiled egg in cold water immediately after cooking it, it is easier to peel: the different thermal expansions of the shell and egg cause the egg to separate from the shell.

Volume Expansion

The change in *volume* of a material which undergoes a temperature change is given by a relation similar to Eq. 17–1a, namely,

$$\Delta V = \beta V_0 \Delta T, \tag{17–2}$$

where ΔT is the change in temperature, V_0 is the original volume, ΔV is the change in volume, and β is the *coefficient of volume expansion*. The units of β are $(\text{C}°)^{-1}$.

Values of β for various materials are given in Table 17–1. Notice that for solids, β is normally equal to approximately 3α. To see why, consider a rectangular solid of length ℓ_0, width W_0, and height H_0. When its temperature is changed by ΔT, its volume changes from $V_0 = \ell_0 W_0 H_0$ to

$$V = \ell_0(1 + \alpha \Delta T)W_0(1 + \alpha \Delta T)H_0(1 + \alpha \Delta T),$$

using Eq. 17–1b and assuming α is the same in all directions. Thus,

$$\Delta V = V - V_0 = V_0(1 + \alpha \Delta T)^3 - V_0 = V_0[3\alpha \Delta T + 3(\alpha \Delta T)^2 + (\alpha \Delta T)^3].$$

If the amount of expansion is much smaller than the original size of the object, then $\alpha \Delta T \ll 1$ and we can ignore all but the first term and obtain

$$\Delta V \approx (3\alpha)V_0 \Delta T.$$

This is Eq. 17–2 with $\beta \approx 3\alpha$. For solids that are not isotropic (having the same properties in all directions), however, the relation $\beta \approx 3\alpha$ is not valid. Note also that linear expansion has no meaning for liquids and gases since they do not have fixed shapes.

EXERCISE B A long thin bar of aluminum at 0°C is 1.0 m long and has a volume of $1.0000 \times 10^{-3} \text{ m}^3$. When heated to 100°C, the length of the bar becomes 1.0025 m. What is the approximate volume of the bar at 100°C? (a) $1.0000 \times 10^{-3} \text{ m}^3$; (b) $1.0025 \times 10^{-3} \text{ m}^3$; (c) $1.0050 \times 10^{-3} \text{ m}^3$; (d) $1.0075 \times 10^{-3} \text{ m}^3$; (e) $2.5625 \times 10^{-3} \text{ m}^3$.

Equations 17–1 and 17–2 are accurate only if $\Delta \ell$ (or ΔV) is small compared to ℓ_0 (or V_0). This is of particular concern for liquids and even more so for gases because of the large values of β. Furthermore, β itself varies substantially with temperature for gases. Therefore, a more convenient way of dealing with gases is needed, and will be discussed starting in Section 17–6.

⊛ **PHYSICS APPLIED**
Opening a tight lid

⊛ **PHYSICS APPLIED**
Peeling a hard-boiled egg

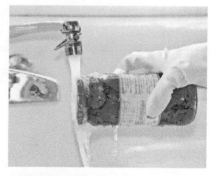

FIGURE 17–11 Example 17–6.

EXAMPLE 17–7 Gas tank in the Sun. The 70-liter (L) steel gas tank of a car is filled to the top with gasoline at 20°C. The car sits in the Sun and the tank reaches a temperature of 40°C (104°F). How much gasoline do you expect to overflow from the tank?

APPROACH Both the gasoline and the tank expand as the temperature increases, and we assume they do so linearly as described by Eq. 17–2. The volume of overflowing gasoline equals the volume increase of the gasoline minus the increase in volume of the tank.

SOLUTION The gasoline expands by

$$\Delta V = \beta V_0 \Delta T = (950 \times 10^{-6}/C°)(70\,L)(40°C - 20°C) = 1.3\,L.$$

The tank also expands. We can think of it as a steel shell that undergoes volume expansion $(\beta \approx 3\alpha = 36 \times 10^{-6}/C°)$. If the tank were solid, the surface layer (the shell) would expand just the same. Thus the tank increases in volume by

$$\Delta V = (36 \times 10^{-6}/C°)(70\,L)(40°C - 20°C) = 0.050\,L,$$

so the tank expansion has little effect. More than a liter of gas could spill out.

NOTE Want to save a few pennies? You pay for gas by volume, so fill your gas tank when it is cool and the gas is denser—more molecules for the same price. But don't fill the tank quite all the way.

Anomalous Behavior of Water Below 4°C

Most substances expand more or less uniformly with an increase in temperature, as long as no phase change occurs. Water, however, does not follow the usual pattern. If water at 0°C is heated, it actually *decreases* in volume until it reaches 4°C. Above 4°C water behaves normally and expands in volume as the temperature is increased, Fig. 17–12. Water thus has its greatest density at 4°C. This anomalous behavior of water is of great importance for the survival of aquatic life during cold winters. When the water in a lake or river is above 4°C and begins to cool by contact with cold air, the water at the surface sinks because of its greater density. It is replaced by warmer water from below. This mixing continues until the temperature reaches 4°C. As the surface water cools further, it remains on the surface because it is less dense than the 4°C water below. Water then freezes first at the surface, and the ice remains on the surface since ice (specific gravity = 0.917) is less dense than water. The water at the bottom remains liquid unless it is so cold that the whole body of water freezes. If water were like most substances, becoming more dense as it cools, the water at the bottom of a lake would be frozen first. Lakes would freeze solid more easily since circulation would bring the warmer water to the surface to be efficiently cooled. The complete freezing of a lake would cause severe damage to its plant and animal life. Because of the unusual behavior of water below 4°C, it is rare for any large body of water to freeze completely, and this is helped by the layer of ice on the surface which acts as an insulator to reduce the flow of heat out of the water into the cold air above. Without this peculiar but wonderful property of water, life on this planet as we know it might not have been possible.

Not only does water expand as it cools from 4°C to 0°C, it expands even more as it freezes to ice. This is why ice cubes float in water and pipes break when water inside them freezes.

FIGURE 17–12 Behavior of water as a function of temperature near 4°C. (a) Volume of 1.00000 g of water, as a function of temperature. (b) Density vs. temperature. [Note the break in each axis.]

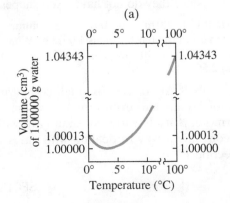

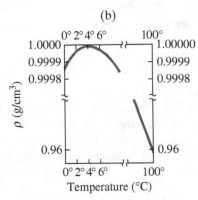

*17–5 Thermal Stresses

In many situations, such as in buildings and roads, the ends of a beam or slab of material are rigidly fixed, which greatly limits expansion or contraction. If the temperature should change, large compressive or tensile stresses, called *thermal stresses*, will occur. The magnitude of such stresses can be calculated using the concept of elastic modulus developed in Chapter 12. To calculate the internal stress, we can think of this process as occurring in two steps: (1) the beam tries to expand (or contract) by an amount $\Delta \ell$ given by Eq. 17–1; (2) the solid in contact with the beam exerts a force to compress (or expand) it, keeping it at its original length. The force F required is given by Eq. 12–4:

$$\Delta \ell = \frac{1}{E} \frac{F}{A} \ell_0,$$

where E is Young's modulus for the material. To calculate the internal stress, F/A, we then set $\Delta \ell$ in Eq. 17–1a equal to $\Delta \ell$ in the equation above and find

$$\alpha \ell_0 \Delta T = \frac{1}{E} \frac{F}{A} \ell_0.$$

Hence, the stress

$$\frac{F}{A} = \alpha E \Delta T.$$

EXAMPLE 17–8 **Stress in concrete on a hot day.** A highway is to be made of blocks of concrete 10 m long placed end to end with no space between them to allow for expansion. If the blocks were placed at a temperature of 10°C, what compressive stress would occur if the temperature reached 40°C? The contact area between each block is 0.20 m². Will fracture occur?

APPROACH We use the expression for the stress F/A we just derived, and find the value of E from Table 12–1. To see if fracture occurs, we compare this stress to the ultimate strength of concrete in Table 12–2.

SOLUTION

$$\frac{F}{A} = \alpha E \Delta T = (12 \times 10^{-6}/\text{C}°)(20 \times 10^9 \, \text{N/m}^2)(30 \, \text{C}°) = 7.2 \times 10^6 \, \text{N/m}^2.$$

This stress is not far from the ultimate strength of concrete under compression (Table 12–2) and exceeds it for tension and shear. If the concrete is not perfectly aligned, part of the force will act in shear, and fracture is likely. This is why soft spacers or expansion joints (Fig. 17–3) are used in concrete sidewalks, highways, and bridges.

EXERCISE C How much space would you allow between the 10-m-long concrete blocks if you expected a temperature range of 0°F to 110°F?

PHYSICS APPLIED
Highway buckling

17–6 The Gas Laws and Absolute Temperature

Equation 17–2 is not very useful for describing the expansion of a gas, partly because the expansion can be so great, and partly because gases generally expand to fill whatever container they are in. Indeed, Eq. 17–2 is meaningful only if the pressure is kept constant. The volume of a gas depends very much on the pressure as well as on the temperature. It is therefore valuable to determine a relation between the volume, the pressure, the temperature, and the mass of a gas. Such a relation is called an **equation of state**. (By the word *state*, we mean the physical condition of the system.)

If the state of a system is changed, we will always wait until the pressure and temperature have reached the same values throughout. We thus consider only **equilibrium states** of a system—when the variables that describe it (such as temperature and pressure) are the same throughout the system and are not changing in time. We also note that the results of this Section are accurate only for gases that are not too dense (the pressure is not too high, on the order of an atmosphere or less) and not close to the liquefaction (boiling) point.

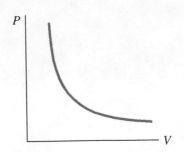

FIGURE 17–13 Pressure vs. volume of a fixed amount of gas at a constant temperature, showing the inverse relationship as given by Boyle's law: as the pressure decreases, the volume increases.

FIGURE 17–14 Volume of a fixed amount of gas as a function of (a) Celsius temperature, and (b) Kelvin temperature, when the pressure is kept constant.

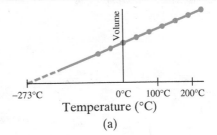

Temperature (°C)

(a)

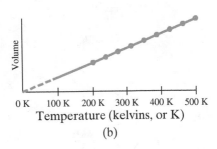

Temperature (kelvins, or K)

(b)

For a given quantity of gas it is found experimentally that, to a good approximation, *the volume of a gas is inversely proportional to the absolute pressure applied to it when the temperature is kept constant.* That is,

$$V \propto \frac{1}{P},$$ [constant T]

where P is the absolute pressure (*not* "gauge pressure"—see Section 13–4). For example, if the pressure on a gas is doubled, the volume is reduced to half its original volume. This relation is known as **Boyle's law**, after Robert Boyle (1627–1691), who first stated it on the basis of his own experiments. A graph of P vs. V for a fixed temperature is shown in Fig. 17–13. Boyle's law can also be written

$$PV = \text{constant}.$$ [constant T]

That is, at constant temperature, if either the pressure or volume of a fixed amount of gas is allowed to vary, the other variable also changes so that the product PV remains constant.

Temperature also affects the volume of a gas, but a quantitative relationship between V and T was not found until more than a century after Boyle's work. The Frenchman Jacques Charles (1746–1823) found that when the pressure is not too high and is kept constant, the volume of a gas increases with temperature at a nearly linear rate, as shown in Fig. 17–14a. However, all gases liquefy at low temperatures (for example, oxygen liquefies at −183°C), so the graph cannot be extended below the liquefaction point. Nonetheless, the graph is essentially a straight line and if projected to lower temperatures, as shown by the dashed line, it crosses the axis at about −273°C.

Such a graph can be drawn for any gas, and the straight line always projects back to −273°C at zero volume. This seems to imply that if a gas could be cooled to −273°C, it would have zero volume, and at lower temperatures a negative volume, which makes no sense. It could be argued that −273°C is the lowest temperature possible; indeed, many other more recent experiments indicate that this is so. This temperature is called the **absolute zero** of temperature. Its value has been determined to be −273.15°C.

Absolute zero forms the basis of a temperature scale known as the **absolute scale** or **Kelvin scale**, and it is used extensively in scientific work. On this scale the temperature is specified as degrees Kelvin or, preferably, simply as *kelvins* (K) without the degree sign. The intervals are the same as for the Celsius scale, but the zero on this scale (0 K) is chosen as absolute zero. Thus the freezing point of water (0°C) is 273.15 K, and the boiling point of water is 373.15 K. Indeed, any temperature on the Celsius scale can be changed to kelvins by adding 273.15 to it:

$$T(\text{K}) = T(°\text{C}) + 273.15.$$

Now let us look at Fig. 17–14b, where the graph of the volume of a gas versus absolute temperature is a straight line that passes through the origin. Thus, to a good approximation, *the volume of a given amount of gas is directly proportional to the absolute temperature when the pressure is kept constant.* This is known as **Charles's law**, and is written

$$V \propto T.$$ [constant P]

A third gas law, known as **Gay-Lussac's law**, after Joseph Gay-Lussac (1778–1850), states that *at constant volume, the absolute pressure of a gas is directly proportional to the absolute temperature:*

$$P \propto T.$$ [constant V]

The laws of Boyle, Charles, and Gay-Lussac are not really laws in the sense that we use this term today (precise, deep, wide-ranging validity). They are really only approximations that are accurate for real gases only as long as the pressure and density of the gas are not too high, and the gas is not too close to liquefaction (condensation). The term *law* applied to these three relationships has become traditional, however, so we have stuck with that usage.

CONCEPTUAL EXAMPLE 17–9 | **Why you should not throw a closed glass jar into a campfire.** What can happen if you did throw an empty glass jar, with the lid on tight, into a fire, and why?

RESPONSE The inside of the jar is not empty. It is filled with air. As the fire heats the air inside, its temperature rises. The volume of the glass jar changes only slightly due to the heating. According to Gay-Lussac's law the pressure P of the air inside the jar can increase dramatically, enough to cause the jar to explode, throwing glass pieces outward.

17–7 The Ideal Gas Law

The gas laws of Boyle, Charles, and Gay-Lussac were obtained by means of a very useful scientific technique: namely, holding one or more variables constant to see clearly the effects on one variable due to changing one other variable. These laws can now be combined into a single more general relation between the absolute pressure, volume, and absolute temperature of a fixed quantity of gas:

$$PV \propto T.$$

This relation indicates how any of the quantities P, V, or T will vary when the other two quantities change. This relation reduces to Boyle's, Charles's, or Gay-Lussac's law when either T, P, or V, respectively, is held constant.

Finally, we must incorporate the effect of the amount of gas present. Anyone who has blown up a balloon knows that the more air forced into the balloon, the bigger it gets (Fig. 17–15). Indeed, careful experiments show that at constant temperature and pressure, the volume V of an enclosed gas increases in direct proportion to the mass m of gas present. Hence we write

$$PV \propto mT.$$

This proportion can be made into an equation by inserting a constant of proportionality. Experiment shows that this constant has a different value for different gases. However, the constant of proportionality turns out to be the same for all gases if, instead of the mass m, we use the number of *moles*.

One **mole** (abbreviated mol) is defined as the amount of substance that contains as many atoms or molecules as there are in precisely 12 grams of carbon 12 (whose atomic mass is exactly 12 u). A simpler but equivalent definition is this: 1 mol is that quantity of substance whose mass in grams is numerically equal to the molecular mass (Section 17–1) of the substance. For example, the molecular mass of hydrogen gas (H_2) is 2.0 u (since each molecule contains two atoms of hydrogen and each atom has an atomic mass of 1.0 u). Thus 1 mol of H_2 has a mass of 2.0 g. Similarly, 1 mol of neon gas has a mass of 20 g, and 1 mol of CO_2 has a mass of $[12 + (2 \times 16)] = 44$ g since oxygen has atomic mass of 16 (see Periodic Table inside the rear cover). The mole is the official unit of amount of substance in the SI system. In general, the number of moles, n, in a given sample of a pure substance is equal to the mass of the sample in grams divided by the molecular mass specified as grams per mole:

$$n\,(\text{mole}) = \frac{\text{mass (grams)}}{\text{molecular mass (g/mol)}}.$$

For example, the number of moles in 132 g of CO_2 (molecular mass 44 u) is

$$n = \frac{132\,\text{g}}{44\,\text{g/mol}} = 3.0\,\text{mole}.$$

FIGURE 17–15 Blowing up a balloon means putting more air (more air molecules) into the balloon, which increases its volume. The pressure is nearly constant (atmospheric) except for the small effect of the balloon's elasticity.

We can now write the proportion discussed above ($PV \propto mT$) as an equation:

$$PV = nRT, \qquad \text{(17–3)}$$

where n represents the number of moles and R is the constant of proportionality. R is called the **universal gas constant** because its value is found experimentally to be the same for all gases. The value of R, in several sets of units (only the first is the proper SI unit), is

$$
\begin{aligned}
R &= 8.314 \, \text{J}/(\text{mol} \cdot \text{K}) & \text{[SI units]}\\
&= 0.0821 \, (\text{L} \cdot \text{atm})/(\text{mol} \cdot \text{K})\\
&= 1.99 \, \text{calories}/(\text{mol} \cdot \text{K}).^{\dagger}
\end{aligned}
$$

Equation 17–3 is called the **ideal gas law**, or the **equation of state for an ideal gas**. We use the term "ideal" because real gases do not follow Eq. 17–3 precisely, particularly at high pressure (and density) or when the gas is near the liquefaction point (= boiling point). However, at pressures less than an atmosphere or so, and when T is not close to the liquefaction point of the gas, Eq. 17–3 is quite accurate and useful for real gases.

Always remember, when using the ideal gas law, that temperatures must be given in kelvins (K) and that the pressure P must always be *absolute* pressure, not gauge pressure (Section 13–4).

⚠ **CAUTION**

Always give T in kelvins and P as absolute (not gauge) pressure

EXERCISE D Return to the Chapter-Opening Question, page 454, and answer it again now. Try to explain why you may have answered differently the first time.

EXERCISE E An ideal gas is contained in a steel sphere at 27.0°C and 1.00 atm absolute pressure. If no gas is allowed to escape and the temperature is raised to 127°C, what will be the new pressure? (*a*) 1.33 atm; (*b*) 0.75 atm; (*c*) 4.7 atm; (*d*) 0.21 atm; (*e*) 1.00 atm.

17–8 Problem Solving with the Ideal Gas Law

The ideal gas law is an extremely useful tool, and we now consider some Examples. We will often refer to "standard conditions" or **standard temperature and pressure (STP)**, which means:

STP

$$T = 273 \, \text{K} \, (0°\text{C}) \quad \text{and} \quad P = 1.00 \, \text{atm} = 1.013 \times 10^5 \, \text{N/m}^2 = 101.3 \, \text{kPa}.$$

EXAMPLE 17–10 **Volume of one mole at STP.** Determine the volume of 1.00 mol of any gas, assuming it behaves like an ideal gas, at STP.

APPROACH We use the ideal gas law, solving for V.

SOLUTION We solve for V in Eq. 17–3:

$$V = \frac{nRT}{P} = \frac{(1.00 \, \text{mol})(8.314 \, \text{J/mol} \cdot \text{K})(273 \, \text{K})}{(1.013 \times 10^5 \, \text{N/m}^2)} = 22.4 \times 10^{-3} \, \text{m}^3.$$

Since 1 liter (L) is $1000 \, \text{cm}^3 = 1.00 \times 10^{-3} \, \text{m}^3$, 1.00 mol of any (ideal) gas has volume $V = 22.4 \, \text{L}$ at STP.

PROBLEM SOLVING

1 mol of gas at STP has $V = 22.4 \, \text{L}$

The value of 22.4 L for the volume of 1 mol of an ideal gas at STP is worth remembering, for it sometimes makes calculation simpler.

EXERCISE F What is the volume of 1.00 mol of ideal gas at 546 K ($= 2 \times 273 \, \text{K}$) and 2.0 atm absolute pressure? (*a*) 11.2 L, (*b*) 22.4 L, (*c*) 44.8 L, (*d*) 67.2 L, (*e*) 89.6 L.

---

†Calories will be defined in Section 19–1; sometimes it is useful to use R as given in terms of calories.

EXAMPLE 17–11 **Helium balloon.** A helium party balloon, assumed to be a perfect sphere, has a radius of 18.0 cm. At room temperature (20°C), its internal pressure is 1.05 atm. Find the number of moles of helium in the balloon and the mass of helium needed to inflate the balloon to these values.

APPROACH We can use the ideal gas law to find n, since we are given P and T, and can find V from the given radius.

SOLUTION We get the volume V from the formula for a sphere:

$$V = \tfrac{4}{3}\pi r^3$$
$$= \tfrac{4}{3}\pi (0.180\,\text{m})^3 = 0.0244\,\text{m}^3.$$

The pressure is given as $1.05\,\text{atm} = 1.064 \times 10^5\,\text{N/m}^2$. The temperature must be expressed in kelvins, so we change 20°C to $(20 + 273)\text{K} = 293\,\text{K}$. Finally, we use the value $R = 8.314\,\text{J/(mol·K)}$ because we are using SI units. Thus

$$n = \frac{PV}{RT} = \frac{(1.064 \times 10^5\,\text{N/m}^2)(0.0244\,\text{m}^3)}{(8.314\,\text{J/mol·K})(293\,\text{K})} = 1.066\,\text{mol}.$$

The mass of helium (atomic mass = 4.00 g/mol as given in the Periodic Table or Appendix F) can be obtained from

$$\text{mass} = n \times \text{molecular mass} = (1.066\,\text{mol})(4.00\,\text{g/mol}) = 4.26\,\text{g}$$

or $4.26 \times 10^{-3}\,\text{kg}$.

EXAMPLE 17–12 **ESTIMATE** **Mass of air in a room.** Estimate the mass of air in a room whose dimensions are 5 m × 3 m × 2.5 m high, at STP.

APPROACH First we determine the number of moles n using the given volume. Then we can multiply by the mass of one mole to get the total mass.

SOLUTION Example 17–10 told us that 1 mol of a gas at 0°C has a volume of 22.4 L. The room's volume is 5 m × 3 m × 2.5 m, so

$$n = \frac{(5\,\text{m})(3\,\text{m})(2.5\,\text{m})}{22.4 \times 10^{-3}\,\text{m}^3} \approx 1700\,\text{mol}.$$

Air is a mixture of about 20% oxygen (O_2) and 80% nitrogen (N_2). The molecular masses are $2 \times 16\,\text{u} = 32\,\text{u}$ and $2 \times 14\,\text{u} = 28\,\text{u}$, respectively, for an average of about 29 u. Thus, 1 mol of air has a mass of about $29\,\text{g} = 0.029\,\text{kg}$, so our room has a mass of air

$$m \approx (1700\,\text{mol})(0.029\,\text{kg/mol}) \approx 50\,\text{kg}.$$

NOTE That is roughly 100 lb of air!

PHYSICS APPLIED
Mass (and weight)
of the air in a room

EXERCISE G At 20°C, would there be (a) more, (b) less, or (c) the same air mass in a room than at 0°C?

Frequently, volume is specified in liters and pressure in atmospheres. Rather than convert these to SI units, we can instead use the value of R given in Section 17–7 as $0.0821\,\text{L·atm/mol·K}$.

In many situations it is not necessary to use the value of R at all. For example, many problems involve a change in the pressure, temperature, and volume of a fixed amount of gas. In this case, $PV/T = nR = \text{constant}$, since n and R remain constant. If we now let P_1, V_1, and T_1 represent the appropriate variables initially, and P_2, V_2, T_2 represent the variables after the change is made, then we can write

PROBLEM SOLVING
Using the ideal gas law as a ratio

$$\frac{P_1 V_1}{T_1} = \frac{P_2 V_2}{T_2}.$$

If we know any five of the quantities in this equation, we can solve for the sixth. Or, if one of the three variables is constant ($V_1 = V_2$, or $P_1 = P_2$, or $T_1 = T_2$) then we can use this equation to solve for one unknown when given the other three quantities.

FIGURE 17–16 Example 17–13.

EXAMPLE 17–13 **Check tires cold.** An automobile tire is filled (Fig. 17–16) to a gauge pressure of 200 kPa at 10°C. After a drive of 100 km, the temperature within the tire rises to 40°C. What is the pressure within the tire now?

APPROACH We do not know the number of moles of gas, or the volume of the tire, but we assume they are constant. We use the ratio form of the ideal gas law.

SOLUTION Since $V_1 = V_2$, then

$$\frac{P_1}{T_1} = \frac{P_2}{T_2}.$$

This is, incidentally, a statement of Gay-Lussac's law. Since the pressure given is the gauge pressure (Section 13–4), we must add atmospheric pressure (= 101 kPa) to get the absolute pressure $P_1 = (200\,\text{kPa} + 101\,\text{kPa}) = 301\,\text{kPa}$. We convert temperatures to kelvins by adding 273 and solve for P_2:

$$P_2 = P_1\left(\frac{T_2}{T_1}\right) = (3.01 \times 10^5\,\text{Pa})\left(\frac{313\,\text{K}}{283\,\text{K}}\right) = 333\,\text{kPa}.$$

Subtracting atmospheric pressure, we find the resulting gauge pressure to be 232 kPa, which is a 16% increase. This Example shows why car manuals suggest checking tire pressure when the tires are cold.

17–9 Ideal Gas Law in Terms of Molecules: Avogadro's Number

The fact that the gas constant, R, has the same value for all gases is a remarkable reflection of simplicity in nature. It was first recognized, although in a slightly different form, by the Italian scientist Amedeo Avogadro (1776–1856). Avogadro stated that *equal volumes of gas at the same pressure and temperature contain equal numbers of molecules*. This is sometimes called **Avogadro's hypothesis**. That this is consistent with R being the same for all gases can be seen as follows. From Eq. 17–3, $PV = nRT$, we see that for the same number of moles, n, and the same pressure and temperature, the volume will be the same for all gases as long as R is the same. Second, the number of molecules in 1 mole is the same for all gases.[†] Thus Avogadro's hypothesis is equivalent to R being the same for all gases.

The number of molecules in one mole of any pure substance is known as **Avogadro's number**, N_A. Although Avogadro conceived the notion, he was not able to actually determine the value of N_A. Indeed, precise measurements were not done until the twentieth century.

A number of methods have been devised to measure N_A, and the accepted value today is

Avogadro's number

$$N_A = 6.02 \times 10^{23}. \qquad \text{[molecules/mole]}$$

Since the total number of molecules, N, in a gas is equal to the number per mole times the number of moles $(N = nN_A)$, the ideal gas law, Eq. 17–3, can be written in terms of the number of molecules present:

$$PV = nRT = \frac{N}{N_A}RT,$$

or

IDEAL GAS LAW
(in terms of molecules)

$$PV = NkT, \qquad (17\text{–}4)$$

where $k = R/N_A$ is called the **Boltzmann constant** and has the value

$$k = \frac{R}{N_A} = \frac{8.314\,\text{J/mol}\cdot\text{K}}{6.02 \times 10^{23}/\text{mol}} = 1.38 \times 10^{-23}\,\text{J/K}.$$

[†]For example, the molecular mass of H_2 gas is 2.0 atomic mass units (u), whereas that of O_2 gas is 32.0 u. Thus 1 mol of H_2 has a mass of 0.0020 kg and 1 mol of O_2 gas, 0.0320 kg. The number of molecules in a mole is equal to the total mass M of a mole divided by the mass m of one molecule; since this ratio (M/m) is the same for all gases by definition of the mole, a mole of any gas must contain the same number of molecules.

EXAMPLE 17–14 **Hydrogen atom mass.** Use Avogadro's number to determine the mass of a hydrogen atom.

APPROACH The mass of one atom equals the mass of 1 mol divided by the number of atoms in 1 mol, N_A.

SOLUTION One mole of hydrogen atoms (atomic mass = 1.008 u, Section 17–1 or Appendix F) has a mass of 1.008×10^{-3} kg and contains 6.02×10^{23} atoms. Thus one atom has a mass

$$m = \frac{1.008 \times 10^{-3} \text{ kg}}{6.02 \times 10^{23}}$$

$$= 1.67 \times 10^{-27} \text{ kg.}$$

EXAMPLE 17–15 **ESTIMATE** **How many molecules in one breath?** Estimate how many molecules you breathe in with a 1.0-L breath of air.

PHYSICS APPLIED
Molecules in a breath

APPROACH We determine what fraction of a mole 1.0 L is by using the result of Example 17–10 that 1 mole has a volume of 22.4 L at STP, and then multiply that by N_A to get the number of molecules in this number of moles.

SOLUTION One mole corresponds to 22.4 L at STP, so 1.0 L of air is $(1.0 \text{ L})/(22.4 \text{ L/mol}) = 0.045$ mol. Then 1.0 L of air contains

$$(0.045 \text{ mol})(6.02 \times 10^{23} \text{ molecules/mol}) \approx 3 \times 10^{22} \text{ molecules.}$$

*17–10 Ideal Gas Temperature Scale— a Standard

It is important to have a very precisely defined temperature scale so that measurements of temperature made at different laboratories around the world can be accurately compared. We now discuss such a scale that has been accepted by the general scientific community.

The standard thermometer for this scale is the constant-volume gas thermometer discussed in Section 17–2. The scale itself is called the **ideal gas temperature scale**, since it is based on the property of an ideal gas that the pressure is directly proportional to the absolute temperature (Gay-Lussac's law). A real gas, which would need to be used in any real constant-volume gas thermometer, approaches this ideal at low density. In other words, the temperature at any point in space is *defined* as being proportional to the pressure in the (nearly) ideal gas used in the thermometer. To set up a scale we need two fixed points. One fixed point will be $P = 0$ at $T = 0$ K. The second fixed point is chosen to be the **triple point** of water, which is that point where water in the solid, liquid, and gas states can coexist in equilibrium. This occurs only at a unique temperature and pressure,[†] and can be reproduced at different laboratories with great precision. The pressure at the triple point of water is 4.58 torr and the temperature is 0.01°C. This temperature corresponds to 273.16 K, since absolute zero is about −273.15°C. In fact, the triple point is now *defined* to be exactly 273.16 K.

[†] Liquid water and steam can coexist (the boiling point) at a range of temperatures depending on the pressure. Water boils at a lower temperature when the pressure is less, such as high in the mountains. The triple point represents a more precisely reproducible fixed point than does either the freezing point or boiling point of water at, say, 1 atm. See Section 18–3 for further discussion.

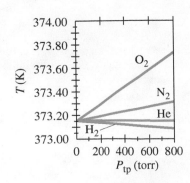

FIGURE 17–17 Temperature readings of a constant-volume gas thermometer for the boiling point of water at 1.00 atm are plotted, for different gases, as a function of the gas pressure in the thermometer at the triple point (P_{tp}). Note that as the amount of gas in the thermometer is reduced, so that $P_{tp} \rightarrow 0$, all gases give the same reading, 373.15 K. For pressure less than 0.10 atm (76 torr), the variation shown is less than 0.07 K.

The absolute or Kelvin temperature T at any point is then defined, using a constant-volume gas thermometer for an ideal gas, as

$$T = (273.16\,\text{K})\left(\frac{P}{P_{tp}}\right). \qquad \text{[ideal gas; constant volume]} \quad \textbf{(17–5a)}$$

In this relation, P_{tp} is the pressure of the gas in the thermometer at the triple point temperature of water, and P is the pressure in the thermometer when it is at the point where T is being determined. Note that if we let $P = P_{tp}$ in this relation, then $T = 273.16\,\text{K}$, as it must.

The definition of temperature, Eq. 17–5a, with a constant-volume gas thermometer filled with a real gas is only approximate because we find that we get different results for the temperature depending on the type of gas that is used in the thermometer. Temperatures determined in this way also vary depending on the amount of gas in the bulb of the thermometer: for example, the boiling point of water at 1.00 atm is found from Eq. 17–5a to be 373.87 K when the gas is O_2 and $P_{tp} = 1000$ torr. If the amount of O_2 in the bulb is reduced so that at the triple point $P_{tp} = 500$ torr, the boiling point of water from Eq. 17–5a is then found to be 373.51 K. If H_2 gas is used instead, the corresponding values are 373.07 K and 373.11 K (see Fig. 17–17). But now suppose we use a particular real gas and make a series of measurements in which the amount of gas in the thermometer bulb is reduced to smaller and smaller amounts, so that P_{tp} becomes smaller and smaller. It is found experimentally that an extrapolation of such data to $P_{tp} = 0$ always gives the *same value* for the temperature of a given system (such as $T = 373.15\,\text{K}$ for the boiling point of water at 1.00 atm) as shown in Fig. 17–17. Thus the temperature T at any point in space, determined using a constant-volume gas thermometer containing a real gas, is defined using this limiting process:

$$T = (273.16\,\text{K})\lim_{P_{tp} \to 0}\left(\frac{P}{P_{tp}}\right). \qquad \text{[constant volume]} \quad \textbf{(17–5b)}$$

This defines the **ideal gas temperature scale**. One of the great advantages of this scale is that the value for T does not depend on the kind of gas used. But the scale does depend on the properties of gases in general. Helium has the lowest condensation point of all gases; at very low pressures it liquefies at about 1 K, so temperatures below this cannot be defined on this scale.

Summary

The atomic theory of matter postulates that all matter is made up of tiny entities called **atoms**, which are typically 10^{-10} m in diameter.

Atomic and **molecular masses** are specified on a scale where ordinary carbon (^{12}C) is arbitrarily given the value 12.0000 u (atomic mass units).

The distinction between solids, liquids, and gases can be attributed to the strength of the attractive forces between the atoms or molecules and to their average speed.

Temperature is a measure of how hot or cold something is. **Thermometers** are used to measure temperature on the **Celsius** (°C), **Fahrenheit** (°F), and **Kelvin** (K) scales. Two standard points on each scale are the freezing point of water (0°C, 32°F, 273.15 K) and the boiling point of water (100°C, 212°F, 373.15 K). A one-kelvin change in temperature equals a change of one Celsius degree or $\frac{9}{5}$ Fahrenheit degrees. Kelvins are related to °C by $T(\text{K}) = T(°\text{C}) + 273.15$.

The change in length, $\Delta \ell$, of a solid, when its temperature changes by an amount ΔT, is directly proportional to the temperature change and to its original length ℓ_0. That is,

$$\Delta \ell = \alpha \ell_0 \Delta T, \qquad \textbf{(17–1a)}$$

where α is the *coefficient of linear expansion*.

The change in volume of most solids, liquids, and gases is proportional to the temperature change and to the original volume V_0:

$$\Delta V = \beta V_0 \Delta T. \qquad \textbf{(17–2)}$$

The *coefficient of volume expansion*, β, is approximately equal to 3α for uniform solids.

Water is unusual because, unlike most materials whose volume increases with temperature, its volume actually decreases as the temperature increases in the range from 0°C to 4°C.

The **ideal gas law**, or **equation of state for an ideal gas**, relates the pressure P, volume V, and temperature T (in kelvins) of n moles of gas by the equation

$$PV = nRT, \qquad \textbf{(17–3)}$$

where $R = 8.314\,\text{J/mol·K}$ for all gases. Real gases obey the ideal gas law quite accurately if they are not at too high a pressure or near their liquefaction point.

One **mole** is that amount of a substance whose mass in grams is numerically equal to the atomic or molecular mass of that substance.

Avogadro's number, $N_A = 6.02 \times 10^{23}$, is the number of atoms or molecules in 1 mol of any pure substance.

The ideal gas law can be written in terms of the number of molecules N in the gas as

$$PV = NkT, \qquad \textbf{(17–4)}$$

where $k = R/N_A = 1.38 \times 10^{-23}\,\text{J/K}$ is Boltzmann's constant.

Questions

1. Which has more atoms: 1 kg of iron or 1 kg of aluminum? See the Periodic Table or Appendix F.
2. Name several properties of materials that could be exploited to make a thermometer.
3. Which is larger, 1C° or 1F°?
4. If system A is in equilibrium with system B, but B is not in equilibrium with system C, what can you say about the temperatures of A, B, and C?
5. Suppose system C is not in equilibrium with system A nor in equilibrium with system B. Does this imply that A and B are not in equilibrium? What can you infer regarding the temperatures of A, B, and C?
6. In the relation $\Delta \ell = \alpha \ell_0 \Delta T$, should ℓ_0 be the initial length, the final length, or does it matter?
7. A flat bimetallic strip consists of a strip of aluminum riveted to a strip of iron. When heated, the strip will bend. Which metal will be on the outside of the curve? Why?
8. Long steam pipes that are fixed at the ends often have a section in the shape of a ∪. Why?
9. A flat uniform cylinder of lead floats in mercury at 0°C. Will the lead float higher or lower if the temperature is raised?
10. Figure 17–18 shows a diagram of a simple **thermostat** used to control a furnace (or other heating or cooling system). The bimetallic strip consists of two strips of different metals bonded together. The electric switch (attached to the bimetallic strip) is a glass vessel containing liquid mercury that conducts electricity when it can flow to touch both contact wires. Explain how this device controls the furnace and how it can be set at different temperatures.

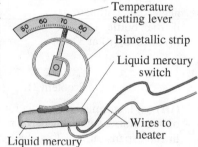

FIGURE 17–18
A thermostat
(Question 10).

11. Explain why it is advisable to add water to an overheated automobile engine only slowly, and only with the engine running.
12. The units for the coefficients of expansion α are $(C°)^{-1}$, and there is no mention of a length unit such as meters. Would the expansion coefficient change if we used feet or millimeters instead of meters?
13. When a cold mercury-in-glass thermometer is first placed in a hot tub of water, the mercury initially descends a bit and then rises. Explain.
14. The principal virtue of Pyrex glass is that its coefficient of linear expansion is much smaller than that for ordinary glass (Table 17–1). Explain why this gives rise to the higher resistance to heat of Pyrex.
15. Will a grandfather clock, accurate at 20°C, run fast or slow on a hot day (30°C)? The clock uses a pendulum supported on a long thin brass rod.
16. Freezing a can of soda will cause its bottom and top to bulge so badly the can will not stand up. What has happened?
17. Why might you expect an alcohol-in-glass thermometer to be more precise than a mercury-in-glass thermometer?
18. Will the buoyant force on an aluminum sphere submerged in water increase, decrease, or remain the same, if the temperature is increased from 20°C to 40°C?
19. If an atom is measured to have a mass of 6.7×10^{-27} kg, what atom do you think it is?
20. From a practical point of view, does it really matter what gas is used in a constant-volume gas thermometer? If so, explain. [*Hint*: See Fig. 17–17.]
21. A ship loaded in sea water at 4°C later sailed up a river into fresh water where it sank in a storm. Explain why a ship might be more likely to sink in fresh water than on the open sea. [*Hint*: Consider the buoyant force due to water.]

Problems

17–1 Atomic Theory

1. (I) How does the number of atoms in a 21.5-g gold ring compare to the number in a silver ring of the same mass?
2. (I) How many atoms are there in a 3.4-g copper penny?

17–2 Temperature and Thermometers

3. (I) (a) "Room temperature" is often taken to be 68°F. What is this on the Celsius scale? (b) The temperature of the filament in a lightbulb is about 1900°C. What is this on the Fahrenheit scale?
4. (I) Among the highest and lowest natural air temperatures recorded are 136°F in the Libyan desert and −129°F in Antarctica. What are these temperatures on the Celsius scale?
5. (I) A thermometer tells you that you have a fever of 39.4°C. What is this in Fahrenheit?
6. (II) In an alcohol-in-glass thermometer, the alcohol column has length 11.82 cm at 0.0°C and length 21.85 cm at 100.0°C. What is the temperature if the column has length (a) 18.70 cm, and (b) 14.60 cm?

17–4 Thermal Expansion

7. (I) The Eiffel Tower (Fig. 17–19) is built of wrought iron approximately 300 m tall. Estimate how much its height changes between January (average temperature of 2°C) and July (average temperature of 25°C). Ignore the angles of the iron beams and treat the tower as a vertical beam.

FIGURE 17–19 Problem 7. The Eiffel Tower in Paris.

8. (I) A concrete highway is built of slabs 12 m long (15°C). How wide should the expansion cracks between the slabs be (at 15°C) to prevent buckling if the range of temperature is −30°C to +50°C?

9. (I) Super Invar™, an alloy of iron and nickel, is a strong material with a very low coefficient of thermal expansion $(0.20 \times 10^{-6}/\text{C}°)$. A 1.6-m-long tabletop made of this alloy is used for sensitive laser measurements where extremely high tolerances are required. How much will this alloy table expand along its length if the temperature increases 5.0 C°? Compare to tabletops made of steel.

10. (II) To what temperature would you have to heat a brass rod for it to be 1.0% longer than it is at 25°C?

11. (II) The density of water at 4°C is $1.00 \times 10^3 \text{ kg/m}^3$. What is water's density at 94°C? Assume a constant coefficient of volume expansion.

12. (II) At a given latitude, ocean water in the so-called "mixed layer" (from the surface to a depth of about 50 m) is at approximately the same temperature due to the mixing action of waves. Assume that because of global warming, the temperature of the mixed layer is everywhere increased by 0.5°C, while the temperature of the deeper portions of the ocean remains unchanged. Estimate the resulting rise in sea level. The ocean covers about 70% of the Earth's surface.

13. (II) To make a secure fit, rivets that are larger than the rivet hole are often used and the rivet is cooled (usually in dry ice) before it is placed in the hole. A steel rivet 1.872 cm in diameter is to be placed in a hole 1.870 cm in diameter in a metal at 20°C. To what temperature must the rivet be cooled if it is to fit in the hole?

14. (II) A uniform rectangular plate of length ℓ and width w has a coefficient of linear expansion α. Show that, if we neglect very small quantities, the change in area of the plate due to a temperature change ΔT is $\Delta A = 2\alpha\ell w \Delta T$. See Fig. 17–20.

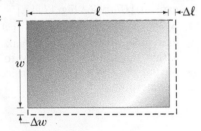

FIGURE 17–20
Problem 14.
A rectangular plate is heated.

15. (II) An aluminum sphere is 8.75 cm in diameter. What will be its change in volume if it is heated from 30°C to 180°C?

16. (II) A typical car has 17 L of liquid coolant circulating at a temperature of 93°C through the engine's cooling system. Assume that, in this normal condition, the coolant completely fills the 3.5-L volume of the aluminum radiator and the 13.5-L internal cavities within the steel engine. When a car overheats, the radiator, engine, and coolant expand and a small reservoir connected to the radiator catches any resultant coolant overflow. Estimate how much coolant overflows to the reservoir if the system is heated from 93°C to 105°C. Model the radiator and engine as hollow shells of aluminum and steel, respectively. The coefficient of volume expansion for coolant is $\beta = 410 \times 10^{-6}/\text{C}°$.

17. (II) It is observed that 55.50 mL of water at 20°C completely fills a container to the brim. When the container and the water are heated to 60°C, 0.35 g of water is lost. (a) What is the coefficient of volume expansion of the container? (b) What is the most likely material of the container? Density of water at 60°C is 0.98324 g/mL.

18. (II) (a) A brass plug is to be placed in a ring made of iron. At 15°C, the diameter of the plug is 8.753 cm and that of the inside of the ring is 8.743 cm. They must both be brought to what common temperature in order to fit? (b) What if the plug were iron and the ring brass?

19. (II) If a fluid is contained in a long narrow vessel so it can expand in essentially one direction only, show that the effective coefficient of linear expansion α is approximately equal to the coefficient of volume expansion β.

20. (II) (a) Show that the change in the density ρ of a substance, when the temperature changes by ΔT, is given by $\Delta\rho = -\beta\rho \Delta T$. (b) What is the fractional change in density of a lead sphere whose temperature decreases from 25°C to −55°C?

21. (II) Wine bottles are never completely filled: a small volume of air is left in the glass bottle's cylindrically shaped neck (inner diameter $d = 18.5$ mm) to allow for wine's fairly large coefficient of thermal expansion. The distance H between the surface of the liquid contents and the bottom of the cork is called the "headspace height" (Fig. 17–21), and is typically $H = 1.5$ cm for a 750-mL bottle filled at 20°C. Due to its alcoholic content, wine's coefficient of volume expansion is about double that of water; in comparison, the thermal expansion of glass can be neglected. Estimate H if the bottle is kept (a) at 10°C, (b) at 30°C.

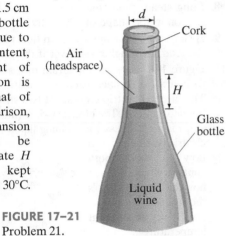

FIGURE 17–21
Problem 21.

22. (III) (a) Determine a formula for the change in surface area of a uniform solid sphere of radius r if its coefficient of linear expansion is α (assumed constant) and its temperature is changed by ΔT. (b) What is the increase in area of a solid iron sphere of radius 60.0 cm if its temperature is raised from 15°C to 275°C?

23. (III) The pendulum in a grandfather clock is made of brass and keeps perfect time at 17°C. How much time is gained or lost in a year if the clock is kept at 28°C? (Assume the frequency dependence on length for a simple pendulum applies.)

24. (III) A 28.4-kg solid aluminum cylindrical wheel of radius 0.41 m is rotating about its axle in frictionless bearings with angular velocity $\omega = 32.8$ rad/s. If its temperature is then raised from 20.0°C to 95.0°C, what is the fractional change in ω?

*17–5 Thermal Stresses

*25. (I) An aluminum bar has the desired length when at 18°C. How much stress is required to keep it at this length if the temperature increases to 35°C?

*26. (II) (a) A horizontal steel I-beam of cross-sectional area 0.041 m² is rigidly connected to two vertical steel girders. If the beam was installed when the temperature was 25°C, what stress is developed in the beam when the temperature drops to −25°C? (b) Is the ultimate strength of the steel exceeded? (c) What stress is developed if the beam is concrete and has a cross-sectional area of 0.13 m²? Will it fracture?

*27. (III) A barrel of diameter 134.122 cm at 20°C is to be enclosed by an iron band. The circular band has an inside diameter of 134.110 cm at 20°C. It is 9.4 cm wide and 0.65 cm thick. (a) To what temperature must the band be heated so that it will fit over the barrel? (b) What will be the tension in the band when it cools to 20°C?

17–6 Gas Laws; Absolute Temperature

28. (I) What are the following temperatures on the Kelvin scale: (a) 66°C, (b) 92°F, (c) −55°C, (d) 5500°C?

29. (I) Absolute zero is what temperature on the Fahrenheit scale?

30. (II) Typical temperatures in the interior of the Earth and Sun are about 4000°C and 15 × 10⁶ °C, respectively. (a) What are these temperatures in kelvins? (b) What percent error is made in each case if a person forgets to change °C to K?

17–7 and 17–8 Ideal Gas Law

31. (I) If 3.80 m³ of a gas initially at STP is placed under a pressure of 3.20 atm, the temperature of the gas rises to 38.0°C. What is the volume?

32. (I) In an internal combustion engine, air at atmospheric pressure and a temperature of about 20°C is compressed in the cylinder by a piston to $\frac{1}{8}$ of its original volume (compression ratio = 8.0). Estimate the temperature of the compressed air, assuming the pressure reaches 40 atm.

33. (II) Calculate the density of nitrogen at STP using the ideal gas law.

34. (II) If 14.00 mol of helium gas is at 10.0°C and a gauge pressure of 0.350 atm, calculate (a) the volume of the helium gas under these conditions, and (b) the temperature if the gas is compressed to precisely half the volume at a gauge pressure of 1.00 atm.

35. (II) A stoppered test tube traps 25.0 cm³ of air at a pressure of 1.00 atm and temperature of 18°C. The cylindrically shaped stopper at the test tube's mouth has a diameter of 1.50 cm and will "pop off" the test tube if a net upward force of 10.0 N is applied to it. To what temperature would one have to heat the trapped air in order to "pop off" the stopper? Assume the air surrounding the test tube is always at a pressure of 1.00 atm.

36. (II) A storage tank contains 21.6 kg of nitrogen (N_2) at an absolute pressure of 3.85 atm. What will the pressure be if the nitrogen is replaced by an equal mass of CO_2 at the same temperature?

37. (II) A storage tank at STP contains 28.5 kg of nitrogen (N_2). (a) What is the volume of the tank? (b) What is the pressure if an additional 25.0 kg of nitrogen is added without changing the temperature?

38. (II) A scuba tank is filled with air to a pressure of 204 atm when the air temperature is 29°C. A diver then jumps into the ocean and, after a short time treading water on the ocean surface, checks the tank's pressure and finds that it is only 194 atm. Assuming the diver has inhaled a negligible amount of air from the tank, what is the temperature of the ocean water?

39. (II) What is the pressure inside a 38.0-L container holding 105.0 kg of argon gas at 20.0°C?

40. (II) A tank contains 30.0 kg of O_2 gas at a gauge pressure of 8.20 atm. If the oxygen is replaced by helium at the same temperature, how many kilograms of the latter will be needed to produce a gauge pressure of 7.00 atm?

41. (II) A sealed metal container contains a gas at 20.0°C and 1.00 atm. To what temperature must the gas be heated for the pressure to double to 2.00 atm? (Ignore expansion of the container.)

42. (II) A tire is filled with air at 15°C to a gauge pressure of 250 kPa. If the tire reaches a temperature of 38°C, what fraction of the original air must be removed if the original pressure of 250 kPa is to be maintained?

43. (II) If 61.5 L of oxygen at 18.0°C and an absolute pressure of 2.45 atm are compressed to 48.8 L and at the same time the temperature is raised to 56.0°C, what will the new pressure be?

44. (II) A helium-filled balloon escapes a child's hand at sea level and 20.0°C. When it reaches an altitude of 3600 m, where the temperature is 5.0°C and the pressure only 0.68 atm, how will its volume compare to that at sea level?

45. (II) A sealed metal container can withstand a pressure difference of 0.50 atm. The container initially is filled with an ideal gas at 18°C and 1.0 atm. To what temperature can you cool the container before it collapses? (Ignore any changes in the container's volume due to thermal expansion.)

46. (II) You buy an "airtight" bag of potato chips packaged at sea level, and take the chips on an airplane flight. When you take the potato chips out of your luggage, you notice it has noticeably "puffed up." Airplane cabins are typically pressurized at 0.75 atm, and assuming the temperature inside an airplane is about the same as inside a potato chip processing plant, by what percentage has the bag "puffed up" in comparison to when it was packaged?

47. (II) A typical scuba tank, when fully charged, contains 12 L of air at 204 atm. Assume an "empty" tank contains air at 34 atm and is connected to an air compressor at sea level. The air compressor intakes air from the atmosphere, compresses it to high pressure, and then inputs this high-pressure air into the scuba tank. If the (average) flow rate of air from the atmosphere into the intake port of the air compressor is 290 L/min, how long will it take to fully charge the scuba tank? Assume the tank remains at the same temperature as the surrounding air during the filling process.

48. (III) A sealed container containing 4.0 mol of gas is squeezed, changing its volume from 0.020 m³ to 0.018 m³. During this process, the temperature decreases by 9.0 K while the pressure increases by 450 Pa. What was the original pressure and temperature of the gas in the container?

49. (III) Compare the value for the density of water vapor at exactly 100°C and 1 atm (Table 13–1) with the value predicted from the ideal gas law. Why would you expect a difference?

50. (III) An air bubble at the bottom of a lake 37.0 m deep has a volume of 1.00 cm³. If the temperature at the bottom is 5.5°C and at the top 18.5°C, what is the volume of the bubble just before it reaches the surface?

17–9 Ideal Gas Law in Terms of Molecules; Avogadro's Number

51. (I) Calculate the number of molecules/m³ in an ideal gas at STP.

52. (I) How many moles of water are there in 1.000 L at STP? How many molecules?

53. (II) What is the pressure in a region of outer space where there is 1 molecule/cm³ and the temperature is 3 K?

54. (II) Estimate the number of (a) moles and (b) molecules of water in all the Earth's oceans. Assume water covers 75% of the Earth to an average depth of 3 km.

55. (II) The lowest pressure attainable using the best available vacuum techniques is about $10^{-12}\,\text{N/m}^2$. At such a pressure, how many molecules are there per cm^3 at $0°\text{C}$?

56. (II) Is a gas mostly empty space? Check by assuming that the spatial extent of common gas molecules is about $\ell_0 = 0.3\,\text{nm}$ so one gas molecule occupies an approximate volume equal to ℓ_0^3. Assume STP.

57. (III) Estimate how many molecules of air are in each 2.0-L breath you inhale that were also in the last breath Galileo took. [*Hint*: Assume the atmosphere is about 10 km high and of constant density.]

*17–10 Ideal Gas Temperature Scale

*58. (I) In a constant-volume gas thermometer, what is the limiting ratio of the pressure at the boiling point of water at 1 atm to that at the triple point? (Keep five significant figures.)

*59. (I) At the boiling point of sulfur ($444.6°\text{C}$) the pressure in a constant-volume gas thermometer is 187 torr. Estimate (*a*) the pressure at the triple point of water, (*b*) the temperature when the pressure in the thermometer is 118 torr.

*60. (II) Use Fig. 17–17 to determine the inaccuracy of a constant-volume gas thermometer using oxygen if it reads a pressure $P = 268$ torr at the boiling point of water at 1 atm. Express answer (*a*) in kelvins and (*b*) as a percentage.

*61. (III) A constant-volume gas thermometer is being used to determine the temperature of the melting point of a substance. The pressure in the thermometer at this temperature is 218 torr; at the triple point of water, the pressure is 286 torr. Some gas is now released from the thermometer bulb so that the pressure at the triple point of water becomes 163 torr. At the temperature of the melting substance, the pressure is 128 torr. Estimate, as accurately as possible, the melting-point temperature of the substance.

General Problems

62. A Pyrex measuring cup was calibrated at normal room temperature. How much error will be made in a recipe calling for 350 mL of cool water, if the water and the cup are hot, at $95°\text{C}$, instead of at room temperature? Neglect the glass expansion.

63. A precise steel tape measure has been calibrated at $15°\text{C}$. At $36°\text{C}$, (*a*) will it read high or low, and (*b*) what will be the percentage error?

64. A cubic box of volume $6.15 \times 10^{-2}\,\text{m}^3$ is filled with air at atmospheric pressure at $15°\text{C}$. The box is closed and heated to $185°\text{C}$. What is the net force on each side of the box?

65. The gauge pressure in a helium gas cylinder is initially 32 atm. After many balloons have been blown up, the gauge pressure has decreased to 5 atm. What fraction of the original gas remains in the cylinder?

66. If a rod of original length ℓ_1 has its temperature changed from T_1 to T_2, determine a formula for its new length ℓ_2 in terms of T_1, T_2, and α. Assume (*a*) $\alpha = \text{constant}$, (*b*) $\alpha = \alpha(T)$ is some function of temperature, and (*c*) $\alpha = \alpha_0 + bT$ where α_0 and b are constants.

67. If a scuba diver fills his lungs to full capacity of 5.5 L when 8.0 m below the surface, to what volume would his lungs expand if he quickly rose to the surface? Is this advisable?

68. (*a*) Use the ideal gas law to show that, for an ideal gas at constant pressure, the coefficient of volume expansion is equal to $\beta = 1/T$, where T is the kelvin temperature. Compare to Table 17–1 for gases at $T = 293\,\text{K}$. (*b*) Show that the bulk modulus (Section 12–4) for an ideal gas held at constant temperature is $B = P$, where P is the pressure.

69. A house has a volume of $870\,\text{m}^3$. (*a*) What is the total mass of air inside the house at $15°\text{C}$? (*b*) If the temperature drops to $-15°\text{C}$, what mass of air enters or leaves the house?

70. Assume that in an alternate universe, the laws of physics are very different from ours and that "ideal" gases behave as follows: (i) At constant temperature, pressure is inversely proportional to the square of the volume. (ii) At constant pressure, the volume varies directly with the $\frac{2}{3}$ power of the temperature. (iii) At 273.15 K and 1.00 atm pressure, 1.00 mole of an ideal gas is found to occupy 22.4 L. Obtain the form of the ideal gas law in this alternate universe, including the value of the gas constant R.

71. An iron cube floats in a bowl of liquid mercury at $0°\text{C}$. (*a*) If the temperature is raised to $25°\text{C}$, will the cube float higher or lower in the mercury? (*b*) By what percent will the fraction of volume submerged change?

72. (*a*) The tube of a mercury thermometer has an inside diameter of 0.140 mm. The bulb has a volume of $0.275\,\text{cm}^3$. How far will the thread of mercury move when the temperature changes from $10.5°\text{C}$ to $33.0°\text{C}$? Take into account expansion of the Pyrex glass. (*b*) Determine a formula for the change in length of the mercury column in terms of relevant variables. Ignore tube volume compared to bulb volume.

73. From the known value of atmospheric pressure at the surface of the Earth, estimate the total number of air molecules in the Earth's atmosphere.

74. Estimate the percent difference in the density of iron at STP, and when it is a solid deep in the Earth where the temperature is $2000°\text{C}$ and under 5000 atm of pressure. Assume the bulk modulus $(90 \times 10^9\,\text{N/m}^2)$ and the coefficient of volume expansion do not vary with temperature and are the same as at STP.

75. What is the average distance between nitrogen molecules at STP?

76. A helium balloon, assumed to be a perfect sphere, has a radius of 22.0 cm. At room temperature $(20°\text{C})$, its internal pressure is 1.06 atm. Determine the number of moles of helium in the balloon, and the mass of helium needed to inflate the balloon to these values.

77. A standard cylinder of oxygen used in a hospital has gauge pressure $= 2000\,\text{psi}$ $(13,800\,\text{kPa})$ and volume $= 14\,\text{L}\,(0.014\,\text{m}^3)$ at $T = 295\,\text{K}$. How long will the cylinder last if the flow rate, measured at atmospheric pressure, is constant at 2.4 L/min?

78. A brass lid screws tightly onto a glass jar at $15°\text{C}$. To help open the jar, it can be placed into a bath of hot water. After this treatment, the temperatures of the lid and the jar are both $75°\text{C}$. The inside diameter of the lid is 8.0 cm. Find the size of the gap (difference in radius) that develops by this procedure.

79. The density of gasoline at $0°\text{C}$ is $0.68 \times 10^3\,\text{kg/m}^3$. (*a*) What is the density on a hot day, when the temperature is $35°\text{C}$? (*b*) What is the percent change in density?

80. A helium balloon has volume V_0 and temperature T_0 at sea level where the pressure is P_0 and the air density is ρ_0. The balloon is allowed to float up in the air to altitude y where the temperature is T_1. (a) Show that the volume occupied by the balloon is then $V = V_0(T_1/T_0)e^{+cy}$ where $c = \rho_0 g/P_0 = 1.25 \times 10^{-4} \, \mathrm{m^{-1}}$. (b) Show that the buoyant force does not depend on altitude y. Assume that the skin of the balloon maintains the helium pressure at a constant factor of 1.05 times greater than the outside pressure. [*Hint:* Assume that the pressure change with altitude is $P = P_0 e^{-cy}$, as in Example 13–5, Chapter 13.]

81. The first real length standard, adopted more than 200 years ago, was a platinum bar with two very fine marks separated by what was defined to be exactly one meter. If this standard bar was to be accurate to within $\pm 1.0 \, \mu\mathrm{m}$, how carefully would the trustees have needed to control the temperature? The coefficient of linear expansion is $9 \times 10^{-6}/\mathrm{C^\circ}$.

82. A scuba tank when fully charged has a pressure of 180 atm at 20°C. The volume of the tank is 11.3 L. (a) What would the volume of the air be at 1.00 atm and at the same temperature? (b) Before entering the water, a person consumes 2.0 L of air in each breath, and breathes 12 times a minute. At this rate, how long would the tank last? (c) At a depth of 20.0 m in sea water at a temperature of 10°C, how long would the same tank last assuming the breathing rate does not change?

83. A temperature controller, designed to work in a steam environment, involves a bimetallic strip constructed of brass and steel, connected at their ends by rivets. Each of the metals is 2.0 mm thick. At 20°C, the strip is 10.0 cm long and straight. Find the radius of curvature r of the assembly at 100°C. See Fig. 17–22.

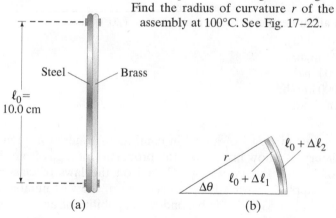

FIGURE 17–22 Problem 83.

84. A copper wire sags 50.0 cm between two utility poles 30.0 m apart when the temperature is −15°C. Estimate the amount of sag when the temperature is +35°C. [*Hint:* An estimate can be made by assuming the shape of the wire is approximately an arc of a circle; hard equations can sometimes be solved by guessing values.]

85. Snorkelers breathe through short tubular "snorkels" while swimming under water very near the surface. One end of the snorkel attaches to the snorkeler's mouth while the other end protrudes above the water's surface. Unfortunately, snorkels cannot support breathing to any great depth: it is said that a typical snorkeler below a water depth of only about 30 cm cannot draw a breath through a snorkel. Based on this claim, what is the approximate fractional change in a typical person's lung volume when drawing a breath? Assume, in equilibrium, the air pressure in a snorkeler's lungs matches that of the surrounding water pressure.

*Numerical/Computer

*86. (II) A thermocouple consists of a junction of two different types of materials that produces a voltage depending on its temperature. A thermocouple's voltages were recorded when at different temperatures as follows:

Temperature (°C)	50	100	200	300
Voltage (mV)	1.41	2.96	5.90	8.92

Use a spreadsheet to fit these data to a cubic equation and determine the temperature when the thermocouple produces 3.21 mV. Get a second value of the temperature by fitting the data to a quadratic equation.

*87. (III) You have a vial of an unknown liquid which might be octane (gasoline), water, glycerin, or ethyl alcohol. You are trying to determine its identity by studying how its volume changes with temperature changes. You fill a Pyrex graduated cylinder to 100.00 mL with the liquid when the liquid and the cylinder are at 0.000°C. You raise the temperature in five-degree increments, allowing the graduated cylinder and liquid to come to equilibrium at each temperature. You read the volumes listed below off the graduated cylinder at each temperature. Take into account the expansion of the Pyrex glass cylinder. Graph the data, possibly using a spreadsheet program, and determine the slope of the line to find the effective (combined) coefficient of volume expansion β. Then determine β for the liquid and which liquid is in the vial.

Temperature (°C)	Volume Reading (apparent mL)
0.000	100.00
5.000	100.24
10.000	100.50
15.000	100.72
20.000	100.96
25.000	101.26
30.000	101.48
35.000	101.71
40.000	101.97
45.000	102.20
50.000	102.46

Answers to Exercises

A: −40°.

B: (d).

C: 8 mm.

D: (i) Higher, (ii) same, (iii) lower.

E: (a).

F: (b).

G: (b) Less.

In this winter scene in Yellowstone Park, we recognize the three states of matter for water: as a liquid, as a solid (snow and ice), and as a gas (steam). In this Chapter we examine the microscopic theory of matter as atoms or molecules that are always in motion, which we call kinetic theory. We will see that the temperature of a gas is directly related to the average translational kinetic energy of its molecules. We will consider ideal gases, but we will also look at real gases and how they change phase, including evaporation, vapor pressure, and humidity.

CHAPTER

18

Kinetic Theory of Gases

CHAPTER-OPENING QUESTION—Guess now!
The typical speed of an air molecule at room temperature (20°C) is

(a) nearly at rest (<10 km/h).
(b) on the order of 10 km/h.
(c) on the order of 100 km/h.
(d) on the order of 1000 km/h.
(e) nearly the speed of light.

The analysis of matter in terms of atoms in continuous random motion is called **kinetic theory**. We now investigate the properties of a gas from the point of view of kinetic theory, which is based on the laws of classical mechanics. But to apply Newton's laws to each one of the vast number of molecules in a gas ($>10^{25}/m^3$ at STP) is far beyond the capability of any present computer. Instead we take a statistical approach and determine averages of certain quantities, and these averages correspond to macroscopic variables. We will, of course, demand that our microscopic description correspond to the macroscopic properties of gases; otherwise our theory would be of little value. Most importantly, we will arrive at an important relation between the average kinetic energy of molecules in a gas and the absolute temperature.

18–1 The Ideal Gas Law and the Molecular Interpretation of Temperature

We make the following assumptions about the molecules in a gas. These assumptions reflect a simple view of a gas, but nonetheless the results they predict correspond well to the essential features of real gases that are at low pressures and far from the liquefaction point. Under these conditions real gases follow the ideal gas law quite closely, and indeed the gas we now describe is referred to as an **ideal gas**.

The assumptions, which represent the basic postulates of the kinetic theory for an ideal gas, are

1. There are a large number of molecules, N, each of mass m, moving in random directions with a variety of speeds. This assumption is in accord with our observation that a gas fills its container and, in the case of air on Earth, is kept from escaping only by the force of gravity.

2. The molecules are, on average, far apart from one another. That is, their average separation is much greater than the diameter of each molecule.

3. The molecules are assumed to obey the laws of classical mechanics, and are assumed to interact with one another only when they collide. Although molecules exert weak attractive forces on each other between collisions, the potential energy associated with these forces is small compared to the kinetic energy, and we ignore it for now.

4. Collisions with another molecule or the wall of the vessel are assumed to be perfectly elastic, like the collisions of perfectly elastic billiard balls (Chapter 9). We assume the collisions are of very short duration compared to the time between collisions. Then we can ignore the potential energy associated with collisions in comparison to the kinetic energy between collisions.

We can see immediately how this kinetic view of a gas can explain Boyle's law (Section 17–6). The pressure exerted on a wall of a container of gas is due to the constant bombardment of molecules. If the volume is reduced by (say) half, the molecules are closer together and twice as many will be striking a given area of the wall per second. Hence we expect the pressure to be twice as great, in agreement with Boyle's law.

Now let us calculate quantitatively the pressure a gas exerts on its container as based on kinetic theory. We imagine that the molecules are inside a rectangular container (at rest) whose ends have area A and whose length is ℓ, as shown in Fig. 18–1a. The pressure exerted by the gas on the walls of its container is, according to our model, due to the collisions of the molecules with the walls. Let us focus our attention on the wall, of area A, at the left end of the container and examine what happens when one molecule strikes this wall, as shown in Fig. 18–1b. This molecule exerts a force on the wall, and according to Newton's third law the wall exerts an equal and opposite force back on the molecule. The magnitude of this force on the molecule, according to Newton's second law, is equal to the molecule's rate of change of momentum, $F = dp/dt$ (Eq. 9–2). Assuming the collision is elastic, only the x component of the molecule's momentum changes, and it changes from $-mv_x$ (it is moving in the negative x direction) to $+mv_x$. Thus the change in the molecule's momentum, $\Delta(mv)$, which is the final momentum minus the initial momentum, is

$$\Delta(mv) = mv_x - (-mv_x) = 2mv_x$$

for one collision. This molecule will make many collisions with the wall, each separated by a time Δt, which is the time it takes the molecule to travel across the container and back again, a distance (x component) equal to 2ℓ. Thus $2\ell = v_x \Delta t$, or

$$\Delta t = \frac{2\ell}{v_x}.$$

The time Δt between collisions is very small, so the number of collisions per second is very large. Thus the average force—averaged over many collisions—will be equal to the momentum change during one collision divided by the time between collisions (Newton's second law):

$$F = \frac{\Delta(mv)}{\Delta t} = \frac{2mv_x}{2\ell/v_x} = \frac{mv_x^2}{\ell}. \qquad \text{[due to one molecule]}$$

During its passage back and forth across the container, the molecule may collide with the tops and sides of the container, but this does not alter its x component of momentum and thus does not alter our result. It may also collide with other molecules, which may change its v_x. However, any loss (or gain) of momentum is acquired by other molecules, and because we will eventually sum over all the molecules, this effect will be included. So our result above is not altered.

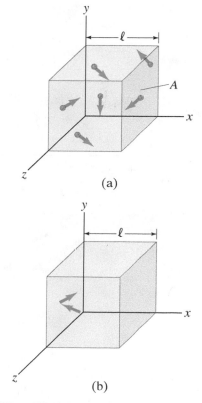

FIGURE 18–1 (a) Molecules of a gas moving about in a rectangular container. (b) Arrows indicate the momentum of one molecule as it rebounds from the end wall.

The actual force due to one molecule is intermittent, but because a huge number of molecules are striking the wall per second, the force is, on average, nearly constant. To calculate the force due to *all* the molecules in the container, we have to add the contributions of each. Thus the net force on the wall is

$$F = \frac{m}{\ell}(v_{x1}^2 + v_{x2}^2 + \cdots + v_{xN}^2),$$

where v_{x1} means v_x for molecule number 1 (we arbitrarily assign each molecule a number) and the sum extends over the total number of molecules N in the container. The average value of the square of the x component of velocity is

$$\overline{v_x^2} = \frac{v_{x1}^2 + v_{x2}^2 + \cdots + v_{xN}^2}{N}, \tag{18-1}$$

where the overbar ($^-$) means "average." Thus we can write the force as

$$F = \frac{m}{\ell} N \overline{v_x^2}.$$

We know that the square of any vector is equal to the sum of the squares of its components (theorem of Pythagoras). Thus $v^2 = v_x^2 + v_y^2 + v_z^2$ for any velocity v. Taking averages, we obtain

$$\overline{v^2} = \overline{v_x^2} + \overline{v_y^2} + \overline{v_z^2}.$$

Since the velocities of the molecules in our gas are assumed to be random, there is no preference to one direction or another. Hence

$$\overline{v_x^2} = \overline{v_y^2} = \overline{v_z^2}.$$

Combining this relation with the one just above, we get

$$\overline{v^2} = 3\overline{v_x^2}.$$

We substitute this into the equation for net force F:

$$F = \frac{m}{\ell} N \frac{\overline{v^2}}{3}.$$

The pressure on the wall is then

$$P = \frac{F}{A} = \frac{1}{3} \frac{N m \overline{v^2}}{A\ell}$$

or

$$P = \frac{1}{3} \frac{N m \overline{v^2}}{V}, \tag{18-2}$$

where $V = \ell A$ is the volume of the container. This is the result we were seeking, the pressure exerted by a gas on its container expressed in terms of molecular properties.

Equation 18–2 can be rewritten in a clearer form by multiplying both sides by V and rearranging the right-hand side:

$$PV = \tfrac{2}{3} N \left(\tfrac{1}{2} m \overline{v^2}\right). \tag{18-3}$$

The quantity $\frac{1}{2} m \overline{v^2}$ is the average translational kinetic energy $\overline{K}$ of the molecules in the gas. If we compare Eq. 18–3 with Eq. 17–4, the ideal gas law $PV = NkT$, we see that the two agree if

$$\tfrac{2}{3}\left(\tfrac{1}{2} m \overline{v^2}\right) = kT,$$

or

$$\overline{K} = \tfrac{1}{2} m \overline{v^2} = \tfrac{3}{2} kT. \qquad\qquad \text{[ideal gas]} \tag{18-4}$$

This equation tells us that

the average translational kinetic energy of molecules in random motion in an ideal gas is directly proportional to the absolute temperature of the gas.

The higher the temperature, according to kinetic theory, the faster the molecules are moving on the average. This relation is one of the triumphs of the kinetic theory.

EXAMPLE 18–1 **Molecular kinetic energy.** What is the average translational kinetic energy of molecules in an ideal gas at 37°C?

APPROACH We use the absolute temperature in Eq. 18–4.

SOLUTION We change 37°C to 310 K and insert into Eq. 18–4:

$$\overline{K} = \tfrac{3}{2}kT = \tfrac{3}{2}(1.38 \times 10^{-23}\,\text{J/K})(310\,\text{K}) = 6.42 \times 10^{-21}\,\text{J}.$$

NOTE A mole of molecules would have a total translational kinetic energy equal to $(6.42 \times 10^{-21}\,\text{J})(6.02 \times 10^{23}) = 3860\,\text{J}$, which equals the kinetic energy of a 1-kg stone traveling almost 90 m/s.

EXERCISE A In a mixture of the gases oxygen and helium, which statement is valid: (*a*) the helium molecules will be moving faster than the oxygen molecules, on average; (*b*) both kinds of molecules will be moving at the same speed; (*c*) the oxygen molecules will, on average, be moving more rapidly than the helium molecules; (*d*) the kinetic energy of the helium will exceed that of the oxygen; (*e*) none of the above.

Equation 18–4 holds not only for gases, but also applies reasonably accurately to liquids and solids. Thus the result of Example 18–1 would apply to molecules within living cells at body temperature (37°C).

We can use Eq. 18–4 to calculate how fast molecules are moving on the average. Notice that the average in Eqs. 18–1 through 18–4 is over the *square* of the speed. The square root of $\overline{v^2}$ is called the **root-mean-square** speed, v_{rms} (since we are taking the square *root* of the *mean* of the *square* of the speed):

$$v_{\text{rms}} = \sqrt{\overline{v^2}} = \sqrt{\frac{3kT}{m}}. \tag{18–5}$$

EXAMPLE 18–2 **Speeds of air molecules.** What is the rms speed of air molecules (O_2 and N_2) at room temperature (20°C)?

APPROACH To obtain v_{rms}, we need the masses of O_2 and N_2 molecules and then apply Eq. 18–5 to oxygen and nitrogen separately, since they have different masses.

SOLUTION The masses of one molecule of O_2 (molecular mass = 32 u) and N_2 (molecular mass = 28 u) are (where $1\,\text{u} = 1.66 \times 10^{-27}\,\text{kg}$)

$$m(O_2) = (32)(1.66 \times 10^{-27}\,\text{kg}) = 5.3 \times 10^{-26}\,\text{kg},$$
$$m(N_2) = (28)(1.66 \times 10^{-27}\,\text{kg}) = 4.6 \times 10^{-26}\,\text{kg}.$$

Thus, for oxygen

$$v_{\text{rms}} = \sqrt{\frac{3kT}{m}} = \sqrt{\frac{(3)(1.38 \times 10^{-23}\,\text{J/K})(293\,\text{K})}{(5.3 \times 10^{-26}\,\text{kg})}} = 480\,\text{m/s},$$

and for nitrogen the result is $v_{\text{rms}} = 510\,\text{m/s}$. These speeds are more than 1700 km/h or 1000 mi/h, and are greater than the speed of sound $\approx 340\,\text{m/s}$ at 20°C (Chapter 16).

NOTE The speed v_{rms} is a magnitude only. The *velocity* of molecules averages to zero: the velocity has direction, and as many molecules move to the right as to the left, as many up as down, as many inward as outward.

EXERCISE B Now you can return to the Chapter-Opening Question, page 476, and answer it correctly. Try to explain why you may have answered differently the first time.

EXERCISE C If you double the volume of a gas while keeping the pressure and number of moles constant, the average (rms) speed of the molecules (*a*) doubles, (*b*) quadruples, (*c*) increases by $\sqrt{2}$, (*d*) is half, (*e*) is $\frac{1}{4}$.

EXERCISE D By what factor must the absolute temperature change to double v_{rms}? (*a*) $\sqrt{2}$; (*b*) 2; (*c*) $2\sqrt{2}$; (*d*) 4; (*e*) 16.

CONCEPTUAL EXAMPLE 18–3 | **Less gas in the tank.** A tank of helium is used to fill balloons. As each balloon is filled, the number of helium atoms remaining in the tank decreases. How does this affect the rms speed of molecules remaining in the tank?

RESPONSE The rms speed is given by Eq. 18–5: $v_{rms} = \sqrt{3kT/m}$. So only the temperature matters, not pressure P or number of moles n. If the tank remains at a constant (ambient) temperature, then the rms speed remains constant even though the pressure of helium in the tank decreases.

In a collection of molecules, the **average speed**, $\bar{v}$, is the average of the magnitudes of the speeds themselves; $\bar{v}$ is generally not equal to v_{rms}. To see the difference between the average speed and the rms speed, consider the following Example.

EXAMPLE 18–4 **Average speed and rms speed.** Eight particles have the following speeds, given in m/s: 1.0, 6.0, 4.0, 2.0, 6.0, 3.0, 2.0, 5.0. Calculate (a) the average speed and (b) the rms speed.

APPROACH In (a) we sum the speeds and divide by $N = 8$. In (b) we square each speed, sum the squares, divide by $N = 8$, and take the square root.

SOLUTION (a) The average speed is

$$\bar{v} = \frac{1.0 + 6.0 + 4.0 + 2.0 + 6.0 + 3.0 + 2.0 + 5.0}{8} = 3.6 \text{ m/s}.$$

(b) The rms speed is (Eq. 18–1):

$$v_{rms} = \sqrt{\frac{(1.0)^2 + (6.0)^2 + (4.0)^2 + (2.0)^2 + (6.0)^2 + (3.0)^2 + (2.0)^2 + (5.0)^2}{8}} \text{ m/s}$$

$$= 4.0 \text{ m/s}.$$

We see in this Example that $\bar{v}$ and v_{rms} are not necessarily equal. In fact, for an ideal gas they differ by about 8%. We will see in the next Section how to calculate $\bar{v}$ for an ideal gas. We already have the tool to calculate v_{rms} (Eq. 18–5).

*Kinetic Energy Near Absolute Zero

Equation 18–4, $\bar{K} = \frac{3}{2}kT$, implies that as the temperature approaches absolute zero, the kinetic energy of molecules approaches zero. Modern quantum theory, however, tells us this is not quite so. Instead, as absolute zero is approached, the kinetic energy approaches a very small nonzero minimum value. Even though all real gases become liquid or solid near 0 K, molecular motion does not cease, even at absolute zero.

18–2 Distribution of Molecular Speeds

The Maxwell Distribution

The molecules in a gas are assumed to be in random motion, which means that many molecules have speeds less than the average speed and others have speeds greater than the average. In 1859, James Clerk Maxwell (1831–1879) worked out a formula for the most probable distribution of speeds in a gas containing N molecules. We will not give a derivation here but merely quote his result:

$$f(v) = 4\pi N \left(\frac{m}{2\pi kT} \right)^{\frac{3}{2}} v^2 e^{-\frac{1}{2}\frac{mv^2}{kT}} \tag{18–6}$$

where $f(v)$ is called the **Maxwell distribution of speeds**, and is plotted in Fig. 18–2. The quantity $f(v) \, dv$ represents the number of molecules that have speed between v and $v + dv$. Notice that $f(v)$ does not give the number of molecules with speed v; $f(v)$ must be multiplied by dv to give the number of molecules (the number of molecules depends on the "width" or "range" of velocities included, dv). In the formula for $f(v)$, m is the mass of a single molecule, T is the absolute temperature, and k is the Boltzmann constant. Since N is the total number of molecules in the gas,

FIGURE 18–2 Distribution of speeds of molecules in an ideal gas. Note that $\bar{v}$ and v_{rms} are not at the peak of the curve. This is because the curve is skewed to the right: it is not symmetrical. The speed at the peak of the curve is the "most probable speed," v_p.

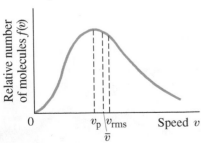

when we sum over all the molecules in the gas we must get N; thus we must have

$$\int_0^\infty f(v)\,dv = N.$$

(Problem 22 is an exercise to show that this is true.)

Experiments to determine the distribution of speeds in real gases, starting in the 1920s, confirmed with considerable accuracy the Maxwell distribution (for gases at not too high a pressure) and the direct proportion between average kinetic energy and absolute temperature, Eq. 18–4.

The Maxwell distribution for a given gas depends only on the absolute temperature. Figure 18–3 shows the distributions for two different temperatures. Just as v_{rms} increases with temperature, so the whole distribution curve shifts to the right at higher temperatures.

Figure 18–3 illustrates how kinetic theory can be used to explain why many chemical reactions, including those in biological cells, take place more rapidly as the temperature increases. Most chemical reactions take place in a liquid solution, and the molecules in a liquid have a distribution of speeds close to the Maxwell distribution. Two molecules may chemically react only if their kinetic energy is great enough so that when they collide, they partially penetrate into each other. The minimum energy required is called the *activation energy*, E_A, and it has a specific value for each chemical reaction. The molecular speed corresponding to a kinetic energy of E_A for a particular reaction is indicated in Fig. 18–3. The relative number of molecules with energy greater than this value is given by the area under the curve to the right of $v(E_A)$, shown in Fig. 18–3 by the two different shadings. We see that the number of molecules that have kinetic energies in excess of E_A increases greatly for only a small increase in temperature. The rate at which a chemical reaction occurs is proportional to the number of molecules with energy greater than E_A, and thus we see why reaction rates increase rapidly with increased temperature.

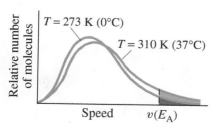

FIGURE 18–3 Distribution of molecular speeds for two different temperatures.

PHYSICS APPLIED
How chemical reactions depend on temperature

*Calculations Using the Maxwell Distribution

Let us see how the Maxwell distribution can be used to obtain some interesting results.

EXAMPLE 18–5 **Determining $\bar{v}$ and v_p.** Determine formulas for (a) the average speed, $\bar{v}$, and (b) the most probable speed, v_p, of molecules in an ideal gas at temperature T.

APPROACH (a) The average value of any quantity is found by multiplying each possible value of the quantity (here, speed) by the number of molecules that have that value, and then summing all these numbers and dividing by N (the total number). For (b), we want to find where the curve of Fig. 18–2 has zero slope; so we set $df/dv = 0$.

SOLUTION (a) We are given a continuous distribution of speeds (Eq. 18–6), so the sum over the speeds becomes an integral over the product of v and the number $f(v)\,dv$ that have speed v:

$$\bar{v} = \frac{\int_0^\infty v\,f(v)\,dv}{N} = 4\pi\left(\frac{m}{2\pi kT}\right)^{\frac{3}{2}}\int_0^\infty v^3 e^{-\frac{1}{2}\frac{mv^2}{kT}}\,dv.$$

We can integrate by parts or look up the definite integral in a Table, and obtain

$$\bar{v} = 4\pi\left(\frac{m}{2\pi kT}\right)^{\frac{3}{2}}\left(\frac{2k^2T^2}{m^2}\right) = \sqrt{\frac{8}{\pi}\frac{kT}{m}} \approx 1.60\sqrt{\frac{kT}{m}}.$$

(b) The *most probable speed* is that speed which occurs more than any others, and thus is that speed where $f(v)$ has its maximum value. At the maximum of the curve, the slope is zero: $df(v)/dv = 0$. Taking the derivative of Eq. 18–6 gives

$$\frac{df(v)}{dv} = 4\pi N\left(\frac{m}{2\pi kT}\right)^{\frac{3}{2}}\left(2v e^{-\frac{mv^2}{2kT}} - \frac{2mv^3}{2kT}e^{-\frac{mv^2}{2kT}}\right) = 0.$$

Solving for v, we find

$$v_p = \sqrt{\frac{2kT}{m}} \approx 1.41\sqrt{\frac{kT}{m}}.$$

(Another solution is $v = 0$, but this corresponds to a minimum, not a maximum.)

In summary,

Most probable speed, v_p
$$v_p = \sqrt{2\frac{kT}{m}} \approx 1.41\sqrt{\frac{kT}{m}} \qquad \textbf{(18–7a)}$$

Average speed, $\bar{v}$
$$\bar{v} = \sqrt{\frac{8}{\pi}\frac{kT}{m}} \approx 1.60\sqrt{\frac{kT}{m}} \qquad \textbf{(18–7b)}$$

and from Eq. 18–5

rms speed, v_{rms}
$$v_{rms} = \sqrt{3\frac{kT}{m}} \approx 1.73\sqrt{\frac{kT}{m}}.$$

These are all indicated in Fig. 18–2. From Eq. 18–6 and Fig. 18–2, it is clear that the speeds of molecules in a gas vary from zero up to many times the average speed, but as can be seen from the graph, most molecules have speeds that are not far from the average. Less than 1% of the molecules exceed four times v_{rms}.

18–3 Real Gases and Changes of Phase

The ideal gas law

$$PV = NkT$$

is an accurate description of the behavior of a real gas as long as the pressure is not too high and as long as the temperature is far from the liquefaction point. But what happens when these two criteria are not satisfied? First we discuss real gas behavior, and then we examine how kinetic theory can help us understand this behavior.

Let us look at a graph of pressure plotted against volume for a given amount of gas. On such a "PV diagram," Fig. 18–4, each point represents an equilibrium state of the given substance. The various curves (labeled A, B, C, and D) show how the pressure varies, as the volume is changed at constant temperature, for several different values of the temperature. The dashed curve A' represents the behavior of a gas as predicted by the ideal gas law; that is, PV = constant. The solid curve A represents the behavior of a real gas at the same temperature. Notice that at high pressure, the volume of a real gas is less than that predicted by the ideal gas law. The curves B and C in Fig. 18–4 represent the gas at successively lower temperatures, and we see that the behavior deviates even more from the curves predicted by the ideal gas law (for example, B'), and the deviation is greater the closer the gas is to liquefying.

To explain this, we note that at higher pressure we expect the molecules to be closer together. And, particularly at lower temperatures, the potential energy associated with the attractive forces between the molecules (which we ignored before) is no longer negligible compared to the now reduced kinetic energy of the molecules. These attractive forces tend to pull the molecules closer together so that at a given pressure, the volume is less than expected from the ideal gas law, as in Fig. 18–4. At still lower temperatures, these forces cause liquefaction, and the molecules become very close together. Section 18–5 discusses in more detail the effect of these attractive molecular forces, as well as the effect of the volume which the molecules themselves occupy.

Curve D represents the situation when liquefaction occurs. At low pressure on curve D (on the right in Fig. 18–4), the substance is a gas and occupies a large volume. As the pressure is increased, the volume decreases until point b is reached. Beyond b, the volume decreases with no change in pressure; the substance is gradually changing from the gas to the liquid phase. At point a, all of the substance has changed to

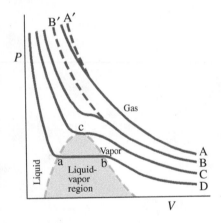

FIGURE 18–4 *PV* diagram for a real substance. Curves A, B, C, and D represent the same substance at different temperatures $(T_A > T_B > T_C > T_D)$.

liquid. Further increase in pressure reduces the volume only slightly—liquids are nearly incompressible—so on the left the curve is very steep as shown. The colored area under the dashed line represents the region where the gas and liquid phases exist together in equilibrium.

Curve C in Fig. 18–4 represents the behavior of the substance at its **critical temperature**; the point c (the one point where curve C is horizontal) is called the **critical point**. At temperatures less than the critical temperature (and this is the definition of the term), a gas will change to the liquid phase if sufficient pressure is applied. Above the critical temperature, no amount of pressure can cause a gas to change phase and become a liquid. The critical temperatures for various gases are given in Table 18–1. Scientists tried for many years to liquefy oxygen without success. Only after the discovery of the behavior of substances associated with the critical point was it realized that oxygen can be liquefied only if first cooled below its critical temperature of $-118°C$.

Often a distinction is made between the terms "gas" and "vapor": a substance below its critical temperature in the gaseous state is called a **vapor**; above the critical temperature, it is called a **gas**.

The behavior of a substance can be diagrammed not only on a PV diagram but also on a PT diagram. A PT diagram, often called a **phase diagram**, is particularly convenient for comparing the different phases of a substance. Figure 18–5 is the phase diagram for water. The curve labeled ℓ-v represents those points where the liquid and vapor phases are in equilibrium—it is thus a graph of the boiling point versus pressure. Note that the curve correctly shows that at a pressure of 1 atm the boiling point is 100°C and that the boiling point is lowered for a decreased pressure. The curve s-ℓ represents points where solid and liquid exist in equilibrium and thus is a graph of the freezing point versus pressure. At 1 atm, the freezing point of water is 0°C, as shown. Notice also in Fig. 18–5 that at a pressure of 1 atm, the substance is in the liquid phase if the temperature is between 0°C and 100°C, but is in the solid or vapor phase if the temperature is below 0°C or above 100°C. The curve labeled s-v is the *sublimation point* versus pressure curve. **Sublimation** refers to the process whereby at low pressures a solid changes directly into the vapor phase without passing through the liquid phase. For water, sublimation occurs if the pressure of the water vapor is less than 0.0060 atm. Carbon dioxide, which in the solid phase is called dry ice, sublimates even at atmospheric pressure (Fig. 18–6).

The intersection of the three curves (in Fig. 18–5) is the **triple point**. For water this occurs at $T = 273.16\,K$ and $P = 6.03 \times 10^{-3}\,atm$. It is only at the triple point that the three phases can exist together in equilibrium. Because the triple point corresponds to a unique value of temperature and pressure, it is precisely reproducible and is often used as a point of reference. For example, the standard of temperature is usually specified as exactly 273.16 K at the triple point of water, rather than 273.15 K at the freezing point of water at 1 atm.

Notice that the solid liquid (s-ℓ) curve for water slopes upward to the left. This is true only of substances that *expand* upon freezing: at a higher pressure, a lower temperature is needed to cause the liquid to freeze. More commonly, substances contract upon freezing and the s-ℓ curve slopes upward to the right, as shown for carbon dioxide (CO_2) in Fig. 18–6.

The phase transitions we have been discussing are the common ones. Some substances, however, can exist in several forms in the solid phase. A transition from one phase to another occurs at a particular temperature and pressure, just like ordinary phase changes. For example, ice has been observed in at least eight forms at very high pressure. Ordinary helium has two distinct liquid phases, called helium I and II. They exist only at temperatures within a few degrees of absolute zero. Helium II exhibits very unusual properties referred to as **superfluidity**. It has essentially zero viscosity and exhibits strange properties such as climbing up the sides of an open container. Also interesting are **liquid crystals** (used for TV and computer monitors, Section 35–11) which can be considered to be in a phase between liquid and solid.

TABLE 18–1 Critical Temperatures and Pressures			
	Critical Temperature		**Critical Pressure (atm)**
Substance	**°C**	**K**	
Water	374	647	218
CO_2	31	304	72.8
Oxygen	−118	155	50
Nitrogen	−147	126	33.5
Hydrogen	−239.9	33.3	12.8
Helium	−267.9	5.3	2.3

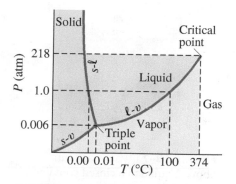

FIGURE 18–5 Phase diagram for water (note that the scales are not linear).

FIGURE 18–6 Phase diagram for carbon dioxide.

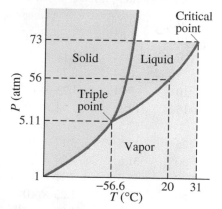

PHYSICS APPLIED
Liquid crystals

18–4 Vapor Pressure and Humidity

Evaporation

If a glass of water is left out overnight, the water level will have dropped by morning. We say the water has evaporated, meaning that some of the water has changed to the vapor or gas phase.

This process of **evaporation** can be explained on the basis of kinetic theory. The molecules in a liquid move past one another with a variety of speeds that follow, approximately, the Maxwell distribution. There are strong attractive forces between these molecules, which is what keeps them close together in the liquid phase. A molecule near the surface of the liquid may, because of its speed, leave the liquid momentarily. But just as a rock thrown into the air returns to the Earth, so the attractive forces of the other molecules can pull the vagabond molecule back to the liquid surface—that is, if its velocity is not too large. A molecule with a high enough velocity, however, will escape the liquid entirely (like an object leaving Earth with a high enough speed, Section 8–7), and become part of the gas phase. Only those molecules that have kinetic energy above a particular value can escape to the gas phase. We have already seen that kinetic theory predicts that the relative number of molecules with kinetic energy above a particular value (such as E_A in Fig. 18–3) increases with temperature. This is in accord with the well-known observation that the evaporation rate is greater at higher temperatures.

Because it is the fastest molecules that escape from the surface, the average speed of those remaining is less. When the average speed is less, the absolute temperature is less. Thus kinetic theory predicts that *evaporation is a cooling process*. You have no doubt noticed this effect when you stepped out of a warm shower and felt cold as the water on your body began to evaporate; and after working up a sweat on a hot day, even a slight breeze makes you feel cool through evaporation.

FIGURE 18–7 Vapor appears above a liquid in a closed container.

Vapor Pressure

Air normally contains water vapor (water in the gas phase), and it comes mainly from evaporation. To look at this process in a little more detail, consider a closed container that is partially filled with water (or another liquid) and from which the air has been removed (Fig. 18–7). The fastest moving molecules quickly evaporate into the empty space above the liquid's surface. As they move about, some of these molecules strike the liquid surface and again become part of the liquid phase: this is called **condensation**. The number of molecules in the vapor increases until a point is reached when the number of molecules returning to the liquid equals the number leaving in the same time interval. Equilibrium then exists, and the space above the liquid surface is said to be *saturated*. The pressure of the vapor when it is saturated is called the **saturated vapor pressure** (or sometimes simply the vapor pressure).

The saturated vapor pressure does not depend on the volume of the container. If the volume above the liquid were reduced suddenly, the density of molecules in the vapor phase would be increased temporarily. More molecules would then be striking the liquid surface per second. There would be a net flow of molecules back to the liquid phase until equilibrium was again reached, and this would occur at the same value of the saturated vapor pressure, as long as the temperature had not changed.

The saturated vapor pressure of any substance depends on the temperature. At higher temperatures, more molecules have sufficient kinetic energy to break from the liquid surface into the vapor phase. Hence equilibrium will be reached at a higher pressure. The saturated vapor pressure of water at various temperatures is given in Table 18–2. Notice that even solids—for example, ice—have a measurable saturated vapor pressure.

In everyday situations, evaporation from a liquid takes place into the air above it rather than into a vacuum. This does not materially alter the discussion above relating to Fig. 18–7. Equilibrium will still be reached when there are sufficient molecules in the gas phase that the number reentering the liquid equals the number leaving. The concentration of particular molecules (such as water) in the gas phase

TABLE 18–2 Saturated Vapor Pressure of Water

Temperature (°C)	Saturated Vapor Pressure	
	torr (= mm-Hg)	Pa (= N/m²)
−50	0.030	4.0
−10	1.95	2.60×10^2
0	4.58	6.11×10^2
5	6.54	8.72×10^2
10	9.21	1.23×10^3
15	12.8	1.71×10^3
20	17.5	2.33×10^3
25	23.8	3.17×10^3
30	31.8	4.24×10^3
40	55.3	7.37×10^3
50	92.5	1.23×10^4
60	149	1.99×10^4
70†	234	3.12×10^4
80	355	4.73×10^4
90	526	7.01×10^4
100‡	760	1.01×10^5
120	1489	1.99×10^5
150	3570	4.76×10^5

†Boiling point on summit of Mt. Everest.
‡Boiling point at sea level.

is not affected by the presence of air, although collisions with air molecules may lengthen the time needed to reach equilibrium. Thus equilibrium occurs at the same value of the saturated vapor pressure as if air were not there.

If the container is large or is not closed, all the liquid may evaporate before saturation is reached. And if the container is not sealed—as, for example, a room in your house—it is not likely that the air will become saturated with water vapor (unless it is raining outside).

Boiling

The saturated vapor pressure of a liquid increases with temperature. When the temperature is raised to the point where the saturated vapor pressure at that temperature equals the external pressure, **boiling** occurs (Fig. 18–8). As the boiling point is approached, tiny bubbles tend to form in the liquid, which indicate a change from the liquid to the gas phase. However, if the vapor pressure inside the bubbles is less than the external pressure, the bubbles immediately are crushed. As the temperature is increased, the saturated vapor pressure inside a bubble eventually becomes equal to or exceeds the external pressure. The bubble will then not collapse but can rise to the surface. Boiling has then begun. *A liquid boils when its saturated vapor pressure equals the external pressure.* This occurs for water at a pressure of 1 atm (760 torr) at 100°C, as can be seen from Table 18–2.

The boiling point of a liquid clearly depends on the external pressure. At high elevations, the boiling point of water is somewhat less than at sea level since the air pressure is less up there. For example, on the summit of Mt. Everest (8850 m) the air pressure is about one-third of what it is at sea level, and from Table 18–2 we can see that water will boil at about 70°C. Cooking food by boiling takes longer at high elevations, since the temperature is less. Pressure cookers, however, reduce cooking time, because they build up a pressure as high as 2 atm, allowing higher boiling temperatures to be attained.

FIGURE 18–8 Boiling: bubbles of water vapor float upward from the bottom (where the temperature is highest).

Partial Pressure and Humidity

When we refer to the weather as being dry or humid, we are referring to the water vapor content of the air. In a gas such as air, which is a mixture of several types of gases, the total pressure is the sum of the *partial pressures* of each gas present.[†] By **partial pressure**, we mean the pressure each gas would exert if it alone were present. The partial pressure of water in the air can be as low as zero and can vary up to a maximum equal to the saturated vapor pressure of water at the given temperature. Thus, at 20°C, the partial pressure of water cannot exceed 17.5 torr (see Table 18–2). The **relative humidity** is defined as the ratio of the partial pressure of water vapor to the saturated vapor pressure at a given temperature. It is usually expressed as a percentage:

$$\text{Relative humidity} = \frac{\text{partial pressure of } H_2O}{\text{saturated vapor pressure of } H_2O} \times 100\%.$$

Thus, when the humidity is close to 100%, the air holds nearly all the water vapor it can.

EXAMPLE 18–6 **Relative humidity.** On a particular hot day, the temperature is 30°C and the partial pressure of water vapor in the air is 21.0 torr. What is the relative humidity?

APPROACH From Table 18–2, we see that the saturated vapor pressure of water at 30°C is 31.8 torr.

SOLUTION The relative humidity is thus

$$\frac{21.0 \text{ torr}}{31.8 \text{ torr}} \times 100\% = 66\%.$$

[†]For example, 78% (by volume) of air molecules are nitrogen and 21% oxygen, with much smaller amounts of water vapor, argon, and other gases. At an air pressure of 1 atm, oxygen exerts a partial pressure of 0.21 atm and nitrogen 0.78 atm.

FIGURE 18–9 Fog or mist settling around a castle where the temperature has dropped below the dew point.

Humans are sensitive to humidity. A relative humidity of 40–50% is generally optimum for both health and comfort. High humidity, particularly on a hot day, reduces the evaporation of moisture from the skin, which is one of the body's vital mechanisms for regulating body temperature. Very low humidity, on the other hand, can dry the skin and mucous membranes.

Air is saturated with water vapor when the partial pressure of water in the air is equal to the saturated vapor pressure at that temperature. If the partial pressure of water exceeds the saturated vapor pressure, the air is said to be **supersaturated**. This situation can occur when a temperature decrease occurs. For example, suppose the temperature is 30°C and the partial pressure of water is 21 torr, which represents a humidity of 66% as we saw in Example 18–6. Suppose now that the temperature falls to, say, 20°C, as might happen at nightfall. From Table 18–2 we see that the saturated vapor pressure of water at 20°C is 17.5 torr. Hence the relative humidity would be greater than 100%, and the supersaturated air cannot hold this much water. The excess water may condense and appear as dew, or as fog or rain (Fig. 18–9).

When air containing a given amount of water is cooled, a temperature is reached where the partial pressure of water equals the saturated vapor pressure. This is called the **dew point**. Measurement of the dew point is the most accurate means of determining the relative humidity. One method uses a polished metal surface in contact with air, which is gradually cooled down. The temperature at which moisture begins to appear on the surface is the dew point, and the partial pressure of water can then be obtained from saturated vapor pressure Tables. If, for example, on a given day the temperature is 20°C and the dew point is 5°C, then the partial pressure of water (Table 18–2) in the 20°C air is 6.54 torr, whereas its saturated vapor pressure is 17.5 torr; hence the relative humidity is 6.54/17.5 = 37%.

EXERCISE E As the air warms up in the afternoon, how would the relative humidity change if there were no further evaporation? It would (*a*) increase, (*b*) decrease, (*c*) stay the same.

CONCEPTUAL EXAMPLE 18–7 | **Dryness in winter.** Why does the air inside heated buildings seem very dry on a cold winter day?

RESPONSE Suppose the relative humidity outside on a −10°C day is 50%. Table 18–2 tells us the partial pressure of water in the air is about 1.0 torr. If this air is brought indoors and heated to +20°C, the relative humidity is (1.0 torr)/(17.5 torr) = 5.7%. Even if the outside air were saturated at a partial pressure of 1.95 torr, the inside relative humidity would be at a low 11%.

*18–5 Van der Waals Equation of State

In Section 18–3, we discussed how real gases deviate from ideal gas behavior, particularly at high densities or when near condensing to a liquid. We would like to understand these deviations using a microscopic (molecular) point of view. J. D. van der Waals (1837–1923) analyzed this problem and in 1873 arrived at an equation of state which fits real gases more accurately than the ideal gas law. His analysis is based on kinetic theory but takes into account: (1) the finite size of molecules (we previously neglected the actual volume of the molecules themselves, compared to the total volume of the container, and this assumption becomes poorer as the density increases and molecules become closer together); (2) the range of the forces between molecules may be greater than the size of the molecules (we previously assumed that intermolecular forces act only during collisions, when the molecules are "in contact"). Let us now look at this analysis and derive the van der Waals equation of state.

Assume the molecules in a gas are spherical with radius r. If we assume these molecules behave like hard spheres, then two molecules collide and bounce off one another if the distance between their centers (Fig. 18–10) gets as small as $2r$. Thus the actual volume in which the molecules can move about is somewhat less than the volume V of the container holding the gas. The amount of "unavailable volume" depends on the number of molecules and on their size. Let b represent the "unavailable volume per mole" of gas.

FIGURE 18–10 Molecules, of radius r, colliding.

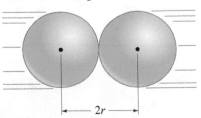

Then in the ideal gas law we replace V by $(V - nb)$, where n is the number of moles, and we obtain

$$P(V - nb) = nRT.$$

If we divide through by n, we have

$$P\left(\frac{V}{n} - b\right) = RT. \tag{18-8}$$

This relation (sometimes called the **Clausius equation of state**) predicts that for a given temperature T and volume V, the pressure P will be greater than for an ideal gas. This makes sense since the reduced "available" volume means the number of collisions with the walls is increased.

Next we consider the effects of attractive forces between molecules, which are responsible for holding molecules in the liquid and solid states at lower temperatures. These forces are electrical in nature and although they act even when molecules are not touching, we assume their range is small—that is, they act mainly between nearest neighbors. Molecules at the edge of the gas, headed toward a wall of the container, are slowed down by a net force pulling them back into the gas. Thus these molecules will exert less force and less pressure on the wall than if there were no attractive forces. The reduced pressure will be proportional to the density of molecules in the layer of gas at the surface, and also to the density in the next layer, which exerts the inward force.[†] Therefore we expect the pressure to be reduced by a factor proportional to the density squared $(n/V)^2$, here written as moles per volume. If the pressure P is given by Eq. 18-8, then we should reduce this by an amount $a(n/V)^2$ where a is a proportionality constant. Thus we have

$$P = \frac{RT}{(V/n) - b} - \frac{a}{(V/n)^2}$$

or

$$\left(P + \frac{a}{(V/n)^2}\right)\left(\frac{V}{n} - b\right) = RT, \tag{18-9}$$

which is the **van der Waals equation of state**.

The constants a and b in the van der Waals equation are different for different gases and are determined by fitting to experimental data for each gas. For CO_2 gas, the best fit is obtained for $a = 0.36\ \text{N·m}^4/\text{mol}^2$ and $b = 4.3 \times 10^{-5}\ \text{m}^3/\text{mol}$. Figure 18-11 shows a typical PV diagram for Eq. 18-9 (a "van der Waals gas") for four different temperatures, with detailed caption, and it should be compared to Fig. 18-4 for real gases.

Neither the van der Waals equation of state nor the many other equations of state that have been proposed are accurate for all gases under all conditions. Yet Eq. 18-9 is a very useful relation. And because it is quite accurate for many situations, its derivation gives us further insight into the nature of gases at the microscopic level. Note that at low densities, $a/(V/n)^2 \ll P$ and $b \ll V/n$, so that the van der Waals equation reduces to the equation of state for an ideal gas, $PV = nRT$.

*18-6 Mean Free Path

If gas molecules were truly point particles, they would have zero cross-section and never collide with one another. If you opened a perfume bottle, you would be able to smell it almost instantaneously across the room, since molecules travel hundreds of meters per second. In reality, it takes time before you detect an odor and, according to kinetic theory, this must be due to collisions between molecules of nonzero size.

If we were to follow the path of a particular molecule, we would expect to see it follow a zigzag path as shown in Fig. 18-12. Between each collision the molecule would move in a straight-line path. (Not quite true if we take account of the small intermolecular forces that act between collisions.) An important parameter for a given situation is the **mean free path**, which is defined as the average distance a molecule travels between collisions. We would expect that the greater the gas density, and the larger the molecules, the shorter the mean free path would be. We now determine the nature of this relationship for an ideal gas.

[†]This is similar to the gravitational force in which the force on mass m_1 due to mass m_2 is proportional to the product of their masses (Newton's law of universal gravitation, Chapter 6).

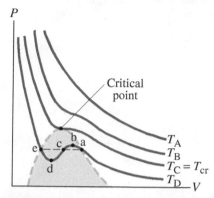

FIGURE 18-11 PV diagram for a van der Waals gas, shown for four different temperatures. For T_A, T_B, and T_C (T_C is chosen equal to the critical temperature), the curves fit experimental data very well for most gases. The curve labeled T_D, a temperature below the critical point, passes through the liquid–vapor region. The maximum (point b) and minimum (point d) would seem to be artifacts, since we usually see constant pressure, as indicated by the horizontal dashed line (and Fig. 18-4). However, for very pure supersaturated vapors or supercooled liquids, the sections ab and ed, respectively, have been observed. (The section bd would be unstable and has not been observed.)

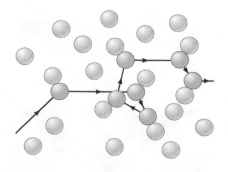

FIGURE 18-12 Zigzag path of a molecule colliding with other molecules.

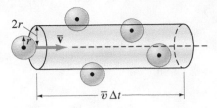

FIGURE 18–13 Molecule at left moves to the right with speed $\bar{v}$. It collides with any molecule whose center is within the cylinder of radius $2r$.

Suppose our gas is made up of molecules which are hard spheres of radius r. A collision will occur whenever the centers of two molecules come within a distance $2r$ of one another. Let us follow a molecule as it traces a straight-line path. In Fig. 18–13, the dashed line represents the path of our particle if it makes no collisions. Also shown is a cylinder of radius $2r$. If the center of another molecule lies within this cylinder, a collision will occur. (Of course, when a collision occurs the particle's path would change direction, as would our imagined cylinder, but our result won't be altered by unbending a zigzag cylinder into a straight one for purposes of calculation.) Assume our molecule is an average one, moving at the mean speed $\bar{v}$ in the gas. For the moment, let us assume that the other molecules are not moving, and that the concentration of molecules (number per unit volume) is N/V. Then the number of molecules whose centers lie within the cylinder of Fig. 18–13 is N/V times the volume of this cylinder, and this also represents the number of collisions that will occur. In a time Δt, our molecule travels a distance $\bar{v}\,\Delta t$, so the length of the cylinder is $\bar{v}\,\Delta t$ and its volume is $\pi(2r)^2\,\bar{v}\,\Delta t$. Hence the number of collisions that occur in a time Δt is $(N/V)\pi(2r)^2\,\bar{v}\,\Delta t$. We define the **mean free path**, ℓ_M, as the average distance between collisions. This distance is equal to the distance traveled ($\bar{v}\,\Delta t$) in a time Δt divided by the number of collisions made in time Δt:

$$\ell_M = \frac{\bar{v}\,\Delta t}{(N/V)\pi(2r)^2\,\bar{v}\,\Delta t} = \frac{1}{4\pi r^2 (N/V)}. \qquad \textbf{(18–10a)}$$

Thus we see that ℓ_M is inversely proportional to the cross-sectional area ($= \pi r^2$) of the molecules and to their concentration (number/volume), N/V. However, Eq. 18–10a is not fully correct since we assumed the other molecules are all at rest. In fact, they are moving, and the number of collisions in a time Δt must depend on the *relative* speed of the colliding molecules, rather than on $\bar{v}$. Hence the number of collisions per second is $(N/V)\pi(2r)^2 v_{rel}\,\Delta t$ (rather than $(N/V)\pi(2r)^2\,\bar{v}\,\Delta t$), where v_{rel} is the average relative speed of colliding molecules. A careful calculation shows that for a Maxwellian distribution of speeds $v_{rel} = \sqrt{2}\bar{v}$. Hence the mean free path is

Mean free path

$$\ell_M = \frac{1}{4\pi\sqrt{2}r^2(N/V)}. \qquad \textbf{(18–10b)}$$

EXAMPLE 18–8 ESTIMATE | **Mean free path of air molecules at STP.** Estimate the mean free path of air molecules at STP, standard temperature and pressure (0°C, 1 atm). The diameter of O_2 and N_2 molecules is about 3×10^{-10} m.

APPROACH We saw in Example 17–10 that 1 mol of an ideal gas occupies a volume of 22.4×10^{-3} m³ at STP. We can thus determine N/V and apply Eq. 18–10b.

SOLUTION

$$\frac{N}{V} = \frac{6.02 \times 10^{23} \text{ molecules}}{22.4 \times 10^{-3} \text{ m}^3} = 2.69 \times 10^{25} \text{ molecules/m}^3.$$

Then

$$\ell_M = \frac{1}{4\pi\sqrt{2}\left(1.5 \times 10^{-10} \text{ m}\right)^2 (2.7 \times 10^{25} \text{ m}^{-3})} \approx 9 \times 10^{-8} \text{ m}.$$

NOTE This is about 300 times the diameter of an air molecule.

At very low densities, such as in an evacuated vessel, the concept of mean free path loses meaning since collisions with the container walls may occur more frequently than collisions with other molecules. For example, in a cubical box that is (say) 20 cm on a side containing air at 10^{-7} torr ($\approx 10^{-10}$ atm), the mean free path would be about 900 m, which means many more collisions are made with the walls than with other molecules. (Note, nonetheless, that the box contains over 10^{12} molecules.) If the concept of mean free path included also collision with the walls, it would be closer to 0.2 m than to the 900 m calculated from Eq. 18–10b.

*18–7 Diffusion

If you carefully place a few drops of food coloring in a container of water as in Fig. 18–14, you will find that the color spreads throughout the water. The process may take some time (assuming you do not shake the glass), but eventually the color will become uniform. This mixing, known as **diffusion**, takes place because of the random movement of the molecules. Diffusion occurs in gases too. Common examples include perfume or smoke (or the odor of something cooking on the stove) diffusing in air, although convection (moving air currents) often plays a greater role in spreading odors than does diffusion. Diffusion depends on concentration, by which we mean the number of molecules or moles per unit volume. In general, *the diffusing substance moves from a region where its concentration is high to one where its concentration is low.*

(a)   (b)   (c)

FIGURE 18–14 A few drops of food coloring (a) dropped into water, (b) spreads slowly throughout the water, eventually (c) becoming uniform.

Diffusion can be readily understood on the basis of kinetic theory and the random motion of molecules. Consider a tube of cross-sectional area A containing molecules in a higher concentration on the left than on the right, Fig. 18–15. We assume the molecules are in random motion. Yet there will be a net flow of molecules to the right. To see why this is true, let us consider the small section of tube of length Δx as shown. Molecules from both regions 1 and 2 cross into this central section as a result of their random motion. The more molecules there are in a region, the more will strike a given area or cross a boundary. Since there is a greater concentration of molecules in region 1 than in region 2, more molecules cross into the central section from region 1 than from region 2. There is, then, a net flow of molecules from left to right, from high concentration toward low concentration. The net flow becomes zero only when the concentrations become equal.

You might expect that the greater the difference in concentration, the greater the flow rate. Indeed, the rate of diffusion, J (number of molecules or moles or kg per second), is directly proportional to the difference in concentration per unit distance, $(C_1 - C_2)/\Delta x$ (which is called the **concentration gradient**), and to the cross-sectional area A (see Fig. 18–15):

$$J = DA\frac{C_1 - C_2}{\Delta x},$$

or, in terms of derivatives,

$$J = DA\frac{dC}{dx}. \tag{18–11}$$

D is a constant of proportionality called the **diffusion constant**. Equation 18–11 is known as the **diffusion equation**, or **Fick's law**. If the concentrations are given in mol/m^3, then J is the number of moles passing a given point per second. If the concentrations are given in kg/m^3, then J is the mass movement per second (kg/s). The length Δx is given in meters. The values of D for a variety of substances are given in Table 18–3.

FIGURE 18–15 Diffusion occurs from a region of high concentration to one of lower concentration (only one type of molecule is shown).

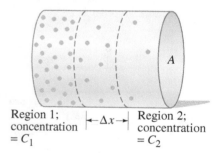

Region 1; concentration $= C_1$ ←Δx→   Region 2; concentration $= C_2$

TABLE 18–3 Diffusion Constants, D (20°C, 1 atm)

Diffusing Molecules	Medium	D (m^2/s)
H_2	Air	6.3×10^{-5}
O_2	Air	1.8×10^{-5}
O_2	Water	100×10^{-11}
Blood hemoglobin	Water	6.9×10^{-11}
Glycine (an amino acid)	Water	95×10^{-11}
DNA (mass 6×10^6 u)	Water	0.13×10^{-11}

EXAMPLE 18-9 ESTIMATE | **Diffusion of ammonia in air.** To get an idea of the time required for diffusion, estimate how long it might take for ammonia (NH_3) to be detected 10 cm from a bottle after it is opened, assuming only diffusion is occurring.

APPROACH This will be an order-of-magnitude calculation. The rate of diffusion J can be set equal to the number of molecules N diffusing across area A in a time t: $J = N/t$. Then the time $t = N/J$, where J is given by Eq. 18–11. We will have to make some assumptions and rough approximations about concentrations to use Eq. 18–11.

SOLUTION Using Eq. 18–11, we find

$$t = \frac{N}{J} = \frac{N}{DA}\frac{\Delta x}{\Delta C}.$$

The average concentration (midway between bottle and nose) can be approximated by $\overline{C} \approx N/V$, where V is the volume over which the molecules move and is roughly of the order of $V \approx A\,\Delta x$, where Δx is $10\,\text{cm} = 0.10\,\text{m}$. We substitute $N = \overline{C}V = \overline{C}A\,\Delta x$ into the above equation:

$$t \approx \frac{(\overline{C}A\,\Delta x)\,\Delta x}{DA\,\Delta C} = \frac{\overline{C}}{\Delta C}\frac{(\Delta x)^2}{D}.$$

The concentration of ammonia is high near the bottle (C) and low near the detecting nose (≈ 0), so $\overline{C} \approx C/2 \approx \Delta C/2$, or $(\overline{C}/\Delta C) \approx \frac{1}{2}$. Since NH_3 molecules have a size somewhere between H_2 and O_2, from Table 18–3 we can estimate $D \approx 4 \times 10^{-5}\,\text{m}^2/\text{s}$. Then

$$t \approx \frac{1}{2}\frac{(0.10\,\text{m})^2}{(4 \times 10^{-5}\,\text{m}^2/\text{s})} \approx 100\,\text{s},$$

or about a minute or two.

NOTE This result seems rather long from experience, suggesting that air currents (convection) are more important than diffusion for transmitting odors.

CONCEPTUAL EXAMPLE 18-10 | **Colored rings on a paper towel.** A child colors a small spot on a wet paper towel with a brown marker. Later, she discovers that instead of a brown spot, there are concentric colored rings around the marked spot. What happened?

RESPONSE The ink in a brown marker is composed of several different inks that mix to make brown. These inks each diffuse at different rates through the wet paper towel. After a period of time the inks have diffused far enough that the differences in distances traveled is sufficient to separate the different colors. Chemists and biochemists use a similar technique, called *chromatography*, to separate substances based on their diffusion rates through a medium.

PHYSICS APPLIED
Diffusion time

PHYSICS APPLIED
Chromatography

Summary

According to the **kinetic theory** of gases, which is based on the idea that a gas is made up of molecules that are moving rapidly and at random, the average translational kinetic energy of the molecules is proportional to the Kelvin temperature T:

$$\overline{K} = \tfrac{1}{2}m\overline{v^2} = \tfrac{3}{2}kT \qquad (18\text{-}4)$$

where k is Boltzmann's constant.

At any moment, there exists a wide distribution of molecular speeds within a gas. The **Maxwell distribution of speeds** is derived from simple kinetic theory assumptions, and is in good accord with experiment for gases at not too high a pressure.

The behavior of real gases at high pressure, and/or when near their liquefaction point, deviates from the ideal gas law due to the finite size of molecules and to the attractive forces between molecules.

Below the **critical temperature**, a gas can change to a liquid if sufficient pressure is applied; but if the temperature is higher than the critical temperature, no amount of pressure will cause a liquid surface to form.

The **triple point** of a substance is that unique temperature and pressure at which all three phases—solid, liquid, and gas—can coexist in equilibrium. Because of its precise reproducibility, the triple point of water is often taken as a standard reference point.

Evaporation of a liquid is the result of the fastest moving molecules escaping from the surface. Because the average molecular velocity is less after the fastest molecules escape, the temperature decreases when evaporation takes place.

Saturated vapor pressure refers to the pressure of the vapor above a liquid when the two phases are in equilibrium. The vapor pressure of a substance (such as water) depends strongly on temperature and is equal to atmospheric pressure at the boiling point.

Relative humidity of air at a given place is the ratio of the partial pressure of water vapor in the air to the saturated vapor pressure at that temperature; it is usually expressed as a percentage.

[*The **van der Waals equation of state** takes into account the finite volume of molecules, and the attractive forces between molecules, to better approximate the behavior of real gases.]

[*The **mean free path** is the average distance a molecule moves between collisions with other molecules.]

[*Diffusion** is the process whereby molecules of a substance move (on average) from one area to another because of a difference in that substance's concentration.]

Questions

1. Why doesn't the size of different molecules enter into the ideal gas law?

2. When a gas is rapidly compressed (say, by pushing down a piston) its temperature increases. When a gas expands against a piston, it cools. Explain these changes in temperature using the kinetic theory, in particular noting what happens to the momentum of molecules when they strike the moving piston.

3. In Section 18–1 we assumed the gas molecules made perfectly elastic collisions with the walls of the container. This assumption is not necessary as long as the walls are at the same temperature as the gas. Why?

4. Explain in words how Charles's law follows from kinetic theory and the relation between average kinetic energy and the absolute temperature.

5. Explain in words how Gay-Lussac's law follows from kinetic theory.

6. As you go higher in the Earth's atmosphere, the ratio of N_2 molecules to O_2 molecules increases. Why?

7. Can you determine the temperature of a vacuum?

8. Is temperature a macroscopic or microscopic variable?

9. Explain why the peak of the curve for 310 K in Fig. 18–3 is not as high as for 273 K. (Assume the total number of molecules is the same for both.)

10. Escape velocity for the Earth refers to the minimum speed an object must have to leave the Earth and never return. (a) The escape velocity for the Moon is about one-fifth what it is for the Earth due to the Moon's smaller mass; explain why the Moon has practically no atmosphere. (b) If hydrogen was once in the Earth's atmosphere, why would it have probably escaped?

11. If a container of gas is at rest, the average velocity of molecules must be zero. Yet the average speed is not zero. Explain.

12. If the pressure in a gas is doubled while its volume is held constant, by what factor do (a) v_{rms} and (b) $\bar{v}$ change?

13. What everyday observation would tell you that not all molecules in a material have the same speed?

14. We saw that the saturated vapor pressure of a liquid (say, water) does not depend on the external pressure. Yet the temperature of boiling does depend on the external pressure. Is there a contradiction? Explain.

15. Alcohol evaporates more quickly than water at room temperature. What can you infer about the molecular properties of one relative to the other?

16. Explain why a hot humid day is far more uncomfortable than a hot dry day at the same temperature.

17. Is it possible to boil water at room temperature (20°C) without heating it? Explain.

18. What exactly does it mean when we say that oxygen boils at −183°C?

19. A length of thin wire is placed over a block of ice (or an ice cube) at 0°C and weights are hung from the ends of the wire. It is found that the wire cuts its way through the ice cube, but leaves a solid block of ice behind it. This process is called *regelation*. Explain how this happens by inferring how the freezing point of water depends on pressure.

20. Consider two days when the air temperature is the same but the humidity is different. Which is more dense, the dry air or the humid air at the same T? Explain.

21. (a) Why does food cook faster in a pressure cooker? (b) Why does pasta or rice need to boil longer at high altitudes? (c) Is it harder to boil water at high altitudes?

22. How do a gas and a vapor differ?

23. (a) At suitable temperatures and pressures, can ice be melted by applying pressure? (b) At suitable temperatures and pressures, can carbon dioxide be melted by applying pressure?

24. Why does dry ice not last long at room temperature?

25. Under what conditions can liquid CO_2 exist? Be specific. Can it exist as a liquid at normal room temperature?

26. Why does exhaled air appear as a little white cloud in the winter (Fig. 18–16)?

FIGURE 18–16
Question 26.

*27. Discuss why sound waves can travel in a gas only if their wavelength is somewhat larger than the mean free path.

*28. Name several ways to reduce the mean free path in a gas.

Problems

18-1 Molecular Interpretation of Temperature

1. (I) (a) What is the average translational kinetic energy of an oxygen molecule at STP? (b) What is the total translational kinetic energy of 1.0 mol of O_2 molecules at 25°C?

2. (I) Calculate the rms speed of helium atoms near the surface of the Sun at a temperature of about 6000 K.

3. (I) By what factor will the rms speed of gas molecules increase if the temperature is increased from 0°C to 180°C?

4. (I) A gas is at 20°C. To what temperature must it be raised to triple the rms speed of its molecules?

5. (I) What speed would a 1.0-g paper clip have if it had the same kinetic energy as a molecule at 15°C?

6. (I) A 1.0-mol sample of helium gas has a temperature of 27°C. (a) What is the total kinetic energy of all the gas atoms in the sample? (b) How fast would a 65-kg person have to run to have the same kinetic energy?

7. (I) Twelve molecules have the following speeds, given in arbitrary units: 6.0, 2.0, 4.0, 6.0, 0.0, 4.0, 1.0, 8.0, 5.0, 3.0, 7.0, and 8.0. Calculate (a) the mean speed, and (b) the rms speed.

8. (II) The rms speed of molecules in a gas at 20.0°C is to be increased by 2.0%. To what temperature must it be raised?

9. (II) If the pressure in a gas is tripled while its volume is held constant, by what factor does v_{rms} change?

10. (II) Show that the rms speed of molecules in a gas is given by $v_{rms} = \sqrt{3P/\rho}$, where P is the pressure in the gas, and ρ is the gas density.

11. (II) Show that for a mixture of two gases at the same temperature, the ratio of their rms speeds is equal to the inverse ratio of the square roots of their molecular masses.

12. (II) What is the rms speed of nitrogen molecules contained in an 8.5-m³ volume at 3.1 atm if the total amount of nitrogen is 1800 mol?

13. (II) (a) For an ideal gas at temperature T show that

$$\frac{dv_{rms}}{dT} = \frac{1}{2}\frac{v_{rms}}{T},$$

and using the approximation $\Delta v_{rms} \approx \dfrac{dv_{rms}}{dT}\Delta T$, show that

$$\frac{\Delta v_{rms}}{v_{rms}} \approx \frac{1}{2}\frac{\Delta T}{T}.$$

(b) If the average air temperature changes from −5°C in winter to 25°C in summer, estimate the percent change in the rms speed of air molecules between these seasons.

14. (II) What is the average distance between oxygen molecules at STP?

15. (II) Two isotopes of uranium, ^{235}U and ^{238}U (the superscripts refer to their atomic masses), can be separated by a gas diffusion process by combining them with fluorine to make the gaseous compound UF_6. Calculate the ratio of the rms speeds of these molecules for the two isotopes, at constant T. Use Appendix F for masses.

16. (II) Can pockets of vacuum persist in an ideal gas? Assume that a room is filled with air at 20°C and that somehow a small spherical region of radius 1 cm within the room becomes devoid of air molecules. Estimate how long it will take for air to refill this region of vacuum. Assume the atomic mass of air is 29 u.

17. (II) Calculate (a) the rms speed of a nitrogen molecule at 0°C and (b) determine how many times per second it would move back and forth across a 5.0-m-long room on the average, assuming it made very few collisions with other molecules.

18. (III) Estimate how many air molecules rebound from a wall in a typical room per second, assuming an ideal gas of N molecules contained in a cubic room with sides of length ℓ at temperature T and pressure P. (a) Show that the frequency f with which gas molecules strike a wall is

$$f = \frac{\bar{v}_x}{2}\frac{P}{kT}\ell^2$$

where $\bar{v}_x$ is the average x component of the molecule's velocity. (b) Show that the equation can then be written as

$$f \approx \frac{P\ell^2}{\sqrt{4mkT}}$$

where m is the mass of a gas molecule. (c) Assume a cubic air-filled room is at sea level, has a temperature 20°C, and has sides of length $\ell = 3$ m. Determine f.

18-2 Distribution of Molecular Speeds

19. (I) If you double the mass of the molecules in a gas, is it possible to change the temperature to keep the velocity distribution from changing? If so, what do you need to do to the temperature?

20. (I) A group of 25 particles have the following speeds: two have speed 10 m/s, seven have 15 m/s, four have 20 m/s, three have 25 m/s, six have 30 m/s, one has 35 m/s, and two have 40 m/s. Determine (a) the average speed, (b) the rms speed, and (c) the most probable speed.

21. (II) A gas consisting of 15,200 molecules, each of mass 2.00×10^{-26} kg, has the following distribution of speeds, which crudely mimics the Maxwell distribution:

Number of Molecules	Speed (m/s)
1600	220
4100	440
4700	660
3100	880
1300	1100
400	1320

(a) Determine v_{rms} for this distribution of speeds. (b) Given your value for v_{rms}, what (effective) temperature would you assign to this gas? (c) Determine the mean speed $\bar{v}$ of this distribution and use this value to assign an (effective) temperature to the gas. Is the temperature you find here consistent with the one you determined in part (b)?

22. (III) Starting from the Maxwell distribution of speeds, Eq. 18-6, show (a) $\int_0^\infty f(v)\, dv = N$, and (b)

$$\int_0^\infty v^2 f(v)\, dv/N = 3kT/m.$$

18-3 Real Gases

23. (I) CO_2 exists in what phase when the pressure is 30 atm and the temperature is 30°C (Fig. 18-6)?

24. (I) (a) At atmospheric pressure, in what phases can CO_2 exist? (b) For what range of pressures and temperatures can CO_2 be a liquid? Refer to Fig. 18-6.

25. (I) Water is in which phase when the pressure is 0.01 atm and the temperature is (a) 90°C, (b) −20°C?

26. (II) You have a sample of water and are able to control temperature and pressure arbitrarily. (a) Using Fig. 18–5, describe the phase changes you would see if you started at a temperature of 85°C, a pressure of 180 atm, and decreased the pressure down to 0.004 atm while keeping the temperature fixed. (b) Repeat part (a) with the temperature at 0.0°C. Assume that you held the system at the starting conditions long enough for the system to stabilize before making further changes.

18–4 Vapor Pressure and Humidity

27. (I) What is the partial pressure of water vapor at 30°C if the humidity is 85%?

28. (I) What is the partial pressure of water on a day when the temperature is 25°C and the relative humidity is 55%?

29. (I) What is the air pressure at a place where water boils at 80°C?

30. (II) What is the dew point if the humidity is 75% on a day when the temperature is 25°C?

31. (II) If the air pressure at a particular place in the mountains is 0.75 atm, estimate the temperature at which water boils.

32. (II) What is the mass of water in a closed room 5.0 m × 6.0 m × 2.4 m when the temperature is 24.0°C and the relative humidity is 65%?

33. (II) What is the approximate pressure inside a pressure cooker if the water is boiling at a temperature of 120°C? Assume no air escaped during the heating process, which started at 12°C.

34. (II) If the humidity in a room of volume 440 m³ at 25°C is 65%, what mass of water can still evaporate from an open pan?

35. (II) A **pressure cooker** is a sealed pot designed to cook food with the steam produced by boiling water somewhat above 100°C. The pressure cooker in Fig. 18–17 uses a weight of mass m to allow steam to escape at a certain pressure through a small hole (diameter d) in the cooker's lid. If d = 3.0 mm, what should m be in order to cook food at 120°C? Assume that atmospheric pressure outside the cooker is 1.01 × 10⁵ Pa.

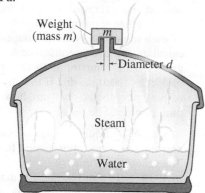

Weight (mass m)

m

Diameter d

Steam

Water

FIGURE 18–17
Problem 35.

36. (II) When using a mercury barometer (Section 13–6), the vapor pressure of mercury is usually assumed to be zero. At room temperature mercury's vapor pressure is about 0.0015 mm-Hg. At sea level, the height h of mercury in a barometer is about 760 mm. (a) If the vapor pressure of mercury is neglected, is the true atmospheric pressure greater or less than the value read from the barometer? (b) What is the percent error? (c) What is the percent error if you use a water barometer and ignore water's saturated vapor pressure at STP?

37. (II) If the humidity is 45% at 30.0°C, what is the dew point? Use linear interpolation to find the temperature of the dew point to the nearest degree.

38. (III) Air that is at its dew point of 5°C is drawn into a building where it is heated to 20°C. What will be the relative humidity at this temperature? Assume constant pressure of 1.0 atm. Take into account the expansion of the air.

39. (III) What is the mathematical relation between water's boiling temperature and atmospheric pressure? (a) Using the data from Table 18–2, in the temperature range from 50°C to 150°C, plot $\ln P$ versus $(1/T)$, where P is water's saturated vapor pressure (Pa) and T is temperature on the Kelvin scale. Show that a straight-line plot results and determine the slope and y-intercept of the line. (b) Show that your result implies

$$P = B e^{-A/T}$$

where A and B are constants. Use the slope and y-intercept from your plot to show that $A \approx 5000\,\text{K}$ and $B \approx 7 \times 10^{10}\,\text{Pa}$.

*18–5 Van der Waals Equation of State

*40. (II) In the van der Waals equation of state, the constant b represents the amount of "unavailable volume" occupied by the molecules themselves. Thus V is replaced by $(V - nb)$, where n is the number of moles. For oxygen, b is about $3.2 \times 10^{-5}\,\text{m}^3/\text{mol}$. Estimate the diameter of an oxygen molecule.

*41. (II) For oxygen gas, the van der Waals equation of state achieves its best fit for $a = 0.14\,\text{N} \cdot \text{m}^4/\text{mol}^2$ and $b = 3.2 \times 10^{-5}\,\text{m}^3/\text{mol}$. Determine the pressure in 1.0 mol of the gas at 0°C if its volume is 0.70 L, calculated using (a) the van der Waals equation, (b) the ideal gas law.

*42. (III) A 0.5-mol sample of O_2 gas is in a large cylinder with a movable piston on one end so it can be compressed. The initial volume is large enough that there is not a significant difference between the pressure given by the ideal gas law and that given by the van der Waals equation. As the gas is slowly compressed at constant temperature (use 300 K), at what volume does the van der Waals equation give a pressure that is 5% different than the ideal gas law pressure? Let $a = 0.14\,\text{N} \cdot \text{m}^4/\text{mol}^2$ and $b = 3.2 \times 10^{-5}\,\text{m}^3/\text{mol}$.

*43. (III) (a) From the van der Waals equation of state, show that the critical temperature and pressure are given by

$$T_{\text{cr}} = \frac{8a}{27bR}, \qquad P_{\text{cr}} = \frac{a}{27b^2}.$$

[Hint: Use the fact that the P versus V curve has an inflection point at the critical point so that the first and second derivatives are zero.] (b) Determine a and b for CO_2 from the measured values of $T_{\text{cr}} = 304\,\text{K}$ and $P_{\text{cr}} = 72.8\,\text{atm}$.

*44. (III) How well does the ideal gas law describe the pressurized air in a scuba tank? (a) To fill a typical scuba tank, an air compressor intakes about 2300 L of air at 1.0 atm and compresses this gas into the tank's 12-L internal volume. If the filling process occurs at 20°C, show that a tank holds about 96 mol of air. (b) Assume the tank has 96 mol of air at 20°C. Use the ideal gas law to predict the air's pressure within the tank. (c) Use the van der Waals equation of state to predict the air's pressure within the tank. For air, the van der Waals constants are $a = 0.1373\,\text{N} \cdot \text{m}^4/\text{mol}^2$ and $b = 3.72 \times 10^{-5}\,\text{m}^3/\text{mol}$. (d) Taking the van der Waals pressure as the true air pressure, show that the ideal gas law predicts a pressure that is in error by only about 3%.

*45. (II) At about what pressure would the mean free path of air molecules be (a) 0.10 m and (b) equal to the diameter of air molecules, $\approx 3 \times 10^{-10}$ m? Assume $T = 20°C$.

*46. (II) Below a certain threshold pressure, the air molecules (0.3-nm diameter) within a research vacuum chamber are in the "collision-free regime," meaning that a particular air molecule is as likely to cross the container and collide first with the opposite wall, as it is to collide with another air molecule. Estimate the threshold pressure for a vacuum chamber of side 1.0 m at 20°C.

*47. (II) A very small amount of hydrogen gas is released into the air. If the air is at 1.0 atm and 15°C, estimate the mean free path for a H_2 molecule. What assumptions did you make?

*48. (II) (a) The mean free path of CO_2 molecules at STP is measured to be about 5.6×10^{-8} m. Estimate the diameter of a CO_2 molecule. (b) Do the same for He gas for which $\ell_M \approx 25 \times 10^{-8}$ m at STP.

*49. (II) (a) Show that the number of collisions a molecule makes per second, called the *collision frequency*, f, is given by $f = \bar{v}/\ell_M$, and thus $f = 4\sqrt{2}\,\pi r^2 \bar{v}N/V$. (b) What is the collision frequency for N_2 molecules in air at $T = 20°C$ and $P = 1.0 \times 10^{-2}$ atm?

*50. (II) We saw in Example 18–8 that the mean free path of air molecules at STP, ℓ_M, is about 9×10^{-8} m. Estimate the collision frequency f, the number of collisions per unit time.

*51. (II) A cubic box 1.80 m on a side is evacuated so the pressure of air inside is 10^{-6} torr. Estimate how many collisions molecules make with each other for each collision with a wall (0°C).

*52. (III) Estimate the maximum allowable pressure in a 32-cm-long cathode ray tube if 98% of all electrons must hit the screen without first striking an air molecule.

*53. (I) Approximately how long would it take for the ammonia of Example 18–9 to be detected 1.0 m from the bottle after it is opened? What does this suggest about the relative importance of diffusion and convection for carrying odors?

*54. (II) Estimate the time needed for a glycine molecule (see Table 18–3) to diffuse a distance of 15 μm in water at 20°C if its concentration varies over that distance from 1.00 mol/m^3 to 0.50 mol/m^3? Compare this "speed" to its rms (thermal) speed. The molecular mass of glycine is about 75 u.

*55. (II) Oxygen diffuses from the surface of insects to the interior through tiny tubes called tracheae. An average trachea is about 2 mm long and has cross-sectional area of 2×10^{-9} m^2. Assuming the concentration of oxygen inside is half what it is outside in the atmosphere, (a) show that the concentration of oxygen in the air (assume 21% is oxygen) at 20°C is about 8.7 mol/m^3, then (b) calculate the diffusion rate J, and (c) estimate the average time for a molecule to diffuse in. Assume the diffusion constant is 1×10^{-5} m^2/s.

General Problems

56. A sample of ideal gas must contain at least $N = 10^6$ molecules in order for the Maxwell distribution to be a valid description of the gas, and to assign it a meaningful temperature. For an ideal gas at STP, what is the smallest length scale ℓ (volume $V = \ell^3$) for which a valid temperature can be assigned?

57. In outer space the density of matter is about one atom per cm^3, mainly hydrogen atoms, and the temperature is about 2.7 K. Calculate the rms speed of these hydrogen atoms, and the pressure (in atmospheres).

58. Calculate approximately the total translational kinetic energy of all the molecules in an *E. coli* bacterium of mass 2.0×10^{-15} kg at 37°C. Assume 70% of the cell, by weight, is water, and the other molecules have an average molecular mass on the order of 10^5 u.

59. (a) Estimate the rms speed of an amino acid, whose molecular mass is 89 u, in a living cell at 37°C. (b) What would be the rms speed of a protein of molecular mass 85,000 u at 37°C?

60. The escape speed from the Earth is 1.12×10^4 m/s, so that a gas molecule travelling away from Earth near the outer boundary of the Earth's atmosphere would, at this speed, be able to escape from the Earth's gravitational field and be lost to the atmosphere. At what temperature is the average speed of (a) oxygen molecules, and (b) helium atoms equal to 1.12×10^4 m/s? (c) Can you explain why our atmosphere contains oxygen but not helium?

61. The second postulate of kinetic theory is that the molecules are, on the average, far apart from one another. That is, their average separation is much greater than the diameter of each molecule. Is this assumption reasonable? To check, calculate the average distance between molecules of a gas at STP, and compare it to the diameter of a typical gas molecule, about 0.3 nm. If the molecules were the diameter of ping-pong balls, say 4 cm, how far away would the next ping-pong ball be on average?

62. A sample of liquid cesium is heated in an oven to 400°C and the resulting vapor is used to produce an atomic beam. The volume of the oven is 55 cm^3, the vapor pressure of Cs at 400°C is 17 mm-Hg, and the diameter of cesium atoms in the vapor is 0.33 nm. (a) Calculate the mean speed of cesium atoms in the vapor. (b) Determine the number of collisions a single Cs atom undergoes with other cesium atoms per second. (c) Determine the total number of collisions per second between all of the cesium atoms in the vapor. Note that a collision involves two Cs atoms and assume the ideal gas law holds.

63. Consider a container of oxygen gas at a temperature of 20°C that is 1.00 m tall. Compare the gravitational potential energy of a molecule at the top of the container (assuming the potential energy is zero at the bottom) with the average kinetic energy of the molecules. Is it reasonable to neglect the potential energy?

64. In humid climates, people constantly *dehumidify* their cellars to prevent rot and mildew. If the cellar in a house (kept at 20°C) has 115 m² of floor space and a ceiling height of 2.8 m, what is the mass of water that must be removed from it in order to drop the humidity from 95% to a more reasonable 40%?

65. Assuming a typical nitrogen or oxygen molecule is about 0.3 nm in diameter, what percent of the room you are sitting in is taken up by the volume of the molecules themselves?

66. A scuba tank has a volume of 3100 cm³. For very deep dives, the tank is filled with 50% (by volume) pure oxygen and 50% pure helium. (*a*) How many molecules are there of each type in the tank if at 20°C the gauge pressure reads 12 atm? (*b*) What is the ratio of the average kinetic energies of the two types of molecule? (*c*) What is the ratio of the rms speeds of the two types of molecule?

67. A space vehicle returning from the Moon enters the atmosphere at a speed of about 42,000 km/h. Molecules (assume nitrogen) striking the nose of the vehicle with this speed correspond to what temperature? (Because of this high temperature, the nose of a space vehicle must be made of special materials; indeed, part of it does vaporize, and this is seen as a bright blaze upon reentry.)

68. At room temperature, it takes approximately 2.45×10^3 J to evaporate 1.00 g of water. Estimate the average speed of evaporating molecules. What multiple of v_{rms} (at 20°C) for water molecules is this? (Assume Eq. 18–4 holds.)

69. Calculate the total water vapor pressure in the air on the following two days: (*a*) a hot summer day, with the temperature 30°C and the relative humidity at 65%; (*b*) a cold winter day, with the temperature 5°C and the relative humidity at 75%.

*70. At 300 K, an 8.50-mol sample of carbon dioxide occupies a volume of 0.220 m³. Calculate the gas pressure, first by assuming the ideal gas law, and then by using the van der Waals equation of state. (The values for *a* and *b* are given in Section 18–5.) In this range of pressure and volume, the van der Waals equation is very accurate. What percent error did you make in assuming ideal-gas-law behavior?

*71. The density of atoms, mostly hydrogen, in interstellar space is about one per cubic centimeter. Estimate the mean free path of the hydrogen atoms, assuming an atomic diameter of 10^{-10} m.

*72. Using the ideal gas law, find an expression for the mean free path ℓ_M that involves pressure and temperature instead of (N/V). Use this expression to find the mean free path for nitrogen molecules at a pressure of 7.5 atm and 300 K.

73. A sauna has 8.5 m³ of air volume, and the temperature is 90°C. The air is perfectly dry. How much water (in kg) should be evaporated if we want to increase the relative humidity from 0% to 10%? (See Table 18–2.)

74. A 0.50-kg trash-can lid is suspended against gravity by tennis balls thrown vertically upward at it. How many tennis balls per second must rebound from the lid elastically, assuming they have a mass of 0.060 kg and are thrown at 12 m/s?

*75. Sound waves in a gas can only propagate if the gas molecules collide with each other on the time scale of the sound wave's period. Thus the highest possible frequency f_{max} for a sound wave in a gas is approximately equal to the inverse of the average collision time between molecules. Assume a gas, composed of molecules with mass *m* and radius *r*, is at pressure *P* and temperature *T*. (*a*) Show that

$$f_{max} \approx 16Pr^2 \sqrt{\frac{\pi}{mkT}}.$$

(*b*) Determine f_{max} for 20°C air at sea level. How many times larger is f_{max} than the highest frequency in the human audio range (20 kHz)?

*## Numerical/Computer

*76. (II) Use a spreadsheet to calculate and graph the fraction of molecules in each 50-m/s speed interval from 100 m/s to 5000 m/s if $T = 300$ K.

*77. (II) Use numerical integration [Section 2–9] to estimate (within 2%) the fraction of molecules in air at 1.00 atm and 20°C that have a speed greater than 1.5 times the most probable speed.

*78. (II) For oxygen gas the van der Waals constants are $a = 0.14$ N·m⁴/mol² and $b = 3.2 \times 10^{-5}$ m³/mol. Using these values, graph six curves of pressure vs. volume between $V = 2 \times 10^{-5}$ m³ to 2.0×10^{-4} m³, for 1 mol of oxygen gas at temperatures of 80 K, 100 K, 120 K, 130 K, 150 K, and 170 K. From the graphs determine approximately the critical temperature for oxygen.

Answers to Exercises

A: (*a*).

B: (*d*).

C: (*c*).

D: (*d*).

E: (*b*).

When it is cold, warm clothes act as insulators to reduce heat loss from the body to the environment by conduction and convection. Heat radiation from a campfire can warm you and your clothes. The fire can also transfer energy directly by heat convection and conduction to what you are cooking. Heat, like work, represents a transfer of energy. Heat is defined as a transfer of energy due to a difference of temperature. Work is a transfer of energy by mechanical means, not due to a temperature difference. The first law of thermodynamics links the two in a general statement of energy conservation: the heat Q added to a system minus the net work W done by the system equals the change in internal energy ΔE_{int} of the system: $\Delta E_{int} = Q - W$. Internal energy E_{int} is the sum total of all the energy of the molecules of the system.

C H A P T E R

19

Heat and the First Law of Thermodynamics

CHAPTER-OPENING QUESTION—Guess now!

A 5-kg cube of warm iron (60°C) is put in thermal contact with a 10-kg cube of cold iron (15°C). Which statement is valid:

(a) Heat flows spontaneously from the warm cube to the cold cube until both cubes have the same heat content.

(b) Heat flows spontaneously from the warm cube to the cold cube until both cubes have the same temperature.

(c) Heat can flow spontaneously from the warm cube to the cold cube, but can also flow spontaneously from the cold cube to the warm cube.

(d) Heat can never flow from a cold object or area to a hot object or area.

(e) Heat flows from the larger cube to the smaller one because the larger one has more internal energy.

When a pot of cold water is placed on a hot burner of a stove, the temperature of the water increases. We say that heat "flows" from the hot burner to the cold water. When two objects at different temperatures are put in contact, heat spontaneously flows from the hotter one to the colder one. The spontaneous flow of heat is in the direction tending to equalize the temperature. If the two objects are kept in contact long enough for their temperatures to become equal, the objects are said to be in thermal equilibrium, and there is no further heat flow between them. For example, when a fever thermometer is first placed in your mouth, heat flows from your mouth to the thermometer. When the thermometer reaches the same temperature as the inside of your mouth, the thermometer and your mouth are then in equilibrium, and no more heat flows.

Heat and temperature are often confused. They are very different concepts and we will make the clear distinction between them. We start this Chapter by defining and using the concept of heat. We also begin our discussion of thermodynamics, which is the name we give to the study of processes in which energy is transferred as heat and as work.

19–1 Heat as Energy Transfer

We use the term "heat" in everyday life as if we knew what we meant. But the term is often used inconsistently, so it is important for us to define heat clearly, and to clarify the phenomena and concepts related to heat.

We commonly speak of the flow of heat—heat flows from a stove burner to a pot of soup, from the Sun to the Earth, from a person's mouth into a fever thermometer. Heat flows spontaneously from an object at higher temperature to one at lower temperature. Indeed, an eighteenth-century model of heat pictured heat flow as movement of a fluid substance called *caloric*. However, the caloric fluid could never be detected. In the nineteenth century, it was found that the various phenomena associated with heat could be described consistently using a new model that views heat as akin to work, as we will discuss in a moment. First we note that a common unit for heat, still in use today, is named after caloric. It is called the **calorie** (cal) and is defined as *the amount of heat necessary to raise the temperature of 1 gram of water by 1 Celsius degree.* [To be precise, the particular temperature range from 14.5°C to 15.5°C is specified because the heat required is very slightly different at different temperatures. The difference is less than 1% over the range 0 to 100°C, and we will ignore it for most purposes.] More often used than the calorie is the **kilocalorie** (kcal), which is 1000 calories. Thus *1 kcal is the heat needed to raise the temperature of 1 kg of water by 1 C°.* Often a kilocalorie is called a **Calorie** (with a capital C), and this Calorie (or the kJ) is used to specify the energy value of food. In the British system of units, heat is measured in British thermal units (Btu). One Btu is defined as the heat needed to raise the temperature of 1 lb of water by 1 F°. It can be shown (Problem 4) that $1 \text{ Btu} = 0.252 \text{ kcal} = 1056 \text{ J}$.

The idea that heat is related to energy transfer was pursued by a number of scientists in the 1800s, particularly by an English brewer, James Prescott Joule (1818–1889). One of Joule's experiments is shown (simplified) in Fig. 19–1. The falling weight causes the paddle wheel to turn. The friction between the water and the paddle wheel causes the temperature of the water to rise slightly (barely measurable, in fact, by Joule). In this and many other experiments (some involving electrical energy), Joule determined that a given amount of work done was always equivalent to a particular amount of heat input. Quantitatively, 4.186 joules (J) of work was found to be equivalent to 1 calorie (cal) of heat. This is known as the **mechanical equivalent of heat**:

$$4.186 \text{ J} = 1 \text{ cal};$$
$$4.186 \text{ kJ} = 1 \text{ kcal}.$$

As a result of these and other experiments, scientists came to interpret heat not as a substance, and not exactly as a form of energy. Rather, heat refers to a *transfer of energy*: when heat flows from a hot object to a cooler one, it is energy that is being transferred from the hot to the cold object. Thus, **heat** is *energy transferred from one object to another because of a difference in temperature.* In SI units, the unit for heat, as for any form of energy, is the joule. Nonetheless, calories and kcal are still sometimes used. Today the calorie is *defined* in terms of the joule (via the mechanical equivalent of heat, above), rather than in terms of the properties of water, as given previously. The latter is still handy to remember: 1 cal raises 1 g of water by 1 C°, or 1 kcal raises 1 kg of water by 1 C°.

Joule's result was crucial because it extended the work-energy principle to include processes involving heat. It also led to the establishment of the law of conservation of energy, which we shall discuss more fully later in this Chapter.

⚠ CAUTION
Heat is not a fluid

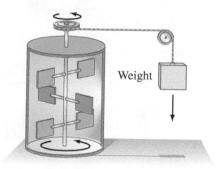

FIGURE 19–1 Joule's experiment on the mechanical equivalent of heat.

⚠ CAUTION
Heat is energy transferred because of a ΔT

EXAMPLE 19–1 ┃ **ESTIMATE** ┃ **Working off the extra calories.** Suppose you throw caution to the wind and eat too much ice cream and cake on the order of 500 Calories. To compensate, you want to do an equivalent amount of work climbing stairs or a mountain. How much total height must you climb?

APPROACH The work W you need to do in climbing stairs equals the change in gravitational potential energy: $W = \Delta PE = mgh$, where h is the vertical height climbed. For this estimate, approximate your mass as $m \approx 60$ kg.

SOLUTION 500 food Calories are 500 kcal, which in joules is

$$(500 \, \text{kcal})(4.186 \times 10^3 \, \text{J/kcal}) = 2.1 \times 10^6 \, \text{J}.$$

The work done to climb a vertical height h is $W = mgh$. We solve for h:

$$h = \frac{W}{mg} = \frac{2.1 \times 10^6 \, \text{J}}{(60 \, \text{kg})(9.80 \, \text{m/s}^2)} = 3600 \, \text{m}.$$

This is a huge elevation change (over 11,000 ft).

NOTE The human body does not transform food energy with 100% efficiency—it is more like 20% efficient. As we shall discuss in the next Chapter, some energy is always "wasted," so you would actually have to climb only about $(0.2)(3600 \, \text{m}) \approx 700 \, \text{m}$, which is more reasonable (about 2300 ft of elevation gain).

19–2 Internal Energy

The sum total of all the energy of all the molecules in an object is called its **internal energy**. (Sometimes **thermal energy** is used to mean the same thing.) We introduce the concept of internal energy now since it will help clarify ideas about heat.

Distinguishing Temperature, Heat, and Internal Energy

⚠ CAUTION
Distinguish heat from internal energy and from temperature

Using the kinetic theory, we can make a clear distinction between temperature, heat, and internal energy. Temperature (in kelvins) is a measure of the *average* kinetic energy of individual molecules. Internal energy refers to the *total* energy of all the molecules within the object. (Thus two equal-mass hot ingots of iron may have the same temperature, but two of them have twice as much internal energy as one does.) Heat, finally, refers to a *transfer* of energy from one object to another because of a difference in temperature.

⚠ CAUTION
Direction of heat flow depends on temperature (not on amount of internal energy)

Notice that the direction of heat flow between two objects depends on their temperatures, not on how much internal energy each has. Thus, if 50 g of water at 30°C is placed in contact (or mixed) with 200 g of water at 25°C, heat flows *from* the water at 30°C *to* the water at 25°C even though the internal energy of the 25°C water is much greater because there is so much more of it.

EXERCISE A Return to the Chapter-Opening Question, page 496, and answer it again now. Try to explain why you may have answered differently the first time.

Internal Energy of an Ideal Gas

Let us calculate the internal energy of n moles of an ideal monatomic (one atom per molecule) gas. The internal energy, E_{int}, is the sum of the translational kinetic energies of all the atoms.[†] This sum is equal to the average kinetic energy per molecule times the total number of molecules, N:

$$E_{\text{int}} = N(\tfrac{1}{2}m\overline{v^2}).$$

Using Eq. 18–4, $\overline{K} = \tfrac{1}{2}m\overline{v^2} = \tfrac{3}{2}kT$, we can write this as

$$E_{\text{int}} = \tfrac{3}{2}NkT \tag{19–1a}$$

[†]The symbol U is used in some books for internal energy. The use of E_{int} avoids confusion with U which stands for potential energy (Chapter 8).

or (recall Section 17–9)

$$E_{int} = \tfrac{3}{2}nRT,$$ [ideal monatomic gas] **(19–1b)**

where n is the number of moles. Thus, the internal energy of an ideal gas depends only on temperature and the number of moles of gas.

If the gas molecules contain more than one atom, then the rotational and vibrational energy of the molecules (Fig. 19–2) must also be taken into account. The internal energy will be greater at a given temperature than for a monatomic gas, but it will still be a function only of temperature for an ideal gas.

The internal energy of real gases also depends mainly on temperature, but where real gases deviate from ideal gas behavior, their internal energy depends also somewhat on pressure and volume (due to atomic potential energy).

The internal energy of liquids and solids is quite complicated, for it includes electrical potential energy associated with the forces (or "chemical" bonds) between atoms and molecules.

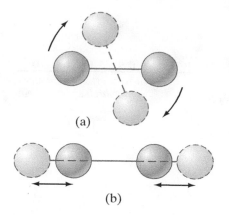

FIGURE 19–2 Besides translational kinetic energy, molecules can have (a) rotational kinetic energy, and (b) vibrational energy (both kinetic and potential).

19–3 Specific Heat

If heat flows into an object, the object's temperature rises (assuming no phase change). But how much does the temperature rise? That depends. As early as the eighteenth century, experimenters had recognized that the amount of heat Q required to change the temperature of a given material is proportional to the mass m of the material present and to the temperature change ΔT. This remarkable simplicity in nature can be expressed in the equation

$$Q = mc\,\Delta T,$$ **(19–2)**

where c is a quantity characteristic of the material called its **specific heat**. Because $c = Q/m\,\Delta T$, specific heat is specified in units[†] of J/kg·C° (the proper SI unit) or kcal/kg·C°. For water at 15°C and a constant pressure of 1 atm, $c = 4.19 \times 10^3$ J/kg·C° or 1.00 kcal/kg·C°, since, by definition of the cal and the joule, it takes 1 kcal of heat to raise the temperature of 1 kg of water by 1 C°. Table 19–1 gives the values of specific heat for other solids and liquids at 20°C. The values of c for solids and liquids depend to some extent on temperature (as well as slightly on pressure), but for temperature changes that are not too great, c can often be considered constant.[‡] Gases are more complicated and are treated in Section 19–8.

EXAMPLE 19–2 **How heat transferred depends on specific heat.** (a) How much heat input is needed to raise the temperature of an empty 20-kg vat made of iron from 10°C to 90°C? (b) What if the vat is filled with 20 kg of water?

APPROACH We apply Eq. 19–2 to the different materials involved.

SOLUTION (a) Our system is the iron vat alone. From Table 19–1, the specific heat of iron is 450 J/kg·C°. The change in temperature is $(90°C - 10°C) = 80$ C°. Thus,

$$Q = mc\,\Delta T = (20\,\text{kg})(450\,\text{J/kg·C°})(80\,\text{C°}) = 7.2 \times 10^5\,\text{J} = 720\,\text{kJ}.$$

(b) Our system is the vat plus the water. The water alone would require

$$Q = mc\,\Delta T = (20\,\text{kg})(4186\,\text{J/kg·C°})(80\,\text{C°}) = 6.7 \times 10^6\,\text{J} = 6700\,\text{kJ},$$

or almost 10 times what an equal mass of iron requires. The total, for the vat plus the water, is $720\,\text{kJ} + 6700\,\text{kJ} = 7400\,\text{kJ}$.

NOTE In (b), the iron vat and the water underwent the same temperature change, $\Delta T = 80$ C°, but their specific heats are different.

[†]Note that J/kg·C° means $\dfrac{\text{J}}{\text{kg·C°}}$ and *not* (J/kg)·C° = J·C°/kg (otherwise we would have written it that way).

[‡]To take into account the dependence of c on T, we can write Eq. 19–2 in differential form: $dQ = mc(T)\,dT$, where $c(T)$ means c is a function of temperature T. Then the heat Q required to change the temperature from T_1 to T_2 is

$$Q = \int_{T_1}^{T_2} mc(T)\,dT.$$

TABLE 19–1 Specific Heats
(at 1 atm constant pressure and 20°C unless otherwise stated)

Substance	Specific Heat, c	
	kcal/kg · C° (= cal/g · C°)	J/kg · C°
Aluminum	0.22	900
Alcohol (ethyl)	0.58	2400
Copper	0.093	390
Glass	0.20	840
Iron or steel	0.11	450
Lead	0.031	130
Marble	0.21	860
Mercury	0.033	140
Silver	0.056	230
Wood	0.4	1700
Water		
Ice (−5°C)	0.50	2100
Liquid (15°C)	1.00	4186
Steam (110°C)	0.48	2010
Human body (average)	0.83	3470
Protein	0.4	1700

If the iron vat in part (*a*) of Example 19–2 had been *cooled* from 90°C to 10°C, 720 kJ of heat would have flowed *out* of the iron. In other words, Eq. 19–2 is valid for heat flow either in or out, with a corresponding increase or decrease in temperature. We saw in part (*b*) that water requires almost 10 times as much heat as an equal mass of iron to make the same temperature change. Water has one of the highest specific heats of all substances, which makes it an ideal substance for hot-water space-heating systems and other uses that require a minimal drop in temperature for a given amount of heat transfer. It is the water content, too, that causes the apples rather than the crust in hot apple pie to burn our tongues, through heat transfer.

PHYSICS APPLIED
Practical effects of water's high specific heat

19–4 Calorimetry—Solving Problems

In discussing heat and thermodynamics, we shall often refer to particular systems. As already mentioned in earlier Chapters, a **system** is any object or set of objects that we wish to consider. Everything else in the universe we will refer to as its "environment" or the "surroundings." There are several categories of systems. A **closed system** is one for which no mass enters or leaves (but energy may be exchanged with the environment). In an **open system**, mass may enter or leave (as may energy). Many (idealized) systems we study in physics are closed systems. But many systems, including plants and animals, are open systems since they exchange materials (food, oxygen, waste products) with the environment. A closed system is said to be **isolated** if no energy in any form passes across its boundaries; otherwise it is not isolated.

When different parts of an isolated system are at different temperatures, heat will flow (energy is transferred) from the part at higher temperature to the part at lower temperature—that is, within the system. If the system is truely isolated, no energy is transferred into or out of it. So the *conservation of energy* again plays an important role for us: the heat lost by one part of the system is equal to the heat gained by the other part:

$$\text{heat lost} = \text{heat gained}$$

or

$$\text{energy out of one part} = \text{energy into another part.}$$

These simple relations are very useful, but depend on the (often very good) approximation that the whole system is isolated (no other energy transfers occur). Let us take an Example.

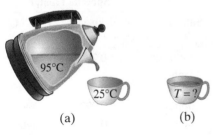

FIGURE 19–3 Example 19–3.

EXAMPLE 19–3 **The cup cools the tea.** If 200 cm^3 of tea at 95°C is poured into a 150-g glass cup initially at 25°C (Fig. 19–3), what will be the common final temperature T of the tea and cup when equilibrium is reached, assuming no heat flows to the surroundings?

APPROACH We apply conservation of energy to our system of tea plus cup, which we are assuming is isolated: all of the heat that leaves the tea flows into the cup. We use the specific heat equation, Eq. 19–2, to determine how the heat flow is related to the temperature changes.

SOLUTION Because tea is mainly water, its specific heat is $4186 \text{ J/kg} \cdot \text{C}°$ (Table 19–1), and its mass m is its density times its volume $(V = 200 \text{ cm}^3 = 200 \times 10^{-6} \text{ m}^3)$: $m = \rho V = (1.0 \times 10^3 \text{ kg/m}^3)(200 \times 10^{-6} \text{ m}^3) = 0.20 \text{ kg}$. We use Eq. 19–2, apply conservation of energy, and let T be the as yet unknown final temperature:

$$\text{heat lost by tea} = \text{heat gained by cup}$$
$$m_{\text{tea}} c_{\text{tea}}(95°C - T) = m_{\text{cup}} c_{\text{cup}}(T - 25°C).$$

Putting in numbers and using Table 19–1 ($c_{\text{cup}} = 840 \text{ J/kg} \cdot \text{C}°$ for glass), we solve for T, and find

$$(0.20 \text{ kg})(4186 \text{ J/kg} \cdot \text{C}°)(95°C - T) = (0.15 \text{ kg})(840 \text{ J/kg} \cdot \text{C}°)(T - 25°C)$$
$$79,500 \text{ J} - (837 \text{ J/C}°)T = (126 \text{ J/C}°)T - 3150 \text{ J}$$
$$T = 86°C.$$

The tea drops in temperature by $9 \text{ C}°$ by coming into equilibrium with the cup.

NOTE The cup increases in temperature by $86°C - 25°C = 61 \text{ C}°$. Its much greater change in temperature (compared with that of the tea water) is due to its much smaller specific heat compared to that of water.

NOTE In this calculation, the ΔT (of Eq. 19–2, $Q = mc\,\Delta T$) is a positive quantity on both sides of our conservation of energy equation. On the left is "heat lost" and ΔT is the initial minus the final temperature ($95°C - T$), whereas on the right is "heat gained" and ΔT is the final minus the initial temperature. But consider the following alternate approach.

Alternate Solution We can set up this Example (and others) by a different approach. We can write that the total heat transferred into or out of the isolated system is zero:

$$\Sigma Q = 0.$$

Then each term is written as $Q = mc(T_f - T_i)$, and $\Delta T = T_f - T_i$ is always the final minus the initial temperature, and each ΔT can be positive or negative. In the present Example:

$$\Sigma Q = m_{cup}c_{cup}(T - 25°C) + m_{tea}c_{tea}(T - 95°C) = 0.$$

The second term is negative because T will be less than 95°C. Solving the algebra gives the same result.

The exchange of energy, as exemplified in Example 19–3, is the basis for a technique known as **calorimetry**, which is the quantitative measurement of heat exchange. To make such measurements, a **calorimeter** is used; a simple water calorimeter is shown in Fig. 19–4. It is very important that the calorimeter be well insulated so that almost no heat is exchanged with the surroundings. One important use of the calorimeter is in the determination of specific heats of substances. In the technique known as the "method of mixtures," a sample of a substance is heated to a high temperature, which is accurately measured, and then quickly placed in the cool water of the calorimeter. The heat lost by the sample will be gained by the water and the calorimeter cup. By measuring the final temperature of the mixture, the specific heat can be calculated, as illustrated in the following Example.

EXAMPLE 19–4 Unknown specific heat determined by calorimetry.
An engineer wishes to determine the specific heat of a new metal alloy. A 0.150-kg sample of the alloy is heated to 540°C. It is then quickly placed in 0.400 kg of water at 10.0°C, which is contained in a 0.200-kg aluminum calorimeter cup. (We do not need to know the mass of the insulating jacket since we assume the air space between it and the cup insulates it well, so that its temperature does not change significantly.) The final temperature of the system is 30.5°C. Calculate the specific heat of the alloy.

APPROACH We apply conservation of energy to our system, which we take to be the alloy sample, the water, and the calorimeter cup. We assume this system is isolated, so the energy lost by the hot alloy equals the energy gained by the water and calorimeter cup.

SOLUTION The heat lost equals the heat gained:

$$\begin{pmatrix}\text{heat lost}\\\text{by alloy}\end{pmatrix} = \begin{pmatrix}\text{heat gained}\\\text{by water}\end{pmatrix} + \begin{pmatrix}\text{heat gained by}\\\text{calorimeter cup}\end{pmatrix}$$

$$m_a c_a \Delta T_a = m_w c_w \Delta T_w + m_{cal} c_{cal} \Delta T_{cal}$$

where the subscripts a, w, and cal refer to the alloy, water, and calorimeter, respectively, and each $\Delta T > 0$. When we put in values and use Table 19–1, this equation becomes

$$(0.150\,\text{kg})(c_a)(540°C - 30.5°C) = (0.400\,\text{kg})(4186\,\text{J/kg}\cdot\text{C}°)(30.5°C - 10.0°C)$$
$$+ (0.200\,\text{kg})(900\,\text{J/kg}\cdot\text{C}°)(30.5°C - 10.0°C)$$
$$(76.4\,\text{kg}\cdot\text{C}°)\,c_a = (34{,}300 + 3690)\,\text{J}$$
$$c_a = 497\,\text{J/kg}\cdot\text{C}°.$$

In making this calculation, we have ignored any heat transferred to the thermometer and the stirrer (which is used to quicken the heat transfer process and thus reduce heat loss to the outside). It can be taken into account by adding additional terms to the right side of the above equation and will result in a slight correction to the value of c_a.

In all Examples and Problems of this sort, be sure to include *all* objects that gain or lose heat (within reason). On the "heat loss" side here, it is only the hot metal alloy. On the "heat gain" side, it is both the water and the aluminum calorimeter cup. For simplicity, we have ignored very small masses, such as the thermometer and the stirrer, which will affect the energy balance only very slightly.

PROBLEM SOLVING
Alternate approach: $\Sigma Q = 0$

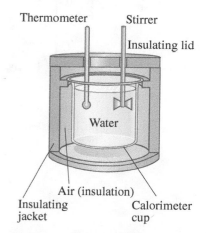

Thermometer   Stirrer

Insulating lid

Water

Air (insulation)

Insulating jacket   Calorimeter cup

FIGURE 19–4 Simple water calorimeter.

PROBLEM SOLVING
Be sure to consider all possible sources of energy transfer

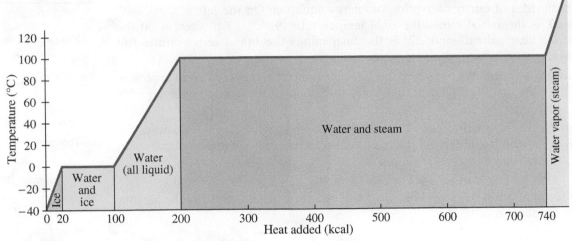

FIGURE 19–5 Temperature as a function of the heat added to bring 1.0 kg of ice at −40°C to steam above 100°C.

19–5 Latent Heat

When a material changes phase from solid to liquid, or from liquid to gas (see also Section 18–3), a certain amount of energy is involved in this **change of phase**. For example, let us trace what happens when a 1.0-kg block of ice at −40°C is heated at a slow steady rate until all the ice has changed to water, then the (liquid) water is heated to 100°C and changed to steam, and heated further above 100°C, all at 1 atm pressure. As shown in the graph of Fig. 19–5, as the ice is heated starting at −40°C, its temperature rises at a rate of about 2 C°/kcal of heat added (for ice, $c \approx 0.50 \, \text{kcal/kg} \cdot \text{C}°$). However, when 0°C is reached, the temperature stops increasing even though heat is still being added. The ice gradually changes to water in the liquid state, with no change in temperature. After about 40 kcal has been added at 0°C, half the ice remains and half has changed to water. After about 80 kcal, or 330 kJ, has been added, all the ice has changed to water, still at 0°C. Continued addition of heat causes the water's temperature to again increase, now at a rate of 1 C°/kcal. When 100°C is reached, the temperature again remains constant as the heat added changes the liquid water to vapor (steam). About 540 kcal (2260 kJ) is required to change the 1.0 kg of water completely to steam, after which the graph rises again, indicating that the temperature of the steam rises as heat is added.

The heat required to change 1.0 kg of a substance from the solid to the liquid state is called the **heat of fusion**; it is denoted by L_F. The heat of fusion of water is 79.7 kcal/kg or, in proper SI units, 333 kJ/kg $(= 3.33 \times 10^5 \, \text{J/kg})$. The heat required to change a substance from the liquid to the vapor phase is called the **heat of vaporization**, L_V. For water it is 539 kcal/kg or 2260 kJ/kg. Other substances follow graphs similar to Fig. 19–5, although the melting-point and boiling-point temperatures are different, as are the specific heats and heats of fusion and vaporization. Values for the heats of fusion and vaporization, which are also called the **latent heats**, are given in Table 19–2 for a number of substances.

The heats of vaporization and fusion also refer to the amount of heat *released* by a substance when it changes from a gas to a liquid, or from a liquid to a solid. Thus, steam releases 2260 kJ/kg when it changes to water, and water releases 333 kJ/kg when it becomes ice.

The heat involved in a change of phase depends not only on the latent heat but also on the total mass of the substance. That is,

$$Q = mL, \tag{19–3}$$

where L is the latent heat of the particular process and substance, m is the mass of the substance, and Q is the heat added or released during the phase change. For example, when 5.00 kg of water freezes at 0°C, $(5.00 \, \text{kg})(3.33 \times 10^5 \, \text{J/kg}) = 1.67 \times 10^6 \, \text{J}$ of energy is released.

TABLE 19–2 Latent Heats (at 1 atm)

Substance	Melting Point (°C)	Heat of Fusion kcal/kg†	Heat of Fusion kJ/kg	Boiling Point (°C)	Heat of Vaporization kcal/kg†	Heat of Vaporization kJ/kg
Oxygen	−218.8	3.3	14	−183	51	210
Nitrogen	−210.0	6.1	26	−195.8	48	200
Ethyl alcohol	−114	25	104	78	204	850
Ammonia	−77.8	8.0	33	−33.4	33	137
Water	0	79.7	333	100	539	2260
Lead	327	5.9	25	1750	208	870
Silver	961	21	88	2193	558	2300
Iron	1808	69.1	289	3023	1520	6340
Tungsten	3410	44	184	5900	1150	4800

†Numerical values in kcal/kg are the same in cal/g.

EXERCISE B A pot of water is boiling on a gas stove, and then you turn up the heat. What happens? (a) The temperature of the water starts increasing. (b) There is a tiny decrease in the rate of water loss by evaporation. (c) The rate of water loss by boiling increases. (d) There is an appreciable increase in both the rate of boiling and the temperature of the water. (e) None of these.

Calorimetry sometimes involves a change of state, as the following Examples show. Indeed, latent heats are often measured using calorimetry.

EXAMPLE 19–5 Will all the ice melt? A 0.50-kg chunk of ice at −10°C is placed in 3.0 kg of "iced" tea at 20°C. At what temperature and in what phase will the final mixture be? The tea can be considered as water. Ignore any heat flow to the surroundings, including the container.

PROBLEM SOLVING

First determine (or estimate) the final state

APPROACH Before we can write down an equation applying conservation of energy, we must first check to see if the final state will be all ice, a mixture of ice and water at 0°C, or all water. To bring the 3.0 kg of water at 20°C down to 0°C would require an energy release of (Eq. 19–2)

$$m_w c_w(20°C - 0°C) = (3.0\,kg)(4186\,J/kg\cdot C°)(20\,C°) = 250\,kJ.$$

On the other hand, to raise the ice from −10°C to 0°C would require

$$m_{ice} c_{ice}[0°C - (-10°C)] = (0.50\,kg)(2100\,J/kg\cdot C°)(10\,C°) = 10.5\,kJ,$$

and to change the ice to water at 0°C would require (Eq. 19–3)

$$m_{ice} L_F = (0.50\,kg)(333\,kJ/kg) = 167\,kJ,$$

for a total of 10.5 kJ + 167 kJ = 177 kJ. This is not enough energy to bring the 3.0 kg of water at 20°C down to 0°C, so we see that the mixture must end up all water, somewhere between 0°C and 20°C.

PROBLEM SOLVING

Then determine the final temperature

SOLUTION To determine the final temperature T, we apply conservation of energy and write: heat gain = heat loss,

$$\begin{pmatrix} \text{heat to raise} \\ 0.50\,kg\,of\,ice \\ \text{from } -10°C \\ \text{to } 0°C \end{pmatrix} + \begin{pmatrix} \text{heat to change} \\ 0.50\,kg \\ \text{of ice} \\ \text{to water} \end{pmatrix} + \begin{pmatrix} \text{heat to raise} \\ 0.50\,kg\,of\,water \\ \text{from } 0°C \\ \text{to } T \end{pmatrix} = \begin{pmatrix} \text{heat lost by} \\ 3.0\,kg\,of \\ \text{water cooling} \\ \text{from } 20°C\,to\,T \end{pmatrix}.$$

Using some of the results from above, we obtain

$$10.5\,kJ + 167\,kJ + (0.50\,kg)(4186\,J/kg\cdot C°)(T - 0°C)$$
$$= (3.0\,kg)(4186\,J/kg\cdot C°)(20°C - T).$$

Solving for T we obtain

$$T = 5.0°C.$$

EXERCISE C How much more ice at −10°C would be needed in Example 19–5 to bring the tea down to 0°C, while just melting all the ice?

Calorimetry

1. Be sure you have sufficient information to apply energy conservation. Ask yourself: **is the system isolated** (or very nearly so, enough to get a good estimate)? Do we know or can we calculate all significant sources of energy transfer?

2. Apply **conservation of energy**:

   heat gained = heat lost.

   For each substance in the system, a heat (energy) term will appear on either the left or right side of this equation. [Alternatively, use $\Sigma Q = 0$.]

3. If **no phase changes** occur, each term in the energy conservation equation (above) will have the form

   $$Q(\text{gain}) = mc(T_f - T_i)$$

   or

   $$Q(\text{lost}) = mc(T_i - T_f)$$

   where T_i and T_f are the initial and final temperatures

of the substance, and m and c are its mass and specific heat, respectively.

4. If **phase changes** do or might occur, there may be terms in the energy conservation equation of the form $Q = mL$, where L is the latent heat. But *before* applying energy conservation, determine (or estimate) in which phase the final state will be, as we did in Example 19–5 by calculating the different contributing values for heat Q.

5. Be sure each term appears on the correct side of the **energy equation** (heat gained or heat lost) and that each ΔT is positive.

6. Note that when the system reaches thermal **equilibrium**, the final **temperature** of each substance will have the *same* value. There is only one T_f.

7. **Solve** your energy equation for the unknown.

EXAMPLE 19–6 **Determining a latent heat.** The specific heat of liquid mercury is 140 J/kg·C°. When 1.0 kg of solid mercury at its melting point of $-39°C$ is placed in a 0.50-kg aluminum calorimeter filled with 1.2 kg of water at 20.0°C, the mercury melts and the final temperature of the combination is found to be 16.5°C. What is the heat of fusion of mercury in J/kg?

APPROACH We follow the Problem Solving Strategy above.

SOLUTION

1. **Is the system isolated?** The mercury is placed in a calorimeter, which we assume is well insulated. Our isolated system is the calorimeter, the water, and the mercury.

2. **Conservation of energy.** The heat gained by the mercury = the heat lost by the water and calorimeter.

3. and 4. **Phase changes.** There is a phase change (of mercury), plus we use specific heat equations. The heat gained by the mercury (Hg) includes a term representing the melting of the Hg,

   $$Q(\text{melt solid Hg}) = m_{Hg}L_{Hg},$$

   plus a term representing the heating of the liquid Hg from $-39°C$ to $+16.5°C$:

   $$Q(\text{heat liquid Hg}) = m_{Hg}c_{Hg}[16.5°C - (-39°C)]$$
   $$= (1.0\,\text{kg})(140\,\text{J/kg·C°})(55.5\,\text{C°}) = 7770\,\text{J}.$$

   All of this heat gained by the mercury is obtained from the water and calorimeter, which cool down:

   $$Q_{cal} + Q_w = m_{cal}c_{cal}(20.0°C - 16.5°C) + m_wc_w(20.0°C - 16.5°C)$$
   $$= (0.50\,\text{kg})(900\,\text{J/kg·C°})(3.5\,\text{C°}) + (1.2\,\text{kg})(4186\,\text{J/kg·C°})(3.5\,\text{C°})$$
   $$= 19{,}200\,\text{J}.$$

5. **Energy equation.** The conservation of energy tells us the heat lost by the water and calorimeter cup must equal the heat gained by the mercury:

   $$Q_{cal} + Q_w = Q(\text{melt solid Hg}) + Q(\text{heat liquid Hg})$$

   or

   $$19{,}200\,\text{J} = m_{Hg}L_{Hg} + 7770\,\text{J}.$$

6. **Equilibrium temperature.** It is given as 16.5°C, and we already used it.

7. Solve. The only unknown in our energy equation (point 5) is L_{Hg}, the latent heat of fusion (or melting) of mercury. We solve for it, putting in $m_{Hg} = 1.0\,kg$:

$$L_{Hg} = \frac{19{,}200\,J - 7770\,J}{1.0\,kg} = 11{,}400\,J/kg \approx 11\,kJ/kg,$$

where we rounded off to 2 significant figures.

Evaporation

The latent heat to change a liquid to a gas is needed not only at the boiling point. Water can change from the liquid to the gas phase even at room temperature. This process is called **evaporation** (see also Section 18–4). The value of the heat of vaporization of water increases slightly with a decrease in temperature: at 20°C, for example, it is 2450 kJ/kg (585 kcal/kg) compared to 2260 kJ/kg ($= 539$ kcal/kg) at 100°C. When water evaporates, the remaining liquid cools, because the energy required (the latent heat of vaporization) comes from the water itself; so its internal energy, and therefore its temperature, must drop.[†]

Evaporation of water from the skin is one of the most important methods the body uses to control its temperature. When the temperature of the blood rises slightly above normal, the hypothalamus region of the brain detects this temperature increase and sends a signal to the sweat glands to increase their production. The energy (latent heat) required to vaporize this water comes from the body, and hence the body cools.

PHYSICS APPLIED
Body temperature

Kinetic Theory of Latent Heats

We can make use of kinetic theory to see why energy is needed to melt or vaporize a substance. At the melting point, the latent heat of fusion does not act to increase the average kinetic energy (and the temperature) of the molecules in the solid, but instead is used to overcome the potential energy associated with the forces between the molecules. That is, work must be done against these attractive forces to break the molecules loose from their relatively fixed positions in the solid so they can freely roll over one another in the liquid phase. Similarly, energy is required for molecules held close together in the liquid phase to escape into the gaseous phase. This process is a more violent reorganization of the molecules than is melting (the average distance between the molecules is greatly increased), and hence the heat of vaporization is generally much greater than the heat of fusion for a given substance.

19–6 The First Law of Thermodynamics

Up to now in this Chapter we have discussed internal energy and heat. But work too is often involved in thermodynamic processes.

In Chapter 8 we saw that work is done when energy is transferred from one object to another by mechanical means. In Section 19–1 we saw that heat is a transfer of energy from one object to a second one at a lower temperature. Thus, heat is much like work. To distinguish them, *heat* is defined as a *transfer of energy due to a difference in temperature*, whereas work is a transfer of energy that is not due to a temperature difference.

In Section 19–2, we defined the internal energy of a system as the sum total of all the energy of the molecules within the system. We would expect that the internal energy of a system would be increased if work was done on the system, or if heat were added to it. Similarly the internal energy would be decreased if heat flowed out of the system or if work were done by the system on something in the surroundings.

[†]According to kinetic theory, evaporation is a cooling process because it is the fastest-moving molecules that escape from the surface. Hence the average speed of the remaining molecules is less, so by Eq. 18–4 the temperature is less.

Thus it is reasonable to extend conservation of energy and propose an important law: the change in internal energy of a closed system, ΔE_{int}, will be equal to the energy added to the system by heating minus the work done by the system on the surroundings. In equation form we write

FIRST LAW OF THERMODYNAMICS

$$\Delta E_{int} = Q - W \qquad\qquad (19\text{–}4)$$

⚠ CAUTION

Heat added is +
Heat lost is −
Work on system is −
Work by system is +

where Q is the net heat *added* to the system and W is the net work done *by* the system.[†] We must be careful and consistent in following the sign conventions for Q and W. Because W in Eq. 19–4 is the work done *by* the system, then if work is done *on* the system, W will be negative and E_{int} will increase. Similarly, Q is positive for heat added to the system, so if heat leaves the system, Q is negative.

Equation 19–4 is known as the **first law of thermodynamics**. It is one of the great laws of physics, and its validity rests on experiments (such as Joule's) to which no exceptions have been seen. Since Q and W represent energy transferred into or out of the system, the internal energy changes accordingly. Thus, the first law of thermodynamics is a great and broad statement of the *law of conservation of energy*.

It is worth noting that the conservation of energy law was not formulated until the nineteenth century, for it depended on the interpretation of heat as a transfer of energy.

Equation 19–4 applies to a closed system. It also applies to an open system (Section 19–4) if we take into account the change in internal energy due to the increase or decrease in the amount of matter. For an isolated system (p. 500), no work is done and no heat enters or leaves the system, so $W = Q = 0$, and hence $\Delta E_{int} = 0$.

A given system at any moment is in a particular state and can be said to have a certain amount of internal energy, E_{int}. But a system does not "have" a certain amount of heat or work. Rather, when work is done on a system (such as compressing a gas), or when heat is added or removed from a system, the state of the system *changes*. Thus, work and heat are involved in *thermodynamic processes* that can change the system from one state to another; they are not characteristic of the state itself. Quantities which describe the state of a system, such as internal energy E_{int}, pressure P, volume V, temperature T, and mass m or number of moles n, are called **state variables**. Q and W are *not* state variables.

Because E_{int} is a *state variable*, which depends only on the state of the system and not on how the system arrived in that state, we can write

$$\Delta E_{int} = E_{int,2} - E_{int,1} = Q - W$$

where $E_{int,1}$ and $E_{int,2}$ represent the internal energy of the system in states 1 and 2, and Q and W are the heat added to the system and work done by the system in going from state 1 to state 2.

It is sometimes useful to write the first law of thermodynamics in differential form:

$$dE_{int} = dQ - dW.$$

Here, dE_{int} represents an infinitesimal change in internal energy when an infinitesimal amount of heat dQ is added to the system, and the system does an infinitesimal amount of work dW.[‡]

[†]This convention relates historically to steam engines: the interest was in the heat *input* and the work *output*, both regarded as positive. In other books you may see the first law of thermodynamics written as $\Delta E_{int} = Q + W$, in which case W refers to the work done *on* the system.

[‡]The differential form of the first law is often written
$$dE_{int} = đQ - đW,$$
where the bars on the differential sign $(đ)$ are used to remind us that W and Q are not functions of the state variables (such as P, V, T, n). Internal energy, E_{int}, is a function of the state variables, and so dE_{int} represents the differential (called an *exact differential*) of some function E_{int}. The differentials $đW$ and $đQ$ are not exact differentials (they are not the differential of some mathematical function); they thus only represent infinitesimal amounts. This issue won't really be of concern in this book.

EXAMPLE 19–7 **Using the first law.** 2500 J of heat is added to a system, and 1800 J of work is done on the system. What is the change in internal energy of the system?

APPROACH We apply the first law of thermodynamics, Eq. 19–4, to our system.

SOLUTION The heat added to the system is $Q = 2500$ J. The work W done *by* the system is -1800 J. Why the minus sign? Because 1800 J done *on* the system (as given) equals -1800 J done *by* the system, and it is the latter we need for the sign conventions we used in Eq. 19–4. Hence

$$\Delta E_{int} = 2500 \, J - (-1800 \, J) = 2500 \, J + 1800 \, J = 4300 \, J.$$

You may have intuitively thought that the 2500 J and the 1800 J would need to be added together, since both refer to energy added to the system. You would have been right.

EXERCISE D What would be the internal energy change in Example 19–7 if 2500 J of heat is added to the system and 1800 J of work is done *by* the system (i.e., as output)?

*The First Law of Thermodynamics Extended

To write the first law of thermodynamics in its complete form, consider a system that has kinetic energy K (there is motion) as well as potential energy U. Then the first law of thermodynamics would have to include these terms and would be written as

$$\Delta K + \Delta U + \Delta E_{int} = Q - W. \qquad (19\text{–}5)$$

EXAMPLE 19–8 **Kinetic energy transformed to thermal energy.** A 3.0-g bullet traveling at a speed of 400 m/s enters a tree and exits the other side with a speed of 200 m/s. Where did the bullet's lost kinetic energy go, and what was the energy transferred?

APPROACH Take the bullet and tree as our system. No potential energy is involved. No work is done on (or by) the system by outside forces, nor is any heat added because no energy was transferred to or from the system due to a temperature difference. Thus the kinetic energy gets transformed into internal energy of the bullet and tree.

SOLUTION From the first law of thermodynamics as given in Eq. 19–5, we are given $Q = W = \Delta U = 0$, so we have

$$\Delta K + \Delta E_{int} = 0$$

or, using subscripts i and f for initial and final velocities

$$\Delta E_{int} = -\Delta K = -(K_f - K_i) = \tfrac{1}{2}m(v_i^2 - v_f^2)$$
$$= \tfrac{1}{2}(3.0 \times 10^{-3} \, kg)[(400 \, m/s)^2 - (200 \, m/s)^2] = 180 \, J.$$

NOTE The internal energy of the bullet and tree both increase, as both experience a rise in temperature. If we had chosen the bullet alone as our system, work would be done on it and heat transfer would occur.

19–7 The First Law of Thermodynamics Applied; Calculating the Work

Let us analyze some simple processes in the light of the first law of thermodynamics.

Isothermal Processes ($\Delta T = 0$)

First we consider an idealized process that is carried out at constant temperature. Such a process is called an **isothermal** process (from the Greek meaning "same temperature"). If the system is an ideal gas, then $PV = nRT$ (Eq. 17–3), so for a fixed amount of gas kept at constant temperature, $PV = $ constant. Thus the process follows a curve like AB on the PV diagram shown in Fig. 19–6, which is a curve for $PV = $ constant. Each point on the curve, such as point A, represents the state of the system at a given moment—that is, its pressure P and volume V. At a lower temperature, another isothermal process would be represented by a curve like A'B' in Fig. 19–6 (the product $PV = nRT = $ constant is less when T is less). The curves shown in Fig. 19–6 are referred to as *isotherms*.

FIGURE 19–6 PV diagram for an ideal gas undergoing isothermal processes at two different temperatures.

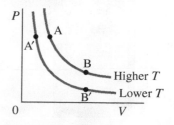

FIGURE 19–7 An ideal gas in a cylinder fitted with a movable piston.

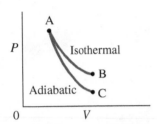

FIGURE 19–8 *PV* diagram for adiabatic (AC) and isothermal (AB) processes on an ideal gas.

FIGURE 19–9 (a) Isobaric ("same pressure") process. (b) Isovolumetric ("same volume") process.

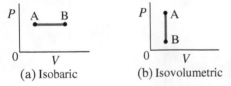

(a) Isobaric   (b) Isovolumetric

FIGURE 19–10 The work done by a gas when its volume increases by $dV = A\,d\ell$ is $dW = P\,dV$.

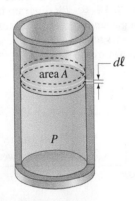

Let us assume that the gas is enclosed in a container fitted with a movable piston, Fig. 19–7, and that the gas is in contact with a **heat reservoir** (a body whose mass is so large that, ideally, its temperature does not change significantly when heat is exchanged with our system). We also assume that the process of compression (volume decreases) or expansion (volume increases) is done **quasistatically** ("almost statically"), by which we mean extremely slowly, so that all of the gas moves between a series of equilibrium states each of which are at the same constant temperature. If an amount of heat Q is added to the system and temperature is to remain constant, the gas will expand and do an amount of work W on the environment (it exerts a force on the piston and moves it through a distance). The temperature and mass are kept constant so, from Eq. 19–1, the internal energy does not change: $\Delta E_{int} = \frac{3}{2}nR\,\Delta T = 0$. Hence, by the first law of thermodynamics, Eq. 19–4, $\Delta E_{int} = Q - W = 0$, so $W = Q$: the work done by the gas in an isothermal process equals the heat added to the gas.

Adiabatic Processes ($Q = 0$)

An **adiabatic** process is one in which no heat is allowed to flow into or out of the system: $Q = 0$. This situation can occur if the system is extremely well insulated, or the process happens so quickly that heat—which flows slowly—has no time to flow in or out. The very rapid expansion of gases in an internal combustion engine is one example of a process that is very nearly adiabatic. A slow adiabatic expansion of an ideal gas follows a curve like that labeled AC in Fig. 19–8. Since $Q = 0$, we have from Eq. 19–4 that $\Delta E_{int} = -W$. That is, the internal energy decreases if the gas expands; hence the temperature decreases as well (because $\Delta E_{int} = \frac{3}{2}nR\,\Delta T$). This is evident in Fig. 19–8 where the product PV ($= nRT$) is less at point C than at point B (curve AB is for an isothermal process, for which $\Delta E_{int} = 0$ and $\Delta T = 0$). In the reverse operation, an adiabatic compression (going from C to A, for example), work is done *on* the gas, and hence the internal energy increases and the temperature rises. In a diesel engine, the fuel–air mixture is rapidly compressed adiabatically by a factor of 15 or more; the temperature rise is so great that the mixture ignites spontaneously.

Isobaric and Isovolumetric Processes

Isothermal and adiabatic processes are just two possible processes that can occur. Two other simple thermodynamic processes are illustrated on the *PV* diagrams of Fig. 19–9: (a) an **isobaric** process is one in which the pressure is kept constant, so the process is represented by a horizontal straight line on the *PV* diagram, Fig. 19–9a; (b) an **isovolumetric** (or *isochoric*) process is one in which the volume does not change (Fig. 19–9b). In these, and in all other processes, the first law of thermodynamics holds.

Work Done in Volume Changes

We often want to calculate the work done in a process. Suppose we have a gas confined to a cylindrical container fitted with a movable piston (Fig. 19–10). We must always be careful to define exactly what our system is. In this case we choose our system to be the gas; so the container's walls and the piston are parts of the environment. Now let us calculate the work done by the gas when it expands quasistatically, so that P and T are defined for the system at all instants.[†] The gas expands against the piston, whose area is A. The gas exerts a force $F = PA$ on the piston, where P is the pressure in the gas. The work done by the gas to move the piston an infinitesimal displacement $d\vec{\ell}$ is

$$dW = \vec{F}\cdot d\vec{\ell} = PA\,d\ell = P\,dV \qquad (19\text{–}6)$$

since the infinitesimal increase in volume is $dV = A\,d\ell$. If the gas was *compressed* so that $d\vec{\ell}$ pointed into the gas, the volume would decrease and $dV < 0$. The work done by the gas in this case would then be negative, which is equivalent to saying that positive work was done *on* the gas, not by it. For a finite change in volume

---

[†] If the gas expands or is compressed quickly, there would be turbulence and different parts would be at different pressure (and temperature).

from V_A to V_B, the work W done by the gas will be

$$W = \int dW = \int_{V_A}^{V_B} P\, dV. \tag{19-7}$$

Equations 19–6 and 19–7 are valid for the work done in any volume change—by a gas, a liquid, or a solid—as long as it is done quasistatically.

In order to integrate Eq. 19–7, we need to know how the pressure varies during the process, and this depends on the type of process. Let us first consider a quasistatic isothermal expansion of an ideal gas. This process is represented by the curve between points A and B on the PV diagram of Fig. 19–11. The work done by the gas in this process, according to Eq. 19–7, is just the area between the PV curve and the V axis, and is shown shaded in Fig. 19–11. We can do the integral in Eq. 19–7 for an ideal gas by using the ideal gas law, $P = nRT/V$. The work done at constant T is

$$W = \int_{V_A}^{V_B} P\, dV = nRT \int_{V_A}^{V_B} \frac{dV}{V} = nRT \ln \frac{V_B}{V_A}. \quad \begin{bmatrix} \text{isothermal process;} \\ \text{ideal gas} \end{bmatrix} \tag{19-8}$$

Let us next consider a different way of taking an ideal gas between the same states A and B. This time, let us lower the pressure in the gas from P_A to P_B, as indicated by the line AD in Fig. 19–12. (In this *isovolumetric* process, heat must be allowed to flow out of the gas so its temperature drops.) Then let the gas expand from V_A to V_B at constant pressure $(= P_B)$, which is indicated by the line DB in Fig. 19–12. (In this *isobaric* process, heat is added to the gas to raise its temperature.) No work is done in the isovolumetric process AD, since $dV = 0$:

$$W = 0. \qquad \text{[isovolumetric process]}$$

In the isobaric process DB the pressure remains constant, so

$$W = \int_{V_A}^{V_B} P\, dV = P_B(V_B - V_A) = P\,\Delta V. \qquad \text{[isobaric process]} \tag{19-9a}$$

The work done is again represented on the PV diagram by the area between the curve (ADB) and the V axis, as indicated by the shading in Fig. 19–12. Using the ideal gas law, we can also write

$$W = P_B(V_B - V_A) = nRT_B\left(1 - \frac{V_A}{V_B}\right). \quad \begin{bmatrix} \text{isobaric process;} \\ \text{ideal gas} \end{bmatrix} \tag{19-9b}$$

As can be seen from the shaded areas in Figs. 19–11 and 19–12, or by putting in numbers in Eqs. 19–8 and 19–9 (try it for $V_B = 2V_A$), the work done in these two processes is different. This is a general result. *The work done in taking a system from one state to another depends not only on the initial and final states but also on the type of process (or "path").*

This result reemphasizes the fact that work cannot be considered a property of a system. The same is true of heat. The heat input required to change the gas from state A to state B depends on the process; for the isothermal process of Fig. 19–11, the heat input turns out to be greater than for the process ADB of Fig. 19–12. In general, *the amount of heat added or removed in taking a system from one state to another depends not only on the initial and final states but also on the path or process.*

CONCEPTUAL EXAMPLE 19–9 **Work in isothermal and adiabatic processes.** In Fig. 19–8 we saw the PV diagrams for a gas expanding in two ways, isothermally and adiabatically. The initial volume V_A was the same in each case, and the final volumes were the same $(V_B = V_C)$. In which process was more work done by the gas?

RESPONSE Our system is the gas. More work was done by the gas in the isothermal process, which we can see in two simple ways by looking at Fig. 19–8. First, the "average" pressure was higher during the isothermal process AB, so $W = \overline{P}\,\Delta V$ was greater (ΔV is the same for both processes). Second, we can look at the area under each curve: the area under curve AB, which represents the work done, was greater (since curve AB is higher) than that under AC.

EXERCISE E Is the work done by the gas in process ADB of Fig. 19–12 greater than, less than, or equal to the work done in the isothermal process AB?

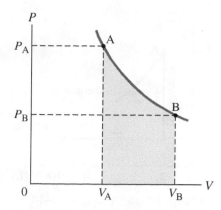

FIGURE 19–11 Work done by an ideal gas in an isothermal process equals the area under the PV curve. Shaded area equals the work done by the gas when it expands from V_A to V_B.

FIGURE 19–12 Process ADB consists of an isovolumetric (AD) and an isobaric (DB) process.

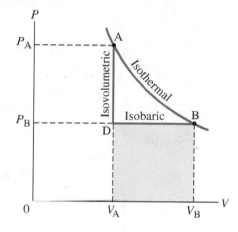

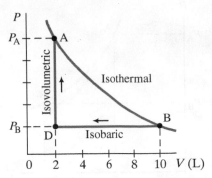

FIGURE 19–13 Example 19–10.

EXAMPLE 19–10 **First law in isobaric and isovolumetric processes.** An ideal gas is slowly compressed at a constant pressure of 2.0 atm from 10.0 L to 2.0 L. This process is represented in Fig. 19–13 as the path B to D. (In this process, some heat flows out of the gas and the temperature drops.) Heat is then added to the gas, holding the volume constant, and the pressure and temperature are allowed to rise (line DA) until the temperature reaches its original value $(T_A = T_B)$. Calculate (a) the total work done by the gas in the process BDA, and (b) the total heat flow into the gas.

APPROACH (a) Work is done only in the compression process BD. In process DA, the volume is constant so $\Delta V = 0$ and no work is done. (b) We use the first law of thermodynamics, Eq. 19–4.

SOLUTION (a) During the compression BD, the pressure is 2.0 atm = $2(1.01 \times 10^5 \,\text{N/m}^2)$ and the work done is (since $1 \,\text{L} = 10^3 \,\text{cm}^3 = 10^{-3} \,\text{m}^3$)

$$W = P\Delta V = (2.02 \times 10^5 \,\text{N/m}^2)(2.0 \times 10^{-3} \,\text{m}^3 - 10.0 \times 10^{-3} \,\text{m}^3)$$
$$= -1.6 \times 10^3 \,\text{J}.$$

The total work done *by* the gas is -1.6×10^3 J, where the minus sign means that $+1.6 \times 10^3$ J of work is done *on* the gas.

(b) Because the temperature at the beginning and at the end of process BDA is the same, there is no change in internal energy: $\Delta E_{int} = 0$. From the first law of thermodynamics we have

$$0 = \Delta E_{int} = Q - W$$

so $Q = W = -1.6 \times 10^3$ J. Because Q is negative, 1600 J of heat flows out of the gas for the whole process, BDA.

EXERCISE F In Example 19–10, if the heat lost from the gas in the process BD is 8.4×10^3 J, what is the change in internal energy of the gas during process BD?

EXAMPLE 19–11 **Work done in an engine.** In an engine, 0.25 mol of an ideal monatomic gas in the cylinder expands rapidly and adiabatically against the piston. In the process, the temperature of the gas drops from 1150 K to 400 K. How much work does the gas do?

APPROACH We take the gas as our system (the piston is part of the surroundings). The pressure is not constant, and its varying value is not given. Instead, we can use the first law of thermodynamics because we can determine ΔE_{int} given $Q = 0$ (the process is adiabatic).

SOLUTION We determine ΔE_{int} from Eq. 19–1 for the internal energy of an ideal monatomic gas, using subscripts f and i for final and initial states:

$$\Delta E_{int} = E_{int,f} - E_{int,i} = \tfrac{3}{2}nR(T_f - T_i)$$
$$= \tfrac{3}{2}(0.25 \,\text{mol})(8.314 \,\text{J/mol·K})(400 \,\text{K} - 1150 \,\text{K})$$
$$= -2300 \,\text{J}.$$

Then, from the first law of thermodynamics, Eq. 19–4,

$$W = Q - \Delta E_{int} = 0 - (-2300 \,\text{J}) = 2300 \,\text{J}.$$

Table 19–3 gives a brief summary of the processes we have discussed.

Free Expansion

One type of adiabatic process is a so-called **free expansion** in which a gas is allowed to expand in volume adiabatically without doing any work. The apparatus to

TABLE 19–3 Simple Thermodynamic Processes and the First Law

Process	What is constant:	The first law predicts:
Isothermal	$T = \text{constant}$	$\Delta T = 0$ makes $\Delta E_{int} = 0$, so $Q = W$
Isobaric	$P = \text{constant}$	$Q = \Delta E_{int} + W = \Delta E_{int} + P\Delta V$
Isovolumetric	$V = \text{constant}$	$\Delta V = 0$ makes $W = 0$, so $Q = \Delta E_{int}$
Adiabatic	$Q = 0$	$\Delta E_{int} = -W$

accomplish a free expansion is shown in Fig. 19–14. It consists of two well-insulated compartments (to ensure no heat flow in or out) connected by a valve or stopcock. One compartment is filled with gas, the other is empty. When the valve is opened, the gas expands to fill both containers. No heat flows in or out $(Q = 0)$, and no work is done because the gas does not move any other object. Thus $Q = W = 0$ and by the first law of thermodynamics, $\Delta E_{int} = 0$. *The internal energy of a gas does not change in a free expansion.* For an ideal gas, $\Delta T = 0$ also, since E_{int} depends only on T (Section 19–2). Experimentally, the free expansion has been used to determine if the internal energy of *real gases* depends only on T. The experiments are very difficult to do accurately, but it has been found that the temperature of a real gas drops very slightly in a free expansion. Thus the internal energy of real gases does depend, a little, on pressure or volume as well as on temperature.

A free expansion can not be plotted on a PV diagram, because the process is rapid, not quasistatic. The intermediate states are not equilibrium states, and hence the pressure (and even the volume at some instants) is not clearly defined.

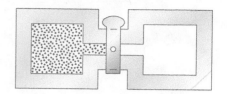

FIGURE 19–14 Free expansion.

19–8 Molar Specific Heats for Gases, and the Equipartition of Energy

In Section 19–3 we discussed the concept of specific heat and applied it to solids and liquids. Much more than for solids and liquids, the values of the specific heat for gases depends on how the process is carried out. Two important processes are those in which either the volume or the pressure is kept constant. Although for solids and liquids it matters little, Table 19–4 shows that the specific heats of gases at constant volume (c_V) and at constant pressure (c_P) are quite different.

Molar Specific Heats for Gases

The difference in specific heats for gases is nicely explained in terms of the first law of thermodynamics and kinetic theory. Our discussion is simplified if we use **molar specific heats**, C_V and C_P, which are defined as the heat required to raise 1 mol of the gas by 1 C° at constant volume and at constant pressure, respectively. That is, in analogy to Eq. 19–2, the heat Q needed to raise the temperature of n moles of gas by ΔT is

$$Q = nC_V \Delta T \qquad \text{[volume constant]} \quad \textbf{(19–10a)}$$

$$Q = nC_P \Delta T. \qquad \text{[pressure constant]} \quad \textbf{(19–10b)}$$

It is clear from the definition of molar specific heat (or by comparing Eqs. 19–2 and 19–10) that

$$C_V = M c_V$$
$$C_P = M c_P,$$

where M is the molecular mass of the gas $(M = m/n$ in grams/mol$)$. The values for molar specific heats are included in Table 19–4, and we see that the values are nearly the same for different gases that have the same number of atoms per molecule.

TABLE 19–4 Specific Heats of Gases at 15°C

Gas	Specific heats (kcal/kg · K)		Molar specific heats (cal/mol · K)		$C_P - C_V$ (cal/mol · K)	$\gamma = \dfrac{C_P}{C_V}$
	c_V	c_P	C_V	C_P		
Monatomic						
He	0.75	1.15	2.98	4.97	1.99	1.67
Ne	0.148	0.246	2.98	4.97	1.99	1.67
Diatomic						
N_2	0.177	0.248	4.96	6.95	1.99	1.40
O_2	0.155	0.218	5.03	7.03	2.00	1.40
Triatomic						
CO_2	0.153	0.199	6.80	8.83	2.03	1.30
H_2O (100°C)	0.350	0.482	6.20	8.20	2.00	1.32

Now we use kinetic theory and imagine that an ideal gas is slowly heated via two different processes—first at constant volume, and then at constant pressure. In both of these processes, we let the temperature increase by the same amount, ΔT. In the process done at constant volume, no work is done since $\Delta V = 0$. Thus, according to the first law of thermodynamics, the heat added (which we denote by Q_V) all goes into increasing the internal energy of the gas:

$$Q_V = \Delta E_{\text{int}}.$$

In the process carried out at constant pressure, work is done, and hence the heat added, Q_P, must not only increase the internal energy but also is used to do the work $W = P\,\Delta V$. Thus, more heat must be added in this process at constant pressure than in the first process at constant volume. For the process at constant pressure, we have from the first law of thermodynamics

$$Q_P = \Delta E_{\text{int}} + P\,\Delta V.$$

Since ΔE_{int} is the same in the two processes (ΔT was chosen to be the same), we can combine the two above equations:

$$Q_P - Q_V = P\,\Delta V.$$

From the ideal gas law, $V = nRT/P$, so for a process at constant pressure we have $\Delta V = nR\,\Delta T/P$. Putting this into the above equation and using Eqs. 19–10, we find

$$nC_P\,\Delta T - nC_V\,\Delta T = P\left(\frac{nR\,\Delta T}{P}\right)$$

or, after cancellations,

$$C_P - C_V = R. \tag{19–11}$$

Since the gas constant $R = 8.314\ \text{J/mol·K} = 1.99\ \text{cal/mol·K}$, our prediction is that C_P will be larger than C_V by about $1.99\ \text{cal/mol·K}$. Indeed, this is very close to what is obtained experimentally, as shown in the next to last column of Table 19–4.

Now we calculate the molar specific heat of a monatomic gas using kinetic theory. In a process carried out at constant volume, no work is done; so the first law of thermodynamics tells us that if heat Q is added to the gas, the internal energy of the gas changes by

$$\Delta E_{\text{int}} = Q.$$

For an ideal monatomic gas, the internal energy E_{int} is the total kinetic energy of all the molecules,

$$E_{\text{int}} = N(\tfrac{1}{2}m\overline{v^2}) = \tfrac{3}{2}nRT$$

as we saw in Section 19–2. Then, using Eq. 19–10a, we can write $\Delta E_{\text{int}} = Q$ in the form

$$\Delta E_{\text{int}} = \tfrac{3}{2}nR\,\Delta T = nC_V\,\Delta T \tag{19–12}$$

or

$$C_V = \tfrac{3}{2}R. \tag{19–13}$$

Since $R = 8.314\ \text{J/mol·K} = 1.99\ \text{cal/mol·K}$, kinetic theory predicts that $C_V = 2.98\ \text{cal/mol·K}$ for an ideal monatomic gas. This is very close to the experimental values for monatomic gases such as helium and neon (Table 19–4). From Eq. 19–11, C_P is predicted to be about $4.97\ \text{cal/mol·K}$, also in agreement with experiment.

Equipartition of Energy

The measured molar specific heats for more complex gases (Table 19–4), such as diatomic (two atoms) and triatomic (three atoms) gases, increase with the increased number of atoms per molecule. We can explain this by assuming that the internal energy includes not only translational kinetic energy but other forms of energy as well. Take, for example, a diatomic gas. As shown in Fig. 19–15 the two atoms can rotate about two different axes (but rotation about a third axis passing through the two atoms would give rise to very little energy since the moment of inertia is so small). The molecules can have rotational as well as translational kinetic energy. It is useful to introduce the idea of **degrees of freedom**, by which we mean the number of independent ways molecules can possess energy. For example, a monatomic gas is said to have three degrees of freedom, since an atom can have velocity along the x axis, the y axis, and the z axis. These are considered to be three independent motions because a change in any one of the components would not affect any of the others. A diatomic molecule has the same three degrees of freedom associated with translational kinetic

FIGURE 19–15 A diatomic molecule can rotate about two different axes.

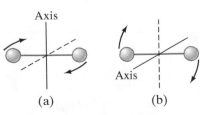

Axis

Axis

(a)   (b)

energy plus two more degrees of freedom associated with rotational kinetic energy, for a total of five degrees of freedom. A quick look at Table 19–4 indicates that the C_V for diatomic gases is about $\frac{5}{3}$ times as great as for a monatomic gas—that is, in the same ratio as their degrees of freedom. This result led nineteenth-century physicists to an important idea, the **principle of equipartition of energy**. This principle states that energy is shared equally among the active degrees of freedom, and in particular each active degree of freedom of a molecule has on the average an energy equal to $\frac{1}{2}kT$. Thus, the average energy for a molecule of a monatomic gas would be $\frac{3}{2}kT$ (which we already knew) and of a diatomic gas $\frac{5}{2}kT$. Hence the internal energy of a diatomic gas would be $E_{\text{int}} = N\left(\frac{5}{2}kT\right) = \frac{5}{2}nRT$, where n is the number of moles. Using the same argument we did for monatomic gases, we see that for diatomic gases the molar specific heat at constant volume would be $\frac{5}{2}R = 4.97\ \text{cal/mol} \cdot \text{K}$, in accordance with measured values. More complex molecules have even more degrees of freedom and thus greater molar specific heats.

The situation was complicated, however, by measurements that showed that for diatomic gases at very low temperatures, C_V has a value of only $\frac{3}{2}R$, as if it had only three degrees of freedom. And at very high temperatures, C_V was about $\frac{7}{2}R$, as if there were seven degrees of freedom. The explanation is that at low temperatures, nearly all molecules have only translational kinetic energy. That is, no energy goes into rotational energy, so only three degrees of freedom are "active." At very high temperatures, on the other hand, all five degrees of freedom are active plus two additional ones. We can interpret the two new degrees of freedom as being associated with the two atoms vibrating as if they were connected by a spring, as shown in Fig. 19–16. One degree of freedom comes from the kinetic energy of the vibrational motion, and the second comes from the potential energy of vibrational motion ($\frac{1}{2}kx^2$). At room temperature, these two degrees of freedom are apparently not active. See Fig. 19–17.

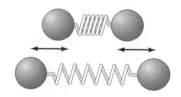

FIGURE 19–16 A diatomic molecule can vibrate, as if the two atoms were connected by a spring. Of course they are not connected by a spring; rather they exert forces on each other that are electrical in nature, but of a form that resembles a spring force.

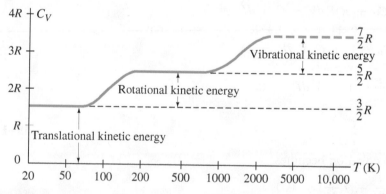

FIGURE 19–17 Molar specific heat C_V as a function of temperature for hydrogen molecules (H_2). As the temperature is increased, some of the translational kinetic energy can be transferred in collisions into rotational kinetic energy and, at still higher temperature, into vibrational kinetic energy. [Note: H_2 dissociates into two atoms at about 3200 K, so the last part of the curve is shown dashed.]

Just why fewer degrees of freedom are "active" at lower temperatures was eventually explained by Einstein using the quantum theory. [According to quantum theory, energy does not take on continuous values but is quantized—it can have only certain values, and there is a certain minimum energy. The minimum rotational and vibrational energies are higher than for simple translational kinetic energy, so at lower temperatures and lower translational kinetic energy, there is not enough energy to excite the rotational or vibrational kinetic energy.] Calculations based on kinetic theory and the principle of equipartition of energy (as modified by the quantum theory) give numerical results in accord with experiment.

*Solids

The principle of equipartition of energy can be applied to solids as well. The molar specific heat of any solid, at high temperature, is close to $3R$ ($6.0\ \text{cal/mol} \cdot \text{K}$), Fig. 19–18. This is called the *Dulong and Petit* value after the scientists who first measured it in 1819. (Note that Table 19–1 gives the specific heats per kilogram, not per mole.) At high temperatures, each atom apparently has six degrees of freedom, although some are not active at low temperatures. Each atom in a crystalline solid can vibrate about its equilibrium position as if it were connected by springs to each of its neighbors. Thus it can have three degrees of freedom for kinetic energy and three more associated with potential energy of vibration in each of the x, y, and z directions, which is in accord with the measured values.

FIGURE 19–18 Molar specific heats of solids as a function of temperature.

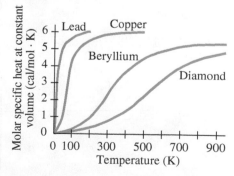

19–9 Adiabatic Expansion of a Gas

The PV curve for the quasistatic (slow) adiabatic expansion $(Q = 0)$ of an ideal gas was shown in Fig. 19–8 (curve AC). It is somewhat steeper than for an isothermal process $(\Delta T = 0)$, which indicates that for the same change in volume the change in pressure will be greater. Hence the temperature of the gas must drop during an adiabatic expansion. Conversely, the temperature rises during an adiabatic compression.

We can derive the relation between the pressure P and the volume V of an ideal gas that is allowed to slowly expand adiabatically. We begin with the first law of thermodynamics, written in differential form:

$$dE_{\text{int}} = dQ - dW = -dW = -P\,dV,$$

since $dQ = 0$ for an adiabatic process. Equation 19–12 gives us a relation between ΔE_{int} and C_V, which is valid for any ideal gas process since E_{int} is a function only of T for an ideal gas. We write this in differential form:

$$dE_{\text{int}} = nC_V\,dT.$$

When we combine these last two equations, we obtain

$$nC_V\,dT + P\,dV = 0.$$

We next take the differential of the ideal gas law, $PV = nRT$, allowing P, V, and T to vary:

$$P\,dV + V\,dP = nR\,dT.$$

We solve for dT in this relation and substitute it into the previous relation and get

$$nC_V\left(\frac{P\,dV + V\,dP}{nR}\right) + P\,dV = 0$$

or, multiplying through by R and rearranging,

$$(C_V + R)P\,dV + C_V V\,dP = 0.$$

We note from Eq. 19–11 that $C_V + R = C_P$, so we have

$$C_P P\,dV + C_V V\,dP = 0,$$

or

$$\frac{C_P}{C_V}P\,dV + V\,dP = 0.$$

We define

$$\gamma = \frac{C_P}{C_V} \qquad\qquad\qquad\qquad \textbf{(19–14)}$$

so that our last equation becomes

$$\frac{dP}{P} + \gamma\frac{dV}{V} = 0.$$

This is integrated to become

$$\ln P + \gamma \ln V = \text{constant}.$$

This simplifies (using the rules for addition and multiplication of logarithms) to

$$PV^{\gamma} = \text{constant}. \qquad \left[\begin{array}{l}\text{quasistatic adiabatic} \\ \text{process; ideal gas}\end{array}\right] \textbf{(19–15)}$$

This is the relation between P and V for a quasistatic adiabatic expansion or contraction. We will find it very useful when we discuss heat engines in the next Chapter. Table 19–4 (p. 511) gives values of γ for some real gases. Figure 19–8 compares an adiabatic expansion (Eq. 19–15) in curve AC to an isothermal expansion $(PV = \text{constant})$ in curve AB. It is important to remember that the ideal gas law, $PV = nRT$, continues to hold even for an adiabatic expansion $(PV^{\gamma} = \text{constant})$; clearly PV is not constant, meaning T is not constant.

EXAMPLE 19–12 **Compressing an ideal gas.** An ideal monatomic gas is compressed starting at point A in the PV diagram of Fig. 19–19, where $P_A = 100\,\text{kPa}$, $V_A = 1.00\,\text{m}^3$, and $T_A = 300\,\text{K}$. The gas is first compressed adiabatically to state B $(P_B = 200\,\text{kPa})$. The gas is then further compressed from point B to point C $(V_C = 0.50\,\text{m}^3)$ in an isothermal process. (a) Determine V_B. (b) Calculate the work done *on* the gas for the whole process.

APPROACH Volume V_B is obtained using Eq. 19–15. The work done *by* a gas is given by Eq. 19–7, $W = \int P\,dV$. The work *on* the gas is the negative of this: $W_{on} = -\int P\,dV$.

SOLUTION In the adiabatic process, Eq. 19–15 tells us $PV^\gamma = $ constant. Therefore, $PV^\gamma = P_A V_A^\gamma = P_B V_B^\gamma$ where for a monatomic gas $\gamma = C_P/C_V = (5/2)/(3/2) = \frac{5}{3}$.

(*a*) Eq. 19–15 gives $V_B = V_A(P_A/P_B)^{\frac{1}{\gamma}} = (1.00\,\text{m}^3)(100\,\text{kPa}/200\,\text{kPa})^{\frac{3}{5}} = 0.66\,\text{m}^3$.

(*b*) The pressure P at any instant during the adiabatic process is given by $P = P_A V_A^\gamma V^{-\gamma}$. The work done on the gas in going from V_A to V_B is

$$W_{AB} = -\int_A^B P\,dV = -P_A V_A^\gamma \int_{V_A}^{V_B} V^{-\gamma}\,dV = -P_A V_A^\gamma \left(\frac{1}{-\gamma+1}\right)(V_B^{1-\gamma} - V_A^{1-\gamma}).$$

Since $\gamma = \frac{5}{3}$, then $-\gamma + 1 = 1 - \gamma = -\frac{2}{3}$, so

$$W_{AB} = -\left(P_A V_A^{\frac{5}{3}}\right)\left(-\frac{3}{2}\right)\left(V_A^{-\frac{2}{3}}\right)\left[\left(\frac{V_B}{V_A}\right)^{-\frac{2}{3}} - 1\right] = +\frac{3}{2} P_A V_A\left[\left(\frac{V_B}{V_A}\right)^{-\frac{2}{3}} - 1\right]$$

$$= +\frac{3}{2}(100\,\text{kPa})(1.00\,\text{m}^3)\left[(0.66)^{-\frac{2}{3}} - 1\right] = +48\,\text{kJ}.$$

For the isothermal process from B to C, the work is done at constant temperature, so the pressure at any instant during the process is $P = nRT_B/V$ and

$$W_{BC} = -\int_B^C P\,dV = -nRT_B \int_{V_B}^{V_C} \frac{dV}{V} = -nRT_B \ln\frac{V_C}{V_B} = -P_B V_B \ln\frac{V_C}{V_B} = +37\,\text{kJ}.$$

The total work done on the gas is $48\,\text{kJ} + 37\,\text{kJ} = 85\,\text{kJ}$.

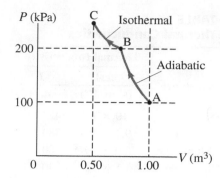

FIGURE 19–19 Example 19–12.

19–10 Heat Transfer: Conduction, Convection, Radiation

Heat is transferred from one place or body to another in three different ways: by *conduction*, *convection*, and *radiation*. We now discuss each of these in turn; but in practical situations, any two or all three may be operating at the same time. We start with conduction.

Conduction

When a metal poker is put in a hot fire, or a silver spoon is placed in a hot bowl of soup, the exposed end of the poker or spoon soon becomes hot as well, even though it is not directly in contact with the source of heat. We say that heat has been conducted from the hot end to the cold end.

Heat **conduction** in many materials can be visualized as being carried out via molecular collisions. As one end of an object is heated, the molecules there move faster and faster. As they collide with slower-moving neighbors, they transfer some of their kinetic energy to these other molecules, which in turn transfer energy by collision with molecules still farther along the object. In metals, collisions of free electrons are mainly responsible for conduction.

Heat conduction from one point to another takes place only if there is a difference in temperature between the two points. Indeed, it is found experimentally that the rate of heat flow through a substance is proportional to the difference in temperature between its ends. The rate of heat flow also depends on the size and shape of the object. To investigate this quantitatively, let us consider the heat flow through a uniform cylinder, as illustrated in Fig. 19–20. It is found experimentally that the heat flow ΔQ over a time interval Δt is given by the relation

$$\frac{\Delta Q}{\Delta t} = kA\frac{T_1 - T_2}{\ell} \tag{19–16a}$$

where A is the cross-sectional area of the object, ℓ is the distance between the two ends, which are at temperatures T_1 and T_2, and k is a proportionality constant called the **thermal conductivity** which is characteristic of the material. From Eq. 19–16a, we see that the rate of heat flow (units of J/s) is directly proportional to the cross-sectional area and to the temperature gradient $(T_1 - T_2)/\ell$.

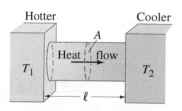

FIGURE 19–20 Heat conduction between areas at temperatures T_1 and T_2. If T_1 is greater than T_2, the heat flows to the right; the rate is given by Eq. 19–16a.

TABLE 19–5
Thermal Conductivities

Substance	Thermal conductivity, k	
	$\dfrac{\text{kcal}}{(\text{s}\cdot\text{m}\cdot\text{C}°)}$	$\dfrac{\text{J}}{(\text{s}\cdot\text{m}\cdot\text{C}°)}$
Silver	10×10^{-2}	420
Copper	9.2×10^{-2}	380
Aluminum	5.0×10^{-2}	200
Steel	1.1×10^{-2}	40
Ice	5×10^{-4}	2
Glass	2.0×10^{-4}	0.84
Brick	2.0×10^{-4}	0.84
Concrete	2.0×10^{-4}	0.84
Water	1.4×10^{-4}	0.56
Human tissue	0.5×10^{-4}	0.2
Wood	0.3×10^{-4}	0.1
Fiberglass	0.12×10^{-4}	0.048
Cork	0.1×10^{-4}	0.042
Wool	0.1×10^{-4}	0.040
Goose down	0.06×10^{-4}	0.025
Polyurethane	0.06×10^{-4}	0.024
Air	0.055×10^{-4}	0.023

FIGURE 19–21 Example 19–13.

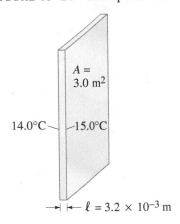

$A = 3.0\ \text{m}^2$

$14.0°\text{C}$ — $15.0°\text{C}$

$\ell = 3.2 \times 10^{-3}\ \text{m}$

(🔬) **PHYSICS APPLIED**
Thermal windows

In some cases (such as when k or A cannot be considered constant) we need to consider the limit of an infinitesimally thin slab of thickness dx. Then Eq. 19–16a becomes

$$\frac{dQ}{dt} = -kA\,\frac{dT}{dx}, \tag{19–16b}$$

where dT/dx is the temperature gradient[†] and the negative sign is included since the heat flow is in the direction opposite to the temperature gradient.

The thermal conductivities, k, for a variety of substances are given in Table 19–5. Substances for which k is large conduct heat rapidly and are said to be good thermal **conductors**. Most metals fall in this category, although there is a wide range even among them, as you may observe by holding the ends of a silver spoon and a stainless-steel spoon immersed in the same hot cup of soup. Substances for which k is small, such as wool, fiberglass, polyurethane, and goose down, are poor conductors of heat and are therefore good thermal **insulators**.

The relative magnitudes of k can explain simple phenomena such as why a tile floor is much colder on the feet than a rug-covered floor at the same temperature. Tile is a better conductor of heat than the rug. Heat that flows from your foot to the rug is not conducted away rapidly, so the rug's surface quickly warms up to the temperature of your foot and feels good. But the tile conducts the heat away rapidly and thus can take more heat from your foot quickly, so your foot's surface temperature drops.

EXAMPLE 19–13 **Heat loss through windows.** A major source of heat loss from a house is through the windows. Calculate the rate of heat flow through a glass window $2.0\ \text{m} \times 1.5\ \text{m}$ in area and $3.2\ \text{mm}$ thick, if the temperatures at the inner and outer surfaces are $15.0°\text{C}$ and $14.0°\text{C}$, respectively (Fig. 19–21).

APPROACH Heat flows by conduction through the glass from the higher inside temperature to the lower outside temperature. We use the heat conduction equation, Eq. 19–16a.

SOLUTION Here $A = (2.0\ \text{m})(1.5\ \text{m}) = 3.0\ \text{m}^2$ and $\ell = 3.2 \times 10^{-3}\ \text{m}$. Using Table 19–5 to get k, we have

$$\frac{\Delta Q}{\Delta t} = kA\,\frac{T_1 - T_2}{\ell} = \frac{(0.84\ \text{J/s}\cdot\text{m}\cdot\text{C}°)(3.0\ \text{m}^2)(15.0°\text{C} - 14.0°\text{C})}{(3.2 \times 10^{-3}\ \text{m})}$$

$$= 790\ \text{J/s}.$$

NOTE This rate of heat flow is equivalent to $(790\ \text{J/s})/(4.19 \times 10^3\ \text{J/kcal}) = 0.19\ \text{kcal/s}$, or $(0.19\ \text{kcal/s}) \times (3600\ \text{s/h}) = 680\ \text{kcal/h}$.

You might notice in Example 19–13 that $15°\text{C}$ is not very warm for the living room of a house. The room itself may indeed be much warmer, and the outside might be colder than $14°\text{C}$. But the temperatures of $15°\text{C}$ and $14°\text{C}$ were specified as those at the window surfaces, and there is usually a considerable drop in temperature of the air in the vicinity of the window both on the inside and the outside. That is, the layer of air on either side of the window acts as an insulator, and normally the major part of the temperature drop between the inside and outside of the house takes place across the air layer. If there is a heavy wind, the air outside a window will constantly be replaced with cold air; the temperature gradient across the glass will be greater and there will be a much greater rate of heat loss. Increasing the width of the air layer, such as using two panes of glass separated by an air gap, will reduce the heat loss more than simply increasing the glass thickness, since the thermal conductivity of air is much less than that for glass.

The insulating properties of clothing come from the insulating properties of air. Without clothes, our bodies in still air would heat the air in contact with the skin and would soon become reasonably comfortable because air is a very good insulator.

[†]Equations 19–16 are quite similar to the relations describing diffusion (Section 18–7) and the flow of fluids through a pipe (Section 13–12). In those cases, the flow of matter was found to be proportional to the concentration gradient dC/dx, or to the pressure gradient $(P_1 - P_2)/\ell$. This close similarity is one reason we speak of the "flow" of heat. Yet we must keep in mind that no substance is flowing in the case of heat—it is energy that is being transferred.

But since air moves—there are breezes and drafts, and people move about—the warm air would be replaced by cold air, thus increasing the temperature difference and the heat loss from the body. Clothes keep us warm by trapping air so it cannot move readily. It is not the cloth that insulates us, but the air that the cloth traps. Goose down is a very good insulator because even a small amount of it fluffs up and traps a great amount of air.

[For practical purposes the thermal properties of building materials, particularly when considered as insulation, are usually specified by R-values (or "thermal resistance"), defined for a given thickness ℓ of material as:

$$R = \ell/k.$$

The R-value of a given piece of material combines the thickness ℓ and the thermal conductivity k in one number. In the United States, R-values are given in British units as $ft^2 \cdot h \cdot F°/Btu$ (for example, R-19 means $R = 19\ ft^2 \cdot h \cdot F°/Btu$). Table 19–6 gives R-values for some common building materials. R-values increase directly with material thickness: for example, 2 inches of fiberglass is R-6, whereas 4 inches is R-12.]

Convection

Although liquids and gases are generally not very good conductors of heat, they can transfer heat quite rapidly by convection. **Convection** is the process whereby heat flows by the mass movement of molecules from one place to another. Whereas conduction involves molecules (and/or electrons) moving only over small distances and colliding, convection involves the movement of large numbers of molecules over large distances.

A forced-air furnace, in which air is heated and then blown by a fan into a room, is an example of *forced convection*. *Natural convection* occurs as well, and one familiar example is that hot air rises. For instance, the air above a radiator (or other type of heater) expands as it is heated (Chapter 17), and hence its density decreases. Because its density is less than that of the surrounding cooler air, it rises, just as a log submerged in water floats upward because its density is less than that of water. Warm or cold ocean currents, such as the balmy Gulf Stream, represent natural convection on a global scale. Wind is another example of convection, and weather in general is strongly influenced by convective air currents.

When a pot of water is heated (Fig. 19–22), convection currents are set up as the heated water at the bottom of the pot rises because of its reduced density. That heated water is replaced by cooler water from above. This principle is used in many heating systems, such as the hot-water radiator system shown in Fig. 19–23. Water is heated in the furnace, and as its temperature increases, it expands and rises as shown. This causes the water to circulate in the heating system. Hot water then enters the radiators, heat is transferred by conduction to the air, and the cooled water returns to the furnace. Thus, the water circulates because of convection; pumps are sometimes used to improve circulation. The air throughout the room also becomes heated as a result of convection. The air heated by the radiators rises and is replaced by cooler air, resulting in convective air currents, as shown by the green arrows in Fig. 19–23.

Other types of furnaces also depend on convection. Hot-air furnaces with registers (openings) near the floor often do not have fans but depend on natural convection, which can be appreciable. In other systems, a fan is used. In either case, it is important that cold air can return to the furnace so that convective currents circulate throughout the room if the room is to be uniformly heated. Convection is not always favorable. Much of the heat from a fireplace, for example, goes up the chimney and not out into the room.

Radiation

Convection and conduction require the presence of matter as a medium to carry the heat from the hotter to the colder region. But a third type of heat transfer occurs without any medium at all. All life on Earth depends on the transfer of energy from the Sun, and this energy is transferred to the Earth over empty (or nearly empty) space. This form of energy transfer is heat—since the Sun's surface temperature is much higher (6000 K) than Earth's—and is referred to as **radiation**. The warmth we receive from a fire is mainly radiant energy.

TABLE 19–6 R-values

Material	Thickness	R-value ($ft^2 \cdot h \cdot F°/Btu$)
Glass	$\frac{1}{8}$ inch	1
Brick	$3\frac{1}{2}$ inches	0.6–1
Plywood	$\frac{1}{2}$ inch	0.6
Fiberglass insulation	4 inches	12

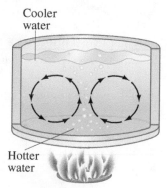

FIGURE 19–22 Convection currents in a pot of water being heated on a stove.

FIGURE 19–23 Convection plays a role in heating a house. The circular arrows show the convective air currents in the rooms.

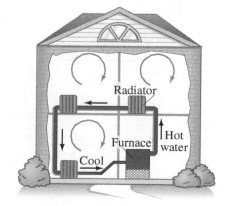

As we shall see in later Chapters, radiation consists essentially of electromagnetic waves. Suffice it to say for now that radiation from the Sun consists of visible light plus many other wavelengths that the eye is not sensitive to, including infrared (IR) radiation.

The rate at which an object radiates energy has been found to be proportional to the fourth power of the Kelvin temperature, T. That is, an object at 2000 K, as compared to one at 1000 K, radiates energy at a rate $2^4 = 16$ times as much. The rate of radiation is also proportional to the area A of the emitting object, so the rate at which energy leaves the object, $\Delta Q / \Delta t$, is

$$\frac{\Delta Q}{\Delta t} = \epsilon \sigma A T^4. \tag{19–17}$$

This is called the **Stefan-Boltzmann equation**, and σ is a universal constant called the **Stefan-Boltzmann constant** which has the value

$$\sigma = 5.67 \times 10^{-8}\,\text{W/m}^2 \cdot \text{K}^4.$$

The factor ϵ (Greek letter epsilon), called the **emissivity**, is a number between 0 and 1 that is characteristic of the surface of the radiating material. Very black surfaces, such as charcoal, have emissivity close to 1, whereas shiny metal surfaces have ϵ close to zero and thus emit correspondingly less radiation. The value depends somewhat on the temperature of the material.

Not only do shiny surfaces emit less radiation, but they absorb little of the radiation that falls upon them (most is reflected). Black and very dark objects are good emitters ($\epsilon \approx 1$), and they also absorb nearly all the radiation that falls on them—which is why light-colored clothing is usually preferable to dark clothing on a hot day. Thus, **a good absorber is also a good emitter**.

Any object not only emits energy by radiation but also absorbs energy radiated by other objects. If an object of emissivity ϵ and area A is at a temperature T_1, it radiates energy at a rate $\epsilon \sigma A T_1^4$. If the object is surrounded by an environment at temperature T_2, the rate at which the surroundings radiate energy is proportional to T_2^4, and the rate that energy is absorbed by the object is proportional to T_2^4. The *net* rate of radiant heat flow from the object is given by

$$\frac{\Delta Q}{\Delta t} = \epsilon \sigma A (T_1^4 - T_2^4), \tag{19–18}$$

where A is the surface area of the object, T_1 its temperature and ϵ its emissivity (at temperature T_1), and T_2 is the temperature of the surroundings. This equation is consistent with the experimental fact that equilibrium between the object and its surroundings is reached when they come to the same temperature. That is, $\Delta Q / \Delta t$ must equal zero when $T_1 = T_2$, so ϵ must be the same for emission and absorption. This confirms the idea that a good emitter is a good absorber. Because both the object and its surroundings radiate energy, there is a net transfer of energy from one to the other unless everything is at the same temperature.

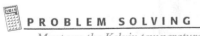
EXAMPLE 19–14 **ESTIMATE** **Cooling by radiation.** An athlete is sitting unclothed in a locker room whose dark walls are at a temperature of 15°C. Estimate his rate of heat loss by radiation, assuming a skin temperature of 34°C and $\epsilon = 0.70$. Take the surface area of the body not in contact with the chair to be 1.5 m².

APPROACH We use Eq. 19–18, with Kelvin temperatures.

SOLUTION We have

$$\frac{\Delta Q}{\Delta t} = \epsilon \sigma A (T_1^4 - T_2^4)$$

$$= (0.70)(5.67 \times 10^{-8}\,\text{W/m}^2 \cdot \text{K}^4)(1.5\,\text{m}^2)\big[(307\,\text{K})^4 - (288\,\text{K})^4\big] = 120\,\text{W}.$$

NOTE The "output" of this resting person is a bit more than what a 100-W lightbulb uses.

A resting person naturally produces heat internally at a rate of about 100 W, which is less than the heat loss by radiation as calculated in Example 19–14. Hence, the person's temperature would drop, causing considerable discomfort. The body responds to excessive heat loss by increasing its metabolic rate, and shivering is one method by which the body increases its metabolism. Naturally, clothes help a lot. Example 19–14 illustrates that a person may be uncomfortable even if the temperature of the air is, say, 25°C, which is quite a warm room. If the walls or floor are cold, radiation to them occurs no matter how warm the air is. Indeed, it is estimated that radiation accounts for about 50% of the heat loss from a sedentary person in a normal room. Rooms are most comfortable when the walls and floor are warm and the air is not so warm. Floors and walls can be heated by means of hot-water conduits or electric heating elements. Such first-rate heating systems are becoming more common today, and it is interesting to note that 2000 years ago the Romans, even in houses in the remote province of Great Britain, made use of hot-water and steam conduits in the floor to heat their houses.

Heating of an object by radiation from the Sun cannot be calculated using Eq. 19–18 since this equation assumes a uniform temperature, T_2, of the environment surrounding the object, whereas the Sun is essentially a point source. Hence the Sun must be treated as a separate source of energy. Heating by the Sun is calculated using the fact that about 1350 J of energy strikes the atmosphere of the Earth from the Sun per second per square meter of area at right angles to the Sun's rays. This number, 1350 W/m², is called the **solar constant**. The atmosphere may absorb as much as 70% of this energy before it reaches the ground, depending on the cloud cover. On a clear day, about 1000 W/m² reaches the Earth's surface. An object of emissivity ϵ with area A facing the Sun absorbs energy from the Sun at a rate, in watts, of about

$$\frac{\Delta Q}{\Delta t} = (1000 \text{ W/m}^2)\,\epsilon\,A\cos\theta, \tag{19–19}$$

where θ is the angle between the Sun's rays and a line perpendicular to the area A (Fig. 19–24). That is, $A\cos\theta$ is the "effective" area, at right angles to the Sun's rays.

The explanation for the **seasons** and the polar ice caps (see Fig. 19–25) depends on this $\cos\theta$ factor in Eq. 19–19. The seasons are *not* a result of how close the Earth is to the Sun—in fact, in the Northern Hemisphere, summer occurs when the Earth is farthest from the Sun. It is the angle (i.e., $\cos\theta$) that really matters. Furthermore, the reason the Sun heats the Earth more at midday than at sunrise or sunset is also related to this $\cos\theta$ factor.

An interesting application of thermal radiation to diagnostic medicine is **thermography**. A special instrument, the thermograph, scans the body, measuring the intensity of radiation from many points and forming a picture that resembles an X-ray (Fig. 19–26). Areas where metabolic activity is high, such as in tumors, can often be detected on a thermogram as a result of their higher temperature and consequent increased radiation.

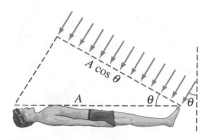

FIGURE 19–24 Radiant energy striking a body at an angle θ.

FIGURE 19–25 (a) Earth's seasons arise from the $23\frac{1}{2}°$ angle Earth's axis makes with its orbit around the Sun. (b) June sunlight makes an angle of about 23° with the equator. Thus θ in the southern United States (A) is near 0° (direct summer sunlight), whereas in the Southern Hemisphere (B), θ is 50° or 60°, and less heat can be absorbed—hence it is winter. Near the poles (C), there is never strong direct sunlight; $\cos\theta$ varies from about $\frac{1}{2}$ in summer to 0 in winter; so with little heating, ice can form.

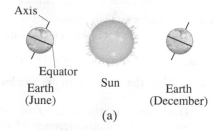

(a)

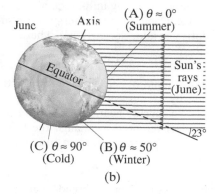

(b)

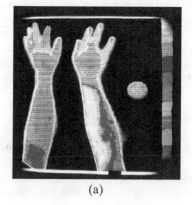

(a)

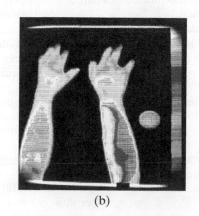

(b)

FIGURE 19–26 Thermograms of a healthy person's arms and hands (a) before and (b) after smoking a cigarette, showing a temperature decrease due to impaired blood circulation associated with smoking. The thermograms have been color-coded according to temperature; the scale on the right goes from blue (cold) to white (hot).

EXAMPLE 19–15 **ESTIMATE** **Star radius.** The giant star Betelgeuse emits radiant energy at a rate 10^4 times greater than our Sun, whereas its surface temperature is only half (2900 K) that of our Sun. Estimate the radius of Betelgeuse, assuming $\epsilon = 1$ for both. The Sun's radius is $r_S = 7 \times 10^8$ m.

APPROACH We assume both Betelgeuse and the Sun are spherical, with surface area $4\pi r^2$.

SOLUTION We solve Eq. 19–17 for A:

$$4\pi r^2 = A = \frac{(\Delta Q/\Delta t)}{\epsilon \sigma T^4}.$$

Then

$$\frac{r_B^2}{r_S^2} = \frac{(\Delta Q/\Delta t)_B}{(\Delta Q/\Delta t)_S} \cdot \frac{T_S^4}{T_B^4} = (10^4)(2^4) = 16 \times 10^4.$$

Hence $r_B = \sqrt{16 \times 10^4}\, r_S = (400)(7 \times 10^8 \text{ m}) \approx 3 \times 10^{11}$ m.

NOTE If Betelgeuse were our Sun, it would envelop us (Earth is 1.5×10^{11} m from the Sun).

EXERCISE G Fanning yourself on a hot day cools you by (*a*) increasing the radiation rate of the skin; (*b*) increasing conductivity; (*c*) decreasing the mean free path of air; (*d*) increasing the evaporation of perspiration; (*e*) none of these.

Summary

Internal energy, E_{int}, refers to the total energy of all the molecules in an object. For an ideal monatomic gas,

$$E_{int} = \tfrac{3}{2} NkT = \tfrac{3}{2} nRT \qquad \text{(19–1)}$$

where N is the number of molecules or n is the number of moles.

Heat refers to the transfer of energy from one object to another because of a difference of temperature. Heat is thus measured in energy units, such as joules.

Heat and internal energy are also sometimes specified in calories or kilocalories (kcal), where

$$1 \text{ kcal} = 4.186 \text{ kJ}$$

is the amount of heat needed to raise the temperature of 1 kg of water by 1 C°.

The **specific heat**, c, of a substance is defined as the energy (or heat) required to change the temperature of unit mass of substance by 1 degree; as an equation,

$$Q = mc\,\Delta T, \qquad \text{(19–2)}$$

where Q is the heat absorbed or given off, ΔT is the temperature increase or decrease, and m is the mass of the substance.

When heat flows between parts of an isolated system, conservation of energy tells us that the heat gained by one part of the system is equal to the heat lost by the other part of the system. This is the basis of **calorimetry**, which is the quantitative measurement of heat exchange.

Exchange of energy occurs, without a change in temperature, whenever a substance changes phase. The **heat of fusion** is the heat required to melt 1 kg of a solid into the liquid phase; it is also equal to the heat given off when the substance changes from liquid to solid. The **heat of vaporization** is the energy required to change 1 kg of a substance from the liquid to the vapor phase; it is also the energy given off when the substance changes from vapor to liquid.

The **first law of thermodynamics** states that the change in internal energy ΔE_{int} of a system is equal to the heat *added to* the system, Q, minus the work, W, done *by* the system:

$$\Delta E_{int} = Q - W. \qquad \text{(19–4)}$$

This important law is a broad restatement of the conservation of energy and is found to hold for all processes.

Two simple thermodynamic processes are **isothermal**, which is a process carried out at constant temperature, and **adiabatic**, a process in which no heat is exchanged. Two more are **isobaric** (a process carried out at constant pressure) and **isovolumetric** (a process at constant volume).

The work done by (or on) a gas to change its volume by dV is $dW = P\,dV$, where P is the pressure.

Work and heat are not functions of the state of a system (as are P, V, T, n, and E_{int}) but depend on the type of process that takes a system from one state to another.

The **molar specific heat** of an ideal gas at constant volume, C_V, and at constant pressure, C_P, are related by

$$C_P - C_V = R, \qquad \text{(19–11)}$$

where R is the gas constant. For a monatomic ideal gas, $C_V = \tfrac{3}{2} R$.

For ideal gases made up of diatomic or more complex molecules, C_V is equal to $\tfrac{1}{2} R$ times the number of **degrees of freedom** of the molecule. Unless the temperature is very high, some of the degrees of freedom may not be active and so do not contribute. According to the **principle of equipartition of energy**, energy is shared equally among the active degrees of freedom in an amount $\tfrac{1}{2} kT$ per molecule on average.

When an ideal gas expands (or contracts) adiabatically ($Q = 0$), the relation $PV^\gamma = $ constant holds, where

$$\gamma = \frac{C_P}{C_V}. \qquad \text{(19–14)}$$

Heat is transferred from one place (or object) to another in three different ways: conduction, convection, and radiation.

In **conduction**, energy is transferred by collisions between molecules or electrons with higher kinetic energy to slower-moving neighbors.

Convection is the transfer of energy by the mass movement of molecules over considerable distances.

Radiation, which does not require the presence of matter, is energy transfer by electromagnetic waves, such as from the Sun.

All objects radiate energy in an amount that is proportional to the fourth power of their Kelvin temperature (T^4) and to their surface area. The energy radiated (or absorbed) also depends on the nature of the surface, which is characterized by the emissivity, ϵ (dark surfaces absorb and radiate more than do bright shiny ones).

Radiation from the Sun arrives at the surface of the Earth on a clear day at a rate of about $1000 \, \text{W/m}^2$.

Questions

1. What happens to the work done on a jar of orange juice when it is vigorously shaken?

2. When a hot object warms a cooler object, does temperature flow between them? Are the temperature changes of the two objects equal? Explain.

3. (a) If two objects of different temperature are placed in contact, will heat naturally flow from the object with higher internal energy to the object with lower internal energy? (b) Is it possible for heat to flow even if the internal energies of the two objects are the same? Explain.

4. In warm regions where tropical plants grow but the temperature may drop below freezing a few times in the winter, the destruction of sensitive plants due to freezing can be reduced by watering them in the evening. Explain.

5. The specific heat of water is quite large. Explain why this fact makes water particularly good for heating systems (that is, hot-water radiators).

6. Why does water in a canteen stay cooler if the cloth jacket surrounding the canteen is kept moist?

7. Explain why burns caused by steam at 100°C on the skin are often more severe than burns caused by water at 100°C.

8. Explain why water cools (its temperature drops) when it evaporates, using the concepts of latent heat and internal energy.

9. Will potatoes cook faster if the water is boiling more vigorously?

10. Very high in the Earth's atmosphere the temperature can be 700°C. Yet an animal there would freeze to death rather than roast. Explain.

11. What happens to the internal energy of water vapor in the air that condenses on the outside of a cold glass of water? Is work done or heat exchanged? Explain.

12. Use the conservation of energy to explain why the temperature of a well-insulated gas increases when it is compressed—say, by pushing down on a piston—whereas the temperature decreases when the gas expands.

13. In an isothermal process, 3700 J of work is done by an ideal gas. Is this enough information to tell how much heat has been added to the system? If so, how much?

14. Explorers on failed Arctic expeditions have survived by covering themselves with snow. Why would they do that?

15. Why is wet sand at the beach cooler to walk on than dry sand?

16. When hot-air furnaces are used to heat a house, why is it important that there be a vent for air to return to the furnace? What happens if this vent is blocked by a bookcase?

17. Is it possible for the temperature of a system to remain constant even though heat flows into or out of it? If so, give examples.

18. Discuss how the first law of thermodynamics can apply to metabolism in humans. In particular, note that a person does work W, but very little heat Q is added to the body (rather, it tends to flow out). Why then doesn't the internal energy drop drastically in time?

19. Explain in words why C_P is greater than C_V.

20. Explain why the temperature of a gas increases when it is adiabatically compressed.

21. An ideal monatomic gas is allowed to expand slowly to twice its volume (1) isothermally; (2) adiabatically; (3) isobarically. Plot each on a PV diagram. In which process is ΔE_{int} the greatest, and in which is ΔE_{int} the least? In which is W the greatest and the least? In which is Q the greatest and the least?

22. Ceiling fans are sometimes reversible, so that they drive the air down in one season and pull it up in another season. Which way should you set the fan for summer? For winter?

23. Goose down sleeping bags and parkas are often specified as so many inches or centimeters of *loft*, the actual thickness of the garment when it is fluffed up. Explain.

24. Microprocessor chips nowadays have a "heat sink" glued on top that looks like a series of fins. Why is it shaped like that?

25. Sea breezes are often encountered on sunny days at the shore of a large body of water. Explain, assuming the temperature of the land rises more rapidly than that of the nearby water.

26. The Earth cools off at night much more quickly when the weather is clear than when cloudy. Why?

27. Explain why air-temperature readings are always taken with the thermometer in the shade.

28. A premature baby in an incubator can be dangerously cooled even when the air temperature in the incubator is warm. Explain.

29. The floor of a house on a foundation under which the air can flow is often cooler than a floor that rests directly on the ground (such as a concrete slab foundation). Explain.

30. Why is the liner of a **thermos bottle** silvered (Fig. 19–27), and why does it have a vacuum between its two walls?

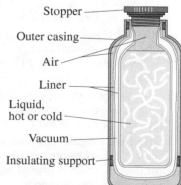

FIGURE 19–27
Question 30.

31. A 22°C day is warm, while a swimming pool at 22°C feels cool. Why?

32. In the Northern Hemisphere the amount of heat required to heat a room where the windows face north is much higher than that required where the windows face south. Explain.

33. Heat loss occurs through windows by the following processes: (1) ventilation around edges; (2) through the frame, particularly if it is metal; (3) through the glass panes; and (4) radiation. (a) For the first three, what is (are) the mechanism(s): conduction, convection, or radiation? (b) Heavy curtains reduce which of these heat losses? Explain in detail.

34. Early in the day, after the Sun has reached the slope of a mountain, there tends to be a gentle upward movement of air. Later, after a slope goes into shadow, there is a gentle downdraft. Explain.

35. A piece of wood lying in the Sun absorbs more heat than a piece of shiny metal. Yet the metal feels hotter than the wood when you pick it up. Explain.

36. An "emergency blanket" is a thin shiny (metal-coated) plastic foil. Explain how it can help to keep an immobile person warm.

37. Explain why cities situated by the ocean tend to have less extreme temperatures than inland cities at the same latitude.

Problems

19–1 Heat as Energy Transfer

1. (I) To what temperature will 8700 J of heat raise 3.0 kg of water that is initially at 10.0°C?

2. (II) When a diver jumps into the ocean, water leaks into the gap region between the diver's skin and her wetsuit, forming a water layer about 0.5 mm thick. Assuming the total surface area of the wetsuit covering the diver is about 1.0 m², and that ocean water enters the suit at 10°C and is warmed by the diver to skin temperature of 35°C, estimate how much energy (in units of candy bars = 300 kcal) is required by this heating process.

3. (II) An average active person consumes about 2500 Cal a day. (a) What is this in joules? (b) What is this in kilowatt-hours? (c) If your power company charges about 10 ¢ per kilowatt-hour, how much would your energy cost per day if you bought it from the power company? Could you feed yourself on this much money per day?

4. (II) A British thermal unit (Btu) is a unit of heat in the British system of units. One Btu is defined as the heat needed to raise 1 lb of water by 1 F°. Show that

$$1\,\text{Btu} = 0.252\,\text{kcal} = 1056\,\text{J}.$$

5. (II) How many joules and kilocalories are generated when the brakes are used to bring a 1200-kg car to rest from a speed of 95 km/h?

6. (II) A small immersion heater is rated at 350 W. Estimate how long it will take to heat a cup of soup (assume this is 250 mL of water) from 15°C to 75°C.

19–3 and 19–4 Specific Heat; Calorimetry

7. (I) An automobile cooling system holds 18 L of water. How much heat does it absorb if its temperature rises from 15°C to 95°C?

8. (I) What is the specific heat of a metal substance if 135 kJ of heat is needed to raise 5.1 kg of the metal from 18.0°C to 37.2°C?

9. (II) (a) How much energy is required to bring a 1.0-L pot of water at 20°C to 100°C? (b) For how long could this amount of energy run a 100-W lightbulb?

10. (II) Samples of copper, aluminum, and water experience the same temperature rise when they absorb the same amount of heat. What is the ratio of their masses?

11. (II) How long does it take a 750-W coffeepot to bring to a boil 0.75 L of water initially at 8.0°C? Assume that the part of the pot which is heated with the water is made of 280 g of aluminum, and that no water boils away.

12. (II) A hot iron horseshoe (mass = 0.40 kg), just forged (Fig. 19–28), is dropped into 1.05 L of water in a 0.30-kg iron pot initially at 20.0°C. If the final equilibrium temperature is 25.0°C, estimate the initial temperature of the hot horseshoe.

FIGURE 19–28
Problem 12.

13. (II) A 31.5-g glass thermometer reads 23.6°C before it is placed in 135 mL of water. When the water and thermometer come to equilibrium, the thermometer reads 39.2°C. What was the original temperature of the water? [Hint: Ignore the mass of fluid inside the glass thermometer.]

14. (II) Estimate the Calorie content of 65 g of candy from the following measurements. A 15-g sample of the candy is placed in a small aluminum container of mass 0.325 kg filled with oxygen. This container is placed in 2.00 kg of water in an aluminum calorimeter cup of mass 0.624 kg at an initial temperature of 15.0°C. The oxygen-candy mixture in the small container is ignited, and the final temperature of the whole system is 53.5°C.

15. (II) When a 290-g piece of iron at 180°C is placed in a 95-g aluminum calorimeter cup containing 250 g of glycerin at 10°C, the final temperature is observed to be 38°C. Estimate the specific heat of glycerin.

16. (II) The *heat capacity, C,* of an object is defined as the amount of heat needed to raise its temperature by 1 C°. Thus, to raise the temperature by ΔT requires heat Q given by

$$Q = C\,\Delta T.$$

(a) Write the heat capacity C in terms of the specific heat, c, of the material. (b) What is the heat capacity of 1.0 kg of water? (c) Of 35 kg of water?

17. (II) The 1.20-kg head of a hammer has a speed of 7.5 m/s just before it strikes a nail (Fig. 19–29) and is brought to rest. Estimate the temperature rise of a 14-g iron nail generated by 10 such hammer blows done in quick succession. Assume the nail absorbs all the energy.

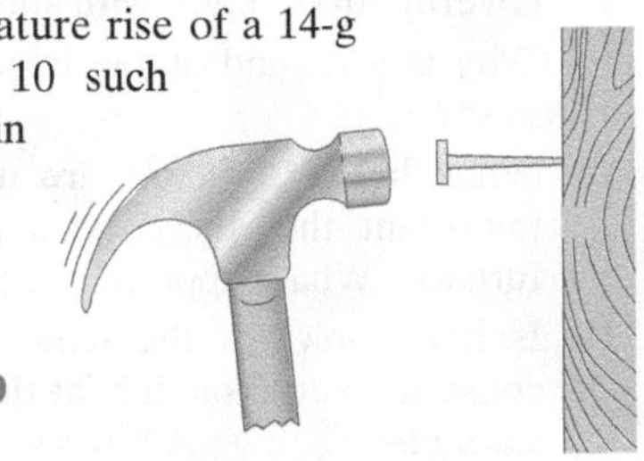

FIGURE 19–29
Problem 17.

19–5 Latent Heat

18. (I) How much heat is needed to melt 26.50 kg of silver that is initially at 25°C?

19. (I) During exercise, a person may give off 180 kcal of heat in 25 min by evaporation of water from the skin. How much water has been lost?

20. (II) A 35-g ice cube at its melting point is dropped into an insulated container of liquid nitrogen. How much nitrogen evaporates if it is at its boiling point of 77 K and has a latent heat of vaporization of 200 kJ/kg? Assume for simplicity that the specific heat of ice is a constant and is equal to its value near its melting point.

21. (II) High-altitude mountain climbers do not eat snow, but always melt it first with a stove. To see why, calculate the energy absorbed from your body if you (a) eat 1.0 kg of −10°C snow which your body warms to body temperature of 37°C. (b) You melt 1.0 kg of −10°C snow using a stove and drink the resulting 1.0 kg of water at 2°C, which your body has to warm to 37°C.

22. (II) An iron boiler of mass 180 kg contains 730 kg of water at 18°C. A heater supplies energy at the rate of 52,000 kJ/h. How long does it take for the water (a) to reach the boiling point, and (b) to all have changed to steam?

23. (II) In a hot day's race, a bicyclist consumes 8.0 L of water over the span of 3.5 hours. Making the approximation that all of the cyclist's energy goes into evaporating this water as sweat, how much energy in kcal did the rider use during the ride? (Since the efficiency of the rider is only about 20%, most of the energy consumed does go to heat, so our approximation is not far off.)

24. (II) The specific heat of mercury is 138 J/kg·C°. Determine the latent heat of fusion of mercury using the following calorimeter data: 1.00 kg of solid Hg at its melting point of −39.0°C is placed in a 0.620-kg aluminum calorimeter with 0.400 kg of water at 12.80°C; the resulting equilibrium temperature is 5.06°C.

25. (II) At a crime scene, the forensic investigator notes that the 7.2-g lead bullet that was stopped in a doorframe apparently melted completely on impact. Assuming the bullet was shot at room temperature (20°C), what does the investigator calculate as the minimum muzzle velocity of the gun?

26. (II) A 58-kg ice-skater moving at 7.5 m/s glides to a stop. Assuming the ice is at 0°C and that 50% of the heat generated by friction is absorbed by the ice, how much ice melts?

19–6 and 19–7 First Law of Thermodynamics

27. (I) Sketch a PV diagram of the following process: 2.0 L of ideal gas at atmospheric pressure are cooled at constant pressure to a volume of 1.0 L, and then expanded isothermally back to 2.0 L, whereupon the pressure is increased at constant volume until the original pressure is reached.

28. (I) A gas is enclosed in a cylinder fitted with a light frictionless piston and maintained at atmospheric pressure. When 1250 kcal of heat is added to the gas, the volume is observed to increase slowly from $12.0 \, m^3$ to $18.2 \, m^3$. Calculate (a) the work done by the gas and (b) the change in internal energy of the gas.

29. (II) The pressure in an ideal gas is cut in half slowly, while being kept in a container with rigid walls. In the process, 365 kJ of heat left the gas. (a) How much work was done during this process? (b) What was the change in internal energy of the gas during this process?

30. (II) A 1.0-L volume of air initially at 3.5 atm of (absolute) pressure is allowed to expand isothermally until the pressure is 1.0 atm. It is then compressed at constant pressure to its initial volume, and lastly is brought back to its original pressure by heating at constant volume. Draw the process on a PV diagram, including numbers and labels for the axes.

31. (II) Consider the following two-step process. Heat is allowed to flow out of an ideal gas at constant volume so that its pressure drops from 2.2 atm to 1.4 atm. Then the gas expands at constant pressure, from a volume of 5.9 L to 9.3 L, where the temperature reaches its original value. See Fig. 19–30. Calculate (a) the total work done by the gas in the process, (b) the change in internal energy of the gas in the process, and (c) the total heat flow into or out of the gas.

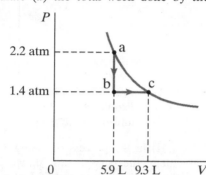

FIGURE 19–30
Problem 31.

32. (II) The PV diagram in Fig. 19–31 shows two possible states of a system containing 1.55 moles of a monatomic ideal gas. $(P_1 = P_2 = 455 \, N/m^2, \quad V_1 = 2.00 \, m^3, \quad V_2 = 8.00 \, m^3.)$ (a) Draw the process which depicts an isobaric expansion from state 1 to state 2, and label this process A. (b) Find the work done by the gas and the change in internal energy of the gas in process A. (c) Draw the two-step process which depicts an isothermal expansion from state 1 to the volume V_2, followed by an isovolumetric increase in temperature to state 2, and label this process B. (d) Find the change in internal energy of the gas for the two-step process B.

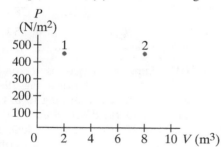

FIGURE 19–31
Problem 32.

33. (II) Suppose 2.60 mol of an ideal gas of volume $V_1 = 3.50 \, m^3$ at $T_1 = 290 \, K$ is allowed to expand isothermally to $V_2 = 7.00 \, m^3$ at $T_2 = 290 \, K$. Determine (a) the work done by the gas, (b) the heat added to the gas, and (c) the change in internal energy of the gas.

34. (II) In an engine, an almost ideal gas is compressed adiabatically to half its volume. In doing so, 2850 J of work is done on the gas. (a) How much heat flows into or out of the gas? (b) What is the change in internal energy of the gas? (c) Does its temperature rise or fall?

35. (II) One and one-half moles of an ideal monatomic gas expand adiabatically, performing 7500 J of work in the process. What is the change in temperature of the gas during this expansion?

36. (II) Determine (a) the work done and (b) the change in internal energy of 1.00 kg of water when it is all boiled to steam at 100°C. Assume a constant pressure of 1.00 atm.

37. (II) How much work is done by a pump to slowly compress, isothermally, 3.50 L of nitrogen at 0°C and 1.00 atm to 1.80 L at 0°C?

38. (II) When a gas is taken from a to c along the curved path in Fig. 19–32, the work done by the gas is $W = -35$ J and the heat added to the gas is $Q = -63$ J. Along path abc, the work done is $W = -54$ J. (a) What is Q for path abc? (b) If $P_c = \frac{1}{2}P_b$, what is W for path cda? (c) What is Q for path cda? (d) What is $E_{int, a} - E_{int, c}$? (e) If $E_{int, d} - E_{int, c} = 12$ J, what is Q for path da?

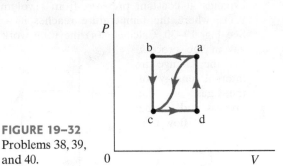

FIGURE 19–32
Problems 38, 39, and 40.

39. (III) In the process of taking a gas from state a to state c along the curved path shown in Fig. 19–32, 85 J of heat leaves the system and 55 J of work is done *on* the system. (a) Determine the change in internal energy, $E_{int, a} - E_{int, c}$. (b) When the gas is taken along the path cda, the work done by the gas is $W = 38$ J. How much heat Q is added to the gas in the process cda? (c) If $P_a = 2.2P_d$, how much work is done by the gas in the process abc? (d) What is Q for path abc? (e) If $E_{int, a} - E_{int, b} = 15$ J, what is Q for the process bc? Here is a summary of what is given:

$$Q_{a \to c} = -85 \text{ J}$$
$$W_{a \to c} = -55 \text{ J}$$
$$W_{cda} = 38 \text{ J}$$
$$E_{int, a} - E_{int, b} = 15 \text{ J}$$
$$P_a = 2.2P_d.$$

40. (III) Suppose a gas is taken clockwise around the rectangular cycle shown in Fig. 19–32, starting at b, then to a, to d, to c, and returning to b. Using the values given in Problem 39, (a) describe each leg of the process, and then calculate (b) the net work done during the cycle, (c) the total internal energy change during the cycle, and (d) the net heat flow during the cycle. (e) What percentage of the *intake* heat was turned into usable work: i.e., how efficient is this "rectangular" cycle (give as a percentage)?

*41. (III) Determine the work done by 1.00 mol of a van der Waals gas (Section 18–5) when it expands from volume V_1 to V_2 isothermally.

19–8 Molecular Specific Heat for Gases; Equipartition of Energy

42. (I) What is the internal energy of 4.50 mol of an ideal diatomic gas at 645 K, assuming all degrees of freedom are active?

43. (I) If a heater supplies 1.8×10^6 J/h to a room 3.5 m × 4.6 m × 3.0 m containing air at 20°C and 1.0 atm, by how much will the temperature rise in one hour, assuming no losses of heat or air mass to the outside? Assume air is an ideal diatomic gas with molecular mass 29.

44. (I) Show that if the molecules of a gas have n degrees of freedom, then theory predicts $C_V = \frac{1}{2}nR$ and $C_P = \frac{1}{2}(n + 2)R$.

45. (II) A certain monatomic gas has specific heat $c_V = 0.0356$ kcal/kg·C°, which changes little over a wide temperature range. What is the atomic mass of this gas? What gas is it?

46. (II) Show that the work done by n moles of an ideal gas when it expands adiabatically is $W = nC_V(T_1 - T_2)$, where T_1 and T_2 are the initial and final temperatures, and C_V is the molar specific heat at constant volume.

47. (II) An audience of 1800 fills a concert hall of volume 22,000 m³. If there were no ventilation, by how much would the temperature of the air rise over a period of 2.0 h due to the metabolism of the people (70 W/person)?

48. (II) The specific heat at constant volume of a particular gas is 0.182 kcal/kg·K at room temperature, and its molecular mass is 34. (a) What is its specific heat at constant pressure? (b) What do you think is the molecular structure of this gas?

49. (II) A 2.00 mole sample of N_2 gas at 0°C is heated to 150°C at constant pressure (1.00 atm). Determine (a) the change in internal energy, (b) the work the gas does, and (c) the heat added to it.

50. (III) A 1.00-mol sample of an ideal diatomic gas at a pressure of 1.00 atm and temperature of 420 K undergoes a process in which its pressure increases linearly with temperature. The final temperature and pressure are 720 K and 1.60 atm. Determine (a) the change in internal energy, (b) the work done by the gas, and (c) the heat added to the gas. (Assume five active degrees of freedom.)

19–9 Adiabatic Expansion of a Gas

51. (I) A 1.00-mol sample of an ideal diatomic gas, originally at 1.00 atm and 20°C, expands adiabatically to 1.75 times its initial volume. What are the final pressure and temperature for the gas? (Assume no molecular vibration.)

52. (II) Show, using Eqs. 19–6 and 19–15, that the work done by a gas that slowly expands adiabatically from pressure P_1 and volume V_1, to P_2 and V_2, is given by $W = (P_1 V_1 - P_2 V_2)/(\gamma - 1)$.

53. (II) A 3.65-mol sample of an ideal diatomic gas expands adiabatically from a volume of 0.1210 m³ to 0.750 m³. Initially the pressure was 1.00 atm. Determine: (a) the initial and final temperatures; (b) the change in internal energy; (c) the heat lost by the gas; (d) the work done *on* the gas. (Assume no molecular vibration.)

54. (II) An ideal monatomic gas, consisting of 2.8 mol of volume 0.086 m³, expands adiabatically. The initial and final temperatures are 25°C and −68°C. What is the final volume of the gas?

55. (III) A 1.00-mol sample of an ideal monatomic gas, originally at a pressure of 1.00 atm, undergoes a three-step process: (1) it is expanded adiabatically from $T_1 = 588$ K to $T_2 = 389$ K; (2) it is compressed at constant pressure until its temperature reaches T_3; (3) it then returns to its original pressure and temperature by a constant-volume process. (a) Plot these processes on a PV diagram. (b) Determine T_3. (c) Calculate the change in internal energy, the work done by the gas, and the heat added to the gas for each process, and (d) for the complete cycle.

56. (III) Consider a **parcel of air** moving to a different altitude y in the Earth's atmosphere (Fig. 19–33). As the parcel changes altitude it acquires the pressure P of the surrounding air. From Eq. 13–4 we have

$$\frac{dP}{dy} = -\rho g$$

where ρ is the parcel's altitude-dependent mass density.

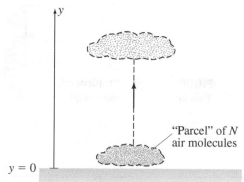

FIGURE 19–33
Problem 56.

During this motion, the parcel's volume will change and, because air is a poor heat conductor, we assume this expansion or contraction will take place adiabatically. (a) Starting with Eq. 19–15, $PV^\gamma = $ constant, show that for an ideal gas undergoing an adiabatic process, $P^{1-\gamma}T^\gamma = $ constant. Then show that the parcel's pressure and temperature are related by

$$(1 - \gamma)\frac{dP}{dy} + \gamma \frac{P}{T}\frac{dT}{dy} = 0$$

and thus

$$(1 - \gamma)(-\rho g) + \gamma \frac{P}{T}\frac{dT}{dy} = 0.$$

(b) Use the ideal gas law with the result from part (a) to show that the change in the parcel's temperature with change in altitude is given by

$$\frac{dT}{dy} = \frac{1 - \gamma}{\gamma}\frac{mg}{k}$$

where m is the average mass of an air molecule and k is the Boltzmann constant. (c) Given that air is a diatomic gas with an average molecular mass of 29, show that $dT/dy = -9.8\,\text{C}°/\text{km}$. This value is called the **adiabatic lapse rate** for dry air. (d) In California, the prevailing westerly winds descend from one of the highest elevations (the 4000-m Sierra Nevada mountains) to one of the lowest elevations (Death Valley, $-100\,\text{m}$) in the continental United States. If a dry wind has a temperature of $-5°\text{C}$ at the top of the Sierra Nevada, what is the wind's temperature after it has descended to Death Valley?

19–10 Conduction, Convection, Radiation

57. (I) (a) How much power is radiated by a tungsten sphere (emissivity $\epsilon = 0.35$) of radius 16 cm at a temperature of 25°C? (b) If the sphere is enclosed in a room whose walls are kept at $-5°\text{C}$, what is the *net* flow rate of energy out of the sphere?

58. (I) One end of a 45-cm-long copper rod with a diameter of 2.0 cm is kept at 460°C, and the other is immersed in water at 22°C. Calculate the heat conduction rate along the rod.

59. (II) How long does it take the Sun to melt a block of ice at 0°C with a flat horizontal area $1.0\,\text{m}^2$ and thickness 1.0 cm? Assume that the Sun's rays make an angle of 35° with the vertical and that the emissivity of ice is 0.050.

60. (II) *Heat conduction to skin.* Suppose 150 W of heat flows by conduction from the blood capillaries beneath the skin to the body's surface area of $1.5\,\text{m}^2$. If the temperature difference is $0.50\,\text{C}°$, estimate the average distance of capillaries below the skin surface.

61. (II) A ceramic teapot ($\epsilon = 0.70$) and a shiny one ($\epsilon = 0.10$) each hold 0.55 L of tea at 95°C. (a) Estimate the rate of heat loss from each, and (b) estimate the temperature drop after 30 min for each. Consider only radiation, and assume the surroundings are at 20°C.

62. (II) A copper rod and an aluminum rod of the same length and cross-sectional area are attached end to end (Fig. 19–34). The copper end is placed in a furnace maintained at a constant temperature of 225°C. The aluminum end is placed in an ice bath held at constant temperature of 0.0°C. Calculate the temperature at the point where the two rods are joined.

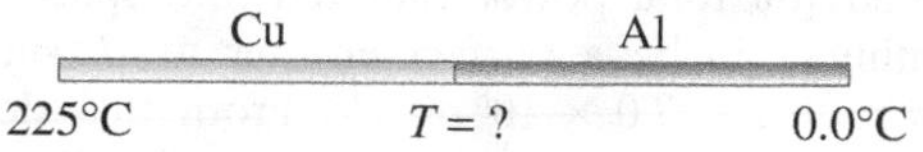

Cu	Al
225°C	$T = ?$	0.0°C

FIGURE 19–34 Problem 62.

63. (II) (a) Using the solar constant, estimate the rate at which the whole Earth receives energy from the Sun. (b) Assume the Earth radiates an equal amount back into space (that is, the Earth is in equilibrium). Then, assuming the Earth is a perfect emitter ($\epsilon = 1.0$), estimate its average surface temperature. [*Hint*: Use area $A = 4\pi r_{\text{E}}^2$, and state why.]

64. (II) A 100-W lightbulb generates 95 W of heat, which is dissipated through a glass bulb that has a radius of 3.0 cm and is 0.50 mm thick. What is the difference in temperature between the inner and outer surfaces of the glass?

65. (III) A house thermostat is normally set to 22°C, but at night it is turned down to 12°C for 9.0 h. Estimate how much more heat would be needed (state as a percentage of daily usage) if the thermostat were not turned down at night. Assume that the outside temperature averages 0°C for the 9.0 h at night and 8°C for the remainder of the day, and that the heat loss from the house is proportional to the difference in temperature inside and out. To obtain an estimate from the data, you will have to make other simplifying assumptions; state what these are.

66. (III) Approximately how long should it take 9.5 kg of ice at 0°C to melt when it is placed in a carefully sealed Styrofoam ice chest of dimensions 25 cm × 35 cm × 55 cm whose walls are 1.5 cm thick? Assume that the conductivity of Styrofoam is double that of air and that the outside temperature is 34°C.

67. (III) A cylindrical pipe has inner radius R_1 and outer radius R_2. The interior of the pipe carries hot water at temperature T_1. The temperature outside is T_2 $(< T_1)$. (a) Show that the rate of heat loss for a length ℓ of pipe is

$$\frac{dQ}{dt} = \frac{2\pi k(T_1 - T_2)\ell}{\ln(R_2/R_1)},$$

where k is the thermal conductivity of the pipe. (b) Suppose the pipe is steel with $R_1 = 3.3$ cm, $R_2 = 4.0$ cm, and $T_2 = 18°C$. If the pipe holds still water at $T_1 = 71°C$, what will be the initial rate of change of its temperature? (c) Suppose water at 71°C enters the pipe and moves at a speed of 8.0 cm/s. What will be its temperature drop per centimeter of travel?

68. (III) Suppose the insulating qualities of the wall of a house come mainly from a 4.0-in. layer of brick and an R-19 layer of insulation, as shown in Fig. 19–35. What is the total rate of heat loss through such a wall, if its total area is 195 ft² and the temperature difference across it is 12 F°?

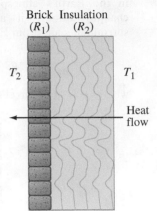

FIGURE 19–35 Problem 68.
Two layers insulating a wall.

General Problems

69. A soft-drink can contains about 0.20 kg of liquid at 5°C. Drinking this liquid can actually consume some of the fat in the body, since energy is needed to warm the liquid to body temperature (37°C). How many food Calories should the drink have so that it is in perfect balance with the heat needed to warm the liquid (essentially water)?

70. (a) Find the total power radiated into space by the Sun, assuming it to be a perfect emitter at $T = 5500$ K. The Sun's radius is 7.0×10^8 m. (b) From this, determine the power per unit area arriving at the Earth, 1.5×10^{11} m away.

71. To get an idea of how much thermal energy is contained in the world's oceans, estimate the heat liberated when a cube of ocean water, 1 km on each side, is cooled by 1 K. (Approximate the ocean water as pure water for this estimate.)

72. A mountain climber wears a goose-down jacket 3.5 cm thick with total surface area 0.95 m². The temperature at the surface of the clothing is −18°C and at the skin is 34°C. Determine the rate of heat flow by conduction through the jacket (a) assuming it is dry and the thermal conductivity k is that of goose down, and (b) assuming the jacket is wet, so k is that of water and the jacket has matted to 0.50 cm thickness.

73. During light activity, a 70-kg person may generate 200 kcal/h. Assuming that 20% of this goes into useful work and the other 80% is converted to heat, estimate the temperature rise of the body after 30 min if none of this heat is transferred to the environment.

74. Estimate the rate at which heat can be conducted from the interior of the body to the surface. Assume that the thickness of tissue is 4.0 cm, that the skin is at 34°C and the interior at 37°C, and that the surface area is 1.5 m². Compare this to the measured value of about 230 W that must be dissipated by a person working lightly. This clearly shows the necessity of convective cooling by the blood.

75. A marathon runner has an average metabolism rate of about 950 kcal/h during a race. If the runner has a mass of 55 kg, estimate how much water she would lose to evaporation from the skin for a race that lasts 2.2 h.

76. A house has well-insulated walls 19.5 cm thick (assume conductivity of air) and area 410 m², a roof of wood 5.5 cm thick and area 280 m², and uncovered windows 0.65 cm thick and total area 33 m². (a) Assuming that heat is lost only by conduction, calculate the rate at which heat must be supplied to this house to maintain its inside temperature at 23°C if the outside temperature is −15°C. (b) If the house is initially at 12°C, estimate how much heat must be supplied to raise the temperature to 23°C within 30 min. Assume that only the air needs to be heated and that its volume is 750 m³. (c) If natural gas costs $0.080 per kilogram and its heat of combustion is 5.4×10^7 J/kg, how much is the monthly cost to maintain the house as in part (a) for 24 h each day, assuming 90% of the heat produced is used to heat the house? Take the specific heat of air to be 0.24 kcal/kg·C°.

77. In a typical game of squash (Fig. 19–36), two people hit a soft rubber ball at a wall until they are about to drop due to dehydration and exhaustion. Assume that the ball hits the wall at a velocity of 22 m/s and bounces back with a velocity of 12 m/s, and that the kinetic energy lost in the process heats the ball. What will be the temperature increase of the ball after one bounce? (The specific heat of rubber is about 1200 J/kg·C°.)

FIGURE 19–36 Problem 77.

78. A bicycle pump is a cylinder 22 cm long and 3.0 cm in diameter. The pump contains air at 20.0°C and 1.0 atm. If the outlet at the base of the pump is blocked and the handle is pushed in very quickly, compressing the air to half its original volume, how hot does the air in the pump become?

79. A microwave oven is used to heat 250 g of water. On its maximum setting, the oven can raise the temperature of the liquid water from 20°C to 100°C in 1 min 45 s (= 105 s). (a) At what rate does the oven input energy to the liquid water? (b) If the power input from the oven to the water remains constant, determine how many grams of water will boil away if the oven is operated for 2 min (rather than just 1 min 45 s).

80. The temperature within the Earth's crust increases about 1.0 C° for each 30 m of depth. The thermal conductivity of the crust is 0.80 W/C°·m. (a) Determine the heat transferred from the interior to the surface for the entire Earth in 1.0 h. (b) Compare this heat to the amount of energy incident on the Earth in 1.0 h due to radiation from the Sun.

81. An ice sheet forms on a lake. The air above the sheet is at −18°C, whereas the water is at 0°C. Assume that the heat of fusion of the water freezing on the lower surface is conducted through the sheet to the air above. How much time will it take to form a sheet of ice 15 cm thick?

82. An iron meteorite melts when it enters the Earth's atmosphere. If its initial temperature was −105°C outside of Earth's atmosphere, calculate the minimum velocity the meteorite must have had before it entered Earth's atmosphere.

83. A scuba diver releases a 3.60-cm-diameter (spherical) bubble of air from a depth of 14.0 m. Assume the temperature is constant at 298 K, and that the air behaves as an ideal gas. (a) How large is the bubble when it reaches the surface? (b) Sketch a PV diagram for the process. (c) Apply the first law of thermodynamics to the bubble, and find the work done by the air in rising to the surface, the change in its internal energy, and the heat added or removed from the air in the bubble as it rises. Take the density of water to be 1000 kg/m³.

84. A reciprocating compressor is a device that compresses air by a back-and-forth straight-line motion, like a piston in a cylinder. Consider a reciprocating compressor running at 150 rpm. During a compression stroke, 1.00 mol of air is compressed. The initial temperature of the air is 390 K, the engine of the compressor is supplying 7.5 kW of power to compress the air, and heat is being removed at the rate of 1.5 kW. Calculate the temperature change per compression stroke.

85. The temperature of the glass surface of a 75-W lightbulb is 75°C when the room temperature is 18°C. Estimate the temperature of a 150-W lightbulb with a glass bulb the same size. Consider only radiation, and assume that 90% of the energy is emitted as heat.

86. Suppose 3.0 mol of neon (an ideal monatomic gas) at STP are compressed slowly and isothermally to 0.22 the original volume. The gas is then allowed to expand quickly and adiabatically back to its original volume. Find the highest and lowest temperatures and pressures attained by the gas, and show on a PV diagram where these values occur.

87. At very low temperatures, the molar specific heat of many substances varies as the cube of the absolute temperature:

$$C = k\frac{T^3}{T_0^3},$$

which is sometimes called Debye's law. For rock salt, $T_0 = 281$ K and $k = 1940$ J/mol·K. Determine the heat needed to raise 2.75 mol of salt from 22.0 K to 48.0 K.

88. A diesel engine accomplishes ignition without a spark plug by an adiabatic compression of air to a temperature above the ignition temperature of the diesel fuel, which is injected into the cylinder at the peak of the compression. Suppose air is taken into the cylinder at 280 K and volume V_1 and is compressed adiabatically to 560°C ($\approx 1000°F$) and volume V_2. Assuming that the air behaves as an ideal gas whose ratio of C_P to C_V is 1.4, calculate the compression ratio V_1/V_2 of the engine.

89. When 6.30×10^5 J of heat is added to a gas enclosed in a cylinder fitted with a light frictionless piston maintained at atmospheric pressure, the volume is observed to increase from 2.2 m³ to 4.1 m³. Calculate (a) the work done by the gas, and (b) the change in internal energy of the gas. (c) Graph this process on a PV diagram.

90. In a cold environment, a person can lose heat by conduction and radiation at a rate of about 200 W. Estimate how long it would take for the body temperature to drop from 36.6°C to 35.6°C if metabolism were nearly to stop. Assume a mass of 70 kg. (See Table 19–1.)

*Numerical/Computer
*91. (II) Suppose 1.0 mol of steam at 100°C of volume 0.50 m³ is expanded isothermally to volume 1.00 m³. Assume steam obeys the van der Waals equation $(P + n^2a/V^2)(V/n - b) = RT$, Eq. 18–9, with $a = 0.55$ N·m⁴/mol² and $b = 3.0 \times 10^{-5}$ m³/mol. Using the expression $dW = P\,dV$, determine numerically the total work done W. Your result should agree within 2% of the result obtained by integrating the expression for dW.

Answers to Exercises

A: (b).

B: (c).

C: 0.21 kg.

D: 700 J.

E: Less.

F: -6.8×10^3 J.

G: (d).

There are many uses for a heat engine, such as old steam trains and modern coal-burning power plants. Steam engines produce steam which does work: on turbines to generate electricity, and on a piston that moves linkage to turn locomotive wheels. The efficiency of any engine—no matter how carefully engineered—is limited by nature as described in the second law of thermodynamics. This great law is best stated in terms of a quantity called entropy, which is unlike any other. Entropy is *not* conserved, but instead is constrained always to increase in any real process. Entropy is a measure of disorder. The second law of thermodynamics tells us that as time moves forward, the disorder in the universe increases.

We discuss many practical matters including heat engines, heat pumps, and refrigeration.

C H A P T E R

20

Second Law of Thermodynamics

CHAPTER-OPENING QUESTION—Guess now!

Fossil-fuel electric generating plants produce "thermal pollution." Part of the heat produced by the burning fuel is not converted to electric energy. The reason for this waste is

(a) The efficiency is higher if some heat is allowed to escape.

(b) Engineering technology has not yet reached the point where 100% waste heat recovery is possible.

(c) Some waste heat *must* be produced: this is a fundamental property of nature when converting heat to useful work.

(d) The plants rely on fossil fuels, not nuclear fuel.

(e) None of the above.

I n this final Chapter on heat and thermodynamics, we discuss the famous second law of thermodynamics, and the quantity "entropy" that arose from this fundamental law and is its quintessential expression. We also discuss heat engines—the engines that transform heat into work in power plants, trains, and motor vehicles—because they first showed us that a new law was needed. Finally, we briefly discuss the third law of thermodynamics.

20–1 The Second Law of Thermodynamics—Introduction

The first law of thermodynamics states that energy is conserved. There are, however, many processes we can imagine that conserve energy but are not observed to occur in nature. For example, when a hot object is placed in contact with a cold object, heat flows from the hotter one to the colder one, never spontaneously the reverse. If heat were to leave the colder object and pass to the hotter one, energy could still be conserved. Yet it does not happen spontaneously.[†] As a second example, consider what happens when you drop a rock and it hits the ground. The initial potential energy of the rock changes to kinetic energy as the rock falls. When the rock hits the ground, this energy in turn is transformed into internal energy of the rock and the ground in the vicinity of the impact; the molecules move faster and the temperature rises slightly. But have you seen the reverse happen—a rock at rest on the ground suddenly rise up in the air because the thermal energy of molecules is transformed into kinetic energy of the rock as a whole? Energy could be conserved in this process, yet we never see it happen.

There are many other examples of processes that occur in nature but whose reverse does not. Here are two more. (1) If you put a layer of salt in a jar and cover it with a layer of similar-sized grains of pepper, when you shake it you get a thorough mixture. But no matter how long you shake it, the mixture does not separate into two layers again. (2) Coffee cups and glasses break spontaneously if you drop them. But they do not go back together spontaneously (Fig. 20–1).

(a) Initial state.   (b) Later: cup reassembles and rises up.   (c) Later still: cup lands on table.

FIGURE 20–1 Have you ever observed this process, a broken cup spontaneously reassembling and rising up onto a table? This process could conserve energy and other laws of mechanics.

The first law of thermodynamics (conservation of energy) would not be violated if any of these processes occurred in reverse. To explain this lack of reversibility, scientists in the latter half of the nineteenth century formulated a new principle known as the second law of thermodynamics.

The **second law of thermodynamics** is a statement about which processes occur in nature and which do not. It can be stated in a variety of ways, all of which are equivalent. One statement, due to R. J. E. Clausius (1822–1888), is that

> **heat can flow spontaneously from a hot object to a cold object; heat will not flow spontaneously from a cold object to a hot object.**

*SECOND LAW OF THERMODYNAMICS
(Clausius statement)*

Since this statement applies to one particular process, it is not obvious how it applies to other processes. A more general statement is needed that will include other possible processes in a more obvious way.

The development of a general statement of the second law of thermodynamics was based partly on the study of heat engines. A **heat engine** is any device that changes thermal energy into mechanical work, such as a steam engine or automobile engine. We now examine heat engines, both from a practical point of view and to show their importance in developing the second law of thermodynamics.

[†]By spontaneously, we mean by itself without input of work of some sort. (A refrigerator does move heat from a cold environment to a warmer one, but only because its motor does work—Section 20–4.)

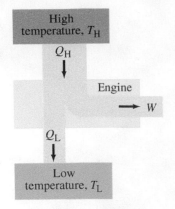

High temperature, T_H

Q_H

Engine

W

Q_L

Low temperature, T_L

FIGURE 20–2 Schematic diagram of energy transfers for a heat engine.

⚠ **CAUTION**

New sign convention:
$Q_H > 0, Q_L > 0, W > 0$

PHYSICS APPLIED

Engines

20–2 Heat Engines

It is easy to produce thermal energy by doing work—for example, by simply rubbing your hands together briskly, or indeed by any frictional process. But to get work from thermal energy is more difficult, and a practical device to do this was invented only about 1700 with the development of the steam engine.

The basic idea behind any heat engine is that mechanical energy can be obtained from thermal energy only when heat is allowed to flow from a high temperature to a low temperature. In the process, some of the heat can then be transformed to mechanical work, as diagrammed schematically in Fig. 20–2. We will be interested only in engines that run in a repeating *cycle* (that is, the system returns repeatedly to its starting point) and thus can run continuously. In each cycle the change in internal energy of the system is $\Delta E_{int} = 0$ because it returns to the starting state. Thus a heat input Q_H at a high temperature T_H is partly transformed into work W and partly exhausted as heat Q_L at a lower temperature T_L (Fig. 20–2). By conservation of energy, $Q_H = W + Q_L$. The high and low temperatures, T_H and T_L, are called the **operating temperatures** of the engine. Note carefully that we are now using a new sign convention: we take Q_H, Q_L, and W as always positive. The direction of each energy transfer is shown by the arrow on the applicable diagram, such as Fig. 20–2.

Steam Engine and Internal Combustion Engine

The operation of a steam engine is illustrated in Fig. 20–3. Steam engines are of two main types, each making use of steam heated by combustion of coal, oil or gas, or by nuclear energy. In a reciprocating engine, Fig. 20–3a, the heated steam passes through the intake valve and expands against a piston, forcing it to move. As the piston returns to its original position, it forces the gases out the exhaust valve. A steam turbine, Fig. 20–3b, is very similar except that the reciprocating piston is replaced by a rotating turbine that resembles a paddlewheel with many sets of blades. Most of our electricity today is generated using steam turbines.[†] The material that is heated and cooled, steam in this case, is called the **working substance**.

[†]Even nuclear power plants utilize steam turbines; the nuclear fuel—uranium—merely serves as fuel to heat the steam.

(a) Reciprocating type

(b) Turbine (boiler and condenser not shown)

FIGURE 20–3 Steam engines.

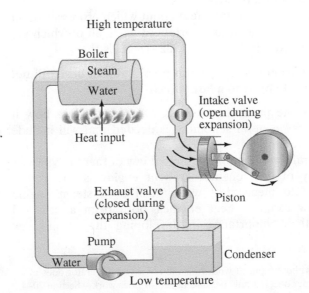

High temperature

Boiler

Steam

Water

Heat input

Intake valve (open during expansion)

Exhaust valve (closed during expansion)

Piston

Pump

Water

Condenser

Low temperature

High-pressure steam, from boiler

Low-pressure steam, exhausted to condenser

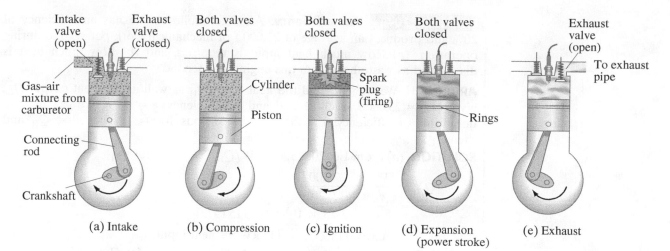

| (a) Intake | (b) Compression | (c) Ignition | (d) Expansion (power stroke) | (e) Exhaust |

In an internal combustion engine (used in most automobiles), the high temperature is achieved by burning the gasoline–air mixture in the cylinder itself (ignited by the spark plug), as described in Fig. 20–4.

Why a ΔT Is Needed to Drive a Heat Engine

To see why a *temperature difference* is required to run an engine, let us examine the steam engine. In the reciprocating engine, for example, suppose there were no condenser or pump (Fig. 20–3a), and that the steam was at the same temperature throughout the system. This would mean that the pressure of the gas being exhausted would be the same as that on intake. Thus, although work would be done by the gas *on* the piston when it expanded, an equal amount of work would have to be done *by* the piston to force the steam out the exhaust; hence, no net work would be done. In a real engine, the exhausted gas is cooled to a lower temperature and condensed so that the exhaust pressure is less than the intake pressure. Thus, although the piston must do work on the gas to expel it on the exhaust stroke, it is less than the work done by the gas on the piston during the intake. So a net amount of work can be obtained—but only if there is a difference of temperature. Similarly, in the gas turbine if the gas isn't cooled, the pressure on each side of the blades would be the same. By cooling the gas on the exhaust side, the pressure on the back side of the blade is less and hence the turbine turns.

Efficiency and the Second Law

The **efficiency**, e, of any heat engine can be defined as the ratio of the work it does, W, to the heat input at the high temperature, Q_H (Fig. 20–2):

$$e = \frac{W}{Q_H}.$$

This is a sensible definition since W is the output (what you get from the engine), whereas Q_H is what you put in and pay for in burned fuel. Since energy is conserved, the heat input Q_H must equal the work done plus the heat that flows out at the low temperature (Q_L):

$$Q_H = W + Q_L.$$

Thus $W = Q_H - Q_L$, and the efficiency of an engine is

$$e = \frac{W}{Q_H} \tag{20–1a}$$

$$= \frac{Q_H - Q_L}{Q_H} = 1 - \frac{Q_L}{Q_H}. \tag{20–1b}$$

To give the efficiency as a percent, we multiply Eqs. 20–1 by 100. Note that e could be 1.0 (or 100%) only if Q_L were zero—that is, only if no heat were exhausted to the environment.

FIGURE 20–4 Four-stroke-cycle internal combustion engine: (a) the gasoline–air mixture flows into the cylinder as the piston moves down; (b) the piston moves upward and compresses the gas; (c) the brief instant when firing of the spark plug ignites the highly compressed gasoline–air mixture, raising it to a high temperature; (d) the gases, now at high temperature and pressure, expand against the piston in this, the power stroke; (e) the burned gases are pushed out to the exhaust pipe; when the piston reaches the top, the exhaust valve closes and the intake valve opens, and the whole cycle repeats. (a), (b), (d), and (e) are the four strokes of the cycle.

EXAMPLE 20–1 **Car efficiency.** An automobile engine has an efficiency of 20% and produces an average of 23,000 J of mechanical work per second during operation. (a) How much heat input is required, and (b) how much heat is discharged as waste heat from this engine, per second?

APPROACH We want to find the heat input Q_H as well as the heat output Q_L, given $W = 23,000$ J each second and an efficiency $e = 0.20$. We can use the definition of efficiency, Eq. 20–1 in its various forms, to find first Q_H and then Q_L.

SOLUTION (a) From Eq. 20–1a, $e = W/Q_H$, we solve for Q_H:

$$Q_H = \frac{W}{e} = \frac{23,000 \text{ J}}{0.20}$$
$$= 1.15 \times 10^5 \text{ J} = 115 \text{ kJ}.$$

The engine requires 115 kJ/s = 115 kW of heat input.

(b) Now we use Eq. 20–1b $(e = 1 - Q_L/Q_H)$ and solve for Q_L:

$$Q_L = (1 - e)Q_H = (0.80)115 \text{ kJ} = 92 \text{ kJ}.$$

The engine discharges heat to the environment at a rate of 92 kJ/s = 92 kW.

NOTE Of the 115 kJ that enters the engine per second, only 23 kJ does useful work whereas 92 kJ is wasted as heat output.

NOTE The problem was stated in terms of energy per unit time. We could just as well have stated it in terms of power, since 1 J/s = 1 W.

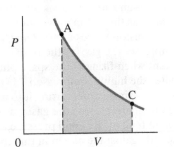

FIGURE 20–5 Adiabatic process, Exercise A.

EXERCISE A An adiabatic process is defined as one in which no heat flows in or out of the system. If an ideal gas expands as shown in Fig. 20–5 (see also Fig. 19–8), the work W done in this expansion equals the area under the graph, shown shaded. The efficiency of this process would be $e = W/Q$, much greater than 100% ($=\infty$ since $Q = 0$). Is this a violation of the second law?

It is clear from Eq. 20–1b, $e = 1 - Q_L/Q_H$, that the efficiency of an engine will be greater if Q_L can be made small. However, from experience with a wide variety of systems, it has not been found possible to reduce Q_L to zero. If Q_L could be reduced to zero we would have a 100% efficient engine, as diagrammed in Fig. 20–6.

FIGURE 20–6 Schematic diagram of a hypothetical perfect heat engine in which all the heat input would be used to do work.

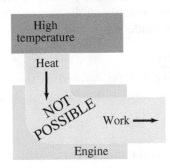

That such a perfect engine (running continuously in a cycle) is not possible is another way of expressing the second law of thermodynamics:

No device is possible whose sole effect is to transform a given amount of heat completely into work.

This is known as the **Kelvin-Planck statement of the second law of thermodynamics**. Said another way, *there can be no perfect (100% efficient) heat engine* such as that diagrammed in Fig. 20–6.

If the second law were not true, so that a perfect engine could be built, some rather remarkable things could happen. For example, if the engine of a ship did not need a low-temperature reservoir to exhaust heat into, the ship could sail across the ocean using the vast resources of the internal energy of the ocean water. Indeed, we would have no fuel problems at all!

20-3 Reversible and Irreversible Processes; the Carnot Engine

In the early nineteenth century, the French scientist N. L. Sadi Carnot (1796–1832) studied in detail the process of transforming heat into mechanical energy. His aim had been to determine how to increase the efficiency of heat engines, but his studies soon led him to investigate the foundations of thermodynamics itself. In 1824, Carnot invented (on paper) an idealized type of engine which we now call the *Carnot engine*. No Carnot engine actually exists, but as a theoretical idea it played an important role in the establishment and understanding of the second law of thermodynamics.

Reversible and Irreversible Processes

The Carnot engine involves *reversible processes*, so before we discuss it we must discuss what is meant by reversible and irreversible processes. A **reversible process** is one that is carried out infinitely slowly, so that the process can be considered as a series of equilibrium states, and the whole process could be done in reverse with no change in magnitude of the work done or heat exchanged. For example, a gas contained in a cylinder fitted with a tight, movable, but frictionless piston could be compressed isothermally in a reversible way if done infinitely slowly. Not all very slow (quasistatic) processes are reversible, however. If there is friction present, for example (as between the movable piston and cylinder just mentioned), the work done in one direction (going from some state A to state B) will not be the negative of the work done in the reverse direction (state B to state A). Such a process would not be considered reversible. A perfectly reversible process is not possible in reality because it would require an infinite time; reversible processes can be approached arbitrarily closely, however, and they are very important theoretically.

All real processes are **irreversible**: they are not done infinitely slowly. There could be turbulence in the gas, friction would be present, and so on. Any process could not be done precisely in reverse since the heat lost to friction would not reverse itself, the turbulence would be different, and so on. For any given volume there would not be a well-defined pressure P and temperature T since the system would not always be in an equilibrium state. Thus a real, irreversible, process cannot be plotted on a PV diagram, except insofar as it may approach an ideal reversible process. But a reversible process (since it is a quasistatic series of equilibrium states) always can be plotted on a PV diagram; and a reversible process, when done in reverse, retraces the same path on a PV diagram. Although all real processes are irreversible, reversible processes are conceptually important, just as the concept of an ideal gas is.

Carnot's Engine

Now let us look at Carnot's idealized engine. The **Carnot engine** makes use of a **reversible cycle**, by which we mean a series of reversible processes that take a given substance (the *working substance*) from an initial equilibrium state through many other equilibrium states and returns it again to the same initial state. In particular, the Carnot engine utilizes the **Carnot cycle**, which is illustrated in Fig. 20-7, with the working substance assumed to be an ideal gas. Let us take point a as the initial state. The gas is first expanded isothermally and reversibly, path ab, at temperature T_H, as heat Q_H is added to it. Next the gas is expanded adiabatically and reversibly, path bc; no heat is exchanged and the temperature of the gas is reduced to T_L. The third step is a reversible isothermal compression, path cd, during which heat Q_L flows out of the working substance. Finally, the gas is compressed adiabatically, path da, back to its original state. Thus a Carnot cycle consists of two isothermal and two adiabatic processes.

The net work done in one cycle by a Carnot engine (or any other type of engine using a reversible cycle) is equal to the area enclosed by the curve representing the cycle on the PV diagram, the curve abcd in Fig. 20-7. (See Section 19-7.)

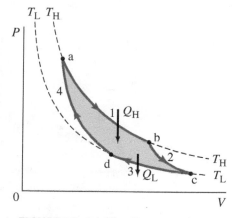

FIGURE 20-7 The Carnot cycle. Heat engines work in a cycle, and the cycle for the Carnot engine begins at point a on this PV diagram. (1) The gas is first expanded isothermally, with the addition of heat Q_H, along the path ab at temperature T_H. (2) Next the gas expands adiabatically from b to c—no heat is exchanged, but the temperature drops to T_L. (3) The gas is then compressed at constant temperature T_L, path cd, and heat Q_L flows out. (4) Finally, the gas is compressed adiabatically, path da, back to its original state. No Carnot engine actually exists, but as a theoretical idea it played an important role in the development of thermodynamics.

Carnot Efficiency and the Second Law of Thermodynamics

The efficiency of a Carnot engine, like any heat engine, is given by Eq. 20–1b:

$$e = 1 - \frac{Q_L}{Q_H}.$$

For a Carnot engine using an ideal gas, however, we can show that the efficiency depends only on the temperatures of the heat reservoirs, T_H and T_L. In the first isothermal process ab in Fig. 20–7, the work done by the gas is (see Eq. 19–8)

$$W_{ab} = nRT_H \ln \frac{V_b}{V_a},$$

where n is the number of moles of the ideal gas used as working substance. Because the internal energy of an ideal gas does not change when the temperature remains constant, the first law of thermodynamics tells us that the heat added to the gas equals the work done by the gas:

$$Q_H = nRT_H \ln \frac{V_b}{V_a}.$$

Similarly, the heat lost by the gas in the isothermal process cd is

$$Q_L = nRT_L \ln \frac{V_c}{V_d}.$$

The paths bc and da are adiabatic, so we have from Eq. 19–15:

$$P_b V_b^\gamma = P_c V_c^\gamma \quad \text{and} \quad P_d V_d^\gamma = P_a V_a^\gamma,$$

where $\gamma = C_P/C_V$ is the ratio of molar specific heats (Eq. 19–14). Also, from the ideal gas law,

$$\frac{P_b V_b}{T_H} = \frac{P_c V_c}{T_L} \quad \text{and} \quad \frac{P_d V_d}{T_L} = \frac{P_a V_a}{T_H}.$$

When we divide these last equations, term by term, into the corresponding set of equations on the line above, we obtain

$$T_H V_b^{\gamma-1} = T_L V_c^{\gamma-1} \quad \text{and} \quad T_L V_d^{\gamma-1} = T_H V_a^{\gamma-1}.$$

Next we divide the equation on the left by the one on the right and obtain

$$\left(\frac{V_b}{V_a} \right)^{\gamma-1} = \left(\frac{V_c}{V_d} \right)^{\gamma-1}$$

or

$$\frac{V_b}{V_a} = \frac{V_c}{V_d}.$$

Inserting this result in our equations for Q_H and Q_L above, we obtain

$$\frac{Q_L}{Q_H} = \frac{T_L}{T_H}. \qquad \text{[Carnot cycle]} \quad \textbf{(20–2)}$$

Hence the efficiency of a reversible Carnot engine can now be written

$$e_{ideal} = 1 - \frac{Q_L}{Q_H}$$

or

$$e_{ideal} = 1 - \frac{T_L}{T_H}. \qquad \left[\begin{array}{l} \text{Carnot efficiency;} \\ \text{Kelvin temperatures} \end{array} \right] \quad \textbf{(20–3)}$$

The temperatures T_L and T_H are the absolute or Kelvin temperatures as measured on the ideal gas temperature scale. Thus the efficiency of a Carnot engine depends only on the temperatures T_L and T_H.

We could imagine other possible reversible cycles that could be used for an ideal reversible engine. According to a theorem stated by Carnot:

> **All reversible engines operating between the same two constant temperatures T_H and T_L have the same efficiency. Any irreversible engine operating between the same two fixed temperatures will have an efficiency less than this.**

This is known as **Carnot's theorem**.[†] It tells us that Eq. 20–3, $e = 1 - (T_L/T_H)$, applies to any ideal reversible engine with fixed input and exhaust temperatures, T_H and T_L, and that this equation represents a maximum possible efficiency for a real (i.e., irreversible) engine.

In practice, the efficiency of real engines is always less than the Carnot efficiency. Well-designed engines reach perhaps 60% to 80% of Carnot efficiency.

EXAMPLE 20–2 A phony claim? An engine manufacturer makes the following claims: An engine's heat input per second is 9.0 kJ at 435 K. The heat output per second is 4.0 kJ at 285 K. Do you believe these claims?

APPROACH The engine's efficiency can be calculated from the definition, Eqs. 20–1. It must be less than the maximum possible, Eq. 20–3.

SOLUTION The claimed efficiency of the engine is (Eq. 20–1b)

$$e = 1 - \frac{Q_L}{Q_H} = 1 - \frac{4.0 \, \text{kJ}}{9.0 \, \text{kJ}} = 0.56,$$

or 56%. However, the maximum possible efficiency is given by the Carnot efficiency, Eq. 20–3:

$$e_{\text{ideal}} = 1 - \frac{T_L}{T_H} = 1 - \frac{285 \, \text{K}}{435 \, \text{K}} = 0.34,$$

or 34%. The manufacturer's claims violate the second law of thermodynamics and cannot be believed.

EXERCISE B A motor is running with an intake temperature $T_H = 400 \, \text{K}$ and an exhaust temperature $T_L = 300 \, \text{K}$. Which of the following is *not* a possible efficiency for the engine? (*a*) 0.10; (*b*) 0.16; (*c*) 0.24; (*d*) 0.30.

It is clear from Eq. 20–3 that a 100% efficient engine is not possible. Only if the exhaust temperature, T_L, were at absolute zero would 100% efficiency be obtainable. But reaching absolute zero is a practical (as well as theoretical) impossibility.[‡] Thus we can state, as we already did in Section 20–2, that **no device is possible whose sole effect is to transform a given amount of heat completely into work**. As we saw in Section 20–2, this is known as the *Kelvin-Planck statement of the second law of thermodynamics*. It tells us that there can be no perfect (100% efficient) heat engine such as the one diagrammed in Fig. 20–6.

EXERCISE C Return to the Chapter-Opening Question, page 528, and answer it again now. Try to explain why you may have answered differently the first time.

*The Otto Cycle

The operation of an automobile internal combustion engine (Fig. 20–4) can be approximated by a reversible cycle known as the *Otto cycle*, whose *PV* diagram is shown in Fig. 20–8. Unlike the Carnot cycle, the input and exhaust temperatures of the Otto cycle are *not* constant. Paths ab and cd are adiabatic, and paths bc and da are at constant volume. The gas (gasoline-air mixture) enters the cylinder at point a and is compressed adiabatically (compression stroke) to point b. At b ignition occurs (spark plug) and the burning of the gas adds heat Q_H to the system at constant volume (approximately in a real engine). The temperature and pressure rise, and then in the power stroke, cd, the gas expands adiabatically. In the exhaust stroke, da, heat Q_L is ejected to the environment (in a real engine, the gas leaves the engine and is replaced by a new mixture of air and fuel).

FIGURE 20–8 The Otto cycle.

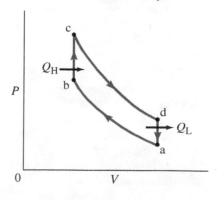

[†]Carnot's theorem can be shown to follow directly from either the Clausius or Kelvin-Planck statements of the second law of thermodynamics.

[‡]This result is known as the *third law of thermodynamics*, as discussed in Section 20–10.

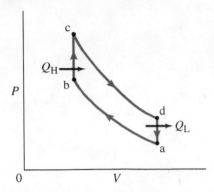

FIGURE 20–8 (repeated for Example 20–3) The Otto cycle.

EXAMPLE 20–3 **The Otto cycle.** (*a*) Show that for an ideal gas as working substance, the efficiency of an Otto cycle engine is

$$e = 1 - \left(\frac{V_a}{V_b}\right)^{1-\gamma}$$

where γ is the ratio of specific heats ($\gamma = C_P/C_V$, Eq. 19–14) and V_a/V_b is the *compression ratio.* (*b*) Calculate the efficiency for a compression ratio $V_a/V_b = 8.0$ assuming a diatomic gas like O_2 and N_2.

APPROACH We use the original definition of efficiency and the results from Chapter 19 for constant volume and adiabatic processes (Sections 19–8 and 19–9).

SOLUTION The heat exchanges take place at constant volume in the ideal Otto cycle, so from Eq. 19–10a:

$$Q_H = nC_V(T_c - T_b) \quad \text{and} \quad Q_L = nC_V(T_d - T_a).$$

Then from Eq. 20–1b,

$$e = 1 - \frac{Q_L}{Q_H} = 1 - \left[\frac{T_d - T_a}{T_c - T_b}\right].$$

To get this in terms of the compression ratio, V_a/V_b, we use the result from Section 19–9, Eq. 19–15, $PV^\gamma = $ constant during the adiabatic processes ab and cd. Thus

$$P_a V_a^\gamma = P_b V_b^\gamma \quad \text{and} \quad P_c V_c^\gamma = P_d V_d^\gamma.$$

We use the ideal gas law, $P = nRT/V$, and substitute P into these two equations

$$T_a V_a^{\gamma-1} = T_b V_b^{\gamma-1} \quad \text{and} \quad T_c V_c^{\gamma-1} = T_d V_d^{\gamma-1}.$$

Then the efficiency (see above) is

$$e = 1 - \left[\frac{T_d - T_a}{T_c - T_b}\right] = 1 - \left[\frac{T_c(V_c/V_d)^{\gamma-1} - T_b(V_b/V_a)^{\gamma-1}}{T_c - T_b}\right].$$

But processes bc and da are at constant volume, so $V_c = V_b$ and $V_d = V_a$. Hence $V_c/V_d = V_b/V_a$ and

$$e = 1 - \left[\frac{(V_b/V_a)^{\gamma-1}(T_c - T_b)}{T_c - T_b}\right] = 1 - \left(\frac{V_b}{V_a}\right)^{\gamma-1} = 1 - \left(\frac{V_a}{V_b}\right)^{1-\gamma}.$$

(*b*) For diatomic molecules (Section 19–8), $\gamma = C_P/C_V = 1.4$ so

$$e = 1 - (8.0)^{1-\gamma} = 1 - (8.0)^{-0.4} = 0.56.$$

Real engines do not reach this high efficiency because they do not follow perfectly the Otto cycle, plus there is friction, turbulence, heat loss and incomplete combustion of the gases.

FIGURE 20–9 Schematic diagram of energy transfers for a refrigerator or air conditioner.

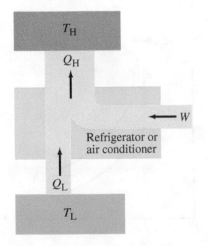

20–4 Refrigerators, Air Conditioners, and Heat Pumps

The operating principle of refrigerators, air conditioners, and heat pumps is just the reverse of a heat engine. Each operates to transfer heat out of a cool environment into a warm environment. As diagrammed in Fig. 20–9, by doing work W, heat is taken from a low-temperature region, T_L (such as inside a refrigerator), and a greater amount of heat is exhausted at a high temperature, T_H (the room). You can often feel this heated air blowing out beneath a refrigerator. The work W is usually done by an electric motor which compresses a fluid, as illustrated in Fig. 20–10.

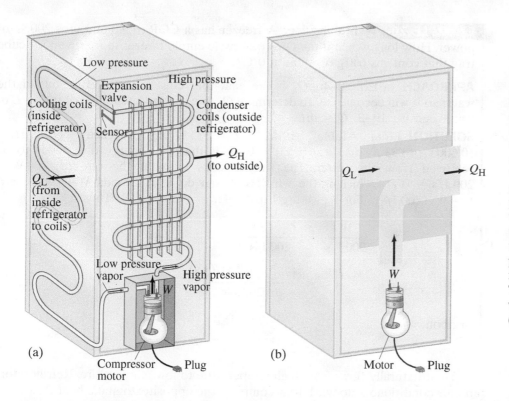

(a)

(b)

FIGURE 20–10 (a) Typical refrigerator system. The electric compressor motor forces a gas at high pressure through a heat exchanger (condenser) on the rear outside wall of the refrigerator where Q_H is given off and the gas cools to become liquid. The liquid passes from a high-pressure region, via a valve, to low-pressure tubes on the inside walls of the refrigerator; the liquid evaporates at this lower pressure and thus absorbs heat (Q_L) from the inside of the refrigerator. The fluid returns to the compressor where the cycle begins again. (b) Schematic diagram, like Fig. 20–9.

A perfect **refrigerator**—one in which no work is required to take heat from the low-temperature region to the high-temperature region—is not possible. This is the **Clausius statement of the second law of thermodynamics**, already mentioned in Section 20–1, which can be stated formally as

> **No device is possible whose sole effect is to transfer heat from one system at a temperature T_L into a second system at a higher temperature T_H.**

To make heat flow from a low-temperature object (or system) to one at a higher temperature, work must be done. Thus, *there can be no perfect refrigerator*.

The **coefficient of performance** (COP) of a refrigerator is defined as the heat Q_L removed from the low-temperature area (inside a refrigerator) divided by the work W done to remove the heat (Fig. 20–9 or 20–10b):

$$\text{COP} = \frac{Q_L}{W}. \qquad \begin{bmatrix}\text{refrigerator and}\\ \text{air conditioner}\end{bmatrix} \quad \textbf{(20–4a)}$$

This makes sense because the more heat Q_L that can be removed from the inside of the refrigerator for a given amount of work, the better (more efficient) the refrigerator is. Energy is conserved, so from the first law of thermodynamics we can write (see Fig. 20–9 or 20–10b) $Q_L + W = Q_H$, or $W = Q_H - Q_L$. Then Eq. 20–4a becomes

$$\text{COP} = \frac{Q_L}{W} = \frac{Q_L}{Q_H - Q_L}. \qquad \begin{bmatrix}\text{refrigerator}\\ \text{air conditioner}\end{bmatrix} \quad \textbf{(20–4b)}$$

For an ideal refrigerator (not a perfect one, which is impossible), the best we could do would be

$$\text{COP}_{\text{ideal}} = \frac{T_L}{T_H - T_L}, \qquad \begin{bmatrix}\text{refrigerator}\\ \text{air conditioner}\end{bmatrix} \quad \textbf{(20–4c)}$$

analagous to an ideal (Carnot) engine (Eqs. 20–2 and 20–3).

An **air conditioner** works very much like a refrigerator, although the actual construction details are different: an air conditioner takes heat Q_L from inside a room or building at a low temperature, and deposits heat Q_H outside to the environment at a higher temperature. Equations 20–4 also describe the coefficient of performance for an air conditioner.

SECOND LAW OF THERMODYNAMICS
(Clausius statement)

PHYSICS APPLIED
Refrigerator

PHYSICS APPLIED
Air conditioner

EXAMPLE 20–4 **Making ice.** A freezer has a COP of 3.8 and uses 200 W of power. How long would it take this otherwise empty freezer to freeze an ice-cube tray that contains 600 g of water at 0°C?

APPROACH In Eq. 20–4b, Q_L is the heat that must be transferred out of the water so it will become ice. To determine Q_L, we use the latent heat of fusion L of water and Eq. 19–3, $Q = mL$.

SOLUTION From Table 19–2, $L = 333 \text{ kJ/kg}$. Hence $Q = mL = (0.600 \text{ kg})(3.33 \times 10^5 \text{ J/kg}) = 2.0 \times 10^5 \text{ J}$ is the total energy that needs to be removed from the water. The freezer does work at the rate of $200 \text{ W} = 200 \text{ J/s} = W/t$, which is the work W it can do in t seconds. We solve for t: $t = W/(200 \text{ J/s})$. For W, we use Eq. 20–4a: $W = Q_L/\text{COP}$. Thus

$$t = \frac{W}{200 \text{ J/s}} = \frac{Q_L/\text{COP}}{200 \text{ J/s}}$$

$$= \frac{(2.0 \times 10^5 \text{ J})/(3.8)}{200 \text{ J/s}} = 260 \text{ s},$$

or about $4\frac{1}{2}$ min.

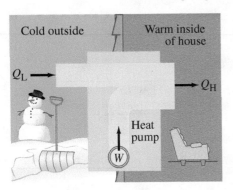

⊕ **PHYSICS APPLIED**

Heat pump

Cold outside

Warm inside of house

$Q_L \rightarrow$

$\rightarrow Q_H$

Heat pump

W

FIGURE 20–11 A heat pump uses an electric motor to "pump" heat from the cold outside to the warm inside of a house.

⚠ **CAUTION**

Heat pumps and air conditioners have different COP definitions

Heat naturally flows from high temperature to low temperature. Refrigerators and air conditioners do work to accomplish the opposite: to make heat flow from cold to hot. We might say they "pump" heat from cold areas to hotter areas, against the natural tendency of heat to flow from hot to cold, just as water can be pumped uphill, against the natural tendency to flow downhill. The term **heat pump** is usually reserved for a device that can heat a house in winter by using an electric motor that does work W to take heat Q_L from the outside at low temperature and delivers heat Q_H to the warmer inside of the house; see Fig. 20–11. As in a refrigerator, there is an indoor and an outdoor heat exchanger (coils of the refrigerator) and an electric compressor motor. The operating principle is like that for a refrigerator or air conditioner; but the objective of a heat pump is to heat (deliver Q_H), rather than to cool (remove Q_L). Thus, the coefficient of performance of a heat pump is defined differently than for an air conditioner because it is the heat Q_H delivered to the inside of the house that is important now:

$$\text{COP} = \frac{Q_H}{W}. \qquad \text{[heat pump]} \quad \textbf{(20–5)}$$

The COP is necessarily greater than 1. Most heat pumps can be "turned around" and used as air conditioners in the summer.

EXAMPLE 20–5 **Heat pump.** A heat pump has a coefficient of performance of 3.0 and is rated to do work at 1500 W. (*a*) How much heat can it add to a room per second? (*b*) If the heat pump were turned around to act as an air conditioner in the summer, what would you expect its coefficient of performance to be, assuming all else stays the same?

APPROACH We use the definitions of coefficient of performance, which are different for the two devices in (*a*) and (*b*).

SOLUTION (*a*) We use Eq. 20–5 for the heat pump, and, since our device does 1500 J of work per second, it can pour heat into the room at a rate of

$$Q_H = \text{COP} \times W = 3.0 \times 1500 \text{ J} = 4500 \text{ J}$$

per second, or at a rate of 4500 W.

(b) If our device is turned around in summer, it can take heat Q_L from inside the house, doing 1500 J of work per second to then dump $Q_H = 4500$ J per second to the hot outside. Energy is conserved, so $Q_L + W = Q_H$ (see Fig. 20–11, but reverse the inside and outside of the house). Then

$$Q_L = Q_H - W = 4500\,\text{J} - 1500\,\text{J} = 3000\,\text{J}.$$

The coefficient of performance as an air conditioner would thus be (Eq. 20–4a)

$$\text{COP} = \frac{Q_L}{W} = \frac{3000\,\text{J}}{1500\,\text{J}} = 2.0.$$

20–5 Entropy

Thus far we have stated the second law of thermodynamics for specific situations. What we really need is a general statement of the second law of thermodynamics that will cover all situations, including those discussed earlier in this Chapter that are not observed in nature even though they would not violate the first law of thermodynamics. It was not until the latter half of the nineteenth century that the second law of thermodynamics was finally stated in a general way—namely, in terms of a quantity called **entropy**, introduced by Clausius in the 1860s. In Section 20–7 we will see that entropy can be interpreted as a measure of the order or disorder of a system.

When we deal with entropy—as with potential energy—it is the *change* in entropy during a process that is important, not the absolute amount. According to Clausius, the change in entropy S of a system, when an amount of heat Q is *added* to it by a reversible process at constant temperature, is given by

$$\Delta S = \frac{Q}{T}, \tag{20–6}$$

where T is the kelvin temperature.

If the temperature is not constant, we define entropy S by the relation

$$dS = \frac{dQ}{T}. \tag{20–7}$$

Then the change in entropy of a system taken reversibly between two states a and b is given by[†]

$$\Delta S = S_b - S_a = \int_a^b dS = \int_a^b \frac{dQ}{T}. \quad \text{[reversible process]} \tag{20–8}$$

A careful analysis (see next page) shows that the change in entropy when a system moves by a reversible process from any state a to another state b does not depend on the process. That is, $\Delta S = S_b - S_a$ depends only on the states a and b of the system. Thus entropy (unlike heat) is a *state variable*. Any system in a given state has a temperature, a volume, a pressure, and also has a particular value of entropy.

It is easy to see why entropy is a state variable for a Carnot cycle. In Eq. 20–2 we saw that $Q_L/Q_H = T_L/T_H$, which we rewrite as

$$\frac{Q_L}{T_L} = \frac{Q_H}{T_H}.$$

In the *PV* diagram for a Carnot cycle, Fig. 20–7, the entropy change $\Delta S = Q/T$ in going from state a to state c along path abc $(= Q_H/T_H + 0)$ is thus the same as going along the path adc. That is, the change in entropy is path independent—it depends only on the initial and final states of the system.

[†]Equation 20–8 says nothing about the absolute value of S; it only gives the change in S. This is much like potential energy (Chapter 8). However, one form of the so-called *third law of thermodynamics* (see also Section 20–10) states that as $T \to 0$, $S \to 0$.

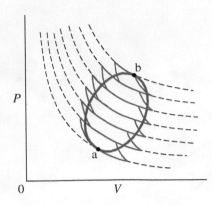

FIGURE 20–12 Any reversible cycle can be approximated as a series of Carnot cycles. (The dashed lines represent isotherms.)

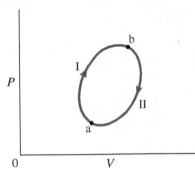

FIGURE 20–13 The integral, $\oint dS$, of the entropy for a reversible cycle is zero. Hence the difference in entropy between states a and b, $S_b - S_a = \int_a^b dS$, is the same for path I as for path II.

*Showing Entropy Is a State Variable

In our study of the Carnot cycle we found (Eq. 20–2) that $Q_L/Q_H = T_L/T_H$. We rewrite this as

$$\frac{Q_H}{T_H} = \frac{Q_L}{T_L}.$$

In this relation, both Q_H and Q_L are positive. But now let us recall our original convention as used in the first law (Section 19–6), that Q is positive when it represents a heat flow into the system (as Q_H) and negative for a heat flow out of the system (as $-Q_L$). Then this relation becomes

$$\frac{Q_H}{T_H} + \frac{Q_L}{T_L} = 0. \qquad \text{[Carnot cycle]} \quad \textbf{(20–9)}$$

Now consider *any* reversible cycle, as represented by the smooth (oval-shaped) curve in Fig. 20–12. Any reversible cycle can be approximated as a series of Carnot cycles. Figure 20–12 shows only six—the isotherms (dashed lines) are connected by adiabatic paths for each—and the approximation becomes better and better if we increase the number of Carnot cycles. Equation 20–9 is valid for each of these cycles, so we can write

$$\Sigma \frac{Q}{T} = 0 \qquad \text{[Carnot cycles]} \quad \textbf{(20–10)}$$

for the sum of all these cycles. But note that the heat output Q_L of one cycle crosses the boundary below it and is approximately equal to the negative of the heat input, Q_H, of the cycle below it (actual equality occurs in the limit of an infinite number of infinitely thin Carnot cycles). Hence the heat flows on the inner paths of all these Carnot cycles cancel out, so the net heat transferred, and the work done, is the same for the series of Carnot cycles as for the original cycle. Hence, in the limit of infinitely many Carnot cycles, Eq. 20–10 applies to any reversible cycle. In this case Eq. 20–10 becomes

$$\oint \frac{dQ}{T} = 0, \qquad \text{[reversible cycle]} \quad \textbf{(20–11)}$$

where dQ represents an infinitesimal heat flow.[†] The symbol $\oint$ means that the integral is taken around a closed path; the integral can be started at any point on the path such as at a or b in Fig. 20–12, and proceed in either direction. If we divide the cycle of Fig. 20–12 into two parts as indicated in Fig. 20–13, then

$$\underbrace{\int_a^b \frac{dQ}{T}}_{\text{I}} + \underbrace{\int_b^a \frac{dQ}{T}}_{\text{II}} = 0.$$

The first term is the integral from point a to point b along path I in Fig. 20–13, and the second term is the integral from b back to a along path II. If path II is taken in reverse, dQ at each point becomes $-dQ$, since the path is reversible. Therefore

$$\underbrace{\int_a^b \frac{dQ}{T}}_{\text{I}} = \underbrace{\int_a^b \frac{dQ}{T}}_{\text{II}}. \qquad \text{[reversible paths]} \quad \textbf{(20–12)}$$

The integral of dQ/T between any two equilibrium states, a and b, does not depend on the path of the process. By defining entropy as $dS = dQ/T$ (Eq. 20–7), we see from Eq. 20–12 that the change in entropy between any two states along a reversible path is *independent of the path between two points a and b*. Thus entropy is a *state variable*—its value depends only on the state of the system, and not on the process or the past history of how it got there.[‡] This is in clear distinction to Q and W which are *not* state variables; their values do depend on the processes undertaken.

[†] dQ is often written $đQ$: see footnote at the end of Section 19–6.

[‡] Real processes are irreversible. Because entropy is a state variable, the change in entropy ΔS for an irreversible process can be determined by calculating ΔS for a reversible process between the same two states.

20–6 Entropy and the Second Law of Thermodynamics

We have defined a new quantity, S, the entropy, which can be used to describe the state of the system, along with P, T, V, E_{int}, and n. But what does this rather abstract quantity have to do with the second law of thermodynamics? To answer this, let us take some examples in which we calculate the entropy changes during particular processes. But note first that Eq. 20–8 can be applied only to reversible processes. How then do we calculate $\Delta S = S_b - S_a$ for a real process that is irreversible? What we can do is this: we figure out some other *reversible* process that takes the system between the same two states, and calculate ΔS for this reversible process. This will equal ΔS for the irreversible process since ΔS depends only on the initial and final states of the system.

If the temperature varies during a process, a summation of the heat flow over the changing temperature can often be calculated using calculus or a computer. However, if the temperature change is not too great, a reasonable approximation can be made using the average value of the temperature, as indicated in the next Example.

EXAMPLE 20–6 ESTIMATE Entropy change when mixing water. A sample of 50.0 kg of water at 20.00°C is mixed with 50.0 kg of water at 24.00°C. Estimate the change in entropy.

APPROACH The final temperature of the mixture will be 22.00°C, since we started with equal amounts of water. We use the specific heat of water and the methods of calorimetry (Sections 19–3 and 19–4) to determine the heat transferred. Then we use the average temperature of each sample of water to estimate the entropy change $(\Delta Q/T)$.

SOLUTION A quantity of heat,

$$Q = mc\,\Delta T = (50.0\,\text{kg})(4186\,\text{J/kg}\cdot\text{C}°)(2.00\,\text{C}°) = 4.186 \times 10^5\,\text{J},$$

flows out of the hot water as it cools down from 24°C to 22°C, and this heat flows into the cold water as it warms from 20°C to 22°C. The total change in entropy, ΔS, will be the sum of the changes in entropy of the hot water, ΔS_H, and that of the cold water, ΔS_C:

$$\Delta S = \Delta S_H + \Delta S_C.$$

We estimate entropy changes by writing $\Delta S = Q/\overline{T}$, where $\overline{T}$ is an "average" temperature for each process, which ought to give a reasonable estimate since the temperature change is small. For the hot water we use an average temperature of 23°C (296 K), and for the cold water an average temperature of 21°C (294 K). Thus

$$\Delta S_H \approx -\frac{4.186 \times 10^5\,\text{J}}{296\,\text{K}} = -1414\,\text{J/K}$$

which is negative because this heat flows out, whereas heat is added to the cold water:

$$\Delta S_C \approx \frac{4.186 \times 10^5\,\text{J}}{294\,\text{K}} = 1424\,\text{J/K}.$$

The entropy of the hot water (S_H) decreases since heat flows out of the hot water. But the entropy of the cold water (S_C) increases by a greater amount. The total change in entropy is

$$\Delta S = \Delta S_H + \Delta S_C \approx -1414\,\text{J/K} + 1424\,\text{J/K} \approx 10\,\text{J/K}.$$

We see that although the entropy of one part of the system decreased, the entropy of the other part increased by a greater amount so that the net change in entropy of the whole system is positive.

We can now show in general that for an isolated system of two objects, the flow of heat from the higher-temperature (T_H) object to the lower-temperature (T_L) object always results in an increase in the total entropy. The two objects eventually come to some intermediate temperature, T_M. The heat lost by the hotter object $(Q_H = -Q,$ where Q is positive) is equal to the heat gained by the colder one $(Q_L = Q)$, so the total change in entropy is

$$\Delta S = \Delta S_H + \Delta S_L = -\frac{Q}{T_{HM}} + \frac{Q}{T_{LM}},$$

where T_{HM} is some intermediate temperature between T_H and T_M for the hot object as it cools from T_H to T_M, and T_{LM} is the counterpart for the cold object. Since the temperature of the hot object is, at all times during the process, greater than that of the cold object, then $T_{HM} > T_{LM}$. Hence

$$\Delta S = Q\left(\frac{1}{T_{LM}} - \frac{1}{T_{HM}}\right) > 0.$$

One object decreases in entropy, while the other gains in entropy, but the *total* change is positive.

EXAMPLE 20–7 **Entropy changes in a free expansion.** Consider the *adiabatic free expansion* of n moles of an ideal gas from volume V_1 to volume V_2, where $V_2 > V_1$ as was discussed in Section 19–7, Fig. 19–14. Calculate the change in entropy (a) of the gas and (b) of the surrounding environment. (c) Evaluate ΔS for 1.00 mole, with $V_2 = 2.00\,V_1$.

APPROACH We saw in Section 19–7 that the gas is initially in a closed container of volume V_1, and, with the opening of a valve, it expands adiabatically into a previously empty container. The total volume of the two containers is V_2. The whole apparatus is thermally insulated from the surroundings, so no heat flows into the gas, $Q = 0$. The gas does no work, $W = 0$, so there is no change in internal energy, $\Delta E_{int} = 0$, and the temperature of the initial and final states is the same, $T_2 = T_1 = T$. The process takes place very quickly, and so is irreversible. Thus we cannot apply Eq. 20–8 to this process. Instead we must think of a reversible process that will take the gas from volume V_1 to V_2 at the same temperature, and use Eq. 20–8 on this reversible process to get ΔS. A reversible isothermal process will do the trick; in such a process, the internal energy does not change, so from the first law,

$$dQ = dW = P\,dV.$$

SOLUTION (a) For the gas,

$$\Delta S_{gas} = \int \frac{dQ}{T} = \frac{1}{T}\int_{V_1}^{V_2} P\,dV.$$

The ideal gas law tells us $P = nRT/V$, so

$$\Delta S_{gas} = \frac{nRT}{T}\int_{V_1}^{V_2}\frac{dV}{V} = nR\ln\frac{V_2}{V_1}.$$

Since $V_2 > V_1$, $\Delta S_{gas} > 0$.

(b) Since no heat is transferred to the surrounding environment, there is no change of the state of the environment due to this process. Hence $\Delta S_{env} = 0$. Note that the total change in entropy, $\Delta S_{gas} + \Delta S_{env}$, is greater than zero.

(c) Since $n = 1.00$ and $V_2 = 2.00\,V_1$, then $\Delta S_{gas} = R\ln 2.00 = 5.76\ \text{J/K}$.

EXAMPLE 20–8 **Heat transfer.** A red-hot 2.00-kg piece of iron at temperature $T_1 = 880\,\mathrm{K}$ is thrown into a huge lake whose temperature is $T_2 = 280\,\mathrm{K}$. Assume the lake is so large that its temperature rise is insignificant. Determine the change in entropy (a) of the iron and (b) of the surrounding environment (the lake).

APPROACH The process is irreversible, but the same entropy change will occur for a reversible process, and we use the concept of specific heat, Eq. 19–2.

SOLUTION (a) We assume the specific heat of the iron is constant at $c = 450\,\mathrm{J/kg \cdot K}$. Then $dQ = mc\,dT$ and in a quasistatic reversible process

$$\Delta S_{iron} = \int \frac{dQ}{T} = mc \int_{T_1}^{T_2} \frac{dT}{T} = mc \ln \frac{T_2}{T_1} = -mc \ln \frac{T_1}{T_2}.$$

Putting in numbers, we find

$$\Delta S_{iron} = -(2.00\,\mathrm{kg})(450\,\mathrm{J/kg \cdot K}) \ln \frac{880\,\mathrm{K}}{280\,\mathrm{K}} = -1030\,\mathrm{J/K}.$$

(b) The initial and final temperatures of the lake are the same, $T = 280\,\mathrm{K}$. The lake receives from the iron an amount of heat

$$Q = mc(T_2 - T_1) = (2.00\,\mathrm{kg})(450\,\mathrm{J/kg \cdot K})(880\,\mathrm{K} - 280\,\mathrm{K}) = 540\,\mathrm{kJ}.$$

Strictly speaking, this is an irreversible process (the lake heats up locally before equilibrium is reached), but is equivalent to a reversible isothermal transfer of heat $Q = 540\,\mathrm{kJ}$ at $T = 280\,\mathrm{K}$. Hence

$$\Delta S_{env} = \frac{540\,\mathrm{kJ}}{280\,\mathrm{K}} = 1930\,\mathrm{J/K}.$$

Thus, although the entropy of the iron actually decreases, the *total* change in entropy of iron plus environment is positive: $1930\,\mathrm{J/K} - 1030\,\mathrm{J/K} = 900\,\mathrm{J/K}$.

EXERCISE D A 1.00-kg piece of ice at $0°\mathrm{C}$ melts very slowly to water at $0°\mathrm{C}$. Assume the ice is in contact with a heat reservoir whose temperature is only infinitesimally greater than $0°\mathrm{C}$. Determine the entropy change of (a) the ice cube and (b) the heat reservoir.

In each of these Examples, the entropy of our system plus that of the environment (or surroundings) either stayed constant or increased. For any *reversible* process, such as that in Exercise D, the total entropy change is zero. This can be seen in general as follows: any reversible process can be considered as a series of quasistatic isothermal transfers of heat ΔQ between a system and the environment, which differ in temperature only by an infinitesimal amount. Hence the change in entropy of either the system or environment is $\Delta Q/T$ and that of the other is $-\Delta Q/T$, so the total is

$$\Delta S = \Delta S_{syst} + \Delta S_{env} = 0. \qquad \text{[any reversible process]}$$

In Examples 20–6, 20–7, and 20–8, we found that the total entropy of system plus environment increases. Indeed, it has been found that for all real (irreversible) processes, the total entropy increases. No exceptions have been found. We can thus make the *general statement of the second law of thermodynamics* as follows:

The entropy of an isolated system never decreases. It either stays constant (reversible processes) or increases (irreversible processes).

Since all real processes are irreversible, we can equally well state the second law as:

The total entropy of any system plus that of its environment increases as a result of any natural process:

$$\Delta S = \Delta S_{syst} + \Delta S_{env} > 0. \qquad (20\text{–}13)$$

SECOND LAW OF THERMODYNAMICS (general statement)

Although the entropy of one part of the universe may decrease in any process (see the Examples above), the entropy of some other part of the universe always increases by a greater amount, so the total entropy always increases.

Now that we finally have a quantitative general statement of the second law of thermodynamics, we can see that it is an unusual law. It differs considerably from other laws of physics, which are typically equalities (such as $F = ma$) or conservation laws (such as for energy and momentum). The second law of thermodynamics introduces a new quantity, the entropy, S, but does not tell us it is conserved. Quite the opposite. Entropy is not conserved in natural processes. Entropy always increases in time.

"Time's Arrow"

The second law of thermodynamics summarizes which processes are observed in nature, and which are not. Or, said another way, it tells us about the *direction* processes go. For the reverse of any of the processes in the last few Examples, the entropy would decrease; and we never observe them. For example, we never observe heat flowing spontaneously from a cold object to a hot object, the reverse of Example 20–8. Nor do we ever observe a gas spontaneously compressing itself into a smaller volume, the reverse of Example 20–7 (gases always expand to fill their containers). Nor do we see thermal energy transform into kinetic energy of a rock so the rock rises spontaneously from the ground. Any of these processes would be consistent with the first law of thermodynamics (conservation of energy). But they are not consistent with the second law of thermodynamics, and this is why we need the second law. If you were to see a movie run backward, you would probably realize it immediately because you would see odd occurrences—such as rocks rising spontaneously from the ground, or air rushing in from the atmosphere to fill an empty balloon (the reverse of free expansion). When watching a movie or video, we are tipped off to a faked reversal of time by observing whether entropy is increasing or decreasing. Hence entropy has been called **time's arrow,** for it can tell us in which direction time is going.

20–7 Order to Disorder

The concept of entropy, as we have discussed it so far, may seem rather abstract. But we can relate it to the more ordinary concepts of *order* and *disorder*. In fact, the entropy of a system can be considered a *measure of the disorder of the system*. Then the second law of thermodynamics can be stated simply as:

Natural processes tend to move toward a state of greater disorder.

Exactly what we mean by disorder may not always be clear, so we now consider a few examples. Some of these will show us how this very general statement of the second law applies beyond what we usually consider as thermodynamics.

Let us look at the simple processes mentioned in Section 20–1. First, a jar containing separate layers of salt and pepper is more orderly than when the salt and pepper are all mixed up. Shaking a jar containing separate layers results in a mixture, and no amount of shaking brings the layers back again. The natural process is from a state of relative order (layers) to one of relative disorder (a mixture), not the reverse. That is, disorder increases. Next, a solid coffee cup is a more "orderly" and useful object than the pieces of a broken cup. Cups break when they fall, but they do not spontaneously mend themselves (as faked in Fig. 20–1). Again, the normal course of events is an increase of disorder.

Let us consider some processes for which we have actually calculated the entropy change, and see that an increase in entropy results in an increase in disorder (or vice versa). When ice melts to water at 0°C, the entropy of the water increases (Exercise D). Intuitively, we can think of solid water, ice, as being more ordered than the less orderly fluid state which can flow all over the place. This change from order to disorder can be seen more clearly from the molecular point of view: the orderly arrangement of water molecules in an ice crystal has changed to the disorderly and somewhat random motion of the molecules in the fluid state.

When a hot object is put in contact with a cold object, heat flows from the high temperature to the low until the two objects reach the same intermediate temperature. At the beginning of the process we can distinguish two classes of molecules: those with a high average kinetic energy (the hot object), and those with a low average kinetic energy (the cooler object). After the process in which heat flows, all the molecules are in one class with the same average kinetic energy. We no longer have the more orderly arrangement of molecules in two classes. Order has gone to disorder. Furthermore, the separate hot and cold objects could serve as the hot- and cold-temperature regions of a heat engine, and thus could be used to obtain useful work. But once the two objects are put in contact and reach the same temperature, no work can be obtained. Disorder has increased, since a system that has the ability to perform work must surely be considered to have a higher order than a system no longer able to do work.

When a stone falls to the ground, its macroscopic kinetic energy is transformed to thermal energy. Thermal energy is associated with the disorderly random motion of molecules, but the molecules in the falling stone all have the same velocity downward in addition to their own random velocities. Thus, the more orderly kinetic energy of the stone as a whole is changed to disordered thermal energy when the stone strikes the ground. Disorder increases in this process, as it does in all processes that occur in nature.

*Biological Evolution

An interesting example of the increase in entropy relates to biological evolution and to growth of organisms. Clearly, a human being is a highly ordered organism. The theory of evolution describes the process from the early macromolecules and simple forms of life to *Homo sapiens*, which is a process of increasing order. So, too, the development of an individual from a single cell to a grown person is a process of increasing order. Do these processes violate the second law of thermodynamics? No, they do not. In the processes of evolution and growth, and even during the mature life of an individual, waste products are eliminated. These small molecules that remain as a result of metabolism are simple molecules without much order. Thus they represent relatively higher disorder or entropy. Indeed, the total entropy of the molecules cast aside by organisms during the processes of evolution and growth is greater than the decrease in entropy associated with the order of the growing individual or evolving species.

PHYSICS APPLIED

Biological Evolution and Development

20–8 Unavailability of Energy; Heat Death

In the process of heat conduction from a hot object to a cold one, we have seen that entropy increases and that order goes to disorder. The separate hot and cold objects could serve as the high- and low-temperature regions for a heat engine and thus could be used to obtain useful work. But after the two objects are put in contact with each other and reach the same uniform temperature, no work can be obtained from them. With regard to being able to do useful work, order has gone to disorder in this process.

The same can be said about a falling rock that comes to rest upon striking the ground. Before hitting the ground, all the kinetic energy of the rock could have been used to do useful work. But once the rock's mechanical kinetic energy becomes thermal energy, doing useful work is no longer possible.

Both these examples illustrate another important aspect of the second law of thermodynamics:

in any natural process, some energy becomes unavailable to do useful work.

In any process, no energy is ever lost (it is always conserved). Rather, energy becomes less useful—it can do less useful work. As time goes on, **energy is degraded**, in a sense; it goes from more orderly forms (such as mechanical) eventually to the least orderly form, internal, or thermal, energy. Entropy is a factor here because the amount of energy that becomes unavailable to do work is proportional to the change in entropy during any process.[†]

[†]It can be shown that the amount of energy that becomes unavailable to do useful work is equal to $T_L \Delta S$, where T_L is the lowest available temperature and ΔS is the total increase in entropy during the process.

A natural outcome of the degradation of energy is the prediction that as time goes on, the universe should approach a state of maximum disorder. Matter would become a uniform mixture, and heat will have flowed from high-temperature regions to low-temperature regions until the whole universe is at one temperature. No work could then be done. All the energy of the universe would have degraded to thermal energy. This prediction, called the **heat death** of the universe, has been much discussed, but would lie very far in the future. It is a complicated subject, and some scientists question whether thermodynamic modeling of the universe is possible or appropriate.

*20–9 Statistical Interpretation of Entropy and the Second Law

The ideas of entropy and disorder are made clearer with the use of a statistical or probabilistic analysis of the molecular state of a system. This statistical approach, which was first applied toward the end of the nineteenth century by Ludwig Boltzmann (1844–1906), makes a clear distinction between the "macrostate" and the "microstate" of a system. The **microstate** of a system would be specified in giving the position and velocity of every particle (or molecule). The **macrostate** of a system is specified by giving the macroscopic properties of the system—the temperature, pressure, number of moles, and so on. In reality, we can know only the macrostate of a system. We could not possibily know the velocity and position of every one of the huge number of molecules in a system at a given moment. Nonetheless, we can hypothesize a great many different microstates that can correspond to the *same* macrostate.

Let us take a very simple example. Suppose you repeatedly shake four coins in your hand and drop them on a table. Specifying the number of heads and the number of tails that appear on a given throw is the macrostate of this system. Specifying each coin as being a head or a tail is the microstate of the system. In the following Table we see how many microstates correspond to each macrostate:

Macrostate	Possible Microstates (H = heads, T = tails)	Number of Microstates
4 heads	H H H H	1
3 heads, 1 tail	H H H T, H H T H, H T H H, T H H H	4
2 heads, 2 tails	H H T T, H T H T, T H H T, H T T H, T H T H, T T H H	6
1 head, 3 tails	T T T H, T T H T, T H T T, H T T T	4
4 tails	T T T T	1

A basic assumption behind the statistical approach is that *each microstate is equally probable*. Thus the number of microstates that give the same macrostate corresponds to the relative probability of that macrostate occurring. The macrostate of two heads and two tails is the most probable one in our case of tossing four coins; out of the total of 16 possible microstates, six correspond to two heads and two tails, so the probability of throwing two heads and two tails is 6 out of 16, or 38%. The probability of throwing one head and three tails is 4 out of 16, or 25%. The probability of four heads is only 1 in 16, or 6%. If you threw the coins 16 times, you might not find that two heads and two tails appear exactly 6 times, or four tails exactly once. These are only probabilities or averages. But if you made 1600 throws, very nearly 38% of them would be two heads and two tails. The greater the number of tries, the closer the percentages are to the calculated probabilities.

EXERCISE E In the Table above, what is the probability that there will be at least two heads? (a) $\frac{1}{2}$; (b) $\frac{1}{16}$; (c) $\frac{1}{8}$; (d) $\frac{3}{8}$; (e) $\frac{11}{16}$.

If we toss more coins—say, 100 all at the same time—the relative probability of throwing all heads (or all tails) is greatly reduced. There is only one microstate corresponding to all heads. For 99 heads and 1 tail, there are 100 microstates since each of the coins could be the one tail. The relative probabilities for other macrostates are given in Table 20–1. About 1.3×10^{30} microstates are possible.[†] Thus the relative probability of finding all heads is 1 in 10^{30}, an incredibly unlikely event! The probability of obtaining 50 heads and 50 tails (see Table 20–1) is $(1.0 \times 10^{29})/1.3 \times 10^{30} = 0.08$ or 8%. The probability of obtaining anything between 45 and 55 heads is over 70%.

TABLE 20–1 Probabilities of Various Macrostates for 100 Coin Tosses

Macrostate		Number of Microstates	Probability
Heads	Tails		
100	0	1	7.9×10^{-31}
99	1	1.0×10^2	7.9×10^{-29}
90	10	1.7×10^{13}	1.4×10^{-17}
80	20	5.4×10^{20}	4.2×10^{-10}
60	40	1.4×10^{28}	0.01
55	45	6.1×10^{28}	0.05
50	50	1.0×10^{29}	0.08
45	55	6.1×10^{28}	0.05
40	60	1.4×10^{28}	0.01
20	80	5.4×10^{20}	4.2×10^{-10}
10	90	1.7×10^{13}	1.4×10^{-17}
1	99	1.0×10^2	7.9×10^{-29}
0	100	1	7.9×10^{-31}

Thus we see that as the number of coins increases, the probability of obtaining the most orderly arrangement (all heads or all tails) becomes extremely unlikely. The least orderly arrangement (half heads, half tails) is the most probable, and the probability of being within, say, 5% of the most probable arrangement greatly increases as the number of coins increases. These same ideas can be applied to the molecules of a system. For example, the most probable state of a gas (say, the air in a room) is one in which the molecules take up the whole space and move about randomly; this corresponds to the Maxwellian distribution, Fig. 20–14a (and see Section 18–2). On the other hand, the very orderly arrangement of all the molecules located in one corner of the room and all moving with the same velocity (Fig. 20–14b) is extremely unlikely.

From these examples, it is clear that probability is directly related to disorder and hence to entropy. That is, the most probable state is the one with greatest entropy or greatest disorder and randomness. Boltzmann showed, consistent with Clausius's definition $(dS = dQ/T)$, that the entropy of a system in a given (macro) state can be written

$$S = k \ln \mathcal{W}, \qquad (20\text{–}14)$$

where k is Boltzmann's constant $(k = R/N_A = 1.38 \times 10^{-23} \text{ J/K})$ and $\mathcal{W}$ is the number of microstates corresponding to the given macrostate. That is, $\mathcal{W}$ is proportional to the probability of occurrence of that state. $\mathcal{W}$ is called the **thermodynamic probability**, or, sometimes, the **disorder parameter**.

[†]Each coin has two possibilities, heads or tails. Then the possible number of microstates is $2 \times 2 \times 2 \times \cdots = 2^{100} = 1.27 \times 10^{30}$ (using a calculator or logarithms).

FIGURE 20–14 (a) Most probable distribution of molecular speeds in a gas (Maxwellian, or random); (b) orderly, but highly unlikely, distribution of speeds in which all molecules have nearly the same speed.

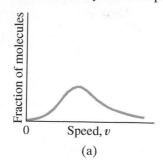

(a)

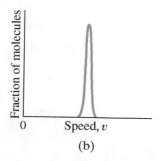

(b)

EXAMPLE 20-9 **Free expansion—statistical determination of entropy.**
Use Eq. 20–14 to determine the change in entropy for the adiabatic *free expansion* of a gas, a calculation we did macroscopically in Example 20–7. Assume $\mathcal{W}$, the number of microstates for each macrostate, is the number of possible positions.

APPROACH We assume the number of moles is $n = 1$, and then the number of molecules is $N = nN_A = N_A$. We let the volume double, just as in Example 20–7. Because the volume doubles, the number of possible positions for each molecule doubles.

SOLUTION When the volume doubles, each molecule has two times as many positions (microstates) available. For two molecules, the number of total microstates increases by $2 \times 2 = 2^2$. For N_A molecules, the total number of microstates increases by a factor of $2 \times 2 \times 2 \times \cdots = 2^{N_A}$. That is

$$\frac{\mathcal{W}_2}{\mathcal{W}_1} = 2^{N_A}.$$

The change in entropy is, from Eq. 20–14,

$$\Delta S = S_2 - S_1 = k(\ln \mathcal{W}_2 - \ln \mathcal{W}_1) = k \ln \frac{\mathcal{W}_2}{\mathcal{W}_1} = k \ln 2^{N_A} = kN_A \ln 2 = R \ln 2$$

which is the same result we obtained in Example 20–7.

In terms of probability, the second law of thermodynamics—which tells us that entropy increases in any process—reduces to the statement that those processes occur which are most probable. The second law thus becomes a trivial statement. However there is an additional element now. The second law in terms of probability does not *forbid* a decrease in entropy. Rather, it says the probability is extremely low. It is not impossible that salt and pepper could separate spontaneously into layers, or that a broken tea cup could mend itself. It is even possible that a lake could freeze over on a hot summer day (that is, heat flow out of the cold lake into the warmer surroundings). But the probability for such events occurring is extremely small. In our coin examples, we saw that increasing the number of coins from 4 to 100 drastically reduced the probability of large deviations from the average, or most probable, arrangement. In ordinary systems we are not dealing with 100 molecules, but with incredibly large numbers of molecules: in 1 mol alone there are 6×10^{23} molecules. Hence the probability of deviation far from the average is incredibly tiny. For example, it has been calculated that the probability that a stone resting on the ground should transform 1 cal of thermal energy into mechanical energy and rise up into the air is much less likely than the probability that a group of monkeys typing randomly would by chance produce the complete works of Shakespeare.

*20-10 Thermodynamic Temperature; Third Law of Thermodynamics

In Section 20–3 we saw for a Carnot cycle that the ratio of the heat absorbed Q_H from the high-temperature reservoir and the heat exhausted Q_L to the low-temperature reservoir is directly related to the ratio of the temperatures of the two reservoirs (Eq. 20–2):

$$\frac{Q_L}{Q_H} = \frac{T_L}{T_H}.$$

This result is valid for any reversible engine and does not depend on the working substance. It can thus serve as the basis for the **Kelvin** or **thermodynamic temperature scale**.

We use this relation and the ideal gas temperature scale (Section 17–10) to complete the definition of the thermodynamic scale: we assign the value

$T_{tp} = 273.16 \text{ K}$ to the triple point of water so that

$$T = (273.16 \text{ K})\left(\frac{Q}{Q_{tp}}\right),$$

where Q and Q_{tp} are the magnitudes of the heats exchanged by a Carnot engine with reservoirs at temperatures T and T_{tp}. Then the thermodynamic scale is identical to the ideal gas scale over the latter's range of validity.

Very low temperatures are difficult to obtain experimentally. The closer the temperature is to absolute zero, the more difficult it is to reduce the temperature further, and it is generally accepted that *it is not possible to reach absolute zero in any finite number of processes*. This last statement is one way to state[†] the **third law of thermodynamics**. Since the maximum efficiency that any heat engine can have is the Carnot efficiency

$$e = 1 - \frac{T_L}{T_H},$$

and since T_L can never be zero, we see that a 100% efficient heat engine is not possible.

FIGURE 20–15 (a) An array of mirrors focuses sunlight on a boiler to produce steam at a solar energy installation. (b) A fossil-fuel steam plant (this one uses forest waste products, biomass). (c) Large cooling towers at an electric generating plant.

(a)

(b)

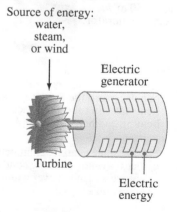

(c)

*20–11 Thermal Pollution, Global Warming, and Energy Resources

Much of the energy we utilize in everyday life—from motor vehicles to most of the electricity produced by power plants—makes use of a heat engine. Electricity produced by falling water at dams, by windmills, or by solar cells (Fig. 20–15a) does not involve a heat engine. But over 90% of the electric energy produced in the U.S. is generated at fossil-fuel steam plants (coal, oil, or gas—see Fig. 20–15b), and they make use of a heat engine (essentially steam engines). In electric power plants, the steam drives the turbines and generators (Fig. 20–16) whose output is electric energy. The various means to turn the turbine are discussed briefly in Table 20–2 (next page), along with some of the advantages and disadvantages of each. Even nuclear power plants use nuclear fuel to run a steam engine.

The heat output Q_L from every heat engine, from power plants to cars, is referred to as **thermal pollution** because this heat (Q_L) must be absorbed by the environment—such as by water from rivers or lakes, or by the air using large cooling towers (Fig. 20–15c). When water is the coolant, this heat raises the temperature of the water, altering the natural ecology of aquatic life (largely because warmer water holds less oxygen). In the case of air cooling towers, the output heat Q_L raises the temperature of the atmosphere, which affects the weather.

FIGURE 20–16 Mechanical energy is transformed to electric energy with a turbine and generator.

Source of energy: water, steam, or wind

Electric generator

Turbine

Electric energy

PHYSICS APPLIED
Heat engines and thermal pollution

[†]See also the statement in the footnote on p. 539.

TABLE 20–2 Electric Energy Resources

Form of Electric Energy Production	% of Production (approx.)		Advantages	Disadvantages
	U.S.	World		
Fossil-fuel steam plants: burn coal, oil, or natural gas to boil water, producing high-pressure steam that turns a turbine of a generator (Figs. 20–3b, 20–16); uses heat engine.	71	66	We know how to build them; for now relatively inexpensive.	Air pollution; thermal pollution; limited efficiency; land devastation from extraction of raw materials (mining); global warming; accidents such as oil spills at sea; limited fuel supply (estimates range from a couple of decades to a few centuries).
Nuclear energy:				
Fission: nuclei of uranium or plutonium atoms split ("fission") with release of energy (Chapter 42) that heats steam; uses heat engine.	20	16	Normally almost no air pollution; less contribution to global warming; relatively inexpensive.	Thermal pollution; accidents can release damaging radioactivity; difficult disposal of radioactive by-products; possible diversion of nuclear material by terrorists; limited fuel supply.
Fusion: energy released when isotopes of hydrogen (or other small nuclei) combine or "fuse" (Chapter 42).	0	0	Relatively "clean"; vast fuel supply (hydrogen in water molecules in oceans); less contribution to global warming.	Not yet workable.
Hydroelectric: falling water turns turbines at the base of a dam.	7	16	No heat engine needed; no air, water, or thermal pollution; relatively inexpensive; high efficiency; dams can control flooding.	Reservoirs behind dams inundate scenic or inhabited land; dams block upstream migration of salmon and other fish for reproduction; few locations remain for new dams; drought.
Geothermal: natural steam from inside the Earth comes to the surface (hot springs, geysers, steam vents); or cold water passed down into contact with hot, dry rock is heated to steam.	<1	<1	No heat engine needed; little air pollution; good efficiency; relatively inexpensive and "clean."	Few appropriate sites; small production; mineral content of spent hot water can pollute.
Wind power: 3-kW to 5-MW windmills (vanes up to 50 m wide) turn a generator.	<1	<1	No heat engine; no air, water, or thermal pollution; relatively inexpensive.	Large array of big windmills might affect weather and be eyesores; hazardous to migratory birds; winds not always strong.
Solar energy:	<1	<1		
Active solar heating: rooftop solar panels absorb the Sun's rays, which heat water in tubes for space heating and hot water supply.			No heat engine needed; no air or thermal pollution; unlimited fuel supply.	Space limitations; may require back-up; relatively expensive; less effective when cloudy.
Passive solar heating: architectural devices—windows along southern exposure, sunshade over windows to keep Sun's rays out in summer.			No heat engine needed; no air or thermal pollution; relatively inexpensive.	Almost none, but other methods needed too.
Solar cells (photovoltaic cells): convert sunlight directly into electricity without use of heat engine.			No heat engine; thermal, air, and water pollution very low; good efficiency (>30% and improving).	Expensive; chemical pollution at manufacture; large land area needed as Sun's energy not concentrated.

Air pollution—by which we mean the chemicals released in the burning of fossil fuels in cars, power plants, and industrial furnaces—gives rise to smog and other problems. Another much talked about issue is the buildup of CO_2 in the Earth's atmosphere due to the burning of fossil fuels. CO_2 absorbs some of the infrared radiation that the Earth naturally emits (Section 19–10) and thus can contribute to **global warming**. Limiting the burning of fossil fuels can help these problems.

Thermal pollution, however, is unavoidable. Engineers can try to design and build engines that are more efficient, but they cannot surpass the Carnot efficiency and must live with T_L being at best the ambient temperature of water or air. The second law of thermodynamics tells us the limit imposed by nature. What we can do, in the light of the second law of thermodynamics, is use less energy and conserve our fuel resources.

PROBLEM SOLVING

Thermodynamics

1. Define the **system** you are dealing with; distinguish the system under study from its surroundings.
2. Be careful of **signs** associated with **work** and **heat**. In the first law, work done *by* the system is positive; work done *on* the system is negative. Heat *added* to the system is positive, but heat *removed* from it is negative. With heat engines, we usually consider the heat intake, the heat exhausted, and the work done as positive.
3. Watch the **units** used for work and heat; work is most often expressed in joules, and heat can be in calories, kilocalories, or joules. Be consistent: choose only one unit for use throughout a given problem.
4. **Temperatures** must generally be expressed in kelvins; temperature *differences* may be expressed in C° or K.
5. **Efficiency** (or coefficient of performance) is a ratio of two energy transfers: useful output divided by required input. Efficiency (but *not* coefficient of performance) is always less than 1 in value, and hence is often stated as a percentage.
6. The **entropy** of a system increases when heat is added to the system, and decreases when heat is removed. If heat is transferred from system A to system B, the change in entropy of A is negative and the change in entropy of B is positive.

Summary

A **heat engine** is a device for changing thermal energy, by means of heat flow, into useful work.

The **efficiency** of a heat engine is defined as the ratio of the work W done by the engine to the heat input Q_H. Because of conservation of energy, the work output equals $Q_H - Q_L$, where Q_L is the heat exhausted to the environment; hence the efficiency

$$e = \frac{W}{Q_H} = 1 - \frac{Q_L}{Q_H}. \qquad (20\text{–}1)$$

Carnot's (idealized) engine consists of two isothermal and two adiabatic processes in a reversible cycle. For a **Carnot engine**, or any reversible engine operating between two temperatures, T_H and T_L (in kelvins), the efficiency is

$$e_{ideal} = 1 - \frac{T_L}{T_H}. \qquad (20\text{–}3)$$

Irreversible (real) engines always have an efficiency less than this.

The operation of **refrigerators** and **air conditioners** is the reverse of that of a heat engine: work is done to extract heat from a cool region and exhaust it to a region at a higher temperature. The coefficient of performance (COP) for either is

$$\text{COP} = \frac{Q_L}{W}, \qquad \begin{bmatrix} \text{refrigerator or} \\ \text{air conditioner} \end{bmatrix} \quad (20\text{–}4a)$$

where W is the work needed to remove heat Q_L from the area with the low temperature.

A **heat pump** does work W to bring heat Q_L from the cold outside and deliver heat Q_H to warm the interior. The coefficient of performance of a heat pump is

$$\text{COP} = \frac{Q_H}{W}. \qquad \text{[heat pump]} \quad (20\text{–}5)$$

The **second law of thermodynamics** can be stated in several equivalent ways:

(a) heat flows spontaneously from a hot object to a cold one, but not the reverse;

(b) there can be no 100% efficient heat engine—that is, one that can change a given amount of heat completely into work;

(c) natural processes tend to move toward a state of greater disorder or greater **entropy**.

Statement (c) is the most general statement of the second law of thermodynamics, and can be restated as: the total entropy, S, of any system plus that of its environment increases as a result of any natural process:

$$\Delta S > 0. \qquad (20\text{–}13)$$

Entropy, which is a state variable, is a quantitative measure of the disorder of a system. The change in entropy of a system during a reversible process is given by $\Delta S = \int dQ/T$.

The second law of thermodynamics tells us in which direction processes tend to proceed; hence entropy is called "time's arrow."

As time goes on, energy is degraded to less useful forms—that is, it is less available to do useful work.

[*All heat engines give rise to **thermal pollution** because they exhaust heat to the environment.]

Questions

1. Can mechanical energy ever be transformed completely into heat or internal energy? Can the reverse happen? In each case, if your answer is no, explain why not; if yes, give one or two examples.

2. Can you warm a kitchen in winter by leaving the oven door open? Can you cool the kitchen on a hot summer day by leaving the refrigerator door open? Explain.

3. Would a definition of heat engine efficiency as $e = W/Q_L$ be useful? Explain.

4. What plays the role of high-temperature and low-temperature areas in (a) an internal combustion engine, and (b) a steam engine? Are they, strictly speaking, heat reservoirs?

5. Which will give the greater improvement in the efficiency of a Carnot engine, a $10 \, C°$ increase in the high-temperature reservoir, or a $10 \, C°$ decrease in the low-temperature reservoir? Explain.

6. The oceans contain a tremendous amount of thermal (internal) energy. Why, in general, is it not possible to put this energy to useful work?

7. Discuss the factors that keep real engines from reaching Carnot efficiency.

8. The expansion valve in a refrigeration system, Fig. 20–10, is crucial for cooling the fluid. Explain how the cooling occurs.

9. Describe a process in nature that is nearly reversible.

10. (a) Describe how heat could be added to a system reversibly. (b) Could you use a stove burner to add heat to a system reversibly? Explain.

11. Suppose a gas expands to twice its original volume (a) adiabatically, (b) isothermally. Which process would result in a greater change in entropy? Explain.

12. Give three examples, other than those mentioned in this Chapter, of naturally occurring processes in which order goes to disorder. Discuss the observability of the reverse process.

13. Which do you think has the greater entropy, 1 kg of solid iron or 1 kg of liquid iron? Why?

14. (a) What happens if you remove the lid of a bottle containing chlorine gas? (b) Does the reverse process ever happen? Why or why not? (c) Can you think of two other examples of irreversibility?

15. You are asked to test a machine that the inventor calls an "in-room air conditioner": a big box, standing in the middle of the room, with a cable that plugs into a power outlet. When the machine is switched on, you feel a stream of cold air coming out of it. How do you know that this machine cannot cool the room?

16. Think up several processes (other than those already mentioned) that would obey the first law of thermodynamics, but, if they actually occurred, would violate the second law.

17. Suppose a lot of papers are strewn all over the floor; then you stack them neatly. Does this violate the second law of thermodynamics? Explain.

18. The first law of thermodynamics is sometimes whimsically stated as, "You can't get something for nothing," and the second law as, "You can't even break even." Explain how these statements could be equivalent to the formal statements.

19. Powdered milk is very slowly (quasistatically) added to water while being stirred. Is this a reversible process? Explain.

20. Two identical systems are taken from state a to state b by two different *irreversible* processes. Will the change in entropy for the system be the same for each process? For the environment? Answer carefully and completely.

21. It can be said that the *total change in entropy during a process is a measure of the irreversibility of the process.* Discuss why this is valid, starting with the fact that $\Delta S_{\text{total}} = \Delta S_{\text{system}} + \Delta S_{\text{environment}} = 0$ for a reversible process.

22. Use arguments, other than the principle of entropy increase, to show that for an adiabatic process, $\Delta S = 0$ if it is done reversibly and $\Delta S > 0$ if done irreversibly.

Problems

20–2 Heat Engines

1. (I) A heat engine exhausts 7800 J of heat while performing 2600 J of useful work. What is the efficiency of this engine?

2. (I) A certain power plant puts out 580 MW of electric power. Estimate the heat discharged per second, assuming that the plant has an efficiency of 35%.

3. (II) A typical compact car experiences a total drag force at 55 mi/h of about 350 N. If this car gets 35 miles per gallon of gasoline at this speed, and a liter of gasoline (1 gal = 3.8 L) releases about 3.2×10^7 J when burned, what is the car's efficiency?

4. (II) A four-cylinder gasoline engine has an efficiency of 0.22 and delivers 180 J of work per cycle per cylinder. The engine fires at 25 cycles per second. (a) Determine the work done per second. (b) What is the total heat input per second from the gasoline? (c) If the energy content of gasoline is 130 MJ per gallon, how long does one gallon last?

5. (II) The burning of gasoline in a car releases about 3.0×10^4 kcal/gal. If a car averages 38 km/gal when driving 95 km/h, which requires 25 hp, what is the efficiency of the engine under those conditions?

6. (II) Figure 20–17 is a PV diagram for a reversible heat engine in which 1.0 mol of argon, a nearly ideal monatomic gas, is initially at STP (point a). Points b and c are on an isotherm at $T = 423$ K. Process ab is at constant volume, process ac at constant pressure. (a) Is the path of the cycle carried out clockwise or counterclockwise? (b) What is the efficiency of this engine?

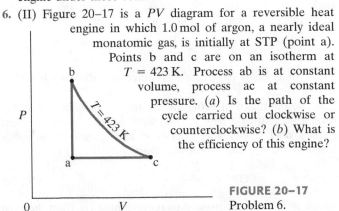

FIGURE 20–17
Problem 6.

7. (III) The operation of a *diesel engine* can be idealized by the cycle shown in Fig. 20–18. Air is drawn into the cylinder during the intake stroke (not part of the idealized cycle). The air is compressed adiabatically, path ab. At point b diesel fuel is injected into the cylinder which immediately burns since the temperature is very high. Combustion is slow, and during the first part of the power stroke, the gas expands at (nearly) constant pressure, path bc. After burning, the rest of the power stroke is adiabatic, path cd. Path da corresponds to the exhaust stroke. (a) Show that, for a quasistatic reversible engine undergoing this cycle using an ideal gas, the ideal efficiency is

$$e = 1 - \frac{(V_a/V_c)^{-\gamma} - (V_a/V_b)^{-\gamma}}{\gamma[(V_a/V_c)^{-1} - (V_a/V_b)^{-1}]},$$

where V_a/V_b is the "compression ratio", V_a/V_c is the "expansion ratio", and γ is defined by Eq. 19–14. (b) If $V_a/V_b = 16$ and $V_a/V_c = 4.5$, calculate the efficiency assuming the gas is diatomic (like N_2 and O_2) and ideal.

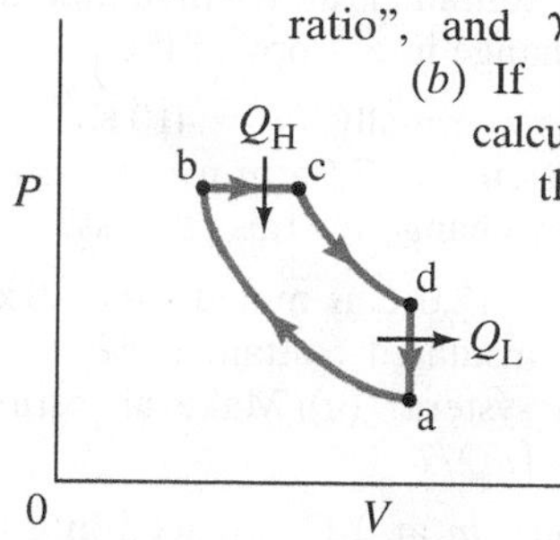

FIGURE 20–18
Problem 7.

20–3 Carnot Engine

8. (I) What is the maximum efficiency of a heat engine whose operating temperatures are 550°C and 365°C?

9. (I) It is not necessary that a heat engine's hot environment be hotter than ambient temperature. Liquid nitrogen (77 K) is about as cheap as bottled water. What would be the efficiency of an engine that made use of heat transferred from air at room temperature (293 K) to the liquid nitrogen "fuel" (Fig. 20–19)?

FIGURE 20–19
Problem 9.

10. (II) A heat engine exhausts its heat at 340°C and has a Carnot efficiency of 38%. What exhaust temperature would enable it to achieve a Carnot efficiency of 45%?

11. (II) (a) Show that the work done by a Carnot engine is equal to the area enclosed by the Carnot cycle on a *PV* diagram, Fig. 20–7. (See Section 19–7.) (b) Generalize this to any reversible cycle.

12. (II) A Carnot engine's operating temperatures are 210°C and 45°C. The engine's power output is 950 W. Calculate the rate of heat output.

13. (II) A nuclear power plant operates at 65% of its maximum theoretical (Carnot) efficiency between temperatures of 660°C and 330°C. If the plant produces electric energy at the rate of 1.2 GW, how much exhaust heat is discharged per hour?

14. (II) A Carnot engine performs work at the rate of 520 kW with an input of 950 kcal of heat per second. If the temperature of the heat source is 560°C, at what temperature is the waste heat exhausted?

15. (II) Assume that a 65 kg hiker needs 4.0×10^3 kcal of energy to supply a day's worth of metabolism. Estimate the maximum height the person can climb in one day, using only this amount of energy. As a rough prediction, treat the person as an isolated heat engine, operating between the internal temperature of 37°C (98.6°F) and the ambient air temperature of 20°C.

16. (II) A particular car does work at the rate of about 7.0 kJ/s when traveling at a steady 20.0 m/s along a level road. This is the work done against friction. The car can travel 17 km on 1 L of gasoline at this speed (about 40 mi/gal). What is the minimum value for T_H if T_L is 25°C? The energy available from 1 L of gas is 3.2×10^7 J.

17. (II) A heat engine utilizes a heat source at 580°C and has a Carnot efficiency of 32%. To increase the efficiency to 38%, what must be the temperature of the heat source?

18. (II) The working substance of a certain Carnot engine is 1.0 mol of an ideal monatomic gas. During the isothermal expansion portion of this engine's cycle, the volume of the gas doubles, while during the adiabatic expansion the volume increases by a factor of 5.7. The work output of the engine is 920 J in each cycle. Compute the temperatures of the two reservoirs between which this engine operates.

19. (III) A Carnot cycle, shown in Fig. 20–7, has the following conditions: $V_a = 7.5$ L, $V_b = 15.0$ L, $T_H = 470$°C, and $T_L = 260$°C. The gas used in the cycle is 0.50 mol of a diatomic gas, $\gamma = 1.4$. Calculate (a) the pressures at a and b; (b) the volumes at c and d. (c) What is the work done along process ab? (d) What is the heat lost along process cd? (e) Calculate the net work done for the whole cycle. (f) What is the efficiency of the cycle, using the definition $e = W/Q_H$? Show that this is the same as given by Eq. 20–3.

20. (III) One mole of monatomic gas undergoes a Carnot cycle with $T_H = 350$°C and $T_L = 210$°C. The initial pressure is 8.8 atm. During the isothermal expansion, the volume doubles. (a) Find the values of the pressure and volume at the points a, b, c, and d (see Fig. 20–7). (b) Determine Q, W, and ΔE_{int} for each segment of the cycle. (c) Calculate the efficiency of the cycle using Eqs. 20–1 and 20–3.

*21. (III) In an engine that approximates the Otto cycle (Fig. 20–8), gasoline vapor must be ignited at the end of the cylinder's adiabatic compression by the spark from a spark plug. The ignition temperature of 87-octane gasoline vapor is about 430°C and, assuming that the working gas is diatomic and enters the cylinder at 25°C, determine the maximum compression ratio of the engine.

20–4 Refrigerators, Air Conditioners, Heat Pumps

22. (I) If an ideal refrigerator keeps its contents at 3.0°C when the house temperature is 22°C, what is its coefficient of performance?

23. (I) The low temperature of a freezer cooling coil is −15°C and the discharge temperature is 33°C. What is the maximum theoretical coefficient of performance?

24. (II) An ideal (Carnot) engine has an efficiency of 38%. If it were possible to run it backward as a heat pump, what would be its coefficient of performance?

25. (II) An ideal heat pump is used to maintain the inside temperature of a house at $T_{in} = 22°C$ when the outside temperature is T_{out}. Assume that when it is operating, the heat pump does work at a rate of 1500 W. Also assume that the house loses heat via conduction through its walls and other surfaces at a rate given by $(650 \text{ W/C°}) (T_{in} - T_{out})$. (a) For what outside temperature would the heat pump have to operate at all times in order to maintain the house at an inside temperature of 22°C? (b) If the outside temperature is 8°C, what percentage of the time does the heat pump have to operate in order to maintain the house at an inside temperature of 22°C?

26. (II) A restaurant refrigerator has a coefficient of performance of 5.0. If the temperature in the kitchen outside the refrigerator is 32°C, what is the lowest temperature that could be obtained inside the refrigerator if it were ideal?

27. (II) A heat pump is used to keep a house warm at 22°C. How much work is required of the pump to deliver 3100 J of heat into the house if the outdoor temperature is (a) 0°C, (b) −15°C? Assume ideal (Carnot) behavior.

28. (II) (a) Given that the coefficient of performance of a refrigerator is defined (Eq. 20–4a) as

$$COP = \frac{Q_L}{W},$$

show that for an ideal (Carnot) refrigerator,

$$COP_{ideal} = \frac{T_L}{T_H - T_L}.$$

(b) Write the COP in terms of the efficiency e of the reversible heat engine obtained by running the refrigerator backward. (c) What is the coefficient of performance for an ideal refrigerator that maintains a freezer compartment at −18°C when the condenser's temperature is 24°C?

29. (II) A "Carnot" refrigerator (reverse of a Carnot engine) absorbs heat from the freezer compartment at a temperature of −17°C and exhausts it into the room at 25°C. (a) How much work must be done by the refrigerator to change 0.40 kg of water at 25°C into ice at −17°C? (b) If the compressor output is 180 W, what minimum time is needed to take 0.40 kg of 25°C water and freeze it at 0°C?

30. (II) A central heat pump operating as an air conditioner draws 33,000 Btu per hour from a building and operates between the temperatures of 24°C and 38°C. (a) If its coefficient of performance is 0.20 that of a Carnot air conditioner, what is the effective coefficient of performance? (b) What is the power (kW) required of the compressor motor? (c) What is the power in terms of hp?

31. (II) What volume of water at 0°C can a freezer make into ice cubes in 1.0 h, if the coefficient of performance of the cooling unit is 7.0 and the power input is 1.2 kilowatt?

20–5 and 20–6 Entropy

32. (I) What is the change in entropy of 250 g of steam at 100°C when it is condensed to water at 100°C?

33. (I) A 7.5-kg box having an initial speed of 4.0 m/s slides along a rough table and comes to rest. Estimate the total change in entropy of the universe. Assume all objects are at room temperature (293 K).

34. (I) What is the change in entropy of 1.00 m³ of water at 0°C when it is frozen to ice at 0°C?

35. (II) If 1.00 m³ of water at 0°C is frozen and cooled to −10°C by being in contact with a great deal of ice at −10°C, estimate the total change in entropy of the process.

36. (II) If 0.45 kg of water at 100°C is changed by a reversible process to steam at 100°C, determine the change in entropy of (a) the water, (b) the surroundings, and (c) the universe as a whole. (d) How would your answers differ if the process were irreversible?

37. (II) An aluminum rod conducts 9.50 cal/s from a heat source maintained at 225°C to a large body of water at 22°C. Calculate the rate at which entropy increases in this process.

38. (II) A 2.8-kg piece of aluminum at 43.0°C is placed in 1.0 kg of water in a Styrofoam container at room temperature (20°C). Estimate the net change in entropy of the system.

39. (II) An ideal gas expands isothermally $(T = 410 \text{ K})$ from a volume of 2.50 L and a pressure of 7.5 atm to a pressure of 1.0 atm. What is the entropy change for this process?

40. (II) When 2.0 kg of water at 12.0°C is mixed with 3.0 kg of water at 38.0°C in a well-insulated container, what is the change in entropy of the system? (a) Make an estimate; (b) use the integral $\Delta S = \int dQ/T$.

41. (II) (a) An ice cube of mass m at 0°C is placed in a large 20°C room. Heat flows (from the room to the ice cube) such that the ice cube melts and the liquid water warms to 20°C. The room is so large that its temperature remains nearly 20°C at all times. Calculate the change in entropy for the (water + room) system due to this process. Will this process occur naturally? (b) A mass m of liquid water at 20°C is placed in a large 20°C room. Heat flows (from the water to the room) such that the liquid water cools to 0°C and then freezes into a 0°C ice cube. The room is so large that its temperature remains 20°C at all times. Calculate the change in entropy for the (water + room) system due to this process. Will this process occur naturally?

42. (II) The temperature of 2.0 mol of an ideal diatomic gas goes from 25°C to 55°C at a constant volume. What is the change in entropy? Use $\Delta S = \int dQ/T$.

43. (II) Calculate the change in entropy of 1.00 kg of water when it is heated from 0°C to 75°C. (a) Make an estimate; (b) use the integral $\Delta S = \int dQ/T$. (c) Does the entropy of the surroundings change? If so, by how much?

44. (II) An ideal gas of n moles undergoes the reversible process ab shown in the PV diagram of Fig. 20–20. The temperature T of the gas is the same at points a and b. Determine the change in entropy of the gas due to this process.

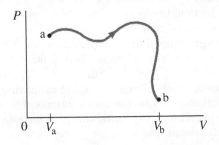

FIGURE 20–20
Problem 44.

45. (II) Two samples of an ideal gas are initially at the same temperature and pressure. They are each compressed reversibly from a volume V to volume $V/2$, one isothermally, the other adiabatically. (a) In which sample is the final pressure greater? (b) Determine the change in entropy of the gas for each process by integration. (c) What is the entropy change of the environment for each process?

46. (II) A 150-g insulated aluminum cup at 15°C is filled with 215 g of water at 100°C. Determine (a) the final temperature of the mixture, and (b) the total change in entropy as a result of the mixing process (use $\Delta S = \int dQ/T$).

47. (II) (a) Why would you expect the total entropy change in a Carnot cycle to be zero? (b) Do a calculation to show that it is zero.

48. (II) 1.00 mole of nitrogen (N_2) gas and 1.00 mole of argon (Ar) gas are in separate, equal-sized, insulated containers at the same temperature. The containers are then connected and the gases (assumed ideal) allowed to mix. What is the change in entropy (a) of the system and (b) of the environment? (c) Repeat part (a) but assume one container is twice as large as the other.

49. (II) Thermodynamic processes are sometimes represented on TS (temperature–entropy) diagrams, rather than PV diagrams. Determine the slope of a constant-volume process on a TS diagram when a system with n moles of an ideal gas with constant-volume molar specific heat C_V is at temperature T.

50. (III) The specific heat per mole of potassium at low temperatures is given by $C_V = aT + bT^3$, where $a = 2.08 \text{ mJ/mol} \cdot K^2$ and $b = 2.57 \text{ mJ/mol} \cdot K^4$. Determine (by integration) the entropy change of 0.15 mol of potassium when its temperature is lowered from 3.0 K to 1.0 K.

51. (III) Consider an ideal gas of n moles with molar specific heats C_V and C_P. (a) Starting with the first law, show that when the temperature and volume of this gas are changed by a reversible process, its change in entropy is given by

$$dS = nC_V \frac{dT}{T} + nR \frac{dV}{V}.$$

(b) Show that the expression in part (a) can be written as

$$dS = nC_V \frac{dP}{P} + nC_P \frac{dV}{V}.$$

(c) Using the expression from part (b), show that if $dS = 0$ for the reversible process (that is, the process is adiabatic), then $PV^\gamma = \text{constant}$, where $\gamma = C_P/C_V$.

20–8 Unavailability of Energy

52. (III) A general theorem states that the amount of energy that becomes unavailable to do useful work in any process is equal to $T_L \Delta S$, where T_L is the lowest temperature available and ΔS is the total change in entropy during the process. Show that this is valid in the specific cases of (a) a falling rock that comes to rest when it hits the ground; (b) the free adiabatic expansion of an ideal gas; and (c) the conduction of heat, Q, from a high-temperature (T_H) reservoir to a low-temperature (T_L) reservoir. [Hint: In part (c) compare to a Carnot engine.]

53. (III) Determine the work available in a 3.5-kg block of copper at 490 K if the surroundings are at 290 K. Use results of Problem 52.

*20–9 **Statistical Interpretation of Entropy**

*54. (I) Use Eq. 20–14 to determine the entropy of each of the five macrostates listed in the Table on page 546.

*55. (II) Suppose that you repeatedly shake six coins in your hand and drop them on the floor. Construct a table showing the number of microstates that correspond to each macrostate. What is the probability of obtaining (a) three heads and three tails and (b) six heads?

*56. (II) Calculate the relative probabilities, when you throw two dice, of obtaining (a) a 7, (b) an 11, (c) a 4.

*57. (II) (a) Suppose you have four coins, all with tails up. You now rearrange them so two heads and two tails are up. What was the change in entropy of the coins? (b) Suppose your system is the 100 coins of Table 20–1; what is the change in entropy of the coins if they are mixed randomly initially, 50 heads and 50 tails, and you arrange them so all 100 are heads? (c) Compare these entropy changes to ordinary thermodynamic entropy changes, such as Examples 20–6, 20–7, and 20–8.

*58. (III) Consider an isolated gas-like system consisting of a box that contains $N = 10$ distinguishable atoms, each moving at the same speed v. The number of unique ways that these atoms can be arranged so that N_L atoms are within the left-hand half of the box and N_R atoms are within the right-hand half of the box is given by $N!/N_L!N_R!$, where, for example, the factorial $4! = 4 \cdot 3 \cdot 2 \cdot 1$ (the only exception is that $0! = 1$). Define each unique arrangement of atoms within the box to be a microstate of this system. Now imagine the following two possible macrostates: state A where all of the atoms are within the left-hand half of the box and none are within the right-hand half; and state B where the distribution is uniform (that is, there is the same number in each half). See Fig. 20–21. (a) Assume the system is initially in state A and, at a later time, is found to be in state B. Determine the system's change in entropy. Can this process occur naturally? (b) Assume the system is initially in state B and, at a later time, is found to be in state A. Determine the system's change in entropy. Can this process occur naturally?

State A ($N_L = 10$, $N_R = 0$)

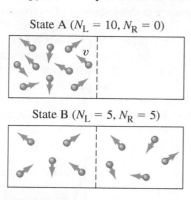

State B ($N_L = 5$, $N_R = 5$)

FIGURE 20–21 Problem 58.

*20–11 **Energy Resources**

*59. (II) Energy may be stored for use during peak demand by pumping water to a high reservoir when demand is low and then releasing it to drive turbines when needed. Suppose water is pumped to a lake 135 m above the turbines at a rate of 1.35×10^5 kg/s for 10.0 h at night. (a) How much energy (kWh) is needed to do this each night? (b) If all this energy is released during a 14-h day, at 75% efficiency, what is the average power output?

*60. (II) If solar cells (Fig. 20–22) can produce about 40 W of electricity per square meter of surface area when directly facing the Sun, how large an area is required to supply the needs of a house that requires 22 kWh/day? Would this fit on the roof of an average house? (Assume the Sun shines about 9 h/day.)

FIGURE 20–22   Problem 60.

*61. (II) Water is stored in an artificial lake created by a dam (Fig. 20–23). The water depth is 38 m at the dam, and a steady flow rate of 32 m³/s is maintained through hydroelectric turbines installed near the base of the dam. How much electrical power can be produced?

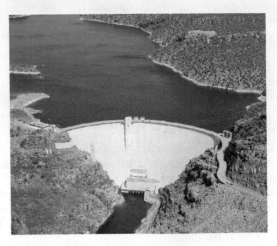

FIGURE 20–23   Problem 61.

General Problems

62. It has been suggested that a heat engine could be developed that made use of the temperature difference between water at the surface of the ocean and water several hundred meters deep. In the tropics, the temperatures may be 27°C and 4°C, respectively. (a) What is the maximum efficiency such an engine could have? (b) Why might such an engine be feasible in spite of the low efficiency? (c) Can you imagine any adverse environmental effects that might occur?

63. A heat engine takes a diatomic gas around the cycle shown in Fig. 20–24. (a) Using the ideal gas law, determine how many moles of gas are in this engine. (b) Determine the temperature at point c. (c) Calculate the heat input into the gas during the constant volume process from points b to c. (d) Calculate the work done by the gas during the isothermal process from points a to b. (e) Calculate the work done by the gas during the adiabatic process from points c to a. (f) Determine the engine's efficiency. (g) What is the maximum efficiency possible for an engine working between T_a and T_c?

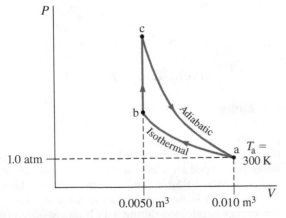

FIGURE 20–24   Problem 63.

64. A 126.5-g insulated aluminum cup at 18.00°C is filled with 132.5 g of water at 46.25°C. After a few minutes, equilibrium is reached. Determine (a) the final temperature, and (b) the total change in entropy.

65. (a) At a steam power plant, steam engines work in pairs, the heat output of the first one being the approximate heat input of the second. The operating temperatures of the first are 710°C and 430°C, and of the second 415°C and 270°C. If the heat of combustion of coal is 2.8×10^7 J/kg, at what rate must coal be burned if the plant is to put out 950 MW of power? Assume the efficiency of the engines is 65% of the ideal (Carnot) efficiency. (b) Water is used to cool the power plant. If the water temperature is allowed to increase by no more than 5.5 C°, estimate how much water must pass through the plant per hour.

66. Refrigeration units can be rated in "tons." A 1-ton air conditioning system can remove sufficient energy to freeze 1 British ton (2000 pounds = 909 kg) of 0°C water into 0°C ice in one 24-h day. If, on a 35°C day, the interior of a house is maintained at 22°C by the continuous operation of a 5-ton air conditioning system, how much does this cooling cost the homeowner per hour? Assume the work done by the refrigeration unit is powered by electricity that costs $0.10 per kWh and that the unit's coefficient of performance is 15% that of an ideal refrigerator. 1 kWh = 3.60×10^6 J.

67. A 35% efficient power plant puts out 920 MW of electrical power. Cooling towers are used to take away the exhaust heat. (a) If the air temperature (15°C) is allowed to rise 7.0 C°, estimate what volume of air (km³) is heated per day. Will the local climate be heated significantly? (b) If the heated air were to form a layer 150 m thick, estimate how large an area it would cover for 24 h of operation. Assume the air has density 1.2 kg/m³ and that its specific heat is about 1.0 kJ/kg·C° at constant pressure.

68. (a) What is the coefficient of performance of an ideal heat pump that extracts heat from 11°C air outside and deposits heat inside your house at 24°C? (b) If this heat pump operates on 1400 W of electrical power, what is the maximum heat it can deliver into your house each hour?

69. The operation of a certain heat engine takes an ideal monatomic gas through a cycle shown as the rectangle on the PV diagram of Fig. 20–25. (a) Determine the efficiency of this engine. Let Q_H and Q_L be the total heat input and total heat exhausted during one cycle of this engine. (b) Compare (as a ratio) the efficiency of this engine to that of a Carnot engine operating between T_H and T_L, where T_H and T_L are the highest and lowest temperatures achieved.

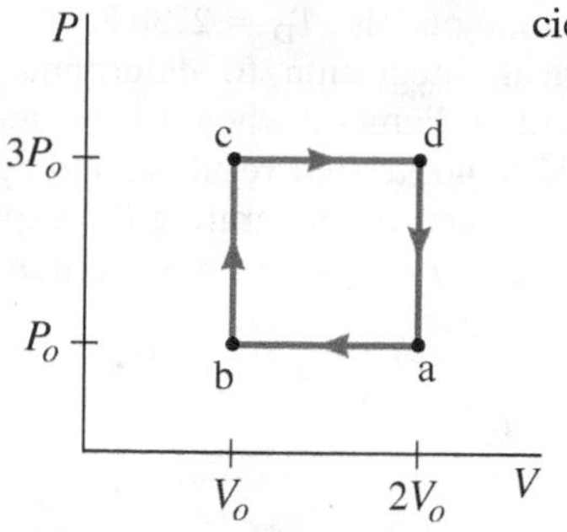

FIGURE 20–25
Problem 69.

70. A car engine whose output power is 155 hp operates at about 15% efficiency. Assume the engine's water temperature of 95°C is its cold-temperature (exhaust) reservoir and 495°C is its thermal "intake" temperature (the temperature of the exploding gas–air mixture). (a) What is the ratio of its efficiency relative to its maximum possible (Carnot) efficiency? (b) Estimate how much power (in watts) goes into moving the car, and how much heat, in joules and in kcal, is exhausted to the air in 1.0 h.

71. Suppose a power plant delivers energy at 850 MW using steam turbines. The steam goes into the turbines superheated at 625 K and deposits its unused heat in river water at 285 K. Assume that the turbine operates as an ideal Carnot engine. (a) If the river's flow rate is $34\,\mathrm{m^3/s}$, estimate the average temperature increase of the river water immediately downstream from the power plant. (b) What is the entropy increase per kilogram of the downstream river water in J/kg·K?

72. 1.00 mole of an ideal monatomic gas at STP first undergoes an isothermal expansion so that the volume at b is 2.5 times the volume at a (Fig. 20–26). Next, heat is extracted at a constant volume so that the pressure drops. The gas is then compressed adiabatically back to the original state. (a) Calculate the pressures at b and c. (b) Determine the temperature at c. (c) Determine the work done, heat input or extracted, and the change in entropy for each process. (d) What is the efficiency of this cycle?

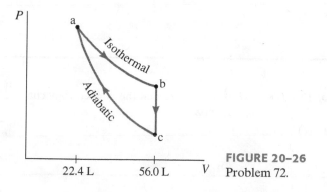

FIGURE 20–26
Problem 72.

73. Two 1100-kg cars are traveling 75 km/h in opposite directions when they collide and are brought to rest. Estimate the change in entropy of the universe as a result of this collision. Assume $T = 15$°C.

74. Metabolizing 1.0 kg of fat results in about 3.7×10^7 J of internal energy in the body. (a) In one day, how much fat does the body burn to maintain the body temperature of a person staying in bed and metabolizing at an average rate of 95 W? (b) How long would it take to burn 1.0-kg of fat this way assuming there is no food intake?

75. A cooling unit for a new freezer has an inner surface area of $6.0\,\mathrm{m^2}$, and is bounded by walls 12 cm thick with a thermal conductivity of 0.050 W/m·K. The inside must be kept at −10°C in a room that is at 20°C. The motor for the cooling unit must run no more than 15% of the time. What is the minimum power requirement of the cooling motor?

76. An ideal air conditioner keeps the temperature inside a room at 21°C when the outside temperature is 32°C. If 3.3 kW of power enters a room through the windows in the form of direct radiation from the Sun, how much electrical power would be saved if the windows were shaded so only 500 W came through them?

77. The *Stirling cycle*, shown in Fig. 20–27, is useful to describe external combustion engines as well as solar-power systems. Find the efficiency of the cycle in terms of the parameters shown, assuming a monatomic gas as the working substance. The processes ab and cd are isothermal whereas bc and da are at constant volume. How does it compare to the Carnot efficiency?

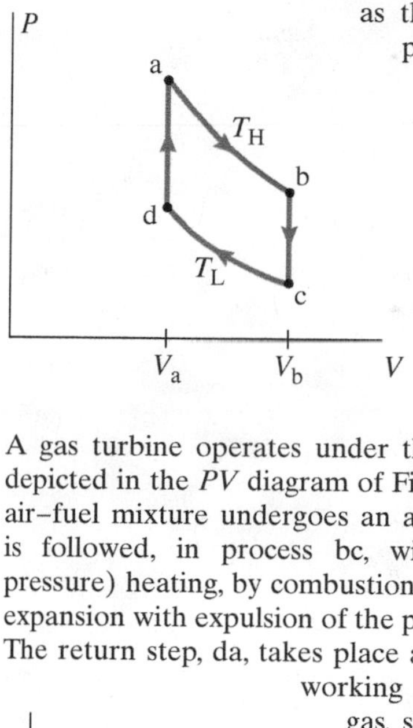

FIGURE 20–27
Problem 77.

78. A gas turbine operates under the *Brayton cycle*, which is depicted in the PV diagram of Fig. 20–28. In process ab the air–fuel mixture undergoes an adiabatic compression. This is followed, in process bc, with an isobaric (constant pressure) heating, by combustion. Process cd is an adiabatic expansion with expulsion of the products to the atmosphere. The return step, da, takes place at constant pressure. If the working gas behaves like an ideal gas, show that the efficiency of the Brayton cycle is

$$e = 1 - \left(\frac{P_b}{P_a}\right)^{\frac{1-\gamma}{\gamma}}.$$

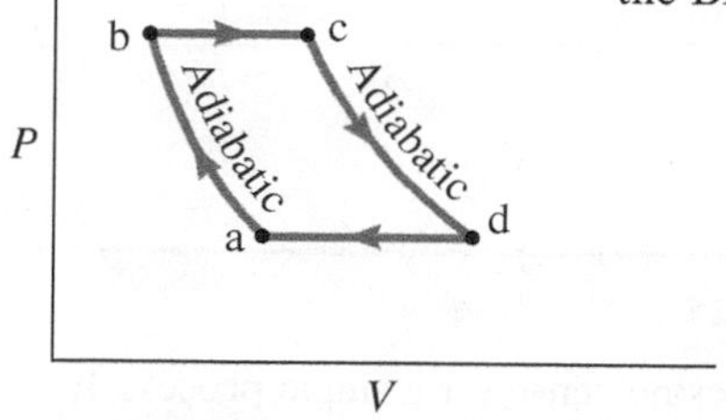

FIGURE 20–28
Problem 78.

79. Thermodynamic processes can be represented not only on PV and PT diagrams; another useful one is a TS (temperature–entropy) diagram. (a) Draw a TS diagram for a Carnot cycle. (b) What does the area within the curve represent?

80. An aluminum can, with negligible heat capacity, is filled with 450 g of water at 0°C and then is brought into thermal contact with a similar can filled with 450 g of water at 50°C. Find the change in entropy of the system if no heat is allowed to exchange with the surroundings. Use $\Delta S = \int dQ/T$.

81. A dehumidifier is essentially a "refrigerator with an open door." The humid air is pulled in by a fan and guided to a cold coil, whose temperature is less than the dew point, and some of the air's water condenses. After this water is extracted, the air is warmed back to its original temperature and sent into the room. In a well-designed dehumidifier, the heat is exchanged between the incoming and outgoing air. Thus the heat that is removed by the refrigerator coil mostly comes from the condensation of water vapor to liquid. Estimate how much water is removed in 1.0 h by an ideal dehumidifier, if the temperature of the room is 25°C, the water condenses at 8°C, and the dehumidifier does work at the rate of 650 W of electrical power.

*82. A bowl contains a large number of red, orange, and green jelly beans. You are to make a line of three jelly beans. (a) Construct a table showing the number of microstates that correspond to each macrostate. Then determine the probability of (b) all 3 beans red, and (c) 2 greens, 1 orange.

*Numerical/Computer

*83. (II) At low temperature the specific heat of diamond varies with absolute temperature T according to the Debye equation $C_V = 1.88 \times 10^3 (T/T_D)^3$ J·mol^{-1}·K^{-1} where the Debye temperature for diamond is $T_D = 2230$ K. Use a spreadsheet and numerical integration to determine the entropy change of 1.00 mol of diamond when it is heated at constant volume from 4 K to 40 K. Your result should agree within 2% of the result obtained by integrating the expression for dS. [Hint: $dS = nC_V \, dT/T$, where n is the number of moles.]

Answers to Exercises

A: No. Efficiency makes no sense for a single process. It is defined (Eqs. 20–1) only for cyclic processes that return to the initial state.

B: (d).

C: (c).

D: 1220 J/K; −1220 J/K. (Note that the *total* entropy change, $\Delta S_{ice} + \Delta S_{res}$, is zero.)

E: (e).

This comb has acquired a static electric charge, either from passing through hair, or being rubbed by a cloth or paper towel. The electrical charge on the comb induces a polarization (separation of charge) in scraps of paper, and thus attracts them.

Our introduction to electricity in this Chapter covers conductors and insulators, and Coulomb's law which relates the force between two point charges as a function of their distance apart. We also introduce the powerful concept of electric field.

Electric Charge and Electric Field

CHAPTER-OPENING QUESTION—Guess now!
Two identical tiny spheres have the same electric charge. If the electric charge on each of them is doubled, and their separation is also doubled, the force each exerts on the other will be

(a) half.
(b) double.
(c) four times larger.
(d) one-quarter as large.
(e) unchanged.

The word "electricity" may evoke an image of complex modern technology: lights, motors, electronics, and computers. But the electric force plays an even deeper role in our lives. According to atomic theory, electric forces between atoms and molecules hold them together to form liquids and solids, and electric forces are also involved in the metabolic processes that occur within our bodies. Many of the forces we have dealt with so far, such as elastic forces, the normal force, and friction and other contact forces (pushes and pulls), are now considered to result from electric forces acting at the atomic level. Gravity, on the other hand, is a separate force.[†]

[†]As we discussed in Section 6–7, physicists in the twentieth century came to recognize four different fundamental forces in nature: (1) gravitational force, (2) electromagnetic force (we will see later that electric and magnetic forces are intimately related), (3) strong nuclear force, and (4) weak nuclear force. The last two forces operate at the level of the nucleus of an atom. Recent theory has combined the electromagnetic and weak nuclear forces so they are now considered to have a common origin known as the electroweak force. We will discuss these forces in later Chapters.

CONTENTS

559

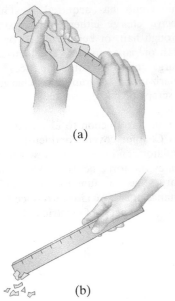

(a)

(b)

FIGURE 21–1 (a) Rub a plastic ruler and (b) bring it close to some tiny pieces of paper.

FIGURE 21–2 Like charges repel one another; unlike charges attract. (Note color coding: positive and negative charged objects are often colored pink and blue-green, respectively, when we want to emphasize them. We use these colors especially for point charges, but not often for real objects.)

(a) Two charged plastic rulers repel

(b) Two charged glass rods repel

(c) Charged glass rod attracts charged plastic ruler

LAW OF CONSERVATION OF ELECTRIC CHARGE

The earliest studies on electricity date back to the ancients, but only in the past two centuries has electricity been studied in detail. We will discuss the development of ideas about electricity, including practical devices, as well as its relation to magnetism, in the next eleven Chapters.

21–1 Static Electricity; Electric Charge and Its Conservation

The word *electricity* comes from the Greek word *elektron*, which means "amber." Amber is petrified tree resin, and the ancients knew that if you rub a piece of amber with a cloth, the amber attracts small pieces of leaves or dust. A piece of hard rubber, a glass rod, or a plastic ruler rubbed with a cloth will also display this "amber effect," or **static electricity** as we call it today. You can readily pick up small pieces of paper with a plastic comb or ruler that you have just vigorously rubbed with even a paper towel. See the photo on the previous page and Fig. 21–1. You have probably experienced static electricity when combing your hair or when taking a synthetic blouse or shirt from a clothes dryer. And you may have felt a shock when you touched a metal doorknob after sliding across a car seat or walking across a nylon carpet. In each case, an object becomes "charged" as a result of rubbing, and is said to possess a net **electric charge**.

Is all electric charge the same, or is there more than one type? In fact, there are *two* types of electric charge, as the following simple experiments show. A plastic ruler suspended by a thread is vigorously rubbed with a cloth to charge it. When a second plastic ruler, which has been charged in the same way, is brought close to the first, it is found that one ruler *repels* the other. This is shown in Fig. 21–2a. Similarly, if a rubbed glass rod is brought close to a second charged glass rod, again a repulsive force is seen to act, Fig. 21–2b. However, if the charged glass rod is brought close to the charged plastic ruler, it is found that they *attract* each other, Fig. 21–2c. The charge on the glass must therefore be different from that on the plastic. Indeed, it is found experimentally that all charged objects fall into one of two categories. Either they are attracted to the plastic and repelled by the glass; or they are repelled by the plastic and attracted to the glass. Thus there seem to be two, and only two, types of electric charge. Each type of charge repels the same type but attracts the opposite type. That is: **unlike charges attract; like charges repel**.

The two types of electric charge were referred to as *positive* and *negative* by the American statesman, philosopher, and scientist Benjamin Franklin (1706–1790). The choice of which name went with which type of charge was arbitrary. Franklin's choice set the charge on the rubbed glass rod to be positive charge, so the charge on a rubbed plastic ruler (or amber) is called negative charge. We still follow this convention today.

Franklin argued that whenever a certain amount of charge is produced on one object, an equal amount of the opposite type of charge is produced on another object. The positive and negative are to be treated *algebraically*, so during any process, the net change in the amount of charge produced is zero. For example, when a plastic ruler is rubbed with a paper towel, the plastic acquires a negative charge and the towel acquires an equal amount of positive charge. The charges are separated, but the sum of the two is zero.

This is an example of a law that is now well established: the **law of conservation of electric charge**, which states that

> **the net amount of electric charge produced in any process is zero;**

or, said another way,

> **no net electric charge can be created or destroyed.**

If one object (or a region of space) acquires a positive charge, then an equal amount of negative charge will be found in neighboring areas or objects. No violations have ever been found, and this conservation law is as firmly established as those for energy and momentum.

21–2 Electric Charge in the Atom

Only within the past century has it become clear that an understanding of electricity originates inside the atom itself. In later Chapters we will discuss atomic structure and the ideas that led to our present view of the atom in more detail. But it will help our understanding of electricity if we discuss it briefly now.

A simplified model of an atom shows it as having a tiny but heavy, positively charged nucleus surrounded by one or more negatively charged electrons (Fig. 21–3). The nucleus contains protons, which are positively charged, and neutrons, which have no net electric charge. All protons and all electrons have exactly the same magnitude of electric charge; but their signs are opposite. Hence neutral atoms, having no net charge, contain equal numbers of protons and electrons. Sometimes an atom may lose one or more of its electrons, or may gain extra electrons, in which case it will have a net positive or negative charge and is called an **ion**.

In solid materials the nuclei tend to remain close to fixed positions, whereas some of the electrons may move quite freely. When an object is *neutral*, it contains equal amounts of positive and negative charge. The charging of a solid object by rubbing can be explained by the transfer of electrons from one object to the other. When a plastic ruler becomes negatively charged by rubbing with a paper towel, the transfer of electrons from the towel to the plastic leaves the towel with a positive charge equal in magnitude to the negative charge acquired by the plastic. In liquids and gases, nuclei or ions can move as well as electrons.

Normally when objects are charged by rubbing, they hold their charge only for a limited time and eventually return to the neutral state. Where does the charge go? Usually the charge "leaks off" onto water molecules in the air. This is because water molecules are **polar**—that is, even though they are neutral, their charge is not distributed uniformly, Fig. 21–4. Thus the extra electrons on, say, a charged plastic ruler can "leak off" into the air because they are attracted to the positive end of water molecules. A positively charged object, on the other hand, can be neutralized by transfer of loosely held electrons from water molecules in the air. On dry days, static electricity is much more noticeable since the air contains fewer water molecules to allow leakage. On humid or rainy days, it is difficult to make any object hold a net charge for long.

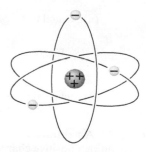

FIGURE 21–3 Simple model of the atom.

FIGURE 21–4 Diagram of a water molecule. Because it has opposite charges on different ends, it is called a "polar" molecule.

21–3 Insulators and Conductors

Suppose we have two metal spheres, one highly charged and the other electrically neutral (Fig. 21–5a). If we now place a metal object, such as a nail, so that it touches both spheres (Fig. 21–5b), the previously uncharged sphere quickly becomes charged. If, instead, we had connected the two spheres by a wooden rod or a piece of rubber (Fig. 21–5c), the uncharged ball would not become noticeably charged. Materials like the iron nail are said to be **conductors** of electricity, whereas wood and rubber are **nonconductors** or **insulators**.

Metals are generally good conductors, whereas most other materials are insulators (although even insulators conduct electricity very slightly). Nearly all natural materials fall into one or the other of these two very distinct categories. However, a few materials (notably silicon and germanium) fall into an intermediate category known as **semiconductors**.

From the atomic point of view, the electrons in an insulating material are bound very tightly to the nuclei. In a good conductor, on the other hand, some of the electrons are bound very loosely and can move about freely within the material (although they cannot *leave* the object easily) and are often referred to as *free electrons* or *conduction electrons*. When a positively charged object is brought close to or touches a conductor, the free electrons in the conductor are attracted by this positively charged object and move quickly toward it. On the other hand, the free electrons move swiftly away from a negatively charged object that is brought close to the conductor. In a semiconductor, there are many fewer free electrons, and in an insulator, almost none.

FIGURE 21–5 (a) A charged metal sphere and a neutral metal sphere. (b) The two spheres connected by a conductor (a metal nail), which conducts charge from one sphere to the other. (c) The original two spheres connected by an insulator (wood); almost no charge is conducted.

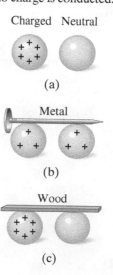

Charged Neutral

(a)

Metal

(b)

Wood

(c)

21–4 Induced Charge; the Electroscope

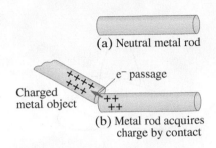

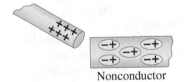

FIGURE 21–6 A neutral metal rod in (a) will acquire a positive charge if placed in contact (b) with a positively charged metal object. (Electrons move as shown by the orange arrow.) This is called charging by conduction.

Suppose a positively charged metal object is brought close to an uncharged metal object. If the two touch, the free electrons in the neutral one are attracted to the positively charged object and some will pass over to it, Fig. 21–6. Since the second object, originally neutral, is now missing some of its negative electrons, it will have a net positive charge. This process is called "charging by conduction," or "by contact," and the two objects end up with the same sign of charge.

Now suppose a positively charged object is brought close to a neutral metal rod, but does not touch it. Although the free electrons of the metal rod do not leave the rod, they still move within the metal toward the external positive charge, leaving a positive charge at the opposite end of the rod (Fig. 21–7). A charge is said to have been *induced* at the two ends of the metal rod. No net charge has been created in the rod: charges have merely been *separated*. The net charge on the metal rod is still zero. However, if the metal is separated into two pieces, we would have two charged objects: one charged positively and one charged negatively.

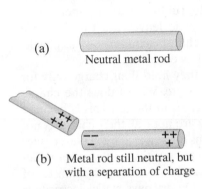

FIGURE 21–7 Charging by induction.

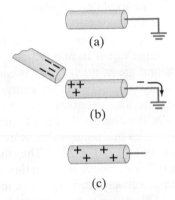

FIGURE 21–8 Inducing a charge on an object connected to ground.

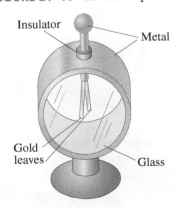

FIGURE 21–9 A charged object brought near an insulator causes a charge separation within the insulator's molecules.

FIGURE 21–10 Electroscope.

Another way to induce a net charge on a metal object is to first connect it with a conducting wire to the ground (or a conducting pipe leading into the ground) as shown in Fig. 21–8a (the symbol ⏚ means connected to "ground"). The object is then said to be "grounded" or "earthed." The Earth, because it is so large and can conduct, easily accepts or gives up electrons; hence it acts like a reservoir for charge. If a charged object—say negative this time—is brought up close to the metal object, free electrons in the metal are repelled and many of them move down the wire into the Earth, Fig. 21–8b. This leaves the metal positively charged. If the wire is now cut, the metal object will have a positive induced charge on it (Fig. 21–8c). If the wire were cut after the negative object was moved away, the electrons would all have moved back into the metal object and it would be neutral.

Charge separation can also be done in nonconductors. If you bring a positively charged object close to a neutral nonconductor as shown in Fig. 21–9, almost no electrons can move about freely within the nonconductor. But they can move slightly within their own atoms and molecules. Each oval in Fig. 21–9 represents a molecule (not to scale); the negatively charged electrons, attracted to the external positive charge, tend to move in its direction within their molecules. Because the negative charges in the nonconductor are nearer to the external positive charge, the nonconductor as a whole is attracted to the external positive charge (see the Chapter-Opening Photo, page 559).

An **electroscope** is a device that can be used for detecting charge. As shown in Fig. 21–10, inside of a case are two movable metal leaves, often made of gold, connected to a metal knob on the outside. (Sometimes only one leaf is movable.)

If a positively charged object is brought close to the knob, a separation of charge is induced: electrons are attracted up into the knob, leaving the leaves positively charged, Fig. 21–11a. The two leaves repel each other as shown, because they are both positively charged. If, instead, the knob is charged by conduction, the whole apparatus acquires a net charge as shown in Fig. 21–11b. In either case, the greater the amount of charge, the greater the separation of the leaves.

Note that you cannot tell the sign of the charge in this way, since negative charge will cause the leaves to separate just as much as an equal amount of positive charge; in either case, the two leaves repel each other. An electroscope can, however, be used to determine the sign of the charge if it is first charged by conduction, say, negatively, as in Fig. 21–12a. Now if a negative object is brought close, as in Fig. 21–12b, more electrons are induced to move down into the leaves and they separate further. If a positive charge is brought close instead, the electrons are induced to flow upward, leaving the leaves less negative and their separation is reduced, Fig. 21–12c.

The electroscope was used in the early studies of electricity. The same principle, aided by some electronics, is used in much more sensitive modern **electrometers**.

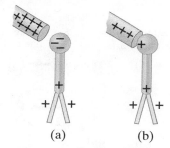

FIGURE 21–11 Electroscope charged (a) by induction, (b) by conduction.

FIGURE 21–12 A previously charged electroscope can be used to determine the sign of a charged object.

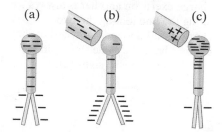

21–5 Coulomb's Law

We have seen that an electric charge exerts a force of attraction or repulsion on other electric charges. What factors affect the magnitude of this force? To find an answer, the French physicist Charles Coulomb (1736–1806) investigated electric forces in the 1780s using a torsion balance (Fig. 21–13) much like that used by Cavendish for his studies of the gravitational force (Chapter 6).

Precise instruments for the measurement of electric charge were not available in Coulomb's time. Nonetheless, Coulomb was able to prepare small spheres with different magnitudes of charge in which the *ratio* of the charges was known.[†] Although he had some difficulty with induced charges, Coulomb was able to argue that the force one tiny charged object exerts on a second tiny charged object is directly proportional to the charge on each of them. That is, if the charge on either one of the objects is doubled, the force is doubled; and if the charge on both of the objects is doubled, the force increases to four times the original value. This was the case when the distance between the two charges remained the same. If the distance between them was allowed to increase, he found that the force decreased with the *square of the distance* between them. That is, if the distance was doubled, the force fell to one-fourth of its original value. Thus, Coulomb concluded, the force one small charged object exerts on a second one is proportional to the product of the magnitude of the charge on one, Q_1, times the magnitude of the charge on the other, Q_2, and inversely proportional to the square of the distance r between them (Fig. 21–14). As an equation, we can write **Coulomb's law** as

$$F = k \frac{Q_1 Q_2}{r^2},$$

[magnitudes] **(21–1)**

where k is a proportionality constant.[‡]

FIGURE 21–13 (below) Coulomb used a torsion balance to investigate how the electric force varies as a function of the magnitude of the charges and of the distance between them. When an external charged sphere is placed close to the charged one on the suspended bar, the bar rotates slightly. The suspending fiber resists the twisting motion, and the angle of twist is proportional to the electric force.

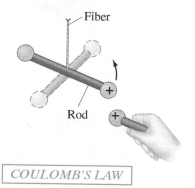

COULOMB'S LAW

FIGURE 21–14 Coulomb's law, Eq. 21–1, gives the force between two point charges, Q_1 and Q_2, a distance r apart.

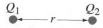

[†] Coulomb reasoned that if a charged conducting sphere is placed in contact with an identical uncharged sphere, the charge on the first would be shared equally by the two of them because of symmetry. He thus had a way to produce charges equal to $\frac{1}{2}$, $\frac{1}{4}$, and so on, of the original charge.

[‡] The validity of Coulomb's law today rests on precision measurements that are much more sophisticated than Coulomb's original experiment. The exponent 2 in Coulomb's law has been shown to be accurate to 1 part in 10^{16} [that is, $2 \pm (1 \times 10^{-16})$].

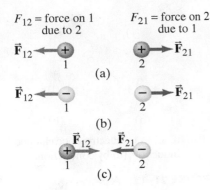

F_{12} = force on 1 due to 2

F_{21} = force on 2 due to 1

$\vec{\mathbf{F}}_{12}$ 1   2 $\vec{\mathbf{F}}_{21}$

(a)

$\vec{\mathbf{F}}_{12}$ 1   2 $\vec{\mathbf{F}}_{21}$

(b)

$\vec{\mathbf{F}}_{12}$ 1   2 $\vec{\mathbf{F}}_{21}$

(c)

FIGURE 21–15 The direction of the static electric force one point charge exerts on another is always along the line joining the two charges, and depends on whether the charges have the same sign as in (a) and (b), or opposite signs (c).

As we just saw, Coulomb's law,

$$F = k\frac{Q_1 Q_2}{r^2}, \qquad \text{[magnitudes]} \quad \textbf{(21–1)}$$

gives the *magnitude* of the electric force that either charge exerts on the other. The *direction* of the electric force *is always along the line joining the two charges*. If the two charges have the same sign, the force on either charge is directed away from the other (they repel each other). If the two charges have opposite signs, the force on one is directed toward the other (they attract). See Fig. 21–15. Notice that the force one charge exerts on the second is equal but opposite to that exerted by the second on the first, in accord with Newton's third law.

The SI unit of charge is the **coulomb** (C).[†] The precise definition of the coulomb today is in terms of electric current and magnetic field, and will be discussed later (Section 28–3). In SI units, the constant k in Coulomb's law has the value

$$k = 8.99 \times 10^9 \, \text{N} \cdot \text{m}^2/\text{C}^2$$

or, when we only need two significant figures,

$$k \approx 9.0 \times 10^9 \, \text{N} \cdot \text{m}^2/\text{C}^2.$$

Thus, 1 C is that amount of charge which, if placed on each of two point objects that are 1.0 m apart, will result in each object exerting a force of $(9.0 \times 10^9 \, \text{N} \cdot \text{m}^2/\text{C}^2)(1.0 \, \text{C})(1.0 \, \text{C})/(1.0 \, \text{m})^2 = 9.0 \times 10^9 \, \text{N}$ on the other. This would be an enormous force, equal to the weight of almost a million tons. We rarely encounter charges as large as a coulomb.

Charges produced by rubbing ordinary objects (such as a comb or plastic ruler) are typically around a microcoulomb $(1 \, \mu\text{C} = 10^{-6} \, \text{C})$ or less. Objects that carry a positive charge have a deficit of electrons, whereas negatively charged objects have an excess of electrons. The charge on one electron has been determined to have a magnitude of about $1.602 \times 10^{-19} \, \text{C}$, and is negative. This is the smallest charge found in nature,[‡] and because it is fundamental, it is given the symbol e and is often referred to as the *elementary charge*:

$$e = 1.602 \times 10^{-19} \, \text{C}.$$

Note that e is defined as a positive number, so the charge on the electron is $-e$. (The charge on a proton, on the other hand, is $+e$.) Since an object cannot gain or lose a fraction of an electron, the net charge on any object must be an integral multiple of this charge. Electric charge is thus said to be **quantized** (existing only in discrete amounts: $1e$, $2e$, $3e$, etc.). Because e is so small, however, we normally do not notice this discreteness in macroscopic charges (1 μC requires about 10^{13} electrons), which thus seem continuous.

Coulomb's law looks a lot like the *law of universal gravitation*, $F = Gm_1 m_2/r^2$, which expresses the gravitational force a mass m_1 exerts on a mass m_2 (Eq. 6–1). Both are inverse square laws $(F \propto 1/r^2)$. Both also have a proportionality to a property of each object—mass for gravity, electric charge for electricity. And both act over a distance (that is, there is no need for contact). A major difference between the two laws is that gravity is always an attractive force, whereas the electric force can be either attractive or repulsive. Electric charge comes in two types, positive and negative; gravitational mass is only positive.

[†]In the once common cgs system of units, k is set equal to 1, and the unit of electric charge is called the *electrostatic unit* (esu) or the statcoulomb. One esu is defined as that charge, on each of two point objects 1 cm apart, that gives rise to a force of 1 dyne.

[‡]According to the standard model of elementary particle physics, subnuclear particles called quarks have a smaller charge than that on the electron, equal to $\frac{1}{3}e$ or $\frac{2}{3}e$. Quarks have not been detected directly as isolated objects, and theory indicates that free quarks may not be detectable.

The constant k in Eq. 21–1 is often written in terms of another constant, ϵ_0, called the **permittivity of free space**. It is related to k by $k = 1/4\pi\epsilon_0$. Coulomb's law can then be written

$$F = \frac{1}{4\pi\epsilon_0}\frac{Q_1 Q_2}{r^2}, \qquad (21\text{–}2)$$

where

$$\epsilon_0 = \frac{1}{4\pi k} = 8.85 \times 10^{-12}\,\text{C}^2/\text{N}\cdot\text{m}^2.$$

COULOMB'S LAW
(in terms of ϵ_0)

Equation 21–2 looks more complicated than Eq. 21–1, but other fundamental equations we haven't seen yet are simpler in terms of ϵ_0 rather than k. It doesn't matter which form we use since Eqs. 21–1 and 21–2 are equivalent. (The latest precise values of e and ϵ_0 are given inside the front cover.)

[Our convention for units, such as $\text{C}^2/\text{N}\cdot\text{m}^2$ for ϵ_0, means m^2 is in the denominator. That is, $\text{C}^2/\text{N}\cdot\text{m}^2$ does *not* mean $(\text{C}^2/\text{N})\cdot\text{m}^2 = \text{C}^2\cdot\text{m}^2/\text{N}$.]

Equations 21–1 and 21–2 apply to objects whose size is much smaller than the distance between them. Ideally, it is precise for **point charges** (spatial size negligible compared to other distances). For finite-sized objects, it is not always clear what value to use for r, particularly since the charge may not be distributed uniformly on the objects. If the two objects are spheres and the charge is known to be distributed uniformly on each, then r is the distance between their centers.

Coulomb's law describes the force between two charges when they are at rest. Additional forces come into play when charges are in motion, and will be discussed in later Chapters. In this Chapter we discuss only charges at rest, the study of which is called **electrostatics**, and Coulomb's law gives the **electrostatic force**.

When calculating with Coulomb's law, we usually ignore the signs of the charges and determine the direction of a force separately based on whether the force is attractive or repulsive.

PROBLEM SOLVING

Use magnitudes in Coulomb's law; find force direction from signs of charges

EXERCISE A Return to the Chapter-Opening Question, page 559, and answer it again now. Try to explain why you may have answered differently the first time.

CONCEPTUAL EXAMPLE 21–1 | **Which charge exerts the greater force?** Two positive point charges, $Q_1 = 50\,\mu\text{C}$ and $Q_2 = 1\,\mu\text{C}$, are separated by a distance ℓ, Fig. 21–16. Which is larger in magnitude, the force that Q_1 exerts on Q_2, or the force that Q_2 exerts on Q_1?

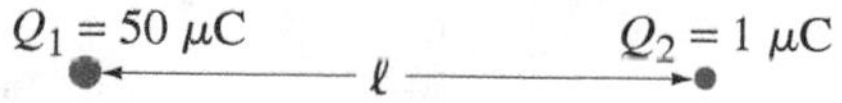

RESPONSE From Coulomb's law, the force on Q_1 exerted by Q_2 is

$$F_{12} = k\frac{Q_1 Q_2}{\ell^2}.$$

The force on Q_2 exerted by Q_1 is

$$F_{21} = k\frac{Q_2 Q_1}{\ell^2}$$

which is the same magnitude. The equation is symmetric with respect to the two charges, so $F_{21} = F_{12}$.

NOTE Newton's third law also tells us that these two forces must have equal magnitude.

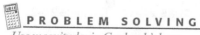

FIGURE 21–16 Example 21–1.

EXERCISE B What is the magnitude of F_{12} (and F_{21}) in Example 21–1 if $\ell = 30\,\text{cm}$?

Keep in mind that Eq. 21–2 (or 21–1) gives the force on a charge due to only *one* other charge. If several (or many) charges are present, the *net force on any one of them will be the vector sum of the forces due to each of the others*. This **principle of superposition** is based on experiment, and tells us that electric force vectors add like any other vector. For continuous distributions of charge, the sum becomes an integral.

EXAMPLE 21–2 **Three charges in a line.** Three charged particles are arranged in a line, as shown in Fig. 21–17. Calculate the net electrostatic force on particle 3 (the $-4.0\,\mu C$ on the right) due to the other two charges.

APPROACH The net force on particle 3 is the vector sum of the force $\vec{F}_{31}$ exerted on 3 by particle 1 and the force $\vec{F}_{32}$ exerted on 3 by particle 2: $\vec{F} = \vec{F}_{31} + \vec{F}_{32}$.

SOLUTION The magnitudes of these two forces are obtained using Coulomb's law, Eq. 21–1:

$$F_{31} = k\frac{Q_3 Q_1}{r_{31}^2}$$

$$= \frac{(9.0 \times 10^9\,\text{N}\cdot\text{m}^2/\text{C}^2)(4.0 \times 10^{-6}\,\text{C})(8.0 \times 10^{-6}\,\text{C})}{(0.50\,\text{m})^2} = 1.2\,\text{N},$$

where $r_{31} = 0.50\,\text{m}$ is the distance from Q_3 to Q_1. Similarly,

$$F_{32} = k\frac{Q_3 Q_2}{r_{32}^2}$$

$$= \frac{(9.0 \times 10^9\,\text{N}\cdot\text{m}^2/\text{C}^2)(4.0 \times 10^{-6}\,\text{C})(3.0 \times 10^{-6}\,\text{C})}{(0.20\,\text{m})^2} = 2.7\,\text{N}.$$

Since we were calculating the magnitudes of the forces, we omitted the signs of the charges. But we must be aware of them to get the direction of each force. Let the line joining the particles be the x axis, and we take it positive to the right. Then, because $\vec{F}_{31}$ is repulsive and $\vec{F}_{32}$ is attractive, the directions of the forces are as shown in Fig. 21–17b: F_{31} points in the positive x direction and F_{32} points in the negative x direction. The net force on particle 3 is then

$$F = -F_{32} + F_{31} = -2.7\,\text{N} + 1.2\,\text{N} = -1.5\,\text{N}.$$

The magnitude of the net force is 1.5 N, and it points to the left.

NOTE Charge Q_1 acts on charge Q_3 just as if Q_2 were not there (this is the principle of superposition). That is, the charge in the middle, Q_2, in no way blocks the effect of charge Q_1 acting on Q_3. Naturally, Q_2 exerts its own force on Q_3.

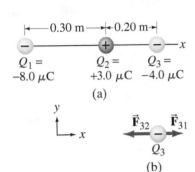

$|{-}0.30\,\text{m}{-}|{-}0.20\,\text{m}{-}|$

$Q_1 = -8.0\,\mu C$ $Q_2 = +3.0\,\mu C$ $Q_3 = -4.0\,\mu C$
(a)

$\vec{F}_{32}$ $\vec{F}_{31}$

Q_3

(b)

FIGURE 21–17 Example 21–2.

⚠ **CAUTION**

Each charge exerts its own force. No charge blocks the effect of the others

| **EXERCISE C** Determine the magnitude and direction of the net force on Q_1 in Fig. 21–17a.

EXAMPLE 21–3 **Electric force using vector components.** Calculate the net electrostatic force on charge Q_3 shown in Fig. 21–18a due to the charges Q_1 and Q_2.

APPROACH We use Coulomb's law to find the magnitudes of the individual forces. The direction of each force will be along the line connecting Q_3 to Q_1 or Q_2. The forces $\vec{F}_{31}$ and $\vec{F}_{32}$ have the directions shown in Fig. 21–18a, since Q_1 exerts an attractive force on Q_3, and Q_2 exerts a repulsive force. The forces $\vec{F}_{31}$ and $\vec{F}_{32}$ are *not* along the same line, so to find the resultant force on Q_3 we resolve $\vec{F}_{31}$ and $\vec{F}_{32}$ into x and y components and perform the vector addition.

SOLUTION The magnitudes of $\vec{F}_{31}$ and $\vec{F}_{32}$ are (ignoring signs of the charges since we know the directions)

$$F_{31} = k\frac{Q_3 Q_1}{r_{31}^2} = \frac{(9.0 \times 10^9\,\text{N}\cdot\text{m}^2/\text{C}^2)(6.5 \times 10^{-5}\,\text{C})(8.6 \times 10^{-5}\,\text{C})}{(0.60\,\text{m})^2} = 140\,\text{N},$$

$$F_{32} = k\frac{Q_3 Q_2}{r_{32}^2} = \frac{(9.0 \times 10^9\,\text{N}\cdot\text{m}^2/\text{C}^2)(6.5 \times 10^{-5}\,\text{C})(5.0 \times 10^{-5}\,\text{C})}{(0.30\,\text{m})^2} = 330\,\text{N}.$$

We resolve $\vec{F}_{31}$ into its components along the x and y axes, as shown in Fig. 21–18a:

$$F_{31x} = F_{31}\cos 30° = (140\,\text{N})\cos 30° = 120\,\text{N},$$

$$F_{31y} = -F_{31}\sin 30° = -(140\,\text{N})\sin 30° = -70\,\text{N}.$$

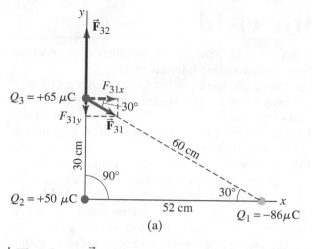

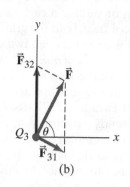

FIGURE 21–18 Determining the forces for Example 21–3. (a) The directions of the individual forces are as shown because $\vec{F}_{32}$ is repulsive (the force on Q_3 is in the direction away from Q_2 because Q_3 and Q_2 are both positive) whereas $\vec{F}_{31}$ is attractive (Q_3 and Q_1 have opposite signs), so $\vec{F}_{31}$ points toward Q_1. (b) Adding $\vec{F}_{32}$ to $\vec{F}_{31}$ to obtain the net force $\vec{F}$.

The force $\vec{F}_{32}$ has only a y component. So the net force $\vec{F}$ on Q_3 has components

$$F_x = F_{31x} = 120\,\text{N},$$
$$F_y = F_{32} + F_{31y} = 330\,\text{N} - 70\,\text{N} = 260\,\text{N}.$$

The magnitude of the net force is

$$F = \sqrt{F_x^2 + F_y^2} = \sqrt{(120\,\text{N})^2 + (260\,\text{N})^2} = 290\,\text{N};$$

and it acts at an angle θ (see Fig. 21–18b) given by

$$\tan\theta = \frac{F_y}{F_x} = \frac{260\,\text{N}}{120\,\text{N}} = 2.2,$$

so $\theta = \tan^{-1}(2.2) = 65°$.

NOTE Because $\vec{F}_{31}$ and $\vec{F}_{32}$ are not along the same line, the magnitude of $\vec{F}_3$ is not equal to the sum (or difference as in Example 21–2) of the separate magnitudes.

| **CONCEPTUAL EXAMPLE 21–4** | **Make the force on Q_3 zero.** In Fig. 21–18, where could you place a fourth charge, $Q_4 = -50\,\mu\text{C}$, so that the net force on Q_3 would be zero?

RESPONSE By the principle of superposition, we need a force in exactly the opposite direction to the resultant $\vec{F}$ due to Q_2 and Q_1 that we calculated in Example 21–3, Fig. 21–18b. Our force must have magnitude 290 N, and must point down and to the left of Q_3 in Fig. 21–18b. So Q_4 must be along this line. See Fig. 21–19.

EXERCISE D (a) Consider two point charges of the same magnitude but opposite sign ($+Q$ and $-Q$), which are fixed a distance d apart. Can you find a location where a third positive charge Q could be placed so that the net electric force on this third charge is zero? (b) What if the first two charges were both $+Q$?

*Vector Form of Coulomb's Law

Coulomb's law can be written in vector form (as we did for Newton's law of universal gravitation in Chapter 6, Section 6–2) as

$$\vec{F}_{12} = k\frac{Q_1 Q_2}{r_{21}^2}\hat{r}_{21},$$

where $\vec{F}_{12}$ is the vector force on charge Q_1 due to Q_2 and $\hat{r}_{21}$ is the unit vector pointing from Q_2 toward Q_1. That is, $\hat{r}_{21}$ points from the "source" charge (Q_2) toward the charge on which we want to know the force (Q_1). See Fig. 21–20. The charges Q_1 and Q_2 can be either positive or negative, and this will affect the direction of the electric force. If Q_1 and Q_2 have the same sign, the product $Q_1 Q_2 > 0$ and the force on Q_1 points away from Q_2—that is, it is repulsive. If Q_1 and Q_2 have opposite signs, $Q_1 Q_2 < 0$ and $\vec{F}_{12}$ points toward Q_2—that is, it is attractive.

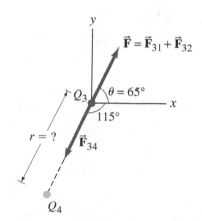

FIGURE 21–19 Example 21–4: Q_4 exerts force ($\vec{F}_{34}$) that makes the net force on Q_3 zero.

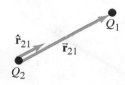

FIGURE 21–20 Determining the force on Q_1 due to Q_2, showing the direction of the unit vector $\hat{r}_{21}$.

21–6 The Electric Field

Many common forces might be referred to as "contact forces," such as your hands pushing or pulling a cart, or a tennis racket hitting a tennis ball.

In contrast, both the gravitational force and the electrical force act over a distance: there is a force between two objects even when the objects are not touching. The idea of a force *acting at a distance* was a difficult one for early thinkers. Newton himself felt uneasy with this idea when he published his law of universal gravitation. A helpful way to look at the situation uses the idea of the **field**, developed by the British scientist Michael Faraday (1791–1867). In the electrical case, according to Faraday, an *electric field* extends outward from every charge and permeates all of space (Fig. 21–21). If a second charge (call it Q_2) is placed near the first charge, it feels a force exerted by the electric field that is there (say, at point P in Fig. 21–21). The electric field at point P is considered to interact directly with charge Q_2 to produce the force on Q_2.

We can in principle investigate the electric field surrounding a charge or group of charges by measuring the force on a small positive **test charge** at rest. By a test charge we mean a charge so small that the force it exerts does not significantly affect the charges that create the field. If a tiny positive test charge q is placed at various locations in the vicinity of a single positive charge Q as shown in Fig. 21–22 (points A, B, C), the force exerted on q is as shown. The force at B is less than at A because B's distance from Q is greater (Coulomb's law); and the force at C is smaller still. In each case, the force on q is directed radially away from Q. The electric field is defined in terms of the force on such a positive test charge. In particular, the **electric field**, $\vec{E}$, at any point in space is defined as the force $\vec{F}$ exerted on a tiny positive test charge placed at that point divided by the magnitude of the test charge q:

$$\vec{E} = \frac{\vec{F}}{q}. \tag{21–3}$$

More precisely, $\vec{E}$ is defined as the limit of $\vec{F}/q$ as q is taken smaller and smaller, approaching zero. That is, q is so tiny that it exerts essentially no force on the other charges which created the field. From this definition (Eq. 21–3), we see that the electric field at any point in space is a vector whose direction is the direction of the force on a tiny positive test charge at that point, and whose magnitude is the *force per unit charge*. Thus $\vec{E}$ has SI units of newtons per coulomb (N/C).

The reason for defining $\vec{E}$ as $\vec{F}/q$ (with $q \to 0$) is so that $\vec{E}$ does not depend on the magnitude of the test charge q. This means that $\vec{E}$ describes only the effect of the charges creating the electric field at that point.

The electric field at any point in space can be measured, based on the definition, Eq. 21–3. For simple situations involving one or several point charges, we can calculate $\vec{E}$. For example, the electric field at a distance r from a single point charge Q would have magnitude

$$E = \frac{F}{q} = \frac{kqQ/r^2}{q}$$

$$E = k\frac{Q}{r^2}; \qquad \text{[single point charge]} \quad \textbf{(21–4a)}$$

or, in terms of ϵ_0 as in Eq. 21–2 $(k = 1/4\pi\epsilon_0)$:

$$E = \frac{1}{4\pi\epsilon_0}\frac{Q}{r^2}. \qquad \text{[single point charge]} \quad \textbf{(21–4b)}$$

Notice that E is independent of the test charge q—that is, E depends only on the charge Q which produces the field, and not on the value of the test charge q. Equations 21–4 are referred to as the electric field form of Coulomb's law.

If we are given the electric field $\vec{E}$ at a given point in space, then we can calculate the force $\vec{F}$ on any charge q placed at that point by writing (see Eq. 21–3):

$$\vec{F} = q\vec{E}. \tag{21–5}$$

This is valid even if q is not small as long as q does not cause the charges creating $\vec{E}$ to move. If q is positive, $\vec{F}$ and $\vec{E}$ point in the same direction. If q is negative, $\vec{F}$ and $\vec{E}$ point in opposite directions. See Fig. 21–23.

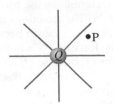

FIGURE 21–21 An electric field surrounds every charge. P is an arbitrary point.

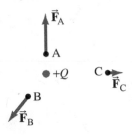

FIGURE 21–22 Force exerted by charge $+Q$ on a small test charge, q, placed at points A, B, and C.

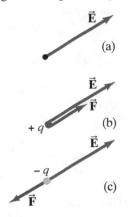

FIGURE 21–23 (a) Electric field at a given point in space. (b) Force on a positive charge at that point. (c) Force on a negative charge at that point.

EXAMPLE 21–5 **Photocopy machine.** A photocopy machine works by arranging positive charges (in the pattern to be copied) on the surface of a drum, then gently sprinkling negatively charged dry toner (ink) particles onto the drum. The toner particles temporarily stick to the pattern on the drum (Fig. 21–24) and are later transferred to paper and "melted" to produce the copy. Suppose each toner particle has a mass of 9.0×10^{-16} kg and carries an average of 20 extra electrons to provide an electric charge. Assuming that the electric force on a toner particle must exceed twice its weight in order to ensure sufficient attraction, compute the required electric field strength near the surface of the drum.

APPROACH The electric force on a toner particle of charge $q = 20e$ is $F = qE$, where E is the needed electric field. This force needs to be at least as great as twice the weight (mg) of the particle.

SOLUTION The minimum value of electric field satisfies the relation

$$qE = 2mg$$

where $q = 20e$. Hence

$$E = \frac{2mg}{q} = \frac{2(9.0 \times 10^{-16}\,\text{kg})(9.8\,\text{m/s}^2)}{20(1.6 \times 10^{-19}\,\text{C})} = 5.5 \times 10^3\,\text{N/C}.$$

EXAMPLE 21–6 **Electric field of a single point charge.** Calculate the magnitude and direction of the electric field at a point P which is 30 cm to the right of a point charge $Q = -3.0 \times 10^{-6}$ C.

APPROACH The magnitude of the electric field due to a single point charge is given by Eq. 21–4. The direction is found using the sign of the charge Q.

SOLUTION The magnitude of the electric field is:

$$E = k\frac{Q}{r^2} = \frac{(9.0 \times 10^9\,\text{N·m}^2/\text{C}^2)(3.0 \times 10^{-6}\,\text{C})}{(0.30\,\text{m})^2} = 3.0 \times 10^5\,\text{N/C}.$$

The direction of the electric field is *toward* the charge Q, to the left as shown in Fig. 21–25a, since we defined the direction as that of the force on a positive test charge which here would be attractive. If Q had been positive, the electric field would have pointed away, as in Fig. 21–25b.

NOTE There is no electric charge at point P. But there is an electric field there. The only real charge is Q.

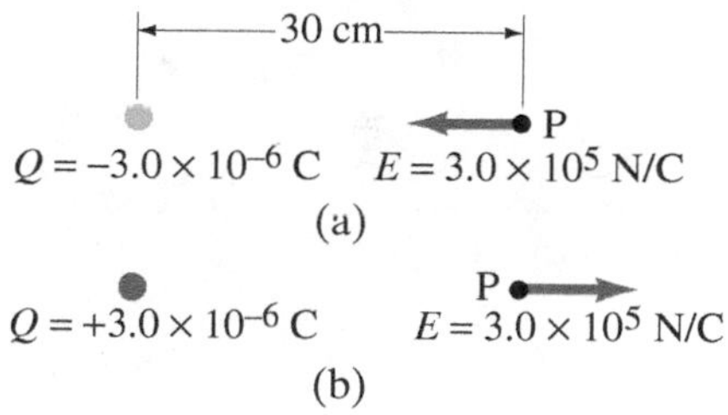

This Example illustrates a general result: The electric field $\vec{E}$ due to a positive charge points away from the charge, whereas $\vec{E}$ due to a negative charge points toward that charge.

EXERCISE E Four charges of equal magnitude, but possibly different sign, are placed on the corners of a square. What arrangement of charges will produce an electric field with the greatest magnitude at the center of the square? (*a*) All four positive charges; (*b*) all four negative charges; (*c*) three positive and one negative; (*d*) two positive and two negative; (*e*) three negative and one positive.

If the electric field at a given point in space is due to more than one charge, the individual fields (call them $\vec{E}_1$, $\vec{E}_2$, etc.) due to each charge are added vectorially to get the total field at that point:

$$\vec{E} = \vec{E}_1 + \vec{E}_2 + \cdots.$$

The validity of this **superposition principle** for electric fields is fully confirmed by experiment.

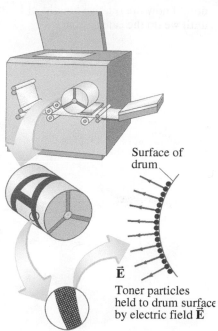

FIGURE 21–24 Example 21–5.

FIGURE 21–25 Example 21–6. Electric field at point P (a) due to a negative charge Q, and (b) due to a positive charge Q, each 30 cm from P.

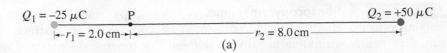

FIGURE 21–26 Example 21–7. In (b), we don't know the relative lengths of $\vec{E}_1$ and $\vec{E}_2$ until we do the calculation.

EXAMPLE 21–7 **E at a point between two charges.** Two point charges are separated by a distance of 10.0 cm. One has a charge of $-25\,\mu C$ and the other $+50\,\mu C$. (a) Determine the direction and magnitude of the electric field at a point P between the two charges that is 2.0 cm from the negative charge (Fig. 21–26a). (b) If an electron (mass $= 9.11 \times 10^{-31}$ kg) is placed at rest at P and then released, what will be its initial acceleration (direction and magnitude)?

APPROACH The electric field at P will be the vector sum of the fields created separately by Q_1 and Q_2. The field due to the negative charge Q_1 points toward Q_1, and the field due to the positive charge Q_2 points away from Q_2. Thus both fields point to the left as shown in Fig. 21–26b and we can add the magnitudes of the two fields together algebraically, ignoring the signs of the charges. In (b) we use Newton's second law $(F = ma)$ to determine the acceleration, where $F = qE$ (Eq. 21–5).

SOLUTION (a) Each field is due to a point charge as given by Eq. 21–4, $E = kQ/r^2$. The total field is

$$E = k\frac{Q_1}{r_1^2} + k\frac{Q_2}{r_2^2} = k\left(\frac{Q_1}{r_1^2} + \frac{Q_2}{r_2^2}\right)$$

$$= (9.0 \times 10^9\,\text{N}\cdot\text{m}^2/\text{C}^2)\left(\frac{25 \times 10^{-6}\,\text{C}}{(2.0 \times 10^{-2}\,\text{m})^2} + \frac{50 \times 10^{-6}\,\text{C}}{(8.0 \times 10^{-2}\,\text{m})^2}\right)$$

$$= 6.3 \times 10^8\,\text{N/C}.$$

(b) The electric field points to the left, so the electron will feel a force to the *right* since it is negatively charged. Therefore the acceleration $a = F/m$ (Newton's second law) will be to the right. The force on a charge q in an electric field E is $F = qE$ (Eq. 21–5). Hence the magnitude of the acceleration is

$$a = \frac{F}{m} = \frac{qE}{m} = \frac{(1.60 \times 10^{-19}\,\text{C})(6.3 \times 10^8\,\text{N/C})}{9.11 \times 10^{-31}\,\text{kg}} = 1.1 \times 10^{20}\,\text{m/s}^2.$$

NOTE By carefully considering the directions of *each* field ($\vec{E}_1$ and $\vec{E}_2$) before doing any calculations, we made sure our calculation could be done simply and correctly.

EXAMPLE 21–8 **$\vec{E}$ above two point charges.** Calculate the total electric field (a) at point A and (b) at point B in Fig. 21–27 due to both charges, Q_1 and Q_2.

APPROACH The calculation is much like that of Example 21–3, except now we are dealing with electric fields instead of force. The electric field at point A is the vector sum of the fields $\vec{E}_{A1}$ due to Q_1, and $\vec{E}_{A2}$ due to Q_2. We find the magnitude of the field produced by each point charge, then we add their components to find the total field at point A. We do the same for point B.

SOLUTION (a) The magnitude of the electric field produced at point A by each of the charges Q_1 and Q_2 is given by $E = kQ/r^2$, so

$$E_{A1} = \frac{(9.0 \times 10^9\,\text{N}\cdot\text{m}^2/\text{C}^2)(50 \times 10^{-6}\,\text{C})}{(0.60\,\text{m})^2} = 1.25 \times 10^6\,\text{N/C},$$

$$E_{A2} = \frac{(9.0 \times 10^9\,\text{N}\cdot\text{m}^2/\text{C}^2)(50 \times 10^{-6}\,\text{C})}{(0.30\,\text{m})^2} = 5.0 \times 10^6\,\text{N/C}.$$

The direction of E_{A1} points from A toward Q_1 (negative charge), whereas E_{A2} points

PROBLEM SOLVING

Ignore signs of charges and determine direction physically, showing directions on diagram

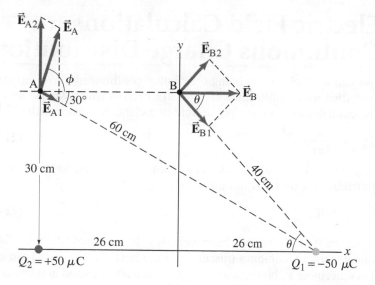

FIGURE 21–27 Calculation of the electric field at points A and B for Example 21–8.

from A away from Q_2, as shown; so the total electric field at A, $\vec{E}_A$, has components
$$E_{Ax} = E_{A1} \cos 30° = 1.1 \times 10^6 \text{ N/C},$$
$$E_{Ay} = E_{A2} - E_{A1} \sin 30° = 4.4 \times 10^6 \text{ N/C}.$$
Thus the magnitude of $\vec{E}_A$ is
$$E_A = \sqrt{(1.1)^2 + (4.4)^2} \times 10^6 \text{ N/C} = 4.5 \times 10^6 \text{ N/C},$$
and its direction is ϕ given by $\tan \phi = E_{Ay}/E_{Ax} = 4.4/1.1 = 4.0$, so $\phi = 76°$.
(b) Because B is equidistant from the two equal charges (40 cm by the Pythagorean theorem), the magnitudes of E_{B1} and E_{B2} are the same; that is,
$$E_{B1} = E_{B2} = \frac{kQ}{r^2} = \frac{(9.0 \times 10^9 \text{ N} \cdot \text{m}^2/\text{C}^2)(50 \times 10^{-6} \text{ C})}{(0.40 \text{ m})^2}$$
$$= 2.8 \times 10^6 \text{ N/C}.$$

Also, because of the symmetry, the y components are equal and opposite, and so cancel out. Hence the total field E_B is horizontal and equals $E_{B1} \cos \theta + E_{B2} \cos \theta = 2E_{B1} \cos \theta$. From the diagram, $\cos \theta = 26 \text{ cm}/40 \text{ cm} = 0.65$. Then
$$E_B = 2E_{B1} \cos \theta = 2(2.8 \times 10^6 \text{ N/C})(0.65)$$
$$= 3.6 \times 10^6 \text{ N/C},$$
and the direction of $\vec{E}_B$ is along the $+x$ direction.
NOTE We could have done part (b) in the same way we did part (a). But symmetry allowed us to solve the problem with less effort.

PROBLEM SOLVING

Use symmetry to save work, when possible

Electrostatics: Electric Forces and Electric Fields

Solving electrostatics problems follows, to a large extent, the general problem-solving procedure discussed in Section 4–8. Whether you use electric field or electrostatic forces, the procedure is similar:

1. **Draw** a careful **diagram**—namely, a free-body diagram for each object, showing all the forces acting on that object, or showing the electric field at a point due to all significant charges present. Determine the **direction** of each force or electric field physically: like charges repel each other, unlike charges attract; fields point away from a + charge, and toward a − charge. Show and label each vector force or field on your diagram.

2. **Apply Coulomb's law** to calculate the magnitude of the force that each contributing charge exerts on a charged object, or the magnitude of the electric field each charge produces at a given point. Deal only with magnitudes of charges (leaving out minus signs), and obtain the magnitude of each force or electric field.

3. **Add vectorially** all the forces on an object, or the contributing fields at a point, to get the resultant. Use **symmetry** (say, in the geometry) whenever possible.

4. **Check** your answer. Is it **reasonable**? If a function of distance, does it give reasonable results in limiting cases?

21–7 Electric Field Calculations for Continuous Charge Distributions

In many cases we can treat charge as being distributed continuously.[†] We can divide up a charge distribution into infinitesimal charges dQ, each of which will act as a tiny point charge. The contribution to the electric field at a distance r from each dQ is

$$dE = \frac{1}{4\pi\epsilon_0}\frac{dQ}{r^2}. \tag{21-6a}$$

Then the electric field, $\vec{E}$, at any point is obtained by summing over all the infinitesimal contributions, which is the integral

$$\vec{E} = \int d\vec{E}. \tag{21-6b}$$

Note that $d\vec{E}$ is a vector (Eq. 21–6a gives its magnitude). [In situations where Eq. 21–6b is difficult to evaluate, other techniques (discussed in the next two Chapters) can often be used instead to determine $\vec{E}$. Numerical integration can also be used in many cases.]

EXAMPLE 21–9 **A ring of charge.** A thin, ring-shaped object of radius a holds a total charge $+Q$ distributed uniformly around it. Determine the electric field at a point P on its axis, a distance x from the center. See Fig. 21–28. Let λ be the charge per unit length (C/m).

APPROACH AND SOLUTION We explicitly follow the steps of the Problem Solving Strategy on page 571.
1. **Draw** a careful **diagram**. The **direction** of the electric field due to one infinitesimal length $d\ell$ of the charged ring is shown in Fig. 21–28.
2. **Apply Coulomb's law.** The electric field, $d\vec{E}$, due to this particular segment of the ring of length $d\ell$ has magnitude

$$dE = \frac{1}{4\pi\epsilon_0}\frac{dQ}{r^2}.$$

The whole ring has length (circumference) of $2\pi a$, so the charge on a length $d\ell$ is

$$dQ = Q\left(\frac{d\ell}{2\pi a}\right) = \lambda\, d\ell$$

where $\lambda = Q/2\pi a$ is the charge per unit length. Now we write dE as

$$dE = \frac{1}{4\pi\epsilon_0}\frac{\lambda\, d\ell}{r^2}.$$

3. **Add vectorially** and use **symmetry**: The vector $d\vec{E}$ has components dE_x along the x axis and $dE_\perp$ perpendicular to the x axis (Fig. 21–28). We are going to sum (integrate) around the entire ring. We note that an equal-length segment diametrically opposite the $d\ell$ shown will produce a $d\vec{E}$ whose component perpendicular to the x axis will just cancel the $dE_\perp$ shown. This is true for all segments of the ring, so by symmetry $\vec{E}$ will have zero y component, and so we need only sum the x components, dE_x. The total field is then

$$E = E_x = \int dE_x = \int dE\cos\theta = \frac{1}{4\pi\epsilon_0}\lambda\int\frac{d\ell}{r^2}\cos\theta.$$

Since $\cos\theta = x/r$, where $r = (x^2 + a^2)^{\frac{1}{2}}$, we have

$$E = \frac{\lambda}{(4\pi\epsilon_0)}\frac{x}{(x^2+a^2)^{\frac{3}{2}}}\int_0^{2\pi a} d\ell = \frac{1}{4\pi\epsilon_0}\frac{\lambda x(2\pi a)}{(x^2+a^2)^{\frac{3}{2}}} = \frac{1}{4\pi\epsilon_0}\frac{Qx}{(x^2+a^2)^{\frac{3}{2}}}.$$

4. To **check reasonableness**, note that at great distances, $x \gg a$, this result reduces to $E = Q/(4\pi\epsilon_0 x^2)$. We would expect this result because at great distances the ring would appear to be a point charge ($1/r^2$ dependence). Also note that our result gives $E = 0$ at $x = 0$, as we might expect because all components will cancel at the center of the circle.

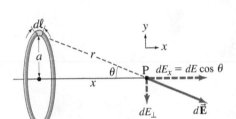

FIGURE 21–28 Example 21–9.

PROBLEM SOLVING

Use symmetry when possible

PROBLEM SOLVING

Check result by noting that at a great distance the ring looks like a point charge

[†]Because we believe there is a minimum charge (e), the treatment here is only for convenience; it is nonetheless useful and accurate since e is usually very much smaller than macroscopic charges.

Note in this Example three important problem-solving techniques that can be used elsewhere: (1) using symmetry to reduce the complexity of the problem; (2) expressing the charge dQ in terms of a charge density (here linear, $\lambda = Q/2\pi a$); and (3) checking the answer at the limit of large r, which serves as an indication (but not proof) of the correctness of the answer—if the result does not check at large r, your result has to be wrong.

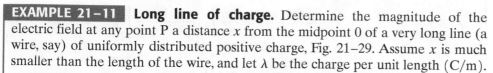

CONCEPTUAL EXAMPLE 21–10 | **Charge at the center of a ring.** Imagine a small positive charge placed at the center of a nonconducting ring carrying a uniformly distributed negative charge. Is the positive charge in equilibrium if it is displaced slightly from the center along the axis of the ring, and if so is it stable? What if the small charge is negative? Neglect gravity, as it is much smaller than the electrostatic forces.

RESPONSE The positive charge is in equilibrium because there is no net force on it, by *symmetry*. If the positive charge moves away from the center of the ring along the axis in either direction, the net force will be back towards the center of the ring and so the charge is in *stable* equilibrium. A negative charge at the center of the ring would feel no net force, but is in *unstable* equilibrium because if it moved along the ring's axis, the net force would be away from the ring and the charge would be pushed farther away.

EXAMPLE 21–11 | **Long line of charge.** Determine the magnitude of the electric field at any point P a distance x from the midpoint 0 of a very long line (a wire, say) of uniformly distributed positive charge, Fig. 21–29. Assume x is much smaller than the length of the wire, and let λ be the charge per unit length (C/m).

APPROACH We set up a coordinate system so the wire is on the y axis with origin 0 as shown. A segment of wire dy has charge $dQ = \lambda \, dy$. The field $d\vec{E}$ at point P due to this length dy of wire (at y) has magnitude

$$dE = \frac{1}{4\pi\epsilon_0} \frac{dQ}{r^2} = \frac{1}{4\pi\epsilon_0} \frac{\lambda \, dy}{(x^2 + y^2)},$$

where $r = (x^2 + y^2)^{\frac{1}{2}}$ as shown in Fig. 21–29. The vector $d\vec{E}$ has components dE_x and dE_y as shown where $dE_x = dE \cos\theta$ and $dE_y = dE \sin\theta$.

SOLUTION Because 0 is at the midpoint of the wire, the y component of $\vec{E}$ will be zero since there will be equal contributions to $E_y = \int dE_y$ from above and below point 0:

$$E_y = \int dE \sin\theta = 0.$$

Thus we have

$$E = E_x = \int dE \cos\theta = \frac{\lambda}{4\pi\epsilon_0} \int \frac{\cos\theta \, dy}{x^2 + y^2}.$$

The integration here is over y, along the wire, with x treated as constant. We must now write θ as a function of y, or y as a function of θ. We do the latter: since $y = x \tan\theta$, then $dy = x \, d\theta/\cos^2\theta$. Furthermore, because $\cos\theta = x/\sqrt{x^2 + y^2}$, then $1/(x^2 + y^2) = \cos^2\theta/x^2$ and our integrand above is $(\cos\theta)(x \, d\theta/\cos^2\theta)(\cos^2\theta/x^2) = \cos\theta \, d\theta/x$. Hence

$$E = \frac{\lambda}{4\pi\epsilon_0} \frac{1}{x} \int_{-\pi/2}^{\pi/2} \cos\theta \, d\theta = \frac{\lambda}{4\pi\epsilon_0 x} (\sin\theta) \Big|_{-\pi/2}^{\pi/2} = \frac{1}{2\pi\epsilon_0} \frac{\lambda}{x},$$

where we have assumed the wire is extremely long in both directions ($y \to \pm\infty$) which corresponds to the limits $\theta = \pm\pi/2$. Thus the field near a long straight wire of uniform charge decreases inversely as the first power of the distance from the wire.

NOTE This result, obtained for an infinite wire, is a good approximation for a wire of finite length as long as x is small compared to the distance of P from the ends of the wire.

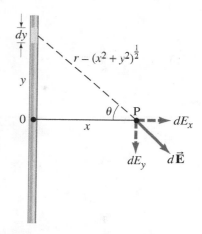

FIGURE 21–29 Example 21–11.

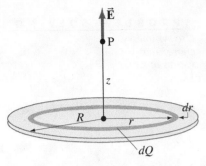

FIGURE 21–30 Example 21–12; a uniformly charged flat disk of radius R.

EXAMPLE 21–12 **Uniformly charged disk.** Charge is distributed uniformly over a thin circular disk of radius R. The charge per unit area (C/m^2) is σ. Calculate the electric field at a point P on the axis of the disk, a distance z above its center, Fig. 21–30.

APPROACH We can think of the disk as a set of concentric rings. We can then apply the result of Example 21–9 to each of these rings, and then sum over all the rings.

SOLUTION For the ring of radius r shown in Fig. 21–30, the electric field has magnitude (see result of Example 21–9)

$$dE = \frac{1}{4\pi\epsilon_0}\frac{z\,dQ}{(z^2 + r^2)^{\frac{3}{2}}}$$

where we have written dE (instead of E) for this thin ring of total charge dQ. The ring has area $(dr)(2\pi r)$ and charge per unit area $\sigma = dQ/(2\pi r\,dr)$. We solve this for dQ ($= \sigma\,2\pi r\,dr$) and insert it in the equation above for dE:

$$dE = \frac{1}{4\pi\epsilon_0}\frac{z\sigma 2\pi r\,dr}{(z^2 + r^2)^{\frac{3}{2}}} = \frac{z\sigma r\,dr}{2\epsilon_0(z^2 + r^2)^{\frac{3}{2}}}.$$

Now we sum over all the rings, starting at $r = 0$ out to the largest with $r = R$:

$$E = \frac{z\sigma}{2\epsilon_0}\int_0^R \frac{r\,dr}{(z^2 + r^2)^{\frac{3}{2}}} = \frac{z\sigma}{2\epsilon_0}\left[-\frac{1}{(z^2 + r^2)^{\frac{1}{2}}}\right]_0^R$$

$$= \frac{\sigma}{2\epsilon_0}\left[1 - \frac{z}{(z^2 + R^2)^{\frac{1}{2}}}\right].$$

This gives the magnitude of $\vec{E}$ at any point z along the axis of the disk. The direction of each $d\vec{E}$ due to each ring is along the z axis (as in Example 21–9), and therefore the direction of $\vec{E}$ is along z. If Q (and σ) are positive, $\vec{E}$ points away from the disk; if Q (and σ) are negative, $\vec{E}$ points toward the disk.

If the radius of the disk in Example 21–12 is much greater than the distance of our point P from the disk (i.e., $z \ll R$) then we can obtain a very useful result: the second term in the solution above becomes very small, so

$$E = \frac{\sigma}{2\epsilon_0}. \qquad\qquad \text{[infinite plane]} \quad \textbf{(21–7)}$$

This result is valid for any point above (or below) an infinite plane of any shape holding a uniform charge density σ. It is also valid for points close to a finite plane, as long as the point is close to the plane compared to the distance to the edges of the plane. Thus the field near a large uniformly charged plane is uniform, and directed outward if the plane is positively charged.

It is interesting to compare here the distance dependence of the electric field due to a point charge $\left(E \sim 1/r^2\right)$, due to a very long uniform line of charge $(E \sim 1/r)$, and due to a very large uniform plane of charge (E does not depend on r).

EXAMPLE 21–13 **Two parallel plates.** Determine the electric field between two large parallel plates or sheets, which are very thin and are separated by a distance d which is small compared to their height and width. One plate carries a uniform surface charge density σ and the other carries a uniform surface charge density $-\sigma$, as shown in Fig. 21–31 (the plates extend upward and downward beyond the part shown).

APPROACH From Eq. 21–7, each plate sets up an electric field of magnitude $\sigma/2\epsilon_0$. The field due to the positive plate points away from that plate whereas the field due to the negative plate points toward that plate.

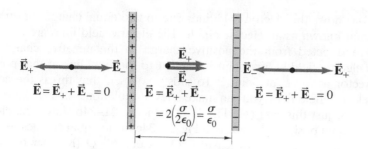

FIGURE 21-31 Example 21-13. (Only the center portion of these large plates is shown: their dimensions are large compared to their separation d.)

SOLUTION In the region between the plates, the fields add together as shown:

$$E = E_+ + E_- = \frac{\sigma}{2\epsilon_0} + \frac{\sigma}{2\epsilon_0} = \frac{\sigma}{\epsilon_0}.$$

The field is uniform, since the plates are very large compared to their separation, so this result is valid for any point, whether near one or the other of the plates, or midway between them as long as the point is far from the ends. Outside the plates, the fields cancel,

$$E = E_+ + E_- = \frac{\sigma}{2\epsilon_0} - \frac{\sigma}{2\epsilon_0} = 0,$$

as shown in Fig. 21-31. These results are valid ideally for infinitely large plates; they are a good approximation for finite plates if the separation is much less than the dimensions of the plate and for points not too close to the edge.

NOTE: These useful and extraordinary results illustrate the principle of superposition and its great power.

21-8 Field Lines

Since the electric field is a vector, it is sometimes referred to as a **vector field**. We could indicate the electric field with arrows at various points in a given situation, such as at A, B, and C in Fig. 21-32. The directions of $\vec{E}_A$, $\vec{E}_B$, and $\vec{E}_C$ are the same as that of the forces shown earlier in Fig. 21-22, but the magnitudes (arrow lengths) are different since we divide $\vec{F}$ in Fig. 21-22 by q to get $\vec{E}$. However, the relative lengths of $\vec{E}_A$, $\vec{E}_B$, and $\vec{E}_C$ are the same as for the forces since we divide by the same q each time. To indicate the electric field in such a way at *many* points, however, would result in many arrows, which might appear complicated or confusing. To avoid this, we use another technique, that of field lines.

To visualize the electric field, we draw a series of lines to indicate the direction of the electric field at various points in space. These **electric field lines** (sometimes called **lines of force**) are drawn so that they indicate the direction of the force due to the given field on a positive test charge. The lines of force due to a single isolated positive charge are shown in Fig. 21-33a, and for a single isolated negative charge in Fig. 21-33b. In part (a) the lines point radially outward from the charge, and in part (b) they point radially inward toward the charge because that is the direction the force would be on a positive test charge in each case (as in Fig. 21-25). Only a few representative lines are shown. We could just as well draw lines in between those shown since the electric field exists there as well. We can draw the lines so that the *number of lines starting on a positive charge, or ending on a negative charge, is proportional to the magnitude of the charge*. Notice that nearer the charge, where the electric field is greater $(F \propto 1/r^2)$, the lines are closer together. This is a general property of electric field lines: *the closer together the lines are, the stronger the electric field in that region*. In fact, field lines can be drawn so that the number of lines crossing unit area perpendicular to $\vec{E}$ is proportional to the magnitude of the electric field.

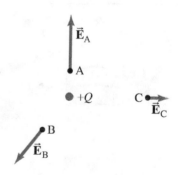

FIGURE 21-32 Electric field vector shown at three points, due to a single point charge Q. (Compare to Fig. 21-22.)

FIGURE 21-33 Electric field lines (a) near a single positive point charge, (b) near a single negative point charge.

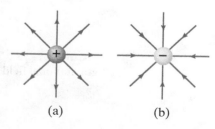

(a)   (b)

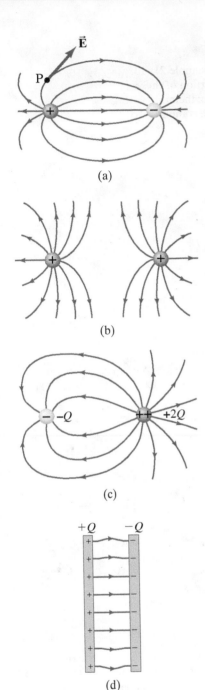

(a)

(b)

$-Q$ $+2Q$

(c)

$+Q$ $-Q$

(d)

FIGURE 21–34 Electric field lines for four arrangements of charges.

Figure 21–34a shows the electric field lines due to two equal charges of opposite sign, a combination known as an **electric dipole**. The electric field lines are curved in this case and are directed from the positive charge to the negative charge. The direction of the electric field at any point is tangent to the field line at that point as shown by the vector arrow $\vec{E}$ at point P. To satisfy yourself that this is the correct pattern for the electric field lines, you can make a few calculations such as those done in Example 21–8 for just this case (see Fig. 21–27). Figure 21–34b shows the electric field lines for two equal positive charges, and Fig. 21–34c for unequal charges, $-Q$ and $+2Q$. Note that twice as many lines leave $+2Q$, as enter $-Q$ (number of lines is proportional to magnitude of Q). Finally, in Fig. 21–34d, we see the field lines between two parallel plates carrying equal but opposite charges. Notice that the electric field lines between the two plates start out perpendicular to the surface of the metal plates (we will see why this is true in the next Section) and go directly from one plate to the other, as we expect because a positive test charge placed between the plates would feel a strong repulsion from the positive plate and a strong attraction to the negative plate. The field lines between two close plates are parallel and equally spaced in the central region, but fringe outward near the edges. Thus, in the central region, the electric field has the same magnitude at all points, and we can write (see Example 21–13)

$$E = \text{constant} = \frac{\sigma}{\epsilon_0}. \quad \begin{bmatrix} \text{between two closely spaced,} \\ \text{oppositely charged, parallel plates} \end{bmatrix} \quad \textbf{(21–8)}$$

The fringing of the field near the edges can often be ignored, particularly if the separation of the plates is small compared to their height and width.

We summarize the properties of field lines as follows:

1. Electric field lines indicate the direction of the electric field; the field points in the direction tangent to the field line at any point.
2. The lines are drawn so that the magnitude of the electric field, E, is proportional to the number of lines crossing unit area perpendicular to the lines. The closer together the lines, the stronger the field.
3. Electric field lines start on positive charges and end on negative charges; and the number starting or ending is proportional to the magnitude of the charge.

Also note that field lines never cross. Why not? Because the electric field can not have two directions at the same point, nor exert more than one force on a test charge.

Gravitational Field

The field concept can also be applied to the gravitational force as mentioned in Chapter 6. Thus we can say that a **gravitational field** exists for every object that has mass. One object attracts another by means of the gravitational field. The Earth, for example, can be said to possess a gravitational field (Fig. 21–35) which is responsible for the gravitational force on objects. The *gravitational field* is defined as the *force per unit mass*. The magnitude of the Earth's gravitational field at any point above the Earth's surface is thus (GM_E/r^2), where M_E is the mass of the Earth, r is the distance of the point from the Earth's center, and G is the gravitational constant (Chapter 6). At the Earth's surface, r is the radius of the Earth and the gravitational field is equal to g, the acceleration due to gravity. Beyond the Earth, the gravitational field can be calculated at any point as a sum of terms due to Earth, Sun, Moon, and other bodies that contribute significantly.

FIGURE 21–35 The Earth's gravitational field.

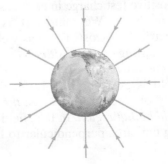

21-9 Electric Fields and Conductors

We now discuss some properties of conductors. First, *the electric field inside a conductor is zero in the static situation*—that is, when the charges are at rest. If there were an electric field within a conductor, there would be a force on the free electrons. The electrons would move until they reached positions where the electric field, and therefore the electric force on them, did become zero.

This reasoning has some interesting consequences. For one, *any net charge on a conductor distributes itself on the surface*. (If there *were* charges inside, there would be an electric field.) For a negatively charged conductor, you can imagine that the negative charges repel one another and race to the surface to get as far from one another as possible. Another consequence is the following. Suppose that a positive charge Q is surrounded by an isolated uncharged metal conductor whose shape is a spherical shell, Fig. 21–36. Because there can be no field within the metal, the lines leaving the central positive charge must end on negative charges on the inner surface of the metal. Thus an equal amount of negative charge, $-Q$, is induced on the inner surface of the spherical shell. Then, since the shell is neutral, a positive charge of the same magnitude, $+Q$, must exist on the outer surface of the shell. Thus, although no field exists in the metal itself, an electric field exists outside of it, as shown in Fig. 21–36, as if the metal were not even there.

A related property of static electric fields and conductors is that *the electric field is always perpendicular to the surface outside of a conductor*. If there were a component of $\vec{E}$ parallel to the surface (Fig. 21–37), it would exert a force on free electrons at the surface, causing the electrons to move along the surface until they reached positions where no net force was exerted on them parallel to the surface—that is, until the electric field was perpendicular to the surface.

These properties apply only to conductors. Inside a nonconductor, which does not have free electrons, a static electric field can exist as we will see in the next Chapter. Also, the electric field outside a nonconductor does not necessarily make an angle of 90° to the surface.

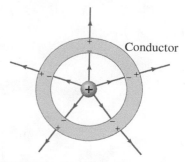

FIGURE 21–36 A charge inside a neutral spherical metal shell induces charge on its surfaces. The electric field exists even beyond the shell, but not within the conductor itself.

FIGURE 21–37 If the electric field $\vec{E}$ at the surface of a conductor had a component parallel to the surface, $\vec{E}_\parallel$, the latter would accelerate electrons into motion. In the static case, $\vec{E}_\parallel$ must be zero, and the electric field must be perpendicular to the conductor's surface: $\vec{E} = \vec{E}_\perp$.

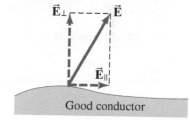

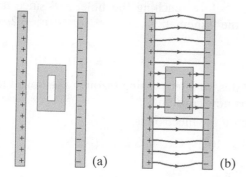

FIGURE 21–38 Example 21–14.

FIGURE 21–39 A strong electric field exists in the vicinity of this "Faraday cage," so strong that stray electrons in the atmosphere are accelerated to the kinetic energy needed to knock electrons out of air atoms, causing an avalanche of charge which flows to (or from) the metal cage. Yet the person inside the cage is not affected.

CONCEPTUAL EXAMPLE 21–14 | **Shielding, and safety in a storm.** A neutral hollow metal box is placed between two parallel charged plates as shown in Fig. 21–38a. What is the field like inside the box?

RESPONSE If our metal box had been solid, and not hollow, free electrons in the box would have redistributed themselves along the surface until all their individual fields would have canceled each other inside the box. The net field inside the box would have been zero. For a hollow box, the external field is not changed since the electrons in the metal can move just as freely as before to the surface. Hence the field inside the hollow metal box is also zero, and the field lines are shown in Fig. 21–38b. A conducting box used in this way is an effective device for shielding delicate instruments and electronic circuits from unwanted external electric fields. We also can see that a relatively safe place to be during a lightning storm is inside a parked car, surrounded by metal. See also Fig. 21–39, where a person inside a porous "cage" is protected from a strong electric discharge.

(Ⓐ) P H Y S I C S   A P P L I E D
Electrical shielding

21–10 Motion of a Charged Particle in an Electric Field

If an object having an electric charge q is at a point in space where the electric field is $\vec{E}$, the force on the object is given by

$$\vec{F} = q\vec{E}$$

(see Eq. 21–5). In the past few Sections we have seen how to determine $\vec{E}$ for some particular situations. Now let us suppose we know $\vec{E}$ and we want to find the force on a charged object and the object's subsequent motion. (We assume no other forces act.)

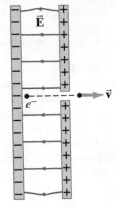

FIGURE 21–40 Example 21–15.

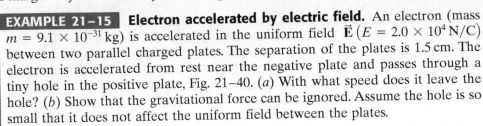

EXAMPLE 21–15 Electron accelerated by electric field. An electron (mass $m = 9.1 \times 10^{-31}$ kg) is accelerated in the uniform field $\vec{E}$ ($E = 2.0 \times 10^4$ N/C) between two parallel charged plates. The separation of the plates is 1.5 cm. The electron is accelerated from rest near the negative plate and passes through a tiny hole in the positive plate, Fig. 21–40. (a) With what speed does it leave the hole? (b) Show that the gravitational force can be ignored. Assume the hole is so small that it does not affect the uniform field between the plates.

APPROACH We can obtain the electron's velocity using the kinematic equations of Chapter 2, after first finding its acceleration from Newton's second law, $F = ma$. The magnitude of the force on the electron is $F = qE$ and is directed to the right.

SOLUTION (a) The magnitude of the electron's acceleration is

$$a = \frac{F}{m} = \frac{qE}{m}.$$

Between the plates $\vec{E}$ is uniform so the electron undergoes uniformly accelerated motion with acceleration

$$a = \frac{(1.6 \times 10^{-19}\,\text{C})(2.0 \times 10^4\,\text{N/C})}{(9.1 \times 10^{-31}\,\text{kg})} = 3.5 \times 10^{15}\,\text{m/s}^2.$$

It travels a distance $x = 1.5 \times 10^{-2}$ m before reaching the hole, and since its initial speed was zero, we can use the kinematic equation, $v^2 = v_0^2 + 2ax$ (Eq. 2–12c), with $v_0 = 0$:

$$v = \sqrt{2ax} = \sqrt{2(3.5 \times 10^{15}\,\text{m/s}^2)(1.5 \times 10^{-2}\,\text{m})} = 1.0 \times 10^7\,\text{m/s}.$$

There is no electric field outside the plates, so after passing through the hole, the electron moves with this speed, which is now constant.

(b) The magnitude of the electric force on the electron is

$$qE = (1.6 \times 10^{-19}\,\text{C})(2.0 \times 10^4\,\text{N/C}) = 3.2 \times 10^{-15}\,\text{N}.$$

The gravitational force is

$$mg = (9.1 \times 10^{-31}\,\text{kg})(9.8\,\text{m/s}^2) = 8.9 \times 10^{-30}\,\text{N},$$

which is 10^{14} times smaller! Note that the electric field due to the electron does not enter the problem (since a particle cannot exert a force on itself).

EXAMPLE 21–16 Electron moving perpendicular to $\vec{E}$. Suppose an electron traveling with speed v_0 enters a uniform electric field $\vec{E}$, which is at right angles to $\vec{v}_0$ as shown in Fig. 21–41. Describe its motion by giving the equation of its path while in the electric field. Ignore gravity.

APPROACH Again we use Newton's second law, with $F = qE$, and the kinematic equations from Chapter 2.

SOLUTION When the electron enters the electric field (at $x = y = 0$) it has velocity $\vec{v}_0 = v_0\hat{i}$ in the x direction. The electric field $\vec{E}$, pointing vertically upward, imparts a uniform vertical acceleration to the electron of

$$a_y = \frac{F}{m} = \frac{qE}{m} = -\frac{eE}{m},$$

where we set $q = -e$ for the electron.

FIGURE 21–41 Example 21–16.

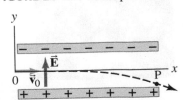

The electron's vertical position is given by Eq. 2–12b,

$$y = \frac{1}{2} a_y t^2 = -\frac{eE}{2m} t^2$$

since the motion is at constant acceleration. The horizontal position is given by

$$x = v_0 t$$

since $a_x = 0$. We eliminate t between these two equations and obtain

$$y = -\frac{eE}{2mv_0^2} x^2,$$

which is the equation of a parabola (just as in projectile motion, Section 3–7).

21–11 Electric Dipoles

The combination of two equal charges of opposite sign, $+Q$ and $-Q$, separated by a distance ℓ, is referred to as an **electric dipole**. The quantity $Q\ell$ is called the **dipole moment** and is represented[†] by the symbol p. The dipole moment can be considered to be a vector $\vec{p}$, of magnitude $Q\ell$, that points from the negative to the positive charge as shown in Fig. 21–42. Many molecules, such as the diatomic molecule CO, have a dipole moment (C has a small positive charge and O a small negative charge of equal magnitude), and are referred to as **polar molecules**. Even though the molecule as a whole is neutral, there is a separation of charge that results from an uneven sharing of electrons by the two atoms.[‡] (Symmetric diatomic molecules, like O_2, have no dipole moment.) The water molecule, with its uneven sharing of electrons (O is negative, the two H are positive), also has a dipole moment—see Fig. 21–43.

Dipole in an External Field

First let us consider a dipole, of dipole moment $p = Q\ell$, that is placed in a uniform electric field $\vec{E}$, as shown in Fig. 21–44. If the field is uniform, the force $Q\vec{E}$ on the positive charge and the force $-Q\vec{E}$ on the negative charge result in no net force on the dipole. There will, however, be a *torque* on the dipole (Fig. 21–44) which has magnitude (calculated about the center, 0, of the dipole)

$$\tau = QE\frac{\ell}{2}\sin\theta + QE\frac{\ell}{2}\sin\theta = pE\sin\theta. \qquad \textbf{(21–9a)}$$

This can be written in vector notation as

$$\vec{\tau} = \vec{p} \times \vec{E}. \qquad \textbf{(21–9b)}$$

The effect of the torque is to try to turn the dipole so $\vec{p}$ is parallel to $\vec{E}$. The work done on the dipole by the electric field to change the angle θ from θ_1 to θ_2 is (see Eq. 10–22)

$$W = \int_{\theta_1}^{\theta_2} \tau \, d\theta.$$

We need to write the torque as $\tau = -pE\sin\theta$ because its direction is opposite to the direction of increasing θ (right-hand rule). Then

$$W = \int_{\theta_1}^{\theta_2} \tau \, d\theta = -pE \int_{\theta_1}^{\theta_2} \sin\theta \, d\theta = pE\cos\theta \Big|_{\theta_1}^{\theta_2} = pE(\cos\theta_2 - \cos\theta_1).$$

Positive work done by the field decreases the potential energy, U, of the dipole in this field. (Recall the relation between work and potential energy, Eq. 8–4, $\Delta U = -W$.) If we choose $U = 0$ when $\vec{p}$ is perpendicular to $\vec{E}$ (that is, choosing $\theta_1 = 90°$ so $\cos\theta_1 = 0$), and setting $\theta_2 = \theta$, then

$$U = -W = -pE\cos\theta = -\vec{p} \cdot \vec{E}. \qquad \textbf{(21–10)}$$

If the electric field is *not* uniform, the force on the $+Q$ of the dipole may not have the same magnitude as on the $-Q$, so there may be a net force as well as a torque.

[†]Be careful not to confuse this p for dipole moment with p for momentum.

[‡]The value of the separated charges may be a fraction of e (say $\pm 0.2e$ or $\pm 0.4e$) but note that such charges do not violate what we said about e being the smallest charge. These charges less than e cannot be isolated and merely represent how much time electrons spend around one atom or the other.

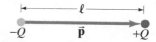

FIGURE 21–42 A dipole consists of equal but opposite charges, $+Q$ and $-Q$, separated by a distance ℓ. The dipole moment is $\vec{p} = Q\vec{\ell}$ and points from the negative to the positive charge.

FIGURE 21–43 In the water molecule (H_2O), the electrons spend more time around the oxygen atom than around the two hydrogen atoms. The net dipole moment $\vec{p}$ can be considered as the vector sum of two dipole moments $\vec{p}_1$ and $\vec{p}_2$ that point from the O toward each H as shown: $\vec{p} = \vec{p}_1 + \vec{p}_2$.

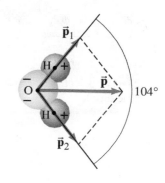

FIGURE 21–44 (below) An electric dipole in a uniform electric field.

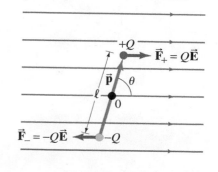

EXAMPLE 21–17 **Dipole in a field.** The dipole moment of a water molecule is 6.1×10^{-30} C·m. A water molecule is placed in a uniform electric field with magnitude 2.0×10^5 N/C. (a) What is the magnitude of the maximum torque that the field can exert on the molecule? (b) What is the potential energy when the torque is at its maximum? (c) In what position will the potential energy take on its greatest value? Why is this different than the position where the torque is maximum?

APPROACH The torque is given by Eq. 21–9 and the potential energy by Eq. 21–10.

SOLUTION (a) From Eq. 21–9 we see that τ is maximized when θ is 90°. Then $\tau = pE = (6.1 \times 10^{-30}\,\text{C·m})(2.0 \times 10^5\,\text{N/C}) = 1.2 \times 10^{-24}\,\text{N·m}$.

(b) The potential energy for $\theta = 90°$ is zero (Eq. 21–10). Note that the potential energy is negative for smaller values of θ, so U is not a minimum for $\theta = 90°$.

(c) The potential energy U will be a maximum when $\cos \theta = -1$ in Eq. 21–10, so $\theta = 180°$, meaning $\vec{\mathbf{E}}$ and $\vec{\mathbf{p}}$ are antiparallel. The potential energy is maximized when the dipole is oriented so that it has to rotate through the largest angle, 180°, to reach the equilibrium position at $\theta = 0°$. The torque on the other hand is maximized when the electric forces are perpendicular to $\vec{\mathbf{p}}$.

Electric Field Produced by a Dipole

We have just seen how an external electric field affects an electric dipole. Now let us suppose that there is no external field, and we want to determine the electric field produced *by* the dipole. For brevity, we restrict ourselves to points that are on the perpendicular bisector of the dipole, such as point P in Fig. 21–45 which is a distance r above the midpoint of the dipole. Note that r in Fig. 21–45 is not the distance from either charge to point P; the latter distance is $(r^2 + \ell^2/4)^{\frac{1}{2}}$ and this is what must be used in Eq. 21–4. The total field at P is

$$\vec{\mathbf{E}} = \vec{\mathbf{E}}_+ + \vec{\mathbf{E}}_-,$$

where $\vec{\mathbf{E}}_+$ and $\vec{\mathbf{E}}_-$ are the fields due to the $+$ and $-$ charges respectively. The magnitudes E_+ and E_- are equal:

$$E_+ = E_- = \frac{1}{4\pi\epsilon_0} \frac{Q}{r^2 + \ell^2/4}.$$

Their y components cancel at point P (*symmetry* again), so the magnitude of the total field $\vec{\mathbf{E}}$ is

$$E = 2E_+ \cos\phi = \frac{1}{2\pi\epsilon_0}\left(\frac{Q}{r^2 + \ell^2/4}\right)\frac{\ell}{2(r^2 + \ell^2/4)^{\frac{1}{2}}}$$

or, setting $Q\ell = p$,

$$E = \frac{1}{4\pi\epsilon_0} \frac{p}{(r^2 + \ell^2/4)^{\frac{3}{2}}}. \qquad \left[\begin{array}{c}\text{on perpendicular bisector}\\\text{of dipole}\end{array}\right] \quad \textbf{(21–11)}$$

Far from the dipole, $r \gg \ell$, this reduces to

$$E = \frac{1}{4\pi\epsilon_0} \frac{p}{r^3}. \qquad \left[\begin{array}{c}\text{on perpendicular bisector}\\\text{of dipole; } r \gg \ell\end{array}\right] \quad \textbf{(21–12)}$$

So the field decreases more rapidly for a dipole than for a single point charge ($1/r^3$ versus $1/r^2$), which we expect since at large distances the two opposite charges appear so close together as to neutralize each other. This $1/r^3$ dependence also applies for points not on the perpendicular bisector (see Problem 67).

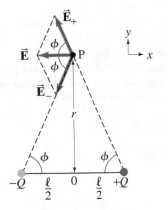

FIGURE 21–45 Electric field due to an electric dipole.

*21–12 Electric Forces in Molecular Biology; DNA

The interior of every biological cell is mainly water. We can imagine a cell as a vast sea of molecules continually in motion (kinetic theory, Chapter 18), colliding with one another with various amounts of kinetic energy. These molecules interact with one another because of *electrostatic attraction* between molecules.

Indeed, cellular processes are now considered to be the result of *random ("thermal") molecular motion plus the ordering effect of the electrostatic force.* As an example, we look at DNA structure and replication. The picture we present has not been seen "in action." Rather, it is a model of what happens based on physical theories and experiment.

The genetic information that is passed on from generation to generation in all living cells is contained in the chromosomes, which are made up of genes. Each gene contains the information needed to produce a particular type of protein molecule, and that information is built into the principal molecule of a chromosome, DNA (deoxyribonucleic acid), Fig. 21–46. DNA molecules are made up of many small molecules known as nucleotide bases which are each polar due to unequal sharing of electrons. There are four types of nucleotide bases in DNA: adenine (A), cytosine (C), guanine (G), and thymine (T).

The DNA of a chromosome generally consists of two long DNA strands wrapped about one another in the shape of a "double helix." The genetic information is contained in the specific order of the four bases (A, C, G, T) along the strand. As shown in Fig. 21–47, the two strands are attracted by electrostatic forces—that is, by the attraction of positive charges to negative charges that exist on parts of the molecules. We see in Fig. 21–47a that an A (adenine) on one strand is always opposite a T on the other strand; similarly, a G is always opposite a C. This important ordering effect occurs because the shapes of A, T, C, and G are such that a T fits closely only into an A, and a G into a C; and only in the case of this close proximity of the charged portions is the electrostatic force great enough to hold them together even for a short time (Fig. 21–47b), forming what are referred to as "weak bonds."

⊛ PHYSICS APPLIED

Inside a cell: kinetic theory plus electrostatic force

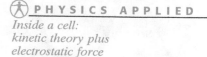

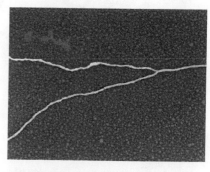

FIGURE 21–46 DNA replicating in a human HeLa cancer cell. This is a false-color image made by a transmission electron microscope (TEM; discussed in Chapter 37).

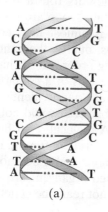

(a)

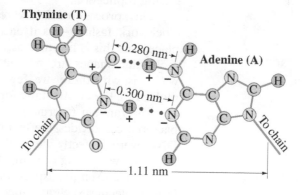

Thymine (T) ⋯⋯ **Adenine (A)**
0.280 nm
0.300 nm
To chain ⋯ To chain
1.11 nm

FIGURE 21–47 (a) Section of a DNA double helix. (b) "Close-up" view of the helix, showing how A and T attract each other and how G and C attract each other through electrostatic forces. The + and − signs represent net charges, usually a fraction of *e*, due to uneven sharing of electrons. The red dots indicate the electrostatic attraction (often called a "weak bond" or "hydrogen bond"—Section 40–3). Note that there are two weak bonds between A and T, and three between C and G.

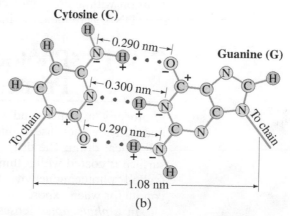

Cytosine (C) ⋯⋯ **Guanine (G)**
0.290 nm
0.300 nm
0.290 nm
To chain ⋯ To chain
1.08 nm

(b)

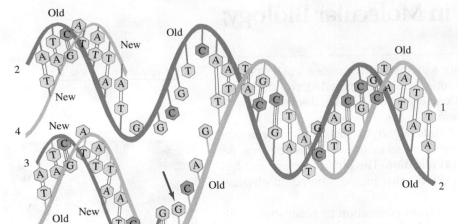

FIGURE 21–48   Replication of DNA.

When the DNA replicates (duplicates) itself just before cell division, the arrangement of A opposite T and G opposite C is crucial for ensuring that the genetic information is passed on accurately to the next generation, Fig. 21–48. The two strands of DNA separate (with the help of enzymes, which also operate via the electrostatic force), leaving the charged parts of the bases exposed. Once replication starts, let us see how the correct order of bases occurs by looking at the G molecule indicated by the red arrow in Fig. 21–48. Many unattached nucleotide bases of all four kinds are bouncing around in the cellular fluid, and the only type that will experience attraction to our G, if it bounces close to it, will be a C. The charges on the other three bases can not get close enough to those on the G to provide a significant attractive force—remember that the force decreases rapidly with distance ($\propto 1/r^2$). Because the G does not attract an A, T, or G appreciably, an A, T, or G will be knocked away by collisions with other molecules before enzymes can attach it to the growing chain (number 3). But the electrostatic force will often hold a C opposite our G long enough so that an enzyme can attach the C to the growing end of the new chain. Thus we see that electrostatic forces are responsible for selecting the bases in the proper order during replication.

This process of DNA replication is often presented as if it occurred in clockwork fashion—as if each molecule knew its role and went to its assigned place. But this is not the case. The forces of attraction are rather weak, and if the molecular shapes are not just right, there is almost no electrostatic attraction, which is why there are few mistakes. Thus, out of the random motion of the molecules, the electrostatic force acts to bring order out of chaos.

The random (thermal) velocities of molecules in a cell affect *cloning*. When a bacterial cell divides, the two new bacteria have nearly identical DNA. Even if the DNA were perfectly identical, the two new bacteria would not end up behaving in the same way. Long protein, DNA, and RNA molecules get bumped into different shapes, and even the expression of genes can thus be different. Loosely held parts of large molecules such as a methyl group (CH_3) can also be knocked off by a strong collision with another molecule. Hence, cloned organisms are not identical, even if their DNA were identical. Indeed, there can not really be genetic determinism.

*21–13   Photocopy Machines and Computer Printers Use Electrostatics

Photocopy machines and laser printers use electrostatic attraction to print an image. They each use a different technique to project an image onto a special cylindrical drum. The drum is typically made of aluminum, a good conductor; its surface is coated with a thin layer of selenium, which has the interesting property (called "photoconductivity") of being an electrical nonconductor in the dark, but a conductor when exposed to light.

In a *photocopier*, lenses and mirrors focus an image of the original sheet of paper onto the drum, much like a camera lens focuses an image on film. Step 1 is

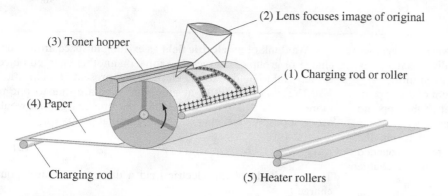

(2) Lens focuses image of original

(3) Toner hopper

(1) Charging rod or roller

(4) Paper

Charging rod

(5) Heater rollers

FIGURE 21–49 Inside a photocopy machine: (1) the selenium drum is given a + charge; (2) the lens focuses image on drum—only dark spots stay charged; (3) toner particles (negatively charged) are attracted to positive areas on drum; (4) the image is transferred to paper; (5) heat binds the image to the paper.

the placing of a uniform positive charge on the drum's selenium layer by a charged rod or roller, done in the dark. In step 2, the image to be copied or printed is projected onto the drum. For simplicity, let us assume the image is a dark letter A on a white background (as on the page of a book) as shown in Fig. 21–49. The letter A on the drum is dark, but all around it is light. At all these light places, the selenium becomes conducting and electrons flow in from the aluminum beneath, neutralizing those positive areas. In the dark areas of the letter A, the selenium is nonconducting and so retains a positive charge, Fig. 21–49. In step 3, a fine dark powder known as *toner* is given a negative charge, and brushed on the drum as it rotates. The negatively charged toner particles are attracted to the positive areas on the drum (the A in our case) and stick only there. In step 4, the rotating drum presses against a piece of paper which has been positively charged more strongly than the selenium, so the toner particles are transferred to the paper, forming the final image. Finally, step 5, the paper is heated to fix the toner particles firmly on the paper.

In a color copier (or printer), this process is repeated for each color—black, cyan (blue), magenta (red), and yellow. Combining these four colors in different proportions produces any desired color.

A *laser printer*, on the other hand, uses a computer output to program the intensity of a laser beam onto the selenium-coated drum. The thin beam of light from the laser is scanned (by a movable mirror) from side to side across the drum in a series of horizontal lines, each line just below the previous line. As the beam sweeps across the drum, the intensity of the beam is varied by the computer output, being strong for a point that is meant to be white or bright, and weak or zero for points that are meant to come out dark. After each sweep, the drum rotates very slightly for additional sweeps, Fig. 21–50, until a complete image is formed on it. The light parts of the selenium become conducting and lose their electric charge, and the toner sticks only to the dark, electrically charged areas. The drum then transfers the image to paper, as in a photocopier.

An *inkjet printer* does not use a drum. Instead nozzles spray tiny droplets of ink directly at the paper. The nozzles are swept across the paper, each sweep just above the previous one as the paper moves down. On each sweep, the ink makes dots on the paper, except for those points where no ink is desired, as directed by the computer. The image consists of a huge number of very tiny dots. The quality or resolution of a printer is usually specified in dots per inch (dpi) in each (linear) direction.

PHYSICS APPLIED
Photocopy machines

PHYSICS APPLIED
Laser printer

PHYSICS APPLIED
Inkjet printer

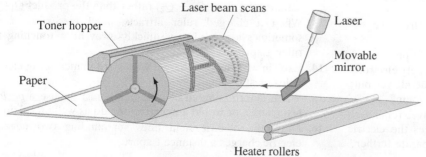

Laser beam scans

Toner hopper

Laser

Paper

Movable mirror

Heater rollers

FIGURE 21–50 Inside a laser printer: A movable mirror sweeps the laser beam in horizontal lines across the drum.

Summary

There are two kinds of **electric charge**, positive and negative. These designations are to be taken algebraically—that is, any charge is plus or minus so many coulombs (C), in SI units.

Electric charge is **conserved**: if a certain amount of one type of charge is produced in a process, an equal amount of the opposite type is also produced; thus the *net* charge produced is zero.

According to atomic theory, electricity originates in the atom, each consisting of a positively charged nucleus surrounded by negatively charged electrons. Each electron has a charge $-e = -1.6 \times 10^{-19}$ C.

Electric **conductors** are those materials in which many electrons are relatively free to move, whereas electric **insulators** are those in which very few electrons are free to move.

An object is negatively charged when it has an excess of electrons, and positively charged when it has less than its normal amount of electrons. The charge on any object is thus a whole number times $+e$ or $-e$. That is, charge is **quantized**.

An object can become charged by rubbing (in which electrons are transferred from one material to another), by conduction (which is transfer of charge from one charged object to another by touching), or by induction (the separation of charge within an object because of the close approach of another charged object but without touching).

Electric charges exert a force on each other. If two charges are of opposite types, one positive and one negative, they each exert an attractive force on the other. If the two charges are the same type, each repels the other.

The magnitude of the force one point charge exerts on another is proportional to the product of their charges, and inversely proportional to the square of the distance between them:

$$F = k\frac{Q_1 Q_2}{r^2} = \frac{1}{4\pi\epsilon_0}\frac{Q_1 Q_2}{r^2}; \qquad \textbf{(21–1, 21–2)}$$

this is **Coulomb's law**. In SI units, k is often written as $1/4\pi\epsilon_0$.

We think of an **electric field** as existing in space around any charge or group of charges. The force on another charged object is then said to be due to the electric field present at its location.

The *electric field*, $\vec{\mathbf{E}}$, at any point in space due to one or more charges, is defined as the force per unit charge that would act on a positive test charge q placed at that point:

$$\vec{\mathbf{E}} = \frac{\vec{\mathbf{F}}}{q}. \qquad \textbf{(21–3)}$$

The magnitude of the electric field a distance r from a point charge Q is

$$E = k\frac{Q}{r^2}. \qquad \textbf{(21–4a)}$$

The total electric field at a point in space is equal to the vector sum of the individual fields due to each contributing charge (**principle of superposition**).

Electric fields are represented by **electric field lines** that start on positive charges and end on negative charges. Their direction indicates the direction the force would be on a tiny positive test charge placed at each point. The lines can be drawn so that the number per unit area is proportional to the magnitude of E.

The static electric field inside a conductor is zero, and the electric field lines just outside a charged conductor are perpendicular to its surface.

An **electric dipole** is a combination of two equal but opposite charges, $+Q$ and $-Q$, separated by a distance ℓ. The **dipole moment** is $p = Q\ell$. A dipole placed in a uniform electric field feels no net force but does feel a net torque (unless $\vec{\mathbf{p}}$ is parallel to $\vec{\mathbf{E}}$). The electric field produced by a dipole decreases as the third power of the distance r from the dipole $(E \propto 1/r^3)$ for r large compared to ℓ.

[*In the replication of DNA, the electrostatic force plays a crucial role in selecting the proper molecules so the genetic information is passed on accurately from generation to generation.]

Questions

1. If you charge a pocket comb by rubbing it with a silk scarf, how can you determine if the comb is positively or negatively charged?

2. Why does a shirt or blouse taken from a clothes dryer sometimes cling to your body?

3. Explain why fog or rain droplets tend to form around ions or electrons in the air.

4. A positively charged rod is brought close to a neutral piece of paper, which it attracts. Draw a diagram showing the separation of charge in the paper, and explain why attraction occurs.

5. Why does a plastic ruler that has been rubbed with a cloth have the ability to pick up small pieces of paper? Why is this difficult to do on a humid day?

6. Contrast the *net charge* on a conductor to the "free charges" in the conductor.

7. Figures 21–7 and 21–8 show how a charged rod placed near an uncharged metal object can attract (or repel) electrons. There are a great many electrons in the metal, yet only some of them move as shown. Why not all of them?

8. When an electroscope is charged, the two leaves repel each other and remain at an angle. What balances the electric force of repulsion so that the leaves don't separate further?

9. The form of Coulomb's law is very similar to that for Newton's law of universal gravitation. What are the differences between these two laws? Compare also gravitational mass and electric charge.

10. We are not normally aware of the gravitational or electric force between two ordinary objects. What is the reason in each case? Give an example where we are aware of each one and why.

11. Is the electric force a conservative force? Why or why not? (See Chapter 8.)

12. What experimental observations mentioned in the text rule out the possibility that the numerator in Coulomb's law contains the sum $(Q_1 + Q_2)$ rather than the product $Q_1 Q_2$?

13. When a charged ruler attracts small pieces of paper, sometimes a piece jumps quickly away after touching the ruler. Explain.

14. Explain why the test charges we use when measuring electric fields must be small.

15. When determining an electric field, must we use a *positive* test charge, or would a negative one do as well? Explain.

16. Draw the electric field lines surrounding two negative electric charges a distance ℓ apart.

17. Assume that the two opposite charges in Fig. 21–34a are 12.0 cm apart. Consider the magnitude of the electric field 2.5 cm from the positive charge. On which side of this charge—top, bottom, left, or right—is the electric field the strongest? The weakest?

18. Consider the electric field at the three points indicated by the letters A, B, and C in Fig. 21–51. First draw an arrow at each point indicating the direction of the net force that a positive test charge would experience if placed at that point, then list the letters in order of *decreasing* field strength (strongest first).

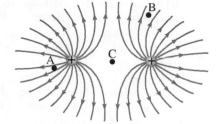

FIGURE 21–51
Question 18.

19. Why can electric field lines never cross?

20. Show, using the three rules for field lines given in Section 21–8, that the electric field lines starting or ending on a single point charge must be symmetrically spaced around the charge.

21. Given two point charges, Q and $2Q$, a distance ℓ apart, is there a point along the straight line that passes through them where $E = 0$ when their signs are (a) opposite, (b) the same? If yes, state roughly where this point will be.

22. Suppose the ring of Fig. 21–28 has a uniformly distributed negative charge Q. What is the magnitude and direction of $\vec{E}$ at point P?

23. Consider a small positive test charge located on an electric field line at some point, such as point P in Fig. 21–34a. Is the direction of the velocity and/or acceleration of the test charge along this line? Discuss.

24. We wish to determine the electric field at a point near a positively charged metal sphere (a good conductor). We do so by bringing a small test charge, q_0, to this point and measure the force F_0 on it. Will F_0/q_0 be greater than, less than, or equal to the electric field $\vec{E}$ as it was at that point before the test charge was present?

25. In what ways does the electron motion in Example 21–16 resemble projectile motion (Section 3–7)? In which ways not?

26. Describe the motion of the dipole shown in Fig. 21–44 if it is released from rest at the position shown.

27. Explain why there can be a net force on an electric dipole placed in a nonuniform electric field.

Problems

21–5 Coulomb's Law

$[1 \text{ mC} = 10^{-3} \text{ C}, \ 1 \mu\text{C} = 10^{-6} \text{ C}, \ 1 \text{ nC} = 10^{-9} \text{ C}.]$

1. (I) What is the magnitude of the electric force of attraction between an iron nucleus $(q = +26e)$ and its innermost electron if the distance between them is 1.5×10^{-12} m?

2. (I) How many electrons make up a charge of $-38.0 \mu\text{C}$?

3. (I) What is the magnitude of the force a $+25 \mu\text{C}$ charge exerts on a $+2.5$ mC charge 28 cm away?

4. (I) What is the repulsive electrical force between two protons 4.0×10^{-15} m apart from each other in an atomic nucleus?

5. (II) When an object such as a plastic comb is charged by rubbing it with a cloth, the net charge is typically a few microcoulombs. If that charge is $3.0 \mu\text{C}$, by what percentage does the mass of a 35-g comb change during charging?

6. (II) Two charged dust particles exert a force of 3.2×10^{-2} N on each other. What will be the force if they are moved so they are only one-eighth as far apart?

7. (II) Two charged spheres are 8.45 cm apart. They are moved, and the force on each of them is found to have been tripled. How far apart are they now?

8. (II) A person scuffing her feet on a wool rug on a dry day accumulates a net charge of $-46 \mu\text{C}$. How many excess electrons does she get, and by how much does her mass increase?

9. (II) What is the total charge of all the electrons in a 15-kg bar of gold? What is the net charge of the bar? (Gold has 79 electrons per atom and an atomic mass of 197 u.)

10. (II) Compare the electric force holding the electron in orbit $(r = 0.53 \times 10^{-10}$ m) around the proton nucleus of the hydrogen atom, with the gravitational force between the same electron and proton. What is the ratio of these two forces?

11. (II) Two positive point charges are a fixed distance apart. The sum of their charges is Q_T. What charge must each have in order to (a) maximize the electric force between them, and (b) minimize it?

12. (II) Particles of charge $+75$, $+48$, and $-85 \mu\text{C}$ are placed in a line (Fig. 21–52). The center one is 0.35 m from each of the others. Calculate the net force on each charge due to the other two.

FIGURE 21–52
Problem 12.

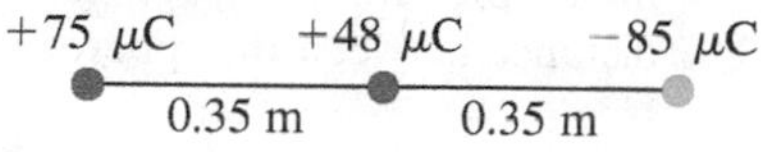

$+75 \mu\text{C}$ $+48 \mu\text{C}$ $-85 \mu\text{C}$

0.35 m   0.35 m

13. (II) Three charged particles are placed at the corners of an equilateral triangle of side 1.20 m (Fig. 21–53). The charges are $+7.0 \mu\text{C}$, $-8.0 \mu\text{C}$, and $-6.0 \mu\text{C}$. Calculate the magnitude and direction of the net force on each due to the other two.

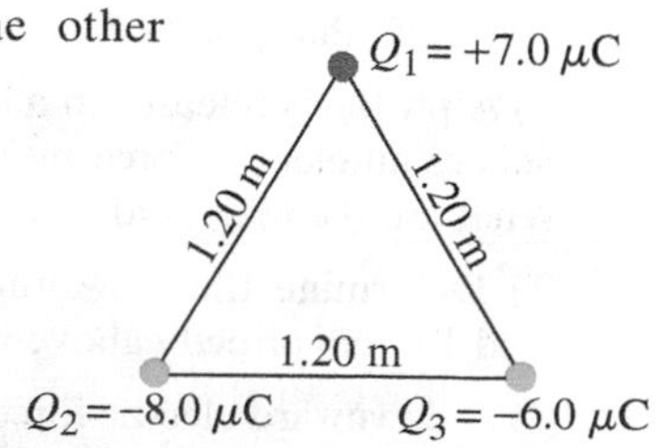

$Q_1 = +7.0 \mu\text{C}$

1.20 m   1.20 m

FIGURE 21–53
Problem 13.

1.20 m

$Q_2 = -8.0 \mu\text{C}$ $Q_3 = -6.0 \mu\text{C}$

14. (II) Two small nonconducting spheres have a total charge of $90.0 \mu\text{C}$. (a) When placed 1.16 m apart, the force each exerts on the other is 12.0 N and is repulsive. What is the charge on each? (b) What if the force were attractive?

15. (II) A charge of 4.15 mC is placed at each corner of a square 0.100 m on a side. Determine the magnitude and direction of the force on each charge.

16. (II) Two negative and two positive point charges (magnitude $Q = 4.15$ mC) are placed on opposite corners of a square as shown in Fig. 21–54. Determine the magnitude and direction of the force on each charge.

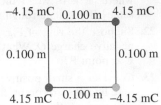

FIGURE 21–54
Problem 16.

17. (II) A charge Q is transferred from an initially uncharged plastic ball to an identical ball 12 cm away. The force of attraction is then 17 mN. How many electrons were transferred from one ball to the other?

18. (III) Two charges, $-Q_0$ and $-4Q_0$, are a distance ℓ apart. These two charges are free to move but do not because there is a third charge nearby. What must be the magnitude of the third charge and its placement in order for the first two to be in equilibrium?

19. (III) Two positive charges $+Q$ are affixed rigidly to the x axis, one at $x = +d$ and the other at $x = -d$. A third charge $+q$ of mass m, which is constrained to move only along the x axis, is displaced from the origin by a small distance $s \ll d$ and then released from rest. (a) Show that (to a good approximation) $+q$ will execute simple harmonic motion and determine an expression for its oscillation period T. (b) If these three charges are each singly ionized sodium atoms $(q = Q = +e)$ at the equilibrium spacing $d = 3 \times 10^{-10}$ m typical of the atomic spacing in a solid, find T in picoseconds.

20. (III) Two small charged spheres hang from cords of equal length ℓ as shown in Fig. 21–55 and make small angles θ_1 and θ_2 with the vertical. (a) If $Q_1 = Q$, $Q_2 = 2Q$, and $m_1 = m_2 = m$, determine the ratio θ_1/θ_2. (b) If $Q_1 = Q$, $Q_2 = 2Q$, $m_1 = m$, and $m_2 = 2m$, determine the ratio θ_1/θ_2. (c) Estimate the distance between the spheres for each case.

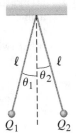

FIGURE 21–55
Problem 20.

21–6 to 21–8 Electric Field, Field Lines

21. (I) What are the magnitude and direction of the electric force on an electron in a uniform electric field of strength 1920 N/C that points due east?

22. (I) A proton is released in a uniform electric field, and it experiences an electric force of 2.18×10^{-14} N toward the south. What are the magnitude and direction of the electric field?

23. (I) Determine the magnitude and direction of the electric field 16.4 cm directly above an isolated 33.0×10^{-6} C charge.

24. (I) A downward electric force of 8.4 N is exerted on a -8.8 μC charge. What are the magnitude and direction of the electric field at the position of this charge?

25. (I) The electric force on a $+4.20$-μC charge is $\vec{F} = (7.22 \times 10^{-4} \text{ N})\hat{j}$. What is the electric field at the position of the charge?

26. (I) What is the electric field at a point when the force on a 1.25-μC charge placed at that point is $\vec{F} = (3.0\hat{i} - 3.9\hat{j}) \times 10^{-3}$ N?

27. (II) Determine the magnitude of the acceleration experienced by an electron in an electric field of 576 N/C. How does the direction of the acceleration depend on the direction of the field at that point?

28. (II) Determine the magnitude and direction of the electric field at a point midway between a -8.0 μC and a $+5.8$ μC charge 8.0 cm apart. Assume no other charges are nearby.

29. (II) Draw, approximately, the electric field lines about two point charges, $+Q$ and $-3Q$, which are a distance ℓ apart.

30. (II) What is the electric field strength at a point in space where a proton experiences an acceleration of 1.8 million "g's"?

31. (II) A long uniformly charged thread (linear charge density $\lambda = 2.5$ C/m) lies along the x axis in Fig. 21–56. A small charged sphere $(Q = -2.0$ C) is at the point $x = 0$ cm, $y = -5.0$ cm. What is the electric field at the point $x = 7.0$ cm, $y = 7.0$ cm? $\vec{E}_{\text{thread}}$ and $\vec{E}_Q$ represent fields due to the long thread and the charge Q, respectively.

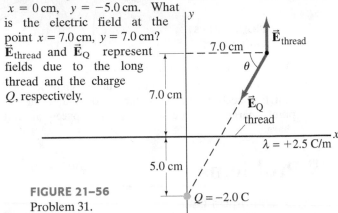

FIGURE 21–56
Problem 31.

32. (II) The electric field midway between two equal but opposite point charges is 586 N/C, and the distance between the charges is 16.0 cm. What is the magnitude of the charge on each?

33. (II) Calculate the electric field at one corner of a square 1.22 m on a side if the other three corners are occupied by 2.25×10^{-6} C charges.

34. (II) Calculate the electric field at the center of a square 52.5 cm on a side if one corner is occupied by a -38.6 μC charge and the other three are occupied by -27.0 μC charges.

35. (II) Determine the direction and magnitude of the electric field at the point P in Fig. 21–57. The charges are separated by a distance $2a$, and point P is a distance x from the midpoint between the two charges. Express your answer in terms of Q, x, a, and k.

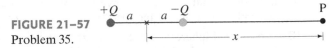

FIGURE 21–57
Problem 35.

36. (II) Two point charges, $Q_1 = -25$ μC and $Q_2 = +45$ μC, are separated by a distance of 12 cm. The electric field at the point P (see Fig. 21–58) is zero. How far from Q_1 is P?

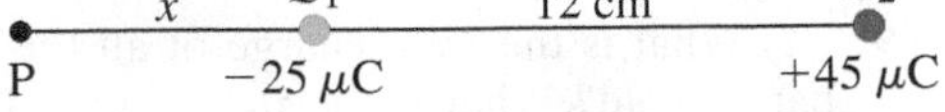

FIGURE 21–58
Problem 36.   P x Q_1 12 cm Q_2
                                  -25 μC $+45$ μC

37. (II) A very thin line of charge lies along the x axis from $x = -\infty$ to $x = +\infty$. Another similar line of charge lies along the y axis from $y = -\infty$ to $y = +\infty$. Both lines have a uniform charge per length λ. Determine the resulting electric field magnitude and direction (relative to the x axis) at a point (x, y) in the first quadrant of the xy plane.

38. (II) (a) Determine the electric field $\vec{E}$ at the origin 0 in Fig. 21–59 due to the two charges at A and B. (b) Repeat, but let the charge at B be reversed in sign.

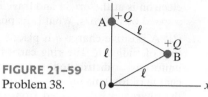

FIGURE 21–59
Problem 38.

39. (II) Draw, approximately, the electric field lines emanating from a uniformly charged straight wire whose length ℓ is not great. The spacing between lines near the wire should be much less than ℓ. [*Hint*: Also consider points very far from the wire.]

40. (II) Two parallel circular rings of radius R have their centers on the x axis separated by a distance ℓ as shown in Fig. 21–60. If each ring carries a uniformly distributed charge Q, find the electric field, $\vec{E}(x)$, at points along the x axis.

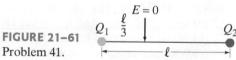

FIGURE 21–60
Problem 40.

41. (II) You are given two unknown point charges, Q_1 and Q_2. At a point on the line joining them, one-third of the way from Q_1 to Q_2, the electric field is zero (Fig. 21–61). What is the ratio Q_1/Q_2?

FIGURE 21–61
Problem 41.

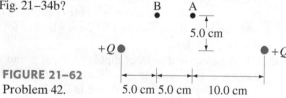

42. (II) Use Coulomb's law to determine the magnitude and direction of the electric field at points A and B in Fig. 21–62 due to the two positive charges $(Q = 5.7\,\mu C)$ shown. Are your results consistent with Fig. 21–34b?

FIGURE 21–62
Problem 42.

43. (II) (a) Two equal charges Q are positioned at points $(x = \ell, y = 0)$ and $(x = -\ell, y = 0)$. Determine the electric field as a function of y for points along the y axis. (b) Show that the field is a maximum at $y = \pm\ell/\sqrt{2}$.

44. (II) At what position, $x = x_M$, is the magnitude of the electric field along the axis of the ring of Example 21–9 a maximum?

45. (II) Estimate the electric field at a point 2.40 cm perpendicular to the midpoint of a uniformly charged 2.00-m-long thin wire carrying a total charge of 4.75 μC.

46. (II) The uniformly charged straight wire in Fig. 21–29 has the length ℓ, where point 0 is at the midpoint. Show that the field at point P, a perpendicular distance x from 0, is given by

$$E = \frac{\lambda}{2\pi\epsilon_0} \frac{\ell}{x(\ell^2 + 4x^2)^{1/2}},$$

where λ is the charge per unit length.

47. (II) Use your result from Problem 46 to find the electric field (magnitude and direction) a distance z above the center of a square loop of wire, each of whose sides has length ℓ and uniform charge per length λ (Fig. 21–63).

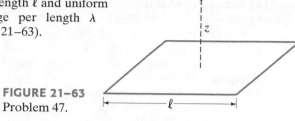

FIGURE 21–63
Problem 47.

48. (II) Determine the direction and magnitude of the electric field at the point P shown in Fig. 21–64. The two charges are separated by a distance of $2a$. Point P is on the perpendicular bisector of the line joining the charges, a distance x from the midpoint between them. Express your answers in terms of Q, x, a, and k.

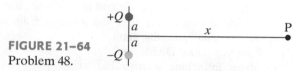

FIGURE 21–64
Problem 48.

49. (III) A thin rod bent into the shape of an arc of a circle of radius R carries a uniform charge per unit length λ. The arc subtends a total angle $2\theta_0$, symmetric about the x axis, as shown in Fig. 21–65. Determine the electric field $\vec{E}$ at the origin 0.

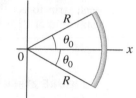

FIGURE 21–65
Problem 49.

50. (III) A thin glass rod is a semicircle of radius R, Fig. 21–66. A charge is nonuniformly distributed along the rod with a linear charge density given by $\lambda = \lambda_0 \sin\theta$, where λ_0 is a positive constant. Point P is at the center of the semicircle. (a) Find the electric field $\vec{E}$ (magnitude and direction) at point P. [*Hint*: Remember $\sin(-\theta) = -\sin\theta$, so the two halves of the rod are oppositely charged.] (b) Determine the acceleration (magnitude and direction) of an electron placed at point P, assuming $R = 1.0$ cm and $\lambda_0 = 1.0\,\mu C/m$.

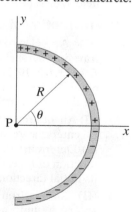

FIGURE 21–66
Problem 50.

51. (III) Suppose a uniformly charged wire starts at point 0 and rises vertically along the positive y axis to a length ℓ. (a) Determine the components of the electric field E_x and E_y at point $(x, 0)$. That is, calculate $\vec{E}$ near one end of a long wire, in the plane perpendicular to the wire. (b) If the wire extends from $y = 0$ to $y = \infty$, so that $\ell = \infty$, show that $\vec{E}$ makes a 45° angle to the horizontal for any x. [*Hint*: See Example 21–11 and Fig. 21–29.]

52. (III) Suppose in Example 21–11 that $x = 0.250\,m$, $Q = 3.15\,\mu C$, and that the uniformly charged wire is only $6.50\,m$ long and extends along the y axis from $y = -4.00\,m$ to $y = +2.50\,m$. (a) Calculate E_x and E_y at point P. (b) Determine what the error would be if you simply used the result of Example 21–11, $E = \lambda/2\pi\epsilon_0 x$. Express this error as $(E_x - E)/E$ and E_y/E.

53. (III) A thin rod of length ℓ carries a total charge Q distributed uniformly along its length. See Fig. 21–67. Determine the electric field along the axis of the rod starting at one end—that is, find $E(x)$ for $x \geq 0$ in Fig. 21–67.

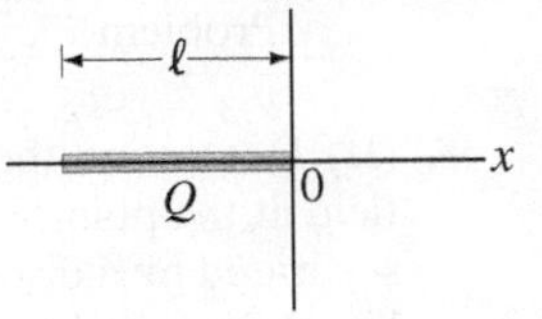

FIGURE 21–67
Problem 53.

54. (III) *Uniform plane of charge.* Charge is distributed uniformly over a large square plane of side ℓ, as shown in Fig. 21–68. The charge per unit area (C/m^2) is σ. Determine the electric field at a point P a distance z above the center of the plane, in the limit $\ell \to \infty$. [*Hint*: Divide the plane into long narrow strips of width dy, and use the result of Example 21–11; then sum the fields due to each strip to get the total field at P.]

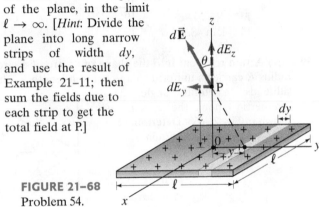

FIGURE 21–68
Problem 54.

55. (III) Suppose the charge Q on the ring of Fig. 21–28 was all distributed uniformly on only the upper half of the ring, and no charge was on the lower half. Determine the electric field $\vec{E}$ at P. (Take y vertically upward.)

21–10 Motion of Charges in an Electric Field

56. (II) An electron with speed $v_0 = 27.5 \times 10^6\,m/s$ is traveling parallel to a uniform electric field of magnitude $E = 11.4 \times 10^3\,N/C$. (a) How far will the electron travel before it stops? (b) How much time will elapse before it returns to its starting point?

57. (II) An electron has an initial velocity $\vec{v}_0 = (8.0 \times 10^4\,m/s)\hat{j}$. It enters a region where $\vec{E} = (2.0\hat{i} + 8.0\hat{j}) \times 10^4\,N/C$. (a) Determine the vector acceleration of the electron as a function of time. (b) At what angle θ is it moving (relative to its initial direction) at $t = 1.0\,ns$?

58. (II) An electron moving to the right at $7.5 \times 10^5\,m/s$ enters a uniform electric field parallel to its direction of motion. If the electron is to be brought to rest in the space of $4.0\,cm$, (a) what direction is required for the electric field, and (b) what is the strength of the field?

59. (II) At what angle will the electrons in Example 21–16 leave the uniform electric field at the end of the parallel plates (point P in Fig. 21–41)? Assume the plates are $4.9\,cm$ long, $E = 5.0 \times 10^3\,N/C$, and $v_0 = 1.00 \times 10^7\,m/s$. Ignore fringing of the field.

60. (II) An electron is traveling through a uniform electric field. The field is constant and given by $\vec{E} = (2.00 \times 10^{-11}\,N/C)\hat{i} - (1.20 \times 10^{-11}\,N/C)\hat{j}$. At $t = 0$, the electron is at the origin and traveling in the x direction with a speed of $1.90\,m/s$. What is its position $2.00\,s$ later?

61. (II) A positive charge q is placed at the center of a circular ring of radius R. The ring carries a uniformly distributed negative charge of total magnitude $-Q$. (a) If the charge q is displaced from the center a small distance x as shown in Fig. 21–69, show that it will undergo simple harmonic motion when released. (b) If its mass is m, what is its period?

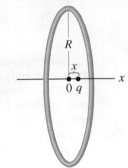

FIGURE 21–69
Problem 61.

21–11 Electric Dipoles

62. (II) A dipole consists of charges $+e$ and $-e$ separated by $0.68\,nm$. It is in an electric field $E = 2.2 \times 10^4\,N/C$. (a) What is the value of the dipole moment? (b) What is the torque on the dipole when it is perpendicular to the field? (c) What is the torque on the dipole when it is at an angle of $45°$ to the field? (d) What is the work required to rotate the dipole from being oriented parallel to the field to being antiparallel to the field?

63. (II) The HCl molecule has a dipole moment of about $3.4 \times 10^{-30}\,C \cdot m$. The two atoms are separated by about $1.0 \times 10^{-10}\,m$. (a) What is the net charge on each atom? (b) Is this equal to an integral multiple of e? If not, explain. (c) What maximum torque would this dipole experience in a $2.5 \times 10^4\,N/C$ electric field? (d) How much energy would be needed to rotate one molecule $45°$ from its equilibrium position of lowest potential energy?

64. (II) Suppose both charges in Fig. 21–45 (for a dipole) were positive. (a) Show that the field on the perpendicular bisector, for $r \gg \ell$, is given by $(1/4\pi\epsilon_0)(2Q/r^2)$. (b) Explain why the field decreases as $1/r^2$ here whereas for a dipole it decreases as $1/r^3$.

65. (II) An electric dipole, of dipole moment p and moment of inertia I, is placed in a uniform electric field $\vec{E}$. (a) If displaced by an angle θ as shown in Fig. 21–44 and released, under what conditions will it oscillate in simple harmonic motion? (b) What will be its frequency?

66. (III) Suppose a dipole $\vec{p}$ is placed in a nonuniform electric field $\vec{E} = E\hat{i}$ that points along the x axis. If $\vec{E}$ depends only on x, show that the net force on the dipole is

$$\vec{F} = \left(\vec{p} \cdot \frac{d\vec{E}}{dx}\right)\hat{i},$$

where $d\vec{E}/dx$ is the gradient of the field in the x direction.

67. (III) (a) Show that at points along the axis of a dipole (along the same line that contains $+Q$ and $-Q$), the electric field has magnitude

$$E = \frac{1}{4\pi\epsilon_0}\frac{2p}{r^3}$$

for $r \gg \ell$ (Fig. 21–45), where r is the distance from a point to the center of the dipole. (b) In what direction does $\vec{E}$ point?

General Problems

68. How close must two electrons be if the electric force between them is equal to the weight of either at the Earth's surface?

69. Given that the human body is mostly made of water, estimate the total amount of positive charge in a 65-kg person.

70. A 3.0-g copper penny has a positive charge of 38 μC. What fraction of its electrons has it lost?

71. Measurements indicate that there is an electric field surrounding the Earth. Its magnitude is about 150 N/C at the Earth's surface and points inward toward the Earth's center. What is the magnitude of the electric charge on the Earth? Is it positive or negative? [*Hint*: The electric field outside a uniformly charged sphere is the same as if all the charge were concentrated at its center.]

72. (*a*) The electric field near the Earth's surface has magnitude of about 150 N/C. What is the acceleration experienced by an electron near the surface of the Earth? (*b*) What about a proton? (*c*) Calculate the ratio of each acceleration to $g = 9.8 \text{ m/s}^2$.

73. A water droplet of radius 0.018 mm remains stationary in the air. If the downward-directed electric field of the Earth is 150 N/C, how many excess electron charges must the water droplet have?

74. Estimate the net force between the CO group and the HN group shown in Fig. 21–70. The C and O have charges $\pm 0.40e$, and the H and N have charges $\pm 0.20e$, where $e = 1.6 \times 10^{-19}$ C. [*Hint*: Do not include the "internal" forces between C and O, or between H and N.]

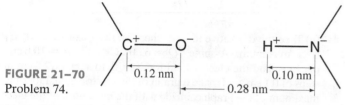

FIGURE 21–70
Problem 74.

75. Suppose that electrical attraction, rather than gravity, were responsible for holding the Moon in orbit around the Earth. If equal and opposite charges Q were placed on the Earth and the Moon, what should be the value of Q to maintain the present orbit? Use data given on the inside front cover of this book. Treat the Earth and Moon as point particles.

76. In a simple model of the hydrogen atom, the electron revolves in a circular orbit around the proton with a speed of 2.2×10^6 m/s. Determine the radius of the electron's orbit. [*Hint*: See Chapter 5 on circular motion.]

77. A positive point charge $Q_1 = 2.5 \times 10^{-5}$ C is fixed at the origin of coordinates, and a negative point charge $Q_2 = -5.0 \times 10^{-6}$ C is fixed to the x axis at $x = +2.0$ m. Find the location of the place(s) along the x axis where the electric field due to these two charges is zero.

78. When clothes are removed from a dryer, a 40-g sock is stuck to a sweater, even with the sock clinging to the sweater's underside. Estimate the minimum attractive force between the sock and the sweater. Then estimate the minimum charge on the sock and the sweater. Assume the charging came entirely from the sock rubbing against the sweater so that they have equal and opposite charges, and approximate the sweater as a flat sheet of uniform charge.

79. A small lead sphere is encased in insulating plastic and suspended vertically from an ideal spring (spring constant $k = 126$ N/m) as in Fig. 21–71. The total mass of the coated sphere is 0.650 kg, and its center lies 15.0 cm above a tabletop when in equilibrium. The sphere is pulled down 5.00 cm below equilibrium, an electric charge $Q = -3.00 \times 10^{-6}$ C is deposited on it, and then it is released. Using what you know about harmonic oscillation, write an expression for the electric field strength as a function of time that would be measured at the point on the tabletop (P) directly below the sphere.

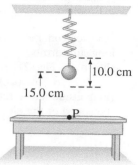

FIGURE 21–71
Problem 79.

80. A large electroscope is made with "leaves" that are 78-cm-long wires with tiny 24-g spheres at the ends. When charged, nearly all the charge resides on the spheres. If the wires each make a 26° angle with the vertical (Fig. 21–72), what total charge Q must have been applied to the electroscope? Ignore the mass of the wires.

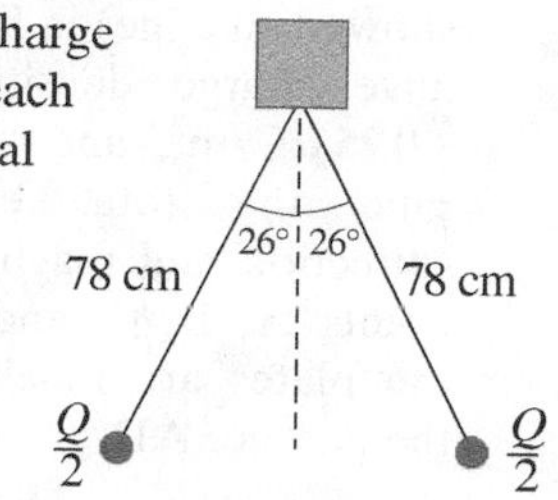

FIGURE 21–72
Problem 80.

81. Dry air will break down and generate a spark if the electric field exceeds about 3×10^6 N/C. How much charge could be packed onto a green pea (diameter 0.75 cm) before the pea spontaneously discharges? [*Hint*: Eqs. 21–4 work outside a sphere if r is measured from its center.]

82. Two point charges, $Q_1 = -6.7 \mu$C and $Q_2 = 1.8 \mu$C, are located between two oppositely charged parallel plates, as shown in Fig. 21–73. The two charges are separated by a distance of $x = 0.34$ m. Assume that the electric field produced by the charged plates is uniform and equal to $E = 73,000$ N/C. Calculate the net electrostatic force on Q_1 and give its direction.

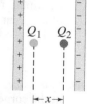

FIGURE 21–73
Problem 82.

83. Packing material made of pieces of foamed polystyrene can easily become charged and stick to each other. Given that the density of this material is about 35 kg/m³, estimate how much charge might be on a 2.0-cm-diameter foamed polystyrene sphere, assuming the electric force between two spheres stuck together is equal to the weight of one sphere.

84. One type of *electric quadrupole* consists of two dipoles placed end to end with their negative charges (say) overlapping; that is, in the center is $-2Q$ flanked (on a line) by a $+Q$ to either side (Fig. 21–74). Determine the electric field $\vec{E}$ at points along the perpendicular bisector and show that E decreases as $1/r^4$. Measure r from the $-2Q$ charge and assume $r \gg \ell$.

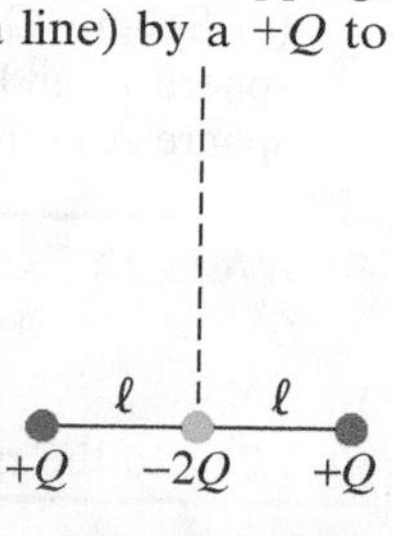

FIGURE 21–74
Problem 84.

85. Suppose electrons enter a uniform electric field midway between two plates at an angle θ_0 to the horizontal, as shown in Fig. 21–75. The path is symmetrical, so they leave at the same angle θ_0 and just barely miss the top plate. What is θ_0? Ignore fringing of the field.

FIGURE 21–75
Problem 85.

|←————6.0 cm————→|
↕1.0 cm
θ_0 $E = 3.8 \times 10^3\,\text{N/C}$ θ_0

86. An electron moves in a circle of radius r around a very long uniformly charged wire in a vacuum chamber, as shown in Fig. 21–76. The charge density on the wire is $\lambda = 0.14\,\mu\text{C/m}$. (a) What is the electric field at the electron (magnitude and direction in terms of r and λ)? (b) What is the speed of the electron?

$\lambda = 0.14\,\mu\text{C/m}$
+++++++++++++++++

FIGURE 21–76
Problem 86.

87. Three very large square planes of charge are arranged as shown (on edge) in Fig. 21–77. From left to right, the planes have charge densities per unit area of $-0.50\,\mu\text{C/m}^2$, $+0.25\,\mu\text{C/m}^2$, and $-0.35\,\mu\text{C/m}^2$. Find the total electric field (direction and magnitude) at the points A, B, C, and D. Assume the plates are much larger than the distance AD.

A B C D

FIGURE 21–77
Problem 87.

88. A point charge ($m = 1.0\,\text{g}$) at the end of an insulating cord of length 55 cm is observed to be in equilibrium in a uniform horizontal electric field of 15,000 N/C, when the pendulum's position is as shown in Fig. 21–78, with the charge 12 cm above the lowest (vertical) position. If the field points to the right in Fig. 21–78, determine the magnitude and sign of the point charge.

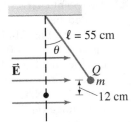

$\ell = 55\,\text{cm}$
θ
$\vec{E}$
Q
m
12 cm

FIGURE 21–78
Problem 88.

89. Four equal positive point charges, each of charge $8.0\,\mu\text{C}$, are at the corners of a square of side 9.2 cm. What charge should be placed at the center of the square so that all charges are at equilibrium? Is this a stable or unstable equilibrium (Section 12–3) in the plane?

90. Two small, identical conducting spheres A and B are a distance R apart; each carries the same charge Q. (a) What is the force sphere B exerts on sphere A? (b) An identical sphere with zero charge, sphere C, makes contact with sphere B and is then moved very far away. What is the net force now acting on sphere A? (c) Sphere C is brought back and now makes contact with sphere A and is then moved far away. What is the force on sphere A in this third case?

91. A point charge of mass 0.210 kg, and net charge $+0.340\,\mu\text{C}$, hangs at rest at the end of an insulating cord above a large sheet of charge. The horizontal sheet of fixed uniform charge creates a uniform vertical electric field in the vicinity of the point charge. The tension in the cord is measured to be 5.18 N. (a) Calculate the magnitude and direction of the electric field due to the sheet of charge (Fig. 21–79). (b) What is the surface charge density $\sigma\,(\text{C/m}^2)$ on the sheet?

↓ $\vec{g}$

$Q = 0.340\,\mu\text{C}$
$m = 0.210\,\text{kg}$

FIGURE 21–79
Problem 91.   Uniform sheet of charge

92. A one-dimensional row of positive ions, each with charge $+Q$ and separated from its neighbors by a distance d, occupies the right-hand half of the x axis. That is, there is a $+Q$ charge at $x = 0$, $x = +d$, $x = +2d$, $x = +3d$, and so on out to ∞. (a) If an electron is placed at the position $x = -d$, determine F, the magnitude of force that this row of charges exerts on the electron. (b) If the electron is instead placed at $x = -3d$, what is the value of F? [Hint: The infinite sum $\sum_{n=1}^{n=\infty} \dfrac{1}{n^2} = \dfrac{\pi^2}{6}$, where n is a positive integer.]

*Numerical/Computer

*93. (III) A thin ring-shaped object of radius a contains a total charge Q uniformly distributed over its length. The electric field at a point on its axis a distance x from its center is given in Example 21–9 as

$$E = \frac{1}{4\pi\epsilon_0} \frac{Qx}{(x^2 + a^2)^{\frac{3}{2}}}.$$

(a) Take the derivative to find where on the x axis ($x > 0$) E_x is a maximum. Assume $Q = 6.00\,\mu\text{C}$ and $a = 10.0\,\text{cm}$. (b) Calculate the electric field for $x = 0$ to $x = +12.0\,\text{cm}$ in steps of 0.1 cm, and make a graph of the electric field. Does the maximum of the graph coincide with the maximum of the electric field you obtained analytically? Also, calculate and graph the electric field (c) due to the ring, and (d) due to a point charge $Q = 6.00\,\mu\text{C}$ at the center of the ring. Make a single graph, from $x = 0$ (or $x = 1.0\,\text{cm}$) out to $x = 50.0\,\text{cm}$ in 1.0 cm steps, with two curves of the electric fields, and show that both fields converge at large distances from the center. (e) At what distance does the electric field of the ring differ from that of the point charge by 10%?

*94. (III) An $8.00\,\mu\text{C}$ charge is on the x axis of a coordinate system at $x = +5.00\,\text{cm}$. A $-2.00\,\mu\text{C}$ charge is at $x = -5.00\,\text{cm}$. (a) Plot the x component of the electric field for points on the x axis from $x = -30.0\,\text{cm}$ to $x = +30.0\,\text{cm}$. The sign of E_x is positive when $\vec{E}$ points to the right and negative when it points to the left. (b) Make a plot of E_x and E_y for points on the y axis from $y = -30.0$ to $+30.0\,\text{cm}$.

Answers to Exercises

A: (e).

B: 5 N.

C: 1.2 N, to the right.

D: (a) No; (b) yes, midway between them.

E: (d), if the two + charges are not at opposite corners (use symmetry).

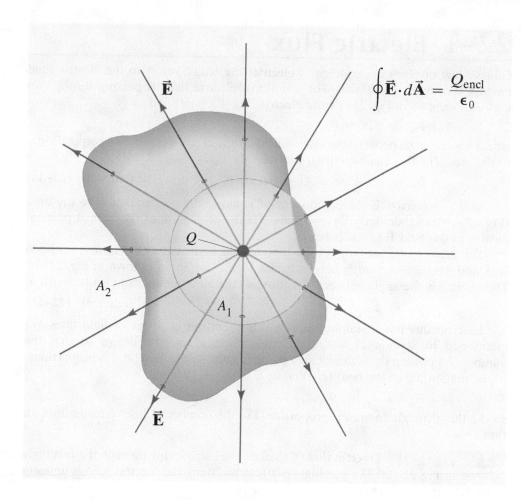

$$\oint \vec{E} \cdot d\vec{A} = \frac{Q_{encl}}{\epsilon_0}$$

Gauss's law is an elegant relation between electric charge and electric field. It is more general than Coulomb's law. Gauss's law involves an integral of the electric field $\vec{E}$ at each point on a closed surface. The surface is only imaginary, and we choose the shape and placement of the surface so that we can evaluate the integral. In this drawing, two different 3-D surfaces are shown (one green, one blue), both enclosing a point charge Q. Gauss's law states that the product $\vec{E} \cdot d\vec{A}$, where $d\vec{A}$ is an infinitesimal area of the surface, integrated over the entire surface, equals the charge enclosed by the surface Q_{encl} divided by ϵ_0. Both surfaces here enclose the same charge Q. Hence $\oint \vec{E} \cdot d\vec{A}$ will give the same result for both surfaces.

Gauss's Law

CHAPTER 22

CHAPTER-OPENING QUESTION—Guess now!

A nonconducting sphere has a uniform charge density throughout. How does the magnitude of the electric field vary inside with distance from the center?

(a) The electric field is zero throughout.
(b) The electric field is constant but nonzero throughout.
(c) The electric field is linearly increasing from the center to the outer edge.
(d) The electric field is exponentially increasing from the center to the outer edge.
(e) The electric field increases quadratically from the center to the outer edge.

The great mathematician Karl Friedrich Gauss (1777–1855) developed an important relation, now known as Gauss's law, which we develop and discuss in this Chapter. It is a statement of the relation between electric charge and electric field and is a more general and elegant form of Coulomb's law.

We can, in principle, determine the electric field due to any given distribution of electric charge using Coulomb's law. The total electric field at any point will be the vector sum (or integral) of contributions from all charges present (see Eq. 21–6). Except for some simple cases, the sum or integral can be quite complicated to evaluate. For situations in which an analytic solution (such as we carried out in the Examples of Sections 21–6 and 21–7) is not possible, a computer can be used.

In some cases, however, the electric field due to a given charge distribution can be calculated more easily or more elegantly using Gauss's law, as we shall see in this Chapter. But the major importance of Gauss's law is that it gives us additional insight into the nature of electrostatic fields, and a more general relationship between charge and field.

Before discussing Gauss's law itself, we first discuss the concept of *flux*.

CONTENTS

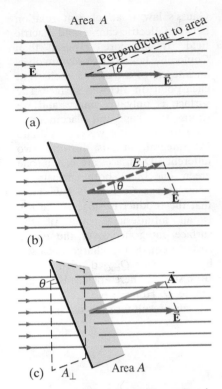

Area A

Perpendicular to area

$\vec{E}$ θ $\vec{E}$

(a)

$E_\perp$ θ $\vec{E}$

(b)

θ $\vec{A}$ $\vec{E}$

(c) $A_\perp$ Area A

FIGURE 22–1 (a) A uniform electric field $\vec{E}$ passing through a flat area A. (b) $E_\perp = E \cos\theta$ is the component of $\vec{E}$ perpendicular to the plane of area A. (c) $A_\perp = A \cos\theta$ is the projection (dashed) of the area A perpendicular to the field $\vec{E}$.

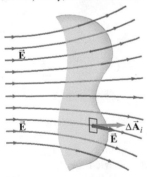

FIGURE 22–2 Electric flux through a curved surface. One small area of the surface, $\Delta\vec{A}_i$, is indicated.

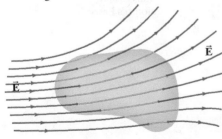

FIGURE 22–3 Electric flux through a closed surface.

22–1 Electric Flux

Gauss's law involves the concept of **electric flux**, which refers to the electric field passing through a given area. For a uniform electric field $\vec{E}$ passing through an area A, as shown in Fig. 22–1a, the electric flux Φ_E is defined as

$$\Phi_E = EA \cos\theta,$$

where θ is the angle between the electric field direction and a line drawn perpendicular to the area. The flux can be written equivalently as

$$\Phi_E = E_\perp A = EA_\perp = EA \cos\theta, \qquad \text{[$\vec{E}$ uniform]} \quad \textbf{(22–1a)}$$

where $E_\perp = E\cos\theta$ is the component of $\vec{E}$ along the perpendicular to the area (Fig. 22–1b) and, similarly, $A_\perp = A\cos\theta$ is the projection of the area A perpendicular to the field $\vec{E}$ (Fig. 22–1c).

The area A of a surface can be represented by a vector $\vec{A}$ whose magnitude is A and whose direction is perpendicular to the surface, as shown in Fig. 22–1c. The angle θ is the angle between $\vec{E}$ and $\vec{A}$, so the electric flux can also be written

$$\Phi_E = \vec{E} \cdot \vec{A}. \qquad \text{[$\vec{E}$ uniform]} \quad \textbf{(22–1b)}$$

Electric flux has a simple intuitive interpretation in terms of field lines. We mentioned in Section 21–8 that field lines can always be drawn so that the number (N) passing through unit area perpendicular to the field ($A_\perp$) is proportional to the magnitude of the field (E): that is, $E \propto N/A_\perp$. Hence,

$$N \propto EA_\perp = \Phi_E,$$

so the flux through an area is proportional to the number of lines passing through that area.

EXAMPLE 22–1 **Electric flux.** Calculate the electric flux through the rectangle shown in Fig. 22–1a. The rectangle is 10 cm by 20 cm, the electric field is uniform at 200 N/C, and the angle θ is 30°.

APPROACH We use the definition of flux, $\Phi_E = \vec{E} \cdot \vec{A} = EA \cos\theta$.

SOLUTION The electric flux is

$$\Phi_E = (200 \, \text{N/C})(0.10 \, \text{m} \times 0.20 \, \text{m}) \cos 30° = 3.5 \, \text{N·m}^2/\text{C}.$$

EXERCISE A Which of the following would cause a change in the electric flux through a circle lying in the xz plane where the electric field is $(10\,\text{N})\hat{\mathbf{j}}$? (a) Changing the magnitude of the electric field. (b) Changing the size of the circle. (c) Tipping the circle so that it is lying in the xy plane. (d) All of the above. (e) None of the above.

In the more general case, when the electric field $\vec{E}$ is not uniform and the surface is not flat, Fig. 22–2, we divide up the chosen surface into n small elements of surface whose areas are $\Delta A_1, \Delta A_2, \cdots, \Delta A_n$. We choose the division so that each ΔA_i is small enough that (1) it can be considered flat, and (2) the electric field varies so little over this small area that it can be considered uniform. Then the electric flux through the entire surface is approximately

$$\Phi_E \approx \sum_{i=1}^{n} \vec{E}_i \cdot \Delta\vec{A}_i,$$

where $\vec{E}_i$ is the field passing through $\Delta\vec{A}_i$. In the limit as we let $\Delta\vec{A}_i \to 0$, the sum becomes an integral over the entire surface and the relation becomes mathematically exact:

$$\Phi_E = \int \vec{E} \cdot d\vec{A}. \qquad \textbf{(22–2)}$$

Gauss's law involves the *total* flux through a *closed* surface—a surface of any shape that completely encloses a volume of space, such as that shown in Fig. 22–3. In this case, the net flux through the enclosing surface is given by

$$\Phi_E = \oint \vec{E} \cdot d\vec{A}, \qquad \textbf{(22–3)}$$

where the integral sign is written $\oint$ to indicate that the integral is over the value of $\vec{E}$ at every point on an enclosing surface.

Up to now we have not been concerned with an ambiguity in the direction of the vector $\vec{A}$ or $d\vec{A}$ that represents a surface. For example, in Fig. 22–1c, the vector $\vec{A}$ could point upward and to the right (as shown) or downward to the left and still be perpendicular to the surface. For a closed surface, we define (arbitrarily) the direction of $\vec{A}$, or of $d\vec{A}$, to point *outward* from the enclosed volume, Fig. 22–4. For an electric field line leaving the enclosed volume (on the right in Fig. 22–4), the angle θ between $\vec{E}$ and $d\vec{A}$ must be less than $\pi/2 (= 90°)$; hence $\cos\theta > 0$. For a line entering the volume (on the left in Fig. 22–4) $\theta > \pi/2$; hence $\cos\theta < 0$. Hence, *flux entering the enclosed volume is negative* $(\int E\cos\theta\, dA < 0)$, whereas *flux leaving the volume is positive*. Consequently, Eq. 22–3 gives the net flux *out of* the volume. If Φ_E is negative, there is a net flux *into* the volume.

In Figs. 22–3 and 22–4, each field line that enters the volume also leaves the volume. Hence $\Phi_E = \oint \vec{E} \cdot d\vec{A} = 0$. There is no net flux into or out of this enclosed surface. The flux, $\oint \vec{E} \cdot d\vec{A}$, will be nonzero only if one or more lines start or end within the surface. Since electric field lines start and stop only on electric charges, the flux will be nonzero only if the surface encloses a net charge. For example, the surface labeled A_1 in Fig. 22–5 encloses a positive charge and there is a net outward flux through this surface $(\Phi_E > 0)$. The surface A_2 encloses an equal magnitude negative charge and there is a net inward flux $(\Phi_E < 0)$. For the configuration shown in Fig. 22–6, the flux through the surface shown is negative (count the lines). The value of Φ_E depends on the charge enclosed by the surface, and this is what Gauss's law is all about.

22–2 Gauss's Law

The precise relation between the electric flux through a closed surface and the net charge Q_{encl} enclosed within that surface is given by **Gauss's law**:

$$\oint \vec{E} \cdot d\vec{A} = \frac{Q_{encl}}{\epsilon_0}, \tag{22–4}$$

where ϵ_0 is the same constant (permittivity of free space) that appears in Coulomb's law. The integral on the left is over the value of $\vec{E}$ on any closed surface, and we choose that surface for our convenience in any given situation. The charge Q_{encl} is the net charge *enclosed* by that surface. It doesn't matter where or how the charge is distributed within the surface. Any charge outside this surface must not be included. A charge outside the chosen surface may affect the position of the electric field lines, but will not affect the net number of lines entering or leaving the surface. For example, Q_{encl} for the gaussian surface A_1 in Fig. 22–5 would be the positive charge enclosed by A_1; the negative charge does contribute to the electric field at A_1 but it is *not* enclosed by surface A_1 and so is not included in Q_{encl}.

Now let us see how Gauss's law is related to Coulomb's law. First, we show that Coulomb's law follows from Gauss's law. In Fig. 22–7 we have a single isolated charge Q. For our "gaussian surface," we choose an imaginary sphere of radius r centered on the charge. Because Gauss's law is supposed to be valid for any surface, we have chosen one that will make our calculation easy. Because of the *symmetry* of this (imaginary) sphere about the charge at its center, we know that $\vec{E}$ must have the same magnitude at any point on the surface, and that $\vec{E}$ points radially outward (inward for a negative charge) parallel to $d\vec{A}$, an element of the surface area. Hence, we write the integral in Gauss's law as

$$\oint \vec{E} \cdot d\vec{A} = \oint E\, dA = E\oint dA = E(4\pi r^2)$$

since the surface area of a sphere of radius r is $4\pi r^2$, and the magnitude of $\vec{E}$ is the same at all points on this spherical surface. Then Gauss's law becomes, with $Q_{encl} = Q$,

$$\frac{Q}{\epsilon_0} = \oint \vec{E} \cdot d\vec{A} = E(4\pi r^2)$$

because $\vec{E}$ and $d\vec{A}$ are both perpendicular to the surface at each point, and $\cos\theta = 1$. Solving for E we obtain

$$E = \frac{Q}{4\pi\epsilon_0 r^2},$$

which is the electric field form of Coulomb's law, Eq. 21–4b.

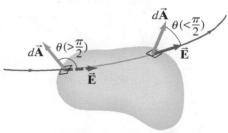

FIGURE 22–4 The direction of an element of area $d\vec{A}$ is taken to point outward from an enclosed surface.

FIGURE 22–5 An electric dipole. Flux through surface A_1 is positive. Flux through A_2 is negative.

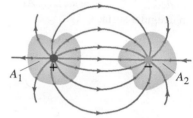

FIGURE 22–6 Net flux through surface A is negative.

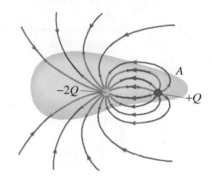

FIGURE 22–7 A single point charge Q at the center of an imaginary sphere of radius r (our "gaussian surface"—that is, the closed surface we choose to use for applying Gauss's law in this case).

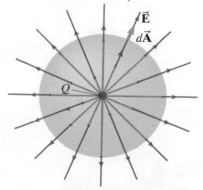

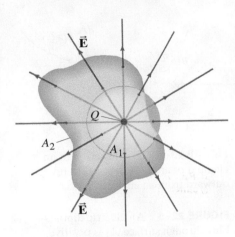

FIGURE 22–8 A single point charge surrounded by a spherical surface, A_1, and an irregular surface, A_2.

Now let us do the reverse, and derive Gauss's law from Coulomb's law for static electric charges[†]. First we consider a single point charge Q surrounded by an imaginary spherical surface as in Fig. 22–7(and shown again, green, in Fig. 22–8). Coulomb's law tells us that the electric field at the spherical surface is $E = (1/4\pi\epsilon_0)(Q/r^2)$. Reversing the argument we just used, we have

$$\oint \vec{E} \cdot d\vec{A} = \oint \frac{1}{4\pi\epsilon_0} \frac{Q}{r^2} dA = \frac{Q}{4\pi\epsilon_0 r^2}(4\pi r^2) = \frac{Q}{\epsilon_0}.$$

This is Gauss's law, with $Q_{encl} = Q$, and we derived it for the special case of a spherical surface enclosing a point charge at its center. But what about some other surface, such as the irregular surface labeled A_2 in Fig. 22–8? The same number of field lines (due to our charge Q) pass through surface A_2, as pass through the spherical surface, A_1. Therefore, because the flux through a surface is proportional to the number of lines through it as we saw in Section 22–1, the flux through A_2 is the same as through A_1:

$$\oint_{A_2} \vec{E} \cdot d\vec{A} = \oint_{A_1} \vec{E} \cdot d\vec{A} = \frac{Q}{\epsilon_0}.$$

Hence, we can expect that

$$\oint \vec{E} \cdot d\vec{A} = \frac{Q}{\epsilon_0}$$

would be valid for *any* surface surrounding a single point charge Q.

Finally, let us look at the case of more than one charge. For each charge, Q_i, enclosed by the chosen surface,

$$\oint \vec{E}_i \cdot d\vec{A} = \frac{Q_i}{\epsilon_0},$$

where $\vec{E}_i$ refers to the electric field produced by Q_i alone. By the superposition principle for electric fields (Section 21–6), the total field $\vec{E}$ is equal to the sum of the fields due to each separate charge, $\vec{E} = \Sigma\vec{E}_i$. Hence

$$\oint \vec{E} \cdot d\vec{A} = \oint (\Sigma\vec{E}_i) \cdot d\vec{A} = \Sigma \frac{Q_i}{\epsilon_0} = \frac{Q_{encl}}{\epsilon_0},$$

where $Q_{encl} = \Sigma Q_i$ is the total net charge enclosed within the surface. Thus we see, based on this simple argument, that Gauss's law follows from Coulomb's law for any distribution of static electric charge enclosed within a closed surface of any shape.

The derivation of Gauss's law from Coulomb's law is valid for electric fields produced by static electric charges. We will see later that electric fields can also be produced by changing magnetic fields. Coulomb's law cannot be used to describe such electric fields. But Gauss's law *is* found to hold also for electric fields produced in any of these ways. Hence *Gauss's law is a more general law than Coulomb's law.* It holds for any electric field whatsoever.

Even for the case of static electric fields that we are considering in this Chapter, it is important to recognize that $\vec{E}$ on the left side of Gauss's law is not necessarily due only to the charge Q_{encl} that appears on the right. For example, in Fig. 22–9 there is an electric field $\vec{E}$ at all points on the imaginary gaussian surface, but it is not due to the charge enclosed by the surface (which is $Q_{encl} = 0$ in this case). The electric field $\vec{E}$ which appears on the left side of Gauss's law is the *total* electric field at each point, on the gaussian surface chosen, not just that due to the charge Q_{encl}, which appears on the right side. Gauss's law has been found to be valid for the total field at any surface. It tells us that any *difference* between the input and output flux of the electric field over any surface is due to charge within that surface.

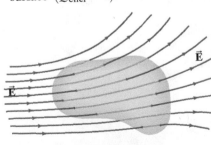

FIGURE 22–9 Electric flux through a closed surface. (Same as Fig. 22–3.) No electric charge is enclosed by this surface ($Q_{encl} = 0$).

[†]Note that Gauss's law would look more complicated in terms of the constant $k = 1/4\pi\epsilon_0$ that we originally used in Coulomb's law (Eqs. 21–1 or 21–4a):

Coulomb's law	Gauss's law
$E = k\dfrac{Q}{r^2}$	$\oint \vec{E} \cdot d\vec{A} = 4\pi kQ$
$E = \dfrac{1}{4\pi\epsilon_0}\dfrac{Q}{r^2}$	$\oint \vec{E} \cdot d\vec{A} = \dfrac{Q}{\epsilon_0}.$

Gauss's law has a simpler form using ϵ_0; Coulomb's law is simpler using k. The normal convention is to use ϵ_0 rather than k because Gauss's law is considered more general and therefore it is preferable to have it in simpler form.

CONCEPTUAL EXAMPLE 22–2 | **Flux from Gauss's law.** Consider the two gaussian surfaces, A_1 and A_2, shown in Fig. 22–10. The only charge present is the charge Q at the center of surface A_1. What is the net flux through each surface, A_1 and A_2?

RESPONSE The surface A_1 encloses the charge $+Q$. By Gauss's law, the net flux through A_1 is then Q/ϵ_0. For surface A_2, the charge $+Q$ is outside the surface. Surface A_2 encloses zero net charge, so the net electric flux through A_2 is zero, by Gauss's law. Note that all field lines that enter the volume enclosed by surface A_2 also leave it.

EXERCISE B A point charge Q is at the center of a spherical gaussian surface A. When a second charge Q is placed just outside A, the total flux through this spherical surface A is (a) unchanged, (b) doubled, (c) halved, (d) none of these.

EXERCISE C Three $2.95\ \mu C$ charges are in a small box. What is the net flux leaving the box? (a) $3.3 \times 10^{12}\ \text{N} \cdot \text{m}^2/\text{C}$, (b) $3.3 \times 10^5\ \text{N} \cdot \text{m}^2/\text{C}$, (c) $1.0 \times 10^{12}\ \text{N} \cdot \text{m}^2/\text{C}$, (d) $1.0 \times 10^6\ \text{N} \cdot \text{m}^2/\text{C}$, (e) $6.7 \times 10^6\ \text{N} \cdot \text{m}^2/\text{C}$.

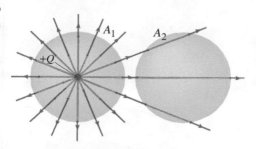

FIGURE 22–10 Example 22–2. Two gaussian surfaces.

We note that the integral in Gauss's law is often rather difficult to carry out in practice. We rarely need to do it except for some fairly simple situations that we now discuss.

22–3 Applications of Gauss's Law

Gauss's law is a very compact and elegant way to write the relation between electric charge and electric field. It also offers a simple way to determine the electric field when the charge distribution is simple and/or possesses a high degree of *symmetry*. In order to apply Gauss's law, however, we must choose the "gaussian" surface very carefully (for the integral on the left side of Gauss's law) so we can determine $\vec{E}$. We normally try to think of a surface that has just the symmetry needed so that E will be constant on all or on parts of its surface. Sometimes we choose a surface so the flux through part of the surface is zero.

EXAMPLE 22–3 **Spherical conductor.** A thin spherical shell of radius r_0 possesses a total net charge Q that is uniformly distributed on it (Fig. 22–11). Determine the electric field at points (a) outside the shell, and (b) inside the shell. (c) What if the conductor were a solid sphere?

APPROACH Because the charge is distributed symmetrically, the electric field must also be *symmetric*. Thus the field outside the sphere must be directed radially outward (inward if $Q < 0$) and must depend only on r, not on angle (spherical coordinates).

SOLUTION (a) The electric field will have the same magnitude at all points on an imaginary gaussian surface, if we choose that surface as a sphere of radius r $(r > r_0)$ concentric with the shell, and shown in Fig. 22–11 as the dashed circle A_1. Because $\vec{E}$ is perpendicular to this surface, the cosine of the angle between $\vec{E}$ and $d\vec{A}$ is always 1. Gauss's law then gives (with $Q_{encl} = Q$ in Eq. 22–4)

$$\oint \vec{E} \cdot d\vec{A} = E(4\pi r^2) = \frac{Q}{\epsilon_0},$$

where $4\pi r^2$ is the surface area of our sphere (gaussian surface) of radius r. Thus

$$E = \frac{1}{4\pi\epsilon_0}\frac{Q}{r^2}. \qquad [r > r_0]$$

Thus the field outside a uniformly charged spherical shell is the same as if all the charge were concentrated at the center as a point charge.

(b) Inside the shell, the electric field must also be symmetric. So E must again have the same value at all points on a spherical gaussian surface (A_2 in Fig. 22–11) concentric with the shell. Thus E can be factored out of the integral and, with $Q_{encl} = 0$ because the charge enclosed within the sphere A_2 is zero, we have

$$\oint \vec{E} \cdot d\vec{A} = E(4\pi r^2) = 0.$$

Hence

$$E = 0 \qquad [r < r_0]$$

inside a uniform spherical shell of charge.

(c) These same results also apply to a uniformly charged solid spherical conductor, since all the charge would lie in a thin layer at the surface.

FIGURE 22–11 Cross-sectional drawing of a thin spherical shell of radius r_0, carrying a net charge Q uniformly distributed. A_1 and A_2 represent two gaussian surfaces we use to determine $\vec{E}$. Example 22–3.

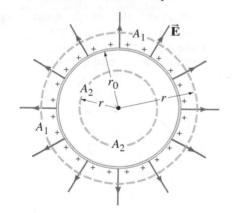

EXAMPLE 22–4 **Solid sphere of charge.** An electric charge Q is distributed uniformly throughout a nonconducting sphere of radius r_0, Fig. 22–12. Determine the electric field (*a*) outside the sphere ($r > r_0$) and (*b*) inside the sphere ($r < r_0$).

APPROACH Since the charge is distributed symmetrically in the sphere, the electric field at all points must again be *symmetric*. $\vec{E}$ depends only on r and is directed radially outward (or inward if $Q < 0$).

SOLUTION (*a*) For our gaussian surface we choose a sphere of radius r ($r > r_0$), labeled A_1 in Fig. 22–12. Since E depends only on r, Gauss's law gives, with $Q_{encl} = Q$,

$$\oint \vec{E} \cdot d\vec{A} = E(4\pi r^2) = \frac{Q}{\epsilon_0}$$

or

$$E = \frac{1}{4\pi\epsilon_0} \frac{Q}{r^2}.$$

Again, the field outside a spherically symmetric distribution of charge is the same as that for a point charge of the same magnitude located at the center of the sphere.

(*b*) Inside the sphere, we choose for our gaussian surface a concentric sphere of radius r ($r < r_0$), labeled A_2 in Fig. 22–12. From symmetry, the magnitude of $\vec{E}$ is the same at all points on A_2, and $\vec{E}$ is perpendicular to the surface, so

$$\oint \vec{E} \cdot d\vec{A} = E(4\pi r^2).$$

We must equate this to Q_{encl}/ϵ_0 where Q_{encl} is the charge enclosed by A_2. Q_{encl} is not the total charge Q but only a portion of it. We define the **charge density**, ρ_E, as the charge per unit volume ($\rho_E = dQ/dV$), and here we are given that $\rho_E = $ constant. So the charge enclosed by the gaussian surface A_2, a sphere of radius r, is

$$Q_{encl} = \left(\frac{\frac{4}{3}\pi r^3 \rho_E}{\frac{4}{3}\pi r_0^3 \rho_E} \right) Q = \frac{r^3}{r_0^3} Q.$$

Hence, from Gauss's law,

$$E(4\pi r^2) = \frac{Q_{encl}}{\epsilon_0} = \frac{r^3}{r_0^3} \frac{Q}{\epsilon_0}$$

or

$$E = \frac{1}{4\pi\epsilon_0} \frac{Q}{r_0^3} r. \qquad\qquad [r < r_0]$$

Thus the field increases linearly with r, until $r = r_0$. It then decreases as $1/r^2$, as plotted in Fig. 22–13.

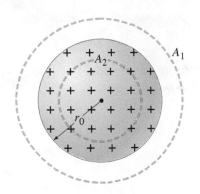

FIGURE 22–12 A solid sphere of uniform charge density. Example 22–4.

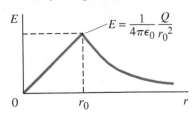

FIGURE 22–13 Magnitude of the electric field as a function of the distance r from the center of a uniformly charged solid sphere.

The results in Example 22–4 would have been difficult to obtain from Coulomb's law by integrating over the sphere. Using Gauss's law and the *symmetry* of the situation, this result is obtained rather easily, and shows the great power of Gauss's law. However, its use in this way is limited mainly to cases where the charge distribution has a high degree of symmetry. In such cases, we *choose* a simple surface on which $E = $ constant, so the integration is simple. Gauss's law holds, of course, for any surface.

EXAMPLE 22–5 **Nonuniformly charged solid sphere.** Suppose the charge density of the solid sphere in Fig. 22–12, Example 22–4, is given by $\rho_E = \alpha r^2$, where α is a constant. (a) Find α in terms of the total charge Q on the sphere and its radius r_0. (b) Find the electric field as a function of r inside the sphere.

APPROACH We divide the sphere up into concentric thin shells of thickness dr as shown in Fig. 22–14, and integrate (a) setting $Q = \int \rho_E \, dV$ and (b) using Gauss's law.

SOLUTION (a) A thin shell of radius r and thickness dr (Fig. 22–14) has volume $dV = 4\pi r^2 \, dr$. The total charge is given by

$$Q = \int \rho_E \, dV = \int_0^{r_0} (\alpha r^2)(4\pi r^2 \, dr) = 4\pi \alpha \int_0^{r_0} r^4 \, dr = \frac{4\pi \alpha}{5} r_0^5.$$

Thus $\alpha = 5Q/4\pi r_0^5$.

(b) To find E inside the sphere at distance r from its center, we apply Gauss's law to an imaginary sphere of radius r which will enclose a charge

$$Q_{\text{encl}} = \int_0^r \rho_E \, dV = \int_0^r (\alpha r^2) \, 4\pi r^2 \, dr = \int_0^r \left(\frac{5Q}{4\pi r_0^5} r^2 \right) 4\pi r^2 \, dr = Q \frac{r^5}{r_0^5}.$$

By *symmetry*, E will be the same at all points on the surface of a sphere of radius r, so Gauss's law gives

$$\oint \vec{E} \cdot d\vec{A} = \frac{Q_{\text{encl}}}{\epsilon_0}$$

$$(E)(4\pi r^2) = Q \frac{r^5}{\epsilon_0 r_0^5},$$

so

$$E = \frac{Qr^3}{4\pi \epsilon_0 r_0^5}.$$

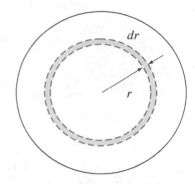

FIGURE 22–14 Example 22–5.

EXAMPLE 22–6 **Long uniform line of charge.** A very long straight wire possesses a uniform positive charge per unit length, λ. Calculate the electric field at points near (but outside) the wire, far from the ends.

APPROACH Because of the *symmetry*, we expect the field to be directed radially outward and to depend only on the perpendicular distance, R, from the wire. Because of the cylindrical symmetry, the field will be the same at all points on a gaussian surface that is a cylinder with the wire along its axis, Fig. 22–15. $\vec{E}$ is perpendicular to this surface at all points. For Gauss's law, we need a closed surface, so we include the flat ends of the cylinder. Since $\vec{E}$ is parallel to the ends, there is no flux through the ends (the cosine of the angle between $\vec{E}$ and $d\vec{A}$ on the ends is $\cos 90° = 0$).

SOLUTION For our chosen gaussian surface Gauss's law gives

$$\oint \vec{E} \cdot d\vec{A} = E(2\pi R \ell) = \frac{Q_{\text{encl}}}{\epsilon_0} = \frac{\lambda \ell}{\epsilon_0},$$

where ℓ is the length of our chosen gaussian surface ($\ell \ll$ length of wire), and $2\pi R$ is its circumference. Hence

$$E = \frac{1}{2\pi \epsilon_0} \frac{\lambda}{R}.$$

NOTE This is the same result we found in Example 21–11 using Coulomb's law (we used x there instead of R), but here it took much less effort. Again we see the great power of Gauss's law.[†]

NOTE Recall from Chapter 10, Fig. 10–2, that we use R for the distance of a particle from an axis (cylindrical symmetry), but lower case r for the distance from a point (usually the origin 0).

FIGURE 22–15 Calculation of $\vec{E}$ due to a very long line of charge. Example 22–6.

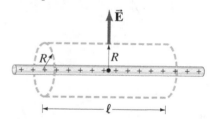

[†]But note that the method of Example 21–11 allows calculation of E also for a short line of charge by using the appropriate limits for the integral, whereas Gauss's law is not readily adapted due to lack of symmetry.

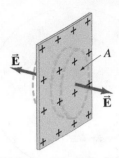

FIGURE 22–16 Calculation of the electric field outside a large uniformly charged nonconducting plane surface. Example 22–7.

EXAMPLE 22–7 **Infinite plane of charge.** Charge is distributed uniformly, with a surface charge density σ (σ = charge per unit area = dQ/dA), over a very large but very thin nonconducting flat plane surface. Determine the electric field at points near the plane.

APPROACH We choose as our gaussian surface a small closed cylinder whose axis is perpendicular to the plane and which extends through the plane as shown in Fig. 22–16. Because of the symmetry, we expect $\vec{E}$ to be directed perpendicular to the plane on both sides as shown, and to be uniform over the end caps of the cylinder, each of whose area is A.

SOLUTION Since no flux passes through the curved sides of our chosen cylindrical surface, all the flux is through the two end caps. So Gauss's law gives

$$\oint \vec{E} \cdot d\vec{A} = 2EA = \frac{Q_{encl}}{\epsilon_0} = \frac{\sigma A}{\epsilon_0},$$

where $Q_{encl} = \sigma A$ is the charge enclosed by our gaussian cylinder. The electric field is then

$$E = \frac{\sigma}{2\epsilon_0}.$$

NOTE This is the same result we obtained much more laboriously in Chapter 21, Eq. 21–7. The field is uniform for points far from the ends of the plane, and close to its surface.

EXAMPLE 22–8 **Electric field near any conducting surface.** Show that the electric field just outside the surface of any good conductor of arbitrary shape is given by

$$E = \frac{\sigma}{\epsilon_0},$$

where σ is the surface charge density on the conductor's surface at that point.

APPROACH We choose as our gaussian surface a small cylindrical box, as we did in the previous Example. We choose the cylinder to be very small in height, so that one of its circular ends is just above the conductor (Fig. 22–17). The other end is just below the conductor's surface, and the sides are perpendicular to it.

SOLUTION The electric field is zero inside a conductor and is perpendicular to the surface just outside it (Section 21–9), so electric flux passes only through the outside end of our cylindrical box; no flux passes through the short sides or inside end. We choose the area A (of the flat cylinder end) small enough so that E is essentially uniform over it. Then Gauss's law gives

$$\oint \vec{E} \cdot d\vec{A} = EA = \frac{Q_{encl}}{\epsilon_0} = \frac{\sigma A}{\epsilon_0},$$

so that

$$E = \frac{\sigma}{\epsilon_0}. \qquad\qquad \text{[at surface of conductor]} \quad \textbf{(22–5)}$$

NOTE This useful result applies for a conductor of any shape.

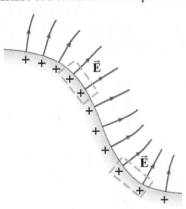

FIGURE 22–17 Electric field near surface of a conductor. Example 22–8.

⚠ **CAUTION**

When is $E = \sigma/\epsilon_0$ and when is $E = \sigma/2\epsilon_0$

Why is it that the field outside a large plane nonconductor is $E = \sigma/2\epsilon_0$ (Example 22–7) whereas outside a conductor it is $E = \sigma/\epsilon_0$ (Example 22–8)? The reason for the factor of 2 comes not from conductor verses nonconductor. It comes instead from how we define charge per unit area σ. For a thin flat nonconductor, Fig. 22–16, the charge may be distributed throughout the volume (not only on the surface, as for a conductor). The charge per unit area σ represents all the charge throughout the thickness of the thin nonconductor. Also our gaussian surface has its ends outside the nonconductor on each side, so as to include all this charge.

For a conductor, on the other hand, the charge accumulates on the outer surfaces only. For a thin flat conductor, as shown in Fig. 22–18, the charge accumulates on both surfaces, and using the same small gaussian surface we did in Fig. 22–17, with one end inside and the other end outside the conductor, we came up with the result, $E = \sigma/\epsilon_0$. If we defined σ for a conductor, as we did for a nonconductor, σ would represent the charge per area for the entire conductor. Then Fig. 22–18 would show $\sigma/2$ as the surface charge on each surface, and Gauss's law would give $\int \vec{E} \cdot d\vec{A} = EA = (\sigma/2)A/\epsilon_0 = \sigma A/2\epsilon_0$ so $E = \sigma/2\epsilon_0$, just as for a nonconductor. We need to be careful about how we define charge per unit area σ.

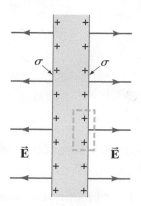

FIGURE 22–18 Thin flat charged conductor with surface charge density σ at each surface. For the conductor as a whole, the charge density is $\sigma' = 2\sigma$.

We saw in Section 21–9 that in the static situation, the electric field inside any conductor must be zero even if it has a net charge. (Otherwise, the free charges in the conductor would move—until the net force on each, and hence $\vec{E}$, were zero.) We also mentioned there that any net electric charge on a conductor must all reside on its outer surface. This is readily shown using Gauss's law. Consider any charged conductor of any shape, such as that shown in Fig. 22–19, which carries a net charge Q. We choose the gaussian surface, shown dashed in the diagram, so that it all lies just below the surface of the conductor and encloses essentially the whole volume of the conductor. Our gaussian surface can be arbitrarily close to the surface, but still *inside* the conductor. The electric field is zero at all points on this gaussian surface since it is inside the conductor. Hence, from Gauss's law, Eq. 22–4, the net charge within the surface must be zero. Thus, there can be no net charge within the conductor. Any net charge must lie on the surface of the conductor.

FIGURE 22–19 An insulated charged conductor of arbitrary shape, showing a gaussian surface (dashed) just below the surface of the conductor.

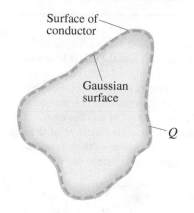

If there is an empty cavity inside a conductor, can charge accumulate on that (inner) surface too? As shown in Fig. 22–20, if we imagine a gaussian surface (shown dashed) just inside the conductor above the cavity, we know that $\vec{E}$ must be zero everywhere on this surface since it is inside the conductor. Hence, by Gauss's law, *there can be no net charge at the surface of the cavity.*

But what if the cavity is not empty and there is a charge inside it?

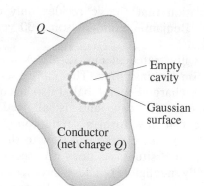

FIGURE 22–20 An empty cavity inside a charged conductor carries zero net charge.

FIGURE 22–21 Example 22–9.

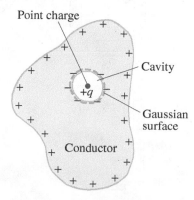

CONCEPTUAL EXAMPLE 22–9 **Conductor with charge inside a cavity.**
Suppose a conductor carries a net charge $+Q$ and contains a cavity, inside of which resides a point charge $+q$. What can you say about the charges on the inner and outer surfaces of the conductor?

RESPONSE As shown in Fig. 22–21, a gaussian surface just inside the conductor surrounding the cavity must contain zero net charge ($E = 0$ in a conductor). Thus a net charge of $-q$ must exist on the cavity surface. The conductor itself carries a net charge $+Q$, so its outer surface must carry a charge equal to $Q + q$. These results apply to a cavity of any shape.

PROBLEM SOLVING

Gauss's Law for Symmetric Charge Distributions

1. First identify the **symmetry** of the charge distribution: spherical, cylindrical, planar. This identification should suggest a gaussian surface for which $\vec{E}$ will be constant and/or zero on all or on parts of the surface: a sphere for spherical symmetry, a cylinder for cylindrical symmetry and a small cylinder or "pillbox" for planar symmetry.

2. Draw the appropriate gaussian surface making sure it passes through the point where you want to know the electric field.

3. Use the symmetry of the charge distribution to determine the direction of $\vec{E}$ at points on the gaussian surface.

4. Evaluate the flux, $\oint \vec{E} \cdot d\vec{A}$. With an appropriate gaussian surface, the dot product $\vec{E} \cdot d\vec{A}$ should be zero or equal to $\pm E\,dA$, with the magnitude of E being constant over all or parts of the surface.

5. Calculate the charge *enclosed* by the gaussian surface. Remember it's the enclosed charge that matters. Ignore all the charge outside the gaussian surface.

6. Equate the flux to the enclosed charge and solve for E.

FIGURE 22–22 (a) A charged conductor (metal ball) is lowered into an insulated metal can (a good conductor) carrying zero net charge. (b) The charged ball is touched to the can and all of its charge quickly flows to the outer surface of the can. (c) When the ball is then removed, it is found to carry zero net charge.

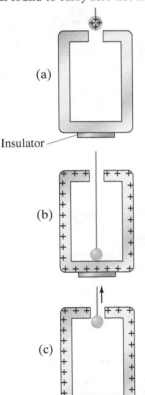

(a)

Insulator

(b)

(c)

*22–4 Experimental Basis of Gauss's and Coulomb's Laws

Gauss's law predicts that any net charge on a conductor must lie only on its surface. But is this true in real life? Let us see how it can be verified experimentally. And in confirming this prediction of Gauss's law, Coulomb's law is also confirmed since the latter follows from Gauss's law, as we saw in Section 22–2. Indeed, the earliest observation that charge resides only on the outside of a conductor was recorded by Benjamin Franklin some 30 years before Coulomb stated his law.

A simple experiment is illustrated in Fig. 22–22. A metal can with a small opening at the top rests on an insulator. The can, a conductor, is initially uncharged (Fig. 22–22a). A charged metal ball (also a conductor) is lowered by an insulating thread into the can, and is allowed to touch the can (Fig. 22–22b). The ball and can now form a single conductor. Gauss's law, as discussed above, predicts that all the charge will flow to the outer surface of the can. (The flow of charge in such situations does not occur instantaneously, but the time involved is usually negligible). These predictions are confirmed in experiments by (1) connecting an electroscope to the can, which will show that the can is charged, and (2) connecting an electroscope to the ball after it has been withdrawn from the can (Fig. 22–22c), which will show that the ball carries zero charge.

The precision with which Coulomb's and Gauss's laws hold can be stated quantitatively by writing Coulomb's law as

$$F = k\frac{Q_1 Q_2}{r^{2+\delta}}.$$

For a perfect inverse-square law, $\delta = 0$. The most recent and precise experiments (1971) give $\delta = (2.7 \pm 3.1) \times 10^{-16}$. Thus Coulomb's and Gauss's laws are found to be valid to an extremely high precision!

Summary

The **electric flux** passing through a flat area A for a uniform electric field $\vec{E}$ is

$$\Phi_E = \vec{E} \cdot \vec{A}. \tag{22–1b}$$

If the field is not uniform, the flux is determined from the integral

$$\Phi_E = \int \vec{E} \cdot d\vec{A}. \tag{22–2}$$

The direction of the vector $\vec{A}$ or $d\vec{A}$ is chosen to be perpendicular to the surface whose area is A or dA, and points outward from an enclosed surface. The flux through a surface is proportional to the number of field lines passing through it.

Gauss's law states that the net flux passing through any closed surface is equal to the net charge Q_{encl} enclosed by the surface divided by ϵ_0:

$$\oint \vec{E} \cdot d\vec{A} = \frac{Q_{encl}}{\epsilon_0}. \tag{22–4}$$

Gauss's law can in principle be used to determine the electric field due to a given charge distribution, but its usefulness is mainly limited to a small number of cases, usually where the charge distribution displays much symmetry. The real importance of Gauss's law is that it is a more general and elegant statement (than Coulomb's law) for the relation between electric charge and electric field. It is one of the basic equations of electromagnetism.

Questions

1. If the electric flux through a closed surface is zero, is the electric field necessarily zero at all points on the surface? Explain. What about the converse: If $\vec{E} = 0$ at all points on the surface is the flux through the surface zero?
2. Is the electric field $\vec{E}$ in Gauss's law, $\oint \vec{E} \cdot d\vec{A} = Q_{encl}/\epsilon_0$, created only by the charge Q_{encl}?
3. A point charge is surrounded by a spherical gaussian surface of radius r. If the sphere is replaced by a cube of side r, will Φ_E be larger, smaller, or the same? Explain.
4. What can you say about the flux through a closed surface that encloses an electric dipole?
5. The electric field $\vec{E}$ is zero at all points on a closed surface; is there necessarily no net charge within the surface? If a surface encloses zero net charge, is the electric field necessarily zero at all points on the surface?
6. Define gravitational flux in analogy to electric flux. Are there "sources" and "sinks" for the gravitational field as there are for the electric field? Discuss.
7. Would Gauss's law be helpful in determining the electric field due to an electric dipole?
8. A spherical basketball (a nonconductor) is given a charge Q distributed uniformly over its surface. What can you say about the electric field inside the ball? A person now steps on the ball, collapsing it, and forcing most of the air out without altering the charge. What can you say about the field inside now?
9. In Example 22–6, it may seem that the electric field calculated is due only to the charge on the wire that is enclosed by the cylinder chosen as our gaussian surface. In fact, the entire charge along the whole length of the wire contributes to the field. Explain how the charge outside the cylindrical gaussian surface of Fig. 22–15 contributes to E at the gaussian surface. [*Hint*: Compare to what the field would be due to a short wire.]

10. Suppose the line of charge in Example 22–6 extended only a short way beyond the ends of the cylinder shown in Fig. 22–15. How would the result of Example 22–6 be altered?
11. A point charge Q is surrounded by a spherical surface of radius r_0, whose center is at C. Later, the charge is moved to the right a distance $\frac{1}{2}r_0$, but the sphere remains where it was, Fig. 22–23. How is the electric flux Φ_E through the sphere changed? Is the electric field at the surface of the sphere changed? For each "yes" answer, describe the change.

FIGURE 22–23
Question 11.

12. A solid conductor carries a net positive charge Q. There is a hollow cavity within the conductor, at whose center is a negative point charge $-q$ (Fig. 22–24). What is the charge on (a) the outer surface of the conductor and (b) the inner surface of the conductor's cavity?

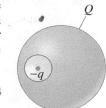

FIGURE 22–24
Question 12.

13. A point charge q is placed at the center of the cavity of a thin metal shell which is neutral. Will a charge Q placed outside the shell feel an electric force? Explain.
14. A small charged ball is inserted into a balloon. The balloon is then blown up slowly. Describe how the flux through the balloon's surface changes as the balloon is blown up. Consider both the total flux and the flux per unit surface area of the balloon.

Problems

22–1 Electric Flux

1. (I) A uniform electric field of magnitude 5.8×10^2 N/C passes through a circle of radius 13 cm. What is the electric flux through the circle when its face is (a) perpendicular to the field lines, (b) at 45° to the field lines, and (c) parallel to the field lines?

2. (I) The Earth possesses an electric field of (average) magnitude 150 N/C near its surface. The field points radially inward. Calculate the net electric flux outward through a spherical surface surrounding, and just beyond, the Earth's surface.

3. (II) A cube of side ℓ is placed in a uniform field E_0 with edges parallel to the field lines. (a) What is the net flux through the cube? (b) What is the flux through each of its six faces?

4. (II) A uniform field $\vec{E}$ is parallel to the axis of a hollow hemisphere of radius r, Fig. 22–25. (a) What is the electric flux through the hemispherical surface? (b) What is the result if $\vec{E}$ is instead perpendicular to the axis?

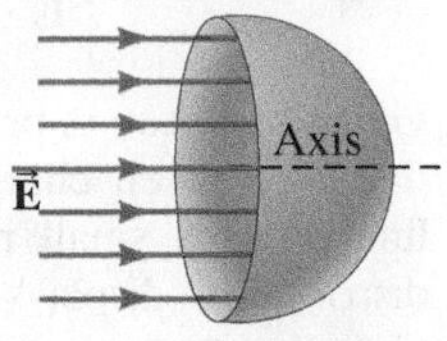

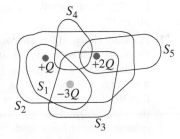

FIGURE 22–25
Problem 4.

22–2 Gauss's Law

5. (I) The total electric flux from a cubical box 28.0 cm on a side is 1.84×10^3 N·m²/C. What charge is enclosed by the box?

6. (I) Figure 22–26 shows five closed surfaces that surround various charges in a plane, as indicated. Determine the electric flux through each surface, S_1, S_2, S_3, S_4, and S_5. The surfaces are flat "pillbox" surfaces that extend only slightly above and below the plane in which the charges lie.

FIGURE 22–26
Problem 6.

7. (II) In Fig. 22–27, two objects, O_1 and O_2, have charges $+1.0\,\mu C$ and $-2.0\,\mu C$ respectively, and a third object, O_3, is electrically neutral. (a) What is the electric flux through the surface A_1 that encloses all the three objects? (b) What is the electric flux through the surface A_2 that encloses the third object only?

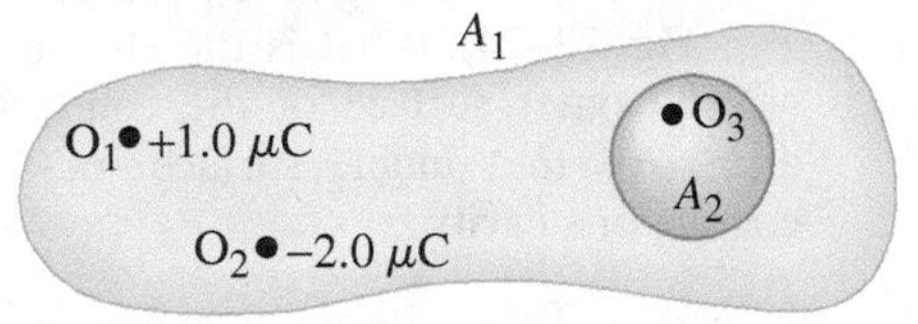

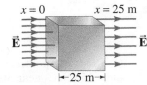

FIGURE 22–27
Problem 7.

8. (II) A ring of charge with uniform charge density is completely enclosed in a hollow donut shape. An exact copy of the ring is completely enclosed in a hollow sphere. What is the ratio of the flux out of the donut shape to that out of the sphere?

9. (II) In a certain region of space, the electric field is constant in direction (say horizontal, in the x direction), but its magnitude decreases from $E = 560$ N/C at $x = 0$ to $E = 410$ N/C at $x = 25$ m. Determine the charge within a cubical box of side $\ell = 25$ m, where the box is oriented so that four of its sides are parallel to the field lines (Fig. 22–28).

FIGURE 22–28
Problem 9.

10. (II) A point charge Q is placed at the center of a cube of side ℓ. What is the flux through one face of the cube?

11. (II) A 15.0-cm-long uniformly charged plastic rod is sealed inside a plastic bag. The total electric flux leaving the bag is 7.3×10^5 N·m²/C. What is the linear charge density on the rod?

22–3 Applications of Gauss's Law

12. (I) Draw the electric field lines around a negatively charged metal egg.

13. (I) The field just outside a 3.50-cm-radius metal ball is 6.25×10^2 N/C and points toward the ball. What charge resides on the ball?

14. (I) Starting from the result of Example 22–3, show that the electric field just outside a uniformly charged spherical conductor is $E = \sigma/\epsilon_0$, consistent with Example 22–8.

15. (I) A long thin wire, hundreds of meters long, carries a uniformly distributed charge of $-7.2\,\mu C$ per meter of length. Estimate the magnitude and direction of the electric field at points (a) 5.0 m and (b) 1.5 m perpendicular from the center of the wire.

16. (I) A metal globe has 1.50 mC of charge put on it at the north pole. Then -3.00 mC of charge is applied to the south pole. Draw the field lines for this system after it has come to equilibrium.

17. (II) A nonconducting sphere is made of two layers. The innermost section has a radius of 6.0 cm and a uniform charge density of -5.0 C/m³. The outer layer has a uniform charge density of $+8.0$ C/m³ and extends from an inner radius of 6.0 cm to an outer radius of 12.0 cm. Determine the electric field for (a) $0 < r < 6.0$ cm, (b) 6.0 cm $< r <$ 12.0 cm, and (c) 12.0 cm $< r <$ 50.0 cm. (d) Plot the magnitude of the electric field for $0 < r < 50.0$ cm. Is the field continuous at the edges of the layers?

18. (II) A solid metal sphere of radius 3.00 m carries a total charge of $-5.50\,\mu C$. What is the magnitude of the electric field at a distance from the sphere's center of (a) 0.250 m, (b) 2.90 m, (c) 3.10 m, and (d) 8.00 m? How would the answers differ if the sphere were (e) a thin shell, or (f) a solid nonconductor uniformly charged throughout?

19. (II) A 15.0-cm-diameter nonconducting sphere carries a total charge of 2.25 μC distributed uniformly throughout its volume. Graph the electric field E as a function of the distance r from the center of the sphere from $r = 0$ to $r = 30.0$ cm.

20. (II) A flat square sheet of thin aluminum foil, 25 cm on a side, carries a uniformly distributed 275 nC charge. What, approximately, is the electric field (a) 1.0 cm above the center of the sheet and (b) 15 m above the center of the sheet?

21. (II) A spherical cavity of radius 4.50 cm is at the center of a metal sphere of radius 18.0 cm. A point charge $Q = 5.50\,\mu C$ rests at the very center of the cavity, whereas the metal conductor carries no net charge. Determine the electric field at a point (a) 3.00 cm from the center of the cavity, (b) 6.00 cm from the center of the cavity, (c) 30.0 cm from the center.

22. (II) A point charge Q rests at the center of an uncharged thin spherical conducting shell. What is the electric field E as a function of r (a) for r less than the radius of the shell, (b) inside the shell, and (c) beyond the shell? (d) Does the shell affect the field due to Q alone? Does the charge Q affect the shell?

23. (II) A solid metal cube has a spherical cavity at its center as shown in Fig. 22–29. At the center of the cavity there is a point charge $Q = +8.00\,\mu\text{C}$. The metal cube carries a net charge $q = -6.10\,\mu\text{C}$ (not including Q). Determine (a) the total charge on the surface of the spherical cavity and (b) the total charge on the outer surface of the cube.

FIGURE 22–29
Problem 23.

24. (II) Two large, flat metal plates are separated by a distance that is very small compared to their height and width. The conductors are given equal but opposite uniform surface charge densities $\pm\sigma$. Ignore edge effects and use Gauss's law to show (a) that for points far from the edges, the electric field between the plates is $E = \sigma/\epsilon_0$ and (b) that outside the plates on either side the field is zero. (c) How would your results be altered if the two plates were nonconductors? (See Fig. 22–30).

FIGURE 22–30
Problems 24, 25, and 26. $\quad +\sigma \;\; -\sigma$

25. (II) Suppose the two conducting plates in Problem 24 have the *same* sign and magnitude of charge. What then will be the electric field (a) between them and (b) outside them on either side? (c) What if the plates are nonconducting?

26. (II) The electric field between two square metal plates is 160 N/C. The plates are 1.0 m on a side and are separated by 3.0 cm, as in Fig. 22–30. What is the charge on each plate? Neglect edge effects.

27. (II) Two thin concentric spherical shells of radii r_1 and r_2 $(r_1 < r_2)$ contain uniform surface charge densities σ_1 and σ_2, respectively (see Fig. 22–31). Determine the electric field for (a) $0 < r < r_1$, (b) $r_1 < r < r_2$, and (c) $r > r_2$. (d) Under what conditions will $E = 0$ for $r > r_2$? (e) Under what conditions will $E = 0$ for $r_1 < r < r_2$? Neglect the thickness of the shells.

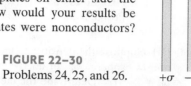

FIGURE 22–31 Two spherical shells (Problem 27).

28. (II) A spherical rubber balloon carries a total charge Q uniformly distributed on its surface. At $t = 0$ the nonconducting balloon has radius r_0 and the balloon is then slowly blown up so that r increases linearly to $2r_0$ in a time T. Determine the electric field as a function of time (a) just outside the balloon surface and (b) at $r = 3.2r_0$.

29. (II) Suppose the nonconducting sphere of Example 22–4 has a spherical cavity of radius r_1 centered at the sphere's center (Fig. 22–32). Assuming the charge Q is distributed uniformly in the "shell" (between $r = r_1$ and $r = r_0$), determine the electric field as a function of r for (a) $0 < r < r_1$, (b) $r_1 < r < r_0$, and (c) $r > r_0$.

FIGURE 22–32
Problems 29, 30, 31, and 44.

30. (II) Suppose in Fig. 22–32, Problem 29, there is also a charge q at the center of the cavity. Determine the electric field for (a) $0 < r < r_1$, (b) $r_1 < r < r_0$, and (c) $r > r_0$.

31. (II) Suppose the thick spherical shell of Problem 29 is a conductor. It carries a total net charge Q and at its center there is a point charge q. What total charge is found on (a) the inner surface of the shell and (b) the outer surface of the shell? Determine the electric field for (c) $0 < r < r_1$, (d) $r_1 < r < r_0$, and (e) $r > r_0$.

32. (II) Suppose that at the center of the cavity inside the shell (charge Q) of Fig. 22–11 (and Example 22–3), there is a point charge q ($\neq \pm Q$). Determine the electric field for (a) $0 < r < r_0$, and for (b) $r > r_0$. What are your answers if (c) $q = Q$ and (d) $q = -Q$?

33. (II) A long cylindrical shell of radius R_0 and length ℓ $(R_0 \ll \ell)$ possesses a uniform surface charge density (charge per unit area) σ (Fig. 22–33). Determine the electric field at points (a) outside the cylinder $(R > R_0)$ and (b) inside the cylinder $(0 < R < R_0)$; assume the points are far from the ends and not too far from the shell $(R \ll \ell)$. (c) Compare to the result for a long line of charge, Example 22–6. Neglect the thickness of shell.

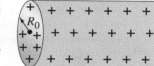

FIGURE 22–33
Problem 33.

34. (II) A very long solid nonconducting cylinder of radius R_0 and length ℓ $(R_0 \ll \ell)$ possesses a uniform volume charge density ρ_E (C/m³), Fig. 22–34. Determine the electric field at points (a) outside the cylinder $(R > R_0)$ and (b) inside the cylinder $(R < R_0)$. Do only for points far from the ends and for which $R \ll \ell$.

FIGURE 22–34
Problem 34.

35. (II) A thin cylindrical shell of radius R_1 is surrounded by a second concentric cylindrical shell of radius R_2 (Fig. 22–35). The inner shell has a total charge $+Q$ and the outer shell $-Q$. Assuming the length ℓ of the shells is much greater than R_1 or R_2, determine the electric field as a function of R (the perpendicular distance from the common axis of the cylinders) for (a) $0 < R < R_1$, (b) $R_1 < R < R_2$, and (c) $R > R_2$. (d) What is the kinetic energy of an electron if it moves between (and concentric with) the shells in a circular orbit of radius $(R_1 + R_2)/2$? Neglect thickness of shells.

FIGURE 22–35
Problems 35, 36, and 37.

36. (II) A thin cylindrical shell of radius $R_1 = 6.5\,\text{cm}$ is surrounded by a second cylindrical shell of radius $R_2 = 9.0\,\text{cm}$, as in Fig. 22–35. Both cylinders are 5.0 m long and the inner one carries a total charge $Q_1 = -0.88\,\mu\text{C}$ and the outer one $Q_2 = +1.56\,\mu\text{C}$. For points far from the ends of the cylinders, determine the electric field at a radial distance R from the central axis of (a) 3.0 cm, (b) 7.0 cm, and (c) 12.0 cm.

37. (II) (a) If an electron $(m = 9.1 \times 10^{-31}\,\text{kg})$ escaped from the surface of the inner cylinder in Problem 36 (Fig. 22–35) with negligible speed, what would be its speed when it reached the outer cylinder? (b) If a proton $(m = 1.67 \times 10^{-27}\,\text{kg})$ revolves in a circular orbit of radius $R = 7.0\,\text{cm}$ about the axis (i.e., between the cylinders), what must be its speed?

38. (II) A very long solid nonconducting cylinder of radius R_1 is uniformly charged with a charge density ρ_E. It is surrounded by a concentric cylindrical tube of inner radius R_2 and outer radius R_3 as shown in Fig. 22–36, and it too carries a uniform charge density ρ_E. Determine the electric field as a function of the distance R from the center of the cylinders for (a) $0 < R < R_1$, (b) $R_1 < R < R_2$, (c) $R_2 < R < R_3$, and (d) $R > R_3$. (e) If $\rho_E = 15\ \mu C/m^3$ and $R_1 = \frac{1}{2}R_2 = \frac{1}{3}R_3 = 5.0\ cm$, plot E as a function of R from $R = 0$ to $R = 20.0\ cm$. Assume the cylinders are very long compared to R_3.

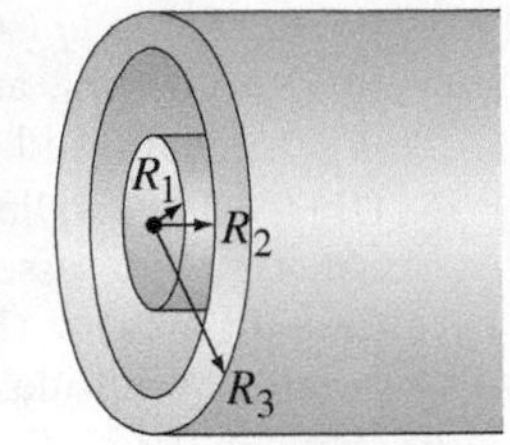

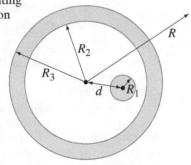

FIGURE 22–36
Problem 38.

39. (II) A nonconducting sphere of radius r_0 is uniformly charged with volume charge density ρ_E. It is surrounded by a concentric metal (conducting) spherical shell of inner radius r_1 and outer radius r_2, which carries a net charge $+Q$. Determine the resulting electric field in the regions (a) $0 < r < r_0$, (b) $r_0 < r < r_1$, (c) $r_1 < r < r_2$, and (d) $r > r_2$ where the radial distance r is measured from the center of the nonconducting sphere.

40. (II) A very long solid nonconducting cylinder of radius R_1 is uniformly charged with charge density ρ_E. It is surrounded by a cylindrical metal (conducting) tube of inner radius R_2 and outer radius R_3, which has no net charge (cross-sectional view shown in Fig. 22–37). If the axes of the two cylinders are parallel, but displaced from each other by a distance d, determine the resulting electric field in the region $R > R_3$, where the radial distance R is measured from the metal cylinder's axis. Assume $d < (R_2 - R_1)$.

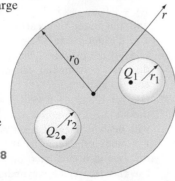

FIGURE 22–37
Problem 40.

41. (II) A flat ring (inner radius R_0, outer radius $4R_0$) is uniformly charged. In terms of the total charge Q, determine the electric field on the axis at points (a) $0.25R_0$ and (b) $75R_0$ from the center of the ring. [*Hint*: The ring can be replaced with two oppositely charged superposed disks.]

42. (II) An uncharged solid conducting sphere of radius r_0 contains two spherical cavities of radii r_1 and r_2, respectively. Point charge Q_1 is then placed within the cavity of radius r_1 and point charge Q_2 is placed within the cavity of radius r_2 (Fig. 22–38). Determine the resulting electric field (magnitude and direction) at locations outside the solid sphere ($r > r_0$), where r is the distance from its center.

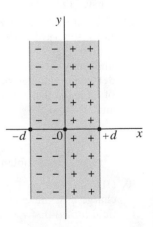

FIGURE 22–38
Problem 42.

43. (III) A very large (i.e., assume infinite) flat slab of nonconducting material has thickness d and a uniform volume charge density $+\rho_E$. (a) Show that a uniform electric field exists outside of this slab. Determine its magnitude E and its direction (relative to the slab's surface). (b) As shown in Fig. 22–39, the slab is now aligned so that one of its surfaces lies on the line $y = x$. At time $t = 0$, a pointlike particle (mass m, charge $+q$) is located at position $\vec{r} = +y_0\hat{j}$ and has velocity $\vec{v} = v_0\hat{i}$. Show that the particle will collide with the slab if $v_0 \geq \sqrt{\sqrt{2}qy_0\rho_E d/\epsilon_0 m}$. Ignore gravity.

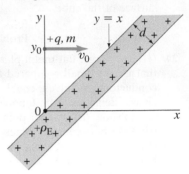

FIGURE 22–39
Problem 43.

44. (III) Suppose the density of charge between r_1 and r_0 of the hollow sphere of Problem 29 (Fig. 22–32) varies as $\rho_E = \rho_0 r_1/r$. Determine the electric field as a function of r for (a) $0 < r < r_1$, (b) $r_1 < r < r_0$, and (c) $r > r_0$. (d) Plot E versus r from $r = 0$ to $r = 2r_0$.

45. (III) Suppose two thin flat plates measure $1.0\ m \times 1.0\ m$ and are separated by $5.0\ mm$. They are oppositely charged with $\pm 15\ \mu C$. (a) Estimate the total force exerted by one plate on the other (ignore edge effects). (b) How much work would be required to move the plates from $5.0\ mm$ apart to $1.00\ cm$ apart?

46. (III) A flat slab of nonconducting material (Fig. 22–40) carries a uniform charge per unit volume, ρ_E. The slab has thickness d which is small compared to the height and breadth of the slab. Determine the electric field as a function of x (a) inside the slab and (b) outside the slab (at distances much less than the slab's height or breadth). Take the origin at the center of the slab.

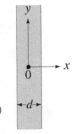

FIGURE 22–40
Problem 46.

47. (III) A flat slab of nonconducting material has thickness $2d$, which is small compared to its height and breadth. Define the x axis to be along the direction of the slab's thickness with the origin at the center of the slab (Fig. 22–41). If the slab carries a volume charge density $\rho_E(x) = -\rho_0$ in the region $-d \leq x < 0$, and $\rho_E(x) = +\rho_0$ in the region $0 < x \leq +d$, determine the electric field $\vec{E}$ as a function of x in the regions (a) outside the slab, (b) $0 < x \leq +d$, and (c) $-d \leq x < 0$. Let ρ_0 be a positive constant.

FIGURE 22–41
Problem 47.

48. (III) An extremely long, solid nonconducting cylinder has a radius R_0. The charge density within the cylinder is a function of the distance R from the axis, given by $\rho_E(R) = \rho_0(R/R_0)^2$. What is the electric field everywhere inside and outside the cylinder (far away from the ends) in terms of ρ_0 and R_0?

49. (III) Charge is distributed within a solid sphere of radius r_0 in such a way that the charge density is a function of the radial position within the sphere of the form: $\rho_E(r) = \rho_0(r/r_0)$. If the total charge within the sphere is Q (and positive), what is the electric field everywhere within the sphere in terms of Q, r_0, and the radial position r?

General Problems

50. A point charge Q is on the axis of a short cylinder at its center. The diameter of the cylinder is equal to its length ℓ (Fig. 22–42). What is the total flux through the curved sides of the cylinder? [*Hint*: First calculate the flux through the ends.]

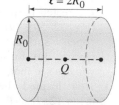

FIGURE 22–42
Problem 50.

51. Write Gauss's law for the gravitational field $\vec{g}$ (see Section 6–6).

52. The Earth is surrounded by an electric field, pointing inward at every point, of magnitude $E \approx 150\,\text{N/C}$ near the surface. (*a*) What is the net charge on the Earth? (*b*) How many excess electrons per square meter on the Earth's surface does this correspond to?

53. A cube of side ℓ has one corner at the origin of coordinates, and extends along the positive x, y, and z axes. Suppose the electric field in this region is given by $\vec{E} = (ay + b)\hat{j}$. Determine the charge inside the cube.

54. A solid nonconducting sphere of radius r_0 has a total charge Q which is distributed according to $\rho_E = br$, where ρ_E is the charge per unit volume, or charge density (C/m^3), and b is a constant. Determine (*a*) b in terms of Q, (*b*) the electric field at points inside the sphere, and (*c*) the electric field at points outside the sphere.

55. A point charge of $9.20\,\text{nC}$ is located at the origin and a second charge of $-5.00\,\text{nC}$ is located on the x axis at $x = 2.75\,\text{cm}$. Calculate the electric flux through a sphere centered at the origin with radius $1.00\,\text{m}$. Repeat the calculation for a sphere of radius $2.00\,\text{m}$.

56. A point charge produces an electric flux of $+235\,\text{N}\cdot\text{m}^2/\text{C}$ through a gaussian sphere of radius $15.0\,\text{cm}$ centered on the charge. (*a*) What is the flux through a gaussian sphere with a radius $27.5\,\text{cm}$? (*b*) What is the magnitude and sign of the charge?

57. A point charge Q is placed a distance $r_0/2$ above the surface of an imaginary spherical surface of radius r_0 (Fig. 22–43). (*a*) What is the electric flux through the sphere? (*b*) What range of values does E have at the surface of the sphere? (*c*) Is $\vec{E}$ perpendicular to the sphere at all points? (*d*) Is Gauss's law useful for obtaining E at the surface of the sphere?

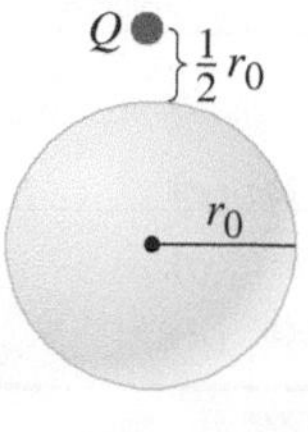

FIGURE 22–43
Problem 57.

58. Three large but thin charged sheets are parallel to each other as shown in Fig. 22–44. Sheet I has a total surface charge density of $6.5\,\text{nC/m}^2$, sheet II a charge of $-2.0\,\text{nC/m}^2$, and sheet III a charge of $5.0\,\text{nC/m}^2$. Estimate the force per unit area on each sheet, in N/m^2.

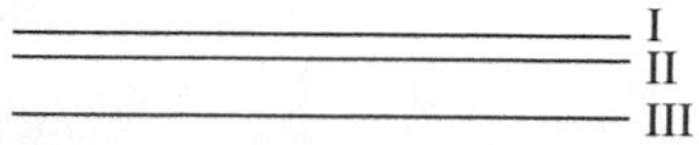

FIGURE 22–44
Problem 58.

59. Neutral hydrogen can be modeled as a positive point charge $+1.6 \times 10^{-19}\,\text{C}$ surrounded by a distribution of negative charge with volume density given by $\rho_E(r) = -Ae^{-2r/a_0}$ where $a_0 = 0.53 \times 10^{-10}\,\text{m}$ is called the *Bohr radius*, A is a constant such that the total amount of negative charge is $-1.6 \times 10^{-19}\,\text{C}$, and $e = 2.718 \cdots$ is the base of the natural log. (*a*) What is the net charge inside a sphere of radius a_0? (*b*) What is the strength of the electric field at a distance a_0 from the nucleus? [*Hint*: Do not confuse the exponential number e with the elementary charge e which uses the same symbol but has a completely different meaning and value $(e = 1.6 \times 10^{-19}\,\text{C})$.]

60. A very large thin plane has uniform surface charge density σ. Touching it on the right (Fig. 22–45) is a long wide slab of thickness d with uniform volume charge density ρ_E. Determine the electric field (*a*) to the left of the plane, (*b*) to the right of the slab, and (*c*) everywhere inside the slab.

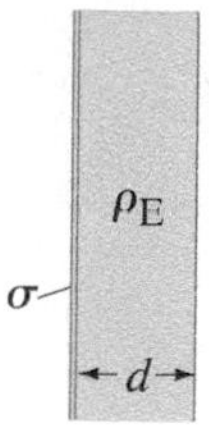

FIGURE 22–45
Problem 60.

61. A sphere of radius r_0 carries a volume charge density ρ_E (Fig. 22–46). A spherical cavity of radius $r_0/2$ is then scooped out and left empty, as shown. (*a*) What is the magnitude and direction of the electric field at point A? (*b*) What is the direction and magnitude of the electric field at point B? Points A and C are at the centers of the respective spheres.

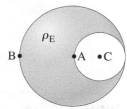

FIGURE 22–46
Problem 61.

62. Dry air will break down and generate a spark if the electric field exceeds about $3 \times 10^6\,\text{N/C}$. How much charge could be packed onto the surface of a green pea (diameter $0.75\,\text{cm}$) before the pea spontaneously discharges?

63. Three very large sheets are separated by equal distances of 15.0 cm (Fig. 22–47). The first and third sheets are very thin and nonconducting and have charge per unit area σ of $+5.00\ \mu C/m^2$ and $-5.00\ \mu C/m^2$ respectively. The middle sheet is conducting but has no net charge. (a) What is the electric field inside the middle sheet? What is the electric field (b) between the left and middle sheets, and (c) between the middle and right sheets? (d) What is the charge density on the surface of the middle sheet facing the left sheet, and (e) on the surface facing the right sheet?

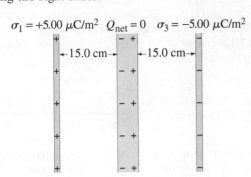

$\sigma_1 = +5.00\ \mu C/m^2 \quad Q_{net} = 0 \quad \sigma_3 = -5.00\ \mu C/m^2$

$\leftarrow$15.0 cm$\rightarrow$ $\leftarrow$15.0 cm$\rightarrow$

FIGURE 22–47 Problem 63.

64. In a cubical volume, 0.70 m on a side, the electric field is

$$\vec{E} = E_0\left(1 + \frac{z}{a}\right)\hat{i} + E_0\left(\frac{z}{a}\right)\hat{j}$$

where $E_0 = 0.125\ N/C$ and $a = 0.70\ m$. The cube has its sides parallel to the coordinate axes, Fig. 22–48. Determine the net charge within the cube.

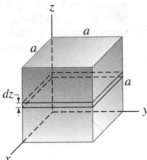

FIGURE 22–48
Problem 64.

65. A conducting spherical shell (Fig. 22–49) has inner radius = 10.0 cm, outer radius = 15.0 cm, and has a $+3.0\ \mu C$ point charge at the center. A charge of $-3.0\ \mu C$ is put on the conductor. (a) Where on the conductor does the $-3.0\ \mu C$ end up? (b) What is the electric field both inside and outside the shell?

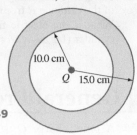

FIGURE 22–49
Problem 65.

66. A hemisphere of radius R is placed in a charge-free region of space where a uniform electric field exists of magnitude E directed perpendicular to the hemisphere's circular base (Fig. 22–50). (a) Using the definition of Φ_E through an "open" surface, calculate (via explicit integration) the electric flux through the hemisphere. [*Hint*: In Fig. 22–50 you can see that, on the surface of a sphere, the infinitesimal area located between the angles θ and $\theta + d\theta$ is $dA = (2\pi R \sin\theta)(R\,d\theta) = 2\pi R^2 \sin\theta\,d\theta$.] (b) Choose an appropriate gaussian surface and use Gauss's law to much more easily obtain the same result for the electric flux through the hemisphere.

$dA = 2\pi R^2 \sin\theta\,d\theta$

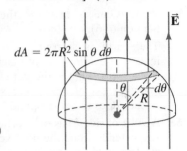

FIGURE 22–50
Problem 66.

*Numerical/Computer

*67. (III) An electric field is given by

$$\mathbf{E} = E_{x0}e^{-\left(\frac{x+y}{a}\right)^2}\hat{i} + E_{y0}e^{-\left(\frac{x+y}{a}\right)^2}\hat{j},$$

where $E_{x0} = 50\ N/C$, $E_{y0} = 25\ N/C$, and $a = 1.0\ m$. Given a cube with sides parallel to the coordinate axes, with one corner at the origin (as in Fig. 22–48), and with sides of length 1.0 m, estimate the flux out of the cube using a spreadsheet or other numerical method. How much total charge is enclosed by the cube?

Answers to Exercises

A: (d).

B: (a).

C: (d).

D: (e).

E: (c).

F: (c).

We are used to voltage in our lives—a 12-volt car battery, 110 V or 220 V at home, 1.5 volt flashlight batteries, and so on. Here we see a Van de Graaff generator, whose voltage may reach 50,000 V or more. Voltage is the same as electric potential difference between two points. Electric potential is defined as the potential energy per unit charge.

The children here, whose hair stands on end because each hair has received the same sign of charge, are not harmed by the voltage because the Van de Graaff cannot provide much current before the voltage drops. (It is current through the body that is harmful, as we will see later.)

23

Electric Potential

CHAPTER-OPENING QUESTION—Guess now!

Consider a pair of parallel plates with equal and opposite charge densities, σ. Which of the following actions will increase the voltage between the plates (assuming fixed charge density)?

(a) Moving the plates closer together.
(b) Moving the plates apart.
(c) Doubling the area of the plates.
(d) Halving the area of the plates.

W e saw in Chapters 7 and 8 that the concept of energy was extremely useful in dealing with the subject of mechanics. The energy point of view is especially useful for electricity. It not only extends the law of conservation of energy, but it gives us another way to view electrical phenomena. Energy is also a powerful tool for solving Problems more easily in many cases than by using forces and electric fields.

CONTENTS

23–1 Electric Potential Energy and Potential Difference

Electric Potential Energy

To apply conservation of energy, we need to define electric potential energy as we did for other types of potential energy. As we saw in Chapter 8, potential energy can be defined only for a conservative force. The work done by a conservative force in moving an object between any two positions is independent of the path taken. The electrostatic force between any two charges (Eq. 21–1, $F = kQ_1Q_2/r^2$) is conservative since the dependence on position is just like the gravitational force, $1/r^2$, which we saw in Section 8–7 is conservative. Hence we can define potential energy U for the electrostatic force.

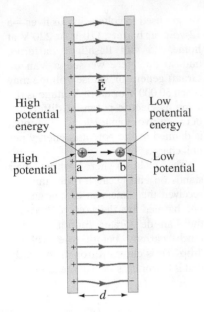

FIGURE 23–1 Work is done by the electric field in moving the positive charge q from position a to position b.

We saw in Chapter 8 that the change in potential energy between two points, a and b, equals the negative of the work done by the conservative force as an object moves from a to b: $\Delta U = -W$.

Thus we define the change in electric potential energy, $U_b - U_a$, when a point charge q moves from some point a to another point b, as the negative of the work done by the electric force as the charge moves from a to b. For example, consider the electric field between two equally but oppositely charged parallel plates; we assume their separation is small compared to their width and height, so the field $\vec{E}$ will be uniform over most of the region, Fig. 23–1. Now consider a tiny positive point charge q placed at point a very near the positive plate as shown. This charge q is so small it has no effect on $\vec{E}$. If this charge q at point a is released, the electric force will do work on the charge and accelerate it toward the negative plate. The work W done by the electric field E to move the charge a distance d is

$$W = Fd = qEd$$

where we used Eq. 21–5, $F = qE$. The change in electric potential energy equals the negative of the work done by the electric force:

$$U_b - U_a = -W = -qEd \qquad \text{[uniform } \vec{E}] \quad \textbf{(23–1)}$$

for this case of uniform electric field $\vec{E}$. In the case illustrated, the potential energy decreases (ΔU is negative); and as the charged particle accelerates from point a to point b in Fig. 23–1, the particle's kinetic energy K increases—by an equal amount. In accord with the conservation of energy, electric potential energy is transformed into kinetic energy, and the total energy is conserved. Note that the positive charge q has its greatest potential energy at point a, near the positive plate.[†] The reverse is true for a negative charge: its potential energy is greatest near the negative plate.

Electric Potential and Potential Difference

In Chapter 21, we found it useful to define the electric field as the force per unit charge. Similarly, it is useful to define the **electric potential** (or simply the **potential** when "electric" is understood) as the *electric potential energy per unit charge*. Electric potential is given the symbol V. If a positive test charge q in an electric field has electric potential energy U_a at some point a (relative to some zero potential energy), the electric potential V_a at this point is

$$V_a = \frac{U_a}{q}. \qquad \textbf{(23–2a)}$$

As we discussed in Chapter 8, only differences in potential energy are physically meaningful. Hence only the **difference in potential**, or the **potential difference**, between two points a and b (such as between a and b in Fig. 23–1) is measurable. When the electric force does positive work on a charge, the kinetic energy increases and the potential energy decreases. The difference in potential energy, $U_b - U_a$, is equal to the negative of the work, W_{ba}, done by the electric field as the charge moves from a to b; so the potential difference V_{ba} is

$$V_{ba} = \Delta V = V_b - V_a = \frac{U_b - U_a}{q} = -\frac{W_{ba}}{q}. \qquad \textbf{(23–2b)}$$

Note that electric potential, like electric field, does not depend on our test charge q. V depends on the other charges that create the field, not on q; q acquires potential energy by being in the potential V due to the other charges.

We can see from our definition that the positive plate in Fig. 23–1 is at a higher potential than the negative plate. Thus a positively charged object moves naturally from a high potential to a low potential. A negative charge does the reverse.

The unit of electric potential, and of potential difference, is joules/coulomb and is given a special name, the **volt**, in honor of Alessandro Volta (1745–1827) who is best known for inventing the electric battery. The volt is abbreviated V, so $1\,\text{V} = 1\,\text{J/C}$. Potential difference, since it is measured in volts, is often referred to as **voltage**.

[†]At this point the charge has its greatest ability to do work (on some other object or system).

If we wish to speak of the potential V_a at some point a, we must be aware that V_a depends on where the potential is chosen to be zero. The zero for electric potential in a given situation can be chosen arbitrarily, just as for potential energy, because only differences in potential energy can be measured. Often the ground, or a conductor connected directly to the ground (the Earth), is taken as zero potential, and other potentials are given with respect to ground. (Thus, a point where the voltage is 50 V is one where the difference of potential between it and ground is 50 V.) In other cases, as we shall see, we may choose the potential to be zero at an infinite distance $(r = \infty)$.

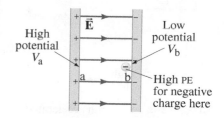

FIGURE 23–2 Central part of Fig. 23–1, showing a negative point charge near the negative plate, where its potential energy (PE) is high. Example 23–1.

CONCEPTUAL EXAMPLE 23–1 | A negative charge. Suppose a negative charge, such as an electron, is placed near the negative plate in Fig. 23–1, at point b, shown here in Fig. 23–2. If the electron is free to move, will its electric potential energy increase or decrease? How will the electric potential change?

RESPONSE An electron released at point b will move toward the positive plate. As the electron moves toward the positive plate, its potential energy *decreases* as its kinetic energy gets larger, so $U_a < U_b$ and $\Delta U = U_a - U_b < 0$. But note that the electron moves from point b at low potential to point a at higher potential: $V_{ab} = V_a - V_b > 0$. (Potentials V_a and V_b are due to the charges on the plates, not due to the electron.) The sign of ΔU and ΔV are opposite because of the negative charge.

⚠ CAUTION

A negative charge has high potential energy when potential V is low

Because the electric potential difference is defined as the potential energy difference per unit charge, then the change in potential energy of a charge q when moved between two points a and b is

$$\Delta U = U_b - U_a = q(V_b - V_a) = qV_{ba}. \qquad \textbf{(23–3)}$$

That is, if an object with charge q moves through a potential difference V_{ba}, its potential energy changes by an amount qV_{ba}. For example, if the potential difference between the two plates in Fig. 23–1 is 6 V, then a +1 C charge moved (say by an external force) from point b to point a will gain $(1\,\text{C})(6\,\text{V}) = 6\,\text{J}$ of electric potential energy. (And it will lose 6 J of electric potential energy if it moves from a to b.) Similarly, a +2 C charge will gain 12 J, and so on. Thus, electric potential difference is a measure of how much energy an electric charge can acquire in a given situation. And, since energy is the ability to do work, the electric potential difference is also a measure of how much work a given charge can do. The exact amount depends both on the potential difference and on the charge.

To better understand electric potential, let's make a comparison to the gravitational case when a rock falls from the top of a cliff. The greater the height, h, of a cliff, the more potential energy $(= mgh)$ the rock has at the top of the cliff, relative to the bottom, and the more kinetic energy it will have when it reaches the bottom. The actual amount of kinetic energy it will acquire, and the amount of work it can do, depends both on the height of the cliff and the mass m of the rock. A large rock and a small rock can be at the same height h (Fig. 23–3a) and thus have the same "gravitational potential," but the larger rock has the greater potential energy (it has more mass). The electrical case is similar (Fig. 23–3b): the potential energy change, or the work that can be done, depends both on the potential difference (corresponding to the height of the cliff) and on the charge (corresponding to mass), Eq. 23–3. But note a significant difference: electric charge comes in two types, + and −, whereas gravitational mass is always +.

Sources of electrical energy such as batteries and electric generators are meant to maintain a potential difference. The actual amount of energy transformed by such a device depends on how much charge flows, as well as the potential difference (Eq. 23–3). For example, consider an automobile headlight connected to a 12.0-V battery. The amount of energy transformed (into light and thermal energy) is proportional to how much charge flows, which depends on how long the light is on. If over a given period of time 5.0 C of charge flows through the light, the total energy transformed is $(5.0\,\text{C})(12.0\,\text{V}) = 60\,\text{J}$. If the headlight is left on twice as long, 10.0 C of charge will flow and the energy transformed is $(10.0\,\text{C})(12.0\,\text{V}) = 120\,\text{J}$. Table 23–1 presents some typical voltages.

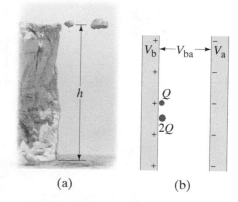

(a)   (b)

FIGURE 23–3 (a) Two rocks are at the same height. The larger rock has more potential energy. (b) Two charges have the same electric potential. The $2Q$ charge has more potential energy.

TABLE 23–1 Some Typical Potential Differences (Voltages)

Source	Voltage (approx.)
Thundercloud to ground	10^8 V
High-voltage power line	10^5–10^6 V
Power supply for TV tube	10^4 V
Automobile ignition	10^4 V
Household outlet	10^2 V
Automobile battery	12 V
Flashlight battery	1.5 V
Resting potential across nerve membrane	10^{-1} V
Potential changes on skin (EKG and EEG)	10^{-4} V

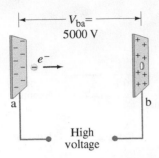

$V_{ba} = 5000\text{ V}$

a

b

High voltage

FIGURE 23–4 Electron accelerated in CRT. Example 23–2.

EXAMPLE 23–2 Electron in CRT. Suppose an electron in a cathode ray tube (Section 23–9) is accelerated from rest through a potential difference $V_b - V_a = V_{ba} = +5000\text{ V}$ (Fig. 23–4). (a) What is the change in electric potential energy of the electron? (b) What is the speed of the electron $(m = 9.1 \times 10^{-31}\text{ kg})$ as a result of this acceleration?

APPROACH The electron, accelerated toward the positive plate, will decrease in potential energy by an amount $\Delta U = qV_{ba}$ (Eq. 23–3). The loss in potential energy will equal its gain in kinetic energy (energy conservation).

SOLUTION (a) The charge on an electron is $q = -e = -1.6 \times 10^{-19}\text{ C}$. Therefore its change in potential energy is

$$\Delta U = qV_{ba} = (-1.6 \times 10^{-19}\text{ C})(+5000\text{ V}) = -8.0 \times 10^{-16}\text{ J}.$$

The minus sign indicates that the potential energy decreases. The potential difference V_{ba} has a positive sign since the final potential V_b is higher than the initial potential V_a. Negative electrons are attracted toward a positive electrode and repelled away from a negative electrode.

(b) The potential energy lost by the electron becomes kinetic energy K. From conservation of energy (Eq. 8–9a), $\Delta K + \Delta U = 0$, so

$$\Delta K = -\Delta U$$
$$\tfrac{1}{2}mv^2 - 0 = -q(V_b - V_a) = -qV_{ba},$$

where the initial kinetic energy is zero since we are given that the electron started from rest. We solve for v:

$$v = \sqrt{-\frac{2qV_{ba}}{m}} = \sqrt{-\frac{2(-1.6 \times 10^{-19}\text{ C})(5000\text{ V})}{9.1 \times 10^{-31}\text{ kg}}} = 4.2 \times 10^7\text{ m/s}.$$

NOTE The electric potential energy does not depend on the mass, only on the charge and voltage. The speed *does* depend on *m*.

23–2 Relation between Electric Potential and Electric Field

The effects of any charge distribution can be described either in terms of electric field or in terms of electric potential. Electric potential is often easier to use because it is a scalar, as compared to electric field which is a vector. There is a crucial connection between the electric potential produced by a given arrangement of charges and the electric field due to those charges, which we now examine.

We start by recalling the relation between a conservative force $\vec{F}$ and the potential energy U associated with that force. As discussed in Section 8–2, the difference in potential energy between any two points in space, a and b, is given by Eq. 8–4:

$$U_b - U_a = -\int_a^b \vec{F} \cdot d\vec{\ell},$$

FIGURE 23–5 To find V_{ba} in a nonuniform electric field $\vec{E}$, we integrate $\vec{E} \cdot d\vec{\ell}$ from point a to point b.

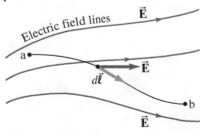

Electric field lines

$\vec{E}$

a

$d\vec{\ell}$

$\vec{E}$

b

$\vec{E}$

where $d\vec{\ell}$ is an infinitesimal increment of displacement, and the integral is taken along any path in space from point a to point b. For the electrical case, we are more interested in the potential difference, given by Eq. 23–2b, $V_{ba} = V_b - V_a = (U_b - U_a)/q$, rather than in the potential energy itself. Also, the electric field $\vec{E}$ at any point in space is defined as the force per unit charge (Eq. 21–3): $\vec{E} = \vec{F}/q$. Putting these two relations in the above equation gives us

$$V_{ba} = V_b - V_a = -\int_a^b \vec{E} \cdot d\vec{\ell}. \qquad \textbf{(23–4a)}$$

This is the general relation between electric field and potential difference. See Fig. 23–5. If we are given the electric field due to some arrangement of electric charge, we can use Eq. 23–4a to determine V_{ba}.

A simple special case is a uniform field. In Fig. 23–1, for example, a path parallel to the electric field lines from point a at the positive plate to point b at the negative plate gives (since $\vec{\mathbf{E}}$ and $d\vec{\boldsymbol{\ell}}$ are in the same direction at each point),

$$V_{ba} = V_b - V_a = -\int_a^b \vec{\mathbf{E}} \cdot d\vec{\boldsymbol{\ell}} = -E \int_a^b d\ell = -Ed$$

or

$$V_{ba} = -Ed \qquad \text{[only if } E \text{ is uniform]} \quad \textbf{(23–4b)}$$

where d is the distance, parallel to the field lines, between points a and b. Be careful not to use Eq. 23–4b unless you are sure the electric field is uniform.

From either of Eqs. 23–4 we can see that the units for electric field intensity can be written as volts per meter (V/m) as well as newtons per coulomb (N/C). These are equivalent in general, since $1\,\text{N/C} = 1\,\text{N·m/C·m} = 1\,\text{J/C·m} = 1\,\text{V/m}$.

EXERCISE A Return to the Chapter-Opening Question, page 607, and answer it again now. Try to explain why you may have answered differently the first time.

EXAMPLE 23–3 **Electric field obtained from voltage.** Two parallel plates are charged to produce a potential difference of 50 V. If the separation between the plates is 0.050 m, calculate the magnitude of the electric field in the space between the plates (Fig. 23–6).

APPROACH We apply Eq. 23–4b to obtain the magnitude of E, assumed uniform.

SOLUTION The electric field magnitude is $E = V_{ba}/d = (50\,\text{V}/0.050\,\text{m}) = 1000\,\text{V/m}$.

EXAMPLE 23–4 **Charged conducting sphere.** Determine the potential at a distance r from the center of a charged conducting sphere of radius r_0 for (a) $r > r_0$, (b) $r = r_0$, (c) $r < r_0$. The total charge on the sphere is Q.

APPROACH The charge Q is distributed over the surface of the sphere since it is a conductor. We saw in Example 22–3 that the electric field outside a conducting sphere is

$$E = \frac{1}{4\pi\epsilon_0}\frac{Q}{r^2} \qquad [r > r_0]$$

and points radially outward (inward if $Q < 0$). Since we know $\vec{\mathbf{E}}$, we can start by using Eq. 23–4a.

SOLUTION (a) We use Eq. 23–4a and integrate along a radial line with $d\vec{\boldsymbol{\ell}}$ parallel to $\vec{\mathbf{E}}$ (Fig. 23–7) between two points which are distances r_a and r_b from the sphere's center:

$$V_b - V_a = -\int_{r_a}^{r_b} \vec{\mathbf{E}} \cdot d\vec{\boldsymbol{\ell}} = -\frac{Q}{4\pi\epsilon_0}\int_{r_a}^{r_b} \frac{dr}{r^2} = \frac{Q}{4\pi\epsilon_0}\left(\frac{1}{r_b} - \frac{1}{r_a}\right)$$

and we set $d\ell = dr$. If we let $V = 0$ for $r = \infty$ (let's choose $V_b = 0$ at $r_b = \infty$), then at any other point r (for $r > r_0$) we have

$$V = \frac{1}{4\pi\epsilon_0}\frac{Q}{r}. \qquad [r > r_0]$$

We will see in the next Section that this same equation applies for the potential a distance r from a single point charge. Thus the electric potential outside a spherical conductor with a uniformly distributed charge is the same as if all the charge were at its center.

(b) As r approaches r_0, we see that

$$V = \frac{1}{4\pi\epsilon_0}\frac{Q}{r_0} \qquad [r = r_0]$$

at the surface of the conductor.

(c) For points within the conductor, $E = 0$. Thus the integral, $\int \vec{\mathbf{E}} \cdot d\vec{\boldsymbol{\ell}}$, between $r = r_0$ and any point within the conductor gives zero change in V. Hence V is constant within the conductor:

$$V = \frac{1}{4\pi\epsilon_0}\frac{Q}{r_0}. \qquad [r \le r_0]$$

The whole conductor, not just its surface, is at this same potential. Plots of both E and V as a function of r are shown in Fig. 23–8 for a positively charged conducting sphere.

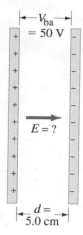

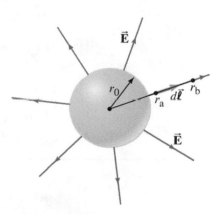

FIGURE 23–6 Example 23–3.

FIGURE 23–7 Example 23–4. Integrating $\vec{\mathbf{E}} \cdot d\vec{\boldsymbol{\ell}}$ for the field outside a spherical conductor.

FIGURE 23–8 (a) E versus r, and (b) V versus r, for a positively charged solid conducting sphere of radius r_0 (the charge distributes itself evenly on the surface); r is the distance from the center of the sphere.

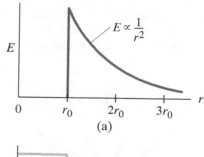

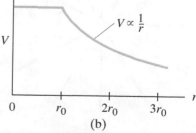

EXAMPLE 23–5 **Breakdown voltage.** In many kinds of equipment, very high voltages are used. A problem with high voltage is that the air can become ionized due to the high electric fields: free electrons in the air (produced by cosmic rays, for example) can be accelerated by such high fields to speeds sufficient to ionize O_2 and N_2 molecules by collision, knocking out one or more of their electrons. The air then becomes conducting and the high voltage cannot be maintained as charge flows. The breakdown of air occurs for electric fields of about 3×10^6 V/m. (a) Show that the breakdown voltage for a spherical conductor in air is proportional to the radius of the sphere, and (b) estimate the breakdown voltage in air for a sphere of diameter 1.0 cm.

APPROACH The electric potential at the surface of a spherical conductor of radius r_0 (Example 23–4), and the electric field just outside its surface, are

$$V = \frac{1}{4\pi\epsilon_0} \frac{Q}{r_0} \quad \text{and} \quad E = \frac{1}{4\pi\epsilon_0} \frac{Q}{r_0^2}.$$

SOLUTION (a) We combine these two equations and obtain

$$V = r_0 E. \qquad \text{[at surface of spherical conductor]}$$

(b) For $r_0 = 5 \times 10^{-3}$ m, the breakdown voltage in air is

$$V = (5 \times 10^{-3} \text{ m})(3 \times 10^6 \text{ V/m}) \approx 15{,}000 \text{ V}.$$

When high voltages are present, a glow may be seen around sharp points, known as a **corona discharge**, due to the high electric fields at these points which ionize air molecules. The light we see is due to electrons jumping down to empty lower states. **Lightning rods**, with their sharp tips, are intended to ionize the surrounding air when a storm cloud is near, and to provide a conduction path to discharge a dangerous high-voltage cloud slowly, over a period of time. Thus lightning rods, connected to the ground, are intended to draw electric charge off threatening clouds before a large buildup of charge results in a swift destructive lightning bolt.

EXERCISE B On a dry day, a person can become electrically charged by rubbing against rugs and other ordinary objects. Suppose you notice a small shock as you reach for a metal doorknob, noting that the shock occurs along with a tiny spark when your hand is about 3.0 mm from the doorknob. As a rough estimate, use Eq. 23–4b to estimate the potential difference between your hand and the doorknob. (a) 9 V; (b) 90 V; (c) 900 V; (d) 9000 V; (e) none of these.

23–3 Electric Potential Due to Point Charges

The electric potential at a distance r from a single point charge Q can be derived directly from Eq. 23–4a, $V_b - V_a = -\int \vec{E} \cdot d\vec{\ell}$. The electric field due to a single point charge has magnitude (Eq. 21–4)

$$E = \frac{1}{4\pi\epsilon_0} \frac{Q}{r^2} \quad \text{or} \quad E = k\frac{Q}{r^2}$$

(where $k = 1/4\pi\epsilon_0 = 8.99 \times 10^9$ N·m²/C²), and is directed radially outward from a positive charge (inward if $Q < 0$). We take the integral in Eq. 23–4a along a (straight) field line (Fig. 23–9) from point a, a distance r_a from Q, to point b, a distance r_b from Q. Then $d\vec{\ell}$ will be parallel to $\vec{E}$ and $d\ell = dr$. Thus

$$V_b - V_a = -\int_{r_a}^{r_b} \vec{E} \cdot d\vec{\ell} = -\frac{Q}{4\pi\epsilon_0} \int_{r_a}^{r_b} \frac{1}{r^2} dr = \frac{1}{4\pi\epsilon_0}\left(\frac{Q}{r_b} - \frac{Q}{r_a}\right).$$

As mentioned earlier, only differences in potential have physical meaning. We are free, therefore, to choose the value of the potential at some one point to

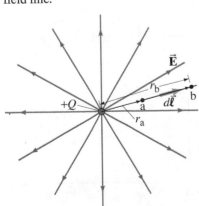

FIGURE 23–9 We integrate Eq. 23–4a along the straight line (shown in black) from point a to point b. The line ab is parallel to a field line.

be whatever we please. It is common to choose the potential to be zero at infinity (let $V_b = 0$ at $r_b = \infty$). Then the electric potential V at a distance r from a single point charge is

$$V = \frac{1}{4\pi\epsilon_0}\frac{Q}{r}.$$ $\begin{bmatrix} \text{single point charge;} \\ V = 0 \text{ at } r = \infty \end{bmatrix}$ **(23–5)**

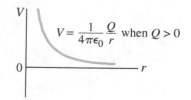

FIGURE 23–10 Potential V as a function of distance r from a single point charge Q when the charge is positive.

FIGURE 23–11 Potential V as a function of distance r from a single point charge Q when the charge is negative.

We can think of V here as representing the absolute potential, where $V = 0$ at $r = \infty$, or we can think of V as the potential difference between r and infinity. Notice that the potential V decreases with the first power of the distance, whereas the electric field (Eq. 21–4) decreases as the *square* of the distance. The potential near a positive charge is large, and it decreases toward zero at very large distances (Fig. 23–10). For a negative charge, the potential is negative and increases toward zero at large distances (Fig. 23–11). Equation 23–5 is sometimes called the **Coulomb potential** (it has its origin in Coulomb's law).

In Example 23–4 we found that the potential due to a uniformly charged sphere is given by the same relation, Eq. 23–5, for points outside the sphere. Thus we see that the potential outside a uniformly charged sphere is the same as if all the charge were concentrated at its center.

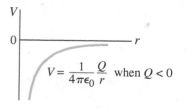

EXERCISE C What is the potential at a distance of 3.0 cm from a point charge $Q = -2.0 \times 10^{-9}$ C? (*a*) 600 V; (*b*) 60 V; (*c*) 6 V; (*d*) −600 V; (*e*) −60 V; (*f*) −6 V.

EXAMPLE 23–6 **Work required to bring two positive charges close together.** What minimum work must be done by an external force to bring a charge $q = 3.00\,\mu$C from a great distance away (take $r = \infty$) to a point 0.500 m from a charge $Q = 20.0\,\mu$C?

APPROACH To find the work we cannot simply multiply the force times distance because the force is not constant. Instead we can set the change in potential energy equal to the (positive of the) work required of an *external* force (Chapter 8), and Eq. 23–3: $W = \Delta U = q(V_b - V_a)$. We get the potentials V_b and V_a using Eq. 23–5.

⚠ **CAUTION**

We cannot use $W = Fd$ when F is not constant

SOLUTION The work required is equal to the change in potential energy:

$$W = q(V_b - V_a)$$

$$= q\left(\frac{kQ}{r_b} - \frac{kQ}{r_a}\right),$$

where $r_b = 0.500$ m and $r_a = \infty$. The right-hand term within the parentheses is zero ($1/\infty = 0$) so

$$W = (3.00 \times 10^{-6}\,\text{C})\frac{(8.99 \times 10^9\,\text{N}\cdot\text{m}^2/\text{C}^2)(2.00 \times 10^{-5}\,\text{C})}{(0.500\,\text{m})} = 1.08\,\text{J}.$$

NOTE We could not use Eq. 23–4b here because it applies *only* to uniform fields. But we did use Eq. 23–3 because it is always valid.

To determine the electric field at points near a collection of two or more point charges requires adding up the electric fields due to each charge. Since the electric field is a vector, this can be time consuming or complicated. To find the electric potential at a point due to a collection of point charges is far easier, since the electric potential is a scalar, and hence you only need to add numbers (with appropriate signs) without concern for direction. This is a major advantage in using electric potential for solving Problems.

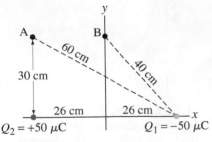

FIGURE 23–12 Example 23–7.
(See also Example 21–8, Fig. 21–27.)

⚠ **CAUTION**

*Potential is a scalar and
has no components*

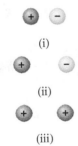

(i)

(ii)

(iii)

FIGURE 23–13 Exercise D.

EXAMPLE 23–7 **Potential above two charges.** Calculate the electric potential (a) at point A in Fig. 23–12 due to the two charges shown, and (b) at point B. [This is the same situation as Example 21–8, Fig. 21–27, where we calculated the electric field at these points.]

APPROACH The total potential at point A (or at point B) is the sum of the potentials at that point due to each of the two charges Q_1 and Q_2. The potential due to each single charge is given by Eq. 23–5. We do not have to worry about directions because electric potential is a scalar quantity. But we do have to keep track of the signs of charges.

SOLUTION (a) We add the potentials at point A due to each charge Q_1 and Q_2, and we use Eq. 23–5 for each:

$$V_A = V_{A2} + V_{A1}$$
$$= k \frac{Q_2}{r_{2A}} + k \frac{Q_1}{r_{1A}}$$

where $r_{1A} = 60$ cm and $r_{2A} = 30$ cm. Then

$$V_A = \frac{(9.0 \times 10^9 \, \text{N·m}^2/\text{C}^2)(5.0 \times 10^{-5} \, \text{C})}{0.30 \, \text{m}}$$
$$+ \frac{(9.0 \times 10^9 \, \text{N·m}^2/\text{C}^2)(-5.0 \times 10^{-5} \, \text{C})}{0.60 \, \text{m}}$$
$$= 1.50 \times 10^6 \, \text{V} - 0.75 \times 10^6 \, \text{V}$$
$$= 7.5 \times 10^5 \, \text{V}.$$

(b) At point B, $r_{1B} = r_{2B} = 0.40$ m, so

$$V_B = V_{B2} + V_{B1}$$
$$= \frac{(9.0 \times 10^9 \, \text{N·m}^2/\text{C}^2)(5.0 \times 10^{-5} \, \text{C})}{0.40 \, \text{m}}$$
$$+ \frac{(9.0 \times 10^9 \, \text{N·m}^2/\text{C}^2)(-5.0 \times 10^{-5} \, \text{C})}{0.40 \, \text{m}}$$
$$= 0 \, \text{V}.$$

NOTE The two terms in the sum in (b) cancel for any point equidistant from Q_1 and Q_2 ($r_{1B} = r_{2B}$). Thus the potential will be zero everywhere on the plane equidistant between the two opposite charges. This plane where V is constant is called an equipotential surface.

Simple summations like these can easily be performed for any number of point charges.

EXERCISE D Consider the three pairs of charges, Q_1 and Q_2, in Fig. 23–13. (a) Which set has a positive potential energy? (b) Which set has the most negative potential energy? (c) Which set requires the most work to separate the charges to infinity? Assume the charges all have the same magnitude.

23–4 Potential Due to Any Charge Distribution

If we know the electric field in a region of space due to any distribution of electric charge, we can determine the difference in potential between two points in the region using Eq. 23–4a, $V_{ba} = -\int_a^b \vec{E} \cdot d\vec{\ell}$. In many cases we don't know $\vec{E}$ as a function of position, and it may be difficult to calculate. We can calculate the potential V due to a given charge distribution in another way, using the potential due to a single point charge, Eq. 23–5:

$$V = \frac{1}{4\pi\epsilon_0} \frac{Q}{r},$$

where we choose $V = 0$ at $r = \infty$. Then we can sum over all the charges.

If we have n individual point charges, the potential at some point a (relative to $V = 0$ at $r = \infty$) is

$$V_a = \sum_{i=1}^{n} V_i = \frac{1}{4\pi\epsilon_0} \sum_{i=1}^{n} \frac{Q_i}{r_{ia}}, \qquad (23\text{–}6a)$$

where r_{ia} is the distance from the ith charge (Q_i) to the point a. (We already used this approach in Example 23–7.) If the charge distribution can be considered continuous, then

$$V = \frac{1}{4\pi\epsilon_0} \int \frac{dq}{r}, \qquad (23\text{–}6b)$$

where r is the distance from a tiny element of charge, dq, to the point where V is being determined.

EXAMPLE 23–8 **Potential due to a ring of charge.** A thin circular ring of radius R has a uniformly distributed charge Q. Determine the electric potential at a point P on the axis of the ring a distance x from its center, Fig. 23–14.

APPROACH We integrate over the ring using Eq. 23–6b.

SOLUTION Each point on the ring is equidistant from point P, and this distance is $(x^2 + R^2)^{\frac{1}{2}}$. So the potential at P is:

$$V = \frac{1}{4\pi\epsilon_0} \int \frac{dq}{r} = \frac{1}{4\pi\epsilon_0} \frac{1}{(x^2 + R^2)^{\frac{1}{2}}} \int dq = \frac{1}{4\pi\epsilon_0} \frac{Q}{(x^2 + R^2)^{\frac{1}{2}}}.$$

NOTE For points very far away from the ring, $x \gg R$, this result reduces to $(1/4\pi\epsilon_0)(Q/x)$, the potential of a point charge, as we should expect.

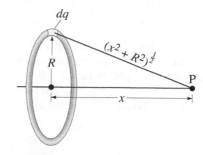

FIGURE 23–14 Example 23–8. Calculating the potential at point P, a distance x from the center of a uniform ring of charge.

FIGURE 23–15 Example 23–9. Calculating the electric potential at point P on the axis of a uniformly charged thin disk.

EXAMPLE 23–9 **Potential due to a charged disk.** A thin flat disk, of radius R_0, has a uniformly distributed charge Q, Fig. 23–15. Determine the potential at a point P on the axis of the disk, a distance x from its center.

APPROACH We divide the disk into thin rings of radius R and thickness dR and use the result of Example 23–8 to sum over the disk.

SOLUTION The charge Q is distributed uniformly, so the charge contained in each ring is proportional to its area. The disk has area πR_0^2 and each thin ring has area $dA = (2\pi R)(dR)$. Hence

$$\frac{dq}{Q} = \frac{2\pi R\, dR}{\pi R_0^2}$$

so

$$dq = Q \frac{(2\pi R)(dR)}{\pi R_0^2} = \frac{2QR\, dR}{R_0^2}.$$

Then the potential at P, using Eq. 23–6b in which r is replaced by $(x^2 + R^2)^{\frac{1}{2}}$, is

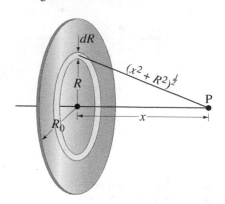

$$V = \frac{1}{4\pi\epsilon_0} \int \frac{dq}{(x^2 + R^2)^{\frac{1}{2}}} = \frac{2Q}{4\pi\epsilon_0 R_0^2} \int_0^{R_0} \frac{R\, dR}{(x^2 + R^2)^{\frac{1}{2}}} = \frac{Q}{2\pi\epsilon_0 R_0^2} (x^2 + R^2)^{\frac{1}{2}} \Big|_{R=0}^{R=R_0}$$

$$= \frac{Q}{2\pi\epsilon_0 R_0^2} \left[(x^2 + R_0^2)^{\frac{1}{2}} - x \right].$$

NOTE For $x \gg R_0$, this formula reduces to

$$V \approx \frac{Q}{2\pi\epsilon_0 R_0^2} \left[x\left(1 + \frac{1}{2} \frac{R_0^2}{x^2} \right) - x \right] = \frac{Q}{4\pi\epsilon_0 x}.$$

This is the formula for a point charge, as we expect.

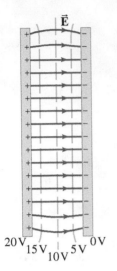

$\vec{E}$

20 V 15 V 10 V 5 V 0 V

FIGURE 23–16 Equipotential lines (the green dashed lines) between two oppositely charged parallel plates. Note that they are perpendicular to the electric field lines (solid red lines).

FIGURE 23–17 Example 23–10. Electric field lines and equipotential surfaces for a point charge.

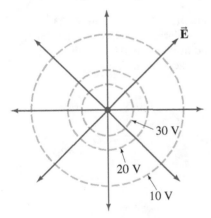

$\vec{E}$

30 V

20 V

10 V

FIGURE 23–18 Equipotential lines (green, dashed) are always perpendicular to the electric field lines (solid red) shown here for two equal but oppositely charged particles.

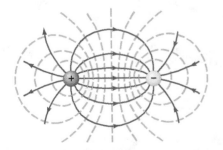

23–5 Equipotential Surfaces

The electric potential can be represented graphically by drawing **equipotential lines** or, in three dimensions, **equipotential surfaces**. An equipotential surface is one on which all points are at the same potential. That is, the potential difference between any two points on the surface is zero, and no work is required to move a charge from one point to the other. An *equipotential surface must be perpendicular to the electric field* at any point. If this were not so—that is, if there were a component of $\vec{E}$ parallel to the surface—it would require work to move the charge along the surface against this component of $\vec{E}$; and this would contradict the idea that it is an equipotential surface. This can also be seen from Eq. 23–4a, $\Delta V = -\int \vec{E} \cdot d\vec{\ell}$. On a surface where V is constant, $\Delta V = 0$, so we must have either $\vec{E} = 0$, $d\vec{\ell} = 0$, or $\cos\theta = 0$ where θ is the angle between $\vec{E}$ and $d\vec{\ell}$. Thus in a region where $\vec{E}$ is not zero, the path $d\vec{\ell}$ along an equipotential must have $\cos\theta = 0$, meaning $\theta = 90°$ and $\vec{E}$ is perpendicular to the equipotential.

The fact that the electric field lines and equipotential surfaces are mutually perpendicular helps us locate the equipotentials when the electric field lines are known. In a normal two-dimensional drawing, we show equipotential *lines*, which are the intersections of equipotential surfaces with the plane of the drawing. In Fig. 23–16, a few of the equipotential lines are drawn (dashed green lines) for the electric field (red lines) between two parallel plates at a potential difference of 20 V. The negative plate is arbitrarily chosen to be zero volts and the potential of each equipotential line is indicated. Note that $\vec{E}$ points toward lower values of V.

EXAMPLE 23–10 **Point charge equipotential surfaces.** For a single point charge with $Q = 4.0 \times 10^{-9}$ C, sketch the equipotential surfaces (or lines in a plane containing the charge) corresponding to $V_1 = 10$ V, $V_2 = 20$ V, and $V_3 = 30$ V.

APPROACH The electric potential V depends on the distance r from the charge (Eq. 23–5).

SOLUTION The electric field for a positive point charge is directed radially outward. Since the equipotential surfaces must be perpendicular to the lines of electric field, they will be spherical in shape, centered on the point charge, Fig. 23–17. From Eq. 23–5 we have $r = (1/4\pi\epsilon_0)(Q/V)$, so that for $V_1 = 10$ V, $r_1 = (9.0 \times 10^9 \text{ N} \cdot \text{m}^2/\text{C}^2)(4.0 \times 10^{-9} \text{ C})/(10 \text{ V}) = 3.6$ m, for $V_2 = 20$ V, $r_2 = 1.8$ m, and for $V_3 = 30$ V, $r_3 = 1.2$ m, as shown.

NOTE The equipotential surface with the largest potential is closest to the positive charge. How would this change if Q were negative?

The equipotential lines for the case of two equal but oppositely charged particles are shown in Fig. 23–18 as green dashed lines. Equipotential lines and surfaces, unlike field lines, are always continuous and never end, and so continue beyond the borders of Figs. 23–16 and 23–18.

We saw in Section 21–9 that there can be no electric field within a conductor in the static case, for otherwise the free electrons would feel a force and would move. Indeed, the entire volume of *a conductor must be entirely at the same potential in the static case*, and the surface of a conductor is then an equipotential surface. (If it weren't, the free electrons at the surface would move, since whenever there is a potential difference between two points, free charges will move.) This is fully consistent with our result, discussed earlier, that the electric field at the surface of a conductor must be perpendicular to the surface.

A useful analogy for equipotential lines is a topographic map: the contour lines are essentially gravitational equipotential lines (Fig. 23–19).

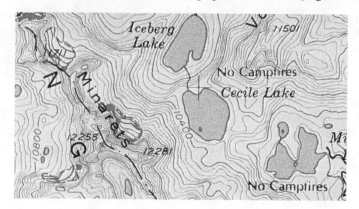

FIGURE 23–19 A topographic map (here, a portion of the Sierra Nevada in California) shows continuous contour lines, each of which is at a fixed height above sea level. Here they are at 80 ft (25 m) intervals. If you walk along one contour line, you neither climb nor descend. If you cross lines, and especially if you climb perpendicular to the lines, you will be changing your gravitational potential (rapidly, if the lines are close together).

23–6 Electric Dipole Potential

Two equal point charges Q, of opposite sign, separated by a distance ℓ, are called an **electric dipole**, as we saw in Section 21–11. Also, the two charges we saw in Figs. 23–12 and 23–18 constitute an electric dipole, and the latter shows the electric field lines and equipotential surfaces for a dipole. Because electric dipoles occur often in physics, as well as in other fields, it is useful to examine them more closely.

The electric potential at an arbitrary point P due to a dipole, Fig. 23–20, is the sum of the potentials due to each of the two charges (we take $V = 0$ at $r = \infty$):

$$V = \frac{1}{4\pi\epsilon_0}\frac{Q}{r} + \frac{1}{4\pi\epsilon_0}\frac{(-Q)}{(r + \Delta r)} = \frac{1}{4\pi\epsilon_0}Q\left(\frac{1}{r} - \frac{1}{r + \Delta r}\right) = \frac{Q}{4\pi\epsilon_0}\frac{\Delta r}{r(r + \Delta r)},$$

where r is the distance from P to the positive charge and $r + \Delta r$ is the distance to the negative charge. This equation becomes simpler if we consider points P whose distance from the dipole is much larger than the separation of the two charges—that is, for $r \gg \ell$. From Fig. 23–20 we see that $\Delta r \approx \ell \cos\theta$; since $r \gg \Delta r = \ell \cos\theta$, we can neglect Δr in the denominator as compared to r. Therefore, we obtain

$$V = \frac{1}{4\pi\epsilon_0}\frac{Q\ell\cos\theta}{r^2} = \frac{1}{4\pi\epsilon_0}\frac{p\cos\theta}{r^2} \qquad \text{[dipole; } r \gg \ell\text{]} \quad \textbf{(23–7)}$$

where $p = Q\ell$ is called the **dipole moment**. We see that the potential decreases as the *square* of the distance from the dipole, whereas for a single point charge the potential decreases with the first power of the distance (Eq. 23–5). It is not surprising that the potential should fall off faster for a dipole; for when you are far from a dipole, the two equal but opposite charges appear so close together as to tend to neutralize each other.

Table 23–2 gives the dipole moments for several molecules. The + and − signs indicate on which atoms these charges lie. The last two entries are a part of many organic molecules and play an important role in molecular biology. A dipole moment has units of coulomb-meters (C·m), although for molecules a smaller unit called a *debye* is sometimes used: 1 debye = 3.33×10^{-30} C·m.

23–7 $\vec{\mathbf{E}}$ Determined from V

We can use Eq. 23–4a, $V_b - V_a = -\int_a^b \vec{\mathbf{E}} \cdot d\vec{\boldsymbol\ell}$, to determine the difference in potential between two points if the electric field is known in the region between those two points. By inverting Eq. 23–4a, we can write the electric field in terms of the potential. Then the electric field can be determined from a knowledge of V. Let us see how to do this.

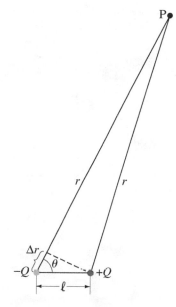

FIGURE 23–20 Electric dipole. Calculation of potential V at point P.

TABLE 23–2 Dipole Moments of Selected Molecules

Molecule	Dipole Moment (C · m)
$H_2^{(+)}O^{(-)}$	6.1×10^{-30}
$H^{(+)}Cl^{(-)}$	3.4×10^{-30}
$N^{(-)}H_3^{(+)}$	5.0×10^{-30}
$>N^{(-)}\!-\!H^{(+)}$	$\approx 3.0^\dagger \times 10^{-30}$
$>C^{(+)}\!=\!O^{(-)}$	$\approx 8.0^\dagger \times 10^{-30}$

† These groups often appear on larger molecules; hence the value for the dipole moment will vary somewhat, depending on the rest of the molecule.

We write Eq. 23–4a in differential form as

$$dV = -\vec{E} \cdot d\vec{\ell} = -E_\ell \, d\ell,$$

where dV is the infinitesimal difference in potential between two points a distance $d\ell$ apart, and E_ℓ is the component of the electric field in the direction of the infinitesimal displacement $d\vec{\ell}$. We can then write

$$E_\ell = -\frac{dV}{d\ell}. \qquad (23-8)$$

Thus *the component of the electric field in any direction is equal to the negative of the rate of change of the electric potential with distance in that direction.* The quantity $dV/d\ell$ is called the gradient of V in a particular direction. If the direction is not specified, the term *gradient* refers to that direction in which V changes most rapidly; this would be the direction of $\vec{E}$ at that point, so we can write

$$E = -\frac{dV}{d\ell}. \qquad \text{[if } d\vec{\ell} \parallel \vec{E}]$$

If $\vec{E}$ is written as a function of x, y, and z, and we let ℓ refer to the x, y, and z axes, then Eq. 23–8 becomes

$$E_x = -\frac{\partial V}{\partial x}, \qquad E_y = -\frac{\partial V}{\partial y}, \qquad E_z = -\frac{\partial V}{\partial z}. \qquad (23-9)$$

Here, $\partial V/\partial x$ is the "partial derivative" of V with respect to x, with y and z held constant.[†] For example, if $V(x, y, z) = (2 \text{ V/m}^2)x^2 + (8 \text{ V/m}^3)y^2 z + (2 \text{ V/m}^2)z^2$, then

$$E_x = -\partial V/\partial x = -(4 \text{ V/m}^2)x,$$
$$E_y = -\partial V/\partial y = -(16 \text{ V/m}^3)yz,$$

and

$$E_z = -\partial V/\partial z = -(8 \text{ V/m}^3)y^2 - (4 \text{ V/m}^2)z.$$

EXAMPLE 23–11 $\vec{E}$ **for ring and disk.** Use electric potential to determine the electric field at point P on the axis of (*a*) a circular ring of charge (Fig. 23–14) and (*b*) a uniformly charged disk (Fig. 23–15).

APPROACH We obtained V as a function of x in Examples 23–8 and 23–9, so we find E by taking derivatives (Eqs. 23–9).

SOLUTION (*a*) From Example 23–8,

$$V = \frac{1}{4\pi\epsilon_0} \frac{Q}{(x^2 + R^2)^{\frac{1}{2}}}.$$

Then

$$E_x = -\frac{\partial V}{\partial x} = \frac{1}{4\pi\epsilon_0} \frac{Qx}{(x^2 + R^2)^{\frac{3}{2}}}.$$

This is the same result we obtained in Example 21–9.

(*b*) From Example 23–9,

$$V = \frac{Q}{2\pi\epsilon_0 R_0^2} \left[(x^2 + R_0^2)^{\frac{1}{2}} - x \right],$$

so

$$E_x = -\frac{\partial V}{\partial x} = \frac{Q}{2\pi\epsilon_0 R_0^2} \left[1 - \frac{x}{(x^2 + R_0^2)^{\frac{1}{2}}} \right].$$

For points very close to the disk, $x \ll R_0$, this can be approximated by

$$E_x \approx \frac{Q}{2\pi\epsilon_0 R_0^2} = \frac{\sigma}{2\epsilon_0}$$

where $\sigma = Q/\pi R_0^2$ is the surface charge density. We also obtained these results in Chapter 21, Example 21–12 and Eq. 21–7.

[†]Equation 23–9 can be written as a vector equation,

$$\vec{E} = -\text{grad } V = -\vec{\nabla}V = -\left(\hat{i}\frac{\partial}{\partial x} + \hat{j}\frac{\partial}{\partial y} + \hat{k}\frac{\partial}{\partial z} \right)V$$

where the symbol $\vec{\nabla}$ is called the *del* or *gradient operator*: $\vec{\nabla} = \hat{i}\frac{\partial}{\partial x} + \hat{j}\frac{\partial}{\partial y} + \hat{k}\frac{\partial}{\partial z}.$

If we compare this last Example with Examples 21–9 and 21–12, we see that here, as for many charge distributions, it is easier to calculate V first, and then $\vec{E}$ from Eq. 23–9, rather than to calculate $\vec{E}$ due to each charge from Coulomb's law. This is because V due to many charges is a scalar sum, whereas $\vec{E}$ is a vector sum.

23–8 Electrostatic Potential Energy; the Electron Volt

Suppose a point charge q is moved between two points in space, a and b, where the electric potential due to other charges is V_a and V_b, respectively. The change in electrostatic potential energy of q in the field of these other charges is, according to Eq. 23–2b,

$$\Delta U = U_b - U_a = q(V_b - V_a).$$

Now suppose we have a system of several point charges. What is the electrostatic potential energy of the system? It is most convenient to choose the electric potential energy to be zero when the charges are very far (ideally infinitely far) apart. A single point charge, Q_1, in isolation, has no potential energy, because if there are no other charges around, no electric force can be exerted on it. If a second point charge Q_2 is brought close to Q_1, the potential due to Q_1 at the position of this second charge is

$$V = \frac{1}{4\pi\epsilon_0} \frac{Q_1}{r_{12}},$$

where r_{12} is the distance between the two. The potential energy of the two charges, relative to $V = 0$ at $r = \infty$, is

$$U = Q_2 V = \frac{1}{4\pi\epsilon_0} \frac{Q_1 Q_2}{r_{12}}. \qquad \text{(23–10)}$$

This represents the work that needs to be done by an external force to bring Q_2 from infinity $(V = 0)$ to a distance r_{12} from Q_1. It is also the negative of the work needed to separate them to infinity.

If the system consists of three charges, the total potential energy will be the work needed to bring all three together. Equation 23–10 represents the work needed to bring Q_2 close to Q_1; to bring a third charge Q_3 so that it is a distance r_{13} from Q_1 and r_{23} from Q_2 requires work equal to

$$\frac{1}{4\pi\epsilon_0} \frac{Q_1 Q_3}{r_{13}} + \frac{1}{4\pi\epsilon_0} \frac{Q_2 Q_3}{r_{23}}.$$

So the potential energy of a system of three point charges is

$$U = \frac{1}{4\pi\epsilon_0} \left(\frac{Q_1 Q_2}{r_{12}} + \frac{Q_1 Q_3}{r_{13}} + \frac{Q_2 Q_3}{r_{23}} \right). \qquad [V = 0 \text{ at } r = \infty]$$

For a system of four charges, the potential energy would contain six such terms, and so on. (Caution must be used when making such sums to avoid double counting of the different pairs.)

The Electron Volt Unit

The joule is a very large unit for dealing with energies of electrons, atoms, or molecules (see Example 23–2), and for this purpose, the unit **electron volt** (eV) is used. One electron volt is defined as the energy acquired by a particle carrying a charge whose magnitude equals that on the electron $(q = e)$ as a result of moving through a potential difference of 1 V. Since $e = 1.6 \times 10^{-19}$ C, and since the change in potential energy equals qV, 1 eV is equal to $(1.6 \times 10^{-19}\text{ C})(1.0\text{ V}) = 1.6 \times 10^{-19}$ J:

$$1\,\text{eV} = 1.6 \times 10^{-19}\,\text{J}.$$

An electron that accelerates through a potential difference of 1000 V will lose 1000 eV of potential energy and will thus gain 1000 eV or 1 keV (kiloelectron volt) of kinetic energy. On the other hand, if a particle with a charge equal to twice the magnitude of the charge on the electron $\left(= 2e = 3.2 \times 10^{-19}\text{ C}\right)$ moves through a potential difference of 1000 V, its energy will change by 2000 eV = 2 keV.

Although the electron volt is handy for *stating* the energies of molecules and elementary particles, it is not a proper SI unit. For calculations it should be converted to joules using the conversion factor given above. In Example 23–2, for example, the electron acquired a kinetic energy of 8.0×10^{-16} J. We normally would quote this energy as 5000 eV ($= 8.0 \times 10^{-16}$ J$/1.6 \times 10^{-19}$ J/eV). But when determining the speed of a particle in SI units, we must use the kinetic energy in J.

EXERCISE E What is the kinetic energy of a He^{2+} ion released from rest and accelerated through a potential difference of 1.0 kV? (a) 1000 eV, (b) 500 eV, (c) 2000 eV, (d) 4000 eV, (e) 250 eV.

EXAMPLE 23–12 **Disassembling a hydrogen atom.** Calculate the work needed to "disassemble" a hydrogen atom. Assume that the proton and electron are initially separated by a distance equal to the "average" radius of the hydrogen atom in its ground state, 0.529×10^{-10} m, and that they end up an infinite distance apart from each other.

APPROACH The work necessary will be equal to the total energy, kinetic plus potential, of the electron and proton as an atom, compared to their total energy when infinitely far apart.

SOLUTION From Eq. 23–10 we have initially

$$U = \frac{1}{4\pi\epsilon_0} \frac{Q_1 Q_2}{r} = \frac{1}{4\pi\epsilon_0} \frac{(e)(-e)}{r} = \frac{-(8.99 \times 10^9 \,\mathrm{N \cdot m^2/C^2})(1.60 \times 10^{-19}\,\mathrm{C})^2}{(0.529 \times 10^{-10}\,\mathrm{m})}$$

$$= -27.2(1.60 \times 10^{-19})\,\mathrm{J} = -27.2\,\mathrm{eV}.$$

This represents the potential energy. The total energy must include also the kinetic energy of the electron moving in an orbit of radius $r = 0.529 \times 10^{-10}$ m. From $F = ma$ for centripetal acceleration, we have

$$\frac{1}{4\pi\epsilon_0}\left(\frac{e^2}{r^2}\right) = \frac{mv^2}{r}.$$

Then

$$K = \tfrac{1}{2}mv^2 = \tfrac{1}{2}\left(\frac{1}{4\pi\epsilon_0}\right)\frac{e^2}{r}$$

which equals $-\tfrac{1}{2}U$ (as calculated above), so $K = +13.6$ eV. The total energy initially is $E = K + U = 13.6\,\mathrm{eV} - 27.2\,\mathrm{eV} = -13.6\,\mathrm{eV}$. To separate a stable hydrogen atom into a proton and an electron at rest very far apart ($U = 0$ at $r = \infty$, $K = 0$ because $v = 0$) requires $+13.6$ eV. This is, in fact, the measured ionization energy for hydrogen.

NOTE To treat atoms properly, we need to use quantum theory (Chapters 37 to 39). But our "classical" calculation does give the correct answer here.

EXERCISE F The kinetic energy of a 1000-kg automobile traveling 20 m/s (70 km/h) would be about (a) 100 GeV, (b) 1000 TeV, (c) 10^6 TeV, (d) 10^{12} TeV, (e) 10^{18} TeV.

*23–9 Cathode Ray Tube: TV and Computer Monitors, Oscilloscope

An important device that makes use of voltage, and that allows us to "visualize" how a voltage changes in time, is the *cathode ray tube* (CRT). A CRT used in this way is an *oscilloscope*. The CRT has also been used for many years as the picture tube of television sets and computer monitors, but LCD (Chapter 35) and other screens are now common.

The operation of a CRT depends on the phenomenon of **thermionic emission** discovered by Thomas Edison (1847–1931). Consider two small plates (electrodes) inside an evacuated "bulb" or "tube" as shown in Fig. 23–21, to which is applied a potential difference. The negative electrode is called the **cathode**, the positive one the **anode**. If the negative cathode is heated (usually by an electric current, as in a lightbulb) so that it becomes hot and glowing, it is found that negative charge leaves the cathode and flows to the positive anode. These negative charges are now called electrons, but originally they were called **cathode rays** since they seemed to come from the cathode (see Section 27–7 on the discovery of the electron).

FIGURE 23–21 If the cathode inside the evacuated glass tube is heated to glowing, negatively charged "cathode rays" (electrons) are "boiled off" and flow across to the anode ($+$) to which they are attracted.

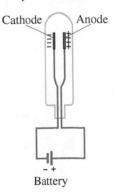

Cathode   Anode

Battery

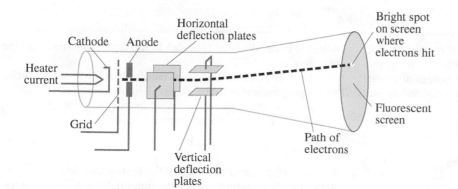

Heater current

Cathode Anode Horizontal deflection plates

Grid

Vertical deflection plates

Path of electrons

Bright spot on screen where electrons hit

Fluorescent screen

FIGURE 23–22 A cathode ray tube. Magnetic deflection coils are often used in place of the electric deflection plates shown here. The relative positions of the elements have been exaggerated for clarity.

The **cathode ray tube** (CRT) derives its name from the fact that inside an evacuated glass tube, a beam of cathode rays (electrons) is directed to various parts of a screen to produce a "picture." A simple CRT is diagrammed in Fig. 23–22. Electrons emitted by the heated cathode are accelerated by a high voltage (5000–50,000 V) applied between the anode and cathode. The electrons pass out of this "electron gun" through a small hole in the anode. The inside of the tube face is coated with a fluorescent material that glows when struck by electrons. A tiny bright spot is thus visible where the electron beam strikes the screen. Two horizontal and two vertical plates can deflect the beam of electrons when a voltage is applied to them. The electrons are deflected toward whichever plate is positive. By varying the voltage on the deflection plates, the bright spot can be placed at any point on the screen. Many CRTs use magnetic deflection coils (Chapter 27) instead of electric plates.

In the picture tube or monitor for a computer or television set, the electron beam is made to sweep over the screen in the manner shown in Fig. 23–23 by changing voltages applied to the deflection plates. For standard television in the United States, 525 lines constitutes a complete sweep in $\frac{1}{30}$ s, over the entire screen. High-definition TV provides more than double this number of lines (1080), giving greater picture sharpness. We see a picture because the image is retained by the fluorescent screen and by our eyes for about $\frac{1}{20}$ s. The picture we see consists of the varied brightness of the spots on the screen, controlled by the grid (a "porous" electrode, such as a wire grid, that allows passage of electrons). The grid limits the flow of electrons by means of the voltage (the "video signal") applied to it: the more negative this voltage, the more electrons are repelled and the fewer pass through. This video signal sent out by the TV station, and received by the TV set, is accompanied by signals that synchronize the grid voltage to the horizontal and vertical sweeps. (More in Chapter 31.)

An **oscilloscope** is a device for amplifying, measuring, and visually observing an electrical signal as a function of time on the screen of a CRT (a "signal" is usually a time-varying voltage). The electron beam is swept horizontally at a uniform rate in time by the horizontal deflection plates. The signal to be displayed is applied (after amplification) to the vertical deflection plates. The visible "trace" on the screen, which could be an electrocardiogram (Fig. 23–24), or a signal from an experiment on nerve conduction, is a plot of the signal voltage (vertically) versus time (horizontally).

PHYSICS APPLIED
CRT, TV and computer monitors

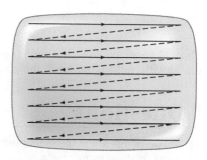

FIGURE 23–23 Electron beam sweeps across a television screen in a succession of horizontal lines. Each horizontal sweep is made by varying the voltage on the horizontal deflection plates. Then the electron beam is moved down a short distance by a change in voltage on the vertical deflection plates, and the process is repeated.

PHYSICS APPLIED
Oscilloscope

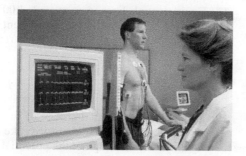

FIGURE 23–24 An electrocardiogram (ECG) trace displayed on a CRT.

Summary

Electric potential is defined as electric potential energy per unit charge. That is, the **electric potential difference** between any two points in space is defined as the difference in potential energy of a test charge q placed at those two points, divided by the charge q:

$$V_{ba} = \frac{U_b - U_a}{q}. \qquad (23\text{--}2b)$$

Potential difference is measured in volts $(1\,\text{V} = 1\,\text{J/C})$ and is sometimes referred to as **voltage**.

The change in potential energy of a charge q when it moves through a potential difference V_{ba} is

$$\Delta U = qV_{ba}. \qquad (23\text{--}3)$$

The potential difference V_{ba} between two points, a and b, is given by the relation

$$V_{ba} = V_b - V_a = -\int_a^b \vec{E} \cdot d\vec{\ell}. \qquad (23\text{--}4a)$$

Thus V_{ba} can be found in any region where $\vec{E}$ is known. If the electric field is uniform, the integral is easy: $V_{ba} = -Ed$,

where d is the distance (parallel to the field lines) between the two points.

An **equipotential line** or **surface** is all at the same potential, and is perpendicular to the electric field at all points.

The electric potential due to a single point charge Q, relative to zero potential at infinity, is given by

$$V = \frac{1}{4\pi\epsilon_0} \frac{Q}{r}. \qquad (23\text{--}5)$$

The potential due to any charge distribution can be obtained by summing (or integrating) over the potentials for all the charges.

The potential due to an **electric dipole** drops off as $1/r^2$. The **dipole moment** is $p = Q\ell$, where ℓ is the distance between the two equal but opposite charges of magnitude Q.

When V is known, the components of $\vec{E}$ can be found from the inverse of Eq. 23–4a, namely

$$E_x = -\frac{\partial V}{\partial x}, \qquad E_y = -\frac{\partial V}{\partial y}, \qquad E_z = -\frac{\partial V}{\partial z}. \qquad (23\text{--}9)$$

[*Television and computer monitors traditionally use a **cathode ray tube** (CRT) that accelerates electrons by high voltage, and sweeps them across the screen in a regular way using deflection plates.]

Questions

1. If two points are at the same potential, does this mean that no work is done in moving a test charge from one point to the other? Does this imply that no force must be exerted? Explain.

2. If a negative charge is initially at rest in an electric field, will it move toward a region of higher potential or lower potential? What about a positive charge? How does the potential energy of the charge change in each instance?

3. State clearly the difference (a) between electric potential and electric field, (b) between electric potential and electric potential energy.

4. An electron is accelerated from rest by a potential difference of, say, 0.10 V. How much greater would its final speed be if it is accelerated with four times as much voltage? Explain.

5. Can a particle ever move from a region of low electric potential to one of high potential and yet have its electric potential energy decrease? Explain.

6. If $V = 0$ at a point in space, must $\vec{E} = 0$? If $\vec{E} = 0$ at some point, must $V = 0$ at that point? Explain. Give examples for each.

7. When dealing with practical devices, we often take the ground (the Earth) to be 0 V. (a) If instead we said the ground was -10 V, how would this affect V and E at other points? (b) Does the fact that the Earth carries a net charge affect the choice of V at its surface?

8. Can two equipotential lines cross? Explain.

9. Draw in a few equipotential lines in Fig. 21–34b and c.

10. What can you say about the electric field in a region of space that has the same potential throughout?

11. A satellite orbits the Earth along a gravitational equipotential line. What shape must the orbit be?

12. Suppose the charged ring of Example 23–8 was not uniformly charged, so that the density of charge was twice as great near the top as near the bottom. Assuming the total charge Q is unchanged, would this affect the potential at point P on the axis (Fig. 23–14)? Would it affect the value of $\vec{E}$ at that point? Is there a discrepancy here? Explain.

13. Consider a metal conductor in the shape of a football. If it carries a total charge Q, where would you expect the charge density σ to be greatest, at the ends or along the flatter sides? Explain. [*Hint:* Near the surface of a conductor, $E = \sigma/\epsilon_0$.]

14. If you know V at a point in space, can you calculate $\vec{E}$ at that point? If you know $\vec{E}$ at a point can you calculate V at that point? If not, what else must be known in each case?

15. A conducting sphere carries a charge Q and a second identical conducting sphere is neutral. The two are initially isolated, but then they are placed in contact. (a) What can you say about the potential of each when they are in contact? (b) Will charge flow from one to the other? If so, how much? (c) If the spheres do not have the same radius, how are your answers to parts (a) and (b) altered?

16. At a particular location, the electric field points due north. In what direction(s) will the rate of change of potential be (a) greatest, (b) least, and (c) zero?

17. Equipotential lines are spaced 1.00 V apart. Does the distance between the lines in different regions of space tell you anything about the relative strengths of $\vec{E}$ in those regions? If so, what?

18. If the electric field $\vec{E}$ is uniform in a region, what can you infer about the electric potential V? If V is uniform in a region of space, what can you infer about $\vec{E}$?

19. Is the electric potential energy of two unlike charges positive or negative? What about two like charges? What is the significance of the sign of the potential energy in each case?

Problems

23-1 Electric Potential

1. (I) What potential difference is needed to stop an electron that has an initial velocity $v = 5.0 \times 10^5$ m/s?

2. (I) How much work does the electric field do in moving a proton from a point with a potential of $+185$ V to a point where it is -55 V?

3. (I) An electron acquires 5.25×10^{-16} J of kinetic energy when it is accelerated by an electric field from plate A to plate B. What is the potential difference between the plates, and which plate is at the higher potential?

4. (II) The work done by an external force to move a $-9.10 \,\mu$C charge from point a to point b is 7.00×10^{-4} J. If the charge was started from rest and had 2.10×10^{-4} J of kinetic energy when it reached point b, what must be the potential difference between a and b?

23-2 Potential Related to Electric Field

5. (I) Thunderclouds typically develop voltage differences of about 1×10^8 V. Given that an electric field of 3×10^6 V/m is required to produce an electrical spark within a volume of air, estimate the length of a thundercloud lightning bolt. [Can you see why, when lightning strikes from a cloud to the ground, the bolt actually has to propagate as a sequence of steps?]

6. (I) The electric field between two parallel plates connected to a 45-V battery is 1300 V/m. How far apart are the plates?

7. (I) What is the maximum amount of charge that a spherical conductor of radius 6.5 cm can hold in air?

8. (I) What is the magnitude of the electric field between two parallel plates 4.0 mm apart if the potential difference between them is 110 V?

9. (I) What minimum radius must a large conducting sphere of an electrostatic generating machine have if it is to be at 35,000 V without discharge into the air? How much charge will it carry?

10. (II) A manufacturer claims that a carpet will not generate more than 5.0 kV of static electricity. What magnitude of charge would have to be transferred between a carpet and a shoe for there to be a 5.0-kV potential difference between the shoe and the carpet. Approximate the shoe and the carpet as large sheets of charge separated by a distance $d = 1.0$ mm.

11. (II) A uniform electric field $\vec{E} = -4.20$ N/C$\hat{i}$ points in the negative x direction as shown in Fig. 23–25. The x and y coordinates of points A, B, and C are given on the diagram (in meters). Determine the differences in potential (a) V_{BA}, (b) V_{CB}, and (c) V_{CA}.

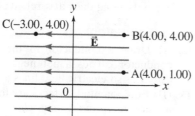

FIGURE 23–25
Problem 11.

12. (II) The electric potential of a very large isolated flat metal plate is V_0. It carries a uniform distribution of charge of surface density σ (C/m^2), or $\sigma/2$ on each surface. Determine V at a distance x from the plate. Consider the point x to be far from the edges and assume x is much smaller than the plate dimensions.

13. (II) The Earth produces an inwardly directed electric field of magnitude 150 V/m near its surface. (a) What is the potential of the Earth's surface relative to $V = 0$ at $r = \infty$? (b) If the potential of the Earth is chosen to be zero, what is the potential at infinity? (Ignore the fact that positive charge in the ionosphere approximately cancels the Earth's net charge; how would this affect your answer?)

14. (II) A 32-cm-diameter conducting sphere is charged to 680 V relative to $V = 0$ at $r = \infty$. (a) What is the surface charge density σ? (b) At what distance will the potential due to the sphere be only 25 V?

15. (II) An insulated spherical conductor of radius r_1 carries a charge Q. A second conducting sphere of radius r_2 and initially uncharged is then connected to the first by a long conducting wire. (a) After the connection, what can you say about the electric potential of each sphere? (b) How much charge is transferred to the second sphere? Assume the connected spheres are far apart compared to their radii. (Why make this assumption?)

16. (II) Determine the difference in potential between two points that are distances R_a and R_b from a very long ($\gg R_a$ or R_b) straight wire carrying a uniform charge per unit length λ.

17. (II) Suppose the end of your finger is charged. (a) Estimate the breakdown voltage in air for your finger. (b) About what surface charge density would have to be on your finger at this voltage?

18. (II) Estimate the electric field in the membrane wall of a living cell. Assume the wall is 10 nm thick and has a potential of 0.10 V across it.

19. (II) A nonconducting sphere of radius r_0 carries a total charge Q distributed uniformly throughout its volume. Determine the electric potential as a function of the distance r from the center of the sphere for (a) $r > r_0$ and (b) $r < r_0$. Take $V = 0$ at $r = \infty$. (c) Plot V versus r and E versus r.

20. (III) Repeat Problem 19 assuming the charge density ρ_E increases as the square of the distance from the center of the sphere, and $\rho_E = 0$ at the center.

21. (III) The volume charge density ρ_E within a sphere of radius r_0 is distributed in accordance with the following spherically symmetric relation

$$\rho_E(r) = \rho_0 \left[1 - \frac{r^2}{r_0^2} \right]$$

where r is measured from the center of the sphere and ρ_0 is a constant. For a point P inside the sphere ($r < r_0$), determine the electric potential V. Let $V = 0$ at infinity.

22. (III) A hollow spherical conductor, carrying a net charge $+Q$, has inner radius r_1 and outer radius $r_2 = 2r_1$ (Fig. 23–26). At the center of the sphere is a point charge $+Q/2$. (a) Write the electric field strength E in all three regions as a function of r. Then determine the potential as a function of r, the distance from the center, for (b) $r > r_2$, (c) $r_1 < r < r_2$, and (d) $0 < r < r_1$. (e) Plot both V and E as a function of r from $r = 0$ to $r = 2r_2$.

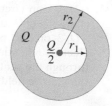

FIGURE 23–26
Problem 22.

23. (III) A very long conducting cylinder (length ℓ) of radius R_0 $(R_0 \ll \ell)$ carries a uniform surface charge density σ (C/m²). The cylinder is at an electric potential V_0. What is the potential, at points far from the end, at a distance R from the center of the cylinder? Determine for (a) $R > R_0$ and (b) $R < R_0$. (c) Is $V = 0$ at $R = \infty$ (assume $\ell = \infty$)? Explain.

23–3 Potential Due to Point Charges

24. (I) A point charge Q creates an electric potential of $+185$ V at a distance of 15 cm. What is Q (let $V = 0$ at $r = \infty$)?

25. (I) (a) What is the electric potential 0.50×10^{-10} m from a proton (charge $+e$)? Let $V = 0$ at $r = \infty$. (b) What is the potential energy of an electron at this point?

26. (II) Two point charges, $3.4 \,\mu$C and $-2.0 \,\mu$C, are placed 5.0 cm apart on the x axis. At what points along the x axis is (a) the electric field zero and (b) the potential zero? Let $V = 0$ at $r = \infty$.

27. (II) A $+25 \,\mu$C point charge is placed 6.0 cm from an identical $+25 \,\mu$C point charge. How much work would be required by an external force to move a $+0.18 \,\mu$C test charge from a point midway between them to a point 1.0 cm closer to either of the charges?

28. (II) Point a is 26 cm north of a $-3.8 \,\mu$C point charge, and point b is 36 cm west of the charge (Fig. 23–27). Determine (a) $V_b - V_a$, and (b) $\vec{E}_b - \vec{E}_a$ (magnitude and direction).

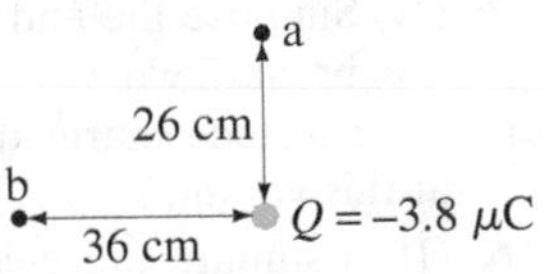

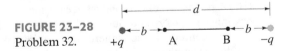

FIGURE 23–27
Problem 28.

29. (II) How much voltage must be used to accelerate a proton (radius 1.2×10^{-15} m) so that it has sufficient energy to just "touch" a silicon nucleus? A silicon nucleus has a charge of $+14e$ and its radius is about 3.6×10^{-15} m. Assume the potential is that for point charges.

30. (II) Two identical $+5.5 \,\mu$C point charges are initially spaced 6.5 cm from each other. If they are released at the same instant from rest, how fast will they be moving when they are very far away from each other? Assume they have identical masses of 1.0 mg.

31. (II) An electron starts from rest 42.5 cm from a fixed point charge with $Q = -0.125$ nC. How fast will the electron be moving when it is very far away?

32. (II) Two equal but opposite charges are separated by a distance d, as shown in Fig. 23–28. Determine a formula for $V_{BA} = V_B - V_A$ for points B and A on the line between the charges situated as shown.

FIGURE 23–28
Problem 32.

23–4 Potential Due to Charge Distribution

33. (II) A thin circular ring of radius R (as in Fig. 23–14) has charge $+Q/2$ uniformly distributed on the top half, and $-Q/2$ on the bottom half. (a) What is the value of the electric potential at a point a distance x along the axis through the center of the circle? (b) What can you say about the electric field $\vec{E}$ at a distance x along the axis? Let $V = 0$ at $r = \infty$.

34. (II) Three point charges are arranged at the corners of a square of side ℓ as shown in Fig. 23–29. What is the potential at the fourth corner (point A), taking $V = 0$ at a great distance?

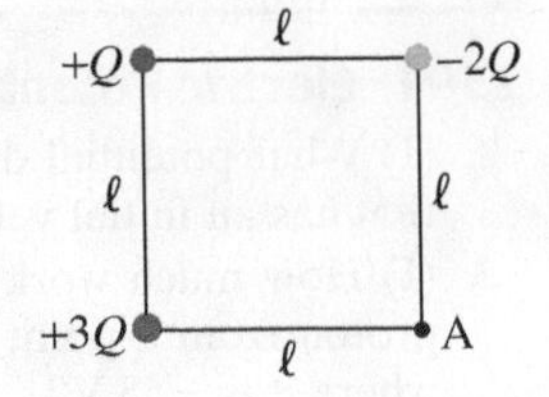

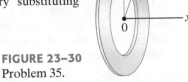

FIGURE 23–29
Problem 34.

35. (II) A flat ring of inner radius R_1 and outer radius R_2, Fig. 23–30, carries a uniform surface charge density σ. Determine the electric potential at points along the axis (the x axis). [Hint: Try substituting variables.]

FIGURE 23–30
Problem 35.

36. (II) A total charge Q is uniformly distributed on a thread of length ℓ. The thread forms a semicircle. What is the potential at the center? (Assume $V = 0$ at large distances.)

37. (II) A 12.0-cm-radius thin ring carries a uniformly distributed $15.0 \,\mu$C charge. A small 7.5-g sphere with a charge of $3.0 \,\mu$C is placed exactly at the center of the ring and given a very small push so it moves along the ring axis ($+x$ axis). How fast will the sphere be moving when it is 2.0 m from the center of the ring (ignore gravity)?

38. (II) A thin rod of length 2ℓ is centered on the x axis as shown in Fig. 23–31. The rod carries a uniformly distributed charge Q. Determine the potential V as a function of y for points along the y axis. Let $V = 0$ at infinity.

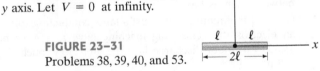

FIGURE 23–31
Problems 38, 39, 40, and 53.

39. (II) Determine the potential $V(x)$ for points along the x axis outside the rod of Fig. 23–31 (Problem 38).

40. (III) The charge on the rod of Fig. 23–31 has a nonuniform linear charge distribution, $\lambda = ax$. Determine the potential V for (a) points along the y axis and (b) points along the x axis outside the rod.

41. (III) Suppose the flat circular disk of Fig. 23–15 (Example 23–9) has a nonuniform surface charge density $\sigma = aR^2$, where R is measured from the center of the disk. Find the potential $V(x)$ at points along the x axis, relative to $V = 0$ at $x = \infty$.

23–5 Equipotentials

42. (I) Draw a conductor in the shape of a football. This conductor carries a net negative charge, $-Q$. Draw in a dozen or so electric field lines and equipotential lines.

43. (II) Equipotential surfaces are to be drawn 100 V apart near a very large uniformly charged metal plate carrying a surface charge density $\sigma = 0.75 \,\mu$C/m². How far apart (in space) are the equipotential surfaces?

44. (II) A metal sphere of radius $r_0 = 0.44$ m carries a charge $Q = 0.50 \,\mu$C. Equipotential surfaces are to be drawn for 100-V intervals outside the sphere. Determine the radius r of (a) the first, (b) the tenth, and (c) the 100th equipotential from the surface.

23-6 Dipoles

45. (II) Calculate the electric potential due to a tiny dipole whose dipole moment is 4.8×10^{-30} C·m at a point 4.1×10^{-9} m away if this point is (a) along the axis of the dipole nearer the positive charge; (b) 45° above the axis but nearer the positive charge; (c) 45° above the axis but nearer the negative charge. Let $V = 0$ at $r = \infty$.

46. (III) The dipole moment, considered as a vector, points from the negative to the positive charge. The water molecule, Fig. 23–32, has a dipole moment $\vec{p}$ which can be considered as the vector sum of the two dipole moments $\vec{p}_1$ and $\vec{p}_2$ as shown. The distance between each H and the O is about 0.96×10^{-10} m; the lines joining the center of the O atom with each H atom make an angle of 104° as shown, and the net dipole moment has been measured to be $p = 6.1 \times 10^{-30}$ C·m. (a) Determine the effective charge q on each H atom. (b) Determine the electric potential, far from the molecule, due to each dipole, $\vec{p}_1$ and $\vec{p}_2$, and show that

$$V = \frac{1}{4\pi\epsilon_0} \frac{p\cos\theta}{r^2},$$

where p is the magnitude of the net dipole moment, $\vec{p} = \vec{p}_1 + \vec{p}_2$, and V is the total potential due to both $\vec{p}_1$ and $\vec{p}_2$. Take $V = 0$ at $r = \infty$.

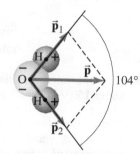

FIGURE 23–32
Problem 46.

23-7 $\vec{E}$ Determined from V

47. (I) Show that the electric field of a single point charge (Eq. 21–4) follows from Eq. 23–5, $V = (1/4\pi\epsilon_0)(Q/r)$.

48. (I) What is the potential gradient just outside the surface of a uranium nucleus $(Q = +92e)$ whose diameter is about 15×10^{-15} m?

49. (II) The electric potential between two parallel plates is given by $V(x) = (8.0\,\text{V/m})x + 5.0\,\text{V}$, with $x = 0$ taken at one of the plates and x positive in the direction toward the other plate. What is the charge density on the plates?

50. (II) The electric potential in a region of space varies as $V = by/(a^2 + y^2)$. Determine $\vec{E}$.

51. (II) In a certain region of space, the electric potential is given by $V = y^2 + 2.5xy - 3.5xyz$. Determine the electric field vector, $\vec{E}$, in this region.

52. (II) A dust particle with mass of 0.050 g and a charge of 2.0×10^{-6} C is in a region of space where the potential is given by $V(x) = (2.0\,\text{V/m}^2)x^2 - (3.0\,\text{V/m}^3)x^3$. If the particle starts at $x = 2.0$ m, what is the initial acceleration of the charge?

53. (III) Use the results of Problems 38 and 39 to determine the electric field due to the uniformly charged rod of Fig. 23–31 for points (a) along the y axis and (b) along the x axis.

23-8 Electrostatic Potential Energy; Electron Volt

54. (I) How much work must be done to bring three electrons from a great distance apart to within 1.0×10^{-10} m from one another (at the corners of an equilateral triangle)?

55. (I) What potential difference is needed to give a helium nucleus $(Q = 3.2 \times 10^{-19}$ C) 125 keV of kinetic energy?

56. (I) What is the speed of (a) a 1.5-keV (kinetic energy) electron and (b) a 1.5-keV proton?

57. (II) Many chemical reactions release energy. Suppose that at the beginning of a reaction, an electron and proton are separated by 0.110 nm, and their final separation is 0.100 nm. How much electric potential energy was lost in this reaction (in units of eV)?

58. (II) An alpha particle (which is a helium nucleus, $Q = +2e$, $m = 6.64 \times 10^{-27}$ kg) is emitted in a radioactive decay with kinetic energy 5.53 MeV. What is its speed?

59. (II) Write the total electrostatic potential energy, U, for (a) four point charges and (b) five point charges. Draw a diagram defining all quantities.

60. (II) Four equal point charges, Q, are fixed at the corners of a square of side b. (a) What is their total electrostatic potential energy? (b) How much potential energy will a fifth charge, Q, have at the center of the square (relative to $V = 0$ at $r = \infty$)? (c) If constrained to remain in that plane, is the fifth charge in stable or unstable equilibrium? (d) If a negative $(-Q)$ charge is at the center, is it in stable equilibrium?

61. (II) An electron starting from rest acquires 1.33 keV of kinetic energy in moving from point A to point B. (a) How much kinetic energy would a proton acquire, starting from rest at B and moving to point A? (b) Determine the ratio of their speeds at the end of their respective trajectories.

62. (II) Determine the total electrostatic potential energy of a conducting sphere of radius r_0 that carries a total charge Q distributed uniformly on its surface.

63. (II) The **liquid-drop model** of the nucleus suggests that high-energy oscillations of certain nuclei can split ("fission") a large nucleus into two unequal fragments plus a few neutrons. Using this model, consider the case of a uranium nucleus fissioning into two spherical fragments, one with a charge $q_1 = +38e$ and radius $r_1 = 5.5 \times 10^{-15}$ m, the other with $q_2 = +54e$ and $r_2 = 6.2 \times 10^{-15}$ m. Calculate the electric potential energy (MeV) of these fragments, assuming that the charge is uniformly distributed throughout the volume of each spherical nucleus and that their surfaces are initially in contact at rest. The electrons surrounding the nuclei can be neglected. This electric potential energy will then be entirely converted to kinetic energy as the fragments repel each other. How does your predicted kinetic energy of the fragments agree with the observed value associated with uranium fission (approximately 200 MeV total)? $[1\,\text{MeV} = 10^6\,\text{eV}.]$

64. (III) Determine the total electrostatic potential energy of a nonconducting sphere of radius r_0 carrying a total charge Q distributed uniformly throughout its volume.

*23-9 CRT

***65.** (I) Use the ideal gas as a model to estimate the rms speed of a free electron in a metal at 273 K, and at 2700 K (a typical temperature of the cathode in a CRT).

***66.** (III) Electrons are accelerated by 6.0 kV in a CRT. The screen is 28 cm wide and is 34 cm from the 2.6-cm-long deflection plates. Over what range must the horizontally deflecting electric field vary to sweep the beam fully across the screen?

***67.** (III) In a given CRT, electrons are accelerated horizontally by 7.2 kV. They then pass through a uniform electric field E for a distance of 2.8 cm which deflects them upward so they reach the top of the screen 22 cm away, 11 cm above the center. Estimate the value of E.

General Problems

68. If the electrons in a single raindrop, 3.5 mm in diameter, could be removed from the Earth (without removing the atomic nuclei), by how much would the potential of the Earth increase?

69. By rubbing a nonconducting material, a charge of 10^{-8} C can readily be produced. If this is done to a sphere of radius 15 cm, estimate the potential produced at the surface. Let $V = 0$ at $r = \infty$.

70. Sketch the electric field and equipotential lines for two charges of the same sign and magnitude separated by a distance d.

71. A $+33\,\mu$C point charge is placed 36 cm from an identical $+33\,\mu$C charge. A $-1.5\,\mu$C charge is moved from point a to point b, Fig. 23–33. What is the change in potential energy?

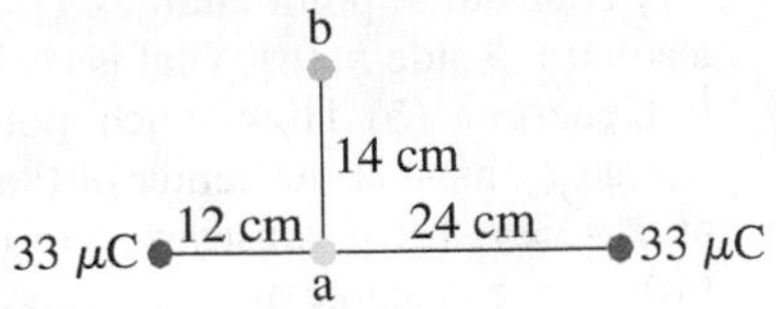

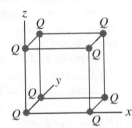

FIGURE 23–33
Problem 71.
33 μC · —12 cm—|— a —24 cm—• 33 μC
14 cm, b

72. At each corner of a cube of side ℓ there is a point charge Q, Fig. 23–34. (a) What is the potential at the center of the cube ($V = 0$ at $r = \infty$)? (b) What is the potential at each corner due to the other seven charges? (c) What is the total potential energy of this system?

FIGURE 23–34
Problem 72.

73. In a television picture tube (CRT), electrons are accelerated by thousands of volts through a vacuum. If a television set is laid on its back, would electrons be able to move upward against the force of gravity? What potential difference, acting over a distance of 3.5 cm, would be needed to balance the downward force of gravity so that an electron would remain stationary? Assume that the electric field is uniform.

74. Four point charges are located at the corners of a square that is 8.0 cm on a side. The charges, going in rotation around the square, are Q, $2Q$, $-3Q$, and $2Q$, where $Q = 3.1\,\mu$C (Fig. 23–35). What is the total electric potential energy stored in the system, relative to $U = 0$ at infinite separation?

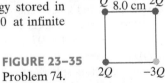

FIGURE 23–35
Problem 74.
Q —8.0 cm— $2Q$
$2Q$ — $-3Q$

75. In a **photocell**, ultraviolet (UV) light provides enough energy to some electrons in barium metal to eject them from the surface at high speed. See Fig. 23–36. To measure the maximum energy of the electrons, another plate above the barium surface is kept at a negative enough potential that the emitted electrons are slowed down and stopped, and return to the barium surface. If the plate voltage is -3.02 V (compared to the barium) when the fastest electrons are stopped, what was the speed of these electrons when they were emitted?

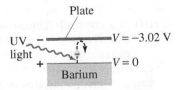

FIGURE 23–36
Problem 75.

76. An electron is accelerated horizontally from rest in a television picture tube by a potential difference of 5500 V. It then passes between two horizontal plates 6.5 cm long and 1.3 cm apart that have a potential difference of 250 V (Fig. 23–37). At what angle θ will the electron be traveling after it passes between the plates?

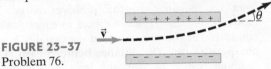

FIGURE 23–37
Problem 76.

77. Three charges are at the corners of an equilateral triangle (side ℓ) as shown in Fig. 23–38. Determine the potential at the midpoint of each of the sides. Let $V = 0$ at $r = \infty$.

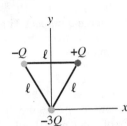

FIGURE 23–38
Problem 77.

78. Near the surface of the Earth there is an electric field of about 150 V/m which points downward. Two identical balls with mass $m = 0.340$ kg are dropped from a height of 2.00 m, but one of the balls is positively charged with $q_1 = 450\,\mu$C, and the second is negatively charged with $q_2 = -450\,\mu$C. Use conservation of energy to determine the difference in the speeds of the two balls when they hit the ground. (Neglect air resistance.)

79. A lightning flash transfers 4.0 C of charge and 4.8 MJ of energy to the Earth. (a) Between what potential difference did it travel? (b) How much water could this energy boil, starting from room temperature? [*Hint*: See Chapter 19.]

80. Determine the components of the electric field, E_x and E_y, as a function of x and y in the xy plane due to a dipole, Fig. 23–39, starting with Eq. 23–7. Assume $r = (x^2 + y^2)^{\frac{1}{2}} \gg \ell$.

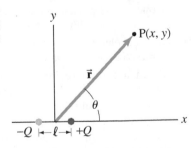

FIGURE 23–39
Problem 80.
$-Q$ |—ℓ—| $+Q$

81. A nonconducting sphere of radius r_2 contains a concentric spherical cavity of radius r_1. The material between r_1 and r_2 carries a uniform charge density ρ_E (C/m³). Determine the electric potential V, relative to $V = 0$ at $r = \infty$, as a function of the distance r from the center for (a) $r > r_2$, (b) $r_1 < r < r_2$, and (c) $0 < r < r_1$. Is V continuous at r_1 and r_2?

82. A thin flat nonconducting disk, with radius R_0 and charge Q, has a hole with a radius $R_0/2$ in its center. Find the electric potential $V(x)$ at points along the symmetry (x) axis of the disk (a line perpendicular to the disk, passing through its center). Let $V = 0$ at $x = \infty$.

83. A **Geiger counter** is used to detect charged particles emitted by radioactive nuclei. It consists of a thin, positively charged central wire of radius R_a surrounded by a concentric conducting cylinder of radius R_b with an equal negative charge (Fig. 23–40). The charge per unit length on the inner wire is λ (units C/m). The interior space between wire and cylinder is filled with low-pressure inert gas. Charged particles ionize some of these gas atoms; the resulting free electrons are attracted toward the positive central wire. If the radial electric field is strong enough, the freed electrons gain enough energy to ionize other atoms, causing an "avalanche" of electrons to strike the central wire, generating an electric "signal." Find the expression for the electric field between the wire and the cylinder, and show that the potential difference between R_a and R_b is

$$V_a - V_b = \left(\frac{\lambda}{2\pi\epsilon_0}\right) \ln\left(\frac{R_b}{R_a}\right).$$

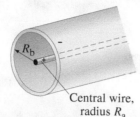

FIGURE 23–40
Problem 83.

Central wire, radius R_a

84. A **Van de Graaff generator** (Fig. 23–41) can develop a very large potential difference, even millions of volts. Electrons are pulled off the belt by the high voltage pointed electrode at A, leaving the belt positively charged. (Recall Example 23–5 where we saw that near sharp points the electric field is high and ionization can occur.) The belt carries the positive charge up inside the spherical shell where electrons from the large conducting sphere are attracted over to the pointed conductor at B, leaving the outer surface of the conducting sphere positively charged. As more charge is brought up, the sphere reaches extremely high voltage. Consider a Van de Graaff generator with a sphere of radius 0.20 m. (a) What is the electric potential on the surface of the sphere when electrical breakdown occurs? (Assume $V = 0$ at $r = \infty$.) (b) What is the charge on the sphere for the potential found in part (a)?

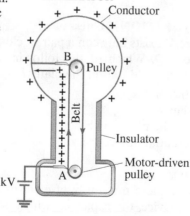

GENERATOR

Conductor

Pulley

B

Belt

Insulator

Motor-driven pulley

A

FIGURE 23–41 50 kV
Problem 84.

85. The potential in a region of space is given by $V = B/(x^2 + R^2)^2$ where $B = 150\ \text{V}\cdot\text{m}^4$ and $R = 0.20\ \text{m}$. (a) Find V at $x = 0.20\ \text{m}$. (b) Find $\vec{E}$ as a function of x. (c) Find $\vec{E}$ at $x = 0.20\ \text{m}$.

86. A charge $-q_1$ of mass m rests on the y axis at a distance b above the x axis. Two positive charges of magnitude $+q_2$ are fixed on the x axis at $x = +a$ and $x = -a$, respectively (Fig. 23–42). If the $-q_1$ charge is given an initial velocity v_0 in the positive y direction, what is the minimum value of v_0 such that the charge escapes to a point infinitely far away from the two positive charges?

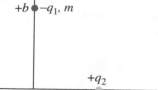

FIGURE 23–42
Problem 86.

$+q_2$ $-a$ $+q_2$ $+a$

Numerical/Computer

*87. (II) A dipole is composed of a $-1.0\ \text{nC}$ charge at $x = -1.0\ \text{cm}$ and a $+1.0\ \text{nC}$ charge at $x = +1.0\ \text{cm}$. (a) Make a plot of V along the x axis from $x = 2.0\ \text{cm}$ to $x = 15\ \text{cm}$. (b) On the same graph, plot the approximate V using Eq. 23–7 from $x = 2.0\ \text{cm}$ to $x = 15\ \text{cm}$. Let $V = 0$ at $x = \infty$.

*88. (II) A thin flat disk of radius R_0 carries a total charge Q that is distributed uniformly over its surface. The electric potential at a distance x on the x axis is given by

$$V(x) = \frac{Q}{2\pi\epsilon_0 R_0^2}\left[(x^2 + R_0^2)^{\frac{1}{2}} - x\right].$$

(See Example 23–9.) Show that the electric field at a distance x on the x axis is given by

$$E(x) = \frac{Q}{2\pi\epsilon_0 R_0^2}\left(1 - \frac{x}{(x^2 + R_0^2)^{\frac{1}{2}}}\right).$$

Make graphs of $V(x)$ and $E(x)$ as a function of x/R_0 for $x/R_0 = 0$ to 4. (Do the calculations in steps of 0.1.) Use $Q = 5.0\ \mu\text{C}$ and $R_0 = 10\ \text{cm}$ for the calculation and graphs.

*89. (III) You are trying to determine an unknown amount of charge using only a voltmeter and a ruler, knowing that it is either a single sheet of charge or a point charge that is creating it. You determine the direction of greatest change of potential, and then measure potentials along a line in that direction. The potential versus position (note that the zero of position is arbitrary, and the potential is measured relative to ground) is measured as follows:

x (cm)	0.0	1.0	2.0	3.0	4.0	5.0	6.0	7.0	8.0	9.0
V (volts)	3.9	3.0	2.5	2.0	1.7	1.5	1.4	1.4	1.2	1.1

(a) Graph V versus position. Do you think the field is caused by a sheet or a point charge? (b) Graph the data in such a way that you can determine the magnitude of the charge and determine that value. (c) Is it possible to determine where the charge is from this data? If so, give the position of the charge.

Answers to Exercises

A: (b).

B: (d).

C: (d).

D: (a) iii, (b) i, (c) i.

E: (c).

F: (d).

Capacitors come in a wide range of sizes and shapes, only a few of which are shown here. A capacitor is basically two conductors that do not touch, and which therefore can store charge of opposite sign on its two conductors. Capacitors are used in a wide variety of circuits, as we shall see in this and later Chapters.

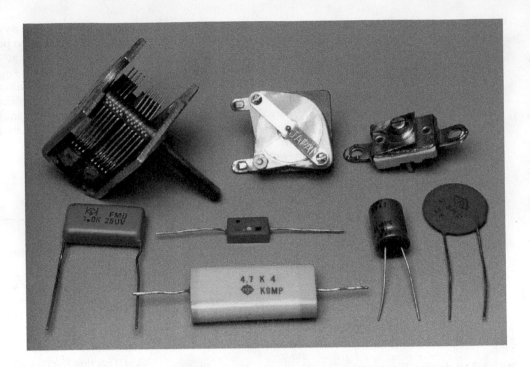

CHAPTER 24

Capacitance, Dielectrics, Electric Energy Storage

CHAPTER-OPENING QUESTION—Guess now!

A fixed potential difference V exists between a pair of close parallel plates carrying opposite charges $+Q$ and $-Q$. Which of the following would not increase the magnitude of charge that you could put on the plates?

(a) Increase the size of the plates.
(b) Move the plates farther apart.
(c) Fill the space between the plates with paper.
(d) Increase the fixed potential difference V.
(e) None of the above.

This Chapter will complete our study of electrostatics. It deals first of all with an important device, the capacitor, which is used in many electronic circuits. We will also discuss electric energy storage and the effects of an insulator, or dielectric, on electric fields and potential differences.

PHYSICS APPLIED
Uses of capacitors

24–1 Capacitors

A **capacitor** is a device that can store electric charge, and normally consists of two conducting objects (usually plates or sheets) placed near each other but not touching. Capacitors are widely used in electronic circuits. They store charge for later use, such as in a camera flash, and as energy backup in computers if the power fails. Capacitors also block surges of charge and energy to protect circuits.

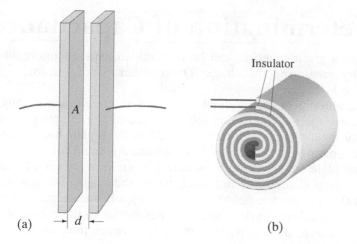

Insulator

(a) d

(b)

Very tiny capacitors serve as memory for the "ones" and "zeros" of the binary code in the random access memory (RAM) of computers. Capacitors serve many other applications, some of which we will discuss.

A simple capacitor consists of a pair of parallel plates of area A separated by a small distance d (Fig. 24–1a). Often the two plates are rolled into the form of a cylinder with plastic, paper, or other insulator separating the plates, Fig. 24–1b. In a diagram, the symbol

$\dashv\vdash$ or $\dashv\vdash$ [capacitor symbol]

represents a capacitor. A battery, which is a source of voltage, is indicated by the symbol:

$\dashv\vdash$ [battery symbol]

with unequal arms.

If a voltage is applied across a capacitor by connecting the capacitor to a battery with conducting wires as in Fig. 24–2, the two plates quickly become charged: one plate acquires a negative charge, the other an equal amount of positive charge. Each battery terminal and the plate of the capacitor connected to it are at the same potential; hence the full battery voltage appears across the capacitor. For a given capacitor, it is found that the amount of charge Q acquired by each plate is proportional to the magnitude of the potential difference V between them:

$$Q = CV. \tag{24–1}$$

The constant of proportionality, C, in the above relation is called the **capacitance** of the capacitor. The unit of capacitance is coulombs per volt and this unit is called a **farad** (F). Common capacitors have capacitance in the range of $1\,\text{pF}$ (picofarad $= 10^{-12}\,\text{F}$) to $10^3\,\mu\text{F}$ (microfarad $= 10^{-6}\,\text{F}$). The relation, Eq. 24–1, was first suggested by Volta in the late eighteenth century. The capacitance C does not in general depend on Q or V. Its value depends only on the size, shape, and relative position of the two conductors, and also on the material that separates them.

In Eq. 24–1, and from now on, we use simply V (in italics) to represent a potential difference, rather than V_{ba}, ΔV, or $V_b - V_a$, as previously. (Be sure not to confuse italic V and C which stand for voltage and capacitance, with non-italic V and C which stand for the units volts and coulombs).

EXERCISE A Graphs for charge versus voltage are shown in Fig. 24–3 for three capacitors, A, B, and C. Which has the greatest capacitance?

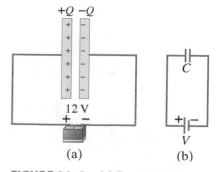

$+Q$ $-Q$

12 V

C

V

(a)   (b)

FIGURE 24–2 (a) Parallel-plate capacitor connected to a battery. (b) Same circuit shown using symbols.

FIGURE 24–3 Exercise A.

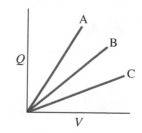

Q

A

B

C

V

⚠ **CAUTION**

V = potential difference from here on

24–2 Determination of Capacitance

The capacitance of a given capacitor can be determined experimentally directly from Eq. 24–1, by measuring the charge Q on either conductor for a given potential difference V.

For capacitors whose geometry is simple, we can determine C analytically, and in this Section we assume the conductors are separated by a vacuum or air. First, we determine C for a parallel-plate capacitor, Fig. 24–4. Each plate has area A and the two plates are separated by a distance d. We assume d is small compared to the dimensions of each plate so that the electric field $\vec{E}$ is uniform between them and we can ignore fringing (lines of $\vec{E}$ not straight) at the edges. We saw earlier (Example 21–13) that the electric field between two closely spaced parallel plates has magnitude $E = \sigma/\epsilon_0$ and its direction is perpendicular to the plates. Since σ is the charge per unit area, $\sigma = Q/A$, then the field between the plates is

$$E = \frac{Q}{\epsilon_0 A}.$$

The relation between electric field and electric potential, as given by Eq. 23–4a, is

$$V = V_{ba} = V_b - V_a = -\int_a^b \vec{E} \cdot d\vec{\ell}.$$

We can take the line integral along a path antiparallel to the field lines, from plate a to plate b; then $\theta = 180°$ and $\cos 180° = -1$, so

$$V = V_b - V_a = -\int_a^b E \, d\ell \cos 180° = +\int_a^b E \, d\ell = \frac{Q}{\epsilon_0 A} \int_a^b d\ell = \frac{Qd}{\epsilon_0 A}.$$

This relates Q to V, and from it we can get the capacitance C in terms of the geometry of the plates:

$$C = \frac{Q}{V} = \epsilon_0 \frac{A}{d}. \qquad \text{[parallel-plate capacitor]} \qquad \textbf{(24–2)}$$

Note from Eq. 24–2 that the value of C does not depend on Q or V, so Q is predicted to be proportional to V as is found experimentally.

EXAMPLE 24–1 **Capacitor calculations.** (a) Calculate the capacitance of a parallel-plate capacitor whose plates are 20 cm × 3.0 cm and are separated by a 1.0-mm air gap. (b) What is the charge on each plate if a 12-V battery is connected across the two plates? (c) What is the electric field between the plates? (d) Estimate the area of the plates needed to achieve a capacitance of 1 F, given the same air gap d.

APPROACH The capacitance is found by using Eq. 24–2, $C = \epsilon_0 A/d$. The charge on each plate is obtained from the definition of capacitance, Eq. 24–1, $Q = CV$. The electric field is uniform, so we can use Eq. 23–4b for the magnitude $E = V/d$. In (d) we use Eq. 24–2 again.

SOLUTION (a) The area $A = (20 \times 10^{-2} \, \text{m})(3.0 \times 10^{-2} \, \text{m}) = 6.0 \times 10^{-3} \, \text{m}^2$. The capacitance C is then

$$C = \epsilon_0 \frac{A}{d} = (8.85 \times 10^{-12} \, \text{C}^2/\text{N} \cdot \text{m}^2) \frac{6.0 \times 10^{-3} \, \text{m}^2}{1.0 \times 10^{-3} \, \text{m}} = 53 \, \text{pF}.$$

(b) The charge on each plate is

$$Q = CV = (53 \times 10^{-12} \, \text{F})(12 \, \text{V}) = 6.4 \times 10^{-10} \, \text{C}.$$

(c) From Eq. 23–4b for a uniform electric field, the magnitude of E is

$$E = \frac{V}{d} = \frac{12 \, \text{V}}{1.0 \times 10^{-3} \, \text{m}} = 1.2 \times 10^4 \, \text{V/m}.$$

(d) We solve for A in Eq. 24–2 and substitute $C = 1.0 \, \text{F}$ and $d = 1.0 \, \text{mm}$ to find that we need plates with an area

$$A = \frac{Cd}{\epsilon_0} \approx \frac{(1 \, \text{F})(1.0 \times 10^{-3} \, \text{m})}{(9 \times 10^{-12} \, \text{C}^2/\text{N} \cdot \text{m}^2)} \approx 10^8 \, \text{m}^2.$$

NOTE This is the area of a square 10^4 m or 10 km on a side. That is the size of a city like San Francisco or Boston! Large-capacitance capacitors will not be simple parallel plates.

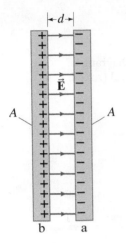

FIGURE 24–4 Parallel-plate capacitor, each of whose plates has area A. Fringing of the field is ignored.

EXERCISE B Two circular plates of radius 5.0 cm are separated by a 0.10-mm air gap. What is the magnitude of the charge on each plate when connected to a 12-V battery?

Not long ago, a capacitance greater than a few mF was unusual. Today capacitors are available that are 1 or 2 F, yet they are just a few cm on a side. Such capacitors are used as power backups, for example, in computer memory and electronics where the time and date can be maintained through tiny charge flow. [Capacitors are superior to rechargable batteries for this purpose because they can be recharged more than 10^5 times with no degradation.] Such high-capacitance capacitors can be made of "activated" carbon which has very high porosity, so that the surface area is very large; one tenth of a gram of activated carbon can have a surface area of $100\ m^2$. Furthermore, the equal and opposite charges exist in an electric "double layer" about $10^{-9}\ m$ thick. Thus, the capacitance of 0.1 g of activated carbon, whose internal area can be $10^2\ m^2$, is equivalent to a parallel-plate capacitor with $C \approx \epsilon_0 A/d = (8.85 \times 10^{-12}\ C^2/N \cdot m^2)(10^2\ m^2)/(10^{-9}\ m) \approx 1\ F.$

One type of computer keyboard operates by capacitance. As shown in Fig. 24–5, each key is connected to the upper plate of a capacitor. The upper plate moves down when the key is pressed, reducing the spacing between the capacitor plates, and increasing the capacitance (Eq. 24–2: smaller d, larger C). The *change* in capacitance results in an electric signal that is detected by an electronic circuit.

The proportionality, $C \propto A/d$ in Eq. 24–2, is valid also for a parallel-plate capacitor that is rolled up into a spiral cylinder, as in Fig. 24–1b. However, the constant factor, ϵ_0, must be replaced if an insulator such as paper separates the plates, as is usual, and this is discussed in Section 24–5. For a true cylindrical capacitor—consisting of two long coaxial cylinders—the result is somewhat different as the next Example shows.

EXAMPLE 24–2 **Cylindrical capacitor.** A cylindrical capacitor consists of a cylinder (or wire) of radius R_b surrounded by a coaxial cylindrical shell of inner radius R_a, Fig. 24–6a. Both cylinders have length ℓ which we assume is much greater than the separation of the cylinders, $R_a - R_b$, so we can neglect end effects. The capacitor is charged (by connecting it to a battery) so that one cylinder has a charge $+Q$ (say, the inner one) and the other one a charge $-Q$. Determine a formula for the capacitance.

APPROACH To obtain $C = Q/V$, we need to determine the potential difference V between the cylinders in terms of Q. We can use our earlier result (Example 21–11 or 22–6) that the electric field outside a long wire is directed radially outward and has magnitude $E = (1/2\pi\epsilon_0)(\lambda/R)$, where R is the distance from the axis and λ is the charge per unit length, Q/ℓ. Then $E = (1/2\pi\epsilon_0)(Q/\ell R)$ for points between the cylinders.

SOLUTION To obtain the potential difference V in terms of Q, we use this result for E in Eq. 23–4a, $V = V_b - V_a = -\int_a^b \vec{E} \cdot d\vec{\ell}$, and write the line integral from the outer cylinder to the inner one (so $V > 0$) along a radial line:[†]

$$V = V_b - V_a = -\int_a^b \vec{E} \cdot d\vec{\ell} = -\frac{Q}{2\pi\epsilon_0 \ell}\int_{R_a}^{R_b} \frac{dR}{R}$$

$$= -\frac{Q}{2\pi\epsilon_0 \ell}\ln\frac{R_b}{R_a} = \frac{Q}{2\pi\epsilon_0 \ell}\ln\frac{R_a}{R_b}.$$

Q and V are proportional, and the capacitance C is

$$C = \frac{Q}{V} = \frac{2\pi\epsilon_0 \ell}{\ln(R_a/R_b)}. \qquad \text{[cylindrical capacitor]}$$

NOTE If the space between cylinders, $R_a - R_b = \Delta R$ is small, we have $\ln(R_a/R_b) = \ln[(R_b + \Delta R)/R_b] = \ln[1 + \Delta R/R_b] \approx \Delta R/R_b$ (see Appendix A–3) so $C \approx 2\pi\epsilon_0 \ell R_b/\Delta R = \epsilon_0 A/\Delta R$ because the area of cylinder b is $A = 2\pi R_b\ell$. This is just Eq. 24–2 ($d = \Delta R$), a nice check.

EXERCISE C What is the capacitance per unit length of a cylindrical capacitor with radii $R_a = 2.5\ mm$ and $R_b = 0.40\ mm$? (a) 30 pF/m; (b) -30 pF/m; (c) 56 pF/m; (d) -56 pF/m; (e) 100 pF/m; (f) -100 pF/m.

[†]Note that $\vec{E}$ points outward in Fig. 24–6b, but $d\vec{\ell}$ points inward for our chosen direction of integration; the angle between $\vec{E}$ and $d\vec{\ell}$ is 180° and cos 180° = -1. Also, $d\ell = -dr$ because dr increases outward. These two minus signs cancel.

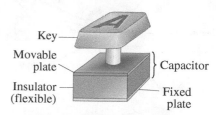
FIGURE 24–5 Key on a computer keyboard. Pressing the key reduces the capacitor spacing thus increasing the capacitance which can be detected electronically.

PHYSICS APPLIED
Computer key

FIGURE 24–6 (a) Cylindrical capacitor consists of two coaxial cylindrical conductors. (b) The electric field lines are shown in cross-sectional view.

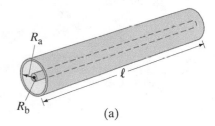

(a)

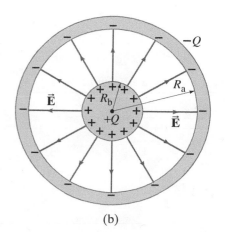

(b)

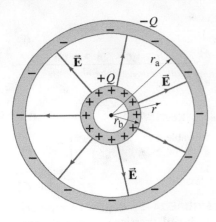

FIGURE 24–7 Cross section through the center of a spherical capacitor. The thin inner shell has radius r_b and the thin outer shell has radius r_a.

PROBLEM SOLVING

Checking with a limiting case

EXAMPLE 24–3 **Spherical capacitor.** A spherical capacitor consists of two thin concentric spherical conducting shells, of radius r_a and r_b as shown in Fig. 24–7. The inner shell carries a uniformly distributed charge Q on its surface, and the outer shell an equal but opposite charge $-Q$. Determine the capacitance of the two shells.

APPROACH In Example 22–3 we used Gauss's law to show that the electric field outside a uniformly charged conducting sphere is $E = Q/4\pi\epsilon_0 r^2$ as if all the charge were concentrated at the center. Now we use Eq. 23–4a, $V = -\int_a^b \vec{E} \cdot d\vec{\ell}$.

SOLUTION We integrate Eq. 23–4a along a radial line to obtain the potential difference between the two conducting shells:

$$V_{ba} = -\int_a^b \vec{E} \cdot d\vec{\ell} = -\frac{Q}{4\pi\epsilon_0}\int_{r_a}^{r_b}\frac{1}{r^2}\,dr$$

$$= \frac{Q}{4\pi\epsilon_0}\left(\frac{1}{r_b} - \frac{1}{r_a}\right) = \frac{Q}{4\pi\epsilon_0}\left(\frac{r_a - r_b}{r_a r_b}\right).$$

Finally,

$$C = \frac{Q}{V_{ba}} = 4\pi\epsilon_0\left(\frac{r_a r_b}{r_a - r_b}\right).$$

NOTE If the separation $\Delta r = r_a - r_b$ is very small, then $C = 4\pi\epsilon_0 r^2/\Delta r \approx \epsilon_0 A/\Delta r$ (since $A = 4\pi r^2$), which is the parallel-plate formula, Eq. 24–2.

A single isolated conductor can also be said to have a capacitance, C. In this case, C can still be defined as the ratio of the charge to absolute potential V on the conductor (relative to $V = 0$ at $r = \infty$), so that the relation

$$Q = CV$$

remains valid. For example, the potential of a single conducting sphere of radius r_b can be obtained from our results in Example 24–3 by letting r_a become infinitely large. As $r_a \to \infty$, then

$$V = \frac{Q}{4\pi\epsilon_0}\left(\frac{1}{r_b} - \frac{1}{r_a}\right) = \frac{1}{4\pi\epsilon_0}\frac{Q}{r_b};$$

so its capacitance is

$$C = \frac{Q}{V} = 4\pi\epsilon_0 r_b.$$

In practical cases, a single conductor may be near other conductors or the Earth (which can be thought of as the other "plate" of a capacitor), and these will affect the value of the capacitance.

EXAMPLE 24–4 **Capacitance of two long parallel wires.** Estimate the capacitance per unit length of two very long straight parallel wires, each of radius R, carrying uniform charges $+Q$ and $-Q$, and separated by a distance d which is large compared to R ($d \gg R$), Fig. 24–8.

FIGURE 24–8 Example 24–4.

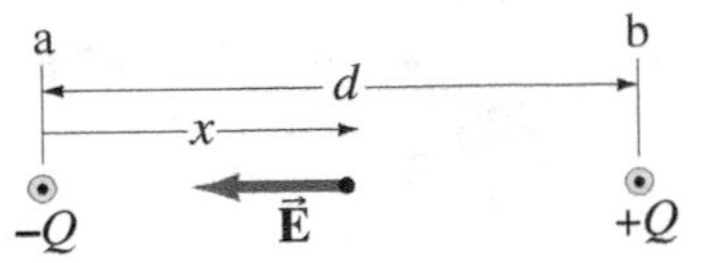

APPROACH We calculate the potential difference between the wires by treating the electric field at any point between them as the superposition of the two fields created by each wire. (The electric field inside each wire conductor is zero.)

SOLUTION The electric field outside of a long straight conductor was found in Examples 21–11 and 22–6 to be radial and given by $E = \lambda/(2\pi\epsilon_0 x)$ where λ is the charge per unit length, $\lambda = Q/\ell$. The total electric field at distance x from the left-hand wire in Fig. 24–8 has magnitude

$$E = \frac{\lambda}{2\pi\epsilon_0 x} + \frac{\lambda}{2\pi\epsilon_0(d - x)},$$

and points to the left (from + to −). Now we find the potential difference between the two wires using Eq. 23–4a and integrating along the straight line from the surface of the negative wire to the surface of the positive wire, noting that $\vec{E}$ and $d\vec{\ell}$ point in opposite directions ($\vec{E} \cdot d\vec{\ell} < 0$):

$$V = V_b - V_a = -\int_a^b \vec{E} \cdot d\vec{\ell} = \left(\frac{\lambda}{2\pi\epsilon_0}\right)\int_R^{d-R}\left[\frac{1}{x} + \frac{1}{(d-x)}\right]dx$$

$$= \left(\frac{\lambda}{2\pi\epsilon_0}\right)\left[\ln(x) - \ln(d-x)\right]\Big|_R^{d-R}$$

$$= \left(\frac{\lambda}{2\pi\epsilon_0}\right)\left[\ln(d-R) - \ln R - \ln R + \ln(d-R)\right]$$

$$= \left(\frac{\lambda}{\pi\epsilon_0}\right)\left[\ln(d-R) - \ln(R)\right] \approx \left(\frac{\lambda}{\pi\epsilon_0}\right)\left[\ln(d) - \ln(R)\right].$$

We are given that $d \gg R$, so

$$V \approx \left(\frac{Q}{\pi\epsilon_0\ell}\right)\left[\ln\left(\frac{d}{R}\right)\right].$$

The capacitance from Eq. 24–1 is $C = Q/V \approx (\pi\epsilon_0\ell)/\ln(d/R)$, so the capacitance per unit length is given approximately by

$$\frac{C}{\ell} \approx \frac{\pi\epsilon_0}{\ln(d/R)}.$$

24–3 Capacitors in Series and Parallel

Capacitors are found in many electric circuits. By electric circuit we mean a closed path of conductors, usually wires connecting capacitors and/or other devices, in which charge can flow and which includes a source of voltage such as a battery. The battery voltage is usually given the symbol V, which means that V represents a potential *difference*. Capacitors can be connected together in various ways. Two common ways are in *series*, or in *parallel*, and we now discuss both.

A circuit containing three capacitors connected in **parallel** is shown in Fig. 24–9. They are in "parallel" because when a battery of voltage V is connected to points a and b, this voltage $V = V_{ab}$ exists across each of the capacitors. That is, since the left-hand plates of all the capacitors are connected by conductors, they all reach the same potential V_a when connected to the battery; and the right-hand plates each reach potential V_b. Each capacitor plate acquires a charge given by $Q_1 = C_1V$, $Q_2 = C_2V$, and $Q_3 = C_3V$. The total charge Q that must leave the battery is then

$$Q = Q_1 + Q_2 + Q_3 = C_1V + C_2V + C_3V.$$

Let us try to find a single equivalent capacitor that will hold the same charge Q at the same voltage $V = V_{ab}$. It will have a capacitance C_{eq} given by

$$Q = C_{eq}V.$$

Combining the two previous equations, we have

$$C_{eq}V = C_1V + C_2V + C_3V = (C_1 + C_2 + C_3)V$$

or

$$C_{eq} = C_1 + C_2 + C_3. \qquad \text{[parallel]} \quad \textbf{(24–3)}$$

The net effect of connecting capacitors in parallel is thus to *increase* the capacitance. This makes sense because we are essentially increasing the area of the plates where charge can accumulate (see, for example, Eq. 24–2).

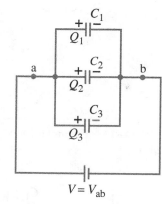

FIGURE 24–9 Capacitors in parallel: $C_{eq} = C_1 + C_2 + C_3$.

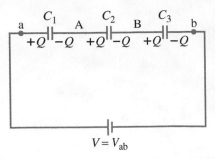

FIGURE 24-10 Capacitors in series:
$$\frac{1}{C_{eq}} = \frac{1}{C_1} + \frac{1}{C_2} + \frac{1}{C_3}.$$

Capacitors can also be connected in **series**: that is, end to end as shown in Fig. 24–10. A charge $+Q$ flows from the battery to one plate of C_1, and $-Q$ flows to one plate of C_3. The regions A and B between the capacitors were originally neutral; so the net charge there must still be zero. The $+Q$ on the left plate of C_1 attracts a charge of $-Q$ on the opposite plate. Because region A must have a zero net charge, there is thus $+Q$ on the left plate of C_2. The same considerations apply to the other capacitors, so we see the charge on each capacitor is the same value Q. A single capacitor that could replace these three in series without affecting the circuit (that is, Q and V the same) would have a capacitance C_{eq} where

$$Q = C_{eq}V.$$

Now the total voltage V across the three capacitors in series must equal the sum of the voltages across each capacitor:

$$V = V_1 + V_2 + V_3.$$

We also have for each capacitor $Q = C_1V_1$, $Q = C_2V_2$, and $Q = C_3V_3$, so we substitute for V, V_1, V_2, and V_3 into the last equation and get

$$\frac{Q}{C_{eq}} = \frac{Q}{C_1} + \frac{Q}{C_2} + \frac{Q}{C_3} = Q\left(\frac{1}{C_1} + \frac{1}{C_2} + \frac{1}{C_3}\right)$$

or

$$\frac{1}{C_{eq}} = \frac{1}{C_1} + \frac{1}{C_2} + \frac{1}{C_3}. \qquad \text{[series]} \quad \textbf{(24–4)}$$

Notice that the equivalent capacitance C_{eq} is smaller than the smallest contributing capacitance.

EXERCISE D Consider two identical capacitors $C_1 = C_2 = 10\,\mu\text{F}$. What are the minimum and maximum capacitances that can be obtained by connecting these in series or parallel combinations? (*a*) $0.2\,\mu\text{F}, 5\,\mu\text{F}$; (*b*) $0.2\,\mu\text{F}, 10\,\mu\text{F}$; (*c*) $0.2\,\mu\text{F}, 20\,\mu\text{F}$; (*d*) $5\,\mu\text{F}, 10\,\mu\text{F}$; (*e*) $5\,\mu\text{F}, 20\,\mu\text{F}$; (*f*) $10\,\mu\text{F}, 20\,\mu\text{F}$.

Other connections of capacitors can be analyzed similarly using charge conservation, and often simply in terms of series and parallel connections.

FIGURE 24-11 Examples 24–5 and 24–6.

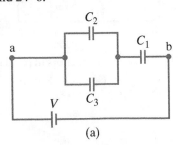

(a)

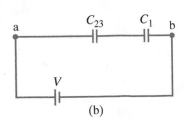

(b)

EXAMPLE 24-5 **Equivalent capacitance.** Determine the capacitance of a single capacitor that will have the same effect as the combination shown in Fig. 24–11a. Take $C_1 = C_2 = C_3 = C$.

APPROACH First we find the equivalent capacitance of C_2 and C_3 in parallel, and then consider that capacitance in series with C_1.

SOLUTION Capacitors C_2 and C_3 are connected in parallel, so they are equivalent to a single capacitor having capacitance

$$C_{23} = C_2 + C_3 = 2C.$$

This C_{23} is in series with C_1, Fig. 24–11b, so the equivalent capacitance of the entire circuit, C_{eq}, is given by

$$\frac{1}{C_{eq}} = \frac{1}{C_1} + \frac{1}{C_{23}} = \frac{1}{C} + \frac{1}{2C} = \frac{3}{2C}.$$

Hence the equivalent capacitance of the entire combination is $C_{eq} = \frac{2}{3}C$, and it is smaller than any of the contributing capacitors, $C_1 = C_2 = C_3 = C$.

EXAMPLE 24–6 **Charge and voltage on capacitors.** Determine the charge on each capacitor in Fig. 24–11a of Example 24–5 and the voltage across each, assuming $C = 3.0\,\mu\text{F}$ and the battery voltage is $V = 4.0\,\text{V}$.

APPROACH We have to work "backward" through Example 24–5. That is, we find the charge Q that leaves the battery, using the equivalent capacitance. Then we find the charge on each separate capacitor and the voltage across each. Each step uses Eq. 24–1, $Q = CV$.

SOLUTION The 4.0-V battery behaves as if it is connected to a capacitance $C_{eq} = \frac{2}{3}C = \frac{2}{3}(3.0\,\mu\text{F}) = 2.0\,\mu\text{F}$. Therefore the charge Q that leaves the battery, by Eq. 24–1, is

$$Q = CV = (2.0\,\mu\text{F})(4.0\,\text{V}) = 8.0\,\mu\text{C}.$$

From Fig. 24–11a, this charge arrives at the negative plate of C_1, so $Q_1 = 8.0\,\mu\text{C}$. The charge Q that leaves the positive plate of the battery is split evenly between C_2 and C_3 (symmetry: $C_2 = C_3$) and is $Q_2 = Q_3 = \frac{1}{2}Q = 4.0\,\mu\text{C}$. Next, the voltages across C_2 and C_3 have to be the same. The voltage across each capacitor is obtained using $V = Q/C$. So

$$V_1 = Q_1/C_1 = (8.0\,\mu\text{C})/(3.0\,\mu\text{F}) = 2.7\,\text{V}$$
$$V_2 = Q_2/C_2 = (4.0\,\mu\text{C})/(3.0\,\mu\text{F}) = 1.3\,\text{V}$$
$$V_3 = Q_3/C_3 = (4.0\,\mu\text{C})/(3.0\,\mu\text{F}) = 1.3\,\text{V}.$$

EXAMPLE 24–7 **Capacitors reconnected.** Two capacitors, $C_1 = 2.2\,\mu\text{F}$ and $C_2 = 1.2\,\mu\text{F}$, are connected in parallel to a 24-V source as shown in Fig. 24–12a. After they are charged they are disconnected from the source and from each other, and then reconnected directly to each other with plates of opposite sign connected together (see Fig. 24–12b). Find the charge on each capacitor and the potential across each after equilibrium is established.

APPROACH We find the charge $Q = CV$ on each capacitor initially. Charge is conserved, although rearranged after the switch. The two new voltages will have to be equal.

SOLUTION First we calculate how much charge has been placed on each capacitor after the power source has charged them fully, using Eq. 24–1:

$$Q_1 = C_1V = (2.2\,\mu\text{F})(24\,\text{V}) = 52.8\,\mu\text{C},$$
$$Q_2 = C_2V = (1.2\,\mu\text{F})(24\,\text{V}) = 28.8\,\mu\text{C}.$$

Next the capacitors are connected in parallel, Fig. 24–12b, and the potential difference across each must quickly equalize. Thus, the charge cannot remain as shown in Fig. 24–12b, but the charge must rearrange itself so that the upper plates at least have the same sign of charge, with the lower plates having the opposite charge as shown in Fig. 24–12c. Equation 24–1 applies for each:

$$q_1 = C_1V' \qquad \text{and} \qquad q_2 = C_2V',$$

where V' is the voltage across each capacitor after the charges have rearranged themselves. We don't know q_1, q_2, or V', so we need a third equation. This is provided by charge conservation. The charges have rearranged themselves between Figs. 24–12b and c. The total charge on the upper plates in those two Figures must be the same, so we have

$$q_1 + q_2 = Q_1 - Q_2 = 24.0\,\mu\text{C}.$$

Combining the last three equations we find:

$$V' = (q_1 + q_2)/(C_1 + C_2) = 24.0\,\mu\text{C}/3.4\,\mu\text{F} = 7.06\,\text{V} \approx 7.1\,\text{V}$$
$$q_1 = C_1V' = (2.2\,\mu\text{F})(7.06\,\text{V}) = 15.5\,\mu\text{C} \approx 16\,\mu\text{C}$$
$$q_2 = C_2V' = (1.2\,\mu\text{F})(7.06\,\text{V}) = 8.5\,\mu\text{C}$$

where we have kept only two significant figures in our final answers.

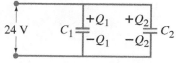

(a) Initial configuration.

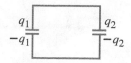

(b) At the instant of reconnection only.

(c) A short time later.

FIGURE 24–12 Example 24–7.

24–4 Electric Energy Storage

A charged capacitor stores electrical energy. The energy stored in a capacitor will be equal to the work done to charge it. The net effect of charging a capacitor is to remove charge from one plate and add it to the other plate. This is what a battery does when it is connected to a capacitor. A capacitor does not become charged instantly. It takes time (Section 26–4). Initially, when the capacitor is uncharged, it requires no work to move the first bit of charge over. When some charge is on each plate, it requires work to add more charge of the same sign because of the electric repulsion. The more charge already on a plate, the more work required to add additional charge. The work needed to add a small amount of charge dq, when a potential difference V is across the plates, is $dW = V\,dq$. Since $V = q/C$ at any moment (Eq. 24–1), where C is the capacitance, the work needed to store a total charge Q is

$$W = \int_0^Q V\,dq = \frac{1}{C}\int_0^Q q\,dq = \frac{1}{2}\frac{Q^2}{C}.$$

Thus we can say that the energy "stored" in a capacitor is

$$U = \frac{1}{2}\frac{Q^2}{C}$$

when the capacitor C carries charges $+Q$ and $-Q$ on its two conductors. Since $Q = CV$, where V is the potential difference across the capacitor, we can also write

$$U = \frac{1}{2}\frac{Q^2}{C} = \frac{1}{2}CV^2 = \frac{1}{2}QV. \tag{24–5}$$

FIGURE 24–13 A camera flash unit.

EXAMPLE 24–8 **Energy stored in a capacitor.** A camera flash unit (Fig. 24–13) stores energy in a 150-μF capacitor at 200 V. (a) How much electric energy can be stored? (b) What is the power output if nearly all this energy is released in 1.0 ms?

APPROACH We use Eq. 24–5 in the form $U = \frac{1}{2}CV^2$ because we are given C and V.

SOLUTION The energy stored is

$$U = \frac{1}{2}CV^2 = \frac{1}{2}(150 \times 10^{-6}\,\text{F})(200\,\text{V})^2 = 3.0\,\text{J}.$$

If this energy is released in $\frac{1}{1000}$ of a second, the power output is $P = U/t = (3.0\,\text{J})/(1.0 \times 10^{-3}\,\text{s}) = 3000\,\text{W}$.

CONCEPTUAL EXAMPLE 24–9 **Capacitor plate separation increased.** A parallel-plate capacitor carries charge Q and is then disconnected from a battery. The two plates are initially separated by a distance d. Suppose the plates are pulled apart until the separation is $2d$. How has the energy stored in this capacitor changed?

RESPONSE If we increase the plate separation d, we decrease the capacitance according to Eq. 24–2, $C = \epsilon_0 A/d$, by a factor of 2. The charge Q hasn't changed. So according to Eq. 24–5, where we choose the form $U = \frac{1}{2}Q^2/C$ because we know Q is the same and C has been halved, the reduced C means the potential energy stored increases by a factor of 2.

NOTE We can see why the energy stored increases from a physical point of view: the two plates are charged equal and opposite, so they attract each other. If we pull them apart, we must do work, so we raise their potential energy.

EXAMPLE 24–10 **Moving parallel capacitor plates.** The plates of a parallel-plate capacitor have area A, separation x, and are connected to a battery with voltage V. While connected to the battery, the plates are pulled apart until they are separated by $3x$. (a) What are the initial and final energies stored in the capacitor? (b) How much work is required to pull the plates apart (assume constant speed)? (c) How much energy is exchanged with the battery?

APPROACH The stored energy is given by Eq. 24–5: $U = \frac{1}{2}CV^2$, where $C = \epsilon_0 A/x$. Unlike Example 24–9, here the capacitor remains connected to the battery. Hence charge and energy can flow to or from the battery, and we can not set the work $W = \Delta U$. Instead, the work can be calculated from Eq. 7–7, $W = \int \vec{F} \cdot d\vec{\ell}$.

SOLUTION (a) When the separation is x, the capacitance is $C_1 = \epsilon_0 A/x$ and the energy stored is

$$U_1 = \tfrac{1}{2} C_1 V^2 = \tfrac{1}{2}\frac{\epsilon_0 A}{x} V^2.$$

When the separation is $3x$, $C_2 = \epsilon_0 A/3x$ and

$$U_2 = \tfrac{1}{2}\frac{\epsilon_0 A}{3x} V^2.$$

Then

$$\Delta U_{\text{cap}} = U_2 - U_1 = -\frac{\epsilon_0 A V^2}{3x}.$$

The potential energy decreases as the oppositely charged plates are pulled apart, which makes sense. The plates remain connected to the battery, so V does not change and C decreases; hence some charge leaves each plate $(Q = CV)$, causing U to decrease.

(b) The work done in pulling the plates apart is $W = \int_x^{3x} F\, d\ell = \int_x^{3x} QE\, d\ell$, where Q is the charge on one plate at a given moment when the plates are a distance ℓ apart, and E is the field due to the other plate at that instant. You might think we could use $E = V/\ell$ where ℓ is the separation of the plates (Eq. 23–4b). But we want the force on one plate (of charge Q) due to the electric field of the other plate only—which is half by *symmetry*: so we take $E = V/2\ell$. The charge at any separation ℓ is given by $Q = CV$, where $C = \epsilon_0 A/\ell$. Substituting, the work is

$$W = \int_{\ell=x}^{\ell=3x} QE\, d\ell = \frac{\epsilon_0 A V^2}{2} \int_x^{3x} \frac{d\ell}{\ell^2} = -\frac{\epsilon_0 A V^2}{2\ell}\Big|_{\ell=x}^{\ell=3x} = \frac{\epsilon_0 A V^2}{2}\left(\frac{-1}{3x} + \frac{1}{x}\right) = \frac{\epsilon_0 A V^2}{3x}.$$

As you might expect, the work required to pull these oppositely charged plates apart is positive.

(c) Even though the work done is positive, the potential energy decreased, which tells us that energy must have gone into the battery (as if charging it). Conservation of energy tells us that the work W done on the system must equal the change in potential energy of the capacitor plus that of the battery (kinetic energy can be assumed to be essentially zero):

$$W = \Delta U_{\text{cap}} + \Delta U_{\text{batt}}.$$

Thus the battery experiences a change in energy of

$$\Delta U_{\text{batt}} = W - \Delta U_{\text{cap}} = \frac{\epsilon_0 A V^2}{3x} + \frac{\epsilon_0 A V^2}{3x} = \frac{2\epsilon_0 A V^2}{3x}.$$

Thus charge flows back into the battery, raising its stored energy. In fact, the battery energy increase is double the work we do.

It is useful to think of the energy stored in a capacitor as being stored in the electric field between the plates. As an example let us calculate the energy stored in a parallel-plate capacitor in terms of the electric field.

We have seen (Eq. 23–4b) that the electric field $\vec{E}$ between two close parallel plates is (approximately) uniform and its magnitude is related to the potential difference by $V = Ed$ where d is the plate separation. Also, Eq. 24–2 tells us $C = \epsilon_0 A/d$ for a parallel-plate capacitor. Thus

$$U = \tfrac{1}{2}CV^2 = \tfrac{1}{2}\left(\frac{\epsilon_0 A}{d}\right)(E^2 d^2)$$
$$= \tfrac{1}{2}\epsilon_0 E^2 A d.$$

The quantity Ad is the volume between the plates in which the electric field E exists. If we divide both sides by the volume, we obtain an expression for the energy per unit volume or **energy density**, u:

$$u = \text{energy density} = \tfrac{1}{2}\epsilon_0 E^2. \qquad \textbf{(24–6)}$$

The *electric energy stored per unit volume in any region of space is proportional to the square of the electric field* in that region. We derived Eq. 24–6 for the special case of a parallel-plate capacitor. But it can be shown to be true for any region of space where there is an electric field. Note that the units check: for $(\epsilon_0 E^2)$ we have $(C^2/N \cdot m^2)(N/C)^2 = N/m^2 = (N \cdot m)/m^3 = J/m^3$.

Health Effects

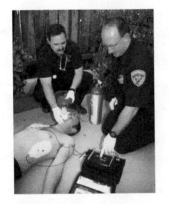

FIGURE 24–14 Heart defibrillator.

The energy stored in a large capacitance can do harm, giving you a burn or a shock. One reason you are warned not to touch a circuit, or the inside of electronic devices, is because capacitors may still be carrying charge even if the external power has been turned off.

On the other hand, the basis of a **heart defibrillator** is a capacitor charged to a high voltage. A heart attack can be characterized by fast irregular beating of the heart, known as *ventricular* (or *cardiac*) *fibrillation*. The heart then does not pump blood to the rest of the body properly, and if it lasts for long, death results. A sudden, brief jolt of charge through the heart from a defibrillator can cause complete heart stoppage, sometimes followed by a resumption of normal beating. The defibrillator capacitor is charged to a high voltage, typically a few thousand volts, and is allowed to discharge very rapidly through the heart via a pair of wide contacts known as "paddles" that spread out the current over the chest (Fig. 24–14).

24–5 Dielectrics

In most capacitors there is an insulating sheet of material, such as paper or plastic, called a **dielectric** between the plates. This serves several purposes. First of all, dielectrics break down (allowing electric charge to flow) less readily than air, so higher voltages can be applied without charge passing across the gap. Furthermore, a dielectric allows the plates to be placed closer together without touching, thus allowing an increased capacitance because d is smaller in Eq. 24–2. Finally, it is found experimentally that if the dielectric fills the space between the two conductors, it increases the capacitance by a factor K which is known as the **dielectric constant**. Thus

$$C = KC_0, \qquad \textbf{(24–7)}$$

where C_0 is the capacitance when the space between the two conductors of the capacitor is a vacuum, and C is the capacitance when the space is filled with a material whose dielectric constant is K.

The values of the dielectric constant for various materials are given in Table 24–1. Also shown in Table 24–1 is the **dielectric strength**, the maximum electric field before breakdown (charge flow) occurs.

For a parallel-plate capacitor (see Eq. 24–2),

$$C = K\epsilon_0 \frac{A}{d} \qquad \text{[parallel-plate capacitor]} \quad \textbf{(24–8)}$$

when the space between the plates is completely filled with a dielectric whose dielectric constant is K. (The situation when the dielectric only partially fills the space will be discussed shortly in Example 24–11.) The quantity $K\epsilon_0$ appears so

TABLE 24–1
Dielectric Constants (at 20°C)

Material	Dielectric constant K	Dielectric strength (V/m)
Vacuum	1.0000	
Air (1 atm)	1.0006	3×10^6
Paraffin	2.2	10×10^6
Polystyrene	2.6	24×10^6
Vinyl (plastic)	2–4	50×10^6
Paper	3.7	15×10^6
Quartz	4.3	8×10^6
Oil	4	12×10^6
Glass, Pyrex	5	14×10^6
Porcelain	6–8	5×10^6
Mica	7	150×10^6
Water (liquid)	80	
Strontium titanate	300	8×10^6

often in formulas that we define a new quantity

$$\epsilon = K\epsilon_0 \qquad (24\text{--}9)$$

called the **permittivity** of a material. Then the capacitance of a parallel-plate capacitor becomes

$$C = \epsilon\, \frac{A}{d}.$$

Note that ϵ_0 represents the permittivity of free space (a vacuum), as in Section 21–5.

The energy density stored in an electric field E (Section 24–4) in a dielectric is given by (see Eq. 24–6)

$$u = \tfrac{1}{2} K\epsilon_0 E^2 = \tfrac{1}{2}\epsilon E^2. \qquad [E \text{ in a dielectric}]$$

| **EXERCISE E** Return to the Chapter-Opening Question, page 628, and answer it again now. Try to explain why you may have answered differently the first time.

Two simple experiments illustrate the effect of a dielectric. In the first, Fig. 24–15a, a battery of voltage V_0 is kept connected to a capacitor as a dielectric is inserted between the plates. If the charge on the plates without dielectric is Q_0, then when the dielectric is inserted, it is found experimentally (first by Faraday) that the charge Q on the plates is increased by a factor K,

$$Q = KQ_0. \qquad [\text{voltage constant}]$$

The capacitance has increased to $C = Q/V_0 = KQ_0/V_0 = KC_0$, which is Eq. 24–7. In a second experiment, Fig. 24–15b, a battery V_0 is connected to a capacitor C_0 which then holds a charge $Q_0 = C_0 V_0$. The battery is then disconnected, leaving the capacitor isolated with charge Q_0 and still at voltage V_0. Next a dielectric is inserted between the plates of the capacitor. The charge remains Q_0 (there is nowhere for the charge to go) but the voltage is found experimentally to drop by a factor K:

$$V = \frac{V_0}{K}. \qquad [\text{charge constant}]$$

Note that the capacitance changes to $C = Q_0/V = Q_0/(V_0/K) = KQ_0/V_0 = KC_0$, so this experiment too confirms Eq. 24–7.

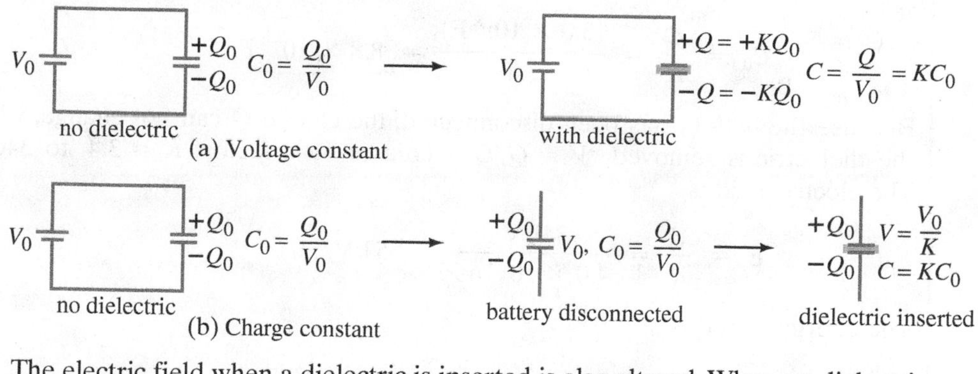

FIGURE 24–15 Two experiments with a capacitor. Dielectric inserted with (a) voltage held constant, (b) charge held constant.

The electric field when a dielectric is inserted is also altered. When no dielectric is present, the electric field between the plates of a parallel-plate capacitor is given by Eq. 23–4b:

$$E_0 = \frac{V_0}{d},$$

where V_0 is the potential difference between the plates and d is their separation. If the capacitor is isolated so that the charge remains fixed on the plates when a dielectric is inserted, filling the space between the plates, the potential difference drops to $V = V_0/K$. So the electric field in the dielectric is

$$E = E_{\mathrm{D}} = \frac{V}{d} = \frac{V_0}{Kd}$$

or

$$E_{\mathrm{D}} = \frac{E_0}{K}. \qquad [\text{in a dielectric}] \quad (24\text{--}10)$$

The electric field in a dielectric is reduced by a factor equal to the dielectric constant. The field in a dielectric (or insulator) is not reduced all the way to zero as in a conductor. Equation 24–10 is valid even if the dielectric's width is smaller than the gap between the capacitor plates.

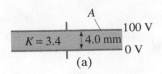

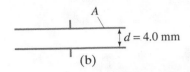

FIGURE 24–16 Example 24–11.

EXAMPLE 24–11 **Dielectric removal.** A parallel-plate capacitor, filled with a dielectric with $K = 3.4$, is connected to a 100-V battery (Fig. 24–16a). After the capacitor is fully charged, the battery is disconnected. The plates have area $A = 4.0 \, \text{m}^2$, and are separated by $d = 4.0 \, \text{mm}$. (a) Find the capacitance, the charge on the capacitor, the electric field strength, and the energy stored in the capacitor. (b) The dielectric is carefully removed, without changing the plate separation nor does any charge leave the capacitor (Fig. 24–16b). Find the new values of capacitance, electric field strength, voltage between the plates, and the energy stored in the capacitor.

APPROACH We use the formulas for parallel-plate capacitance and electric field with and without a dielectric.

SOLUTION (a) First we find the capacitance, with dielectric:

$$C = \frac{K\epsilon_0 A}{d} = \frac{3.4(8.85 \times 10^{-12} \, \text{C}^2/\text{N} \cdot \text{m}^2)(4.0 \, \text{m}^2)}{4.0 \times 10^{-3} \, \text{m}}$$
$$= 3.0 \times 10^{-8} \, \text{F}.$$

The charge Q on the plates is

$$Q = CV = (3.0 \times 10^{-8} \, \text{F})(100 \, \text{V}) = 3.0 \times 10^{-6} \, \text{C}.$$

The electric field between the plates is

$$E = \frac{V}{d} = \frac{100 \, \text{V}}{4.0 \times 10^{-3} \, \text{m}} = 25 \, \text{kV/m}.$$

Finally, the total energy stored in the capacitor is

$$U = \tfrac{1}{2}CV^2 = \tfrac{1}{2}(3.0 \times 10^{-8} \, \text{F})(100 \, \text{V})^2 = 1.5 \times 10^{-4} \, \text{J}.$$

(b) The capacitance without dielectric decreases by a factor $K = 3.4$:

$$C_0 = \frac{C}{K} = \frac{(3.0 \times 10^{-8} \, \text{F})}{3.4} = 8.8 \times 10^{-9} \, \text{F}.$$

Because the battery has been disconnected, the charge Q can not change; when the dielectric is removed, $V = Q/C$ increases by a factor $K = 3.4$ to 340 V. The electric field is

$$E = \frac{V}{d} = \frac{340 \, \text{V}}{4.0 \times 10^{-3} \, \text{m}} = 85 \, \text{kV/m}.$$

The energy stored is

$$U = \tfrac{1}{2}CV^2 = \tfrac{1}{2}(8.8 \times 10^{-9} \, \text{F})(340 \, \text{V})^2$$
$$= 5.1 \times 10^{-4} \, \text{J}.$$

NOTE Where did all this extra energy come from? The energy increased because work had to be done to remove the dielectric. The work required was $W = (5.1 \times 10^{-4} \, \text{J}) - (1.5 \times 10^{-4} \, \text{J}) = 3.6 \times 10^{-4} \, \text{J}$. (We will see in the next Section that work is required because of the force of attraction between induced charge on the dielectric and the charges on the plates, Fig. 24–17c.)

*24–6 Molecular Description of Dielectrics

Let us examine, from the molecular point of view, why the capacitance of a capacitor should be larger when a dielectric is between the plates. A capacitor whose plates are separated by an air gap has a charge $+Q$ on one plate and $-Q$ on the other (Fig. 24–17a). Assume it is isolated (not connected to a battery) so charge cannot flow to or from the plates. The potential difference between the plates, V_0, is given by Eq. 24–1:

$$Q = C_0 V_0,$$

where the subscripts refer to air between the plates. Now we insert a dielectric between the plates (Fig. 24–17b). Because of the electric field between the capacitor plates, the dielectric molecules will tend to become oriented as shown in Fig. 24–17b. If the dielectric molecules are *polar*, the positive end is attracted to the negative plate and vice versa. Even if the dielectric molecules are not polar, electrons within them will tend to move slightly toward the positive capacitor plate, so the effect is the same. The net effect of the aligned dipoles is a net negative charge on the outer edge of the dielectric facing the positive plate, and a net positive charge on the opposite side, as shown in Fig. 24–17c.

Some of the electric field lines, then, do not pass through the dielectric but instead end on charges induced on the surface of the dielectric as shown in Fig. 24–17c. Hence the electric field within the dielectric is less than in air. That is, the electric field between the capacitor plates, assumed filled by the dielectric, has been reduced by some factor K. The voltage across the capacitor is reduced by the same factor K because $V = Ed$ (Eq. 23–4b) and hence, by Eq. 24–1, $Q = CV$, the capacitance C must increase by that same factor K to keep Q constant.

As shown in Fig. 24–17d, the electric field within the dielectric E_D can be considered as the vector sum of the electric field $\vec{E}_0$ due to the "free" charges on the conducting plates, and the field $\vec{E}_{ind}$ due to the induced charge on the surfaces of the dielectric. Since these two fields are in opposite directions, the net field within the dielectric, $E_0 - E_{ind}$, is less than E_0. The precise relationship is given by Eq. 24–10, even if the dielectric does not fill the gap between the plates:

$$E_D = E_0 - E_{ind} = \frac{E_0}{K},$$

so

$$E_{ind} = E_0\left(1 - \frac{1}{K}\right).$$

The electric field between two parallel plates is related to the surface charge density, σ, by $E = \sigma/\epsilon_0$ (Example 21–13 or 22–8). Thus

$$E_0 = \sigma/\epsilon_0$$

where $\sigma = Q/A$ is the surface charge density on the conductor; Q is the net charge on the conductor and is often called the **free charge** (since charge is free to move in a conductor). Similarly, we define an equivalent induced surface charge density σ_{ind} on the dielectric; then

$$E_{ind} = \sigma_{ind}/\epsilon_0$$

where E_{ind} is the electric field due to the induced charge $Q_{ind} = \sigma_{ind} A$ on the surface of the dielectric, Fig. 24–17d. Q_{ind} is often called the **bound charge**, since it is on an insulator and is not free to move. Since $E_{ind} = E_0(1 - 1/K)$ as shown above, we now have

$$\sigma_{ind} = \sigma\left(1 - \frac{1}{K}\right) \tag{24–11a}$$

and

$$Q_{ind} = Q\left(1 - \frac{1}{K}\right). \tag{24–11b}$$

Since K is always greater than 1, we see that the charge induced on the dielectric is always less than the free charge on each of the capacitor plates.

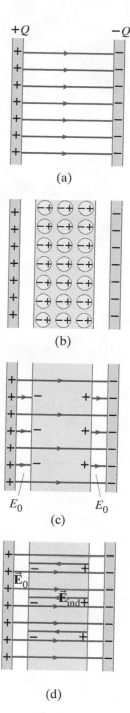

FIGURE 24–17 Molecular view of the effects of a dielectric.

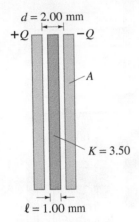

$d = 2.00$ mm

$+Q$ $-Q$

A

$K = 3.50$

$\ell = 1.00$ mm

FIGURE 24–18 Example 24–12.

EXAMPLE 24–12 **Dielectric partially fills capacitor.** A parallel-plate capacitor has plates of area $A = 250 \text{ cm}^2$ and separation $d = 2.00$ mm. The capacitor is charged to a potential difference $V_0 = 150$ V. Then the battery is disconnected (the charge Q on the plates then won't change), and a dielectric sheet ($K = 3.50$) of the same area A but thickness $\ell = 1.00$ mm is placed between the plates as shown in Fig. 24–18. Determine (a) the initial capacitance of the air-filled capacitor, (b) the charge on each plate before the dielectric is inserted, (c) the charge induced on each face of the dielectric after it is inserted, (d) the electric field in the space between each plate and the dielectric, (e) the electric field in the dielectric, (f) the potential difference between the plates after the dielectric is added, and (g) the capacitance after the dielectric is in place.

APPROACH We use the expressions for capacitance and charge developed in this Section plus (part e), Eq. 23–4a, $V = -\int \vec{\mathbf{E}} \cdot d\vec{\boldsymbol{\ell}}$.

SOLUTION (a) Before the dielectric is in place, the capacitance is

$$C_0 = \epsilon_0 \frac{A}{d} = (8.85 \times 10^{-12} \text{ C}^2/\text{N} \cdot \text{m}^2)\left(\frac{2.50 \times 10^{-2} \text{ m}^2}{2.00 \times 10^{-3} \text{ m}}\right) = 111 \text{ pF}.$$

(b) The charge on each plate is

$$Q = C_0 V_0 = (1.11 \times 10^{-10} \text{ F})(150 \text{ V}) = 1.66 \times 10^{-8} \text{ C}.$$

(c) Equations 24–10 and 24–11 are valid even when the dielectric does not fill the gap, so (Eq. 24–11b)

$$Q_{\text{ind}} = Q\left(1 - \frac{1}{K}\right) = (1.66 \times 10^{-8} \text{ C})\left(1 - \frac{1}{3.50}\right) = 1.19 \times 10^{-8} \text{ C}.$$

(d) The electric field in the gaps between the plates and the dielectric (see Fig. 24–17c) is the same as in the absence of the dielectric since the charge on the plates has not been altered. The result of Example 21–13 can be used here, which gives $E_0 = \sigma/\epsilon_0$. [Or we can note that, in the absence of the dielectric, $E_0 = V_0/d = Q/C_0 d$ (since $V_0 = Q/C_0$) $= Q/\epsilon_0 A$ (since $C_0 = \epsilon_0 A/d$) which is the same result.] Thus

$$E_0 = \frac{Q}{\epsilon_0 A} = \frac{1.66 \times 10^{-8} \text{ C}}{(8.85 \times 10^{-12} \text{ C}^2/\text{N} \cdot \text{m}^2)(2.50 \times 10^{-2} \text{ m}^2)} = 7.50 \times 10^4 \text{ V/m}.$$

(e) In the dielectric the electric field is (Eq. 24–10)

$$E_D = \frac{E_0}{K} = \frac{7.50 \times 10^4 \text{ V/m}}{3.50} = 2.14 \times 10^4 \text{ V/m}.$$

(f) To obtain the potential difference in the presence of the dielectric we use Eq. 23–4a, and integrate from the surface of one plate to the other along a straight line parallel to the field lines:

$$V = -\int \vec{\mathbf{E}} \cdot d\vec{\boldsymbol{\ell}} = E_0(d - \ell) + E_D \ell,$$

which can be simplified to

$$V = E_0\left(d - \ell + \frac{\ell}{K}\right)$$

$$= (7.50 \times 10^4 \text{ V/m})\left(1.00 \times 10^{-3} \text{ m} + \frac{1.00 \times 10^{-3} \text{ m}}{3.50}\right)$$

$$= 96.4 \text{ V}.$$

(g) In the presence of the dielectric, the capacitance is

$$C = \frac{Q}{V} = \frac{1.66 \times 10^{-8} \text{ C}}{96.4 \text{ V}} = 172 \text{ pF}.$$

NOTE If the dielectric filled the space between the plates, the answers to (f) and (g) would be 42.9 V and 387 pF, respectively.

Summary

A **capacitor** is a device used to store charge (and electric energy), and consists of two nontouching conductors. The two conductors generally hold equal and opposite charges of magnitude Q. The ratio of this charge Q to the potential difference V between the conductors is called the **capacitance**, C:

$$C = \frac{Q}{V} \quad \text{or} \quad Q = CV. \qquad (24\text{-}1)$$

The capacitance of a parallel-plate capacitor is proportional to the area A of each plate and inversely proportional to their separation d:

$$C = \epsilon_0 \frac{A}{d}. \qquad (24\text{-}2)$$

When capacitors are connected in **parallel**, the equivalent capacitance is the sum of the individual capacitances:

$$C_{eq} = C_1 + C_2 + \cdots. \qquad (24\text{-}3)$$

When capacitors are connected in **series**, the reciprocal of the equivalent capacitance equals the sum of the reciprocals of the individual capacitances:

$$\frac{1}{C_{eq}} = \frac{1}{C_1} + \frac{1}{C_2} + \cdots. \qquad (24\text{-}4)$$

A charged capacitor stores an amount of electric energy given by

$$U = \tfrac{1}{2}QV = \tfrac{1}{2}CV^2 = \tfrac{1}{2}\frac{Q^2}{C}. \qquad (24\text{-}5)$$

This energy can be thought of as stored in the electric field between the plates. In any electric field $\vec{E}$ in free space the **energy density** u (energy per unit volume) is

$$u = \tfrac{1}{2}\epsilon_0 E^2. \qquad (24\text{-}6)$$

The space between the conductors contains a nonconducting material such as air, paper, or plastic. These materials are referred to as **dielectrics**, and the capacitance is proportional to a property of dielectrics called the **dielectric constant**, K (nearly equal to 1 for air). For a parallel-plate capacitor

$$C = K\epsilon_0 \frac{A}{d} = \epsilon \frac{A}{d} \qquad (24\text{-}8)$$

where $\epsilon = K\epsilon_0$ is called the **permittivity** of the dielectric material. When a dielectric is present, the energy density is

$$u = \tfrac{1}{2}K\epsilon_0 E^2 = \tfrac{1}{2}\epsilon E^2.$$

Questions

1. Suppose two nearby conductors carry the same negative charge. Can there be a potential difference between them? If so, can the definition of capacitance, $C = Q/V$, be used here?

2. Suppose the separation of plates d in a parallel-plate capacitor is not very small compared to the dimensions of the plates. Would you expect Eq. 24–2 to give an overestimate or underestimate of the true capacitance? Explain.

3. Suppose one of the plates of a parallel-plate capacitor was moved so that the area of overlap was reduced by half, but they are still parallel. How would this affect the capacitance?

4. When a battery is connected to a capacitor, why do the two plates acquire charges of the same magnitude? Will this be true if the two conductors are different sizes or shapes?

5. Describe a simple method of measuring ϵ_0 using a capacitor.

6. Suppose three identical capacitors are connected to a battery. Will they store more energy if connected in series or in parallel?

7. A large copper sheet of thickness ℓ is placed between the parallel plates of a capacitor, but does not touch the plates. How will this affect the capacitance?

8. The parallel plates of an isolated capacitor carry opposite charges, Q. If the separation of the plates is increased, is a force required to do so? Is the potential difference changed? What happens to the work done in the pulling process?

9. How does the energy in a capacitor change if (a) the potential difference is doubled, (b) the charge on each plate is doubled, and (c) the separation of the plates is doubled, as the capacitor remains connected to a battery in each case?

10. If the voltage across a capacitor is doubled, the amount of energy it can store (a) doubles; (b) is halved; (c) is quadrupled; (d) is unaffected; (e) none of these.

11. An isolated charged capacitor has horizontal plates. If a thin dielectric is inserted a short way between the plates, Fig. 24–19, will it move left or right when it is released?

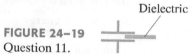

FIGURE 24–19
Question 11.

12. Suppose a battery remains connected to the capacitor in Question 11. What then will happen when the dielectric is released?

13. How does the energy stored in a capacitor change when a dielectric is inserted if (a) the capacitor is isolated so Q does not change; (b) the capacitor remains connected to a battery so V does not change?

14. For dielectrics consisting of polar molecules, how would you expect the dielectric constant to change with temperature?

15. A dielectric is pulled out from between the plates of a capacitor which remains connected to a battery. What changes occur to the capacitance, charge on the plates, potential difference, energy stored in the capacitor, and electric field?

16. We have seen that the capacitance C depends on the size, shape, and position of the two conductors, as well as on the dielectric constant K. What then did we mean when we said that C is a constant in Eq. 24–1?

17. What value might we assign to the dielectric constant for a good conductor? Explain.

Problems

24–1 Capacitors

1. (I) The two plates of a capacitor hold $+2800\,\mu C$ and $-2800\,\mu C$ of charge, respectively, when the potential difference is 930 V. What is the capacitance?

2. (I) How much charge flows from a 12.0-V battery when it is connected to a 12.6-μF capacitor?

3. (I) The potential difference between two short sections of parallel wire in air is 24.0 V. They carry equal and opposite charge of magnitude 75 pC. What is the capacitance of the two wires?

4. (I) The charge on a capacitor increases by 26 μC when the voltage across it increases from 28 V to 78 V. What is the capacitance of the capacitor?

5. (II) A 7.7-μF capacitor is charged by a 125-V battery (Fig. 24–20a) and then is disconnected from the battery. When this capacitor (C_1) is then connected (Fig. 24–20b) to a second (initially uncharged) capacitor, C_2, the final voltage on each capacitor is 15 V. What is the value of C_2? [*Hint:* Charge is conserved.]

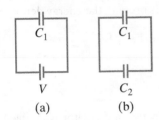

(a)   (b)

FIGURE 24–20 Problems 5 and 48.

6. (II) An isolated capacitor C_1 carries a charge Q_0. Its wires are then connected to those of a second capacitor C_2, previously uncharged. What charge will each carry now? What will be the potential difference across each?

7. (II) It takes 15 J of energy to move a 0.20-mC charge from one plate of a 15-μF capacitor to the other. How much charge is on each plate?

8. (II) A 2.70-μF capacitor is charged to 475 V and a 4.00-μF capacitor is charged to 525 V. (a) These capacitors are then disconnected from their batteries, and the positive plates are now connected to each other and the negative plates are connected to each other. What will be the potential difference across each capacitor and the charge on each? (b) What is the voltage and charge for each capacitor if plates of opposite sign are connected?

9. (II) Compact "ultracapacitors" with capacitance values up to several thousand farads are now commercially available. One application for ultracapacitors is in providing power for electrical circuits when other sources (such as a battery) are turned off. To get an idea of how much charge can be stored in such a component, assume a 1200-F ultracapacitor is initially charged to 12.0 V by a battery and is then disconnected from the battery. If charge is then drawn off the plates of this capacitor at a rate of 1.0 mC/s, say, to power the backup memory of some electrical gadget, how long (in days) will it take for the potential difference across this capacitor to drop to 6.0 V?

10. (II) In a **dynamic random access memory (DRAM)** computer chip, each memory cell chiefly consists of a capacitor for charge storage. Each of these cells represents a single binary-bit value of 1 when its 35-fF capacitor ($1\text{ fF} = 10^{-15}\text{ F}$) is charged at 1.5 V, or 0 when uncharged at 0 V. (a) When it is fully charged, how many excess electrons are on a cell capacitor's negative plate? (b) After charge has been placed on a cell capacitor's plate, it slowly "leaks" off (through a variety of mechanisms) at a constant rate of 0.30 fC/s. How long does it take for the potential difference across this capacitor to decrease by 1.0% from its fully charged value? (Because of this leakage effect, the charge on a DRAM capacitor is "refreshed" many times per second.)

24–2 Determination of Capacitance

11. (I) To make a 0.40-μF capacitor, what area must the plates have if they are to be separated by a 2.8-mm air gap?

12. (I) What is the capacitance per unit length (F/m) of a coaxial cable whose inner conductor has a 1.0-mm diameter and the outer cylindrical sheath has a 5.0-mm diameter? Assume the space between is filled with air.

13. (I) Determine the capacitance of the Earth, assuming it to be a spherical conductor.

14. (II) Use Gauss's law to show that $\vec{E} = 0$ inside the inner conductor of a cylindrical capacitor (see Fig. 24–6 and Example 24–2) as well as outside the outer cylinder.

15. (II) Dry air will break down if the electric field exceeds about 3.0×10^6 V/m. What amount of charge can be placed on a capacitor if the area of each plate is 6.8 cm^2?

16. (II) An electric field of 4.80×10^5 V/m is desired between two parallel plates, each of area 21.0 cm^2 and separated by 0.250 cm of air. What charge must be on each plate?

17. (II) How strong is the electric field between the plates of a 0.80-μF air-gap capacitor if they are 2.0 mm apart and each has a charge of 92 μC?

18. (II) A large metal sheet of thickness ℓ is placed between, and parallel to, the plates of the parallel-plate capacitor of Fig. 24–4. It does not touch the plates, and extends beyond their edges. (a) What is now the net capacitance in terms of A, d, and ℓ? (b) If $\ell = 0.40\,d$, by what factor does the capacitance change when the sheet is inserted?

19. (III) Small distances are commonly measured capacitively. Consider an air-filled parallel-plate capacitor with fixed plate area $A = 25$ mm^2 and a variable plate-separation distance x. Assume this capacitor is attached to a capacitance-measuring instrument which can measure capacitance C in the range 1.0 pF to 1000.0 pF with an accuracy of $\Delta C = 0.1$ pF. (a) If C is measured while x is varied, over what range $(x_{min} \le x \le x_{max})$ can the plate-separation distance (in μm) be determined by this setup? (b) Define Δx to be the accuracy (magnitude) to which x can be determined, and determine a formula for Δx. (c) Determine the percent accuracy to which x_{min} and x_{max} can be measured.

20. (III) In an **electrostatic air cleaner ("precipitator")**, the strong nonuniform electric field in the central region of a cylindrical capacitor (with outer and inner cylindrical radii R_a and R_b) is used to create ionized air molecules for use in charging dust and soot particles (Fig. 24–21). Under standard atmospheric conditions, if air is subjected to an electric field magnitude that exceeds its dielectric strength $E_S = 2.7 \times 10^6$ N/C, air molecules will dissociate into positively charged ions and free electrons. In a precipitator, the region within which air is ionized (the *corona discharge* region) occupies a cylindrical volume of radius R that is typically five times that of the inner cylinder. Assume a particular precipitator is constructed with $R_b = 0.10$ mm and $R_a = 10.0$ cm. In order to create a corona discharge region with radius $R = 5.0\,R_b$, what potential difference V should be applied between the precipitator's inner and outer conducting cylinders? [Besides dissociating air, the charged inner cylinder repels the resulting positive ions from the corona discharge region, where they are put to use in charging dust particles, which are then "collected" on the negatively charged outer cylinder.]

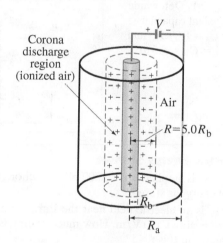

FIGURE 24–21   Problem 20.

24–3 Capacitors in Series and Parallel

21. (I) The capacitance of a portion of a circuit is to be reduced from 2900 pF to 1600 pF. What capacitance can be added to the circuit to produce this effect without removing existing circuit elements? Must any existing connections be broken to accomplish this?

22. (I) (a) Six 3.8-μF capacitors are connected in parallel. What is the equivalent capacitance? (b) What is their equivalent capacitance if connected in series?

23. (II) Given three capacitors, $C_1 = 2.0\,\mu$F, $C_2 = 1.5\,\mu$F, and $C_3 = 3.0\,\mu$F, what arrangement of parallel and series connections with a 12-V battery will give the minimum voltage drop across the 2.0-μF capacitor? What is the minimum voltage drop?

24. (II) Suppose three parallel-plate capacitors, whose plates have areas A_1, A_2, and A_3 and separations d_1, d_2, and d_3, are connected in parallel. Show, using only Eq. 24–2, that Eq. 24–3 is valid.

25. (II) An electric circuit was accidentally constructed using a 5.0-μF capacitor instead of the required 16-μF value. Without removing the 5.0-μF capacitor, what can a technician add to correct this circuit?

26. (II) Three conducting plates, each of area A, are connected as shown in Fig. 24–22. (a) Are the two capacitors thus formed connected in series or in parallel? (b) Determine C as a function of d_1, d_2, and A. Assume $d_1 + d_2$ is much less than the dimensions of the plates. (c) The middle plate can be moved (changing the values of d_1 and d_2), so as to vary the capacitance. What are the minimum and maximum values of the net capacitance?

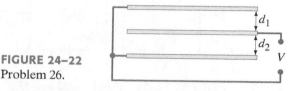

FIGURE 24–22
Problem 26.

27. (II) Consider three capacitors, of capacitance 3600 pF, 5800 pF, and 0.0100 μF. What maximum and minimum capacitance can you form from these? How do you make the connection in each case?

28. (II) A 0.50-μF and a 0.80-μF capacitor are connected in series to a 9.0-V battery. Calculate (a) the potential difference across each capacitor and (b) the charge on each. (c) Repeat parts (a) and (b) assuming the two capacitors are in parallel.

29. (II) In Fig. 24–23, suppose $C_1 = C_2 = C_3 = C_4 = C$. (a) Determine the equivalent capacitance between points a and b. (b) Determine the charge on each capacitor and the potential difference across each in terms of V.

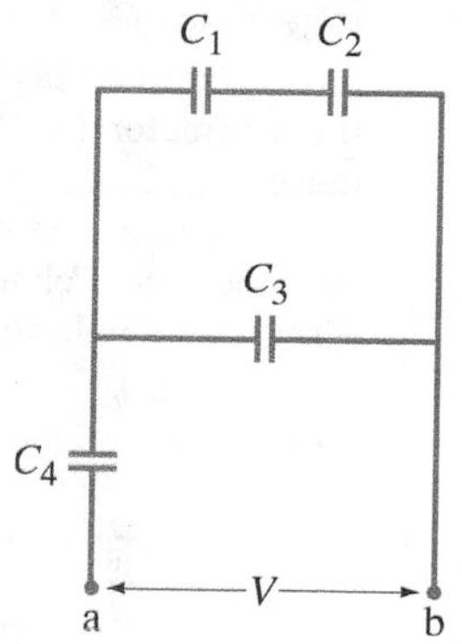

FIGURE 24–23
Problems 29 and 30.

30. (II) Suppose in Fig. 24–23 that $C_1 = C_2 = C_3 = 16.0\,\mu$F and $C_4 = 28.5\,\mu$F. If the charge on C_2 is $Q_2 = 12.4\,\mu$C, determine the charge on each of the other capacitors, the voltage across each capacitor, and the voltage V_{ab} across the entire combination.

31. (II) The switch S in Fig. 24–24 is connected downward so that capacitor C_2 becomes fully charged by the battery of voltage V_0. If the switch is then connected upward, determine the charge on each capacitor after the switching.

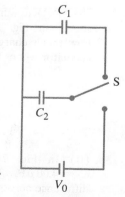

FIGURE 24–24
Problem 31.

32. (II) (a) Determine the equivalent capacitance between points a and b for the combination of capacitors shown in Fig. 24–25. (b) Determine the charge on each capacitor and the voltage across each if $V_{ba} = V$.

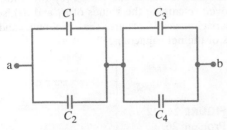

FIGURE 24–25 Problems 32 and 33.

33. (II) Suppose in Problem 32, Fig. 24–25, that $C_1 = C_3 = 8.0 \, \mu F$, $C_2 = C_4 = 16 \, \mu F$, and $Q_3 = 23 \, \mu C$. Determine (a) the charge on each of the other capacitors, (b) the voltage across each capacitor, and (c) the voltage V_{ba} across the combination.

34. (II) Two capacitors connected in parallel produce an equivalent capacitance of $35.0 \, \mu F$ but when connected in series the equivalent capacitance is only $5.5 \, \mu F$. What is the individual capacitance of each capacitor?

35. (II) In the **capacitance bridge** shown in Fig. 24–26, a voltage V_0 is applied and the variable capacitor C_1 is adjusted until there is zero voltage between points a and b as measured on the voltmeter ($\bullet\!\!-\!\!\text{V}\!\!-\!\!\bullet$). Determine the unknown capacitance C_x if $C_1 = 8.9 \, \mu F$ and the fixed capacitors have $C_2 = 18.0 \, \mu F$ and $C_3 = 4.8 \, \mu F$. Assume no charge flows through the voltmeter.

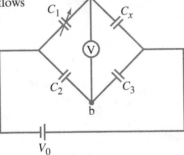

FIGURE 24–26 Problem 35.

36. (II) Two capacitors, $C_1 = 3200 \, pF$ and $C_2 = 1800 \, pF$, are connected in series to a 12.0-V battery. The capacitors are later disconnected from the battery and connected directly to each other, positive plate to positive plate, and negative plate to negative plate. What then will be the charge on each capacitor?

37. (II) (a) Determine the equivalent capacitance of the circuit shown in Fig. 24–27. (b) If $C_1 = C_2 = 2C_3 = 24.0 \, \mu F$, how much charge is stored on each capacitor when $V = 35.0 \, V$?

FIGURE 24–27
Problems 37, 38, and 45.

38. (II) In Fig. 24–27, let $C_1 = 2.00 \, \mu F$, $C_2 = 3.00 \, \mu F$, $C_3 = 4.00 \, \mu F$, and $V = 24.0 \, V$. What is the potential difference across each capacitor?

39. (III) Suppose one plate of a parallel-plate capacitor is tilted so it makes a small angle θ with the other plate, as shown in Fig. 24–28. Determine a formula for the capacitance C in terms of A, d, and θ, where A is the area of each plate and θ is small. Assume the plates are square. [*Hint*: Imagine the capacitor as many infinitesimal capacitors in parallel.]

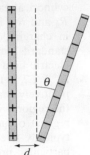

FIGURE 24–28
Problem 39.

40. (III) A voltage V is applied to the capacitor network shown in Fig. 24–29. (a) What is the equivalent capacitance? [*Hint*: Assume a potential difference V_{ab} exists across the network as shown; write potential differences for various pathways through the network from a to b in terms of the charges on the capacitors and the capacitances.] (b) Determine the equivalent capacitance if $C_2 = C_4 = 8.0 \, \mu F$ and $C_1 = C_3 = C_5 = 4.5 \, \mu F$.

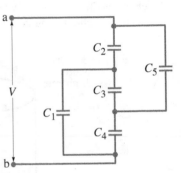

FIGURE 24–29
Problem 40.

24–4 Electric Energy Storage

41. (I) 2200 V is applied to a 2800-pF capacitor. How much electric energy is stored?

42. (I) There is an electric field near the Earth's surface whose intensity is about 150 V/m. How much energy is stored per cubic meter in this field?

43. (I) How much energy is stored by the electric field between two square plates, 8.0 cm on a side, separated by a 1.3-mm air gap? The charges on the plates are equal and opposite and of magnitude $420 \, \mu C$.

44. (II) A parallel-plate capacitor has fixed charges $+Q$ and $-Q$. The separation of the plates is then tripled. (a) By what factor does the energy stored in the electric field change? (b) How much work must be done to increase the separation of the plates from d to $3.0d$? The area of each plate is A.

45. (II) In Fig. 24–27, let $V = 10.0 \, V$ and $C_1 = C_2 = C_3 = 22.6 \, \mu F$. How much energy is stored in the capacitor network?

46. (II) How much energy must a 28-V battery expend to charge a $0.45\text{-}\mu F$ and a $0.20\text{-}\mu F$ capacitor fully when they are placed (a) in parallel, (b) in series? (c) How much charge flowed from the battery in each case?

47. (II) (a) Suppose the outer radius R_a of a cylindrical capacitor was tripled, but the charge was kept constant. By what factor would the stored energy change? Where would the energy come from? (b) Repeat part (a), assuming the voltage remains constant.

48. (II) A $2.20\text{-}\mu F$ capacitor is charged by a 12.0-V battery. It is disconnected from the battery and then connected to an uncharged $3.50\text{-}\mu F$ capacitor (Fig. 24–20). Determine the total stored energy (a) before the two capacitors are connected, and (b) after they are connected. (c) What is the change in energy?

49. (II) How much work would be required to remove a metal sheet from between the plates of a capacitor (as in Problem 18a), assuming: (a) the battery remains connected so the voltage remains constant; (b) the battery is disconnected so the charge remains constant?

50. (II) (a) Show that each plate of a parallel-plate capacitor exerts a force

$$F = \frac{1}{2}\frac{Q^2}{\epsilon_0 A}$$

on the other, by calculating dW/dx where dW is the work needed to increase the separation by dx. (b) Why does using $F = QE$, with E being the electric field between the plates, give the wrong answer?

51. (II) Show that the electrostatic energy stored in the electric field outside an isolated spherical conductor of radius r_0 carrying a net charge Q is

$$U = \frac{1}{8\pi\epsilon_0}\frac{Q^2}{r_0}.$$

Do this in three ways: (a) Use Eq. 24–6 for the energy density in an electric field [Hint: Consider spherical shells of thickness dr]; (b) use Eq. 24–5 together with the capacitance of an isolated sphere (Section 24–2); (c) by calculating the work needed to bring all the charge Q up from infinity in infinitesimal bits dq.

52. (II) When two capacitors are connected in parallel and then connected to a battery, the total stored energy is 5.0 times greater than when they are connected in series and then connected to the same battery. What is the ratio of the two capacitances? (Before the battery is connected in each case, the capacitors are fully discharged.)

53. (II) For commonly used **CMOS** (complementary metal oxide semiconductor) digital circuits, the charging of the component capacitors C to their working potential difference V accounts for the major contribution of its energy input requirements. Thus, if a given logical operation requires such circuitry to charge its capacitors N times, we can assume that the operation requires an energy of $N(\frac{1}{2}CV^2)$. In the past 20 years, the capacitance in digital circuits has been reduced by a factor of about 20 and the voltage to which these capacitors are charged has been reduced from 5.0 V to 1.5 V. Also, present-day alkaline batteries hold about five times the energy of older batteries. Two present-day AA alkaline cells, each of which measures 1 cm diameter by 4 cm long, can power the logic circuitry of a hand-held **personal digital assistant** (PDA) with its display turned off for about two months. If an attempt was made to construct a similar PDA (i.e., same digital capabilities so N remains constant) 20 years ago, how many (older) AA batteries would have been required to power its digital circuitry for two months? Would this PDA fit in a pocket or purse?

24–5 Dielectrics

54. (I) What is the capacitance of two square parallel plates 4.2 cm on a side that are separated by 1.8 mm of paraffin?

55. (II) Suppose the capacitor in Example 24–11 remains connected to the battery as the dielectric is removed. What will be the work required to remove the dielectric in this case?

56. (II) How much energy would be stored in the capacitor of Problem 43 if a mica dielectric is placed between the plates? Assume the mica is 1.3 mm thick (and therefore fills the space between the plates).

57. (II) In the DRAM computer chip of Problem 10, the cell capacitor's two conducting parallel plates are separated by a 2.0-nm thick insulating material with dielectric constant $K = 25$. (a) Determine the area A (in μm^2) of the cell capacitor's plates. (b) In (older) "planar" designs, the capacitor was mounted on a silicon-wafer surface with its plates parallel to the plane of the wafer. Assuming the plate area A accounts for half of the area of each cell, estimate how many megabytes of memory can be placed on a 3.0-cm^2 silicon wafer with the planar design? (1 byte = 8 bits.)

58. (II) A 3500-pF air-gap capacitor is connected to a 32-V battery. If a piece of mica fills the space between the plates, how much charge will flow from the battery?

59. (II) Two different dielectrics each fill half the space between the plates of a parallel-plate capacitor as shown in Fig. 24–30. Determine a formula for the capacitance in terms of K_1, K_2, the area A of the plates, and the separation d. [Hint: Can you consider this capacitor as two capacitors in series or in parallel?]

FIGURE 24–30
Problem 59.

60. (II) Two different dielectrics fill the space between the plates of a parallel-plate capacitor as shown in Fig. 24–31. Determine a formula for the capacitance in terms of K_1, K_2, the area A, of the plates, and the separation $d_1 = d_2 = d/2$. [Hint: Can you consider this capacitor as two capacitors in series or in parallel?]

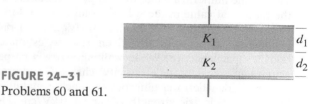

FIGURE 24–31
Problems 60 and 61.

61. (II) Repeat Problem 60 (Fig. 24–31) but assume the separation $d_1 \neq d_2$.

62. (II) Two identical capacitors are connected in parallel and each acquires a charge Q_0 when connected to a source of voltage V_0. The voltage source is disconnected and then a dielectric $(K = 3.2)$ is inserted to fill the space between the plates of one of the capacitors. Determine (a) the charge now on each capacitor, and (b) the voltage now across each capacitor.

63. (III) A slab of width d and dielectric constant K is inserted a distance x into the space between the square parallel plates (of side ℓ) of a capacitor as shown in Fig. 24–32. Determine, as a function of x, (a) the capacitance, (b) the energy stored if the potential difference is V_0, and (c) the magnitude and direction of the force exerted on the slab (assume V_0 is constant).

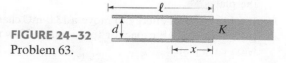

FIGURE 24–32
Problem 63.

64. (III) The quantity of liquid (such as cryogenic liquid nitrogen) available in its storage tank is often monitored by a capacitive level sensor. This sensor is a vertically aligned cylindrical capacitor with outer and inner conductor radii R_a and R_b, whose length ℓ spans the height of the tank. When a nonconducting liquid fills the tank to a height h ($\leq \ell$) from the tank's bottom, the dielectric in the lower and upper region between the cylindrical conductors is the liquid (K_{liq}) and its vapor (K_V), respectively (Fig. 24–33). (a) Determine a formula for the fraction F of the tank filled by liquid in terms of the level-sensor capacitance C. [Hint: Consider the sensor as a combination of two capacitors.] (b) By connecting a capacitance-measuring instrument to the level sensor, F can be monitored. Assume the sensor dimensions are $\ell = 2.0$ m, $R_a = 5.0$ mm, and $R_b = 4.5$ mm. For liquid nitrogen ($K_{liq} = 1.4$, $K_V = 1.0$), what values of C (in pF) will correspond to the tank being completely full and completely empty?

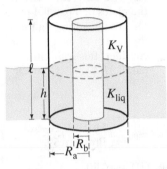

FIGURE 24–33
Problem 64.

*24–6 Molecular Description of Dielectrics

*65. (II) Show that the capacitor in Example 24–12 with dielectric inserted can be considered as equivalent to three capacitors in series, and using this assumption show that the same value for the capacitance is obtained as was obtained in part (g) of the Example.

*66. (II) Repeat Example 24–12 assuming the battery remains connected when the dielectric is inserted. Also, what is the free charge on the plates after the dielectric is added (let this be part (h) of this Problem)?

*67. (II) Using Example 24–12 as a model, derive a formula for the capacitance of a parallel-plate capacitor whose plates have area A, separation d, with a dielectric of dielectric constant K and thickness ℓ ($\ell < d$) placed between the plates.

*68. (II) In Example 24–12 what percent of the stored energy is stored in the electric field in the dielectric?

*69. (III) The capacitor shown in Fig. 24–34 is connected to a 90.0-V battery. Calculate (and sketch) the electric field everywhere between the capacitor plates. Find both the free charge on the capacitor plate and the induced charge on the faces of the glass dielectric plate.

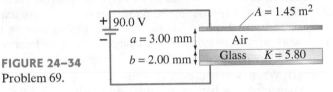

FIGURE 24–34
Problem 69.

General Problems

70. (a) A general rule for estimating the capacitance C of an isolated conducting sphere with radius r is C (in pF) $\approx r$ (in cm). That is, the numerical value of C in pF is about the same as the numerical value of the sphere's radius in cm. Justify this rule. (b) Modeling the human body as a 1-m-radius conducting sphere, use the given rule to estimate your body's capacitance. (c) While walking across a carpet, you acquire an excess "static electricity" charge Q and produce a 0.5-cm spark when reaching out to touch a metallic doorknob. The dielectric strength of air is 30 kV/cm. Use this information to estimate Q (in μC).

71. A *cardiac defibrillator* is used to shock a heart that is beating erratically. A capacitor in this device is charged to 7.5 kV and stores 1200 J of energy. What is its capacitance?

72. A homemade capacitor is assembled by placing two 9-in. pie pans 5.0 cm apart and connecting them to the opposite terminals of a 9-V battery. Estimate (a) the capacitance, (b) the charge on each plate, (c) the electric field halfway between the plates, and (d) the work done by the battery to charge the plates. (e) Which of the above values change if a dielectric is inserted?

73. An uncharged capacitor is connected to a 34.0-V battery until it is fully charged, after which it is disconnected from the battery. A slab of paraffin is then inserted between the plates. What will now be the voltage between the plates?

74. It takes 18.5 J of energy to move a 13.0-mC charge from one plate of a 17.0-μF capacitor to the other. How much charge is on each plate?

75. A huge 3.0-F capacitor has enough stored energy to heat 3.5 kg of water from 22°C to 95°C. What is the potential difference across the plates?

76. A coaxial cable, Fig. 24–35, consists of an inner cylindrical conducting wire of radius R_b surrounded by a dielectric insulator. Surrounding the dielectric insulator is an outer conducting sheath of radius R_a, which is usually "grounded." (a) Determine an expression for the capacitance per unit length of a cable whose insulator has dielectric constant K. (b) For a given cable, $R_b = 2.5$ mm and $R_a = 9.0$ mm. The dielectric constant of the dielectric insulator is $K = 2.6$. Suppose that there is a potential of 1.0 kV between the inner conducting wire and the outer conducting sheath. Find the capacitance per meter of the cable.

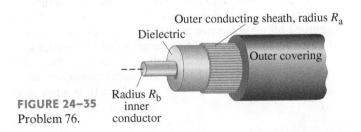

FIGURE 24–35
Problem 76.

Outer conducting sheath, radius R_a
Dielectric
Outer covering
Radius R_b inner conductor

77. The electric field between the plates of a paper-separated ($K = 3.75$) capacitor is 9.21×10^4 V/m. The plates are 1.95 mm apart and the charge on each plate is 0.675 μC. Determine the capacitance of this capacitor and the area of each plate.

78. Capacitors can be used as "electric charge counters." Consider an initially uncharged capacitor of capacitance C with its bottom plate grounded and its top plate connected to a source of electrons. (a) If N electrons flow onto the capacitor's top plate, show that the resulting potential difference V across the capacitor is directly proportional to N. (b) Assume the voltage-measuring device can accurately resolve voltage changes of about 1 mV. What value of C would be necessary to detect each new collected electron? (c) Using modern semiconductor technology, a micron-size capacitor can be constructed with parallel conducting plates separated by an insulating oxide of dielectric constant $K = 3$ and thickness $d = 100$ nm. To resolve the arrival of an individual electron on the plate of such a capacitor, determine the required value of ℓ (in μm) assuming square plates of side length ℓ.

79. A parallel-plate capacitor is isolated with a charge $\pm Q$ on each plate. If the separation of the plates is halved and a dielectric (constant K) is inserted in place of air, by what factor does the energy storage change? To what do you attribute the change in stored potential energy? How does the new value of the electric field between the plates compare with the original value?

80. In lightning storms, the potential difference between the Earth and the bottom of the thunderclouds can be as high as 35,000,000 V. The bottoms of thunderclouds are typically 1500 m above the Earth, and may have an area of 120 km². Modeling the Earth–cloud system as a huge capacitor, calculate (a) the capacitance of the Earth–cloud system, (b) the charge stored in the "capacitor," and (c) the energy stored in the "capacitor."

81. A multilayer film capacitor has a maximum voltage rating of 100 V and a capacitance of 1.0 μF. It is made from alternating sheets of metal foil connected together, separated by films of polyester dielectric. The sheets are 12.0 mm by 14.0 mm and the total thickness of the capacitor is 6.0 mm (not counting the thickness of the insulator on the outside). The metal foil is actually a very thin layer of metal deposited directly on the dielectric, so most of the thickness of the capacitor is due to the dielectric. The dielectric strength of the polyester is about 30×10^6 V/m. Estimate the dielectric constant of the polyester material in the capacitor.

82. A 3.5-μF capacitor is charged by a 12.4-V battery and then is disconnected from the battery. When this capacitor (C_1) is then connected to a second (initially uncharged) capacitor, C_2, the voltage on the first drops to 5.9 V. What is the value of C_2?

83. The power supply for a pulsed nitrogen laser has a 0.080-μF capacitor with a maximum voltage rating of 25 kV. (a) Estimate how much energy could be stored in this capacitor. (b) If 15% of this stored electrical energy is converted to light energy in a pulse that is 4.0-μs long, what is the power of the laser pulse?

84. A parallel-plate capacitor has square plates 12 cm on a side separated by 0.10 mm of plastic with a dielectric constant of $K = 3.1$. The plates are connected to a battery, causing them to become oppositely charged. Since the oppositely charged plates attract each other, they exert a pressure on the dielectric. If this pressure is 40.0 Pa, what is the battery voltage?

85. The variable capacitance of an old radio tuner consists of four plates connected together placed alternately between four other plates, also connected together (Fig. 24–36). Each plate is separated from its neighbor by 1.6 mm of air. One set of plates can move so that the area of overlap of each plate varies from 2.0 cm² to 9.0 cm². (a) Are these seven capacitors connected in series or in parallel? (b) Determine the range of capacitance values.

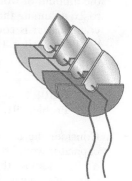

FIGURE 24–36
Problems 85 and 86.

86. A high-voltage supply can be constructed from a variable capacitor with interleaving plates which can be rotated as in Fig. 24–36. A version of this type of capacitor with more plates has a capacitance which can be varied from 10 pF to 1 pF. (a) Initially, this capacitor is charged by a 7500-V power supply when the capacitance is 8.0 pF. It is then disconnected from the power supply and the capacitance reduced to 1.0 pF by rotating the plates. What is the voltage across the capacitor now? (b) What is a major disadvantage of this as a high-voltage power supply?

87. A 175-pF capacitor is connected in series with an unknown capacitor, and as a series combination they are connected to a 25.0-V battery. If the 175-pF capacitor stores 125 pC of charge on its plates, what is the unknown capacitance?

88. A parallel-plate capacitor with plate area 2.0 cm² and air-gap separation 0.50 mm is connected to a 12-V battery, and fully charged. The battery is then disconnected. (a) What is the charge on the capacitor? (b) The plates are now pulled to a separation of 0.75 mm. What is the charge on the capacitor now? (c) What is the potential difference across the plates now? (d) How much work was required to pull the plates to their new separation?

89. In the circuit shown in Fig. 24–37, $C_1 = 1.0\ \mu$F, $C_2 = 2.0\ \mu$F, $C_3 = 2.4\ \mu$F, and a voltage $V_{ab} = 24$ V is applied across points a and b. After C_1 is fully charged the switch is thrown to the right. What is the final charge and potential difference on each capacitor?

FIGURE 24–37
Problem 89.

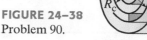

90. The long cylindrical capacitor shown in Fig. 24–38 consists of four concentric cylinders, with respective radii R_a, R_b, R_c, and R_d. The cylinders b and c are joined by metal strips. Determine the capacitance per unit length of this arrangement. (Assume equal and opposite charges are placed on the innermost and outermost cylinders.)

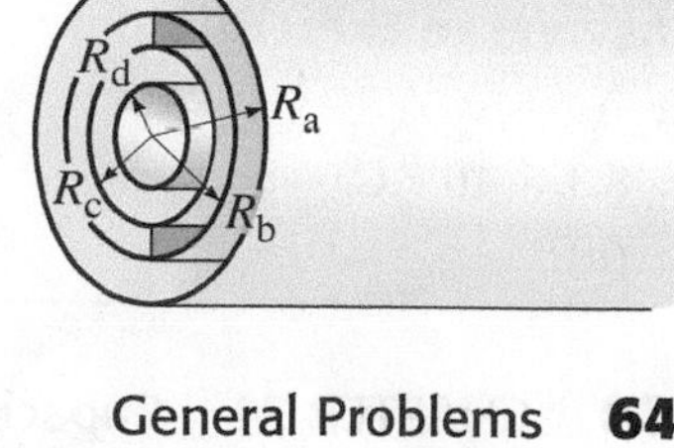

FIGURE 24–38
Problem 90.

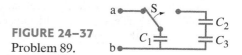

91. A parallel-plate capacitor has plate area A, plate separation x, and has a charge Q stored on its plates (Fig. 24–39). Find the amount of work required to double the plate separation to $2x$, assuming the charge remains constant at Q. Show that your answer is consistent with the change in energy stored by the capacitor. (*Hint*: See Example 24–10.)

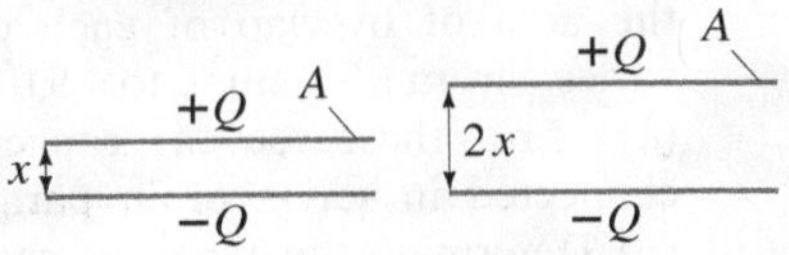

FIGURE 24–39
Problem 91.

x $+Q$ A $-Q$ $+Q$ A $2x$ $-Q$

92. Consider the use of capacitors as memory cells. A charged capacitor would represent a one and an uncharged capacitor a zero. Suppose these capacitors were fabricated on a silicon chip and each has a capacitance of 30 femto-farads $(1\,\text{fF} = 10^{-15}\,\text{F.})$ The dielectric filling the space between the parallel plates has dielectric constant $K = 25$ and a dielectric strength of $1.0 \times 10^9\,\text{V/m}$. (*a*) If the operating voltage is 1.5 V, how many electrons would be stored on one of these capacitors when charged? (*b*) If no safety factor is allowed, how thin a dielectric layer could we use for operation at 1.5 V? (*c*) Using the layer thickness from your answer to part (*b*), what would be the area of the capacitor plates?

93. To get an idea how big a farad is, suppose you want to make a 1-F air-filled parallel-plate capacitor for a circuit you are building. To make it a reasonable size, suppose you limit the plate area to $1.0\,\text{cm}^2$. What would the gap have to be between the plates? Is this practically achievable?

94. A student wearing shoes with thin insulating soles is standing on a grounded metal floor when he puts his hand flat against the screen of a CRT computer monitor. The voltage inside the monitor screen, 6.3 mm from his hand, is 25,000 V. The student's hand and the monitor form a capacitor; the student is a conductor, and there is another capacitor between the floor and his feet. Using reasonable numbers for hand and foot areas, estimate the student's voltage relative to the floor. Assume vinyl-soled shoes 1 cm thick.

95. A parallel-plate capacitor with plate area $A = 2.0\,\text{m}^2$ and plate separation $d = 3.0\,\text{mm}$ is connected to a 45-V battery (Fig. 24–40a). (*a*) Determine the charge on the capacitor, the electric field, the capacitance, and the energy stored in the capacitor. (*b*) With the capacitor still connected to the battery, a slab of plastic with dielectric strength $K = 3.2$ is placed between the plates of the capacitor, so that the gap is completely filled with the dielectric. What are the new values of charge, electric field, capacitance, and the energy U stored in the capacitor?

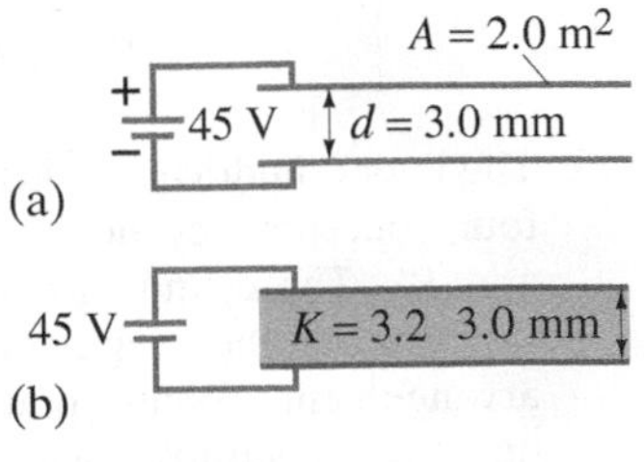

FIGURE 24–40
Problem 95.

(a) $+$ $-$ 45 V $\quad$ $A = 2.0\,\text{m}^2$ $\quad d = 3.0\,\text{mm}$

(b) 45 V $\quad$ $K = 3.2$ $\quad 3.0\,\text{mm}$

96. Let us try to estimate the maximum "static electricity" charge that might result during each walking step across an insulating floor. Assume the sole of a person's shoe has area $A \approx 150\,\text{cm}^2$, and when the foot is lifted from the ground during each step, the sole acquires an excess charge Q from rubbing contact with the floor. (*a*) Model the sole as a plane conducting surface with Q uniformly distributed across it as the foot is lifted from the ground. If the dielectric strength of the air between the sole and floor as the foot is lifted is $E_S = 3 \times 10^6\,\text{N/C}$, determine Q_{max}, the maximum possible excess charge that can be transferred to the sole during each step. (*b*) Modeling a person as an isolated conducting sphere of radius $r \approx 1\,\text{m}$, estimate a person's capacitance. (*c*) After lifting the foot from the floor, assume the excess charge Q quickly redistributes itself over the entire surface area of the person. Estimate the maximum potential difference that the person can develop with respect to the floor.

97. Paper has a dielectric constant $K = 3.7$ and a dielectric strength of $15 \times 10^6\,\text{V/m}$. Suppose that a typical sheet of paper has a thickness of 0.030 mm. You make a "homemade" capacitor by placing a sheet of $21 \times 14\,\text{cm}$ paper between two aluminum foil sheets (Fig. 24–41). The thickness of the aluminum foil is 0.040 mm. (*a*) What is the capacitance C_0 of your device? (*b*) About how much charge could you store on your capacitor before it would break down? (*c*) Show in a sketch how you could overlay sheets of paper and aluminum for a parallel combination. If you made 100 such capacitors, and connected the edges of the sheets in parallel so that you have a single large capacitor of capacitance $100\,C_0$, how thick would your new large capacitor be? (*d*) What is the maximum voltage you can apply to this $100\,C_0$ capacitor without breakdown?

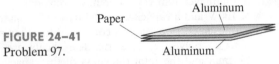

FIGURE 24–41
Problem 97.

Paper / Aluminum / Aluminum

*Numerical/Computer

*98. (II) Six physics students were each given an air filled capacitor. Although the areas were different, the spacing between the plates, d, was the same for all six capacitors, but was unknown. Each student made a measurement of the area A and capacitance C of their capacitor. Below is a Table for their data. Using the combined data and a graphing program or spreadsheet, determine the spacing d between the plates.

Area (m^2)	Capacitance (pF)
0.01	90
0.03	250
0.04	340
0.06	450
0.09	800
0.12	1050

Answers to Exercises

A: A.

B: $8.3 \times 10^{-9}\,\text{C}$.

C: (*a*).

D: (*e*).

E: (*b*).

The glow of the thin wire filament of a lightbulb is caused by the electric current passing through it. Electric energy is transformed to thermal energy (via collisions between moving electrons and atoms of the wire), which causes the wire's temperature to become so high that it glows. Electric current and electric power in electric circuits are of basic importance in everyday life. We examine both dc and ac in this Chapter, and include the microscopic analysis of electric current.

Electric Currents and Resistance

CHAPTER-OPENING QUESTION—Guess now!

The conductors shown are all made of copper and are at the same temperature. Which conductor would have the greatest resistance to the flow of charge entering from the left? Which would offer the least resistance?

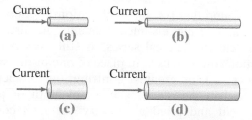

Current (a)   Current (b)

Current (c)   Current (d)

CONTENTS

I n the previous four Chapters we have been studying static electricity: electric charges at rest. In this Chapter we begin our study of charges in motion, and we call a flow of charge an electric current.

In everyday life we are familiar with electric currents in wires and other conductors. Indeed, most practical electrical devices depend on electric current: current through a lightbulb, current in the heating element of a stove or electric heater, and currents in electronic devices. Electric currents can exist in conductors such as wires, and also in other devices such as the CRT of a television or computer monitor whose charged electrons flow through space (Section 23–9).

FIGURE 25–1 Alessandro Volta. In this portrait, Volta exhibits his battery to Napoleon in 1801.

In electrostatic situations, we saw in Sections 21–9 and 22–3 that the electric field must be zero inside a conductor (if it weren't, the charges would move). But when charges are *moving* in a conductor, there usually *is* an electric field in the conductor. Indeed, an electric field is needed to set charges into motion, and to keep them in motion in any normal conductor. We can control the flow of charge using electric fields and electric potential (voltage), concepts we have just been discussing. In order to have a current in a wire, a potential difference is needed, which can be provided by a battery.

We first look at electric current from a macroscopic point of view: that is, current as measured in a laboratory. Later in the Chapter we look at currents from a microscopic (theoretical) point of view as a flow of electrons in a wire.

Until the year 1800, the technical development of electricity consisted mainly of producing a static charge by friction. It all changed in 1800 when Alessandro Volta (1745–1827; Fig. 25–1) invented the electric battery, and with it produced the first steady flow of electric charge—that is, a steady electric current.

25–1 The Electric Battery

The events that led to the discovery of the battery are interesting. For not only was this an important discovery, but it also gave rise to a famous scientific debate.

In the 1780s, Luigi Galvani (1737–1798), professor at the University of Bologna, carried out a series of experiments on the contraction of a frog's leg muscle through electricity produced by static electricity. Galvani found that the muscle also contracted when dissimilar metals were inserted into the frog. Galvani believed that the source of the electric charge was in the frog muscle or nerve itself, and that the metal merely transmitted the charge to the proper points. When he published his work in 1791, he termed this charge "animal electricity." Many wondered, including Galvani himself, if he had discovered the long-sought "life-force."

Volta, at the University of Pavia 200 km away, was skeptical of Galvani's results, and came to believe that the source of the electricity was not in the animal itself, but rather in the *contact between the dissimilar metals*. Volta realized that a moist conductor, such as a frog muscle or moisture at the contact point of two dissimilar metals, was necessary in the circuit if it was to be effective. He also saw that the contracting frog muscle was a sensitive instrument for detecting electric "tension" or "electromotive force" (his words for what we now call potential), in fact more sensitive than the best available electroscopes (Section 21–4) that he and others had developed.[†]

FIGURE 25–2 A voltaic battery, from Volta's original publication.

Volta's research found that certain combinations of metals produced a greater effect than others, and, using his measurements, he listed them in order of effectiveness. (This "electrochemical series" is still used by chemists today.) He also found that carbon could be used in place of one of the metals.

Volta then conceived his greatest contribution to science. Between a disc of zinc and one of silver, he placed a piece of cloth or paper soaked in salt solution or dilute acid and piled a "battery" of such couplings, one on top of another, as shown in Fig. 25–2. This "pile" or "battery" produced a much increased potential difference. Indeed, when strips of metal connected to the two ends of the pile were brought close, a spark was produced. Volta had designed and built the first electric battery; he published his discovery in 1800.

[†]Volta's most sensitive electroscope measured about 40 V per degree (angle of leaf separation). Nonetheless, he was able to estimate the potential differences produced by dissimilar metals in contact: for a silver–zinc contact he got about 0.7 V, remarkably close to today's value of 0.78 V.

Electric Cells and Batteries

A battery produces electricity by transforming chemical energy into electrical energy. Today a great variety of electric cells and batteries are available, from flashlight batteries to the storage battery of a car. The simplest batteries contain two plates or rods made of dissimilar metals (one can be carbon) called **electrodes**. The electrodes are immersed in a solution, such as a dilute acid, called the **electrolyte**. Such a device is properly called an **electric cell**, and several cells connected together is a **battery**, although today even a single cell is called a battery. The chemical reactions involved in most electric cells are quite complicated. Here we describe how one very simple cell works, emphasizing the physical aspects.

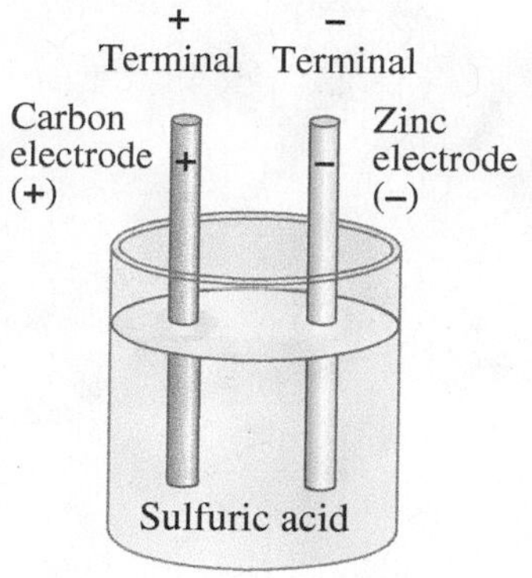

The cell shown in Fig. 25–3 uses dilute sulfuric acid as the electrolyte. One of the electrodes is made of carbon, the other of zinc. That part of each electrode outside the solution is called the **terminal**, and connections to wires and circuits are made here. The acid tends to dissolve the zinc electrode. Each zinc atom leaves two electrons behind on the electrode and enters the solution as a positive ion. The zinc electrode thus acquires a negative charge. As the electrolyte becomes positively charged, electrons are pulled off the carbon electrode by the electrolyte. Thus the carbon electrode becomes positively charged. Because there is an opposite charge on the two electrodes, there is a potential difference between the two terminals.

In a cell whose terminals are not connected, only a small amount of the zinc is dissolved, for as the zinc electrode becomes increasingly negative, any new positive zinc ions produced are attracted back to the electrode. Thus, a particular potential difference (or voltage) is maintained between the two terminals. If charge is allowed to flow between the terminals, say, through a wire (or a lightbulb), then more zinc can be dissolved. After a time, one or the other electrode is used up and the cell becomes "dead."

The voltage that exists between the terminals of a battery depends on what the electrodes are made of and their relative ability to be dissolved or give up electrons.

When two or more cells are connected so that the positive terminal of one is connected to the negative terminal of the next, they are said to be connected in *series* and their voltages add up. Thus, the voltage between the ends of two 1.5-V flashlight batteries connected in series is 3.0 V, whereas the six 2-V cells of an automobile storage battery give 12 V. Figure 25–4a shows a diagram of a common "dry cell" or "flashlight battery" used in portable radios and CD players, flashlights, etc., and Fig. 25–4b shows two smaller ones in series, connected to a flashlight bulb. A lightbulb consists of a thin, coiled wire (filament) inside an evacuated glass bulb, as shown in Fig. 25–5 and in the large photo opening this Chapter, page 651. The filament gets very hot (3000 K) and glows when charge passes through it.

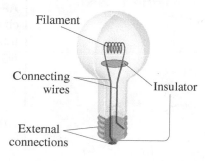

FIGURE 25–3 Simple electric cell.

FIGURE 25–4 (a) Diagram of an ordinary dry cell (like a D-cell or AA). The cylindrical zinc cup is covered on the sides; its flat bottom is the negative terminal. (b) Two dry cells (AA type) connected in series. Note that the positive terminal of one cell pushes against the negative terminal of the other.

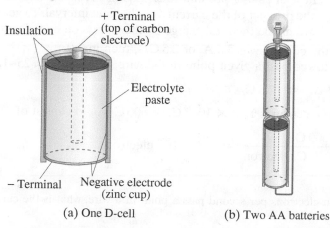

(a) One D-cell   (b) Two AA batteries

FIGURE 25–5 A lightbulb: the fine wire of the filament becomes so hot that it glows. This type of lightbulb is called an incandescent bulb (as compared, say, to a fluorescent bulb).

25–2 Electric Current

The purpose of a battery is to produce a potential difference, which can then make charges move. When a continuous conducting path is connected between the terminals of a battery, we have an electric **circuit**, Fig. 25–6a. On any diagram of a circuit, as in Fig. 25–6b, we use the symbol

   [battery symbol]

to represent a battery. The device connected to the battery could be a lightbulb, a heater, a radio, or whatever. When such a circuit is formed, charge can flow through the wires of the circuit, from one terminal of the battery to the other, as long as the conducting path is continuous. Any flow of charge such as this is called an **electric current**.

More precisely, the electric current in a wire is defined as the net amount of charge that passes through the wire's full cross section at any point per unit time. Thus, the average current $\overline{I}$ is defined as

$$\overline{I} = \frac{\Delta Q}{\Delta t}, \tag{25–1a}$$

where ΔQ is the amount of charge that passes through the conductor at any location during the time interval Δt. The instantaneous current is defined by the derivative limit

$$I = \frac{dQ}{dt}. \tag{25–1b}$$

Electric current is measured in coulombs per second; this is given a special name, the **ampere** (abbreviated amp or A), after the French physicist André Ampère (1775–1836). Thus, $1\,A = 1\,C/s$. Smaller units of current are often used, such as the milliampere $(1\,mA = 10^{-3}\,A)$ and microampere $(1\,\mu A = 10^{-6}\,A)$.

A current can flow in a circuit only if there is a *continuous* conducting path. We then have a **complete circuit**. If there is a break in the circuit, say, a cut wire, we call it an **open circuit** and no current flows. In any single circuit, with only a single path for current to follow such as in Fig. 25–6b, a steady current at any instant is the same at one point (say, point A) as at any other point (such as B). This follows from the conservation of electric charge: charge doesn't disappear. A battery does not create (or destroy) any net charge, nor does a lightbulb absorb or destroy charge.

(a)

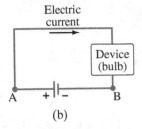

(b)

FIGURE 25–6 (a) A simple electric circuit. (b) Schematic drawing of the same circuit, consisting of a battery, connecting wires (thick gray lines), and a lightbulb or other device.

⚠ **CAUTION**

A battery does not create charge; a lightbulb does not destroy charge

---

EXAMPLE 25–1 **Current is flow of charge.** A steady current of 2.5 A exists in a wire for 4.0 min. (*a*) How much total charge passed by a given point in the circuit during those 4.0 min? (*b*) How many electrons would this be?

APPROACH Current is flow of charge per unit time, Eqs. 25–1, so the amount of charge passing a point is the product of the current and the time interval. To get the number of electrons (*b*), we divide the total charge by the charge on one electron.

SOLUTION (*a*) Since the current was 2.5 A, or 2.5 C/s, then in 4.0 min (= 240 s) the total charge that flowed past a given point in the wire was, from Eq. 25–1a,

$$\Delta Q = I\,\Delta t = (2.5\,C/s)(240\,s) = 600\,C.$$

(*b*) The charge on one electron is $1.60 \times 10^{-19}\,C$, so 600 C would consist of

$$\frac{600\,C}{1.60 \times 10^{-19}\,C/electron} = 3.8 \times 10^{21}\ \text{electrons}.$$

EXERCISE A If 1 million electrons per second pass a point in a wire, what is the current in amps?

CONCEPTUAL EXAMPLE 25–2 | **How to connect a battery.** What is wrong with each of the schemes shown in Fig. 25–7 for lighting a flashlight bulb with a flashlight battery and a single wire?

RESPONSE (*a*) There is no closed path for charge to flow around. Charges might briefly start to flow from the battery toward the lightbulb, but there they run into a "dead end," and the flow would immediately come to a stop.

(*b*) Now there is a closed path passing to and from the lightbulb; but the wire touches only one battery terminal, so there is no potential difference in the circuit to make the charge move.

(*c*) Nothing is wrong here. This is a complete circuit: charge can flow out from one terminal of the battery, through the wire and the bulb, and into the other terminal. This scheme will light the bulb.

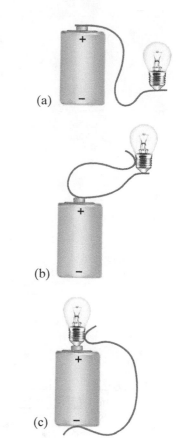

(a)

(b)

(c)

FIGURE 25–7 Example 25–2.

FIGURE 25–8 Conventional current from + to − is equivalent to a negative electron flow from − to +.

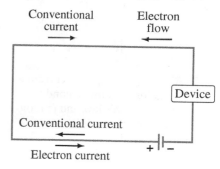

In many real circuits, wires are connected to a common conductor that provides continuity. This common conductor is called **ground**, usually represented as ⏚ or ⏚, and really is connected to the ground in a building or house. In a car, one terminal of the battery is called "ground," but is not connected to the ground—it is connected to the frame of the car, as is one connection to each light-bulb and other devices. Thus the car frame is a conductor in each circuit, ensuring a continuous path for charge flow.

We saw in Chapter 21 that conductors contain many free electrons. Thus, if a continuous conducting wire is connected to the terminals of a battery, negatively charged electrons flow in the wire. When the wire is first connected, the potential difference between the terminals of the battery sets up an electric field inside the wire[†] and parallel to it. Free electrons at one end of the wire are attracted into the positive terminal, and at the same time other electrons leave the negative terminal of the battery and enter the wire at the other end. There is a continuous flow of electrons throughout the wire that begins as soon as the wire is connected to *both* terminals. However, when the conventions of positive and negative charge were invented two centuries ago, it was assumed that positive charge flowed in a wire. For nearly all purposes, positive charge flowing in one direction is exactly equivalent to negative charge flowing in the opposite direction,[‡] as shown in Fig. 25–8. Today, we still use the historical convention of positive charge flow when discussing the direction of a current. So when we speak of the current direction in a circuit, we mean the direction positive charge would flow. This is sometimes referred to as **conventional current**. When we want to speak of the direction of electron flow, we will specifically state it is the electron current. In liquids and gases, both positive and negative charges (ions) can move.

25–3 Ohm's Law: Resistance and Resistors

To produce an electric current in a circuit, a difference in potential is required. One way of producing a potential difference along a wire is to connect its ends to the opposite terminals of a battery. It was Georg Simon Ohm (1787–1854) who established experimentally that the current in a metal wire is proportional to the potential difference V applied to its two ends:

$$I \propto V.$$

If, for example, we connect a wire to the two terminals of a 6-V battery, the current flow will be twice what it would be if the wire were connected to a 3-V battery. It is also found that reversing the sign of the voltage does not affect the magnitude of the current.

[†]This does not contradict what was said in Section 21–9 that in the *static* case, there can be no electric field within a conductor since otherwise the charges would move. Indeed, when there is an electric field in a conductor, charges do move, and we get an electric current.

[‡]An exception is discussed in Section 27–8.

A useful analogy compares the flow of electric charge in a wire to the flow of water in a river, or in a pipe, acted on by gravity. If the river or pipe is nearly level, the flow rate is small. But if one end is somewhat higher than the other, the flow rate—or current—is greater. The greater the difference in height, the swifter the current. We saw in Chapter 23 that electric potential is analogous, in the gravitational case, to the height of a cliff. This applies in the present case to the height through which the fluid flows. Just as an increase in height can cause a greater flow of water, so a greater electric potential difference, or voltage, causes a greater electric current.

Exactly how large the current is in a wire depends not only on the voltage but also on the resistance the wire offers to the flow of electrons. The walls of a pipe, or the banks of a river and rocks in the middle, offer resistance to the water current. Similarly, electron flow is impeded because of interactions with the atoms of the wire. The higher this resistance, the less the current for a given voltage V. We then define electrical *resistance* so that the current is inversely proportional to the resistance: that is,

$$I = \frac{V}{R} \qquad\qquad (25\text{-}2a)$$

where R is the **resistance** of a wire or other device, V is the potential difference applied across the wire or device, and I is the current through it. Equation 25–2a is often written as

$$V = IR. \qquad\qquad (25\text{-}2b)$$

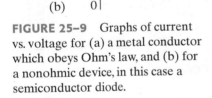

OHM'S "LAW"

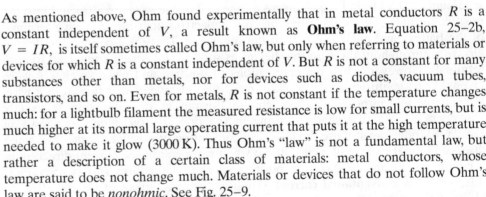

(a)

$$\frac{\Delta I}{\Delta V} = \frac{1}{R}$$

(b)

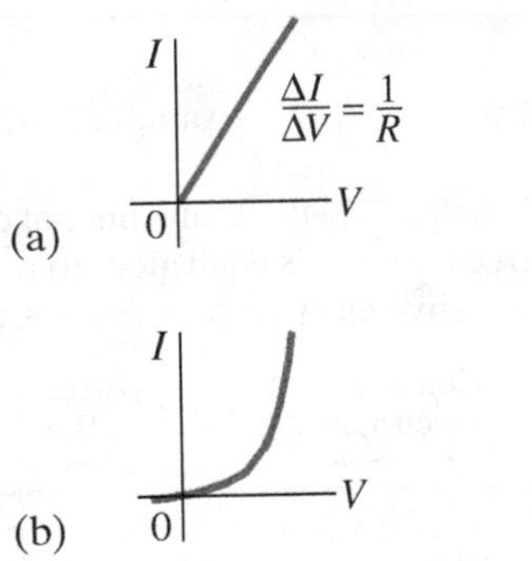

FIGURE 25–9 Graphs of current vs. voltage for (a) a metal conductor which obeys Ohm's law, and (b) for a nonohmic device, in this case a semiconductor diode.

As mentioned above, Ohm found experimentally that in metal conductors R is a constant independent of V, a result known as **Ohm's law**. Equation 25–2b, $V = IR$, is itself sometimes called Ohm's law, but only when referring to materials or devices for which R is a constant independent of V. But R is not a constant for many substances other than metals, nor for devices such as diodes, vacuum tubes, transistors, and so on. Even for metals, R is not constant if the temperature changes much: for a lightbulb filament the measured resistance is low for small currents, but is much higher at its normal large operating current that puts it at the high temperature needed to make it glow (3000 K). Thus Ohm's "law" is not a fundamental law, but rather a description of a certain class of materials: metal conductors, whose temperature does not change much. Materials or devices that do not follow Ohm's law are said to be *nonohmic*. See Fig. 25–9.

The unit for resistance is called the **ohm** and is abbreviated Ω (Greek capital letter omega). Because $R = V/I$, we see that $1.0\,\Omega$ is equivalent to $1.0\,\text{V/A}$.

FIGURE 25–10 Example 25–3.

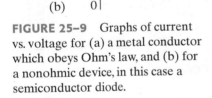

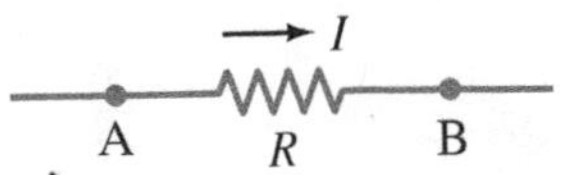

$$\xrightarrow{\ I\ }$$

A   R   B

| CONCEPTUAL EXAMPLE 25–3 | **Current and potential.** Current I enters a resistor R as shown in Fig. 25–10. (a) Is the potential higher at point A or at point B? (b) Is the current greater at point A or at point B?

RESPONSE (a) Positive charge always flows from + to −, from high potential to low potential. Think again of the gravitational analogy: a mass will fall down from high gravitational potential to low. So for positive current I, point A is at a higher potential than point B.

(b) Conservation of charge requires that whatever charge flows into the resistor at point A, an equal amount of charge emerges at point B. Charge or current does not get "used up" by a resistor, just as an object that falls through a gravitational potential difference does not gain or lose mass. So the current is the same at A and B.

An electric potential decrease, as from point A to point B in Example 25–3, is often called a **potential drop** or a **voltage drop**.

EXAMPLE 25-4 **Flashlight bulb resistance.** A small flashlight bulb (Fig. 25–11) draws 300 mA from its 1.5-V battery. (a) What is the resistance of the bulb? (b) If the battery becomes weak and the voltage drops to 1.2 V, how would the current change?

APPROACH We can apply Ohm's law to the bulb, where the voltage applied across it is the battery voltage.

SOLUTION (a) We change 300 mA to 0.30 A and use Eq. 25–2a or b:

$$R = \frac{V}{I} = \frac{1.5\,V}{0.30\,A} = 5.0\,\Omega.$$

(b) If the resistance stays the same, the current would be

$$I = \frac{V}{R} = \frac{1.2\,V}{5.0\,\Omega} = 0.24\,A = 240\,mA,$$

or a decrease of 60 mA.

NOTE With the smaller current in part (b), the bulb filament's temperature would be lower and the bulb less bright. Also, resistance does depend on temperature (Section 25–4), so our calculation is only a rough approximation.

FIGURE 25–11 Flashlight (Example 25–4). Note how the circuit is completed along the side strip.

EXERCISE B What resistance should be connected across a 9.0-V battery to make a 10-mA current? (a) 9 Ω, (b) 0.9 Ω, (c) 900 Ω, (d) 1.1 Ω, (e) 0.11 Ω.

All electric devices, from heaters to lightbulbs to stereo amplifiers, offer resistance to the flow of current. The filaments of lightbulbs (Fig. 25–5) and electric heaters are special types of wires whose resistance results in their becoming very hot. Generally, the connecting wires have very low resistance in comparison to the resistance of the wire filaments or coils, so the connecting wires usually have a minimal effect on the magnitude of the current. In many circuits, particularly in electronic devices, **resistors** are used to control the amount of current. Resistors have resistances ranging from less than an ohm to millions of ohms (see Figs. 25–12 and 25–13). The main types are "wire-wound" resistors which consist of a coil of fine wire, "composition" resistors which are usually made of carbon, and thin carbon or metal films.

When we draw a diagram of a circuit, we use the symbol

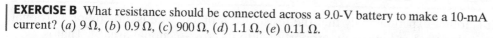

[resistor symbol]

to indicate a resistance. Wires whose resistance is negligible, however, are shown simply as straight lines.

FIGURE 25–12 Photo of resistors (striped), plus other devices on a circuit board.

Resistor Color Code

Color	Number	Multiplier	Tolerance
Black	0	1	
Brown	1	10^1	1%
Red	2	10^2	2%
Orange	3	10^3	
Yellow	4	10^4	
Green	5	10^5	
Blue	6	10^6	
Violet	7	10^7	
Gray	8	10^8	
White	9	10^9	
Gold		10^{-1}	5%
Silver		10^{-2}	10%
No color			20%

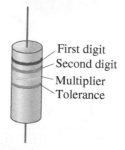

First digit
Second digit
Multiplier
Tolerance

FIGURE 25–13 The resistance value of a given resistor is written on the exterior, or may be given as a color code as shown above and in the Table: the first two colors represent the first two digits in the value of the resistance, the third color represents the power of ten that it must be multiplied by, and the fourth is the manufactured tolerance. For example, a resistor whose four colors are red, green, yellow, and silver has a resistance of $25 \times 10^4\,\Omega = 250{,}000\,\Omega = 250\,k\Omega$, plus or minus 10%. An alternate example of a simple code is a number such as 104, which means $R = 1.0 \times 10^4\,\Omega$.

Some Helpful Clarifications

Here we briefly summarize some possible misunderstandings and clarifications. Batteries do not put out a constant current. Instead, batteries are intended to maintain a constant potential difference, or very nearly so. (Details in the next Chapter.) Thus a battery should be considered a source of voltage. The voltage is applied *across* a wire or device.

Electric current passes *through* a wire or device (connected to a battery), and its magnitude depends on that device's resistance. The resistance is a *property* of the wire or device. The voltage, on the other hand, is external to the wire or device, and is applied across the two ends of the wire or device. The current through the device might be called the "response": the current increases if the voltage increases or the resistance decreases, as $I = V/R$.

In a wire, the direction of the current is always parallel to the wire, no matter how the wire curves, just like water in a pipe. The direction of conventional (positive) current is from high potential $(+)$ toward lower potential $(-)$.

Current and charge do not increase or decrease or get "used up" when going through a wire or other device. The amount of charge that goes in at one end comes out at the other end.

25–4 Resistivity

It is found experimentally that the resistance R of any wire is directly proportional to its length ℓ and inversely proportional to its cross-sectional area A. That is,

$$R = \rho \frac{\ell}{A}, \tag{25–3}$$

where ρ, the constant of proportionality, is called the **resistivity** and depends on the material used. Typical values of ρ, whose units are $\Omega \cdot m$ (see Eq. 25–3), are given for various materials in the middle column of Table 25–1, which is divided into the categories *conductors*, *insulators*, and *semiconductors* (see Section 21–3). The values depend somewhat on purity, heat treatment, temperature, and other factors. Notice that silver has the lowest resistivity and is thus the best conductor (although it is expensive). Copper is close, and much less expensive, which is why most wires are made of copper. Aluminum, although it has a higher resistivity, is much less dense than copper; it is thus preferable to copper in some situations, such as for transmission lines, because its resistance for the same weight is less than that for copper.

TABLE 25–1 Resistivity and Temperature Coefficients (at 20°C)

Material	Resistivity, ρ $(\Omega \cdot m)$	Temperature Coefficient, α $(C°)^{-1}$
Conductors		
Silver	1.59×10^{-8}	0.0061
Copper	1.68×10^{-8}	0.0068
Gold	2.44×10^{-8}	0.0034
Aluminum	2.65×10^{-8}	0.00429
Tungsten	5.6×10^{-8}	0.0045
Iron	9.71×10^{-8}	0.00651
Platinum	10.6×10^{-8}	0.003927
Mercury	98×10^{-8}	0.0009
Nichrome (Ni, Fe, Cr alloy)	100×10^{-8}	0.0004
Semiconductors[†]		
Carbon (graphite)	$(3-60) \times 10^{-5}$	-0.0005
Germanium	$(1-500) \times 10^{-3}$	-0.05
Silicon	$0.1-60$	-0.07
Insulators		
Glass	$10^{9}-10^{12}$	
Hard rubber	$10^{13}-10^{15}$	

[†] Values depend strongly on the presence of even slight amounts of impurities.

The reciprocal of the resistivity, called the **conductivity** σ, is

$$\sigma = \frac{1}{\rho} \qquad (25-4)$$

and has units of $(\Omega \cdot m)^{-1}$.

EXERCISE C Return to the Chapter-Opening Question, page 651, and answer it again now. Try to explain why you may have answered differently the first time.

EXERCISE D A copper wire has a resistance of $10\,\Omega$. What will its resistance be if it is only half as long? (a) $20\,\Omega$, (b) $10\,\Omega$, (c) $5\,\Omega$, (d) $1\,\Omega$, (e) none of these.

EXAMPLE 25–5 **Speaker wires.** Suppose you want to connect your stereo to remote speakers (Fig. 25–14). (a) If each wire must be 20 m long, what diameter copper wire should you use to keep the resistance less than $0.10\,\Omega$ per wire? (b) If the current to each speaker is 4.0 A, what is the potential difference, or voltage drop, across each wire?

APPROACH We solve Eq. 25–3 to get the area A, from which we can calculate the wire's radius using $A = \pi r^2$. The diameter is $2r$. In (b) we can use Ohm's law, $V = IR$.

SOLUTION (a) We solve Eq. 25–3 for the area A and find ρ for copper in Table 25–1:

$$A = \rho \frac{\ell}{R} = \frac{(1.68 \times 10^{-8}\,\Omega \cdot m)(20\,m)}{(0.10\,\Omega)} = 3.4 \times 10^{-6}\,m^2.$$

The cross-sectional area A of a circular wire is $A = \pi r^2$. The radius must then be at least

$$r = \sqrt{\frac{A}{\pi}} = 1.04 \times 10^{-3}\,m = 1.04\,mm.$$

The diameter is twice the radius and so must be at least $2r = 2.1\,mm$.
(b) From $V = IR$ we find that the voltage drop across each wire is

$$V = IR = (4.0\,A)(0.10\,\Omega) = 0.40\,V.$$

NOTE The voltage drop across the wires reduces the voltage that reaches the speakers from the stereo amplifier, thus reducing the sound level a bit.

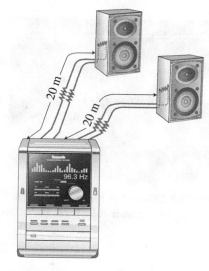

FIGURE 25–14 Example 25–5.

CONCEPTUAL EXAMPLE 25–6 **Stretching changes resistance.** Suppose a wire of resistance R could be stretched uniformly until it was twice its original length. What would happen to its resistance?

RESPONSE If the length ℓ doubles, then the cross-sectional area A is halved, because the volume $(V = A\ell)$ of the wire remains the same. From Eq. 25–3 we see that the resistance would increase by a factor of four $(2/\frac{1}{2} = 4)$.

EXERCISE E Copper wires in houses typically have a diameter of about 1.5 mm. How long a wire would have a 1.0-Ω resistance?

Temperature Dependence of Resistivity

The resistivity of a material depends somewhat on temperature. The resistance of metals generally increases with temperature. This is not surprising, for at higher temperatures, the atoms are moving more rapidly and are arranged in a less orderly fashion. So they might be expected to interfere more with the flow of electrons. If the temperature change is not too great, the resistivity of metals usually increases nearly linearly with temperature. That is,

$$\rho_T = \rho_0 \left[1 + \alpha (T - T_0) \right] \qquad (25-5)$$

where ρ_0 is the resistivity at some reference temperature T_0 (such as $0°C$ or $20°C$), ρ_T is the resistivity at a temperature T, and α is the *temperature coefficient of resistivity*. Values for α are given in Table 25–1. Note that the temperature coefficient for semiconductors can be negative. Why? It seems that at higher temperatures, some of the electrons that are normally not free in a semiconductor become free and can contribute to the current. Thus, the resistance of a semiconductor can decrease with an increase in temperature.

FIGURE 25–15 A thermistor shown next to a millimeter ruler for scale.

EXAMPLE 25–7 **Resistance thermometer.** The variation in electrical resistance with temperature can be used to make precise temperature measurements. Platinum is commonly used since it is relatively free from corrosive effects and has a high melting point. Suppose at 20.0°C the resistance of a platinum resistance thermometer is 164.2 Ω. When placed in a particular solution, the resistance is 187.4 Ω. What is the temperature of this solution?

APPROACH Since the resistance R is directly proportional to the resistivity ρ, we can combine Eq. 25–3 with Eq. 25–5 to find R as a function of temperature T, and then solve that equation for T.

SOLUTION We multiply Eq. 25–5 by (ℓ/A) to obtain (see also Eq. 25–3)

$$R = R_0[1 + \alpha(T - T_0)].$$

Here $R_0 = \rho_0 \ell/A$ is the resistance of the wire at $T_0 = 20.0$°C. We solve this equation for T and find (see Table 25–1 for α)

$$T = T_0 + \frac{R - R_0}{\alpha R_0} = 20.0°C + \frac{187.4 \ \Omega - 164.2 \ \Omega}{(3.927 \times 10^{-3}(C°)^{-1})(164.2 \ \Omega)} = 56.0°C.$$

NOTE Resistance thermometers have the advantage that they can be used at very high or low temperatures where gas or liquid thermometers would be useless.

NOTE More convenient for some applications is a *thermistor* (Fig. 25–15), which consists of a metal oxide or semiconductor whose resistance also varies in a repeatable way with temperature. Thermistors can be made quite small and respond very quickly to temperature changes.

EXERCISE F The resistance of the tungsten filament of a common incandescent lightbulb is how many times greater at its operating temperature of 3000 K than its resistance at room temperature? (*a*) Less than 1% greater; (*b*) roughly 10% greater; (*c*) about 2 times greater; (*d*) roughly 10 times greater; (*e*) more than 100 times greater.

The value of α in Eq. 25–5 itself can depend on temperature, so it is important to check the temperature range of validity of any value (say, in a handbook of physical data). If the temperature range is wide, Eq. 25–5 is not adequate and terms proportional to the square and cube of the temperature are needed, but they are generally very small except when $T - T_0$ is large.

25–5 Electric Power

Electric energy is useful to us because it can be easily transformed into other forms of energy. Motors transform electric energy into mechanical energy, and are examined in Chapter 27.

In other devices such as electric heaters, stoves, toasters, and hair dryers, electric energy is transformed into thermal energy in a wire resistance known as a "heating element." And in an ordinary lightbulb, the tiny wire filament (Fig. 25–5 and Chapter-opening photo) becomes so hot it glows; only a few percent of the energy is transformed into visible light, and the rest, over 90%, into thermal energy. Lightbulb filaments and heating elements (Fig. 25–16) in household appliances have resistances typically of a few ohms to a few hundred ohms.

Electric energy is transformed into thermal energy or light in such devices, and there are many collisions between the moving electrons and the atoms of the wire. In each collision, part of the electron's kinetic energy is transferred to the atom with which it collides. As a result, the kinetic energy of the wire's atoms increases and hence the temperature of the wire element increases. The increased thermal energy can be transferred as heat by conduction and convection to the air in a heater or to food in a pan, by radiation to bread in a toaster, or radiated as light.

To find the power transformed by an electric device, recall that the energy transformed when an infinitesimal charge dq moves through a potential difference V is $dU = V \, dq$ (Eq. 23–3). Let dt be the time required for an amount of charge dq

FIGURE 25–16 Hot electric stove burner glows because of energy transformed by electric current.

to move through a potential difference V. Then the power P, which is the rate energy is transformed, is

$$P = \frac{dU}{dt} = \frac{dq}{dt}V.$$

The charge that flows per second, dq/dt, is the electric current I. Thus we have

$$P = IV. \tag{25-6}$$

This general relation gives us the power transformed by any device, where I is the current passing through it and V is the potential difference across it. It also gives the power delivered by a source such as a battery. The SI unit of electric power is the same as for any kind of power, the **watt** $(1\,W = 1\,J/s)$.

The rate of energy transformation in a resistance R can be written in two other ways, starting with the general relation $P = IV$ and substituting in $V = IR$:

$$P = IV = I(IR) = I^2R \tag{25-7a}$$

$$P = IV = \left(\frac{V}{R}\right)V = \frac{V^2}{R}. \tag{25-7b}$$

Equations 25–7a and b apply only to resistors, whereas Eq. 25–6, $P = IV$, is more general and applies to any device, including a resistor.

EXAMPLE 25–8 **Headlights.** Calculate the resistance of a 40-W automobile headlight designed for 12 V (Fig. 25–17).

APPROACH We solve Eq. 25–7b for R.

SOLUTION From Eq. 25–7b,

$$R = \frac{V^2}{P} = \frac{(12\,V)^2}{(40\,W)} = 3.6\,\Omega.$$

NOTE This is the resistance when the bulb is burning brightly at 40 W. When the bulb is cold, the resistance is much lower, as we saw in Eq. 25–5. Since the current is high when the resistance is low, lightbulbs burn out most often when first turned on.

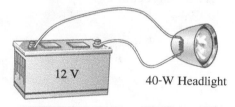

FIGURE 25–17 Example 25–8.

PHYSICS APPLIED
Why lightbulbs burn out when first turned on

⚠ CAUTION
You pay for energy, which is power × time, not for power

It is energy, not power, that you pay for on your electric bill. Since power is the *rate* energy is transformed, the total energy used by any device is simply its power consumption multiplied by the time it is on. If the power is in watts and the time is in seconds, the energy will be in joules since $1\,W = 1\,J/s$. Electric companies usually specify the energy with a much larger unit, the **kilowatt-hour** (kWh). One kWh $= (1000\,W)(3600\,s) = 3.60 \times 10^6\,J$.

EXAMPLE 25–9 **Electric heater.** An electric heater draws a steady 15.0 A on a 120-V line. How much power does it require and how much does it cost per month (30 days) if it operates 3.0 h per day and the electric company charges 9.2 cents per kWh?

APPROACH We use Eq. 25–6, $P = IV$, to find the power. We multiply the power (in kW) by the time (h) used in a month and by the cost per energy unit, \$0.092 per kWh, to get the cost per month.

SOLUTION The power is

$$P = IV = (15.0\,A)(120\,V) = 1800\,W$$

or 1.80 kW. The time (in hours) the heater is used per month is $(3.0\,h/d)(30\,d) = 90\,h$, which at 9.2¢/kWh would cost $(1.80\,kW)(90\,h)(\$0.092/kWh) = \$15$.

NOTE Household current is actually alternating (ac), but our solution is still valid assuming the given values for V and I are the proper averages (rms) as we discuss in Section 25–7.

FIGURE 25–18 Example 25–10. A lightning bolt.

EXAMPLE 25–10 **ESTIMATE** **Lightning bolt.** Lightning is a spectacular example of electric current in a natural phenomenon (Fig. 25–18). There is much variability to lightning bolts, but a typical event can transfer 10^9 J of energy across a potential difference of perhaps 5×10^7 V during a time interval of about 0.2 s. Use this information to estimate (a) the total amount of charge transferred between cloud and ground, (b) the current in the lightning bolt, and (c) the average power delivered over the 0.2 s.

APPROACH We estimate the charge Q, recalling that potential energy change equals the potential difference ΔV times the charge Q, Eq. 23–3. We equate ΔU with the energy transferred, $\Delta U \approx 10^9$ J. Next, the current I is Q/t (Eq. 25–1a) and the power P is energy/time.

SOLUTION (a) From Eq. 23–3, the energy transformed is $\Delta U = Q \, \Delta V$. We solve for Q:

$$Q = \frac{\Delta U}{\Delta V} \approx \frac{10^9 \, \text{J}}{5 \times 10^7 \, \text{V}} = 20 \, \text{coulombs}.$$

(b) The current during the 0.2 s is about

$$I = \frac{Q}{t} \approx \frac{20 \, \text{C}}{0.2 \, \text{s}} = 100 \, \text{A}.$$

(c) The average power delivered is

$$P = \frac{\text{energy}}{\text{time}} = \frac{10^9 \, \text{J}}{0.2 \, \text{s}} = 5 \times 10^9 \, \text{W} = 5 \, \text{GW}.$$

We can also use Eq. 25–6:

$$P = IV = (100 \, \text{A})(5 \times 10^7 \, \text{V}) = 5 \, \text{GW}.$$

NOTE Since most lightning bolts consist of several stages, it is possible that individual parts could carry currents much higher than the 100 A calculated above.

25–6 Power in Household Circuits

The electric wires that carry electricity to lights and other electric appliances have some resistance, although usually it is quite small. Nonetheless, if the current is large enough, the wires will heat up and produce thermal energy at a rate equal to I^2R, where R is the wire's resistance. One possible hazard is that the current-carrying wires in the wall of a building may become so hot as to start a fire. Thicker wires have less resistance (see Eq. 25–3) and thus can carry more current without becoming too hot. When a wire carries more current than is safe, it is said to be "overloaded." To prevent overloading, *fuses* or *circuit breakers* are installed in circuits. They are basically switches (Fig. 25–19)

FIGURE 25–19 (a) Fuses. When the current exceeds a certain value, the metallic ribbon melts and the circuit opens. Then the fuse must be replaced. (b) One type of circuit breaker. The electric current passes through a bimetallic strip. When the current exceeds a safe level, the heating of the bimetallic strip causes the strip to bend so far to the left that the notch in the spring-loaded metal strip drops down over the end of the bimetallic strip; (c) the circuit then opens at the contact points (one is attached to the metal strip) and the outside switch is also flipped. As soon as the bimetallic strip cools down, it can be reset using the outside switch. Magnetic-type circuit breakers are discussed in Chapters 28 and 29.

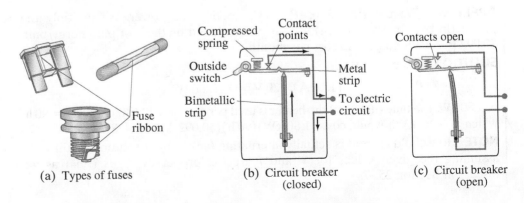

(a) Types of fuses

(b) Circuit breaker (closed)

(c) Circuit breaker (open)

that open the circuit when the current exceeds some particular value. A 20-A fuse or circuit breaker, for example, opens when the current passing through it exceeds 20 A. If a circuit repeatedly burns out a fuse or opens a circuit breaker, there are two possibilities: there may be too many devices drawing current in that circuit; or there is a fault somewhere, such as a "short." A short, or "short circuit," means that two wires have touched that should not have (perhaps because the insulation has worn through) so the resistance is much reduced and the current becomes very large. Short circuits should be remedied immediately.

Household circuits are designed with the various devices connected so that each receives the standard voltage (usually 120 V in the United States) from the electric company (Fig. 25–20). Circuits with the devices arranged as in Fig. 25–20 are called *parallel circuits*, as we will discuss in the next Chapter. When a fuse blows or circuit breaker opens, it is important to check the total current being drawn on that circuit, which is the sum of the currents in each device.

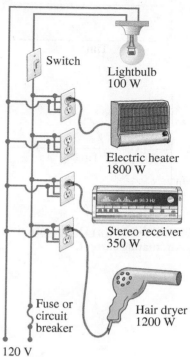

EXAMPLE 25–11 Will a fuse blow? Determine the total current drawn by all the devices in the circuit of Fig. 25–20.

APPROACH Each device has the same 120-V voltage across it. The current each draws from the source is found from $I = P/V$, Eq. 25–6.

SOLUTION The circuit in Fig. 25–20 draws the following currents: the lightbulb draws $I = P/V = 100 \text{ W}/120 \text{ V} = 0.8 \text{ A}$; the heater draws $1800 \text{ W}/120 \text{ V} = 15.0 \text{ A}$; the stereo draws a maximum of $350 \text{ W}/120 \text{ V} = 2.9 \text{ A}$; and the hair dryer draws $1200 \text{ W}/120 \text{ V} = 10.0 \text{ A}$. The total current drawn, if all devices are used at the same time, is

$$0.8 \text{ A} + 15.0 \text{ A} + 2.9 \text{ A} + 10.0 \text{ A} = 28.7 \text{ A}.$$

NOTE The heater draws as much current as 18 100-W lightbulbs. For safety, the heater should probably be on a circuit by itself.

FIGURE 25–20 Connection of household appliances.

If the circuit in Fig. 25–20 is designed for a 20-A fuse, the fuse should blow, and we hope it will, to prevent overloaded wires from getting hot enough to start a fire. Something will have to be turned off to get this circuit below 20 A. (Houses and apartments usually have several circuits, each with its own fuse or circuit breaker; try moving one of the devices to another circuit.) If the circuit is designed with heavier wire and a 30-A fuse, the fuse shouldn't blow—if it does, a short may be the problem. (The most likely place for a short is in the cord of one of the devices.) Proper fuse size is selected according to the wire used to supply the current. A properly rated fuse should *never* be replaced by a higher-rated one. A fuse blowing or a circuit breaker opening is acting like a switch, making an "open circuit." By an open circuit, we mean that there is no longer a complete conducting path, so no current can flow; it is as if $R = \infty$.

CONCEPTUAL EXAMPLE 25–12 A dangerous extension cord. Your 1800-W portable electric heater is too far from your desk to warm your feet. Its cord is too short, so you plug it into an extension cord rated at 11 A. Why is this dangerous?

RESPONSE 1800 W at 120 V draws a 15-A current. The wires in the extension cord rated at 11 A could become hot enough to melt the insulation and cause a fire.

EXERCISE G How many 60-W 120-V lightbulbs can operate on a 20-A line? (*a*) 2; (*b*) 3; (*c*) 6; (*d*) 20; (*e*) 40.

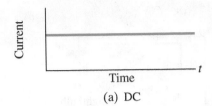

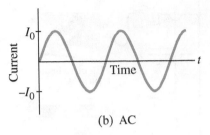

FIGURE 25–21 (a) Direct current. (b) Alternating current.

25–7 Alternating Current

When a battery is connected to a circuit, the current moves steadily in one direction. This is called a **direct current**, or **dc**. Electric generators at electric power plants, however, produce **alternating current**, or **ac**. (Sometimes capital letters are used, DC and AC.) An alternating current reverses direction many times per second and is commonly sinusoidal, as shown in Fig. 25–21. The electrons in a wire first move in one direction and then in the other. The current supplied to homes and businesses by electric companies is ac throughout virtually the entire world. We will discuss and analyze ac circuits in detail in Chapter 30. But because ac circuits are so common in real life, we will discuss some of their basic aspects here.

The voltage produced by an ac electric generator is sinusoidal, as we shall see later. The current it produces is thus sinusoidal (Fig. 25–21b). We can write the voltage as a function of time as

$$V = V_0 \sin 2\pi f t = V_0 \sin \omega t.$$

The potential V oscillates between $+V_0$ and $-V_0$, and V_0 is referred to as the **peak voltage**. The frequency f is the number of complete oscillations made per second, and $\omega = 2\pi f$. In most areas of the United States and Canada, f is 60 Hz (the unit "hertz," as we saw in Chapters 10 and 14, means cycles per second). In many other countries, 50 Hz is used.

Equation 25–2, $V = IR$, works also for ac: if a voltage V exists across a resistance R, then the current I through the resistance is

$$I = \frac{V}{R} = \frac{V_0}{R} \sin \omega t = I_0 \sin \omega t. \tag{25–8}$$

The quantity $I_0 = V_0/R$ is the **peak current**. The current is considered positive when the electrons flow in one direction and negative when they flow in the opposite direction. It is clear from Fig. 25–21b that an alternating current is as often positive as it is negative. Thus, the average current is zero. This does not mean, however, that no power is needed or that no heat is produced in a resistor. Electrons do move back and forth, and do produce heat. Indeed, the power transformed in a resistance R at any instant is

$$P = I^2 R = I_0^2 R \sin^2 \omega t.$$

FIGURE 25–22 Power transformed in a resistor in an ac circuit.

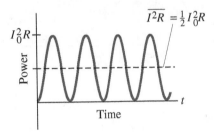

Because the current is squared, we see that the power is always positive, as graphed in Fig. 25–22. The quantity $\sin^2 \omega t$ varies between 0 and 1; and it is not too difficult to show[†] that its average value is $\frac{1}{2}$, as indicated in Fig. 25–22. Thus, the *average power* transformed, $\overline{P}$, is

$$\overline{P} = \frac{1}{2} I_0^2 R.$$

Since power can also be written $P = V^2/R = (V_0^2/R) \sin^2 \omega t$, we also have that the average power is

$$\overline{P} = \frac{1}{2} \frac{V_0^2}{R}.$$

The average or mean value of the *square* of the current or voltage is thus what is important for calculating average power: $\overline{I^2} = \frac{1}{2} I_0^2$ and $\overline{V^2} = \frac{1}{2} V_0^2$. The square root of each of these is the **rms** (root-mean-square) value of the current or voltage:

$$I_{\text{rms}} = \sqrt{\overline{I^2}} = \frac{I_0}{\sqrt{2}} = 0.707 I_0, \tag{25–9a}$$

$$V_{\text{rms}} = \sqrt{\overline{V^2}} = \frac{V_0}{\sqrt{2}} = 0.707 V_0. \tag{25–9b}$$

The rms values of V and I are sometimes called the *effective values*.

[†]A graph of $\cos^2 \omega t$ versus t is identical to that for $\sin^2 \omega t$ in Fig. 25–22, except that the points are shifted (by $\frac{1}{4}$ cycle) on the time axis. Hence the average value of $\sin^2$ and $\cos^2$, averaged over one or more full cycles, will be the same: $\overline{\sin^2 \omega t} = \overline{\cos^2 \omega t}$. From the trigonometric identity $\sin^2 \theta + \cos^2 \theta = 1$, we can write

$$\overline{(\sin^2 \omega t)} + \overline{(\cos^2 \omega t)} = 2\overline{(\sin^2 \omega t)} = 1.$$

Hence the average value of $\sin^2 \omega t$ is $\frac{1}{2}$.

They are useful because they can be substituted directly into the power formulas, Eqs. 25–6 and 25–7, to get the average power:

$$\overline{P} = I_{rms}V_{rms} \qquad\qquad (25-10a)$$

$$\overline{P} = \tfrac{1}{2}I_0^2 R = I_{rms}^2 R \qquad\qquad (25-10b)$$

$$\overline{P} = \tfrac{1}{2}\frac{V_0^2}{R} = \frac{V_{rms}^2}{R}. \qquad\qquad (25-10c)$$

Thus, a direct current whose values of I and V equal the rms values of I and V for an alternating current will produce the same power. Hence it is usually the rms value of current and voltage that is specified or measured. For example, in the United States and Canada, standard line voltage[†] is 120-V ac. The 120 V is V_{rms}; the peak voltage V_0 is

$$V_0 = \sqrt{2}\,V_{rms} = 170\text{ V}.$$

In much of the world (Europe, Australia, Asia) the rms voltage is 240 V, so the peak voltage is 340 V.

EXAMPLE 25–13 Hair dryer. (a) Calculate the resistance and the peak current in a 1000-W hair dryer (Fig. 25–23) connected to a 120-V line. (b) What happens if it is connected to a 240-V line in Britain?

APPROACH We are given $\overline{P}$ and V_{rms}, so $I_{rms} = \overline{P}/V_{rms}$ (Eq. 25–10a or 25–6), and $I_0 = \sqrt{2}\,I_{rms}$. Then we find R from $V = IR$.

SOLUTION (a) We solve Eq. 25–10a for the rms current:

$$I_{rms} = \frac{\overline{P}}{V_{rms}} = \frac{1000\text{ W}}{120\text{ V}} = 8.33\text{ A}.$$

Then

$$I_0 = \sqrt{2}\,I_{rms} = 11.8\text{ A}.$$

The resistance is

$$R = \frac{V_{rms}}{I_{rms}} = \frac{120\text{ V}}{8.33\text{ A}} = 14.4\ \Omega.$$

The resistance could equally well be calculated using peak values:

$$R = \frac{V_0}{I_0} = \frac{170\text{ V}}{11.8\text{ A}} = 14.4\ \Omega.$$

(b) When connected to a 240-V line, more current would flow and the resistance would change with the increased temperature (Section 25–4). But let us make an estimate of the power transformed based on the same 14.4-Ω resistance. The average power would be

$$\overline{P} = \frac{V_{rms}^2}{R} = \frac{(240\text{ V})^2}{(14.4\ \Omega)} = 4000\text{ W}.$$

This is four times the dryer's power rating and would undoubtedly melt the heating element or the wire coils of the motor.

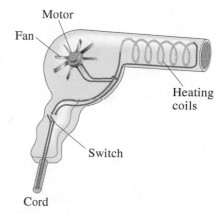

FIGURE 25–23 A hair dryer. Most of the current goes through the heating coils, a pure resistance; a small part goes to the motor to turn the fan. Example 25–13.

EXERCISE H Each channel of a stereo receiver is capable of an average power output of 100 W into an 8-Ω loudspeaker (see Fig. 25–14). What are the rms voltage and the rms current fed to the speaker (a) at the maximum power of 100 W, and (b) at 1.0 W when the volume is turned down?

[†]The line voltage can vary, depending on the total load; the frequency of 60 Hz or 50 Hz, however, remains extremely steady.

25–8 Microscopic View of Electric Current: Current Density and Drift Velocity

FIGURE 25–24 Electric field $\vec{E}$ in a uniform wire of cross-sectional area A carrying a current I. The current density $j = I/A$.

Up to now in this Chapter we have dealt mainly with a macroscopic view of electric current. We saw, however, that according to atomic theory, the electric current in metal wires is carried by negatively charged electrons, and that in liquid solutions current can also be carried by positive and/or negative ions. Let us now look at this microscopic picture in more detail.

When a potential difference is applied to the two ends of a wire of uniform cross section, the direction of the electric field $\vec{E}$ is parallel to the walls of the wire (Fig. 25–24). The existence of $\vec{E}$ within the conducting wire does not contradict our earlier result that $\vec{E} = 0$ inside a conductor in the electrostatic case, as we are no longer dealing with the static case. Charges are free to move in a conductor, and hence can move under the action of the electric field. If all the charges are at rest, then $\vec{E}$ must be zero (electrostatics).

We now define a new microscopic quantity, the **current density**, $\vec{j}$. It is defined as the *electric current per unit cross-sectional area* at any point in space. If the current density $\vec{j}$ in a wire of cross-sectional area A is uniform over the cross section, then j is related to the electric current by

$$j = \frac{I}{A} \quad \text{or} \quad I = jA. \tag{25–11}$$

If the current density is not uniform, then the general relation is

$$I = \int \vec{j} \cdot d\vec{A}, \tag{25–12}$$

where $d\vec{A}$ is an element of surface and I is the current through the surface over which the integration is taken. The direction of the current density at any point is the direction that a positive charge would move when placed at that point—that is, the direction of $\vec{j}$ at any point is generally the same as the direction of $\vec{E}$, Fig. 25–24. The current density exists for any *point* in space. The current I, on the other hand, refers to a conductor as a whole, and hence is a macroscopic quantity.

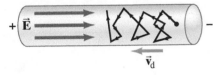

FIGURE 25–25 Electric field $\vec{E}$ in a wire gives electrons in random motion a drift velocity v_d.

The direction of $\vec{j}$ is chosen to represent the direction of net flow of positive charge. In a conductor, it is negatively charged electrons that move, so they move in the direction of $-\vec{j}$, or $-\vec{E}$ (to the left in Fig. 25–24). We can imagine the free electrons as moving about randomly at high speeds, bouncing off the atoms of the wire (somewhat like the molecules of a gas—Chapter 18). When an electric field exists in the wire, Fig. 25–25, the electrons feel a force and initially begin to accelerate. But they soon reach a more or less steady average velocity in the direction of $\vec{E}$, known as their **drift velocity**, $\vec{v}_d$ (collisions with atoms in the wire keep them from accelerating further). The drift velocity is normally very much smaller than the electrons' average random speed.

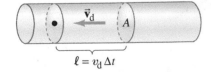

FIGURE 25–26 Electrons in the volume $A\ell$ will all pass through the cross section indicated in a time Δt, where $\ell = v_d \Delta t$.

We can relate the drift velocity v_d to the macroscopic current I in the wire. In a time Δt, the electrons will travel a distance $\ell = v_d \Delta t$ on average. Suppose the wire has cross-sectional area A. Then in time Δt, electrons in a volume $V = A\ell = Av_d \Delta t$ will pass through the cross section A of wire, as shown in Fig. 25–26. If there are n free electrons (each of charge $-e$) per unit volume ($n = N/V$), then the total charge ΔQ that passes through the area A in a time Δt is

$$\Delta Q = (\text{no. of charges, } N) \times (\text{charge per particle})$$
$$= (nV)(-e) = -(nAv_d \Delta t)(e).$$

The current I in the wire is thus

$$I = \frac{\Delta Q}{\Delta t} = -neAv_d. \tag{25–13}$$

The current density, $j = I/A$, is

$$j = -nev_d. \tag{25–14}$$

In vector form, this is written

$$\vec{j} = -ne\vec{v}_d, \tag{25–15}$$

where the minus sign indicates that the direction of (positive) current flow is opposite to the drift velocity of electrons.

We can generalize Eq. 25–15 to any type of charge flow, such as flow of ions in an electrolyte. If there are several types of ions (which can include free electrons), each of density n_i (number per unit volume), charge q_i ($q_i = -e$ for electrons) and drift velocity $\vec{v}_{di}$, then the net current density at any point is

$$\vec{j} = \sum_i n_i q_i \vec{v}_{di}. \tag{25-16}$$

The total current I passing through an area A perpendicular to a uniform $\vec{j}$ is then

$$I = \sum_i n_i q_i v_{di} A.$$

EXAMPLE 25–14 Electron speeds in a wire. A copper wire 3.2 mm in diameter carries a 5.0-A current. Determine (a) the current density in the wire, and (b) the drift velocity of the free electrons. (c) Estimate the rms speed of electrons assuming they behave like an ideal gas at 20°C. Assume that one electron per Cu atom is free to move (the others remain bound to the atom).

APPROACH For (a) $j = I/A = I/\pi r^2$. For (b) we can apply Eq. 25–14 to find v_d if we can determine the number n of free electrons per unit volume. Since we assume there is one free electron per atom, the density of free electrons, n, is the same as the density of Cu atoms. The atomic mass of Cu is 63.5 u (see Periodic Table inside the back cover), so 63.5 g of Cu contains one mole or 6.02×10^{23} free electrons. The mass density of copper (Table 13–1) is $\rho_D = 8.9 \times 10^3 \, \text{kg/m}^3$, where $\rho_D = m/V$. (We use ρ_D to distinguish it here from ρ for resistivity.) In (c) we use $K = \frac{3}{2}kT$, Eq. 18–4. (Do not confuse V for volume with V for voltage.)

SOLUTION (a) The current density is (with $r = \frac{1}{2}(3.2 \, \text{mm}) = 1.6 \times 10^{-3} \, \text{m}$)

$$j = \frac{I}{A} = \frac{I}{\pi r^2} = \frac{5.0 \, \text{A}}{\pi(1.6 \times 10^{-3} \, \text{m})^2} = 6.2 \times 10^5 \, \text{A/m}^2.$$

(b) The number of free electrons per unit volume, $n = N/V$ (where $V = m/\rho_D$), is

$$n = \frac{N}{V} = \frac{N}{m/\rho_D} = \frac{N(1 \, \text{mole})}{m(1 \, \text{mole})} \rho_D$$

$$n = \left(\frac{6.02 \times 10^{23} \, \text{electrons}}{63.5 \times 10^{-3} \, \text{kg}}\right)(8.9 \times 10^3 \, \text{kg/m}^3) = 8.4 \times 10^{28} \, \text{m}^{-3}.$$

Then, by Eq. 25–14, the drift velocity has magnitude

$$v_d = \frac{j}{ne} = \frac{6.2 \times 10^5 \, \text{A/m}^2}{(8.4 \times 10^{28} \, \text{m}^{-3})(1.6 \times 10^{-19} \, \text{C})} = 4.6 \times 10^{-5} \, \text{m/s} \approx 0.05 \, \text{mm/s}.$$

(c) If we model the free electrons as an ideal gas (a rather rough approximation), we use Eq. 18–5 to estimate the random rms speed of an electron as it darts around:

$$v_{rms} = \sqrt{\frac{3kT}{m}} = \sqrt{\frac{3(1.38 \times 10^{-23} \, \text{J/K})(293 \, \text{K})}{9.11 \times 10^{-31} \, \text{kg}}} = 1.2 \times 10^5 \, \text{m/s}.$$

The drift velocity (average speed in the direction of the current) is very much less than the rms thermal speed of the electrons, by a factor of about 10^9.

NOTE The result in (c) is an underestimate. Quantum theory calculations, and experiments, give the rms speed in copper to be about $1.6 \times 10^6 \, \text{m/s}$.

The drift velocity of electrons in a wire is very slow, only about 0.05 mm/s (Example 25–14 above), which means it takes an electron $20 \times 10^3 \, \text{s}$, or $5\frac{1}{2} \, \text{h}$, to travel only 1 m. This is not, of course, how fast "electricity travels": when you flip a light switch, the light—even if many meters away—goes on nearly instantaneously. Why? Because electric fields travel essentially at the speed of light ($3 \times 10^8 \, \text{m/s}$). We can think of electrons in a wire as being like a pipe full of water: when a little water enters one end of the pipe, almost immediately some water comes out at the other end.

*Electric Field Inside a Wire

Equation 25–2b, $V = IR$, can be written in terms of microscopic quantities as follows. We write the resistance R in terms of the resistivity ρ:

$$R = \rho \frac{\ell}{A};$$

and we write V and I as

$$I = jA \qquad \text{and} \qquad V = E\ell.$$

The last relation follows from Eqs. 23–4, where we assume the electric field is uniform within the wire and ℓ is the length of the wire (or a portion of the wire) between whose ends the potential difference is V. Thus, from $V = IR$, we have

$$E\ell = (jA)\left(\rho \frac{\ell}{A}\right) = j\rho\ell$$

so

$$j = \frac{1}{\rho} E = \sigma E, \tag{25–17}$$

where $\sigma = 1/\rho$ is the *conductivity* (Eq. 25–4). For a metal conductor, ρ and σ do not depend on V (and hence not on E). Therefore the current density $\vec{\mathbf{j}}$ is proportional to the electrical field $\vec{\mathbf{E}}$ in the conductor. This is the "microscopic" statement of Ohm's law. Equation 25–17, which can be written in vector form as

$$\vec{\mathbf{j}} = \sigma \vec{\mathbf{E}} = \frac{1}{\rho} \vec{\mathbf{E}},$$

is sometimes taken as the definition of conductivity σ and resistivity ρ.

EXAMPLE 25–15 **Electric field inside a wire.** What is the electric field inside the wire of Example 25–14?

APPROACH We use Eq. 25–17 and $\rho = 1.68 \times 10^{-8}\ \Omega \cdot \text{m}$ for copper.

SOLUTION Example 25–14 gives $j = 6.2 \times 10^5\ \text{A/m}^2$, so

$$E = \rho j = (1.68 \times 10^{-8}\ \Omega \cdot \text{m})(6.2 \times 10^5\ \text{A/m}^2) = 1.0 \times 10^{-2}\ \text{V/m}.$$

NOTE For comparison, the electric field between the plates of a capacitor is often much larger; in Example 24–1, for example, E is on the order of 10^4 V/m. Thus we see that only a modest electric field is needed for current flow in practical cases.

*25–9 Superconductivity

At very low temperatures, well below 0°C, the resistivity (Section 25–4) of certain metals and certain compounds or alloys becomes zero as measured by the highest-precision techniques. Materials in such a state are said to be **superconducting**. It was first observed by H. K. Onnes (1853–1926) in 1911 when he cooled mercury below 4.2 K (-269°C) and found that the resistance of mercury suddenly dropped to zero. In general, superconductors become superconducting only below a certain *transition temperature* or *critical temperature*, T_C, which is usually within a few degrees of absolute zero. Current in a ring-shaped superconducting material has been observed to flow for years in the absence of a potential difference, with no measurable decrease. Measurements show that the resistivity ρ of superconductors is less than $4 \times 10^{-25}\ \Omega \cdot \text{m}$, which is over 10^{16} times smaller than that for copper, and is considered to be zero in practice. See Fig. 25–27.

Before 1986 the highest temperature at which a material was found to super-conduct was 23 K, which required liquid helium to keep the material cold. In 1987, a compound of yttrium, barium, copper, and oxygen (YBCO) was developed that can be superconducting at 90 K. This was an important breakthrough since liquid nitrogen, which boils at 77 K (sufficiently cold to keep the material superconducting), is more easily and cheaply obtained than the liquid helium needed for conventional superconductors. Superconductivity at temperatures as high as 160 K has been reported, though in fragile compounds.

FIGURE 25–27 A superconducting material has zero resistivity when its temperature is below T_C, its "critical temperature." At T_C, the resistivity jumps to a "normal" nonzero value and increases with temperature as most materials do (Eq. 25–5).

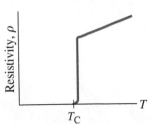

Most applications today use a bismuth-strontium-calcium-copper oxide, known (for short) as BSCCO. A major challenge is how to make a useable, bendable wire out of the BSCCO, which is very brittle. (One solution is to embed tiny filaments of the high-T_C superconductor in a metal alloy, which is not resistanceless, but the resistance is much less than that of a conventional copper cable.)

*25-10 Electrical Conduction in the Nervous System

The flow of electric charge in the human nervous system provides us the means for being aware of the world. Although the detailed functioning is not well understood, we do have a reasonable understanding of how messages are transmitted within the nervous system: they are electrical signals passing along the basic element of the nervous system, the *neuron*.

Neurons are living cells of unusual shape (Fig. 25–28). Attached to the main cell body are several small appendages known as *dendrites* and a long tail called the *axon*. Signals are received by the dendrites and are propagated along the axon. When a signal reaches the nerve endings, it is transmitted to the next neuron or to a muscle at a connection called a *synapse*.

A neuron, before transmitting an electrical signal, is in the so-called "resting state." Like nearly all living cells, neurons have a net positive charge on the outer surface of the cell membrane and a negative charge on the inner surface. This difference in charge, or "dipole layer," means that a potential difference exists across the cell membrane. When a neuron is not transmitting a signal, this "resting potential," normally stated as

$$V_{inside} - V_{outside},$$

is typically $-60\,\text{mV}$ to $-90\,\text{mV}$, depending on the type of organism. The most common ions in a cell are K^+, Na^+, and Cl^-. There are large differences in the concentrations of these ions inside and outside a cell, as indicated by the typical values given in Table 25–2. Other ions are also present, so the fluids both inside and outside the axon are electrically neutral. Because of the differences in concentration, there is a tendency for ions to diffuse across the membrane (see Section 18–7 on diffusion). However, in the resting state the cell membrane prevents any net flow of Na^+ (through a mechanism of "active pumping" of Na^+ out of the cell). But it does allow the flow of Cl^- ions, and less so of K^+ ions, and it is these two ions that produce the dipole charge layer on the membrane. Because there is a greater concentration of K^+ inside the cell than outside, more K^+ ions tend to diffuse outward across the membrane than diffuse inward. A K^+ ion that passes through the membrane becomes attached to the outer surface of the membrane, and leaves behind an equal negative charge that lies on the inner surface of the membrane (Fig. 25–29). Independently, Cl^- ions tend to diffuse *into* the cell since their concentration outside is higher. Both K^+ and Cl^- diffusion tends to charge the interior surface of the membrane negatively and the outside positively. As charge accumulates on the membrane surface, it becomes increasingly difficult for more ions to diffuse: K^+ ions trying to move outward, for example, are repelled by the positive charge already there. Equilibrium is reached when the tendency to diffuse because of the concentration difference is just balanced by the electrical potential difference across the membrane. The greater the concentration difference, the greater the potential difference across the membrane ($-60\,\text{mV}$ to $-90\,\text{mV}$).

The most important aspect of a neuron is not that it has a resting potential (most cells do), but rather that it can respond to a stimulus and conduct an electrical signal along its length. The stimulus could be thermal (when you touch a hot stove) or chemical (as in taste buds); it could be pressure (as on the skin or at the eardrum), or light (as in the eye); or it could be the electric stimulus of a signal coming from the brain or another neuron. In the laboratory, the stimulus is usually electrical and is applied by a tiny probe at some point on the neuron. If the stimulus exceeds some threshold, a voltage pulse will travel down the axon. This voltage pulse can be detected at a point on the axon using a voltmeter or an oscilloscope connected as in Fig. 25–30.

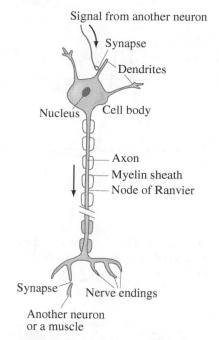

FIGURE 25–28 A simplified sketch of a typical neuron.

TABLE 25–2
Concentrations of Ions Inside and Outside a Typical Axon

	Concentration inside axon (mol/m³)	Concentration outside axon (mol/m³)
K^+	140	5
Na^+	15	140
Cl^-	9	125

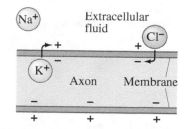

FIGURE 25–29 How a dipole layer of charge forms on a cell membrane.

FIGURE 25–30 Measuring the potential difference between the inside and outside of a nerve cell.

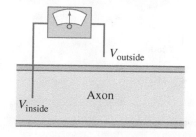

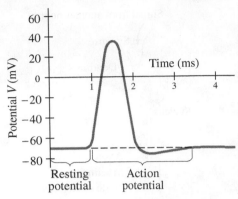

FIGURE 25–31   Action potential.

FIGURE 25–32   Propagation of an action potential along an axon membrane.

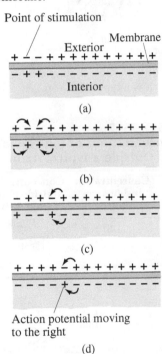

This voltage pulse has the shape shown in Fig. 25–31, and is called an **action potential**. As can be seen, the potential increases from a resting potential of about −70 mV and becomes a positive 30 mV or 40 mV. The action potential lasts for about 1 ms and travels down an axon with a speed of 30 m/s to 150 m/s. When an action potential is stimulated, the nerve is said to have "fired."

What causes the action potential? Apparently, the cell membrane has the ability to alter its permeability properties. At the point where the stimulus occurs, the membrane suddenly becomes much more permeable to Na^+ than to K^+ and Cl^- ions. Thus, Na^+ ions rush into the cell and the inner surface of the wall becomes positively charged, and the potential difference quickly swings positive ($\approx +35$ mV in Fig. 25–31). Just as suddenly, the membrane returns to its original characteristics: it becomes impermeable to Na^+ and in fact pumps out Na^+ ions. The diffusion of Cl^- and K^+ ions again predominates and the original resting potential is restored (−70 mV in Fig. 25–31).

What causes the action potential to travel along the axon? The action potential occurs at the point of stimulation, as shown in Fig. 25–32a. The membrane momentarily is positive on the inside and negative on the outside at this point. Nearby charges are attracted toward this region, as shown in Fig. 25–32b. The potential in these adjacent regions then drops, causing an action potential there. Thus, as the membrane returns to normal at the original point, nearby it experiences an action potential, so the action potential moves down the axon (Figs. 25–32c and d).

You may wonder if the number of ions that pass through the membrane would significantly alter the concentrations. The answer is no; and we can show why by treating the axon as a capacitor in the following Example.

EXAMPLE 25–16   ESTIMATE   Capacitance of an axon. (a) Do an order-of-magnitude estimate for the capacitance of an axon 10 cm long of radius 10 μm. The thickness of the membrane is about 10^{-8} m, and the dielectric constant is about 3. (b) By what factor does the concentration (number of ions per volume) of Na^+ ions in the cell change as a result of one action potential?

APPROACH We model the membrane of an axon as a cylindrically shaped parallel-plate capacitor, with opposite charges on each side. The separation of the "plates" is the thickness of the membrane, $d \approx 10^{-8}$ m. We first calculate the area of the cylinder and then can use Eq. 24–8, $C = K\epsilon_0 A/d$, to find the capacitance. In (b), we use the voltage change during one action potential to find the amount of charge moved across the membrane.

SOLUTION (a) The area A is the area of a cylinder of radius r and length ℓ:
$$A = 2\pi r \ell \approx (6.28)(10^{-5}\,\text{m})(0.1\,\text{m}) \approx 6 \times 10^{-6}\,\text{m}^2.$$
From Eq. 24–8, we have
$$C = K\epsilon_0 \frac{A}{d} \approx (3)(8.85 \times 10^{-12}\,\text{C}^2/\text{N}\cdot\text{m}^2)\frac{6 \times 10^{-6}\,\text{m}^2}{10^{-8}\,\text{m}} \approx 10^{-8}\,\text{F}.$$

(b) Since the voltage changes from −70 mV to about +30 mV, the total change is about 100 mV. The amount of charge that moves is then
$$Q = CV \approx (10^{-8}\,\text{F})(0.1\,\text{V}) = 10^{-9}\,\text{C}.$$

Each ion carries a charge $e = 1.6 \times 10^{-19}$ C, so the number of ions that flow per action potential is $Q/e = (10^{-9}\,\text{C})/(1.6 \times 10^{-19}\,\text{C}) \approx 10^{10}$. The volume of our cylindrical axon is
$$V = \pi r^2 \ell \approx (3)(10^{-5}\,\text{m})^2(0.1\,\text{m}) = 3 \times 10^{-11}\,\text{m}^3,$$

and the concentration of Na^+ ions inside the cell (Table 25–2) is 15 mol/m^3 = $15 \times 6.02 \times 10^{23}$ ions/m^3 $\approx 10^{25}$ ions/m^3. Thus, the cell contains $(10^{25}\,\text{ions/m}^3) \times (3 \times 10^{-11}\,\text{m}^3) \approx 3 \times 10^{14}\,Na^+$ ions. One action potential, then, will change the concentration of Na^+ ions by about $10^{10}/(3 \times 10^{14}) = \frac{1}{3} \times 10^{-4}$, or 1 part in 30,000. This tiny change would not be measurable.

Thus, even 1000 action potentials will not alter the concentration significantly. The sodium pump does not, therefore, have to remove Na^+ ions quickly after an action potential, but can operate slowly over time to maintain a relatively constant concentration.

Summary

An electric **battery** serves as a source of nearly constant potential difference by transforming chemical energy into electric energy. A simple battery consists of two electrodes made of different metals immersed in a solution or paste known as an electrolyte.

Electric current, I, refers to the rate of flow of electric charge and is measured in **amperes** (A): 1 A equals a flow of 1 C/s past a given point.

The direction of **conventional current** is that of positive charge flow. In a wire, it is actually negatively charged electrons that move, so they flow in a direction opposite to the conventional current. A positive charge flow in one direction is almost always equivalent to a negative charge flow in the opposite direction. Positive conventional current always flows from a high potential to a low potential.

The **resistance** R of a device is defined by the relation

$$V = IR, \qquad (25\text{--}2)$$

where I is the current in the device when a potential difference V is applied across it. For materials such as metals, R is a constant independent of V (thus $I \propto V$), a result known as **Ohm's law**. Thus, the current I coming from a battery of voltage V depends on the resistance R of the circuit connected to it.

Voltage is applied *across* a device or between the ends of a wire. Current passes *through* a wire or device. Resistance is a property *of* the wire or device.

The unit of resistance is the **ohm** (Ω), where $1\,\Omega = 1\,\text{V/A}$. See Table 25–3.

TABLE 25–3 Summary of Units

Current	$1\,\text{A} = 1\,\text{C/s}$
Potential difference	$1\,\text{V} = 1\,\text{J/C}$
Power	$1\,\text{W} = 1\,\text{J/s}$
Resistance	$1\,\Omega = 1\,\text{V/A}$

The resistance R of a wire is inversely proportional to its cross-sectional area A, and directly proportional to its length ℓ and to a property of the material called its resistivity:

$$R = \frac{\rho \ell}{A}. \qquad (25\text{--}3)$$

The **resistivity**, ρ, increases with temperature for metals, but for semiconductors it may decrease.

The rate at which energy is transformed in a resistance R from electric to other forms of energy (such as heat and light) is equal to the product of current and voltage. That is, the **power** transformed, measured in watts, is given by

$$P = IV, \qquad (25\text{--}6)$$

which for resistors can be written as

$$P = I^2 R = \frac{V^2}{R}. \qquad (25\text{--}7)$$

The SI unit of power is the **watt** ($1\,\text{W} = 1\,\text{J/s}$).

The total electric energy transformed in any device equals the product of the power and the time during which the device is operated. In SI units, energy is given in joules ($1\,\text{J} = 1\,\text{W·s}$), but electric companies use a larger unit, the **kilowatt-hour** ($1\,\text{kWh} = 3.6 \times 10^6\,\text{J}$).

Electric current can be **direct current** (**dc**), in which the current is steady in one direction; or it can be **alternating current** (**ac**), in which the current reverses direction at a particular frequency f, typically 60 Hz. Alternating currents are typically sinusoidal in time,

$$I = I_0 \sin \omega t, \qquad (25\text{--}8)$$

where $\omega = 2\pi f$, and are produced by an alternating voltage.

The **rms** values of sinusoidally alternating currents and voltages are given by

$$I_{\text{rms}} = \frac{I_0}{\sqrt{2}} \quad \text{and} \quad V_{\text{rms}} = \frac{V_0}{\sqrt{2}}, \qquad (25\text{--}9)$$

respectively, where I_0 and V_0 are the **peak** values. The power relationship, $P = IV = I^2 R = V^2/R$, is valid for the average power in alternating currents when the rms values of V and I are used.

Current density $\vec{j}$ is the current per cross-sectional area. From a microscopic point of view, the current density is related to the number of charge carriers per unit volume, n, their charge, q, and their **drift velocity**, $\vec{v}_d$, by

$$\vec{j} = nq\vec{v}_d. \qquad (25\text{--}16)$$

The electric field within a wire is related to $\vec{j}$ by $\vec{j} = \sigma \vec{E}$ where $\sigma = 1/\rho$ is the **conductivity**.

[*At very low temperatures certain materials become **superconducting**, which means their electrical resistance becomes zero.]

[*The human nervous system operates via electrical conduction: when a nerve "fires," an electrical signal travels as a voltage pulse known as an **action potential**.]

Questions

1. What quantity is measured by a battery rating given in ampere-hours (A·h)?

2. When an electric cell is connected to a circuit, electrons flow away from the negative terminal in the circuit. But within the cell, electrons flow *to* the negative terminal. Explain.

3. When a flashlight is operated, what is being used up: battery current, battery voltage, battery energy, battery power, or battery resistance? Explain.

4. One terminal of a car battery is said to be connected to "ground." Since it is not really connected to the ground, what is meant by this expression?

5. When you turn on a water faucet, the water usually flows immediately. You don't have to wait for water to flow from the faucet valve to the spout. Why not? Is the same thing true when you connect a wire to the terminals of a battery?

6. Can a copper wire and an aluminum wire of the same length have the same resistance? Explain.

7. The equation $P = V^2/R$ indicates that the power dissipated in a resistor decreases if the resistance is increased, whereas the equation $P = I^2 R$ implies the opposite. Is there a contradiction here? Explain.

8. What happens when a lightbulb burns out?

9. If the resistance of a small immersion heater (to heat water for tea or soup, Fig. 25–33) was increased, would it speed up or slow down the heating process? Explain.

FIGURE 25–33
Question 9.

10. If a rectangular solid made of carbon has sides of lengths $a, 2a$, and $3a$, how would you connect the wires from a battery so as to obtain (a) the least resistance, (b) the greatest resistance?

11. Explain why lightbulbs almost always burn out just as they are turned on and not after they have been on for some time.

12. Which draws more current, a 100-W lightbulb or a 75-W bulb? Which has the higher resistance?

13. Electric power is transferred over large distances at very high voltages. Explain how the high voltage reduces power losses in the transmission lines.

14. A 15-A fuse blows repeatedly. Why is it dangerous to replace this fuse with a 25-A fuse?

15. When electric lights are operated on low-frequency ac (say, 5 Hz), they flicker noticeably. Why?

16. Driven by ac power, the same electrons pass back and forth through your reading lamp over and over again. Explain why the light stays lit instead of going out after the first pass of electrons.

17. The heating element in a toaster is made of Nichrome wire. Immediately after the toaster is turned on, is the current (I_{rms}) in the wire increasing, decreasing, or staying constant? Explain.

18. Is current used up in a resistor? Explain.

19. Compare the drift velocities and electric currents in two wires that are geometrically identical and the density of atoms is similar, but the number of free electrons per atom in the material of one wire is twice that in the other.

20. A voltage V is connected across a wire of length ℓ and radius r. How is the electron drift velocity affected if (a) ℓ is doubled, (b) r is doubled, (c) V is doubled?

21. Why is it more dangerous to turn on an electric appliance when you are standing outside in bare feet than when you are inside wearing shoes with thick soles?

Problems

25–2 and 25–3 Electric Current, Resistance, Ohm's Law
(*Note:* The charge on one electron is 1.60×10^{-19} C.)

1. (I) A current of 1.30 A flows in a wire. How many electrons are flowing past any point in the wire per second?

2. (I) A service station charges a battery using a current of 6.7-A for 5.0 h. How much charge passes through the battery?

3. (I) What is the current in amperes if 1200 Na$^+$ ions flow across a cell membrane in 3.5 μs? The charge on the sodium is the same as on an electron, but positive.

4. (I) What is the resistance of a toaster if 120 V produces a current of 4.2 A?

5. (II) An electric clothes dryer has a heating element with a resistance of 8.6 Ω. (a) What is the current in the element when it is connected to 240 V? (b) How much charge passes through the element in 50 min? (Assume direct current.)

6. (II) A hair dryer draws 9.5 A when plugged into a 120-V line. (a) What is its resistance? (b) How much charge passes through it in 15 min? (Assume direct current.)

7. (II) A 4.5-V battery is connected to a bulb whose resistance is 1.6 Ω. How many electrons leave the battery per minute?

8. (II) A bird stands on a dc electric transmission line carrying 3100 A (Fig. 25–34). The line has 2.5×10^{-5} Ω resistance per meter, and the bird's feet are 4.0 cm apart. What is the potential difference between the bird's feet?

FIGURE 25–34
Problem 8.

9. (II) A 12-V battery causes a current of 0.60 A through a resistor. (a) What is its resistance, and (b) how many joules of energy does the battery lose in a minute?

10. (II) An electric device draws 6.50 A at 240 V. (a) If the voltage drops by 15%, what will be the current, assuming nothing else changes? (b) If the resistance of the device were reduced by 15%, what current would be drawn at 240 V?

25–4 Resistivity

11. (I) What is the diameter of a 1.00-m length of tungsten wire whose resistance is 0.32 Ω?

12. (I) What is the resistance of a 4.5-m length of copper wire 1.5 mm in diameter?

13. (II) Calculate the ratio of the resistance of 10.0 m of aluminum wire 2.0 mm in diameter, to 20.0 m of copper wire 1.8 mm in diameter.

14. (II) Can a 2.2-mm-diameter copper wire have the same resistance as a tungsten wire of the same length? Give numerical details.

15. (II) A sequence of potential differences V is applied across a wire (diameter = 0.32 mm, length = 11 cm) and the resulting currents I are measured as follows:

V (V)	0.100	0.200	0.300	0.400	0.500
I (mA)	72	144	216	288	360

(a) If this wire obeys Ohm's law, graphing I vs. V will result in a straight-line plot. Explain why this is so and determine the theoretical predictions for the straight line's slope and y-intercept. (b) Plot I vs. V. Based on this plot, can you conclude that the wire obeys Ohm's law (i.e., did you obtain a straight line with the expected y-intercept)? If so, determine the wire's resistance R. (c) Calculate the wire's resistivity and use Table 25–1 to identify the solid material from which it is composed.

16. (II) How much would you have to raise the temperature of a copper wire (originally at 20°C) to increase its resistance by 15%?

17. (II) A certain copper wire has a resistance of 10.0 Ω. At what point along its length must the wire be cut so that the resistance of one piece is 4.0 times the resistance of the other? What is the resistance of each piece?

18. (II) Determine at what temperature aluminum will have the same resistivity as tungsten does at 20°C.

19. (II) A 100-W lightbulb has a resistance of about 12 Ω when cold (20°C) and 140 Ω when on (hot). Estimate the temperature of the filament when hot assuming an average temperature coefficient of resistivity $\alpha = 0.0045\ (C°)^{-1}$.

20. (II) Compute the voltage drop along a 26-m length of household no. 14 copper wire (used in 15-A circuits). The wire has diameter 1.628 mm and carries a 12-A current.

21. (II) Two aluminum wires have the same resistance. If one has twice the length of the other, what is the ratio of the diameter of the longer wire to the diameter of the shorter wire?

22. (II) A rectangular solid made of carbon has sides of lengths 1.0 cm, 2.0 cm, and 4.0 cm, lying along the x, y, and z axes, respectively (Fig. 25–35). Determine the resistance for current that passes through the solid in (a) the x direction, (b) the y direction, and (c) the z direction. Assume the resistivity is $\rho = 3.0 \times 10^{-5}\ \Omega \cdot m$.

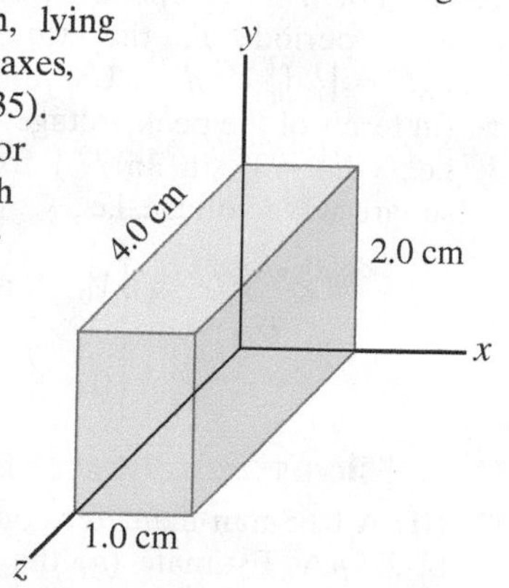

FIGURE 25–35
Problem 22.

23. (II) A length of aluminum wire is connected to a precision 10.00-V power supply, and a current of 0.4212 A is precisely measured at 20.0°C. The wire is placed in a new environment of unknown temperature where the measured current is 0.3818 A. What is the unknown temperature?

24. (II) Small changes in the length of an object can be measured using a **strain gauge** sensor, which is a wire with undeformed length ℓ_0, cross-sectional area A_0, and resistance R_0. This sensor is rigidly affixed to the object's surface, aligning its length in the direction in which length changes are to be measured. As the object deforms, the length of the wire sensor changes by $\Delta\ell$, and the resulting change ΔR in the sensor's resistance is measured. Assuming that as the solid wire is deformed to a length ℓ, its density (and volume) remains constant (only approximately valid), show that the strain $(= \Delta\ell/\ell_0)$ of the wire sensor, and thus of the object to which it is attached, is $\Delta R/2R_0$.

25. (II) A length of wire is cut in half and the two lengths are wrapped together side by side to make a thicker wire. How does the resistance of this new combination compare to the resistance of the original wire?

26. (III) For some applications, it is important that the value of a resistance not change with temperature. For example, suppose you made a 3.70-kΩ resistor from a carbon resistor and a Nichrome wire-wound resistor connected together so the total resistance is the sum of their separate resistances. What value should each of these resistors have (at 0°C) so that the combination is temperature independent?

27. (III) Determine a formula for the total resistance of a spherical shell made of material whose conductivity is σ and whose inner and outer radii are r_1 and r_2. Assume the current flows radially outward.

28. (III) The filament of a lightbulb has a resistance of 12 Ω at 20°C and 140 Ω when hot (as in Problem 19). (a) Calculate the temperature of the filament when it is hot, and take into account the change in length and area of the filament due to thermal expansion (assume tungsten for which the thermal expansion coefficient is $\approx 5.5 \times 10^{-6}\ (C°)^{-1}$). (b) In this temperature range, what is the percentage change in resistance due to thermal expansion, and what is the percentage change in resistance due solely to the change in ρ? Use Eq. 25–5.

29. (III) A 10.0-m length of wire consists of 5.0 m of copper followed by 5.0 m of aluminum, both of diameter 1.4 mm. A voltage difference of 85 mV is placed across the composite wire. (a) What is the total resistance (sum) of the two wires? (b) What is the current through the wire? (c) What are the voltages across the aluminum part and across the copper part?

30. (III) A hollow cylindrical resistor with inner radius r_1 and outer radius r_2, and length ℓ, is made of a material whose resistivity is ρ (Fig. 25–36). (a) Show that the resistance is given by

$$R = \frac{\rho}{2\pi\ell} \ln \frac{r_2}{r_1}$$

for current that flows radially outward. [*Hint*: Divide the resistor into concentric cylindrical shells and integrate.] (b) Evaluate the resistance R for such a resistor made of carbon whose inner and outer radii are 1.0 mm and 1.8 mm and whose length is 2.4 cm. (Choose $\rho = 15 \times 10^{-5}\ \Omega \cdot m$.) (c) What is the resistance in part (b) for current flowing *parallel* to the axis?

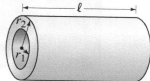

FIGURE 25–36
Problem 30.

25–5 and 25–6 Electric Power

31. (I) What is the maximum power consumption of a 3.0-V portable CD player that draws a maximum of 270 mA of current?

32. (I) The heating element of an electric oven is designed to produce 3.3 kW of heat when connected to a 240-V source. What must be the resistance of the element?

33. (I) What is the maximum voltage that can be applied across a 3.3-kΩ resistor rated at $\frac{1}{4}$ watt?

34. (I) (a) Determine the resistance of, and current through, a 75-W lightbulb connected to its proper source voltage of 110 V. (b) Repeat for a 440-W bulb.

35. (II) An electric power plant can produce electricity at a fixed power P, but the plant operator is free to choose the voltage V at which it is produced. This electricity is carried as an electric current I through a transmission line (resistance R) from the plant to the user, where it provides the user with electric power P'. (a) Show that the reduction in power $\Delta P = P - P'$ due to transmission losses is given by $\Delta P = P^2 R/V^2$. (b) In order to reduce power losses during transmission, should the operator choose V to be as large or as small as possible?

36. (II) A 120-V hair dryer has two settings: 850 W and 1250 W. (a) At which setting do you expect the resistance to be higher? After making a guess, determine the resistance at (b) the lower setting; and (c) the higher setting.

37. (II) A 115-V fish-tank heater is rated at 95 W. Calculate (a) the current through the heater when it is operating, and (b) its resistance.

38. (II) You buy a 75-W lightbulb in Europe, where electricity is delivered to homes at 240 V. If you use the lightbulb in the United States at 120 V (assume its resistance does not change), how bright will it be relative to 75-W 120-V bulbs? [Hint: Assume roughly that brightness is proportional to power consumed.]

39. (II) How many kWh of energy does a 550-W toaster use in the morning if it is in operation for a total of 6.0 min? At a cost of 9.0 cents/kWh, estimate how much this would add to your monthly electric energy bill if you made toast four mornings per week.

40. (II) At $0.095/kWh, what does it cost to leave a 25-W porch light on day and night for a year?

41. (II) What is the total amount of energy stored in a 12-V, 75-A·h car battery when it is fully charged?

42. (II) An ordinary flashlight uses two D-cell 1.5-V batteries connected in series as in Fig. 25–4b (Fig. 25–37). The bulb draws 380 mA when turned on. (a) Calculate the resistance of the bulb and the power dissipated. (b) By what factor would the power increase if four D-cells in series were used with the same bulb? (Neglect heating effects of the filament.) Why shouldn't you try this?

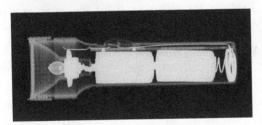

FIGURE 25–37 Problem 42.

43. (II) How many 75-W lightbulbs, connected to 120 V as in Fig. 25–20, can be used without blowing a 15-A fuse?

44. (II) An extension cord made of two wires of diameter 0.129 cm (no. 16 copper wire) and of length 2.7 m (9 ft) is connected to an electric heater which draws 15.0 A on a 120-V line. How much power is dissipated in the cord?

45. (II) A power station delivers 750 kW of power at 12,000 V to a factory through wires with total resistance 3.0 Ω. How much less power is wasted if the electricity is delivered at 50,000 V rather than 12,000 V?

46. (III) A small immersion heater can be used in a car to heat a cup of water for coffee or tea. If the heater can heat 120 mL of water from 25°C to 95°C in 8.0 min, (a) approximately how much current does it draw from the car's 12-V battery, and (b) what is its resistance? Assume the manufacturer's claim of 75% efficiency.

47. (III) The current in an electromagnet connected to a 240-V line is 17.5 A. At what rate must cooling water pass over the coils if the water temperature is to rise by no more than 6.50 C°?

48. (III) A 1.0-m-long round tungsten wire is to reach a temperature of 3100 K when a current of 15.0 A flows through it. What diameter should the wire be? Assume the wire loses energy only by radiation (emissivity $\epsilon = 1.0$, Section 19–10) and the surrounding temperature is 20°C.

25–7 Alternating Current

49. (I) Calculate the peak current in a 2.7-kΩ resistor connected to a 220-V rms ac source.

50. (I) An ac voltage, whose peak value is 180 V, is across a 380-Ω resistor. What are the rms and peak currents in the resistor?

51. (II) Estimate the resistance of the 120-V_{rms} circuits in your house as seen by the power company, when (a) everything electrical is unplugged, and (b) there are two 75-W lightbulbs burning.

52. (II) The peak value of an alternating current in a 1500-W device is 5.4 A. What is the rms voltage across it?

53. (II) An 1800-W arc welder is connected to a 660-V_{rms} ac line. Calculate (a) the peak voltage and (b) the peak current.

54. (II) (a) What is the maximum instantaneous power dissipated by a 2.5-hp pump connected to a 240-V_{rms} ac power source? (b) What is the maximum current passing through the pump?

55. (II) A heater coil connected to a 240-V_{rms} ac line has a resistance of 44 Ω. (a) What is the average power used? (b) What are the maximum and minimum values of the instantaneous power?

56. (II) For a time-dependent voltage $V(t)$, which is periodic with period T, the rms voltage is defined to be $V_{rms} = \left[\frac{1}{T}\int_0^T V^2 \, dt\right]^{\frac{1}{2}}$. Use this definition to determine V_{rms} (in terms of the peak voltage V_0) for (a) a sinusoidal voltage, i.e., $V(t) = V_0 \sin(2\pi t/T)$ for $0 \le t \le T$; and (b) a positive square-wave voltage, i.e.,

$$V(t) = \begin{cases} V_0 & 0 \le t \le \dfrac{T}{2} \\ 0 & \dfrac{T}{2} \le t \le T \end{cases}.$$

25–8 Microscopic View of Electric Current

57. (II) A 0.65-mm-diameter copper wire carries a tiny current of 2.3 μA. Estimate (a) the electron drift velocity, (b) the current density, and (c) the electric field in the wire.

58. (II) A 5.80-m length of 2.0-mm-diameter wire carries a 750-mA current when 22.0 mV is applied to its ends. If the drift velocity is 1.7×10^{-5} m/s, determine (a) the resistance R of the wire, (b) the resistivity ρ, (c) the current density j, (d) the electric field inside the wire, and (e) the number n of free electrons per unit volume.

59. (II) At a point high in the Earth's atmosphere, He²⁺ ions in a concentration of $2.8 \times 10^{12}/m^3$ are moving due north at a speed of 2.0×10^6 m/s. Also, a $7.0 \times 10^{11}/m^3$ concentration of O₂⁻ ions is moving due south at a speed of 6.2×10^6 m/s. Determine the magnitude and direction of the current density $\vec{j}$ at this point.

*25–10 Nerve Conduction

*60. (I) What is the magnitude of the electric field across an axon membrane 1.0×10^{-8} m thick if the resting potential is −70 mV?

*61. (II) A neuron is stimulated with an electric pulse. The action potential is detected at a point 3.40 cm down the axon 0.0052 s later. When the action potential is detected 7.20 cm from the point of stimulation, the time required is 0.0063 s. What is the speed of the electric pulse along the axon? (Why are two measurements needed instead of only one?)

*62. (III) During an action potential, Na⁺ ions move into the cell at a rate of about 3×10^{-7} mol/m²·s. How much power must be produced by the "active Na⁺ pumping" system to produce this flow against a +30-mV potential difference? Assume that the axon is 10 cm long and 20 μm in diameter.

General Problems

63. A person accidentally leaves a car with the lights on. If each of the two headlights uses 40 W and each of the two taillights 6 W, for a total of 92 W, how long will a fresh 12-V battery last if it is rated at 85 A·h? Assume the full 12 V appears across each bulb.

64. How many coulombs are there in 1.00 ampere-hour?

65. You want to design a portable electric blanket that runs on a 1.5-V battery. If you use copper wire with a 0.50-mm diameter as the heating element, how long should the wire be if you want to generate 15 W of heating power? What happens if you accidentally connect the blanket to a 9.0-V battery?

66. What is the average current drawn by a 1.0-hp 120-V motor? (1 hp = 746 W.)

67. The *conductance* G of an object is defined as the reciprocal of the resistance R; that is, $G = 1/R$. The unit of conductance is a *mho* $(= \text{ohm}^{-1})$, which is also called the *siemens* (S). What is the conductance (in siemens) of an object that draws 480 mA of current at 3.0 V?

68. The heating element of a 110-V, 1500-W heater is 3.5 m long. If it is made of iron, what must its diameter be?

69. (a) A particular household uses a 1.8-kW heater 2.0 h/day ("on" time), four 100-W lightbulbs 6.0 h/day, a 3.0-kW electric stove element for a total of 1.0 h/day, and miscellaneous power amounting to 2.0 kWh/day. If electricity costs $0.105 per kWh, what will be their monthly bill (30 d)? (b) How much coal (which produces 7500 kcal/kg) must be burned by a 35%-efficient power plant to provide the yearly needs of this household?

70. A small city requires about 15 MW of power. Suppose that instead of using high-voltage lines to supply the power, the power is delivered at 120 V. Assuming a two-wire line of 0.50-cm-diameter copper wire, estimate the cost of the energy lost to heat per hour per meter. Assume the cost of electricity is about 9.0 cents per kWh.

71. A 1400-W hair dryer is designed for 117 V. (a) What will be the percentage change in power output if the voltage drops to 105 V? Assume no change in resistance. (b) How would the actual change in resistivity with temperature affect your answer?

72. The wiring in a house must be thick enough so it does not become so hot as to start a fire. What diameter must a copper wire be if it is to carry a maximum current of 35 A and produce no more than 1.5 W of heat per meter of length?

73. Determine the resistance of the tungsten filament in a 75-W 120-V incandescent lightbulb (a) at its operating temperature of about 3000 K, (b) at room temperature.

74. Suppose a current is given by the equation $I = 1.80 \sin 210t$, where I is in amperes and t in seconds. (a) What is the frequency? (b) What is the rms value of the current? (c) If this is the current through a 24.0-Ω resistor, write the equation that describes the voltage as a function of time.

75. A microwave oven running at 65% efficiency delivers 950 W to the interior. Find (a) the power drawn from the source, and (b) the current drawn. Assume a source voltage of 120 V.

76. A 1.00-Ω wire is stretched uniformly to 1.20 times its original length. What is its resistance now?

77. 220 V is applied to two different conductors made of the same material. One conductor is twice as long and twice the diameter of the second. What is the ratio of the power transformed in the first relative to the second?

78. An electric heater is used to heat a room of volume 54 m³. Air is brought into the room at 5°C and is completely replaced twice per hour. Heat loss through the walls amounts to approximately 850 kcal/h. If the air is to be maintained at 20°C, what minimum wattage must the heater have? (The specific heat of air is about 0.17 kcal/kg·C°.)

79. A 2800-W oven is connected to a 240-V source. (a) What is the resistance of the oven? (b) How long will it take to bring 120 mL of 15°C water to 100°C assuming 75% efficiency? (c) How much will this cost at 11 cents/kWh?

80. A proposed electric vehicle makes use of storage batteries as its source of energy. Its mass is 1560 kg and it is powered by 24 batteries, each 12 V, 95 A·h. Assume that the car is driven on level roads at an average speed of 45 km/h, and the average friction force is 240 N. Assume 100% efficiency and neglect energy used for acceleration. No energy is consumed when the vehicle is stopped, since the engine doesn't need to idle. (a) Determine the horsepower required. (b) After approximately how many kilometers must the batteries be recharged?

81. A 12.5-Ω resistor is made from a coil of copper wire whose total mass is 15.5 g. What is the diameter of the wire, and how long is it?

82. A fish-tank heater is rated at 95 W when connected to 120 V. The heating element is a coil of Nichrome wire. When uncoiled, the wire has a total length of 3.8 m. What is the diameter of the wire?

83. A 100-W, 120-V lightbulb has a resistance of 12 Ω when cold (20°C) and 140 Ω when on (hot). Calculate its power consumption (a) at the instant it is turned on, and (b) after a few moments when it is hot.

84. In an automobile, the system voltage varies from about 12 V when the car is off to about 13.8 V when the car is on and the charging system is in operation, a difference of 15%. By what percentage does the power delivered to the headlights vary as the voltage changes from 12 V to 13.8 V? Assume the headlight resistance remains constant.

85. The Tevatron accelerator at Fermilab (Illinois) is designed to carry an 11-mA beam of protons traveling at very nearly the speed of light $(3.0 \times 10^8 \text{ m/s})$ around a ring 6300 m in circumference. How many protons are in the beam?

86. Lightbulb A is rated at 120 V and 40 W for household applications. Lightbulb B is rated at 12 V and 40 W for automotive applications. (a) What is the current through each bulb? (b) What is the resistance of each bulb? (c) In one hour, how much charge passes through each bulb? (d) In one hour, how much energy does each bulb use? (e) Which bulb requires larger diameter wires to connect its power source and the bulb?

87. An air conditioner draws 14 A at 220-V ac. The connecting cord is copper wire with a diameter of 1.628 mm. (a) How much power does the air conditioner draw? (b) If the total length of wire is 15 m, how much power is dissipated in the wiring? (c) If no. 12 wire, with a diameter of 2.053 mm, was used instead, how much power would be dissipated in the wiring? (d) Assuming that the air conditioner is run 12 h per day, how much money per month (30 days) would be saved by using no. 12 wire? Assume that the cost of electricity is 12 cents per kWh.

88. Copper wire of diameter 0.259 cm is used to connect a set of appliances at 120 V, which draw 1750 W of power total. (a) What power is wasted in 25.0 m of this wire? (b) What is your answer if wire of diameter 0.412 cm is used?

89. Battery-powered electricity is very expensive compared with that available from a wall receptacle. Estimate the cost per kWh of (a) an alkaline D-cell (cost $1.70) and (b) an alkaline AA-cell (cost $1.25). These batteries can provide a continuous current of 25 mA for 820 h and 120 h, respectively, at 1.5 V. Compare to normal 120-V ac house current at $0.10/kWh.

90. How far does an average electron move along the wires of a 550-W toaster during an alternating current cycle? The power cord has copper wires of diameter 1.7 mm and is plugged into a standard 60-Hz 120-V ac outlet. [*Hint*: The maximum current in the cycle is related to the maximum drift velocity. The maximum velocity in an oscillation is related to the maximum displacement; see Chapter 14.]

91. A copper pipe has an inside diameter of 3.00 cm and an outside diameter of 5.00 cm (Fig. 25–38). What is the resistance of a 10.0-m length of this pipe?

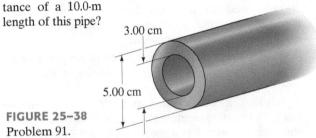

3.00 cm

5.00 cm

FIGURE 25–38
Problem 91.

92. For the wire in Fig. 25–39, whose diameter varies uniformly from a to b as shown, suppose a current $I = 2.0$ A enters at a. If $a = 2.5$ mm and $b = 4.0$ mm, what is the current density (assume uniform) at each end?

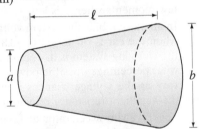

ℓ

a

b

FIGURE 25–39
Problems 92 and 93.

93. The cross section of a portion of wire increases uniformly as shown in Fig. 25–39 so it has the shape of a truncated cone. The diameter at one end is a and at the other it is b, and the total length along the axis is ℓ. If the material has resistivity ρ, determine the resistance R between the two ends in terms of a, b, ℓ, and ρ. Assume that the current flows uniformly through each section, and that the taper is small, i.e., $(b - a) \ll \ell$.

94. A tungsten filament used in a flashlight bulb operates at 0.20 A and 3.2 V. If its resistance at 20°C is 1.5 Ω, what is the temperature of the filament when the flashlight is on?

95. The level of liquid helium (temperature ≤ 4 K) in its storage tank can be monitored using a vertically aligned niobium–titanium (NbTi) wire, whose length ℓ spans the height of the tank. In this level-sensing setup, an electronic circuit maintains a constant electrical current I at all times in the NbTi wire and a voltmeter monitors the voltage difference V across this wire. Since the superconducting transition temperature for NbTi is 10 K, the portion of the wire immersed in the liquid helium is in the superconducting state, while the portion above the liquid (in helium vapor with temperature above 10 K) is in the normal state. Define $f = x/\ell$ to be the fraction of the tank filled with liquid helium (Fig. 25–40) and V_0 to be the value of V when the tank is empty ($f = 0$). Determine the relation between f and V (in terms of V_0).

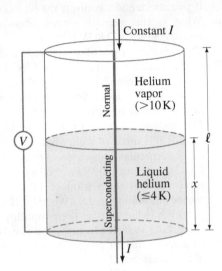

Constant I

Normal

Helium vapor (>10 K)

Superconducting

V

Liquid helium (≤ 4 K)

ℓ

x

I

FIGURE 25–40
Problem 95.

*Numerical/Computer

***96.** (II) The resistance, R, of a particular thermistor as a function of temperature T is shown in this Table:

T (°C)	R (Ω)	T (°C)	R (Ω)
20	126,740	36	60,743
22	115,190	38	55,658
24	104,800	40	51,048
26	95,447	42	46,863
28	87,022	44	43,602
30	79,422	46	39,605
32	72,560	48	36,458
34	66,356	50	33,591

Determine what type of best-fit equation (linear, quadratic, exponential, other) describes the variation of R with T. The resistance of the thermistor is 57,641 Ω when embedded in a substance whose temperature is unknown. Based on your equation, what is the unknown temperature?

Answers to Exercises

A: 1.6×10^{-13} A.

B: (c).

C: (b), (c).

D: (c).

E: 110 m.

F: (d).

G: (e).

H: (a) 28 V, 3.5 A; (b) 2.8 V, 0.35 A.

These MP3 players contain circuits that are dc, at least in part. (The audio signal is ac.) The circuit diagram below shows a possible amplifier circuit for each stereo channel. We have already met two of the circuit elements shown: resistors and capacitors, and we discuss them in circuits in this Chapter. (The large triangle is an amplifier chip containing transistors.) We also discuss voltmeters and ammeters, and how they are built and used to make measurements.

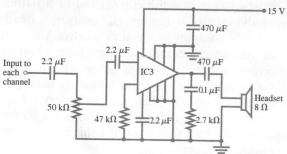

DC Circuits

C H A P T E R

26

CHAPTER-OPENING QUESTION—Guess now!

The automobile headlight bulbs shown in the circuits here are identical. The connection which produces more light is

(a) circuit 1.
(b) circuit 2.
(c) both the same.
(d) not enough information.

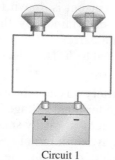

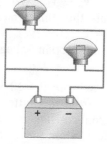

Circuit 1   Circuit 2

CONTENTS

E lectric circuits are basic parts of all electronic devices from radio and TV sets to computers and automobiles. Scientific measurements, from physics to biology and medicine, make use of electric circuits. In Chapter 25, we discussed the basic principles of electric current. Now we will apply these principles to analyze dc circuits involving combinations of batteries, resistors, and capacitors. We also study the operation of some useful instruments.[†]

[†]AC circuits that contain only a voltage source and resistors can be analyzed like the dc circuits in this Chapter. However, ac circuits that contain capacitors and other circuit elements are more complicated, and we discuss them in Chapter 30.

TABLE 26–1 Symbols for Circuit Elements

Symbol	Device
—⊣⊢—	Battery
—⊣⊢— or —⊣(—	Capacitor
—◁◁◁—	Resistor
———	Wire with negligible resistance
—◞—	Switch
⏚ or ↓	Ground

⚠ **CAUTION**

Why battery voltage isn't perfectly constant

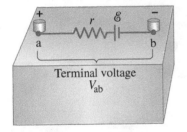

FIGURE 26–1 Diagram for an electric cell or battery.

FIGURE 26–2 Example 26–1.

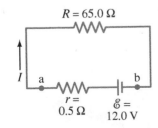

When we draw a diagram for a circuit, we represent batteries, capacitors, and resistors by the symbols shown in Table 26–1. Wires whose resistance is negligible compared with other resistance in the circuit are drawn simply as straight lines. Some circuit diagrams show a ground symbol (⏚ or ↓) which may mean a real connection to the ground, perhaps via a metal pipe, or it may simply mean a common connection, such as the frame of a car.

For the most part in this Chapter, except in Section 26–5 on *RC* circuits, we will be interested in circuits operating in their steady state. That is, we won't be looking at a circuit at the moment a change is made in it, such as when a battery or resistor is connected or disconnected, but rather later when the currents have reached their steady values.

26–1 EMF and Terminal Voltage

To have current in an electric circuit, we need a device such as a battery or an electric generator that transforms one type of energy (chemical, mechanical, or light, for example) into electric energy. Such a device is called a **source** of **electromotive force** or of **emf**. (The term "electromotive force" is a misnomer since it does not refer to a "force" that is measured in newtons. Hence, to avoid confusion, we prefer to use the abbreviation, emf.) The *potential difference* between the terminals of such a source, when no current flows to an external circuit, is called the **emf** of the source. The symbol $\mathscr{E}$ is usually used for emf (don't confuse it with E for electric field), and its unit is volts.

A battery is not a source of constant current—the current out of a battery varies according to the resistance in the circuit. A battery *is*, however, a nearly constant voltage source, but not perfectly constant as we now discuss. You may have noticed in your own experience that when a current is drawn from a battery, the potential difference (voltage) across its terminals drops below its rated emf. For example, if you start a car with the headlights on, you may notice the headlights dim. This happens because the starter draws a large current, and the battery voltage drops as a result. The voltage drop occurs because the chemical reactions in a battery (Section 25–1) cannot supply charge fast enough to maintain the full emf. For one thing, charge must move (within the electrolyte) between the electrodes of the battery, and there is always some hindrance to completely free flow. Thus, a battery itself has some resistance, which is called its **internal resistance**; it is usually designated r.

A real battery is modeled as if it were a perfect emf $\mathscr{E}$ in series with a resistor r, as shown in Fig. 26–1. Since this resistance r is inside the battery, we can never separate it from the battery. The two points a and b in the diagram represent the two terminals of the battery. What we measure is the **terminal voltage** $V_{ab} = V_a - V_b$. When no current is drawn from the battery, the terminal voltage equals the emf, which is determined by the chemical reactions in the battery: $V_{ab} = \mathscr{E}$. However, when a current I flows naturally from the battery there is an internal drop in voltage equal to Ir. Thus the terminal voltage (the actual voltage) is[†]

$$V_{ab} = \mathscr{E} - Ir. \tag{26–1}$$

For example, if a 12-V battery has an internal resistance of 0.1 Ω, then when 10 A flows from the battery, the terminal voltage is 12 V − (10 A)(0.1 Ω) = 11 V. The internal resistance of a battery is usually small. For example, an ordinary flashlight battery when fresh may have an internal resistance of perhaps 0.05 Ω. (However, as it ages and the electrolyte dries out, the internal resistance increases to many ohms.) Car batteries have lower internal resistance.

EXAMPLE 26–1 **Battery with internal resistance.** A 65.0-Ω resistor is connected to the terminals of a battery whose emf is 12.0 V and whose internal resistance is 0.5 Ω, Fig. 26–2. Calculate (*a*) the current in the circuit, (*b*) the terminal voltage of the battery, V_{ab}, and (*c*) the power dissipated in the resistor R and in the battery's internal resistance r.

APPROACH We first consider the battery as a whole, which is shown in Fig. 26–2 as an emf $\mathscr{E}$ and internal resistance r between points a and b. Then we apply $V = IR$ to the circuit itself.

[†]When a battery is being charged, a current is forced to pass through it; we then have to write
$$V_{ab} = \mathscr{E} + Ir.$$
See Section 26–4 or Problem 28 and Fig. 26–46.

SOLUTION (a) From Eq. 26–1, we have

$$V_{ab} = \mathscr{E} - Ir.$$

We apply Ohm's law (Eqs. 25–2) to this battery and the resistance R of the circuit: $V_{ab} = IR$. Hence $IR = \mathscr{E} - Ir$ or $\mathscr{E} = I(R + r)$, and so

$$I = \frac{\mathscr{E}}{R + r} = \frac{12.0\,\text{V}}{65.0\,\Omega + 0.5\,\Omega} = \frac{12.0\,\text{V}}{65.5\,\Omega} = 0.183\,\text{A}.$$

(b) The terminal voltage is

$$V_{ab} = \mathscr{E} - Ir = 12.0\,\text{V} - (0.183\,\text{A})(0.5\,\Omega) = 11.9\,\text{V}.$$

(c) The power dissipated (Eq. 25–7) in R is

$$P_R = I^2R = (0.183\,\text{A})^2(65.0\,\Omega) = 2.18\,\text{W},$$

and in r is

$$P_r = I^2r = (0.183\,\text{A})^2(0.5\,\Omega) = 0.02\,\text{W}.$$

EXERCISE A Repeat Example 26–1 assuming now that the resistance $R = 10.0\,\Omega$, whereas $\mathscr{E}$ and r remain as before.

In much of what follows, unless stated otherwise, we assume that the battery's internal resistance is negligible, and that the battery voltage given is its terminal voltage, which we will usually write simply as V rather than V_{ab}. Be careful not to confuse V (italic) for voltage and V (not italic) for the volt unit.

26–2 Resistors in Series and in Parallel

When two or more resistors are connected end to end along a single path as shown in Fig. 26–3a, they are said to be connected in **series**. The resistors could be simple resistors as were pictured in Fig. 25–12, or they could be lightbulbs (Fig. 26–3b), or heating elements, or other resistive devices. Any charge that passes through R_1 in Fig. 26–3a will also pass through R_2 and then R_3. Hence the same current I passes through each resistor. (If it did not, this would imply that either charge was not conserved, or that charge was accumulating at some point in the circuit, which does not happen in the steady state.)

We let V represent the potential difference (voltage) across all three resistors in Fig. 26–3a. We assume all other resistance in the circuit can be ignored, so V equals the terminal voltage supplied by the battery. We let V_1, V_2, and V_3 be the potential differences across each of the resistors, R_1, R_2, and R_3, respectively. From Ohm's law, $V = IR$, we can write $V_1 = IR_1$, $V_2 = IR_2$, and $V_3 = IR_3$. Because the resistors are connected end to end, energy conservation tells us that the total voltage V is equal to the sum of the voltages[†] across each resistor:

$$V = V_1 + V_2 + V_3 = IR_1 + IR_2 + IR_3. \qquad \text{[series]} \quad \textbf{(26–2)}$$

Now let us determine the equivalent single resistance R_{eq} that would draw the same current I as our combination of three resistors in series; see Fig. 26–3c. Such a single resistance R_{eq} would be related to V by

$$V = IR_{eq}.$$

We equate this expression with Eq. 26–2, $V = I(R_1 + R_2 + R_3)$, and find

$$R_{eq} = R_1 + R_2 + R_3. \qquad \text{[series]} \quad \textbf{(26–3)}$$

This is, in fact, what we expect. When we put several resistances in series, the total or equivalent resistance is the sum of the separate resistances. (Sometimes we may also call it the "net resistance.") This sum applies to any number of resistances in series. Note that when you add more resistance to the circuit, the current through the circuit will decrease. For example, if a 12-V battery is connected to a 4-Ω resistor, the current will be 3 A. But if the 12-V battery is connected to three 4-Ω resistors in series, the total resistance is 12 Ω and the current through the entire circuit will be only 1 A.

[†]To see in more detail why this is true, note that an electric charge q passing through R_1 loses an amount of potential energy equal to qV_1. In passing through R_2 and R_3, the potential energy U decreases by qV_2 and qV_3, for a total $\Delta U = qV_1 + qV_2 + qV_3$; this sum must equal the energy given to q by the battery, qV, so that energy is conserved. Hence $qV = q(V_1 + V_2 + V_3)$, and so $V = V_1 + V_2 + V_3$, which is Eq. 26–2.

FIGURE 26–3 (a) Resistances connected in series. (b) Resistances could be lightbulbs, or any other type of resistance. (c) Equivalent single resistance R_{eq} that draws the same current: $R_{eq} = R_1 + R_2 + R_3$.

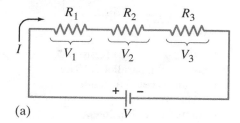

(a)

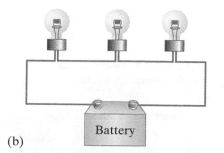

(b)

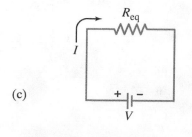

(c)

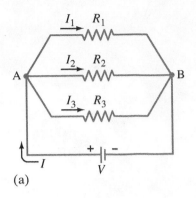

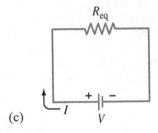

FIGURE 26–4 (a) Resistances connected in parallel. (b) The resistances could be lightbulbs. (c) The equivalent circuit with R_{eq} obtained from Eq. 26–4:
$$\frac{1}{R_{eq}} = \frac{1}{R_1} + \frac{1}{R_2} + \frac{1}{R_3}.$$

FIGURE 26–5 Water pipes in parallel—analogy to electric currents in parallel.

Another simple way to connect resistors is in **parallel** so that the current from the source splits into separate branches or paths, as shown in Fig. 26–4a and b. The wiring in houses and buildings is arranged so all electric devices are in parallel, as we already saw in Chapter 25, Fig. 25–20. With parallel wiring, if you disconnect one device (say, R_1 in Fig. 26–4a), the current to the other devices is not interrupted. Compare to a series circuit, where if one device (say, R_1 in Fig. 26–3a) is disconnected, the current *is* stopped to all the others.

In a parallel circuit, Fig. 26–4a, the total current I that leaves the battery splits into three separate paths. We let I_1, I_2, and I_3 be the currents through each of the resistors, R_1, R_2, and R_3, respectively. Because *electric charge is conserved*, the current I flowing into junction A (where the different wires or conductors meet, Fig. 26–4a) must equal the current flowing out of the junction. Thus

$$I = I_1 + I_2 + I_3. \qquad \text{[parallel]}$$

When resistors are connected in parallel, each has the same voltage across it. (Indeed, any two points in a circuit connected by a wire of negligible resistance are at the same potential.) Hence the full voltage of the battery is applied to each resistor in Fig. 26–4a. Applying Ohm's law to each resistor, we have

$$I_1 = \frac{V}{R_1}, \qquad I_2 = \frac{V}{R_2}, \qquad \text{and} \qquad I_3 = \frac{V}{R_3}.$$

Let us now determine what single resistor R_{eq} (Fig. 26–4c) will draw the same current I as these three resistances in parallel. This equivalent resistance R_{eq} must satisfy Ohm's law too:

$$I = \frac{V}{R_{eq}}.$$

We now combine the equations above:

$$I = I_1 + I_2 + I_3,$$
$$\frac{V}{R_{eq}} = \frac{V}{R_1} + \frac{V}{R_2} + \frac{V}{R_3}.$$

When we divide out the V from each term, we have

$$\frac{1}{R_{eq}} = \frac{1}{R_1} + \frac{1}{R_2} + \frac{1}{R_3}. \qquad \text{[parallel]} \quad (26\text{–}4)$$

For example, suppose you connect two 4-Ω loudspeakers to a single set of output terminals of your stereo amplifier or receiver. (Ignore the other channel for a moment—our two speakers are both connected to the left channel, say.) The equivalent resistance of the two 4-Ω "resistors" in parallel is

$$\frac{1}{R_{eq}} = \frac{1}{4\,\Omega} + \frac{1}{4\,\Omega} = \frac{2}{4\,\Omega} = \frac{1}{2\,\Omega},$$

and so $R_{eq} = 2\,\Omega$. Thus the net (or equivalent) resistance is *less* than each single resistance. This may at first seem surprising. But remember that when you connect resistors in parallel, you are giving the current additional paths to follow. Hence the net resistance will be less.

Equations 26–3 and 26–4 make good sense. Recalling Eq. 25–3 for resistivity, $R = \rho\ell/A$, we see that placing resistors in series increases the length and therefore the resistance; putting resistors in parallel increases the area through which current flows, thus reducing the overall resistance.

An analogy may help here. Consider two identical pipes taking in water near the top of a dam and releasing it below as shown in Fig. 26–5. The gravitational potential difference, proportional to the height h, is the same for both pipes, just as the voltage is the same for parallel resistors. If both pipes are open, rather than only one, twice as much water will flow through. That is, with two equal pipes open, the net resistance to the flow of water will be reduced, by half, just as for electrical resistors in parallel. Note that if both pipes are closed, the dam offers infinite resistance to the flow of water. This corresponds in the electrical case to an open circuit—when the path is not continuous and no current flows—so the electrical resistance is infinite.

EXERCISE B You have a 10-Ω and a 15-Ω resistor. What is the smallest and largest equivalent resistance that you can make with these two resistors?

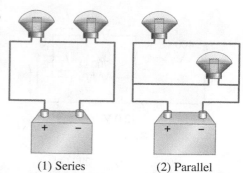

CONCEPTUAL EXAMPLE 26–2 **Series or parallel?** (*a*) The lightbulbs in Fig. 26–6 are identical. Which configuration produces more light? (*b*) Which way do you think the headlights of a car are wired? Ignore change of filament resistance *R* with current.

RESPONSE (*a*) The equivalent resistance of the parallel circuit is found from Eq. 26–4, $1/R_{eq} = 1/R + 1/R = 2/R$. Thus $R_{eq} = R/2$. The parallel combination then has lower resistance ($= R/2$) than the series combination ($R_{eq} = R + R = 2R$). There will be more total current in the parallel configuration (2), since $I = V/R_{eq}$ and *V* is the same for both circuits. The total power transformed, which is related to the light produced, is $P = IV$, so the greater current in (2) means more light produced.
(*b*) Headlights are wired in parallel (2), because if one bulb goes out, the other bulb can stay lit. If they were in series (1), when one bulb burned out (the filament broke), the circuit would be open and no current would flow, so neither bulb would light.

NOTE When you answered the Chapter-Opening Question on page 677, was your answer circuit 2? Can you express any misconceptions you might have had?

(1) Series   (2) Parallel
FIGURE 26–6 Example 26–2.

FIGURE 26–7 Example 26–3.

CONCEPTUAL EXAMPLE 26–3 **An illuminating surprise.** A 100-W, 120-V lightbulb and a 60-W, 120-V lightbulb are connected in two different ways as shown in Fig. 26–7. In each case, which bulb glows more brightly? Ignore change of filament resistance with current (and temperature).

RESPONSE (*a*) These are normal lightbulbs with their power rating given for 120 V. They both receive 120 V, so the 100-W bulb is naturally brighter.
(*b*) The resistance of the 100-W bulb is less than that of the 60-W bulb (calculated from $P = V^2/R$ at constant 120 V). Here they are connected in series and receive the same current. Hence, from $P = I^2R$ (*I* = constant) the higher-resistance "60-W" bulb will transform more power and thus be brighter.

NOTE When connected in series as in (*b*), the two bulbs do *not* dissipate 60 W and 100 W because neither bulb receives 120 V.

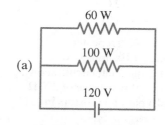

(a)

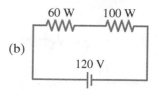

(b)

Note that whenever a group of resistors is replaced by the equivalent resistance, current and voltage and power in the rest of the circuit are unaffected.

EXAMPLE 26–4 **Circuit with series and parallel resistors.** How much current is drawn from the battery shown in Fig. 26–8a?

APPROACH The current *I* that flows out of the battery all passes through the 400-Ω resistor, but then it splits into I_1 and I_2 passing through the 500-Ω and 700-Ω resistors. The latter two resistors are in parallel with each other. We look for something that we already know how to treat. So let's start by finding the equivalent resistance, R_p, of the parallel resistors, 500 Ω and 700 Ω. Then we can consider this R_p to be in series with the 400-Ω resistor.

SOLUTION The equivalent resistance, R_p, of the 500-Ω and 700-Ω resistors in parallel is given by

$$\frac{1}{R_P} = \frac{1}{500\ \Omega} + \frac{1}{700\ \Omega} = 0.0020\ \Omega^{-1} + 0.0014\ \Omega^{-1} = 0.0034\ \Omega^{-1}.$$

This is $1/R_P$, so we take the reciprocal to find R_P. It is a common mistake to forget to take this reciprocal. Notice that the units of reciprocal ohms, Ω^{-1}, are a reminder. Thus

$$R_P = \frac{1}{0.0034\ \Omega^{-1}} = 290\ \Omega.$$

This 290 Ω is the equivalent resistance of the two parallel resistors, and is in series with the 400-Ω resistor as shown in the equivalent circuit of Fig. 26–8b. To find the total equivalent resistance R_{eq}, we add the 400-Ω and 290-Ω resistances together, since they are in series, and find

$$R_{eq} = 400\ \Omega + 290\ \Omega = 690\ \Omega.$$

The total current flowing from the battery is then

$$I = \frac{V}{R_{eq}} = \frac{12.0\ V}{690\ \Omega} = 0.0174\ A \approx 17\ mA.$$

NOTE This *I* is also the current flowing through the 400-Ω resistor, but not through the 500-Ω and 700-Ω resistors (both currents are less—see the next Example).

NOTE Complex resistor circuits can often be analyzed in this way, considering the circuit as a combination of series and parallel resistances.

FIGURE 26–8 (a) Circuit for Examples 26–4 and 26–5. (b) Equivalent circuit, showing the equivalent resistance of 290 Ω for the two parallel resistors in (a).

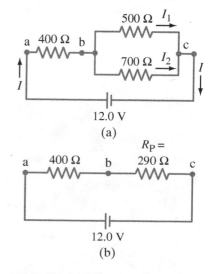

(a)

(b)

⚠ **C A U T I O N**
Remember to take the reciprocal

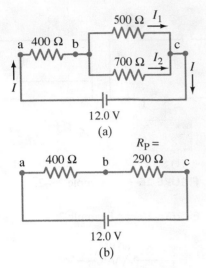

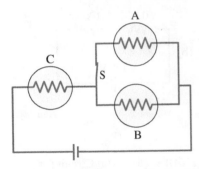

FIGURE 26–8 (repeated)
(a) Circuit for Examples 26–4 and 26–5. (b) Equivalent circuit, showing the equivalent resistance of 290 Ω for the two parallel resistors in (a).

FIGURE 26–9 Example 26–6, three identical lightbulbs. Each yellow circle with ‑⌇⌇‑ inside represents a lightbulb and its resistance.

EXAMPLE 26–5 **Current in one branch.** What is the current through the 500-Ω resistor in Fig. 26–8a?

APPROACH We need to find the voltage across the 500-Ω resistor, which is the voltage between points b and c in Fig. 26–8a, and we call it V_{bc}. Once V_{bc} is known, we can apply Ohm's law, $V = IR$, to get the current. First we find the voltage across the 400-Ω resistor, V_{ab}, since we know that 17.4 mA passes through it (Example 26–4).

SOLUTION V_{ab} can be found using $V = IR$:
$$V_{ab} = (0.0174 \text{ A})(400 \text{ } \Omega) = 7.0 \text{ V}.$$
Since the total voltage across the network of resistors is $V_{ac} = 12.0$ V, then V_{bc} must be $12.0 \text{ V} - 7.0 \text{ V} = 5.0$ V. Then Ohm's law applied to the 500-Ω resistor tells us that the current I_1 through that resistor is
$$I_1 = \frac{5.0 \text{ V}}{500 \text{ } \Omega} = 1.0 \times 10^{-2} \text{ A} = 10 \text{ mA}.$$
This is the answer we wanted. We can also calculate the current I_2 through the 700-Ω resistor since the voltage across it is also 5.0 V:
$$I_2 = \frac{5.0 \text{ V}}{700 \text{ } \Omega} = 7 \text{ mA}.$$

NOTE When I_1 combines with I_2 to form the total current I (at point c in Fig. 26–8a), their sum is $10 \text{ mA} + 7 \text{ mA} = 17 \text{ mA}$. This equals the total current I as calculated in Example 26–4, as it should.

CONCEPTUAL EXAMPLE 26–6 **Bulb brightness in a circuit.** The circuit shown in Fig. 26–9 has three identical lightbulbs, each of resistance R. (a) When switch S is closed, how will the brightness of bulbs A and B compare with that of bulb C? (b) What happens when switch S is opened? Use a minimum of mathematics in your answers.

RESPONSE (a) With switch S closed, the current that passes through bulb C must split into two equal parts when it reaches the junction leading to bulbs A and B. It splits into equal parts because the resistance of bulb A equals that of B. Thus, bulbs A and B each receive half of C's current; A and B will be equally bright, but they will be less bright than bulb C ($P = I^2R$). (b) When the switch S is open, no current can flow through bulb A, so it will be dark. We now have a simple one-loop series circuit, and we expect bulbs B and C to be equally bright. However, the equivalent resistance of this circuit ($= R + R$) is greater than that of the circuit with the switch closed. When we open the switch, we increase the resistance and reduce the current leaving the battery. Thus, bulb C will be dimmer when we open the switch. Bulb B gets more current when the switch is open (you may have to use some mathematics here), and so it will be brighter than with the switch closed; and B will be as bright as C.

EXAMPLE 26–7 **ESTIMATE** **A two-speed fan.** One way a multiple-speed ventilation fan for a car can be designed is to put resistors in series with the fan motor. The resistors reduce the current through the motor and make it run more slowly. Suppose the current in the motor is 5.0 A when it is connected directly across a 12-V battery. (a) What series resistor should be used to reduce the current to 2.0 A for low-speed operation? (b) What power rating should the resistor have?

APPROACH An electric motor in series with a resistor can be treated as two resistors in series. The power comes from $P = IV$.

SOLUTION (a) When the motor is connected to 12 V and drawing 5.0 A, its resistance is $R = V/I = (12 \text{ V})/(5.0 \text{ A}) = 2.4 \text{ } \Omega$. We will assume that this is the motor's resistance for all speeds. (This is an approximation because the current through the motor depends on its speed.) Then, when a current of 2.0 A is flowing, the voltage across the motor is $(2.0 \text{ A})(2.4 \text{ } \Omega) = 4.8$ V. The remaining $12.0 \text{ V} - 4.8 \text{ V} = 7.2$ V must appear across the series resistor. When 2.0 A flows through the resistor, its resistance must be $R = (7.2 \text{ V})/(2.0 \text{ A}) = 3.6 \text{ } \Omega$. (b) The power dissipated by the resistor is $P = (7.2 \text{ V})(2.0 \text{ A}) = 14.4$ W. To be safe, a power rating of 20 W would be appropriate.

EXAMPLE 26–8 **Analyzing a circuit.** A 9.0-V battery whose internal resistance r is 0.50 Ω is connected in the circuit shown in Fig. 26–10a. (*a*) How much current is drawn from the battery? (*b*) What is the terminal voltage of the battery? (*c*) What is the current in the 6.0-Ω resistor?

APPROACH To find the current out of the battery, we first need to determine the equivalent resistance R_{eq} of the entire circuit, including r, which we do by identifying and isolating simple series or parallel combinations of resistors. Once we find I from Ohm's law, $I = \mathcal{E}/R_{eq}$, we get the terminal voltage using $V_{ab} = \mathcal{E} - Ir$. For (*c*) we apply Ohm's law to the 6.0-Ω resistor.

SOLUTION (*a*) We want to determine the equivalent resistance of the circuit. But where do we start? We note that the 4.0-Ω and 8.0-Ω resistors are in parallel, and so have an equivalent resistance R_{eq1} given by

$$\frac{1}{R_{eq1}} = \frac{1}{8.0\,\Omega} + \frac{1}{4.0\,\Omega} = \frac{3}{8.0\,\Omega};$$

so $R_{eq1} = 2.7\,\Omega$. This 2.7 Ω is in series with the 6.0-Ω resistor, as shown in the equivalent circuit of Fig. 26–10b. The net resistance of the lower arm of the circuit is then

$$R_{eq2} = 6.0\,\Omega + 2.7\,\Omega = 8.7\,\Omega,$$

as shown in Fig. 26–10c. The equivalent resistance R_{eq3} of the 8.7-Ω and 10.0-Ω resistances in parallel is given by

$$\frac{1}{R_{eq3}} = \frac{1}{10.0\,\Omega} + \frac{1}{8.7\,\Omega} = 0.21\,\Omega^{-1},$$

so $R_{eq3} = (1/0.21\,\Omega^{-1}) = 4.8\,\Omega$. This 4.8 Ω is in series with the 5.0-Ω resistor and the 0.50-Ω internal resistance of the battery (Fig. 26–10d), so the total equivalent resistance R_{eq} of the circuit is $R_{eq} = 4.8\,\Omega + 5.0\,\Omega + 0.50\,\Omega = 10.3\,\Omega$. Hence the current drawn is

$$I = \frac{\mathcal{E}}{R_{eq}} = \frac{9.0\,\text{V}}{10.3\,\Omega} = 0.87\,\text{A}.$$

(*b*) The terminal voltage of the battery is

$$V_{ab} = \mathcal{E} - Ir = 9.0\,\text{V} - (0.87\,\text{A})(0.50\,\Omega) = 8.6\,\text{V}.$$

(*c*) Now we can work back and get the current in the 6.0-Ω resistor. It must be the same as the current through the 8.7 Ω shown in Fig. 26–10c (why?). The voltage across that 8.7 Ω will be the emf of the battery minus the voltage drops across r and the 5.0-Ω resistor: $V_{8.7} = 9.0\,\text{V} - (0.87\,\text{A})(0.50\,\Omega + 5.0\,\Omega)$. Applying Ohm's law, we get the current (call it I')

$$I' = \frac{9.0\,\text{V} - (0.87\,\text{A})(0.50\,\Omega + 5.0\,\Omega)}{8.7\,\Omega} = 0.48\,\text{A}.$$

This is the current through the 6.0-Ω resistor.

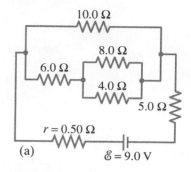

(a)

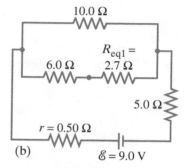

(b)

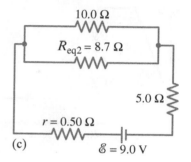

(c)

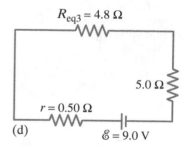

(d)

FIGURE 26–10 Circuit for Example 26–8, where r is the internal resistance of the battery.

26–3 Kirchhoff's Rules

In the last few Examples we have been able to find the currents in circuits by combining resistances in series and parallel, and using Ohm's law. This technique can be used for many circuits. However, some circuits are too complicated for that analysis. For example, we cannot find the currents in each part of the circuit shown in Fig. 26–11 simply by combining resistances as we did before.

To deal with such complicated circuits, we use Kirchhoff's rules, devised by G. R. Kirchhoff (1824–1887) in the mid-nineteenth century. There are two rules, and they are simply convenient applications of the laws of conservation of charge and energy.

FIGURE 26–11 Currents can be calculated using Kirchhoff's rules.

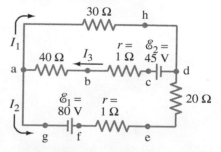

Kirchhoff's first rule or **junction rule** is based on the conservation of electric charge that we already used to derive the rule for parallel resistors. It states that

at any junction point, the sum of all currents entering the junction must equal the sum of all currents leaving the junction.

That is, whatever charge goes in must come out. We already saw an instance of this in the NOTE at the end of Example 26–5.

Kirchhoff's second rule or **loop rule** is based on the conservation of energy. It states that

the sum of the changes in potential around any closed loop of a circuit must be zero.

To see why this rule should hold, consider a rough analogy with the potential energy of a roller coaster on its track. When the roller coaster starts from the station, it has a particular potential energy. As it climbs the first hill, its potential energy increases and reaches a maximum at the top. As it descends the other side, its potential energy decreases and reaches a local minimum at the bottom of the hill. As the roller coaster continues on its path, its potential energy goes through more changes. But when it arrives back at the starting point, it has exactly as much potential energy as it had when it started at this point. Another way of saying this is that there was as much uphill as there was downhill.

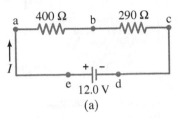

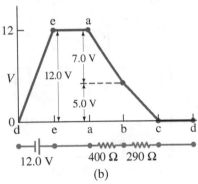

FIGURE 26–12 Changes in potential around the circuit in (a) are plotted in (b).

Similar reasoning can be applied to an electric circuit. We will analyze the circuit of Fig. 26–11 shortly but first we consider the simpler circuit in Fig. 26–12. We have chosen it to be the same as the equivalent circuit of Fig. 26–8b already discussed. The current in this circuit is $I = (12.0 \text{ V})/(690 \, \Omega) = 0.0174 \text{ A}$, as we calculated in Example 26–4. (We keep an extra digit in I to reduce rounding errors.) The positive side of the battery, point e in Fig. 26–12a, is at a high potential compared to point d at the negative side of the battery. That is, point e is like the top of a hill for a roller coaster. We follow the current around the circuit starting at any point. We choose to start at point d and follow a positive test charge completely around this circuit. As we go, we note all changes in potential. When the test charge returns to point d, the potential will be the same as when we started (total change in potential around the circuit is zero). We plot the changes in potential around the circuit in Fig. 26–12b; point d is arbitrarily taken as zero.

As our positive test charge goes from point d, which is the negative or low potential side of the battery, to point e, which is the positive terminal (high potential side) of the battery, the potential increases by 12.0 V. (This is like the roller coaster being pulled up the first hill.) That is,

$$V_{ed} = +12.0 \text{ V}.$$

When our test charge moves from point e to point a, there is no change in potential since there is no source of emf and we assume negligible resistance in the connecting wires. Next, as the charge passes through the 400-Ω resistor to get to point b, there is a decrease in potential of $V = IR = (0.0174 \text{ A})(400 \, \Omega) = 7.0 \text{ V}$. The positive test charge is flowing "downhill" since it is heading toward the negative terminal of the battery, as indicated in the graph of Fig. 26–12b. Because this is a *decrease* in potential, we use a *negative* sign:

$$V_{ba} = V_b - V_a = -7.0 \text{ V}.$$

As the charge proceeds from b to c there is another potential decrease (a "voltage drop") of $(0.0174 \text{ A}) \times (290 \, \Omega) = 5.0 \text{ V}$, and this too is a decrease in potential:

$$V_{cb} = -5.0 \text{ V}.$$

There is no change in potential as our test charge moves from c to d as we assume negligible resistance in the wires.

The sum of all the changes in potential around the circuit of Fig. 26–12 is

$$+12.0 \text{ V} - 7.0 \text{ V} - 5.0 \text{ V} = 0.$$

This is exactly what Kirchhoff's loop rule said it would be.

Kirchhoff's Rules

1. **Label the current** in each separate branch of the given circuit with a different subscript, such as I_1, I_2, I_3 (see Fig. 26–11 or 26–13). Each current refers to a segment between two junctions. Choose the direction of each current, using an arrow. The direction can be chosen arbitrarily: if the current is actually in the opposite direction, it will come out with a minus sign in the solution.

2. **Identify the unknowns.** You will need as many independent equations as there are unknowns. You may write down more equations than this, but you will find that some of the equations will be redundant (that is, not be independent in the sense of providing new information). You may use $V = IR$ for each resistor, which sometimes will reduce the number of unknowns.

3. **Apply Kirchhoff's junction rule** at one or more junctions.

4. **Apply Kirchhoff's loop rule** for one or more loops: follow each loop in one direction only. Pay careful attention to subscripts, and to signs:
   (a) For a resistor, apply Ohm's law; the potential difference is negative (a decrease) if your chosen loop direction is the same as the chosen current direction through that resistor; the potential difference is positive (an increase) if your chosen loop direction is opposite to the chosen current direction.
   (b) For a battery, the potential difference is positive if your chosen loop direction is from the negative terminal toward the positive terminal; the potential difference is negative if the loop direction is from the positive terminal toward the negative terminal.

5. **Solve the equations** algebraically for the unknowns. Be careful when manipulating equations not to err with signs. At the end, check your answers by plugging them into the original equations, or even by using any additional loop or junction rule equations not used previously.

EXAMPLE 26–9 **Using Kirchhoff's rules.** Calculate the currents I_1, I_2, and I_3 in the three branches of the circuit in Fig. 26–13 (which is the same as Fig. 26–11).

APPROACH AND SOLUTION

1. **Label the currents** and their directions. Figure 26–13 uses the labels I_1, I_2, and I_3 for the current in the three separate branches. Since (positive) current tends to move away from the positive terminal of a battery, we choose I_2 and I_3 to have the directions shown in Fig. 26–13. The direction of I_1 is not obvious in advance, so we arbitrarily chose the direction indicated. If the current actually flows in the opposite direction, our answer will have a negative sign.

2. **Identify the unknowns.** We have three unknowns and therefore we need three equations, which we get by applying Kirchhoff's junction and loop rules.

3. **Junction rule:** We apply Kirchhoff's junction rule to the currents at point a, where I_3 enters and I_2 and I_1 leave:

$$I_3 = I_1 + I_2. \qquad (a)$$

This same equation holds at point d, so we get no new information by writing an equation for point d.

4. **Loop rule:** We apply Kirchhoff's loop rule to two different closed loops. First we apply it to the upper loop ahdcba. We start (and end) at point a. From a to h we have a potential decrease $V_{ha} = -(I_1)(30\,\Omega)$. From h to d there is no change, but from d to c the potential increases by 45 V: that is, $V_{cd} = +45$ V. From c to a the potential decreases through the two resistances by an amount $V_{ac} = -(I_3)(40\,\Omega + 1\,\Omega) = -(41\,\Omega)I_3$. Thus we have $V_{ha} + V_{cd} + V_{ac} = 0$, or

$$-30I_1 + 45 - 41I_3 = 0, \qquad (b)$$

where we have omitted the units (volts and amps) so we can more easily do the algebra. For our second loop, we take the outer loop ahdefga. (We could have chosen the lower loop abcdefga instead.) Again we start at point a and have $V_{ha} = -(I_1)(30\,\Omega)$, and $V_{dh} = 0$. But when we take our positive test charge from d to e, it actually is going uphill, against the current—or at least against the *assumed* direction of the current, which is what counts in this calculation. Thus $V_{ed} = I_2(20\,\Omega)$ has a *positive* sign. Similarly, $V_{fe} = I_2(1\,\Omega)$. From f to g there is a decrease in potential of 80 V since we go from the high potential terminal of the battery to the low. Thus $V_{gf} = -80$ V. Finally, $V_{ag} = 0$, and the sum of the potential changes around this loop is

$$-30I_1 + (20 + 1)I_2 - 80 = 0. \qquad (c)$$

Our major work is done. The rest is algebra.

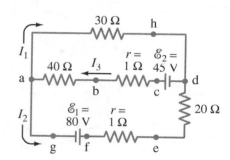

FIGURE 26–13 Currents can be calculated using Kirchhoff's rules. See Example 26–9.

5. Solve the equations. We have three equations—labeled (a), (b), and (c)—and three unknowns. From Eq. (c) we have

$$I_2 = \frac{80 + 30I_1}{21} = 3.8 + 1.4I_1. \qquad (d)$$

From Eq. (b) we have

$$I_3 = \frac{45 - 30I_1}{41} = 1.1 - 0.73I_1. \qquad (e)$$

We substitute Eqs. (d) and (e) into Eq. (a):

$$I_1 = I_3 - I_2 = 1.1 - 0.73I_1 - 3.8 - 1.4I_1.$$

We solve for I_1, collecting terms:

$$3.1I_1 = -2.7$$
$$I_1 = -0.87 \text{ A}.$$

The negative sign indicates that the direction of I_1 is actually opposite to that initially assumed and shown in Fig. 26–13. The answer automatically comes out in amperes because all values were in volts and ohms. From Eq. (d) we have

$$I_2 = 3.8 + 1.4I_1 = 3.8 + 1.4(-0.87) = 2.6 \text{ A},$$

and from Eq. (e)

$$I_3 = 1.1 - 0.73I_1 = 1.1 - 0.73(-0.87) = 1.7 \text{ A}.$$

This completes the solution.

NOTE The unknowns in different situations are not necessarily currents. It might be that the currents are given and we have to solve for unknown resistance or voltage. The variables are then different, but the technique is the same.

EXERCISE C Write the equation for the lower loop abcdefga of Example 26–9 and show, assuming the currents calculated in this Example, that the potentials add to zero for this lower loop.

26–4 Series and Parallel EMFs; Battery Charging

When two or more sources of emf, such as batteries, are arranged in series as in Fig. 26–14a, the total voltage is the algebraic sum of their respective voltages. On the other hand, when a 20-V and a 12-V battery are connected oppositely, as shown in Fig. 26–14b, the net voltage V_{ca} is 8 V (ignoring voltage drop across internal resistances). That is, a positive test charge moved from a to b gains in potential by 20 V, but when it passes from b to c it drops by 12 V. So the net change is $20 \text{ V} - 12 \text{ V} = 8 \text{ V}$. You might think that connecting batteries in reverse like this would be wasteful. For most purposes that would be true. But such a reverse arrangement is precisely how a battery charger works. In Fig. 26–14b, the 20-V source is charging up the 12-V battery. Because of its greater voltage, the 20-V source is forcing charge back into the 12-V battery: electrons are being forced into its negative terminal and removed from its positive terminal.

An automobile alternator keeps the car battery charged in the same way. A voltmeter placed across the terminals of a (12-V) car battery with the engine running fairly fast can tell you whether or not the alternator is charging the battery. If it is, the voltmeter reads 13 or 14 V. If the battery is not being charged, the voltage will be 12 V, or less if the battery is discharging. Car batteries can be recharged, but other batteries may not be rechargeable, since the chemical reactions in many cannot be reversed. In such cases, the arrangement of Fig. 26–14b would simply waste energy.

Sources of emf can also be arranged in parallel, Fig. 26–14c. With equal emfs, a parallel arrangement can provide more energy when large currents are needed. Each of the cells in parallel has to produce only a fraction of the total current, so the energy loss due to internal resistance is less than for a single cell; and the batteries will go dead less quickly.

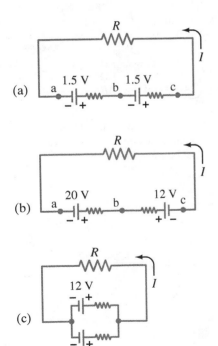

FIGURE 26–14 Batteries in series (a) and (b), and in parallel (c).

EXAMPLE 26–10 **Jump starting a car.** A good car battery is being used to jump start a car with a weak battery. The good battery has an emf of 12.5 V and internal resistance 0.020 Ω. Suppose the weak battery has an emf of 10.1 V and internal resistance 0.10 Ω. Each copper jumper cable is 3.0 m long and 0.50 cm in diameter, and can be attached as shown in Fig. 26–15. Assume the starter motor can be represented as a resistor $R_s = 0.15$ Ω. Determine the current through the starter motor (a) if only the weak battery is connected to it, and (b) if the good battery is also connected, as shown in Fig. 26–15.

APPROACH We apply Kirchhoff's rules, but in (b) we will first need to determine the resistance of the jumper cables using their dimensions and the resistivity ($\rho = 1.68 \times 10^{-8}$ Ω·m for copper) as discussed in Section 25–4.

SOLUTION (a) The circuit with only the weak battery and no jumper cables is simple: an emf of 10.1 V connected to two resistances in series, 0.10 Ω $+ 0.15$ Ω $= 0.25$ Ω. Hence the current is $I = V/R = (10.1$ V$)/(0.25$ Ω$) = 40$ A.

(b) We need to find the resistance of the jumper cables that connect the good battery. From Eq. 25–3, each has resistance $R_J = \rho \ell/A = (1.68 \times 10^{-8}$ Ω·m$)(3.0$ m$)/(\pi)(0.25 \times 10^{-2}$ m$)^2 = 0.0026$ Ω. Kirchhoff's loop rule for the full outside loop gives

$$12.5 \text{ V} - I_1(2R_J + r_1) - I_3 R_S = 0$$
$$12.5 \text{ V} - I_1(0.025 \text{ Ω}) - I_3(0.15 \text{ Ω}) = 0 \qquad (a)$$

since $(2R_J + r) = (0.0052$ Ω $+ 0.020$ Ω$) = 0.025$ Ω.
The loop rule for the lower loop, including the weak battery and the starter, gives

$$10.1 \text{ V} - I_3(0.15 \text{ Ω}) - I_2(0.10 \text{ Ω}) = 0. \qquad (b)$$

The junction rule at point B gives

$$I_1 + I_2 = I_3. \qquad (c)$$

We have three equations in three unknowns. From Eq. (c), $I_1 = I_3 - I_2$ and we substitute this into Eq. (a):

$$12.5 \text{ V} - (I_3 - I_2)(0.025 \text{ Ω}) - I_3(0.15 \text{ Ω}) = 0,$$
$$12.5 \text{ V} - I_3(0.175 \text{ Ω}) + I_2(0.025 \text{ Ω}) = 0.$$

Combining this last equation with (b) gives $I_3 = 71$ A, quite a bit better than in (a). The other currents are $I_2 = -5$ A and $I_1 = 76$ A. Note that $I_2 = -5$ A is in the opposite direction from that assumed in Fig. 26–15. The terminal voltage of the weak 10.1-V battery is now $V_{BA} = 10.1$ V $- (-5$ A$)(0.10$ Ω$) = 10.6$ V.

NOTE The circuit shown in Fig. 26–15, without the starter motor, is how a battery can be charged. The stronger battery pushes charge back into the weaker battery.

EXERCISE D If the jumper cables of Example 26–10 were mistakenly connected in reverse, the positive terminal of each battery would be connected to the negative terminal of the other battery (Fig. 26–16). What would be the current I even before the starter motor is engaged (the switch S in Fig. 26–16 is open)? Why could this cause the batteries to explode?

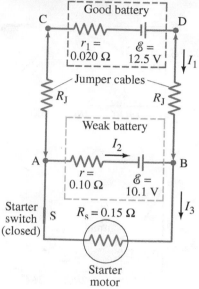

FIGURE 26–15 Example 26–10, a jump start.

FIGURE 26–16 Exercise D.

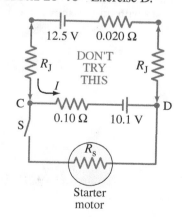

26–5 Circuits Containing Resistor and Capacitor (*RC* Circuits)

Our study of circuits in this Chapter has, until now, dealt with steady currents that do not change in time. Now we examine circuits that contain both resistance and capacitance. Such a circuit is called an ***RC* circuit**. *RC* circuits are common in everyday life: they are used to control the speed of a car's windshield wiper, and the timing of the change of traffic lights. They are used in camera flashes, in heart pacemakers, and in many other electronic devices. In *RC* circuits, we are not so interested in the final "steady state" voltage and charge on the capacitor, but rather in how these variables change in time.

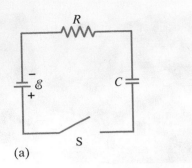

(a)

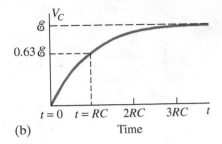

(b)

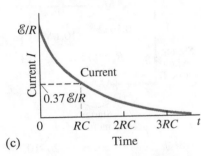

(c)

FIGURE 26–17 After the switch S closes in the RC circuit shown in (a), the voltage across the capacitor increases with time as shown in (b), and the current through the resistor decreases with time as shown in (c).

Let us now examine the RC circuit shown in Fig. 26–17a. When the switch S is closed, current immediately begins to flow through the circuit. Electrons will flow out from the negative terminal of the battery, through the resistor R, and accumulate on the upper plate of the capacitor. And electrons will flow into the positive terminal of the battery, leaving a positive charge on the other plate of the capacitor. As charge accumulates on the capacitor, the potential difference across it increases $(V_C = Q/C)$, and the current is reduced until eventually the voltage across the capacitor equals the emf of the battery, $\mathscr{E}$. There is then no potential difference across the resistor, and no further current flows. Potential difference V_C across the capacitor thus increases in time as shown in Fig. 26–17b. The mathematical form of this curve—that is, V_C as a function of time—can be derived using conservation of energy (or Kirchhoff's loop rule). The emf $\mathscr{E}$ of the battery will equal the sum of the voltage drops across the resistor (IR) and the capacitor (Q/C):

$$\mathscr{E} = IR + \frac{Q}{C}. \tag{26–5}$$

The resistance R includes all resistance in the circuit, including the internal resistance of the battery; I is the current in the circuit at any instant, and Q is the charge on the capacitor at that same instant. Although $\mathscr{E}$, R, and C are constants, both Q and I are functions of time. The rate at which charge flows through the resistor $(I = dQ/dt)$ is equal to the rate at which charge accumulates on the capacitor. Thus we can write

$$\mathscr{E} = R\frac{dQ}{dt} + \frac{1}{C}Q.$$

This equation can be solved by rearranging it:

$$\frac{dQ}{C\mathscr{E} - Q} = \frac{dt}{RC}.$$

We now integrate from $t = 0$, when $Q = 0$, to time t when a charge Q is on the capacitor:

$$\int_0^Q \frac{dQ}{C\mathscr{E} - Q} = \frac{1}{RC}\int_0^t dt$$

$$-\ln(C\mathscr{E} - Q)\Big|_0^Q = \frac{t}{RC}\Big|_0^t$$

$$-\ln(C\mathscr{E} - Q) - (-\ln C\mathscr{E}) = \frac{t}{RC}$$

$$\ln(C\mathscr{E} - Q) - \ln(C\mathscr{E}) = -\frac{t}{RC}$$

$$\ln\left(1 - \frac{Q}{C\mathscr{E}}\right) = -\frac{t}{RC}.$$

We take the exponential[†] of both sides

$$1 - \frac{Q}{C\mathscr{E}} = e^{-t/RC}$$

or

$$Q = C\mathscr{E}(1 - e^{-t/RC}). \tag{26–6a}$$

The potential difference across the capacitor is $V_C = Q/C$, so

$$V_C = \mathscr{E}(1 - e^{-t/RC}). \tag{26–6b}$$

From Eqs. 26–6 we see that the charge Q on the capacitor, and the voltage V_C across it, increase from zero at $t = 0$ to maximum values $Q_{max} = C\mathscr{E}$ and $V_C = \mathscr{E}$ after a very long time. The quantity RC that appears in the exponent is called the **time constant** τ of the circuit:

$$\tau = RC. \tag{26–7}$$

It represents the time[‡] required for the capacitor to reach $(1 - e^{-1}) = 0.63$ or 63% of its full charge and voltage. Thus the product RC is a measure of how quickly the

---

[†]The constant e, known as the base for natural logarithms, has the value $e = 2.718\cdots$. Do not confuse this e with e for the charge on the electron.

[‡]The units of RC are $\Omega\cdot F = (V/A)(C/V) = C/(C/s) = s$.

capacitor gets charged. In a circuit, for example, where $R = 200\,\text{k}\Omega$ and $C = 3.0\,\mu\text{F}$, the time constant is $(2.0 \times 10^5\,\Omega)(3.0 \times 10^{-6}\,\text{F}) = 0.60\,\text{s}$. If the resistance is much lower, the time constant is much smaller. This makes sense, since a lower resistance will retard the flow of charge less. All circuits contain some resistance (if only in the connecting wires), so a capacitor never can be charged instantaneously when connected to a battery.

From Eqs. 26–6, it appears that Q and V_C never quite reach their maximum values within a finite time. However, they reach 86% of maximum in $2RC$, 95% in $3RC$, 98% in $4RC$, and so on. Q and V_C approach their maximum values asymptotically. For example, if $R = 20\,\text{k}\Omega$ and $C = 0.30\,\mu\text{F}$, the time constant is $(2.0 \times 10^4\,\Omega)(3.0 \times 10^{-7}\,\text{F}) = 6.0 \times 10^{-3}\,\text{s}$. So the capacitor is more than 98% charged in less than $\frac{1}{40}$ of a second.

The current I through the circuit of Fig. 26–17a at any time t can be obtained by differentiating Eq. 26–6a:

$$I = \frac{dQ}{dt} = \frac{\mathscr{E}}{R}e^{-t/RC}. \tag{26-8}$$

Thus, at $t = 0$, the current is $I = \mathscr{E}/R$, as expected for a circuit containing only a resistor (there is not yet a potential difference across the capacitor). The current then drops exponentially in time with a time constant equal to RC, as the voltage across the capacitor increases. This is shown in Fig. 26–17c. The time constant RC represents the time required for the current to drop to $1/e \approx 0.37$ of its initial value.

EXAMPLE 26–11 *RC* **circuit, with emf.** The capacitance in the circuit of Fig. 26–17a is $C = 0.30\,\mu\text{F}$, the total resistance is $20\,\text{k}\Omega$, and the battery emf is 12 V. Determine (a) the time constant, (b) the maximum charge the capacitor could acquire, (c) the time it takes for the charge to reach 99% of this value, (d) the current I when the charge Q is half its maximum value, (e) the maximum current, and (f) the charge Q when the current I is 0.20 its maximum value.

APPROACH We use Fig. 26–17 and Eqs. 26–5, 6, 7, and 8.

SOLUTION (a) The time constant is $RC = (2.0 \times 10^4\,\Omega)(3.0 \times 10^{-7}\,\text{F}) = 6.0 \times 10^{-3}\,\text{s}$.

(b) The maximum charge would be $Q = C\mathscr{E} = (3.0 \times 10^{-7}\,\text{F})(12\,\text{V}) = 3.6\,\mu\text{C}$.

(c) In Eq. 26–6a, we set $Q = 0.99C\mathscr{E}$:

$$0.99C\mathscr{E} = C\mathscr{E}(1 - e^{-t/RC}),$$

or

$$e^{-t/RC} = 1 - 0.99 = 0.01.$$

Then

$$\frac{t}{RC} = -\ln(0.01) = 4.6$$

so

$$t = 4.6RC = 28 \times 10^{-3}\,\text{s}$$

or 28 ms (less than $\frac{1}{30}\,\text{s}$).

(d) From part (b) the maximum charge is $3.6\,\mu\text{C}$. When the charge is half this value, $1.8\,\mu\text{C}$, the current I in the circuit can be found using the original differential equation, or Eq. 26–5:

$$I = \frac{1}{R}\left(\mathscr{E} - \frac{Q}{C}\right) = \frac{1}{2.0 \times 10^4\,\Omega}\left(12\,\text{V} - \frac{1.8 \times 10^{-6}\,\text{C}}{0.30 \times 10^{-6}\,\text{F}}\right) = 300\,\mu\text{A}.$$

(e) The current is a maximum when there is no charge on the capacitor $(Q = 0)$:

$$I_{max} = \frac{\mathscr{E}}{R} = \frac{12\,\text{V}}{2.0 \times 10^4\,\Omega} = 600\,\mu\text{A}.$$

(f) Again using Eq. 26–5, now with $I = 0.20I_{max} = 120\,\mu\text{A}$, we have

$$Q = C(\mathscr{E} - IR)$$
$$= (3.0 \times 10^{-7}\,\text{F})[12\,\text{V} - (1.2 \times 10^{-4}\,\text{A})(2.0 \times 10^4\,\Omega)] = 2.9\,\mu\text{C}.$$

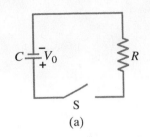

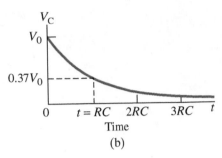

FIGURE 26–18 For the RC circuit shown in (a), the voltage V_C across the capacitor decreases with time, as shown in (b), after the switch S is closed at $t = 0$. The charge on the capacitor follows the same curve since $V_C \propto Q$.

The circuit just discussed involved the *charging* of a capacitor by a battery through a resistance. Now let us look at another situation: when a capacitor is already charged (say to a voltage V_0), and it is then allowed to *discharge* through a resistance R as shown in Fig. 26–18a. (In this case there is no battery.) When the switch S is closed, charge begins to flow through resistor R from one side of the capacitor toward the other side, until the capacitor is fully discharged. The voltage across the resistor at any instant equals that across the capacitor:

$$IR = \frac{Q}{C}.$$

The rate at which charge leaves the capacitor equals the negative of the current in the resistor, $I = -dQ/dt$, because the capacitor is discharging (Q is decreasing). So we write the above equation as

$$-\frac{dQ}{dt} R = \frac{Q}{C}.$$

We rearrange this to

$$\frac{dQ}{Q} = -\frac{dt}{RC}$$

and integrate it from $t = 0$ when the charge on the capacitor is Q_0, to some time t later when the charge is Q:

$$\ln \frac{Q}{Q_0} = -\frac{t}{RC}$$

or

$$Q = Q_0 e^{-t/RC}. \tag{26–9a}$$

The voltage across the capacitor $(V_C = Q/C)$ as a function of time is

$$V_C = V_0 e^{-t/RC}, \tag{26–9b}$$

where the initial voltage $V_0 = Q_0/C$. Thus the charge on the capacitor, and the voltage across it, decrease exponentially in time with a time constant RC. This is shown in Fig. 26–18b. The current is

$$I = -\frac{dQ}{dt} = \frac{Q_0}{RC} e^{-t/RC} = I_0 e^{-t/RC}, \tag{26–10}$$

and it too is seen to decrease exponentially in time with the same time constant RC. The charge on the capacitor, the voltage across it, and the current in the resistor all decrease to 37% of their original value in one time constant $t = \tau = RC$.

EXERCISE E In 10 time constants, the charge on the capacitor in Fig. 26–18 will be about (a) $Q_0/20,000$, (b) $Q_0/5000$, (c) $Q_0/1000$, (d) $Q_0/10$, (e) $Q_0/3$?

FIGURE 26–19 Example 26–12.

EXAMPLE 26–12 **Discharging RC circuit.** In the RC circuit shown in Fig. 26–19, the battery has fully charged the capacitor, so $Q_0 = C\mathscr{E}$. Then at $t = 0$ the switch is thrown from position a to b. The battery emf is 20.0 V, and the capacitance $C = 1.02\,\mu\text{F}$. The current I is observed to decrease to 0.50 of its initial value in 40 μs. (a) What is the value of Q, the charge on the capacitor, at $t = 0$? (b) What is the value of R? (c) What is Q at $t = 60\,\mu\text{s}$?

APPROACH At $t = 0$, the capacitor has charge $Q_0 = C\mathscr{E}$, and then the battery is removed from the circuit and the capacitor begins discharging through the resistor, as in Fig. 26–18. At any time t later (Eq. 26–9a) we have

$$Q = Q_0 e^{-t/RC} = C\mathscr{E} e^{-t/RC}.$$

SOLUTION (a) At $t = 0$,

$$Q = Q_0 = C\mathcal{E} = (1.02 \times 10^{-6}\,\text{F})(20.0\,\text{V}) = 2.04 \times 10^{-5}\,\text{C} = 20.4\,\mu\text{C}.$$

(b) To find R, we are given that at $t = 40\,\mu\text{s}$, $I = 0.50I_0$. Hence

$$0.50I_0 = I_0 e^{-t/RC}.$$

Taking natural logs on both sides $(\ln 0.50 = -0.693)$:

$$0.693 = \frac{t}{RC}$$

so

$$R = \frac{t}{(0.693)C} = \frac{(40 \times 10^{-6}\,\text{s})}{(0.693)(1.02 \times 10^{-6}\,\text{F})} = 57\,\Omega.$$

(c) At $t = 60\,\mu\text{s}$,

$$Q = Q_0 e^{-t/RC} = (20.4 \times 10^{-6}\,\text{C})e^{-\frac{60 \times 10^{-6}\,\text{s}}{(57\,\Omega)(1.02 \times 10^{-6}\,\text{F})}} = 7.3\,\mu\text{C}.$$

CONCEPTUAL EXAMPLE 26–13 | **Bulb in *RC* circuit.** In the circuit of Fig. 26–20, the capacitor is originally uncharged. Describe the behavior of the lightbulb from the instant switch S is closed until a long time later.

RESPONSE When the switch is first closed, the current in the circuit is high and the lightbulb burns brightly. As the capacitor charges, the voltage across the capacitor increases causing the current to be reduced, and the lightbulb dims. As the potential difference across the capacitor approaches the same voltage as the battery, the current decreases toward zero and the lightbulb goes out.

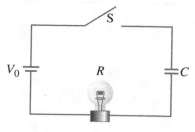

FIGURE 26–20 Example 26–13.

*Applications of *RC* Circuits

The charging and discharging in an *RC* circuit can be used to produce voltage pulses at a regular frequency. The charge on the capacitor increases to a particular voltage, and then discharges. One way of initiating the discharge of the capacitor is by the use of a gas-filled tube which has an electrical breakdown when the voltage across it reaches a certain value V_0. After the discharge is finished, the tube no longer conducts current and the recharging process repeats itself, starting at a lower voltage V_0'. Figure 26–21 shows a possible circuit, and the "sawtooth" voltage it produces.

A simple blinking light can be an application of a sawtooth oscillator circuit. Here the emf is supplied by a battery; the neon bulb flashes on at a rate of perhaps 1 cycle per second. The main component of a "flasher unit" is a moderately large capacitor.

The intermittent windshield wipers of a car can also use an *RC* circuit. The *RC* time constant, which can be changed using a multi-positioned switch for different values of R with fixed C, determines the rate at which the wipers come on.

PHYSICS APPLIED
Sawtooth, blinkers, windshield wipers

FIGURE 26–21 (a) An *RC* circuit, coupled with a gas-filled tube as a switch, can produce a repeating "sawtooth" voltage, as shown in (b).

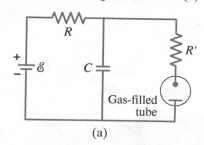

(a)

EXAMPLE 26–14 | **ESTIMATE** | **Resistor in a turn signal.** Estimate the order of magnitude of the resistor in a turn-signal circuit.

APPROACH A typical turn signal flashes perhaps twice per second, so the time constant is on the order of 0.5 s. A moderate capacitor might have $C = 1\,\mu\text{F}$.

SOLUTION Setting $\tau = RC = 0.5\,\text{s}$, we find

$$R = \frac{\tau}{C} = \frac{0.5\,\text{s}}{1 \times 10^{-6}\,\text{F}} \approx 500\,\text{k}\Omega.$$

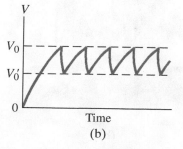

(b)

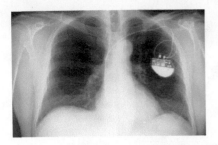
FIGURE 26–22 Electronic battery-powered pacemaker can be seen on the rib cage in this X-ray.

PHYSICS APPLIED
Dangers of electricity

FIGURE 26–23 A person receives an electric shock when the circuit is completed.

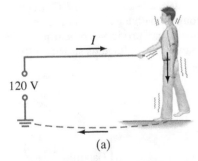

(a)

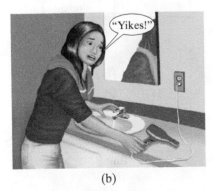

"Yikes!"

(b)

An interesting medical use of an *RC* circuit is the electronic heart pacemaker, which can make a stopped heart start beating again by applying an electric stimulus through electrodes attached to the chest. The stimulus can be repeated at the normal heartbeat rate if necessary. The heart itself contains *pacemaker* cells, which send out tiny electric pulses at a rate of 60 to 80 per minute. These signals induce the start of each heartbeat. In some forms of heart disease, the natural pacemaker fails to function properly, and the heart loses its beat. Such patients use *electronic pacemakers* which produce a regular voltage pulse that starts and controls the frequency of the heartbeat. The electrodes are implanted in or near the heart (Fig. 26–22), and the circuit contains a capacitor and a resistor. The charge on the capacitor increases to a certain point and then discharges a pulse to the heart. Then it starts charging again. The pulsing rate depends on the values of *R* and *C*.

26–6 Electric Hazards

Excess electric current can heat wires in buildings and cause fires, as discussed in Section 25–6. Electric current can also damage the human body or even be fatal. Electric current through the human body can cause damage in two ways: (1) Electric current heats tissue and can cause burns; (2) electric current stimulates nerves and muscles, and we feel a "shock." The severity of a shock depends on the magnitude of the current, how long it acts, and through what part of the body it passes. A current passing through vital organs such as the heart or brain is especially serious for it can interfere with their operation.

Most people can "feel" a current of about 1 mA. Currents of a few mA cause pain but rarely cause much damage in a healthy person. Currents above 10 mA cause severe contraction of the muscles, and a person may not be able to let go of the source of the current (say, a faulty appliance or wire). Death from paralysis of the respiratory system can occur. Artificial respiration, however, can sometimes revive a victim. If a current above about 80 to 100 mA passes across the torso, so that a portion passes through the heart for more than a second or two, the heart muscles will begin to contract irregularly and blood will not be properly pumped. This condition is called **ventricular fibrillation**. If it lasts for long, death results. Strangely enough, if the current is much larger, on the order of 1 A, death by heart failure may be less likely,[†] but such currents can cause serious burns, especially if concentrated through a small area of the body.

The seriousness of a shock depends on the applied voltage and on the effective resistance of the body. Living tissue has low resistance since the fluid of cells contains ions that can conduct quite well. However, the outer layer of skin, when dry, offers high resistance and is thus protective. The effective resistance between two points on opposite sides of the body when the skin is dry is in the range of 10^4 to $10^6 \, \Omega$. But when the skin is wet, the resistance may be $10^3 \, \Omega$ or less. A person who is barefoot or wearing thin-soled shoes will be in good contact with the ground, and touching a 120-V line with a wet hand can result in a current

$$ I = \frac{120 \, \text{V}}{1000 \, \Omega} = 120 \, \text{mA}. $$

As we saw, this could be lethal.

A person who has received a shock has become part of a complete circuit. Figure 26–23 shows two ways the circuit might be completed when a person

[†]Larger currents apparently bring the entire heart to a standstill. Upon release of the current, the heart returns to its normal rhythm. This may not happen when fibrillation occurs because, once started, it can be hard to stop. Fibrillation may also occur as a result of a heart attack or during heart surgery. A device known as a *defibrillator* (described in Section 24–4) can apply a brief high current to the heart, causing complete heart stoppage which is often followed by resumption of normal beating.

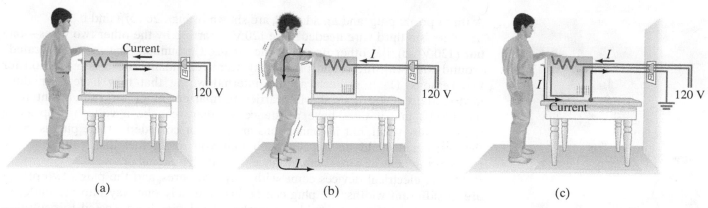

(a)   (b)   (c)

FIGURE 26–24 (a) An electric oven operating normally with a 2-prong plug.
(b) Short to the case with ungrounded case: shock. (c) Short to the case with the case
grounded by a 3-prong plug.

accidentally touches a "hot" electric wire—"hot" meaning a high potential such
as 120 V (normal U.S. household voltage) relative to ground. The other wire of
building wiring is connected to ground—either by a wire connected to a buried
conductor, or via a metal water pipe into the ground. In Fig. 26–23a, the current passes
from the high-voltage wire, through the person, to the ground through his bare
feet, and back along the ground (a fair conductor) to the ground terminal of the
source. If the person stands on a good insulator—thick rubber-soled shoes or a
dry wood floor—there will be much more resistance in the circuit and consequently much less current through the person. If the person stands with bare feet
on the ground, or is in a bathtub, there is lethal danger because the resistance is
much less and the current greater. In a bathtub (or swimming pool), not only are
you wet, which reduces your resistance, but the water is in contact with the drain
pipe (typically metal) that leads to the ground. It is strongly recommended that
you not touch anything electrical when wet or in bare feet. Building codes that
require the use of non-metal pipes would be protective.

In Fig. 26–23b, a person touches a faulty "hot" wire with one hand, and the
other hand touches a sink faucet (connected to ground via the pipe). The current is
particularly dangerous because it passes across the chest, through the heart and
lungs. A useful rule: if one hand is touching something electrical, keep your other
hand in your pocket (don't use it!), and wear thick rubber-soled shoes. It is also a
good idea to remove metal jewelry, especially rings (your finger is usually moist
under a ring).

You can come into contact with a hot wire by touching a bare wire whose
insulation has worn off, or from a bare wire inside an appliance when you're
tinkering with it. (Always unplug an electrical device before investigating[†] its
insides!) Another possibility is that a wire inside a device may break or lose
its insulation and come in contact with the case. If the case is metal, it will
conduct electricity. A person could then suffer a severe shock merely by touching
the case, as shown in Fig. 26–24b. To prevent an accident, metal cases are
supposed to be connected directly to ground by a separate ground wire. Then if a
"hot" wire touches the grounded case, a short circuit to ground immediately
occurs internally, as shown in Fig. 26–24c, and most of the current passes through
the low-resistance ground wire rather than through the person. Furthermore,
the high current should open the fuse or circuit breaker. Grounding a metal
case is done by a separate ground wire connected to the third (round)
prong of a 3-prong plug. Never cut off the third prong of a plug—it could save your life.

⚠ **CAUTION**

*Keep one hand in your pocket
when other touches electricity*

🚶 **PHYSICS APPLIED**

Grounding and shocks

[†]Even then you can get a bad shock from a capacitor that hasn't been discharged until you
touch it.

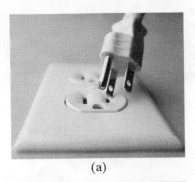

(a)

(b)

(c)

FIGURE 26–25 (a) A 3-prong plug, and (b) an adapter (gray) for old-fashioned 2-prong outlets—be sure to screw down the ground tab. (c) A polarized 2-prong plug.

FIGURE 26–26 Four wires entering a typical house. The color codes for wires are not always as shown here—be careful!

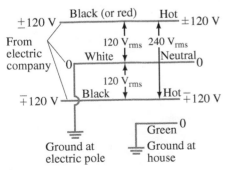

A three-prong plug, and an adapter, are shown in Figs. 26–25a and b.

Why is a third wire needed? The 120 V is carried by the other two wires—one **hot** (120 V ac), the other **neutral**, which is itself grounded. The third "dedicated" ground wire with the round prong may seem redundant. But it is protection for two reasons: (1) it protects against internal wiring that may have been done incorrectly; (2) the neutral wire carries normal current ("return" current from the 120 V) and it does have resistance; so there can be a voltage drop along it—normally small, but if connections are poor or corroded, or the plug is loose, the resistance could be large enough that you might feel that voltage if you touched the neutral wire some distance from its grounding point.

Some electrical devices come with only two wires, and the plug's two prongs are of different widths; the plug can be inserted only one way into the outlet so that the intended neutral (wider prong) in the device is connected to neutral in the wiring (Fig. 26–25c). For example, the screw threads of a lightbulb are meant to be connected to neutral (and the base contact to hot), to avoid shocks when changing a bulb in a possibly protruding socket. Devices with 2-prong plugs do *not* have their cases grounded; they are supposed to have double electric insulation. Take extra care anyway.

The insulation on a wire may be color coded. Hand-held meters may have red (hot) and black (ground) lead wires. But in a house, black is usually hot (or it may be red), whereas white is neutral and green is the dedicated ground, Fig. 26–26. But beware: these color codes cannot always be trusted. [In the U.S., three wires normally enter a house: two *hot* wires at 120 V each (which add together to 240 V for appliances or devices that run on 240 V) plus the grounded *neutral* (carrying return current for the two hots). See Fig. 26–26. The "dedicated" *ground* wire (non-current carrying) is a fourth wire that does not come from the electric company but enters the house from a nearby heavy stake in the ground or a buried metal pipe. The two hot wires can feed separate 120-V circuits in the house, so each 120-V circuit inside the house has only three wires, including ground.]

Normal circuit breakers (Sections 25–6 and 28–8) protect equipment and buildings from overload and fires. They protect humans only in some circumstances, such as the very high currents that result from a short, if they respond quickly enough. *Ground fault circuit interrupters* (GFCI), described in Section 29–8, are designed to protect people from the much lower currents (10 mA to 100 mA) that are lethal but would not throw a 15-A circuit breaker or blow a 20-A fuse.

It is current that harms, but it is voltage that drives the current. 30 volts is sometimes said to be the threshhold for danger. But even a 12-V car battery (which can supply large currents) can cause nasty burns and shock.

Another danger is **leakage current**, by which we mean a current along an unintended path. Leakage currents are often "capacitively coupled." For example, a wire in a lamp forms a capacitor with the metal case; charges moving in one conductor attract or repel charge in the other, so there is a current. Typical electrical codes limit leakage currents to 1 mA for any device. A 1-mA leakage current is usually harmless. It can be very dangerous, however, to a hospital patient with implanted electrodes connected to ground through the apparatus. This is due to the absence of the protective skin layer and because the current can pass directly through the heart as compared to the usual situation where the current enters at the hands and spreads out through the body. Although 100 mA may be needed to cause heart fibrillation when entering through the hands (very little of it actually passes through the heart), as little as 0.02 mA has been known to cause fibrillation when passing directly to the heart. Thus, a "wired" patient is in considerable danger from leakage current even from as simple an act as touching a lamp.

Finally, don't touch a downed power line (lethal!) or even get near it. A hot power line is at thousands of volts. A huge current can flow along the ground or pavement, from where the high-voltage wire touches the ground along its path to the grounding point of the neutral line, enough that the voltage between your two feet could be large. Tip: stand on one foot or run (only one foot touching the ground at a time).

*26–7 Ammeters and Voltmeters

An **ammeter** is used to measure current, and a **voltmeter** measures potential difference or voltage. Measurements of current and voltage are made with meters that are of two types: (1) *analog* meters, which display numerical values by the position of a pointer that can move across a scale (Fig. 26–27a); and (2) *digital* meters, which display the numerical value in numbers (Fig. 26–27b). We now discuss the meters themselves and how they work, then how they are connected to circuits to make measurements. Finally we will discuss how using meters affects the circuit being measured, possibly causing erroneous results—and what to do about it.

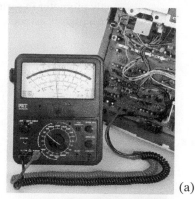

(a)

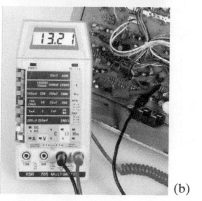

(b)

FIGURE 26–27 (a) An analog multimeter being used as a voltmeter. (b) An electronic digital meter.

*Analog Ammeters and Voltmeters

The crucial part of an analog ammeter or voltmeter, in which the reading is by a pointer on a scale (Fig. 26–27a), is a *galvanometer*. The galvanometer works on the principle of the force between a magnetic field and a current-carrying coil of wire, and will be discussed in Chapter 27. For now, we merely need to know that the deflection of the needle of a galvanometer is proportional to the current flowing through it. The *full-scale current sensitivity* of a galvanometer, I_m, is the electric current needed to make the needle deflect full scale.

A galvanometer can be used directly to measure small dc currents. For example, a galvanometer whose sensitivity I_m is 50 μA can measure currents from about 1 μA (currents smaller than this would be hard to read on the scale) up to 50 μA. To measure larger currents, a resistor is placed in parallel with the galvanometer. Thus, an analog **ammeter**, represented by the symbol •-Ⓐ-•, consists of a galvanometer (•-Ⓖ-•) in parallel with a resistor called the **shunt resistor**, as shown in Fig. 26–28. ("Shunt" is a synonym for "in parallel.") The shunt resistance is R_{sh}, and the resistance of the galvanometer coil, through which current passes, is r. The value of R_{sh} is chosen according to the full-scale deflection desired; R_{sh} is normally very small—giving an ammeter a very small net resistance—so most of the current passes through R_{sh} and very little ($\lesssim 50 \mu$A) passes through the galvanometer to deflect the needle.

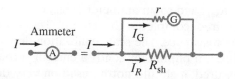

FIGURE 26–28 An ammeter is a galvanometer in parallel with a (shunt) resistor with low resistance, R_{sh}.

EXAMPLE 26–15 **Ammeter design.** Design an ammeter to read 1.0 A at full scale using a galvanometer with a full-scale sensitivity of 50 μA and a resistance $r = 30 \Omega$. Check if the scale is linear.

APPROACH Only 50 μA $(= I_G = 0.000050$ A$)$ of the 1.0-A current must pass through the galvanometer to give full-scale deflection. The rest of the current $(I_R = 0.999950$ A$)$ passes through the small shunt resistor, R_{sh}, Fig. 26–28. The potential difference across the galvanometer equals that across the shunt resistor (they are in parallel). We apply Ohm's law to find R_{sh}.

SOLUTION Because $I = I_G + I_R$, when $I = 1.0$ A flows into the meter, we want I_R through the shunt resistor to be $I_R = 0.999950$ A. The potential difference across the shunt is the same as across the galvanometer, so Ohm's law tells us

$$I_R R_{sh} = I_G r;$$

then

$$R_{sh} = \frac{I_G r}{I_R} = \frac{(5.0 \times 10^{-5} \text{ A})(30 \Omega)}{(0.999950 \text{ A})} = 1.5 \times 10^{-3} \Omega,$$

or 0.0015 Ω. The shunt resistor must thus have a very low resistance and most of the current passes through it.

Because $I_G = I_R(R_{sh}/r)$ and (R_{sh}/r) is constant, we see that the scale is linear.

An analog **voltmeter** (•ⓥ•) also consists of a galvanometer and a resistor. But the resistor R_{ser} is connected in series, Fig. 26–29, and it is usually large, giving a voltmeter a high internal resistance.

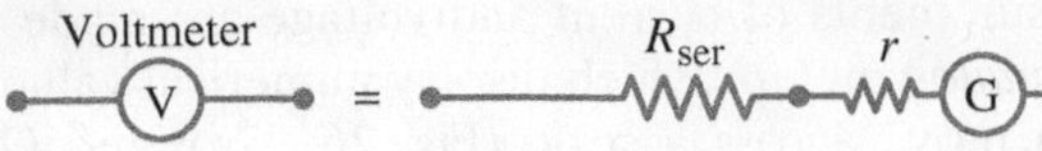

FIGURE 26–29 A voltmeter is a galvanometer in series with a resistor with high resistance, R_{ser}.

Voltmeter: •ⓥ• = •R_{ser}—r—ⓖ•

EXAMPLE 26–16 Voltmeter design. Using a galvanometer with internal resistance $r = 30\,\Omega$ and full-scale current sensitivity of $50\,\mu A$, design a voltmeter that reads from 0 to 15 V. Is the scale linear?

APPROACH When a potential difference of 15 V exists across the terminals of our voltmeter, we want $50\,\mu A$ to be passing through it so as to give a full-scale deflection.

SOLUTION From Ohm's law, $V = IR$, we have (see Fig. 26–29)

$$15\,V = (50\,\mu A)(r + R_{ser}),$$

so

$$R_{ser} = \frac{15\,V}{5.0 \times 10^{-5}\,A} - r = 300\,k\Omega - 30\,\Omega = 300\,k\Omega.$$

Notice that $r = 30\,\Omega$ is so small compared to the value of R_{ser} that it doesn't influence the calculation significantly. The scale will again be linear: if the voltage to be measured is 6.0 V, the current passing through the voltmeter will be $(6.0\,V)/(3.0 \times 10^5\,\Omega) = 2.0 \times 10^{-5}\,A$, or $20\,\mu A$. This will produce two-fifths of full-scale deflection, as required $(6.0\,V/15.0\,V = 2/5)$.

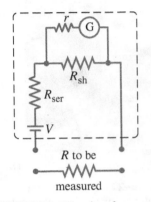

FIGURE 26–30 An ohmmeter.

FIGURE 26–31 Measuring current and voltage.

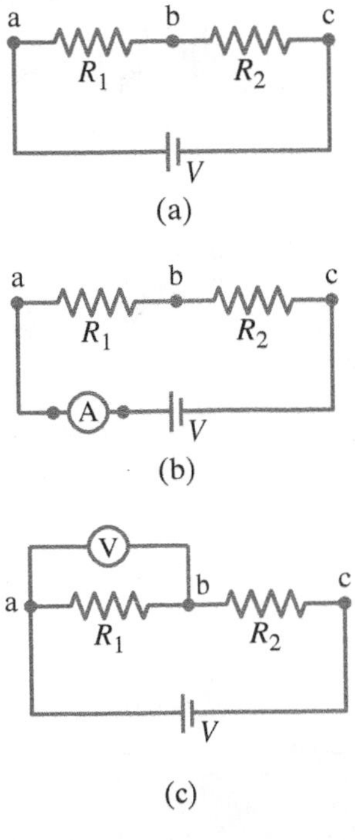

(a)

(b)

(c)

The meters just described are for direct current. A dc meter can be modified to measure ac (alternating current, Section 25–7) with the addition of diodes (Chapter 40), which allow current to flow in one direction only. An ac meter can be calibrated to read rms or peak values.

Voltmeters and ammeters can have several series or shunt resistors to offer a choice of range. **Multimeters** can measure voltage, current, and resistance. Sometimes a multimeter is called a VOM (Volt-Ohm-Meter or Volt-Ohm-Milliammeter).

An **ohmmeter** measures resistance, and must contain a battery of known voltage connected in series to a resistor (R_{ser}) and to an ammeter (Fig. 26–30). The resistor whose resistance is to be measured completes the circuit. The needle deflection is inversely proportional to the resistance. The scale calibration depends on the value of the series resistor. Because an ohmmeter sends a current through the device whose resistance is to be measured, it should not be used on very delicate devices that could be damaged by the current.

The **sensitivity** of a meter is generally specified on the face. It may be given as so many ohms per volt, which indicates how many ohms of resistance there are in the meter per volt of full-scale reading. For example, if the sensitivity is 30,000 Ω/V, this means that on the 10-V scale the meter has a resistance of 300,000 Ω, whereas on a 100-V scale the meter resistance is 3 MΩ. The full-scale current sensitivity, I_m, discussed earlier, is just the reciprocal of the sensitivity in Ω/V.

*How to Connect Meters

Suppose you wish to determine the current I in the circuit shown in Fig. 26–31a, and the voltage V across the resistor R_1. How exactly are ammeters and voltmeters connected to the circuit being measured?

Because an ammeter is used to measure the current flowing in the circuit, it must be inserted directly into the circuit, in series with the other elements, as shown in Fig. 26–31b. The smaller its internal resistance, the less it affects the circuit.

A voltmeter, on the other hand, is connected "externally," in parallel with the circuit element across which the voltage is to be measured. It is used to measure the potential difference between two points. Its two wire leads (connecting wires) are connected to the two points, as shown in Fig. 26–31c, where the voltage across R_1 is being measured. The larger its internal resistance, $(R_{ser} + r)$ in Fig. 26–29, the less it affects the circuit being measured.

*Effects of Meter Resistance

It is important to know the sensitivity of a meter, for in many cases the resistance of the meter can seriously affect your results. Take the following Example.

PHYSICS APPLIED
Correcting for meter resistance

EXAMPLE 26–17 **Voltage reading versus true voltage.** Suppose you are testing an electronic circuit which has two resistors, R_1 and R_2, each 15 kΩ, connected in series as shown in Fig. 26–32a. The battery maintains 8.0 V across them and has negligible internal resistance. A voltmeter whose sensitivity is 10,000 Ω/V is put on the 5.0-V scale. What voltage does the meter read when connected across R_1, Fig. 26–32b, and what error is caused by the finite resistance of the meter?

APPROACH The meter acts as a resistor in parallel with R_1. We use parallel and series resistor analyses and Ohm's law to find currents and voltages.

SOLUTION On the 5.0-V scale, the voltmeter has an internal resistance of $(5.0 \text{ V})(10,000 \text{ } \Omega/\text{V}) = 50,000 \text{ } \Omega$. When connected across R_1, as in Fig. 26–32b, we have this 50 kΩ in parallel with $R_1 = 15$ kΩ. The net resistance R_{eq} of these two is given by

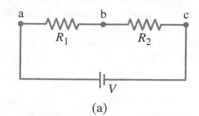

$$\frac{1}{R_{eq}} = \frac{1}{50 \text{ k}\Omega} + \frac{1}{15 \text{ k}\Omega} = \frac{13}{150 \text{ k}\Omega};$$

so $R_{eq} = 11.5$ kΩ. This $R_{eq} = 11.5$ kΩ is in series with $R_2 = 15$ kΩ, so the total resistance of the circuit is now 26.5 kΩ (instead of the original 30 kΩ). Hence the current from the battery is

$$I = \frac{8.0 \text{ V}}{26.5 \text{ k}\Omega} = 3.0 \times 10^{-4} \text{ A} = 0.30 \text{ mA}.$$

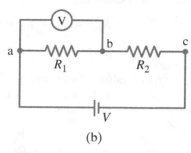

FIGURE 26–32 Example 26–17.

Then the voltage drop across R_1, which is the same as that across the voltmeter, is $(3.0 \times 10^{-4} \text{ A})(11.5 \times 10^3 \text{ } \Omega) = 3.5 \text{ V}$. [The voltage drop across R_2 is $(3.0 \times 10^{-4} \text{ A})(15 \times 10^3 \text{ } \Omega) = 4.5 \text{ V}$, for a total of 8.0 V.] If we assume the meter is precise, it will read 3.5 V. In the original circuit, without the meter, $R_1 = R_2$ so the voltage across R_1 is half that of the battery, or 4.0 V. Thus the voltmeter, because of its internal resistance, gives a low reading. In this case it is off by 0.5 V, or more than 10%.

Example 26–17 illustrates how seriously a meter can affect a circuit and give a misleading reading. If the resistance of a voltmeter is much higher than the resistance of the circuit, however, it will have little effect and its readings can be trusted, at least to the manufactured precision of the meter, which for ordinary analog meters is typically 3% to 4% of full-scale deflection. An ammeter also can interfere with a circuit, but the effect is minimal if its resistance is much less than that of the circuit as a whole. For both voltmeters and ammeters, the more sensitive the galvanometer, the less effect it will have. A 50,000-Ω/V meter is far better than a 1000-Ω/V meter.

*Digital Meters

Digital meters (see Fig. 26–27b) are used in the same way as analog meters: they are inserted directly into the circuit, in series, to measure current (Fig. 26–31b), and connected "outside," in parallel with the circuit, to measure voltage (Fig. 26–31c).

The internal construction of digital meters, however, is different from that of analog meters in that digital meters do not use a galvanometer. The electronic circuitry and digital readout are more sensitive than a galvanometer, and have less effect on the circuit to be measured. When we measure dc voltages, a digital meter's resistance is very high, commonly on the order of 10 to 100 MΩ $(10^7 – 10^8 \text{ } \Omega)$, and doesn't change significantly when different voltage scales are selected. A 100-MΩ digital meter draws off very little current when connected across even a 1-MΩ resistance.

The precision of digital meters is exceptional, often one part in 10^4 ($= 0.01\%$) or better. This precision is not the same as accuracy, however. A precise meter of internal resistance $10^8 \text{ } \Omega$ will not give accurate results if used to measure a voltage across a 10^8-Ω resistor—in which case it is necessary to do a calculation like that in Example 26–17.

Whenever we make a measurement on a circuit, to some degree we affect that circuit (Example 26–17). This is true for other types of measurement as well: when we make a measurement on a system, we affect that system in some way. On a temperature measurement, for example, the thermometer can exchange heat with the system, thus altering its temperature. It is important to be able to make needed corrections, as we saw in Example 26–17.

Summary

A device that transforms another type of energy into electrical energy is called a **source** of **emf**. A battery behaves like a source of emf in series with an **internal resistance**. The emf is the potential difference determined by the chemical reactions in the battery and equals the terminal voltage when no current is drawn. When a current is drawn, the voltage at the battery's terminals is less than its emf by an amount equal to the potential decrease Ir across the internal resistance.

When resistances are connected in **series** (end to end in a single linear path), the equivalent resistance is the sum of the individual resistances:

$$R_{eq} = R_1 + R_2 + \cdots . \qquad (26\text{-}3)$$

In a series combination, R_{eq} is greater than any component resistance.

When resistors are connected in **parallel**, the reciprocal of the equivalent resistance equals the sum of the reciprocals of the individual resistances:

$$\frac{1}{R_{eq}} = \frac{1}{R_1} + \frac{1}{R_2} + \cdots . \qquad (26\text{-}4)$$

In a parallel connection, the net resistance is less than any of the individual resistances.

Kirchhoff's rules are helpful in determining the currents and voltages in circuits. Kirchhoff's **junction rule** is based on conservation of electric charge and states that the sum of all currents entering any junction equals the sum of all currents leaving that junction. The second, or **loop rule**, is based on conservation of energy and states that the algebraic sum of the changes in potential around any closed path of the circuit must be zero.

When an **RC circuit** containing a resistor R in series with a capacitance C is connected to a dc source of emf, the voltage across the capacitor rises gradually in time characterized by an exponential of the form $(1 - e^{-t/RC})$, where the **time constant**,

$$\tau = RC, \qquad (26\text{-}7)$$

is the time it takes for the voltage to reach 63 percent of its maximum value. The current through the resistor decreases as $e^{-t/RC}$.

A capacitor discharging through a resistor is characterized by the same time constant: in a time $\tau = RC$, the voltage across the capacitor drops to 37 percent of its initial value. The charge on the capacitor, and voltage across it, decreases as $e^{-t/RC}$, as does the current.

Electric shocks are caused by current passing through the body. To avoid shocks, the body must not become part of a complete circuit by allowing different parts of the body to touch objects at different potentials. Commonly, shocks are caused by one part of the body touching ground and another part touching a high electric potential.

[*An **ammeter** measures current. An analog ammeter consists of a galvanometer and a parallel **shunt resistor** that carries most of the current. An analog **voltmeter** consists of a galvanometer and a series resistor. An ammeter is inserted *into* the circuit whose current is to be measured. A voltmeter is external, being connected in parallel to the element whose voltage is to be measured. Digital voltmeters have greater internal resistance and affect the circuit to be measured less than do analog meters.]

Questions

1. Explain why birds can sit on power lines safely, whereas leaning a metal ladder up against a power line to fetch a stuck kite is extremely dangerous.

2. Discuss the advantages and disadvantages of Christmas tree lights connected in parallel versus those connected in series.

3. If all you have is a 120-V line, would it be possible to light several 6-V lamps without burning them out? How?

4. Two lightbulbs of resistance R_1 and R_2 $(R_2 > R_1)$ and a battery are all connected in series. Which bulb is brighter? What if they are connected in parallel? Explain.

5. Household outlets are often double outlets. Are these connected in series or parallel? How do you know?

6. With two identical lightbulbs and two identical batteries, how would you arrange the bulbs and batteries in a circuit to get the maximum possible total power to the lightbulbs? (Assume the batteries have negligible internal resistance.)

7. If two identical resistors are connected in series to a battery, does the battery have to supply more power or less power than when only one of the resistors is connected? Explain.

8. You have a single 60-W bulb on in your room. How does the overall resistance of your room's electric circuit change when you turn on an additional 100-W bulb?

9. When applying Kirchhoff's loop rule (such as in Fig. 26–33), does the sign (or direction) of a battery's emf depend on the direction of current through the battery? What about the terminal voltage?

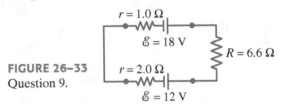

FIGURE 26–33
Question 9.

10. Compare and discuss the formulas for resistors and for capacitors when connected in series and in parallel.

11. For what use are batteries connected in series? For what use are they connected in parallel? Does it matter if the batteries are nearly identical or not in either case?

12. Can the terminal voltage of a battery ever exceed its emf? Explain.

13. Explain in detail how you could measure the internal resistance of a battery.

14. In an RC circuit, current flows from the battery until the capacitor is completely charged. Is the total energy supplied by the battery equal to the total energy stored by the capacitor? If not, where does the extra energy go?

15. Given the circuit shown in Fig. 26–34, use the words "increases," "decreases," or "stays the same" to complete the following statements:

(a) If R_7 increases, the potential difference between A and E ____. Assume no resistance in Ⓐ and Ⓔ.

(b) If R_7 increases, the potential difference between A and E ____. Assume Ⓐ and Ⓔ have resistance.

(c) If R_7 increases, the voltage drop across R_4 _____.

(d) If R_2 decreases, the current through R_1 _____.

(e) If R_2 decreases, the current through R_6 _____.

(f) If R_2 decreases, the current through R_3 ____.

(g) If R_5 increases, the voltage drop across R_2 ____.

(h) If R_5 increases, the voltage drop across R_4 ____.

(i) If R_2, R_5, and R_7 increase, $\mathscr{E}$ ($r = 0$) ____.

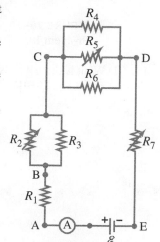

FIGURE 26–34

Question 15. R_2, R_5, and R_7 are *variable* resistors (you can change their resistance), given the symbol ─W─.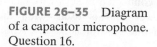

16. Figure 26–35 is a diagram of a capacitor (or condenser) **microphone**. The changing air pressure in a sound wave causes one plate of the capacitor C to move back and forth. Explain how a current of the same frequency as the sound wave is produced.

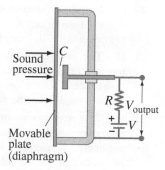

FIGURE 26–35 Diagram of a capacitor microphone. Question 16.

17. Design a circuit in which two different switches of the type shown in Fig. 26–36 can be used to operate the same lightbulb from opposite sides of a room.

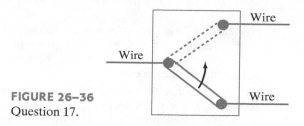

FIGURE 26–36
Question 17.

*18. What is the main difference between an analog voltmeter and an analog ammeter?

*19. What would happen if you mistakenly used an ammeter where you needed to use a voltmeter?

*20. Explain why an ideal ammeter would have zero resistance and an ideal voltmeter infinite resistance.

*21. A voltmeter connected across a resistor always reads *less* than the actual voltage across the resistor when the meter is not present. Explain.

*22. A small battery-operated flashlight requires a single 1.5-V battery. The bulb is barely glowing, but when you take the battery out and check it with a voltmeter, it registers 1.5 V. How would you explain this?

23. Different lamps might have batteries connected in either of the two arrangements shown in Fig. 26–37. What would be the advantages of each scheme?

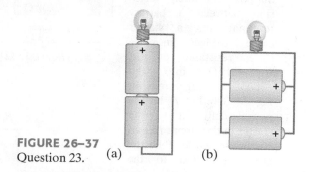

FIGURE 26–37
Question 23. (a)   (b)

Problems

26–1 Emf and Terminal Voltage

1. (I) Calculate the terminal voltage for a battery with an internal resistance of $0.900 \, \Omega$ and an emf of 6.00 V when the battery is connected in series with (a) an 81.0-Ω resistor, and (b) an 810-Ω resistor.

2. (I) Four 1.50-V cells are connected in series to a 12-Ω lightbulb. If the resulting current is 0.45 A, what is the internal resistance of each cell, assuming they are identical and neglecting the resistance of the wires?

3. (II) A 1.5-V dry cell can be tested by connecting it to a low-resistance ammeter. It should be able to supply at least 25 A. What is the internal resistance of the cell in this case, assuming it is much greater than that of the ammeter?

4. (II) What is the internal resistance of a 12.0-V car battery whose terminal voltage drops to 8.4 V when the starter draws 95 A? What is the resistance of the starter?

26–2 Resistors in Series and Parallel

In these Problems neglect the internal resistance of a battery unless the Problem refers to it.

5. (I) A 650-Ω and a 2200-Ω resistor are connected in series with a 12-V battery. What is the voltage across the 2200-Ω resistor?

6. (I) Three 45-Ω lightbulbs and three 65-Ω lightbulbs are connected in series. (a) What is the total resistance of the circuit? (b) What is the total resistance if all six are wired in parallel?

7. (I) Suppose that you have a 680-Ω, a 720-Ω, and a 1.20-kΩ resistor. What is (a) the maximum, and (b) the minimum resistance you can obtain by combining these?

8. (I) How many 10-Ω resistors must be connected in series to give an equivalent resistance to five 100-Ω resistors connected in parallel?

9. (II) Suppose that you have a 9.0-V battery and you wish to apply a voltage of only 4.0 V. Given an unlimited supply of 1.0-Ω resistors, how could you connect them so as to make a "voltage divider" that produces a 4.0-V output for a 9.0-V input?

10. (II) Three 1.70-kΩ resistors can be connected together in four different ways, making combinations of series and/or parallel circuits. What are these four ways, and what is the net resistance in each case?

11. (II) A battery with an emf of 12.0 V shows a terminal voltage of 11.8 V when operating in a circuit with two light-bulbs, each rated at 4.0 W (at 12.0 V), which are connected in parallel. What is the battery's internal resistance?

12. (II) Eight identical bulbs are connected in series across a 110-V line. (a) What is the voltage across each bulb? (b) If the current is 0.42 A, what is the resistance of each bulb, and what is the power dissipated in each?

13. (II) Eight bulbs are connected in parallel to a 110-V source by two long leads of total resistance 1.4 Ω. If 240 mA flows through each bulb, what is the resistance of each, and what fraction of the total power is wasted in the leads?

14. (II) The performance of the starter circuit in an automobile can be significantly degraded by a small amount of corrosion on a battery terminal. Figure 26–38a depicts a properly functioning circuit with a battery (12.5-V emf, 0.02-Ω internal resistance) attached via corrosion-free cables to a starter motor of resistance $R_S = 0.15 \, \Omega$. Suppose that later, corrosion between a battery terminal and a starter cable introduces an extra series resistance of just $R_C = 0.10 \, \Omega$ into the circuit as suggested in Fig. 26–38b. Let P_0 be the power delivered to the starter in the circuit free of corrosion, and let P be the power delivered to the circuit with corrosion. Determine the ratio P/P_0.

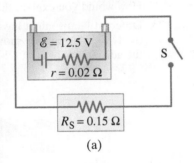

(a)

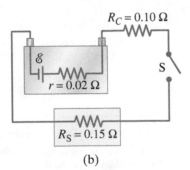

(b)

FIGURE 26–38
Problem 14.

15. (II) A close inspection of an electric circuit reveals that a 480-Ω resistor was inadvertently soldered in the place where a 370-Ω resistor is needed. How can this be fixed without removing anything from the existing circuit?

16. (II) Determine (a) the equivalent resistance of the circuit shown in Fig. 26–39, and (b) the voltage across each resistor.

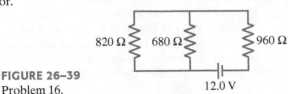

FIGURE 26–39
Problem 16.

17. (II) A 75-W, 110-V bulb is connected in parallel with a 25-W, 110-V bulb. What is the net resistance?

18. (II) (a) Determine the equivalent resistance of the "ladder" of equal 125-Ω resistors shown in Fig. 26–40. In other words, what resistance would an ohmmeter read if connected between points A and B? (b) What is the current through each of the three resistors on the left if a 50.0-V battery is connected between points A and B?

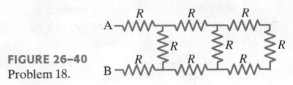

FIGURE 26–40
Problem 18.

19. (II) What is the net resistance of the circuit connected to the battery in Fig. 26–41?

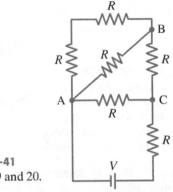

FIGURE 26–41
Problems 19 and 20.

20. (II) Calculate the current through each resistor in Fig. 26–41 if each resistance $R = 1.20 \, k\Omega$ and $V = 12.0 \, V$. What is the potential difference between points A and B?

21. (II) The two terminals of a voltage source with emf $\mathscr{E}$ and internal resistance r are connected to the two sides of a load resistance R. For what value of R will the maximum power be delivered from the source to the load?

22. (II) Two resistors when connected in series to a 110-V line use one-fourth the power that is used when they are connected in parallel. If one resistor is 3.8 kΩ, what is the resistance of the other?

23. (III) Three equal resistors (R) are connected to a battery as shown in Fig. 26–42. Qualitatively, what happens to (a) the voltage drop across each of these resistors, (b) the current flow through each, and (c) the terminal voltage of the battery, when the switch S is opened, after having been closed for a long time? (d) If the emf of the battery is 9.0 V, what is its terminal voltage when the switch is closed if the internal resistance r is 0.50 Ω and $R = 5.50 \, \Omega$? (e) What is the terminal voltage when the switch is open?

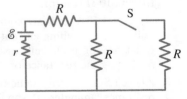

FIGURE 26–42
Problem 23.

24. (III) A 2.8-kΩ and a 3.7-kΩ resistor are connected in parallel; this combination is connected in series with a 1.8-kΩ resistor. If each resistor is rated at $\frac{1}{2}$ W (maximum without overheating), what is the maximum voltage that can be applied across the whole network?

25. (III) Consider the network of resistors shown in Fig. 26–43. Answer qualitatively: (a) What happens to the voltage across each resistor when the switch S is closed? (b) What happens to the current through each when the switch is closed? (c) What happens to the power output of the battery when the switch is closed? (d) Let $R_1 = R_2 = R_3 = R_4 = 125\ \Omega$ and $V = 22.0\ \text{V}$. Determine the current through each resistor before and after closing the switch. Are your qualitative predictions confirmed?

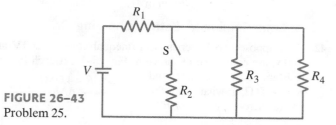

FIGURE 26–43
Problem 25.

26. (III) You are designing a wire resistance heater to heat an enclosed volume of gas. For the apparatus to function properly, this heater must transfer heat to the gas at a very constant rate. While in operation, the resistance of the heater will always be close to the value $R = R_0$, but may fluctuate slightly causing its resistance to vary a small amount $\Delta R\ (\ll R_0)$. To maintain the heater at constant power, you design the circuit shown in Fig. 26–44, which includes two resistors, each of resistance r. Determine the value for r so that the heater power will remain constant even if its resistance R fluctuates by a small amount. [*Hint:* If $\Delta R \ll R_0$, then $\Delta P \approx \Delta R \dfrac{dP}{dR}\Big|_{R=R_0}$.]

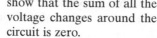

FIGURE 26–44
Problem 26.

26–3 Kirchhoff's Rules

27. (I) Calculate the current in the circuit of Fig. 26–45, and show that the sum of all the voltage changes around the circuit is zero.

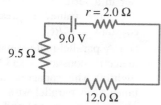

FIGURE 26–45
Problem 27.

28. (II) Determine the terminal voltage of each battery in Fig. 26–46.

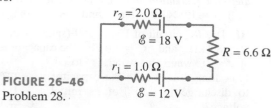

FIGURE 26–46
Problem 28.

29. (II) For the circuit shown in Fig. 26–47, find the potential difference between points a and b. Each resistor has $R = 130\ \Omega$ and each battery is 1.5 V.

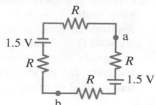

FIGURE 26–47
Problem 29.

30. (II) (a) A network of five equal resistors R is connected to a battery $\mathscr{E}$ as shown in Fig. 26–48. Determine the current I that flows out of the battery. (b) Use the value determined for I to find the single resistor R_{eq} that is equivalent to the five-resistor network.

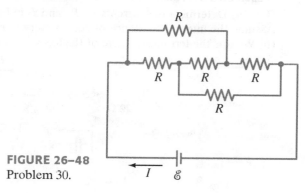

FIGURE 26–48
Problem 30.

31. (II) (a) What is the potential difference between points a and d in Fig. 26–49 (similar to Fig. 26–13, Example 26–9), and (b) what is the terminal voltage of each battery?

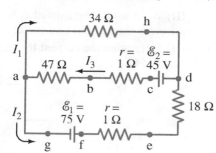

FIGURE 26–49
Problem 31.

32. (II) Calculate the currents in each resistor of Fig. 26–50.

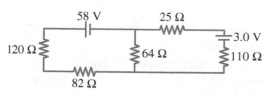

FIGURE 26–50   Problem 32.

33. (II) Determine the magnitudes and directions of the currents through R_1 and R_2 in Fig. 26–51.

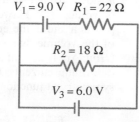

FIGURE 26–51
Problem 33.

34. (II) Determine the magnitudes and directions of the currents in each resistor shown in Fig. 26–52. The batteries have emfs of $\mathcal{E}_1 = 9.0\,\text{V}$ and $\mathcal{E}_2 = 12.0\,\text{V}$ and the resistors have values of $R_1 = 25\,\Omega$, $R_2 = 48\,\Omega$, and $R_3 = 35\,\Omega$. (a) Ignore internal resistance of the batteries. (b) Assume each battery has internal resistance $r = 1.0\,\Omega$.

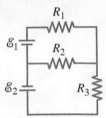

FIGURE 26–52
Problem 34.

35. (II) A voltage V is applied to n identical resistors connected in parallel. If the resistors are instead all connected in series with the applied voltage, show that the power transformed is decreased by a factor n^2.

36. (III) (a) Determine the currents I_1, I_2, and I_3 in Fig. 26–53. Assume the internal resistance of each battery is $r = 1.0\,\Omega$. (b) What is the terminal voltage of the 6.0-V battery?

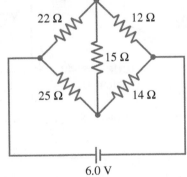

FIGURE 26–53
Problems 36 and 37.

37. (III) What would the current I_1 be in Fig. 26–53 if the 12-Ω resistor is shorted out (resistance = 0)? Let $r = 1.0\,\Omega$.

38. (III) Determine the current through each of the resistors in Fig. 26–54.

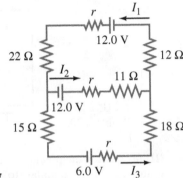

FIGURE 26–54
Problems 38 and 39.

39. (III) If the 25-Ω resistor in Fig. 26–54 is shorted out (resistance = 0), what then would be the current through the 15-Ω resistor?

40. (III) Twelve resistors, each of resistance R, are connected as the edges of a cube as shown in Fig. 26–55. Determine the equivalent resistance (a) between points a and b, the ends of a side; (b) between points a and c, the ends of a face diagonal; (c) between points a and d, the ends of the volume diagonal. [*Hint:* Apply an emf and determine currents; use symmetry at junctions.]

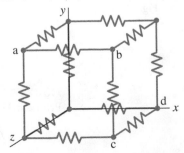

FIGURE 26–55
Problem 40.

41. (III) Determine the net resistance in Fig. 26–56 (a) between points a and c, and (b) between points a and b. Assume $R' \neq R$. [*Hint:* Apply an emf and determine currents; use symmetry at junctions.]

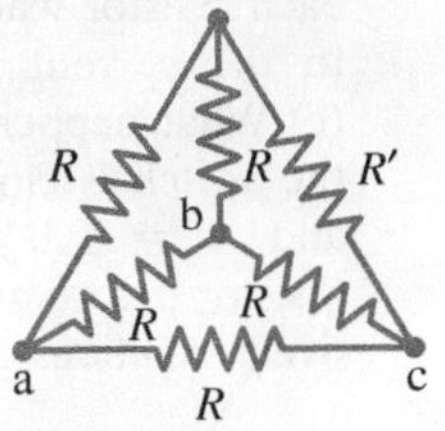

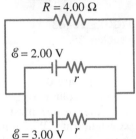

FIGURE 26–56
Problem 41.

26–4 Emfs Combined, Battery Charging

42. (II) Suppose two batteries, with unequal emfs of 2.00 V and 3.00 V, are connected as shown in Fig. 26–57. If each internal resistance is $r = 0.450\,\Omega$, and $R = 4.00\,\Omega$, what is the voltage across the resistor R?

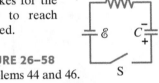

FIGURE 26–57
Problem 42.

26–5 RC Circuits

43. (I) Estimate the range of resistance needed to make a variable timer for typical intermittent windshield wipers if the capacitor used is on the order of $1\,\mu\text{F}$.

44. (II) In Fig. 26–58 (same as Fig. 26–17a), the total resistance is $15.0\,\text{k}\Omega$, and the battery's emf is 24.0 V. If the time constant is measured to be $24.0\,\mu\text{s}$, calculate (a) the total capacitance of the circuit and (b) the time it takes for the voltage across the resistor to reach 16.0 V after the switch is closed.

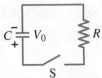

FIGURE 26–58
Problems 44 and 46.

45. (II) Two 3.8-μF capacitors, two 2.2-kΩ resistors, and a 12.0-V source are connected in series. Starting from the uncharged state, how long does it take for the current to drop from its initial value to 1.50 mA?

46. (II) How long does it take for the energy stored in a capacitor in a series RC circuit (Fig. 26–58) to reach 75% of its maximum value? Express answer in terms of the time constant $\tau = RC$.

47. (II) A parallel-plate capacitor is filled with a dielectric of dielectric constant K and high resistivity ρ (it conducts very slightly). This capacitor can be modeled as a pure capacitance C in parallel with a resistance R. Assume a battery places a charge $+Q$ and $-Q$ on the capacitor's opposing plates and is then disconnected. Show that the capacitor discharges with a time constant $\tau = K\varepsilon_0\rho$ (known as the *dielectric relaxation time*). Evaluate τ if the dielectric is glass with $\rho = 1.0 \times 10^{12}\,\Omega\cdot\text{m}$ and $K = 5.0$.

48. (II) The RC circuit of Fig. 26–59 (same as Fig. 26–18a) has $R = 8.7\,\text{k}\Omega$ and $C = 3.0\,\mu\text{F}$. The capacitor is at voltage V_0 at $t = 0$, when the switch is closed. How long does it take the capacitor to discharge to 0.10% of its initial voltage?

FIGURE 26–59
Problem 48.

49. (II) Consider the circuit shown in Fig. 26–60, where all resistors have the same resistance R. At $t = 0$, with the capacitor C uncharged, the switch is closed. (a) At $t = 0$, the three currents can be determined by analyzing a simpler, but equivalent, circuit. Identify this simpler circuit and use it to find the values of I_1, I_2, and I_3 at $t = 0$. (b) At $t = \infty$, the currents can be determined by analyzing a simpler, equivalent, circuit. Identify this simpler circuit and implement it in finding the values of I_1, I_2, and I_3 at $t = \infty$. (c) At $t = \infty$, what is the potential difference across the capacitor?

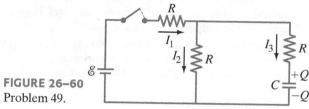

FIGURE 26–60
Problem 49.

50. (III) Determine the time constant for charging the capacitor in the circuit of Fig. 26–61. [*Hint:* Use Kirchhoff's rules.] (b) What is the maximum charge on the capacitor?

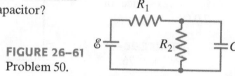

FIGURE 26–61
Problem 50.

51. (III) Two resistors and two uncharged capacitors are arranged as shown in Fig. 26–62. Then a potential difference of 24 V is applied across the combination as shown. (a) What is the potential at point a with switch S open? (Let $V = 0$ at the negative terminal of the source.) (b) What is the potential at point b with the switch open? (c) When the switch is closed, what is the final potential of point b? (d) How much charge flows through the switch S after it is closed?

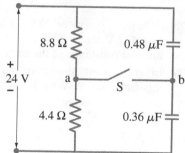

FIGURE 26–62
Problems 51 and 52.

52. (III) Suppose the switch S in Fig. 26–62 is closed. What is the time constant (or time constants) for charging the capacitors after the 24 V is applied?

*26–7 Ammeters and Voltmeters

*53. (I) An ammeter has a sensitivity of 35,000 Ω/V. What current in the galvanometer produces full-scale deflection?

*54. (I) What is the resistance of a voltmeter on the 250-V scale if the meter sensitivity is 35,000 Ω/V?

*55. (II) A galvanometer has a sensitivity of 45 kΩ/V and internal resistance 20.0 Ω. How could you make this into (a) an ammeter that reads 2.0 A full scale, or (b) a voltmeter reading 1.00 V full scale?

*56. (II) A galvanometer has an internal resistance of 32 Ω and deflects full scale for a 55-μA current. Describe how to use this galvanometer to make (a) an ammeter to read currents up to 25 A, and (b) a voltmeter to give a full scale deflection of 250 V.

*57. (II) A particular digital meter is based on an electronic module that has an internal resistance of 100 MΩ and a full-scale sensitivity of 400 mV. Two resistors connected as shown in Fig. 26–63 can be used to change the voltage range. Assume $R_1 = 10$ MΩ. Find the value of R_2 that will result in a voltmeter with a full-scale range of 40 V.

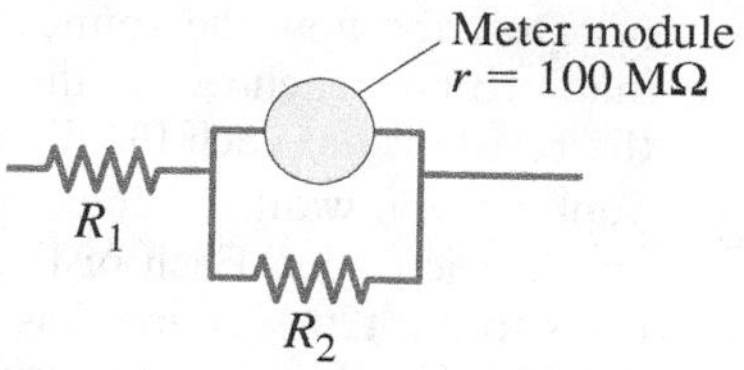

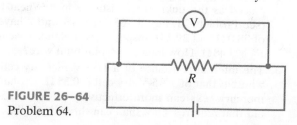

FIGURE 26–63
Problem 57.

*58. (II) A milliammeter reads 25 mA full scale. It consists of a 0.20-Ω resistor in parallel with a 33 Ω galvanometer. How can you change this ammeter to a voltmeter giving a full scale reading of 25 V without taking the ammeter apart? What will be the sensitivity (Ω/V) of your voltmeter?

*59. (II) A 45-V battery of negligible internal resistance is connected to a 44-kΩ and a 27-kΩ resistor in series. What reading will a voltmeter, of internal resistance 95 kΩ, give when used to measure the voltage across each resistor? What is the percent inaccuracy due to meter resistance for each case?

*60. (II) An ammeter whose internal resistance is 53 Ω reads 5.25 mA when connected in a circuit containing a battery and two resistors in series whose values are 650 Ω and 480 Ω. What is the actual current when the ammeter is absent?

*61. (II) A battery with $\mathscr{E} = 12.0$ V and internal resistance $r = 1.0$ Ω is connected to two 7.5-kΩ resistors in series. An ammeter of internal resistance 0.50 Ω measures the current, and at the same time a voltmeter with internal resistance 15 kΩ measures the voltage across one of the 7.5-kΩ resistors in the circuit. What do the ammeter and voltmeter read?

*62. (II) A 12.0-V battery (assume the internal resistance = 0) is connected to two resistors in series. A voltmeter whose internal resistance is 18.0 kΩ measures 5.5 V and 4.0 V, respectively, when connected across each of the resistors. What is the resistance of each resistor?

*63. (III) Two 9.4-kΩ resistors are placed in series and connected to a battery. A voltmeter of sensitivity 1000 Ω/V is on the 3.0-V scale and reads 2.3 V when placed across either resistor. What is the emf of the battery? (Ignore its internal resistance.)

*64. (III) When the resistor R in Fig. 26–64 is 35 Ω, the high-resistance voltmeter reads 9.7 V. When R is replaced by a 14.0-Ω resistor, the voltmeter reading drops to 8.1 V. What are the emf and internal resistance of the battery?

FIGURE 26–64
Problem 64.

General Problems

65. Suppose that you wish to apply a 0.25-V potential difference between two points on the human body. The resistance is about 1800 Ω, and you only have a 1.5-V battery. How can you connect up one or more resistors to produce the desired voltage?

66. A **three-way lightbulb** can produce 50 W, 100 W, or 150 W, at 120 V. Such a bulb contains two filaments that can be connected to the 120 V individually or in parallel. (a) Describe how the connections to the two filaments are made to give each of the three wattages. (b) What must be the resistance of each filament?

67. Suppose you want to run some apparatus that is 65 m from an electric outlet. Each of the wires connecting your apparatus to the 120-V source has a resistance per unit length of 0.0065 Ω/m. If your apparatus draws 3.0 A, what will be the voltage drop across the connecting wires and what voltage will be applied to your apparatus?

68. For the circuit shown in Fig. 26–18a, show that the decrease in energy stored in the capacitor from $t = 0$ until one time constant has elapsed equals the energy dissipated as heat in the resistor.

69. A heart pacemaker is designed to operate at 72 beats/min using a 6.5-μF capacitor in a simple RC circuit. What value of resistance should be used if the pacemaker is to fire (capacitor discharge) when the voltage reaches 75% of maximum?

70. Suppose that a person's body resistance is 950 Ω. (a) What current passes through the body when the person accidentally is connected to 110 V? (b) If there is an alternative path to ground whose resistance is 35 Ω, what current passes through the person? (c) If the voltage source can produce at most 1.5 A, how much current passes through the person in case (b)?

71. A **Wheatstone bridge** is a type of "bridge circuit" used to make measurements of resistance. The unknown resistance to be measured, R_x, is placed in the circuit with accurately known resistances R_1, R_2, and R_3 (Fig. 26–65). One of these, R_3, is a variable resistor which is adjusted so that when the switch is closed momentarily, the ammeter Ⓐ shows zero current flow. (a) Determine R_x in terms of R_1, R_2, and R_3. (b) If a Wheatstone bridge is "balanced" when $R_1 = 630\,Ω$, $R_2 = 972\,Ω$, and $R_3 = 78.6\,Ω$, what is the value of the unknown resistance?

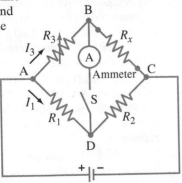

FIGURE 26–65
Problems 71 and 72.
Wheatstone bridge.

72. An unknown length of platinum wire 1.22 mm in diameter is placed as the unknown resistance in a Wheatstone bridge (see Problem 71, Fig. 26–65). Arms 1 and 2 have resistance of 38.0 Ω and 29.2 Ω, respectively. Balance is achieved when R_3 is 3.48 Ω. How long is the platinum wire?

73. The internal resistance of a 1.35-V mercury cell is 0.030 Ω, whereas that of a 1.5-V dry cell is 0.35 Ω. Explain why three mercury cells can more effectively power a 2.5-W hearing aid that requires 4.0 V than can three dry cells.

74. How many $\frac{1}{2}$-W resistors, each of the same resistance, must be used to produce an equivalent 3.2-kΩ, 3.5-W resistor? What is the resistance of each, and how must they be connected? Do not exceed $P = \frac{1}{2}$ W in each resistor.

75. A solar cell, 3.0 cm square, has an output of 350 mA at 0.80 V when exposed to full sunlight. A solar panel that delivers close to 1.3 A of current at an emf of 120 V to an external load is needed. How many cells will you need to create the panel? How big a panel will you need, and how should you connect the cells to one another? How can you optimize the output of your solar panel?

76. A power supply has a fixed output voltage of 12.0 V, but you need $V_T = 3.0\,V$ output for an experiment. (a) Using the voltage divider shown in Fig. 26–66, what should R_2 be if R_1 is 14.5 Ω? (b) What will the terminal voltage V_T be if you connect a load to the 3.0-V output, assuming the load has a resistance of 7.0 Ω?

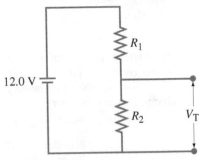

FIGURE 26–66
Problem 76.

77. The current through the 4.0-kΩ resistor in Fig. 26–67 is 3.10 mA. What is the terminal voltage V_{ba} of the "unknown" battery? (There are two answers. Why?)

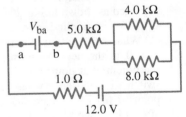

FIGURE 26–67
Problem 77.

78. A battery produces 40.8 V when 7.40 A is drawn from it, and 47.3 V when 2.80 A is drawn. What are the emf and internal resistance of the battery?

79. In the circuit shown in Fig. 26–68, the 33-Ω resistor dissipates 0.80 W. What is the battery voltage?

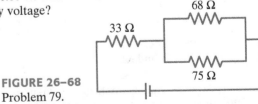

FIGURE 26–68
Problem 79.

80. The current through the 20-Ω resistor in Fig. 26–69 does not change whether the two switches S_1 and S_2 are both open or both closed. Use this clue to determine the value of the unknown resistance R.

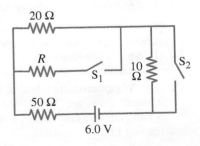

FIGURE 26–69
Problem 80.

*81. (a) A voltmeter and an ammeter can be connected as shown in Fig. 26–70a to measure a resistance R. If V is the voltmeter reading, and I is the ammeter reading, the value of R will not quite be V/I (as in Ohm's law) because some of the current actually goes through the voltmeter. Show that the actual value of R is given by

$$\frac{1}{R} = \frac{I}{V} - \frac{1}{R_V},$$

where R_V is the voltmeter resistance. Note that $R \approx V/I$ if $R_V \gg R$. (b) A voltmeter and an ammeter can also be connected as shown in Fig. 26–70b to measure a resistance R. Show in this case that

$$R = \frac{V}{I} - R_A,$$

where V and I are the voltmeter and ammeter readings and R_A is the resistance of the ammeter. Note that $R \approx V/I$ if $R_A \ll R$.

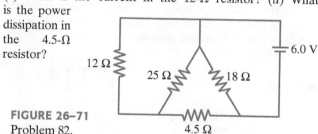

(a)   (b)

FIGURE 26–70 Problem 81.

82. (a) What is the equivalent resistance of the circuit shown in Fig. 26–71? (b) What is the current in the 18-Ω resistor? (c) What is the current in the 12-Ω resistor? (d) What is the power dissipation in the 4.5-Ω resistor?

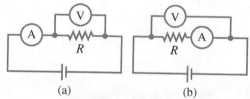

FIGURE 26–71
Problem 82.

83. A flashlight bulb rated at 2.0 W and 3.0 V is operated by a 9.0-V battery. To light the bulb at its rated voltage and power, a resistor R is connected in series as shown in Fig. 26–72. What value should the resistor have?

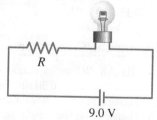

FIGURE 26–72
Problem 83.

84. Some light-dimmer switches use a variable resistor as shown in Fig. 26–73. The slide moves from position $x = 0$ to $x = 1$, and the resistance up to slide position x is proportional to x (the total resistance is $R_{var} = 150\,\Omega$ at $x = 1$). What is the power expended in the lightbulb if (a) $x = 1.00$, (b) $x = 0.65$, (c) $x = 0.35$?

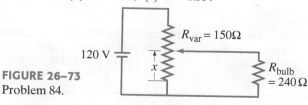

FIGURE 26–73
Problem 84.

85. A **potentiometer** is a device to precisely measure potential differences or emf, using a "null" technique. In the simple potentiometer circuit shown in Fig. 26–74, R' represents the total resistance of the resistor from A to B (which could be a long uniform "slide" wire), whereas R represents the resistance of only the part from A to the movable contact at C. When the unknown emf to be measured, $\mathscr{E}_x$, is placed into the circuit as shown, the movable contact C is moved until the galvanometer G gives a null reading (i.e., zero) when the switch S is closed. The resistance between A and C for this situation we call R_x. Next, a standard emf, $\mathscr{E}_s$, which is known precisely, is inserted into the circuit in place of $\mathscr{E}_x$ and again the contact C is moved until zero current flows through the galvanometer when the switch S is closed. The resistance between A and C now is called R_s. (a) Show that the unknown emf is given by

$$\mathscr{E}_x = \left(\frac{R_x}{R_s}\right)\mathscr{E}_s$$

where R_x, R_s, and $\mathscr{E}_s$ are all precisely known. The working battery is assumed to be fresh and to give a constant voltage. (b) A slide-wire potentiometer is balanced against a 1.0182-V standard cell when the slide wire is set at 33.6 cm out of a total length of 100.0 cm. For an unknown source, the setting is 45.8 cm. What is the emf of the unknown? (c) The galvanometer of a potentiometer has an internal resistance of 35 Ω and can detect a current as small as 0.012 mA. What is the minimum uncertainty possible in measuring an unknown voltage? (d) Explain the advantage of using this "null" method of measuring emf.

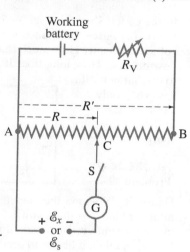

FIGURE 26–74
Potentiometer circuit.
Problem 85.

86. Electronic devices often use an RC circuit to protect against power outages as shown in Fig. 26–75. (a) If the protector circuit is supposed to keep the supply voltage at least 75% of full voltage for as long as 0.20 s, how big a resistance R is needed? The capacitor is 8.5 μF. Assume the attached "electronics" draws negligible current. (b) Between which two terminals should the device be connected, a and b, b and c, or a and c?

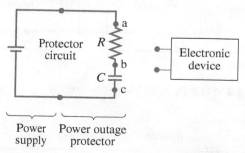

FIGURE 26–75
Problem 86.

87. The circuit shown in Fig. 26–76 is a primitive 4-bit **digital-to-analog converter (DAC)**. In this circuit, to represent each digit (2^n) of a binary number, a "1" has the nth switch closed whereas zero ("0") has the switch open. For example, 0010 is represented by closing switch $n = 1$, while all other switches are open. Show that the voltage V across the 1.0-Ω resistor for the binary numbers 0001, 0010, 0100, and 1010 (which represent 1, 2, 4, 10) follows the pattern that you expect for a 4-bit DAC.

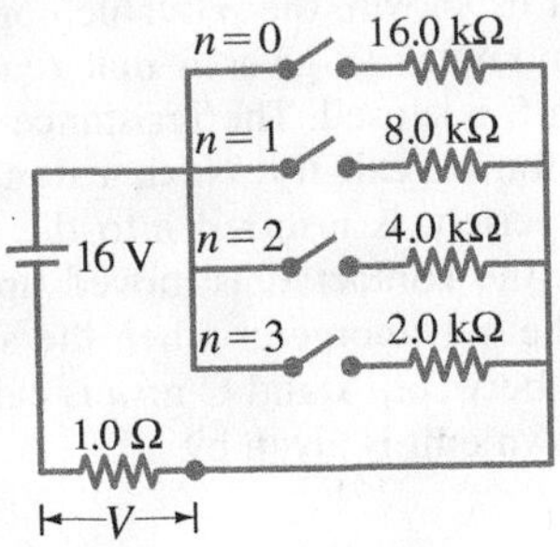

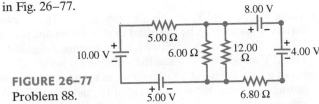

FIGURE 26–76
Problem 87.

88. Determine the current in each resistor of the circuit shown in Fig. 26–77.

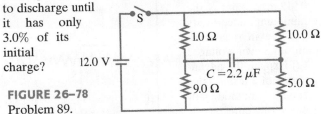

FIGURE 26–77
Problem 88.

89. In the circuit shown in Fig. 26–78, switch S is closed at time $t = 0$. (a) After the capacitor is fully charged, what is the voltage across it? How much charge is on it? (b) Switch S is now opened. How long does it now take for the capacitor to discharge until it has only 3.0% of its initial charge?

12.0 V

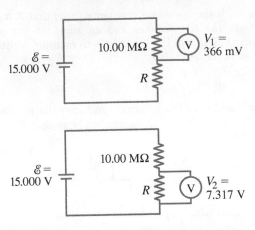

FIGURE 26–78
Problem 89.

90. Figure 26–79 shows the circuit for a simple **sawtooth oscillator**. At time $t = 0$, its switch S is closed. The neon bulb has initially infinite resistance until the voltage across it reaches 90.0 V, and then it begins to conduct with very little resistance (essentially zero). It stops conducting (its resistance becomes essentially infinite) when the voltage drops down to 65.0 V. (a) At what time t_1 does the neon bulb reach 90.0 V and start conducting? (b) At what time t_2 does the bulb reach 90.0 V for a second time and again become conducting? (c) Sketch the sawtooth waveform between $t = 0$ and $t = 0.70$ s.

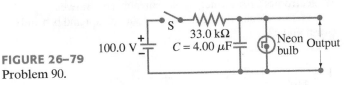

FIGURE 26–79
Problem 90.

*91. Measurements made on circuits that contain large resistances can be confusing. Consider a circuit powered by a battery $\mathcal{E} = 15.000$ V with a 10.00-MΩ resistor in series with an unknown resistor R. As shown in Fig. 26–80, a particular voltmeter reads $V_1 = 366$ mV when connected across the 10.00-MΩ resistor, and this meter reads $V_2 = 7.317$ V when connected across R. Determine the value of R. [*Hint*: Define R_V as the voltmeter's internal resistance.]

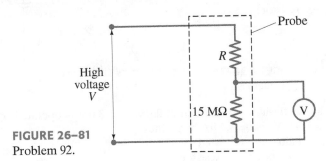

FIGURE 26–80   Problem 91.

*92. A typical voltmeter has an internal resistance of 10 MΩ and can only measure voltage differences of up to several hundred volts. Figure 26–81 shows the design of a probe to measure a very large voltage difference V using a voltmeter. If you want the voltmeter to read 50 V when $V = 50$ kV, what value R should be used in this probe?

FIGURE 26–81
Problem 92.

*Numerical/Computer

*93. (II) An RC series circuit contains a resistor $R = 15$ kΩ, a capacitor $C = 0.30$ μF, and a battery of emf $\mathcal{E} = 9.0$ V. Starting at $t = 0$, when the battery is connected, determine the charge Q on the capacitor and the current I in the circuit from $t = 0$ to $t = 10.0$ ms (at 0.1-ms intervals). Make graphs showing how the charge Q and the current I change with time within this time interval. From the graphs find the time at which the charge attains 63% of its final value, $C\mathcal{E}$, and the current drops to 37% of its initial value, $\mathcal{E}/R$.

Answers to Exercises

A: (a) 1.14 A; (b) 11.4 V; (c) $P_R = 13.1$ W, $P_r = 0.65$ W.

B: 6 Ω and 25 Ω.

C: $41I_3 - 45 + 21I_2 - 80 = 0$.

D: 180 A; this high current through the batteries could cause them to become very hot: the power dissipated in the weak battery would be $P = I^2r = (180 \text{ A})^2(0.10 \Omega) = 3200$ W!

E: (a).

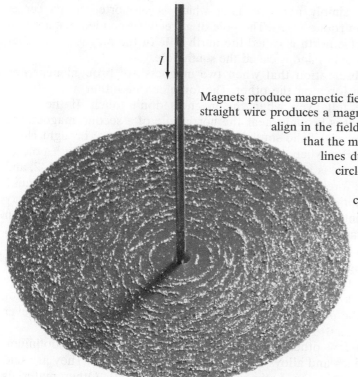

Magnets produce magnetic fields, but so do electric currents. An electric current flowing in this straight wire produces a magnetic field which causes the tiny pieces of iron (iron "filings") to align in the field. We shall see in this Chapter how magnetic field is defined, and that the magnetic field direction is along the iron filings. The magnetic field lines due to the electric current in this long wire are in the shape of circles around the wire.

We also discuss how magnetic fields exert forces on electric currents and on charged particles, as well as useful applications of the interaction between magnetic fields and electric currents and moving electric charges.

Magnetism

C H A P T E R

27

CHAPTER-OPENING QUESTION—Guess now!

Which of the following can experience a force when placed in the magnetic field of a magnet?

(a) An electric charge at rest.
(b) An electric charge moving.
(c) An electric current in a wire.
(d) Another magnet.

The history of magnetism begins thousands of years ago. In a region of Asia Minor known as Magnesia, rocks were found that could attract each other. These rocks were called "magnets" after their place of discovery. Not until the nineteenth century, however, was it seen that magnetism and electricity are closely related. A crucial discovery was that electric currents produce magnetic effects (we will say "magnetic fields") like magnets do. All kinds of practical devices depend on magnetism, from compasses to motors, loudspeakers, computer memory, and electric generators.

CONTENTS

27–1 Magnets and Magnetic Fields

We have all observed a magnet attract paper clips, nails, and other objects made of iron, Fig. 27–1. Any magnet, whether it is in the shape of a bar or a horseshoe, has two ends or faces, called **poles**, which is where the magnetic effect is strongest. If a bar magnet is suspended from a fine thread, it is found that one pole of the magnet will always point toward the north. It is not known for sure when this fact was discovered, but it is known that the Chinese were making use of it as an aid to navigation by the eleventh century and perhaps earlier. This is the principle of a compass.

FIGURE 27–1 A horseshoe magnet attracts iron tacks and paper clips.

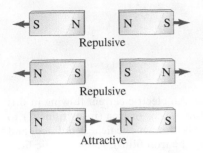

FIGURE 27–2 Like poles of a magnet repel; unlike poles attract. Red arrows indicate force direction.

FIGURE 27–3 If you split a magnet, you won't get isolated north and south poles; instead, two new magnets are produced, each with a north and a south pole.

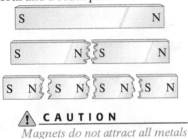

⚠ CAUTION

Magnets do not attract all metals

FIGURE 27–4 (a) Visualizing magnetic field lines around a bar magnet, using iron filings and compass needles. The red end of the bar magnet is its north pole. The N pole of a nearby compass needle points away from the north pole of the magnet. (b) Magnetic field lines for a bar magnet.

⚠ CAUTION

Magnetic field lines form closed loops, unlike electric field lines

A compass needle is simply a bar magnet which is supported at its center of gravity so that it can rotate freely. The pole of a freely suspended magnet that points toward geographic north is called the **north pole** of the magnet. The other pole points toward the south and is called the **south pole**.

It is a familiar observation that when two magnets are brought near one another, each exerts a force on the other. The force can be either attractive or repulsive and can be felt even when the magnets don't touch. If the north pole of one bar magnet is brought near the north pole of a second magnet, the force is repulsive. Similarly, if the south poles of two magnets are brought close, the force is repulsive. But when a north pole is brought near the south pole of another magnet, the force is attractive. These results are shown in Fig. 27–2, and are reminiscent of the forces between electric charges: like poles repel, and unlike poles attract. *But do not confuse magnetic poles with electric charge.* They are very different. One important difference is that a positive or negative electric charge can easily be isolated. But an isolated single magnetic pole has never been observed. If a bar magnet is cut in half, you do not obtain isolated north and south poles. Instead, two new magnets are produced, Fig. 27–3, each with north (N) and south (S) poles. If the cutting operation is repeated, more magnets are produced, each with a north and a south pole. Physicists have searched for isolated single magnetic poles (monopoles), but no **magnetic monopole** has ever been observed.

Only iron and a few other materials, such as cobalt, nickel, gadolinium, and some of their oxides and alloys, show strong magnetic effects. They are said to be **ferromagnetic** (from the Latin word *ferrum* for iron). Other materials show some slight magnetic effect, but it is very weak and can be detected only with delicate instruments. We will look in more detail at ferromagnetism in Section 28–7.

In Chapter 21, we used the concept of an electric field surrounding an electric charge. In a similar way, we can picture a **magnetic field** surrounding a magnet. The force one magnet exerts on another can then be described as the interaction between one magnet and the magnetic field of the other. Just as we drew electric field lines, we can also draw **magnetic field lines**. They can be drawn, as for electric field lines, so that (1) the direction of the magnetic field is tangent to a field line at any point, and (2) the number of lines per unit area is proportional to the strength of the magnetic field.

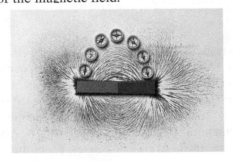
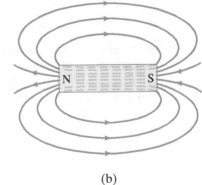

(a)   (b)

The *direction* of the magnetic field at a given point can be defined as the direction that the north pole of a compass needle would point if placed at that point. (A more precise definition will be given in Section 27–3.) Figure 27–4a shows how thin iron filings (acting like tiny magnets) reveal the magnetic field lines by lining up like the compass needles. The magnetic field determined in this way for the field surrounding a bar magnet is shown in Fig. 27–4b. Notice that because of our definition, the lines always point out from the north pole and in toward the south pole of a magnet (the north pole of a magnetic compass needle is attracted to the south pole of the magnet).

Magnetic field lines continue inside a magnet, as indicated in Fig. 27–4b. Indeed, given the lack of single magnetic poles, magnetic field lines always form closed loops, unlike electric field lines that begin on positive charges and end on negative charges.

Earth's Magnetic Field

The Earth's magnetic field is shown in Fig. 27–5. The pattern of field lines is as if there were an imaginary bar magnet inside the Earth. Since the north pole (N) of a compass needle points north, the Earth's magnetic pole which is in the geographic north is magnetically a south pole, as indicated in Fig. 27–5 by the S on the schematic bar magnet inside the Earth. Remember that the north pole of one magnet is attracted to the south pole of another magnet. Nonetheless, Earth's pole in the north is still often called the "north magnetic pole," or "geomagnetic north," simply because it is in the north. Similarly, the Earth's southern magnetic pole, which is near the geographic south pole, is magnetically a north pole (N). The Earth's magnetic poles do not coincide with the *geographic* poles, which are on the Earth's axis of rotation. The north magnetic pole, for example, is in the Canadian Arctic,[†] about 900 km from the geographic north pole, or "true north." This difference must be taken into account when you use a compass (Fig. 27–6). The angular difference between magnetic north and true (geographical) north is called the **magnetic declination**. In the U.S. it varies from 0° to about 20°, depending on location.

Notice in Fig. 27–5 that the Earth's magnetic field at most locations is not tangent to the Earth's surface. The angle that the Earth's magnetic field makes with the horizontal at any point is referred to as the **angle of dip**.

| **EXERCISE A** Does the Earth's magnetic field have a greater magnitude near the poles or near the equator? [*Hint*: Note the field lines in Fig. 27–5.]

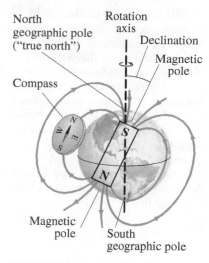

FIGURE 27–5 The Earth acts like a huge magnet; but its magnetic poles are not at the geographic poles, which are on the Earth's rotation axis.

PHYSICS APPLIED
Use of a compass

FIGURE 27–6 Using a map and compass in the wilderness. First you align the compass case so the needle points away from true north (N) exactly the number of degrees of declination as stated on the map (15° for the place shown on this topographic map of a part of California). Then align the map with true north, as shown, *not* with the compass needle.

Uniform Magnetic Field

The simplest magnetic field is one that is uniform—it doesn't change in magnitude or direction from one point to another. A perfectly uniform field over a large area is not easy to produce. But the field between two flat parallel pole pieces of a magnet is nearly uniform if the area of the pole faces is large compared to their separation, as shown in Fig. 27–7. At the edges, the field "fringes" out somewhat: the magnetic field lines are no longer quite parallel and uniform. The parallel evenly spaced field lines in the central region of the gap indicate that the field is uniform at points not too near the edges, much like the electric field between two parallel plates (Fig. 23–16).

FIGURE 27–7 Magnetic field between two wide poles of a magnet is nearly uniform, except near the edges.

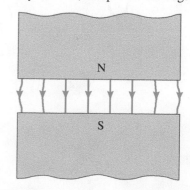

[†]Magnetic north is moving many kilometers a year at present. Magnetism in rocks suggests that the Earth's poles have not only moved significantly over geologic time, but have also reversed direction 400 times over the last 330 million years.

FIGURE 27–8 **FIGURE 27–8** (a) Deflection of compass needles near a current-carrying wire, showing the presence and direction of the magnetic field. (b) Magnetic field lines around an electric current in a straight wire. See also the Chapter-Opening photo. (c) Right-hand rule for remembering the direction of the magnetic field: when the thumb points in the direction of the conventional current, the fingers wrapped around the wire point in the direction of the magnetic field.

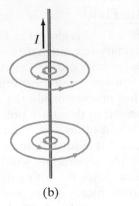

(a)   (b)   (c)

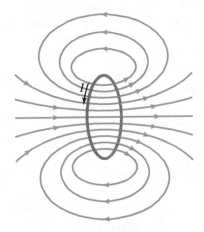

FIGURE 27–9 Magnetic field lines due to a circular loop of wire.

Right-hand-rule 1: magnetic field direction produced by electric current

FIGURE 27–10 Right-hand rule for determining the direction of the magnetic field relative to the current.

I Magnetic field

27–2 Electric Currents Produce Magnetic Fields

During the eighteenth century, many scientists sought to find a connection between electricity and magnetism. A stationary electric charge and a magnet were shown to have no influence on each other. But in 1820, Hans Christian Oersted (1777–1851) found that when a compass needle is placed near a wire, the needle deflects as soon as the two ends of the wire are connected to the terminals of a battery and the wire carries an electric current. As we have seen, a compass needle is deflected by a magnetic field. So Oersted's experiment showed that **an electric current produces a magnetic field**. He had found a connection between electricity and magnetism.

A compass needle placed near a straight section of current-carrying wire experiences a force, causing the needle to align tangent to a circle around the wire, Fig. 27–8a. Thus, the magnetic field lines produced by a current in a straight wire are in the form of circles with the wire at their center, Fig. 27–8b. The direction of these lines is indicated by the north pole of the compasses in Fig. 27–8a. There is a simple way to remember the direction of the magnetic field lines in this case. It is called a **right-hand rule**: grasp the wire with your right hand so that your thumb points in the direction of the conventional (positive) current; then your fingers will encircle the wire in the direction of the magnetic field, Fig. 27–8c.

The magnetic field lines due to a circular loop of current-carrying wire can be determined in a similar way using a compass. The result is shown in Fig. 27–9. Again the right-hand rule can be used, as shown in Fig. 27–10. Unlike the uniform field shown in Fig. 27–7, the magnetic fields shown in Figs. 27–8 and 27–9 are *not* uniform—the fields are different in magnitude and direction at different points.

EXERCISE B A straight wire carries a current directly toward you. In what direction are the magnetic field lines surrounding the wire?

27–3 Force on an Electric Current in a Magnetic Field; Definition of $\vec{\mathbf{B}}$

In Section 27–2 we saw that an electric current exerts a force on a magnet, such as a compass needle. By Newton's third law, we might expect the reverse to be true as well: we should expect that *a magnet exerts a force on a current-carrying wire*. Experiments indeed confirm this effect, and it too was first observed by Oersted.

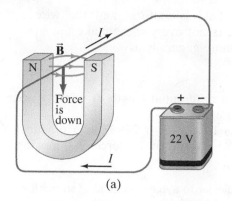

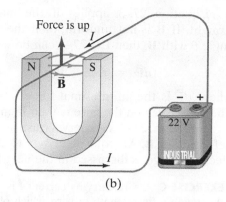

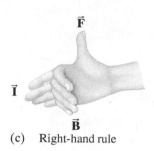

(a)   (b)   (c)   Right-hand rule

Suppose a straight wire is placed in the magnetic field between the poles of a horseshoe magnet as shown in Fig. 27–11. When a current flows in the wire, experiment shows that a force is exerted on the wire. But this force is *not* toward one or the other pole of the magnet. Instead, the force is directed at right angles to the magnetic field direction, downward in Fig. 27–11a. If the current is reversed in direction, the force is in the opposite direction, upward as shown in Fig. 27–11b. Experiments show that *the direction of the force is always perpendicular to the direction of the current and also perpendicular to the direction of the magnetic field*, $\vec{B}$.

The direction of the force is given by another **right-hand rule**, as illustrated in Fig. 27–11c. Orient your right hand until your outstretched fingers can point in the direction of the conventional current I, and when you bend your fingers they point in the direction of the magnetic field lines, $\vec{B}$. Then your outstretched thumb will point in the direction of the force $\vec{F}$ on the wire.

This right-hand rule describes the direction of the force. What about the magnitude of the force on the wire? It is found experimentally that the magnitude of the force is directly proportional to the current I in the wire, and to the length ℓ of wire exposed to the magnetic field (assumed uniform). Furthermore, if the magnetic field B is made stronger, the force is found to be proportionally greater. The force also depends on the angle θ between the current direction and the magnetic field (Fig. 27–12), being proportional to $\sin\theta$. Thus, the force on a wire carrying a current I with length ℓ in a uniform magnetic field B is given by

$$F \propto I\ell B \sin\theta.$$

When the current is perpendicular to the field lines ($\theta = 90°$), the force is strongest. When the wire is parallel to the magnetic field lines ($\theta = 0°$), there is no force at all.

Up to now we have not defined the magnetic field strength precisely. In fact, the magnetic field B can be conveniently defined in terms of the above proportion so that the proportionality constant is precisely 1. Thus we have

$$F = I\ell B \sin\theta. \qquad \textbf{(27–1)}$$

If the direction of the current is perpendicular to the field $\vec{B}$ ($\theta = 90°$), then the force is

$$F_{max} = I\ell B. \qquad [\text{current} \perp \vec{B}] \quad \textbf{(27–2)}$$

If the current is parallel to the field ($\theta = 0°$), the force is zero. The magnitude of $\vec{B}$ can be defined using Eq. 27–2 as $B = F_{max}/I\ell$, where F_{max} is the magnitude of the force on a straight length ℓ of wire carrying a current I when the wire is perpendicular to $\vec{B}$.

The relation between the force $\vec{F}$ on a wire carrying current I, and the magnetic field $\vec{B}$ that causes the force, can be written as a vector equation. To do so, we recall that the direction of $\vec{F}$ is given by the right-hand rule (Fig. 27–11c), and the magnitude by Eq. 27–1. This is consistent with the definition of the vector cross product (see Section 11–2), so we can write

$$\vec{F} = I\vec{\ell} \times \vec{B}; \qquad \textbf{(27–3)}$$

here, $\vec{\ell}$ is a vector whose magnitude is the length of the wire and its direction is along the wire (assumed straight) in the direction of the conventional (positive) current.

FIGURE 27–11 (a) Force on a current-carrying wire placed in a magnetic field $\vec{B}$; (b) same, but current reversed; (c) right-hand rule for setup in (b).

Right-hand-rule 2:
force on current exerted by $\vec{B}$

FIGURE 27–12 Current-carrying wire in a magnetic field. Force on the wire is directed into the page.

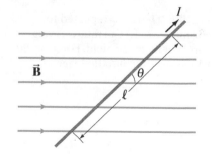

Equation 27–3 applies if the magnetic field is uniform and the wire is straight. If $\vec{\mathbf{B}}$ is not uniform, or if the wire does not everywhere make the same angle θ with $\vec{\mathbf{B}}$, then Eq. 27–3 can be written more generally as

$$d\vec{\mathbf{F}} = I\,d\vec{\boldsymbol{\ell}} \times \vec{\mathbf{B}}, \qquad\qquad (27\text{–}4)$$

where $d\vec{\mathbf{F}}$ is the infinitesimal force acting on a differential length $d\vec{\boldsymbol{\ell}}$ of the wire. The total force on the wire is then found by integrating.

Equation 27–4 can serve (just as well as Eq. 27–2 or 27–3) as a practical definition of $\vec{\mathbf{B}}$. An equivalent way to define $\vec{\mathbf{B}}$, in terms of the force on a moving electric charge, is discussed in the next Section.

EXERCISE C A wire carrying current I is perpendicular to a magnetic field of strength B. Assuming a fixed length of wire, which of the following changes will result in decreasing the force on the wire by a factor of 2? (a) Decrease the angle from 90° to 45°; (b) decrease the angle from 90° to 30°; (c) decrease the current in the wire to $I/2$; (d) decrease the magnetic field strength to $B/2$; (e) none of these will do it.

The SI unit for magnetic field B is the **tesla** (T). From Eqs. 27–1, 2, 3, or 4, we see that $1\,\text{T} = 1\,\text{N/A}\cdot\text{m}$. An older name for the tesla is the "weber per meter squared" $\left(1\,\text{Wb/m}^2 = 1\,\text{T}\right)$. Another unit sometimes used to specify magnetic field is a cgs unit, the **gauss** (G): $1\,\text{G} = 10^{-4}\,\text{T}$. A field given in gauss should always be changed to teslas before using with other SI units. To get a "feel" for these units, we note that the magnetic field of the Earth at its surface is about $\frac{1}{2}\,\text{G}$ or $0.5 \times 10^{-4}\,\text{T}$. On the other hand, the field near a small magnet attached to your refrigerator may be $100\,\text{G}$ $(0.01\,\text{T})$ whereas strong electromagnets can produce fields on the order of $2\,\text{T}$ and superconducting magnets can produce over $10\,\text{T}$.

EXAMPLE 27–1 **Magnetic force on a current-carrying wire.** A wire carrying a 30-A current has a length $\ell = 12\,\text{cm}$ between the pole faces of a magnet at an angle $\theta = 60°$ (Fig. 27–12). The magnetic field is approximately uniform at $0.90\,\text{T}$. We ignore the field beyond the pole pieces. What is the magnitude of the force on the wire?

APPROACH We use Eq. 27–1, $F = I\ell B \sin\theta$.

SOLUTION The force F on the 12-cm length of wire within the uniform field B is

$$F = I\ell B \sin\theta = (30\,\text{A})(0.12\,\text{m})(0.90\,\text{T})(0.866) = 2.8\,\text{N}.$$

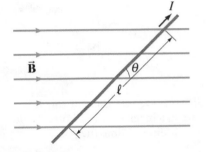

FIGURE 27–12 (Repeated for Example 27–1.) Current-carrying wire in a magnetic field. Force on the wire is directed into the page.

EXERCISE D A straight power line carries 30 A and is perpendicular to the Earth's magnetic field of $0.50 \times 10^{-4}\,\text{T}$. What magnitude force is exerted on 100 m of this power line?

On a diagram, when we want to represent an electric current or a magnetic field that is pointing out of the page (toward us) or into the page, we use $\odot$ or $\times$, respectively. The $\odot$ is meant to resemble the tip of an arrow pointing directly toward the reader, whereas the $\times$ or $\otimes$ resembles the tail of an arrow moving away. (See Figs. 27–13 and 27–14.)

EXAMPLE 27–2 **Measuring a magnetic field.** A rectangular loop of wire hangs vertically as shown in Fig. 27–13. A magnetic field $\vec{\mathbf{B}}$ is directed horizontally, perpendicular to the wire, and points out of the page at all points as represented by the symbol $\odot$. The magnetic field $\vec{\mathbf{B}}$ is very nearly uniform along the horizontal portion of wire ab (length $\ell = 10.0\,\text{cm}$) which is near the center of the gap of a large magnet producing the field. The top portion of the wire loop is free of the field. The loop hangs from a balance which measures a downward magnetic force (in addition to the gravitational force) of $F = 3.48 \times 10^{-2}\,\text{N}$ when the wire carries a current $I = 0.245\,\text{A}$. What is the magnitude of the magnetic field B?

APPROACH Three straight sections of the wire loop are in the magnetic field: a horizontal section and two vertical sections. We apply Eq. 27–1 to each section and use the right-hand rule.

SOLUTION The magnetic force on the left vertical section of wire points to the left; the force on the vertical section on the right points to the right. These two forces are equal and in opposite directions and so add up to zero. Hence, the net magnetic force on the loop is that on the horizontal section ab, whose length is $\ell = 0.100$ m. The angle θ between $\vec{B}$ and the wire is $\theta = 90°$, so $\sin \theta = 1$. Thus Eq. 27–1 gives

$$B = \frac{F}{I\ell} = \frac{3.48 \times 10^{-2}\,\text{N}}{(0.245\,\text{A})(0.100\,\text{m})} = 1.42\,\text{T}.$$

NOTE This technique can be a precise means of determining magnetic field strength.

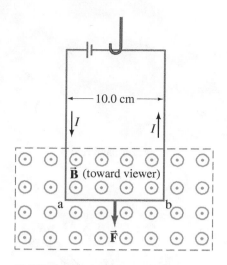

FIGURE 27–13 Measuring a magnetic field $\vec{B}$. Example 27–2.

EXAMPLE 27–3 **Magnetic force on a semicircular wire.** A rigid wire, carrying a current I, consists of a semicircle of radius R and two straight portions as shown in Fig. 27–14. The wire lies in a plane perpendicular to a uniform magnetic field $\vec{B}_0$. Note choice of x and y axis. The straight portions each have length ℓ within the field. Determine the net force on the wire due to the magnetic field $\vec{B}_0$.

APPROACH The forces on the two straight sections are equal $(= I\ell B_0)$ and in opposite directions, so they cancel. Hence the net force is that on the semicircular portion.

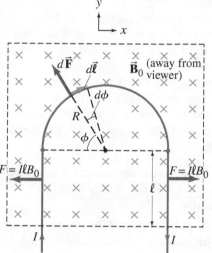

FIGURE 27–14 Example 27–3.

SOLUTION We divide the semicircle into short lengths $d\ell = R\,d\phi$ as indicated in Fig. 27–14, and use Eq. 27–4, $d\vec{F} = I\,d\vec{\ell} \times \vec{B}$, to find

$$dF = IB_0 R\,d\phi,$$

where dF is the force on the length $d\ell = R\,d\phi$, and the angle between $d\vec{\ell}$ and $\vec{B}_0$ is $90°$ (so $\sin\theta = 1$ in the cross product). The x component of the force $d\vec{F}$ on the segment $d\vec{\ell}$ shown, and the x component of $d\vec{F}$ for a symmetrically located $d\vec{\ell}$ on the other side of the semicircle, will cancel each other. Thus for the entire semicircle there will be no x component of force. Hence we need be concerned only with the y components, each equal to $dF\sin\phi$, and the total force will have magnitude

$$F = \int_0^\pi dF\sin\phi = IB_0 R \int_0^\pi \sin\phi\,d\phi = -IB_0 R\cos\phi\Big|_0^\pi = 2IB_0 R,$$

with direction vertically upward along the y axis in Fig. 27–14.

27–4 Force on an Electric Charge Moving in a Magnetic Field

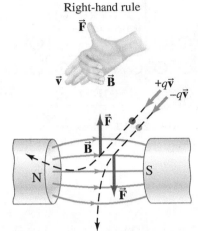

Right-hand rule

FIGURE 27–15 Force on charged particles due to a magnetic field is perpendicular to the magnetic field direction. If $\vec{v}$ is horizontal, then $\vec{F}$ is vertical.

Right-hand-rule 3:
force on moving charge exerted by $\vec{B}$

We have seen that a current-carrying wire experiences a force when placed in a magnetic field. Since a current in a wire consists of moving electric charges, we might expect that freely moving charged particles (not in a wire) would also experience a force when passing through a magnetic field. Indeed, this is the case.

From what we already know we can predict the force on a single moving electric charge. If N such particles of charge q pass by a given point in time t, they constitute a current $I = Nq/t$. We let t be the time for a charge q to travel a distance ℓ in a magnetic field $\vec{B}$; then $\vec{\ell} = \vec{v}t$ where $\vec{v}$ is the velocity of the particle. Thus, the force on these N particles is, by Eq. 27–3, $\vec{F} = I\vec{\ell} \times \vec{B} = (Nq/t)(\vec{v}t) \times \vec{B} = Nq\vec{v} \times \vec{B}$. The force on *one* of the N particles is then

$$\vec{F} = q\vec{v} \times \vec{B}. \qquad (27\text{–}5a)$$

This basic and important result can be considered as an alternative way of defining the magnetic field $\vec{B}$, in place of Eq. 27–4 or 27–3. The magnitude of the force in Eq. 27–5a is

$$F = qvB \sin \theta. \qquad (27\text{–}5b)$$

This gives the magnitude of the force on a particle of charge q moving with velocity $\vec{v}$ at a point where the magnetic field has magnitude B. The angle between $\vec{v}$ and $\vec{B}$ is θ. The force is greatest when the particle moves perpendicular to $\vec{B}$ ($\theta = 90°$):

$$F_{max} = qvB. \qquad [\vec{v} \perp \vec{B}]$$

The force is *zero* if the particle moves *parallel* to the field lines ($\theta = 0°$). The *direction* of the force is perpendicular to the magnetic field $\vec{B}$ and to the velocity $\vec{v}$ of the particle. It is given again by a **right-hand rule** (as for any cross product): you orient your right hand so that your outstretched fingers point along the direction of the particle's velocity ($\vec{v}$), and when you bend your fingers they must point along the direction of $\vec{B}$. Then your thumb will point in the direction of the force. This is true only for *positively* charged particles, and will be "up" for the positive particle shown in Fig. 27–15. For negatively charged particles, the force is in exactly the opposite direction, "down" in Fig. 27–15.

CONCEPTUAL EXAMPLE 27–4 | **Negative charge near a magnet.** A negative charge $-Q$ is placed at rest near a magnet. Will the charge begin to move? Will it feel a force? What if the charge were positive, $+Q$?

RESPONSE No to all questions. A charge at rest has velocity equal to zero. Magnetic fields exert a force only on moving electric charges (Eqs. 27–5).

EXERCISE E Return to the Chapter-Opening Question, page 707, and answer it again now. Try to explain why you may have answered differently the first time.

EXAMPLE 27–5 **Magnetic force on a proton.** A magnetic field exerts a force of 8.0×10^{-14} N toward the west on a proton moving vertically upward at a speed of 5.0×10^6 m/s (Fig. 27–16a). When moving horizontally in a northerly direction, the force on the proton is zero (Fig. 27–16b). Determine the magnitude and direction of the magnetic field in this region. (The charge on a proton is $q = +e = 1.6 \times 10^{-19}$ C.)

APPROACH Since the force on the proton is zero when moving north, the field must be in a north–south direction. In order to produce a force to the west when the proton moves upward, the right-hand rule tells us that $\vec{B}$ must point toward the north. (Your thumb points west and the outstretched fingers of your right hand point upward only when your bent fingers point north.) The magnitude of $\vec{B}$ is found using Eq. 27–5b.

SOLUTION Equation 27–5b with $\theta = 90°$ gives

$$B = \frac{F}{qv} = \frac{8.0 \times 10^{-14}\,\text{N}}{(1.6 \times 10^{-19}\,\text{C})(5.0 \times 10^6\,\text{m/s})} = 0.10\,\text{T}.$$

FIGURE 27–16 Example 27–5.

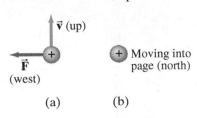

(a) (b)

EXAMPLE 27-6 ESTIMATE Magnetic force on ions during a nerve pulse.

Estimate the magnetic force due to the Earth's magnetic field on ions crossing a cell membrane during an action potential. Assume the speed of the ions is 10^{-2} m/s (Section 25–10).

APPROACH Using $F = qvB$, set the magnetic field of the Earth to be roughly $B \approx 10^{-4}$ T, and the charge $q \approx e \approx 10^{-19}$ C.

SOLUTION $F \approx (10^{-19}\,\text{C})(10^{-2}\,\text{m/s})(10^{-4}\,\text{T}) = 10^{-25}$ N.

NOTE This is an extremely small force. Yet it is thought migrating animals do somehow detect the Earth's magnetic field, and this is an area of active research.

The path of a charged particle moving in a plane perpendicular to a uniform magnetic field is a circle as we shall now show. In Fig. 27–17 the magnetic field is directed *into* the paper, as represented by ×'s. An electron at point P is moving to the right, and the force on it at this point is downward as shown (use the right-hand rule and reverse the direction for negative charge). The electron is thus deflected toward the page bottom. A moment later, say, when it reaches point Q, the force is still perpendicular to the velocity and is in the direction shown. Because the force is always perpendicular to $\vec{v}$, the magnitude of $\vec{v}$ does not change—the electron moves at constant speed. We saw in Chapter 5 that if the force on a particle is always perpendicular to its velocity $\vec{v}$, the particle moves in a circle and has a centripetal acceleration $a = v^2/r$ (Eq. 5–1). Thus a charged particle moves in a circular path with constant centripetal acceleration in a uniform magnetic field (see Example 27–7). The electron moves clockwise in Fig. 27–17. A positive particle in this field would feel a force in the opposite direction and would thus move counterclockwise.

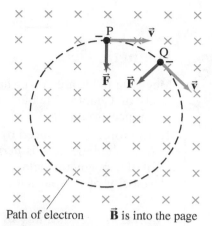

Path of electron   **B** is into the page

FIGURE 27–17 Force exerted by a uniform magnetic field on a moving charged particle (in this case, an electron) produces a circular path.

EXAMPLE 27-7 Electron's path in a uniform magnetic field.

An electron travels at 2.0×10^7 m/s in a plane perpendicular to a uniform 0.010-T magnetic field. Describe its path quantitatively.

APPROACH The electron moves at speed v in a curved path and so must have a centripetal acceleration $a = v^2/r$ (Eq. 5–1). We find the radius of curvature using Newton's second law. The force is given by Eq. 27–5b with $\sin \theta = 1$: $F = qvB$.

SOLUTION We insert F and a into Newton's second law:

$$\Sigma F = ma$$
$$qvB = \frac{mv^2}{r}.$$

We solve for r and find

$$r = \frac{mv}{qB}.$$

Since $\vec{F}$ is perpendicular to $\vec{v}$, the magnitude of $\vec{v}$ doesn't change. From this equation we see that if $\vec{B}$ = constant, then r = constant, and the curve must be a circle as we claimed above. To get r we put in the numbers:

$$r = \frac{(9.1 \times 10^{-31}\,\text{kg})(2.0 \times 10^7\,\text{m/s})}{(1.6 \times 10^{-19}\,\text{C})(0.010\,\text{T})} = 1.1 \times 10^{-2}\,\text{m} = 1.1\,\text{cm}.$$

NOTE See Fig. 27–18.

FIGURE 27–18 The blue ring inside the glass tube is the glow of a beam of electrons that ionize the gas molecules. The red coils of current-carrying wire produce a nearly uniform magnetic field, illustrating the circular path of charged particles in a uniform magnetic field.

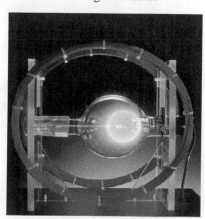

The time T required for a particle of charge q moving with constant speed v to make one circular revolution in a uniform magnetic field $\vec{B}$ ($\perp \vec{v}$) is $T = 2\pi r/v$, where $2\pi r$ is the circumference of its circular path. From Example 27–7, $r = mv/qB$, so

$$T = \frac{2\pi m}{qB}.$$

Since T is the period of rotation, the frequency of rotation is

$$f = \frac{1}{T} = \frac{qB}{2\pi m}. \tag{27-6}$$

This is often called the **cyclotron frequency** of a particle in a field because this is the frequency at which particles revolve in a cyclotron (see Problem 66).

CONCEPTUAL EXAMPLE 27–8 | Stopping charged particles. Can a magnetic field be used to stop a single charged particle, as an electric field can?

RESPONSE No, because the force is always *perpendicular* to the velocity of the particle and thus cannot change the magnitude of its velocity. It also means the magnetic force cannot do work on the particle and so cannot change the kinetic energy of the particle.

PROBLEM SOLVING

Magnetic Fields

Magnetic fields are somewhat analogous to the electric fields of Chapter 21, but there are several important differences to recall:

1. The force experienced by a charged particle moving in a magnetic field is *perpendicular* to the direction of the magnetic field (and to the direction of the velocity of the particle), whereas the force exerted by an electric field is *parallel* to the direction of the field (and unaffected by the velocity of the particle).

2. The *right-hand rule*, in its different forms, is intended to help you determine the directions of magnetic field, and the forces they exert, and/or the directions of electric current or charged particle velocity. The right-hand rules (Table 27–1) are designed to deal with the "perpendicular" nature of these quantities.

TABLE 27–1 Summary of Right-hand Rules (= RHR)

Physical Situation	Example	How to Orient Right Hand	Result
1. Magnetic field produced by current (RHR-1)	I $\vec{B}$ Fig. 27–8c	Wrap fingers around wire with thumb pointing in direction of current I	Fingers point in direction of $\vec{B}$
2. Force on electric current I due to magnetic field (RHR-2)	$\vec{F}$ $\vec{I}$ $\vec{B}$ Fig. 27–11c	Fingers point straight along current I, then bend along magnetic field $\vec{B}$	Thumb points in direction of the force $\vec{F}$
3. Force on electric charge $+q$ due to magnetic field (RHR-3)	$\vec{F}$ $\vec{v}$ $\vec{B}$ Fig. 27–15	Fingers point along particle's velocity $\vec{v}$, then along $\vec{B}$	Thumb points in direction of the force $\vec{F}$

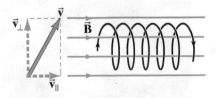

FIGURE 27–19 Example 27–9.

CONCEPTUAL EXAMPLE 27–9 | A helical path. What is the path of a charged particle in a uniform magnetic field if its velocity is *not* perpendicular to the magnetic field?

RESPONSE The velocity vector can be broken down into components parallel and perpendicular to the field. The velocity component parallel to the field lines experiences no force ($\theta = 0$), so this component remains constant. The velocity component perpendicular to the field results in circular motion about the field lines. Putting these two motions together produces a helical (spiral) motion around the field lines as shown in Fig. 27–19.

EXERCISE F What is the sign of the charge in Fig. 27–19? How would you modify the drawing if the sign were reversed?

*Aurora Borealis

Charged ions approach the Earth from the Sun (the "solar wind") and enter the atmosphere mainly near the poles, sometimes causing a phenomenon called the **aurora borealis** or "northern lights" in northern latitudes. To see why, consider Example 27–9 and Fig. 27–20 (see also Fig. 27–19). In Fig. 27–20 we imagine a stream of charged particles approaching the Earth. The velocity component *perpendicular* to the field for each particle becomes a circular orbit around the field lines, whereas the velocity component *parallel* to the field carries the particle along the field lines toward the poles. As a particle approaches the N pole, the magnetic field is stronger and the radius of the helical path becomes smaller.

A high concentration of charged particles ionizes the air, and as the electrons recombine with atoms, light is emitted (Chapter 37) which is the aurora. Auroras are especially spectacular during periods of high sunspot activity when the solar wind brings more charged particles toward Earth.

Lorentz Equation

If a particle of charge q moves with velocity $\vec{v}$ in the presence of both a magnetic field $\vec{B}$ and an electric field $\vec{E}$, it will feel a force

$$\vec{F} = q(\vec{E} + \vec{v} \times \vec{B}) \qquad (27\text{–}7)$$

where we have made use of Eqs. 21–3 and 27–5a. Equation 27–7 is often called the **Lorentz equation** and is considered one of the basic equations in physics.

CONCEPTUAL EXAMPLE 27–10 **Velocity selector, or filter: Crossed $\vec{E}$ and $\vec{B}$ fields.** Some electronic devices and experiments need a beam of charged particles all moving at nearly the same velocity. This can be achieved using both a uniform electric field and a uniform magnetic field, arranged so they are at right angles to each other. As shown in Fig. 27–21a, particles of charge q pass through slit S_1 and enter the region where $\vec{B}$ points into the page and $\vec{E}$ points down from the positive plate toward the negative plate. If the particles enter with different velocities, show how this device "selects" a particular velocity, and determine what this velocity is.

RESPONSE After passing through slit S_1, each particle is subject to two forces as shown in Fig. 27–21b. If q is positive, the magnetic force is upwards and the electric force downwards. (Vice versa if q is negative.) The exit slit, S_2, is assumed to be directly in line with S_1 and the particles' velocity $\vec{v}$. Depending on the magnitude of $\vec{v}$, some particles will be bent upwards and some downwards. The only ones to make it through the slit S_2 will be those for which the net force is zero: $\Sigma F = qvB - qE = 0$. Hence this device selects particles whose velocity is

$$v = \frac{E}{B}. \qquad (27\text{–}8)$$

This result does not depend on the sign of the charge q.

EXERCISE G A particle in a velocity selector as diagrammed in Fig. 27–21 hits below the exit hole, S_2. This means that the particle (a) is going faster than the selected speed; (b) is going slower than the selected speed; (c) answer a is true if $q > 0$, b is true if $q < 0$; (d) answer a is true if $q < 0$, b is true if $q > 0$.

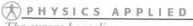

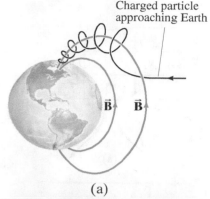

Charged particle approaching Earth

(a)

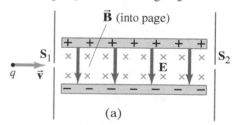

(b)

FIGURE 27–20 (a) Diagram showing a negatively charged particle that approaches the Earth and is "captured" by the magnetic field of the Earth. Such particles follow the field lines toward the poles as shown. (b) Photo of aurora borealis (here, in Kansas, where it is a rare sight).

FIGURE 27–21 A velocity selector: if $v = E/B$, the particles passing through S_1 make it through S_2.

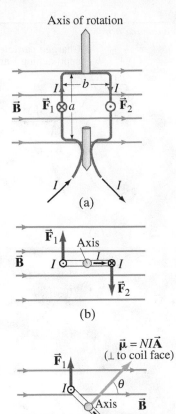

Axis of rotation

(a)

(b)

$$\vec{\boldsymbol{\mu}} = NI\vec{\mathbf{A}}$$
($\perp$ to coil face)

(c)

FIGURE 27–22 Calculating the torque on a current loop in a magnetic field $\vec{\mathbf{B}}$. (a) Loop face parallel to $\vec{\mathbf{B}}$ field lines; (b) top view; (c) loop makes an angle to $\vec{\mathbf{B}}$, reducing the torque since the lever arm is reduced.

27–5 Torque on a Current Loop; Magnetic Dipole Moment

When an electric current flows in a closed loop of wire placed in an external magnetic field, as shown in Fig. 27–22, the magnetic force on the current can produce a torque. This is the principle behind a number of important practical devices, including motors and analog voltmeters and ammeters, which we discuss in the next Section. The interaction between a current and a magnetic field is important in other areas as well, including atomic physics.

Current flows through the rectangular loop in Fig. 27–22a, whose face we assume is parallel to $\vec{\mathbf{B}}$. $\vec{\mathbf{B}}$ exerts no force and no torque on the horizontal segments of wire because they are parallel to the field and $\sin\theta = 0$ in Eq. 27–1. But the magnetic field does exert a force on each of the vertical sections of wire as shown, $\vec{\mathbf{F}}_1$ and $\vec{\mathbf{F}}_2$ (see also top view, Fig. 27–22b). By right-hand-rule 2 (Fig. 27–11c or Table 27–1) the direction of the force on the upward current on the left is in the opposite direction from the equal magnitude force $\vec{\mathbf{F}}_2$ on the downward current on the right. These forces give rise to a net torque that acts to rotate the coil about its vertical axis.

Let us calculate the magnitude of this torque. From Eq. 27–2 (current $\perp \vec{\mathbf{B}}$), the force $F = IaB$, where a is the length of the vertical arm of the coil. The lever arm for each force is $b/2$, where b is the width of the coil and the "axis" is at the midpoint. The torques produced by $\vec{\mathbf{F}}_1$ and $\vec{\mathbf{F}}_2$ act in the same direction, so the total torque is the sum of the two torques:

$$\tau = IaB\frac{b}{2} + IaB\frac{b}{2} = IabB = IAB,$$

where $A = ab$ is the area of the coil. If the coil consists of N loops of wire, the current is then NI, so the torque becomes

$$\tau = NIAB.$$

If the coil makes an angle θ with the magnetic field, as shown in Fig. 27–22c, the forces are unchanged, but each lever arm is reduced from $\frac{1}{2}b$ to $\frac{1}{2}b\sin\theta$. Note that the angle θ is taken to be the angle between $\vec{\mathbf{B}}$ and the perpendicular to the face of the coil, Fig. 27–22c. So the torque becomes

$$\tau = NIAB\sin\theta. \tag{27–9}$$

This formula, derived here for a rectangular coil, is valid for any shape of flat coil.

The quantity NIA is called the **magnetic dipole moment** of the coil and is considered a vector:

$$\vec{\boldsymbol{\mu}} = NI\vec{\mathbf{A}}, \tag{27–10}$$

where the direction of $\vec{\mathbf{A}}$ (and therefore of $\vec{\boldsymbol{\mu}}$) is *perpendicular* to the plane of the coil (the green arrow in Fig. 27–22c) consistent with the right-hand rule (cup your right hand so your fingers wrap around the loop in the direction of current flow, then your thumb points in the direction of $\vec{\boldsymbol{\mu}}$ and $\vec{\mathbf{A}}$). With this definition of $\vec{\boldsymbol{\mu}}$, we can rewrite Eq. 27–9 in vector form:

$$\vec{\boldsymbol{\tau}} = NI\vec{\mathbf{A}} \times \vec{\mathbf{B}}$$

or

$$\vec{\boldsymbol{\tau}} = \vec{\boldsymbol{\mu}} \times \vec{\mathbf{B}}, \tag{27–11}$$

which gives the correct magnitude and direction for the torque $\vec{\boldsymbol{\tau}}$.

Equation 27–11 has the same form as Eq. 21–9b for an electric dipole (with electric dipole moment $\vec{\mathbf{p}}$) in an electric field $\vec{\mathbf{E}}$, which is $\vec{\boldsymbol{\tau}} = \vec{\mathbf{p}} \times \vec{\mathbf{E}}$. And just as an electric dipole has potential energy given by $U = -\vec{\mathbf{p}}\cdot\vec{\mathbf{E}}$ when in an electric field, we expect a similar form for a magnetic dipole in a magnetic field. In order to rotate a current loop (Fig. 27–22) so as to increase θ, we must do work against the torque due to the magnetic field.

Hence the potential energy depends on angle (see Eq. 10–22, the work-energy principle for rotational motion) as

$$U = \int \tau \, d\theta = \int NIAB \sin\theta \, d\theta = -\mu B \cos\theta + C.$$

If we choose $U = 0$ at $\theta = \pi/2$, then the arbitrary constant C is zero and the potential energy is

$$U = -\mu B \cos\theta = -\vec{\mu} \cdot \vec{B}, \tag{27–12}$$

as expected (compare Eq. 21–10). Bar magnets and compass needles, as well as current loops, can be considered as magnetic dipoles. Note the striking similarities of the fields produced by a bar magnet and a current loop, Figs. 27–4b and 27–9.

EXAMPLE 27–11 Torque on a coil. A circular coil of wire has a diameter of 20.0 cm and contains 10 loops. The current in each loop is 3.00 A, and the coil is placed in a 2.00-T external magnetic field. Determine the maximum and minimum torque exerted on the coil by the field.

APPROACH Equation 27–9 is valid for any shape of coil, including circular loops. Maximum and minimum torque are determined by the angle θ the coil makes with the magnetic field.

SOLUTION The area of one loop of the coil is

$$A = \pi r^2 = \pi(0.100\,\text{m})^2 = 3.14 \times 10^{-2}\,\text{m}^2.$$

The maximum torque occurs when the coil's face is parallel to the magnetic field, so $\theta = 90°$ in Fig. 27–22c, and $\sin\theta = 1$ in Eq. 27–9:

$$\tau = NIAB \sin\theta = (10)(3.00\,\text{A})(3.14 \times 10^{-2}\,\text{m}^2)(2.00\,\text{T})(1) = 1.88\,\text{N·m}.$$

The minimum torque occurs if $\sin\theta = 0$, for which $\theta = 0°$, and then $\tau = 0$ from Eq. 27–9.

NOTE If the coil is free to turn, it will rotate toward the orientation with $\theta = 0°$.

EXAMPLE 27–12 Magnetic moment of a hydrogen atom. Determine the magnetic dipole moment of the electron orbiting the proton of a hydrogen atom at a given instant, assuming (in the Bohr model) it is in its ground state with a circular orbit of radius $0.529 \times 10^{-10}\,\text{m}$. [This is a very rough picture of atomic structure, but nonetheless gives an accurate result.]

APPROACH We start by setting the electrostatic force on the electron due to the proton equal to $ma = mv^2/r$ since the electron's acceleration is centripetal.

SOLUTION The electron is held in its orbit by the coulomb force, so Newton's second law, $F = ma$, gives

$$\frac{e^2}{4\pi\epsilon_0 r^2} = \frac{mv^2}{r};$$

so

$$v = \sqrt{\frac{e^2}{4\pi\epsilon_0 mr}}$$

$$= \sqrt{\frac{(8.99 \times 10^9\,\text{N·m}^2/\text{C}^2)(1.60 \times 10^{-19}\,\text{C})^2}{(9.11 \times 10^{-31}\,\text{kg})(0.529 \times 10^{-10}\,\text{m})}} = 2.19 \times 10^6\,\text{m/s}.$$

Since current is the electric charge that passes a given point per unit time, the revolving electron is equivalent to a current

$$I = \frac{e}{T} = \frac{ev}{2\pi r},$$

where $T = 2\pi r/v$ is the time required for one orbit. Since the area of the orbit is $A = \pi r^2$, the magnetic dipole moment is

$$\mu = IA = \frac{ev}{2\pi r}(\pi r^2) = \tfrac{1}{2}evr$$

$$= \tfrac{1}{2}(1.60 \times 10^{-19}\,\text{C})(2.19 \times 10^6\,\text{m/s})(0.529 \times 10^{-10}\,\text{m}) = 9.27 \times 10^{-24}\,\text{A·m}^2,$$

or $9.27 \times 10^{-24}\,\text{J/T}$.

*27–6 Applications: Motors, Loudspeakers, Galvanometers

*Electric Motors

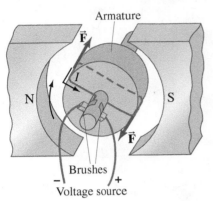

FIGURE 27–23 Diagram of a simple dc motor.

An **electric motor** changes electric energy into (rotational) mechanical energy. A motor works on the principle that a torque is exerted on a coil of current-carrying wire suspended in the magnetic field of a magnet, described in Section 27–5. The coil is mounted on a large cylinder called the **rotor** or **armature**, Fig. 27–23, so that it can rotate continuously in one direction. Actually, there are several coils, although only one is indicated in the Figure. The armature is mounted on a shaft or axle. When the armature is in the position shown in Fig. 27–23, the magnetic field exerts forces on the current in the loop as shown (perpendicular to $\vec{B}$ and to the current direction). However, when the coil, which is rotating clockwise in Fig. 27–23, passes beyond the vertical position, the forces would then act to return the coil back to vertical if the current remained the same. But if the current could somehow be reversed at that critical moment, the forces would reverse, and the coil would continue rotating in the same direction. Thus, alternation of the current is necessary if a motor is to turn continuously in one direction. This can be achieved in a **dc motor** with the use of **commutators** and **brushes**: as shown in Fig. 27–24, input current passes through stationary brushes that rub against the conducting commutators mounted on the motor shaft. At every half revolution, each commutator changes its connection over to the other brush. Thus the current in the coil reverses every half revolution as required for continuous rotation.

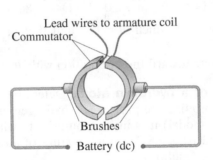

FIGURE 27–24 The commutator-brush arrangement in a dc motor ensures alternation of the current in the armature to keep rotation continuous. The commutators are attached to the motor shaft and turn with it, whereas the brushes remain stationary.

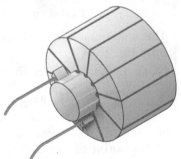

FIGURE 27–25 Motor with many windings.

Most motors contain several coils, called *windings*, each located in a different place on the armature, Fig. 27–25. Current flows through each coil only during a small part of a revolution, at the time when its orientation results in the maximum torque. In this way, a motor produces a much steadier torque than can be obtained from a single coil.

An **ac motor**, with ac current as input, can work without commutators since the current itself alternates. Many motors use wire coils to produce the magnetic field (electromagnets) instead of a permanent magnet. Indeed the design of most motors is more complex than described here, but the general principles remain the same.

*Loudspeakers

FIGURE 27–26 Loudspeaker.

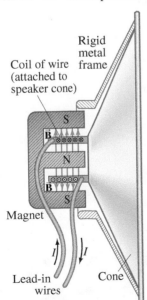

A **loudspeaker** also works on the principle that a magnet exerts a force on a current-carrying wire. The electrical output of a stereo or TV set is connected to the wire leads of the speaker. The speaker leads are connected internally to a coil of wire, which is itself attached to the speaker cone, Fig. 27–26. The speaker cone is usually made of stiffened cardboard and is mounted so that it can move back and forth freely. A permanent magnet is mounted directly in line with the coil of wire. When the alternating current of an audio signal flows through the wire coil, which is free to move within the magnet, the coil experiences a force due to the magnetic field of the magnet. (The force is to the right at the instant shown in Fig. 27–26.)

As the current alternates at the frequency of the audio signal, the coil and attached speaker cone move back and forth at the same frequency, causing alternate compressions and rarefactions of the adjacent air, and sound waves are produced. A speaker thus changes electrical energy into sound energy, and the frequencies and intensities of the emitted sound waves can be an accurate reproduction of the electrical input.

*Galvanometer

The basic component of analog meters (those with pointer and dial), including analog ammeters, voltmeters, and ohmmeters, is a galvanometer. We have already seen how these meters are designed (Section 26–7), and now we can examine how the crucial element, a galvanometer, works. As shown in Fig. 27–27, a **galvanometer** consists of a coil of wire (with attached pointer) suspended in the magnetic field of a permanent magnet. When current flows through the loop of wire, the magnetic field exerts a torque on the loop, as given by Eq. 27–9,

$$\tau = NIAB \sin \theta.$$

This torque is opposed by a spring which exerts a torque τ_s approximately proportional to the angle ϕ through which it is turned (Hooke's law). That is,

$$\tau_s = k\phi,$$

where k is the stiffness constant of the spring. The coil and attached pointer rotate to the angle where the torques balance. When the needle is in equilibrium at rest, the torques are equal: $k\phi = NIAB \sin \theta$, or

$$\phi = \frac{NIAB \sin \theta}{k}.$$

The deflection of the pointer, ϕ, is directly proportional to the current I flowing in the coil, but also depends on the angle θ the coil makes with $\vec{\mathbf{B}}$. For a useful meter we need ϕ to depend only on the current I, independent of θ. To solve this problem, magnets with curved pole pieces are used and the galvanometer coil is wrapped around a cylindrical iron core as shown in Fig. 27–28. The iron tends to concentrate the magnetic field lines so that $\vec{\mathbf{B}}$ always points parallel to the face of the coil at the wire outside the core. The force is then always perpendicular to the face of the coil, and the torque will not vary with angle. Thus ϕ will be proportional to I as required.

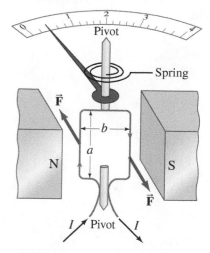

FIGURE 27–27 Galvanometer.

FIGURE 27–28 Galvanometer coil wrapped on an iron core.

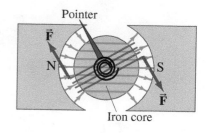

27–7 Discovery and Properties of the Electron

The electron plays a basic role in our understanding of electricity and magnetism today. But its existence was not suggested until the 1890s. We discuss it here because magnetic fields were crucial for measuring its properties.

Toward the end of the nineteenth century, studies were being done on the discharge of electricity through rarefied gases. One apparatus, diagrammed in Fig. 27–29, was a glass tube fitted with electrodes and evacuated so only a small amount of gas remained inside. When a very high voltage was applied to the electrodes, a dark space seemed to extend outward from the cathode (negative electrode) toward the opposite end of the tube; and that far end of the tube would glow. If one or more screens containing a small hole was inserted as shown, the glow was restricted to a tiny spot on the end of the tube. It seemed as though something being emitted by the cathode traveled to the opposite end of the tube. These "somethings" were named **cathode rays**.

There was much discussion at the time about what these rays might be. Some scientists thought they might resemble light. But the observation that the bright spot at the end of the tube could be deflected to one side by an electric or magnetic field suggested that cathode rays could be charged particles; and the direction of the deflection was consistent with a negative charge. Furthermore, if the tube contained certain types of rarefied gas, the path of the cathode rays was made visible by a slight glow.

FIGURE 27–29 Discharge tube. In some models, one of the screens is the anode (positive plate).

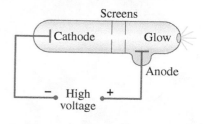

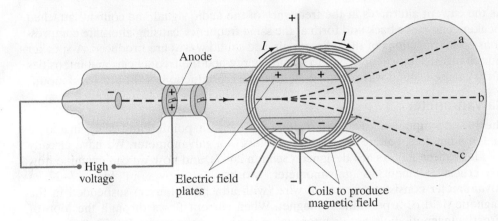

FIGURE 27–30 Cathode rays deflected by electric and magnetic fields.

Anode

High voltage

Electric field plates

Coils to produce magnetic field

Estimates of the charge e of the (assumed) cathode-ray particles, as well as of their charge-to-mass ratio e/m, had been made by 1897. But in that year, J. J. Thomson (1856–1940) was able to measure e/m directly, using the apparatus shown in Fig. 27–30. Cathode rays are accelerated by a high voltage and then pass between a pair of parallel plates built into the tube. The voltage applied to the plates produces an electric field, and a pair of coils produces a magnetic field. When only the electric field is present, say with the upper plate positive, the cathode rays are deflected upward as in path a in Fig. 27–30. If only a magnetic field exists, say inward, the rays are deflected downward along path c. These observations are just what is expected for a negatively charged particle. The force on the rays due to the magnetic field is $F = evB$, where e is the charge and v is the velocity of the cathode rays. In the absence of an electric field, the rays are bent into a curved path, so we have, from $F = ma$,

$$evB = m\frac{v^2}{r},$$

and thus

$$\frac{e}{m} = \frac{v}{Br}.$$

The radius of curvature r can be measured and so can B. The velocity v can be found by applying an electric field in addition to the magnetic field. The electric field E is adjusted so that the cathode rays are undeflected and follow path b in Fig. 27–30. This is just like the velocity selector of Example 27–10 where the force due to the electric field, $F = eE$, is balanced by the force due to the magnetic field, $F = evB$. Thus $eE = evB$ and $v = E/B$. Combining this with the above equation we have

$$\frac{e}{m} = \frac{E}{B^2 r}. \tag{27–13}$$

The quantities on the right side can all be measured so that although e and m could not be determined separately, the ratio e/m could be determined. The accepted value today is $e/m = 1.76 \times 10^{11}$ C/kg. Cathode rays soon came to be called **electrons**.

It is worth noting that the "discovery" of the electron, like many others in science, is not quite so obvious as discovering gold or oil. Should the discovery of the electron be credited to the person who first saw a glow in the tube? Or to the person who first called them cathode rays? Perhaps neither one, for they had no conception of the electron as we know it today. In fact, the credit for the discovery is generally given to Thomson, but not because he was the first to see the glow in the tube. Rather it is because he believed that this phenomenon was due to tiny negatively charged particles and made careful measurements on them. Furthermore he argued that these particles were constituents of atoms, and not ions or atoms themselves as many thought, and he developed an electron theory of matter. His view is close to what we accept today, and this is why Thomson is credited with the "discovery." Note, however, that neither he nor anyone else ever actually saw an electron itself. We discuss this briefly, for it illustrates the fact that discovery in science is not always a clear-cut matter. In fact some philosophers of science think the word "discovery" is often not appropriate, such as in this case.

Thomson believed that an electron was not an atom, but rather a constituent, or part, of an atom. Convincing evidence for this came soon with the determination of the charge and the mass of the cathode rays. Thomson's student J. S. Townsend made the first direct (but rough) measurements of e in 1897. But it was the more refined **oil-drop experiment** of Robert A. Millikan (1868–1953) that yielded a precise value for the charge on the electron and showed that charge comes in discrete amounts. In this experiment, tiny droplets of mineral oil carrying an electric charge were allowed to fall under gravity between two parallel plates, Fig. 27–31. The electric field E between the plates was adjusted until the drop was suspended in midair. The downward pull of gravity, mg, was then just balanced by the upward force due to the electric field. Thus $qE = mg$, so the charge $q = mg/E$. The mass of the droplet was determined by measuring its terminal velocity in the absence of the electric field. Sometimes the drop was charged negatively, and sometimes positively, suggesting that the drop had acquired or lost electrons (by friction, leaving the atomizer). Millikan's painstaking observations and analysis presented convincing evidence that any charge was an integral multiple of a smallest charge, e, that was ascribed to the electron, and that the value of e was 1.6×10^{-19} C. This value of e, combined with the measurement of e/m, gives the mass of the electron to be $(1.6 \times 10^{-19}\,\text{C})/(1.76 \times 10^{11}\,\text{C/kg}) = 9.1 \times 10^{-31}$ kg. This mass is less than a thousandth the mass of the smallest atom, and thus confirmed the idea that the electron is only a part of an atom. The accepted value today for the mass of the electron is $m_e = 9.11 \times 10^{-31}$ kg.

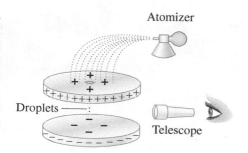

FIGURE 27–31 Millikan's oil-drop experiment.

CRT, Revisited

The cathode ray tube (CRT), which can serve as the picture tube of TV sets, oscilloscopes, and computer monitors, was discussed in Chapter 23. There, in Fig. 23–22, we saw a design using electric deflection plates to maneuver the electron beam. Many CRTs, however, make use of the magnetic field produced by coils to maneuver the electron beam. They operate much like the coils shown in Fig. 27–30.

27–8 The Hall Effect

When a current-carrying conductor is held fixed in a magnetic field, the field exerts a sideways force on the charges moving in the conductor. For example, if electrons move to the right in the rectangular conductor shown in Fig. 27–32a, the inward magnetic field will exert a downward force on the electrons $\vec{F}_B = -e\vec{v}_d \times \vec{B}$, where $\vec{v}_d$ is the drift velocity of the electrons (Section 25–8). Thus the electrons will tend to move nearer to face D than face C. There will thus be a potential difference between faces C and D of the conductor. This potential difference builds up until the electric field $\vec{E}_H$ that it produces exerts a force, $e\vec{E}_H$, on the moving charges that is equal and opposite to the magnetic force. This effect is called the **Hall effect** after E. H. Hall, who discovered it in 1879. The difference of potential produced is called the **Hall emf**.

The electric field due to the separation of charge is called the *Hall field*, $\vec{E}_H$, and points downward in Fig. 27–32a, as shown. In equilibrium, the force due to this electric field is balanced by the magnetic force $e v_d B$, so

$$eE_H = ev_d B.$$

Hence $E_H = v_d B$. The Hall emf is then (Eq. 23–4b, assuming the conductor is long and thin so E_H is uniform)

$$\mathscr{E}_H = E_H d = v_d B d, \qquad \textbf{(27–14)}$$

where d is the width of the conductor.

A current of negative charges moving to the right is equivalent to positive charges moving to the left, at least for most purposes. But the Hall effect can distinguish these two. As can be seen in Fig. 27–32b, positive particles moving to the left are deflected downward, so that the bottom surface is positive relative to the top surface. This is the reverse of part (a). Indeed, the direction of the emf in the Hall effect first revealed that it is negative particles that move in metal conductors.

FIGURE 27–32 The Hall effect. (a) Negative charges moving to the right as the current. (b) Positive charges moving to the left as the current.

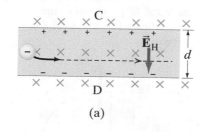

(a)

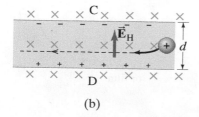

(b)

The magnitude of the Hall emf is proportional to the strength of the magnetic field. The Hall effect can thus be used to measure magnetic field strengths. First the conductor, called a *Hall probe*, is calibrated with known magnetic fields. Then, for the same current, its emf output will be a measure of B. Hall probes can be made very small and are convenient and accurate to use.

The Hall effect can also be used to measure the drift velocity of charge carriers when the external magnetic field B is known. Such a measurement also allows us to determine the density of charge carriers in the material.

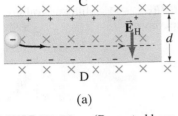

FIGURE 27–32a (Repeated here for Example 27–13.)

EXAMPLE 27–13 **Drift velocity using the Hall effect.** A long copper strip 1.8 cm wide and 1.0 mm thick is placed in a 1.2-T magnetic field as in Fig. 27–32a. When a steady current of 15 A passes through it, the Hall emf is measured to be 1.02 μV. Determine the drift velocity of the electrons and the density of free (conducting) electrons (number per unit volume) in the copper.

APPROACH We use Eq. 27–14 to obtain the drift velocity, and Eq. 25–13 of Chapter 25 to find the density of conducting electrons.

SOLUTION The drift velocity (Eq. 27–14) is

$$v_d = \frac{\mathscr{E}_H}{Bd} = \frac{1.02 \times 10^{-6}\,\text{V}}{(1.2\,\text{T})(1.8 \times 10^{-2}\,\text{m})} = 4.7 \times 10^{-5}\,\text{m/s}.$$

The density of charge carriers n is obtained from Eq. 25–13, $I = nev_d A$, where A is the cross-sectional area through which the current I flows. Then

$$n = \frac{I}{ev_d A} = \frac{15\,\text{A}}{(1.6 \times 10^{-19}\,\text{C})(4.7 \times 10^{-5}\,\text{m/s})(1.8 \times 10^{-2}\,\text{m})(1.0 \times 10^{-3}\,\text{m})}$$

$$= 11 \times 10^{28}\,\text{m}^{-3}.$$

This value for the density of free electrons in copper, $n = 11 \times 10^{28}$ per m³, is the experimentally measured value. It represents *more* than one free electron per atom, which as we saw in Example 25–14 is $8.4 \times 10^{28}\,\text{m}^{-3}$.

*27–9 Mass Spectrometer

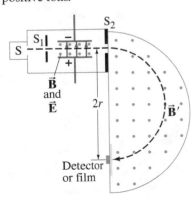

PHYSICS APPLIED

The mass spectrometer

FIGURE 27–33 Bainbridge-type mass spectrometer. The magnetic fields B and B' point out of the paper (indicated by the dots), for positive ions.

A **mass spectrometer** is a device to measure masses of atoms. It is used today not only in physics but also in chemistry, geology, and medicine, often to identify atoms (and their concentration) in given samples. As shown in Fig. 27–33, ions are produced by heating, or by an electric current, in the source or sample S. The particles, of mass m and electric charge q, pass through slit S_1 and enter crossed electric and magnetic fields. Ions follow a straight-line path in this "velocity selector" (as in Example 27–10) if the electric force qE is balanced by the magnetic force qvB: that is, if $qE = qvB$, or $v = E/B$. Thus only those ions whose speed is $v = E/B$ will pass through undeflected and emerge through slit S_2. In the semicircular region, after S_2, there is only a magnetic field, B', so the ions follow a circular path. The radius of the circular path is found from their mark on film (or detectors) if B' is fixed; or else r is fixed by the position of a detector and B' is varied until detection occurs. Newton's second law, $\Sigma F = ma$, applied to an ion moving in a circle under the influence only of the magnetic field B' gives $qvB' = mv^2/r$. Since $v = E/B$, we have

$$m = \frac{qB'r}{v} = \frac{qBB'r}{E}.$$

All the quantities on the right side are known or can be measured, and thus m can be determined.

Historically, the masses of many atoms were measured this way. When a pure substance was used, it was sometimes found that two or more closely spaced marks would appear on the film. For example, neon produced two marks whose radii corresponded to atoms of mass 20 and 22 atomic mass units (u). Impurities were ruled out and it was concluded that there must be two types of neon with different masses. These different forms were called **isotopes**. It was soon found that most elements are mixtures of isotopes, and the difference in mass is due to different numbers of neutrons (discussed in Chapter 41).

EXAMPLE 27–14 **Mass spectrometry.** Carbon atoms of atomic mass 12.0 u are found to be mixed with another, unknown, element. In a mass spectrometer with fixed B', the carbon traverses a path of radius 22.4 cm and the unknown's path has a 26.2-cm radius. What is the unknown element? Assume the ions of both elements have the same charge.

APPROACH The carbon and unknown atoms pass through the same electric and magnetic fields. Hence their masses are proportional to the radius of their respective paths (see equation on previous page).

SOLUTION We write a ratio for the masses, using the equation at the bottom of the previous page:

$$\frac{m_x}{m_C} = \frac{qBB'r_x/E}{qBB'r_C/E} = \frac{26.2 \text{ cm}}{22.4 \text{ cm}} = 1.17.$$

Thus $m_x = 1.17 \times 12.0 \text{ u} = 14.0 \text{ u}$. The other element is probably nitrogen (see the Periodic Table, inside the back cover).

NOTE The unknown could also be an isotope such as carbon-14 ($^{14}_6\text{C}$). See Appendix F. Further physical or chemical analysis would be needed.

Summary

A magnet has two **poles**, north and south. The north pole is that end which points toward geographic north when the magnet is freely suspended. Like poles of two magnets repel each other, whereas unlike poles attract.

We can picture that a **magnetic field** surrounds every magnet. The SI unit for magnetic field is the **tesla** (T).

Electric currents produce magnetic fields. For example, the lines of magnetic field due to a current in a straight wire form circles around the wire, and the field exerts a force on magnets (or currents) near it.

A magnetic field exerts a force on an electric current. The force on an infinitesimal length of wire $d\vec{\ell}$ carrying a current I in a magnetic field $\vec{B}$ is

$$d\vec{F} = I\,d\vec{\ell} \times \vec{B}. \tag{27–4}$$

If the field $\vec{B}$ is uniform over a straight length $\vec{\ell}$ of wire, then the force is

$$\vec{F} = I\vec{\ell} \times \vec{B} \tag{27–3}$$

which has magnitude

$$F = I\ell B \sin\theta \tag{27–1}$$

where θ is the angle between magnetic field $\vec{B}$ and the wire. The direction of the force is perpendicular to the wire and to the magnetic field, and is given by the right-hand rule. This relation serves as the definition of magnetic field $\vec{B}$.

Similarly, a magnetic field $\vec{B}$ exerts a force on a charge q moving with velocity $\vec{v}$ given by

$$\vec{F} = q\vec{v} \times \vec{B}. \tag{27–5a}$$

The magnitude of the force is

$$F = qvB \sin\theta, \tag{27–5b}$$

where θ is the angle between $\vec{v}$ and $\vec{B}$.

The path of a charged particle moving perpendicular to a uniform magnetic field is a circle.

If both electric and magnetic fields ($\vec{E}$ and $\vec{B}$) are present, the force on a charge q moving with velocity $\vec{v}$ is

$$\vec{F} = q\vec{E} + q\vec{v} \times \vec{B}. \tag{27–7}$$

The torque on a current loop in a magnetic field $\vec{B}$ is

$$\vec{\tau} = \vec{\mu} \times \vec{B}, \tag{27–11}$$

where $\vec{\mu}$ is the **magnetic dipole moment** of the loop:

$$\vec{\mu} = NI\vec{A}. \tag{27–10}$$

Here N is the number of coils carrying current I in the loop and $\vec{A}$ is a vector perpendicular to the plane of the loop (use right-hand rule, fingers along current in loop) and has magnitude equal to the area of the loop.

The measurement of the charge-to-mass ratio (e/m) of the electron was done using magnetic and electric fields. The charge e on the electron was first measured in the Millikan oil-drop experiment and then its mass was obtained from the measured value of the e/m ratio.

[*In the **Hall effect**, moving charges in a conductor placed in a magnetic field are forced to one side, producing an emf between the two sides of the conductor.]

[*A **mass spectrometer** uses magnetic and electric fields to measure the mass of ions.]

Questions

1. A compass needle is not always balanced parallel to the Earth's surface, but one end may dip downward. Explain.

2. Draw the magnetic field lines around a straight section of wire carrying a current horizontally to the left.

3. A horseshoe magnet is held vertically with the north pole on the left and south pole on the right. A wire passing between the poles, equidistant from them, carries a current directly away from you. In what direction is the force on the wire?

4. In the relation $\vec{\mathbf{F}} = I\vec{\boldsymbol{\ell}} \times \vec{\mathbf{B}}$, which pairs of the vectors $(\vec{\mathbf{F}}, \vec{\boldsymbol{\ell}}, \vec{\mathbf{B}})$ are always at 90°? Which can be at other angles?

5. The magnetic field due to current in wires in your home can affect a compass. Discuss the effect in terms of currents, including if they are ac or dc.

6. If a negatively charged particle enters a region of uniform magnetic field which is perpendicular to the particle's velocity, will the kinetic energy of the particle increase, decrease, or stay the same? Explain your answer. (Neglect gravity and assume there is no electric field.)

7. In Fig. 27–34, charged particles move in the vicinity of a current-carrying wire. For each charged particle, the arrow indicates the direction of motion of the particle, and the + or – indicates the sign of the charge. For each of the particles, indicate the direction of the magnetic force due to the magnetic field produced by the wire.

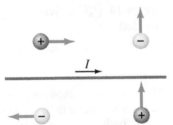

FIGURE 27–34
Question 7.

8. A positively charged particle in a nonuniform magnetic field follows the trajectory shown in Fig. 27–35. Indicate the direction of the magnetic field at points near the path, assuming the path is always in the plane of the page, and indicate the relative magnitudes of the field in each region.

FIGURE 27–35
Question 8.

9. Note that the pattern of magnetic field lines surrounding a bar magnet is similar to that of the electric field around an electric dipole. From this fact, predict how the magnetic field will change with distance (a) when near one pole of a very long bar magnet, and (b) when far from a magnet as a whole.

10. Explain why a strong magnet held near a CRT television screen causes the picture to become distorted. Also, explain why the picture sometimes goes completely black where the field is the strongest. [But don't risk damage to your TV by trying this.]

11. Describe the trajectory of a negatively charged particle in the velocity selector of Fig. 27–21 if its speed exceeds E/B. What is its trajectory if $v < E/B$? Would it make any difference if the particle were positively charged?

12. Can you set a resting electron into motion with a steady magnetic field? With an electric field? Explain.

13. A charged particle is moving in a circle under the influence of a uniform magnetic field. If an electric field that points in the same direction as the magnetic field is turned on, describe the path the charged particle will take.

14. The force on a particle in a magnetic field is the idea behind **electromagnetic pumping**. It is used to pump metallic fluids (such as sodium) and to pump blood in artificial heart machines. The basic design is shown in Fig. 27–36. An electric field is applied perpendicular to a blood vessel and to a magnetic field. Explain how ions are caused to move. Do positive and negative ions feel a force in the same direction?

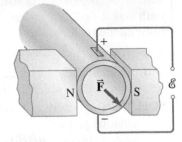

FIGURE 27–36
Electromagnetic pumping in a blood vessel.
Question 14.

15. A beam of electrons is directed toward a horizontal wire carrying a current from left to right (Fig. 27–37). In what direction is the beam deflected?

FIGURE 27–37
Question 15.
Electron direction

16. A charged particle moves in a straight line through a particular region of space. Could there be a nonzero magnetic field in this region? If so, give two possible situations.

17. If a moving charged particle is deflected sideways in some region of space, can we conclude, for certain, that $\vec{\mathbf{B}} \neq 0$ in that region? Explain.

18. How could you tell whether moving electrons in a certain region of space are being deflected by an electric field or by a magnetic field (or by both)?

19. How can you make a compass without using iron or other ferromagnetic material?

20. Describe how you could determine the dipole moment of a bar magnet or compass needle.

21. In what positions (if any) will a current loop placed in a uniform magnetic field be in (a) stable equilibrium, and (b) unstable equilibrium?

*22. A rectangular piece of semiconductor is inserted in a magnetic field and a battery is connected to its ends as shown in Fig. 27–38. When a sensitive voltmeter is connected between points a and b, it is found that point a is at a higher potential than b. What is the sign of the charge carriers in this semiconductor material?

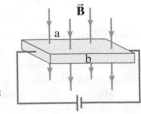

FIGURE 27–38
Question 22.

*23. Two ions have the same mass, but one is singly ionized and the other is doubly ionized. How will their positions on the film of the mass spectrometer of Fig. 27–33 differ?

Problems

27–3 Force on Electric Current in Magnetic Field

1. (I) (a) What is the force per meter of length on a straight wire carrying a 9.40-A current when perpendicular to a 0.90-T uniform magnetic field? (b) What if the angle between the wire and field is 35.0°?

2. (I) Calculate the magnitude of the magnetic force on a 240-m length of wire stretched between two towers and carrying a 150-A current. The Earth's magnetic field of 5.0×10^{-5} T makes an angle of 68° with the wire.

3. (I) A 1.6-m length of wire carrying 4.5 A of current toward the south is oriented horizontally. At that point on the Earth's surface, the dip angle of the Earth's magnetic field makes an angle of 41° to the wire. Estimate the magnitude of the magnetic force on the wire due to the Earth's magnetic field of 5.5×10^{-5} T at this point.

4. (II) The magnetic force per meter on a wire is measured to be only 25 percent of its maximum possible value. Sketch the relationship of the wire and the field if the force had been a maximum, and sketch the relationship as it actually is, calculating the angle between the wire and the magnetic field.

5. (II) The force on a wire is a maximum of 7.50×10^{-2} N when placed between the pole faces of a magnet. The current flows horizontally to the right and the magnetic field is vertical. The wire is observed to "jump" toward the observer when the current is turned on. (a) What type of magnetic pole is the top pole face? (b) If the pole faces have a diameter of 10.0 cm, estimate the current in the wire if the field is 0.220 T. (c) If the wire is tipped so that it makes an angle of 10.0° with the horizontal, what force will it now feel?

6. (II) Suppose a straight 1.00-mm-diameter copper wire could just "float" horizontally in air because of the force due to the Earth's magnetic field $\vec{B}$, which is horizontal, perpendicular to the wire, and of magnitude 5.0×10^{-5} T. What current would the wire carry? Does the answer seem feasible? Explain briefly.

7. (II) A stiff wire 50.0 cm long is bent at a right angle in the middle. One section lies along the z axis and the other is along the line $y = 2x$ in the xy plane. A current of 20.0 A flows in the wire—down the z axis and out the line in the xy plane. The wire passes through a uniform magnetic field given by $\vec{B} = (0.318\hat{i})$T. Determine the magnitude and direction of the total force on the wire.

8. (II) A long wire stretches along the x axis and carries a 3.0-A current to the right $(+x)$. The wire is in a uniform magnetic field $\vec{B} = (0.20\hat{i} - 0.36\hat{j} + 0.25\hat{k})$ T. Determine the components of the force on the wire per cm of length.

9. (II) A current-carrying circular loop of wire (radius r, current I) is partially immersed in a magnetic field of constant magnitude B_0 directed out of the page as shown in Fig. 27–39. Determine the net force on the loop due to the field in terms of θ_0. (Note that θ_0 points to the dashed line, above which $B = 0$.)

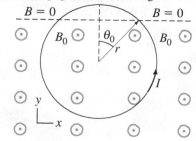

FIGURE 27–39
Problem 9.

10. (II) A 2.0-m-long wire carries a current of 8.2 A and is immersed within a uniform magnetic field $\vec{B}$. When this wire lies along the $+x$ axis, a magnetic force $\vec{F} = (-2.5\hat{j})$ N acts on the wire, and when it lies on the $+y$ axis, the force is $\vec{F} = (2.5\hat{i} - 5.0\hat{k})$ N. Find $\vec{B}$.

11. (III) A curved wire, connecting two points a and b, lies in a plane perpendicular to a uniform magnetic field $\vec{B}$ and carries a current I. Show that the resultant magnetic force on the wire, no matter what its shape, is the same as that on a straight wire connecting the two points carrying the same current I. See Fig. 27–40.

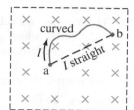

FIGURE 27–40
Problem 11.

12. (III) A circular loop of wire, of radius r, carries current I. It is placed in a magnetic field whose straight lines seem to diverge from a point a distance d below the loop on its axis. (That is, the field makes an angle θ with the loop at all points, Fig. 27–41, where $\tan\theta = r/d$.) Determine the force on the loop.

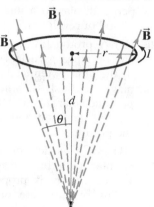

FIGURE 27–41
Problem 12.

27–4 Force on Charge Moving in Magnetic Field

13. (I) Determine the magnitude and direction of the force on an electron traveling 8.75×10^5 m/s horizontally to the east in a vertically upward magnetic field of strength 0.45 T.

14. (I) An electron is projected vertically upward with a speed of 1.70×10^6 m/s into a uniform magnetic field of 0.480 T that is directed horizontally away from the observer. Describe the electron's path in this field.

15. (I) Alpha particles of charge $q = +2e$ and mass $m = 6.6 \times 10^{-27}$ kg are emitted from a radioactive source at a speed of 1.6×10^7 m/s. What magnetic field strength would be required to bend them into a circular path of radius $r = 0.18$ m?

16. (I) Find the direction of the force on a negative charge for each diagram shown in Fig. 27–42, where $\vec{v}$ (green) is the velocity of the charge and $\vec{B}$ (blue) is the direction of the magnetic field. ($\otimes$ means the vector points inward. $\odot$ means it points outward, toward you.)

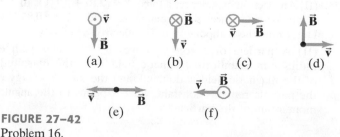

FIGURE 27–42
Problem 16.

17. (I) Determine the direction of $\vec{B}$ for each case in Fig. 27–43, where $\vec{F}$ represents the maximum magnetic force on a positively charged particle moving with velocity $\vec{v}$.

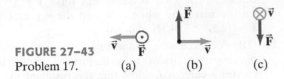

FIGURE 27–43
Problem 17. (a)   (b)   (c)

28. (II) An electron enters a uniform magnetic field $B = 0.28$ T at a $45°$ angle to $\vec{B}$. Determine the radius r and pitch p (distance between loops) of the electron's helical path assuming its speed is 3.0×10^6 m/s. See Fig. 27–44.

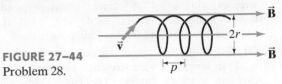

FIGURE 27–44
Problem 28.

18. (II) What is the velocity of a beam of electrons that goes undeflected when passing through perpendicular electric and magnetic fields of magnitude 8.8×10^3 V/m and 7.5×10^{-3} T, respectively? What is the radius of the electron orbit if the electric field is turned off?

19. (II) A doubly charged helium atom whose mass is 6.6×10^{-27} kg is accelerated by a voltage of 2700 V. (a) What will be its radius of curvature if it moves in a plane perpendicular to a uniform 0.340-T field? (b) What is its period of revolution?

20. (II) A proton (mass m_p), a deuteron $(m = 2m_p, Q = e)$, and an alpha particle $(m = 4m_p, Q = 2e)$ are accelerated by the same potential difference V and then enter a uniform magnetic field $\vec{B}$, where they move in circular paths perpendicular to $\vec{B}$. Determine the radius of the paths for the deuteron and alpha particle in terms of that for the proton.

21. (II) For a particle of mass m and charge q moving in a circular path in a magnetic field B, (a) show that its kinetic energy is proportional to r^2, the square of the radius of curvature of its path, and (b) show that its angular momentum is $L = qBr^2$, about the center of the circle.

22. (II) An electron moves with velocity $\vec{v} = (7.0\hat{i} - 6.0\hat{j}) \times 10^4$ m/s in a magnetic field $\vec{B} = (-0.80\hat{i} + 0.60\hat{j})$ T. Determine the magnitude and direction of the force on the electron.

23. (II) A 6.0-MeV (kinetic energy) proton enters a 0.20-T field, in a plane perpendicular to the field. What is the radius of its path? See Section 23–8.

24. (II) An electron experiences the greatest force as it travels 2.8×10^6 m/s in a magnetic field when it is moving northward. The force is vertically upward and of magnitude 8.2×10^{-13} N. What is the magnitude and direction of the magnetic field?

25. (II) A proton moves through a region of space where there is a magnetic field $\vec{B} = (0.45\hat{i} + 0.38\hat{j})$ T and an electric field $\vec{E} = (3.0\hat{i} - 4.2\hat{j}) \times 10^3$ V/m. At a given instant, the proton's velocity is $\vec{v} = (6.0\hat{i} + 3.0\hat{j} - 5.0\hat{k}) \times 10^3$ m/s. Determine the components of the total force on the proton.

26. (II) An electron experiences a force $\vec{F} = (3.8\hat{i} - 2.7\hat{j}) \times 10^{-13}$ N when passing through a magnetic field $\vec{B} = (0.85$ T$)\hat{k}$. Determine the components of the electron's velocity.

27. (II) A particle of charge q moves in a circular path of radius r in a uniform magnetic field $\vec{B}$. If the magnitude of the magnetic field is doubled, and the kinetic energy of the particle remains constant, what happens to the angular momentum of the particle?

29. (II) A particle with charge q and momentum p, initially moving along the x axis, enters a region where a uniform magnetic field $\vec{B} = B_0\hat{k}$ extends over a width $x = \ell$ as shown in Fig. 27–45. The particle is deflected a distance d in the $+y$ direction as it traverses the field. Determine (a) whether q is positive or negative, and (b) the magnitude of its momentum p.

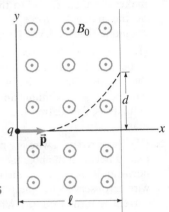

FIGURE 27–45
Problem 29.

30. (II) The path of protons emerging from an accelerator must be bent by $90°$ by a "bending magnet" so as not to strike a barrier in their path a distance d from their exit hole in the accelerator. Show that the field $\vec{B}$ in the bending magnet, which we assume is uniform and can extend over an area $d \times d$, must have magnitude $B \geq (2mK/e^2d^2)^{\frac{1}{2}}$, where m is the mass of a proton and K is its kinetic energy.

31. (III) Suppose the Earth's magnetic field at the equator has magnitude 0.50×10^{-4} T and a northerly direction at all points. Estimate the speed a singly ionized uranium ion $(m = 238$ u, $q = e)$ would need to circle the Earth 5.0 km above the equator. Can you ignore gravity? [Ignore relativity.]

32. (III) A 3.40-g bullet moves with a speed of 155 m/s perpendicular to the Earth's magnetic field of 5.00×10^{-5} T. If the bullet possesses a net charge of 18.5×10^{-9} C, by what distance will it be deflected from its path due to the Earth's magnetic field after it has traveled 1.00 km?

33. (III) A proton moving with speed $v = 1.3 \times 10^5$ m/s in a field-free region abruptly enters an essentially uniform magnetic field $B = 0.850$ T $(\vec{B} \perp \vec{v})$. If the proton enters the magnetic field region at a $45°$ angle as shown in Fig. 27–46, (a) at what angle does it leave, and (b) at what distance x does it exit the field?

FIGURE 27–46
Problem 33.

34. (III) A particle with charge $+q$ and mass m travels in a uniform magnetic field $\vec{\mathbf{B}} = B_0\hat{\mathbf{k}}$. At time $t = 0$, the particle's speed is v_0 and its velocity vector lies in the xy plane directed at an angle of 30° with respect to the y axis as shown in Fig. 27–47. At a later time $t = t_\alpha$, the particle will cross the x axis at $x = \alpha$. In terms of q, m, v_0, and B_0, determine (a) α, and (b) t_α.

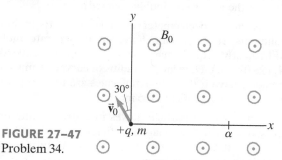

FIGURE 27–47
Problem 34.

27–5 Torque on a Current Loop; Magnetic Moment

35. (I) How much work is required to rotate the current loop (Fig. 27–22) in a uniform magnetic field $\vec{\mathbf{B}}$ from (a) $\theta = 0°$ ($\vec{\boldsymbol{\mu}} \| \vec{\mathbf{B}}$) to $\theta = 180°$, (b) $\theta = 90°$ to $\theta = -90°$?

36. (I) A 13.0-cm-diameter circular loop of wire is placed with the plane of the loop parallel to the uniform magnetic field between the pole pieces of a large magnet. When 4.20 A flows in the coil, the torque on it is 0.185 m·N. What is the magnetic field strength?

37. (II) A circular coil 18.0 cm in diameter and containing twelve loops lies flat on the ground. The Earth's magnetic field at this location has magnitude 5.50×10^{-5} T and points into the Earth at an angle of 66.0° below a line pointing due north. If a 7.10-A clockwise current passes through the coil, determine (a) the torque on the coil, and (b) which edge of the coil rises up, north, east, south, or west.

38. (II) Show that the magnetic dipole moment μ of an electron orbiting the proton nucleus of a hydrogen atom is related to the orbital momentum L of the electron by

$$\mu = \frac{e}{2m}L.$$

39. (II) A 15-loop circular coil 22 cm in diameter lies in the xy plane. The current in each loop of the coil is 7.6 A clockwise, and an external magnetic field $\vec{\mathbf{B}} = (0.55\hat{\mathbf{i}} + 0.60\hat{\mathbf{j}} - 0.65\hat{\mathbf{k}})$ T passes through the coil. Determine (a) the magnetic moment of the coil, $\vec{\boldsymbol{\mu}}$; (b) the torque on the coil due to the external magnetic field; (c) the potential energy U of the coil in the field (take the same zero for U as we did in our discussion of Fig. 27–22).

40. (III) Suppose a nonconducting rod of length d carries a uniformly distributed charge Q. It is rotated with angular velocity ω about an axis perpendicular to the rod at one end, Fig. 27–48. Show that the magnetic dipole moment of this rod is $\frac{1}{6}Q\omega d^2$. [*Hint*: Consider the motion of each infinitesimal length of the rod.]

FIGURE 27–48
Problem 40.   Axis
$\overset{\longleftarrow d \longrightarrow}{}$

*27–6 Motors, Galvanometers

*41. (I) If the current to a motor drops by 12%, by what factor does the output torque change?

*42. (I) A galvanometer needle deflects full scale for a 63.0-μA current. What current will give full-scale deflection if the magnetic field weakens to 0.800 of its original value?

*43. (I) If the restoring spring of a galvanometer weakens by 15% over the years, what current will give full-scale deflection if it originally required 46 μA?

27–7 Discovery of Electron

44. (I) What is the value of q/m for a particle that moves in a circle of radius 8.0 mm in a 0.46-T magnetic field if a crossed 260-V/m electric field will make the path straight?

45. (II) An oil drop whose mass is determined to be 3.3×10^{-15} kg is held at rest between two large plates separated by 1.0 cm as in Fig. 27–31. If the potential difference between the plates is 340 V, how many excess electrons does this drop have?

27–8 Hall Effect

46. (II) A Hall probe, consisting of a rectangular slab of current-carrying material, is calibrated by placing it in a known magnetic field of magnitude 0.10 T. When the field is oriented normal to the slab's rectangular face, a Hall emf of 12 mV is measured across the slab's width. The probe is then placed in a magnetic field of unknown magnitude B, and a Hall emf of 63 mV is measured. Determine B assuming that the angle θ between the unknown field and the plane of the slab's rectangular face is (a) $\theta = 90°$, and (b) $\theta = 60°$.

47. (II) A Hall probe used to measure magnetic field strengths consists of a rectangular slab of material (free-electron density n) with width d and thickness t, carrying a current I along its length ℓ. The slab is immersed in a magnetic field of magnitude B oriented perpendicular to its rectangular face (of area ℓd), so that a Hall emf $\mathscr{E}_H$ is produced across its width d. The probe's magnetic sensitivity, defined as $K_H = \mathscr{E}_H/IB$, indicates the magnitude of the Hall emf achieved for a given applied magnetic field and current. A slab with a large K_H is a good candidate for use as a Hall probe. (a) Show that $K_H = 1/ent$. Thus, a good Hall probe has small values for both n and t. (b) As possible candidates for the material used in a Hall probe, consider (i) a typical metal ($n \approx 1 \times 10^{29}/\text{m}^3$) and (ii) a (doped) semiconductor ($n \approx 3 \times 10^{22}/\text{m}^3$). Given that a semiconductor slab can be manufactured with a thickness of 0.15 mm, how thin (nm) should a metal slab be to yield a K_H value equal to that of the semiconductor slab? Compare this metal slab thickness with the 0.3-nm size of a typical metal atom. (c) For the typical semiconductor slab described in part (b), what is the expected value for $\mathscr{E}_H$ when $I = 100$ mA and $B = 0.1$ T?

48. (II) A rectangular sample of a metal is 3.0 cm wide and 680 μm thick. When it carries a 42-A current and is placed in a 0.80-T magnetic field it produces a 6.5-μV Hall emf. Determine: (a) the Hall field in the conductor; (b) the drift speed of the conduction electrons; (c) the density of free electrons in the metal.

49. (II) In a probe that uses the Hall effect to measure magnetic fields, a 12.0-A current passes through a 1.50-cm-wide 1.30-mm-thick strip of sodium metal. If the Hall emf is 1.86 μV, what is the magnitude of the magnetic field (take it perpendicular to the flat face of the strip)? Assume one free electron per atom of Na, and take its specific gravity to be 0.971.

50. (II) The Hall effect can be used to measure blood flow rate because the blood contains ions that constitute an electric current. (a) Does the sign of the ions influence the emf? (b) Determine the flow velocity in an artery 3.3 mm in diameter if the measured emf is 0.13 mV and B is 0.070 T. (In actual practice, an alternating magnetic field is used.)

*27–9 Mass Spectrometer

*51. (I) In a mass spectrometer, germanium atoms have radii of curvature equal to 21.0, 21.6, 21.9, 22.2, and 22.8 cm. The largest radius corresponds to an atomic mass of 76 u. What are the atomic masses of the other isotopes?

*52. (II) One form of mass spectrometer accelerates ions by a voltage V before they enter a magnetic field B. The ions are assumed to start from rest. Show that the mass of an ion is $m = qB^2R^2/2V$, where R is the radius of the ions' path in the magnetic field and q is their charge.

*53. (II) Suppose the electric field between the electric plates in the mass spectrometer of Fig. 27–33 is 2.48×10^4 V/m and the magnetic fields are $B = B' = 0.58$ T. The source contains carbon isotopes of mass numbers 12, 13, and 14 from a long dead piece of a tree. (To estimate atomic masses, multiply by 1.66×10^{-27} kg.) How far apart are the lines formed by the singly charged ions of each type on the photographic film? What if the ions were doubly charged?

*54. (II) A mass spectrometer is being used to monitor air pollutants. It is difficult, however, to separate molecules with nearly equal mass such as CO (28.0106 u) and N_2 (28.0134 u). How large a radius of curvature must a spectrometer have if these two molecules are to be separated at the film or detectors by 0.65 mm?

*55. (II) An unknown particle moves in a straight line through crossed electric and magnetic fields with $E = 1.5$ kV/m and $B = 0.034$ T. If the electric field is turned off, the particle moves in a circular path of radius $r = 2.7$ cm. What might the particle be?

General Problems

56. Protons move in a circle of radius 5.10 cm in a 0.625-T magnetic field. What value of electric field could make their paths straight? In what direction must the electric field point?

57. Protons with momentum 3.8×10^{-16} kg·m/s are magnetically steered clockwise in a circular path 2.0 km in diameter at Fermi National Accelerator Laboratory in Illinois. Determine the magnitude and direction of the field in the magnets surrounding the beam pipe.

58. A proton and an electron have the same kinetic energy upon entering a region of constant magnetic field. What is the ratio of the radii of their circular paths?

59. Two stiff parallel wires a distance d apart in a horizontal plane act as rails to support a light metal rod of mass m (perpendicular to each rail), Fig. 27–49. A magnetic field $\vec{B}$, directed vertically upward (outward in diagram), acts throughout. At $t = 0$, a constant current I begins to flow through the system. Determine the speed of the rod, which starts from rest at $t = 0$, as a function of time (a) assuming no friction between the rod and the rails, and (b) if the coefficient of friction is μ_k. (c) In which direction does the rod move, east or west, if the current through it heads north?

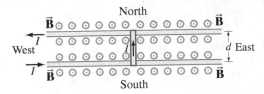

North

West I

d East

South

FIGURE 27–49 Looking down on a rod sliding on rails. Problems 59 and 60.

60. Suppose the rod in Fig. 27–49 (Problem 59) has mass $m = 0.40$ kg and length 22 cm and the current through it is $I = 36$ A. If the coefficient of static friction is $\mu_s = 0.50$, determine the minimum magnetic field $\vec{B}$ (not necessarily vertical) that will just cause the rod to slide. Give the magnitude of $\vec{B}$ and its direction relative to the vertical (outwards towards us).

61. Near the equator, the Earth's magnetic field points almost horizontally to the north and has magnitude $B = 0.50 \times 10^{-4}$ T. What should be the magnitude and direction for the velocity of an electron if its weight is to be exactly balanced by the magnetic force?

62. Calculate the magnetic force on an airplane which has acquired a net charge of 1850 μC and moves with a speed of 120 m/s perpendicular to the Earth's magnetic field of 5.0×10^{-5} T.

63. A motor run by a 9.0-V battery has a 20 turn square coil with sides of length 5.0 cm and total resistance 24 Ω. When spinning, the magnetic field felt by the wire in the coil is 0.020 T. What is the maximum torque on the motor?

64. Estimate the approximate maximum deflection of the electron beam near the center of a CRT television screen due to the Earth's 5.0×10^{-5} T field. Assume the screen is 18 cm from the electron gun, where the electrons are accelerated (a) by 2.0 kV, or (b) by 28 kV. Note that in color TV sets, the beam must be directed accurately to within less than 1 mm in order to strike the correct phosphor. Because the Earth's field is significant here, mu-metal shields are used to reduce the Earth's field in the CRT. (See Section 23–9.)

65. The rectangular loop of wire shown in Fig. 27–22 has mass m and carries current I. Show that if the loop is oriented at an angle $\theta \ll 1$ (in radians), then when it is released it will execute simple harmonic motion about $\theta = 0$. Calculate the period of the motion.

66. The **cyclotron** (Fig. 27–50) is a device used to accelerate elementary particles such as protons to high speeds. Particles starting at point A with some initial velocity travel in circular orbits in the magnetic field B. The particles are accelerated to higher speeds each time they pass in the gap between the metal "dees," where there is an electric field E. (There is no electric field within the hollow metal dees.) The electric field changes direction each half-cycle, due to an ac voltage $V = V_0 \sin 2\pi f t$, so that the particles are increased in speed at each passage through the gap. (a) Show that the frequency f of the voltage must be $f = Bq/2\pi m$, where q is the charge on the particles and m their mass. (b) Show that the kinetic energy of the particles increases by $2qV_0$ each revolution, assuming that the gap is small. (c) If the radius of the cyclotron is 0.50 m and the magnetic field strength is 0.60 T, what will be the maximum kinetic energy of accelerated protons in MeV?

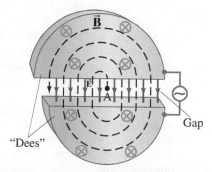

FIGURE 27–50
A cyclotron.
"Dees"
Problem 66.

67. Magnetic fields are very useful in particle accelerators for "beam steering"; that is, magnetic fields can be used to change the beam's direction without altering its speed (Fig. 27–51). Show how this could work with a beam of protons. What happens to protons that are not moving with the speed that the magnetic field is designed for? If the field extends over a region 5.0 cm wide and has a magnitude of 0.38 T, by approximately what angle will a beam of protons traveling at 0.85×10^7 m/s be bent?

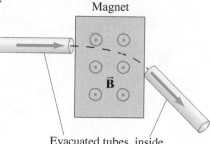

Magnet

$\vec{B}$

Evacuated tubes, inside of which the protons move with velocity indicated by the green arrows

FIGURE 27–51
Problem 67.

68. A square loop of aluminum wire is 20.0 cm on a side. It is to carry 15.0 A and rotate in a uniform 1.35-T magnetic field as shown in Fig. 27–52. (a) Determine the minimum diameter of the wire so that it will not fracture from tension or shear. Assume a safety factor of 10. (See Table 12–2.) (b) What is the resistance of a single loop of this wire?

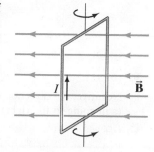

I $\vec{B}$

FIGURE 27–52
Problem 68.

69. A sort of "projectile launcher" is shown in Fig. 27–53. A large current moves in a closed loop composed of fixed rails, a power supply, and a very light, almost frictionless bar touching the rails. A 1.8 T magnetic field is perpendicular to the plane of the circuit. If the rails are a distance $d = 24$ cm apart, and the bar has a mass of 1.5 g, what constant current flow is needed to accelerate the bar from rest to 25 m/s in a distance of 1.0 m? In what direction must the field point?

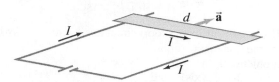

d $\vec{a}$
I
I
I

FIGURE 27–53   Problem 69.

70. (a) What value of magnetic field would make a beam of electrons, traveling to the right at a speed of 4.8×10^6 m/s, go undeflected through a region where there is a uniform electric field of 8400 V/m pointing vertically up? (b) What is the direction of the magnetic field if it is known to be perpendicular to the electric field? (c) What is the frequency of the circular orbit of the electrons if the electric field is turned off?

71. In a certain cathode ray tube, electrons are accelerated horizontally by 25 kV. They then pass through a uniform magnetic field B for a distance of 3.5 cm, which deflects them upward so they reach the top of the screen 22 cm away, 11 cm above the center. Estimate the value of B.

72. **Zeeman effect.** In the Bohr model of the hydrogen atom, the electron is held in its circular orbit of radius r about its proton nucleus by electrostatic attraction. If the atoms are placed in a weak magnetic field $\vec{B}$, the rotation frequency of electrons rotating in a plane perpendicular to $\vec{B}$ is changed by an amount

$$\Delta f = \pm \frac{eB}{4\pi m}$$

where e and m are the charge and mass of an electron. (a) Derive this result, assuming the force due to $\vec{B}$ is much less than that due to electrostatic attraction of the nucleus. (b) What does the $\pm$ sign indicate?

73. A proton follows a spiral path through a gas in a magnetic field of 0.018 T, perpendicular to the plane of the spiral, as shown in Fig. 27–54. In two successive loops, at points P and Q, the radii are 10.0 mm and 8.5 mm, respectively. Calculate the change in the kinetic energy of the proton as it travels from P to Q.

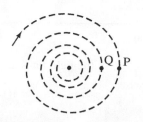

Q   P

FIGURE 27–54   Problem 73.

74. The net force on a current loop whose face is perpendicular to a uniform magnetic field is zero, since contributions to the net force from opposite sides of the loop cancel. However, if the field varies in magnitude from one side of the loop to the other, then there can be a net force on the loop. Consider a square loop with sides whose length is a, located with one side at $x = b$ in the xy plane (Fig. 27–55). A magnetic field is directed along z, with a magnitude that varies with x according to

$$ B = B_0\left(1 - \frac{x}{b}\right). $$

If the current in the loop circulates counterclockwise (that is, the magnetic dipole moment of the loop is along the z axis), find an expression for the net force on the loop.

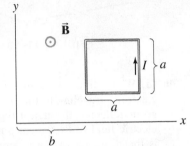

FIGURE 27–55
Problem 74.

75. The power cable for an electric trolley (Fig. 27–56) carries a horizontal current of 330 A toward the east. The Earth's magnetic field has a strength 5.0×10^{-5} T and makes an angle of dip of 22° at this location. Calculate the magnitude and direction of the magnetic force on a 5.0-m length of this cable.

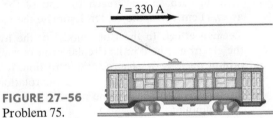

FIGURE 27–56
Problem 75.

76. A uniform conducting rod of length d and mass m sits atop a fulcrum, which is placed a distance $d/4$ from the rod's left-hand end and is immersed in a uniform magnetic field of magnitude B directed into the page (Fig. 27–57). An object whose mass M is 8.0 times greater than the rod's mass is hung from the rod's left-hand end. What current (direction and magnitude) should flow through the rod in order for it to be "balanced" (i.e., be at rest horizontally) on the fulcrum? (Flexible connecting wires which exert negligible force on the rod are not shown.)

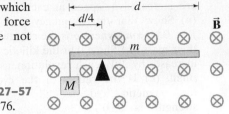

FIGURE 27–57
Problem 76.

77. In a simple device for measuring the magnitude B of a magnetic field, a conducting rod (length $d = 1.0$ m, mass $m = 150$ g) hangs from a friction-free pivot and is oriented so that its axis of rotation is aligned with the direction of the magnetic field to be measured. Thin flexible wires (which exert negligible force on the rod) carry a current $I = 12$ A, which causes the rod to deflect an angle θ with respect to the vertical, where it remains at rest (Fig. 27–58). (a) Is the current flowing upward (toward the pivot) or downward in Fig. 27–58? (b) If $\theta = 13°$, determine B. (c) What is the largest magnetic field magnitude that can be measured using this device?

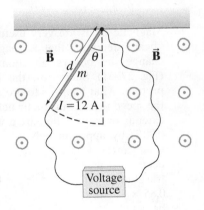

FIGURE 27–58
Problem 77.

Answers to Exercises

A: Near the poles, where the field lines are closer together.

B: Counterclockwise.

C: (b), (c), (d).

D: 0.15 N.

E: (b), (c), (d).

F: Negative; the direction of the helical path would be reversed (still going to the right).

G: (d).

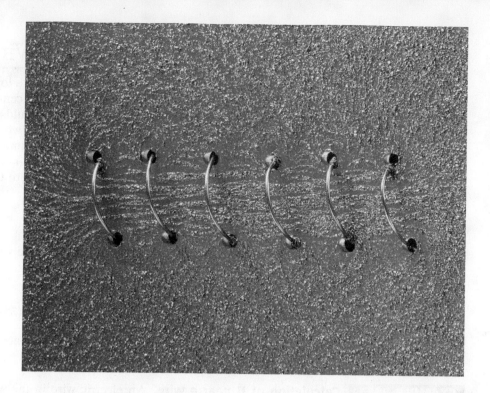

A long coil of wire with many closely spaced loops is called a solenoid. When a long solenoid carries an electric current, a nearly uniform magnetic field is produced within the loops as suggested by the alignment of the iron filings in this photo. The magnitude of the field inside a solenoid is readily found using Ampère's law, one of the great general laws of electromagnetism, relating magnetic fields and electric currents. We examine these connections in detail in this Chapter, as well as other means for producing magnetic fields.

28

Sources of Magnetic Field

CHAPTER-OPENING QUESTION—Guess now!
Which of the following will produce a magnetic field?

(a) An electric charge at rest.
(b) A moving electric charge.
(c) An electric current.
(d) The voltage of a battery not connected to anything.
(e) Any piece of iron.
(f) A piece of any metal.

I n the previous Chapter, we discussed the effects (forces and torques) that a magnetic field has on electric currents and on moving electric charges. We also saw that magnetic fields are produced not only by magnets but also by electric currents (Oersted's great discovery). It is this aspect of magnetism, the production of magnetic fields, that we discuss in this Chapter. We will now see how magnetic field strengths are determined for some simple situations, and discuss some general relations between magnetic fields and their sources, electric current. Most elegant is Ampère's law. We also study the Biot-Savart Law, which can be very helpful for solving practical problems.

CONTENTS

28–1 Magnetic Field Due to a Straight Wire

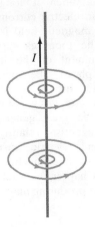

FIGURE 28–1 Same as Fig. 27–8b. Magnetic field lines around a long straight wire carrying an electric current I.

FIGURE 28–2 Example 28–1.

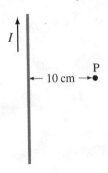

⚠ **CAUTION**

A compass, near a current, may not point north

We saw in Section 27–2 that the magnetic field due to the electric current in a long straight wire is such that the field lines are circles with the wire at the center (Fig. 28–1). You might expect that the field strength at a given point would be greater if the current flowing in the wire were greater; and that the field would be less at points farther from the wire. This is indeed the case. Careful experiments show that the magnetic field B due to a long straight wire at a point near it is directly proportional to the current I in the wire and inversely proportional to the distance r from the wire:

$$B \propto \frac{I}{r}.$$

This relation $B \propto I/r$ is valid as long as r, the perpendicular distance to the wire, is much less than the distance to the ends of the wire (i.e., the wire is long).

The proportionality constant is written[†] as $\mu_0/2\pi$; thus,

$$B = \frac{\mu_0}{2\pi}\frac{I}{r}. \qquad \text{[near a long straight wire]} \quad \textbf{(28–1)}$$

The value of the constant μ_0, which is called the **permeability of free space**, is $\mu_0 = 4\pi \times 10^{-7}\,\text{T·m/A}$.

EXAMPLE 28–1 **Calculation of $\vec{B}$ near a wire.** An electric wire in the wall of a building carries a dc current of 25 A vertically upward. What is the magnetic field due to this current at a point P, 10 cm due north of the wire (Fig. 28–2)?

APPROACH We assume the wire is much longer than the 10-cm distance to the point P so we can apply Eq. 28–1.

SOLUTION According to Eq. 28–1:

$$B = \frac{\mu_0 I}{2\pi r} = \frac{(4\pi \times 10^{-7}\,\text{T·m/A})(25\,\text{A})}{(2\pi)(0.10\,\text{m})} = 5.0 \times 10^{-5}\,\text{T},$$

or 0.50 G. By the right-hand rule (Table 27–1, page 716), the field due to the current points to the west (into the page in Fig. 28–2) at point P.

NOTE The wire's field has about the same magnitude as Earth's magnetic field, so a compass at P would not point north but in a northwesterly direction.

NOTE Most electrical wiring in buildings consists of cables with two wires in each cable. Since the two wires carry current in opposite directions, their magnetic fields cancel to a large extent, but may still affect sensitive electronic devices.

EXERCISE A In Example 25–10 we saw that a typical lightning bolt produces a 100-A current for 0.2 s. Estimate the magnetic field 10 m from a lightning bolt. Would it have a significant effect on a compass?

FIGURE 28–3 Example 28–2. Wire 1 carrying current I_1 out towards us, and wire 2 carrying current I_2 into the page, produce magnetic fields whose lines are circles around their respective wires.

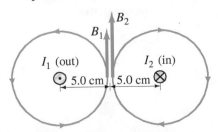

EXAMPLE 28–2 **Magnetic field midway between two currents.** Two parallel straight wires 10.0 cm apart carry currents in opposite directions (Fig. 28–3). Current $I_1 = 5.0\,\text{A}$ is out of the page, and $I_2 = 7.0\,\text{A}$ is into the page. Determine the magnitude and direction of the magnetic field halfway between the two wires.

APPROACH The magnitude of the field produced by each wire is calculated from Eq. 28–1. The direction of *each* wire's field is determined with the right-hand rule. The total field is the vector sum of the two fields at the midway point.

SOLUTION The magnetic field lines due to current I_1 form circles around the wire of I_1, and right-hand-rule-1 (Fig. 27–8c) tells us they point counterclockwise around the wire. The field lines due to I_2 form circles around the wire of I_2 and point clockwise, Fig. 28–3. At the midpoint, both fields point upward as shown, and so add together.

[†]The constant is chosen in this complicated way so that Ampère's law (Section 28–4), which is considered more fundamental, will have a simple and elegant form.

The midpoint is 0.050 m from each wire, and from Eq. 28–1 the magnitudes of B_1 and B_2 are

$$B_1 = \frac{\mu_0 I_1}{2\pi r} = \frac{(4\pi \times 10^{-7}\,\text{T}\cdot\text{m/A})(5.0\,\text{A})}{2\pi(0.050\,\text{m})} = 2.0 \times 10^{-5}\,\text{T};$$

$$B_2 = \frac{\mu_0 I_2}{2\pi r} = \frac{(4\pi \times 10^{-7}\,\text{T}\cdot\text{m/A})(7.0\,\text{A})}{2\pi(0.050\,\text{m})} = 2.8 \times 10^{-5}\,\text{T}.$$

The total field is *up* with a magnitude of

$$B = B_1 + B_2 = 4.8 \times 10^{-5}\,\text{T}.$$

EXERCISE B Suppose both I_1 and I_2 point into the page in Fig. 28–3. What then is the field midway between the two wires?

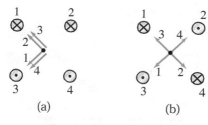

FIGURE 28–4 Example 28–3.

CONCEPTUAL EXAMPLE 28–3 **Magnetic field due to four wires.** Figure 28–4 shows four long parallel wires which carry equal currents into or out of the page as shown. In which configuration, (a) or (b), is the magnetic field greater at the center of the square?

RESPONSE It is greater in (a). The arrows illustrate the directions of the field produced by each wire; check it out, using the right-hand rule to confirm these results. The net field at the center is the superposition of the four fields, which will point to the left in (a) and is zero in (b).

28–2 Force between Two Parallel Wires

We have seen that a wire carrying a current produces a magnetic field (magnitude given by Eq. 28–1 for a long straight wire). Also, a current-carrying wire feels a force when placed in a magnetic field (Section 27–3, Eq. 27–1). Thus, we expect that two current-carrying wires will exert a force on each other.

Consider two long parallel wires separated by a distance d, as in Fig. 28–5a. They carry currents I_1 and I_2, respectively. Each current produces a magnetic field that is "felt" by the other, so each must exert a force on the other. For example, the magnetic field B_1 produced by I_1 in Fig. 28–5 is given by Eq. 28–1, which at the location of wire 2 is

$$B_1 = \frac{\mu_0}{2\pi}\frac{I_1}{d}.$$

See Fig. 28–5b, where the field due *only* to I_1 is shown. According to Eq. 27–2, the force F_2 exerted by B_1 on a length ℓ_2 of wire 2, carrying current I_2, is

$$F_2 = I_2 B_1 \ell_2.$$

Note that the force on I_2 is due only to the field produced by I_1. Of course, I_2 also produces a field, but it does not exert a force on itself. We substitute B_1 into the formula for F_2 and find that the force on a length ℓ_2 of wire 2 is

$$F_2 = \frac{\mu_0}{2\pi}\frac{I_1 I_2}{d}\ell_2. \qquad \text{[parallel wires]} \quad \textbf{(28–2)}$$

If we use right-hand-rule-1 of Fig. 27–8c, we see that the lines of B_1 are as shown in Fig. 28–5b. Then using right-hand-rule-2 of Fig. 27–11c, we see that the force exerted on I_2 will be to the left in Fig. 28–5b. That is, I_1 exerts an attractive force on I_2 (Fig. 28–6a). This is true as long as the currents are in the same direction. If I_2 is in the opposite direction, the right-hand rule indicates that the force is in the opposite direction. That is, I_1 exerts a repulsive force on I_2 (Fig. 28–6b).

Reasoning similar to that above shows that the magnctic field produced by I_2 exerts an equal but opposite force on I_1. We expect this to be true also from Newton's third law. Thus, as shown in Fig. 28–6, parallel currents in the same direction attract each other, whereas parallel currents in opposite directions repel.

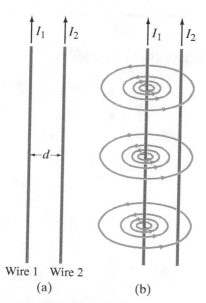

FIGURE 28–5 (a) Two parallel conductors carrying currents I_1 and I_2. (b) Magnetic field $\vec{B}_1$ produced by I_1. (Field produced by I_2 is not shown.) $\vec{B}_1$ points into page at position of I_2.

FIGURE 28–6 (a) Parallel currents in the same direction exert an attractive force on each other. (b) Antiparallel currents (in opposite directions) exert a repulsive force on each other.

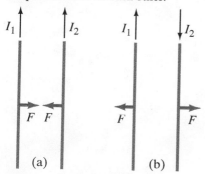

EXAMPLE 28–4 **Force between two current-carrying wires.** The two wires of a 2.0-m-long appliance cord are 3.0 mm apart and carry a current of 8.0 A dc. Calculate the force one wire exerts on the other.

APPROACH Each wire is in the magnetic field of the other when the current is on, so we can apply Eq. 28–2.

SOLUTION Equation 28–2 gives

$$F = \frac{(4\pi \times 10^{-7}\,\text{T·m/A})(8.0\,\text{A})^2(2.0\,\text{m})}{(2\pi)(3.0 \times 10^{-3}\,\text{m})} = 8.5 \times 10^{-3}\,\text{N}.$$

The currents are in opposite directions (one toward the appliance, the other away from it), so the force would be repulsive and tend to spread the wires apart.

EXAMPLE 28–5 **Suspending a wire with a current.** A horizontal wire carries a current $I_1 = 80$ A dc. A second parallel wire 20 cm below it (Fig. 28–7) must carry how much current I_2 so that it doesn't fall due to gravity? The lower wire has a mass of 0.12 g per meter of length.

APPROACH If wire 2 is not to fall under gravity, which acts downward, the magnetic force on it must be upward. This means that the current in the two wires must be in the same direction (Fig. 28–6). We can find the current I_2 by equating the magnitudes of the magnetic force and the gravitational force on the wire.

SOLUTION The force of gravity on wire 2 is downward. For each 1.0 m of wire length, the gravitational force has magnitude

$$F = mg = (0.12 \times 10^{-3}\,\text{kg/m})(1.0\,\text{m})(9.8\,\text{m/s}^2) = 1.18 \times 10^{-3}\,\text{N}.$$

The magnetic force on wire 2 must be upward, and Eq. 28–2 gives

$$F = \frac{\mu_0}{2\pi}\frac{I_1 I_2}{d}\ell$$

where $d = 0.20$ m and $I_1 = 80$ A. We solve this for I_2 and set the two force magnitudes equal (letting $\ell = 1.0$ m):

$$I_2 = \frac{2\pi d}{\mu_0 I_1}\left(\frac{F}{\ell}\right) = \frac{2\pi(0.20\,\text{m})}{(4\pi \times 10^{-7}\,\text{T·m/A})(80\,\text{A})}\frac{(1.18 \times 10^{-3}\,\text{N/m})}{(1.0\,\text{m})} = 15\,\text{A}.$$

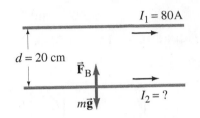

FIGURE 28–7 Example 28–5.

28–3 Definitions of the Ampere and the Coulomb

You may have wondered how the constant μ_0 in Eq. 28–1 could be exactly $4\pi \times 10^{-7}$ T·m/A. Here is how it happened. With an older definition of the ampere, μ_0 was measured experimentally to be very close to this value. Today, μ_0 is *defined* to be exactly $4\pi \times 10^{-7}$ T·m/A. This could not be done if the ampere were defined independently. The ampere, the unit of current, is now defined in terms of the magnetic field B it produces using the defined value of μ_0.

In particular, we use the force between two parallel current-carrying wires, Eq. 28–2, to define the ampere precisely. If $I_1 = I_2 = 1$ A exactly, and the two wires are exactly 1 m apart, then

$$\frac{F}{\ell} = \frac{\mu_0}{2\pi}\frac{I_1 I_2}{d} = \frac{(4\pi \times 10^{-7}\,\text{T·m/A})}{(2\pi)}\frac{(1\,\text{A})(1\,\text{A})}{(1\,\text{m})} = 2 \times 10^{-7}\,\text{N/m}.$$

Thus, *one* **ampere** *is defined as that current flowing in each of two long parallel wires 1 m apart, which results in a force of exactly 2×10^{-7} N per meter of length of each wire.*

This is the precise definition of the ampere. The **coulomb** is then defined as being *exactly* one ampere-second: $1 \text{ C} = 1 \text{ A} \cdot \text{s}$. The value of k or ϵ_0 in Coulomb's law (Section 21–5) is obtained from experiment.

This may seem a rather roundabout way of defining quantities. The reason behind it is the desire for **operational definitions** of quantities—that is, definitions of quantities that can actually be measured given a definite set of operations to carry out. For example, the unit of charge, the coulomb, could be defined in terms of the force between two equal charges after defining a value for ϵ_0 or k in Eqs. 21–1 or 21–2. However, to carry out an actual experiment to measure the force between two charges is very difficult. For one thing, any desired amount of charge is not easily obtained precisely; and charge tends to leak from objects into the air. The amount of current in a wire, on the other hand, can be varied accurately and continuously (by putting a variable resistor in a circuit). Thus the force between two current-carrying conductors is far easier to measure precisely. This is why we first define the ampere, and then define the coulomb in terms of the ampere. At the National Institute of Standards and Technology in Maryland, precise measurement of current is made using circular coils of wire rather than straight lengths because it is more convenient and accurate.

Electric and magnetic field strengths are also defined operationally: the electric field in terms of the measurable force on a charge, via Eq. 21–3; and the magnetic field in terms of the force per unit length on a current-carrying wire, via Eq. 27–2.

28–4 Ampère's Law

In Section 28–1 we saw that Eq. 28–1 gives the relation between the current in a long straight wire and the magnetic field it produces. This equation is valid *only* for a long straight wire. Is there a general relation between a current in a wire of any shape and the magnetic field around it? The answer is yes: the French scientist André Marie Ampère (1775–1836) proposed such a relation shortly after Oersted's discovery. Consider an arbitrary closed path around a current as shown in Fig. 28–8, and imagine this path as being made up of short segments each of length $\Delta\ell$. First, we take the product of the length of each segment times the component of $\vec{\mathbf{B}}$ parallel to that segment (call this component $B_\parallel$). If we now sum all these terms, according to Ampère, the result will be equal to μ_0 times the net current I_{encl} that passes through the surface enclosed by the path:

$$\sum B_\parallel \, \Delta\ell = \mu_0 I_{\text{encl}}.$$

The lengths $\Delta\ell$ are chosen so that $B_\parallel$ is essentially constant along each length. The sum must be made over a *closed path*; and I_{encl} is the net current passing through the surface bounded by this closed path (orange in Fig. 28–8). In the limit $\Delta\ell \to 0$, this relation becomes

$$\oint \vec{\mathbf{B}} \cdot d\vec{\boldsymbol{\ell}} = \mu_0 I_{\text{encl}}, \tag{28–3}$$

where $d\vec{\boldsymbol{\ell}}$ is an infinitesimal length vector and the vector dot product assures that the parallel component of $\vec{\mathbf{B}}$ is taken. Equation 28–3 is known as **Ampère's law**. The integrand in Eq. 28–3 is taken around a closed path, and I_{encl} is the current passing through the space enclosed by the chosen path or loop.

FIGURE 28–8 Arbitrary path enclosing a current, for Ampère's law. The path is broken down into segments of equal length $\Delta\ell$.

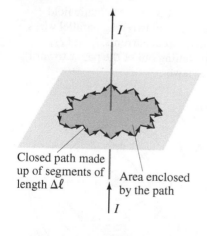

Closed path made up of segments of length $\Delta\ell$

Area enclosed by the path

AMPÈRE'S LAW

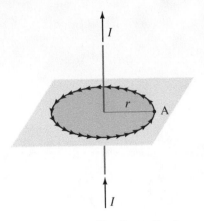

FIGURE 28–9 Circular path of radius r.

To understand Ampère's law better, let us apply it to the simple case of a single long straight wire carrying a current I which we've already examined, and which served as an inspiration for Ampère himself. Suppose we want to find the magnitude of $\vec{B}$ at some point A which is a distance r from the wire (Fig. 28–9). We know the magnetic field lines are circles with the wire at their center. So to apply Eq. 28–3 we choose as our path of integration a circle of radius r. The choice of path is ours, so we choose one that will be convenient: at any point on this circular path, $\vec{B}$ will be tangent to the circle. Furthermore, since all points on the path are the same distance from the wire, by symmetry we expect B to have the same magnitude at each point. Thus for any short segment of the circle (Fig. 28–9), $\vec{B}$ will be parallel to that segment, and (setting $I_{\text{encl}} = I$)

$$\mu_0 I = \oint \vec{B} \cdot d\vec{\ell}$$

$$= \oint B\, d\ell = B \oint d\ell = B(2\pi r),$$

where $\oint d\ell = 2\pi r$, the circumference of the circle. We solve for B and obtain

$$B = \frac{\mu_0 I}{2\pi r}.$$

This is just Eq. 28–1 for the field near a long straight wire as discussed earlier.

Ampère's law thus works for this simple case. A great many experiments indicate that Ampère's law is valid in general. However, as with Gauss's law for the electric field, its practical value as a means to calculate the magnetic field is limited mainly to simple or symmetric situations. Its importance is that it relates the magnetic field to the current in a direct and mathematically elegant way. Ampère's law is thus considered one of the basic laws of electricity and magnetism. It is valid for any situation where the currents and fields are steady and not changing in time, and no magnetic materials are present.

We now can see why the constant in Eq. 28–1 is written $\mu_0/2\pi$. This is done so that only μ_0 appears in Eq. 28–3, rather than, say, $2\pi k$ if we had used k in Eq. 28–1. In this way, the more fundamental equation, Ampère's law, has the simpler form.

It should be noted that the $\vec{B}$ in Ampère's law is not necessarily due only to the current I_{encl}. Ampère's law, like Gauss's law for the electric field, is valid in general. $\vec{B}$ is the field at each point in space along the chosen path due to all sources—including the current I enclosed by the path, but also due to any other sources. For example, the field surrounding two parallel current-carrying wires is the vector sum of the fields produced by each, and the field lines are shown in Fig. 28–10. If the path chosen for the integral (Eq. 28–3) is a circle centered on one of the wires with radius less than the distance between the wires (the dashed line in Fig. 28–10), only the current (I_1) in the encircled wire is included on the right side of Eq. 28–3. $\vec{B}$ on the left side of the equation must be the total $\vec{B}$ at each point due to both wires. Note also that $\oint \vec{B} \cdot d\vec{\ell}$ for the path shown in Fig. 28–10 is the same whether the second wire is present or not (in both cases, it equals $\mu_0 I_1$ according to Ampère's law). How can this be? It can be so because the fields due to the two wires partially cancel one another at some points between them, such as point C in the diagram ($\vec{B} = 0$ at a point midway between the wires if $I_1 = I_2$); at other points, such as D in Fig. 28–10, the fields add together to produce a larger field. In the *sum*, $\oint \vec{B} \cdot d\vec{\ell}$, these effects just balance so that $\oint \vec{B} \cdot d\vec{\ell} = \mu_0 I_1$, whether the second wire is there or not. The integral $\oint \vec{B} \cdot d\vec{\ell}$ will be the same in each case, even though $\vec{B}$ will not be the same at every point for each of the two cases.

FIGURE 28–10 Magnetic field lines around two long parallel wires whose equal currents, I_1 and I_2, are coming out of the paper toward the viewer.

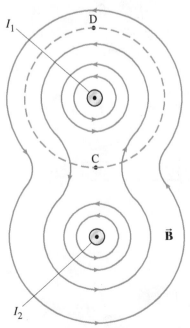

EXAMPLE 28-6 **Field inside and outside a wire.** A long straight cylindrical wire conductor of radius R carries a current I of uniform current density in the conductor. Determine the magnetic field due to this current at (a) points outside the conductor $(r > R)$, and (b) points inside the conductor $(r < R)$. See Fig. 28–11. Assume that r, the radial distance from the axis, is much less than the length of the wire. (c) If $R = 2.0$ mm and $I = 60$ A, what is B at $r = 1.0$ mm, $r = 2.0$ mm, and $r = 3.0$ mm?

APPROACH We can use *symmetry*: Because the wire is long, straight, and cylindrical, we expect from symmetry that the magnetic field must be the same at all points that are the same distance from the center of the conductor. There is no reason why any such point should have preference over others at the same distance from the wire (they are physically equivalent). So B must have the same value at all points the same distance from the center. We also expect $\vec{B}$ to be tangent to circles around the wire (Fig. 28–1), so we choose a circular path of integration as we did in Fig. 28–9.

SOLUTION (a) We apply Ampère's law, integrating around a circle $(r > R)$ centered on the wire (Fig. 28–11a), and then $I_{encl} = I$:

$$\oint \vec{B} \cdot d\vec{\ell} = B(2\pi r) = \mu_0 I_{encl}$$

or

$$B = \frac{\mu_0 I}{2\pi r}, \qquad\qquad [r > R]$$

which is the same result as for a thin wire.

(b) Inside the wire $(r < R)$, we again choose a circular path concentric with the cylinder; we expect $\vec{B}$ to be tangential to this path, and again, because of the symmetry, it will have the same magnitude at all points on the circle. The current enclosed in this case is less than I by a factor of the ratio of the areas:

$$I_{encl} = I \frac{\pi r^2}{\pi R^2}.$$

So Ampère's law gives

$$\oint \vec{B} \cdot d\vec{\ell} = \mu_0 I_{encl}$$

$$B(2\pi r) = \mu_0 I \left(\frac{\pi r^2}{\pi R^2} \right)$$

so

$$B = \frac{\mu_0 I r}{2\pi R^2}. \qquad\qquad [r < R]$$

The field is zero at the center of the conductor and increases linearly with r until $r = R$; beyond $r = R$, B decreases as $1/r$. This is shown in Fig. 28–11b. Note that these results are valid only for points close to the center of the conductor as compared to its length. For a current to flow, there must be connecting wires (to a battery, say), and the field due to these conducting wires, if not very far away, will destroy the assumed symmetry.

(c) At $r = 2.0$ mm, the surface of the wire, $r = R$, so

$$B = \frac{\mu_0 I}{2\pi R} = \frac{(4\pi \times 10^{-7}\,\text{T·m/A})(60\,\text{A})}{(2\pi)(2.0 \times 10^{-3}\,\text{m})} = 6.0 \times 10^{-3}\,\text{T}.$$

We saw in (b) that inside the wire B is linear in r. So at $r = 1.0$ mm, B will be half what it is at $r = 2.0$ mm or 3.0×10^{-3} T. Outside the wire, B falls off as $1/r$, so at $r = 3.0$ mm it will be two-thirds as great as at $r = 2.0$ mm, or $B = 4.0 \times 10^{-3}$ T. To check, we use our result in (a), $B = \mu_0 I/2\pi r$, which gives the same result.

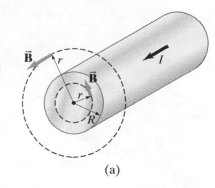

(a)

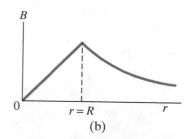

(b)

FIGURE 28-11 Magnetic field inside and outside a cylindrical conductor (Example 28–6).

⚠ **CAUTION**
Connecting wires can destroy assumed symmetry

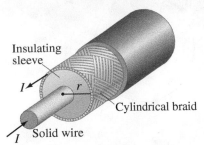

FIGURE 28–12 Coaxial cable. Example 28–7.

FIGURE 28–13 Exercise C.

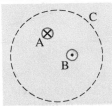

FIGURE 28–14 Example 28–8.

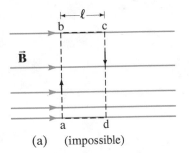

(a)   (impossible)

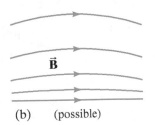

(b)   (possible)

CONCEPTUAL EXAMPLE 28–7 | **Coaxial cable.** A *coaxial cable* is a single wire surrounded by a cylindrical metallic braid, as shown in Fig. 28–12. The two conductors are separated by an insulator. The central wire carries current to the other end of the cable, and the outer braid carries the return current and is usually considered ground. Describe the magnetic field (*a*) in the space between the conductors, and (*b*) outside the cable.

RESPONSE (*a*) In the space between the conductors, we can apply Ampère's law for a circular path around the center wire, just as we did for the case shown in Figs. 28–9 and 28–11. The magnetic field lines will be concentric circles centered on the center of the wire, and the magnitude is given by Eq. 28–1. The current in the outer conductor has no bearing on this result. (Ampère's law uses only the current enclosed *inside* the path; as long as the currents outside the path don't affect the *symmetry* of the field, they do not contribute to the field along the path at all). (*b*) Outside the cable, we can draw a similar circular path, for we expect the field to have the same cylindrical symmetry. Now, however, there are two currents enclosed by the path, and they add up to zero. The field outside the cable is zero.

The nice feature of coaxial cables is that they are self-shielding: no stray magnetic fields exist outside the cable. The outer cylindrical conductor also shields external electric fields from coming in (see also Example 21–14). This makes them ideal for carrying signals near sensitive equipment. Audiophiles use coaxial cables between stereo equipment components and even to the loudspeakers.

EXERCISE C In Fig. 28–13, A and B are wires each carrying a 3.0-A current but in opposite directions. On the circle C, which statement is true? (*a*) $B = 0$; (*b*) $\oint \vec{B} \cdot d\vec{\ell} = 0$; (*c*) $B = 3\mu_0$; (*d*) $B = -3\mu_0$; (*e*) $\oint \vec{B} \cdot d\vec{\ell} = 6\mu_0$.

EXAMPLE 28–8 **A nice use for Ampère's law.** Use Ampère's law to show that in any region of space where there are no currents the magnetic field cannot be both unidirectional and nonuniform as shown in Fig. 28–14a.

APPROACH The wider spacing of lines near the top of Fig. 28–14a indicates the field $\vec{B}$ has a smaller magnitude at the top than it does lower down. We apply Ampère's law to the rectangular path abcd shown dashed in Fig. 28–14a.

SOLUTION Because no current is enclosed by the chosen path, Ampère's law gives

$$\oint \vec{B} \cdot d\vec{\ell} = 0.$$

The integral along sections ab and cd is zero, since $\vec{B} \perp d\vec{\ell}$. Thus

$$\oint \vec{B} \cdot d\vec{\ell} = B_{bc}\ell - B_{da}\ell = (B_{bc} - B_{da})\ell,$$

which is not zero since the field B_{bc} along the path bc is less than the field B_{da} along path da. Hence we have a contradiction: $\oint \vec{B} \cdot d\vec{\ell}$ cannot be both zero (since $I = 0$) and nonzero. Thus we have shown that a nonuniform unidirectional field is not consistent with Ampère's law. A nonuniform field whose direction also changes, as in Fig. 28–14b, is consistent with Ampère's law (convince yourself this is so), and possible. The fringing of a permanent magnet's field (Fig. 27–7) has this shape.

PROBLEM SOLVING

Ampère's Law

1. Ampère's law, like Gauss's law, is always a valid statement. But as a calculation tool it is limited mainly to systems with a high degree of symmetry. The first step in applying Ampère's law is to identify useful **symmetry**.

2. Choose an integration path that reflects the symmetry (see the Examples). Search for paths where B has constant magnitude along the entire path or along segments of the path. Make sure your integration path passes through the point where you wish to evaluate the magnetic field.

3. Use symmetry to determine the direction of $\vec{B}$ along the integration path. With a smart choice of path, $\vec{B}$ will be either parallel or perpendicular to the path.

4. Determine the enclosed current, I_{encl}. Be careful with signs. Let the fingers of your right hand curl along the direction of $\vec{B}$ so that your thumb shows the direction of positive current. If you have a solid conductor and your integration path does not enclose the full current, you can use the current density (current per unit area) multiplied by the enclosed area (as in Example 28–6).

28–5 Magnetic Field of a Solenoid and a Toroid

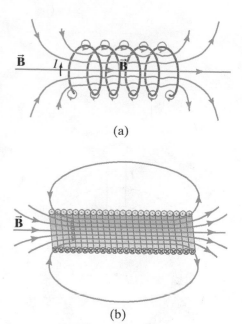

FIGURE 28–15 Magnetic field due to a solenoid: (a) loosely spaced turns, (b) closely spaced turns.

A long coil of wire consisting of many loops is called a **solenoid**. Each loop produces a magnetic field as was shown in Fig. 27–9. In Fig. 28–15a, we see the field due to a solenoid when the coils are far apart. Near each wire, the field lines are very nearly circles as for a straight wire (that is, at distances that are small compared to the curvature of the wire). Between any two wires, the fields due to each loop tend to cancel. Toward the center of the solenoid, the fields add up to give a field that can be fairly large and fairly uniform. For a long solenoid with closely packed coils, the field is nearly uniform and parallel to the solenoid axis within the entire cross section, as shown in Fig. 28–15b. The field outside the solenoid is very small compared to the field inside, except near the ends. Note that the same number of field lines that are concentrated inside the solenoid, spread out into the vast open space outside.

We now use Ampère's law to determine the magnetic field inside a very long (ideally, infinitely long) closely packed solenoid. We choose the path abcd shown in Fig. 28–16, far from either end, for applying Ampère's law. We will consider this path as made up of four segments, the sides of the rectangle: ab, bc, cd, da. Then the left side of Eq. 28–3, Ampère's law, becomes

$$\oint \vec{B} \cdot d\vec{\ell} = \int_a^b \vec{B} \cdot d\vec{\ell} + \int_b^c \vec{B} \cdot d\vec{\ell} + \int_c^d \vec{B} \cdot d\vec{\ell} + \int_d^a \vec{B} \cdot d\vec{\ell}.$$

The field outside the solenoid is so small as to be negligible compared to the field inside. Thus the first term in this sum will be zero. Furthermore, $\vec{B}$ is perpendicular to the segments bc and da inside the solenoid, and is nearly zero between and outside the coils,

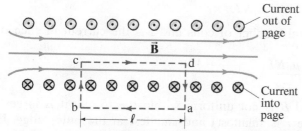

Current out of page

Current into page

FIGURE 28–16 Cross-sectional view into a solenoid. The magnetic field inside is straight except at the ends. Red dashed lines indicate the path chosen for use in Ampère's law. $\odot$ and $\otimes$ are electric current direction (in the wire loops) out of the page and into the page.

so these terms too are zero. Therefore we have reduced the integral to the segment cd where $\vec{B}$ is the nearly uniform field inside the solenoid, and is parallel to $d\vec{\ell}$, so

$$\oint \vec{B} \cdot d\vec{\ell} = \int_c^d \vec{B} \cdot d\vec{\ell} = B\ell,$$

where ℓ is the length cd. Now we determine the current enclosed by this loop for the right side of Ampère's law, Eq. 28–3. If a current I flows in the wire of the solenoid, the total current enclosed by our path abcd is NI where N is the number of loops our path encircles (five in Fig. 28–16). Thus Ampère's law gives us

$$B\ell = \mu_0 NI.$$

If we let $n = N/\ell$ be the *number of loops per unit length*, then

$$B = \mu_0 nI. \qquad \text{[solenoid]} \quad (28\text{–}4)$$

This is the magnitude of the magnetic field within a solenoid. Note that B depends only on the number of loops per unit length, n, and the current I. The field does not depend on position within the solenoid, so B is uniform. This is strictly true only for an infinite solenoid, but it is a good approximation for real ones for points not close to the ends.

EXAMPLE 28–9 **Field inside a solenoid.** A thin 10-cm-long solenoid used for fast electromechanical switching has a total of 400 turns of wire and carries a current of 2.0 A. Calculate the field inside near the center.

APPROACH We use Eq. 28–4, where the number of turns per unit length is $n = 400/0.10 \text{ m} = 4.0 \times 10^3 \text{ m}^{-1}$.

SOLUTION $B = \mu_0 nI = (4\pi \times 10^{-7} \text{ T} \cdot \text{m/A})(4.0 \times 10^3 \text{ m}^{-1})(2.0 \text{ A}) = 1.0 \times 10^{-2} \text{ T}.$

A close look at Fig. 28–15 shows that the field outside of a solenoid is much like that of a bar magnet (Fig. 27–4). Indeed, a solenoid acts like a magnet, with one end acting as a north pole and the other as south pole, depending on the direction of the current in the loops. Since magnetic field lines leave the north pole of a magnet, the north poles of the solenoids in Fig. 28–15 are on the right.

Solenoids have many practical applications, and we discuss some of them later in the Chapter, in Section 28–8.

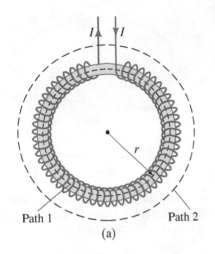

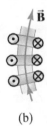

(b)

FIGURE 28–17 (a) A toroid. (b) A section of the toroid showing direction of the current for three loops: ⊙ means current toward you, ⊗ means current away from you.

EXAMPLE 28–10 **Toroid.** Use Ampère's law to determine the magnetic field (a) inside and (b) outside a toroid, which is like a solenoid bent into the shape of a circle as shown in Fig. 28–17a.

APPROACH The magnetic field lines inside the toroid will be circles concentric with the toroid. (If you think of the toroid as a solenoid bent into a circle, the field lines bend along with the solenoid.) The direction of $\vec{\mathbf{B}}$ is clockwise. We choose as our path of integration one of these field lines of radius r inside the toroid as shown by the dashed line labeled "path 1" in Fig. 28–17a. We make this choice to use the *symmetry* of the situation, so B will be tangent to the path and will have the same magnitude at all points along the path (although it is not necessarily the same across the whole cross section of the toroid). This chosen path encloses *all* the coils; if there are N coils, each carrying current I, then $I_{encl} = NI$.

SOLUTION (a) Ampère's law applied along this path gives

$$\oint \vec{\mathbf{B}} \cdot d\vec{\boldsymbol{\ell}} = \mu_0 I_{encl}$$

$$B(2\pi r) = \mu_0 NI,$$

where N is the total number of coils and I is the current in each of the coils. Thus

$$B = \frac{\mu_0 NI}{2\pi r}.$$

The magnetic field B is not uniform within the toroid: it is largest along the inner edge (where r is smallest) and smallest at the outer edge. However, if the toroid is large, but thin (so that the difference between the inner and outer radii is small compared to the average radius), the field will be essentially uniform within the toroid. In this case, the formula for B reduces to that for a straight solenoid $B = \mu_0 nI$ where $n = N/(2\pi r)$ is the number of coils per unit length. (b) Outside the toroid, we choose as our path of integration a circle concentric with the toroid, "path 2" in Fig. 28–17a. This path encloses N loops carrying current I in one direction and N loops carrying the same current in the opposite direction. (Figure 28–17b shows the directions of the current for the parts of the loop on the inside and outside of the toroid.) Thus the net current enclosed by path 2 is zero. For a very tightly packed toroid, all points on path 2 are equidistant from the toroid and equivalent, so we expect B to be the same at all points along the path. Hence, Ampère's law gives

$$\oint \vec{\mathbf{B}} \cdot d\vec{\boldsymbol{\ell}} = \mu_0 I_{encl}$$

$$B(2\pi r) = 0$$

or

$$B = 0.$$

The same is true for a path taken at a radius smaller than that of the toroid. So there is no field exterior to a very tightly wound toroid. It is all inside the loops.

28–6 Biot-Savart Law

The usefulness of Ampère's law for determining the magnetic field $\vec{\mathbf{B}}$ due to particular electric currents is restricted to situations where the symmetry of the given currents allows us to evaluate $\oint \vec{\mathbf{B}} \cdot d\vec{\boldsymbol{\ell}}$ readily. This does not, of course, invalidate Ampère's law nor does it reduce its fundamental importance. Recall the electric case, where Gauss's law is considered fundamental but is limited in its use for actually calculating $\vec{\mathbf{E}}$. We must often determine the electric field $\vec{\mathbf{E}}$ by another method summing over contributions due to infinitesimal charge elements dq via Coulomb's law: $dE = (1/4\pi\epsilon_0)(dq/r^2)$. A magnetic equivalent to this infinitesimal form of Coulomb's law would be helpful for currents that do not have great symmetry. Such a law was developed by Jean Baptiste Biot (1774–1862) and Felix Savart (1791–1841) shortly after Oersted's discovery in 1820 that a current produces a magnetic field.

According to Biot and Savart, a current I flowing in any path can be considered as many tiny (infinitesimal) current elements, such as in the wire of Fig. 28–18. If $d\vec{\boldsymbol{\ell}}$ represents any infinitesimal length along which the current is flowing, then the magnetic field, $d\vec{\mathbf{B}}$, at any point P in space, due to this element of current, is given by

$$d\vec{\mathbf{B}} = \frac{\mu_0 I}{4\pi} \frac{d\vec{\boldsymbol{\ell}} \times \hat{\mathbf{r}}}{r^2}, \qquad (28\text{–}5) \qquad \textit{Biot-Savart law}$$

where $\vec{\mathbf{r}}$ is the displacement vector from the element $d\vec{\boldsymbol{\ell}}$ to the point P, and $\hat{\mathbf{r}} - \vec{\mathbf{r}}/r$ is the unit vector (magnitude = 1) in the direction of $\vec{\mathbf{r}}$ (see Fig. 28–18).

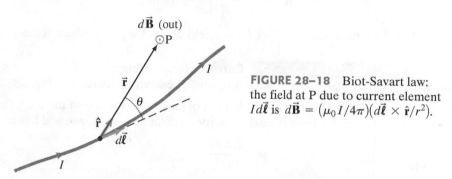

FIGURE 28–18 Biot-Savart law: the field at P due to current element $I d\vec{\boldsymbol{\ell}}$ is $d\vec{\mathbf{B}} = (\mu_0 I/4\pi)(d\vec{\boldsymbol{\ell}} \times \hat{\mathbf{r}}/r^2)$.

Equation 28–5 is known as the **Biot-Savart law**. The magnitude of $d\vec{\mathbf{B}}$ is

$$dB = \frac{\mu_0 I \, d\ell \sin\theta}{4\pi r^2}, \qquad (28\text{–}6)$$

where θ is the angle between $d\vec{\boldsymbol{\ell}}$ and $\vec{\mathbf{r}}$ (Fig. 28–18). The total magnetic field at point P is then found by summing (integrating) over all current elements:

$$\vec{\mathbf{B}} = \int d\vec{\mathbf{B}} = \frac{\mu_0 I}{4\pi} \int \frac{d\vec{\boldsymbol{\ell}} \times \hat{\mathbf{r}}}{r^2}.$$

Note that this is a *vector* sum. The Biot-Savart law is the magnetic equivalent of Coulomb's law in its infinitesimal form. It is even an inverse square law, like Coulomb's law.

An important difference between the Biot-Savart law and Ampère's law (Eq. 28–3) is that in Ampère's law $\left[\oint \vec{\mathbf{B}} \cdot d\vec{\boldsymbol{\ell}} = \mu_0 I_{\text{encl}}\right]$, $\vec{\mathbf{B}}$ is not necessarily due only to the current enclosed by the path of integration. But in the Biot-Savart law the field $d\vec{\mathbf{B}}$ in Eq. 28–5 is due only, and entirely, to the current element $I d\vec{\boldsymbol{\ell}}$. To find the total $\vec{\mathbf{B}}$ at any point in space, it is necessary to include *all* currents.

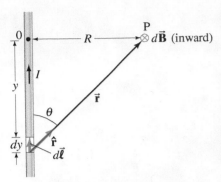

FIGURE 28–19 Determining $\vec{B}$ due to a long straight wire using the Biot-Savart law.

EXAMPLE 28–11 $\vec{B}$ **due to current I in straight wire.** For the field near a long straight wire carrying a current I, show that the Biot-Savart law gives the same result as Eq. 28–1, $B = \mu_0 I / 2\pi r$.

APPROACH We calculate the magnetic field in Fig. 28–19 at point P, which is a perpendicular distance R from an infinitely long wire. The current is moving upwards, and both $d\vec{\ell}$ and $\hat{r}$, which appear in the cross product of Eq. 28–5, are in the plane of the page. Hence the direction of the field $d\vec{B}$ due to each element of current must be directed into the plane of the page as shown (right-hand rule for the cross product $d\vec{\ell} \times \hat{r}$). Thus all the $d\vec{B}$ have the same direction at point P, and add up to give $\vec{B}$ the same direction consistent with our previous results (Figs. 28–1 and 28–11).

SOLUTION The magnitude of $\vec{B}$ will be

$$B = \frac{\mu_0 I}{4\pi} \int_{y=-\infty}^{+\infty} \frac{dy \sin \theta}{r^2},$$

where $dy = d\ell$ and $r^2 = R^2 + y^2$. Note that we are integrating over y (the length of the wire) so R is considered constant. Both y and θ are variables, but they are not independent. In fact, $y = -R/\tan \theta$. Note that we measure y as positive upward from point 0, so for the current element we are considering $y < 0$. Then

$$dy = +R \csc^2 \theta \, d\theta = \frac{R \, d\theta}{\sin^2 \theta} = \frac{R \, d\theta}{(R/r)^2} = \frac{r^2 \, d\theta}{R}.$$

From Fig. 28–19 we can see that $y = -\infty$ corresponds to $\theta = 0$ and that $y = +\infty$ corresponds to $\theta = \pi$ radians. So our integral becomes

$$B = \frac{\mu_0 I}{4\pi} \frac{1}{R} \int_{\theta=0}^{\pi} \sin \theta \, d\theta = -\frac{\mu_0 I}{4\pi R} \cos \theta \Big|_0^{\pi} = \frac{\mu_0 I}{2\pi R}.$$

This is just Eq. 28–1 for the field near a long wire, where R has been used instead of r.

FIGURE 28–20 Determining $\vec{B}$ due to a current loop.

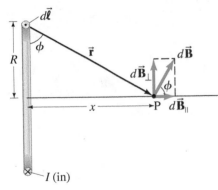

EXAMPLE 28–12 **Current loop.** Determine $\vec{B}$ for points on the axis of a circular loop of wire of radius R carrying a current I, Fig. 28–20.

APPROACH For an element of current at the top of the loop, the magnetic field $d\vec{B}$ at point P on the axis is perpendicular to $\vec{r}$ as shown, and has magnitude (Eq. 28–5)

$$dB = \frac{\mu_0 I \, d\ell}{4\pi r^2}$$

since $d\vec{\ell}$ is perpendicular to $\vec{r}$ so $|d\vec{\ell} \times \hat{r}| = d\ell$. We can break $d\vec{B}$ down into components $dB_{\parallel}$ and $dB_{\perp}$, which are parallel and perpendicular to the axis as shown.

SOLUTION When we sum over all the elements of the loop, *symmetry* tells us that the perpendicular components will cancel on opposite sides, so $B_{\perp} = 0$. Hence, the total $\vec{B}$ will point along the axis, and will have magnitude

$$B = B_{\parallel} = \int dB \cos \phi = \int dB \frac{R}{r} = \int dB \frac{R}{(R^2 + x^2)^{\frac{1}{2}}},$$

where x is the distance of P from the center of the ring, and $r^2 = R^2 + x^2$. Now we put in dB from the equation above and integrate around the current loop, noting that all segments $d\vec{\ell}$ of current are the same distance, $(R^2 + x^2)^{\frac{1}{2}}$, from point P:

$$B = \frac{\mu_0 I}{4\pi} \frac{R}{(R^2 + x^2)^{\frac{3}{2}}} \int d\ell = \frac{\mu_0 I R^2}{2(R^2 + x^2)^{\frac{3}{2}}}$$

since $\int d\ell = 2\pi R$, the circumference of the loop.

NOTE At the very center of the loop (where $x = 0$) the field has its maximum value

$$B = \frac{\mu_0 I}{2R}. \qquad \text{[at center of current loop]}$$

Recall from Section 27–5 that a current loop, such as that just discussed (Fig. 28–20), is considered a **magnetic dipole**. We saw there that a current loop has a magnetic dipole moment

$$\mu = NIA,$$

where A is the area of the loop and N is the number of coils in the loop, each carrying current I. We also saw in Chapter 27 that a magnetic dipole placed in an external magnetic field experiences a torque and possesses potential energy, just like an electric dipole. In Example 28–12, we looked at another aspect of a magnetic dipole: the magnetic field *produced by* a magnetic dipole has magnitude, along the dipole axis, of

$$B = \frac{\mu_0 I R^2}{2(R^2 + x^2)^{\frac{3}{2}}}.$$

We can write this in terms of the magnetic dipole moment $\mu = IA = I\pi R^2$ (for a single loop $N = 1$):

$$B = \frac{\mu_0}{2\pi} \frac{\mu}{(R^2 + x^2)^{\frac{3}{2}}}. \qquad \text{[magnetic dipole]} \quad \textbf{(28–7a)}$$

(Be careful to distinguish μ for dipole moment from μ_0, the magnetic permeability constant.) For distances far from the loop, $x \gg R$, this becomes

$$B \approx \frac{\mu_0}{2\pi} \frac{\mu}{x^3}. \qquad \left[\begin{matrix} \text{on axis,} \\ \text{magnetic dipole, } x \gg R \end{matrix} \right] \quad \textbf{(28–7b)}$$

The magnetic field on the axis of a magnetic dipole decreases with the cube of the distance, just as the electric field does for an electric dipole. B decreases as the cube of the distance also for points not on the axis, although the multiplying factor is not the same. The magnetic field due to a current loop can be determined at various points using the Biot-Savart law and the results are in accord with experiment. The field lines around a current loop are shown in Fig. 28–21.

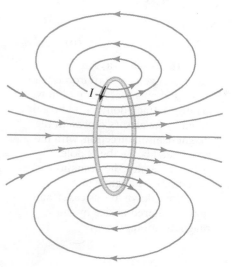

FIGURE 28–21 Magnetic field due to a circular loop of wire. (Same as Fig. 27–9.)

EXAMPLE 28–13 $\vec{\mathbf{B}}$ **due to a wire segment.** One quarter of a circular loop of wire carries a current I as shown in Fig. 28–22. The current I enters and leaves on straight segments of wire, as shown; the straight wires are along the radial direction from the center C of the circular portion. Find the magnetic field at point C.

APPROACH The current in the straight sections produces no magnetic field at point C because $d\vec{\ell}$ and $\hat{\mathbf{r}}$ in the Biot-Savart law (Eq. 28–5) are parallel and therefore $d\vec{\ell} \times \hat{\mathbf{r}} = 0$. Each piece $d\vec{\ell}$ of the curved section of wire produces a field $d\vec{\mathbf{B}}$ that points into the page at C (right-hand rule).

SOLUTION The magnitude of each $d\vec{\mathbf{B}}$ due to each $d\ell$ of the circular portion of wire is (Eq. 28–6)

$$dB = \frac{\mu_0 I \, d\ell}{4\pi R^2}$$

where $r = R$ is the radius of the curved section, and $\sin\theta$ in Eq. 28–6 is $\sin 90° = 1$. With $r = R$ for all pieces $d\vec{\ell}$, we integrate over a quarter of a circle.

$$B = \int dB = \frac{\mu_0 I}{4\pi R^2} \int d\ell = \frac{\mu_0 I}{4\pi R^2} \left(\frac{1}{4} 2\pi R \right) = \frac{\mu_0 I}{8R}.$$

FIGURE 28–22 Example 28–13.

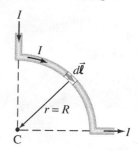

28-7 Magnetic Materials—Ferromagnetism

Magnetic fields can be produced (1) by magnetic materials (magnets) and (2) by electric currents. Common magnetic materials include ordinary magnets, iron cores in motors and electromagnets, recording tape, computer hard drives and magnetic stripes on credit cards. We saw in Section 27–1 that iron (and a few other materials) can be made into strong magnets. These materials are said to be **ferromagnetic**. We now look into the sources of ferromagnetism.

A bar magnet, with its two opposite poles near either end, resembles an electric dipole (equal-magnitude positive and negative charges separated by a distance). Indeed, a bar magnet is sometimes referred to as a "magnetic dipole." There are opposite "poles" separated by a distance. And the magnetic field lines of a bar magnet form a pattern much like that for the electric field of an electric dipole: compare Fig. 21–34a with Fig. 27–4 (or 28–24).

Microscopic examination reveals that a piece of iron is made up of tiny regions known as **domains**, less than 1 mm in length or width. Each domain behaves like a tiny magnet with a north and a south pole. In an unmagnetized piece of iron, these domains are arranged randomly, as shown in Fig. 28–23a. The magnetic effects of the domains cancel each other out, so this piece of iron is not a magnet. In a magnet, the domains are preferentially aligned in one direction as shown in Fig. 28–23b (downward in this case). A magnet can be made from an unmagnetized piece of iron by placing it in a strong magnetic field. (You can make a needle magnetic, for example, by stroking it with one pole of a strong magnet.) The magnetization direction of domains may actually rotate slightly to be more nearly parallel to the external field, and the borders of domains may move so domains with magnetic orientation parallel to the external field grow larger (compare Figs. 28–23a and b).

We can now explain how a magnet can pick up unmagnetized pieces of iron like paper clips. The field of the magnet's south pole (say) causes a slight realignment of the domains in the unmagnetized object, which then becomes a temporary magnet with its north pole facing the south pole of the permanent magnet; thus, attraction results. Similarly, elongated iron filings in a magnetic field acquire aligned domains and align themselves to reveal the shape of the magnetic field, Fig. 28–24.

An iron magnet can remain magnetized for a long time, and is referred to as a "permanent magnet." But if you drop a magnet on the floor or strike it with a hammer, you can jar the domains into randomness and the magnet loses some or all of its magnetism. Heating a permanent magnet can also cause loss of magnetism, for raising the temperature increases the random thermal motion of atoms, which tends to randomize the domains. Above a certain temperature known as the **Curie temperature** (1043 K for iron), a magnet cannot be made at all. Iron, nickel, cobalt, gadolinium, and certain alloys are ferromagnetic at room temperature; several other elements and alloys have low Curie temperature and thus are ferromagnetic only at low temperatures. Most other metals, such as aluminum and copper, do not show any noticeable magnetic effect (but see Section 28–10).

The striking similarity between the fields produced by a bar magnet and by a loop of electric current (Figs. 27–4b and 28–21) offers a clue that perhaps magnetic fields produced by electric currents may have something to do with ferromagnetism. According to modern atomic theory, atoms can be visualized as having electrons that orbit around a central nucleus. The electrons are charged, and so constitute an electric current and therefore produce a magnetic field; but the fields due to orbiting electrons generally all add up to zero. Electrons themselves produce an additional magnetic field, as if they and their electric charge were spinning about their own axes. It is the magnetic field due to electron **spin**[†] that is believed to produce ferromagnetism in most ferromagnetic materials.

It is believed today that *all* magnetic fields are caused by electric currents. This means that magnetic field lines always form closed loops, unlike electric field lines which begin on positive charges and end on negative charges.

[†]The name "spin" comes from an early suggestion that this intrinsic magnetic moment arises from the electron "spinning" on its axis (as well as "orbiting" the nucleus) to produce the extra field. However this view of a spinning electron is oversimplified and not valid.

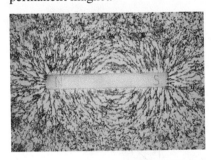

FIGURE 28–23 (a) An unmagnetized piece of iron is made up of domains that are randomly arranged. Each domain is like a tiny magnet; the arrows represent the magnetization direction, with the arrowhead being the N pole. (b) In a magnet, the domains are preferentially aligned in one direction (down in this case), and may be altered in size by the magnetization process.

FIGURE 28–24 Iron filings line up along magnetic field lines due to a permanent magnet.

⚠ **CAUTION**

$\vec{\mathbf{B}}$ *lines form closed loops,*
$\vec{\mathbf{E}}$ *start on* ⊕ *and end on* ⊖

EXERCISE D Return to the Chapter-Opening Question, page 733, and answer it again now. Try to explain why you may have answered differently the first time.

*28–8 Electromagnets and Solenoids—Applications

A long coil of wire consisting of many loops of wire, as discussed in Section 28–5, is called a solenoid. The magnetic field within a solenoid can be fairly large since it will be the sum of the fields due to the current in each loop (see Fig. 28–25). The solenoid acts like a magnet; one end can be considered the north pole and the other the south pole, depending on the direction of the current in the loops (use the right-hand rule). Since the magnetic field lines leave the north pole of a magnet, the north pole of the solenoid in Fig. 28–25 is on the right.

If a piece of iron is placed inside a solenoid, the magnetic field is increased greatly because the domains of the iron are aligned by the magnetic field produced by the current. The resulting magnetic field is the sum of that due to the current and that due to the iron, and can be hundreds or thousands of times larger than that due to the current alone (see Section 28–9). This arrangement is called an **electromagnet**. The alloys of iron used in electromagnets acquire and lose their magnetism quite readily when the current is turned on or off, and so are referred to as "soft iron." (It is "soft" only in a magnetic sense.) Iron that holds its magnetism even when there is no externally applied field is called "hard iron." Hard iron is used in permanent magnets. Soft iron is usually used in electromagnets so that the field can be turned on and off readily. Whether iron is hard or soft depends on heat treatment, type of alloy, and other factors.

Electromagnets have many practical applications, from use in motors and generators to producing large magnetic fields for research. Sometimes an iron core is not present—the magnetic field comes only from the current in the wire coils. When the current flows continuously in a normal electromagnet, a great deal of waste heat (I^2R power) can be produced. Cooling coils, which are tubes carrying water, are needed to absorb the heat in larger installations.

For some applications, the current-carrying wires are made of superconducting material kept below the transition temperature (Section 25–9). Very high fields can be produced with superconducting wire without an iron core. No electric power is needed to maintain large current in the superconducting coils, which means large savings of electricity; nor must huge amounts of heat be dissipated. It is not a free ride, though, because energy is needed to keep the superconducting coils at the necessary low temperature.

Another useful device consists of a solenoid into which a rod of iron is partially inserted. This combination is also referred to as a solenoid. One simple use is as a doorbell (Fig. 28–26). When the circuit is closed by pushing the button, the coil effectively becomes a magnet and exerts a force on the iron rod. The rod is pulled into the coil and strikes the bell. A large solenoid is used in the starters of cars; when you engage the starter, you are closing a circuit that not only turns the starter motor, but activates a solenoid that first moves the starter into direct contact with the gears on the engine's flywheel. Solenoids are used as switches in many devices. They have the advantage of moving mechanical parts quickly and accurately.

*Magnetic Circuit Breakers

Modern circuit breakers that protect houses and buildings from overload and fire contain not only a "thermal" part (bimetallic strip as described in Section 25–6, Fig. 25–19) but also a magnetic sensor. If the current is above a certain level, the magnetic field it produces pulls an iron plate that breaks the same contact points as in Fig. 25–19b and c. In more sophisticated circuit breakers, including ground fault circuit interrupters (GFCIs—discussed in Section 29–8), a solenoid is used. The iron rod of Fig. 28–26, instead of striking a bell, strikes one side of a pair of points, opening them and opening the circuit. Magnetic circuit breakers react quickly (<10 msec), and for buildings are designed to react to the high currents of shorts (but not shut off for the start-up surges of motors).

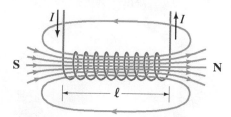

FIGURE 28–25 Magnetic field of a solenoid. The north pole of this solenoid, thought of as a magnet, is on the right, and the south pole is on the left.

PHYSICS APPLIED
Electromagnets and solenoids

PHYSICS APPLIED
Doorbell, car starter

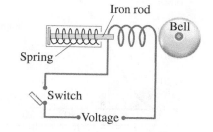

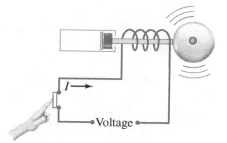

FIGURE 28–26 Solenoid used as a doorbell.

PHYSICS APPLIED
Magnetic circuit breakers

*28–9 Magnetic Fields in Magnetic Materials; Hysteresis

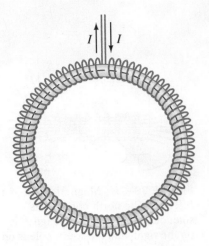

FIGURE 28–27 Iron-core toroid.

FIGURE 28–28 Total magnetic field B in an iron-core toroid as a function of the external field B_0 (B_0 is caused by the current I in the coil).

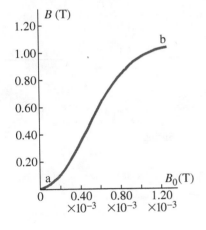

FIGURE 28–29 Hysteresis curve.

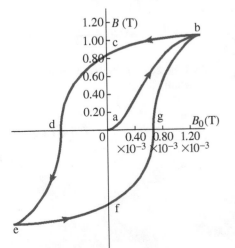

The field of a long solenoid is directly proportional to the current. Indeed, Eq. 28–4 tells us that the field B_0 inside a solenoid is given by

$$B_0 = \mu_0 n I.$$

This is valid if there is only air inside the coil. If we put a piece of iron or other ferromagnetic material inside the solenoid, the field will be greatly increased, often by hundreds or thousands of times. This occurs because the domains in the iron become preferentially aligned by the external field. The resulting magnetic field is the sum of that due to the current and that due to the iron. It is sometimes convenient to write the total field in this case as a sum of two terms:

$$\vec{B} = \vec{B}_0 + \vec{B}_M. \qquad (28\text{–}8)$$

Here, $\vec{B}_0$ refers to the field due only to the current in the wire (the "external field"). It is the field that would be present in the absence of a ferromagnetic material. Then $\vec{B}_M$ represents the additional field due to the ferromagnetic material itself; often $\vec{B}_M \gg \vec{B}_0$.

The total field inside a solenoid in such a case can also be written by replacing the constant μ_0 in Eq. 28–4 by another constant, μ, characteristic of the material inside the coil:

$$B = \mu n I; \qquad (28\text{–}9)$$

μ is called the **magnetic permeability** of the material (do not confuse it with $\vec{\mu}$ for magnetic dipole moment). For ferromagnetic materials, μ is much greater than μ_0. For all other materials, its value is very close to μ_0 (Section 28–10). The value of μ, however, is not constant for ferromagnetic materials; it depends on the value of the external field B_0, as the following experiment shows.

Measurements on magnetic materials are generally done using a toroid, which is essentially a long solenoid bent into the shape of a circle (Fig. 28–27), so that practically all the lines of $\vec{B}$ remain within the toroid. Suppose the toroid has an iron core that is initially unmagnetized and there is no current in the windings of the toroid. Then the current I is slowly increased, and B_0 increases linearly with I. The total field B also increases, but follows the curved line shown in the graph of Fig. 28–28. (Note the different scales: $B \gg B_0$.) Initially, point a, the domains (Section 28–7) are randomly oriented. As B_0 increases, the domains become more and more aligned until at point b, nearly all are aligned. The iron is said to be approaching **saturation**. Point b is typically 70% of full saturation. (If B_0 is increased further, the curve continues to rise very slowly, and reaches 98% saturation only when B_0 reaches a value about a thousandfold above that at point b; the last few domains are very difficult to align.) Next, suppose the external field B_0 is reduced by decreasing the current in the toroid coils. As the current is reduced to zero, shown as point c in Fig. 28–29, the domains do not become completely random. Some permanent magnetism remains. If the current is then reversed in direction, enough domains can be turned around so $B = 0$ (point d). As the reverse current is increased further, the iron approaches saturation in the opposite direction (point e). Finally, if the current is again reduced to zero and then increased in the original direction, the total field follows the path efgb, again approaching saturation at point b.

Notice that the field did not pass through the origin (point a) in this cycle. The fact that the curves do not retrace themselves on the same path is called **hysteresis**. The curve bcdefgb is called a **hysteresis loop**. In such a cycle, much energy is transformed to thermal energy (friction) due to realigning of the domains. It can be shown that the energy dissipated in this way is proportional to the area of the hysteresis loop.

At points c and f, the iron core is magnetized even though there is no current in the coils. These points correspond to a permanent magnet. For a permanent magnet, it is desired that ac and af be as large as possible. Materials for which this is true are said to have high **retentivity**.

Materials with a broad hysteresis curve as in Fig. 28–29 are said to be magnetically "hard" and make good permanent magnets. On the other hand, a hysteresis curve such as that in Fig. 28–30 occurs for "soft" iron, which is preferred for electromagnets and transformers (Section 29–6) since the field can be more readily switched off, and the field can be reversed with less loss of energy.

A ferromagnetic material can be demagnetized—that is, made unmagnetized. This can be done by reversing the magnetizing current repeatedly while decreasing its magnitude. This results in the curve of Fig. 28–31. The heads of a tape recorder are demagnetized in this way. The alternating magnetic field acting at the heads due to a handheld demagnetizer is strong when the demagnetizer is placed near the heads and decreases as it is moved slowly away. Video and audio tapes themselves can be erased and ruined by a magnetic field, as can computer hard disks, other magnetic storage devices, and the magnetic stripes on credit cards.

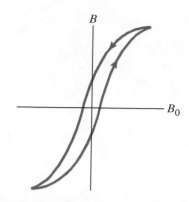

FIGURE 28–30 Hysteresis curve for soft iron.

FIGURE 28–31 Successive hysteresis loops during demagnetization.

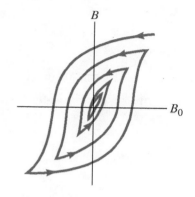

*28–10 Paramagnetism and Diamagnetism

All materials are magnetic to at least a tiny extent. Nonferromagnetic materials fall into two principal classes: *paramagnetic*, in which the magnetic permeability μ is very slightly greater than μ_0; and *diamagnetic*, in which μ is very slightly less than μ_0. The ratio of μ to μ_0 for any material is called the **relative permeability** K_m:

$$K_m = \frac{\mu}{\mu_0}.$$

Another useful parameter is the **magnetic susceptibility** χ_m defined as

$$\chi_m = K_m - 1.$$

Paramagnetic substances have $K_m > 1$ and $\chi_m > 0$, whereas diamagnetic substances have $K_m < 1$ and $\chi_m < 0$. See Table 28–1, and note how small the effect is.

TABLE 28–1 Paramagnetism and Diamagnetism: Magnetic Susceptibilities

Paramagnetic substance	χ_m	Diamagnetic substance	χ_m
Aluminum	2.3×10^{-5}	Copper	-9.8×10^{-6}
Calcium	1.9×10^{-5}	Diamond	-2.2×10^{-5}
Magnesium	1.2×10^{-5}	Gold	-3.6×10^{-5}
Oxygen (STP)	2.1×10^{-6}	Lead	-1.7×10^{-5}
Platinum	2.9×10^{-4}	Nitrogen (STP)	-5.0×10^{-9}
Tungsten	6.8×10^{-5}	Silicon	-4.2×10^{-6}

The difference between paramagnetic and diamagnetic materials can be understood theoretically at the molecular level on the basis of whether or not the molecules have a permanent magnetic dipole moment. One type of **paramagnetism** occurs in materials whose molecules (or ions) have a permanent magnetic dipole moment.[†] In the absence of an external field, the molecules are randomly oriented and no magnetic effects are observed. However, when an external magnetic field is applied, say, by putting the material in a solenoid, the applied field exerts a torque on the magnetic dipoles (Section 27–5), tending to align them parallel to the field. The total magnetic field (external plus that due to aligned magnetic dipoles) will be slightly greater than B_0. The thermal motion of the molecules reduces the alignment, however.

[†] Other types of paramagnetism also occur whose origin is different from that described here, such as in metals where free electrons can contribute.

A useful quantity is the **magnetization vector**, $\vec{M}$, defined as the magnetic dipole moment per unit volume,

$$\vec{M} = \frac{\vec{\mu}}{V},$$

where $\vec{\mu}$ is the magnetic dipole moment of the sample and V its volume. It is found experimentally that M is directly proportional to the external magnetic field (tending to align the dipoles) and inversely proportional to the kelvin temperature T (tending to randomize dipole directions). This is called *Curie's law*, after Pierre Curie (1859–1906), who first noted it:

$$M = C\frac{B}{T},$$

where C is a constant. If the ratio B/T is very large (B very large or T very small) Curie's law is no longer accurate; as B is increased (or T decreased), the magnetization approaches some maximum value, M_{max}. This makes sense, of course, since M_{max} corresponds to complete alignment of all the permanent magnetic dipoles. However, even for very large magnetic fields, $\approx 2.0\,\mathrm{T}$, deviations from Curie's law are normally noted only at very low temperatures, on the order of a few kelvins.

Ferromagnetic materials, as mentioned in Section 28–7, are no longer ferromagnetic above a characteristic temperature called the Curie temperature (1043 K for iron). Above this Curie temperature, they generally are paramagnetic.

Diamagnetic materials (for which μ_m is slightly less than μ_0) are made up of molecules that have no permanent magnetic dipole moment. When an external magnetic field is applied, magnetic dipoles are induced, but the induced magnetic dipole moment is in the direction opposite to that of the field. Hence the total field will be slightly less than the external field. The effect of the external field—in the crude model of electrons orbiting nuclei—is to increase the "orbital" speed of electrons revolving in one direction, and to decrease the speed of electrons revolving in the other direction; the net result is a net dipole moment opposing the external field. Diamagnetism is present in all materials, but is weaker even than paramagnetism and so is overwhelmed by paramagnetic and ferromagnetic effects in materials that display these other forms of magnetism.

Summary

The magnetic field B at a distance r from a long straight wire is directly proportional to the current I in the wire and inversely proportional to r:

$$B = \frac{\mu_0}{2\pi}\frac{I}{r}. \tag{28–1}$$

The magnetic field lines are circles centered at the wire.

The force that one long current-carrying wire exerts on a second parallel current-carrying wire 1 m away serves as the definition of the ampere unit, and ultimately of the coulomb as well.

Ampère's law states that the line integral of the magnetic field $\vec{B}$ around any closed loop is equal to μ_0 times the total net current I_{encl} enclosed by the loop:

$$\oint \vec{B} \cdot d\vec{\ell} = \mu_0 I_{encl}. \tag{28–3}$$

The magnetic field inside a long tightly wound solenoid is

$$B = \mu_0 n I \tag{28–4}$$

where n is the number of coils per unit length and I is the current in each coil.

The **Biot-Savart law** is useful for determining the magnetic field due to a known arrangement of currents. It states that

$$d\vec{B} = \frac{\mu_0 I}{4\pi}\frac{d\vec{\ell} \times \hat{r}}{r^2}, \tag{28–5}$$

where $d\vec{B}$ is the contribution to the total field at some point P due to a current I along an infinitesimal length $d\vec{\ell}$ of its path, and $\hat{r}$ is the unit vector along the direction of the displacement vector $\vec{r}$ from $d\vec{\ell}$ to P. The total field $\vec{B}$ will be the integral over all $d\vec{B}$.

Iron and a few other materials can be made into strong permanent magnets. They are said to be **ferromagnetic**. Ferromagnetic materials are made up of tiny **domains**—each a tiny magnet—which are preferentially aligned in a permanent magnet, but randomly aligned in a nonmagnetized sample.

[*When a ferromagnetic material is placed in a magnetic field B_0 due to a current, say inside a solenoid or toroid, the material becomes magnetized. When the current is turned off, however, the material remains magnetized, and when the current is increased in the opposite direction (and then again reversed), a graph of the total field B versus B_0 is a **hysteresis loop**, and the fact that the curves do not retrace themselves is called **hysteresis**.]

[*All materials exhibit some magnetic effects. Nonferromagnetic materials have much smaller paramagnetic or diamagnetic properties.]

Questions

1. The magnetic field due to current in wires in your home can affect a compass. Discuss the problem in terms of currents, depending on whether they are ac or dc, and their distance away.

2. Compare and contrast the magnetic field due to a long straight current and the electric field due to a long straight line of electric charge at rest (Section 21–7).

3. Two insulated long wires carrying equal currents I cross at right angles to each other. Describe the magnetic force one exerts on the other.

4. A horizontal wire carries a large current. A second wire carrying a current in the same direction is suspended below it. Can the current in the upper wire hold the lower wire in suspension against gravity? Under what conditions will the lower wire be in equilibrium?

5. A horizontal current-carrying wire, free to move in Earth's gravitational field, is suspended directly above a second, parallel, current-carrying wire. (a) In what direction is the current in the lower wire? (b) Can the upper wire be held in stable equilibrium due to the magnetic force of the lower wire? Explain.

6. (a) Write Ampère's law for a path that surrounds both conductors in Fig. 28–10. (b) Repeat, assuming the lower current, I_2, is in the opposite direction $(I_2 = -I_1)$.

7. Suppose the cylindrical conductor of Fig. 28–11a has a concentric cylindrical hollow cavity inside it (so it looks like a pipe). What can you say about $\vec{B}$ in the cavity?

8. Explain why a field such as that shown in Fig. 28–14b is consistent with Ampère's law. Could the lines curve upward instead of downward?

9. What would be the effect on B inside a long solenoid if (a) the diameter of all the loops was doubled, or (b) the spacing between loops was doubled, or (c) the solenoid's length was doubled along with a doubling in the total number of loops.

10. Use the Biot-Savart law to show that the field of the current loop in Fig. 28–21 is correct as shown for points off the axis.

11. Do you think $\vec{B}$ will be the same for all points in the plane of the current loop of Fig. 28–21? Explain.

12. Why does twisting the lead-in wires to electrical devices reduce the magnetic effects of the leads?

13. Compare the Biot-Savart law with Coulomb's law. What are the similarities and differences?

14. How might you define or determine the magnetic pole strength (the magnetic equivalent of a single electric charge) for (a) a bar magnet, (b) a current loop?

15. How might you measure the magnetic dipole moment of the Earth?

16. A type of magnetic switch similar to a solenoid is a **relay** (Fig. 28–32). A relay is an electromagnet (the iron rod inside the coil does not move) which, when activated, attracts a piece of iron on a pivot. Design a relay to close an electrical switch. A relay is used when you need to switch on a circuit carrying a very large current but you do not want that large current flowing through the main switch. For example, the starter switch of a car is connected to a relay so that the large current needed for the starter doesn't pass to the dashboard switch.

FIGURE 28–32
Question 16.

17. A heavy magnet attracts, from rest, a heavy block of iron. Before striking the magnet the block has acquired considerable kinetic energy. (a) What is the source of this kinetic energy? (b) When the block strikes the magnet, some of the latter's domains may be jarred into randomness; describe the energy transformations.

18. Will a magnet attract any metallic object, such as those made of aluminum, or only those made of iron? (Try it and see.) Why is this so?

19. An unmagnetized nail will not attract an unmagnetized paper clip. However, if one end of the nail is in contact with a magnet, the other end *will* attract a paper clip. Explain.

20. Can an iron rod attract a magnet? Can a magnet attract an iron rod? What must you consider to answer these questions?

21. How do you suppose the first magnets found in Magnesia were formed?

22. Why will either pole of a magnet attract an unmagnetized piece of iron?

23. Suppose you have three iron rods, two of which are magnetized but the third is not. How would you determine which two are the magnets without using any additional objects?

24. Two iron bars attract each other no matter which ends are placed close together. Are both magnets? Explain.

*25. Describe the magnetization curve for (a) a paramagnetic substance and (b) a diamagnetic substance, and compare to that for a ferromagnetic substance (Fig. 28–29).

*26. Can all materials be considered (a) diamagnetic, (b) paramagnetic, (c) ferromagnetic? Explain.

Problems

28–1 and 28–2 Straight Wires, Magnetic Field, and Force

1. (I) Jumper cables used to start a stalled vehicle often carry a 65-A current. How strong is the magnetic field 3.5 cm from one cable? Compare to the Earth's magnetic field $(5.0 \times 10^{-5}\,\text{T})$.

2. (I) If an electric wire is allowed to produce a magnetic field no larger than that of the Earth $(0.50 \times 10^{-4}\,\text{T})$ at a distance of 15 cm from the wire, what is the maximum current the wire can carry?

3. (I) Determine the magnitude and direction of the force between two parallel wires 25 m long and 4.0 cm apart, each carrying 35 A in the same direction.

4. (I) A vertical straight wire carrying an upward 28-A current exerts an attractive force per unit length of 7.8×10^{-4} N/m on a second parallel wire 7.0 cm away. What current (magnitude and direction) flows in the second wire?

5. (I) In Fig. 28–33, a long straight wire carries current I out of the page toward the viewer. Indicate, with appropriate arrows, the direction of $\vec{B}$ at each of the points C, D, and E in the plane of the page.

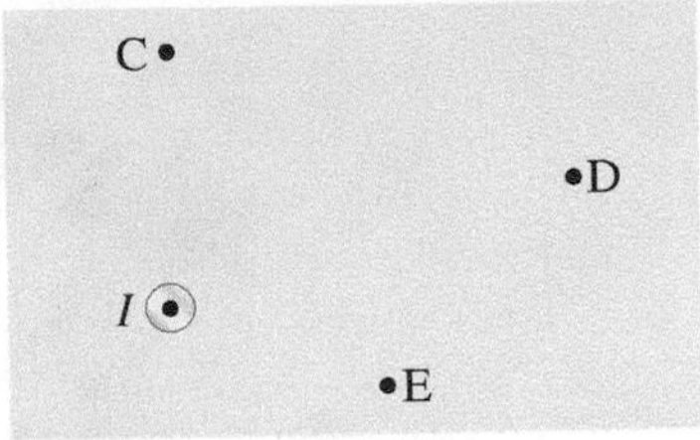

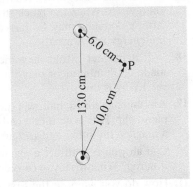

FIGURE 28–33
Problem 5.

6. (II) An experiment on the Earth's magnetic field is being carried out 1.00 m from an electric cable. What is the maximum allowable current in the cable if the experiment is to be accurate to $\pm 2.0\%$?

7. (II) Two long thin parallel wires 13.0 cm apart carry 35-A currents in the same direction. Determine the magnetic field vector at a point 10.0 cm from one wire and 6.0 cm from the other (Fig. 28–34).

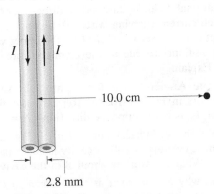

FIGURE 28–34
Problem 7.

8. (II) A horizontal compass is placed 18 cm due south from a straight vertical wire carrying a 43-A current downward. In what direction does the compass needle point at this location? Assume the horizontal component of the Earth's field at this point is 0.45×10^{-4} T and the magnetic declination is $0°$.

9. (II) A long horizontal wire carries 24.0 A of current due north. What is the net magnetic field 20.0 cm due west of the wire if the Earth's field there points downward, $44°$ below the horizontal, and has magnitude 5.0×10^{-5} T?

10. (II) A straight stream of protons passes a given point in space at a rate of 2.5×10^9 protons/s. What magnetic field do they produce 2.0 m from the beam?

11. (II) Determine the magnetic field midway between two long straight wires 2.0 cm apart in terms of the current I in one when the other carries 25 A. Assume these currents are (a) in the same direction, and (b) in opposite directions.

12. (II) Two straight parallel wires are separated by 6.0 cm. There is a 2.0-A current flowing in the first wire. If the magnetic field strength is found to be zero between the two wires at a distance of 2.2 cm from the first wire, what is the magnitude and direction of the current in the second wire?

13. (II) Two long straight wires each carry a current I out of the page toward the viewer, Fig. 28–35. Indicate, with appropriate arrows, the direction of $\vec{B}$ at each of the points 1 to 6 in the plane of the page. State if the field is zero at any of the points.

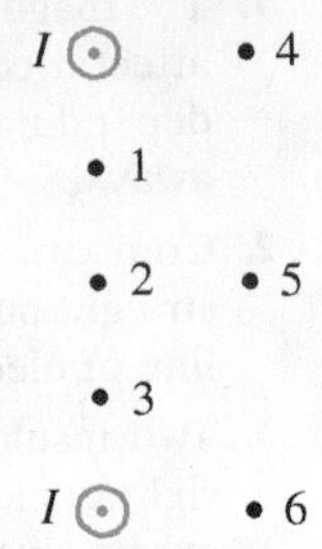

$I \odot$ •4

•1

•2 •5

•3

FIGURE 28–35
Problem 13. $I \odot$ •6

14. (II) A long pair of insulated wires serves to conduct 28.0 A of dc current to and from an instrument. If the wires are of negligible diameter but are 2.8 mm apart, what is the magnetic field 10.0 cm from their midpoint, in their plane (Fig. 28–36)? Compare to the magnetic field of the Earth.

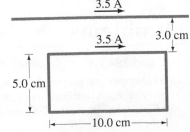

FIGURE 28–36   Problems 14 and 15.

15. (II) A third wire is placed in the plane of the two wires shown in Fig. 28–36 parallel and just to the right. If it carries 25.0 A upward, what force per meter of length does it exert on each of the other two wires? Assume it is 2.8 mm from the nearest wire, center to center.

16. (II) A power line carries a current of 95 A west along the tops of 8.5-m-high poles. (a) What is the magnitude and direction of the magnetic field produced by this wire at the ground directly below? How does this compare with the Earth's field of about $\frac{1}{2}$ G? (b) Where would the line's field cancel the Earth's?

17. (II) A compass needle points $28°$ E of N outdoors. However, when it is placed 12.0 cm to the east of a vertical wire inside a building, it points $55°$ E of N. What is the magnitude and direction of the current in the wire? The Earth's field there is 0.50×10^{-4} T and is horizontal.

18. (II) A rectangular loop of wire is placed next to a straight wire, as shown in Fig. 28–37. There is a current of 3.5 A in both wires. Determine the magnitude and direction of the net force on the loop.

3.5 A

3.5 A   3.0 cm

5.0 cm

FIGURE 28–37
Problem 18.   ├──10.0 cm──┤

19. (II) Let two long parallel wires, a distance d apart, carry equal currents I in the same direction. One wire is at $x = 0$, the other at $x = d$, Fig. 28–38. Determine $\vec{B}$ along the x axis between the wires as a function of x.

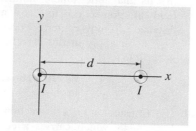

FIGURE 28–38
Problems 19 and 20.

20. (II) Repeat Problem 19 if the wire at $x = 0$ carries twice the current $(2I)$ as the other wire, and in the opposite direction.

21. (II) Two long wires are oriented so that they are perpendicular to each other. At their closest, they are 20.0 cm apart (Fig. 28–39). What is the magnitude of the magnetic field at a point midway between them if the top one carries a current of 20.0 A and the bottom one carries 12.0 A?

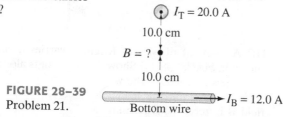

FIGURE 28–39
Problem 21.

22. (II) Two long parallel wires 8.20 cm apart carry 16.5-A currents in the same direction. Determine the magnetic field vector at a point P, 12.0 cm from one wire and 13.0 cm from the other. See Fig. 28–40.
[*Hint*: Use the law of cosines.]

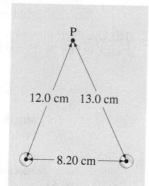

FIGURE 28–40
Problem 22.

23. (III) A very long flat conducting strip of width d and negligible thickness lies in a horizontal plane and carries a uniform current I across its cross section. (a) Show that at points a distance y directly above its center, the field is given by

$$B = \frac{\mu_0 I}{\pi d} \tan^{-1} \frac{d}{2y},$$

assuming the strip is infinitely long. [*Hint*: Divide the strip into many thin "wires," and sum (integrate) over these.] (b) What value does B approach for $y \gg d$? Does this make sense? Explain.

24. (III) A triangular loop of side length a carries a current I (Fig. 28–41). If this loop is placed a distance d away from a very long straight wire carrying a current I', determine the force on the loop.

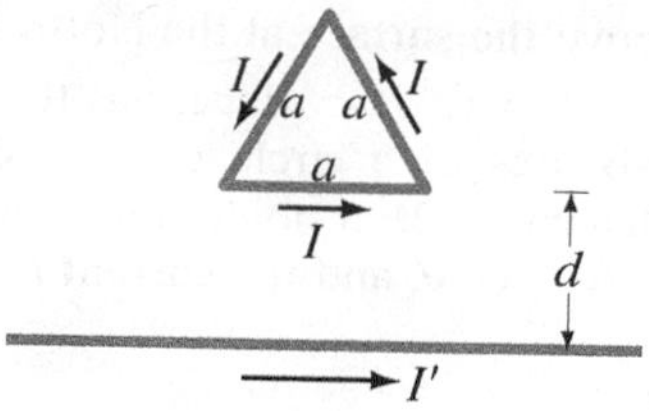

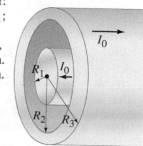

FIGURE 28–41
Problem 24.

28–4 and 28–5 Ampère's Law, Solenoids and Toroids

25. (I) A 40.0-cm-long solenoid 1.35 cm in diameter is to produce a field of 0.385 mT at its center. How much current should the solenoid carry if it has 765 turns of wire?

26. (I) A 32-cm-long solenoid, 1.8 cm in diameter, is to produce a 0.30-T magnetic field at its center. If the maximum current is 4.5 A, how many turns must the solenoid have?

27. (I) A 2.5-mm-diameter copper wire carries a 33-A current (uniform across its cross section). Determine the magnetic field: (a) at the surface of the wire; (b) inside the wire, 0.50 mm below the surface; (c) outside the wire 2.5 mm from the surface.

28. (II) A toroid (Fig. 28–17) has a 50.0-cm inner diameter and a 54.0-cm outer diameter. It carries a 25.0 A current in its 687 coils. Determine the range of values for B inside the toroid.

29. (II) A 20.0-m-long copper wire, 2.00 mm in diameter including insulation, is tightly wrapped in a single layer with adjacent coils touching, to form a solenoid of diameter 2.50 cm (outer edge). What is (a) the length of the solenoid and (b) the field at the center when the current in the wire is 16.7 A?

30. (II) (a) Use Eq. 28–1, and the vector nature of $\vec{B}$, to show that the magnetic field lines around two long parallel wires carrying equal currents $I_1 = I_2$ are as shown in Fig. 28–10. (b) Draw the equipotential lines around two stationary positive electric charges. (c) Are these two diagrams similar? Identical? Why or why not?

31. (II) A coaxial cable consists of a solid inner conductor of radius R_1, surrounded by a concentric cylindrical tube of inner radius R_2 and outer radius R_3 (Fig. 28–42). The conductors carry equal and opposite currents I_0 distributed uniformly across their cross sections. Determine the magnetic field at a distance R from the axis for: (a) $R < R_1$; (b) $R_1 < R < R_2$; (c) $R_2 < R < R_3$; (d) $R > R_3$. (e) Let $I_0 = 1.50$ A, $R_1 = 1.00$ cm, $R_2 = 2.00$ cm, and $R_3 = 2.50$ cm. Graph B from $R = 0$ to $R = 3.00$ cm.

FIGURE 28–42
Problems 31 and 32.

32. (III) Suppose the current in the coaxial cable of Problem 31, Fig. 28–42, is not uniformly distributed, but instead the current density j varies linearly with distance from the center: $j_1 = C_1 R$ for the inner conductor and $j_2 = C_2 R$ for the outer conductor. Each conductor still carries the same total current I_0, in opposite directions. Determine the magnetic field in terms of I_0 in the same four regions of space as in Problem 31.

28-6 Biot-Savart Law

33. (I) The Earth's magnetic field is essentially that of a magnetic dipole. If the field near the North Pole is about 1.0×10^{-4} T, what will it be (approximately) 13,000 km above the surface at the North Pole?

34. (II) A wire, in a plane, has the shape shown in Fig. 28–43, two arcs of a circle connected by radial lengths of wire. Determine $\vec{\mathbf{B}}$ at point C in terms of R_1, R_2, θ, and the current I.

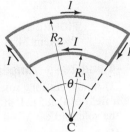

FIGURE 28–43
Problem 34.

35. (II) A circular conducting ring of radius R is connected to two exterior straight wires at two ends of a diameter (Fig. 28–44). The current I splits into unequal portions (as shown) while passing through the ring. What is $\vec{\mathbf{B}}$ at the center of the ring?

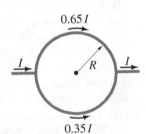

FIGURE 28–44
Problem 35.

36. (II) A small loop of wire of radius 1.8 cm is placed at the center of a wire loop with radius 25.0 cm. The planes of the loops are perpendicular to each other, and a 7.0-A current flows in each. Estimate the torque the large loop exerts on the smaller one. What simplifying assumption did you make?

37. (II) A wire is formed into the shape of two half circles connected by equal-length straight sections as shown in Fig. 28–45. A current I flows in the circuit clockwise as shown. Determine (a) the magnitude and direction of the magnetic field at the center, C, and (b) the magnetic dipole moment of the circuit.

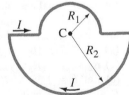

FIGURE 28–45
Problem 37.

38. (II) A single point charge q is moving with velocity $\vec{\mathbf{v}}$. Use the Biot-Savart law to show that the magnetic field $\vec{\mathbf{B}}$ it produces at a point P, whose position vector relative to the charge is $\vec{\mathbf{r}}$ (Fig. 28–46), is given by

$$\vec{\mathbf{B}} = \frac{\mu_0}{4\pi} \frac{q\vec{\mathbf{v}} \times \vec{\mathbf{r}}}{r^3}.$$

(Assume v is much less than the speed of light.)

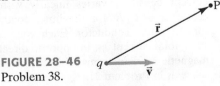

FIGURE 28–46
Problem 38.

39. (II) A nonconducting circular disk, of radius R, carries a uniformly distributed electric charge Q. The plate is set spinning with angular velocity ω about an axis perpendicular to the plate through its center (Fig. 28–47). Determine (a) its magnetic dipole moment and (b) the magnetic field at points on its axis a distance x from its center; (c) does Eq. 28–7b apply in this case for $x \gg R$?

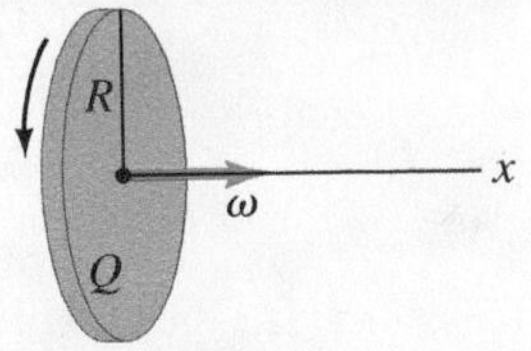

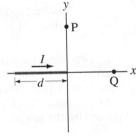

FIGURE 28–47
Problem 39.

40. (II) Consider a straight section of wire of length d, as in Fig. 28–48, which carries a current I. (a) Show that the magnetic field at a point P a distance R from the wire along its perpendicular bisector is

$$B = \frac{\mu_0 I}{2\pi R} \frac{d}{(d^2 + 4R^2)^{\frac{1}{2}}}.$$

(b) Show that this is consistent with Example 28–11 for an infinite wire.

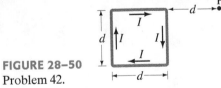

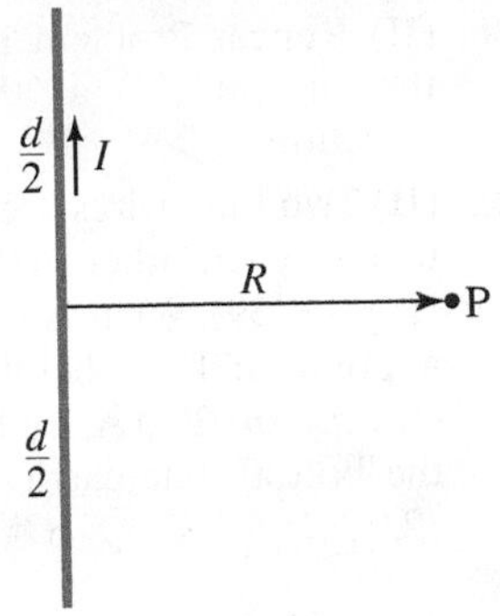

FIGURE 28–48
Problem 40.

41. (II) A segment of wire of length d carries a current I as shown in Fig. 28–49. (a) Show that for points along the positive x axis (the axis of the wire), such as point Q, the magnetic field $\vec{\mathbf{B}}$ is zero. (b) Determine a formula for the field at points along the y axis, such as point P.

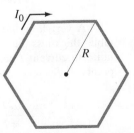

FIGURE 28–49
Problem 41.

42. (III) Use the result of Problem 41 to find the magnetic field at point P in Fig. 28–50 due to the current in the square loop.

FIGURE 28–50
Problem 42.

43. (III) A wire is bent into the shape of a regular polygon with n sides whose vertices are a distance R from the center. (See Fig. 28–51, which shows the special case of $n = 6$.) If the wire carries a current I_0, (a) determine the magnetic field at the center; (b) if n is allowed to become very large ($n \to \infty$), show that the formula in part (a) reduces to that for a circular loop (Example 28–12).

FIGURE 28–51
Problem 43.

44. (III) Start with the result of Example 28–12 for the magnetic field along the axis of a single loop to obtain the field inside a very long solenoid with n turns per meter (Eq. 28–4) that stretches from $+\infty$ to $-\infty$.

45. (III) A single rectangular loop of wire, with sides a and b, carries a current I. An xy coordinate system has its origin at the lower left corner of the rectangle with the x axis parallel to side b (Fig. 28–52) and the y axis parallel to side a. Determine the magnetic field B at all points (x, y) within the loop.

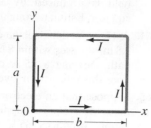

FIGURE 28–52
Problem 45.

46. (III) A square loop of wire, of side d, carries a current I. (a) Determine the magnetic field B at points on a line perpendicular to the plane of the square which passes through the center of the square (Fig. 28–53). Express B as a function of x, the distance along the line from the center of the square. (b) For $x \gg d$, does the square appear to be a magnetic dipole? If so, what is its dipole moment?

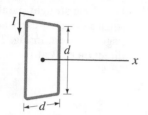

FIGURE 28–53
Problem 46.

28–7 Magnetic Materials—Ferromagnetism

47. (II) An iron atom has a magnetic dipole moment of about $1.8 \times 10^{-23}\,\text{A} \cdot \text{m}^2$. (a) Determine the dipole moment of an iron bar 9.0 cm long, 1.2 cm wide, and 1.0 cm thick, if it is 100 percent saturated. (b) What torque would be exerted on this bar when placed in a 0.80-T field acting at right angles to the bar?

*28–9 Magnetic Materials; Hysteresis

*48. (I) The following are some values of B and B_0 for a piece of annealed iron as it is being magnetized:

$B_0(10^{-4}\,\text{T})$	0.0	0.13	0.25	0.50	0.63	0.78	1.0	1.3
$B(\text{T})$	0.0	0.0042	0.010	0.028	0.043	0.095	0.45	0.67
$B_0(10^{-4}\,\text{T})$	1.9	2.5	6.3	13.0	130	1300	10,000	
$B(\text{T})$	1.01	1.18	1.44	1.58	1.72	2.26	3.15	

Determine the magnetic permeability μ for each value and plot a graph of μ versus B_0.

*49. (I) A large thin toroid has 285 loops of wire per meter, and a 3.0-A current flows through the wire. If the relative permeability of the iron is $\mu/\mu_0 = 2200$, what is the total field B inside the toroid?

*50. (II) An iron-core solenoid is 38 cm long and 1.8 cm in diameter, and has 640 turns of wire. The magnetic field inside the solenoid is 2.2 T when 48 A flows in the wire. What is the permeability μ at this high field strength?

General Problems

51. Three long parallel wires are 3.5 cm from one another. (Looking along them, they are at three corners of an equilateral triangle.) The current in each wire is 8.00 A, but its direction in wire M is opposite to that in wires N and P (Fig. 28–54). Determine the magnetic force per unit length on each wire due to the other two.

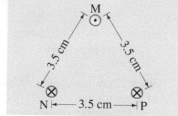

FIGURE 28–54
Problems 51, 52, and 53.

52. In Fig. 28–54, determine the magnitude and direction of the magnetic field midway between points M and N.

53. In Fig. 28–54 the top wire is 1.00-mm-diameter copper wire and is suspended in air due to the two magnetic forces from the bottom two wires. The current is 40.0 A in each of the two bottom wires. Calculate the required current flow in the suspended wire.

54. An electron enters a large solenoid at a 7.0° angle to the axis. If the field is a uniform $3.3 \times 10^{-2}\,\text{T}$, determine the radius and pitch (distance between loops) of the electron's helical path if its speed is $1.3 \times 10^7\,\text{m/s}$.

55. Two long straight parallel wires are 15 cm apart. Wire A carries 2.0-A current. Wire B's current is 4.0 A in the same direction. (a) Determine the magnetic field due to wire A at the position of wire B. (b) Determine the magnetic field due to wire B at the position of wire A. (c) Are these two magnetic fields equal and opposite? Why or why not? (d) Determine the force per unit length on wire A due to wire B, and that on wire B due to wire A. Are these two forces equal and opposite? Why or why not?

56. A rectangular loop of wire carries a 2.0-A current and lies in a plane which also contains a very long straight wire carrying a 10.0-A current as shown in Fig. 28–55. Determine (a) the net force and (b) the net torque on the loop due to the straight wire.

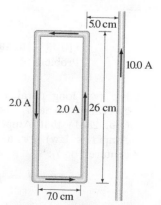

FIGURE 28–55
Problem 56.

57. A very large flat conducting sheet of thickness t carries a uniform current density $\vec{\mathbf{j}}$ throughout (Fig. 28–56). Determine the magnetic field (magnitude and direction) at a distance y above the plane. (Assume the plane is infinitely long and wide.)

FIGURE 28–56
Problem 57.

58. A long horizontal wire carries a current of 48 A. A second wire, made of 1.00-mm-diameter copper wire and parallel to the first, is kept in suspension magnetically 5.0 cm below (Fig. 28–57). (a) Determine the magnitude and direction of the current in the lower wire. (b) Is the lower wire in stable equilibrium? (c) Repeat parts (a) and (b) if the second wire is suspended 5.0 cm *above* the first due to the first's magnetic field.

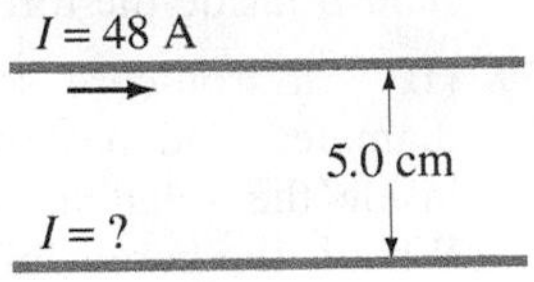

$I = 48$ A

5.0 cm

$I = \,?$

FIGURE 28–57
Problem 58.

59. A square loop of wire, of side d, carries a current I. Show that the magnetic field at the center of the square is

$$B = \frac{2\sqrt{2}\,\mu_0 I}{\pi d}.$$

[*Hint*: Determine $\vec{\mathbf{B}}$ for each segment of length d.]

60. In Problem 59, if you reshaped the square wire into a circle, would B increase or decrease at the center? Explain.

61. Helmholtz coils are two identical circular coils having the same radius R and the same number of turns N, separated by a distance equal to the radius R and carrying the same current I in the same direction. (See Fig. 28–58.) They are used in scientific instruments to generate nearly uniform magnetic fields.(They can be seen in the photo, Fig. 27–18.) (a) Determine the magnetic field B at points x along the line joining their centers. Let $x = 0$ at the center of one coil, and $x = R$ at the center of the other. (b) Show that the field midway between the coils is particularly uniform by showing that $\dfrac{dB}{dx} = 0$ and $\dfrac{d^2B}{dx^2} = 0$ at the midpoint between the coils. (c) If $R = 10.0$ cm, $N = 250$ turns and $I = 2.0$ A, what is the field at the midpoint between the coils, $x = R/2$?

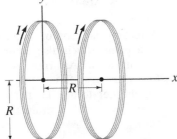

FIGURE 28–58
Problem 61.

62. For two long parallel wires separated by a distance d, carrying currents I_1 and I_2 as in Fig. 28–10, show directly (Eq. 28–1) that Ampère's law is valid (but do not use Ampère's law) for a circular path of radius r ($r < d$) centered on I_1:

$$\oint \vec{\mathbf{B}} \cdot d\vec{\boldsymbol{\ell}} = \mu_0 I_1.$$

63. Near the Earth's poles the magnetic field is about 1 G $(1 \times 10^{-4}\,\text{T})$. Imagine a simple model in which the Earth's field is produced by a single current loop around the equator. Estimate roughly the current this loop would carry.

64. A 175-g model airplane charged to 18.0 mC and traveling at 2.8 m/s passes within 8.6 cm of a wire, nearly parallel to its path, carrying a 25-A current. What acceleration (in g's) does this interaction give the airplane?

65. Suppose that an electromagnet uses a coil 2.0 m in diameter made from square copper wire 2.0 mm on a side; the power supply produces 35 V at a maximum power output of 1.0 kW. (a) How many turns are needed to run the power supply at maximum power? (b) What is the magnetic field strength at the center of the coil? (c) If you use a greater number of turns and this same power supply, will a greater magnetic field result? Explain.

66. Four long straight parallel wires located at the corners of a square of side d carry equal currents I_0 perpendicular to the page as shown in Fig. 28–59. Determine the magnitude and direction of $\vec{\mathbf{B}}$ at the center C of the square.

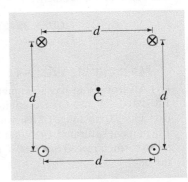

FIGURE 28–59
Problem 66.

67. Determine the magnetic field at the point P due to a very long wire with a square bend as shown in Fig. 28–60. The point P is halfway between the two corners. [*Hint*: You can use the results of Problems 40 and 41.]

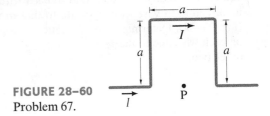

FIGURE 28–60
Problem 67.

68. A thin 12-cm-long solenoid has a total of 420 turns of wire and carries a current of 2.0 A. Calculate the field inside the solenoid near the center.

69. A 550-turn solenoid is 15 cm long. The current into it is 33 A. A 3.0-cm-long straight wire cuts through the center of the solenoid, along a diameter. This wire carries a 22-A current downward (and is connected by other wires that don't concern us). What is the force on this wire assuming the solenoid's field points due east?

70. You have 1.0 kg of copper and want to make a practical solenoid that produces the greatest possible magnetic field for a given voltage. Should you make your copper wire long and thin, short and fat, or something else? Consider other variables, such as solenoid diameter, length, and so on.

71. A small solenoid (radius r_a) is inside a larger solenoid (radius $r_b > r_a$). They are coaxial with n_a and n_b turns per unit length, respectively. The solenoids carry the same current, but in opposite directions. Let r be the radial distance from the common axis of the solenoids. If the magnetic field inside the inner solenoid $(r < r_a)$ is to be in the opposite direction as the field between the solenoids $(r_a < r < r_b)$, but have half the magnitude, determine the required ratio n_b/n_a.

72. Find B at the center of the 4.0-cm-radius semicircle in Fig. 28–61. The straight wires extend a great distance outward to the left and carry a current $I = 6.0A$.

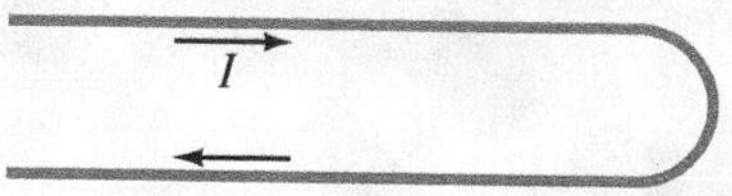

FIGURE 28–61
Problem 72.

73. The design of a magneto-optical atom trap requires a magnetic field B that is directly proportional to position x along an axis. Such a field perturbs the absorption of laser light by atoms in the manner needed to spatially confine atoms in the trap. Let us demonstrate that "anti-Helmholtz" coils will provide the required field $B = Cx$, where C is a constant. Anti-Helmholtz coils consist of two identical circular wire coils, each with radius R and N turns, carrying current I in opposite directions (Fig. 28–62). The coils share a common axis (defined as the x axis with $x = 0$ at the midpoint (0) between the coils). Assume that the centers of the coils are separated by a distance equal to the radius R of the coils. (a) Show that the magnetic field at position x along the x axis is given by

$$B(x) = \frac{4\mu_0 NI}{R}\left\{\left[4 + \left(1 - \frac{2x}{R}\right)^2\right]^{-\frac{3}{2}} - \left[4 + \left(1 + \frac{2x}{R}\right)^2\right]^{-\frac{3}{2}}\right\}.$$

(b) For small excursions from the origin where $|x| \ll R$, show that the magnetic field is given by $B \approx Cx$, where the constant $C = 48\mu_0 NI/25\sqrt{5}\,R^2$. (c) For optimal atom trapping, dB/dx should be about 0.15 T/m. Assume an atom trap uses anti-Helmholtz coils with $R = 4.0$ cm and $N = 150$. What current should flow through the coils? [Coil separation equal to coil radius, as assumed in this problem, is not a strict requirement for anti-Helmholtz coils.]

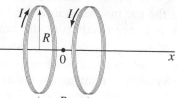

FIGURE 28–62
Problem 75.

74. You want to get an idea of the magnitude of magnetic fields produced by overhead power lines. You estimate that a transmission wire is about 12 m above the ground. The local power company tells you that the line operates at 15 kV and provide a maximum of 45 MW to the local area. Estimate the maximum magnetic field you might experience walking under such a power line, and compare to the Earth's field. [For an ac current, values are rms, and the magnetic field will be changing.]

*Numerical/Computer

* 75. (II) A circular current loop of radius 15 cm containing 250 turns carries a current of 2.0 A. Its center is at the origin and its axis lies along the x axis. Calculate the magnetic field B at a point x on the x axis for $x = -40$ cm to $+40$ cm in steps of 2 cm and make a graph of B as a function of x.

* 76. (III) A set of Helmholtz coils (see Problem 61, Fig. 28–58) have a radius $R = 10.0$ cm and are separated by a distance $R = 10.0$ cm. Each coil has 250 loops carrying a current $I = 2.0$ A. (a) Determine the total magnetic field B along the x axis (the center line for the two coils) in steps of 0.2 cm from the center of one coil $(x = 0)$ to the center of the other $(x = R)$. (b) Graph B as a function of x. (c) By what % does B vary from $x = 5.0$ cm to $x = 6.0$ cm?

Answers to Exercises

A: 2×10^{-6} T; not at this distance, and then only briefly.

B: 0.8×10^{-5} T, up.

C: (b).

D: (b), (c).

One of the great laws of physics is Faraday's law of induction, which says that a changing magnetic flux produces an induced emf. This photo shows a bar magnet moving inside a coil of wire, and the galvanometer registers an induced current. This phenomenon of electromagnetic induction is the basis for many practical devices, including generators, alternators, transformers, tape recording, and computer memory.

C H A P T E R

29

Electromagnetic Induction and Faraday's Law

CHAPTER-OPENING QUESTION—Guess now!
In the photograph above, the bar magnet is inserted into the coil of wire, and is left there for 1 minute; then it is removed from the coil. What would an observer watching the galvanometer see?

(a) No change; without a battery there is no current to detect.
(b) A small current flows while the magnet is inside the coil of wire.
(c) A current spike as the magnet enters the coil, and then nothing.
(d) A current spike as the magnet enters the coil, and then a steady small current.
(e) A current spike as the magnet enters the coil, then nothing, and then a current spike in the opposite direction as the magnet leaves the coil.

I n Chapter 27, we discussed two ways in which electricity and magnetism are related: (1) an electric current produces a magnetic field; and (2) a magnetic field exerts a force on an electric current or moving electric charge. These discoveries were made in 1820–1821. Scientists then began to wonder: if electric currents produce a magnetic field, is it possible that a magnetic field can produce an electric current? Ten years later the American Joseph Henry (1797–1878) and the Englishman Michael Faraday (1791–1867) independently found that it was possible. Henry actually made the discovery first. But Faraday published his results earlier and investigated the subject in more detail. We now discuss this phenomenon and some of its world-changing applications including the electric generator.

29–1 Induced EMF

In his attempt to produce an electric current from a magnetic field, Faraday used an apparatus like that shown in Fig. 29–1. A coil of wire, X, was connected to a battery. The current that flowed through X produced a magnetic field that was intensified by the ring-shaped iron core around which the wire was wrapped. Faraday hoped that a strong steady current in X would produce a great enough magnetic field to produce a current in a second coil Y wrapped on the same iron ring. This second circuit, Y, contained a galvanometer to detect any current but contained no battery.

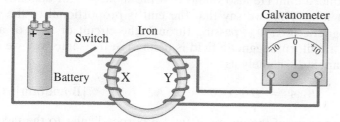

FIGURE 29–1 Faraday's experiment to induce an emf.

He met no success with constant currents. But the long-sought effect was finally observed when Faraday noticed the galvanometer in circuit Y deflect strongly at the moment he closed the switch in circuit X. And the galvanometer deflected strongly in the opposite direction when he opened the switch in X. A constant current in X produced a constant magnetic field which produced *no* current in Y. Only when the current in X was starting or stopping was a current produced in Y.

Faraday concluded that although a constant magnetic field produces no current in a conductor, a *changing* magnetic field can produce an electric current. Such a current is called an **induced current**. When the magnetic field through coil Y changes, a current occurs in Y as if there were a source of emf in circuit Y. We therefore say that

a changing magnetic field induces an emf.

Faraday did further experiments on **electromagnetic induction**, as this phenomenon is called. For example, Fig. 29–2 shows that if a magnet is moved quickly into a coil of wire, a current is induced in the wire. If the magnet is quickly removed, a current is induced in the opposite direction ($\vec{B}$ through the coil decreases). Furthermore, if the magnet is held steady and the coil of wire is moved toward or away from the magnet, again an emf is induced and a current flows. Motion or change is required to induce an emf. It doesn't matter whether the magnet or the coil moves. It is their *relative motion* that counts.

⚠ **CAUTION**
Changing $\vec{B}$, not $\vec{B}$ itself, induces current

⚠ **CAUTION**
Relative motion—magnet or coil moving induces current

FIGURE 29–2 (a) A current is induced when a magnet is moved toward a coil, momentarily increasing the magnetic field through the coil. (b) The induced current is opposite when the magnet is moved away from the coil ($\vec{B}$ decreases). Note that the galvanometer zero is at the center of the scale and the needle deflects left or right, depending on the direction of the current. In (c), no current is induced if the magnet does not move relative to the coil. It is the relative motion that counts here: the magnet can be held steady and the coil moved, which also induces an emf.

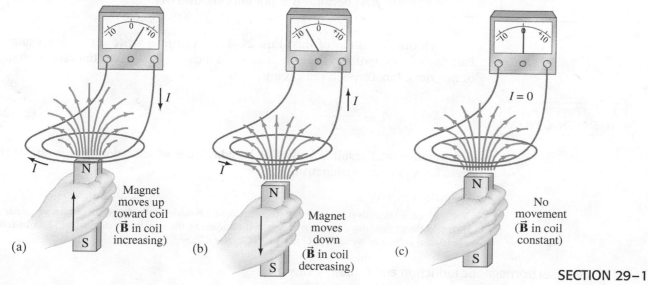

(a) Magnet moves up toward coil ($\vec{B}$ in coil increasing)

(b) Magnet moves down ($\vec{B}$ in coil decreasing)

(c) No movement ($\vec{B}$ in coil constant)

EXERCISE A Return to the Chapter-Opening Question, page 758, and answer it again now. Try to explain why you may have answered differently the first time.

29–2 Faraday's Law of Induction; Lenz's Law

Faraday investigated quantitatively what factors influence the magnitude of the emf induced. He found first of all that the more rapidly the magnetic field changes, the greater the induced emf. He also found that the induced emf depends on the area of the circuit loop. Thus we say that the emf is proportional to the rate of change of the **magnetic flux**, Φ_B, passing through the circuit or loop of area A. Magnetic flux for a uniform magnetic field is defined in the same way we did for electric flux in Chapter 22, namely as

$$\Phi_B = B_\perp A = BA\cos\theta = \vec{B}\cdot\vec{A}. \qquad [\vec{B}\ \text{uniform}] \quad (29\text{–}1a)$$

Here $B_\perp$ is the component of the magnetic field $\vec{B}$ perpendicular to the face of the loop, and θ is the angle between $\vec{B}$ and the vector $\vec{A}$ (representing the area) whose direction is perpendicular to the face of the loop. These quantities are shown in Fig. 29–3 for a square loop of side ℓ whose area is $A = \ell^2$. If the area is of some other shape, or $\vec{B}$ is not uniform, the magnetic flux can be written[†]

$$\Phi_B = \int \vec{B}\cdot d\vec{A}. \qquad (29\text{–}1b)$$

As we saw in Chapter 27, the lines of $\vec{B}$ (like lines of $\vec{E}$) can be drawn such that the number of lines per unit area is proportional to the field strength. Then the flux Φ_B can be thought of as being proportional to the *total number of lines passing through the area enclosed by the loop*. This is illustrated in Fig. 29–4, where the loop is viewed from the side (on edge). For $\theta = 90°$, no magnetic field lines pass through the loop and $\Phi_B = 0$, whereas Φ_B is a maximum when $\theta = 0°$. The unit of magnetic flux is the tesla-meter²; this is called a **weber**: $1\ \text{Wb} = 1\ \text{T}\cdot\text{m}^2$.

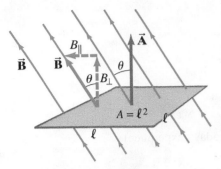

FIGURE 29–3 Determining the flux through a flat loop of wire. This loop is square, of side ℓ and area $A = \ell^2$.

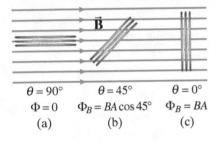

FIGURE 29–4 Magnetic flux Φ_B is proportional to the number of lines of $\vec{B}$ that pass through the loop.

$$\begin{array}{ccc} \theta = 90° & \theta = 45° & \theta = 0° \\ \Phi = 0 & \Phi_B = BA\cos 45° & \Phi_B = BA \\ (a) & (b) & (c) \end{array}$$

FIGURE 29–5 Example 29–1.

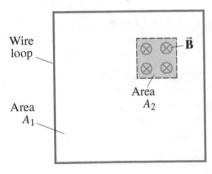

Wire loop

Area A_2

Area A_1

CONCEPTUAL EXAMPLE 29–1 **Determining flux.** A square loop of wire encloses area A_1 as shown in Fig. 29–5. A uniform magnetic field $\vec{B}$ perpendicular to the loop extends over the area A_2. What is the magnetic flux through the loop A_1?

RESPONSE We assume that the magnetic field is zero outside the area A_2. The total magnetic flux through area A_1 is the flux through area A_2, which by Eq. 29–1a for a uniform field is BA_2, plus the flux through the remaining area $(= A_1 - A_2)$, which is zero because $B = 0$. So the total flux is $\Phi_B = BA_2 + 0(A_1 - A_2) = BA_2$. It is *not* equal to BA_1 because $\vec{B}$ is not uniform over A_1.

With our definition of flux, Eqs. 29–1, we can now write down the results of Faraday's investigations: The emf induced in a circuit is equal to the rate of change of magnetic flux through the circuit:

$$\mathcal{E} = -\frac{d\Phi_B}{dt}. \qquad (29\text{–}2a)$$

FARADAY'S LAW
OF INDUCTION

This fundamental result is known as **Faraday's law of induction**, and is one of the basic laws of electromagnetism.

[†]The integral is taken over an open surface—that is, one bounded by a closed curve such as a circle or square. In the present discussion, the area is that enclosed by the loop under discussion. The area is not an enclosed surface as we used in Gauss's law, Chapter 22.

If the circuit contains N loops that are closely wrapped so the same flux passes through each, the emfs induced in each loop add together, so

$$\mathscr{E} = -N\frac{d\Phi_B}{dt}. \qquad\qquad \text{[N loops]} \quad \textbf{(29–2b)}$$

EXAMPLE 29–2 **A loop of wire in a magnetic field.** A square loop of wire of side $\ell = 5.0$ cm is in a uniform magnetic field $B = 0.16$ T. What is the magnetic flux in the loop (a) when $\vec{\mathbf{B}}$ is perpendicular to the face of the loop and (b) when $\vec{\mathbf{B}}$ is at an angle of $30°$ to the area $\vec{\mathbf{A}}$ of the loop? (c) What is the magnitude of the average current in the loop if it has a resistance of $0.012\,\Omega$ and it is rotated from position (b) to position (a) in 0.14 s?

APPROACH We use the definition $\Phi_B = \vec{\mathbf{B}} \cdot \vec{\mathbf{A}}$ to calculate the magnetic flux. Then we use Faraday's law of induction to find the induced emf in the coil, and from that the induced current ($I = \mathscr{E}/R$).

SOLUTION The area of the coil is $A = \ell^2 = (5.0 \times 10^{-2}\,\text{m})^2 = 2.5 \times 10^{-3}\,\text{m}^2$, and the direction of $\vec{\mathbf{A}}$ is perpendicular to the face of the loop (Fig. 29–3).
(a) $\vec{\mathbf{B}}$ is perpendicular to the coil's face, and thus parallel to $\vec{\mathbf{A}}$ (Fig. 29–3), so

$$\Phi_B = \vec{\mathbf{B}} \cdot \vec{\mathbf{A}}$$
$$= BA\cos 0° = (0.16\,\text{T})(2.5 \times 10^{-3}\,\text{m}^2)(1) = 4.0 \times 10^{-4}\,\text{Wb}.$$

(b) The angle between $\vec{\mathbf{B}}$ and $\vec{\mathbf{A}}$ is $30°$, so

$$\Phi_B = \vec{\mathbf{B}} \cdot \vec{\mathbf{A}}$$
$$= BA\cos\theta = (0.16\,\text{T})(2.5 \times 10^{-3}\,\text{m}^2)\cos 30° = 3.5 \times 10^{-4}\,\text{Wb}.$$

(c) The magnitude of the induced emf is

$$\mathscr{E} = \frac{\Delta\Phi_B}{\Delta t} = \frac{(4.0 \times 10^{-4}\,\text{Wb}) - (3.5 \times 10^{-4}\,\text{Wb})}{0.14\,\text{s}} = 3.6 \times 10^{-4}\,\text{V}.$$

The current is then

$$I = \frac{\mathscr{E}}{R} = \frac{3.6 \times 10^{-4}\,\text{V}}{0.012\,\Omega} = 0.030\,\text{A} = 30\,\text{mA}.$$

The minus signs in Eqs. 29–2a and b are there to remind us in which direction the induced emf acts. Experiments show that

a current produced by an induced emf moves in a direction so that the magnetic field created by that current opposes the original change in flux.

This is known as **Lenz's law.** Be aware that we are now discussing two distinct magnetic fields: (1) the changing magnetic field or flux that induces the current, and (2) the magnetic field produced by the induced current (all currents produce a field). The second field opposes the change in the first.

Lenz's law can be said another way, valid even if no current can flow (as when a circuit is not complete):

An induced emf is always in a direction that opposes the original change in flux that caused it.

⚠ **CAUTION**

Distinguish two different magnetic fields

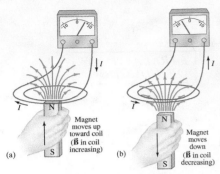

FIGURE 29–2 (repeated).

Let us apply Lenz's law to the relative motion between a magnet and a coil, Fig. 29–2. The changing flux through the coil induces an emf in the coil, producing a current. This induced current produces its own magnetic field. In Fig. 29–2a the distance between the coil and the magnet decreases. The magnet's magnetic field (and number of field lines) through the coil increases, and therefore the flux increases. The magnetic field of the magnet points upward. To oppose the upward increase, the magnetic field inside the coil produced by the induced current needs to point *downward*. Thus, Lenz's law tells us that the current moves as shown (use the right-hand rule). In Fig. 29–2b, the flux *decreases* (because the magnet is moved away and B decreases), so the induced current in the coil produces an *upward* magnetic field through the coil that is "trying" to maintain the status quo. Thus the current in Fig. 29–2b is in the opposite direction from Fig. 29–2a.

It is important to note that an emf is induced whenever there is a change in *flux* through the coil, and we now consider some more possibilities.

FIGURE 29–6 A current can be induced by changing the area of the coil, even though B doesn't change. Here the area is reduced by pulling on its sides: the *flux* through the coil is reduced as we go from (a) to (b). Here the brief induced current acts in the direction shown so as to try to maintain the original flux ($\Phi = BA$) by producing its own magnetic field into the page. That is, as the area A decreases, the current acts to increase B in the original (inward) direction.

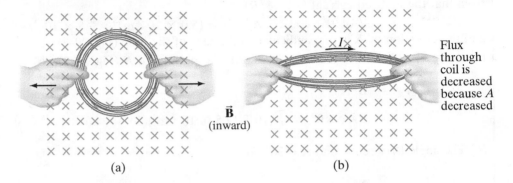

Since magnetic flux $\Phi_B = \int \vec{B} \cdot d\vec{A} = \int B \cos \theta \, dA$, we see that an emf can be induced in three ways: (1) by a changing magnetic field B; (2) by changing the area A of the loop in the field; or (3) by changing the loop's orientation θ with respect to the field. Figures 29–1 and 29–2 illustrated case 1. Examples of cases 2 and 3 are illustrated in Figs. 29–6 and 29–7, respectively.

FIGURE 29–7 A current can be induced by rotating a coil in a magnetic field. The flux through the coil changes from (a) to (b) because θ (in Eq. 29–1a, $\Phi = BA \cos \theta$) went from $0°$ ($\cos \theta = 1$) to $90°$ ($\cos \theta = 0$).

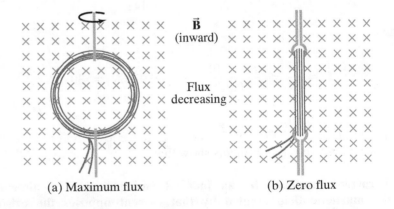

(a) Maximum flux (b) Zero flux

FIGURE 29–8 Example 29–3: An induction stove.

CONCEPTUAL EXAMPLE 29–3 | **Induction stove.** In an induction stove (Fig. 29–8), an ac current exists in a coil that is the "burner" (a burner that never gets hot). Why will it heat a metal pan but not a glass container?

RESPONSE The ac current sets up a changing magnetic field that passes through the pan bottom. This changing magnetic field induces a current in the pan bottom, and since the pan offers resistance, electric energy is transformed to thermal energy which heats the pot and its contents. A glass container offers such high resistance that little current is induced and little energy is transferred ($P = V^2/R$).

Lenz's Law

Lenz's law is used to determine the direction of the (conventional) electric current induced in a loop due to a change in magnetic flux inside the loop. To produce an induced current you need

(a) a closed conducting loop, and

(b) an external magnetic flux through the loop that is changing in time.

1. Determine whether the magnetic flux ($\Phi_B = BA \cos \theta$) inside the loop is decreasing, increasing, or unchanged.

2. The magnetic field due to the induced current: (a) points in the same direction as the external field if the flux is decreasing; (b) points in the opposite direction from the external field if the flux is increasing; or (c) is zero if the flux is not changing.

3. Once you know the direction of the induced magnetic field, use the right-hand rule to find the direction of the induced current.

4. Always keep in mind that there are two magnetic fields: (1) an external field whose flux must be changing if it is to induce an electric current, and (2) a magnetic field produced by the induced current.

FIGURE 29–9 Example 29–4.

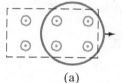
(a)
Pulling a round loop to the right out of a magnetic field which points out of the page

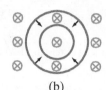
(b)
Shrinking a loop in a magnetic field pointing into the page

(c)
S magnetic pole moving from below, up toward the loop

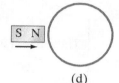
(d)
N magnetic pole moving toward loop in the plane of the page

(e)
Rotating the loop by pulling the left side toward us and pushing the right side in; the magnetic field points from right to left

CONCEPTUAL EXAMPLE 29–4 | **Practice with Lenz's law.** In which direction is the current induced in the circular loop for each situation in Fig. 29–9?

RESPONSE (*a*) Initially, the magnetic field pointing out of the page passes through the loop. If you pull the loop out of the field, magnetic flux through the loop decreases; so the induced current will be in a direction to maintain the decreasing flux through the loop: the current will be counterclockwise to produce a magnetic field outward (toward the reader).

(*b*) The external field is into the page. The coil area gets smaller, so the flux will decrease; hence the induced current will be clockwise, producing its own field into the page to make up for the flux decrease.

(*c*) Magnetic field lines point into the S pole of a magnet, so as the magnet moves toward us and the loop, the magnet's field points into the page and is getting stronger. The current in the loop will be induced in the counterclockwise direction in order to produce a field $\vec{B}$ *out* of the page.

(*d*) The field is in the plane of the loop, so no magnetic field lines pass through the loop and the flux through the loop is zero throughout the process; hence there is no change in external magnetic flux with time, and there will be no induced emf or current in the loop.

(*e*) Initially there is no flux through the loop. When you start to rotate the loop, the external field through the loop begins increasing to the left. To counteract this change in flux, the loop will have current induced in a counterclockwise direction so as to produce its own field to the right.

⚠ **CAUTION**

Magnetic field created by induced current opposes change in external flux, not necessarily opposing the external field

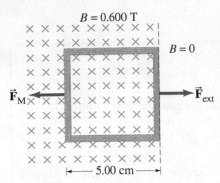

$B = 0.600\,\text{T}$

$B = 0$

$\vec{F}_M$

$\vec{F}_{ext}$

|← 5.00 cm →|

FIGURE 29–10 Example 29–5. The square coil in a magnetic field $B = 0.600\,\text{T}$ is pulled abruptly to the right to a region where $B = 0$.

FIGURE 29–11 Exercise B.

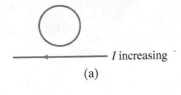

I increasing

(a)

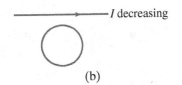

I decreasing

(b)

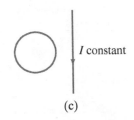

I constant

(c)

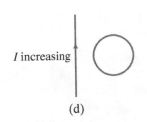

I increasing

(d)

EXAMPLE 29–5 Pulling a coil from a magnetic field. A 100-loop square coil of wire, with side $\ell = 5.00\,\text{cm}$ and total resistance $100\,\Omega$, is positioned perpendicular to a uniform 0.600-T magnetic field, as shown in Fig. 29–10. It is quickly pulled from the field at constant speed (moving perpendicular to $\vec{B}$) to a region where B drops abruptly to zero. At $t = 0$, the right edge of the coil is at the edge of the field. It takes 0.100 s for the whole coil to reach the field-free region. Find (a) the rate of change in flux through the coil, and (b) the emf and current induced. (c) How much energy is dissipated in the coil? (d) What was the average force required (F_{ext})?

APPROACH We start by finding how the magnetic flux, $\Phi_B = BA$, changes during the time interval $\Delta t = 0.100\,\text{s}$. Faraday's law then gives the induced emf and Ohm's law gives the current.

SOLUTION (a) The area of the coil is $A = \ell^2 = (5.00 \times 10^{-2}\,\text{m})^2 = 2.50 \times 10^{-3}\,\text{m}^2$. The flux through one loop is initially $\Phi_B = BA = (0.600\,\text{T})(2.50 \times 10^{-3}\,\text{m}^2) = 1.50 \times 10^{-3}\,\text{Wb}$. After 0.100 s, the flux is zero. The rate of change in flux is constant (because the coil is square), equal to

$$\frac{\Delta\Phi_B}{\Delta t} = \frac{0 - (1.50 \times 10^{-3}\,\text{Wb})}{0.100\,\text{s}} = -1.50 \times 10^{-2}\,\text{Wb/s}.$$

(b) The emf induced (Eq. 29–2) in the 100-loop coil during this 0.100-s interval is

$$\mathscr{E} = -N\frac{\Delta\Phi_B}{\Delta t} = -(100)(-1.50 \times 10^{-2}\,\text{Wb/s}) = 1.50\,\text{V}.$$

The current is found by applying Ohm's law to the 100-Ω coil:

$$I = \frac{\mathscr{E}}{R} = \frac{1.50\,\text{V}}{100\,\Omega} = 1.50 \times 10^{-2}\,\text{A} = 15.0\,\text{mA}.$$

By Lenz's law, the current must be clockwise to produce more $\vec{B}$ into the page and thus oppose the decreasing flux into the page.

(c) The total energy dissipated in the coil is the product of the power $(= I^2R)$ and the time:

$$E = Pt = I^2Rt = (1.50 \times 10^{-2}\,\text{A})^2(100\,\Omega)(0.100\,\text{s}) = 2.25 \times 10^{-3}\,\text{J}.$$

(d) We can use the result of part (c) and apply the work-energy principle: the energy dissipated E is equal to the work W needed to pull the coil out of the field (Chapters 7 and 8). Because $W = \bar{F}d$ where $d = 5.00\,\text{cm}$, then

$$\bar{F} = \frac{W}{d} = \frac{2.25 \times 10^{-3}\,\text{J}}{5.00 \times 10^{-2}\,\text{m}} = 0.0450\,\text{N}.$$

Alternate Solution (d) We can also calculate the force directly using $\vec{F} = I\vec{\ell} \times \vec{B}$, Eq. 27–3, which here for constant $\vec{B}$ is $F = I\ell B$. The force the magnetic field exerts on the top and bottom sections of the square coil of Fig. 29–10 are in opposite directions and cancel each other. The magnetic force $\vec{F}_M$ exerted on the left vertical section of the square coil acts to the left as shown because the current is up (clockwise). The right side of the loop is in the region where $\vec{B} = 0$. Hence the external force, to the right, needed to just overcome the magnetic force to the left (on $N = 100$ loops) is

$$F_{ext} = NI\ell B = (100)(0.0150\,\text{A})(0.0500\,\text{m})(0.600\,\text{T}) = 0.0450\,\text{N},$$

which is the same answer, confirming our use of energy conservation above.

EXERCISE B What is the direction of the induced current in the circular loop due to the current shown in each part of Fig. 29–11?

29–3 EMF Induced in a Moving Conductor

Another way to induce an emf is shown in Fig. 29–12a, and this situation helps illuminate the nature of the induced emf. Assume that a uniform magnetic field $\vec{B}$ is perpendicular to the area bounded by the U-shaped conductor and the movable rod resting on it. If the rod is made to move at a speed v, it travels a distance $dx = v\,dt$ in a time dt. Therefore, the area of the loop increases by an amount $dA = \ell\,dx = \ell v\,dt$ in a time dt. By Faraday's law there is an induced emf $\mathscr{E}$ whose magnitude is given by

$$\mathscr{E} = \frac{d\Phi_B}{dt} = \frac{B\,dA}{dt} = \frac{B\ell v\,dt}{dt} = B\ell v. \tag{29–3}$$

Equation 29–3 is valid as long as B, ℓ, and v are mutually perpendicular. (If they are not, we use only the components of each that are mutually perpendicular.) An emf induced on a conductor moving in a magnetic field is sometimes called *motional emf*.

We can also obtain Eq. 29–3 without using Faraday's law. We saw in Chapter 27 that a charged particle moving perpendicular to a magnetic field B with speed v experiences a force $\vec{F} = q\vec{v} \times \vec{B}$ (Eq. 27–5a). When the rod of Fig. 29–12a moves to the right with speed v, the electrons in the rod also move with this speed. Therefore, since $\vec{v} \perp \vec{B}$, each electron feels a force $F = qvB$, which acts up the page as shown in Fig. 29–12b. If the rod was not in contact with the U-shaped conductor, electrons would collect at the upper end of the rod, leaving the lower end positive (see signs in Fig. 29–12b). There must thus be an induced emf. If the rod is in contact with the U-shaped conductor (Fig. 29–12a), the electrons will flow into the U. There will then be a clockwise (conventional) current in the loop. To calculate the emf, we determine the work W needed to move a charge q from one end of the rod to the other against this potential difference: $W = \text{force} \times \text{distance} = (qvB)(\ell)$. The emf equals the work done per unit charge, so $\mathscr{E} = W/q = qvB\ell/q = B\ell v$, the same result[†] as from Faraday's law above, Eq. 29–3.

EXERCISE C In what direction will the electrons flow in Fig. 29–12 if the rod moves to the left, decreasing the area of the current loop?

EXAMPLE 29–6 **ESTIMATE** **Does a moving airplane develop a large emf?** An airplane travels 1000 km/h in a region where the Earth's magnetic field is about 5×10^{-5} T and is nearly vertical (Fig. 29–13). What is the potential difference induced between the wing tips that are 70 m apart?

APPROACH We consider the wings to be a 70-m-long conductor moving through the Earth's magnetic field. We use Eq. 29–3 to get the emf.

SOLUTION Since $v = 1000$ km/h $= 280$ m/s, and $\vec{v} \perp \vec{B}$, we have

$$\mathscr{E} = B\ell v = (5 \times 10^{-5}\,\text{T})(70\,\text{m})(280\,\text{m/s}) \approx 1\,\text{V}.$$

NOTE Not much to worry about.

EXAMPLE 29–7 **Electromagnetic blood-flow measurement.** The rate of blood flow in our body's vessels can be measured using the apparatus shown in Fig. 29–14, since blood contains charged ions. Suppose that the blood vessel is 2.0 mm in diameter, the magnetic field is 0.080 T, and the measured emf is 0.10 mV. What is the flow velocity v of the blood?

APPROACH The magnetic field $\vec{B}$ points horizontally from left to right (N pole toward S pole). The induced emf acts over the width $\ell = 2.0$ mm of the blood vessel, perpendicular to $\vec{B}$ and $\vec{v}$ (Fig. 29–14), just as in Fig. 29–12. We can then use Eq. 29–3 to get v. ($\vec{v}$ in Fig. 29–14 corresponds to $\vec{v}$ in Fig. 29–12.)

SOLUTION We solve for v in Eq. 29–3:

$$v = \frac{\mathscr{E}}{B\ell} = \frac{(1.0 \times 10^{-4}\,\text{V})}{(0.080\,\text{T})(2.0 \times 10^{-3}\,\text{m})} = 0.63\,\text{m/s}.$$

NOTE In actual practice, an alternating current is used to produce an alternating magnetic field. The induced emf is then alternating.

[†]This force argument, which is basically the same as for the Hall effect (Section 27–8), explains this one way of inducing an emf. It does not explain the general case of electromagnetic induction.

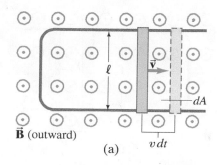

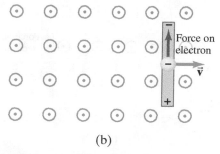

(a)

(b)

FIGURE 29–12 (a) A conducting rod is moved to the right on a U-shaped conductor in a uniform magnetic field $\vec{B}$ that points out of the page. The induced current is clockwise. (b) Upward force on an electron in the metal rod (moving to the right) due to $\vec{B}$ pointing out of the page; hence electrons can collect at top of rod, leaving + charge at bottom.

FIGURE 29–13 Example 29–6.

PHYSICS APPLIED
Blood-flow measurement

FIGURE 29–14 Measurement of blood velocity from the induced emf. Example 29–7.

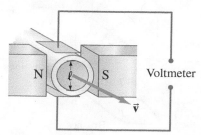

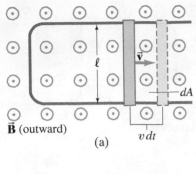

$\vec{\mathbf{B}}$ (outward)

(a)

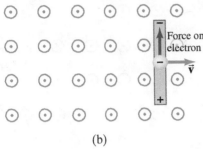

(b)

FIGURE 29–12 (repeated)
(a) A conducting rod is moved to the right on a U-shaped conductor in a uniform magnetic field $\vec{\mathbf{B}}$ that points out of the page. The induced current is clockwise. (b) Upward force on an electron in the metal rod (moving to the right) due to $\vec{\mathbf{B}}$ pointing out of the page; hence electrons can collect at top of rod, leaving + charge at bottom.

EXAMPLE 29–8 **Force on the rod.** To make the rod of Fig. 29–12a move to the right at constant speed v, you need to apply an external force on the rod to the right. (a) Explain and determine the magnitude of the required force. (b) What external power is needed to move the rod? (Do not confuse this external force on the rod with the upward force on the electrons shown in Fig. 29–12b.)

APPROACH When the rod moves to the right, electrons flow upward in the rod according to the right-hand rule. So the conventional current is downward in the rod. We can see this also from Lenz's law: the outward magnetic flux through the loop is increasing, so the induced current must oppose the increase. Thus the current is clockwise so as to produce a magnetic field into the page (right-hand rule). The magnetic force on the moving rod is $\vec{\mathbf{F}} = I\vec{\boldsymbol{\ell}} \times \vec{\mathbf{B}}$ for a constant $\vec{\mathbf{B}}$ (Eq. 27–3). The right-hand rule tells us this magnetic force is to the left, and is thus a "drag force" opposing our effort to move the rod to the right.

SOLUTION (a) The magnitude of the external force, to the right, needs to balance the magnetic force $F = I\ell B$, to the left. The current $I = \mathcal{E}/R = B\ell v/R$ (see Eq. 29–3), and the resistance R is that of the whole circuit: the rod and the U-shaped conductor. The force F required to move the rod is thus

$$F = I\ell B = \left(\frac{B\ell v}{R}\right)\ell B = \frac{B^2\ell^2}{R}\,v.$$

If B, ℓ, and R are constant, then a constant speed v is produced by a constant external force. (Constant R implies that the parallel rails have negligible resistance.)

(b) The external power needed to move the rod for constant R is

$$P_{\text{ext}} = Fv = \frac{B^2\ell^2v^2}{R}.$$

The power dissipated in the resistance is $P = I^2R$. With $I = \mathcal{E}/R = B\ell v/R$,

$$P_R = I^2R = \frac{B^2\ell^2v^2}{R},$$

so the power input equals the power dissipated in the resistance at any moment.

29–4 Electric Generators

We discussed alternating currents (ac) briefly in Section 25–7. Now we examine how ac is generated: by an **electric generator** or **dynamo**, one of the most important practical results of Faraday's great discovery. A generator transforms mechanical energy into electric energy, just the opposite of what a motor does. A simplified diagram of an **ac generator** is shown in Fig. 29–15. A generator consists of many loops of wire (only one is shown) wound on an *armature* that can rotate in a magnetic field. The axle is turned by some mechanical means (falling water, steam turbine, car motor belt), and an emf is induced in the rotating coil. An electric current is thus the *output* of a generator. Suppose in Fig. 29–15 that the armature is rotating clockwise; then $\vec{\mathbf{F}} = q\vec{\mathbf{v}} \times \vec{\mathbf{B}}$ applied to charged particles in the wire (or Lenz's law) tells us that the (conventional) current in the wire labeled b on the armature is outward, toward us; therefore the current is outward from brush b. (Each brush is fixed and presses against a continuous slip ring that rotates with the armature.) After one-half revolution, wire b will be where wire a is now in the drawing, and the current then at brush b will be inward. Thus the current produced is alternating.

FIGURE 29–15 An ac generator.

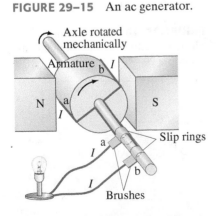

Let us assume the loop is being made to rotate in a uniform magnetic field $\vec{B}$ with constant angular velocity ω. From Faraday's law (Eq. 29–2a), the induced emf is

$$\mathcal{E} = -\frac{d\Phi_B}{dt} = -\frac{d}{dt}\int \vec{B}\cdot d\vec{A} = -\frac{d}{dt}[BA\cos\theta]$$

where A is the area of the loop and θ is the angle between $\vec{B}$ and $\vec{A}$. Since $\omega = d\theta/dt$, then $\theta = \theta_0 + \omega t$. We arbitrarily take $\theta_0 = 0$, so

$$\mathcal{E} = -BA\frac{d}{dt}(\cos\omega t) = BA\omega\sin\omega t.$$

If the rotating coil contains N loops,

$$\mathcal{E} = NBA\omega\sin\omega t$$
$$= \mathcal{E}_0\sin\omega t. \qquad\qquad\textbf{(29–4)}$$

Thus the output emf is sinusoidal (Fig. 29–16) with amplitude $\mathcal{E}_0 = NBA\omega$. Such a rotating coil in a magnetic field is the basic operating principle of an ac generator.

The frequency $f\,(=\omega/2\pi)$ is 60 Hz for general use in the United States and Canada, whereas 50 Hz is used in many countries. Most of the power generated in the United States is done at steam plants, where the burning of fossil fuels (coal, oil, natural gas) boils water to produce high-pressure steam that turns a turbine connected to the generator axle. Falling water from the top of a dam (hydroelectric) is also common (Fig. 29–17). At nuclear power plants, the nuclear energy released is used to produce steam to turn turbines. Indeed, a heat engine (Chapter 20) connected to a generator is the principal means of generating electric power. The frequency of 60 Hz or 50 Hz is maintained very precisely by power companies, and in doing Problems, we will assume it is at least as precise as other numbers given.

EXAMPLE 29–9 **An ac generator.** The armature of a 60-Hz ac generator rotates in a 0.15-T magnetic field. If the area of the coil is $2.0\times10^{-2}\,\text{m}^2$, how many loops must the coil contain if the peak output is to be $\mathcal{E}_0 = 170\,\text{V}$?

APPROACH From Eq. 29–4 we see that the maximum emf is $\mathcal{E}_0 = NBA\omega$.

SOLUTION We solve Eq. 29–4 for N with $\omega = 2\pi f = (6.28)(60\,\text{s}^{-1}) = 377\,\text{s}^{-1}$:

$$N = \frac{\mathcal{E}_0}{BA\omega} = \frac{170\,\text{V}}{(0.15\,\text{T})(2.0\times10^{-2}\,\text{m}^2)(377\,\text{s}^{-1})} = 150\ \text{turns}.$$

A **dc generator** is much like an ac generator, except the slip rings are replaced by split-ring commutators, Fig. 29–18a, just as in a dc motor (Section 27–6). The output of such a generator is as shown and can be smoothed out by placing a capacitor in parallel with the output (Section 26–5). More common is the use of many armature windings, as in Fig. 29–18b, which produces a smoother output.

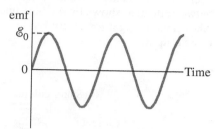

FIGURE 29–16 An ac generator produces an alternating current. The output emf $\mathcal{E} = \mathcal{E}_0\sin\omega t$, where $\mathcal{E}_0 = NAB\omega$ (Eq. 29–4).

PHYSICS APPLIED
Power plants

FIGURE 29–17 Water-driven generators at the base of Bonneville Dam, Oregon.

PHYSICS APPLIED
DC generator

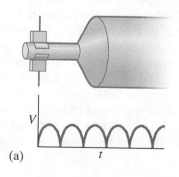

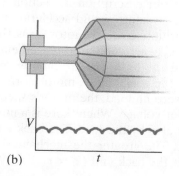

FIGURE 29–18 (a) A dc generator with one set of commutators, and (b) a dc generator with many sets of commutators and windings.

FIGURE 29–19 (a) Simplified schematic diagram of an alternator. The input current to the rotor from the battery is connected through continuous slip rings. Sometimes the rotor electromagnet is replaced by a permanent magnet. (b) Actual shape of an alternator. The rotor is made to turn by a belt from the engine. The current in the wire coil of the rotor produces a magnetic field inside it on its axis that points horizontally from left to right, thus making north and south poles of the plates attached at either end. These end plates are made with triangular fingers that are bent over the coil—hence there are alternating N and S poles quite close to one another, with magnetic field lines between them as shown by the blue lines. As the rotor turns, these field lines pass through the fixed stator coils (shown on the right for clarity, but in operation the rotor rotates within the stator), inducing a current in them, which is the output.

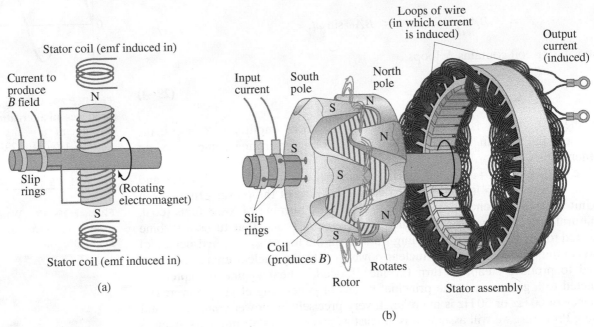

(a)

(b)

PHYSICS APPLIED

Alternators

Automobiles used to use dc generators. Today they mainly use **alternators**, which avoid the problems of wear and electrical arcing (sparks) across the split-ring commutators of dc generators. Alternators differ from generators in that an electromagnet, called the *rotor*, is fed by current from the battery and is made to rotate by a belt from the engine. The magnetic field of the turning rotor passes through a surrounding set of stationary coils called the *stator* (Fig. 29–19), inducing an alternating current in the stator coils, which is the output. This ac output is changed to dc for charging the battery by the use of semiconductor diodes, which allow current flow in one direction only.

*29–5 Back EMF and Counter Torque; Eddy Currents

*Back EMF, in a Motor

A motor turns and produces mechanical energy when a current is made to flow in it. From our description in Section 27–6 of a simple dc motor, you might expect that the armature would accelerate indefinitely due to the torque on it. However, as the armature of the motor turns, the magnetic flux through the coil changes and an emf is generated. This induced emf acts to oppose the motion (Lenz's law) and is called the **back emf** or **counter emf**. The greater the speed of the motor, the greater the back emf. A motor normally turns and does work on something, but if there were no load, the motor's speed would increase until the back emf equaled the input voltage. When there is a mechanical load, the speed of the motor may be limited also by the load. The back emf will then be less than the external applied voltage. The greater the mechanical load, the slower the motor rotates and the lower is the back emf ($\mathscr{E} \propto \omega$, Eq. 29–4).

EXAMPLE 29–10 **Back emf in a motor.** The armature windings of a dc motor have a resistance of 5.0 Ω. The motor is connected to a 120-V line, and when the motor reaches full speed against its normal load, the back emf is 108 V. Calculate (a) the current into the motor when it is just starting up, and (b) the current when the motor reaches full speed.

APPROACH As the motor is just starting up, it is turning very slowly, so there is no induced back emf. The only voltage is the 120-V line. The current is given by Ohm's law with $R = 5.0\,\Omega$. At full speed, we must include as emfs both the 120-V applied emf and the opposing back emf.

SOLUTION (a) At start up, the current is controlled by the 120 V applied to the coil's 5.0-Ω resistance. By Ohm's law,

$$I = \frac{V}{R} = \frac{120\,\text{V}}{5.0\,\Omega} = 24\,\text{A}.$$

(b) When the motor is at full speed, the back emf must be included in the equivalent circuit shown in Fig. 29–20. In this case, Ohm's law (or Kirchhoff's rule) gives

$$120\,\text{V} - 108\,\text{V} = I(5.0\,\Omega).$$

Therefore

$$I = \frac{12\,\text{V}}{5.0\,\Omega} = 2.4\,\text{A}.$$

NOTE This result shows that the current can be very high when a motor first starts up. This is why the lights in your house may dim when the motor of the refrigerator (or other large motor) starts up. The large initial current causes the voltage to the lights and at the outlets to drop, since the house wiring has resistance and there is some voltage drop across it when large currents are drawn.

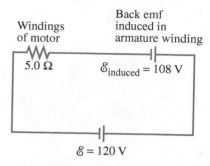

FIGURE 29–20 Circuit of a motor showing induced back emf. Example 29–10.

CONCEPTUAL EXAMPLE 29–11 **Motor overload.** When using an appliance such as a blender, electric drill, or sewing machine, if the appliance is overloaded or jammed so that the motor slows appreciably or stops while the power is still connected, the device can burn out and be ruined. Explain why this happens.

RESPONSE The motors are designed to run at a certain speed for a given applied voltage, and the designer must take the expected back emf into account. If the rotation speed is reduced, the back emf will not be as high as expected ($\mathscr{E} \propto \omega$, Eq. 29–4), and the current will increase, and may become large enough that the windings of the motor heat up to the point of ruining the motor.

*Counter Torque

In a generator, the situation is the reverse of that for a motor. As we saw, the mechanical turning of the armature induces an emf in the loops, which is the output. If the generator is not connected to an external circuit, the emf exists at the terminals but there is no current. In this case, it takes little effort to turn the armature. But if the generator *is* connected to a device that draws current, then a current flows in the coils of the armature. Because this current-carrying coil is in an external magnetic field, there will be a torque exerted on it (as in a motor), and this torque opposes the motion (use the right-hand rule for the force on a wire in Fig. 29–15). This is called a **counter torque**. The greater the electrical load—that is, the more current that is drawn—the greater will be the counter torque. Hence the external applied torque will have to be greater to keep the generator turning. This makes sense from the conservation of energy principle. More mechanical-energy input is needed to produce more electrical-energy output.

EXERCISE D A bicycle headlight is powered by a generator that is turned by the bicycle wheel. (a) If you pedal faster, how does the power to the light change? (b) Does the generator resist being turned as the bicycle's speed increases, and if so how?

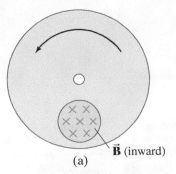

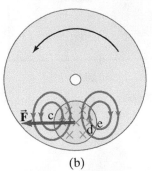

(a)

(b)

FIGURE 29–21 Production of eddy currents in a rotating wheel. The grey lines in (b) indicate induced current.

FIGURE 29–22 Airport metal detector.

PHYSICS APPLIED

Airport metal detector

FIGURE 29–23 Repairing a step-down transformer on a utility pole.

*Eddy Currents

Induced currents are not always confined to well-defined paths such as in wires. Consider, for example, the rotating metal wheel in Fig. 29–21a. An external magnetic field is applied to a limited area of the wheel as shown and points into the page. The section of wheel in the magnetic field has an emf induced in it because the conductor is moving, carrying electrons with it. The flow of induced (conventional) current in the wheel is upward in the region of the magnetic field (Fig. 29–21b), and the current follows a downward return path outside that region. Why? According to Lenz's law, the induced currents oppose the change that causes them. Consider the part of the wheel labeled c in Fig. 29–21b, where the magnetic field is zero but is just about to enter a region where $\vec{B}$ points into the page. To oppose this inward increase in magnetic field, the induced current is counterclockwise to produce a field pointing out of the page (right-hand-rule 1). Similarly, region d is about to move to e, where $\vec{B}$ is zero; hence the current is clockwise to produce an inward field opposed to this decreasing flux inward. These currents are referred to as **eddy currents**. They can be present in any conductor that is moving across a magnetic field or through which the magnetic flux is changing.

In Fig. 29–21b, the magnetic field exerts a force $\vec{F}$ on the induced currents it has created, and that force opposes the rotational motion. Eddy currents can be used in this way as a smooth braking device on, say, a rapid-transit car. In order to stop the car, an electromagnet can be turned on that applies its field either to the wheels or to the moving steel rail below. Eddy currents can also be used to dampen (reduce) the oscillation of a vibrating system. Eddy currents, however, can be a problem. For example, eddy currents induced in the armature of a motor or generator produce heat $(P = I\mathscr{E})$ and waste energy. To reduce the eddy currents, the armatures are *laminated*; that is, they are made of very thin sheets of iron that are well insulated from one another. The total path length of the eddy currents is confined to each slab, which increases the total resistance; hence the current is less and there is less wasted energy.

Walk-through metal detectors at airports (Fig. 29–22) detect metal objects using electromagnetic induction and eddy currents. Several coils are situated in the walls of the walk-through at different heights. In a technique called "pulse induction," the coils are given repeated brief pulses of current (on the order of microseconds), hundreds or thousands of times a second. Each pulse in a coil produces a magnetic field for a very brief period of time. When a passenger passes through the walk-through, any metal object being carried will have eddy currents induced in it. The eddy currents persist briefly after each input pulse, and the small magnetic field produced by the persisting eddy current (before the next external pulse) can be detected, setting off an alert or alarm. Stores and libraries sometimes use similar systems to discourage theft.

29–6 Transformers and Transmission of Power

A transformer is a device for increasing or decreasing an ac voltage. Transformers are found everywhere: on utility poles (Fig. 29–23) to reduce the high voltage from the electric company to a usable voltage in houses (120 V or 240 V), in chargers for cell phones, laptops, and other electronic devices, in CRT monitors and in your car to give the needed high voltage (to the spark plugs), and in many other applications. A **transformer** consists of two coils of wire known as the **primary** and **secondary** coils. The two coils can be interwoven (with insulated wire); or they can be linked by an iron core which is laminated to minimize eddy-current losses (Section 29–5), as shown in Fig. 29–24. Transformers are designed so that (nearly) all the magnetic flux produced by the current in the primary coil also passes through the secondary coil, and we assume this is true in what follows. We also assume that energy losses (in resistance and hysteresis) can be ignored—a good approximation for real transformers, which are often better than 99% efficient.

When an ac voltage is applied to the primary coil, the changing magnetic field it produces will induce an ac voltage of the same frequency in the secondary coil. However, the voltage will be different according to the number of loops in each coil. From Faraday's law, the voltage or emf induced in the secondary coil is

$$V_S = N_S \frac{d\Phi_B}{dt},$$

where N_S is the number of turns in the secondary coil, and $d\Phi_B/dt$ is the rate at which the magnetic flux changes.

The input primary voltage, V_P, is related to the rate at which the flux changes through it,

$$V_P = N_P \frac{d\Phi_B}{dt},$$

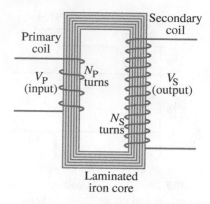

FIGURE 29–24 Step-up transformer $(N_P = 4, N_S = 12)$.

where N_P is the number of turns in the primary coil. This follows because the changing flux produces a back emf, $N_P \, d\Phi_B/dt$, in the primary that exactly balances the applied voltage V_P if the resistance of the primary can be ignored (Kirchhoff's rules). We divide these two equations, assuming little or no flux is lost, to find

$$\frac{V_S}{V_P} = \frac{N_S}{N_P}. \qquad (29–5)$$

This **transformer equation** tells how the secondary (output) voltage is related to the primary (input) voltage; V_S and V_P in Eq. 29–5 can be the rms values (Section 25–7) for both, or peak values for both. DC voltages don't work in a transformer because there would be no changing magnetic flux.

If the secondary coil contains more loops than the primary coil $(N_S > N_P)$, we have a **step-up transformer**. The secondary voltage is greater than the primary voltage. For example, if the secondary coil has twice as many turns as the primary coil, then the secondary voltage will be twice that of the primary voltage. If N_S is less than N_P, we have a **step-down transformer**.

Although ac voltage can be increased (or decreased) with a transformer, we don't get something for nothing. Energy conservation tells us that the power output can be no greater than the power input. A well-designed transformer can be greater than 99% efficient, so little energy is lost to heat. The power output thus essentially equals the power input. Since power $P = IV$ (Eq. 25–6), we have

$$I_P V_P = I_S V_S,$$

or

$$\frac{I_S}{I_P} = \frac{N_P}{N_S}. \qquad (29–6)$$

EXAMPLE 29–12 **Cell phone charger.** The charger for a cell phone contains a transformer that reduces 120-V (or 240-V) ac to 5.0-V ac to charge the 3.7-V battery (Section 26–4). (It also contains diodes to change the 5.0-V ac to 5.0-V dc.) Suppose the secondary coil contains 30 turns and the charger supplies 700 mA. Calculate (a) the number of turns in the primary coil, (b) the current in the primary, and (c) the power transformed.

APPROACH We assume the transformer is ideal, with no flux loss, so we can use Eq. 29–5 and then Eq. 29–6.

SOLUTION (a) This is a step-down transformer, and from Eq. 29–5 we have

$$N_P = N_S \frac{V_P}{V_S} = \frac{(30)(120\,\text{V})}{(5.0\,\text{V})} = 720\ \text{turns}.$$

(b) From Eq. 29–6

$$I_P = I_S \frac{N_S}{N_P} = (0.70\,\text{A})\left(\frac{30}{720}\right) = 29\ \text{mA}.$$

(c) The power transformed is

$$P = I_S V_S = (0.70\,\text{A})(5.0\,\text{V}) = 3.5\,\text{W}.$$

NOTE The power in the primary coil, $P = (0.029\,\text{A})(120\,\text{V}) = 3.5\,\text{W}$, is the same as the power in the secondary coil. There is 100% efficiency in power transfer for our ideal transformer.

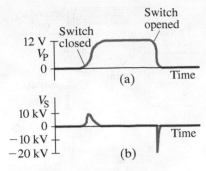

FIGURE 29–25 A dc voltage turned on and off as shown in (a) produces voltage pulses in the secondary (b). Voltage scales in (a) and (b) are not the same.

PHYSICS APPLIED

Transformers help power transmission

A transformer operates only on ac. A dc current in the primary coil does not produce a changing flux and therefore induces no emf in the secondary. However, if a dc voltage is applied to the primary through a switch, at the instant the switch is opened or closed there will be an induced voltage in the secondary. For example, if the dc is turned on and off as shown in Fig. 29–25a, the voltage induced in the secondary is as shown in Fig. 29–25b. Notice that the secondary voltage drops to zero when the dc voltage is steady. This is basically how, in the **ignition system** of an automobile, the high voltage is created to produce the spark across the gap of a spark plug that ignites the gas-air mixture. The transformer is referred to simply as an "ignition coil," and transforms the 12 V of the battery (when switched off in the primary) into a spike of as much as 30 kV in the secondary.

Transformers play an important role in the transmission of electricity. Power plants are often situated some distance from metropolitan areas, so electricity must then be transmitted over long distances (Fig. 29–26). There is always some power loss in the transmission lines, and this loss can be minimized if the power is transmitted at high voltage, using transformers, as the following Example shows.

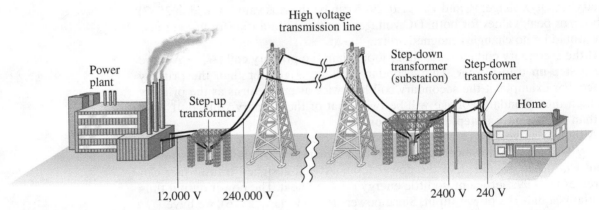

FIGURE 29–26 The transmission of electric power from power plants to homes makes use of transformers at various stages.

EXAMPLE 29–13 **Transmission lines.** An average of 120 kW of electric power is sent to a small town from a power plant 10 km away. The transmission lines have a total resistance of 0.40 Ω. Calculate the power loss if the power is transmitted at (*a*) 240 V and (*b*) 24,000 V.

APPROACH We cannot use $P = V^2/R$ because if R is the resistance of the transmission lines, we don't know the voltage drop along them; the given voltages are applied across the lines plus the load (the town). But we can determine the current I in the lines ($= P/V$), and then find the power loss from $P_L = I^2R$, for both cases (*a*) and (*b*).

SOLUTION (*a*) If 120 kW is sent at 240 V, the total current will be

$$I = \frac{P}{V} = \frac{1.2 \times 10^5 \, \text{W}}{2.4 \times 10^2 \, \text{V}} = 500 \, \text{A}.$$

The power loss in the lines, P_L, is then

$$P_L = I^2R = (500 \, \text{A})^2(0.40 \, \Omega) = 100 \, \text{kW}.$$

Thus, over 80% of all the power would be wasted as heat in the power lines!

(b) If 120 kW is sent at 24,000 V, the total current will be

$$I = \frac{P}{V} = \frac{1.2 \times 10^5 \, \text{W}}{2.4 \times 10^4 \, \text{V}} = 5.0 \, \text{A}.$$

The power loss in the lines is then

$$P_L = I^2 R = (5.0 \, \text{A})^2 (0.40 \, \Omega) = 10 \, \text{W},$$

which is less than $\frac{1}{100}$ of 1%: a far better efficiency!

NOTE We see that the higher voltage results in less current, and thus less power is wasted as heat in the transmission lines. It is for this reason that power is usually transmitted at very high voltages, as high as 700 kV.

The great advantage of ac, and a major reason it is in nearly universal use, is that the voltage can easily be stepped up or down by a transformer. The output voltage of an electric generating plant is stepped up prior to transmission. Upon arrival in a city, it is stepped down in stages at electric substations prior to distribution. The voltage in lines along city streets is typically 2400 V or 7200 V (but sometimes less), and is stepped down to 240 V or 120 V for home use by transformers (Figs. 29–23 and 29–26).

Fluorescent lights require a very high voltage initially to ionize the gas inside the bulb. The high voltage is obtained using a step-up transformer, called a ballast, and can be replaced independently of the bulb in many fluorescent light fixtures. When the ballast starts to fail, the tube is slow to light. Replacing the bulb will not solve the problem. In newer compact fluorescent bulbs designed to replace incandescent bulbs, the ballast (transformer) is part of the bulb, and is very small.

PHYSICS APPLIED
Fluorescent lightbulb ballast

29–7 A Changing Magnetic Flux Produces an Electric Field

We have seen in earlier Chapters (especially Chapter 25, Section 25–8) that when an electric current flows in a wire, there is an electric field in the wire that does the work of moving the electrons in the wire. In this Chapter we have seen that a changing magnetic flux induces a current in the wire, which implies that there is an electric field in the wire induced by the changing magnetic flux. Thus we come to the important conclusion that

a changing magnetic flux produces an electric field.

This result applies not only to wires and other conductors, but is actually a general result that applies to any region in space. Indeed, an electric field will be produced at any point in space where there is a changing magnetic field.

Faraday's Law—General Form

We can put these ideas into mathematical form by generalizing our relation between an electric field and the potential difference between two points a and b: $V_{ab} = \int_a^b \vec{E} \cdot d\vec{\ell}$ (Eq. 23–4a) where $d\vec{\ell}$ is an element of displacement along the path of integration. The emf $\mathscr{E}$ induced in a circuit is equal to the work done per unit charge by the electric field, which equals the integral of $\vec{E} \cdot d\vec{\ell}$ around the closed path:

$$\mathscr{E} = \oint \vec{E} \cdot d\vec{\ell}. \tag{29–7}$$

We combine this with Eq. 29–2a, to obtain a more elegant and general form of Faraday's law

$$\oint \vec{E} \cdot d\vec{\ell} = -\frac{d\Phi_B}{dt} \tag{29–8}$$

*FARADAY'S LAW
(general form)*

which relates the changing magnetic flux to the electric field it produces. The integral on the left is taken around a path enclosing the area through which the magnetic flux Φ_B is changing. This more elegant statement of Faraday's law (Eq. 29–8) is valid not only in conductors, but in any region of space. To illustrate this, let us take an Example.

FIGURE 29–27 Example 29–14.
(a) Side view of nearly constant $\vec{B}$.
(b) Top view, for determining the
electric field $\vec{E}$ at point P. (c) Lines of
$\vec{E}$ produced by increasing $\vec{B}$ (pointing
outward). (d) Graph of E vs. r.

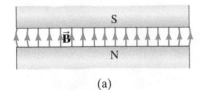

(a)

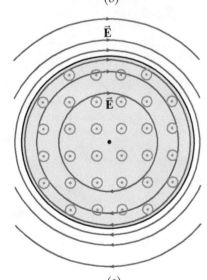

(b)

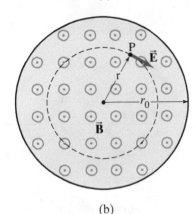

(c)

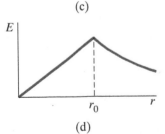

(d)

EXAMPLE 29–14 $\vec{E}$ **produced by changing** $\vec{B}$**.** A magnetic field $\vec{B}$ between the pole faces of an electromagnet is nearly uniform at any instant over a circular area of radius r_0 as shown in Figs. 29–27a and b. The current in the windings of the electromagnet is increasing in time so that $\vec{B}$ changes in time at a constant rate $d\vec{B}/dt$ at each point. Beyond the circular region $(r > r_0)$, we assume $\vec{B} = 0$ at all times. Determine the electric field $\vec{E}$ at any point P a distance r from the center of the circular area due to the changing $\vec{B}$.

APPROACH The changing magnetic flux through a circle of radius r, shown dashed in Fig. 29–27b, will produce an emf around this circle. Because all points on the dashed circle are equivalent physically, the electric field too will show this symmetry and will be in the plane perpendicular to $\vec{B}$. Thus we can expect $\vec{E}$ to be perpendicular to $\vec{B}$ and to be tangent to the circle of radius r. The direction of $\vec{E}$ will be as shown in Fig. 29–27b and c, since by Lenz's law the induced $\vec{E}$ needs to be capable of producing a current that generates a magnetic field opposing the original change in $\vec{B}$. By *symmetry*, we also expect $\vec{E}$ to have the same magnitude at all points on the circle of radius r.

SOLUTION We take the circle shown in Fig 29–27b as our path of integration in Eq. 29–8. We ignore the minus sign so we can concentrate on magnitude since we already found the direction of $\vec{E}$ from Lenz's law, and obtain

$$E(2\pi r) = (\pi r^2)\frac{dB}{dt}, \qquad [r < r_0]$$

since $\Phi_B = BA = B(\pi r^2)$ at any instant. We solve for E and obtain

$$E = \frac{r}{2}\frac{dB}{dt}. \qquad [r < r_0]$$

This expression is valid up to the edge of the circle $(r \leq r_0)$, beyond which $\vec{B} = 0$. If we now consider a point where $r > r_0$, the flux through a circle of radius r is $\Phi_B = \pi r_0^2 B$. Then Eq. 29–8 gives

$$E(2\pi r) = \pi r_0^2\frac{dB}{dt} \qquad [r > r_0]$$

or

$$E = \frac{r_0^2}{2r}\frac{dB}{dt}. \qquad [r > r_0]$$

Thus the magnitude of the induced electric field increases linearly from zero at the center of the magnet to $E = (dB/dt)(r_0/2)$ at the edge, and then decreases inversely with distance in the region beyond the edge of the magnetic field. The electric field lines are circles as shown in Fig. 29–27c. A graph of E vs. r is shown in Fig. 29–27d.

EXERCISE E Consider the magnet shown in Fig. 29–27 with a radius $r_0 = 6.0\,\text{cm}$. If the magnetic field changes uniformly from $0.040\,\text{T}$ to $0.090\,\text{T}$ in $0.18\,\text{s}$, what is the magnitude of the resulting electric field at (a) $r = 3.0\,\text{cm}$ and (b) $r = 9.0\,\text{cm}$?

*Forces Due to Changing $\vec{B}$ are Nonconservative

Example 29–14 illustrates an important difference between electric fields produced by changing magnetic fields and electric fields produced by electric charges at rest (electrostatic fields). Electric field lines produced in the electrostatic case (Chapters 21 to 24) start and stop on electric charges. But the electric field lines produced by a changing magnetic field are continuous; they form closed loops. This distinction goes even further and is an important one. In the electrostatic case, the potential difference between two points is given by (Eq. 23–4a)

$$V_{ba} = V_b - V_a = -\int_a^b \vec{E}\cdot d\vec{\ell}.$$

If the integral is around a closed loop, so points a and b are the same, then $V_{ba} = 0$.

Hence the integral of $\vec{\mathbf{E}} \cdot d\vec{\boldsymbol{\ell}}$ around a closed path is zero:

$$\oint \vec{\mathbf{E}} \cdot d\vec{\boldsymbol{\ell}} = 0. \qquad \text{[electrostatic field]}$$

This followed from the fact that the electrostatic force (Coulomb's law) is a conservative force, and so a potential energy function could be defined. Indeed, the relation above, $\oint \vec{\mathbf{E}} \cdot d\vec{\boldsymbol{\ell}} = 0$, tells us that the work done per unit charge around any closed path is zero (or the work done between any two points is independent of path—see Chapter 8), which is a property only of a conservative force. But in the nonelectrostatic case, when the electric field is produced by a changing magnetic field, the integral around a closed path is *not* zero, but is given by Eq. 29–8:

$$\oint \vec{\mathbf{E}} \cdot d\vec{\boldsymbol{\ell}} = -\frac{d\Phi_B}{dt}.$$

We thus come to the conclusion that the forces due to changing magnetic fields are *nonconservative*. We are not able therefore to define a potential energy, or potential function, at a given point in space for the nonelectrostatic case. Although static electric fields are *conservative fields*, the electric field produced by a changing magnetic field is a **nonconservative field**.

*29-8 Applications of Induction: Sound Systems, Computer Memory, Seismograph, GFCI

*Microphone

There are various types of *microphones*, and many operate on the principle of induction. In one form, a microphone is just the inverse of a loudspeaker (Section 27–6). A small coil connected to a membrane is suspended close to a small permanent magnet, as shown in Fig. 29–28. The coil moves in the magnetic field when sound waves strike the membrane and this motion induces an emf. The frequency of the induced emf will be just that of the impinging sound waves, and this emf is the "signal" that can be amplified and sent to loudspeakers, or sent to a recorder.

*Read/Write on Tape and Disks

Recording and playback on tape or disks is done by magnetic *heads*. Recording tapes for use in audio and video tape recorders contain a thin layer of magnetic oxide on a thin plastic tape. During recording, the audio and/or video signal voltage is sent to the recording head, which acts as a tiny electromagnet (Fig. 29–29) that magnetizes the tiny section of tape passing over the narrow gap in the head at each instant. In playback, the changing magnetism of the moving tape at the gap causes corresponding changes in the magnetic field within the soft-iron head, which in turn induces an emf in the coil (Faraday's law). This induced emf is the output signal that can be amplified and sent to a loudspeaker (audio) or to the picture tube (video). In audio and video recorders, the signals may be *analog*—they vary continuously in amplitude over time. The variation in degree of magnetization of the tape at any point reflects the variation in amplitude and frequency of the audio or video signal.

Digital information, such as used on computer hard drives or on magnetic computer tape and some types of digital tape recorders, is read and written using heads that are basically the same as just described (Fig. 29–29). The essential difference is in the signals, which are not analog, but are digital, and in particular binary, meaning that only two values are possible for each of the extremely high number of predetermined spaces on the tape or disk. The two possible values are usually referred to as 1 and 0. The signal voltage does not vary continuously but rather takes on only two values, $+5$ V and 0 V, for example, corresponding to the 1 or 0. Thus, information is carried as a series of **bits**, each of which can have only one of two values, 1 or 0.

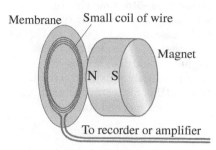

FIGURE 29–28 Diagram of a microphone that works by induction.

FIGURE 29–29 (a) Read/Write (playback/recording) head for tape or disk. In writing or recording, the electric input signal to the head, which acts as an electromagnet, magnetizes the passing tape or disk. In reading or playback, the changing magnetic field of the passing tape or disk induces a changing magnetic field in the head, which in turn induces in the coil an emf that is the output signal. (b) Photo of a hard drive showing several platters and read/write heads that can quickly move from the edge of the disk to the center.

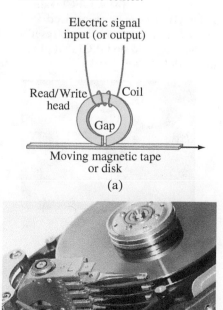

(a)

(b)

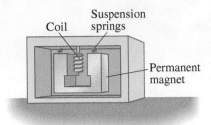

FIGURE 29–30 One type of seismograph, in which the coil is fixed to the case and moves with the Earth. The magnet, suspended by springs, has inertia and does not move instantaneously with the coil (and case), so there is relative motion between magnet and coil.

*Credit Card Swipe

When you swipe your credit card at a store or gas station, the magnetic stripe on the back of the card passes over a read head just as in a tape recorder or computer. The magnetic stripe contains personal information about your account and connects by telephone line for approval if your account is in order.

*Seismograph

In geophysics, a **seismograph** measures the intensity of earthquake waves using a magnet and a coil of wire. Either the magnet or the coil is fixed to the case, and the other is inertial (suspended by a spring; Fig. 29–30). The relative motion of magnet and coil when the Earth shakes induces an emf output.

*Ground Fault Circuit Interrupter (GFCI)

Fuses and circuit breakers (Sections 25–6 and 28–8) protect buildings from fire, and apparatus from damage, due to undesired high currents. But they do not turn off the current until it is very much greater than that which causes permanent damage to humans or death (≈ 100 mA). If fast enough, they may protect in case of a short. A *ground fault circuit interrupter* (GFCI) is meant to protect humans; GFCIs can react to currents as small as 5 mA.

FIGURE 29–31 A ground fault circuit interrupter (GFCI).

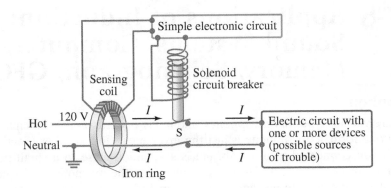

FIGURE 29–32 (a) A GFCI wall outlet. GFCIs can be recognized because they have "test" and "reset" buttons. (b) Add-on GFCI that plugs into outlet.

(a)

(b)

Electromagnetic induction is the physical basis of a GFCI. As shown in Fig. 29–31, the two conductors of a power line leading to an electrical circuit or device (red) pass through a small iron ring. Around the ring are many loops of thin wire that serve as a sensing coil. Under normal conditions (no ground fault), the current moving in the hot wire is exactly balanced by the returning current in the neutral wire. If something goes wrong and the hot wire touches the ungrounded metal case of the device or appliance, some of the entering current can pass through a person who touches the case and then to ground (a *ground fault*). Then the return current in the neutral wire will be less than the entering current in the hot wire, so there is a *net current* passing through the GFCI's iron ring. Because the current is ac, it is changing and the current difference produces a changing magnetic field in the iron, thus inducing an emf in the sensing coil wrapped around the iron. For example, if a device draws 8.0 A, and there is a ground fault through a person of 100 mA ($= 0.1$ A), then 7.9 A will appear in the neutral wire. The emf induced in the sensing coil by this 100-mA difference is amplified by a simple transistor circuit and sent to its own solenoid circuit breaker that opens the circuit at the switch S, thus protecting your life.

If the case of the faulty device is grounded, the current difference is even higher when there is a fault, and the GFCI trips immediately.

GFCIs can sense currents as low as 5 mA and react in 1 msec, saving lives. They can be small enough to fit as a wall outlet (Fig. 29–32a), or as a plug-in unit into which you plug a hair dryer or toaster (Fig. 29–32b). It is especially important to have GFCIs installed in kitchens, bathrooms, outdoors, and near swimming pools, where people are most in danger of touching ground. GFCIs always have a "test" button (to be sure it works) and a "reset" button (after it goes off).

Summary

The **magnetic flux** passing through a loop is equal to the product of the area of the loop times the perpendicular component of the (uniform) magnetic field: $\Phi_B = B_\perp A = BA \cos\theta$. If $\vec{B}$ is not uniform, then

$$\Phi_B = \int \vec{B} \cdot d\vec{A}. \qquad (29\text{–}1b)$$

If the magnetic flux through a coil of wire changes in time, an emf is induced in the coil. The magnitude of the induced emf equals the time rate of change of the magnetic flux through the loop times the number N of loops in the coil:

$$\mathscr{E} = -N \frac{d\Phi_B}{dt}. \qquad (29\text{–}2b)$$

This is **Faraday's law of induction**.

The induced emf can produce a current whose magnetic field opposes the original change in flux (**Lenz's law**).

We can also see from Faraday's law that a straight wire of length ℓ moving with speed v perpendicular to a magnetic field of strength B has an emf induced between its ends equal to:

$$\mathscr{E} = B\ell v. \qquad (29\text{–}3)$$

Faraday's law also tells us that *a changing magnetic field produces an electric field*. The mathematical relation is

$$\oint \vec{E} \cdot d\vec{\ell} = -\frac{d\Phi_B}{dt} \qquad (29\text{–}8)$$

and is the general form of Faraday's law. The integral on the left is taken around the loop through which the magnetic flux Φ_B is changing.

An electric **generator** changes mechanical energy into electrical energy. Its operation is based on Faraday's law: a coil of wire is made to rotate uniformly by mechanical means in a magnetic field, and the changing flux through the coil induces a sinusoidal current, which is the output of the generator.

[*A motor, which operates in the reverse of a generator, acts like a generator in that a **back emf** is induced in its rotating coil; since this counter emf opposes the input voltage, it can act to limit the current in a motor coil. Similarly, a generator acts somewhat like a motor in that a **counter torque** acts on its rotating coil.]

A **transformer**, which is a device to change the magnitude of an ac voltage, consists of a primary coil and a secondary coil. The changing flux due to an ac voltage in the primary coil induces an ac voltage in the secondary coil. In a 100% efficient transformer, the ratio of output to input voltages (V_S/V_P) equals the ratio of the number of turns N_S in the secondary to the number N_P in the primary:

$$\frac{V_S}{V_P} = \frac{N_S}{N_P}. \qquad (29\text{–}5)$$

The ratio of secondary to primary current is in the inverse ratio of turns:

$$\frac{I_S}{I_P} = \frac{N_P}{N_S}. \qquad (29\text{–}6)$$

[*Microphones, ground fault circuit interrupters, seismographs, and read/write heads for computer drives and tape recorders are applications of electromagnetic induction.]

Questions

1. What would be the advantage, in Faraday's experiments (Fig. 29–1), of using coils with many turns?

2. What is the difference between magnetic flux and magnetic field?

3. Suppose you are holding a circular ring of wire and suddenly thrust a magnet, south pole first, away from you toward the center of the circle. Is a current induced in the wire? Is a current induced when the magnet is held steady within the ring? Is a current induced when you withdraw the magnet? In each case, if your answer is yes, specify the direction.

4. Two loops of wire are moving in the vicinity of a very long straight wire carrying a steady current as shown in Fig. 29–33. Find the direction of the induced current in each loop.

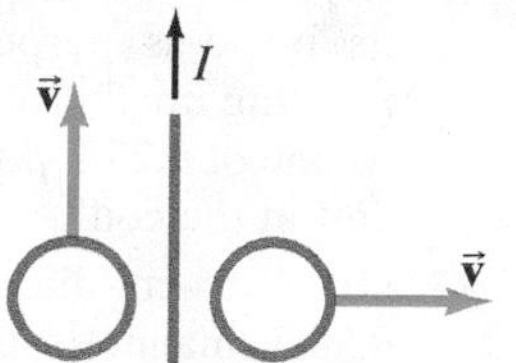

FIGURE 29–33
Questions 4 and 5.

5. Is there a force between the two loops discussed in Question 4? If so, in what direction?

6. Suppose you are looking along a line through the centers of two circular (but separate) wire loops, one behind the other. A battery is suddenly connected to the front loop, establishing a clockwise current. (*a*) Will a current be induced in the second loop? (*b*) If so, when does this current start? (*c*) When does it stop? (*d*) In what direction is this current? (*e*) Is there a force between the two loops? (*f*) If so, in what direction?

7. The battery mentioned in Question 6 is disconnected. Will a current be induced in the second loop? If so, when does it start and stop? In what direction is this current?

8. In what direction will the current flow in Fig. 29–12a if the rod moves to the left, which decreases the area of the loop to the left?

9. In Fig. 29–34, determine the direction of the induced current in resistor R_A (*a*) when coil B is moved toward coil A, (*b*) when coil B is moved away from A, (*c*) when the resistance R_B is increased.

 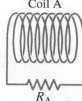

Coil B   Coil A

FIGURE 29–34
Question 9. R_B R_A

10. In situations where a small signal must travel over a distance, a *shielded cable* is used in which the signal wire is surrounded by an insulator and then enclosed by a cylindrical conductor carrying the return current (Fig. 28–12). Why is a "shield" necessary?

11. What is the advantage of placing the two insulated electric wires carrying ac close together or even twisted about each other?

12. Which object will fall faster in a nonuniform magnetic field, a conducting loop with radius ℓ or a straight wire of length $\ell/2$?

13. A region where no magnetic field is desired is surrounded by a sheet of low-resistivity metal. (*a*) Will this sheet shield the interior from a rapidly changing magnetic field outside? Explain. (*b*) Will it act as a shield to a static magnetic field? (*c*) What if the sheet is superconducting (resistivity = 0)?

14. A cell phone charger contains a transformer. Why can't you just buy one universal charger to charge your old cell phone, your new cell phone, your drill, and your toy electric train?

15. An enclosed transformer has four wire leads coming from it. How could you determine the ratio of turns on the two coils without taking the transformer apart? How would you know which wires paired with which?

16. The use of higher-voltage lines in homes—say, 600 V or 1200 V—would reduce energy waste. Why are they not used?

17. A transformer designed for a 120-V ac input will often "burn out" if connected to a 120-V dc source. Explain. [*Hint*: The resistance of the primary coil is usually very low.]

*18. Explain why, exactly, the lights may dim briefly when a refrigerator motor starts up. When an electric heater is turned on, the lights may stay dimmed as long as the heater is on. Explain the difference.

*19. Use Fig. 29–15 plus the right-hand rules to show why the counter torque in a generator *opposes* the motion.

*20. Will an eddy current brake (Fig. 29–21) work on a copper or aluminum wheel, or must the wheel be ferromagnetic? Explain.

*21. It has been proposed that eddy currents be used to help sort solid waste for recycling. The waste is first ground into tiny pieces and iron removed with a dc magnet. The waste then is allowed to slide down an incline over permanent magnets. How will this aid in the separation of nonferrous metals (Al, Cu, Pb, brass) from nonmetallic materials?

*22. The pivoted metal bar with slots in Fig. 29–35 falls much more quickly through a magnetic field than does a solid bar. Explain.

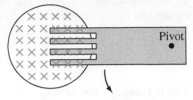

FIGURE 29–35
Question 22.

*23. If an aluminum sheet is held between the poles of a large bar magnet, it requires some force to pull it out of the magnetic field even though the sheet is not ferromagnetic and does not touch the pole faces. Explain.

*24. A bar magnet falling inside a vertical metal tube reaches a terminal velocity even if the tube is evacuated so that there is no air resistance. Explain.

*25. A metal bar, pivoted at one end, oscillates freely in the absence of a magnetic field; but in a magnetic field, its oscillations are quickly damped out. Explain. (This *magnetic damping* is used in a number of practical devices.)

*26. Since a magnetic microphone is basically like a loudspeaker, could a loudspeaker (Section 27–6) actually serve as a microphone? That is, could you speak into a loudspeaker and obtain an output signal that could be amplified? Explain. Discuss, in light of your response, how a microphone and loudspeaker differ in construction.

Problems

29–1 and 29–2 Faraday's Law of Induction

1. (I) The magnetic flux through a coil of wire containing two loops changes at a constant rate from −58 Wb to +38 Wb in 0.42 s. What is the emf induced in the coil?

2. (I) The north pole of the magnet in Fig. 29–36 is being inserted into the coil. In which direction is the induced current flowing through the resistor R?

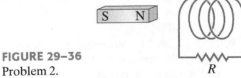

FIGURE 29–36
Problem 2.

3. (I) The rectangular loop shown in Fig. 29–37 is pushed into the magnetic field which points inward. In what direction is the induced current?

FIGURE 29–37
Problem 3.

4. (I) A 22.0-cm-diameter loop of wire is initially oriented perpendicular to a 1.5-T magnetic field. The loop is rotated so that its plane is parallel to the field direction in 0.20 s. What is the average induced emf in the loop?

5. (II) A circular wire loop of radius $r = 12$ cm is immersed in a uniform magnetic field $B = 0.500$ T with its plane normal to the direction of the field. If the field magnitude then decreases at a constant rate of −0.010 T/s, at what rate should r increase so that the induced emf within the loop is zero?

6. (II) A 10.8-cm-diameter wire coil is initially oriented so that its plane is perpendicular to a magnetic field of 0.68 T pointing up. During the course of 0.16 s, the field is changed to one of 0.25 T pointing down. What is the average induced emf in the coil?

7. (II) A 16-cm-diameter circular loop of wire is placed in a 0.50-T magnetic field. (*a*) When the plane of the loop is perpendicular to the field lines, what is the magnetic flux through the loop? (*b*) The plane of the loop is rotated until it makes a 35° angle with the field lines. What is the angle θ in Eq. 29–1a for this situation? (*c*) What is the magnetic flux through the loop at this angle?

8. (II) (a) If the resistance of the resistor in Fig. 29–38 is slowly increased, what is the direction of the current induced in the small circular loop inside the larger loop? (b) What would it be if the small loop were placed outside the larger one, to the left?

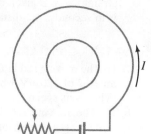

FIGURE 29–38
Problem 8.

9. (II) If the solenoid in Fig. 29–39 is being pulled away from the loop shown, in what direction is the induced current in the loop?

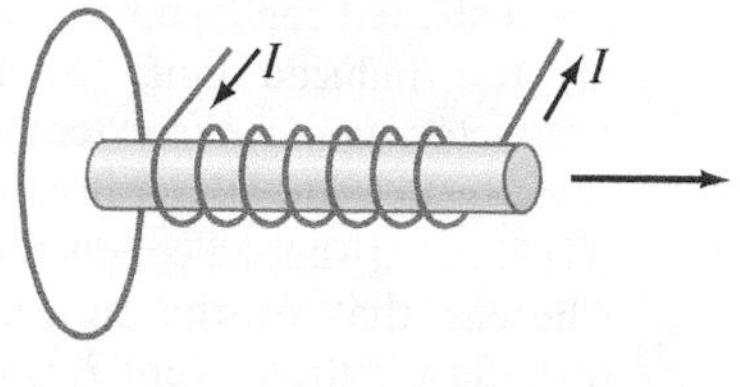

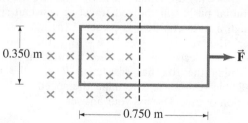

FIGURE 29–39
Problem 9.

10. (II) The magnetic field perpendicular to a circular wire loop 8.0 cm in diameter is changed from +0.52 T to −0.45 T in 180 ms, where + means the field points away from an observer and − toward the observer. (a) Calculate the induced emf. (b) In what direction does the induced current flow?

11. (II) A circular loop in the plane of the paper lies in a 0.75-T magnetic field pointing into the paper. If the loop's diameter changes from 20.0 cm to 6.0 cm in 0.50 s, (a) what is the direction of the induced current, (b) what is the magnitude of the average induced emf, and (c) if the coil resistance is 2.5 Ω, what is the average induced current?

12. (II) Part of a single rectangular loop of wire with dimensions shown in Fig. 29–40 is situated inside a region of uniform magnetic field of 0.650 T. The total resistance of the loop is 0.280 Ω. Calculate the force required to pull the loop from the field (to the right) at a constant velocity of 3.40 m/s. Neglect gravity.

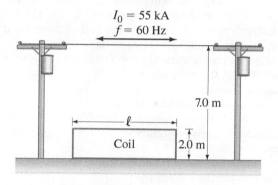

FIGURE 29–40   Problem 12.

13. (II) While demonstrating Faraday's law to her class, a physics professor inadvertently moves the gold ring on her finger from a location where a 0.80-T magnetic field points along her finger to a zero-field location in 45 ms. The 1.5-cm-diameter ring has a resistance and mass of 55 $\mu\Omega$ and 15 g, respectively. (a) Estimate the thermal energy produced in the ring due to the flow of induced current. (b) Find the temperature rise of the ring, assuming all of the thermal energy produced goes into increasing the ring's temperature. The specific heat of gold is 129 J/kg·C°.

14. (II) A 420-turn solenoid, 25 cm long, has a diameter of 2.5 cm. A 15-turn coil is wound tightly around the center of the solenoid. If the current in the solenoid increases uniformly from 0 to 5.0 A in 0.60 s, what will be the induced emf in the short coil during this time?

15. (II) A 22.0-cm-diameter coil consists of 28 turns of circular copper wire 2.6 mm in diameter. A uniform magnetic field, perpendicular to the plane of the coil, changes at a rate of 8.65×10^{-3} T/s. Determine (a) the current in the loop, and (b) the rate at which thermal energy is produced.

16. (II) A power line carrying a sinusoidally varying current with frequency $f = 60$ Hz and peak value $I_0 = 55$ kA runs at a height of 7.0 m across a farmer's land (Fig. 29–41). The farmer constructs a vertically oriented 2.0-m-high 10-turn rectangular wire coil below the power line. The farmer hopes to use the induced voltage in this coil to power 120-Volt electrical equipment, which requires a sinusoidally varying voltage with frequency $f = 60$ Hz and peak value $V_0 = 170$ V. What should the length ℓ of the coil be? Would this be unethical?

FIGURE 29–41   Problem 16.

17. (II) The magnetic field perpendicular to a single 18.2-cm-diameter circular loop of copper wire decreases uniformly from 0.750 T to zero. If the wire is 2.35 mm in diameter, how much charge moves past a point in the coil during this operation?

18. (II) The magnetic flux through each loop of a 75-loop coil is given by $(8.8t - 0.51t^3) \times 10^{-2}$ T·m², where the time t is in seconds. (a) Determine the emf $\mathscr{E}$ as a function of time. (b) What is $\mathscr{E}$ at $t = 1.0$ s and $t = 4.0$ s?

19. (II) A 25-cm-diameter circular loop of wire has a resistance of 150 Ω. It is initially in a 0.40-T magnetic field, with its plane perpendicular to $\vec{\mathbf{B}}$, but is removed from the field in 120 ms. Calculate the electric energy dissipated in this process.

20. (II) The area of an elastic circular loop decreases at a constant rate, $dA/dt = -3.50 \times 10^{-2}$ m²/s. The loop is in a magnetic field $B = 0.28$ T whose direction is perpendicular to the plane of the loop. At $t = 0$, the loop has area $A = 0.285$ m². Determine the induced emf at $t = 0$, and at $t = 2.00$ s.

21. (II) Suppose the radius of the elastic loop in Problem 20 increases at a constant rate, $dr/dt = 4.30$ cm/s. Determine the emf induced in the loop at $t = 0$ and at $t = 1.00$ s.

22. (II) A single circular loop of wire is placed inside a long solenoid with its plane perpendicular to the axis of the solenoid. The area of the loop is A_1 and that of the solenoid, which has n turns per unit length, is A_2. A current $I = I_0 \cos \omega t$ flows in the solenoid turns. What is the induced emf in the small loop?

23. (II) We are looking down on an elastic conducting loop with resistance $R = 2.0\,\Omega$, immersed in a magnetic field. The field's magnitude is uniform spatially, but varies with time t according to $B(t) = \alpha t$, where $\alpha = 0.60\,\text{T/s}$. The area A of the loop also increases at a constant rate, according to $A(t) = A_0 + \beta t$, where $A_0 = 0.50\,\text{m}^2$ and $\beta = 0.70\,\text{m}^2/\text{s}$. Find the magnitude and direction (clockwise or counterclockwise, when viewed from above the page) of the induced current within the loop at time $t = 2.0\,\text{s}$ if the magnetic field (a) is parallel to the plane of the loop to the right; (b) is perpendicular to the plane of the loop, down.

24. (II) Inductive battery chargers, which allow transfer of electrical power without the need for exposed electrical contacts, are commonly used in appliances that need to be safely immersed in water, such as electric toothbrushes. Consider the following simple model for the power transfer in an inductive charger (Fig. 29–42). Within the charger's plastic base, a primary coil of diameter d with n_P turns per unit length is connected to a home's ac wall outlet so that a current $I = I_0 \sin(2\pi ft)$ flows within it. When the toothbrush is seated on the base, an N-turn secondary coil inside the toothbrush has a diameter only slightly greater than d and is centered on the primary. Find an expression for the emf induced in the secondary coil. [This induced emf recharges the battery.]

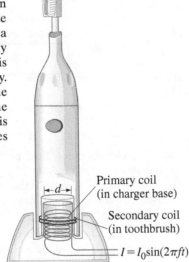

Primary coil (in charger base)

Secondary coil (in toothbrush)

$I = I_0 \sin(2\pi ft)$

FIGURE 29–42
Problem 24.

25. (III) (a) Determine the magnetic flux through a square loop of side a (Fig. 29–43) if one side is parallel to, and a distance b from, a straight wire that carries a current I. (b) If the loop is pulled away from the wire at speed v, what emf is induced in it? (c) Does the induced current flow clockwise or counterclockwise? (d) Determine the force F required to pull the loop away.

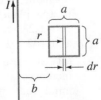

FIGURE 29–43
Problems 25 and 26.

26. (III) Determine the emf induced in the square loop in Fig. 29–43 if the loop stays at rest and the current in the straight wire is given by $I(t) = (15.0\,\text{A}) \sin(2500 t)$ where t is in seconds. The distance a is 12.0 cm, and b is 15.0 cm.

29–3 Motional EMF

27. (I) The moving rod in Fig. 29–12b is 13.2 cm long and generates an emf of 120 mV while moving in a 0.90-T magnetic field. What is its speed?

28. (I) The moving rod in Fig. 29–12b is 12.0 cm long and is pulled at a speed of 15.0 cm/s. If the magnetic field is 0.800 T, calculate the emf developed.

29. (II) In Fig. 29–12a, the rod moves to the right with a speed of 1.3 m/s and has a resistance of 2.5 Ω. The rail separation is $\ell = 25.0$ cm. The magnetic field is 0.35 T, and the resistance of the U-shaped conductor is 25.0 Ω at a given instant. Calculate (a) the induced emf, (b) the current in the U-shaped conductor, and (c) the external force needed to keep the rod's velocity constant at that instant.

30. (II) If the U-shaped conductor in Fig. 29–12a has resistivity ρ, whereas that of the moving rod is negligible, derive a formula for the current I as a function of time. Assume the rod starts at the bottom of the U at $t = 0$, and moves with uniform speed v in the magnetic field B. The cross-sectional area of the rod and all parts of the U is A.

31. (II) Suppose that the U-shaped conductor and connecting rod in Fig. 29–12a are oriented vertically (but still in contact) so that the rod is falling due to the gravitational force. Find the terminal speed of the rod if it has mass $m = 3.6$ grams, length $\ell = 18$ cm, and resistance $R = 0.0013\,\Omega$. It is falling in a uniform horizontal field $B = 0.060\,\text{T}$. Neglect the resistance of the U-shaped conductor.

32. (II) When a car drives through the Earth's magnetic field, an emf is induced in its vertical 75.0-cm-long radio antenna. If the Earth's field $(5.0 \times 10^{-5}\,\text{T})$ points north with a dip angle of 45°, what is the maximum emf induced in the antenna and which direction(s) will the car be moving to produce this maximum value? The car's speed is 30.0 m/s on a horizontal road.

33. (II) A conducting rod rests on two long frictionless parallel rails in a magnetic field $\vec{B}$ ($\perp$ to the rails and rod) as in Fig. 29–44. (a) If the rails are horizontal and the rod is given an initial push, will the rod travel at constant speed even though a magnetic field is present? (b) Suppose at $t = 0$, when the rod has speed $v = v_0$, the two rails are connected electrically by a wire from point a to point b. Assuming the rod has resistance R and the rails have negligible resistance, determine the speed of the rod as a function of time. Discuss your answer.

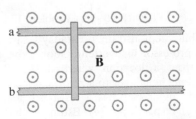

FIGURE 29–44 Problems 33 and 34.

34. (III) Suppose a conducting rod (mass m, resistance R) rests on two frictionless and resistanceless parallel rails a distance ℓ apart in a uniform magnetic field $\vec{\mathbf{B}}$ ($\perp$ to the rails and to the rod) as in Fig. 29–44. At $t = 0$, the rod is at rest and a source of emf is connected to the points a and b. Determine the speed of the rod as a function of time if (a) the source puts out a constant current I, (b) the source puts out a constant emf $\mathscr{E}_0$. (c) Does the rod reach a terminal speed in either case? If so, what is it?

35. (III) A short section of wire, of length a, is moving with velocity $\vec{\mathbf{v}}$, parallel to a very long wire carrying a current I as shown in Fig. 29–45. The near end of the wire section is a distance b from the long wire. Assuming the vertical wire is very long compared to $a + b$, determine the emf between the ends of the short section. Assume $\vec{\mathbf{v}}$ is (a) in the same direction as I, (b) in the opposite direction to I.

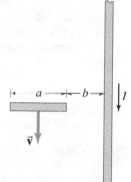

FIGURE 29–45
Problem 35.

29–4 Generators

36. (I) The generator of a car idling at 875-rpm produces 12.4 V. What will the output be at a rotation speed of 1550 rpm assuming nothing else changes?

37. (I) A simple generator is used to generate a peak output voltage of 24.0 V. The square armature consists of windings that are 5.15 cm on a side and rotates in a field of 0.420 T at a rate of 60.0 rev/s. How many loops of wire should be wound on the square armature?

38. (II) A simple generator has a 480-loop square coil 22.0 cm on a side. How fast must it turn in a 0.550-T field to produce a 120-V peak output?

39. (II) Show that the rms output of an ac generator is $V_{rms} = NAB\omega/\sqrt{2}$ where $\omega = 2\pi f$.

40. (II) A 250-loop circular armature coil with a diameter of 10.0 cm rotates at 120 rev/s in a uniform magnetic field of strength 0.45 T. What is the rms voltage output of the generator? What would you do to the rotation frequency in order to double the rms voltage output?

*29–5 Back EMF, Counter Torque; Eddy Current

***41.** (I) The back emf in a motor is 72 V when operating at 1200 rpm. What would be the back emf at 2500 rpm if the magnetic field is unchanged?

***42.** (I) A motor has an armature resistance of 3.05 Ω. If it draws 7.20 A when running at full speed and connected to a 120-V line, how large is the back emf?

***43.** (II) What will be the current in the motor of Example 29–10 if the load causes it to run at half speed?

***44.** (II) The back emf in a motor is 85 V when the motor is operating at 1100 rpm. How would you change the motor's magnetic field if you wanted to reduce the back emf to 75 V when the motor was running at 2300 rpm?

***45.** (II) A dc generator is rated at 16 kW, 250 V, and 64 A when it rotates at 1000 rpm. The resistance of the armature windings is 0.40 Ω. (a) Calculate the "no-load" voltage at 1000 rpm (when there is no circuit hooked up to the generator). (b) Calculate the full-load voltage (i.e. at 64 A) when the generator is run at 750 rpm. Assume that the magnitude of the magnetic field remains constant.

29–6 Transformers

[Assume 100% efficiency, unless stated otherwise.]

46. (I) A transformer has 620 turns in the primary coil and 85 in the secondary coil. What kind of transformer is this, and by what factor does it change the voltage? By what factor does it change the current?

47. (I) Neon signs require 12 kV for their operation. To operate from a 240-V line, what must be the ratio of secondary to primary turns of the transformer? What would the voltage output be if the transformer were connected backward?

48. (II) A model-train transformer plugs into 120-V ac and draws 0.35 A while supplying 7.5 A to the train. (a) What voltage is present across the tracks? (b) Is the transformer step-up or step-down?

49. (II) The output voltage of a 75-W transformer is 12 V, and the input current is 22 A. (a) Is this a step-up or a step-down transformer? (b) By what factor is the voltage multiplied?

50. (II) If 65 MW of power at 45 kV (rms) arrives at a town from a generator via 3.0-Ω transmission lines, calculate (a) the emf at the generator end of the lines, and (b) the fraction of the power generated that is wasted in the lines.

51. (II) Assume a voltage source supplies an ac voltage of amplitude V_0 between its output terminals. If the output terminals are connected to an external circuit, and an ac current of amplitude I_0 flows out of the terminals, then the equivalent resistance of the external circuit is $R_{eq} = V_0/I_0$. (a) If a resistor R is connected directly to the output terminals, what is R_{eq}? (b) If a transformer with N_P and N_S turns in its primary and secondary, respectively, is placed between the source and the resistor as shown in Fig. 29–46, what is R_{eq}? [Transformers can be used in ac circuits to alter the apparent resistance of circuit elements, such as loud speakers, in order to maximize transfer of power.]

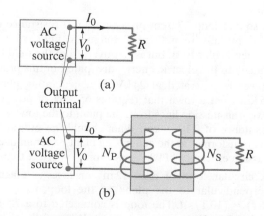

FIGURE 29–46 Problem 51.

52. (III) Design a dc transmission line that can transmit 225 MW of electricity 185 km with only a 2.0% loss. The wires are to be made of aluminum and the voltage is 660 kV.

53. (III) Suppose 85 kW is to be transmitted over two 0.100-Ω lines. Estimate how much power is saved if the voltage is stepped up from 120 V to 1200 V and then down again, rather than simply transmitting at 120 V. Assume the transformers are each 99% efficient.

29–7 Changing Φ_B Produces $\vec{E}$

54. (II) In a circular region, there is a uniform magnetic field $\vec{B}$ pointing into the page (Fig. 29–47). An xy coordinate system has its origin at the circular region's center. A free positive point charge $+Q = 1.0\,\mu\text{C}$ is initially at rest at a position $x = +10$ cm on the x axis. If the magnitude of the magnetic field is now decreased at a rate of -0.10 T/s, what force (magnitude and direction) will act on $+Q$?

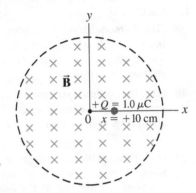

FIGURE 29–47
Problem 54.

55. (II) The **betatron**, a device used to accelerate electrons to high energy, consists of a circular vacuum tube placed in a magnetic field (Fig. 29–48), into which electrons are injected. The electromagnet produces a field that (1) keeps the electrons in their circular orbit inside the tube, and (2) increases the speed of the electrons when B changes. (a) Explain how the electrons are accelerated. (See Fig. 29–48.) (b) In what direction are the electrons moving in Fig. 29–48 (give directions as if looking down from above)? (c) Should B increase or decrease to accelerate the electrons? (d) The magnetic field is actually 60 Hz ac; show that the electrons can be accelerated only during $\frac{1}{4}$ of a cycle $\left(\frac{1}{240}\text{ s}\right)$. (During this time they make hundreds of thousands of revolutions and acquire very high energy.)

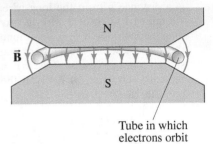

FIGURE 29–48
Problems 55 and 56.

Tube in which electrons orbit

56. (III) Show that the electrons in a betatron, Problem 55 and Fig. 29–48, are accelerated at constant radius if the magnetic field B_0 at the position of the electron orbit in the tube is equal to half the average value of the magnetic field (B_{avg}) over the area of the circular orbit at each moment: $B_0 = \frac{1}{2}B_{\text{avg}}$. (This is the reason the pole faces have a rather odd shape, as indicated in Fig. 29–48.)

57. (III) Find a formula for the net electric field in the moving rod of Problem 34 as a function of time for each case, (a) and (b).

General Problems

58. Suppose you are looking at two current loops in the plane of the page as shown in Fig. 29–49. When the switch S is closed in the left-hand coil, (a) what is the direction of the induced current in the other loop? (b) What is the situation after a "long" time? (c) What is the direction of the induced current in the right-hand loop if that loop is quickly pulled horizontally to the right (S having been closed for a long time)?

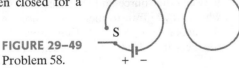

FIGURE 29–49
Problem 58.

59. A square loop 27.0 cm on a side has a resistance of 7.50 Ω. It is initially in a 0.755-T magnetic field, with its plane perpendicular to $\vec{B}$, but is removed from the field in 40.0 ms. Calculate the electric energy dissipated in this process.

60. Power is generated at 24 kV at a generating plant located 85 km from a town that requires 65 MW of power at 12 kV. Two transmission lines from the plant to the town each have a resistance of 0.10 Ω/km. What should the output voltage of the transformer at the generating plant be for an overall transmission efficiency of 98.5%, assuming a perfect transformer?

61. A circular loop of area 12 m^2 encloses a magnetic field perpendicular to the plane of the loop; its magnitude is $B(t) = (10\text{ T/s})t$. The loop is connected to a 7.5-Ω resistor and a 5.0-pF capacitor in series. When fully charged, how much charge is stored on the capacitor?

62. The primary windings of a transformer which has an 85% efficiency are connected to 110-V ac. The secondary windings are connected across a 2.4-Ω, 75-W lightbulb. (a) Calculate the current through the primary windings of the transformer. (b) Calculate the ratio of the number of primary windings of the transformer to the number of secondary windings of the transformer.

63. A pair of power transmission lines each have a 0.80-Ω resistance and carry 740 A over 9.0 km. If the rms input voltage is 42 kV, calculate (a) the voltage at the other end, (b) the power input, (c) power loss in the lines, and (d) the power output.

64. Show that the power loss in transmission lines, P_L, is given by $P_L = (P_T)^2 R_L/V^2$, where P_T is the power transmitted to the user, V is the delivered voltage, and R_L is the resistance of the power lines.

65. A high-intensity desk lamp is rated at 35 W but requires only 12 V. It contains a transformer that converts 120-V household voltage. (a) Is the transformer step-up or step-down? (b) What is the current in the secondary coil when the lamp is on? (c) What is the current in the primary coil? (d) What is the resistance of the bulb when on?

66. Two resistanceless rails rest 32 cm apart on a 6.0° ramp. They are joined at the bottom by a 0.60-Ω resistor. At the top a copper bar of mass 0.040 kg (ignore its resistance) is laid across the rails. The whole apparatus is immersed in a vertical 0.55-T field. What is the terminal (steady) velocity of the bar as it slides frictionlessly down the rails?

67. A coil with 150 turns, a radius of 5.0 cm, and a resistance of 12 Ω surrounds a solenoid with 230 turns/cm and a radius of 4.5 cm; see Fig. 29–50. The current in the solenoid changes at a constant rate from 0 to 2.0 A in 0.10 s. Calculate the magnitude and direction of the induced current in the 150-turn coil.

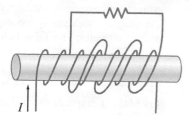

FIGURE 29–50
Problem 67.

68. A **search coil** for measuring B (also called a **flip coil**) is a small coil with N turns, each of cross-sectional area A. It is connected to a so-called **ballistic galvanometer**, which is a device to measure the total charge Q that passes through it in a short time. The flip coil is placed in the magnetic field to be measured with its face perpendicular to the field. It is then quickly rotated 180° about a diameter. Show that the total charge Q that flows in the induced current during this short "flip" time is proportional to the magnetic field B. In particular, show that B is given by

$$B = \frac{QR}{2NA}$$

where R is the total resistance of the circuit, including that of the coil and that of the ballistic galvanometer which measures the charge Q.

69. A ring with a radius of 3.0 cm and a resistance of 0.025 Ω is rotated about an axis through its diameter by 90° in a magnetic field of 0.23 T perpendicular to that axis. What is the largest number of electrons that would flow past a fixed point in the ring as this process is accomplished?

70. A flashlight can be made that is powered by the induced current from a magnet moving through a coil of wire. The coil and magnet are inside a plastic tube that can be shaken causing the magnet to move back and forth through the coil. Assume the magnet has a maximum field strength of 0.05 T. Make reasonable assumptions and specify the size of the coil and the number of turns necessary to light a standard 1-watt, 3-V flashlight bulb.

*71. A small electric car overcomes a 250-N friction force when traveling 35 km/h. The electric motor is powered by ten 12-V batteries connected in series and is coupled directly to the wheels whose diameters are 58 cm. The 270 armature coils are rectangular, 12 cm by 15 cm, and rotate in a 0.60-T magnetic field. (a) How much current does the motor draw to produce the required torque? (b) What is the back emf? (c) How much power is dissipated in the coils? (d) What percent of the input power is used to drive the car?

72. What is the energy dissipated as a function of time in a circular loop of 18 turns of wire having a radius of 10.0 cm and a resistance of 2.0 Ω if the plane of the loop is perpendicular to a magnetic field given by

$$B(t) = B_0 e^{-t/\tau}$$

with $B_0 = 0.50$ T and $\tau = 0.10$ s?

73. A thin metal rod of length ℓ rotates with angular velocity ω about an axis through one end (Fig. 29–51). The rotation axis is perpendicular to the rod and is parallel to a uniform magnetic field $\vec{B}$. Determine the emf developed between the ends of the rod.

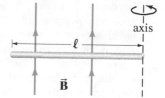

FIGURE 29–51
Problem 73.

*74. The magnetic field of a "shunt-wound" dc motor is produced by field coils placed in parallel with the armature coils. Suppose that the field coils have a resistance of 36.0 Ω and the armature coils 3.00 Ω. The back emf at full speed is 105 V when the motor is connected to 115 V dc. (a) Draw the equivalent circuit for the situations when the motor is just starting and when it is running full speed. (b) What is the total current drawn by the motor at start up? (c) What is the total current drawn when the motor runs at full speed?

75. Apply Faraday's law, in the form of Eq. 29–8, to show that the static electric field between the plates of a parallel-plate capacitor cannot drop abruptly to zero at the edges, but must, in fact, fringe. Use the path shown dashed in Fig. 29–52.

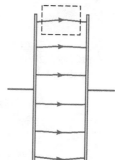

FIGURE 29–52
Problem 75.

76. A circular metal disk of radius R rotates with angular velocity ω about an axis through its center perpendicular to its face. The disk rotates in a uniform magnetic field B whose direction is parallel to the rotation axis. Determine the emf induced between the center and the edges.

77. What is the magnitude and direction of the electric field at each point in the rotating disk of Problem 76?

78. A circular-shaped circuit of radius r, containing a resistance R and capacitance C, is situated with its plane perpendicular to a spatially uniform magnetic field $\vec{B}$ directed into the page (Fig. 29–53). Starting at time $t = 0$, the voltage difference $V_{ba} = V_b - V_a$ across the capacitor plates is observed to increase with time t according to $V_{ba} = V_0(1 - e^{-t/\tau})$, where V_0 and τ are positive constants. Determine dB/dt, the rate at which the magnetic field magnitude changes with time. Is B becoming larger or smaller as time increases?

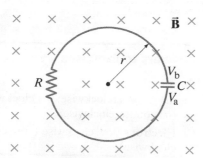

FIGURE 29–53
Problem 78.

79. In a certain region of space near Earth's surface, a uniform horizontal magnetic field of magnitude B exists above a level defined to be $y = 0$. Below $y = 0$, the field abruptly becomes zero (Fig. 29–54). A vertical square wire loop has resistivity ρ, mass density ρ_m, diameter d, and side length ℓ. It is initially at rest with its lower horizontal side at $y = 0$ and is then allowed to fall under gravity, with its plane perpendicular to the direction of the magnetic field. (a) While the loop is still partially immersed in the magnetic field (as it falls into the zero-field region), determine the magnetic "drag" force that acts on it at the moment when its speed is v. (b) Assume that the loop achieves a terminal velocity v_T before its upper horizontal side exits the field. Determine a formula for v_T. (c) If the loop is made of copper and $B = 0.80\,\text{T}$, find v_T.

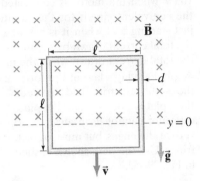

FIGURE 29–54
Problem 79.

*80. (III) In an experiment, a coil was mounted on a low-friction cart that moved through the magnetic field B of a permanent magnet. The speed of the cart v and the induced voltage V were simultaneously measured, as the cart moved through the magnetic field, using a computer-interfaced motion sensor and a voltmeter. The Table below shows the collected data:

Speed, v (m/s)	0.367	0.379	0.465	0.623	0.630
Induced voltage, V (V)	0.128	0.135	0.164	0.221	0.222

(a) Make a graph of the induced voltage, V, vs. the speed, v. Determine a best-fit linear equation for the data. Theoretically, the relationship between V and v is given by $V = BN\ell v$ where N is the number of turns of the coil, B is the magnetic field, and ℓ is the average of the inside and outside widths of the coil. In the experiment, $B = 0.126\,\text{T}$, $N = 50$, and $\ell = 0.0561\,\text{m}$. (b) Find the % error between the slope of the experimental graph and the theoretical value for the slope. (c) For each of the measured speeds v, determine the theoretical value of V and find the % error of each.

Answers to Exercises

A: (e).

B: (a) Counterclockwise; (b) clockwise; (c) zero; (d) counterclockwise.

C: Electrons flow clockwise (conventional current counterclockwise).

D: (a) increases; (b) yes; increases (counter torque).

E: (a) $4.2 \times 10^{-3}\,\text{V/m}$; (b) $5.6 \times 10^{-3}\,\text{V/m}$.

A spark plug in a car receives a high voltage, which produces a high enough electric field in the air across its gap to pull electrons off the atoms in the air–gasoline mixture and form a spark. The high voltage is produced, from the basic 12 V of the car battery, by an induction coil which is basically a transformer or mutual inductance. Any coil of wire has a self-inductance, and a changing current in it causes an emf to be induced. Such inductors are useful in many circuits.

Inductance, Electromagnetic Oscillations, and AC Circuits

CHAPTER-OPENING QUESTION—Guess now!

Consider a circuit with only a capacitor C and a coil of many loops of wire (called an inductor, L) as shown. If the capacitor is initially charged $(Q = Q_0)$, what will happen when the switch S is closed?

(a) Nothing will happen—the capacitor will remain charged with charge $Q = Q_0$.

(b) The capacitor will quickly discharge and remain discharged $(Q = 0)$.

(c) Current will flow until the positive charge is on the opposite plate of the capacitor, and then will reverse—back and forth.

(d) The energy initially in the capacitor $(U_E = \frac{1}{2}Q_0^2/C)$ will all transfer to the coil and then remain that way.

(e) The system will quickly transfer half of the capacitor energy to the coil and then remain that way.

W e discussed in the last Chapter how a changing magnetic flux through a circuit induces an emf in that circuit. Before that we saw that an electric current produces a magnetic field. Combining these two ideas, we could predict that a changing current in one circuit ought to induce an emf and a current in a second nearby circuit, and even induce an emf in itself. We already saw an example in the previous Chapter (transformers), but now we will treat this effect in a more general way in terms of what we will call mutual inductance and self-inductance. The concept of inductance also gives us a springboard to treat energy storage in a magnetic field. This Chapter concludes with an analysis of circuits that contain inductance as well as resistance and/or capacitance.

CONTENTS

30–1 Mutual Inductance

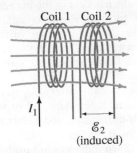

Coil 1 Coil 2

I_1

$\mathcal{E}_2$
(induced)

FIGURE 30–1 A changing current in one coil will induce a current in the second coil.

If two coils of wire are placed near each other, as in Fig. 30–1, a changing current in one will induce an emf in the other. According to Faraday's law, the emf $\mathcal{E}_2$ induced in coil 2 is proportional to the rate of change of magnetic flux passing through it. This flux is due to the current I_1 in coil 1, and it is often convenient to express the emf in coil 2 in terms of the current in coil 1.

We let Φ_{21} be the magnetic flux in each loop of coil 2 created by the current in coil 1. If coil 2 contains N_2 closely wrapped loops, then $N_2 \Phi_{21}$ is the total flux passing through coil 2. If the two coils are fixed in space, $N_2 \Phi_{21}$ is proportional to the current I_1 in coil 1; the proportionality constant is called the **mutual inductance**, M_{21}, defined by

$$M_{21} = \frac{N_2 \Phi_{21}}{I_1}. \tag{30–1}$$

The emf $\mathcal{E}_2$ induced in coil 2 due to a changing current in coil 1 is, by Faraday's law,

$$\mathcal{E}_2 = -N_2 \frac{d\Phi_{21}}{dt}.$$

We combine this with Eq. 30–1 rewritten as $\Phi_{21} = M_{21} I_1 / N_2$ (and take its derivative) and obtain

$$\mathcal{E}_2 = -M_{21} \frac{dI_1}{dt}. \tag{30–2}$$

This relates the change in current in coil 1 to the emf it induces in coil 2. The mutual inductance of coil 2 with respect to coil 1, M_{21}, is a "constant" in that it does not depend on I_1; M_{21} depends on "geometric" factors such as the size, shape, number of turns, and relative positions of the two coils, and also on whether iron (or some other ferromagnetic material) is present. For example, if the two coils in Fig. 30–1 are farther apart, fewer lines of flux can pass through coil 2, so M_{21} will be less. For some arrangements, the mutual inductance can be calculated (see Example 30–1). More often it is determined experimentally.

Suppose, now, we consider the reverse situation: when a changing current in coil 2 induces an emf in coil 1. In this case,

$$\mathcal{E}_1 = -M_{12} \frac{dI_2}{dt}$$

where M_{12} is the mutual inductance of coil 1 with respect to coil 2. It is possible to show, although we will not prove it here, that $M_{12} = M_{21}$. Hence, for a given arrangement we do not need the subscripts and we can let

$$M = M_{12} = M_{21},$$

so that

$$\mathcal{E}_1 = -M \frac{dI_2}{dt} \tag{30–3a}$$

and

$$\mathcal{E}_2 = -M \frac{dI_1}{dt}. \tag{30–3b}$$

The SI unit for mutual inductance is the henry (H), where $1\,\text{H} = 1\,\text{V·s/A} = 1\,\Omega\cdot\text{s}$.

EXERCISE A Two coils which are close together have a mutual inductance of 330 mH. (a) If the emf in coil 1 is 120 V, what is the rate of change of the current in coil 2? (b) If the rate of change of current in coil 1 is 36 A/s, what is the emf in coil 2?

EXAMPLE 30–1 **Solenoid and coil.** A long thin solenoid of length ℓ and cross-sectional area A contains N_1 closely packed turns of wire. Wrapped around it is an insulated coil of N_2 turns, Fig. 30–2. Assume all the flux from coil 1 (the solenoid) passes through coil 2, and calculate the mutual inductance.

APPROACH We first determine the flux produced by the solenoid, all of which passes uniformly through coil N_2, using Eq. 28–4 for the magnetic field inside the solenoid:

$$B = \mu_0 \frac{N_1}{\ell} I_1,$$

where $n = N_1/\ell$ is the number of loops in the solenoid per unit length, and I_1 is the current in the solenoid.

SOLUTION The solenoid is closely packed, so we assume that all the flux in the solenoid stays inside the secondary coil. Then the flux Φ_{21} through coil 2 is

$$\Phi_{21} = BA = \mu_0 \frac{N_1}{\ell} I_1 A.$$

Then the mutual inductance is

$$M = \frac{N_2 \Phi_{21}}{I_1} = \frac{\mu_0 N_1 N_2 A}{\ell}.$$

NOTE We calculated M_{21}; if we had tried to calculate M_{12}, it would have been difficult. Given $M_{12} = M_{21} = M$, we did the simpler calculation to obtain M. Note again that M depends only on geometric factors, and not on the currents.

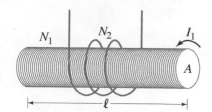

FIGURE 30–2   Example 30–1.

CONCEPTUAL EXAMPLE 30–2 | **Reversing the coils.** How would Example 30–1 change if the coil with N_2 turns was inside the solenoid rather than outside the solenoid?

RESPONSE The magnetic field inside the solenoid would be unchanged. The flux through the coil would be BA where A is the area of the coil, not of the solenoid as in Example 30–1. Solving for M would give the same formula except that A would refer to the coil, and would be smaller.

EXERCISE B Which solenoid and coil combination shown in Fig. 30–3 has the largest mutual inductance? Assume each solenoid is the same.

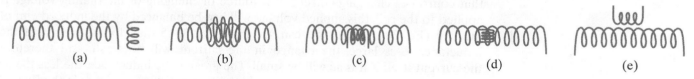

(a)   (b)   (c)   (d)   (e)

FIGURE 30–3   Exercise B.

A transformer is an example of mutual inductance in which the coupling is maximized so that nearly all flux lines pass through both coils. Mutual inductance has other uses as well, including some types of *pacemakers* used to maintain blood flow in heart patients (Section 26–5). Power in an external coil is transmitted via mutual inductance to a second coil in the pacemaker at the heart. This type has the advantage over battery-powered pacemakers in that surgery is not needed to replace a battery when it wears out.

Mutual inductance can sometimes be a problem, however. Any changing current in a circuit can induce an emf in another part of the same circuit or in a different circuit even though the conductors are not in the shape of a coil. The mutual inductance M is usually small unless coils with many turns and/or iron cores are involved. However, in situations where small voltages are being used, problems due to mutual inductance often arise. Shielded cable, in which an inner conductor is surrounded by a cylindrical grounded conductor (Fig. 28–12), is often used to reduce the problem.

PHYSICS APPLIED
Pacemaker

30–2 Self-Inductance

The concept of inductance applies also to a single isolated coil of N turns. When a changing current passes through a coil (or solenoid), a changing magnetic flux is produced inside the coil, and this in turn induces an emf in that same coil. This induced emf opposes the change in flux (Lenz's law). For example, if the current through the coil is increasing, the increasing magnetic flux induces an emf that opposes the original current and tends to retard its increase. If the current is decreasing in the coil, the decreasing flux induces an emf in the same direction as the current, thus tending to maintain the original current.

The magnetic flux Φ_B passing through the N turns of a coil is proportional to the current I in the coil, so we define the **self-inductance** L (in analogy to mutual inductance, Eq. 30–1) as

$$L = \frac{N\Phi_B}{I}. \tag{30–4}$$

Then the emf $\mathscr{E}$ induced in a coil of self-inductance L is, from Faraday's law,

$$\mathscr{E} = -N\frac{d\Phi_B}{dt} = -L\frac{dI}{dt}. \tag{30–5}$$

Like mutual inductance, self-inductance is measured in henrys. The magnitude of L depends on the geometry and on the presence of a ferromagnetic material. Self-inductance (inductance, for short) can be defined, as above, for any circuit or part of a circuit.

Circuits always contain some inductance, but often it is quite small unless the circuit contains a coil of many turns. A coil that has significant self-inductance L is called an **inductor**. Inductance is shown on circuit diagrams by the symbol

—⁓⁓⁓—;   [inductor symbol]

any resistance an inductor has should also be shown separately. Inductance can serve a useful purpose in certain circuits. Often, however, inductance is to be avoided in a circuit. Precision resistors are normally wire wound and thus would have inductance as well as resistance. The inductance can be minimized by winding the insulated wire back on itself in the opposite sense so that the current going in opposite directions produces little net magnetic flux; this is called a **noninductive winding**.

If an inductor has negligible resistance, it is the inductance (or induced emf) that controls a changing current. If a source of changing or alternating voltage is applied to the coil, this applied voltage will just be balanced by the induced emf of the coil (Eq. 30–5). Thus we can see from Eq. 30–5 that, for a given $\mathscr{E}$, if the inductance L is large, the change in the current will be small, and therefore the current itself if it is ac will be small. The greater the inductance, the less the ac current. An inductance thus acts something like a resistance to impede the flow of alternating current. We use the term *reactance* or *impedance* for this quality of an inductor. We will discuss reactance and impedance more fully in Sections 30–7 and 30–8. We shall see that reactance depends not only on the inductance L, but also on the frequency. Here we mention one example of its importance. The resistance of the primary in a transformer is usually quite small, perhaps less than $1\,\Omega$. If resistance alone limited the current in a transformer, tremendous currents would flow when a high voltage was applied. Indeed, a dc voltage applied to a transformer can burn it out. It is the induced emf (or reactance) of the coil that limits the current to a reasonable value.

Common inductors have inductances in the range from about $1\,\mu\text{H}$ to about $1\,\text{H}$ (where $1\,\text{H} = 1\,\text{henry} = 1\,\Omega\cdot\text{s}$).

EXAMPLE 30–3 **Solenoid inductance.** (*a*) Determine a formula for the self-inductance L of a tightly wrapped and long solenoid containing N turns of wire in its length ℓ and whose cross-sectional area is A. (*b*) Calculate the value of L if $N = 100$, $\ell = 5.0\,\text{cm}$, $A = 0.30\,\text{cm}^2$ and the solenoid is air filled.

APPROACH To determine the inductance L, it is usually simplest to start with Eq. 30–4, so we need to first determine the flux.

SOLUTION (a) According to Eq. 28–4, the magnetic field inside a solenoid (ignoring end effects) is constant: $B = \mu_0 n I$ where $n = N/\ell$. The flux is $\Phi_B = BA = \mu_0 N I A/\ell$, so

$$L = \frac{N\Phi_B}{I} = \frac{\mu_0 N^2 A}{\ell}.$$

(b) Since $\mu_0 = 4\pi \times 10^{-7}\,\text{T}\cdot\text{m/A}$, then

$$L = \frac{(4\pi \times 10^{-7}\,\text{T}\cdot\text{m/A})(100)^2(3.0 \times 10^{-5}\,\text{m}^2)}{(5.0 \times 10^{-2}\,\text{m})} = 7.5\,\mu\text{H}.$$

NOTE Magnetic field lines "stray" out of the solenoid (see Fig. 28–15), especially near the ends, so our formula is only an approximation.

CONCEPTUAL EXAMPLE 30–4 **Direction of emf in inductor.** Current passes through the coil in Fig. 30–4 from left to right as shown. (a) If the current is increasing with time, in which direction is the induced emf? (b) If the current is decreasing in time, what then is the direction of the induced emf?

RESPONSE (a) From Lenz's law we know that the induced emf must oppose the change in magnetic flux. If the current is increasing, so is the magnetic flux. The induced emf acts to oppose the increasing flux, which means it acts like a source of emf that opposes the outside source of emf driving the current. So the induced emf in the coil acts to oppose I in Fig. 30–4a. In other words, the inductor might be thought of as a battery with a positive terminal at point A (tending to block the current entering at A), and negative at point B. (b) If the current is decreasing, then by Lenz's law the induced emf acts to bolster the flux—like a source of emf reinforcing the external emf. The induced emf acts to increase I in Fig. 30–4b, so in this situation you can think of the induced emf as a battery with its negative terminal at point A to attract more ($+$) current to move to the right.

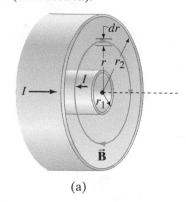

FIGURE 30–4 Example 30–4. The $+$ and $-$ signs refer to the induced emf due to the changing current, as if points A and B were the terminals of a battery (and the coiled loops were the inside of the battery).

EXAMPLE 30–5 **Coaxial cable inductance.** Determine the inductance per unit length of a coaxial cable whose inner conductor has a radius r_1 and the outer conductor has a radius r_2, Fig. 30–5. Assume the conductors are thin hollow tubes so there is no magnetic field within the inner conductor, and the magnetic field inside both thin conductors can be ignored. The conductors carry equal currents I in opposite directions.

APPROACH We need to find the magnetic flux, $\Phi_B = \int \vec{B} \cdot d\vec{A}$, between the conductors. The lines of $\vec{B}$ are circles surrounding the inner conductor (only one is shown in Fig. 30–5a). From Ampère's law, $\oint \vec{B} \cdot d\vec{\ell} = \mu_0 I$, the magnitude of the field along the circle at a distance r from the center, when the inner conductor carries a current I, is (Example 28–6):

$$B = \frac{\mu_0 I}{2\pi r}.$$

The magnetic flux through a rectangle of width dr and length ℓ (along the cable, Fig. 30–5b), a distance r from the center, is

$$d\Phi_B = B(\ell\,dr) = \frac{\mu_0 I}{2\pi r}\ell\,dr.$$

SOLUTION The total flux in a length ℓ of cable is

$$\Phi_B = \int d\Phi_B = \frac{\mu_0 I\ell}{2\pi}\int_{r_1}^{r_2}\frac{dr}{r} = \frac{\mu_0 I\ell}{2\pi}\ln\frac{r_2}{r_1}.$$

Since the current I all flows in one direction in the inner conductor, and the same current I all flows in the opposite direction in the outer conductor, we have only one turn, so $N = 1$ in Eq. 30–4. Hence the self-inductance for a length ℓ is

$$L = \frac{\Phi_B}{I} = \frac{\mu_0 \ell}{2\pi}\ln\frac{r_2}{r_1}.$$

The inductance per unit length is

$$\frac{L}{\ell} = \frac{\mu_0}{2\pi}\ln\frac{r_2}{r_1}.$$

Note that L depends only on geometric factors and not on the current I.

FIGURE 30–5 Example 30–5. Coaxial cable: (a) end view, (b) side view (cross section).

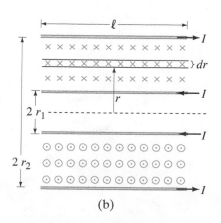

30–3 Energy Stored in a Magnetic Field

When an inductor of inductance L is carrying a current I which is changing at a rate dI/dt, energy is being supplied to the inductor at a rate

$$P = I\mathscr{E} = LI\frac{dI}{dt}$$

where P stands for power and we used[†] Eq. 30–5. Let us calculate the work needed to increase the current in an inductor from zero to some value I. Using this last equation, the work dW done in a time dt is

$$dW = P\,dt = LI\,dI.$$

Then the total work done to increase the current from zero to I is

$$W = \int dW = \int_0^I LI\,dI = \tfrac{1}{2}LI^2.$$

This work done is equal to the energy U stored in the inductor when it is carrying a current I (and we take $U = 0$ when $I = 0$):

$$U = \tfrac{1}{2}LI^2. \tag{30–6}$$

This can be compared to the energy stored in a capacitor, C, when the potential difference across it is V (see Section 24–4):

$$U = \tfrac{1}{2}CV^2.$$

EXERCISE C What is the inductance of an inductor if it has a stored energy of 1.5 J when there is a current of 2.5 A in it? (a) 0.48 H, (b) 1.2 H, (c) 2.1 H, (d) 4.7 H, (e) 19 H.

Just as the energy stored in a capacitor can be considered to reside in the electric field between its plates, so the energy in an inductor can be considered to be stored in its magnetic field. To write the energy in terms of the magnetic field, let us use the result of Example 30–3, that the inductance of an ideal solenoid (end effects ignored) is $L = \mu_0 N^2 A/\ell$. Because the magnetic field B in a solenoid is related to the current I by $B = \mu_0 NI/\ell$, we have

$$U = \tfrac{1}{2}LI^2 = \frac{1}{2}\left(\frac{\mu_0 N^2 A}{\ell}\right)\left(\frac{B\ell}{\mu_0 N}\right)^2$$

$$= \frac{1}{2}\frac{B^2}{\mu_0}A\ell.$$

We can think of this energy as residing in the volume enclosed by the windings, which is $A\ell$. Then the energy per unit volume or **energy density** is

$$u = \text{energy density} = \frac{1}{2}\frac{B^2}{\mu_0}. \tag{30–7}$$

This formula, which was derived for the special case of a solenoid, can be shown to be valid for any region of space where a magnetic field exists. If a ferromagnetic material is present, μ_0 is replaced by μ. This equation is analogous to that for an electric field, $\tfrac{1}{2}\epsilon_0 E^2$, Eq. 24–6.

30–4 *LR* Circuits

Any inductor will have some resistance. We represent this situation by drawing its inductance L and its resistance R separately, as in Fig. 30–6a. The resistance R could also include any other resistance present in the circuit. Now we ask, what happens when a battery or other source of dc voltage V_0 is connected in series to such an LR circuit?

[†]No minus sign here because we are supplying power to oppose the emf of the inductor.

At the instant the switch connecting the battery is closed, the current starts to flow. It is opposed by the induced emf in the inductor which means point B in Fig. 30–6a is positive relative to point C. However, as soon as current starts to flow, there is also a voltage drop of magnitude IR across the resistance. Hence the voltage applied across the inductance is reduced and the current increases less rapidly. The current thus rises gradually as shown in Fig. 30–6b, and approaches the steady value $I_{max} = V_0/R_0$, for which all the voltage drop is across the resistance.

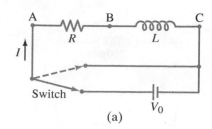

We can show this analytically by applying Kirchhoff's loop rule to the circuit of Fig. 30–6a. The emfs in the circuit are the battery voltage V_0 and the emf $\mathcal{E} = -L(dI/dt)$ in the inductor opposing the increasing current. Hence the sum of the potential changes around the loop is

$$V_0 - IR - L\frac{dI}{dt} = 0,$$

where I is the current in the circuit at any instant. We rearrange this to obtain

$$L\frac{dI}{dt} + RI = V_0. \tag{30–8}$$

This is a linear differential equation and can be integrated in the same way we did in Section 26–5 for an RC circuit. We rewrite Eq. 30–8 and then integrate:

$$\int_{I=0}^{I} \frac{dI}{V_0 - IR} = \int_0^t \frac{dt}{L}.$$

Then

$$-\frac{1}{R}\ln\left(\frac{V_0 - IR}{V_0}\right) = \frac{t}{L}$$

or

$$I = \frac{V_0}{R}\left(1 - e^{-t/\tau}\right) \tag{30–9}$$

where

$$\tau = \frac{L}{R} \tag{30–10}$$

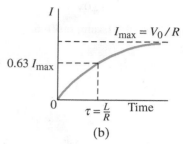

FIGURE 30–6 (a) LR circuit; (b) growth of current when connected to battery.

is the **time constant** of the LR circuit. The symbol τ represents the time required for the current I to reach $(1 - 1/e) = 0.63$ or 63% of its maximum value (V_0/R). Equation 30–9 is plotted in Fig. 30–6b. (Compare to the RC circuit, Section 26–5.)

| **EXERCISE D** Show that L/R does have dimensions of time. (See Section 1–7.)

Now let us flip the switch in Fig. 30–6a so that the battery is taken out of the circuit, and points A and C are connected together as shown in Fig. 30–7 at the moment when the switching occurs (call it $t = 0$) and the current is I_0. Then the differential equation (Eq. 30–8) becomes (since $V_0 = 0$):

$$L\frac{dI}{dt} + RI = 0.$$

We rearrange this equation and integrate:

$$\int_{I_0}^{I} \frac{dI}{I} = -\int_0^t \frac{R}{L}\,dt$$

where $I = I_0$ at $t = 0$, and $I = I$ at time t.

We integrate this last equation to obtain

$$\ln\frac{I}{I_0} = -\frac{R}{L}t$$

or

$$I = I_0 e^{-t/\tau} \tag{30–11}$$

where again the time constant is $\tau = L/R$. The current thus decays exponentially to zero as shown in Fig. 30–8.

This analysis shows that there is always some "reaction time" when an electromagnet, for example, is turned on or off. We also see that an LR circuit has properties similar to an RC circuit (Section 26–5). Unlike the capacitor case, however, the time constant here is *inversely* proportional to R.

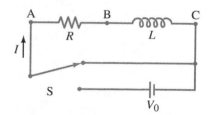

FIGURE 30–7 The switch is flipped quickly so the battery is removed but we still have a circuit. The current at this moment (call it $t = 0$) is I_0.

FIGURE 30–8 Decay of the current in Fig. 30–7 in time after the battery is switched out of the circuit.

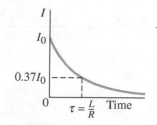

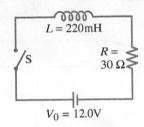

$L = 220\,\text{mH}$

S

$R = 30\,\Omega$

$V_0 = 12.0\,\text{V}$

FIGURE 30–9 Example 30–6.

EXAMPLE 30–6 **An *LR* circuit.** At $t = 0$, a 12.0-V battery is connected in series with a 220-mH inductor and a total of 30-Ω resistance, as shown in Fig. 30–9. (*a*) What is the current at $t = 0$? (*b*) What is the time constant? (*c*) What is the maximum current? (*d*) How long will it take the current to reach half its maximum possible value? (*e*) At this instant, at what rate is energy being delivered by the battery, and (*f*) at what rate is energy being stored in the inductor's magnetic field?

APPROACH We have the situation shown in Figs. 30–6a and b, and we can apply the equations we just developed.

SOLUTION (*a*) The current cannot instantaneously jump from zero to some other value when the switch is closed because the inductor opposes the change $\left(\mathcal{E}_L = -L(dI/dt)\right)$. Hence just after the switch is closed, I is still zero at $t = 0$ and then begins to increase.

(*b*) The time constant is, from Eq. 30–10, $\tau = L/R = (0.22\,\text{H})/(30\,\Omega) = 7.3\,\text{ms}$.

(*c*) The current reaches its maximum steady value after a long time, when $dI/dt = 0$ so $I_{max} = V_0/R = 12.0\,\text{V}/30\,\Omega = 0.40\,\text{A}$.

(*d*) We set $I = \frac{1}{2}I_{max} = V_0/2R$ in Eq. 30–9, which gives us

$$1 - e^{-t/\tau} = \tfrac{1}{2}$$

or

$$e^{-t/\tau} = \tfrac{1}{2}.$$

We solve for t:

$$t = \tau \ln 2 = (7.3 \times 10^{-3}\,\text{s})(0.69) = 5.0\,\text{ms}.$$

(*e*) At this instant, $I = I_{max}/2 = 200\,\text{mA}$, so the power being delivered by the battery is

$$P = IV = (0.20\,\text{A})(12\,\text{V}) = 2.4\,\text{W}.$$

(*f*) From Eq. 30–6, the energy stored in an inductor L at any instant is

$$U = \tfrac{1}{2}LI^2$$

where I is the current in the inductor at that instant. The *rate* at which the energy changes is

$$\frac{dU}{dt} = LI\frac{dI}{dt}.$$

We can differentiate Eq. 30–9 to obtain dI/dt, or use the differential equation, Eq. 30–8, directly:

$$\frac{dU}{dt} = I\left(L\frac{dI}{dt}\right) = I(V_0 - RI)$$
$$= (0.20\,\text{A})[12\,\text{V} - (30\,\Omega)(0.20\,\text{A})] = 1.2\,\text{W}.$$

Since only part of the battery's power is feeding the inductor at this instant, where is the rest going?

EXERCISE E A resistor in series with an inductor has a time constant of 10 ms. When the same resistor is placed in series with a 5-μF capacitor, the time constant is $5 \times 10^{-6}\,\text{s}$. What is the value of the inductor? (*a*) 5 μH; (*b*) 10 μH; (*c*) 5 mH; (*d*) 10 mH; (*e*) not enough information to determine it.

PHYSICS APPLIED
Surge protection

An inductor can act as a "surge protector" for sensitive electronic equipment that can be damaged by high currents. If equipment is plugged into a standard wall plug, a sudden "surge," or increase, in voltage will normally cause a corresponding large change in current and damage the electronics. However, if there is an inductor in series with the voltage to the device, the sudden change in current produces an opposing emf preventing the current from reaching dangerous levels.

30–5 LC Circuits and Electromagnetic Oscillations

In any electric circuit, there can be three basic components: resistance, capacitance, and inductance, in addition to a source of emf. (There can also be more complex components, such as diodes or transistors.) We have previously discussed both RC and LR circuits. Now we look at an LC circuit, one that contains only a capacitance C and an inductance, L, Fig. 30–10. This is an idealized circuit in which we assume there is no resistance; in the next Section we will include resistance. Let us suppose the capacitor in Fig. 30–10 is initially charged so that one plate has charge Q_0 and the other plate has charge $-Q_0$, and the potential difference across it is $V = Q/C$ (Eq. 24–1). Suppose that at $t = 0$, the switch is closed. The capacitor immediately begins to discharge. As it does so, the current I through the inductor increases. We now apply Kirchhoff's loop rule (sum of potential changes around a loop is zero):

$$-L\frac{dI}{dt} + \frac{Q}{C} = 0.$$

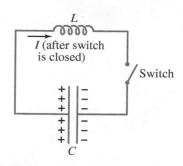

FIGURE 30–10 An LC circuit.

Because charge leaves the positive plate on the capacitor to produce the current I as shown in Fig. 30–10, the charge Q on the (positive) plate of the capacitor is decreasing, so $I = -dQ/dt$. We can then rewrite the above equation as

$$\frac{d^2Q}{dt^2} + \frac{Q}{LC} = 0. \tag{30–12}$$

This is a familiar differential equation. It has the same form as the equation for simple harmonic motion (Chapter 14, Eq. 14–3). The solution of Eq. 30–12 can be written as

$$Q = Q_0 \cos(\omega t + \phi) \tag{30–13}$$

where Q_0 and ϕ are constants that depend on the initial conditions. We insert Eq. 30–13 into Eq. 30–12, noting that $d^2Q/dt^2 = -\omega^2 Q_0 \cos(\omega t + \phi)$; thus

$$-\omega^2 Q_0 \cos(\omega t + \phi) + \frac{1}{LC} Q_0 \cos(\omega t + \phi) = 0$$

or

$$\left(-\omega^2 + \frac{1}{LC}\right)\cos(\omega t + \phi) = 0.$$

This relation can be true for all times t only if $\left(-\omega^2 + 1/LC\right) = 0$, which tells us that

$$\omega = 2\pi f = \sqrt{\frac{1}{LC}}. \tag{30–14}$$

Equation 30–13 shows that the charge on the capacitor in an LC circuit oscillates sinusoidally. The current in the inductor is

$$I = -\frac{dQ}{dt} = \omega Q_0 \sin(\omega t + \phi)$$

$$= I_0 \sin(\omega t + \phi); \tag{30–15}$$

so the current too is sinusoidal. The maximum value of I is $I_0 = \omega Q_0 = Q_0/\sqrt{LC}$. Equations 30–13 and 30–15 for Q and I when $\phi = 0$ are plotted in Fig. 30–11.

FIGURE 30–11 Charge Q and current I in an LC circuit. The period $T = \frac{1}{f} = \frac{2\pi}{\omega} = 2\pi\sqrt{LC}$.

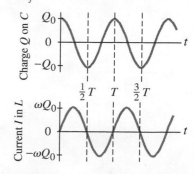

Now let us look at *LC* oscillations from the point of view of energy. The energy stored in the electric field of the capacitor at any time t is (see Eq. 24–5):

$$U_E = \frac{1}{2}\frac{Q^2}{C} = \frac{Q_0^2}{2C}\cos^2(\omega t + \phi).$$

The energy stored in the magnetic field of the inductor at the same instant is (Eq. 30–6)

$$U_B = \frac{1}{2}LI^2 = \frac{L\omega^2 Q_0^2}{2}\sin^2(\omega t + \phi) = \frac{Q_0^2}{2C}\sin^2(\omega t + \phi)$$

where we used Eq. 30–14. If we let $\phi = 0$, then at times $t = 0$, $t = \frac{1}{2}T$, $t = T$, and so on (where T is the period $= 1/f = 2\pi/\omega$), we have $U_E = Q_0^2/2C$ and $U_B = 0$. That is, all the energy is stored in the electric field of the capacitor. But at $t = \frac{1}{4}T, \frac{3}{4}T$, and so on, $U_E = 0$ and $U_B = Q_0^2/2C$, and so all the energy is stored in the magnetic field of the inductor. At any time t, the total energy is

$$U = U_E + U_B = \frac{1}{2}\frac{Q^2}{C} + \frac{1}{2}LI^2$$

$$= \frac{Q_0^2}{2C}\left[\cos^2(\omega t + \phi) + \sin^2(\omega t + \phi)\right] = \frac{Q_0^2}{2C}. \quad \textbf{(30–16)}$$

Hence the total energy is constant, and energy is conserved.

What we have in this *LC* circuit is an **LC oscillator** or **electromagnetic oscillation**. The charge Q oscillates back and forth, from one plate of the capacitor to the other, and repeats this continuously. Likewise, the current oscillates back and forth as well. They are also energy oscillations: when Q is a maximum, the energy is all stored in the electric field of the capacitor; but when Q reaches zero, the current I is a maximum and all the energy is stored in the magnetic field of the inductor. Thus the energy oscillates between being stored in the electric field of the capacitor and in the magnetic field of the inductor. See Fig. 30–12.

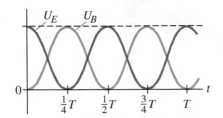

FIGURE 30–12 Energy U_E (red line) and U_B (blue line) stored in the capacitor and the inductor as a function of time. Note how the energy oscillates between electric and magnetic. The dashed line at the top is the (constant) total energy $U = U_E + U_B$.

EXERCISE F Return to the Chapter-Opening Question, page 785, and answer it again now. Try to explain why you may have answered differently the first time.

EXAMPLE 30–7 *LC* **circuit.** A 1200-pF capacitor is fully charged by a 500-V dc power supply. It is disconnected from the power supply and is connected, at $t = 0$, to a 75-mH inductor. Determine: (*a*) the initial charge on the capacitor; (*b*) the maximum current; (*c*) the frequency f and period T of oscillation; and (*d*) the total energy oscillating in the system.

APPROACH We use the analysis above, and the definition of capacitance $Q = CV$ (Chapter 24).

SOLUTION (*a*) The 500-V power supply, before being disconnected, charged the capacitor to a charge of

$$Q_0 = CV = (1.2 \times 10^{-9}\,\text{F})(500\,\text{V}) = 6.0 \times 10^{-7}\,\text{C}.$$

(*b*) The maximum current, I_{max}, is (see Eqs. 30-14 and 30–15)

$$I_{max} = \omega Q_0 = \frac{Q_0}{\sqrt{LC}} = \frac{(6.0 \times 10^{-7}\,\text{C})}{\sqrt{(0.075\,\text{H})(1.2 \times 10^{-9}\,\text{F})}} = 63\,\text{mA}.$$

(*c*) Equation 30–14 gives us the frequency:

$$f = \frac{\omega}{2\pi} = \frac{1}{(2\pi\sqrt{LC})} = 17\,\text{kHz},$$

and the period T is

$$T = \frac{1}{f} = 6.0 \times 10^{-5}\,\text{s}.$$

(*d*) Finally the total energy (Eq. 30–16) is

$$U = \frac{Q_0^2}{2C} = \frac{(6.0 \times 10^{-7}\,\text{C})^2}{2(1.2 \times 10^{-9}\,\text{F})} = 1.5 \times 10^{-4}\,\text{J}.$$

30–6 LC Oscillations with Resistance (LRC Circuit)

The *LC* circuit discussed in the previous Section is an idealization. There is always some resistance *R* in any circuit, and so we now discuss such a simple *LRC* circuit, Fig. 30–13.

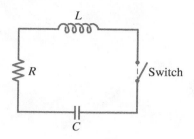

Suppose again that the capacitor is initially given a charge Q_0 and the battery or other source is then removed from the circuit. The switch is closed at $t = 0$. Since there is now a resistance in the circuit, we expect some of the energy to be converted to thermal energy, and so we don't expect undamped oscillations as in a pure *LC* circuit. Indeed, if we use Kirchhoff's loop rule around this circuit, we obtain

$$-L\frac{dI}{dt} - IR + \frac{Q}{C} = 0,$$

FIGURE 30–13 An *LRC* circuit.

which is the same equation we had in Section 30–5 with the addition of the voltage drop *IR* across the resistor. Since $I = -dQ/dt$, as we saw in Section 30–5, this equation becomes

$$L\frac{d^2Q}{dt^2} + R\frac{dQ}{dt} + \frac{1}{C}Q = 0. \qquad (30\text{–}17)$$

This second-order differential equation in the variable *Q* has precisely the same form as that for the damped harmonic oscillator, Eq. 14–15:

$$m\frac{d^2x}{dt^2} + b\frac{dx}{dt} + kx = 0.$$

Hence we can analyze our *LRC* circuit in the same way as for damped harmonic motion, Section 14–7. Our system may undergo damped oscillations, curve A in Fig. 30–14 (underdamped system), or it may be critically damped (curve B), or overdamped (curve C), depending on the relative values of *R*, *L*, and *C*. Using the results of Section 14–7, with *m* replaced by *L*, *b* by *R*, and *k* by C^{-1}, we find that the system will be underdamped when

$$R^2 < \frac{4L}{C},$$

and overdamped for $R^2 > 4L/C$. Critical damping (curve B in Fig. 30–14) occurs when $R^2 = 4L/C$. If *R* is smaller than $\sqrt{4L/C}$, the angular frequency, ω', will be

$$\omega' = \sqrt{\frac{1}{LC} - \frac{R^2}{4L^2}} \qquad (30\text{–}18)$$

(compare to Eq. 14–18). And the charge *Q* as a function of time will be

$$Q = Q_0 e^{-\frac{R}{2L}t}\cos(\omega't + \phi) \qquad (30\text{–}19)$$

FIGURE 30–14 Charge *Q* on the capacitor in an *LRC* circuit as a function of time: curve A is for underdamped oscillation $(R^2 < 4L/C)$, curve B is for critically damped $(R^2 = 4L/C)$, and curve C is for overdamped $(R^2 > 4L/C)$.

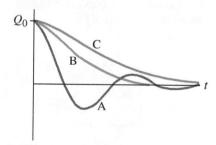

where ϕ is a phase constant (compare to Eq. 14–19).

Oscillators are an important element in many electronic devices: radios and television sets use them for tuning, tape recorders use them (the "bias frequency") when recording, and so on. Because some resistance is always present, electrical oscillators generally need a periodic input of power to compensate for the energy converted to thermal energy in the resistance.

in series with a resistance $R = 3.0 \, \Omega$ and a charged capacitor $C = 4.8 \, \mu F$.
(a) Show that this circuit will oscillate. (b) Determine the frequency. (c) What is
the time required for the charge amplitude to drop to half its starting value?
(d) What value of R will make the circuit nonoscillating?

APPROACH We first check R^2 vs. $4L/C$; then use Eqs. 30–18 and 30–19.

SOLUTION (a) In order to oscillate, the circuit must be underdamped, so we must
have $R^2 < 4L/C$. Since $R^2 = 9.0 \, \Omega^2$ and $4L/C = 4(0.040 \, \text{H})/(4.8 \times 10^{-6} \, \text{F}) = 3.3 \times 10^4 \, \Omega^2$, this relation is satisfied, so the circuit will oscillate.

(b) We use Eq. 30–18:

$$f' = \frac{\omega'}{2\pi} = \frac{1}{2\pi}\sqrt{\frac{1}{LC} - \frac{R^2}{4L^2}} = 3.6 \times 10^2 \, \text{Hz}.$$

(c) From Eq. 30–19, the amplitude will be half when

$$e^{-\frac{R}{2L}t} = \tfrac{1}{2}$$

or

$$t = \frac{2L}{R} \ln 2 = 18 \, \text{ms}.$$

(d) To make the circuit critically damped or overdamped, we must use the criterion
$R^2 \geq 4L/C = 3.3 \times 10^4 \, \Omega^2$. Hence we must have $R \geq 180 \, \Omega$.

30–7 AC Circuits with AC Source

We have previously discussed circuits that contain combinations of resistor, capacitor,
and inductor, but only when they are connected to a dc source of emf or to no source.
Now we discuss these circuit elements when they are connected to a source of
alternating voltage that produces an alternating current (ac).

First we examine, one at a time, how a resistor, a capacitor, and an inductor
behave when connected to a source of alternating voltage, represented by the symbol

$$\bullet\!-\!\!\sim\!\!-\!\bullet \qquad\qquad \text{[alternating voltage]}$$

which produces a sinusoidal voltage of frequency f. We assume in each case that
the emf gives rise to a current

$$I = I_0 \cos 2\pi ft = I_0 \cos \omega t \qquad\qquad \textbf{(30–20)}$$

where t is time and I_0 is the peak current. Remember (Section 25–7) that
$V_{\text{rms}} = V_0/\sqrt{2}$ and $I_{\text{rms}} = I_0/\sqrt{2}$ (Eqs. 25–9).

Resistor

When an ac source is connected to a resistor as in Fig. 30–15a, the current
increases and decreases with the alternating voltage according to Ohm's law

$$V = IR = I_0 R \cos \omega t = V_0 \cos \omega t$$

where $V_0 = I_0 R$ is the peak voltage as a function of time. Figure 30–15b shows
the voltage (red curve) and the current (blue curve). Because the current is zero
when the voltage is zero and the current reaches a peak when the voltage does, we
say that the current and voltage are **in phase**. Energy is transformed into heat
(Section 25–7), at an average rate

$$\overline{P} = \overline{IV} = I_{\text{rms}}^2 R = V_{\text{rms}}^2/R.$$

Inductor

In Fig. 30–16a an inductor of inductance L (symbol $-\!\text{ooo}\!-$) is connected to the
ac source. We ignore any resistance it might have (it is usually small). The voltage
applied to the inductor will be equal to the "back" emf generated in the inductor by the
changing current as given by Eq. 30–5. This is because the sum of the electric potential
changes around any closed circuit must add up to zero, according to Kirchhoff's rule.

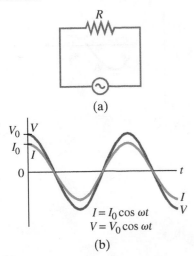

FIGURE 30–15 (a) Resistor
connected to an ac source.
(b) Current (blue curve) is in phase
with the voltage (red) across a
resistor.

Thus

$$V - L\frac{dI}{dt} = 0$$

or (inserting Eq. 30–20)

$$V = L\frac{dI}{dt} = -\omega L I_0 \sin \omega t. \tag{30–21}$$

Using the identity $\sin\theta = -\cos(\theta + 90°)$ we can write

$$V = \omega L I_0 \cos(\omega t + 90°) = V_0 \cos(\omega t + 90°) \tag{30–22a}$$

where

$$V_0 = I_0 \omega L \tag{30–22b}$$

is the peak voltage. The current I and voltage V as a function of time are graphed for the inductor in Fig. 30–16b. It is clear from this graph, as well as from Eqs. 30–22, that the current and voltage are out of phase by a quarter cycle, which is equivalent to $\pi/2$ radians or 90°. We see from the graph that

the current lags the voltage by 90° in an inductor.

That is, the current in an inductor reaches its peaks a quarter cycle later than the voltage does. Alternatively, we can say that the voltage leads the current by 90°.

Because the current and voltage in an inductor are out of phase by 90°, the product IV (= power) is as often positive as it is negative (Fig. 30–16b). So no energy is transformed in an inductor on the average; and no energy is dissipated as thermal energy.

Just as a resistor impedes the flow of charge, so too an inductor impedes the flow of charge in an alternating current due to the back emf produced. For a resistor R, the peak current and peak voltage are related by $V_0 = I_0 R$. We can write a similar relation for an inductor:

$$V_0 = I_0 X_L \qquad \left[\begin{array}{c}\text{maximum or rms values,} \\ \text{not at any instant}\end{array}\right] \tag{30–23a}$$

where, from Eq. 30–22b (and using $\omega = 2\pi f$ where f is the frequency of the ac),

$$X_L = \omega L = 2\pi f L. \tag{30–23b}$$

The term X_L is called the **inductive reactance** of the inductor, and has units of ohms. The greater X_L is, the more it impedes the flow of charge and the smaller the current. X_L is larger for higher frequencies f and larger inductance L.

Equation 30–23a is valid for peak values I_0 and V_0; it is also valid for rms values, $V_{rms} = I_{rms} X_L$. Because the peak values of current and voltage are not reached at the same time, Eq. 30–23a is *not valid at a particular instant*, as is the case for a resistor $(V = IR)$.

Note from Eq. 30–23b that if $\omega = 2\pi f = 0$ (so the current is dc), there is no back emf and no impedance to the flow of charge.

EXAMPLE 30–9 Reactance of a coil. A coil has a resistance $R = 1.00\,\Omega$ and an inductance of 0.300 H. Determine the current in the coil if (*a*) 120-V dc is applied to it, (*b*) 120-V ac (rms) at 60.0 Hz is applied.

APPROACH When the voltage is dc, there is no inductive reactance $(X_L = 2\pi f L = 0$ since $f = 0)$, so we apply Ohm's law for the resistance. When the voltage is ac, we calculate the reactance X_L and then use Eq. 30–23a.

SOLUTION (*a*) With dc, we have no X_L so we simply apply Ohm's law:

$$I = \frac{V}{R} = \frac{120\,\text{V}}{1.00\,\Omega} = 120\,\text{A}.$$

(*b*) The inductive reactance is

$$X_L = 2\pi f L = (6.283)(60.0\,\text{s}^{-1})(0.300\,\text{H}) = 113\,\Omega.$$

In comparison to this, the resistance can be ignored. Thus,

$$I_{rms} = \frac{V_{rms}}{X_L} = \frac{120\,\text{V}}{113\,\Omega} = 1.06\,\text{A}.$$

NOTE It might be tempting to say that the total impedance is $113\,\Omega + 1\,\Omega = 114\,\Omega$. This might imply that about 1% of the voltage drop is across the resistor, or about 1 V; and that across the inductance is 119 V. Although the 1 V across the resistor is correct, the other statements are not true because of the alteration in phase in an inductor. This will be discussed in the next Section.

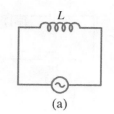

(a)

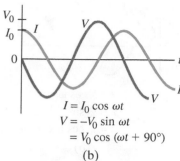

$$I = I_0 \cos \omega t$$
$$V = -V_0 \sin \omega t$$
$$= V_0 \cos(\omega t + 90°)$$

(b)

FIGURE 30–16 (a) Inductor connected to an ac source. (b) Current (blue curve) lags voltage (red curve) by a quarter cycle or 90°.

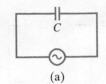

(a)

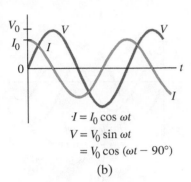

$I = I_0 \cos \omega t$

$V = V_0 \sin \omega t$

$\quad = V_0 \cos(\omega t - 90°)$

(b)

FIGURE 30–17 (a) Capacitor connected to an ac source. (b) Current leads voltage by a quarter cycle, or 90°.

Capacitor

When a capacitor is connected to a battery, the capacitor plates quickly acquire equal and opposite charges; but no steady current flows in the circuit. A capacitor prevents the flow of a dc current. But if a capacitor is connected to an alternating source of voltage, as in Fig. 30–17a, an alternating current will flow continuously. This can happen because when the ac voltage is first turned on, charge begins to flow and one plate acquires a negative charge and the other a positive charge. But when the voltage reverses itself, the charges flow in the opposite direction. Thus, for an alternating applied voltage, an ac current is present in the circuit continuously.

Let us look at this in more detail. By Kirchhoff's loop rule, the applied source voltage must equal the voltage V across the capacitor at any moment:

$$V = \frac{Q}{C}$$

where C is the capacitance and Q is the charge on the capacitor plates. The current I at any instant (given as $I = I_0 \cos \omega t$, Eq. 30–20) is

$$I = \frac{dQ}{dt} = I_0 \cos \omega t.$$

Hence the charge Q on the plates at any instant is given by

$$Q = \int_0^t dQ = \int_0^t I_0 \cos \omega t \, dt = \frac{I_0}{\omega} \sin \omega t.$$

Then the voltage across the capacitor is

$$V = \frac{Q}{C} = I_0 \left(\frac{1}{\omega C}\right) \sin \omega t.$$

Using the trigonometric identity $\sin \theta = \cos(90° - \theta) = \cos(\theta - 90°)$, we can rewrite this as

$$V = I_0 \left(\frac{1}{\omega C}\right) \cos(\omega t - 90°) = V_0 \cos(\omega t - 90°) \qquad \textbf{(30–24a)}$$

where

$$V_0 = I_0 \left(\frac{1}{\omega C}\right) \qquad \textbf{(30–24b)}$$

is the peak voltage. The current $I \left(= I_0 \cos \omega t\right)$ and voltage V (Eq. 30–24a) across the capacitor are graphed in Fig. 30–17b. It is clear from this graph, as well as a comparison of Eq. 30–24a with Eq. 30–20, that the current and voltage are out of phase by a quarter cycle or 90° ($\pi/2$ radians):

The current leads the voltage across a capacitor by 90°.

Alternatively we can say that the voltage lags the current by 90°. This is the opposite of what happens for an inductor.

Because the current and voltage are out of phase by 90°, the average power dissipated is zero, just as for an inductor. Energy from the source is fed to the capacitor, where it is stored in the electric field between its plates. As the field decreases, the energy returns to the source. Thus *only a resistance will dissipate energy* as thermal energy in an ac circuit.

A relationship between the applied voltage and the current in a capacitor can be written just as for an inductance:

$$V_0 = I_0 X_C \qquad \left[\begin{array}{c}\text{maximum or rms values,} \\ \text{not at any instant}\end{array}\right] \qquad \textbf{(30–25a)}$$

where X_C is the **capacitive reactance** of the capacitor, and has units of ohms; X_C is given by (see Eq. 30–24b):

$$X_C = \frac{1}{\omega C} = \frac{1}{2\pi f C}. \qquad \textbf{(30–25b)}$$

When frequency f and/or capacitance C are smaller, X_C is larger and thus impedes the flow of charge more. That is, when X_C is larger, the current is smaller (Eq. 30–25a). In the next Section we use the term **impedance** to represent reactances and resistance.

Equation 30–25a relates the peak values of V and I, or the rms values $(V_{rms} = I_{rms} X_C)$. But it is not valid at a particular instant because I and V are not in phase.

Note from Eq. 30–25b that for dc conditions, $\omega = 2\pi f = 0$ and X_C becomes infinite. This is as it should be, since a pure capacitor does not pass dc current. Also, note that the reactance of an inductor increases with frequency, but that of a capacitor decreases with frequency.

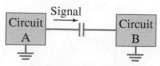

Signal

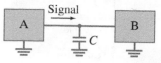

(a) High-pass filter

EXAMPLE 30–10 **Capacitor reactance.** What is the rms current in the circuit of Fig. 30–17a if $C = 1.0\,\mu\text{F}$ and $V_{\text{rms}} = 120\,\text{V}$? Calculate (a) for $f = 60\,\text{Hz}$, and then (b) for $f = 6.0 \times 10^5\,\text{Hz}$.

APPROACH We find the reactance using Eq. 30–25b, and solve for current in the equivalent form of Ohm's law, Eq. 30–25a.

SOLUTION (a) $X_C = 1/2\pi fC = 1/(6.28)(60\,\text{s}^{-1})(1.0 \times 10^{-6}\,\text{F}) = 2.7\,\text{k}\Omega$. The rms current is (Eq. 30–25a):

$$I_{\text{rms}} = \frac{V_{\text{rms}}}{X_C} = \frac{120\,\text{V}}{2.7 \times 10^3\,\Omega} = 44\,\text{mA}.$$

(b) For $f = 6.0 \times 10^5\,\text{Hz}$, X_C will be $0.27\,\Omega$ and $I_{\text{rms}} = 440\,\text{A}$, vastly larger!

NOTE The dependence on f is dramatic. For high frequencies, the capacitive reactance is very small, and the current can be large.

(b) Low-pass filter

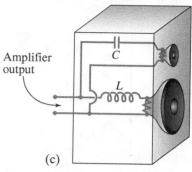

Amplifier output

(c)

Two common applications of capacitors are illustrated in Fig. 30–18a and b. In Fig. 30–18a, circuit A is said to be capacitively coupled to circuit B. The purpose of the capacitor is to prevent a dc voltage from passing from A to B but allowing an ac signal to pass relatively unimpeded (if C is sufficiently large, Eq. 30–25b). The capacitor in Fig. 30–18a is called a **high-pass filter** because it allows high-frequency ac to pass easily, but not dc.

In Fig. 30–18b, the capacitor passes ac to ground. In this case, a dc voltage can be maintained between circuits A and B, but an ac signal leaving A passes to ground instead of into B. Thus the capacitor in Fig. 30–18b acts like a **low-pass filter** when a constant dc voltage is required; any high-frequency variation in voltage will pass to ground instead of into circuit B. (Very low-frequency ac will also be able to reach circuit B, at least in part.)

Loudspeakers having separate "woofer" (low-frequency speaker) and "tweeter" (high-frequency speaker) may use a simple "cross-over" that consists of a capacitor in the tweeter circuit to impede low-frequency signals, and an inductor in the woofer circuit to impede high-frequency signals $(X_L = 2\pi fL)$. Hence mainly low-frequency sounds reach and are emitted by the woofer. See Fig. 30–18c.

FIGURE 30–18 (a) and (b) Two common uses for a capacitor as a filter. (c) Simple loudspeaker cross-over.

(X) PHYSICS APPLIED
Capacitors as filters

(X) PHYSICS APPLIED
Loudspeaker cross-over

EXERCISE G At what frequency is the reactance of a 1.0-μF capacitor equal to 500 Ω? (a) 320 Hz, (b) 500 Hz, (c) 640 Hz, (d) 2000 Hz, (e) 4000 Hz.

EXERCISE H At what frequency is the reactance of a 1.0-μH inductor equal to 500 Ω? (a) 80 Hz, (b) 500 Hz, (c) 80 MHz, (d) 160 MHz, (e) 500 MHz.

30–8 *LRC* Series AC Circuit

Let us examine a circuit containing all three elements in series: a resistor R, an inductor L, and a capacitor C, Fig. 30–19. If a given circuit contains only two of these elements, we can still use the results of this Section by setting $R = 0$, $X_L = 0$, or $X_C = 0$, as needed. We let V_R, V_L, and V_C represent the voltage across each element at a *given instant* in time; and V_{R0}, V_{L0}, and V_{C0} represent the *maximum* (peak) values of these voltages. The voltage across each of the elements will follow the phase relations we discussed in the previous Section. At any instant the voltage V supplied by the source will be, by Kirchhoff's loop rule,

$$V = V_R + V_L + V_C. \tag{30–26}$$

Because the various voltages are not in phase, they do not reach their peak values at the same time, so the peak voltage of the source V_0 will *not* equal $V_{R0} + V_{L0} + V_{C0}$.

FIGURE 30–19 An *LRC* circuit.

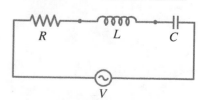

⚠ CAUTION
Peak voltages do not add to yield source voltage

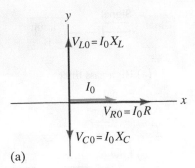

(a)

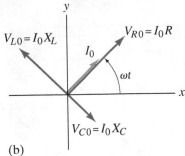

(b)

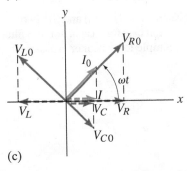

(c)

FIGURE 30–20 Phasor diagram for a series *LRC* circuit at (a) $t = 0$, (b) a time t later. (c) Projections on x axis reflect Eqs. 30–20, 30–22a, and 30–24a.

FIGURE 30–21 Phasor diagram for a series *LRC* circuit showing the sum vector, V_0.

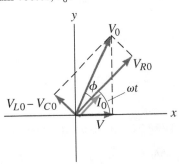

Let us now find the impedance of an *LRC* circuit as a whole (the effect of R, X_C, and X_L), as well as the peak current I_0, and the phase relation between V and I. The current at any instant must be the same at all points in the circuit. Thus the *currents in each element are in phase with each other, even though the voltages are not*. We choose our origin in time $(t = 0)$ so that the current I at any time t is (as in Eq. 30–20)

$$I = I_0 \cos \omega t.$$

We analyze an *LRC* circuit using[†] a **phasor diagram**. Arrows (treated like vectors) are drawn in an xy coordinate system to represent each voltage. The *length of each arrow represents the magnitude of the peak voltage across each element*:

$$V_{R0} = I_0 R, \qquad V_{L0} = I_0 X_L, \qquad \text{and} \qquad V_{C0} = I_0 X_C.$$

V_{R0} is in phase with the current and is initially $(t = 0)$ drawn along the positive x axis, as is the current (Fig. 30–20a). V_{L0} leads the current by 90°, so it leads V_{R0} by 90° and is initially drawn along the positive y axis. V_{C0} lags the current by 90°, so V_{C0} is drawn initially along the negative y axis, Fig. 30–20a.

If we let the vector diagram rotate counterclockwise at frequency f, we get the diagram shown in Fig. 30–20b; after a time, t, each arrow has rotated through an angle ωt. Then the *projections of each arrow on the x axis represent the voltages across each element* at the instant t (Fig. 30–20c). For example $I = I_0 \cos \omega t$. Compare Eqs. 30–22a and 30–24a with Fig. 30–20c to confirm the validity of the phasor diagram.

The sum of the projections of the three voltage vectors represents the instantaneous voltage across the whole circuit, V. Therefore, the vector sum of these vectors will be the vector that represents the peak source voltage, V_0, as shown in Fig. 30–21 where it is seen that V_0 makes an angle ϕ with I_0 and V_{R0}. As time passes, V_0 rotates with the other vectors, so the instantaneous voltage V (projection of V_0 on the x axis) is (see Fig. 30–21)

$$V = V_0 \cos(\omega t + \phi).$$

The voltage V across the whole circuit must equal the source voltage (Fig. 30–19). Thus the voltage from the source is out of phase[‡] with the current by an angle ϕ.

From this analysis we can now determine the total **impedance** Z of the circuit, which is defined in analogy to resistance and reactance as

$$V_{\text{rms}} = I_{\text{rms}} Z, \qquad \text{or} \qquad V_0 = I_0 Z. \qquad (30\text{–}27)$$

From Fig. 30–21 we see, using the Pythagorean theorem (V_0 is the hypotenuse of a right triangle), that

$$V_0 = \sqrt{V_{R0}^2 + (V_{L0} - V_{C0})^2}$$

$$= I_0 \sqrt{R^2 + (X_L - X_C)^2}.$$

Thus, from Eq. 30–27, the total impedance Z is

$$Z = \sqrt{R^2 + (X_L - X_C)^2} \qquad (30\text{–}28a)$$

$$= \sqrt{R^2 + \left(\omega L - \frac{1}{\omega C}\right)^2}. \qquad (30\text{–}28b)$$

Also from Fig. 30–21, we can find the phase angle ϕ between voltage and current:

$$\tan \phi = \frac{V_{L0} - V_{C0}}{V_{R0}} = \frac{I_0(X_L - X_C)}{I_0 R} = \frac{X_L - X_C}{R}. \qquad (30\text{–}29a)$$

[†]We could instead do our analysis by rewriting Eq. 30–26 as a differential equation (setting $V_C = Q/C$, $V_R = IR = (dQ/dt)R$, and $V_L = L\, dI/dt$) and trying to solve the differential equation. The differential equation we would get would look like Eq. 14–21 in Section 14–8 (on forced vibrations), and would be solved in the same way. Phasor diagrams are easier, and at the same time give us some physical insight.

[‡]As a check, note that if $R = X_C = 0$, then $\phi = 90°$, and V_0 would lead the current by 90°, as it must for an inductor alone. Similarly, if $R = L = 0$, $\phi = -90°$ and V_0 would lag the current by 90°, as it must for a capacitor alone.

We can also write

$$\cos\phi = \frac{V_{R0}}{V_0} = \frac{I_0 R}{I_0 Z} = \frac{R}{Z}. \tag{30–29b}$$

Figure 30–21 was drawn for the case $X_L > X_C$, and the current lags the source voltage by ϕ. When the reverse is true, $X_L < X_C$, then ϕ in Eqs. 30–29 is less than zero, and the current leads the source voltage.

We saw earlier that power is dissipated only by a resistance; none is dissipated by inductance or capacitance. Therefore, the average power $\overline{P} = I_{rms}^2 R$. But from Eq. 30–29b, $R = Z\cos\phi$. Therefore

$$\overline{P} = I_{rms}^2 Z\cos\phi = I_{rms} V_{rms}\cos\phi. \tag{30–30}$$

The factor $\cos\phi$ is referred to as the **power factor** of the circuit. For a pure resistor, $\cos\phi = 1$ and $\overline{P} = I_{rms} V_{rms}$. For a capacitor or inductor alone, $\phi = -90°$ or $+90°$, respectively, so $\cos\phi = 0$ and no power is dissipated.

EXAMPLE 30–11 *LRC* **circuit.** Suppose $R = 25.0\,\Omega$, $L = 30.0\,mH$, and $C = 12.0\,\mu F$ in Fig. 30–19, and they are connected in series to a 90.0-V ac (rms) 500-Hz source. Calculate (*a*) the current in the circuit, (*b*) the voltmeter readings (rms) across each element, (*c*) the phase angle ϕ, and (*d*) the power dissipated in the circuit.

APPROACH To obtain the current we need to determine the impedance (Eq. 30–28 plus Eqs. 30–23b and 30–25b), and then use $I_{rms} = V_{rms}/Z$. Voltage drops across each element are found using Ohm's law or equivalent for each element: $V_R = IR$, $V_L = IX_L$, and $V_C = IX_C$.

SOLUTION (*a*) First, we find the reactance of the inductor and capacitor at $f = 500\,Hz = 500\,s^{-1}$:

$$X_L = 2\pi f L = 94.2\,\Omega, \qquad X_C = \frac{1}{2\pi f C} = 26.5\,\Omega.$$

Then the total impedance is

$$Z = \sqrt{R^2 + (X_L - X_C)^2} = \sqrt{(25.0\,\Omega)^2 + (94.2\,\Omega - 26.5\,\Omega)^2} = 72.2\,\Omega.$$

From the impedance version of Ohm's law, Eq. 30–27,

$$I_{rms} = \frac{V_{rms}}{Z} = \frac{90.0\,V}{72.2\,\Omega} = 1.25\,A.$$

(*b*) The rms voltage across each element is

$$(V_R)_{rms} = I_{rms} R = (1.25\,A)(25.0\,\Omega) = 31.2\,V$$
$$(V_L)_{rms} = I_{rms} X_L = (1.25\,A)(94.2\,\Omega) = 118\,V$$
$$(V_C)_{rms} = I_{rms} X_C = (1.25\,A)(26.5\,\Omega) = 33.1\,V.$$

NOTE These voltages do *not* add up to the source voltage, 90.0 V (rms). Indeed, the rms voltage across the inductance *exceeds* the source voltage. This can happen because the different voltages are out of phase with each other, and at any instant one voltage can be negative, to compensate for a large positive voltage of another. The rms voltages, however, are always positive by definition. Although the rms voltages need not add up to the source voltage, the instantaneous voltages at any time must add up to the source voltage at that instant.

⚠ **C A U T I O N**

Individual peak or rms voltages do NOT add up to source voltage (due to phase differences)

(*c*) The phase angle ϕ is given by Eq. 30–29b,

$$\cos\phi = \frac{R}{Z} = \frac{25.0\,\Omega}{72.2\,\Omega} = 0.346,$$

so $\phi = 69.7°$. Note that ϕ is positive because $X_L > X_C$ in this case, so $V_{L0} > V_{C0}$ in Fig. 30–21.

(*d*) $\overline{P} = I_{rms} V_{rms}\cos\phi = (1.25\,A)(90.0\,V)(25.0\,\Omega/72.2\,\Omega) = 39.0\,W.$

30–9 Resonance in AC Circuits

The rms current in an LRC series circuit is given by (see Eqs. 30–27 and 30–28b):

$$I_{rms} = \frac{V_{rms}}{Z} = \frac{V_{rms}}{\sqrt{R^2 + \left(\omega L - \frac{1}{\omega C}\right)^2}}. \qquad (30\text{–}31)$$

Because the reactance of inductors and capacitors depends on the frequency f ($= \omega/2\pi$) of the source, the current in an LRC circuit will depend on frequency. From Eq. 30–31 we can see that the current will be maximum at a frequency that satisfies

$$\left(\omega L - \frac{1}{\omega C}\right) = 0.$$

We solve this for ω and call the solution ω_0:

$$\omega_0 = \sqrt{\frac{1}{LC}}. \qquad \text{[resonance]} \quad (30\text{–}32)$$

When $\omega = \omega_0$, the circuit is in **resonance**, and $f_0 = \omega_0/2\pi$ is the **resonant frequency** of the circuit. At this frequency, $X_C = X_L$, so the impedance is purely resistive and $\cos\phi = 1$. A graph of I_{rms} versus ω is shown in Fig. 30–22 for particular values of R, L, and C. For small R compared to X_L and X_C, the resonance peak will be higher and sharper. When R is very small, the circuit approaches the pure LC circuit we discussed in Section 30–5. When R is large compared to X_L and X_C, the resonance curve is relatively flat—there is little frequency dependence.

This electrical resonance is analogous to mechanical resonance, which we discussed in Chapter 14. The energy transferred to the system by the source is a maximum at resonance whether it is electrical resonance, the oscillation of a spring, or pushing a child on a swing (Section 14–8). That this is true in the electrical case can be seen from Eq. 30–30; at resonance, $\cos\phi = 1$, and power $\overline{P}$ is a maximum. A graph of power versus frequency peaks like that for the current, Fig. 30–22.

Electric resonance is used in many circuits. Radio and TV sets, for example, use resonant circuits for tuning in a station. Many frequencies reach the circuit, but a significant current flows only for those at or near the resonant frequency. Either L or C is variable so that different stations can be tuned in.

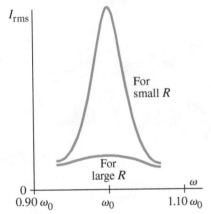

FIGURE 30–22 Current in LRC circuit as a function of angular frequency, ω, showing resonance peak at $\omega = \omega_0 = \sqrt{1/LC}$.

*30–10 Impedance Matching

It is common to connect one electric circuit to a second circuit. For example, a TV antenna is connected to a TV receiver, an amplifier is connected to a loudspeaker; electrodes for an electrocardiogram are connected to a recorder. Maximum power is transferred from one to the other, with a minimum of loss, when the output impedance of the one device matches the input impedance of the second.

To show why, we consider simple circuits that contain only resistance. In Fig. 30–23 the source in circuit 1 could represent the signal from an antenna or a laboratory probe, and R_1 represents its resistance including internal resistance of the source. R_1 is called the output impedance (or resistance) of circuit 1. The output of circuit 1 is across the terminals a and b which are connected to the input of circuit 2 which may be very complicated. We let R_2 be the equivalent "input resistance" of circuit 2.

FIGURE 30–23 Output of the circuit on the left is input to the circuit on the right.

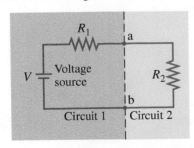

The power delivered to circuit 2 is $P = I^2 R_2$ where $I = V/(R_1 + R_2)$. Thus

$$P = I^2 R_2 = \frac{V^2 R_2}{(R_1 + R_2)^2}.$$

If the resistance of the source is R_1, what value should R_2 have so that the maximum power is transferred to circuit 2? To determine this, we take the derivative of P with respect to R_2 and set it equal to zero, which gives

$$V^2 \left[\frac{1}{(R_1 + R_2)^2} - \frac{2R_2}{(R_1 + R_2)^3} \right] = 0$$

or

$$R_2 = R_1.$$

Thus, the maximum power is transmitted when the *output impedance* of one device *equals the input impedance* of the second. This is called **impedance matching**.

In an ac circuit that contains capacitors and inductors, the different phases are important and the analysis is more complicated. However, the same result holds: to maximize power transfer it is important to match impedances $(Z_2 = Z_1)$.

In addition, it is possible to seriously distort a signal if impedances do not match, and this can lead to meaningless or erroneous experimental results.

⚠ **CAUTION**

Erroneous results can occur if impedances don't match

*30–11 Three-Phase AC

Transmission lines typically consist of four wires, rather than two. One of these wires is the ground; the remaining three are used to transmit three-phase ac power which is a superposition of three ac voltages 120° out of phase with each other:

$$V_1 = V_0 \sin \omega t$$
$$V_2 = V_0 \sin(\omega t + 2\pi/3)$$
$$V_3 = V_0 \sin(\omega t + 4\pi/3).$$

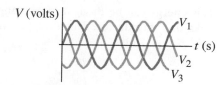

FIGURE 30–24 The three voltages, out of phase by 120° ($= \frac{2}{3}\pi$ radians), in a three-phase power line.

(See Fig. 30–24.) Why is three-phase power used? We saw in Fig. 25–22 that single-phase ac (i.e., the voltage V_1 by itself) delivers power to the load in pulses. A much smoother flow of power can be delivered using three-phase power. Suppose that each of the three voltages making up the three-phase source is hooked up to a resistor R. Then the power delivered is:

$$P = \frac{1}{R} (V_1^2 + V_2^2 + V_3^2).$$

You can show that this power is a constant equal to $3V_0^2/2R$, which is three times the rms power delivered by a single-phase source. This smooth flow of power makes electrical equipment run smoothly. Although houses use single-phase ac power, most industrial-grade machinery is wired for three-phase power.

EXAMPLE 30–12 **Three-phase circuit.** In a three-phase circuit, 266 V rms exists between line 1 and ground. What is the rms voltage between lines 2 and 3?
SOLUTION We are given $V_{rms} = V_0/\sqrt{2} = 266$ V. Hence $V_0 = 376$ V. Now $V_3 - V_2 = V_0 [\sin(\omega t + 4\pi/3) - \sin(\omega t + 2\pi/3)] = 2V_0 \sin\frac{1}{2}(\frac{2\pi}{3}) \cos\frac{1}{2}(2\omega t)$ where we used the identity: $\sin A - \sin B = 2 \sin\frac{1}{2}(A - B) \cos\frac{1}{2}(A + B)$. The rms voltage is

$$(V_3 - V_2)_{rms} = \frac{1}{\sqrt{2}} 2V_0 \sin\frac{\pi}{3} = \sqrt{2}(376 \text{ V})(0.866) = 460 \text{ V (rms)}.$$

Summary

A changing current in a coil of wire will induce an emf in a second coil placed nearby. The **mutual inductance**, M, is defined as the proportionality constant between the induced emf $\mathscr{E}_2$ in the second coil and the time rate of change of current in the first:

$$\mathscr{E}_2 = -M \, dI_1/dt. \tag{30-3b}$$

We can also write M as

$$M = \frac{N_2 \Phi_{21}}{I_1} \tag{30-1}$$

where Φ_{21} is the magnetic flux through coil 2 with N_2 loops, produced by the current I_1 in another coil (coil 1).

Within a single coil, a changing current induces an opposing emf, $\mathscr{E}$, so a coil has a **self-inductance** L defined by

$$\mathscr{E} = -L \, dI/dt. \tag{30-5}$$

This induced emf acts as an *impedance* to the flow of an alternating current. We can also write L as

$$L = N\frac{\Phi_B}{I} \tag{30-4}$$

where Φ_B is the flux through the inductance when a current I flows in its N loops.

When the current in an inductance L is I, the energy stored in the inductance is given by

$$U = \tfrac{1}{2}LI^2. \tag{30-6}$$

This energy can be thought of as being stored in the magnetic field of the inductor. The energy density u in any magnetic field B is given by

$$u = \frac{1}{2}\frac{B^2}{\mu_0}, \tag{30-7}$$

where μ_0 is replaced by μ if a ferromagnetic material is present.

When an inductance L and resistor R are connected in series to a constant source of emf, V_0, the current rises according to an exponential of the form

$$I = \frac{V_0}{R}\left(1 - e^{-t/\tau}\right), \tag{30-9}$$

where

$$\tau = L/R \tag{30-10}$$

is the **time constant**. The current eventually levels out at $I = V_0/R$. If the battery is suddenly switched out of the **LR circuit**, and the circuit remains complete, the current drops exponentially, $I = I_0 e^{-t/\tau}$, with the same time constant τ.

The current in a pure **LC circuit** (or charge on the capacitor) would oscillate sinusoidally. The energy too would oscillate back and forth between electric and magnetic, from the capacitor to the inductor, and back again. If such a circuit has resistance (LRC), and the capacitor at some instant is charged, it can undergo damped oscillations or exhibit critically damped or overdamped behavior.

Capacitance and inductance offer *impedance* to the flow of alternating current just as resistance does. This impedance is referred to as **reactance**, X, and is defined (as for resistors) as the proportionality constant between voltage and current (either the rms or peak values). Across an inductor,

$$V_0 = I_0 X_L, \tag{30-23a}$$

and across a capacitor,

$$V_0 = I_0 X_C. \tag{30-25a}$$

The reactance of an inductor increases with frequency:

$$X_L = \omega L. \tag{30-23b}$$

where $\omega = 2\pi f$ and f is the frequency of the ac. The reactance of a capacitor decreases with frequency:

$$X_C = \frac{1}{\omega C}. \tag{30-25b}$$

Whereas the current through a resistor is always in phase with the voltage across it, this is not true for inductors and capacitors: in an inductor, the current lags the voltage by 90°, and in a capacitor the current leads the voltage by 90°.

In an ac **LRC series circuit**, the total **impedance** Z is defined by the equivalent of $V = IR$ for resistance: namely $V_0 = I_0 Z$ or $V_{\text{rms}} = I_{\text{rms}}Z$. The impedance Z is related to R, C, and L by

$$Z = \sqrt{R^2 + (X_L - X_C)^2}. \tag{30-28a}$$

The current in the circuit lags (or leads) the source voltage by an angle ϕ given by $\cos\phi = R/Z$. Only the resistor in an ac LRC circuit dissipates energy, and at a rate

$$\overline{P} = I_{\text{rms}}^2 Z \cos\phi \tag{30-30}$$

where the factor $\cos\phi$ is referred to as the **power factor**.

An LRC series circuit **resonates** at a frequency given by

$$\omega_0 = \sqrt{\frac{1}{LC}}. \tag{30-32}$$

The rms current in the circuit is largest when the applied voltage has a frequency equal to $f_0 \,(= \omega_0/2\pi)$. The lower the resistance R, the higher and sharper the resonance peak.

Questions

1. How would you arrange two flat circular coils so that their mutual inductance was (a) greatest, (b) least (without separating them by a great distance)?

2. Suppose the second coil of N_2 turns in Fig. 30–2 were moved so it was near the end of the solenoid. How would this affect the mutual inductance?

3. Would two coils with mutual inductance also have self-inductance? Explain.

4. Is the energy density inside a solenoid greatest near the ends of the solenoid or near its center?

5. If you are given a fixed length of wire, how would you shape it to obtain the greatest self-inductance? The least?

6. Does the emf of the battery in Fig. 30–6a affect the time needed for the LR circuit to reach (a) a given fraction of its maximum possible current, (b) a given value of current?

7. A circuit with large inductive time constant carries a steady current. If a switch is opened, there can be a very large (and sometimes dangerous) spark or "arcing over." Explain.

8. At the instant the battery is connected into the LR circuit of Fig. 30–6a, the emf in the inductor has its maximum value even though the current is zero. Explain.

9. What keeps an LC circuit oscillating even after the capacitor has discharged completely?

10. Is the ac current in the inductor always the same as the current in the resistor of the LRC circuit of Fig. 30–13?

11. When an ac generator is connected to an LRC circuit, where does the energy come from ultimately? Where does it go? How do the values of L, C, and R affect the energy supplied by the generator?

12. In an ac LRC circuit, if $X_L > X_C$, the circuit is said to be predominantly "inductive." And if $X_C > X_L$, the circuit is said to be predominantly "capacitive." Discuss the reasons for these terms. In particular, do they say anything about the relative values of L and C at a given frequency?

13. Do the results of Section 30–8 approach the proper expected results when ω approaches zero? What are the expected results?

14. Under what conditions is the impedance in an LRC circuit a minimum?

15. Is it possible for the instantaneous power output of an ac generator connected to an LRC circuit ever to be negative? Explain.

16. In an ac LRC circuit, does the power factor, $\cos \phi$, depend on frequency? Does the power dissipated depend on frequency?

17. Describe briefly how the frequency of the source emf affects the impedance of (a) a pure resistance, (b) a pure capacitance, (c) a pure inductance, (d) an LRC circuit near resonance (R small), (e) an LRC circuit far from resonance (R small).

18. Discuss the response of an LRC circuit as $R \to 0$ when the frequency is (a) at resonance, (b) near resonance, (c) far from resonance. Is there energy dissipation in each case? Discuss the transformations of energy that occur in each case.

19. An LRC resonant circuit is often called an *oscillator* circuit. What is it that oscillates?

20. Compare the oscillations of an LRC circuit to the vibration of a mass m on a spring. What do L and C correspond to in the mechanical system?

Problems

30–1 Mutual Inductance

1. (II) A 2.44-m-long coil containing 225 loops is wound on an iron core (average $\mu = 1850\mu_0$) along with a second coil of 115 loops. The loops of each coil have a radius of 2.00 cm. If the current in the first coil drops uniformly from 12.0 A to zero in 98.0 ms, determine: (a) the mutual inductance M; (b) the emf induced in the second coil.

2. (II) Determine the mutual inductance per unit length between two long solenoids, one inside the other, whose radii are r_1 and r_2 $(r_2 < r_1)$ and whose turns per unit length are n_1 and n_2.

3. (II) A small thin coil with N_2 loops, each of area A_2, is placed inside a long solenoid, near its center. The solenoid has N_1 loops in its length ℓ and has area A_1. Determine the mutual inductance as a function of θ, the angle between the plane of the small coil and the axis of the solenoid.

4. (III) A long straight wire and a small rectangular wire loop lie in the same plane, Fig. 30–25. Determine the mutual inductance in terms of ℓ_1, ℓ_2, and w. Assume the wire is very long compared to ℓ_1, ℓ_2, and w, and that the rest of its circuit is very far away compared to ℓ_1, ℓ_2, and w.

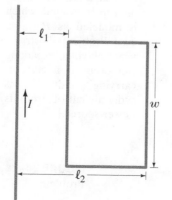

FIGURE 30–25
Problem 4.

30–2 Self-Inductance

5. (I) If the current in a 280-mH coil changes steadily from 25.0 A to 10.0 A in 360 ms, what is the magnitude of the induced emf?

6. (I) How many turns of wire would be required to make a 130-mH inductance out of a 30.0-cm-long air-filled coil with a diameter of 4.2 cm?

7. (I) What is the inductance of a coil if the coil produces an emf of 2.50 V when the current in it changes from -28.0 mA to $+25.0$ mA in 12.0 ms?

8. (II) An air-filled cylindrical inductor has 2800 turns, and it is 2.5 cm in diameter and 21.7 cm long. (a) What is its inductance? (b) How many turns would you need to generate the same inductance if the core were filled with iron of magnetic permeability 1200 times that of free space?

9. (II) A coil has 3.25-Ω resistance and 440-mH inductance. If the current is 3.00 A and is increasing at a rate of 3.60 A/s, what is the potential difference across the coil at this moment?

10. (II) If the outer conductor of a coaxial cable has radius 3.0 mm, what should be the radius of the inner conductor so that the inductance per unit length does not exceed 55 nH per meter?

11. (II) To demonstrate the large size of the henry unit, a physics professor wants to wind an air-filled solenoid with self-inductance of 1.0 H on the outside of a 12-cm diameter plastic hollow tube using copper wire with a 0.81-mm diameter. The solenoid is to be tightly wound with each turn touching its neighbor (the wire has a thin insulating layer on its surface so the neighboring turns are not in electrical contact). How long will the plastic tube need to be and how many kilometers of copper wire will be required? What will be the resistance of this solenoid?

12. (II) The wire of a tightly wound solenoid is unwound and used to make another tightly wound solenoid of 2.5 times the diameter. By what factor does the inductance change?

13. (II) A toroid has a rectangular cross section as shown in Fig. 30–26. Show that the self-inductance is

$$L = \frac{\mu_0 N^2 h}{2\pi} \ln \frac{r_2}{r_1}$$

where N is the total number of turns and r_1, r_2, and h are the dimensions shown in Fig. 30–26. [*Hint*: Use Ampère's law to get B as a function of r inside the toroid, and integrate.]

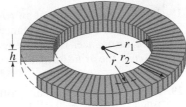

FIGURE 30–26
Problems 13 and 19.
A toroid of rectangular cross section, with N turns carrying a current I.

14. (II) Ignoring any mutual inductance, what is the equivalent inductance of two inductors connected (*a*) in series, (*b*) in parallel?

30–3 Magnetic Energy Storage

15. (I) The magnetic field inside an air-filled solenoid 38.0 cm long and 2.10 cm in diameter is 0.600 T. Approximately how much energy is stored in this field?

16. (I) Typical large values for electric and magnetic fields attained in laboratories are about 1.0×10^4 V/m and 2.0 T. (*a*) Determine the energy density for each field and compare. (*b*) What magnitude electric field would be needed to produce the same energy density as the 2.0-T magnetic field?

17. (II) What is the energy density at the center of a circular loop of wire carrying a 23.0-A current if the radius of the loop is 28.0 cm?

18. (II) Calculate the magnetic and electric energy densities at the surface of a 3.0-mm-diameter copper wire carrying a 15-A current.

19. (II) For the toroid of Fig. 30–26, determine the energy density in the magnetic field as a function of r $(r_1 < r < r_2)$ and integrate this over the volume to obtain the total energy stored in the toroid, which carries a current I in each of its N loops.

20. (II) Determine the total energy stored per unit length in the magnetic field between the coaxial cylinders of a coaxial cable (Fig. 30–5) by using Eq. 30–7 for the energy density and integrating over the volume.

21. (II) A long straight wire of radius R carries current I uniformly distributed across its cross-sectional area. Find the magnetic energy stored per unit length in the interior of this wire.

30–4 *LR* Circuits

22. (II) After how many time constants does the current in Fig. 30–6 reach within (*a*) 5.0%, (*b*) 1.0%, and (*c*) 0.10% of its maximum value?

23. (II) How many time constants does it take for the potential difference across the resistor in an *LR* circuit like that in Fig. 30–7 to drop to 3.0% of its original value?

24. (II) It takes 2.56 ms for the current in an *LR* circuit to increase from zero to 0.75 its maximum value. Determine (*a*) the time constant of the circuit, (*b*) the resistance of the circuit if $L = 31.0$ mH.

25. (II) (*a*) Determine the energy stored in the inductor L as a function of time for the *LR* circuit of Fig. 30–6a. (*b*) After how many time constants does the stored energy reach 99.9% of its maximum value?

26. (II) In the circuit of Fig. 30–27, determine the current in each resistor (I_1, I_2, I_3) at the moment (*a*) the switch is closed, (*b*) a long time after the switch is closed. After the switch has been closed for a long time, and then reopened, what is each current (*c*) just after it is opened, (*d*) after a long time?

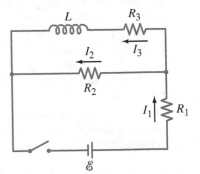

FIGURE 30–27
Problem 26.

27. (II) (*a*) In Fig. 30–28a, assume that the switch S has been in position A for sufficient time so that a steady current $I_0 = V_0/R$ flows through the resistor R. At time $t = 0$, the switch is quickly switched to position B and the current through R decays according to $I = I_0 e^{-t/\tau}$. Show that the maximum emf $\mathscr{E}_{max}$ induced in the inductor during this time period equals the battery voltage V_0. (*b*) In Fig. 30–28b, assume that the switch has been in position A for sufficient time so that a steady current $I_0 = V_0/R$ flows through the resistor R. At time $t = 0$, the switch is quickly switched to position B and the current decays through resistor R' (which is much greater than R) according to $I = I_0 e^{-t/\tau'}$. Show that the maximum emf $\mathscr{E}_{max}$ induced in the inductor during this time period is $(R'/R)V_0$. If $R' = 55R$ and $V_0 = 120$ V, determine $\mathscr{E}_{max}$. [When a mechanical switch is opened, a high-resistance air gap is created, which is modeled as R' here. This Problem illustrates why high-voltage sparking can occur if a current-carrying inductor is suddenly cut off from its power source.]

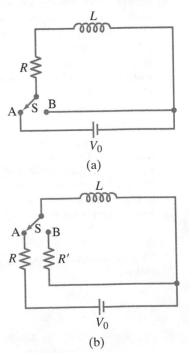

FIGURE 30–28
Problem 27.

28. (II) You want to turn on the current through a coil of self-inductance L in a controlled manner, so you place it in series with a resistor $R = 2200\,\Omega$, a switch, and a dc voltage source $V_0 = 240\,\text{V}$. After closing the switch, you find that the current through the coil builds up to its steady-state value with a time constant τ. You are pleased with the current's steady-state value, but want τ to be half as long. What new values should you use for R and V_0?

29. (II) A 12-V battery has been connected to an LR circuit for sufficient time so that a steady current flows through the resistor $R = 2.2\,\text{k}\Omega$ and inductor $L = 18\,\text{mH}$. At $t = 0$, the battery is removed from the circuit and the current decays exponentially through R. Determine the emf $\mathscr{E}$ across the inductor as time t increases. At what time is $\mathscr{E}$ greatest and what is this maximum value (V)?

30. (III) Two tightly wound solenoids have the same length and circular cross-sectional area. But solenoid 1 uses wire that is 1.5 times as thick as solenoid 2. (a) What is the ratio of their inductances? (b) What is the ratio of their inductive time constants (assuming no other resistance in the circuits)?

30–5 LC Circuits and Oscillations

31. (I) The variable capacitor in the tuner of an AM radio has a capacitance of 1350 pF when the radio is tuned to a station at 550 kHz. (a) What must be the capacitance for a station at 1600 kHz? (b) What is the inductance (assumed constant)? Ignore resistance.

32. (I) (a) If the initial conditions of an LC circuit were $I = I_0$ and $Q = 0$ at $t = 0$, write Q as a function of time. (b) Practically, how could you set up these initial conditions?

33. (II) In some experiments, short distances are measured by using capacitance. Consider forming an LC circuit using a parallel-plate capacitor with plate area A, and a known inductance L. (a) If charge is found to oscillate in this circuit at frequency $f = \omega/2\pi$ when the capacitor plates are separated by distance x, show that $x = 4\pi^2 A \epsilon_0 f^2 L$. (b) When the plate separation is changed by Δx, the circuit's oscillation frequency will change by Δf. Show that $\Delta x/x \approx 2(\Delta f/f)$. (c) If f is on the order of 1 MHz and can be measured to a precision of $\Delta f = 1\,\text{Hz}$, with what percent accuracy can x be determined? Assume fringing effects at the capacitor's edges can be neglected.

34. (II) A 425-pF capacitor is charged to 135 V and then quickly connected to a 175-mH inductor. Determine (a) the frequency of oscillation, (b) the peak value of the current, and (c) the maximum energy stored in the magnetic field of the inductor.

35. (II) At $t = 0$, let $Q = Q_0$, and $I = 0$ in an LC circuit. (a) At the first moment when the energy is shared equally by the inductor and the capacitor, what is the charge on the capacitor? (b) How much time has elapsed (in terms of the period T)?

30–6 LC Oscillations with Resistance

36. (II) A damped LC circuit loses 3.5% of its electromagnetic energy per cycle to thermal energy. If $L = 65\,\text{mH}$ and $C = 1.00\,\mu\text{F}$, what is the value of R?

37. (II) In an oscillating LRC circuit, how much time does it take for the energy stored in the fields of the capacitor and inductor to fall to 75% of the initial value? (See Fig. 30–13; assume $R \ll \sqrt{4L/C}$.)

38. (III) How much resistance must be added to a pure LC circuit ($L = 350\,\text{mH}$, $C = 1800\,\text{pF}$) to change the oscillator's frequency by 0.25%? Will it be increased or decreased?

30–7 AC Circuits; Reactance

39. (I) At what frequency will a 32.0-mH inductor have a reactance of $660\,\Omega$?

40. (I) What is the reactance of a 9.2-μF capacitor at a frequency of (a) 60.0 Hz, (b) 1.00 MHz?

41. (I) Plot a graph of the reactance of a 1.0-μF capacitor as a function of frequency from 10 Hz to 1000 Hz.

42. (I) Calculate the reactance of, and rms current in, a 36.0-mH radio coil connected to a 250-V (rms) 33.3-kHz ac line. Ignore resistance.

43. (II) A resistor R is in parallel with a capacitor C, and this parallel combination is in series with a resistor R'. If connected to an ac voltage source of frequency ω, what is the equivalent impedance of this circuit at the two extremes in frequency (a) $\omega = 0$, and (b) $\omega = \infty$?

44. (II) What is the inductance L of the primary of a transformer whose input is 110 V at 60 Hz and the current drawn is 3.1 A? Assume no current in the secondary.

45. (II) (a) What is the reactance of a 0.086-μF capacitor connected to a 22-kV (rms), 660-Hz line? (b) Determine the frequency and the peak value of the current.

46. (II) A capacitor is placed in parallel with some device, B, as in Fig. 30–18b, to filter out stray high-frequency signals, but to allow ordinary 60-Hz ac to pass through with little loss. Suppose that circuit B in Fig. 30–18b is a resistance $R = 490\,\Omega$ connected to ground, and that $C = 0.35\,\mu\text{F}$. What percent of the incoming current will pass through C rather than R if it is (a) 60 Hz; (b) 60,000 Hz?

47. (II) A current $I = 1.80 \cos 377t$ (I in amps, t in seconds, and the "angle" is in radians) flows in a series LR circuit in which $L = 3.85\,\text{mH}$ and $R = 1.35\,\text{k}\Omega$. What is the average power dissipation?

30–8 LRC Series AC Circuit

48. (I) A 10.0-kΩ resistor is in series with a 26.0-mH inductor and an ac source. Calculate the impedance of the circuit if the source frequency is (a) 55.0 Hz; (b) 55,000 Hz.

49. (I) A 75-Ω resistor and a 6.8-μF capacitor are connected in series to an ac source. Calculate the impedance of the circuit if the source frequency is (a) 60 Hz; (b) 6.0 MHz.

50. (I) For a 120-V, 60-Hz voltage, a current of 70 mA passing through the body for 1.0 s could be lethal. What must be the impedance of the body for this to occur?

51. (II) A 2.5-kΩ resistor in series with a 420-mH inductor is driven by an ac power supply. At what frequency is the impedance double that of the impedance at 60 Hz?

52. (II) (a) What is the rms current in a series RC circuit if $R = 3.8\,\text{k}\Omega$, $C = 0.80\,\mu\text{F}$, and the rms applied voltage is 120 V at 60.0 Hz? (b) What is the phase angle between voltage and current? (c) What is the power dissipated by the circuit? (d) What are the voltmeter readings across R and C?

53. (II) An ac voltage source is connected in series with a 1.0-μF capacitor and a 750-Ω resistor. Using a digital ac voltmeter, the amplitude of the voltage source is measured to be 4.0 V rms, while the voltages across the resistor and across the capacitor are found to be 3.0 V rms and 2.7 V rms, respectively. Determine the frequency of the ac voltage source. Why is the voltage measured across the voltage source not equal to the sum of the voltages measured across the resistor and across the capacitor?

54. (II) Determine the total impedance, phase angle, and rms current in an LRC circuit connected to a 10.0-kHz, 725-V (rms) source if $L = 32.0\,\text{mH}$, $R = 8.70\,\text{k}\Omega$, and $C = 6250\,\text{pF}$.

55. (II) (a) What is the rms current in a series LR circuit when a 60.0-Hz, 120-V rms ac voltage is applied, where $R = 965\,\Omega$ and $L = 225\,\text{mH}$? (b) What is the phase angle between voltage and current? (c) How much power is dissipated? (d) What are the rms voltage readings across R and L?

56. (II) A 35-mH inductor with 2.0-Ω resistance is connected in series to a 26-μF capacitor and a 60-Hz, 45-V (rms) source. Calculate (a) the rms current, (b) the phase angle, and (c) the power dissipated in this circuit.

57. (II) A 25-mH coil whose resistance is $0.80\,\Omega$ is connected to a capacitor C and a 360-Hz source voltage. If the current and voltage are to be in phase, what value must C have?

58. (II) A 75-W lightbulb is designed to operate with an applied ac voltage of 120 V rms. The bulb is placed in series with an inductor L, and this series combination is then connected to a 60-Hz 240-V rms voltage source. For the bulb to operate properly, determine the required value for L. Assume the bulb has resistance R and negligible inductance.

59. (II) In the LRC circuit of Fig. 30–19, suppose $I = I_0 \sin \omega t$ and $V = V_0 \sin(\omega t + \phi)$. Determine the instantaneous power dissipated in the circuit from $P = IV$ using these equations and show that on the average, $\overline{P} = \frac{1}{2} V_0 I_0 \cos \phi$, which confirms Eq. 30–30.

60. (II) An LRC series circuit with $R = 150\,\Omega$, $L = 25\,\text{mH}$, and $C = 2.0\,\mu\text{F}$ is powered by an ac voltage source of peak voltage $V_0 = 340\,\text{V}$ and frequency $f = 660\,\text{Hz}$. (a) Determine the peak current that flows in this circuit. (b) Determine the phase angle of the source voltage relative to the current. (c) Determine the peak voltage across R and its phase angle relative to the source voltage. (d) Determine the peak voltage across L and its phase angle relative to the source voltage. (e) Determine the peak voltage across C and its phase angle relative to the source voltage.

61. (II) An LR circuit can be used as a "phase shifter." Assume that an "input" source voltage $V = V_0 \sin(2\pi f t + \phi)$ is connected across a series combination of an inductor $L = 55\,\text{mH}$ and resistor R. The "output" of this circuit is taken across the resistor. If $V_0 = 24\,\text{V}$ and $f = 175\,\text{Hz}$, determine the value of R so that the output voltage V_R lags the input voltage V by 25°. Compare (as a ratio) the peak output voltage with V_0.

30–9 Resonance in AC Circuits

62. (I) A 3800-pF capacitor is connected in series to a 26.0-μH coil of resistance $2.00\,\Omega$. What is the resonant frequency of this circuit?

63. (I) What is the resonant frequency of the LRC circuit of Example 30–11? At what rate is energy taken from the generator, on the average, at this frequency?

64. (II) An LRC circuit has $L = 4.15\,\text{mH}$ and $R = 3.80\,\text{k}\Omega$. (a) What value must C have to produce resonance at 33.0 kHz? (b) What will be the maximum current at resonance if the peak external voltage is 136 V?

65. (II) The frequency of the ac voltage source (peak voltage V_0) in an LRC circuit is tuned to the circuit's resonant frequency $f_0 = 1/(2\pi\sqrt{LC})$. (a) Show that the peak voltage across the capacitor is $V_{C0} = V_0 T_0/2\pi\,\tau$), where $T_0(= 1/f_0)$ is the period of the resonant frequency and $\tau = RC$ is the time constant for charging the capacitor C through a resistor R. (b) Define $\beta = T_0/(2\pi\tau)$ so that $V_{C0} = \beta V_0$. Then β is the "amplification" of the source voltage across the capacitor. If a particular LRC circuit contains a 2.0-nF capacitor and has a resonant frequency of 5.0 kHz, what value of R will yield $\beta = 125$?

66. (II) Capacitors made from piezoelectric materials are commonly used as sound transducers ("speakers"). They often require a large operating voltage. One method for providing the required voltage is to include the speaker as part of an LRC circuit as shown in Fig. 30–29, where the speaker is modeled electrically as the capacitance $C = 1.0\,\text{nF}$. Take $R = 35\,\Omega$ and $L = 55\,\text{mH}$. (a) What is the resonant frequency f_0 for this circuit? (b) If the voltage source has peak amplitude $V_0 = 2.0\,\text{V}$ at frequency $f = f_0$, find the peak voltage V_{C0} across the speaker (i.e., the capacitor C). (c) Determine the ratio V_{C0}/V_0.

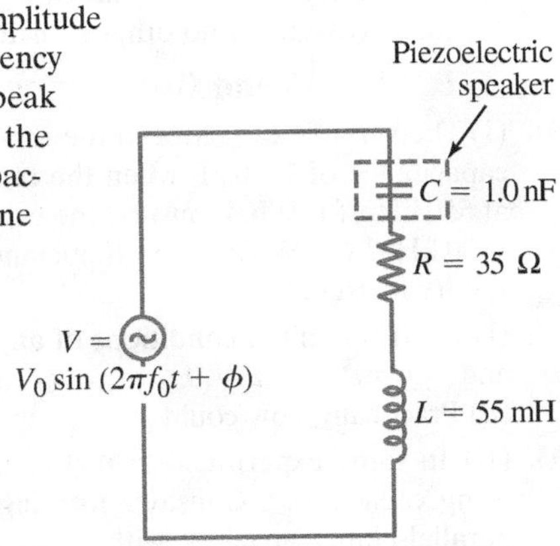

FIGURE 30–29
Problem 66.

67. (II) (a) Determine a formula for the average power $\overline{P}$ dissipated in an LRC circuit in terms of L, R, C, ω, and V_0. (b) At what frequency is the power a maximum? (c) Find an approximate formula for the width of the resonance peak in average power, $\Delta\omega$, which is the difference in the two (angular) frequencies where $\overline{P}$ has half its maximum value. Assume a sharp peak.

68. (II) (a) Show that oscillation of charge Q on the capacitor of an LRC circuit has amplitude

$$Q_0 = \frac{V_0}{\sqrt{(\omega R)^2 + \left(\omega^2 L - \dfrac{1}{C}\right)^2}}.$$

(b) At what angular frequency, ω', will Q_0 be a maximum? (c) Compare to a forced damped harmonic oscillator (Chapter 14), and discuss. (See also Question 20 in this Chapter.)

69. (II) A resonant circuit using a 220-nF capacitor is to resonate at 18.0 kHz. The air-core inductor is to be a solenoid with closely packed coils made from 12.0 m of insulated wire 1.1 mm in diameter. How many loops will the inductor contain?

*30–10 Impedance Matching

*70. (II) The output of an electrocardiogram amplifier has an impedance of 45 kΩ. It is to be connected to an 8.0-Ω loudspeaker through a transformer. What should be the turns ratio of the transformer?

General Problems

71. A 2200-pF capacitor is charged to 120 V and then quickly connected to an inductor. The frequency of oscillation is observed to be 17 kHz. Determine (a) the inductance, (b) the peak value of the current, and (c) the maximum energy stored in the magnetic field of the inductor.

72. At $t = 0$, the current through a 60.0-mH inductor is 50.0 mA and is increasing at the rate of 78.0 mA/s. What is the initial energy stored in the inductor, and how long does it take for the energy to increase by a factor of 5.0 from the initial value?

73. At time $t = 0$, the switch in the circuit shown in Fig. 30–30 is closed. After a sufficiently long time, steady currents I_1, I_2, and I_3 flow through resistors R_1, R_2, and R_3, respectively. Determine these three currents.

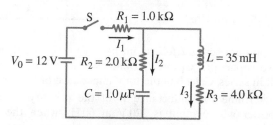

FIGURE 30–30 Problem 73.

74. (a) Show that the self-inductance L of a toroid (Fig. 30–31) of radius r_0 containing N loops each of diameter d is

$$L \approx \frac{\mu_0 N^2 d^2}{8r_0}$$

if $r_0 \gg d$. Assume the field is uniform inside the toroid; is this actually true? Is this result consistent with L for a solenoid? Should it be? (b) Calculate the inductance L of a large toroid if the diameter of the coils is 2.0 cm and the diameter of the whole ring is 66 cm. Assume the field inside the toroid is uniform. There are a total of 550 loops of wire.

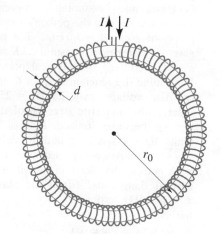

FIGURE 30–31
A toroid.
Problem 74.

75. A pair of straight parallel thin wires, such as a lamp cord, each of radius r, are a distance ℓ apart and carry current to a circuit some distance away. Ignoring the field within each wire, show that the inductance per unit length is $(\mu_0/\pi) \ln[(\ell - r)/r]$.

76. Assuming the Earth's magnetic field averages about 0.50×10^{-4} T near the surface of the Earth, estimate the total energy stored in this field in the first 5.0 km above the Earth's surface.

77. (a) For an underdamped LRC circuit, determine a formula for the energy $U = U_E + U_B$ stored in the electric and magnetic fields as a function of time. Give answer in terms of the initial charge Q_0 on the capacitor. (b) Show how dU/dt is related to the rate energy is transformed in the resistor, I^2R.

78. An electronic device needs to be protected against sudden surges in current. In particular, after the power is turned on the current should rise to no more than 7.5 mA in the first 75 μs. The device has resistance 150 Ω and is designed to operate at 33 mA. How would you protect this device?

79. The circuit shown in Fig. 30–32a can integrate (in the calculus sense) the input voltage V_{in}, if the time constant L/R is large compared with the time during which V_{in} varies. Explain how this integrator works and sketch its output for the square wave signal input shown in Fig. 30–32b. [*Hint:* Write Kirchhoff's loop rule for the circuit. Multiply each term in this differential equation (in I) by a factor $e^{Rt/L}$ to make it easier to integrate.]

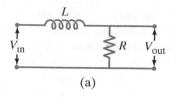

(a)

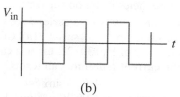

FIGURE 30–32
Problem 79.   (b)

80. Suppose circuit B in Fig. 30–18a consists of a resistance $R = 550 \, \Omega$. The filter capacitor has capacitance $C = 1.2 \, \mu$F. Will this capacitor act to eliminate 60-Hz ac but pass a high-frequency signal of frequency 6.0 kHz? To check this, determine the voltage drop across R for a 130-mV signal of frequency (a) 60 Hz; (b) 6.0 kHz.

81. An ac voltage source $V = V_0 \sin(\omega t + 90°)$ is connected across an inductor L and current $I = I_0 \sin(\omega t)$ flows in this circuit. Note that the current and source voltage are 90° out of phase. (a) Directly calculate the average power delivered by the source over one period T of its sinusoidal cycle via the integral $\overline{P} = \int_0^T VI \, dt/T$. (b) Apply the relation $\overline{P} = I_{rms}V_{rms} \cos \phi$ to this circuit and show that the answer you obtain is consistent with that found in part (a). Comment on your results.

82. A circuit contains two elements, but it is not known if they are L, R, or C. The current in this circuit when connected to a 120-V 60-Hz source is 5.6 A and lags the voltage by 65°. What are the two elements and what are their values?

83. A 3.5-kΩ resistor in series with a 440-mH inductor is driven by an ac power supply. At what frequency is the impedance double that of the impedance at 60 Hz?

84. (a) What is the rms current in an RC circuit if $R = 5.70\,k\Omega$, $C = 1.80\,\mu F$, and the rms applied voltage is $120\,V$ at $60.0\,Hz$? (b) What is the phase angle between voltage and current? (c) What is the power dissipated by the circuit? (d) What are the voltmeter readings across R and C?

85. An inductance coil draws $2.5\,A$ dc when connected to a 45-V battery. When connected to a 60-Hz 120-V (rms) source, the current drawn is $3.8\,A$ (rms). Determine the inductance and resistance of the coil.

86. The **Q-value** of a resonance circuit can be defined as the ratio of the voltage across the capacitor (or inductor) to the voltage across the resistor, at resonance. The larger the Q factor, the sharper the resonance curve will be and the sharper the tuning. (a) Show that the Q factor is given by the equation $Q = (1/R)\sqrt{L/C}$. (b) At a resonant frequency $f_0 = 1.0\,MHz$, what must be the value of L and R to produce a Q factor of 350? Assume that $C = 0.010\,\mu F$.

87. Show that the fraction of electromagnetic energy lost (to thermal energy) per cycle in a lightly damped $(R^2 \ll 4L/C)$ LRC circuit is approximately

$$\frac{\Delta U}{U} = \frac{2\pi R}{L\omega} = \frac{2\pi}{Q}.$$

The quantity Q can be defined as $Q = L\omega/R$, and is called the Q-value, or quality factor, of the circuit and is a measure of the damping present. A high Q-value means smaller damping and less energy input required to maintain oscillations.

88. In a series LRC circuit, the inductance is $33\,mH$, the capacitance is $55\,nF$, and the resistance is $1.50\,k\Omega$. At what frequencies is the power factor equal to 0.17?

89. In our analysis of a series LRC circuit, Fig. 30–19, suppose we chose $V = V_0 \sin \omega t$. (a) Construct a phasor diagram, like that of Fig. 30–21, for this case. (b) Write a formula for the current I, defining all terms.

90. A voltage $V = 0.95 \sin 754t$ is applied to an LRC circuit (I is in amperes, t is in seconds, V is in volts, and the "angle" is in radians) which has $L = 22.0\,mH$, $R = 23.2\,k\Omega$, and $C = 0.42\,\mu F$. (a) What is the impedance and phase angle? (b) How much power is dissipated in the circuit? (c) What is the rms current and voltage across each element?

91. *Filter circuit.* Figure 30–33 shows a simple filter circuit designed to pass dc voltages with minimal attenuation and to remove, as much as possible, any ac components (such as 60-Hz line voltage that could cause hum in a stereo receiver, for example). Assume $V_{in} = V_1 + V_2$ where V_1 is dc and $V_2 = V_{20} \sin \omega t$, and that any resistance is very small. (a) Determine the current through the capacitor: give amplitude and phase (assume $R = 0$ and $X_L > X_C$). (b) Show that the ac component of the output voltage, $V_{2\,out}$, equals $(Q/C) - V_1$, where Q is the charge on the capacitor at any instant, and determine the amplitude and phase of $V_{2\,out}$. (c) Show that the attenuation of the ac voltage is greatest when $X_C \ll X_L$, and calculate the ratio of the output to input ac voltage in this case. (d) Compare the dc output voltage to input voltage.

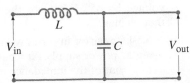

FIGURE 30–33
Problems 91 and 92.

92. Show that if the inductor L in the filter circuit of Fig. 30–33 (Problem 91) is replaced by a large resistor R, there will still be significant attenuation of the ac voltage and little attenuation of the dc voltage if the input dc voltage is high and the current (and power) are low.

93. A resistor R, capacitor C, and inductor L are connected in parallel across an ac generator as shown in Fig. 30–34. The source emf is $V = V_0 \sin \omega t$. Determine the current as a function of time (including amplitude and phase): (a) in the resistor, (b) in the inductor, (c) in the capacitor. (d) What is the total current leaving the source? (Give amplitude I_0 and phase.) (e) Determine the impedance Z defined as $Z = V_0/I_0$. (f) What is the power factor?

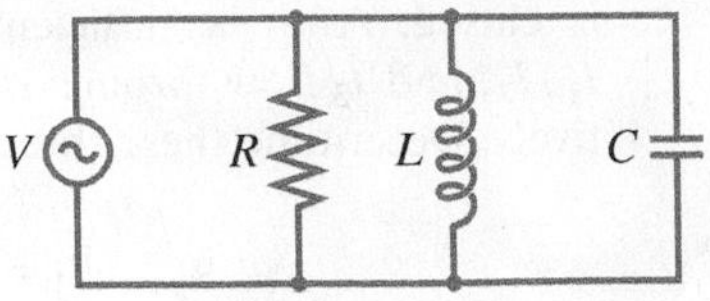

FIGURE 30–34
Problem 93.

94. Suppose a series LRC circuit has two resistors, R_1 and R_2, two capacitors, C_1 and C_2, and two inductors, L_1 and L_2, all in series. Calculate the total impedance of the circuit.

95. Determine the inductance L of the primary of a transformer whose input is $220\,V$ at $60\,Hz$ when the current drawn is $4.3\,A$. Assume no current in the secondary.

96. In a *plasma globe*, a hollow glass sphere is filled with low-pressure gas and a small spherical metal electrode is located at its center. Assume an ac voltage source of peak voltage V_0 and frequency f is applied between the metal sphere and the ground, and that a person is touching the outer surface of the globe with a fingertip, whose approximate area is $1.0\,cm^2$. The equivalent circuit for this situation is shown in Fig. 30–35, where R_G and R_P are the resistances of the gas and the person, respectively, and C is the capacitance formed by the gas, glass, and finger. (a) Determine C assuming it is a parallel-plate capacitor. The conductive gas and the person's fingertip form the opposing plates of area $A = 1.0\,cm^2$. The plates are separated by glass (dielectric constant $K = 5.0$) of thickness $d = 2.0\,mm$. (b) In a typical plasma globe, $f = 12\,kHz$. Determine the reactance X_C of C at this frequency in $M\Omega$. (c) The voltage may be $V_0 = 2500\,V$. With this high voltage, the dielectric strength of the gas is exceeded and the gas becomes ionized. In this "plasma" state, the gas emits light ("sparks") and is highly conductive so that $R_G \ll X_C$. Assuming also that $R_P \ll X_C$, estimate the peak current that flows in the given circuit. Is this level of current dangerous? (d) If the plasma globe operated at $f = 1.0\,MHz$, estimate the peak current that would flow in the given circuit. Is this level of current dangerous?

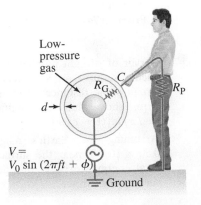

FIGURE 30–35
Problem 96.

97. You have a small electromagnet that consumes 350 W from a residential circuit operating at 120 V at 60 Hz. Using your ac multimeter, you determine that the unit draws 4.0 A rms. What are the values of the inductance and the internal resistance?

98. An inductor L in series with a resistor R, driven by a sinusoidal voltage source, responds as described by the following differential equation:

$$V_0 \sin \omega t = L\frac{dI}{dt} + RI.$$

Show that a current of the form $I = I_0 \sin(\omega t - \phi)$ flows through the circuit by direct substitution into the differential equation. Determine the amplitude of the current (I_0) and the phase difference ϕ between the current and the voltage source.

99. In a certain LRC series circuit, when the ac voltage source has a particular frequency f, the peak voltage across the inductor is 6.0 times greater than the peak voltage across the capacitor. Determine f in terms of the resonant frequency f_0 of this circuit.

100. For the circuit shown in Fig. 30–36, $V = V_0 \sin \omega t$. Calculate the current in each element of the circuit, as well as the total impedance. [*Hint*: Try a trial solution of the form $I = I_0 \sin(\omega t + \phi)$ for the current leaving the source.]

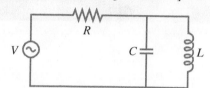

FIGURE 30–36
Problem 100.

101. To detect vehicles at traffic lights, wire loops with dimensions on the order of 2 m are often buried horizontally under roadways. Assume the self-inductance of such a loop is $L = 5.0\,\text{mH}$ and that it is part of an LRC circuit as shown in Fig. 30–37 with $C = 0.10\,\mu\text{F}$ and $R = 45\,\Omega$. The ac voltage has frequency f and rms voltage V_{rms}. (a) The frequency f is chosen to match the resonant frequency f_0 of the circuit. Find f_0 and determine what the rms voltage $(V_R)_{\text{rms}}$ across the resistor will be when $f = f_0$. (b) Assume that f, C, and R never change, but that, when a car is located above the buried loop, the loop's self-inductance decreases by 10% (due to induced eddy currents in the car's metal parts). Determine by what factor the voltage $(V_R)_{\text{rms}}$ decreases in this situation in comparison to no car above the loop. [Monitoring $(V_R)_{\text{rms}}$ detects the presence of a car.]

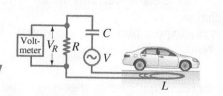

FIGURE 30–37
Problem 101.

102. For the circuit shown in Fig. 30–38, show that if the condition $R_1 R_2 = L/C$ is satisfied then the potential difference between points a and b is zero for all frequencies.

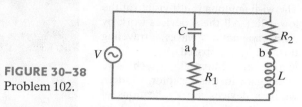

FIGURE 30–38
Problem 102.

*Numerical/Computer

*103. (II) The RC circuit shown in Fig. 30–39 is called a **low-pass filter** because it passes low-frequency ac signals with less attenuation than high-frequency ac signals. (a) Show that the voltage gain is $A = V_{\text{out}}/V_{\text{in}} = 1/(4\pi^2 f^2 R^2 C^2 + 1)^{\frac{1}{2}}$. (b) Discuss the behavior of the gain A for $f \to 0$ and $f \to \infty$. (c) Choose $R = 850\,\Omega$ and $C = 1.0 \times 10^{-6}\,\text{F}$, and graph log A versus log f with suitable scales to show the behavior of the circuit at low and high frequencies.

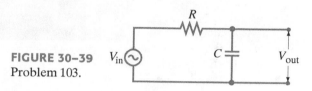

FIGURE 30–39
Problem 103.

*104. (II) The RC circuit shown in Fig. 30–40 is called a **high-pass filter** because it passes high-frequency ac signals with less attenuation than low-frequency ac signals. (a) Show that the voltage gain is $A = V_{\text{out}}/V_{\text{in}} = 2\pi f RC/(4\pi^2 f^2 R^2 C^2 + 1)^{\frac{1}{2}}$. (b) Discuss the behavior of the gain A for $f \to 0$ and $f \to \infty$. (c) Choose $R = 850\,\Omega$ and $C = 1.0 \times 10^{-6}\,\text{F}$, and then graph log A versus log f with suitable scales to show the behavior of the circuit at high and low frequencies.

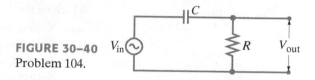

FIGURE 30–40
Problem 104.

*105. (III) Write a computer program or use a spreadsheet program to plot I_{rms} for an ac LRC circuit with a sinusoidal voltage source (Fig. 30–19) with $V_{\text{rms}} = 0.100\,\text{V}$. For $L = 50\,\mu\text{H}$ and $C = 50\,\mu\text{F}$, plot the I_{rms} graph for (a) $R = 0.10\,\Omega$, and (b) $R = 1.0\,\Omega$ from $\omega = 0.1\omega_0$ to $\omega = 3.0\omega_0$ on the same graph.

Answers to Exercises

A: (a) 360 A/s; (b) 12 V.

B: (b).

C: (a).

D: From Eq. 30–5, L has dimensions VT/A so (L/R) has dimensions $(VT/A)/(V/A) = T$.

E: (d).

F: (c)

G: (a).

H: (c).

Wireless technology is all around us: in this photo we see a Bluetooth earpiece for wireless telephone communication and a wi-fi computer. The wi-fi antenna is just visible at the lower left. All these devices work by electromagnetic waves traveling through space, based on the great work of Maxwell which we investigate in this Chapter. Modern wireless devices are applications of Marconi's development of long distance transmission of information a century ago.

We will see in this Chapter that Maxwell predicted the existence of EM waves from his famous equations. Maxwell's equations themselves are a magnificent summary of electromagnetism. We will also examine how EM waves carry energy and momentum.

CHAPTER 31

Maxwell's Equations and Electromagnetic Waves

CONTENTS

CHAPTER-OPENING QUESTION—Guess now!

Which of the following best describes the difference between radio waves and X-rays?

(a) X-rays are radiation while radio waves are electromagnetic waves.

(b) Both can be thought of as electromagnetic waves. They differ only in wavelength and frequency.

(c) X-rays are pure energy. Radio waves are made of fields, not energy.

(d) Radio waves come from electric currents in an antenna. X-rays are not related to electric charge.

(e) The fact that X-rays can expose film, and radio waves cannot, means they are fundamentally different.

The culmination of electromagnetic theory in the nineteenth century was the prediction, and the experimental verification, that waves of electromagnetic fields could travel through space. This achievement opened a whole new world of communication: first the wireless telegraph, then radio and television, and more recently cell phones, remote-control devices, wi-fi, and Bluetooth. Most important was the spectacular prediction that visible light is an electromagnetic wave.

The theoretical prediction of electromagnetic waves was the work of the Scottish physicist James Clerk Maxwell (1831–1879; Fig. 31–1), who unified, in one magnificent theory, all the phenomena of electricity and magnetism.

The development of electromagnetic theory in the early part of the nineteenth century by Oersted, Ampère, and others was not actually done in terms of electric and magnetic fields. The idea of the field was introduced somewhat later by Faraday, and was not generally used until Maxwell showed that all electric and magnetic phenomena could be described using only four equations involving electric and magnetic fields. These equations, known as **Maxwell's equations**, are the basic equations for all electromagnetism. They are fundamental in the same sense that Newton's three laws of motion and the law of universal gravitation are for mechanics. In a sense, they are even more fundamental, since they are consistent with the theory of relativity (Chapter 36), whereas Newton's laws are not. Because all of electromagnetism is contained in this set of four equations, Maxwell's equations are considered one of the great triumphs of human intellect.

Before we discuss Maxwell's equations and electromagnetic waves, we first need to discuss a major new prediction of Maxwell's, and, in addition, Gauss's law for magnetism.

FIGURE 31–1 James Clerk Maxwell (1831–1879).

31–1 Changing Electric Fields Produce Magnetic Fields; Ampère's Law and Displacement Current

Ampère's Law

That a magnetic field is produced by an electric current was discovered by Oersted, and the mathematic relation is given by Ampère's law (Eq. 28–3):

$$\oint \vec{B} \cdot d\vec{\ell} = \mu_0 I_{encl}.$$

Is it possible that magnetic fields could be produced in another way as well? For if a changing magnetic field produces an electric field, as discussed in Section 29–7, then perhaps the reverse might be true as well: that *a changing electric field will produce a magnetic field*. If this were true, it would signify a beautiful *symmetry* in nature.

To back up this idea that a changing electric field might produce a magnetic field, we use an indirect argument that goes something like this. According to Ampère's law, we divide any chosen closed path into short segments $d\vec{\ell}$, take the dot product of each $d\vec{\ell}$ with the magnetic field $\vec{B}$ at that segment, and sum (integrate) all these products over the chosen closed path. That sum will equal μ_0 times the total current I that passes through a surface bounded by the path of the line integral. When we applied Ampère's law to the field around a straight wire (Section 28–4), we imagined the current as passing through the circular area enclosed by our circular loop, and that area is the flat surface 1 shown in Fig. 31–2. However, we could just as well use the sackshaped surface 2 in Fig. 31–2 as the surface for Ampère's law, since the same current I passes through it.

Now consider the closed circular path for the situation of Fig. 31–3, where a capacitor is being discharged. Ampère's law works for surface 1 (current I passes through surface 1), but it does not work for surface 2, since no current passes through surface 2. There is a magnetic field around the wire, so the left side of Ampère's law ($\int \vec{B} \cdot d\vec{\ell}$) is not zero; yet no current flows through surface 2, so the right side of Ampère's law *is* zero. We seem to have a contradiction of Ampère's law.

There is a magnetic field present in Fig. 31–3, however, only if charge is flowing to or away from the capacitor plates. The changing charge on the plates means that the electric field between the plates is changing in time. Maxwell resolved the problem of no current through surface 2 in Fig. 31–3 by proposing that there needs to be an extra term on the right in Ampère's law involving the changing electric field.

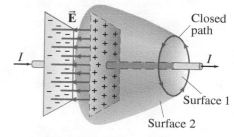

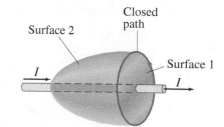

FIGURE 31–2 Ampère's law applied to two different surfaces bounded by the same closed path.

FIGURE 31–3 A capacitor discharging. A conduction current passes through surface 1, but no conduction current passes through surface 2. An extra term is needed in Ampère's law.

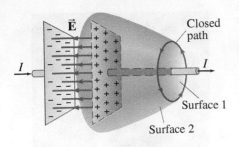

FIGURE 31-3 (repeated) See text.

Ampère's law
(general form)

Let us see what this term should be by determining it for the changing electric field between the capacitor plates in Fig. 31–3. The charge Q on a capacitor of capacitance C is $Q = CV$ where V is the potential difference between the plates (Eq. 24–1). Also recall that $V = Ed$ (Eq. 23–4) where d is the (small) separation of the plates and E is the (uniform) electric field strength between them, if we ignore any fringing of the field. Also, for a parallel-plate capacitor, $C = \epsilon_0 A/d$, where A is the area of each plate (Eq. 24–2). We combine these to obtain:

$$Q = CV = \left(\epsilon_0 \frac{A}{d}\right)(Ed) = \epsilon_0 AE.$$

If the charge on each plate changes at a rate dQ/dt, the electric field changes at a proportional rate. That is, by differentiating this expression for Q, we have:

$$\frac{dQ}{dt} = \epsilon_0 A \frac{dE}{dt}.$$

Now dQ/dt is also the current I flowing into or out of the capacitor:

$$I = \frac{dQ}{dt} = \epsilon_0 A \frac{dE}{dt} = \epsilon_0 \frac{d\Phi_E}{dt}$$

where $\Phi_E = EA$ is the **electric flux** through the closed path (surface 2 in Fig. 31–3). In order to make Ampère's law work for surface 2 in Fig. 31–3, as well as for surface 1 (where current I flows), we therefore write:

$$\oint \vec{B} \cdot d\vec{\ell} = \mu_0 I_{\text{encl}} + \mu_0 \epsilon_0 \frac{d\Phi_E}{dt}. \qquad (31-1)$$

This equation represents the general form of **Ampère's law,**[†] and embodies Maxwell's idea that a magnetic field can be caused not only by an ordinary electric current, but also by a changing electric field or changing electric flux. Although we arrived at it for a special case, Eq. 31–1 has proved valid in general. The last term on the right in Eq. 31–1 is usually very small, and not easy to measure experimentally.

EXAMPLE 31–1 Charging capacitor. A 30-pF air-gap capacitor has circular plates of area $A = 100\,\text{cm}^2$. It is charged by a 70-V battery through a 2.0-Ω resistor. At the instant the battery is connected, the electric field between the plates is changing most rapidly. At this instant, calculate (a) the current into the plates, and (b) the rate of change of electric field between the plates. (c) Determine the magnetic field induced between the plates. Assume $\vec{E}$ is uniform between the plates at any instant and is zero at all points beyond the edges of the plates.

APPROACH In Section 26–5 we discussed RC circuits and saw that the charge on a capacitor being charged, as a function of time, is

$$Q = CV_0(1 - e^{-t/RC}),$$

where V_0 is the voltage of the battery. To find the current at $t = 0$, we differentiate this and substitute the values $V_0 = 70\,\text{V}$, $C = 30\,\text{pF}$, $R = 2.0\,\Omega$.

SOLUTION (a) We take the derivative of Q and evaluate it at $t = 0$:

$$\left.\frac{dQ}{dt}\right|_{t=0} = \left.\frac{CV_0}{RC} e^{-t/RC}\right|_{t=0} = \frac{V_0}{R} = \frac{70\,\text{V}}{2.0\,\Omega} = 35\,\text{A}.$$

This is the rate at which charge accumulates on the capacitor and equals the current flowing in the circuit at $t = 0$.

(b) The electric field between two closely spaced conductors is given by (Eq. 21–8)

$$E = \frac{\sigma}{\epsilon_0} = \frac{Q/A}{\epsilon_0}$$

as we saw in Chapter 21 (see Example 21–13).

[†]Actually, there is a third term on the right for the case when a magnetic field is produced by magnetized materials. This can be accounted for by changing μ_0 to μ, but we will mainly be interested in cases where no magnetic material is present. In the presence of a dielectric, ϵ_0 is replaced by $\epsilon = K\epsilon_0$ (see Section 24–5).

Hence

$$\frac{dE}{dt} = \frac{dQ/dt}{\epsilon_0 A} = \frac{35 \text{ A}}{(8.85 \times 10^{-12} \text{ C}^2/\text{N} \cdot \text{m}^2)(1.0 \times 10^{-2} \text{ m}^2)} = 4.0 \times 10^{14} \text{ V/m} \cdot \text{s}.$$

(c) Although we will not prove it, we might expect the lines of $\vec{B}$, because of *symmetry*, to be circles, and to be perpendicular to $\vec{E}$, as shown in Fig. 31–4; this is the same symmetry we saw for the inverse situation of a changing magnetic field producing an electric field (Section 29–7, see Fig. 29–27). To determine the magnitude of B between the plates we apply Ampère's law, Eq. 31–1, with the current $I_{encl} = 0$:

$$\oint \vec{B} \cdot d\vec{\ell} = \mu_0 \epsilon_0 \frac{d\Phi_E}{dt}.$$

We choose our path to be a circle of radius r, centered at the center of the plate, and thus following a magnetic field line such as the one shown in Fig. 31–4. For $r \leq r_0$ (the radius of plate) the flux through a circle of radius r is $E(\pi r^2)$ since E is assumed uniform between the plates at any moment. So from Ampère's law we have

$$B(2\pi r) = \mu_0 \epsilon_0 \frac{d}{dt}(\pi r^2 E)$$

$$= \mu_0 \epsilon_0 \pi r^2 \frac{dE}{dt}.$$

Hence

$$B = \frac{\mu_0 \epsilon_0}{2} r \frac{dE}{dt}. \qquad [r \leq r_0]$$

We assume $\vec{E} = 0$ for $r > r_0$, so for points beyond the edge of the plates all the flux is contained within the plates (area $= \pi r_0^2$) and $\Phi_E = E\pi r_0^2$. Thus Ampère's law gives

$$B(2\pi r) = \mu_0 \epsilon_0 \frac{d}{dt}(\pi r_0^2 E)$$

$$= \mu_0 \epsilon_0 \pi r_0^2 \frac{dE}{dt}$$

or

$$B = \frac{\mu_0 \epsilon_0 r_0^2}{2r} \frac{dE}{dt}. \qquad [r \geq r_0]$$

B has its maximum value at $r = r_0$ which, from either relation above (using $r_0 = \sqrt{A/\pi} = 5.6$ cm), is

$$B_{max} = \frac{\mu_0 \epsilon_0 r_0}{2} \frac{dE}{dt}$$

$$= \tfrac{1}{2}(4\pi \times 10^{-7} \text{ T} \cdot \text{m/A})(8.85 \times 10^{-12} \text{ C}^2/\text{N} \cdot \text{m}^2)(5.6 \times 10^{-2} \text{ m})(4.0 \times 10^{14} \text{ V/m} \cdot \text{s})$$

$$= 1.2 \times 10^{-4} \text{ T}.$$

This is a very small field and lasts only briefly (the time constant $RC = 6.0 \times 10^{-11}$ s) and so would be very difficult to measure.

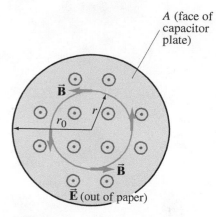

FIGURE 31–4 Frontal view of a circular plate of a parallel-plate capacitor. $\vec{E}$ between plates points out toward viewer; lines of $\vec{B}$ are circles. (Example 31–1.)

Let us write the magnetic field B outside the capacitor plates of Example 31–1 in terms of the current I that leaves the plates. The electric field between the plates is $E = \sigma/\epsilon_0 = Q/(\epsilon_0 A)$, as we saw in part b, so $dE/dt = I/(\epsilon_0 A)$. Hence B for $r > r_0$ is,

$$B = \frac{\mu_0 \epsilon_0 r_0^2}{2r} \frac{dE}{dt} = \frac{\mu_0 \epsilon_0 r_0^2}{2r} \frac{I}{\epsilon_0 \pi r_0^2} = \frac{\mu_0 I}{2\pi r}.$$

This is the same formula for the field that surrounds a wire (Eq. 28–1). Thus the B field outside the capacitor is the same as that outside the wire. In other words, the magnetic field produced by the changing electric field between the plates is the same as that produced by the current in the wire.

Displacement Current

Maxwell interpreted the second term on the right in Eq. 31–1 as being *equivalent* to an electric current. He called it a **displacement current**, I_D. An ordinary current I is then called a **conduction current**. Ampère's law can then be written

$$\oint \vec{B} \cdot d\vec{\ell} = \mu_0 (I + I_D)_{encl} \tag{31-2}$$

where

Displacement current

$$I_D = \epsilon_0 \frac{d\Phi_E}{dt}. \tag{31-3}$$

The term "displacement current" was based on an old discarded theory. Don't let it confuse you: I_D does not represent a flow of electric charge[†], nor is there a displacement.

31–2 Gauss's Law for Magnetism

We are almost in a position to state Maxwell's equations, but first we need to discuss the magnetic equivalent of Gauss's law. As we saw in Chapter 29, for a magnetic field $\vec{B}$ the *magnetic flux* Φ_B through a surface is defined as

$$\Phi_B = \int \vec{B} \cdot d\vec{A}$$

where the integral is over the area of either an open or a closed surface. The magnetic flux through a closed surface—that is, a surface which completely encloses a volume—is written

$$\Phi_B = \oint \vec{B} \cdot d\vec{A}.$$

In the electric case, we saw in Section 22–2 that the electric flux Φ_E through a closed surface is equal to the total net charge Q enclosed by the surface, divided by ϵ_0 (Eq. 22–4):

$$\oint \vec{E} \cdot d\vec{A} = \frac{Q}{\epsilon_0}.$$

This relation is Gauss's law for electricity.

We can write a similar relation for the magnetic flux. We have seen, however, that in spite of intense searches, no isolated magnetic poles (monopoles)—the magnetic equivalent of single electric charges—have ever been observed. Hence, **Gauss's law for magnetism** is

$$\oint \vec{B} \cdot d\vec{A} = 0. \tag{31-4}$$

FIGURE 31–5 Magnetic field lines for a bar magnet.

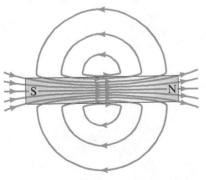

In terms of magnetic field lines, this relation tells us that as many lines enter the enclosed volume as leave it. If, indeed, magnetic monopoles do not exist, then there are no "sources" or "sinks" for magnetic field lines to start or stop on, corresponding to electric field lines starting on positive charges and ending on negative charges. Magnetic field lines must then be continuous. Even for a bar magnet, a magnetic field $\vec{B}$ exists inside as well as outside the magnetic material, and the lines of $\vec{B}$ are closed loops as shown in Fig. 31–5.

[†]The interpretation of the changing electric field as a current does fit in well with our discussion in Chapter 30 where we saw that an alternating current can be said to pass through a capacitor (although charge doesn't). It also means that Kirchhoff's junction rule will be valid even at a capacitor plate: conduction current flows into the plate, but no conduction current flows out of the plate—instead a "displacement current" flows out of one plate (toward the other plate).

31–3 Maxwell's Equations

With the extension of Ampère's law given by Eq. 31–1, plus Gauss's law for magnetism (Eq. 31–4), we are now ready to state all four of Maxwell's equations. We have seen them all before in the past ten Chapters. In the absence of dielectric or magnetic materials, **Maxwell's equations** are:

$$\oint \vec{E} \cdot d\vec{A} = \frac{Q}{\epsilon_0} \tag{31–5a}$$

$$\oint \vec{B} \cdot d\vec{A} = 0 \tag{31–5b}$$

$$\oint \vec{E} \cdot d\vec{\ell} = -\frac{d\Phi_B}{dt} \tag{31–5c}$$

$$\oint \vec{B} \cdot d\vec{\ell} = \mu_0 I + \mu_0 \epsilon_0 \frac{d\Phi_E}{dt}. \tag{31–5d}$$

The first two of Maxwell's equations are the same as Gauss's law for electricity (Chapter 22, Eq. 22–4) and Gauss's law for magnetism (Section 31–2, Eq. 31–4). The third is Faraday's law (Chapter 29, Eq. 29–8) and the fourth is Ampère's law as modified by Maxwell (Eq. 31–1). (We dropped the subscripts on Q_{encl} and I_{encl} for simplicity.)

They can be summarized in words: (1) a generalized form of Coulomb's law relating electric field to its sources, electric charges; (2) the same for the magnetic field, except that if there are no magnetic monopoles, magnetic field lines are continuous—they do not begin or end (as electric field lines do on charges); (3) an electric field is produced by a changing magnetic field; (4) a magnetic field is produced by an electric current or by a changing electric field.

Maxwell's equations are the basic equations for all electromagnetism, and are as fundamental as Newton's three laws of motion and the law of universal gravitation. Maxwell's equations can also be written in differential form; see Appendix E.

In earlier Chapters, we have seen that we can treat electric and magnetic fields separately if they do not vary in time. But we cannot treat them independently if they do change in time. For a changing magnetic field produces an electric field; and a changing electric field produces a magnetic field. An important outcome of these relations is the production of electromagnetic waves.

31–4 Production of Electromagnetic Waves

A magnetic field will be produced in empty space if there is a changing electric field. A changing magnetic field produces an electric field that is itself changing. This changing electric field will, in turn, produce a magnetic field, which will be changing, and so it too will produce a changing electric field; and so on. Maxwell found that the net result of these interacting changing fields was a *wave* of electric and magnetic fields that can propagate (travel) through space! We now examine, in a simplified way, how such **electromagnetic waves** can be produced.

Consider two conducting rods that will serve as an "antenna" (Fig. 31–6a). Suppose these two rods are connected by a switch to the opposite terminals of a battery. When the switch is closed, the upper rod quickly becomes positively charged and the lower one negatively charged. Electric field lines are formed as indicated by the lines in Fig. 31–6b. While the charges are flowing, a current exists whose direction is indicated by the black arrows. A magnetic field is therefore produced near the antenna. The magnetic field lines encircle the rod-like antenna and therefore, in Fig. 31–6, $\vec{B}$ points into the page ($\otimes$) on the right and out of the page ($\odot$) on the left. How far out do these electric and magnetic fields extend? In the static case, the fields extend outward indefinitely far. However, when the switch in Fig. 31–6 is closed, the fields quickly appear nearby, but it takes time for them to reach distant points. Both electric and magnetic fields store energy, and this energy cannot be transferred to distant points at infinite speed.

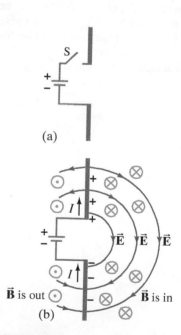

FIGURE 31–6 Fields produced by charge flowing into conductors. It takes time for the $\vec{E}$ and $\vec{B}$ fields to travel outward to distant points. The fields are shown to the right of the antenna, but they move out in all directions, symmetrically about the (vertical) antenna.

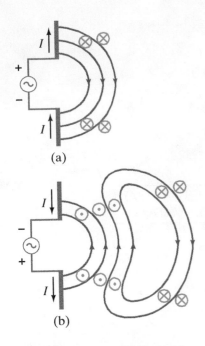

FIGURE 31–7 Sequence showing electric and magnetic fields that spread outward from oscillating charges on two conductors (the antenna) connected to an ac source (see the text).

(a)

(b)

FIGURE 31–8 (a) The radiation fields (far from the antenna) produced by a sinusoidal signal on the antenna. The red closed loops represent electric field lines. The magnetic field lines, perpendicular to the page and represented by blue $\otimes$ and $\odot$, also form closed loops. (b) Very far from the antenna the wave fronts (field lines) are essentially flat over a fairly large area, and are referred to as *plane waves*.

Now we look at the situation of Fig. 31–7 where our antenna is connected to an ac generator. In Fig. 31–7a, the connection has just been completed. Charge starts building up and fields form just as in Fig. 31–6. The + and − signs in Fig. 31–7a indicate the net charge on each rod at a given instant. The black arrows indicate the direction of the current. The electric field is represented by the red lines in the plane of the page; and the magnetic field, according to the right-hand rule, is into ($\otimes$) or out of ($\odot$) the page, in blue. In Fig. 31–7b, the voltage of the ac generator has reversed in direction; the current is reversed and the new magnetic field is in the opposite direction. Because the new fields have changed direction, the old lines fold back to connect up to some of the new lines and form closed loops as shown.[†] The old fields, however, don't suddenly disappear; they are on their way to distant points. Indeed, because a changing magnetic field produces an electric field, and a changing electric field produces a magnetic field, this combination of changing electric and magnetic fields moving outward is self-supporting, no longer depending on the antenna charges.

The fields not far from the antenna, referred to as the *near field*, become quite complicated, but we are not so interested in them. We are instead mainly interested in the fields far from the antenna (they are generally what we detect), which we refer to as the **radiation field**, or *far field*. The electric field lines form loops, as shown in Fig. 31–8, and continue moving outward. The magnetic field lines also form closed loops, but are not shown since they are perpendicular to the page. Although the lines are shown only on the right of the source, fields also travel in other directions. The field strengths are greatest in directions perpendicular to the oscillating charges; and they drop to zero along the direction of oscillation—above and below the antenna in Fig. 31–8.

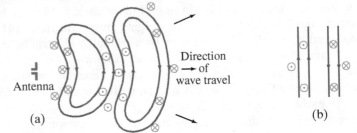

Antenna

Direction of wave travel

(a)

(b)

The magnitudes of both $\vec{E}$ and $\vec{B}$ in the radiation field are found to decrease with distance as $1/r$. (Compare this to the static electric field given by Coulomb's law where $\vec{E}$ decreases as $1/r^2$.) The energy carried by the electromagnetic wave is proportional (as for any wave, Chapter 15) to the square of the amplitude, E^2 or B^2, as will be discussed further in Section 31–8, so the intensity of the wave decreases as $1/r^2$.

Several things about the radiation field can be noted from Fig. 31–8. First, *the electric and magnetic fields at any point are perpendicular to each other, and to the direction of wave travel.* Second, we can see that the fields alternate in direction ($\vec{B}$ is into the page at some points and out of the page at others; $\vec{E}$ points up at some points and down at others). Thus, the field strengths vary from a maximum in one direction, to zero, to a maximum in the other direction. The electric and magnetic fields are "in phase": that is, they each are zero at the same points and reach their maxima at the same points in space. Finally, very far from the antenna (Fig. 31–8b) the field lines are quite flat over a reasonably large area, and the waves are referred to as **plane waves**.

If the source voltage varies sinusoidally, then the electric and magnetic field strengths in the radiation field will also vary sinusoidally. The sinusoidal character of the waves is diagrammed in Fig. 31–9, which shows the field directions and magnitudes plotted as a function of position. Notice that $\vec{B}$ and $\vec{E}$ are perpendicular to each other and to the direction of travel (= the direction of the wave velocity $\vec{v}$). The direction of $\vec{v}$ can be had from a right-hand rule using $\vec{E} \times \vec{B}$: fingers along $\vec{E}$, then along $\vec{B}$, gives $\vec{v}$ along thumb.

[†]We are considering waves traveling through empty space. There are no charges for lines of $\vec{E}$ to start or stop on, so they form closed loops. Magnetic field lines always form closed loops.

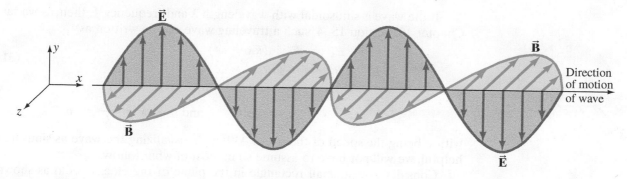

We call these waves electromagnetic (EM) waves. They are *transverse* waves because the amplitude is perpendicular to the direction of wave travel. However, EM waves are always waves of *fields*, not of matter (like waves on water or a rope). Because they are fields, EM waves can propagate in empty space.

As we have seen, EM waves are produced by electric charges that are oscillating, and hence are undergoing acceleration. In fact, we can say in general that

accelerating electric charges give rise to electromagnetic waves.

Electromagnetic waves can be produced in other ways as well, requiring description at the atomic and nuclear levels, as we will discuss later.

EXERCISE A At a particular instant in time, a wave has its electric field pointing north and its magnetic field pointing up. In which direction is the wave traveling? (*a*) South, (*b*) west, (*c*) east, (*d*) down, (*e*) not enough information.

31–5 Electromagnetic Waves, and Their Speed, Derived from Maxwell's Equations

Let us now examine how the existence of EM waves follows from Maxwell's equations. We will see that Maxwell's prediction of the existence of EM waves was startling. Equally startling was the speed at which they were predicted to travel.

We begin by considering a region of free space, where there are *no charges or conduction currents*—that is, far from the source so that the wave fronts (the field lines in Fig. 31–8) are essentially flat over a reasonable area. We call them **plane waves**, as we saw, because at any instant $\vec{\mathbf{E}}$ and $\vec{\mathbf{B}}$ are uniform over a reasonably large plane perpendicular to the direction of propagation. We choose a coordinate system, so that the wave is traveling in the x direction with velocity $\vec{\mathbf{v}} = v\hat{\mathbf{i}}$, with $\vec{\mathbf{E}}$ parallel to the y axis and $\vec{\mathbf{B}}$ parallel to the z axis, as in Fig. 31–9.

Maxwell's equations, with $Q = I = 0$, become

$$\oint \vec{\mathbf{E}} \cdot d\vec{\mathbf{A}} = 0 \tag{31–6a}$$

$$\oint \vec{\mathbf{B}} \cdot d\vec{\mathbf{A}} = 0 \tag{31–6b}$$

$$\oint \vec{\mathbf{E}} \cdot d\vec{\boldsymbol{\ell}} = -\frac{d\Phi_B}{dt} \tag{31–6c}$$

$$\oint \vec{\mathbf{B}} \cdot d\vec{\boldsymbol{\ell}} = \mu_0 \epsilon_0 \frac{d\Phi_E}{dt}. \tag{31–6d}$$

Notice the beautiful *symmetry* of these equations. The term on the right in the last equation, conceived by Maxwell, is essential for this symmetry. It is also essential if electromagnetic waves are to be produced, as we will now see.

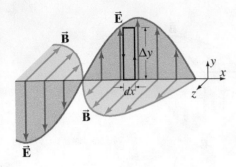

FIGURE 31–10 Applying Faraday's law to the rectangle $(\Delta y)(dx)$.

If the wave is sinusoidal with wavelength λ and frequency f, then, as we saw in Chapter 15, Section 15–4, such a traveling wave can be written as

$$E = E_y = E_0 \sin(kx - \omega t)$$
$$B = B_z = B_0 \sin(kx - \omega t)$$

(31–7)

where

$$k = \frac{2\pi}{\lambda}, \quad \omega = 2\pi f, \quad \text{and} \quad f\lambda = \frac{\omega}{k} = v,$$

(31–8)

with v being the speed of the wave. Although visualizing the wave as sinusoidal is helpful, we will not have to assume so in most of what follows.

Consider now a small rectangle in the plane of the electric field as shown in Fig. 31–10. This rectangle has a finite height Δy, and a very thin width which we take to be the infinitesimal distance dx. First we show that $\vec{E}$, $\vec{B}$, and $\vec{v}$ are in the orientation shown by applying Lenz's law to this rectangular loop. The changing magnetic flux through this loop is related to the electric field around the loop by Faraday's law (Maxwell's third equation, Eq. 31–6c). For the case shown, B through the loop is decreasing in time (the wave is moving to the right). So the electric field must be in a direction to oppose this change, meaning E must be greater on the right side of the loop than on the left, as shown (so it could produce a counterclockwise current whose magnetic field would act to oppose the change in Φ_B—but of course there is no current). This brief argument shows that the orientation of $\vec{E}$, $\vec{B}$, and $\vec{v}$ are in the correct relation as shown. That is, $\vec{v}$ is in the direction of $\vec{E} \times \vec{B}$. Now let us apply Faraday's law, which is Maxwell's third equation (Eq. 31–6c),

$$\oint \vec{E} \cdot d\vec{\ell} = -\frac{d\Phi_B}{dt}$$

to the rectangle of height Δy and width dx shown in Fig. 31–10. First we consider $\oint \vec{E} \cdot d\vec{\ell}$. Along the short top and bottom sections of length dx, $\vec{E}$ is perpendicular to $d\vec{\ell}$, so $\vec{E} \cdot d\vec{\ell} = 0$. Along the vertical sides, we let E be the electric field along the left side, and on the right side where it will be slightly larger, it is $E + dE$. Thus, if we take our loop counterclockwise,

$$\oint \vec{E} \cdot d\vec{\ell} = (E + dE) \, \Delta y - E \, \Delta y = dE \, \Delta y.$$

For the right side of Faraday's law, the magnetic flux through the loop changes as

$$\frac{d\Phi_B}{dt} = \frac{dB}{dt} dx \, \Delta y,$$

since the area of the loop, $(dx)(\Delta y)$, is not changing. Thus, Faraday's law gives us

$$dE \, \Delta y = -\frac{dB}{dt} dx \, \Delta y$$

or

$$\frac{dE}{dx} = -\frac{dB}{dt}.$$

Actually, both E and B are functions of position x and time t. We should therefore use partial derivatives:

$$\frac{\partial E}{\partial x} = -\frac{\partial B}{\partial t}$$

(31–9)

where $\partial E/\partial x$ means the derivative of E with respect to x while t is held fixed, and $\partial B/\partial t$ is the derivative of B with respect to t while x is kept fixed.

We can obtain another important relation between E and B in addition to Eq. 31–9. To do so, we consider now a small rectangle in the plane of $\vec{B}$, whose length and width are Δz and dx as shown in Fig. 31–11. To this rectangular loop we apply Maxwell's fourth equation (the extension of Ampère's law), Eq. 31–6d:

$$\oint \vec{B} \cdot d\vec{\ell} = \mu_0 \epsilon_0 \frac{d\Phi_E}{dt}$$

where we have taken $I = 0$ since we assume the absence of conduction currents.

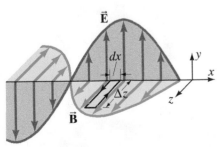

FIGURE 31–11 Applying Maxwell's fourth equation to the rectangle $(\Delta z)(dx)$.

Along the short sides (dx), $\vec{B} \cdot d\vec{\ell}$ is zero since $\vec{B}$ is perpendicular to $d\vec{\ell}$. Along the longer sides (Δz), we let B be the magnetic field along the left side of length Δz, and $B + dB$ be the field along the right side. We again integrate counterclockwise, so

$$\oint \vec{B} \cdot d\vec{\ell} = B \, \Delta z - (B + dB) \, \Delta z = -dB \, \Delta z.$$

The right side of Maxwell's fourth equation is

$$\mu_0 \epsilon_0 \frac{d\Phi_E}{dt} = \mu_0 \epsilon_0 \frac{dE}{dt} \, dx \, \Delta z.$$

Equating the two expressions, we obtain

$$-dB \, \Delta z = \mu_0 \epsilon_0 \frac{dE}{dt} \, dx \, \Delta z$$

or

$$\frac{\partial B}{\partial x} = -\mu_0 \epsilon_0 \frac{\partial E}{\partial t} \qquad\qquad (31\text{--}10)$$

where we have replaced dB/dx and dE/dt by the proper partial derivatives as before.

We can use Eqs. 31–9 and 31–10 to obtain a relation between the magnitudes of $\vec{E}$ and $\vec{B}$, and the speed v. Let E and B be given by Eqs. 31–7 as a function of x and t. When we apply Eq. 31–9, taking the derivatives of E and B as given by Eqs. 31–7, we obtain

$$k E_0 \cos(kx - \omega t) = \omega B_0 \cos(kx - \omega t)$$

or

$$\frac{E_0}{B_0} = \frac{\omega}{k} = v,$$

since $v = \omega / k$ (see Eq. 31–8 or 15–12). Since E and B are in phase, we see that E and B are related by

$$\frac{E}{B} = v \qquad\qquad (31\text{--}11)$$

at any point in space, where v is the velocity of the wave.

Now we apply Eq. 31–10 to the sinusoidal fields (Eqs. 31–7) and we obtain

$$k B_0 \cos(kx - \omega t) = \mu_0 \epsilon_0 \omega E_0 \cos(kx - \omega t)$$

or

$$\frac{B_0}{E_0} = \frac{\mu_0 \epsilon_0 \omega}{k} = \mu_0 \epsilon_0 v.$$

We just saw that $B_0 / E_0 = 1/v$, so

$$\mu_0 \epsilon_0 v = \frac{1}{v}.$$

Solving for v we find

$$v = c = \frac{1}{\sqrt{\epsilon_0 \mu_0}}, \qquad\qquad (31\text{--}12)$$

where c is the special symbol for the speed of electromagnetic waves in free space. We see that c is a constant, independent of the wavelength or frequency. If we put in values for ϵ_0 and μ_0 we find

$$c = \frac{1}{\sqrt{\epsilon_0 \mu_0}} = \frac{1}{\sqrt{(8.85 \times 10^{-12}\,\mathrm{C^2/N \cdot m^2})(4\pi \times 10^{-7}\,\mathrm{T \cdot m/A})}}$$

$$= 3.00 \times 10^8 \,\mathrm{m/s}.$$

This is a remarkable result. For this is precisely equal to the measured speed of light!

SECTION 31–5   Electromagnetic Waves, and Their Speed, Derived from Maxwell's Equations   **821**

EXAMPLE 31–2 Determining $\vec{E}$ and $\vec{B}$ in EM waves. Assume a 60.0-Hz EM wave is a sinusoidal wave propagating in the z direction with $\vec{E}$ pointing in the x direction, and $E_0 = 2.00 \text{ V/m}$. Write vector expressions for $\vec{E}$ and $\vec{B}$ as functions of position and time.

APPROACH We find λ from $\lambda f = v = c$. Then we use Fig. 31–9 and Eqs. 31–7 and 31–8 for the mathematical form of traveling electric and magnetic fields of an EM wave.

SOLUTION The wavelength is

$$\lambda = \frac{c}{f} = \frac{3.00 \times 10^8 \text{ m/s}}{60.0 \text{ s}^{-1}} = 5.00 \times 10^6 \text{ m}.$$

From Eq. 31–8 we have

$$k = \frac{2\pi}{\lambda} = \frac{2\pi}{5.00 \times 10^6 \text{ m}} = 1.26 \times 10^{-6} \text{ m}^{-1}$$

$$\omega = 2\pi f = 2\pi(60.0 \text{ Hz}) = 377 \text{ rad/s}.$$

From Eq. 31–11 with $v = c$, we find that

$$B_0 = \frac{E_0}{c} = \frac{2.00 \text{ V/m}}{3.00 \times 10^8 \text{ m/s}} = 6.67 \times 10^{-9} \text{ T}.$$

The direction of propagation is that of $\vec{E} \times \vec{B}$, as in Fig. 31–9. With $\vec{E}$ pointing in the x direction, and the wave propagating in the z direction, $\vec{B}$ must point in the y direction. Using Eqs. 31–7 we find:

$$\vec{E} = \hat{i}(2.00 \text{ V/m}) \sin\left[(1.26 \times 10^{-6} \text{ m}^{-1})z - (377 \text{ rad/s})t\right]$$

$$\vec{B} = \hat{j}(6.67 \times 10^{-9} \text{ T}) \sin\left[(1.26 \times 10^{-6} \text{ m}^{-1})z - (377 \text{ rad/s})t\right]$$

*Derivation of Speed of Light (General)

We can derive the speed of EM waves without having to assume sinusoidal waves by combining Eqs. 31–9 and 31–10 as follows. We take the derivative, with respect to t of Eq. 31–10

$$\frac{\partial^2 B}{\partial t\, \partial x} = -\mu_0 \epsilon_0 \frac{\partial^2 E}{\partial t^2}.$$

We next take the derivative of Eq. 31–9 with respect to x:

$$\frac{\partial^2 E}{\partial x^2} = -\frac{\partial^2 B}{\partial t\, \partial x}.$$

Since $\partial^2 B/\partial t\, \partial x$ appears in both relations, we obtain

$$\frac{\partial^2 E}{\partial t^2} = \frac{1}{\mu_0 \epsilon_0} \frac{\partial^2 E}{\partial x^2}. \qquad \textbf{(31–13a)}$$

By taking other derivatives of Eqs. 31–9 and 31–10 we obtain the same relation for B:

$$\frac{\partial^2 B}{\partial t^2} = \frac{1}{\mu_0 \epsilon_0} \frac{\partial^2 B}{\partial x^2}. \qquad \textbf{(31–13b)}$$

Both of Eqs. 31–13 have the form of the **wave equation** for a plane wave traveling in the x direction, as discussed in Section 15–5 (Eq. 15–16):

$$\frac{\partial^2 D}{\partial t^2} = v^2 \frac{\partial^2 D}{\partial x^2},$$

where D stands for any type of displacement. We see that the velocity v for Eqs. 31–13 is given by

$$v^2 = \frac{1}{\mu_0 \epsilon_0}$$

in agreement with Eq. 31–12. Thus we see that a natural outcome of Maxwell's equations is that E and B obey the wave equation for waves traveling with speed $v = 1/\sqrt{\mu_0 \epsilon_0}$. It was on this basis that Maxwell predicted the existence of electromagnetic waves and predicted their speed.

31–6 Light as an Electromagnetic Wave and the Electromagnetic Spectrum

The calculations in Section 31–5 gave the result that Maxwell himself determined: that the speed of EM waves in empty space is given by

$$c = \frac{E}{B} = \frac{1}{\sqrt{\epsilon_0 \mu_0}} = 3.00 \times 10^8 \, \text{m/s},$$

the same as the measured speed of light in vacuum.

Light had been shown some 60 years previously to behave like a wave (we'll discuss this in Chapter 34). But nobody knew what kind of wave it was. What is it that is oscillating in a light wave? Maxwell, on the basis of the calculated speed of EM waves, argued that light must be an electromagnetic wave. This idea soon came to be generally accepted by scientists, but not fully until after EM waves were experimentally detected. EM waves were first generated and detected experimentally by Heinrich Hertz (1857–1894) in 1887, eight years after Maxwell's death. Hertz used a spark-gap apparatus in which charge was made to rush back and forth for a short time, generating waves whose frequency was about 10^9 Hz. He detected them some distance away using a loop of wire in which an emf was produced when a changing magnetic field passed through. These waves were later shown to travel at the speed of light, 3.00×10^8 m/s, and to exhibit all the characteristics of light such as reflection, refraction, and interference. The only difference was that they were not visible. Hertz's experiment was a strong confirmation of Maxwell's theory.

The wavelengths of visible light were measured in the first decade of the nineteenth century, long before anyone imagined that light was an electromagnetic wave. The wavelengths were found to lie between 4.0×10^{-7} m and 7.5×10^{-7} m, or 400 nm to 750 nm $(1 \, \text{nm} = 10^9 \, \text{m})$. The frequencies of visible light can be found using Eq. 15–1 or 31–8, which we rewrite here:

$$c = \lambda f, \tag{31–14}$$

where f and λ are the frequency and wavelength, respectively, of the wave. Here, c is the speed of light, 3.00×10^8 m/s; it gets the special symbol c because of its universality for all EM waves in free space. Equation 31–14 tells us that the frequencies of visible light are between 4.0×10^{14} Hz and 7.5×10^{14} Hz. (Recall that $1 \, \text{Hz} = 1$ cycle per second $= 1 \, \text{s}^{-1}$.)

But visible light is only one kind of EM wave. As we have seen, Hertz produced EM waves of much lower frequency, about 10^9 Hz. These are now called **radio waves**, because frequencies in this range are used to transmit radio and TV signals. Electromagnetic waves, or EM radiation as we sometimes call it, have been produced or detected over a wide range of frequencies. They are usually categorized as shown in Fig. 31–12, which is known as the **electromagnetic spectrum**.

FIGURE 31–12
Electromagnetic spectrum.

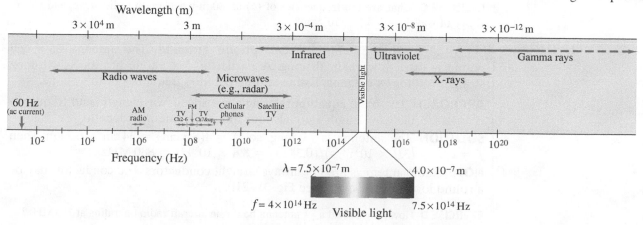

Radio waves and microwaves can be produced in the laboratory using electronic equipment (Fig. 31–7). Higher-frequency waves are very difficult to produce electronically. These and other types of EM waves are produced in natural processes, as emission from atoms, molecules, and nuclei (more on this later). EM waves can be produced by the acceleration of electrons or other charged particles, such as electrons in the antenna of Fig. 31–7. Another example is X-rays, which are produced (Chapter 35) when fast-moving electrons are rapidly decelerated upon striking a metal target. Even the visible light emitted by an ordinary incandescent light is due to electrons undergoing acceleration within the hot filament.

We will meet various types of EM waves later. However, it is worth mentioning here that infrared (IR) radiation (EM waves whose frequency is just less than that of visible light) is mainly responsible for the heating effect of the Sun. The Sun emits not only visible light but substantial amounts of IR and UV (ultraviolet) as well. The molecules of our skin tend to "resonate" at infrared frequencies, so it is these that are preferentially absorbed and thus warm us up. We humans experience EM waves differently, depending on their wavelengths: Our eyes detect wavelengths between about 4×10^{-7} m and 7.5×10^{-7} m (visible light), whereas our skin detects longer wavelengths (IR). Many EM wavelengths we don't detect directly at all.

EXERCISE B Return to the Chapter-Opening Question, page 812, and answer it again now. Try to explain why you may have answered differently the first time.

CAUTION

Sound and EM waves are different

Light and other electromagnetic waves travel at a speed of 3×10^8 m/s. Compare this to sound, which travels (see Chapter 16) at a speed of about 300 m/s in air, a million times slower; or to typical freeway speeds of a car, 30 m/s (100 km/h, or 60 mi/h), 10 million times slower than light. EM waves differ from sound waves in another big way: sound waves travel in a medium such as air, and involve motion of air molecules; EM waves do not involve any material—only fields, and they can travel in empty space.

EXAMPLE 31–3 **Wavelengths of EM waves.** Calculate the wavelength (a) of a 60-Hz EM wave, (b) of a 93.3-MHz FM radio wave, and (c) of a beam of visible red light from a laser at frequency 4.74×10^{14} Hz.

APPROACH All of these waves are electromagnetic waves, so their speed is $c = 3.00 \times 10^8$ m/s. We solve for λ in Eq. 31–14: $\lambda = c/f$.

SOLUTION (a) $\lambda = \dfrac{c}{f} = \dfrac{3.00 \times 10^8 \text{ m/s}}{60 \text{ s}^{-1}} = 5.0 \times 10^6$ m,

or 5000 km. 60 Hz is the frequency of ac current in the United States, and, as we see here, one wavelength stretches all the way across the continental USA.

(b) $\lambda = \dfrac{3.00 \times 10^8 \text{ m/s}}{93.3 \times 10^6 \text{ s}^{-1}} = 3.22$ m.

The length of an FM antenna is about half this ($\frac{1}{2}\lambda$), or $1\frac{1}{2}$ m.

(c) $\lambda = \dfrac{3.00 \times 10^8 \text{ m/s}}{4.74 \times 10^{14} \text{ s}^{-1}} = 6.33 \times 10^{-7}$ m ($= 633$ nm).

EXERCISE C What are the frequencies of (a) an 80-m-wavelength radio wave, and (b) an X-ray of wavelength 5.5×10^{-11} m?

EXAMPLE 31–4 **ESTIMATE** **Cell phone antenna.** The antenna of a cell phone is often $\frac{1}{4}$ wavelength long. A particular cell phone has an 8.5-cm-long straight rod for its antenna. Estimate the operating frequency of this phone.

APPROACH The basic equation relating wave speed, wavelength, and frequency is $c = \lambda f$; the wavelength λ equals four times the antenna's length.

SOLUTION The antenna is $\frac{1}{4}\lambda$ long, so $\lambda = 4(8.5 \text{ cm}) = 34 \text{ cm} = 0.34$ m. Then $f = c/\lambda = (3.0 \times 10^8 \text{ m/s})/(0.34 \text{ m}) = 8.8 \times 10^8$ Hz $= 880$ MHz.

NOTE Radio antennas are not always straight conductors. The conductor may be a round loop to save space. See Fig. 31–21b.

EXERCISE D How long should a $\frac{1}{4}\lambda$ antenna be for an aircraft radio operating at 165 MHz?

Electromagnetic waves can travel along transmission lines as well as in empty space. When a source of emf is connected to a transmission line—be it two parallel wires or a coaxial cable (Fig. 31–13)—the electric field within the wire is not set up immediately at all points along the wires. This is based on the same argument we used in Section 31–4 with reference to Fig. 31–7. Indeed, it can be shown that if the wires are separated by empty space or air, the electrical signal travels along the wires at the speed $c = 3.0 \times 10^8$ m/s. For example, when you flip a light switch, the light actually goes on a tiny fraction of a second later. If the wires are in a medium whose electric permittivity is ϵ and magnetic permeability is μ (Sections 24–5 and 28–9, respectively), the speed is not given by Eq. 31–12, but by

FIGURE 31–13   Coaxial cable.

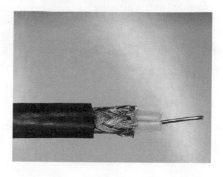

$$v = \frac{1}{\sqrt{\epsilon \mu}}.$$

EXAMPLE 31–5   ESTIMATE   **Phone call time lag.** You make a telephone call from New York to a friend in London. Estimate how long it will take the electrical signal generated by your voice to reach London, assuming the signal is (a) carried on a telephone cable under the Atlantic Ocean, and (b) sent via satellite 36,000 km above the ocean. Would this cause a noticeable delay in either case?

APPROACH The signal is carried on a telephone wire or in the air via satellite. In either case it is an electromagnetic wave. Electronics as well as the wire or cable slow things down, but as a rough estimate we take the speed to be $c = 3.0 \times 10^8$ m/s.

SOLUTION The distance from New York to London is about 5000 km.
(a) The time delay via the cable is $t = d/c \approx (5 \times 10^6 \text{ m})/(3.0 \times 10^8 \text{ m/s}) = 0.017$ s.
(b) Via satellite the time would be longer because communications satellites, which are usually geosynchronous (Example 6–6), move at a height of 36,000 km. The signal would have to go up to the satellite and back down, or about 72,000 km. The actual distance the signal would travel would be a little more than this as the signal would go up and down on a diagonal. Thus $t = d/c \approx 7.2 \times 10^7 \text{ m}/(3 \times 10^8 \text{ m/s}) = 0.24$ s.

NOTE When the signal travels via the underwater cable, there is only a hint of a delay and conversations are fairly normal. When the signal is sent via satellite, the delay *is* noticeable. The length of time between the end of when you speak and your friend receives it and replies, and then you hear the reply, is about a half second beyond the normal time in a conversation. This is enough to be noticeable, and you have to adjust for it so you don't start talking again while your friend's reply is on the way back to you.

EXERCISE E If you are on the phone via satellite to someone only 100 km away, would you hear the same effect?

EXERCISE F If your voice traveled as a sound wave, how long would it take to go from New York to London?

31–7   Measuring the Speed of Light

Galileo attempted to measure the speed of light by trying to measure the time required for light to travel a known distance between two hilltops. He stationed an assistant on one hilltop and himself on another, and ordered the assistant to lift the cover from a lamp the instant he saw a flash from Galileo's lamp. Galileo measured the time between the flash of his lamp and when he received the light from his assistant's lamp. The time was so short that Galileo concluded it merely represented human reaction time, and that the speed of light must be extremely high.

The first successful determination that the speed of light is finite was made by the Danish astronomer Ole Roemer (1644–1710). Roemer had noted that the carefully measured orbital period of Io, a moon of Jupiter with an average period of 42.5 h, varied slightly, depending on the relative position of Earth and Jupiter. He attributed this variation in the apparent period to the change in distance between the Earth and Jupiter during one of Io's periods, and the time it took light to travel the extra distance. Roemer concluded that the speed of light—though great—is finite.

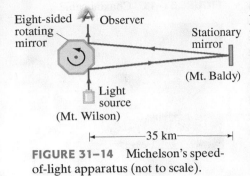

FIGURE 31–14 Michelson's speed-of-light apparatus (not to scale).

Eight-sided rotating mirror

Observer

Stationary mirror

(Mt. Baldy)

Light source

(Mt. Wilson)

|←————35 km————→|

Since then a number of techniques have been used to measure the speed of light. Among the most important were those carried out by the American Albert A. Michelson (1852–1931). Michelson used the rotating mirror apparatus diagrammed in Fig. 31–14 for a series of high-precision experiments carried out from 1880 to the 1920s. Light from a source would hit one face of a rotating eight-sided mirror. The reflected light traveled to a stationary mirror a large distance away and back again as shown. If the rotating mirror was turning at just the right rate, the returning beam of light would reflect from one of the eight mirrors into a small telescope through which the observer looked. If the speed of rotation was only slightly different, the beam would be deflected to one side and would not be seen by the observer. From the required speed of the rotating mirror and the known distance to the stationary mirror, the speed of light could be calculated. In the 1920s, Michelson set up the rotating mirror on the top of Mt. Wilson in southern California and the stationary mirror on Mt. Baldy (Mt. San Antonio) 35 km away. He later measured the speed of light in vacuum using a long evacuated tube.

Today the speed of light, c, in vacuum is taken as

$$c = 2.99792458 \times 10^8 \text{ m/s},$$

and is defined to be this value. This means that the standard for length, the meter, is no longer defined separately. Instead, as we noted in Section 1–4, the meter is now formally defined as the distance light travels in vacuum in 1/299,792,458 of a second. We usually round off c to

$$c = 3.00 \times 10^8 \text{ m/s}$$

when extremely precise results are not required. In air, the speed is only slightly less.

31–8 Energy in EM Waves; the Poynting Vector

Electromagnetic waves carry energy from one region of space to another. This energy is associated with the moving electric and magnetic fields. In Section 24–4, we saw that the energy density u_E (J/m^3) stored in an electric field E is $u_E = \frac{1}{2}\epsilon_0 E^2$ (Eq. 24–6). The energy density stored in a magnetic field B, as we discussed in Section 30–3, is given by $u_B = \frac{1}{2}B^2/\mu_0$ (Eq. 30–7). Thus, the total energy stored per unit volume in a region of space where there is an electromagnetic wave is

$$u = u_E + u_B = \frac{1}{2}\epsilon_0 E^2 + \frac{1}{2}\frac{B^2}{\mu_0}. \qquad \textbf{(31–15)}$$

In this equation, E and B represent the electric and magnetic field strengths of the wave at any instant in a small region of space. We can write Eq. 31–15 in terms of the E field alone, using Eqs. 31–11 $(B = E/c)$ and 31–12 $(c = 1/\sqrt{\epsilon_0 \mu_0})$ to obtain

$$u = \frac{1}{2}\epsilon_0 E^2 + \frac{1}{2}\frac{\epsilon_0 \mu_0 E^2}{\mu_0} = \epsilon_0 E^2. \qquad \textbf{(31–16a)}$$

Note here that the energy density associated with the B field equals that due to the E field, and each contributes half to the total energy. We can also write the energy density in terms of the B field only:

$$u = \epsilon_0 E^2 = \epsilon_0 c^2 B^2 = \frac{B^2}{\mu_0}, \qquad \textbf{(31–16b)}$$

or in one term containing both E and B,

$$u = \epsilon_0 E^2 = \epsilon_0 E c B = \frac{\epsilon_0 E B}{\sqrt{\epsilon_0 \mu_0}} = \sqrt{\frac{\epsilon_0}{\mu_0}} E B. \qquad \textbf{(31–16c)}$$

Equations 31–16 give the energy density in any region of space at any instant.

Now let us determine the energy the wave transports per unit time per unit area. This is given by a vector $\vec{\mathbf{S}}$, which is called the **Poynting vector**.[†] The units of $\vec{\mathbf{S}}$ are W/m^2. The direction of $\vec{\mathbf{S}}$ is the direction in which the energy is transported, which is the direction in which the wave is moving.

[†]After J. H. Poynting (1852–1914).

Let us imagine the wave is passing through an area A perpendicular to the x axis as shown in Fig. 31–15. In a short time dt, the wave moves to the right a distance $dx = c\,dt$ where c is the wave speed. The energy that passes through A in the time dt is the energy that occupies the volume $dV = A\,dx = Ac\,dt$. The energy density u is $u = \epsilon_0 E^2$ where E is the electric field in this volume at the given instant. So the total energy dU contained in this volume dV is the energy density u times the volume: $dU = u\,dV = (\epsilon_0 E^2)(Ac\,dt)$. Therefore the energy crossing the area A per time dt is

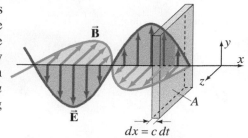

FIGURE 31–15 Electromagnetic wave carrying energy through area A.

$$S = \frac{1}{A}\frac{dU}{dt} = \epsilon_0 c E^2. \qquad (31\text{–}17)$$

Since $E = cB$ and $c = 1/\sqrt{\epsilon_0 \mu_0}$, this can also be written:

$$S = \epsilon_0 c E^2 = \frac{cB^2}{\mu_0} = \frac{EB}{\mu_0}.$$

The direction of $\vec{\mathbf{S}}$ is along $\vec{\mathbf{v}}$, perpendicular to $\vec{\mathbf{E}}$ and $\vec{\mathbf{B}}$, so the Poynting vector $\vec{\mathbf{S}}$ can be written

$$\vec{\mathbf{S}} = \frac{1}{\mu_0}(\vec{\mathbf{E}} \times \vec{\mathbf{B}}). \qquad (31\text{–}18)$$

Equation 31–17 or 31–18 gives the energy transported per unit area per unit time at any *instant*. We often want to know the *average* over an extended period of time since the frequencies are usually so high we don't detect the rapid time variation. If E and B are sinusoidal, then $\overline{E^2} = E_0^2/2$, just as for electric currents and voltages (Section 25–7), where E_0 is the *maximum* value of E. Thus we can write for the magnitude of the Poynting vector, on the average,

$$\overline{S} = \frac{1}{2}\epsilon_0 c E_0^2 = \frac{1}{2}\frac{c}{\mu_0}B_0^2 = \frac{E_0 B_0}{2\mu_0}, \qquad (31\text{–}19\text{a})$$

where B_0 is the maximum value of B. This time averaged value of $\vec{\mathbf{S}}$ is the **intensity**, defined as the average power transferred across unit area (Section 15–3). We can also write for the average value of S:

$$\overline{S} = \frac{E_{\text{rms}} B_{\text{rms}}}{\mu_0} \qquad (31\text{–}19\text{b})$$

where E_{rms} and B_{rms} are the rms values $\left(E_{\text{rms}} = \sqrt{\overline{E^2}},\ B_{\text{rms}} = \sqrt{\overline{B^2}}\right)$.

EXAMPLE 31–6 E **and** B **from the Sun.** Radiation from the Sun reaches the Earth (above the atmosphere) at a rate of about $1350\,\text{J/s·m}^2\,(= 1350\,\text{W/m}^2)$. Assume that this is a single EM wave, and calculate the maximum values of E and B.

APPROACH We solve Eq. 31–19a $\left(\overline{S} = \frac{1}{2}\epsilon_0 c E_0^2\right)$ for E_0 in terms of $\overline{S}$ using $\overline{S} = 1350\,\text{J/s·m}^2$.

SOLUTION $E_0 = \sqrt{\dfrac{2\overline{S}}{\epsilon_0 c}} = \sqrt{\dfrac{2(1350\,\text{J/s·m}^2)}{(8.85 \times 10^{-12}\,\text{C}^2/\text{N·m}^2)(3.00 \times 10^8\,\text{m/s})}}$

$ = 1.01 \times 10^3\,\text{V/m}.$

From Eq. 31–11, $B = E/c$, so

$$B_0 = \frac{E_0}{c} = \frac{1.01 \times 10^3\,\text{V/m}}{3.00 \times 10^8\,\text{m/s}} = 3.37 \times 10^{-6}\,\text{T}.$$

NOTE Although B has a small numerical value compared to E (because of the way the different units for E and B are defined), B contributes the same energy to the wave as E does, as we saw earlier (Eqs. 31–15 and 16).

31–9 Radiation Pressure

If electromagnetic waves carry energy, then we might expect them to also carry linear momentum. When an electromagnetic wave encounters the surface of an object, a force will be exerted on the surface as a result of the momentum transfer $(F = dp/dt)$, just as when a moving object strikes a surface. The force per unit area exerted by the waves is called **radiation pressure**, and its existence was predicted by Maxwell. He showed that if a beam of EM radiation (light, for example) is completely absorbed by an object, then the momentum transferred is

$$\Delta p = \frac{\Delta U}{c} \qquad \begin{bmatrix} \text{radiation} \\ \text{fully} \\ \text{absorbed} \end{bmatrix} \quad \textbf{(31–20a)}$$

where ΔU is the energy absorbed by the object in a time Δt, and c is the speed of light.[†] If instead, the radiation is fully reflected (suppose the object is a mirror), then the momentum transferred is twice as great, just as when a ball bounces elastically off a surface:

$$\Delta p = \frac{2\,\Delta U}{c}. \qquad \begin{bmatrix} \text{radiation} \\ \text{fully} \\ \text{reflected} \end{bmatrix} \quad \textbf{(31–20b)}$$

If a surface absorbs some of the energy, and reflects some of it, then $\Delta p = a\,\Delta U/c$, where a is a factor between 1 and 2.

Using Newton's second law we can calculate the force and the pressure exerted by radiation on the object. The force F is given by

$$F = \frac{dp}{dt}.$$

The average rate that energy is delivered to the object is related to the Poynting vector by

$$\frac{dU}{dt} = \bar{S}A,$$

where A is the cross-sectional area of the object which intercepts the radiation. The radiation pressure P (assuming full absorption) is given by (see Eq. 31–20a)

$$P = \frac{F}{A} = \frac{1}{A}\frac{dp}{dt} = \frac{1}{Ac}\frac{dU}{dt} = \frac{\bar{S}}{c}. \qquad \begin{bmatrix} \text{fully} \\ \text{absorbed} \end{bmatrix} \quad \textbf{(31–21a)}$$

If the light is fully reflected, the pressure is twice as great (Eq. 31–20b):

$$P = \frac{2\bar{S}}{c}. \qquad \begin{bmatrix} \text{fully} \\ \text{reflected} \end{bmatrix} \quad \textbf{(31–21b)}$$

EXAMPLE 31–7 ESTIMATE **Solar pressure.** Radiation from the Sun that reaches the Earth's surface (after passing through the atmosphere) transports energy at a rate of about $1000\,\text{W/m}^2$. Estimate the pressure and force exerted by the Sun on your outstretched hand.

APPROACH The radiation is partially reflected and partially absorbed, so let us estimate simply $P = \bar{S}/c$.

SOLUTION $P \approx \dfrac{\bar{S}}{c} = \dfrac{1000\,\text{W/m}^2}{3 \times 10^8\,\text{m/s}} \approx 3 \times 10^{-6}\,\text{N/m}^2.$

An estimate of the area of your outstretched hand might be about 10 cm by 20 cm, so $A = 0.02\,\text{m}^2$. Then the force is

$$F = PA \approx (3 \times 10^{-6}\,\text{N/m}^2)(0.02\,\text{m}^2) \approx 6 \times 10^{-8}\,\text{N}.$$

NOTE These numbers are tiny. The force of gravity on your hand, for comparison, is maybe a half pound, or with $m = 0.2\,\text{kg}$, $mg \approx (0.2\,\text{kg})(9.8\,\text{m/s}^2) \approx 2\,\text{N}$. The radiation pressure on your hand is imperceptible compared to gravity.

[†]Very roughly, if we think of light as particles (and we do—see Chapter 37), the force that would be needed to bring such a particle moving at speed c to "rest" (i.e. absorption) is $F = \Delta p/\Delta t$. But F is also related to energy by Eq. 8–7, $F = \Delta U/\Delta x$, so $\Delta p = F\,\Delta t = \Delta U/(\Delta x/\Delta t) = \Delta U/c$ where we identify $(\Delta x/\Delta t)$ with the speed of light c.

EXAMPLE 31–8 ESTIMATE | **A solar sail.** Proposals have been made to use the radiation pressure from the Sun to help propel spacecraft around the solar system. (*a*) About how much force would be applied on a 1 km × 1 km highly reflective sail, and (*b*) by how much would this increase the speed of a 5000-kg spacecraft in one year? (*c*) If the spacecraft started from rest, about how far would it travel in a year?

APPROACH Pressure P is force per unit area, so $F = PA$. We use the estimate of Example 31–7, doubling it for a reflecting surface $P = 2\overline{S}/c$. We find the acceleration from Newton's second law, and assume it is constant, and then find the speed from $v = v_0 + at$. The distance traveled is given by $x = \frac{1}{2}at^2$.

SOLUTION (*a*) Doubling the result of Example 31–7, the solar pressure is $2\overline{S}/c = 6 \times 10^{-6}\,\text{N/m}^2$. Then the force is $F \approx PA = (6 \times 10^{-6}\,\text{N/m}^2)(10^6\,\text{m}^2) \approx 6\,\text{N}$. (*b*) The acceleration is $a \approx F/m \approx (6\,\text{N})/(5000\,\text{kg}) \approx 1.2 \times 10^{-3}\,\text{m/s}^2$. The speed increase is $v - v_0 = at = (1.2 \times 10^{-3}\,\text{m/s}^2)(365\,\text{days})(24\,\text{hr/day})(3600\,\text{s/hr}) \approx 4 \times 10^4\,\text{m/s}$ ($\approx 150{,}000\,\text{km/h}$!). (*c*) Starting from rest, this acceleration would result in a distance of about $\frac{1}{2}at^2 \approx 6 \times 10^{11}\,\text{m}$ in a year, about four times the Sun-Earth distance. The starting point should be far from the Earth so the Earth's gravitational force is small compared to 6 N.

NOTE A large sail providing a small force over a long time can result in a lot of motion.

Although you cannot directly feel the effects of radiation pressure, the phenomenon is quite dramatic when applied to atoms irradiated by a finely focused laser beam. An atom has a mass on the order of $10^{-27}\,\text{kg}$, and a laser beam can deliver energy at a rate of $1000\,\text{W/m}^2$. This is the same intensity used in Example 31–7, but here a radiation pressure of $10^{-6}\,\text{N/m}^2$ would be very significant on a molecule whose mass might be 10^{-23} to $10^{-26}\,\text{kg}$. It is possible to move atoms and molecules around by steering them with a laser beam, in a device called "optical tweezers." Optical tweezers have some remarkable applications. They are of great interest to biologists, especially since optical tweezers can manipulate live microorganisms, and components within a cell, without damaging them. Optical tweezers have been used to measure the elastic properties of DNA by pulling each end of the molecule with such a laser "tweezers."

PHYSICS APPLIED
Optical tweezers

31–10 Radio and Television; Wireless Communication

PHYSICS APPLIED
Wireless transmission

Electromagnetic waves offer the possibility of transmitting information over long distances. Among the first to realize this and put it into practice was Guglielmo Marconi (1874–1937) who, in the 1890s, invented and developed wireless communication. With it, messages could be sent at the speed of light without the use of wires. The first signals were merely long and short pulses that could be translated into words by a code, such as the "dots" and "dashes" of the Morse code: they were digital wireless, believe it or not. In 1895 Marconi sent wireless signals a kilometer or two in Italy. By 1901 he had sent test signals 3000 km across the ocean from Newfoundland, Canada, to Cornwall, England. In 1903 he sent the first practical commercial messages from Cape Cod, Massachusetts, to England: the London *Times* printed news items sent from its New York correspondent. 1903 was also the year of the first powered airplane flight by the Wright brothers. The hallmarks of the modern age—wireless communication and flight—date from the same year. Our modern world of wireless communication, including radio, television, cordless phones, cell phones, Bluetooth, wi-fi, and satellite communication, are simply modern applications of Marconi's pioneering work.

The next decade saw the development of vacuum tubes. Out of this early work radio and television were born. We now discuss briefly (1) how radio and TV signals are transmitted, and (2) how they are received at home.

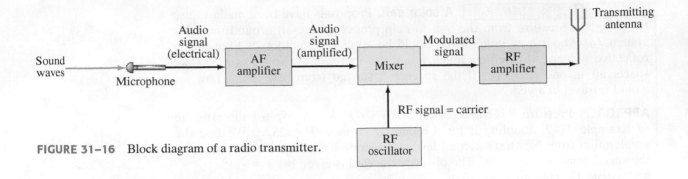

FIGURE 31–16 Block diagram of a radio transmitter.

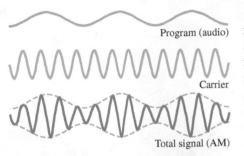

Program (audio)

Carrier

Total signal (AM)

FIGURE 31–17 In amplitude modulation (AM), the amplitude of the carrier signal is made to vary in proportion to the audio signal's amplitude.

FIGURE 31–18 In frequency modulation (FM), the frequency of the carrier signal is made to change in proportion to the audio signal's amplitude. This method is used by FM radio and television.

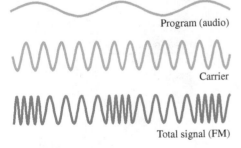

Program (audio)

Carrier

Total signal (FM)

The process by which a radio station transmits information (words and music) is outlined in Fig. 31–16. The audio (sound) information is changed into an electrical signal of the same frequencies by, say, a microphone or magnetic read/write head. This electrical signal is called an audiofrequency (AF) signal, since the frequencies are in the audio range (20 to 20,000 Hz). The signal is amplified electronically and is then mixed with a radio-frequency (RF) signal called its **carrier frequency**, which represents that station. AM radio stations have carrier frequencies from about 530 kHz to 1700 kHz. For example, "710 on your dial" means a station whose carrier frequency is 710 kHz. FM radio stations have much higher carrier frequencies, between 88 MHz and 108 MHz. The carrier frequencies for broadcast TV stations in the United States lie between 54 MHz and 72 MHz, between 76 MHz and 88 MHz, between 174 MHz and 216 MHz, and between 470 MHz and 698 MHz.

The mixing of the audio and carrier frequencies is done in two ways. In **amplitude modulation** (AM), the amplitude of the high-frequency carrier wave is made to vary in proportion to the amplitude of the audio signal, as shown in Fig. 31–17. It is called "amplitude modulation" because the *amplitude* of the carrier is altered ("modulate" means to change or alter). In **frequency modulation** (FM), the *frequency* of the carrier wave is made to change in proportion to the audio signal's amplitude, as shown in Fig. 31–18. The mixed signal is amplified further and sent to the transmitting antenna, where the complex mixture of frequencies is sent out in the form of EM waves. In digital communication, the signal is put into a digital form (Section 29–8) which modulates the carrier.

A television transmitter works in a similar way, using FM for audio and AM for video; both audio and video signals (see Section 23–9) are mixed with carrier frequencies.

Now let us look at the other end of the process, the reception of radio and TV programs at home. A simple radio receiver is diagrammed in Fig. 31–19. The EM waves sent out by all stations are received by the antenna. The signals the antenna detects and sends to the receiver are very small and contain frequencies from many different stations. The receiver selects out a particular RF frequency (actually a narrow range of frequencies) corresponding to a particular station using a resonant *LC* circuit (Sections 30–6 and 30–9).

FIGURE 31–19 Block diagram of a simple radio receiver.

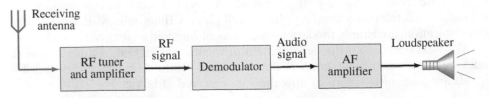

A simple way of tuning a station is shown in Fig. 31–20. A particular station is "tuned in" by adjusting C and/or L so that the resonant frequency of the circuit equals that of the station's carrier frequency. The signal, containing both audio and carrier frequencies, next goes to the *demodulator*, or *detector* (Fig. 31–19), where "demodulation" takes place—that is, the RF carrier frequency is separated from the audio signal. The audio signal is amplified and sent to a loudspeaker or headphones.

Modern receivers have more stages than those shown. Various means are used to increase the sensitivity and selectivity (ability to detect weak signals and distinguish them from other stations), and to minimize distortion of the original signal.[†]

A television receiver does similar things to both the audio and the video signals. The audio signal goes finally to the loudspeaker, and the video signal to the monitor, such as a *cathode ray tube* (CRT) or LCD screen (Sections 23–9 and 35–12).

One kind of antenna consists of one or more conducting rods; the electric field in the EM waves exerts a force on the electrons in the conductor, causing them to move back and forth at the frequencies of the waves (Fig. 31–21a). A second type of antenna consists of a tubular coil of wire which detects the magnetic field of the wave: the changing B field induces an emf in the coil (Fig. 31–21b).

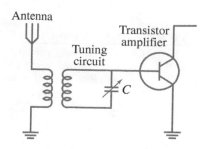

FIGURE 31–20 Simple tuning stage of a radio.

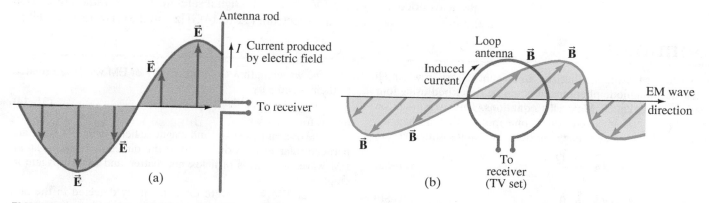

FIGURE 31–21 Antennas. (a) Electric field of EM wave produces a current in an antenna consisting of straight wire or rods. (b) Changing magnetic field induces an emf and current in a loop antenna.

A satellite dish (Fig. 31–22) consists of a parabolic reflector that focuses the EM waves onto a "horn," similar to a concave mirror telescope (Fig. 33–38).

FIGURE 31–22 A satellite dish.

EXAMPLE 31–9 **Tuning a station.** Calculate the transmitting wavelength of an FM radio station that transmits at 100 MHz.

APPROACH Radio is transmitted as an EM wave, so the speed is $c = 3.0 \times 10^8$ m/s. The wavelength is found from Eq. 31–14, $\lambda = c/f$.

SOLUTION The carrier frequency is $f = 100$ MHz $= 1.0 \times 10^8$ s^{-1}, so

$$\lambda = \frac{c}{f} = \frac{(3.0 \times 10^8 \text{ m/s})}{(1.0 \times 10^8 \text{ s}^{-1})} = 3.0 \text{ m}.$$

NOTE The wavelengths of other FM signals (88 MHz to 108 MHz) are close to the 3.0-m wavelength of this station. FM antennas are typically 1.5 m long, or about a half wavelength. This length is chosen so that the antenna reacts in a resonant fashion and thus is more sensitive to FM frequencies. AM radio antennas would have to be very long to be either $\frac{1}{2}\lambda$ or $\frac{1}{4}\lambda$.

[†]For *FM stereo broadcasting*, two signals are carried by the carrier wave. One signal contains frequencies up to about 15 kHz, which includes most audio frequencies. The other signal includes the same range of frequencies, but 19 kHz is added to it. A stereo receiver subtracts this 19,000-Hz signal and distributes the two signals to the left and right channels. The first signal consists of the sum of left and right channels (L + R), so mono radios detect all the sound. The second signal is the difference between left and right (L − R). Hence the receiver must add and subtract the two signals to get pure left and right signals for each channel.

Other EM Wave Communications

The various regions of the radio-wave spectrum are assigned by governmental agencies for various purposes. Besides those mentioned above, there are "bands" assigned for use by ships, airplanes, police, military, amateurs, satellites and space, and radar. Cell phones, for example, are complete radio transmitters and receivers. In the U.S., CDMA cell phones function on two different bands: 800 MHz and 1900 MHz (= 1.9 GHz). Europe, Asia, and much of the rest of the world use a different system: the international standard called GSM (Global System for Mobile Communication), on 900-MHz and 1800-MHz bands. The U.S. now also has the GSM option (at 850 MHz and 1.9 GHz), as does much of the rest of the Americas. A 700-MHz band is now being made available for cell phones (it used to carry TV broadcast channels 52–69, now no longer used). Radio-controlled toys (cars, sailboats, robotic animals, etc.) can use various frequencies from 27 MHz to 75 MHz. Automobile remote (keyless) entry may operate around 300 MHz or 400 MHz.

Cable TV channels are carried as electromagnetic waves along a coaxial cable (see Fig. 31–13) rather than being broadcast and received through the "air." The channels are in the same part of the EM spectrum, hundreds of MHz, but some are at frequencies not available for TV broadcast. Digital satellite TV and radio are carried in the microwave portion of the spectrum (12 to 14 GHz and 2.3 GHz, respectively).

Summary

James Clerk Maxwell synthesized an elegant theory in which all electric and magnetic phenomena could be described using four equations, now called **Maxwell's equations**. They are based on earlier ideas, but Maxwell added one more—that a changing electric field produces a magnetic field. Maxwell's equations are

$$\oint \vec{E} \cdot d\vec{A} = \frac{Q}{\epsilon_0} \tag{31–5a}$$

$$\oint \vec{B} \cdot d\vec{A} = 0 \tag{31–5b}$$

$$\oint \vec{E} \cdot d\vec{\ell} = -\frac{d\Phi_B}{dt} \tag{31–5c}$$

$$\oint \vec{B} \cdot d\vec{\ell} = \mu_0 I + \mu_0 \epsilon_0 \frac{d\Phi_E}{dt}. \tag{31–5d}$$

The first two are Gauss's laws for electricity and for magnetism; the other two are Faraday's law and Ampère's law (as extended by Maxwell), respectively.

Maxwell's theory predicted that transverse **electromagnetic (EM) waves** would be produced by accelerating electric charges, and these waves would propagate through space at the speed of light c, given by

$$c = \frac{1}{\sqrt{\epsilon_0 \mu_0}} = 3.00 \times 10^8 \, \text{m/s}. \tag{31–12}$$

The wavelength λ and frequency f of EM waves are related to their speed c by

$$c = \lambda f, \tag{31–14}$$

just as for other waves.

The oscillating electric and magnetic fields in an EM wave are perpendicular to each other and to the direction of propagation. EM waves are waves of fields, not matter, and can propagate in empty space.

After EM waves were experimentally detected in the late 1800s, the idea that light is an EM wave (although of much higher frequency than those detected directly) became generally accepted. The **electromagnetic spectrum** includes EM waves of a wide variety of wavelengths, from microwaves and radio waves to visible light to X-rays and gamma rays, all of which travel through space at a speed $c = 3.00 \times 10^8 \, \text{m/s}$.

The energy carried by EM waves can be described by the **Poynting vector**

$$\vec{S} = \frac{1}{\mu_0} \vec{E} \times \vec{B} \tag{31–18}$$

which gives the rate energy is carried across unit area per unit time when the electric and magnetic fields in an EM wave in free space are $\vec{E}$ and $\vec{B}$.

EM waves carry momentum and exert a **radiation pressure** proportional to the intensity S of the wave.

Questions

1. An electric field $\vec{E}$ points away from you, and its magnitude is increasing. Will the induced magnetic field be clockwise or counterclockwise? What if $\vec{E}$ points toward you and is decreasing?

2. What is the direction of the displacement current in Fig. 31–3? (*Note*: The capacitor is discharging.)

3. Why is it that the magnetic field of a displacement current in a capacitor is so much harder to detect than the magnetic field of a conduction current?

4. Are there any good reasons for calling the term $\mu_0 \epsilon_0 \, d\Phi_E/dt$ in Eq. 31–1 as being due to a "current"? Explain.

5. The electric field in an EM wave traveling north oscillates in an east–west plane. Describe the direction of the magnetic field vector in this wave.

6. Is sound an electromagnetic wave? If not, what kind of wave is it?

7. Can EM waves travel through a perfect vacuum? Can sound waves?

8. When you flip a light switch, does the overhead light go on immediately? Explain.

9. Are the wavelengths of radio and television signals longer or shorter than those detectable by the human eye?

10. What does the wavelength calculated in Example 31–2 tell you about the phase of a 60-Hz ac current that starts at a power plant as compared to its phase at a house 200 km away?

11. When you connect two loudspeakers to the output of a stereo amplifier, should you be sure the lead wires are equal in length so that there will not be a time lag between speakers? Explain.

12. In the electromagnetic spectrum, what type of EM wave would have a wavelength of 10^3 km; 1 km; 1 m; 1 cm; 1 mm; 1 μm?

13. Can radio waves have the same frequencies as sound waves (20 Hz–20,000 Hz)?

14. Discuss how cordless telephones make use of EM waves. What about cellular telephones?

15. Can two radio or TV stations broadcast on the same carrier frequency? Explain.

16. If a radio transmitter has a vertical antenna, should a receiver's antenna (rod type) be vertical or horizontal to obtain best reception?

17. The carrier frequencies of FM broadcasts are much higher than for AM broadcasts. On the basis of what you learned about diffraction in Chapter 15, explain why AM signals can be detected more readily than FM signals behind low hills or buildings.

18. A lost person may signal by flashing a flashlight on and off using Morse code. This is actually a modulated EM wave. Is it AM or FM? What is the frequency of the carrier, approximately?

Problems

31–1 $\vec{B}$ Produced by Changing $\vec{E}$

1. (I) Determine the rate at which the electric field changes between the round plates of a capacitor, 6.0 cm in diameter, if the plates are spaced 1.1 mm apart and the voltage across them is changing at a rate of 120 V/s.

2. (I) Calculate the displacement current I_D between the square plates, 5.8 cm on a side, of a capacitor if the electric field is changing at a rate of 2.0×10^6 V/m·s.

3. (II) At a given instant, a 2.8-A current flows in the wires connected to a parallel-plate capacitor. What is the rate at which the electric field is changing between the plates if the square plates are 1.60 cm on a side?

4. (II) A 1500-nF capacitor with circular parallel plates 2.0 cm in diameter is accumulating charge at the rate of 38.0 mC/s at some instant in time. What will be the induced magnetic field strength 10.0 cm radially outward from the center of the plates? What will be the value of the field strength after the capacitor is fully charged?

5. (II) Show that the displacement current through a parallel-plate capacitor can be written $I_D = C \, dV/dt$, where V is the voltage across the capacitor at any instant.

6. (II) Suppose an air-gap capacitor has circular plates of radius $R = 2.5$ cm and separation $d = 1.6$ mm. A 76.0-Hz emf, $\mathscr{E} = \mathscr{E}_0 \cos \omega t$, is applied to the capacitor. The maximum displacement current is 35 μA. Determine (a) the maximum conduction current I, (b) the value of $\mathscr{E}_0$, (c) the maximum value of $d\Phi_E/dt$ between the plates. Neglect fringing.

7. (III) Suppose that a circular parallel-plate capacitor has radius $R_0 = 3.0$ cm and plate separation $d = 5.0$ mm. A sinusoidal potential difference $V = V_0 \sin(2\pi ft)$ is applied across the plates, where $V_0 = 150$ V and $f = 60$ Hz. (a) In the region between the plates, show that the magnitude of the induced magnetic field is given by $B = B_0(R) \cos(2\pi ft)$, where R is the radial distance from the capacitor's central axis. (b) Determine the expression for the amplitude $B_0(R)$ of this time-dependent (sinusoidal) field when $R \le R_0$, and when $R > R_0$. (c) Plot $B_0(R)$ in tesla for the range $0 \le R \le 10$ cm.

31–5 EM Waves

8. (I) If the electric field in an EM wave has a peak magnitude of 0.57×10^{-4} V/m, what is the peak magnitude of the magnetic field strength?

9. (I) If the magnetic field in a traveling EM wave has a peak magnitude of 12.5 nT, what is the peak magnitude of the electric field?

10. (I) In an EM wave traveling west, the B field oscillates vertically and has a frequency of 80.0 kHz and an rms strength of 7.75×10^{-9} T. Determine the frequency and rms strength of the electric field. What is its direction?

11. (II) The electric field of a plane EM wave is given by $E_x = E_0 \cos(kz + \omega t)$, $E_y = E_z = 0$. Determine (a) the direction of propagation and (b) the magnitude and direction of $\vec{B}$.

12. (III) Consider two possible candidates $E(x, t)$ as solutions of the wave equation for an EM wave's electric field. Let A and α be constants. Show that (a) $E(x, t) = Ae^{-\alpha(x-vt)^2}$ satisfies the wave equation, and that (b) $E(x, t) = Ae^{-(\alpha x^2 - vt)}$ does not satisfy the wave equation.

31–6 Electromagnetic Spectrum

13. (I) What is the frequency of a microwave whose wavelength is 1.50 cm?

14. (I) (a) What is the wavelength of a 25.75×10^9 Hz radar signal? (b) What is the frequency of an X-ray with wavelength 0.12 nm?

15. (I) How long does it take light to reach us from the Sun, 1.50×10^8 km away?

16. (I) An EM wave has frequency 8.56×10^{14} Hz. What is its wavelength, and how would we classify it?

17. (I) Electromagnetic waves and sound waves can have the same frequency. (a) What is the wavelength of a 1.00-kHz electromagnetic wave? (b) What is the wavelength of a 1.00-kHz sound wave? (The speed of sound in air is 341 m/s.) (c) Can you hear a 1.00-kHz electromagnetic wave?

18. (II) Pulsed lasers used for science and medicine produce very brief bursts of electromagnetic energy. If the laser light wavelength is 1062 nm (Neodymium–YAG laser), and the pulse lasts for 38 picoseconds, how many wavelengths are found within the laser pulse? How brief would the pulse need to be to fit only one wavelength?

19. (II) How long would it take a message sent as radio waves from Earth to reach Mars (a) when nearest Earth, (b) when farthest from Earth?

20. (II) An electromagnetic wave has an electric field given by
$$\vec{E} = \hat{i}(225 \text{ V/m}) \sin[(0.077 \text{ m}^{-1})z - (2.3 \times 10^7 \text{ rad/s})t].$$
(a) What are the wavelength and frequency of the wave? (b) Write down an expression for the magnetic field.

31-7 Speed of Light

21. (II) What is the minimum angular speed at which Michelson's eight-sided mirror would have had to rotate to reflect light into an observer's eye by succeeding mirror faces (1/8 of a revolution, Fig. 31–14)?

31-8 EM Wave Energy; Poynting Vector

22. (I) The $\vec{E}$ field in an EM wave has a peak of 26.5 mV/m. What is the average rate at which this wave carries energy across unit area per unit time?

23. (II) The magnetic field in a traveling EM wave has an rms strength of 22.5 nT. How long does it take to deliver 335 J of energy to 1.00 cm^2 of a wall that it hits perpendicularly?

24. (II) How much energy is transported across a 1.00 cm^2 area per hour by an EM wave whose E field has an rms strength of 32.8 mV/m?

25. (II) A spherically spreading EM wave comes from a 1500-W source. At a distance of 5.0 m, what is the intensity, and what is the rms value of the electric field?

26. (II) If the amplitude of the B field of an EM wave is 2.5×10^{-7} T, (a) what is the amplitude of the E field? (b) What is the average power per unit area of the EM wave?

27. (II) What is the energy contained in a 1.00-m^3 volume near the Earth's surface due to radiant energy from the Sun? See Example 31–6.

28. (II) A 15.8-mW laser puts out a narrow beam 2.00 mm in diameter. What are the rms values of E and B in the beam?

29. (II) Estimate the average power output of the Sun, given that about 1350 W/m^2 reaches the upper atmosphere of the Earth.

30. (II) A high-energy pulsed laser emits a 1.0-ns-long pulse of average power 1.8×10^{11} W. The beam is 2.2×10^{-3} m in radius. Determine (a) the energy delivered in each pulse, and (b) the rms value of the electric field.

31. (II) How practical is solar power for various devices? Assume that on a sunny day, sunlight has an intensity of 1000 W/m^2 at the surface of Earth and that, when illuminated by that sunlight, a solar-cell panel can convert 10% of the sunlight's energy into electric power. For each device given below, calculate the area A of solar panel needed to power it. (a) A calculator consumes 50 mW. Find A in cm^2. Is A small enough so that the solar panel can be mounted directly on the calculator that it is powering? (b) A hair dryer consumes 1500 W. Find A in m^2. Assuming no other electronic devices are operating within a house at the same time, is A small enough so that the hair dryer can be powered by a solar panel mounted on the house's roof? (c) A car requires 20 hp for highway driving at constant velocity (this car would perform poorly in situations requiring acceleration). Find A in m^2. Is A small enough so that this solar panel can be mounted directly on the car and power it in "real time"?

32. (III) (a) Show that the Poynting vector $\vec{S}$ points radially inward toward the center of a circular parallel-plate capacitor when it is being charged as in Example 31–1. (b) Integrate $\vec{S}$ over the cylindrical boundary of the capacitor gap to show that the rate at which energy enters the capacitor is equal to the rate at which electrostatic energy is being stored in the electric field of the capacitor (Section 24–4). Ignore fringing of $\vec{E}$.

33. (III) The Arecibo radio telescope in Puerto Rico can detect a radio wave with an intensity as low as 1×10^{-23} W/m^2. As a "best-case" scenario for communication with extraterrestrials, consider the following: suppose an advanced civilization located at point A, a distance x away from Earth, is somehow able to harness the entire power output of a Sun-like star, converting that power completely into a radio-wave signal which is transmitted uniformly in all directions from A. (a) In order for Arecibo to detect this radio signal, what is the maximum value for x in light-years (1 ly $\approx 10^{16}$ m)? (b) How does this maximum value compare with the 100,000-ly size of our Milky Way galaxy? The intensity of sunlight at Earth's orbital distance from the Sun is 1350 W/m^2.

31-9 Radiation Pressure

34. (II) Estimate the radiation pressure due to a 75-W bulb at a distance of 8.0 cm from the center of the bulb. Estimate the force exerted on your fingertip if you place it at this point.

35. (II) Laser light can be focused (at best) to a spot with a radius r equal to its wavelength λ. Suppose that a 1.0-W beam of green laser light ($\lambda = 5 \times 10^{-7}$ m) is used to form such a spot and that a cylindrical particle of about that size (let the radius and height equal r) is illuminated by the laser as shown in Fig. 31–23. Estimate the acceleration of the particle, if its density equals that of water and it absorbs the radiation. [This order-of-magnitude calculation convinced researchers of the feasibility of "optical tweezers," p. 829.]

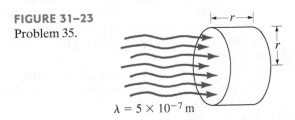

FIGURE 31–23
Problem 35.

$\lambda = 5 \times 10^{-7}$ m

36. (II) The powerful laser used in a laser light show provides a 3-mm diameter beam of green light with a power of 3 W. When a space-walking astronaut is outside the Space Shuttle, her colleague inside the Shuttle playfully aims such a laser beam at the astronaut's space suit. The masses of the suited astronaut and the Space Shuttle are 120 kg and 103,000 kg, respectively. (a) Assuming the suit is perfectly reflecting, determine the "radiation-pressure" force exerted on the astronaut by the laser beam. (b) Assuming the astronaut is separated from the Shuttle's center of mass by 20 m, model the Shuttle as a sphere in order to estimate the gravitation force it exerts on the astronaut. (c) Which of the two forces is larger, and by what factor?

37. (II) What size should the solar panel on a satellite orbiting Jupiter be if it is to collect the same amount of radiation from the Sun as a 1.0-m^2 solar panel on a satellite orbiting Earth?

38. (I) What is the range of wavelengths for (a) FM radio (88 MHz to 108 MHz) and (b) AM radio (535 kHz to 1700 kHz)?

39. (I) Estimate the wavelength for 1.9-GHz cell phone reception.

40. (I) The variable capacitor in the tuner of an AM radio has a capacitance of 2200 pF when the radio is tuned to a station at 550 kHz. What must the capacitance be for a station near the other end of the dial, 1610 kHz?

41. (II) A certain FM radio tuning circuit has a fixed capacitor $C = 620$ pF. Tuning is done by a variable inductance. What range of values must the inductance have to tune stations from 88 MHz to 108 MHz?

42. (II) A satellite beams microwave radiation with a power of 12 kW toward the Earth's surface, 550 km away. When the beam strikes Earth, its circular diameter is about 1500 m. Find the rms electric field strength of the beam at the surface of the Earth.

General Problems

43. A 1.60-m-long FM antenna is oriented parallel to the electric field of an EM wave. How large must the electric field be to produce a 1.00-mV (rms) voltage between the ends of the antenna? What is the rate of energy transport per square meter?

44. Who will hear the voice of a singer first: a person in the balcony 50.0 m away from the stage (see Fig. 31–24), or a person 1500 km away at home whose ear is next to the radio listening to a live broadcast? Roughly how much sooner? Assume the microphone is a few centimeters from the singer and the temperature is 20°C.

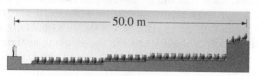

FIGURE 31–24 Problem 44.

45. Light is emitted from an ordinary lightbulb filament in wave-train bursts about 10^{-8} s in duration. What is the length in space of such wave trains?

46. Radio-controlled clocks throughout the United States receive a radio signal from a transmitter in Fort Collins, Colorado, that accurately (within a microsecond) marks the beginning of each minute. A slight delay, however, is introduced because this signal must travel from the transmitter to the clocks. Assuming Fort Collins is no more than 3000 km from any point in the U.S., what is the longest travel-time delay?

47. A radio voice signal from the *Apollo* crew on the Moon (Fig. 31–25) was beamed to a listening crowd from a radio speaker. If you were standing 25 m from the loudspeaker, what was the total time lag between when you heard the sound and when the sound entered a microphone on the Moon and traveled to Earth?

FIGURE 31–25
Problem 47.

48. Cosmic microwave background radiation fills all space with an average energy density of 4×10^{-14} J/m³. (a) Find the rms value of the electric field associated with this radiation. (b) How far from a 7.5-kW radio transmitter emitting uniformly in all directions would you find a comparable value?

49. What are E_0 and B_0 2.00 m from a 75-W light source? Assume the bulb emits radiation of a single frequency uniformly in all directions.

50. Estimate the rms electric field in the sunlight that hits Mars, knowing that the Earth receives about 1350 W/m² and that Mars is 1.52 times farther from the Sun (on average) than is the Earth.

51. At a given instant in time, a traveling EM wave is noted to have its maximum magnetic field pointing west and its maximum electric field pointing south. In which direction is the wave traveling? If the rate of energy flow is 560 W/m², what are the maximum values for the two fields?

52. How large an emf (rms) will be generated in an antenna that consists of a circular coil 2.2 cm in diameter having 320 turns of wire, when an EM wave of frequency 810 kHz transporting energy at an average rate of 1.0×10^{-4} W/m² passes through it? [*Hint*: you can use Eq. 29–4 for a generator, since it could be applied to an observer moving with the coil so that the magnetic field is oscillating with the frequency $f = \omega/2\pi$.]

53. The average intensity of a particular TV station's signal is 1.0×10^{-13} W/m² when it arrives at a 33-cm-diameter satellite TV antenna. (a) Calculate the total energy received by the antenna during 6.0 hours of viewing this station's programs. (b) What are the amplitudes of the E and B fields of the EM wave?

54. A radio station is allowed to broadcast at an average power not to exceed 25 kW. If an electric field amplitude of 0.020 V/m is considered to be acceptable for receiving the radio transmission, estimate how many kilometers away you might be able to hear this station.

55. A point source emits light energy uniformly in all directions at an average rate P_0 with a single frequency f. Show that the peak electric field in the wave is given by

$$E_0 = \sqrt{\frac{\mu_0 c P_0}{2\pi r^2}}.$$

56. Suppose a 35-kW radio station emits EM waves uniformly in all directions. (a) How much energy per second crosses a 1.0-m² area 1.0 km from the transmitting antenna? (b) What is the rms magnitude of the $\vec{\mathbf{E}}$ field at this point, assuming the station is operating at full power? What is the rms voltage induced in a 1.0-m-long vertical car antenna (c) 1.0 km away, (d) 50 km away?

57. What is the maximum power level of a radio station so as to avoid electrical breakdown of air at a distance of 0.50 m from the transmitting antenna? Assume the antenna is a point source. Air breaks down in an electric field of about 3×10^6 V/m.

58. In free space ("vacuum"), where the net charge and current flow is zero, the speed of an EM wave is given by $v = 1/\sqrt{\epsilon_0 \mu_0}$. If, instead, an EM wave travels in a nonconducting ("dielectric") material with dielectric constant K, then $v = 1/\sqrt{K\epsilon_0 \mu_0}$. For frequencies corresponding to the visible spectrum (near 5×10^{14} Hz), the dielectric constant of water is 1.77. Predict the speed of light in water and compare this value (as a percentage) with the speed of light in a vacuum.

59. The metal walls of a microwave oven form a cavity of dimensions 37 cm $\times$ 37 cm $\times$ 20 cm. When 2.45-GHz microwaves are continuously introduced into this cavity, reflection of incident waves from the walls set up standing waves with nodes at the walls. Along the 37-cm dimension of the oven, how many nodes exist (excluding the nodes at the wall) and what is the distance between adjacent nodes? [Because no heating occurs at these nodes, most microwaves rotate food while operating.]

60. Imagine that a steady current I flows in a straight cylindrical wire of radius R_0 and resistivity ρ. (a) If the current is then changed at a rate dI/dt, show that a displacement current I_D exists in the wire of magnitude $\epsilon_0 \rho (dI/dt)$. (b) If the current in a copper wire is changed at the rate of 1.0 A/ms, determine the magnitude of I_D. (c) Determine the magnitude of the magnetic field B_D (T) created by I_D at the surface of a copper wire with $R_0 = 1.0$ mm. Compare (as a ratio) B_D with the field created at the surface of the wire by a steady current of 1.0 A.

61. The electric field of an EM wave pulse traveling along the x axis in free space is given by $E_y = E_0 \exp[-\alpha^2 x^2 - \beta^2 t^2 + 2\alpha\beta xt]$, where E_0, α, and β are positive constants. (a) Is the pulse moving in the $+x$ or $-x$ direction? (b) Express β in terms of α and c (speed of light in free space). (c) Determine the expression for the magnetic field of this EM wave.

62. Suppose that a right-moving EM wave overlaps with a left-moving EM wave so that, in a certain region of space, the total electric field in the y direction and magnetic field in the z direction are given by $E_y = E_0 \sin(kx - \omega t) + E_0 \sin(kx + \omega t)$ and $B_z = B_0 \sin(kx - \omega t) - B_0 \sin(kx + \omega t)$. (a) Find the mathematical expression that represents the standing electric and magnetic waves in the y and z directions, respectively. (b) Determine the Poynting vector and find the x locations at which it is zero at all times.

63. The electric and magnetic fields of a certain EM wave in free space are given by $\vec{E} = E_0 \sin(kx - \omega t)\hat{j} + E_0 \cos(kx - \omega t)\hat{k}$ and $\vec{B} = B_0 \cos(kx - \omega t)\hat{j} - B_0 \sin(kx - \omega t)\hat{k}$. (a) Show that $\vec{E}$ and $\vec{B}$ are perpendicular to each other at all times. (b) For this wave, $\vec{E}$ and $\vec{B}$ are in a plane parallel to the yz plane. Show that the wave moves in a direction perpendicular to both $\vec{E}$ and $\vec{B}$. (c) At any arbitrary choice of position x and time t, show that the magnitudes of $\vec{E}$ and $\vec{B}$ always equal E_0 and B_0, respectively. (d) At $x = 0$, draw the orientation of $\vec{E}$ and $\vec{B}$ in the yz plane at $t = 0$. Then qualitatively describe the motion of these vectors in the yz plane as time increases. [Note: The EM wave in this Problem is "circularly polarized."]

Answers to Exercises

A: (c).

B: (b).

C: (a) 3.8×10^6 Hz; (b) 5.5×10^{18} Hz.

D: 45 cm.

E: Yes; the signal still travels 72,000 km.

F: Over 4 hours.

Mathematical Formulas

A–1 Quadratic Formula

If $\qquad ax^2 + bx + c = 0$

then $\qquad x = \dfrac{-b \pm \sqrt{b^2 - 4ac}}{2a}$

A–2 Binomial Expansion

$$(1 \pm x)^n = 1 \pm nx + \frac{n(n-1)}{2!}x^2 \pm \frac{n(n-1)(n-2)}{3!}x^3 + \cdots$$

$$(x + y)^n = x^n\left(1 + \frac{y}{x}\right)^n = x^n\left(1 + n\frac{y}{x} + \frac{n(n-1)}{2!}\frac{y^2}{x^2} + \cdots\right)$$

A–3 Other Expansions

$$e^x = 1 + x + \frac{x^2}{2!} + \frac{x^3}{3!} + \cdots$$

$$\ln(1 + x) = x - \frac{x^2}{2} + \frac{x^3}{3} - \frac{x^4}{4} + \cdots$$

$$\sin\theta = \theta - \frac{\theta^3}{3!} + \frac{\theta^5}{5!} - \cdots$$

$$\cos\theta = 1 - \frac{\theta^2}{2!} + \frac{\theta^4}{4!} - \cdots$$

$$\tan\theta = \theta + \frac{\theta^3}{3} + \frac{2}{15}\theta^5 + \cdots \qquad |\theta| < \frac{\pi}{2}$$

In general: $\quad f(x) = f(0) + \left(\dfrac{df}{dx}\right)_0 x + \left(\dfrac{d^2f}{dx^2}\right)_0 \dfrac{x^2}{2!} + \cdots$

A–4 Exponents

$$(a^n)(a^m) = a^{n+m}$$
$$(a^n)(b^n) = (ab)^n$$
$$(a^n)^m = a^{nm}$$

$$\frac{1}{a^n} = a^{-n}$$
$$a^n a^{-n} = a^0 = 1$$
$$a^{\frac{1}{2}} = \sqrt{a}$$

A–5 Areas and Volumes

Object	Surface area	Volume
Circle, radius r	πr^2	—
Sphere, radius r	$4\pi r^2$	$\frac{4}{3}\pi r^3$
Right circular cylinder, radius r, height h	$2\pi r^2 + 2\pi rh$	$\pi r^2 h$
Right circular cone, radius r, height h	$\pi r^2 + \pi r\sqrt{r^2 + h^2}$	$\frac{1}{3}\pi r^2 h$

A-6 Plane Geometry

1. *Equal angles:*

FIGURE A–1 If line a_1 is parallel to line a_2, then $\theta_1 = \theta_2$.

2. *Equal angles:*

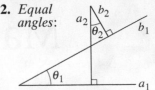

FIGURE A–2 If $a_1 \perp a_2$ and $b_1 \perp b_2$, then $\theta_1 = \theta_2$.

3. The sum of the angles in any plane triangle is 180°.

4. *Pythagorean theorem:*

In any right triangle (one angle = 90°) of sides $a, b,$ and c:

$$a^2 + b^2 = c^2$$

FIGURE A–3

where c is the length of the hypotenuse (opposite the 90° angle).

5. *Similar triangles:* Two triangles are said to be similar if all three of their angles are equal (in Fig. A–4, $\theta_1 = \phi_1, \theta_2 = \phi_2,$ and $\theta_3 = \phi_3$). Similar triangles can have different sizes and different orientations.

(*a*) Two triangles are similar if any two of their angles are equal. (This follows because the third angles must also be equal since the sum of the angles of a triangle is 180°.)

(*b*) The ratios of corresponding sides of two similar triangles are equal (Fig. A–4):

$$\frac{a_1}{b_1} = \frac{a_2}{b_2} = \frac{a_3}{b_3}.$$

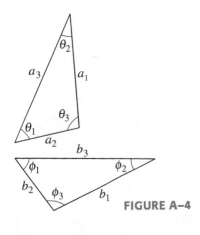

FIGURE A–4

6. *Congruent triangles:* Two triangles are congruent if one can be placed precisely on top of the other. That is, they are similar triangles and they have the same size. Two triangles are congruent if any of the following holds:

(*a*) The three corresponding sides are equal.

(*b*) Two sides and the enclosed angle are equal ("side-angle-side").

(*c*) Two angles and the enclosed side are equal ("angle-side-angle").

A-7 Logarithms

Logarithms are defined in the following way:

$$\text{if} \quad y = A^x, \quad \text{then} \quad x = \log_A y.$$

That is, the logarithm of a number y to the base A is that number which, as the exponent of A, gives back the number y. For **common logarithms**, the base is 10, so

$$\text{if} \quad y = 10^x, \quad \text{then} \quad x = \log y.$$

The subscript 10 on $\log_{10}$ is usually omitted when dealing with common logs. Another important base is the exponential base $e = 2.718\ldots$, a natural number. Such logarithms are called **natural logarithms** and are written ln. Thus,

$$\text{if} \quad y = e^x, \quad \text{then} \quad x = \ln y.$$

For any number y, the two types of logarithm are related by

$$\ln y = 2.3026 \log y.$$

Some simple rules for logarithms are as follows:

$$\log(ab) = \log a + \log b, \tag{i}$$

which is true because if $a = 10^n$ and $b = 10^m$, then $ab = 10^{n+m}$. From the definition of logarithm, $\log a = n$, $\log b = m$, and $\log(ab) = n + m$; hence, $\log(ab) = n + m = \log a + \log b$. In a similar way, we can show that

$$\log\left(\frac{a}{b}\right) = \log a - \log b \qquad \text{(ii)}$$

and

$$\log a^n = n \log a. \qquad \text{(iii)}$$

These three rules apply to any kind of logarithm.

If you do not have a calculator that calculates logs, you can easily use a **log table**, such as the small one shown here (Table A–1): the number N whose log we want is given to two digits. The first digit is in the vertical column to the left, the second digit is in the horizontal row across the top. For example, Table A–1 tells us that $\log 1.0 = 0.000$, $\log 1.1 = 0.041$, and $\log 4.1 = 0.613$. Table A–1 does not include the decimal point. The Table gives logs for numbers between 1.0 and 9.9. For larger or smaller numbers, we use rule (i) above, $\log(ab) = \log a + \log b$. For example, $\log(380) = \log(3.8 \times 10^2) = \log(3.8) + \log(10^2)$. From the Table, $\log 3.8 = 0.580$; and from rule (iii) above $\log(10^2) = 2\log(10) = 2$, since $\log(10) = 1$. [This follows from the definition of the logarithm: if $10 = 10^1$, then $1 = \log(10)$.] Thus,

$$\log(380) = \log(3.8) + \log(10^2)$$
$$= 0.580 + 2$$
$$= 2.580.$$

Similarly,

$$\log(0.081) = \log(8.1) + \log(10^{-2})$$
$$= 0.908 - 2 = -1.092.$$

The reverse process of finding the number N whose log is, say, 2.670, is called "taking the **antilogarithm**." To do so, we separate our number 2.670 into two parts, making the separation at the decimal point:

$$\log N = 2.670 = 2 + 0.670$$
$$= \log 10^2 + 0.670.$$

We now look at Table A–1 to see what number has its log equal to 0.670; none does, so we must **interpolate**: we see that $\log 4.6 = 0.663$ and $\log 4.7 = 0.672$. So the number we want is between 4.6 and 4.7, and closer to the latter by $\frac{7}{9}$. Approximately we can say that $\log 4.68 = 0.670$. Thus

$$\log N = 2 + 0.670$$
$$= \log(10^2) + \log(4.68) = \log(4.68 \times 10^2),$$

so $N = 4.68 \times 10^2 = 468$.

If the given logarithm is negative, say, -2.180, we proceed as follows:

$$\log N = -2.180 = -3 + 0.820$$
$$= \log 10^{-3} + \log 6.6 = \log 6.6 \times 10^{-3},$$

so $N = 6.6 \times 10^{-3}$. Notice that we added to our given logarithm the next largest integer (3 in this case) so that we have an integer, plus a decimal number between 0 and 1.0 whose antilogarithm can be looked up in the Table.

TABLE A–1 Short Table of Common Logarithms

N	0.0	0.1	0.2	0.3	0.4	0.5	0.6	0.7	0.8	0.9
1	000	041	079	114	146	176	204	230	255	279
2	301	322	342	362	380	398	415	431	447	462
3	477	491	505	519	531	544	556	568	580	591
4	602	613	623	633	643	653	663	672	681	690
5	699	708	716	724	732	740	748	756	763	771
6	778	785	792	799	806	813	820	826	833	839
7	845	851	857	863	869	875	881	886	892	898
8	903	908	914	919	924	929	935	940	944	949
9	954	959	964	968	973	978	982	987	991	996

A–8 Vectors

Vector addition is covered in Sections 3–2 to 3–5.
Vector multiplication is covered in Sections 3–3, 7–2, and 11–2.

A–9 Trigonometric Functions and Identities

The trigonometric functions are defined as follows (see Fig. A–5, o = side opposite, a = side adjacent, h = hypotenuse. Values are given in Table A–2):

$$\sin\theta = \frac{o}{h} \qquad\qquad \csc\theta = \frac{1}{\sin\theta} = \frac{h}{o}$$

$$\cos\theta = \frac{a}{h} \qquad\qquad \sec\theta = \frac{1}{\cos\theta} = \frac{h}{a}$$

$$\tan\theta = \frac{o}{a} = \frac{\sin\theta}{\cos\theta} \qquad \cot\theta = \frac{1}{\tan\theta} = \frac{a}{o}$$

and recall that

$$a^2 + o^2 = h^2 \qquad\qquad \text{[Pythagorean theorem].}$$

Figure A–6 shows the signs (+ or −) that cosine, sine, and tangent take on for angles θ in the four quadrants (0° to 360°). Note that angles are measured counterclockwise from the x axis as shown; negative angles are measured from *below* the x axis, clockwise: for example, −30° = +330°, and so on.

The following are some useful identities among the trigonometric functions:

$$\sin^2\theta + \cos^2\theta = 1$$

$$\sec^2\theta - \tan^2\theta = 1, \quad \csc^2\theta - \cot^2\theta = 1$$

$$\sin 2\theta = 2\sin\theta\cos\theta$$

$$\cos 2\theta = \cos^2\theta - \sin^2\theta = 2\cos^2\theta - 1 = 1 - 2\sin^2\theta$$

$$\tan 2\theta = \frac{2\tan\theta}{1 - \tan^2\theta}$$

$$\sin(A \pm B) = \sin A\cos B \pm \cos A\sin B$$

$$\cos(A \pm B) = \cos A\cos B \mp \sin A\sin B$$

$$\tan(A \pm B) = \frac{\tan A \pm \tan B}{1 \mp \tan A\tan B}$$

$$\sin(180° - \theta) = \sin\theta$$

$$\cos(180° - \theta) = -\cos\theta$$

$$\sin(90° - \theta) = \cos\theta$$

$$\cos(90° - \theta) = \sin\theta$$

$$\sin(-\theta) = -\sin\theta$$

$$\cos(-\theta) = \cos\theta$$

$$\tan(-\theta) = -\tan\theta$$

$$\sin\tfrac{1}{2}\theta = \sqrt{\frac{1 - \cos\theta}{2}}, \quad \cos\tfrac{1}{2}\theta = \sqrt{\frac{1 + \cos\theta}{2}}, \quad \tan\tfrac{1}{2}\theta = \sqrt{\frac{1 - \cos\theta}{1 + \cos\theta}}$$

$$\sin A \pm \sin B = 2\sin\left(\frac{A \pm B}{2}\right)\cos\left(\frac{A \mp B}{2}\right).$$

For any triangle (see Fig. A–7):

$$\frac{\sin\alpha}{a} = \frac{\sin\beta}{b} = \frac{\sin\gamma}{c} \qquad\qquad \text{[Law of sines]}$$

$$c^2 = a^2 + b^2 - 2ab\cos\gamma. \qquad\qquad \text{[Law of cosines]}$$

Values of sine, cosine, tangent are given in Table A–2.

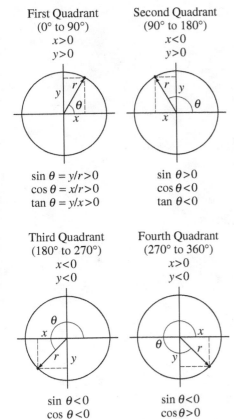

FIGURE A–5

FIGURE A–6

First Quadrant
(0° to 90°)
$x > 0$
$y > 0$

$\sin\theta = y/r > 0$
$\cos\theta = x/r > 0$
$\tan\theta = y/x > 0$

Second Quadrant
(90° to 180°)
$x < 0$
$y > 0$

$\sin\theta > 0$
$\cos\theta < 0$
$\tan\theta < 0$

Third Quadrant
(180° to 270°)
$x < 0$
$y < 0$

$\sin\theta < 0$
$\cos\theta < 0$
$\tan\theta > 0$

Fourth Quadrant
(270° to 360°)
$x > 0$
$y < 0$

$\sin\theta < 0$
$\cos\theta > 0$
$\tan\theta < 0$

FIGURE A–7

TABLE A–2 Trigonometric Table: Numerical Values of Sin, Cos, Tan

Angle in Degrees	Angle in Radians	Sine	Cosine	Tangent	Angle in Degrees	Angle in Radians	Sine	Cosine	Tangent
0°	0.000	0.000	1.000	0.000					
1°	0.017	0.017	1.000	0.017	46°	0.803	0.719	0.695	1.036
2°	0.035	0.035	0.999	0.035	47°	0.820	0.731	0.682	1.072
3°	0.052	0.052	0.999	0.052	48°	0.838	0.743	0.669	1.111
4°	0.070	0.070	0.998	0.070	49°	0.855	0.755	0.656	1.150
5°	0.087	0.087	0.996	0.087	50°	0.873	0.766	0.643	1.192
6°	0.105	0.105	0.995	0.105	51°	0.890	0.777	0.629	1.235
7°	0.122	0.122	0.993	0.123	52°	0.908	0.788	0.616	1.280
8°	0.140	0.139	0.990	0.141	53°	0.925	0.799	0.602	1.327
9°	0.157	0.156	0.988	0.158	54°	0.942	0.809	0.588	1.376
10°	0.175	0.174	0.985	0.176	55°	0.960	0.819	0.574	1.428
11°	0.192	0.191	0.982	0.194	56°	0.977	0.829	0.559	1.483
12°	0.209	0.208	0.978	0.213	57°	0.995	0.839	0.545	1.540
13°	0.227	0.225	0.974	0.231	58°	1.012	0.848	0.530	1.600
14°	0.244	0.242	0.970	0.249	59°	1.030	0.857	0.515	1.664
15°	0.262	0.259	0.966	0.268	60°	1.047	0.866	0.500	1.732
16°	0.279	0.276	0.961	0.287	61°	1.065	0.875	0.485	1.804
17°	0.297	0.292	0.956	0.306	62°	1.082	0.883	0.469	1.881
18°	0.314	0.309	0.951	0.325	63°	1.100	0.891	0.454	1.963
19°	0.332	0.326	0.946	0.344	64°	1.117	0.899	0.438	2.050
20°	0.349	0.342	0.940	0.364	65°	1.134	0.906	0.423	2.145
21°	0.367	0.358	0.934	0.384	66°	1.152	0.914	0.407	2.246
22°	0.384	0.375	0.927	0.404	67°	1.169	0.921	0.391	2.356
23°	0.401	0.391	0.921	0.424	68°	1.187	0.927	0.375	2.475
24°	0.419	0.407	0.914	0.445	69°	1.204	0.934	0.358	2.605
25°	0.436	0.423	0.906	0.466	70°	1.222	0.940	0.342	2.747
26°	0.454	0.438	0.899	0.488	71°	1.239	0.946	0.326	2.904
27°	0.471	0.454	0.891	0.510	72°	1.257	0.951	0.309	3.078
28°	0.489	0.469	0.883	0.532	73°	1.274	0.956	0.292	3.271
29°	0.506	0.485	0.875	0.554	74°	1.292	0.961	0.276	3.487
30°	0.524	0.500	0.866	0.577	75°	1.309	0.966	0.259	3.732
31°	0.541	0.515	0.857	0.601	76°	1.326	0.970	0.242	4.011
32°	0.559	0.530	0.848	0.625	77°	1.344	0.974	0.225	4.331
33°	0.576	0.545	0.839	0.649	78°	1.361	0.978	0.208	4.705
34°	0.593	0.559	0.829	0.675	79°	1.379	0.982	0.191	5.145
35°	0.611	0.574	0.819	0.700	80°	1.396	0.985	0.174	5.671
36°	0.628	0.588	0.809	0.727	81°	1.414	0.988	0.156	6.314
37°	0.646	0.602	0.799	0.754	82°	1.431	0.990	0.139	7.115
38°	0.663	0.616	0.788	0.781	83°	1.449	0.993	0.122	8.144
39°	0.681	0.629	0.777	0.810	84°	1.466	0.995	0.105	9.514
40°	0.698	0.643	0.766	0.839	85°	1.484	0.996	0.087	11.43
41°	0.716	0.656	0.755	0.869	86°	1.501	0.998	0.070	14.301
42°	0.733	0.669	0.743	0.900	87°	1.518	0.999	0.052	19.081
43°	0.750	0.682	0.731	0.933	88°	1.536	0.999	0.035	28.636
44°	0.768	0.695	0.719	0.966	89°	1.553	1.000	0.017	57.290
45°	0.785	0.707	0.707	1.000	90°	1.571	1.000	0.000	∞

Derivatives and Integrals

B–1 Derivatives: General Rules

(See also Section 2–3.)

$$\frac{dx}{dx} = 1$$

$$\frac{d}{dx}[af(x)] = a\frac{df}{dx} \quad [a = \text{constant}]$$

$$\frac{d}{dx}[f(x) + g(x)] = \frac{df}{dx} + \frac{dg}{dx}$$

$$\frac{d}{dx}[f(x)g(x)] = \frac{df}{dx}g + f\frac{dg}{dx}$$

$$\frac{d}{dx}[f(y)] = \frac{df}{dy}\frac{dy}{dx} \quad [\text{chain rule}]$$

$$\frac{dx}{dy} = \frac{1}{\left(\frac{dy}{dx}\right)} \quad \text{if } \frac{dy}{dx} \neq 0.$$

B–2 Derivatives: Particular Functions

$$\frac{da}{dx} = 0 \quad [a = \text{constant}]$$

$$\frac{d}{dx}x^n = nx^{n-1}$$

$$\frac{d}{dx}\sin ax = a\cos ax$$

$$\frac{d}{dx}\cos ax = -a\sin ax$$

$$\frac{d}{dx}\tan ax = a\sec^2 ax$$

$$\frac{d}{dx}\ln ax = \frac{1}{x}$$

$$\frac{d}{dx}e^{ax} = ae^{ax}$$

B–3 Indefinite Integrals: General Rules

(See also Section 7–3.)

$$\int dx = x$$

$$\int a f(x)\, dx = a\int f(x)\, dx \quad [a = \text{constant}]$$

$$\int [f(x) + g(x)]\, dx = \int f(x)\, dx + \int g(x)\, dx$$

$$\int u\, dv = uv - \int v\, du \quad [\text{integration by parts: see also B–6}]$$

B–4 Indefinite Integrals: Particular Functions

(An arbitrary constant can be added to the right side of each equation.)

$$\int a\,dx = ax \qquad [a = \text{constant}]$$

$$\int x^m\,dx = \frac{1}{m+1}x^{m+1} \qquad [m \neq -1]$$

$$\int \sin ax\,dx = -\frac{1}{a}\cos ax$$

$$\int \cos ax\,dx = \frac{1}{a}\sin ax$$

$$\int \tan ax\,dx = \frac{1}{a}\ln|\sec ax|$$

$$\int \frac{1}{x}\,dx = \ln x$$

$$\int e^{ax}\,dx = \frac{1}{a}e^{ax}$$

$$\int \frac{dx}{\sqrt{x^2 \pm a^2}} = \ln(x + \sqrt{x^2 \pm a^2})$$

$$\int \frac{dx}{\sqrt{a^2 - x^2}} = \sin^{-1}\left(\frac{x}{a}\right) = -\cos^{-1}\left(\frac{x}{a}\right) \qquad [\text{if } x^2 \leq a^2]$$

$$\int \frac{dx}{(x^2 \pm a^2)^{\frac{3}{2}}} = \frac{\pm x}{a^2\sqrt{x^2 \pm a^2}}$$

$$\int \frac{x\,dx}{(x^2 \pm a^2)^{\frac{3}{2}}} = \frac{-1}{\sqrt{x^2 \pm a^2}}$$

$$\int \sin^2 ax\,dx = \frac{x}{2} - \frac{\sin 2ax}{4a}$$

$$\int xe^{-ax}\,dx = -\frac{e^{-ax}}{a^2}(ax + 1)$$

$$\int x^2 e^{-ax}\,dx = -\frac{e^{-ax}}{a^3}(a^2x^2 + 2ax + 2)$$

$$\int \frac{dx}{x^2 + a^2} = \frac{1}{a}\tan^{-1}\frac{x}{a}$$

$$\int \frac{dx}{x^2 - a^2} = \frac{1}{2a}\ln\left(\frac{x - a}{x + a}\right) \qquad [x^2 > a^2]$$

$$= -\frac{1}{2a}\ln\left(\frac{a + x}{a - x}\right) \qquad [x^2 < a^2]$$

B–5 A Few Definite Integrals

$$\int_0^\infty x^n e^{-ax}\,dx = \frac{n!}{a^{n+1}}$$

$$\int_0^\infty e^{-ax^2}\,dx = \sqrt{\frac{\pi}{4a}}$$

$$\int_0^\infty xe^{-ax^2}\,dx = \frac{1}{2a}$$

$$\int_0^\infty x^2 e^{-ax^2}\,dx = \sqrt{\frac{\pi}{16a^3}}$$

$$\int_0^\infty x^3 e^{-ax^2}\,dx = \frac{1}{2a^2}$$

$$\int_0^\infty x^{2n} e^{-ax^2}\,dx = \frac{1\cdot 3\cdot 5\cdots(2n-1)}{2^{n+1}a^n}\sqrt{\frac{\pi}{a}}$$

B–6 Integration by Parts

Sometimes a difficult integral can be simplified by carefully choosing the functions u and v in the identity:

$$\int u\,dv = uv - \int v\,du. \qquad [\text{Integration by parts}]$$

This identity follows from the property of derivatives

$$\frac{d}{dx}(uv) = u\frac{dv}{dx} + v\frac{du}{dx}$$

or as differentials: $d(uv) = u\,dv + v\,du$.

For example $\int xe^{-x}\,dx$ can be integrated by choosing $u = x$ and $dv = e^{-x}\,dx$ in the "integration by parts" equation above:

$$\int xe^{-x}\,dx = (x)(-e^{-x}) + \int e^{-x}\,dx$$

$$= -xe^{-x} - e^{-x} = -(x + 1)e^{-x}.$$

More on Dimensional Analysis

An important use of dimensional analysis (Section 1–7) is to obtain the *form* of an equation: how one quantity depends on others. To take a concrete example, let us try to find an expression for the period T of a simple pendulum. First, we try to figure out what T could depend on, and make a list of these variables. It might depend on its length ℓ, on the mass m of the bob, on the angle of swing θ, and on the acceleration due to gravity, g. It might also depend on air resistance (we would use the viscosity of air), the gravitational pull of the Moon, and so on; but everyday experience suggests that the Earth's gravity is the major force involved, so we ignore the other possible forces. So let us assume that T is a function of ℓ, m, θ, and g, and that each of these factors is present to some power:

$$T = C\ell^w m^x \theta^y g^z.$$

C is a dimensionless constant, and w, x, y, and z are exponents we want to solve for. We now write down the dimensional equation (Section 1–7) for this relationship:

$$[T] = [L]^w [M]^x [L/T^2]^z.$$

Because θ has no dimensions (a radian is a length divided by a length—see Eq. 10–1a), it does not appear. We simplify and obtain

$$[T] = [L]^{w+z} [M]^x [T]^{-2z}$$

To have dimensional consistency, we must have

$$1 = -2z$$
$$0 = w + z$$
$$0 = x.$$

We solve these equations and find that $z = -\frac{1}{2}, w = \frac{1}{2}$, and $x = 0$. Thus our desired equation must be

$$T = C\sqrt{\ell/g}\, f(\theta), \tag{C–1}$$

where $f(\theta)$ is some function of θ that we cannot determine using this technique. Nor can we determine in this way the dimensionless constant C. (To obtain C and f, we would have to do an analysis such as that in Chapter 14 using Newton's laws, which reveals that $C = 2\pi$ and $f \approx 1$ for small θ). But look what we *have* found, using only dimensional consistency. We obtained the form of the expression that relates the period of a simple pendulum to the major variables of the situation, ℓ and g (see Eq. 14–12c), and saw that it does not depend on the mass m.

How did we do it? And how useful is this technique? Basically, we had to use our intuition as to which variables were important and which were not. This is not always easy, and often requires a lot of insight. As to usefulness, the final result in our example could have been obtained from Newton's laws, as in Chapter 14. But in many physical situations, such a derivation from other laws cannot be done. In those situations, dimensional analysis can be a powerful tool.

In the end, any expression derived by the use of dimensional analysis (or by any other means, for that matter) must be checked against experiment. For example, in our derivation of Eq. C–1, we can compare the periods of two pendulums of different lengths, ℓ_1 and ℓ_2, whose amplitudes (θ) are the same. For, using Eq. C–1, we would have

$$\frac{T_1}{T_2} = \frac{C\sqrt{\ell_1/g}\, f(\theta)}{C\sqrt{\ell_2/g}\, f(\theta)} = \sqrt{\frac{\ell_1}{\ell_2}}.$$

Because C and $f(\theta)$ are the same for both pendula, they cancel out, so we can experimentally determine if the ratio of the periods varies as the ratio of the square roots of the lengths. This comparison to experiment checks our derivation, at least in part; C and $f(\theta)$ could be determined by further experiments.

D Gravitational Force due to a Spherical Mass Distribution

In Chapter 6 we stated that the gravitational force exerted by or on a uniform sphere acts as if all the mass of the sphere were concentrated at its center, if the other object (exerting or feeling the force) is outside the sphere. In other words, the gravitational force that a uniform sphere exerts on a particle outside it is

$$F = G\frac{mM}{r^2},\qquad\qquad\text{[m outside sphere of mass M]}$$

where m is the mass of the particle, M the mass of the sphere, and r the distance of m from the center of the sphere. Now we will derive this result. We will use the concepts of infinitesimally small quantities and integration.

First we consider a very thin, uniform spherical shell (like a thin-walled basketball) of mass M whose thickness t is small compared to its radius R (Fig. D–1). The force on a particle of mass m at a distance r from the center of the shell can be calculated as the vector sum of the forces due to all the particles of the shell. We imagine the shell divided up into thin (infinitesimal) circular strips so that all points on a strip are equidistant from our particle m. One of these circular strips, labeled AB, is shown in Fig. D–1. It is $R\,d\theta$ wide, t thick, and has a radius $R\sin\theta$. The force on our particle m due to a tiny piece of the strip at point A is represented by the vector $\vec{F}_A$ shown. The force due to a tiny piece of the strip at point B, which is diametrically opposite A, is the force $\vec{F}_B$. We take the two pieces at A and B to be of equal mass, so $F_A = F_B$. The horizontal components of $\vec{F}_A$ and $\vec{F}_B$ are each equal to

$$F_A \cos\phi$$

and point toward the center of the shell. The vertical components of $\vec{F}_A$ and $\vec{F}_B$ are of equal magnitude and point in opposite directions, and so cancel. Since for every point on the strip there is a corresponding point diametrically opposite (as with A and B), we see that the net force due to the entire strip points toward the center of the shell. Its magnitude will be

$$dF = G\frac{m\,dM}{\ell^2}\cos\phi,$$

where dM is the mass of the entire circular strip and ℓ is the distance from all points on the strip to m, as shown. We write dM in terms of the density ρ; by density we mean the mass per unit volume (Section 13–2). Hence, $dM = \rho\,dV$, where dV is the volume of the strip and equals $(2\pi R\sin\theta)(t)(R\,d\theta)$. Then the force dF due to the circular strip shown is

$$dF = G\frac{m\rho 2\pi R^2 t\sin\theta\,d\theta}{\ell^2}\cos\phi. \qquad\qquad \textbf{(D–1)}$$

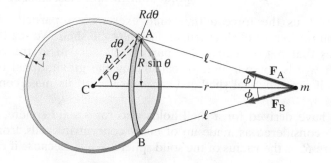

FIGURE D–1 Calculating the gravitational force on a particle of mass m due to a uniform spherical shell of radius R and mass M.

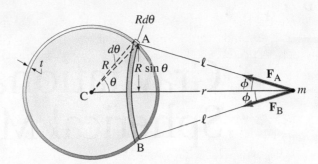

FIGURE D–1 (repeated)
Calculating the gravitational force
on a particle of mass m due to a
uniform spherical shell of radius R
and mass M.

To get the total force F that the entire shell exerts on the particle m, we must integrate over all the circular strips: that is, we integrate

$$dF = G \frac{m\rho 2\pi R^2 t \sin\theta \, d\theta}{\ell^2} \cos\phi \qquad \textbf{(D–1)}$$

from $\theta = 0°$ to $\theta = 180°$. But our expression for dF contains ℓ and ϕ, which are functions of θ. From Fig. D–1 we can see that

$$\ell \cos\phi = r - R\cos\theta.$$

Furthermore, we can write the law of cosines for triangle CmA:

$$\cos\theta = \frac{r^2 + R^2 - \ell^2}{2rR}. \qquad \textbf{(D–2)}$$

With these two expressions we can reduce our three variables (ℓ, θ, ϕ) to only one, which we take to be ℓ. We do two things with Eq. D–2: (1) We put it into the equation for $\ell \cos\phi$ above:

$$\cos\phi = \frac{1}{\ell}(r - R\cos\theta) = \frac{r^2 + \ell^2 - R^2}{2r\ell}.$$

and (2) we take the differential of both sides of Eq. D–2 (because $\sin\theta \, d\theta$ appears in the expression for dF, Eq. D–1), considering r and R to be constants when summing over the strips:

$$-\sin\theta \, d\theta = -\frac{2\ell \, d\ell}{2rR} \qquad \text{or} \qquad \sin\theta \, d\theta = \frac{\ell \, d\ell}{rR}.$$

We insert these into Eq. D–1 for dF and find

$$dF = Gm\rho\pi t \frac{R}{r^2}\left(1 + \frac{r^2 - R^2}{\ell^2}\right) d\ell.$$

Now we integrate to get the net force on our thin shell of radius R. To integrate over all the strips ($\theta = 0°$ to $180°$), we must go from $\ell = r - R$ to $\ell = r + R$ (see Fig. D–1). Thus,

$$F = Gm\rho\pi t \frac{R}{r^2}\left[\ell - \frac{r^2 - R^2}{\ell}\right]_{\ell=r-R}^{\ell=r+R}$$

$$= Gm\rho\pi t \frac{R}{r^2}(4R).$$

The volume V of the spherical shell is its area $(4\pi R^2)$ times the thickness t. Hence the mass $M = \rho V = \rho 4\pi R^2 t$, and finally

$$F = G \frac{mM}{r^2}. \qquad \left[\begin{array}{l}\text{particle of mass } m \text{ outside a} \\ \text{thin uniform spherical shell of mass } M\end{array}\right]$$

This result gives us the force a thin shell exerts on a particle of mass m a distance r from the center of the shell, and *outside* the shell. We see that the force is the same as that between m and a particle of mass M at the center of the shell. In other words, for purposes of calculating the gravitational force exerted on or by a uniform spherical shell, we can consider all its mass concentrated at its center.

What we have derived for a shell holds also for a solid sphere, since a solid sphere can be considered as made up of many concentric shells, from $R = 0$ to $R = R_0$, where R_0 is the radius of the solid sphere. Why? Because if each shell has mass dM, we write for each shell, $dF = Gm \, dM/r^2$, where r is the distance from the center C to mass m and is the same for all shells. Then the total force equals the sum or integral over dM, which gives the total mass M. Thus the result

$$F = G\frac{mM}{r^2} \qquad \begin{bmatrix} \text{particle of mass } m \text{ outside} \\ \text{solid sphere of mass } M \end{bmatrix} \quad \textbf{(D–3)}$$

is valid for a solid sphere of mass M even if the density varies with distance from the center. (It is not valid if the density varies within each shell—that is, depends not only on R.) Thus the gravitational force exerted on or by spherical objects, including nearly spherical objects like the Earth, Sun, and Moon, can be considered to act as if the objects were point particles.

This result, Eq. D–3, is true only if the mass m is outside the sphere. Let us next consider a point mass m that is located inside the spherical shell of Fig. D–1. Here, r would be less than R, and the integration over ℓ would be from $\ell = R - r$ to $\ell = R + r$, so

$$\left[\ell - \frac{r^2 - R^2}{\ell} \right]_{R-r}^{R+r} = 0.$$

Thus the force on any mass inside the shell would be zero. This result has particular importance for the electrostatic force, which is also an inverse square law. For the gravitational situation, we see that at points within a solid sphere, say 1000 km below the Earth's surface, only the mass up to that radius contributes to the net force. The outer shells beyond the point in question contribute zero net gravitational effect.

The results we have obtained here can also be reached using the gravitational analog of Gauss's law for electrostatics (Chapter 22).

Differential Form of Maxwell's Equations

Maxwell's equations can be written in another form that is often more convenient than Eqs. 31–5. This material is usually covered in more advanced courses, and is included here simply for completeness.

We quote here two theorems, without proof, that are derived in vector analysis textbooks. The first is called **Gauss's theorem** or the **divergence theorem**. It relates the integral over a surface of any vector function $\vec{F}$ to a volume integral over the volume enclosed by the surface:

$$\oint_{\text{Area } A} \vec{F} \cdot d\vec{A} = \int_{\text{Volume } V} \vec{\nabla} \cdot \vec{F} \, dV.$$

The operator $\vec{\nabla}$ is the **del operator**, defined in Cartesian coordinates as

$$\vec{\nabla} = \hat{\mathbf{i}} \frac{\partial}{\partial x} + \hat{\mathbf{j}} \frac{\partial}{\partial y} + \hat{\mathbf{k}} \frac{\partial}{\partial z}.$$

The quantity

$$\vec{\nabla} \cdot \vec{F} = \frac{\partial F_x}{\partial x} + \frac{\partial F_y}{\partial y} + \frac{\partial F_z}{\partial z}$$

is called the **divergence** of $\vec{F}$. The second theorem is **Stokes's theorem**, and relates a line integral around a closed path to a surface integral over any surface enclosed by that path:

$$\oint_{\text{Line}} \vec{F} \cdot d\vec{\ell} = \int_{\text{Area } A} \vec{\nabla} \times \vec{F} \cdot d\vec{A}.$$

The quantity $\vec{\nabla} \times \vec{F}$ is called the **curl** of $\vec{F}$. (See Section 11–2 on the vector product.)

We now use these two theorems to obtain the differential form of Maxwell's equations in free space. We apply Gauss's theorem to Eq. 31–5a (Gauss's law):

$$\oint_A \vec{E} \cdot d\vec{A} = \int \vec{\nabla} \cdot \vec{E} \, dV = \frac{Q}{\epsilon_0}.$$

Now the charge Q can be written as a volume integral over the charge density ρ: $Q = \int \rho \, dV$. Then

$$\int \vec{\nabla} \cdot \vec{E} \, dV = \frac{1}{\epsilon_0} \int \rho \, dV.$$

Both sides contain volume integrals over the same volume, and for this to be true over *any* volume, whatever its size or shape, the integrands must be equal:

$$\vec{\nabla} \cdot \vec{E} = \frac{\rho}{\epsilon_0}. \tag{E–1}$$

This is the differential form of Gauss's law. The second of Maxwell's equations, $\oint \vec{B} \cdot d\vec{A} = 0$, is treated in the same way, and we obtain

$$\vec{\nabla} \cdot \vec{B} = 0. \tag{E–2}$$

Next, we apply Stokes's theorem to the third of Maxwell's equations,

$$\oint \vec{\mathbf{E}} \cdot d\vec{\boldsymbol{\ell}} \;=\; \int \vec{\boldsymbol{\nabla}} \times \vec{\mathbf{E}} \cdot d\vec{\mathbf{A}} \;=\; -\frac{d\Phi_B}{dt}.$$

Since the magnetic flux $\Phi_B = \int \vec{\mathbf{B}} \cdot d\vec{\mathbf{A}}$, we have

$$\int \vec{\boldsymbol{\nabla}} \times \vec{\mathbf{E}} \cdot d\vec{\mathbf{A}} \;=\; -\frac{\partial}{\partial t} \int \vec{\mathbf{B}} \cdot d\vec{\mathbf{A}}$$

where we use the partial derivative, $\partial \vec{\mathbf{B}}/\partial t$, since B may also depend on position. These are surface integrals over the same area, and to be true over any area, even a very small one, we must have

$$\vec{\boldsymbol{\nabla}} \times \vec{\mathbf{E}} \;=\; -\frac{\partial \vec{\mathbf{B}}}{\partial t}. \qquad\qquad \textbf{(E–3)}$$

This is the third of Maxwell's equations in differential form. Finally, to the last of Maxwell's equations,

$$\oint \vec{\mathbf{B}} \cdot d\vec{\boldsymbol{\ell}} \;=\; \mu_0 I + \mu_0 \epsilon_0 \frac{d\Phi_E}{dt},$$

we apply Stokes's theorem and write $\Phi_E = \int \vec{\mathbf{E}} \cdot d\vec{\mathbf{A}}$:

$$\int \vec{\boldsymbol{\nabla}} \times \vec{\mathbf{B}} \cdot d\vec{\mathbf{A}} \;=\; \mu_0 I + \mu_0 \epsilon_0 \frac{\partial}{\partial t} \int \vec{\mathbf{E}} \cdot d\vec{\mathbf{A}}.$$

The conduction current I can be written in terms of the current density $\vec{\mathbf{j}}$, using Eq. 25–12:

$$I \;=\; \int \vec{\mathbf{j}} \cdot d\vec{\mathbf{A}}.$$

Then Maxwell's fourth equation becomes:

$$\int \vec{\boldsymbol{\nabla}} \times \vec{\mathbf{B}} \cdot d\vec{\mathbf{A}} \;=\; \mu_0 \int \vec{\mathbf{j}} \cdot d\vec{\mathbf{A}} + \mu_0 \epsilon_0 \frac{\partial}{\partial t} \int \vec{\mathbf{E}} \cdot d\vec{\mathbf{A}}.$$

For this to be true over any area A, whatever its size or shape, the integrands on each side of the equation must be equal:

$$\vec{\boldsymbol{\nabla}} \times \vec{\mathbf{B}} \;=\; \mu_0 \vec{\mathbf{j}} + \mu_0 \epsilon_0 \frac{\partial \vec{\mathbf{E}}}{\partial t}. \qquad\qquad \textbf{(E–4)}$$

Equations E–1, 2, 3, and 4 are Maxwell's equations in differential form for free space. They are summarized in Table E–1.

TABLE E–1 Maxwell's Equations in Free Space[†]

Integral form	Differential form
$\oint \vec{\mathbf{E}} \cdot d\vec{\mathbf{A}} = \dfrac{Q}{\epsilon_0}$	$\vec{\boldsymbol{\nabla}} \cdot \vec{\mathbf{E}} = \dfrac{\rho}{\epsilon_0}$
$\oint \vec{\mathbf{B}} \cdot d\vec{\mathbf{A}} = 0$	$\vec{\boldsymbol{\nabla}} \cdot \vec{\mathbf{B}} = 0$
$\oint \vec{\mathbf{E}} \cdot d\vec{\boldsymbol{\ell}} = -\dfrac{d\Phi_B}{dt}$	$\vec{\boldsymbol{\nabla}} \times \vec{\mathbf{E}} = -\dfrac{\partial \vec{\mathbf{B}}}{\partial t}$
$\oint \vec{\mathbf{B}} \cdot d\vec{\boldsymbol{\ell}} = \mu_0 I + \mu_0 \epsilon_0 \dfrac{d\Phi_E}{dt}$	$\vec{\boldsymbol{\nabla}} \times \vec{\mathbf{B}} = \mu_0 \vec{\mathbf{j}} + \mu_0 \epsilon_0 \dfrac{\partial \vec{\mathbf{E}}}{\partial t}$

[†] $\vec{\boldsymbol{\nabla}}$ stands for the *del operator* $\vec{\boldsymbol{\nabla}} = \hat{\mathbf{i}}\frac{\partial}{\partial x} + \hat{\mathbf{j}}\frac{\partial}{\partial y} + \hat{\mathbf{k}}\frac{\partial}{\partial z}$ in Cartesian coordinates.

F Selected Isotopes

(1) Atomic Number Z	(2) Element	(3) Symbol	(4) Mass Number A	(5) Atomic Mass[†]	(6) % Abundance (or Radioactive Decay[‡] Mode)	(7) Half-life (if radioactive)
0	(Neutron)	n	1	1.008665	β^-	10.23 min
1	Hydrogen	H	1	1.007825	99.9885%	
	Deuterium	d or D	2	2.014082	0.0115%	
	Tritium	t or T	3	3.016049	β^-	12.312 yr
2	Helium	He	3	3.016029	0.000137%	
			4	4.002603	99.999863%	
3	Lithium	Li	6	6.015123	7.59%	
			7	7.016005	92.41%	
4	Beryllium	Be	7	7.016930	EC, γ	53.22 days
			9	9.012182	100%	
5	Boron	B	10	10.012937	19.9%	
			11	11.009305	80.1%	
6	Carbon	C	11	11.011434	β^+, EC	20.370 min
			12	12.000000	98.93%	
			13	13.003355	1.07%	
			14	14.003242	β^-	5730 yr
7	Nitrogen	N	13	13.005739	β^+, EC	9.9670 min
			14	14.003074	99.632%	
			15	15.000109	0.368%	
8	Oxygen	O	15	15.003066	β^+, EC	122.5 min
			16	15.994915	99.757%	
			18	17.999161	0.205%	
9	Fluorine	F	19	18.998403	100%	
10	Neon	Ne	20	19.992440	90.48%	
			22	21.991385	9.25%	
11	Sodium	Na	22	21.994436	β^+, EC, γ	2.6027 yr
			23	22.989769	100%	
			24	23.990963	β^-, γ	14.9574 h
12	Magnesium	Mg	24	23.985042	78.99%	
13	Aluminum	Al	27	26.981539	100%	
14	Silicon	Si	28	27.976927	92.2297%	
			31	30.975363	β^-, γ	157.3 min
15	Phosphorus	P	31	30.973762	100%	
			32	31.973907	β^-	14.284 days

[†] The masses given in column (5) are those for the neutral atom, including the Z electrons.

[‡] Chapter 41; EC = electron capture.

(1) Atomic Number Z	(2) Element	(3) Symbol	(4) Mass Number A	(5) Atomic Mass	(6) % Abundance (or Radioactive Decay Mode)	(7) Half-life (if radioactive)
16	Sulfur	S	32	31.972071	94.9%	
			35	34.969032	β^-	87.32 days
17	Chlorine	Cl	35	34.968853	75.78%	
			37	36.965903	24.22%	
18	Argon	Ar	40	39.962383	99.600%	
19	Potassium	K	39	38.963707	93.258%	
			40	39.963998	0.0117%	
					β^-, EC, γ, β^+	1.265×10^9 yr
20	Calcium	Ca	40	39.962591	96.94%	
21	Scandium	Sc	45	44.955912	100%	
22	Titanium	Ti	48	47.947946	73.72%	
23	Vanadium	V	51	50.943960	99.750%	
24	Chromium	Cr	52	51.940508	83.789%	
25	Manganese	Mn	55	54.938045	100%	
26	Iron	Fe	56	55.934938	91.75%	
27	Cobalt	Co	59	58.933195	100%	
			60	59.933817	β^-, γ	5.2710 yr
28	Nickel	Ni	58	57.935343	68.077%	
			60	59.930786	26.223%	
29	Copper	Cu	63	62.929598	69.17%	
			65	64.927790	30.83%	
30	Zinc	Zn	64	63.929142	48.6%	
			66	65.926033	27.9%	
31	Gallium	Ga	69	68.925574	60.108%	
32	Germanium	Ge	72	71.922076	27.5%	
			74	73.921178	36.3%	
33	Arsenic	As	75	74.921596	100%	
34	Selenium	Se	80	79.916521	49.6%	
35	Bromine	Br	79	78.918337	50.69%	
36	Krypton	Kr	84	83.911507	57.00%	
37	Rubidium	Rb	85	84.911790	72.17%	
38	Strontium	Sr	86	85.909260	9.86%	
			88	87.905612	82.58%	
			90	89.907738	β^-	28.80 yr
39	Yttrium	Y	89	88.905848	100%	
40	Zirconium	Zr	90	89.904704	51.4%	
41	Niobium	Nb	93	92.906378	100%	
42	Molybdenum	Mo	98	97.905408	24.1%	
43	Technetium	Tc	98	97.907216	β^-, γ	4.2×10^6 yr
44	Ruthenium	Ru	102	101.904349	31.55%	
45	Rhodium	Rh	103	102.905504	100%	
46	Palladium	Pd	106	105.903486	27.33%	
47	Silver	Ag	107	106.905097	51.839%	
			109	108.904752	48.161%	
48	Cadmium	Cd	114	113.903359	28.7%	
49	Indium	In	115	114.903878	95.71%; β^-	4.41×10^{14} yr
50	Tin	Sn	120	119.902195	32.58%	
51	Antimony	Sb	121	120.903816	57.21%	

(1) Atomic Number Z	(2) Element	(3) Symbol	(4) Mass Number A	(5) Atomic Mass	(6) % Abundance (or Radioactive Decay Mode)	(7) Half-life (if radioactive)
52	Tellurium	Te	130	129.906224	34.1%; $\beta^-\beta^-$	$>9.7 \times 10^{22}$ yr
53	Iodine	I	127	126.904473	100%	
			131	130.906125	β^- , γ	8.0233 days
54	Xenon	Xe	132	131.904154	26.89%	
			136	135.907219	8.87%; $\beta^-\beta^-$	$>8.5 \times 10^{21}$ yr
55	Cesium	Cs	133	132.905452	100%	
56	Barium	Ba	137	136.905827	11.232%	
			138	137.905247	71.70%	
57	Lanthanum	La	139	138.906353	99.910%	
58	Cerium	Ce	140	139.905439	88.45%	
59	Praseodymium	Pr	141	140.907653	100%	
60	Neodymium	Nd	142	141.907723	27.2%	
61	Promethium	Pm	145	144.912749	EC, α	17.7 yr
62	Samarium	Sm	152	151.919732	26.75%	
63	Europium	Eu	153	152.921230	52.19%	
64	Gadolinium	Gd	158	157.924104	24.84%	
65	Terbium	Tb	159	158.925347	100%	
66	Dysprosium	Dy	164	163.929175	28.2%	
67	Holmium	Ho	165	164.930322	100%	
68	Erbium	Er	166	165.930293	33.6%	
69	Thulium	Tm	169	168.934213	100%	
70	Ytterbium	Yb	174	173.938862	31.8%	
71	Lutetium	Lu	175	174.940772	97.41%	
72	Hafnium	Hf	180	179.946550	35.08%	
73	Tantalum	Ta	181	180.947996	99.988%	
74	Tungsten (wolfram)	W	184	183.950931	30.64%; α	$>8.9 \times 10^{21}$ yr
75	Rhenium	Re	187	186.955753	62.60%; β^-	4.35×10^{10} yr
76	Osmium	Os	191	190.960930	β^-, γ	15.4 days
			192	191.961481	40.78%	
77	Iridium	Ir	191	190.960594	37.3%	
			193	192.962926	62.7%	
78	Platinum	Pt	195	194.964791	33.832%	
79	Gold	Au	197	196.966569	100%	
80	Mercury	Hg	199	198.968280	16.87%	
			202	201.970643	29.9%	
81	Thallium	Tl	205	204.974428	70.476%	
82	Lead	Pb	206	205.974465	24.1%	
			207	206.975897	22.1%	
			208	207.976652	52.4%	
			210	209.984188	β^-, γ, α	22.23 yr
			211	210.988737	β^-, γ	36.1 min
			212	211.991898	β^-, γ	10.64 h
			214	213.999805	β^-, γ	26.8 min
83	Bismuth	Bi	209	208.980399	100%	
			211	210.987269	α, γ, β^-	2.14 min
84	Polonium	Po	210	209.982874	α, γ, EC	138.376 days
			214	213.995201	α, γ	162.3 μs
85	Astatine	At	218	218.008694	α, β^-	1.4 s

(1) Atomic Number Z	(2) Element	(3) Symbol	(4) Mass Number A	(5) Atomic Mass	(6) % Abundance (or Radioactive Decay Mode)	(7) Half-life (if radioactive)
86	Radon	Rn	222	222.017578	α, γ	3.8232 days
87	Francium	Fr	223	223.019736	β^-, γ, α	22.00 min
88	Radium	Ra	226	226.025410	α, γ	1600 yr
89	Actinium	Ac	227	227.027752	β^-, γ, α	21.772 yr
90	Thorium	Th	228	228.028741	α, γ	698.60 days
			232	232.038055	100%; α, γ	1.405×10^{10} yr
91	Protactinium	Pa	231	231.035884	α, γ	3.276×10^4 yr
92	Uranium	U	232	232.037156	α, γ	68.9 yr
			233	233.039635	α, γ	1.592×10^5 yr
			235	235.043930	0.720%; α, γ	7.04×10^8 yr
			236	236.045568	α, γ	2.342×10^7 yr
			238	238.050788	99.274%; α, γ	4.468×10^9 yr
			239	239.054293	β^-, γ	23.46 min
93	Neptunium	Np	237	237.048173	α, γ	2.144×10^6 yr
			239	239.052939	β^-, γ	2.356 days
94	Plutonium	Pu	239	239.052163	α, γ	24,100 yr
			244	244.064204	α	8.00×10^7 yr
95	Americium	Am	243	243.061381	α, γ	7370 yr
96	Curium	Cm	247	247.070354	α, γ	1.56×10^7 yr
97	Berkelium	Bk	247	247.070307	α, γ	1380 yr
98	Californium	Cf	251	251.079587	α, γ	898 yr
99	Einsteinium	Es	252	252.082980	α, EC, γ	471.7 days
100	Fermium	Fm	257	257.095105	α, γ	100.5 days
101	Mendelevium	Md	258	258.098431	α, γ	51.5 days
102	Nobelium	No	259	259.10103	α, EC	58 min
103	Lawrencium	Lr	262	262.10963	α, EC, fission	≈ 4 h
104	Rutherfordium	Rf	263	263.11255	fission	10 min
105	Dubnium	Db	262	262.11408	α, fission, EC	35 s
106	Seaborgium	Sg	266	266.12210	α, fission	≈ 21 s
107	Bohrium	Bh	264	264.12460	α	≈ 0.44 s
108	Hassium	Hs	269	269.13406	α	≈ 10 s
109	Meitnerium	Mt	268	268.13870	α	21 ms
110	Darmstadtium	Ds	271	271.14606	α	≈ 70 ms
111	Roentgenium	Rg	272	272.15360	α	3.8 ms
112		Uub	277	277.16394	α	≈ 0.7 ms

Preliminary evidence (unconfirmed) has been reported for elements 113, 114, 115, 116 and 118.

Answers to Odd-Numbered Problems

CHAPTER 13

1. 3×10^{11} kg.
3. 6.7×10^2 kg.
5. 0.8547.
7. (a) 5510 kg/m^3;
   (b) 5520 kg/m^3, 0.3%.
9. (a) 8.1×10^7 N/m^2;
   (b) 2×10^5 N/m^2.
11. 13 m.
13. 6990 kg.
15. (a) 2.8×10^7 N, 1.2×10^5 N/m^2;
    (b) 1.2×10^5 N/m^2.
17. 683 kg/m^3.
19. 3.35×10^4 N/m^2.
21. (a) 1.32×10^5 Pa;
    (b) 9.7×10^4 Pa.
23. (c) $0.38h$, no.
27. 2990 kg/m^3.
29. 920 kg.
31. Iron or steel.
33. 1.1×10^{-2} m^3.
35. 10.5%.
37. (b) Above.
39. 3600 balloons.
43. 2.8 m/s.
45. 1.0×10^1 m/s.
47. 1.8×10^5 N/m^2.
49. 1.2×10^5 N.
51. 9.7×10^4 Pa.
57. $\frac{1}{2}$.
59. (b) $h = \left[\sqrt{h_0} - t\sqrt{\dfrac{gA_1^2}{2(A_2^2 - A_1^2)}}\right]^2$
    (c) 92 s.
63. 7.9×10^{-2} Pa·s.
65. 6.9×10^3 Pa.
67. 0.10 m.
69. (a) Laminar;
    (b) turbulent.
71. 1.0 m.
73. 0.012 N.
75. 1.5 mm.
79. (a) 0.75 m;
    (b) 0.65 m;
    (c) 1.1 m.
81. 0.047 atm.
83. 0.24 N.
85. 1.0 m.

87. 5.3 km.
89. (a) 88 Pa/s;
    (b) 5.0×10^1 s.
91. 5×10^{18} kg.
93. (a) 8.5 m/s;
    (b) 0.24 L/s;
    (c) 0.85 m/s.
95. $d\left(\dfrac{v_0^2}{v_0^2 + 2gy}\right)^{\frac{1}{4}}$.
97. 170 m/s.
99. 1.2×10^4 N.
101. 4.9 s.

CHAPTER 17

1. $N_{Au} = 0.548 N_{Ag}$.
3. (a) 20°C;
   (b) 3500°F.
5. 102.9°F.
7. 0.08 m.
9. 1.6×10^{-6} m for Super Invar™,
   9.6×10^{-5} m for steel, steel is
   $60\times$ as much.
11. 981 kg/m^3.
13. −69°C.
15. 3.9 cm^3.
17. (a) 5.0×10^{-5}/C°;
    (b) copper.
21. (a) 2.7 cm;
    (b) 0.3 cm.
23. 55 min.
25. 3.0×10^7 N/m^2.
27. (a) 27°C;
    (b) 5500 N.
29. −459.67°F.
31. 1.35 m^3.
33. 1.25 kg/m^3.
35. 181°C.
37. (a) 22.8 m^3;
    (b) 1.88 atm.
39. 1660 atm.
41. 313°C.
43. 3.49 atm.

45. −130°C.
47. 7.0 min.
49. Ideal = 0.588 m^3,
    actual = 0.598 m^3 (nonideal
    behavior).
51. 2.69×10^{25} molecules/m^3.
53. 4×10^{-17} Pa.
55. 300 molecules/cm^3.
57. 19 molecules/breath.
59. (a) 71.2 torr;
    (b) 180°C.
61. 223 K.
63. (a) Low;
    (b) 0.025%.
65. 20%.
67. 9.9 L, not advisable.
69. (a) 1100 kg;
    (b) 100 kg.
71. (a) Lower;
    (b) 0.36%.
73. 1.1×10^{44} molecules.
75. 3.34 nm.
77. 13 h.
79. (a) 0.66×10^3 kg/m^3;
    (b) −3%.
81. ± 0.11 C°.
83. 3.6 m.
85. 3% increase.
87.

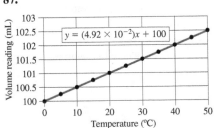

Slope of the line: 4.92×10^{-2} ml/°C,
relative β: 492×10^{-6}/°C,
β for the liquid: 501×10^{-6}/°C,
which liquid: glycerin.

CHAPTER 18

1. (a) 5.65×10^{-21} J;
   (b) 3.7×10^3 J.
3. 1.29.
5. 3.5×10^{-9} m/s.
7. (a) 4.5;
   (b) 5.2.
9. $\sqrt{3}$.
13. (b) 5.6%.
15. 1.004.
17. (a) 493 m/s;
    (b) 28 round trips/s.
19. Double the temperature.
21. (a) 710 m/s;
    (b) 240 K;
    (c) 650 m/s, 240 K, yes.
23. Vapor.
25. (a) Vapor;
    (b) solid.
27. 3600 Pa.
29. 355 torr or 4.73×10^4 Pa or 0.466 atm.
31. 92°C.
33. 1.99×10^5 Pa or 1.97 atm.
35. 70 g.
37. 16.6°C.
39. (a) Slope $= -5.00 \times 10^3$ K,
    y intercept $= 24.9$.
    Let $P_0 = 1$ Pa in this graph:

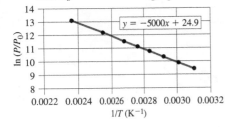

41. (a) 3.1×10^6 Pa;
    (b) 3.2×10^6 Pa.
43. (b) $a = 0.365$ N·m^4/mol^2,
    $b = 4.28 \times 10^{-5}$ m^3/mol.
45. (a) 0.10 Pa;
    (b) 3×10^7 Pa.
47. 2.1×10^{-7} m, stationary targets, effective radius of $r_{H_2} + r_{air}$.
49. (b) 4.7×10^7 s^{-1}.
51. $\frac{1}{40}$.
53. 3.5 h, convection is much more important than diffusion.
55. (b) 4×10^{-11} mol/s;
    (c) 0.6 s.
57. 260 m/s, 3.7×10^{-22} atm.
59. (a) 290 m/s;
    (b) 9.5 m/s.
61. 50 cm.
63. Kinetic energy $= 6.07 \times 10^{-21}$ J, potential energy $= 5.21 \times 10^{-25}$ J, yes, potential energy can be neglected.
65. 0.07%.
67. 1.5×10^5 K.
69. (a) 2800 Pa;
    (b) 650 Pa.
71. 2×10^{13} m.
73. 0.36 kg.
75. (b) 4.6×10^9 Hz, 2.3×10^5 times larger.
77. 0.21.

CHAPTER 19

1. 10.7°C.
3. (a) 1.0×10^7 J;
   (b) 2.9 kWh;
   (c) $0.29 per day, no.
5. 4.2×10^5 J, 1.0×10^2 kcal.
7. 6.0×10^6 J.
9. (a) 3.3×10^5 J;
   (b) 56 min.
11. 6.9 min.
13. 39.9°C.

15. 2.3×10^3 J/kg·C°.
17. 54 C°.
19. 0.31 kg.
21. (a) 5.1×10^5 J;
    (b) 1.5×10^5 J.
23. 4700 kcal.
25. 360 m/s.
27.

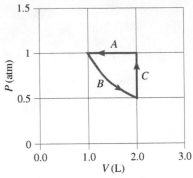

29. (a) 0;
    (b) −365 kJ.
31. (a) 480 J;
    (b) 0;
    (c) 480 J into gas.
33. (a) 4350 J;
    (b) 4350 J;
    (c) 0.
35. -4.0×10^2 K.
37. 236 J.
39. (a) 3.0×10^1 J;
    (b) 68 J;
    (c) −84 J;
    (d) −114 J;
    (e) −15 J.
41. $RT \ln \dfrac{(V_2 - b)}{(V_1 - b)} + a\left(\dfrac{1}{V_2} - \dfrac{1}{V_1}\right)$.
43. 43 C°.
45. 83.7 g/mol, krypton.
47. 48 C°.
49. (a) 6230 J;
    (b) 2490 J;
    (c) 8720 J.
51. 0.457 atm, −39°C.
53. (a) 404 K, 195 K;
    (b) -1.59×10^4 J;
    (c) 0;
    (d) -1.59×10^4 J.

55. (a)

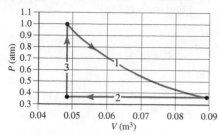

(b) 209 K;

(c) $Q_{1 \to 2} = 0$,
$\Delta E_{1 \to 2} = -2480$ J,
$W_{1 \to 2} = 2480$ J,
$Q_{2 \to 3} = -3740$ J,
$\Delta E_{2 \to 3} = -2240$ J,
$W_{2 \to 3} = -1490$ J,
$Q_{3 \to 1} = 4720$ J,
$\Delta E_{3 \to 1} = 4720$ J,
$W_{3 \to 1} = 0$;

(d) $Q_{cycle} = 990$ J,
$\Delta E_{cycle} = 0$,
$W_{cycle} = 990$ J.

57. (a) 5.0×10^1 W;

(b) 17 W.

59. 21 h.

61. (a) Ceramic: 14 W, shiny: 2.0 W;

(b) ceramic: 11 C°, shiny: 1.6 C°.

63. (a) 1.73×10^{17} W;

(b) 278 K or 5°C.

65. 28%.

67. (b) 4.8 C°/s;

(c) 0.60 C°/cm.

69. 6.4 Cal.

71. 4×10^{15} J.

73. 1 C°.

75. 3.6 kg.

77. 0.14 C°.

79. (a) 800 W;

(b) 5.3 g.

81. 1.1 days.

83. (a) 4.79 cm;

(b)

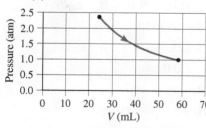

(c) $Q = 4.99$ J, $\Delta E = 0$, $W = 4.99$ J.

85. 110°C.

87. 305 J.

89. (a) 1.9×10^5 J;

(b) 4.4×10^5 J;

(c)

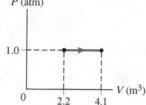

91. 2200 J.

CHAPTER 20

1. 0.25.

3. 0.16.

5. 0.21.

7. (b) 0.55.

9. 0.74.

13. 1.4×10^{13} J/h.

15. 1400 m.

17. 660°C.

19. (a) 4.1×10^5 Pa, 2.1×10^5 Pa;

(b) 34 L, 17 L;

(c) 2100 J;

(d) −1500 J;

(e) 600 J;

(f) 0.3.

21. 8.55.

23. 5.4.

25. (a) −4°C;

(b) 29%.

27. (a) 230 J;

(b) 390 J.

29. (a) 3.1×10^4 J;

(b) 2.7 min.

31. 91 L.

33. 0.20 J/K.

35. 5×10^4 J/K.

37. $5.49 \times 10^{-2} \dfrac{J/K}{s}$.

39. 9.3 J/K.

41. (a) 93 m J/K, yes;

(b) −93 m J/K, no; m in kg (SI).

43. (a) 1010 J/K;

(b) 1020 J/K;

(c) -9.0×10^2 J/K.

45. (a) Adiabatic;

(b) $\Delta S_{adiabatic} = 0$,
$\Delta S_{isothermal} = -nR \ln 2$;

(c) $\Delta S_{environment\ adiabatic} = 0$,
$\Delta S_{environment\ isothermal} = nR \ln 2$.

47. (a) All processes are reversible.

49. $\dfrac{T}{nC_V}$.

53. 2.1×10^5 J.

55. (a) $\frac{5}{16}$;

(b) $\frac{1}{64}$.

57. (a) 2.47×10^{-23} J/K;

(b) -9.2×10^{-22} J/K;

(c) these are many orders of magnitude smaller, due to the relatively small number of microstates for the coins.

59. (a) 1.79×10^6 kWh;

(b) 9.6×10^4 kW.

61. 12 MW.

63. (a) 0.41 mol;

(b) 396 K;

(c) 810 J;

(d) −700 J;

(e) 810 J;

(f) 0.13;

(g) 0.24.

65. (a) 110 kg/s;

(b) 9.3×10^7 gal/h.

67. (a) 18 km³/days;

(b) 120 km².

69. (a) 0.19;

(b) 0.23.

71. (a) 5.0 C°;

(b) 72.8 J/kg·K.

73. 1700 J/K.

75. 57 W or 0.076 hp.

77. $e_{Sterling} =$
$$\left(\frac{T_H - T_L}{T_H}\right)\left[\frac{\ln\left(\frac{V_b}{V_a}\right)}{\ln\left(\frac{V_b}{V_a}\right) + \frac{3}{2}\left(\frac{T_H - T_L}{T_H}\right)}\right],$$
$e_{Sterling} < e_{Carnot}$.

79. (a)

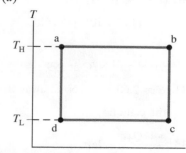

(b) W_{net}.

81. 16 kg.

83. 3.61×10^{-2} J/K.

1. 2.7×10^{-3} N.

3. 7200 N.

5. $(4.9 \times 10^{-14})\%$.

7. 4.88 cm.

9. -5.8×10^{8} C, 0.

11. (a) $q_1 = q_2 = \frac{1}{2}Q_T$;

(b) $q_1 = 0$, $q_2 = Q_T$.

13. $F_1 = 0.53$ N at 265°,

$F_2 = 0.33$ N at 112°,

$F_3 = 0.26$ N at 53°.

15. $F = 2.96 \times 10^{7}$ N, away from

center of square.

17. 1.0×10^{12} electrons.

19. (a) $\pi\sqrt{\dfrac{md^3}{kQq}}$;

(b) 0.2 ps.

21. 3.08×10^{-16} N west.

23. 1.10×10^{7} N/C up.

25. $(172\,\hat{\mathbf{j}})$ N/C.

27. 1.01×10^{14} m/s², opposite to the

field.

29.

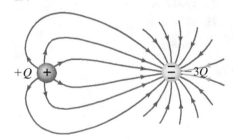

31. $(-4.7 \times 10^{11}\,\hat{\mathbf{i}})$ N/C

$- (1.6 \times 10^{11}\,\hat{\mathbf{j}})$ N/C;

or

5.0×10^{11} N/C at 199°.

33. $E = 2.60 \times 10^{4}$ N/C, away from

the center.

35. $\dfrac{4kQxa}{(x^2 - a^2)^2}$, left.

37. $\dfrac{\lambda}{2\pi\varepsilon_0}\sqrt{\dfrac{1}{x^2} + \dfrac{1}{y^2}}$, $\tan^{-1}\dfrac{x}{y}$.

39.

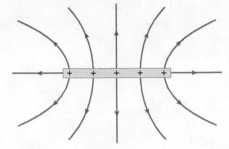

41. $\frac{1}{4}$.

43. (a) $\dfrac{Qy}{2\pi\varepsilon_0(y^2 + \ell^2)^{3/2}}$.

45. 1.8×10^{6} N/C, away from the wire.

47. $\dfrac{8\lambda\ell z}{\pi\varepsilon_0(\ell^2 + 4z^2)\sqrt{4z^2 + 2\ell^2}}$, vertical.

49. $-\dfrac{2\lambda\sin\theta_0}{4\pi\varepsilon_0 R}\,\hat{\mathbf{i}}$.

51. (a) $\dfrac{\lambda}{4\pi\varepsilon_0 x(x^2 + \ell^2)^{1/2}}$

$\times (\ell\hat{\mathbf{i}} + [x - (x^2 + \ell^2)^{1/2}]\hat{\mathbf{j}})$.

53. $\dfrac{Q}{4\pi\varepsilon_0 x(x + \ell)}$.

55. $\dfrac{Q(x\hat{\mathbf{i}} - \frac{2a}{\pi}\hat{\mathbf{j}})}{4\pi\varepsilon_0(x^2 + a^2)^{3/2}}$.

57. (a) $(-3.5 \times 10^{15}$ m/s²$)\,\hat{\mathbf{i}}$

$- (1.41 \times 10^{16}$ m/s²$)\,\hat{\mathbf{j}}$;

(b) 166° counterclockwise from the

initial direction.

59. $-23°$.

61. (b) $2\pi\sqrt{\dfrac{4\pi\varepsilon_0 mR^3}{qQ}}$.

63. (a) 3.4×10^{-20} C;

(b) no;

(c) 8.5×10^{-26} m·N;

(d) 2.5×10^{-26} J.

65. (a) θ very small;

(b) $\dfrac{1}{2\pi}\sqrt{\dfrac{pE}{I}}$.

67. (a) In the direction of the dipole.

69. 3.5×10^{9} C.

71. 6.8×10^{5} C, negative.

73. 1.0×10^{7} electrons.

75. 5.71×10^{13} C.

77. 1.6 m from Q_2, 3.6 m from Q_1.

79. $\dfrac{1.08 \times 10^{7}}{[3.00 - \cos(13.9t)]^2}$ N/C (upwards).

81. 5×10^{-9} C.

83. 8.0×10^{-9} C.

85. 18°.

87. $E_A = 3.4 \times 10^{4}$ N/C, to the right;

$E_B = 2.3 \times 10^{4}$ N/C, to the left;

$E_C = 5.6 \times 10^{3}$ N/C, to the right;

$E_D = 3.4 \times 10^{3}$ N/C, to the left.

89. -7.66×10^{-6} C, unstable.

91. (a) 9.18×10^{6} N/C, down;

(b) 1.63×10^{-4} C/m².

93. (a) $\dfrac{a}{\sqrt{2}} = 7.07$ cm;

(b) yes;

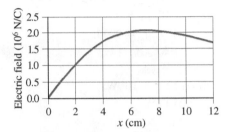

(c) and (d)

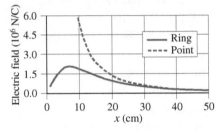

(e) 37 cm.

CHAPTER 22

1. (a) 31 N·m²/C;

(b) 22 N·m²/C;

(c) 0.

3. (a) 0;

(b) 0, 0, 0, 0, $E_0\ell^2$, $-E_0\ell^2$.

5. 1.63×10^{-8} C.

7. (a) -1.1×10^{5} N·m²/C;

(b) 0.

9. -8.3×10^{-7} C.

11. 4.3×10^{-5} C/m.

13. -8.52×10^{-11} C.

15. (a) -2.6×10^{4} N/C (toward wire);

(b) -8.6×10^{4} N/C (toward wire).

17. (a) $-(1.9 \times 10^{11}\,\text{N/C}\cdot\text{m})r$;

(b) $-(1.1 \times 10^8\,\text{N}\cdot\text{m}^2/\text{C})/r^2$
$+ (3.0 \times 10^{11}\,\text{N/C}\cdot\text{m})r$;

(c) $(4.1 \times 10^8\,\text{N}\cdot\text{m}^2/\text{C})/r^2$;

(d) yes.

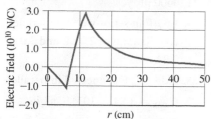

19.

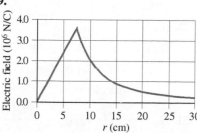

21. (a) $5.5 \times 10^7\,\text{N/C}$ (outward);

(b) 0;

(c) $5.5 \times 10^5\,\text{N/C}$ (outward).

23. (a) $-8.00\,\mu\text{C}$;

(b) $+1.90\,\mu\text{C}$.

25. (a) 0;

(b) $\dfrac{\sigma}{\varepsilon_0}$ (outward, if both plates are positive);

(c) same.

27. (a) 0;

(b) $\dfrac{r_1^2\sigma_1}{\varepsilon_0 r^2}$;

(c) $\dfrac{(r_1^2\sigma_1 + r_2^2\sigma_2)}{\varepsilon_0 r^2}$;

(d) $\sigma_1 = -\left(\dfrac{r_2}{r_1}\right)^2\sigma_2$;

(e) $\sigma_1 = 0$, or place $Q = -4\pi\sigma_1 r_1^2$ inside r_1.

29. (a) 0;

(b) $\dfrac{Q}{4\pi\varepsilon_0}\left(\dfrac{1}{r_0^3 - r_1^3}\right)\left(\dfrac{r^3 - r_1^3}{r^2}\right)$;

(c) $\dfrac{kQ}{r^2}$.

31. (a) $-q$;

(b) $Q + q$;

(c) $\dfrac{kq}{r^2}$;

(d) 0;

(e) $\dfrac{k(q + Q)}{r^2}$.

33. (a) $\dfrac{\sigma R_0}{\varepsilon_0 R}$, radially outward;

(b) 0;

(c) same for $R > R_0$ if $\lambda = 2\pi R_0\sigma$.

35. (a) 0;

(b) $\dfrac{1}{2\pi\varepsilon_0}\dfrac{(Q/\ell)}{r}$;

(c) 0;

(d) $\dfrac{e}{4\pi\varepsilon_0}\left(\dfrac{Q}{\ell}\right)$.

37. (a) $1.9 \times 10^7\,\text{m/s}$;

(b) $5.5 \times 10^5\,\text{m/s}$.

39. (a) $\dfrac{\rho_E r}{3\varepsilon_0}$;

(b) $\dfrac{\rho_E r_0^3}{3\varepsilon_0 r^2}$;

(c) 0;

(d) $\left(\dfrac{\rho_E r_0^3}{3\varepsilon_0} + \dfrac{Q}{4\pi\varepsilon_0}\right)\dfrac{1}{r^2}$.

41. (a) 0;

(b) $\dfrac{Q}{2500\pi\varepsilon_0 R_0^2}$.

43. (a) $\dfrac{\rho_E d}{2\varepsilon_0}$ away from surface.

45. (a) 13 N (attractive);

(b) 0.064 J.

47. (a) 0;

(b) $-\dfrac{\rho_0(d - x)}{\varepsilon_0}\hat{\mathbf{i}}$;

(c) $-\dfrac{\rho_0(d + x)}{\varepsilon_0}\hat{\mathbf{i}}$.

49. $\dfrac{Q}{4\pi\varepsilon_0}\dfrac{r^2}{r_0^4}$, radially outward.

51. $\Phi = \oint \vec{\mathbf{g}}\cdot d\vec{\mathbf{A}} = -4\pi G M_{\text{enc}}$.

53. $a\ell^3\varepsilon_0$.

55. $475\,\text{N}\cdot\text{m}^2/\text{C}$, $475\,\text{N}\cdot\text{m}^2/\text{C}$.

57. (a) 0;

(b) $E_{\max} = \dfrac{Q}{\pi\varepsilon_0 r_0^2}$, $E_{\min} = \dfrac{Q}{25\pi\varepsilon_0 r_0^2}$;

(c) no;

(d) no.

59. (a) $1.1 \times 10^{-19}\,\text{C}$;

(b) $3.5 \times 10^{11}\,\text{N/C}$.

61. (a) $\dfrac{\rho_E r_0}{6\varepsilon_0}$, right;

(b) $\dfrac{17}{54}\dfrac{\rho_E r_0}{\varepsilon_0}$, left.

63. (a) 0;

(b) $5.65 \times 10^5\,\text{N/C}$, right;

(c) $5.65 \times 10^5\,\text{N/C}$, right;

(d) $-5.00 \times 10^{-6}\,\text{C/m}^3$;

(e) $+5.00 \times 10^{-6}\,\text{C/m}^3$.

65. (a) On inside surface of shell.

(b) $r < 0.10\,\text{m}$,

$E = \left(\dfrac{2.7 \times 10^4}{r^2}\right)\text{N/C}$;

$r > 0.10\,\text{m}$, $E = 0$.

67. $-46\,\text{N}\cdot\text{m}^2/\text{C}$, $-4.0 \times 10^{-10}\,\text{C}$.

CHAPTER 23

1. $-0.71\,\text{V}$.

3. 3280 V, plate B has a higher potential.

5. 30 m.

7. $1.4\,\mu\text{C}$.

9. 1.2 cm, 46 nC.

11. (a) 0;

(b) $-29.4\,\text{V}$;

(c) $-29.4\,\text{V}$.

13. (a) $-9.6 \times 10^8\,\text{V}$;

(b) $9.6 \times 10^8\,\text{V}$.

15. (a) They are equal;

(b) $Q\left(\dfrac{r_2}{r_1 + r_2}\right)$.

17. (a) 10–20 kV;

(b) $30\,\mu\text{C/m}^2$.

19. (a) $\dfrac{Q}{4\pi\varepsilon_0 r}$;

(b) $\dfrac{Q}{8\pi\varepsilon_0 r_0}\left(3 - \dfrac{r^2}{r_0^2}\right)$;

(c) Let $V_0 = V$ at $r = r_0$, and $E_0 = E$ at $r = r_0$:

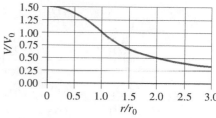

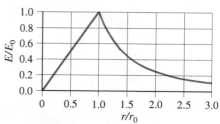

21. $\dfrac{\rho_0}{\varepsilon_0}\left(\dfrac{r_0^2}{4} - \dfrac{r^2}{6} + \dfrac{r^4}{20 r_0^2}\right)$.

23. (a) $\dfrac{R_0\sigma}{\varepsilon_0}\ln\left(\dfrac{R_0}{R}\right) + V_0$;

(b) V_0;

(c) no, from part (a) $V \to -\infty$ due to length of wire.

25. (a) 29 V;

(b) $-4.6 \times 10^{-18}\,\text{J}$.

27. 0.34 J.

29. 4.2 MV.

31. 9.64×10^5 m/s.

33. (a) 0;

   (b) $E_x = 0$,

$$E_y = \frac{Q}{4\pi\varepsilon_0} \frac{R}{(x^2 + R^2)^{3/2}},\ \text{looks}$$

   like a dipole.

35. $\frac{\sigma}{2\varepsilon_0}\left(\sqrt{R_2^2 + x^2} - \sqrt{R_1^2 + x^2}\right)$.

37. 29 m/s.

39. $\frac{Q}{8\pi\varepsilon_0 \ell} \ln\left(\frac{x + \ell}{x - \ell}\right)$.

41. $\frac{a}{6\varepsilon_0}\left(R^2 - 2x^2\right)\sqrt{R^2 + x^2} + \frac{a|x|^3}{3\varepsilon_0}$.

43. 2 mm.

45. (a) 2.6 mV;

   (b) 1.8 mV;

   (c) −1.8 mV.

49. -7.1×10^{-11} C/m^2 on $x = 0$ plate, 7.1×10^{-11} C/m^2 on other plate.

51. $(-2.5y + 3.5yz)\hat{\mathbf{i}}$
   $+ (-2y - 2.5x + 3.5xz)\hat{\mathbf{j}}$
   $+ (3.5xy)\hat{\mathbf{k}}$.

53. (a) $\frac{Q}{4\pi\varepsilon_0}\left(\frac{1}{y\sqrt{\ell^2 + y^2}}\right)\hat{\mathbf{j}}$;

   (b) $\frac{Q}{4\pi\varepsilon_0}\left(\frac{1}{x^2 - \ell^2}\right)\hat{\mathbf{i}}$.

55. −62.5 kV.

57. 1.3 eV.

59. (a) $\frac{1}{4\pi\varepsilon_0}\left(\frac{Q_1Q_2}{r_{12}} + \frac{Q_1Q_3}{r_{13}} + \frac{Q_1Q_4}{r_{14}}\right.$

$$\left. + \frac{Q_2Q_3}{r_{23}} + \frac{Q_2Q_4}{r_{24}} + \frac{Q_3Q_4}{r_{34}}\right);$$

   (b) $\frac{1}{4\pi\varepsilon_0}\left(\frac{Q_1Q_2}{r_{12}} + \frac{Q_1Q_3}{r_{13}} + \frac{Q_1Q_4}{r_{14}}\right.$

$$+ \frac{Q_1Q_5}{r_{15}} + \frac{Q_2Q_3}{r_{23}} + \frac{Q_2Q_4}{r_{24}}$$

$$+ \frac{Q_2Q_5}{r_{25}} + \frac{Q_3Q_4}{r_{34}} + \frac{Q_3Q_5}{r_{35}}$$

$$\left. + \frac{Q_4Q_5}{r_{45}}\right).$$

61. (a) 1.33 keV;

   (b) $v_e/v_p = 42.8$.

63. 250 MeV, same order of magnitude as observed values.

65. 1.11×10^5 m/s, 3.5×10^5 m/s.

67. 0.26 MV/m.

69. 600 V.

71. 1.5 J.

73. Yes, 2.0 pV.

75. 1.03×10^6 m/s.

77. $-\frac{\sqrt{3}Q}{2\pi\varepsilon_0 \ell}, \frac{Q}{\pi\varepsilon_0 \ell}\left(\frac{\sqrt{3}}{6} - 2\right)$,

$$-\frac{Q}{\pi\varepsilon_0 \ell}\left(1 + \frac{\sqrt{3}}{6}\right).$$

79. (a) 1.2 MV;

   (b) 1.8 kg.

81. (a) $\frac{\rho_E(r_2^3 - r_1^3)}{3\varepsilon_0 r}$;

   (b) $\frac{\rho_E}{\varepsilon_0}\left(\frac{r_2^2}{2} - \frac{r^2}{6} - \frac{r_1^3}{3r}\right)$;

   (c) $\frac{\rho_E}{2\varepsilon_0}(r_2^2 - r_1^2)$; yes.

83. $\vec{\mathbf{E}} = \frac{\lambda}{2\pi\varepsilon_0 R}$, radially outward.

85. (a) 23 kV;

   (b) $\frac{4Bx\hat{\mathbf{i}}}{(x^2 + R^2)^3}$;

   (c) $(2.3 \times 10^5\,\text{N/C})\hat{\mathbf{i}}$.

87. (a) and (b):

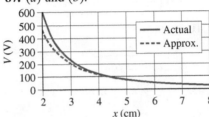

89. (a) Point charge;

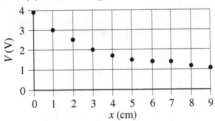

   (b) 1.5×10^{-11} C;

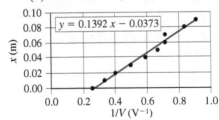

   (c) $x = -3.7$ cm.

CHAPTER 24

1. 3.0 μF.

3. 3.1 pF.

5. 56 μF.

7. 1.1 C.

9. 83 days.

11. 130 m^2.

13. 7.10×10^{-4} F.

15. 18 nC.

17. 5.8×10^4 V/m.

19. (a) $0.22\,\mu\text{m} \le x \le 220\,\mu\text{m}$;

   (b) $\frac{x^2 \Delta C}{\varepsilon_0 A}$;

   (c) 0.01%, 10%.

21. 3600 pF, yes.

23. 1.5 μF in series with the parallel combination of 2.0 μF and 3.0 μF, 2.8 V.

25. Add 11 μF connected in parallel.

27. $C_{max} = 1.94 \times 10^{-8}$ F, all in parallel, $C_{min} = 1.8 \times 10^{-9}$ F, all in series.

29. (a) $\frac{3}{5}C$;

   (b) $Q_1 = Q_2 = \frac{1}{5}CV, Q_3 = \frac{2}{5}CV$,

$$Q_4 = \frac{3}{5}CV, V_1 = V_2 = \frac{1}{5}V,$$

$$V_3 = \frac{2}{5}V, V_4 = \frac{3}{5}V.$$

31. $Q_1 = \frac{C_1C_2}{C_1 + C_2}V_0, Q_2 = \frac{C_2^2}{C_1 + C_2}V_0$.

33. (a) $Q_1 = 23\,\mu\text{C}, Q_2 = Q_4 = 46\,\mu\text{C}$;

   (b) $V_1 = V_2 = V_3 = V_4 = 2.9$ V;

   (c) 5.8 V.

35. 2.4 μF.

37. (a) $C_1 + \frac{C_2C_3}{C_2 + C_3}$;

   (b) $Q_1 = 8.40 \times 10^{-4}$ C,

$$Q_2 = Q_3 = 2.80 \times 10^{-4}\,\text{C}.$$

39. $C = \frac{\varepsilon_0 A}{d}\left(1 - \frac{\theta\sqrt{A}}{2d}\right)$.

41. 6.8×10^{-3} J.

43. 2.0×10^3 J.

45. 1.70×10^{-3} J.

47. (a) $\frac{U_f}{U_i} = \frac{\ln\left(\frac{3R_a}{R_b}\right)}{\ln\left(\frac{R_a}{R_b}\right)} > 1$,

   work done to enlarge cylinder;

   (b) $\frac{U_f}{U_i} = \frac{\ln\left(\frac{R_a}{R_b}\right)}{\ln\left(\frac{3R_a}{R_b}\right)} < 1$,

   charge moved to battery.

49. (a) $-\frac{\varepsilon_0 A\ell V_0^2}{2d(d - \ell)}$;

   (b) $\frac{\varepsilon_0 A\ell V_0^2}{2(d - \ell)^2}$.

53. 2200 batteries, no.

55. 1.1×10^{-4} J.

57. (a) $0.32 \, \mu\text{m}^2$;

    (b) 59 megabytes.

59. $\dfrac{\varepsilon_0 A}{2d}(K_1 + K_2)$.

61. $\dfrac{\varepsilon_0 A K_1 K_2}{(d_1 K_2 + d_2 K_1)}$.

63. (a) $\dfrac{\varepsilon_0 \ell^2}{d}\left[1 + (K-1)\dfrac{x}{\ell}\right]$;

    (b) $\dfrac{V_0^2 \varepsilon_0 \ell^2}{2d}\left[1 + (K-1)\dfrac{x}{\ell}\right]$;

    (c) $\dfrac{V_0^2 \varepsilon_0 \ell}{2d}(K-1)$, left.

67. $\dfrac{\varepsilon_0 A}{d - \ell + \dfrac{\ell}{K}}$.

69. $E_{\text{air}} = 2.69 \times 10^4 \, \text{V/m}$,

    $E_{\text{glass}} = 4.64 \times 10^3 \, \text{V/m}$,

    $Q_{\text{free}} = 0.345 \, \mu\text{C}$, $Q_{\text{ind}} = 0.286 \, \mu\text{C}$.

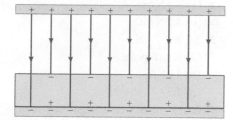

71. $43 \, \mu\text{F}$.

73. 15 V.

75. 840 V.

77. 3.76×10^{-9} F, $0.221 \, \text{m}^2$.

79. $\dfrac{1}{2K}$, work done by the electric

    field, $\dfrac{1}{K}$.

81. 1.2.

83. (a) 25 J;

    (b) 940 kW.

85. (a) Parallel;

    (b) 7.7 pF to 35 pF.

87. 5.15 pF.

89. $Q_1 = 11 \, \mu\text{C}$, $Q_2 = 13 \, \mu\text{C}$,

    $Q_3 = 13 \, \mu\text{C}$, $V_1 = 11 \, \text{V}$,

    $V_2 = 6.3 \, \text{V}$, $V_3 = 5.2 \, \text{V}$.

91. $\dfrac{Q^2 x}{2\varepsilon_0 A}$.

93. 9×10^{-16} m, no.

95. (a) $0.27 \, \mu\text{C}$, 15 kV/m, 5.9 nF,

    $6.0 \, \mu\text{J}$;

    (b) $0.85 \, \mu\text{C}$, 15 kV/m, 19 nF, $19 \, \mu\text{J}$.

97. (a) 32 nF;

    (b) $14 \, \mu\text{C}$;

    (c) 7.0 mm;

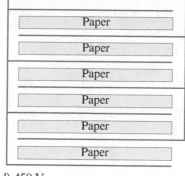

    (d) 450 V.

CHAPTER 25

1. 8.13×10^{18} electrons/s.

3. 5.5×10^{-11} A.

5. (a) 28 A;

    (b) 8.4×10^4 C.

7. 1.1×10^{21} electrons/min.

9. (a) $2.0 \times 10^1 \, \Omega$;

    (b) 430 J.

11. 0.47 mm.

13. 0.64.

15. (a) Slope $= 1/R$, y-intercept $= 0$;

    (b) yes, $R = 1.39 \, \Omega$;

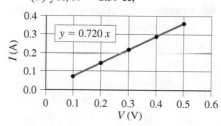

    (c) $1.0 \times 10^{-6} \, \Omega \cdot \text{m}$, nichrome.

17. At 1/5.0 of its length, $2.0 \, \Omega$, $8.0 \, \Omega$.

19. 2400°C.

21. $\sqrt{2}$.

23. 44.1°C.

25. One-quarter of the original.

27. $\dfrac{1}{4\pi\sigma}\left(\dfrac{1}{r_1} - \dfrac{1}{r_2}\right)$.

29. (a) $0.14 \, \Omega$;

    (b) 0.60 A;

    (c) $V_{\text{Al}} = 52 \, \text{mV}$, $V_{\text{Cu}} = 33 \, \text{mV}$.

31. 0.81 W.

33. 29 V.

35. (b) As large as possible.

37. (a) 0.83 A;

    (b) $140 \, \Omega$.

39. 0.055 kWh, 7.9 cents/month.

41. 0.90 kWh $= 3.2 \times 10^6$ J.

43. 24 lightbulbs.

45. 11 kW.

47. 0.15 kg/s $= 150$ mL/s.

49. 0.12 A.

51. (a) ∞;

    (b) $96 \, \Omega$.

53. (a) 930 V;

    (b) 3.9 A.

55. (a) 1.3 kW;

    (b) max $= 2.6$ kW, min $= 0$.

57. (a) 5.1×10^{-10} m/s;

    (b) $6.9 \, \text{A/m}^2$;

    (c) 1.2×10^{-7} V/m.

59. $2.5 \, \text{A/m}^2$, north.

61. 35 m/s, delay time from stimulus to action.

63. 11 hr.

65. 1.8 m, it would generate 540 W of heat and could start a fire.

67. 0.16 S.

69. (a) \$35/month;

    (b) 1300 kg/year.

71. (a) -19% change;

    (b) % change would be slightly less.

73. (a) $190 \, \Omega$;

    (b) $15 \, \Omega$.

75. (a) 1500 W;

    (b) 12 A.

77. 2:1.

79. (a) $21 \, \Omega$;

    (b) 2.0×10^1 s;

    (c) 0.17 cents.

81. 36.0 m, 0.248 mm.

83. (a) 1200 W;

    (b) 100 W.

85. 1.4×10^{12} protons.

87. (a) 3.1 kW;

    (b) 24 W;

    (c) 15 W;

    (d) 38 cents/month.

89. (a) \$55/kWh;

    (b) \$280/kWh, D-cells and AA-cells are $550\times$ and $2800\times$, respectively, more expensive.

91. $1.34 \times 10^{-4} \, \Omega$.

93. $\dfrac{4\ell\rho}{ab\pi}$.

95. $f = 1 - \dfrac{V}{V_0}$.

CHAPTER 26

1. (a) 5.93 V;
   (b) 5.99 V.

3. 0.060 Ω.

5. 9.3 V.

7. (a) 2.60 kΩ;
   (b) 270 Ω.

9. Connect nine 1.0-Ω resistors in series with battery; then connect output voltage circuit across four consecutive resistors.

11. 0.3 Ω.

13. 450 Ω, 0.024.

15. Solder a 1.6-kΩ resistor in parallel with 480-Ω resistor.

17. 120 Ω.

19. $\frac{13}{8} R$.

21. $R = r$.

23. (a) V_{left} decreases,
      V_{middle} increases,
      $V_{\text{right}} = 0$;
   (b) I_{left} decreases,
      I_{middle} increases,
      $I_{\text{right}} = 0$;
   (c) terminal voltage increases;
   (d) 8.5 V;
   (e) 8.6 V.

25. (a) V_1 and V_2 increase, V_3 and V_4 decrease;
   (b) I_1 and I_2 increase, I_3 and I_4 decrease;
   (c) increases;
   (d) before: $I_1 = 117\,\text{mA}$, $I_2 = 0$,
      $I_3 = I_4 = 59\,\text{mA}$;
      after: $I_1 = 132\,\text{mA}$,
      $I_2 = I_3 = I_4 = 44\,\text{mA}$, yes.

27. 0.38 A.

29. 0.

31. (a) 29 V;
   (b) 43 V, 73 V.

33. $I_1 = 0.68$ A left, $I_2 = 0.33$ A left.

37. 0.70 A.

39. 0.17 A.

41. (a) $\dfrac{R(5R' + 3R)}{8(R' + R)}$;
   (b) $\dfrac{R}{2}$.

43. 1–15 MΩ.

45. 5.0 ms.

47. 44 s.

49. (a) $I_1 = \dfrac{2\mathscr{E}}{3R}$, $I_2 = I_3 = \dfrac{\mathscr{E}}{3R}$;
   (b) $I_1 = I_2 = \dfrac{\mathscr{E}}{2R}$, $I_3 = 0$;
   (c) $\dfrac{\mathscr{E}}{2}$.

51. (a) 8.0 V;
   (b) 14 V;
   (c) 8.0 V;
   (d) 4.8 μC.

53. 29 μA.

55. (a) Place in parallel with 0.22-mΩ shunt resistor;
   (b) place in series with 45-kΩ resistor.

57. 100 kΩ.

59. $V_{44} = 24$ V, $V_{27} = 15$ V;
   -15%, -15%.

61. 0.960 mA, 4.8 V.

63. 12 V.

65. Connect a 9.0-kΩ resistor in series with human body and battery.

67. 2.5 V, 117 V.

69. 92 kΩ.

71. (a) $\dfrac{R_2 R_3}{R_1}$;
   (b) 121 Ω.

73. Terminal voltage of mercury cell (3.99 V) is closer to 4.0 V than terminal voltage of dry cell (3.84 V).

75. 150 cells, 0.54 m², connect in series; connect four such sets in parallel to total 600 cells and deliver 120 V.

77. Counterclockwise current: -24 V, clockwise current: $+48$ V.

79. 10.7 V.

83. 9.0 Ω.

85. (b) 1.39 V;
   (c) 0.42 mV;
   (d) no current from "working" battery is needed to "power" galvanometer.

87. 1.0 mV, 2.0 mV, 4.0 mV, 10.0 mV.

89. (a) 6.8 V, 15 μC;
   (b) 48 μs.

91. 200 MΩ.

93. 4.5 ms.

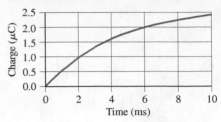

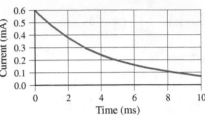

CHAPTER 27

1. (a) 8.5 N/m;
   (b) 4.9 N/m.

3. 2.6×10^{-4} N.

5. (a) South pole;
   (b) 3.41 A;
   (c) 7.39×10^{-2} N.

7. 2.13 N, 41.8° below negative y axis.

9. $\left(-2IrB_0 \sin\theta_0\right)\hat{\mathbf{j}}$.

13. 6.3×10^{-14} N, north.

15. 1.8 T.

17. (a) Downward;
   (b) into page;
   (c) right.

19. (a) 0.031 m;
   (b) 3.8×10^{-7} s.

23. 1.8 m.

25. $(0.78\hat{\mathbf{i}} - 1.0\hat{\mathbf{j}} + 0.1\hat{\mathbf{k}}) \times 10^{-15}$ N.

27. $L_{\text{final}} = \frac{1}{2} L_{\text{initial}}$.

29. (a) Negative;
   (b) $qB_0\left(\dfrac{\ell^2 + d^2}{2d}\right)$.

31. 1.3×10^8 m/s, yes.

33. (a) 45°;
   (b) 2.3×10^{-3} m.

35. (a) $2NIAB$;
   (b) 0.

37. (a) 4.85×10^{-5} m·N;
   (b) north.

39. (a) $(-4.3\,\hat{\mathbf{k}})$ A·m²;
   (b) $(2.6\hat{\mathbf{i}} - 2.4\hat{\mathbf{j}})$ m·N;
   (c) -2.8 J.

41. 12%.

43. 39 μA.

45. 6 electrons.

47. (b) 0.05 nm, about $\frac{1}{6}$ the size of a typical metal atom;
(c) 10 mV.

49. 0.820 T.

51. 70 u, 72 u, 73 u, and 74 u.

53. 1.5 mm, 1.5 mm, 0.77 mm, 0.77 mm.

55. $^2_1$H, $^4_2$He.

57. 2.4 T, upwards.

59. (a) $\dfrac{IBd}{m}t$;

(b) $\left(\dfrac{IBd}{m} - \mu_k g\right)t$;

(c) east.

61. 1.1×10^{-6} m/s, west.

63. 3.8×10^{-4} m·N.

65. $\pi\left[\dfrac{mb(3a + b)}{3NIBa(a + b)}\right]^{1/2}$.

67. They do not enter second tube, 12°.

69. 1.1 A, down.

71. 7.3×10^{-3} T.

73. -6.9×10^{-20} J.

75. 0.083 N, northerly and 68° above the horizontal.

77. (a) Downward;
(b) 28 mT;
(c) 0.12 T.

CHAPTER 28

1. 0.37 mT, 7.4 times larger.

3. 0.15 N, toward other wire.

7. 0.12 mT, 82° above directly right.

9. 3.8×10^{-5} T, 17° below the horizontal to north.

11. (a) $(2.0 \times 10^{-5})(25 - I)$ T;
(b) $(2.0 \times 10^{-5})(25 + I)$ T.

15. Closer wire: 0.050 N/m, attractive, farther wire: 0.025 N/m, repulsive.

17. 17 A, downward.

19. $\dfrac{\mu_0 I}{2\pi}\left(\dfrac{d - 2x}{x(d - x)}\right)\hat{\mathbf{j}}$.

21. 46.6 μT.

23. (b) $\dfrac{\mu_0 I}{2\pi y}$, yes, looks like B from long straight wire.

25. 0.160 A.

27. (a) 5.3 mT;
(b) 3.2 mT;
(c) 1.8 mT.

29. (a) 0.554 m;
(b) 10.5 mT.

31. (a) $\dfrac{\mu_0 I_0 R}{2\pi R_1^2}$;

(b) $\dfrac{\mu_0 I_0}{2\pi R}$;

(c) $\dfrac{\mu_0 I_0}{2\pi R}\left(\dfrac{R_3^2 - R^2}{R_3^2 - R_2^2}\right)$;

(d) 0;

(e)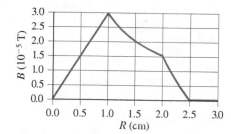

33. 3.6×10^{-6} T.

35. $0.075\,\mu_0 I/R$.

37. (a) $\dfrac{\mu_0 I}{4}\left(\dfrac{1}{R_1} + \dfrac{1}{R_2}\right)$, into the page;

(b) $\dfrac{\pi I(R_1^2 + R_2^2)}{2}$, into the page.

39. (a) $\dfrac{Q\omega R^2}{4}\hat{\mathbf{i}}$;

(b) $\dfrac{\mu_0 Q\omega}{2\pi R^2}\left(\dfrac{R^2 + 2x^2}{\sqrt{R^2 + x^2}} - 2x\right)\hat{\mathbf{i}}$;

(c) yes.

41. (b) $\dfrac{\mu_0 I}{4\pi y}\left(\dfrac{d}{\sqrt{d^2 + y^2}}\right)\hat{\mathbf{k}}$.

43. (a) $\dfrac{n\mu_0 I \tan(\pi/n)}{2\pi R}$, into the page.

45. $\dfrac{\mu_0 I}{4\pi}\left[\dfrac{\sqrt{x^2 + y^2}}{xy} + \dfrac{\sqrt{y^2 + (b - x)^2}}{(b - x)y}\right.$
$\left. + \dfrac{\sqrt{(a - y)^2 + (b - x)^2}}{(a - y)(b - x)}\right.$
$\left. + \dfrac{\sqrt{(a - y)^2 + x^2}}{x(a - y)}\right]$,
out of page.

47. (a) 16 A·m²;
(b) 13 m·N.

49. 2.4 T.

51. $(\vec{\mathbf{F}}/\ell)_M = 6.3 \times 10^{-4}$ N/m at 90°,
$(\vec{\mathbf{F}}/\ell)_N = 3.7 \times 10^{-4}$ N/m at 300°,
$(\vec{\mathbf{F}}/\ell)_P = 3.7 \times 10^{-4}$ N/m at 240°.

53. 170 A.

55. (a) 2.7×10^{-6} T;
(b) 5.3×10^{-6} T;
(c) no, no Newton's third-law-type of relationship;
(d) both 1.1×10^{-5} N/m, yes, Newton's third law holds.

57. $\dfrac{\mu_0 t j}{2}$, to the left above sheet (with current coming toward you).

61. (a) $\dfrac{N\mu_0 I R^2}{2}$

$\times \left(\dfrac{1}{(R^2 + x^2)^{3/2}} + \dfrac{1}{(R^2 + (x - R)^2)^{3/2}}\right)$;

(b) 4.5 mT.

63. 3×10^9 A.

65. (a) 46 turns;
(b) 0.83 mT;
(c) no.

67. $\dfrac{\mu_0 I \sqrt{5}}{2\pi a}$, into the page.

69. 0.10 N, south.

71. $\frac{2}{3}$.

73. (c) 1.5 A.

75.

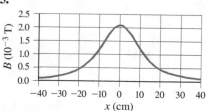

CHAPTER 29

1. -460 V.

3. Counterclockwise.

5. 1.2 mm/s.

7. (a) 0.010 Wb;
(b) 55°;
(c) 5.8 mWb.

9. Counterclockwise.

11. (a) Clockwise;
(b) 43 mV;
(c) 17 mA.

13. (a) 8.1 mJ;
(b) 4.2×10^{-3} C°.

15. (a) 0.15 A;
(b) 1.4 mW.

17. 8.81 C.

19. 21 μJ.

21. 23 mV, 26 mV.

23. (a) 0;
(b) 0.99 A, counterclockwise.

25. (a) $\dfrac{\mu_0 I a}{2\pi} \ln\left(1 + \dfrac{a}{b}\right)$;

    (b) $\dfrac{\mu_0 I a^2 v}{2\pi b(a + b)}$;

    (c) clockwise;

    (d) $\dfrac{\mu_0^2 I^2 a^4 v}{4\pi^2 b^2 (a + b)^2 R}$.

27. 1.0 m/s.

29. (a) 0.11 V;

    (b) 4.1 mA;

    (c) 0.36 mN.

31. 0.39 m/s.

33. (a) Yes;

    (b) $v_0 e^{-B^2 \ell^2 t / mR}$.

35. (a) $\dfrac{v \mu_0 I}{2\pi} \ln\left(1 + \dfrac{a}{b}\right)$;

    (b) $-\dfrac{v \mu_0 I}{2\pi} \ln\left(1 + \dfrac{a}{b}\right)$.

37. 57.2 loops.

41. 150 V.

43. 13 A.

45. (a) 2.4 kV;

    (b) 190 V.

47. 50, 4.8 V.

49. (a) Step-up;

    (b) 3.5.

51. (a) R;

    (b) $\left(\dfrac{N_\text{P}}{N_\text{S}}\right)^2 R$.

53. 98 kW.

55. (b) Clockwise;

    (c) increase.

57. (a) $\dfrac{IR}{\ell}$;

    (b) $\dfrac{\mathscr{E}_0}{\ell} e^{-B^2 \ell^2 t / mR}$.

59. 10.1 mJ.

61. 0.6 nC.

63. (a) 41 kV;

    (b) 31 MW;

    (c) 0.88 MW;

    (d) 3.0×10^7 W.

65. (a) Step-down;

    (b) 2.9 A;

    (c) 0.29 A;

    (d) 4.1 Ω.

67. 46 mA, left to right through resistor.

69. 2.3×10^{17} electrons.

71. (a) 25 A;

    (b) 98 V;

    (c) 600 W;

    (d) 81%.

73. $\frac{1}{2} B \omega \ell^2$.

77. $B \omega R$, radially in toward axis.

79. (a) $\dfrac{\pi d^2 B^2 \ell v}{16\rho}$;

    (b) $16 \rho \rho_\text{m} g / B^2$;

    (c) 3.7 cm/s.

CHAPTER 30

1. (a) 31.0 mH;

    (b) 3.79 V.

3. $\dfrac{\mu_0 N_1 N_2 A_2 \sin \theta}{\ell}$.

5. 12 V.

7. 0.566 H.

9. 11.3 V.

11. 46 m, 21 km, 0.70 kΩ.

15. 18.9 J.

17. 1.06×10^{-3} J/m³.

19. $\dfrac{\mu_0 N^2 I^2}{8\pi^2 r^2}$, $\dfrac{\mu_0 N^2 I^2 h}{4\pi} \ln\left(\dfrac{r_2}{r_1}\right)$.

21. $\dfrac{\mu_0 I^2}{16\pi}$.

23. 3.5 time constants.

25. (a) $\dfrac{L V_0^2}{2R^2}\left(1 - e^{-t/\tau}\right)^2$;

    (b) 7.6 time constants.

27. (b) 6600 V.

29. $(12\,\text{V})e^{-t/8.2\,\mu\text{s}}$, 0, 12 V.

31. (a) 0.16 nF;

    (b) 62 μH.

33. (c) $(2 \times 10^{-4})\%$.

35. (a) $\dfrac{Q_0}{\sqrt{2}}$;

    (b) $\frac{1}{8} T$.

37. $\dfrac{L}{R} \ln\left(\frac{4}{3}\right) = (0.29)\dfrac{L}{R}$.

39. 3300 Hz.

41.

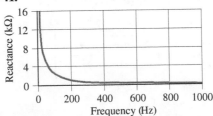

43. (a) $R + R'$;

    (b) R'.

45. (a) 2800 Ω;

    (b) 660 Hz, 11 A.

47. 2190 W.

49. (a) 0.40 kΩ;

    (b) 75 Ω.

51. 1600 Hz.

53. 240 Hz, voltages are out of phase.

55. (a) 0.124 A;

    (b) 5.02°;

    (c) 14.8 W;

    (d) 0.120 kV, 10.5 V.

57. 7.8 μF.

59. $I_0 V_0 \sin \omega t \sin (\omega t + \phi)$.

61. 130 Ω, 0.91.

63. 265 Hz, 324 W.

65. (b) 130 Ω.

67. (a) $\dfrac{V_0^2 R}{2\left[R^2 + \left(\omega L - \dfrac{1}{\omega C}\right)^2\right]}$;

    (b) $\dfrac{1}{2\pi}\sqrt{\dfrac{1}{LC}}$;

    (c) $\dfrac{R}{L}$.

69. 37 loops.

71. (a) 0.040 H;

    (b) 28 mA;

    (c) 16 μJ.

73. 2.4 mA, 0, 2.4 mA.

77. (a) $\dfrac{Q_0^2}{2C} e^{-Rt/L}$;

    (b) $\dfrac{dU}{dt} = -I^2 R$.

79.

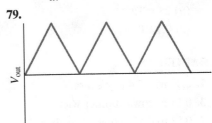

81. (a) 0;

    (b) 0, 90° out of phase.

83. 2.2 kHz.

85. 69 mH, 18 Ω.

89. (a)

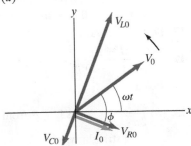

    (b) $\dfrac{V_0}{\sqrt{R^2 + \left(\omega L - \dfrac{1}{\omega C}\right)^2}} \sin(\omega t - \phi)$,

    $\phi = \tan^{-1} \dfrac{\omega L - \dfrac{1}{\omega C}}{R}$.

91. (a) $\left(\dfrac{V_{20}}{\omega L - \dfrac{1}{\omega C}}\right)\sin(\omega t - \tfrac{1}{2}\pi)$;

(b) $\left(\dfrac{V_{20}}{\omega^2 LC - 1}\right)\sin(\omega t - \pi)$;

(c) $\dfrac{1}{\omega^2 LC}$;

(d) $V_{1\,\text{out}} = V_1$.

93. (a) $\dfrac{V_0}{R}\sin\omega t$;

(b) $\dfrac{V_0}{X_L}\sin(\omega t - \tfrac{1}{2}\pi)$;

(c) $\dfrac{V_0}{X_C}\sin(\omega t + \tfrac{1}{2}\pi)$

(d) $\dfrac{V_0}{R}\sqrt{1 + \left(R\omega C - \dfrac{R}{\omega L}\right)^2}\sin(\omega t + \phi)$,

$\phi = \tan^{-1}\left(R\omega C - \dfrac{R}{\omega L}\right)$;

(e) $\dfrac{R}{\sqrt{1 + \left(R\omega C - \dfrac{R}{\omega L}\right)^2}}$;

(f) $\dfrac{1}{\sqrt{1 + \left(R\omega C - \dfrac{R}{\omega L}\right)^2}}$.

95. 0.14 H.

97. 54 mH, 22 Ω.

99. $\sqrt{6.0}\,f_0 = 2.4 f_0$.

101. (a) 7.1 kHz, V_{rms};
(b) 0.90.

103. (b) For $f \to 0$ $A \to 1$;
for $f \to \infty$, $A \to 0$;

(c) f is in s^{-1}:

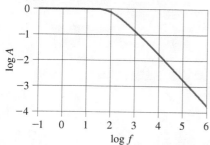

105.

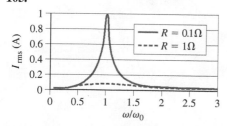

CHAPTER 31

1. 110 kV/m·s.

3. 1.2×10^{15} V/m·s.

7. (b) With R in meters, for $R \le R_0$,
$B_0 = (6.3 \times 10^{-11}\ \text{T/m})R$;
for $R > R_0$, $B_0 = \dfrac{5.7 \times 10^{-14}\ \text{T·m}}{R}$.

(c)

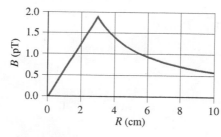

9. 3.75 V/m.

11. (a) $-\hat{\mathbf{k}}$;

(b) $\dfrac{E_0}{c}$, $-\hat{\mathbf{j}}$.

13. 2.00×10^{10} Hz.

15. 5.00×10^2 s = 8.33 min.

17. (a) 3.00×10^5 m;

(b) 34.1 cm;

(c) no.

19. (a) 261 s;

(b) 1260 s.

21. 3.4 krad/s.

23. 2.77×10^7 s.

25. 4.8 W/m², 42 V/m.

27. 4.50 μJ.

29. 3.80×10^{26} W.

31. (a) 5 cm², yes;

(b) 20 m², yes;

(c) 100 m², no.

33. (a) 2×10^8 ly;

(b) 2000 times larger.

35. 8×10^6 m/s².

37. 27 m².

39. 16 cm.

41. 3.5 nH to 5.3 nH.

43. 6.25×10^{-4} V/m;
1.04×10^{-9} W/m².

45. 3 m.

47. 1.35 s.

49. 34 V/m, 0.11 μT.

51. Down, 2.2 μT, 650 V/m.

53. (a) 0.18 nJ;

(b) 8.7 μV/m, 2.9×10^{-14} T.

57. 4×10^{10} W.

59. 5 nodes, 6.1 cm.

61. (a) $+x$;

(b) $\beta = \alpha c$;

(c) $\dfrac{E_0}{c}\,e^{-(\alpha x - \beta t)^2}$.

63. (d) Both $\vec{\mathbf{E}}$ and $\vec{\mathbf{B}}$ rotate counterclockwise.

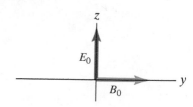

Index

Hooke, Robert, 318, 910 *fn*
Hooke's law, 170, 188, 318, 370
Horizon, 1216
    event, 1209
Horizontal (*defn*), 92 *fn*
Horizontal range (*defn*), 68
Horsepower, 202–3
Hot air balloons, 454
Hot wire, 693, 694
Household circuits, 662–63
H–R diagram, 1199, 1204
HST (*see* Hubble Space Telescope)
Hubble, Edwin, 979, 1196, 1210
Hubble age, 1213
Hubble parameter, 1210, 1213
Hubble Space Telescope (HST), 930, 1207, 1211
Hubble Ultra Deep Field, 1211
Hubble's constant, 1210
Hubble's law, 1210, 1213, 1223
Humidity, 485–86
Huygens, C., 901
Huygens' principle, 901–3
Hydraulic brake, 346
Hydraulic lift, 346
Hydraulic press, 364 *pr*
Hydrodynamics, 352
Hydroelectric power, 550
Hydrogen atom:
    Bohr theory of, 1003–9
    magnetic moment of, 719
    populations in, 1070 *pr*
    quantum mechanics of, 1045–51
    spectrum of, 936, 1002–3
Hydrogen bomb, 1141, 1144
Hydrogen bond, 581, 1077, 1079
Hydrogen isotopes, 1105
Hydrogen molecule, 1072–75, 1080, 1083
Hydrogen-like atoms, 1004 *fn*, 1008, 1010
Hydrometer, 351
Hyperopia, 883
Hysteresis, 748–49
    hysteresis loop, 748

Ice skater, 284, 286, 309 *pr*
Ideal gas, 465–70, 476 *ff*, 1089
    kinetic theory of, 476–90, 1089
Ideal gas law, 465–66, 482
    internal energy of, 498–99
    in terms of molecules, 468–69
Ideal gas temperature scale, 469–70, 534
Identical (electrons), 1053
Ignition:
    automobile, 609, 772
    fusion, 1145
ILC, 1170
Illuminance, 915
Image:
    CAT scan, 1153–54, 1156
    false-color, 1154
    formed by lens, 867 *ff*
    formed by plane mirror, 838–41
    formed by spherical mirror, 842–49, 889
    MRI, 1107, 1158–59
    NMR, 1107, 1156–59
    PET and SPECT, 1156
    real, 840, 844, 869
    seeing, 847, 848, 869

as tiny diffraction pattern, 929–30
    ultrasound, 445–46
    virtual, 840, 870
Image artifact, 878
Image distance, 840, 845, 857, 870–71
Imaging, medical, 445–46, 1107, 1152–59
Imbalance, rotational, 296–97
Impedance, 798, 800–3
Impedance matching, 802–3
Impulse, 220–21
Impulsive forces, 221
Inanimate object, force exerted by, 90
Inch (in.) (unit), 6
Incidence, angle of, 410, 415, 838, 850
Incident waves, 410, 415
Inclines, motion on, 101
Incoherent source of light, 906
Indefinite integrals, A-6–A-7
Indeterminacy principle, 1021 (*see* Uncertainty principle)
Index of refraction, 850
    dependence on wavelength (dispersion), 853
    in Snell's law, 851
Induced current, 758–76, 785 *ff*
Induced electric charge, 562–63, 641
Induced emf, 758–66, 789
    counter, 768–69
    in electric generator, 766–68
    in transformer, 770–73
Inductance, 786–89
    in ac circuits, 790–803
    of coaxial cable, 789
    mutual, 786–87
    self-, 788–89
Induction:
    charging by, 562–63
    electromagnetic, 758 *ff*
    Faraday's law of, 760–61, 773–74, 817
Induction stove, 762
Inductive battery charger, 780 *pr*
Inductive reactance, 797
Inductor, 788, 1098
    in circuits, 790–803
    energy stored in, 790
    reactance of, 797
Inelastic collisions, 222, 225–29
Inelastic scattering, 1135
Inertia, 85
    moment of, 258–60
Inertial confinement, 1145, 1146
Inertial forces, 300–1
Inertial mass, 155, 1205–6
Inertial reference frame, 85, 88, 137 *pr*, 300, 952 *ff*
    Earth as, 85, 137 *pr*, 145–46
    equivalence of all, 952–53, 957
    transformations between, 968–71
Infinitely deep square well potential, 1030–34
Inflationary scenario, 1217, 1219–21
Infrared (IR) radiation, 823–24, 852, 936
Infrasonic waves, 426
Initial conditions, 373
Inkjet printer, 583
In-phase waves, 411, 904, 910–14, 933
Instantaneous acceleration, 27–28, 60–61
Instantaneous acceleration vector, 60
Instantaneous axis, 268

Instantaneous velocity, 22–24, 60
Instantaneous velocity vector, 60
Insulators:
    electrical, 561, 658, 1091–92
    thermal, 516, 1091–92
Integrals, 39–43, 169–70, A-6, A-7, A-12, A-13, inside back cover
    definite, A-7
    Fourier, 408
    indefinite, A-6, A-7
    line, 169
    surface, A-13
    volume, A-12
Integrated circuits, 1098
Integration by parts, 1034, 1050, A-6, A-7
Intensity, 402–3, 427 *ff*
    in interference and diffraction patterns, 906–9, 924–28
    of light, 915, 1019
    of Poynting vector, 827
    of sound, 427–31
Interference, 410–11, 437–8, 903–14
    constructive, 410–11, 437, 904, 913, 914, 1072
    destructive, 410, 437, 904, 913, 914, 1072
    as distinguished from diffraction, 929
    of electrons, 1019–20, 1072
    of light waves, 903–14, 928–29
    of sound waves, 437–39
    by thin films, 909–14
    of water waves, 411
    wave-phenomenon, 903
    of waves on a string, 410
Interference factor, 928
Interference fringes, 904–6, 956, 1065
Interference pattern:
    double-slit, 903–9, 1019–20
        including diffraction, 927–29
    multiple slit, 933–36
Interferometers, 914, 954–57
Intermodulation distortion, 408 *fn*
Internal combustion engine, 530–31, 532
Internal conversion, 1117
Internal energy, 196, 498–99
    distinguished from heat and temperature, 498
    of an ideal gas, 498–99
Internal reflection, total, 421 *pr*, 854–56
Internal resistance, 678–79
International Linear Collider (ILC), 1170
International Thermonuclear Experimental Reactor (ITER), 1131, 1146
Interpolation, A-3
Interstellar dust, 1196
Intrinsic luminosity, 1197, 1204
Intrinsic semiconductor, 1091, 1093
Invariant quantity, 977
Inverse square law, 140 *ff*, 403, 429, 563–4
Inverted population, 1062–63
Ion (*defn*), 561
Ionic bonds, 1073, 1075, 1085, 1086
Ionic cohesive energy, 1086
Ionization energy, 1006, 1008
Ionizing radiation (*defn*), 1146
IR radiation, 823–24, 852, 936
Iris, 882

Photo Credits

Press–Gamma **42-12** Corbis/Bettmann **42-19a** Robert Turgeon, Cornell University **42-19b** Courtesy of Brookhaven National Laboratory **42-20b** Sovereign/Phototake NYC **42-24a** Martin M. Rotker **42-24b** Scott Camazine/Alamy Images **42-27** ISM/Phototake NYC **42-31b** Southern Illinois University/Peter Arnold, Inc. **42-33** Sovereign/Phototake NYC **CO-43** Fermilab/Science Photo Library/Photo Researchers, Inc. **43-1** Smithsonian Institution, Science Service Collection, photograph by Watson Davis/Ernest Orlando Lawrence Berkeley National Laboratory, University of California, Berkeley, courtesy AIP Emilio Segrè Visual Archives, Fermi Film **43-3a/b** Fermilab Visual Media Services **43-5** CERN/ Science Photo Library/Photo Researchers, Inc. **43-6** ATLAS Experiment/CERN–European Organization for Nuclear Research **43-10a/b** Science Photo Library/Photo Researchers **43-12a** Brookhaven National Laboratory **43-13** Lawrence Berkeley National Laboratory **CO-44** WMAP Science Team/NASA Headquarters **44-1a** Space Telescope Science Institute **44-1b** Allan Morton/ Dennis Milon/Science Photo Library/Photo Researchers, Inc. **44-2c** NASA/Johnson Space Center **44-3** U.S. Naval Observatory Photo/NASA Headquarters **44-4** National Optical Astronomy Observatories **44-5a** Reginald J. Dufour, Rice University **44-5b** U.S. Naval Observatory **44-5c** National Optical Astronomy Observatories **44-9a/b** © Anglo-Australian Observatory **44-9c** The Hubble Heritage Team (AURA/STScI/ NASA) **44-9c (inset)** STScI/NASA/Science Source/Photo Researchers, Inc. **44-15a** NASA Headquarters **44-22** NASA, ESA, S. Beckwith (STScI) and the HUDF Team **44-22 (inset)** NASA, ESA, R. Bouwens and G. Illingworth (University of California, Santa Cruz) **44-24** © Roger Ressmeyer/CORBIS All Rights Reserved **44-26** Fredrik Persson/AP Wide World Photos **44-27** NASA/ WMAP Science Team

Table of Contents Photos p. iii left © Reuters/Corbis; **right** Agence Zoom/Getty Images **p. iv left** Ben Margot/AP Wide World Photos; **right** Kai Pfaffenbach/Reuters Limited **p. v** Jerry Driendl/Taxi/Getty Images **p. vi left** Richard Price/Photographer's Choice/Getty Images; **right** Frank Herholdt/Stone/Getty Images **p. viii** Richard Megna/Fundamental Photographs, NYC **p. ix left** Richard Megna/Fundamental Photographs, NYC; **right** Giuseppe Molesini, Istituto Nazionale di Ottica Florence **p. x** © Richard Cummins/Corbis **p. xi left** Fermilab/Science Photo Library/Photo Researchers, Inc.; **right** The Microwave Sky: NASA/WMAP Science Team **p. xvii** Douglas C. Giancoli

Useful Geometry Formulas—Areas, Volumes

Circumference of circle $C = \pi d = 2\pi r$

Area of circle $A = \pi r^2 = \dfrac{\pi d^2}{4}$

Area of rectangle $A = \ell w$

Area of parallelogram $A = bh$

Area of triangle $A = \frac{1}{2} hb$

Right triangle (Pythagoras) $c^2 = a^2 + b^2$

Sphere: surface area $A = 4\pi r^2$
          volume $V = \frac{4}{3}\pi r^3$

Rectangular solid: volume $V = \ell w h$

Cylinder (right):
        surface area $A = 2\pi r\ell + 2\pi r^2$
        volume $V = \pi r^2 \ell$

Right circular cone:
        surface area $A = \pi r^2 + \pi r \sqrt{r^2 + h^2}$
        volume $V = \frac{1}{3}\pi r^2 h$

Quadratic Formula

Equation with unknown x, in the form

$$ax^2 + bx + c = 0,$$

has solutions

$$x = \frac{-b \pm \sqrt{b^2 - 4ac}}{2a}.$$

Exponents

$(a^n)(a^m) = a^{n+m}$ [Example: $(a^3)(a^2) = a^5$]
$(a^n)(b^n) = (ab)^n$ [Example: $(a^3)(b^3) = (ab)^3$]
$(a^n)^m = a^{nm}$ $\begin{bmatrix}\text{Example: } (a^3)^2 = a^6 \\ \text{Example: } (a^{\frac{1}{4}})^4 = a\end{bmatrix}$

$a^{-1} = \dfrac{1}{a}$ $\quad a^{-n} = \dfrac{1}{a^n}$ $\quad a^0 = 1$

$a^{\frac{1}{2}} = \sqrt{a}$ $\quad a^{\frac{1}{4}} = \sqrt{\sqrt{a}}$

$(a^n)(a^{-m}) = \dfrac{a^n}{a^m} = a^{n-m}$ [Ex.: $(a^5)(a^{-2}) = a^3$]

$\dfrac{a^n}{b^n} = \left(\dfrac{a}{b}\right)^n$

Logarithms [Appendix A–7; Table A–1]

If $y = 10^x$, then $x = \log_{10} y = \log y$.
If $y = e^x$, then $x = \log_e y = \ln y$.

$\log(ab) = \log a + \log b$

$\log\left(\dfrac{a}{b}\right) = \log a - \log b$

$\log a^n = n \log a$

Some Derivatives and Integrals†

$\dfrac{d}{dx} x^n = nx^{n-1}$ $\qquad \displaystyle\int \sin ax\, dx = -\dfrac{1}{a}\cos ax$

$\dfrac{d}{dx} \sin ax = a \cos ax$ $\qquad \displaystyle\int \cos ax\, dx = \dfrac{1}{a}\sin ax$

$\dfrac{d}{dx} \cos ax = -a \sin ax$ $\qquad \displaystyle\int \dfrac{1}{x}\, dx = \ln x$

$\displaystyle\int x^m\, dx = \dfrac{1}{m+1} x^{m+1}$ $\qquad \displaystyle\int e^{ax}\, dx = \dfrac{1}{a} e^{ax}$

† See Appendix B for more.

Binomial Expansion

$$(1 \pm x)^n = 1 \pm nx + \frac{n(n-1)}{2\cdot 1}x^2 \pm \frac{n(n-1)(n-2)}{3\cdot 2\cdot 1}x^3 + \cdots \quad [\text{for } x^2 < 1]$$

$$\approx 1 \pm nx \quad [\text{for } x \ll 1]$$

Trigonometric Formulas [Appendix A–9]

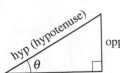

opp (opposite)

hyp (hypotenuse)

adj (adjacent)

$\sin \theta = \dfrac{\text{opp}}{\text{hyp}}$

$\cos \theta = \dfrac{\text{adj}}{\text{hyp}}$

$\tan \theta = \dfrac{\text{opp}}{\text{adj}}$

$\text{adj}^2 + \text{opp}^2 = \text{hyp}^2$ (Pythagorean theorem)

$\tan \theta = \dfrac{\sin \theta}{\cos \theta}$

$\sin^2 \theta + \cos^2 \theta = 1$

$\sin 2\theta = 2 \sin \theta \cos \theta$

$\cos 2\theta = (\cos^2 \theta - \sin^2 \theta) = (1 - 2\sin^2 \theta) = (2\cos^2 \theta - 1)$

$\sin(180° - \theta) = \sin \theta$ $\qquad \cos(180° - \theta) = -\cos \theta$
$\sin(90° - \theta) = \cos \theta$
$\cos(90° - \theta) = \sin \theta$
$\sin \frac{1}{2}\theta = \sqrt{(1 - \cos \theta)/2}$ $\qquad \cos \frac{1}{2}\theta = \sqrt{(1 + \cos \theta)/2}$
$\sin \theta \approx \theta$ [for small $\theta \lesssim 0.2$ rad]
$\cos \theta \approx 1 - \dfrac{\theta^2}{2}$ [for small $\theta \lesssim 0.2$ rad]
$\sin(A \pm B) = \sin A \cos B \pm \cos A \sin B$
$\cos(A \pm B) = \cos A \cos B \mp \sin A \sin B$

For any triangle:
$c^2 = a^2 + b^2 - 2ab \cos \gamma$ (law of cosines)
$\dfrac{\sin \alpha}{a} = \dfrac{\sin \beta}{b} = \dfrac{\sin \gamma}{c}$ (law of sines)